Second Canadian Edition

Focus on Health

DALE B. HAHN, Ph.D.
Ball State University

WAYNE A. PAYNE, Ed.D.
Ball State University

MARGARET GALLANT, BSc., BEd., MSc.
St. Francis Xavier University

PAULA C. FLETCHER, Ph.D.
Wilfrid Laurier University

Toronto Montréal Boston Burr Ridge, IL Dubuque, IA Madison, WI New York San Francisco St. Louis Bangkok Bogotá Caracas Kuala Lumpur Lisbon London Madrid Mexico City Milan New Delhi Santiago Seoul Singapore Sydney Taipei

FOCUS ON HEALTH
SECOND CANADIAN EDITION

ISBN: 0-07-087736-X

1 2 3 4 5 6 7 8 9 10 QPV 0 9 8 7 6

Printed and bound in the United States of America

Executive Sponsoring Editor: James Buchanan
Sponsoring Editor: Karen Noxon
Developmental Editor: Christine Gilbert
Marketing Manager: Marc Trudel
Manager, Editorial Services: Kelly Dickson
Supervising Editor: Joanne Limebeer
Copy Editor: Karen Rolfe
Senior Production Coordinator: Paula Brown
Page Layout: Pronk&Associates Inc.
Cover Design: Pronk&Associates Inc.
Cover Photo: © John Kelly/Getty Images
Printer: Quebecor Printing Versailles

Library and Archives Canada Cataloguing in Publication Data

Focus on health / Dale B. Hahn ... [et al.].—2nd. Canadian ed.

Includes bibliographical references and index.
ISBN 0-07-087736-X

1. Health—Textbooks. I. Hahn, Dale B.

RA776.F62 2006 fol. 613 C2005-906304-1

Contents in Brief

Contents

Part Three SUBSTANCE ABUSE AND ADDICTION

JIM WISECARVER
1951 1998
Wayne Erik Larsen
DAYTON-CHILD 1957-1991

Preface

As a health educator, you already know that the personal health course is one of the most exciting courses a college or university student will take. Today's media-oriented students are aware of today's critical health issues. They hear about substance abuse, sexually transmitted infections, fitness, and nutrition virtually every day. The value of the personal health course is its potential to expand students' knowledge of these and other health topics. Students will then be able to examine their attitudes toward health issues and modify their behaviour to improve their health and perhaps even prevent or delay the onset of certain health conditions.

Focus on Health, Second Canadian Edition, accomplishes this task with a carefully composed, well-documented text written by four health educators who teach the personal health course to several hundred students each year. They understand the teaching issues you face daily in the classroom and have written this text with your concerns in mind.

Written for the diverse group of students in the undergraduate personal health course, *Focus on Health*, Second Canadian Edition offers an engaging writing style and proactive features that invite readers to make positive changes in their health behaviour. The text integrates coverage of health care services within the discussion of personal health issues such as fitness, chronic conditions, and substance abuse. Extensive technology is also integrated into the text through Online Learning Centre boxes, HealthQuest Activities, and "Health on the Web" boxes.

HALLMARKS OF THE TEXT

Focus on Health, Second Canadian Edition, has several unique features and themes that set it apart from other personal health texts and continue to enhance student learning.

A Text for All Canadian Students

This book is written for Canadian college and university students in a wide variety of settings, from community colleges to large universities. The content is carefully constructed to be meaningful to both traditional- and non-traditional-age students. The authors have paid special attention to the increasing numbers of non-traditional-age students (those over age 25) who have decided to pursue a college or university education. The topics covered in the text often address the particular needs of these non-traditional-age students. *Focus on Health* continues to encourage students of all ages and backgrounds in their goals.

Two Central Themes

Two central themes—the multiple dimensions of health and the developmental tasks—are presented in Chapter 1. These give students a foundation for understanding their own health and achieving positive behaviour change.

Flexible Organization

The Second Canadian Edition of *Focus on Health* has 17 chapters. The first stands alone as an introductory chapter that explains the focus of the book. Of course, instructors can choose to cover the chapters in any sequence that suits the needs of their course.

Wellness and Disease Prevention

Throughout this new edition, students are continually urged to be proactive in shaping their future health. For example, Chapter 5, Understanding Nutrition and Diet, explains the health benefits of following a low-fat diet. Even the chapter titles invite students to take control of their own health behaviour.

The Second Canadian Edition of *Focus on Health* has been thoroughly updated with the latest information, statistics, and findings.

Updated Coverage

As experienced health educators, the authors know how important it is to provide students with the most current information available. Throughout each chapter the authors have included the very latest information, Canadian statistics, and findings.

New or Expanded Topics for the Second Canadian Edition

All weblinks have been revised and updated, as well as all end-of-chapter material. Following is a sampling of topics that are either completely new to this edition or are covered in greater depth than in the previous edition:

Chapter 1—Charting a Plan for Behaviour Change

- Updated Canadian statistics and data
- Stages of Change section added to chapter
- Content completely revised and updated

Chapter 2—Achieving Psychological Wellness

- Information added on psychological health, suicide intervention, and electroconvulsive theory
- Expanded sections on exercise and depression, humour, and risk factors for suicide
- New section on general anxiety disorders

Chapter 3—Managing Stress

- New information on flight-or-fight response and the costs and benefits of stress
- Section on alarm stage expanded
- Pedagogical features revised and updated, i.e., Exploring Your Spirituality

Chapter 4—Becoming Physically Fit

- Chapter title revised to better reflect content
- More emphasis added to physical activity
- Chapter completely revised and updated with the latest available Canadian data and statistics

Chapter 5—Understanding Nutrition and Diet

- Updated Canadian statistics and data
- Tips for reducing fat added (Changing for the Better)
- New information added on making better fast-food choices and on food safety
- New Focus On article about Mad Cow Disease

Chapter 6—Maintaining a Healthy Weight

- New data and statistics on BMI and body weight added
- New information added on binge-eating disorders, chewing and spitting out food syndrome, and night eating syndrome
- Updated statistics and data throughout

Chapter 7—Making Decisions About Drug Use

- Section on narcotics revised and updated
- Updated statistics and data throughout
- Chapter completely revised and updated from previous edition

Chapter 8—Taking Control of Alcohol Use

- Updated statistics and data throughout
- Section added on differences between Canadian and American students' drinking habits
- Chapter completely revised and updated from previous edition

Chapter 9—Rejecting Tobacco Use

- Updated statistics and data throughout
- New information added on cigar smoking and its effects
- New data on established and suspected health effects of cigarette smoking
- Updated information on efforts in Canada to ban smoking (Making Headlines box)

Chapter 10—Reducing Your Risk for Chronic Disease

- New information added concerning race and heart disease, risk factors for cardiovascular disease, alternate treatments for cancer, women and heart disease, and tips for healthy eating for Type 2 diabetics
- Updated data and statistics throughout
- New sections on managing heart health and risk reduction

Chapter 11—Preventing Infectious Diseases

- New section on the immune response
- Updated and expanded section on AIDS
- New information added on SARS, Lyme Disease, Hantavirus Pulmonary Syndrome, and West Nile virus
- Updated data and statistics throughout
- New Focus On article concerning many changes in regards to infectious diseases

Chapter 12—Sexuality and Relationships

- Updated data and statistics throughout
- Updated Sexual Orientation section
- Chapter title changed to better reflect content
- Updated information on endometriosis

Chapter 13—Managing Your Fertility

- New information added on contraception
- New Focus On article on reproductive technologies

Chapter 14—Aging and the End of Life

- Updated Canadian data and statistics
- Expanded section on falls and how the problem is increasing
- Updated information on organ donation

Chapter 15—Becoming an Informed Health Care Consumer

- New Star Box on therapeutic drugs and how they are identified
- Updated Canadian statistics and data throughout
- New information added on massage and massotherapy
- New information on buying drugs over the Internet (Changing for the Better)

Chapter 16—Protecting Your Safety

- Updated Canadian statistics and data throughout
- New information added on harassment
- Updated information on violent crime across the country
- New Focus On article on using cellular phones while driving
- New section on identity theft and reducing your risk of becoming a victim

Chapter 17—The Environment and Your Health

- Updated Canadian data and statistics throughout
- Expanded discussion on human population growth
- New information added on tsunamis, laws of ecology, reducing risk of waterborne illness while travelling, and the high-tech revolution and electronic waste
- New Personal Assessment on your awareness of how you affect the environment

STUDENT-FRIENDLY CHAPTER PEDAGOGY

Each chapter of *Focus on Health* is rich with pedagogical features that offer a variety of ways to address new and emerging health issues and to pique student interest in particular topics. New to this edition, over half of the boxes have been revised and updated, and Chapter Objectives have been added to each chapter.

Chapter Objectives

Each chapter begins with a set of clear objectives that help students distill the most important concepts in the pages that follow.

HealthQuest Activities

These activities allow students to assess their health behaviour in each of nine different areas. HealthQuest's interactive approach will encourage students to learn about topics such as condom use, cancer prevention, and healthy eating behaviour as they complete the activities. These boxes direct you to the text's Online Learning Centre at **www.mcgrawhill.ca/college/hahn**.

Health on the Web Behaviour Change Activities

Today's computer-savvy students can find reliable health information at their fingertips when they search the World Wide Web. For each activity, students explore a Web site and then complete a quiz or self-assessment offered at the site. These activities help students think critically about valuable health information.

Taking Charge of Your Health

Taking Charge of Your Health behaviour change objectives, listed at the end of each chapter, help students apply what they have learned in the text. These objectives reinforce the concept of self-responsibility and positive behaviour change.

Online Learning Centre (OLC) Boxes

Online Learning Centre boxes, found on the opening page of each chapter, direct students toward the useful resources available on the Online Learning Centre that accompanies this text. These resources include learning objectives, interactive exercises, and self-scoring chapter quizzes. The Online Learning Centre boxes also list some of the Weblinks that students will find on the OLC.

Media Pulse

Face it—a student's world revolves around media of all types, especially the Web. Students get most of their health information not from instructors and textbooks, but from television, self-help books, popular news magazines, the Web, and radio. To meet students on this familiar ground, we've included Media Pulse boxes, which take a critical look at these media sources of health information. This feature appears on the first page of each chapter.

Exploring Your Spirituality

Spirituality has become an important focus in health courses. Exploring Your Spirituality boxes highlight the spiritual dimension of health and its effect on overall wellness. The boxes cover topics such as making decisions about sex and having an enjoyable social life without abusing alcohol or other drugs.

Changing for the Better

These unique question-and-answer boxes show students how to put health concepts into practice. Each box begins with a real-life question, followed by helpful tips and practical advice for initiating behaviour change and staying motivated to follow a healthy lifestyle.

Learning From Our Diversity

These boxes expose students to alternate viewpoints and highlight what we can learn from the differences that make us unique. Topics include alcohol abuse, prevention of infectious diseases, and dietary supplements.

Making Headlines

These boxes highlight current or recent topics in the news from around the world with regards to various health issues such as the effects of supplemental antioxidant nutrients and tobacco consumption legislation.

Talking Points

Interspersed throughout each chapter, Talking Points offer students opportunities to explore how they might start a dialogue about specific health-related issues and situations.

Star Boxes

Special material in Star Boxes encourages students to delve into a particular topic or closely examine an important health issue.

Personal Assessment Inventories

Most chapters contain at least one Personal Assessment inventory, beginning with a comprehensive health assessment just before Chapter 1. These self-assessment exercises serve three important functions: they capture students' attention, serve as a basis for introspection and behaviour change, and provide suggestions for carrying the applications further.

Definition Boxes

Key terms are set in boldface type and are defined in corresponding boxes. Pronunciation guides are provided where appropriate. Other important terms in the text are set in italics for emphasis. Both approaches facilitate student vocabulary comprehension.

Comprehensive Glossary

At the end of the text, all terms defined in boxes, as well as pertinent italicized terms, are merged into a comprehensive glossary.

Chapter Summaries

Each chapter concludes with a bulleted summary of key concepts and their significance or application. The student can then return to any topic in the chapter for clarification or study.

Review Questions

A set of questions appears at the end of each chapter to aid the student in review and analysis of chapter content.

Think About This ...

These engaging questions encourage students to apply what they have learned in the chapter by analyzing their own health habits and finding appropriate solutions to the issues raised.

Suggested Readings

Because some students want to know more about a particular topic, a list of annotated readings is given at the end of each chapter.

Comprehensive Discussion of Sexuality

The biological and psychosocial origins of sexuality, sexual behaviour, and intimate relationships are presented in a single, comprehensive chapter. This organization gives the student a better framework for studying these complex topics.

Personal Safety Chapter

With good reason, students are more concerned than ever about issues related to violence and safety both on and off campus. Chapter 16, Protecting Your Safety, probes critically important current issues such as homicide; domestic violence; hate crimes; sexual victimization; and recreational, residential, and motor vehicle safety.

Focus On Articles

Focus On articles examine current issues that students are hearing about in today's news, such as alcohol and violence, volunteering, smokers' rights, and even sex on the Internet. These often controversial health-related topics are a perfect starting point for class or group discussions. Because these essays are set at the end of each chapter, they can be covered or not at the instructor's option.

Exam Prep Guide

An exam preparation section is included at the back of the book. The multiple-choice questions test students' retention of the material they have read. The critical thinking questions allow students to integrate the concepts introduced in the text with the information presented in class lectures and discussions. This built-in study guide is a good value for students.

INSTRUCTOR'S RESOURCES

Integrated Learning

Your Integrated Learning (*i*Learning) Sales Specialist is a McGraw-Hill Ryerson representative who has the experience, product knowledge, training, and support to help you assess and integrate any of the below-noted products, technology, and services into your course for optimum teaching and learning performance. Whether it's using our test bank software, helping your students improve their grades, or putting your entire course online, your *i*Learning Sales Specialist is there to help you do it. Contact your local *i*Learning Sales Specialist today to learn how to maximize all of McGraw-Hill Ryerson's resources!

*i*Learning Services Program

McGraw-Hill Ryerson offers a unique *i*Services program designed for Canadian faculty. For additional information visit **www.mcgrawhill.ca/highereducation/iservices**.

PageOut and WebCT

Visit **www.mhhe.com/pageout** to create a Web page for your course using our resources. **PageOut** is the McGraw-Hill Ryerson Web site development centre. This Web page–generation software is free to adopters and is designed to help faculty create an online course, complete with assignments, quizzes, links to relevant Web sites, and more—all in a matter of minutes.

In addition, content cartridges are available for the course management systems **WebCT and Blackboard**. These platforms provide instructors with user-friendly, flexible teaching tools. Please contact your local McGraw-Hill Ryerson *i*Learning Sales Specialist for details.

The Instructor Online Learning Centre (OLC)

The OLC at **www.mcgrawhill.ca/college/hahn** includes a password-protected Web site for instructors. The site offers a downloadable Instructor's Manual/Course Integrator Guide and access to PageOut, the McGraw-Hill Ryerson Web site development centre.

Computerized Test Bank

This easy-to-use electronic testing program allows instructors to create tests from book-specific test banks and to add their own questions. It accommodates a wide range of question types, and multiple versions of the test can be created.

STUDENT RESOURCES

Student Online Learning Centre (OLC)

This powerful electronic learning aid, located at **www.mcgrawhill.ca/college/hahn**, includes quizzes, Weblinks, bonus material, and much more.

PowerWeb

A unique online tool that provides access to course-related journal articles, weekly updates, timely world news, Weblinks, a discipline-specific search engine, study tools, and interactive exercises.

OTHER RESOURCES AVAILABLE

Video Library

The McGraw-Hill Video Library contains many quality videotapes, including selected Films for Humanities and all videos from the award-winning series *Healthy Living: Road to Wellness*. Digitized video clips are also available (see Healthy Living Video Clips CD-ROM). The library also features Students on Health Video, a unique video filmed on college campuses that includes eight brief (8 to 10 minute) segments featuring students involved in discussion and role-play on health issues. Lastly, a new video—McGraw-Hill Health Video—is available. This video features brief clips on a wide range of topics of interest in personal health courses. Talk with your local McGraw-Hill Ryerson *i*Learning Sales Specialist about eligibility to receive videos.

Fitness and Nutrition Log

This logbook helps students track their diet and exercise programs. It serves as a diary to help students monitor their behaviours. It can be packaged with any McGraw-Hill Ryerson textbook for a small additional fee.

You Can Make a Difference: Be Environmentally Responsible, Second Edition, by Judith Getis

This handy text is organized around the three parts of the biosphere: land, water, and air. Each section contains descriptions of the environmental problems associated with that part of the biosphere. Immediately following the problems, or "challenges," are suggested ways in which individuals and communities can help solve or alleviate them.

Annual Editions

Annual Editions is an ever-enlarging series of more than 70 volumes; each designed to provide convenient, low-cost access to a wide range of current, carefully selected articles from some of the most important magazines, newspapers, and journals published today. Prominent scholars, researchers, and commentators write the articles, drawn from more than 400 periodical sources. All Annual Editions have common organizational features, such as annotated tables of contents, topic guides, unit overviews, and indexes. In addition, a list of annotated Web sites is included. An Instructor's Resource Guide with testing suggestions for each volume is available to qualified instructors.

Taking Sides

www.dushkin.com/takingsides

McGraw-Hill/Dushkin's Taking Sides series currently comprises 22 volumes with an instructor's guide with testing material available for each volume. The Taking Sides approach brings together the arguments of leading social and behavioural scientists, educators, and contemporary commentators, forming 18 to 20 debates, or issues, that present the pros and cons of current controversies in an area of study. An Issue Introduction that precedes the two opposing viewpoints gives students the proper context and historical background for each debate. After reading the debate, students are given other viewpoints to consider in the Issue Postscript, which also offers recommendations for further reading. Taking Sides fosters critical thinking in students and encourages them to develop a concern for serious social dialogue.

ACKNOWLEDGEMENTS

Extensive feedback from numerous reviews and the valuable suggestions provided by that process helped us to develop this Second Canadian Edition. Thank you to the following colleagues for their invaluable advice:

Lara Lauzon
University of Victoria

Lucie Lévesque
Queen's University

Susan M. M. Todd
Langara College

Coreen Fleming
Centennial College

Elaine Craig
Humber College

Candace Johnson Redden
Brock University

Lorne J. Adams
Brock University

Mark Lund
Grant MacEwan College

Kelly Nicol Bower
Dalhousie University

Jacqueline Cottingham
Confederation College

Celine Homsy
John Abbott College

Anne-Marie McAllister
Georgian College

Diane Potvin
University of New Brunswick

David Thomas
Fanshawe College

Jayne Smitten
Grant MacEwan College

Manju P. Acharya
University of Lethbridge

We would like to thank and acknowledge the support of our Copy Editor, Karen Rolfe; our Supervising Editor, Joanne Limebeer; and our Developmental Editor, Christine Gilbert for her tireless efforts throughout this process.

Peggy would like to give a special thanks to her husband Leo Gallant for his support, advice, and encouragement.

Paula would like to acknowledge the support of her family, particularly her partner, best friend, and confidante, Stan—thank you for always being in my corner.

Margaret (Peggy) Gallant
St. Francis Xavier University

Paula Fletcher
Wilfrid Laurier University

A Visual Guide to *Focus on Health*

Whether you're trying to get in shape, looking for sound health advice, trying to interpret the health information you see in the media, or just working toward a good grade, *Focus on Health* is designed to help you succeed. Here's a brief guide to some of the useful and eye-opening features you'll find inside.

Part Four

Chapter **10**

Reducing Your Risk for Chronic Disease

Chapter Objectives

Each chapter opens with a set of clear learning goals; check them out before you begin reading the chapter, and use them for review once you've completed it.

Chapter Objectives

After reading this chapter, you should be able to

- Describe the prevalence of cardiovascular disease compared to other diseases.
- List the cardiovascular disease risk factors and distinguish between those that can vs. those that cannot be modified.
- Explain how each of the modifiable cardiovascular disease risk factors can be changed.
- Explain the signs of a heart attack and the recommended action that should be taken.
- Explain how coronary heart disease is diagnosed and treated.
- Explain the recommendations for prevention and treatment of hypertension.
- Distinguish between the different types of stroke.
- Describe different types of cancers and specific early-detection methods for each.
- List diagnosis tools and treatments for different types of cancer.
- Offer several lifestyle choices that effectively reduce your risk for cancer.
- Describe diabetes and diabetes treatments.

Online Learning Centre Resources

A wealth of study aids and other resources to help you prepare for exams and improve your grades are available at **www.mcgrawhill.ca/college/hahn**.

Online Learning Centre Resources
www.mcgrawhill.ca/college/hahn

Log on to our Online Learning Centre (OLC) for access to Web links for study and exploration of health topics. Here are some examples of what you'll find:

- **www.cancer.ca** This site offers links to provincial branches of the Canadian Cancer Society, along with answers to frequently asked questions about cancer. You can also find annual lists of cancer statistics.
- **www.hc-sc.gc.ca/english/ahc_asc** Search "diabetes" and learn all about Health Canada's Diabetes Strategy and find out more about your own risk for this increasingly common condition by visiting the Health Canada Web pages.
- **www.heartandstroke.ca** Find hundreds of topics related to cardiovascular health and disease, including prevention, nutrition, smoking cessation, and other lifestyle considerations.

Media Pulse

Curious about all those ads you see for various drugs? Wondering about the reliability of the health information you find on the Internet? This feature investigates the way that written, broadcast, and electronic media shape our perceptions about health, health care, and wellness.

Media Pulse
Support Is Just a Click Away

Health support groups are composed of people who come together to help each other through the demands of a chronic health condition. These groups have traditionally been organized by institutions in the local health care community, such as hospitals; by the provincial and local affiliates of national organizations, such as the Canadian Cancer Society; or by citizens who have the same chronic condition. Increasingly common today, however, are support groups whose members are connected, not by physical proximity, but by the Internet.

Health self-help groups on the Internet develop in one of two ways. The first occurs when a brick-and-mortar organization, such as a national agency or health care institution, develops a support group for its homepage. The second occurs when a person with the condition (or a family member of that person) organizes an online group.

You can find a health support group simply by surfing the Internet. Or you can be referred to a site by a health care professional. You can also go to the homepage of a medical institution or a national agency to find out if it provides a support group link.

Health on the Web Behaviour Change Activities

Surfing the Web can be good for your health! These activities guide you to interactive self-assessments on the Web. How much stress are you under? What form of contraception is best for you? Log on and find out!

Health on the Web
Behaviour Change Activities

Following a Healthy Lifestyle

Students who take a personal health course usually want to improve their health behaviour. *Prevention* magazine offers an excellent general health Web site that addresses subjects such as health, weight loss and fitness, food, and community. The content varies, but it's always useful. Click on **www.prevention.com**, and choose a path that interests you.

Exploring Lifestyle Links

If you're seeking information on a multitude of lifestyle choices, this is the site for you. Topics include fitness,

HealthQuest Activities

This feature provides activities to help you explore HealthQuest and assess your health behaviour in areas like cancer prevention, fitness, and nutrition. Go to the text's Online Learning Centre at **www.mcgrawhill.ca/college/hahn** for these useful exercises.

HealthQuest Activities
www.mcgrawhill.ca/college/hahn

- The *How Fit Are You?* exercise in the Fitness Module will help you determine your current level of fitness in four major areas: cardiorespiratory capacity, muscular strength, flexibility, and body composition. Complete the series of questions about how much you exercise, what types of training you do, how intensely you exercise, and your body size. After you complete the questions, *HealthQuest* will give you feedback in each of the four areas mentioned above. Then develop an individual plan for improving or maintaining your current fitness level.
- The *Exercise Interest Inventory* in the Fitness Module allows you to rate your feelings about certain aspects of exercise. *HealthQuest* provides feedback about the activities and exercises you would most enjoy, based on your individual needs and preferences. First, write down the five fitness activities that you like best or those you participate in most often. After each one, indicate your motivation for engaging in that particular activity. For example, you could list "enjoyment," "habit," or "convenience." When you have completed the *Exercise Interest Inventory*, compare the two lists. Are there any surprises? What factors had you not considered to be influential in your choice of exercise?

Changing *for the Better*

When Do Headaches Need Attention?

I never used to get headaches, but now I seem to have them a lot, especially around midterm and exam weeks.Is this something to be concerned about?

An estimated 45 million North Americans have frequent,

Migraine

Description

Throbbing pain on one side of the head, usually preceded by visual disturbances. Sensitivity to lights and sounds; nausea and dizziness. More common in women. Can last from a few hours to two days

Changing for the Better

Learn to put health concepts into practice by following these useful tips. This feature provides practical advice for making positive changes and staying motivated to follow a healthy lifestyle.

Exploring Your Spirituality

Solitude: Time to Reflect, Regroup, Renew

Have you taken a moment today to be quiet and just be with yourself? Time alone can help you step away from a busy, fragmented world and draw inward for renewal. It provides an opportunity to reflect and to have new and deeper observations. Having strengthened awareness of yourself in both mind and body allows you to

at a coffee shop, in the library, or in the garden. Go for a walk, listen to music, weed the garden, write a letter to a friend, paint, read a poem, or just be still and concentrate on your breathing. All of these are solitary actions that, in the end, reconnect you to a life force and to others. Pretty soon you may feel that your

Exploring Your Spirituality

A healthy body and a healthy mind go hand in hand. This feature will help you tap into your spiritual side to improve your self-esteem, foster good relationships with others, and jump-start your physical health.

TALKING POINTS • How would you speak honestly with a friend who seems chronically angry and cynical?

Talking Points

Throughout each chapter, you'll find these tips for starting a dialogue about sensitive health topics.

Learning from Our Diversity

Do You Eat Real Ethnic Food?

The typical diets in many other countries tend to contain more high-carbohydrate foods and fewer foods high in animal fats than the common North American diet. Moreover, when ethnic foods are prepared in Canada and the United States, especially in restaurants, they are

Italian

- *Traditional:* Large mound of pasta with tomato-based sauce containing small amounts of meat or meatballs on the side; pizza with an extra-thick crust and a mere sprinkle of tomato sauce,

Learning from Our Diversity

These unique boxes invite you to explore the rich diversity of your own campus, and to gain perspective on the way such characteristics as age, ethnic background, physical abilities, and sexual orientation can shape individuals' lives and well-being.

Taking Charge of Your Health

- Investigate the resources available on your campus that you could use to determine your healthy weight and body composition profile.
- Evaluate your eating behaviours to find out if you are using food to cope with stress. If you are, develop a plan to use nonfood options, such as exercise or interaction with friends or family members, to deal with stress.
- Formulate a realistic set of goals for altering your weight and body composition in a time frame that allows you to do so in a healthy way.
- Establish a daily schedule that lets you make any necessary dietary and physical activity adjustments.
- Keep a daily journal of your weight-management efforts.
- Monitor your progress toward meeting your weight-management goals.

Taking Charge of Your Health

How would you approach a doctor, family member, friend, or partner about a specific health problem? Where do you stand on today's controversial health issues? Are you honest with yourself about your own health? Use these boxes to role-play and sharpen your communication skills.

Personal Assessment

Do you eat too much fat? What's the best method of birth control for you if you are sexually active? Are you a perfectionist? Each chapter in *Focus on Health* includes an assessment to help you learn the answers to these and many other questions.

Focus on

MEAT SAFETY: IS IT SAFE TO EAT CANADIAN BEEF?

Focus On ...

Every day you hear the buzz about hot health topics ranging from prescription drug abuse to food safety. Read these articles and decide where you stand on these controversial issues.

Chapter **16**

Protecting Your Safety

Personal Safety Chapter

In today's world, you are more concerned than ever before about issues related to violence and safety both on and off campus. This chapter probes such critically important issues as sexual victimization, hate crimes, domestic violence, and recreational safety.

Comprehensive Health Assessment

SOCIAL AND OCCUPATIONAL HEALTH

	Not true/ rarely	Somewhat true/ sometimes	Mostly true/ usually	Very true/ always
1. I feel loved and supported by my family.	1	2	3	4
2. I establish friendships with ease and enjoyment.	1	2	3	4
3. I establish friendships with people of both genders and all ages.	1	2	3	4
4. I sustain relationships by communicating with and caring about my family and friends.	1	2	3	4
5. I feel comfortable and confident when meeting people for the first time.	1	2	3	4
6. I practise social skills to facilitate the process of forming new relationships.	1	2	3	4
7. I seek opportunities to meet and interact with new people.	1	2	3	4
8. I talk with, rather than at, people.	1	2	3	4
9. I am open to developing or sustaining intimate relationships.	1	2	3	4
10. I appreciate the importance of parenting the next generation and am committed to supporting it in ways that reflect my own resources.	1	2	3	4
11. I recognize the strengths and weaknesses of my parents' childrearing skills and feel comfortable modifying them if I choose to become a parent.	1	2	3	4
12. I attempt to be tolerant of others whether or not I approve of their behaviour or beliefs.	1	2	3	4
13. I understand and appreciate the contribution that cultural diversity makes to the quality of living.	1	2	3	4
14. I understand and appreciate the difference between being educated and being trained.	1	2	3	4
15. My work gives me a sense of self-sufficiency and an opportunity to contribute.	1	2	3	4
16. I have equal respect for the roles of leader and subordinate within the workplace.	1	2	3	4
17. I have chosen an occupation that suits my interests and temperament.	1	2	3	4
18. I have chosen an occupation that does not compromise my physical or psychological health.	1	2	3	4
19. I get along well with my coworkers most of the time.	1	2	3	4
20. When I have a disagreement with a coworker, I try to resolve it directly and constructively.	1	2	3	4

Points __________

SPIRITUAL AND PSYCHOLOGICAL HEALTH

	Not true/ rarely	Somewhat true/ sometimes	Mostly true/ usually	Very true/ always
1. I have a deeply held belief system or personal theology.	1	2	3	4
2. I recognize the contribution that membership in a community of faith can make to a person's overall quality of life.	1	2	3	4
3. I seek experiences with nature and reflect on nature's contribution to my quality of life.	1	2	3	4
4. My spirituality is a resource that helps me remain calm and strong during times of stress.	1	2	3	4
5. I have found appropriate ways to express my spirituality.	1	2	3	4
6. I respect the diversity of spiritual expression and am tolerant of those whose beliefs differ from my own.	1	2	3	4
7. I take adequate time to reflect on my own life and my relationships with others and the institutions of society.	1	2	3	4
8. I routinely undertake new experiences.	1	2	3	4
9. I receive adequate support from others.	1	2	3	4
10. I look for opportunities to support others, even occasionally at the expense of my own goals and aspirations.	1	2	3	4
11. I recognize that emotional and psychological health are as important as physical health.	1	2	3	4
12. I express my feelings and opinions comfortably, yet am capable of keeping them to myself when appropriate.	1	2	3	4
13. I see myself as a person of worth and feel comfortable with my own strengths and limitations.	1	2	3	4
14. I establish realistic goals and work to achieve them.	1	2	3	4
15. I understand the differences between the normal range of emotions and the signs of clinical depression.	1	2	3	4
16. I know how to recognize signs of suicidal thoughts and am willing to intervene.	1	2	3	4
17. I regularly assess my own behaviour patterns and beliefs and would seek professional assistance for any emotional dysfunction.	1	2	3	4
18. I accept the reality of aging and view it as an opportunity for positive change.	1	2	3	4
19. I accept the reality of death and view it as a normal and inevitable part of life.	1	2	3	4
20. I have made decisions about my own death to ensure that I die with dignity when the time comes.	1	2	3	4

Points ___________

STRESS MANAGEMENT

	Not true/ rarely	Somewhat true/ sometimes	Mostly true/ usually	Very true/ always
1. I accept the reality of change while maintaining the necessary stability in my daily activities.	1	2	3	4
2. I seek change when it is necessary or desirable to do so.	1	2	3	4
3. I know what stress-management services are offered on campus, through my employer, or in my community.	1	2	3	4
4. When necessary, I use the stress-management services to which I have access.	1	2	3	4
5. I employ stress-reduction practices in anticipation of stressful events, such as job interviews and final examinations.	1	2	3	4
6. I reevaluate the way in which I handled stressful events so that I can better cope with similar events in the future.	1	2	3	4

7. I turn to relatives and friends during periods of disruption in my life.	1	2	3	4
8. I avoid using alcohol or other drugs during periods of stress.	1	2	3	4
9. I refrain from behaving aggressively or abusively during periods of stress.	1	2	3	4
10. I sleep enough to maintain a high level of health and cope successfully with daily challenges.	1	2	3	4
11. I avoid sleeping excessively as a response to stressful change.	1	2	3	4
12. My diet is conducive to good health and stress management.	1	2	3	4
13. I participate in physical activity to relieve stress.	1	2	3	4
14. I practise stress-management skills, such as diaphragmatic breathing and yoga.	1	2	3	4
15. I manage my time effectively.	1	2	3	4

Points ___________

FITNESS

	Not true/ rarely	Somewhat true/ sometimes	Mostly true/ usually	Very true/ always
1. I participate in recreational and fitness activities both to minimize stress and to improve or maintain my level of physical fitness.	1	2	3	4
2. I select some recreational activities that are strenuous rather than sedentary in nature.	1	2	3	4
3. I include various types of aerobic conditioning activities among the wider array of recreational and fitness activities in which I engage.	1	2	3	4
4. I engage in aerobic activities with appropriate frequency, intensity, and duration to provide a training effect for my heart and lungs.	1	2	3	4
5. I routinely include strength-training activities among the wider array of fitness activities in which I engage.	1	2	3	4
6. I routinely vary the types of strength-training activities in which I participate in order to minimize injury and strengthen all of the important muscle groups.	1	2	3	4
7. I do exercises specifically designed to maintain joint range of motion.	1	2	3	4
8. I believe that recreational and fitness activities can help me improve my physical health and my emotional and social well-being.	1	2	3	4
9. I include a variety of fitness activities in my overall plan for physical fitness.	1	2	3	4
10. I take appropriate steps to avoid injuries when participating in recreational and fitness activities.	1	2	3	4
11. I seek appropriate treatment for all injuries that result from fitness activities.	1	2	3	4
12. I believe that older adults should undertake appropriately chosen fitness activities.	1	2	3	4
13. My body composition is consistent with a high level of health.	1	2	3	4
14. I warm up before beginning vigorous activity, and I cool down afterward.	1	2	3	4
15. I select properly designed and well-maintained equipment and clothing for each activity.	1	2	3	4

16. I avoid using performance-enhancing substances that are known to be dangerous and those whose influence on the body is not fully understood.	1	2	3	4
17. I sleep seven to eight hours daily.	1	2	3	4
18. I refrain from using over-the-counter sleep-inducing aids.	1	2	3	4
19. I follow sound dietary practices as an important adjunct to a health-enhancing physical activity program.	1	2	3	4
20. My current level of fitness allows me to participate fully and effortlessly in my daily activities.	1	2	3	4

Points __________

NUTRITION AND WEIGHT MANAGEMENT

	Not true/ rarely	Somewhat true/ sometimes	Mostly true/ usually	Very true/ always
1. I balance my caloric intake with my caloric expenditure.	1	2	3	4
2. I obtain the recommended number of servings from each of the food groups.	1	2	3	4
3. I select a wide variety of foods chosen from each of the food groups.	1	2	3	4
4. I understand the amount of a particular food that constitutes a single serving.	1	2	3	4
5. I often try new foods, particularly when I know them to be healthy.	1	2	3	4
6. I select breads, cereals, fresh fruits, and vegetables in preference to pastries, candies, soft drinks, and fruits canned in heavy syrup.	1	2	3	4
7. I limit the amount of sugar that I add to foods during preparation and at the table.	1	2	3	4
8. I consume an appropriate percentage of my total daily calories from carbohydrates.	1	2	3	4
9. I select primarily nonmeat sources of protein, such as peas, beans, and peanut butter, while limiting my consumption of red meat and high-fat dairy products.	1	2	3	4
10. I consume an appropriate percentage of my total daily calories from protein.	1	2	3	4
11. I select foods prepared with unsaturated vegetable oils while reducing my consumption of red meat, high-fat dairy products, and foods prepared with lard (animal fat) or butter.	1	2	3	4
12. I carefully limit the amount of fast food that I consume during a typical week.	1	2	3	4
13. I consume an appropriate percentage of my total daily calories from fat.	1	2	3	4
14. I select nutritious foods when I snack.	1	2	3	4
15. I limit my use of salt during food preparation and at the table.	1	2	3	4
16. I consume adequate amounts of fibre.	1	2	3	4
17. I routinely consider the nutrient density of individual food items when choosing foods.	1	2	3	4
18. I maintain my weight without reliance on over-the-counter or prescription diet pills.	1	2	3	4
19. I maintain my weight without reliance on fad diets or liquid weight-loss beverages.	1	2	3	4
20. I exercise regularly to help maintain my weight.	1	2	3	4

Points __________

ALCOHOL, TOBACCO, AND OTHER DRUG USE

	Not true/ rarely	Somewhat true/ sometimes	Mostly true/ usually	Very true/ always
1. I abstain or drink in moderation when offered alcoholic beverages.	1	2	3	4
2. I abstain from using illegal psychoactive (mind-altering) drugs.	1	2	3	4
3. I do not consume alcoholic beverages or psychoactive drugs rapidly or in large quantities.	1	2	3	4
4. I do not use alcohol or psychoactive drugs in a way that causes me to behave inappropriately.	1	2	3	4
5. My use of alcohol or other drugs does not compromise my academic performance.	1	2	3	4
6. I refrain from drinking alcoholic beverages or using psychoactive drugs when engaging in recreational activities that require strength, speed, or coordination.	1	2	3	4
7. I refrain from drinking alcoholic beverages while participating in occupational activities, regardless of the nature of those activities.	1	2	3	4
8. My use of alcohol or other drugs does not generate financial concerns for myself or for others.	1	2	3	4
9. I refrain from drinking alcohol or using psychoactive drugs when driving a motor vehicle or operating heavy equipment.	1	2	3	4
10. I do not drink alcohol or use psychoactive drugs when I am alone.	1	2	3	4
11. I avoid riding with people who have been drinking alcohol or using psychoactive drugs.	1	2	3	4
12. My use of alcohol or other drugs does not cause family dysfunction.	1	2	3	4
13. I do not use marijuana.	1	2	3	4
14. I do not use hallucinogens.	1	2	3	4
15. I do not use heroin or other illegal intravenous drugs.	1	2	3	4
16. I do not experience blackouts when I drink alcohol.	1	2	3	4
17. I do not become abusive or violent when I drink alcohol or use psychoactive drugs.	1	2	3	4
18. I use potentially addictive prescription medication in complete compliance with my physician's directions.	1	2	3	4
19. I do not smoke cigarettes.	1	2	3	4
20. I do not use tobacco products in any other form.	1	2	3	4
21. I minimize my exposure to secondhand smoke.	1	2	3	4
22. I am concerned about the effect that alcohol, tobacco, and other drug use is known to have on developing fetuses.	1	2	3	4
23. I am concerned about the effect that alcohol, tobacco, and other drug use is known to have on the health of other people.	1	2	3	4
24. I seek natural, health-enhancing highs rather than relying on alcohol, tobacco, and illegal drugs.	1	2	3	4
25. I take prescription medication only as instructed, and I use over-the-counter medication in accordance with directions.	1	2	3	4

Points ___________

DISEASE PREVENTION

	Not true/ rarely	Somewhat true/ sometimes	Mostly true/ usually	Very true/ always
1. My diet includes foods rich in phytochemicals.	1	2	3	4
2. My diet includes foods rich in folic acid.	1	2	3	4
3. My diet includes foods that are good sources of dietary fibre.	1	2	3	4
4. My diet is low in dietary cholesterol.	1	2	3	4
5. I follow food preparation practices that minimize the risk of food-borne illness.	1	2	3	4
6. I engage in regular physical activity and am able to control my weight effectively.	1	2	3	4
7. I do not use tobacco products.	1	2	3	4
8. I abstain from alcohol or drink only in moderation.	1	2	3	4
9. I do not use intravenously administered illegal drugs.	1	2	3	4
10. I use safer sex practices intended to minimize my risk of exposure to sexually transmitted infections, including HIV and HPV.	1	2	3	4
11. I take steps to limit my risk of exposure to the bacterium that causes Lyme disease and to the virus that causes hantavirus pulmonary syndrome.	1	2	3	4
12. I control my blood pressure with weight management and physical fitness activities.	1	2	3	4
13. I minimize my exposure to allergens, including those that trigger asthma attacks.	1	2	3	4
14. I wash my hands frequently and thoroughly.	1	2	3	4
15. I use preventive medical care services appropriately.	1	2	3	4
16. I use appropriate cancer self-screening practices, such as breast self-examination and testicular self-examination.	1	2	3	4
17. I know which chronic illnesses and diseases are part of my family history.	1	2	3	4
18. I know which inherited conditions are part of my family history and will seek preconceptional counselling regarding these conditions.	1	2	3	4
19. I am fully immunized against infectious diseases.	1	2	3	4
20. I take prescribed medications, particularly antibiotics, exactly as instructed by my physician.	1	2	3	4

Points ___________

SEXUAL HEALTH

	Not true/ rarely	Somewhat true/ sometimes	Mostly true/ usually	Very true/ always
1. I know how sexually transmitted infections are spread.	1	2	3	4
2. I can recognize the symptoms of sexually transmitted infections.	1	2	3	4
3. I know how sexually transmitted infection transmission can be prevented.	1	2	3	4
4. I know how safer sex practices reduce the risk of contracting sexually transmitted infections.	1	2	3	4
5. I follow safer sex practices.	1	2	3	4
6. I recognize the symptoms of premenstrual syndrome and understand how it is prevented and treated.	1	2	3	4
7. I recognize the symptoms of endometriosis and understand the relationship of its symptoms to hormonal cycles.	1	2	3	4
8. I understand the physiological basis of menopause and recognize that it is a normal part of the aging process in women.	1	2	3	4
9. I understand and accept the range of human sexual orientations.	1	2	3	4

10. I encourage the development of flexible sex roles (androgyny) in children.	1	2	3	4
11. I take a mature approach to dating and mate selection.	1	2	3	4
12. I recognize that marriage and other types of long-term relationships can be satisfying.	1	2	3	4
13. I recognize that a celibate lifestyle is appropriate and satisfying for some people.	1	2	3	4
14. I affirm the sexuality of older adults and am comfortable with its expression.	1	2	3	4
15. I am familiar with the advantages and disadvantages of a wide range of birth control methods.	1	2	3	4
16. I understand how each birth control method works and how effective it is.	1	2	3	4
17. I use my birth control method consistently and appropriately.	1	2	3	4
18. I am familiar with the wide range of procedures now available to treat infertility.	1	2	3	4
19. I accept that others may disagree with my feelings about pregnancy termination.	1	2	3	4
20. I am familiar with alternatives available to infertile couples, including adoption.	1	2	3	4

Points ___________

SAFETY PRACTICES AND VIOLENCE PREVENTION

	Not true/ rarely	**Somewhat true/ sometimes**	**Mostly true/ usually**	**Very true/ always**
1. I attempt to identify sources of risk or danger in each new setting or activity.	1	2	3	4
2. I learn proper procedures and precautions before undertaking new recreational or occupational activities.	1	2	3	4
3. I select appropriate clothing and equipment for all activities and maintain equipment in good working order.	1	2	3	4
4. I curtail my participation in activities when I am not feeling well or am distracted by other demands.	1	2	3	4
5. I repair dangerous conditions or report them to those responsible for maintenance.	1	2	3	4
6. I use common sense and observe the laws governing nonmotorized vehicles when I ride a bicycle.	1	2	3	4
7. I operate all motor vehicles as safely as possible, including using seat belts and other safety equipment.	1	2	3	4
8. I refrain from driving an automobile or boat when I have been drinking alcohol or taking drugs or medications.	1	2	3	4
9. I try to anticipate the risk of falling and maintain my environment to minimize this risk.	1	2	3	4
10. I maintain my environment to minimize the risk of fire, and I have a well-rehearsed plan to exit my residence in case of fire.	1	2	3	4
11. I am a competent swimmer and could save myself or rescue someone who was drowning.	1	2	3	4
12. I refrain from sexually aggressive behaviour toward my partner or others.	1	2	3	4
13. I would report an incident of sexual harassment or date rape whether or not I was the victim.	1	2	3	4
14. I would seek help from others if I were the victim or perpetrator of domestic violence.	1	2	3	4

15. I practise gun safety and encourage other gun owners to do so.	1	2	3	4
16. I drive at all times in a way that will minimize my risk of being carjacked.	1	2	3	4
17. I have taken steps to protect my home from intruders.	1	2	3	4
18. I use campus security services as much as possible when they are available.	1	2	3	4
19. I know what to do if I am being stalked.	1	2	3	4
20. I have a well-rehearsed plan to protect myself from the aggressive behaviour of other people in my place of residence.	1	2	3	4

Points ___________

HEALTH-CARE CONSUMERISM

	Not true/ rarely	Somewhat true/ sometimes	Mostly true/ usually	Very true/ always
1. I know how to obtain valid health information.	1	2	3	4
2. I accept health information that has been deemed valid by the established scientific community.	1	2	3	4
3. I am skeptical of claims that guarantee the effectiveness of a particular health-care service or product.	1	2	3	4
4. I am skeptical of practitioners or clinics who advertise or offer services at rates substantially lower than those charged by reputable providers.	1	2	3	4
5. I am not swayed by advertisements that present unhealthy behaviour in an attractive manner.	1	2	3	4
6. I can afford proper medical care, including hospitalization.	1	2	3	4
7. I can afford adequate extended coverage health insurance if necessary.	1	2	3	4
8. I understand the concept of publicly funded health-care plans.	1	2	3	4
9. I know how to select health-care providers who are highly qualified and appropriate for my current health-care needs.	1	2	3	4
10. I seek a second or third opinion when surgery or other costly therapies are recommended.	1	2	3	4
11. I have told my physician which hospital I would prefer to use should the need arise.	1	2	3	4
12. I understand my rights and responsibilities as a patient when admitted to a hospital.	1	2	3	4
13. I practise adequate self-care to reduce my health-care expenditures and my reliance on health-care providers.	1	2	3	4
14. I am open-minded about alternative health-care practices and support current efforts to determine their appropriate role in effective health care.	1	2	3	4
15. I have a well-established relationship with a pharmacist and have transmitted all necessary information regarding medication and use.	1	2	3	4
16. I carefully follow labels and directions when using health-care products, such as over-the-counter medications.	1	2	3	4
17. I finish all prescription medications as directed, rather than stopping use when symptoms subside.	1	2	3	4
18. I report to the appropriate agencies any providers of health-care services, information, or products that use deceptive advertising or fraudulent methods of operation.	1	2	3	4
19. I pursue my rights as fully as possible in matters of misrepresentation or consumer dissatisfaction.	1	2	3	4
20. I follow current health-care issues in the news and voice my opinion to my elected representatives.	1	2	3	4

Points ___________

ENVIRONMENTAL HEALTH

	Not true/ rarely	Somewhat true/ sometimes	Mostly true/ usually	Very true/ always
1. I avoid use of and exposure to pesticides as much as possible.	1	2	3	4
2. I avoid use of and exposure to herbicides as much as possible.	1	2	3	4
3. I am willing to spend the extra money and time required to obtain organically grown produce.	1	2	3	4
4. I reduce environmental pollutants by minimizing my use of the automobile.	1	2	3	4
5. I avoid the use of products that contribute to indoor air pollution.	1	2	3	4
6. I limit my exposure to ultraviolet radiation by avoiding excessive sun exposure.	1	2	3	4
7. I limit my exposure to radon gas by using a radon gas detector.	1	2	3	4
8. I limit my exposure to radiation by promptly eliminating radon gas within my home.	1	2	3	4
9. I limit my exposure to radiation by agreeing to undergo medical radiation procedures only when absolutely necessary for the diagnosis and treatment of an illness or disease.	1	2	3	4
10. I avoid the use of potentially unsafe water, particularly when travelling in a foreign country or when a municipal water supply or bottled water is unavailable.	1	2	3	4
11. I avoid noise pollution by limiting my exposure to loud noise or by using ear protection.	1	2	3	4
12. I avoid air pollution by carefully selecting the environments in which I live, work, and recreate.	1	2	3	4
13. I do not knowingly use or improperly dispose of personal care products that can harm the environment.	1	2	3	4
14. I reuse as many products as possible so that they can avoid the recycling bins for as long as possible.	1	2	3	4
15. I participate fully in my community's recycling efforts.	1	2	3	4
16. I encourage the increased use of recycled materials in the design and manufacturing of new products.	1	2	3	4
17. I dispose of residential toxic substances safely and properly.	1	2	3	4
18. I follow environmental issues in the news and voice my opinion to my elected representatives.	1	2	3	4
19. I am aware of and involved in environmental issues in my local area.	1	2	3	4
20. I perceive myself as a steward of the environment for the generations to come, rather than as a person with a right to use (and misuse) the environment to meet my immediate needs.	1	2	3	4

Points __________

YOUR TOTAL POINTS __________

INTERPRETATION

770–880 points

Congratulations! Your health behaviour is very supportive of high-level health. Continue to practise your positive health habits, and look for areas in which you can become even stronger. Encourage others to follow your example, and support their efforts in any way you can.

550–769 points

Good job! Your health behaviour is relatively supportive of high-level health. You scored well in several areas; however, you can improve in some ways. Identify your weak areas and chart a plan for behaviour change, as explained in Chapter 1. Then pay close attention as you learn more about health in the weeks ahead.

330–549 points

Caution! Your relatively low score indicates that your behaviour may be compromising your health. Review your responses to this assessment carefully, noting the areas in which you scored poorly. Then chart a detailed plan for behaviour change, as outlined in Chapter 1. Be sure to set realistic goals that you can work toward steadily as you complete this course.

Below 330

Red flag! Your low score suggests that your health behaviour is destructive. Immediate changes in your behaviour are needed to put you back on track. Review your responses to this assessment carefully. Then begin to make changes in the most critical areas, such as harmful alcohol or other drug use patterns. Seek help promptly for any difficulties that you are not prepared to deal with alone, such as domestic violence or suicidal thoughts. The information you read in this textbook and learn in this course could have a significant effect on your future health. Remember, it's not too late to improve your health!

TO CARRY THIS FURTHER . . .

Most of us can improve our health behaviour in a number of ways. We hope this assessment will help you identify areas in which you can make positive changes and serve as a motivator as you implement your plan for behaviour change (see Chapter 1). If you scored well, give yourself a pat on the back. If your score was not as high as you would have liked, take heart. This textbook and your instructor can help you get started on the road to wellness. Good luck!

Chapter **1**

Charting a Plan for Behaviour Change

Chapter Objectives

Upon completing this chapter, you should be able to

- Understand how your health affects your lifestyle.
- Recognize how the delivery of health care influences definitions of health.
- Suggest reasons health behaviour change is difficult, beyond those outlined in your text.
- Speculate on strategies for encouraging health behaviour change, and explain why health behaviour change is difficult.
- List Prochaska's six stages of change.
- Describe and compare the range of traditional and nontraditional students on your campus.
- Describe the developmental tasks of adulthood, and assess your current level of progress in mastering them.
- Monitor your own activities, and list the dimensions of health from which resources were drawn.
- Compare wellness and health promotion, noting both the differences and the similarities between the two concepts.
- Describe your text's definition of health, and compare it with definitions of episodic health care and health promotion.

Online Learning Centre Resources

www.mcgrawhill.ca/college/hahn

Log on to our Online Learning Centre (OLC) for access to Web links for study and exploration of health topics. Here are some examples of what you'll find:

- **www.yahoo.ca** Research hundreds of health-related links and use the Yahoo search engine to zero in on sites of interest.
- **www.canadian-health-network.ca** This government-sponsored Web site includes comprehensive links to information and support across a wide array of health issues. The 26 different health centres and their links are managed by responsible organizations in the health field from across Canada.
- **www.healthfinder.gov** Check out this gateway for consumer health and human services information from the U.S. government.
- **www.HealthAtoZ.com** Look here for a searchable database of health information sites that are rated for quality.

Media Pulse

Where Does our Health Information Come From?

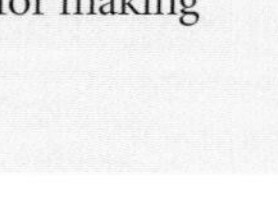

Today our health information comes from a variety of media—some more reliable than others. The following six media groups convey health-related information. Because Media Pulse will appear in each chapter of this text, this introduction is limited to an overview of these sources. Later chapters will deal with the important issue of which ones are good (in other words, valid and reliable) sources for learning about health.

Radio and Television

When you think of radio, the first thing that may come to mind is your favourite music. But two areas of radio are especially important for news and information: talk radio and the Canadian Broadcasting Corporation (CBC). Talk radio raises the question of validity of information. For example, if you're listening to a talk show about HIV exposure, the perceptions and opinions of the host (which may be strong or even extreme) are an important part of the show. When this point of view is combined with the opinions of callers, whose "facts" may come from unauthoritative sources, what you're hearing is probably not solid information. It's certainly not a good basis for making your health decisions.

Media Pulse *continued*

The CBC, on the other hand, takes a scholarly approach to news, featuring experts who do not always agree on an issue. In general, the news reports on CBC are long enough to present an in-depth, balanced treatment of health-related topics.

Newspapers and Magazines

Let's assume that most people read only one or two newspapers a day—their local paper and perhaps a national newspaper such as *The Globe and Mail* or the *National Post*. If so, the health information they are receiving is typically from wire services like the Associated Press or the Canadian Press; it is condensed and simplified but accurate within these limitations. When health-related information in newspapers is accompanied by illustrations and original source information (such as a professional journal), it is more helpful to the reader.

Unlike newspapers, magazines are so diverse in terms of ownership, intended audience, and standards of validity that it is difficult to determine the reliability of their health-related content. In general, the national news magazines, such as *Time* and *Maclean's*, are very careful about the accuracy of their reporting, often including primary (original) sources. Their content is considered "state of the art." In contrast, the checkout-lane tabloids, such as *The Globe* and *The National Enquirer*, are known for printing stories with "health" content that few readers take seriously. Between these two extremes is a wide array of general content magazines, such as *The Saturday Evening Post*, and health-oriented magazines, such as *Prevention*, that vary greatly in validity and reliability.

Professional Journals

Your college or university library probably offers a broad selection of professional journals. Through these publications, the members of an academic discipline share the latest developments and issues in their field with their colleagues and other readers. Because the study of health is so multifaceted, drawing on different disciplines for information, health-related journals are plentiful. The vast majority of articles that appear in publications such as *The New England Journal of Medicine* and *The Journal of the American Dietetic Association* are peer-reviewed. This means that professionals in the particular field review and judge the content of a submitted article to determine whether or not it should be published. Then, if a study being reported was not carefully controlled, or if its underlying theory seems to be flawed, the article is returned to the author(s) for refinement. This process greatly reduces the risk of publishing invalid information. Currently, journals are beginning to appear in fields such as complementary (alternative) health care. When reading such publications, you need to consider whether they are backed by a peer-review process.

Government Documents

Each year various departments of the federal government, particularly Health Canada, release the results of research being done under the oversight of its many divisions and agencies. These documents, such as *Toward a Healthy Future: Second Report on the Health of Canadians*,[1] become the source of much of the health-related news reported by other media sources, including textbooks

CHARTING A PLAN FOR BEHAVIOUR CHANGE

As you begin to study health, this is a good time to commit to a health behaviour change project. When thinking about making such a change, some students know exactly which behaviour they want to alter. Other students are uncertain about which behaviour to choose and need to do some self-assessment before they start (Figure 1–1).

Whether or not you think you know how you want to begin, it's a good idea to take the Comprehensive Health Assessment on p. xx. After you've finished the assessment and calculated your score, you'll know the areas in which you need the most improvement. Knowing that much will at least start to give you a focus. Then browse through this text and take a look at the Personal Assessments in each chapter. For example, if you are thinking about a behaviour change in weight management, see the Personal Assessment titled "Is It Time for a Weight-Loss Program?" on p. 133.

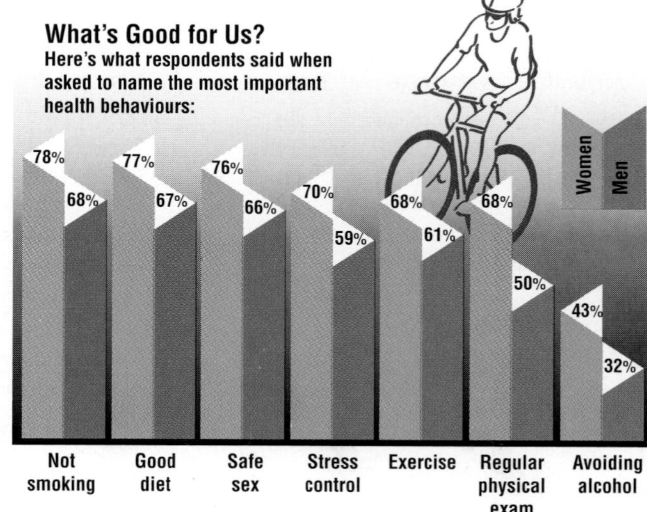

Figure 1–1 People have different ideas about what's good for our health. Which behaviours do you think are most important?

Media Pulse *continued*

and professional journals. These publications generally can be purchased from the government printing office. They are also available through urban public libraries and large university libraries. With few exceptions, the information in these publications is reviewed by the most respected authorities in each field.

Books

Books continue to be a vast source of information on health-related topics. Today's health books, in addition to academic health textbooks such as *Focus on Health*, fall into three categories: reference books, medical encyclopedias, and single-topic trade (retail) books.

Included in the category of reference books are important professional publications such as *The Merck Manual* and the *Physicians' Desk Reference*. These books, intended for professionals in various health fields, contain the most current information on specific aspects of health. Although these books can be purchased by the general public, their content is technical and complex, and their language is often difficult for nonprofessional readers to follow.

More valuable to the typical North American household are the various medical (health) encyclopedias, such as *The Johns Hopkins Home Medical Handbook* and *The Mayo Clinic Family Health Book*. Such books usually include a wide array of medical conditions and offer valuable information about health promotion and disease prevention. Their clear writing styles and highly valid information make these books excellent home references.

Single-topic health-related trade books, such as those about diets and health problems, are readily available from retail outlets like bookstores and the Internet. Like magazines, these books are difficult to assess because of their quantity and the varying backgrounds of the authors. Some are very sound in terms of content and philosophy. Others may be misleading and may contain advice that could be dangerous to your health. Included in this group are self-help books, the best-selling health books of all.

The Internet

Canadians are among the most "connected" in the world. Almost 70% of citizens have access to the Internet and they spend an average of nine hours per week on the Internet. In addition, 81% of Canadians consider the use of information technology by government to be a move in the right direction. Internet access is also available through libraries, educational institutions, and the workplace. With just a few clicks, you can reach many health-related Web sites that offer a wide range of health information. Chat rooms provide a forum for individuals to share their personal health experiences. Because the Internet is such an important source of health information for both professionals and the general public, this text highlights helpful Web sites in all chapters. To learn about criteria for assessing the validity and reliability of Internet information, see Chapter 15 (pp. 362–363).

TALKING POINTS • Would you be hesitant to talk to your doctor about health advice you found on the Internet? How would you approach the subject?

Some of the health behaviours students typically want to change are

- To gain or lose weight
- To stop smoking
- To stop using smokeless tobacco
- To eliminate or reduce caffeine consumption
- To develop better sleeping patterns
- To reduce levels of stress
- To improve physical fitness
- To reduce alcohol consumption
- To eat more nutritiously
- To develop more friendships
- To enhance the spiritual dimension of health

WHY BEHAVIOUR CHANGE IS OFTEN DIFFICULT

Several factors can strongly influence a person's desire to change high health-risk behaviours. Individuals must

1. Know that a particular behavioural pattern is clearly associated with (or even causes) a particular health problem. For example: Cigarette smoking is the primary cause of lung cancer.
2. Believe (accept) that their behavioural pattern will make (or has made) them susceptible to this particular health problem. For example: My cigarette smoking will significantly increase my risk of developing lung cancer.
3. Recognize that risk-reduction intervention strategies exist and that should they adopt these in a compliant manner they will reduce their risk for a particular health condition. For example: Smoking cessation programs exist, and following such a program could help me quit smoking.
4. Believe that benefits of newly adopted health-enhancing behaviours will be more reinforcing than the behaviours being given up. For example: The improved health, lowered risk, and freedom from dependence resulting from no longer smoking are

better than the temporary pleasures provided by smoking.

5. Feel that significant others in their lives truly want them to alter their high-risk health behaviours and will support their efforts. For example: My friends who are cigarette smokers will make a concerted effort to not smoke in my presence and will help me avoid being around people who smoke.

When one or more of the conditions listed above is not in place, the likelihood that individuals will be successful in reducing health-risk behaviours will be greatly diminished.

STAGES OF CHANGE

The process of behavioural change unfolds over time and progresses through defined stages.[2,3] James Prochaska, John Norcross, and Carol DiClemente outlined six predictable stages of change. They studied thousands of individuals who were changing long-standing problems such as alcohol abuse, smoking, and gambling. While these people used different strategies to change their behaviour, they all proceeded through six consistent stages of change in the process referred to as **Prochaska's stages of change**.[4]

Precontemplation Stage

The first stage of change is called *precontemplation*, during which a person might think about making a change, but ultimately finds it too difficult and avoids doing it. For example, during this phase a smoker might tell friends, "Eventually I will quit," but have no real intention of stopping within the next six months.

Contemplation Stage

For many, however, progress toward change begins as they move into a *contemplation* stage, during which they might develop the desire to change but have little understanding of how to go about it. Typically, they see themselves taking action within the next six months.

Preparation Stage

Following the contemplation stage, a *preparation* begins, during which change begins to appear to be not only desirable but possible as well. A smoker might begin making plans to quit during this stage, setting a quit date for the very near future (a few days to a month), and perhaps enrolling in a smoking cessation program.

Action Stage

Plans for change are implemented during the *action* stage, during which changes are made and sustained for a period of about six months.

Maintenance Stage

The fifth stage is the *maintenance* stage, during which new habits are consolidated and practised for an additional six months.

Termination Stage

The sixth and final stage is called *termination*, which refers to the point at which new habits are well established and so efforts to change are complete.

As you plan to change your behaviour, using the following 10-step program as a guide can be very helpful:

1. *Establish some baseline data about your behaviour. Baseline data* is information about your current health and behaviour that you can use later for comparison. For example, if you want to lose weight, weigh yourself for three consecutive days early in the morning to pinpoint your starting weight. If you plan to stop smoking, keep track of your smoking patterns for a few days. If you are changing your diet, write down everything you eat for three or four days in a row. It's also a good idea to keep a journal and record your activities and your feelings about the behaviour.
2. *Summarize your baseline data.* Identify any patterns you see. Accept this information as an accurate indicator of your current health behaviour. Use this text to find information about your behaviour that can help you plan behaviour-change strategies.
3. *Establish some specific goals.* Begin with small steps. For example, if you plan to lose weight, start out with a goal of losing half a kilogram (one pound) per week for the next three weeks. If you plan to stop smoking, begin by cutting down on your daily intake by five cigarettes. Try to make gradual progress toward your goals.
4. *Make a personal contract to accomplish your goals.* Write down both the starting and ending dates. To help you focus on specific activities for reaching your goals, use the Changing for the Better boxes found in each chapter. Identify any milestones along the way to your goal. Specify the time, personal resources, and energy you will need to commit to this project.
5. *Devise a plan of action.* As you develop your strategy, adjust your environment to help you replace old cues with new ones. For example, if you are trying to get more sleep, calm yourself before bedtime by reading rather than listening to loud music or watching a TV drama. If you want to improve your eating behaviour, change your walking route so that you avoid passing the campus snack bar.
6. *Chart your progress in your diary or journal.* From day 1, keep a record of how you are doing. Consider making this record visible. For instance, posting an eating record on the refrigerator door is a good motivator for some people.

Changing *for the Better*

The Importance of Risk Reduction

I find that I'm getting lazy about good health habits. How can I start to refocus my thoughts and actions on good health?

Prescriptions for good health usually place considerable importance on *risk reduction.* Health care professionals stress the importance of identifying behavioural patterns and biomedical indexes that suggest the potential for illness or death. Each of us has the opportunity to receive information, counselling, behaviour-change strategies, and medical therapies designed to lower our risk. The extent to which we act on this opportunity is our degree of *compliance.*

Some risk factors cannot be reduced. For example, gender, race, age, and genetic predisposition make developing certain conditions more likely. Being aware of these risk factors is important.

To refocus on good health, concentrate on these actions, which can reduce risk factors:

- *Refrain from using tobacco in any form.* This rule is so critically important that the surgeon general of the United States has identified smoking as the single most important reversible factor contributing to illness and early death.
- *If you drink alcohol, do so in moderation.* This is particularly important for people who must drive or operate machinery, women who are pregnant or planning to become pregnant, and people taking certain medications.
- *Engage in regular exercise designed to train the cardiorespiratory system as well as maintain muscle strength.* You can use a wide array of exercises as the basis of a fitness program, and you can develop specific programs around recommendations about frequency, duration, and intensity of activity.
- *Eat a balanced diet that includes a wide array of choices from each of the food groups.* Pay attention to the recommended amounts of carbohydrate, protein, and fat, as well as the specific food items that supply these three nutrients.
- *Develop effective coping techniques for use in moderating the effects of stress.* Effective coping can reduce the duration of physiological challenge the body faces during periods of unexpected change. Remember, however, that some forms of coping can themselves be sources of additional stress.
- *Maintain normal body weight.* Persons who are excessively overweight or underweight may experience abnormal structural or functional changes, predispose themselves to chronic illnesses, and unnecessarily shorten their lives. Lifelong weight management is preferable to intermittent periods of weight gain and loss.
- *Receive regular preventive health care from competent professionals.* This care should include routine screening and risk-reducing lifestyle management, early diagnosis, and effective treatment if needed.
- *Maintain an optimistic outlook.* Anger, cynicism, and a pessimistic outlook on life can erode the holistic basis on which high-level health is built. Several chronic conditions, including cardiovascular diseases and cancers, occur more frequently in individuals who lack a positive outlook on their own lives and life in general.
- *Establish a personally meaningful belief system.* Over the course of a long life the presence of such a system and the supportive faith community usually associated with it may prove to be the most beneficial health resource we will possess.

7. *Encourage your family and friends to help you.* Social support is important in any attempt at behaviour change. Your friends may want to join you and change their own behaviour. Then you can support each other. But some friends or family members might misunderstand your efforts. They might actually discourage you. If possible, avoid these people—at least while your project is under way.
8. *Set up a reward system.* Rewards tend to motivate people. They can be used to reinforce your positive changes. If you achieve success at a particular point in your plan, reward yourself with a special meal, new clothes, or a weekend trip. Pat yourself on the back occasionally for your efforts. Relish your success.
9. *Prepare for obstacles along the way.* No one who achieved anything of importance did it without a few setbacks, so prepare yourself mentally for an occasional obstacle. For example, if you neglect your fitness plan during a long holiday weekend, try to get back on course as soon as possible. Work through your setbacks with a "forgive and forget" attitude.
10. *Revise your plan as necessary.* Try to be flexible in your approach to behaviour change. A strategy that works for a while might not work as well after a month or two. So be prepared to reevaluate your goals and try new techniques when necessary.

Now that we've outlined a plan for behaviour change, let's determine why behaviour change is so difficult.

Key Term

Prochaska's stages of change
The six predictable stages—precontemplation, contemplation, preparation, action, maintenance, and termination—people go through in establishing new habits and patterns of behaviour.

HEALTH CONCERNS OF THE PRESENT DECADE

As we move further into the new millennium, traditionally defined health problems—heart disease, cancer, accidents, drug use, and mental illness—will continue to be important concerns. Environmental pollution, violence, health care costs, acquired immunodeficiency syndrome (AIDS), and sexually transmitted diseases will also continue to be significantly important. World hunger, population control, and the threat of terrorism involving nuclear and biological weapons will be great concerns for your generation and those to follow.

Many health conditions can be prevented or managed successfully. As you learn more about health, you'll find out how to lower your risk for many of them. Your behaviour is within your control, and the choices you make will certainly affect your health. Select a plan of healthy living that incorporates a sound diet, proper exercise, adequate rest, periodic medical checkups, and elimination (or moderation) of drug use (including tobacco and alcohol). This text is designed to provide you with the information and motivation to help you select the lifestyle that will make you a happy and healthy person.

DEFINITIONS OF HEALTH

What Is Health?

In the 1940s, the World Health Organization (WHO) defined health as "a complete state of physical, mental and social well being" and not simply "the absence of disease or infirmity." This was a controversial declaration, as the medical community at the time believed itself to be uniquely responsible for people's health, and naturally felt that it could not deliver on such a broad and inclusive definition. But is health something that should be the sole responsibility of medical practitioners and the health care system? It has only been fairly recently in the history of humankind that health has been seen as something that comes from a professional service.

Primitive societies believed that the spirits were responsible for health. Personal behaviour or failings might be suggested as the reason the spirits were displeased, and so the resolution of ill health required appealing to the spirits involved. Special elders such as witch doctors and shamans were summoned to those whose health was poor. Their treatments usually involved an elaborate ritual that invoked a strong belief in their power to appease the offended spirit. Modern medicine

Table 1–1 Life Expectancy[1]

	Life expectancy at birth, 2002			Life expectancy at age 65, 2002		
	Both sexes	Men	Women	Both sexes	Men	Women
		years			years	
Canada	**79.7**	**77.2**	**82.1**	**19.1**	**17.2**	**20.6**
Newfoundland and Labrador	78.3	75.7	80.9	17.6	15.8	19.3
Prince Edward Island	78.8	76.2	81.3	18.0	16.3	19.5
Nova Scotia	79.0	76.4	81.5	18.3	16.4	20.0
New Brunswick	79.3	76.5	82.0	18.5	16.6	20.2
Quebec	79.4	76.6	82.0	18.8	16.6	20.5
Ontario	80.1	77.7	82.2	19.1	17.5	20.6
Manitoba	78.7	76.2	81.1	18.8	16.9	20.4
Saskatchewan	79.1	76.3	82.0	19.1	16.8	21.2
Alberta	79.7	77.4	81.9	19.3	17.6	20.8
British Columbia	80.6	78.2	82.9	19.8	18.2	21.1
Yukon[2]	76.7	73.9	80.3	17.3	15.6	19.5
Northwest Territories[2]	75.8	73.2	79.6	16.2	14.5	19.2
Nunavut[2]	68.5	67.2	69.6	11.9	12.3	11.2

[1] Life expectancy is calculated from birth and death data that exclude the following: stillbirths; births and deaths of non-residents of Canada and residents of Canada whose province or territory of residence was unknown; and deaths for which the age of the decedent was unknown. The difference in life expectancy between men and women was calculated on unrounded figures.

[2] Life expectancy for Yukon, the Northwest Territories, and Nunavut should be interpreted with caution because of underlying counts of births and deaths.

and alternative therapies also include elaborate rituals such as tests and medication regimes that, in their own way, invoke a belief in the power of the intervention.

With industrialization, and the migration of huge numbers of people from rural farmlands to cities in order to work in the factories, health problems associated with overcrowding and an inadequate food supply became prominent. Infectious diseases such as cholera and typhoid spread readily due to a lack of clean water, poor sewage removal, and life in close quarters with people and animals. The growing trade between countries moved diseases from one to the other, usually starting in the port towns, then spreading across the nation. There was little understanding of the source of these infectious diseases. Miasma, or the mist (likely the odour!) that rose above bodies of water was commonly blamed.

The major health advances of the 18th and 19th centuries came from engineering innovations. Advances in the delivery of clean water and effective sewage control enabled populations in urban centres to avoid coming into contact with the pathogens that were so often fatal. Road building and the development of more sophisticated farming and food preservation techniques made it possible for larger amounts of safer food to be delivered to the cities at a lower cost. This allowed more people to have healthier diets, thereby strengthening their bodies against infection as well as preventing the diseases of malnutrition.

When the sources of infectious diseases were discovered in the early 1900s, it became easier to control the spread of disease, and public health became a major factor in human well-being. People were educated not to spit, to wash their hands after using the toilet, and to use care in preserving and preparing their food. But it was the adoption of vaccinations and, with WWII, the development of antibiotics that finally allowed Western society to gain control over the major causes of **morbidity** and **mortality**—infectious diseases such as tuberculosis, diphtheria, pneumonia, syphilis, and tetanus. Within the span of a lifetime, people could avoid or be cured of a disease that only recently may have killed others in their family. People began to expect that modern medicine could conquer any illness that came their way.

The medical approach to health that we are familiar with today is still very much embedded in the belief that there are single causes for most diseases and when we are not well, an expert, through tests, medications, surgery, or other intervention, can "fix it."

Through the middle of the 20th century, with the eradication of infectious diseases as major health concerns, chronic diseases such as cardiovascular disease and cancers became more prominent causes of illness and death. Research was unable to identify single causes, such as pathogens, underlying these diseases, but identified risk factors that appeared more frequently among those who fell ill than in those who stayed healthy. Many of these risk factors were within the realm of a person's "lifestyle." That is, they were consciously chosen behaviours, such as smoking, eating fatty foods, not exercising, etc. While the medical focus remained on treatment or management of these diseases (as you will see in Chapter 10, chronic diseases are not always curable), an emphasis on **health education** began to emerge. This education involved health agencies informing people about what behaviours are unhealthy and why.

Health education was relatively successful at improving the behaviours of those people in higher income and education brackets. They were able to read the brochures and posters, and to find ways to successfully change their behaviour. However, it has become clear that for many people, their behaviour is not entirely based on free choice. Nor is their failure to change behaviour due to a lack of motivation. It may be that the circumstances of their life make it very difficult to change. Table 1–1[5] shows the life expectancy Canadians currently enjoy at birth. The average of 77 to 82 years is much higher than at any other time in history.

The contemporary approach to health in Canada considers both medicine and personal behaviour as important, but also adds a third crucial element, the psychosocial environment. This "environment" includes your family, your friends and other social support, your neighbourhood, your education, your income, your feelings of self-worth, your job, your success at college or university, and your sense of the future, among others. Many of these factors are called *determinants of population health.*

In 1986, the WHO expanded its definition of health at the first International Conference on Health Promotion, held in Ottawa. Known as the Ottawa Charter, it stated

> [I]n order to reach a state of complete physical, mental and social well-being, an individual or group must be able to identify and realize aspirations, to satisfy needs,

Key Terms

morbidity
Illness or disease.

mortality
Death.

health education
A movement in which knowledge, practices, and values are transmitted to people for use in lengthening their lives, reducing the incidence of illness, and feeling better.

The State of Canada's Youth

Toward a Healthy Future: Second Report on the Health of Canadians summarizes the most current information we have on the health of Canadians and the factors that influence health. It suggests several priority areas for action; one of these is the need to invest in Canada's youth.

A number of things are going well for young Canadians. For example, youth volunteering has increased dramatically and the number of young women completing post-secondary levels of education is at its highest point ever. At the same time, *Toward a Healthy Future* alerts us to some conditions affecting the psychosocial well-being of Canada's youth.

Here are some of the highlights:

- In contrast to the high levels of physical health enjoyed by most young people, psychological well-being is, on average, lowest among this age group. Young Canadians aged 18 and 19 were the most likely to report high stress levels (37%) and to report being depressed. Young women aged 15 to 19 were the most likely of any age–sex group to show signs of depression (9%).
- The 1996 suicide rate of 19 per 100 000 among young men aged 15 to 19 was almost twice as high as the 1970 rate. Suicide rates among young men aged 20 to 24 were even higher (29 per 100 000). The suicide rate for Aboriginal youth is much higher than for their peers in the general population. As in the case of the population at large, young men are the most likely to commit suicide.
- Young women aged 12 to 17 are particularly vulnerable to sexual abuse by a family member or date. Young women aged 18 to 24 are most likely of all age groups to report being assaulted by an intimate partner.
- Despite recent high-profile events of youth violence, in 1997, the percentage of young people aged 12 to 17 charged with Criminal Code offences dropped 7% from the previous year. The 1997 rate, however, was still more than double that of a decade ago.
- Teenagers are the only age group in which smoking levels continue to increase. Young women aged 12 to 17 are more likely than young men the same age to smoke. Many of them report that they smoke to manage stress and control their weight.
- Underage drinking and the combined use of alcohol, tobacco, and cannabis increased dramatically between 1991 and 1998 in several provinces.
- In 1996–97, almost 50% of sexually active young people aged 20 to 24 and 40% of young people aged 15 to 19 reported an inconsistent or non-use of condoms.

> and to change or cope with the environment. Health is, therefore, seen as a resource for everyday life ... Health is a positive concept emphasizing social and personal resources, as well as physical capacities.[6]

There are additional ways of viewing health and the activities around it. If you asked a room full of people to define health, you'd probably get a variety of responses. Even the experts don't agree on this issue. This section explores the main approaches to this question—both traditional and nontraditional.

Episodic Medicine

When people become ill or are injured, they commonly visit a health care provider for diagnosis and treatment. They are experiencing an "episode" of unhealthyness. Once this period is over, they feel healthy again. Only in this context, therefore, health can be defined as *the absence of illness, disease, or injury*.

Preventive Medicine

In **preventive medicine,** patients who are well visit their physicians to identify any potential for illness. By using various tests, the physician attempts to identify and manage early indicators of risk. The goal is to prevent illness from occurring, delay its onset, or lessen its severity. This concept of **risk factor** reduction leads to defining health as *the absence of high-level risk for future illness or disease.*

Health Promotion and Prevention

Health promotion is a process of enabling people to increase control over and to improve their health. This can be accomplished through enabling people to take control over those things that determine their health. Health promotion involves educating people and developing their skills. It also includes social action, by which people work with each other to make a difference in their community. Finally, it involves activities at a much higher level, for example, policy and legislative changes, that make it possible for people to successfully achieve healthy living.

Prevention or preventive health care is often categorized into three levels. *Primary prevention* involves assisting people to develop or maintain behaviours that enable health. The goal is preventing or avoiding risk factors for chronic diseases.

Enabling people to alter their behaviours to healthy ones, often by identifying those at risk through screening processes, is called *secondary prevention.* In this level of prevention, the aim is to reduce the likelihood that an individual at high risk will progress to having one or more fully developed chronic diseases.

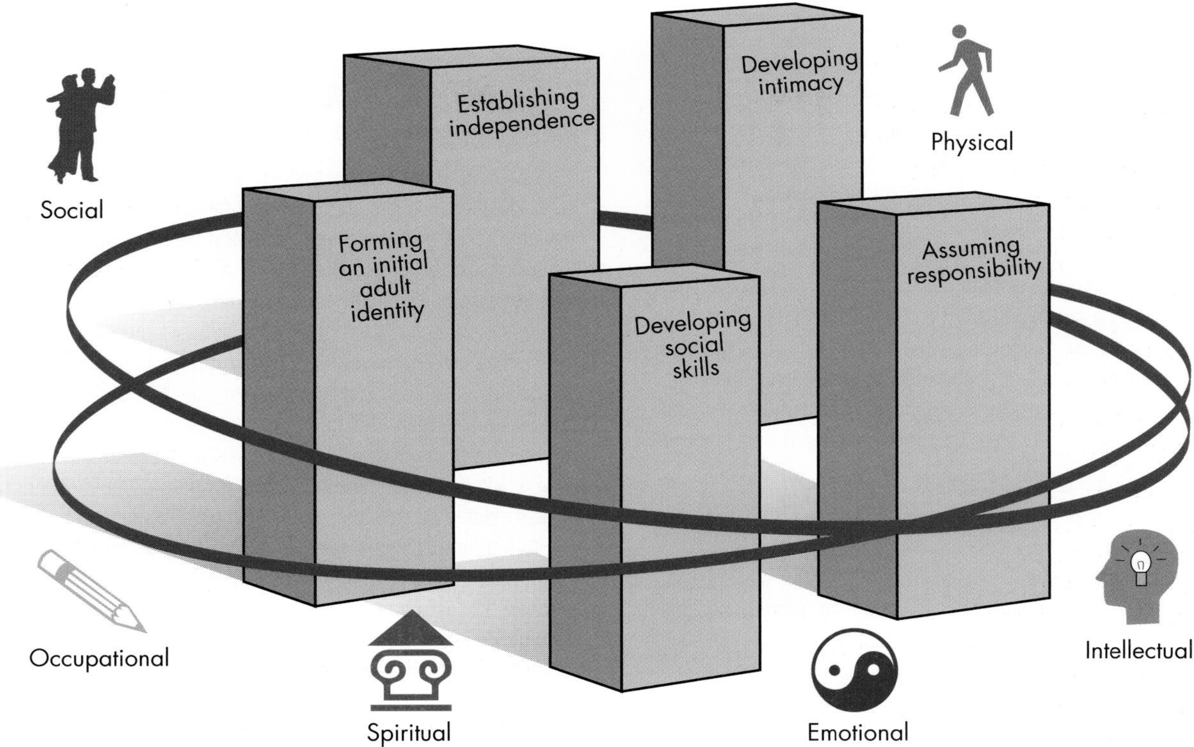

Figure 1–2 Mastery of the developmental tasks through a balanced involvement of the six dimensions of health will lead to your enjoying a more productive and satisfying life. Choose one developmental task you would like to focus on, such as assuming responsibility, and plan the steps you can follow to progress in this area.

Tertiary prevention involves helping to ensure that chronic diseases, once developed, do not progress further in an individual. This often involves rehabilitation and aggressive preventive measures aimed at risk factors and disease indicators.

DEVELOPMENTAL TASKS FOR TODAY'S POST-SECONDARY STUDENTS

Now that we've looked at different ways of defining health, it's time to consider the various aspects of your life that are made possible by high-level health. This is a multidimensional, or *holistic*, form of health that *empowers* you to grow and develop (Figure 1–2).

Whether you are a nontraditional-age or traditional-age student, the following are important questions to consider:

1. Compared with your friends, do you see yourself as a fully functioning adult? What new experiences do you need to reach that level and stay there?
2. How independent do you want to be in the future? What decisions do you need to make to reach that point?
3. What is your current level of responsibility—for yourself and for others? What must you do to expand that responsibility to the adult level?
4. Are you developing the social skills necessary to develop comfortable and productive relationships with others in a culturally diverse society?
5. What are your expectations for intimate relationships, such as marriage, long-term friendships, and mentor relationships? Can you handle the responsibilities necessary to sustain them?

Key Terms

preventive or prospective medicine
Physician-centred medical care in which areas of risk for chronic illnesses are identified so that they might be lowered.

risk factor
A biomedical index such as serum cholesterol level, or a behavioural pattern such as smoking, associated with a chronic illness.

health promotion
Movement in which knowledge, practices, and values are transmitted to people for use in lengthening their lives, reducing the incidence of illness, and feeling better.

Why Men Die Young

The extra longevity of women in our society is well established. In fact, the difference in life expectancy for male and female infants born today is projected to be 82 years for females, but only 77 for males. This five-year difference has commonly been attributed to genetic factors. However, new evidence demonstrates that this discrepancy may be affected more by male behaviour rather than genetic traits.

Men outrank women in all of the top 15 causes of death except for Alzheimer's disease. Men's death rates are twice as high for suicide, homicide, and cirrhosis of the liver. In every age group, American males have poorer health and higher risk of mortality than do females. Common increased risks include

- More men than women smoke.
- Men are twice as likely to be heavy drinkers, or to engage in other risky behaviours such as abusing drugs and driving without a seatbelt.
- More men work in dangerous settings than women, and men account for 90% of on-the-job fatalities.
- More men drive SUVs that are rollover prone, and suffer more fatalities in motorcycle accidents.

Perhaps some of these increased risks are associated with deep-seated cultural beliefs about men's bravery and machismo, which reward them for taking risks and facing danger head-on. This "macho" attitude seems to extend to the care that men take of their own physical and mental health. Women are twice as likely to visit their doctor on an annual basis and explore preventive medical treatments than are men. Men are more likely to ignore symptoms and less likely to schedule checkups or seek follow-up treatment. Psychologically, men tend to internalize their feelings or stressors, or even self-medicate to deal with stress, while women tend to seek psychological help. Almost all stress-related diseases are more common in men.

In the final analysis, men and women alike must be responsible for their own health and well-being. By making sound choices regarding diet, exercise, medical care, and **high-risk behaviours**, both genders can attempt to maximize the full potential of their life expectancy.

Today's college and university student population is diverse, with ages ranging from 18 to 40 and beyond. In fact, the rapidly growing percentage of nontraditional-age students is changing the sequence and duration of the traditional areas of growth and development. The lock-step progression toward adulthood that was seen among earlier generations of post-secondary students is giving way to a more flexible, nontraditional type of passage.

Of the five developmental tasks discussed here (Figure 1–2), the first four (involving the nurturing of one's adult identity, level of independence, level of responsibility, and social skill development) seem especially pertinent to the traditional-age college or university student. The remaining task, developing intimate relationships, often unfolds later.

Forming an Initial Adult Identity

During your youth, you were viewed by the adults in your neighbourhood or community as someone's son or daughter. That stage is rapidly passing. Both you and society are beginning to look at each other in new ways.

As a maturing adult, you'd probably like to present a unique identity to society. Internally, you're constructing a perception of yourself as the person you wish to be. Externally, you're forming the behavioural patterns to project this identity to others.

The completion of this first developmental task is necessary to have a productive and satisfying life. As you work toward achieving an adult identity, you'll eventually be able to answer the central question of young adulthood: "Who am I?" Many nontraditional-age students are also asking this question as they progress through post-secondary education.

Establishing Independence

During childhood and adolescence, the primary responsibility for socialization rests with the family. For many years your family was the primary contributor to your knowledge, values, and behaviour. By this time, however, you should be demonstrating an interest in moving away from that dependent relationship.

Travel, peer relationships, marriage, military service, and post-secondary education have been traditional avenues for disengagement from the family. Your ability and willingness to follow one or more of these paths will help you to establish your independence. Your success in these endeavours depends on your willingness to use the resources you have. You will need to draw on various strengths—physical, emotional, social, intellectual, spiritual, and occupational—to undertake the new experiences that will lead you to an increasing level of independence. In a sense, your family laid the foundation for the resources and experiences you will now use to draw yourself away from them.

Assuming Responsibility

Assuming increasing levels of responsibility is your third developmental task. The opportunity to assume responsibility can come from a variety of sources. You may sometimes accept responsibility voluntarily, such as when you join organizations or establish new friendships. Other responsibilities are placed on you by family members, professors, friends, dating partners, and employers. You may also accept responsibility for doing a particular task for the benefit of someone else, such as when you donate a unit of blood during a campus blood drive.

Developing Social Skills

A fourth developmental task seems especially relevant to traditional-age post-secondary students—developing appropriate and dependable social skills. The college or university experience has traditionally prepared students very well socially, but the interactions involved in friendships, work relationships, or parenting may require that you make an effort to refine a variety of social skills, including communication, listening, and conflict management.

Developing Intimate Relationships

After formal studies have been completed, the nearly universal developmental task of establishing one or more intimate relationships becomes important. When defined broadly, intimacy reflects open, deep, caring relationships between you and another in the context of true friendships, marriage or other close relationships, and mentor relationships in the workplace.

People vary in terms of the number of intimate relationships they engage in and the depth of those relationships. Some have several close relationships at the same time, while others seem interested in, or capable of, sustaining only one at a time. What is important is that each person have someone with whom to share close personal thoughts, feelings, and emotions. This connection is helpful throughout life but especially important in the later years, when isolation can become a significant problem.

Once familiar with the five developmental tasks, you will see considerable overlap in their accomplishment. For example, developing and refining your social skills can also enhance your independence from your family. Your willingness to accept increasing responsibility may influence your ability to develop an intimate relationship with someone.

Related Stages

Although not considered developmental tasks, two stages related to them need attention. The first stage, entering or advancing in a career or profession, is generally pursued in the years immediately following the completion of formal studies. Post-secondary coursework leading to an earned degree or diploma, strong recommendations from field-experienced supervisors, and a carefully nurtured network of people already in your field of interest are often required for opening doors into a chosen career path. Professions such as medicine and dentistry also require their own plan for the transition from student to practitioner.

Good physical health helps you develop all the other dimensions of your health.

The second stage is making parenting decisions. Regardless of one's ability or desire to reproduce, a wide range of decisions must be made by adults about their role in sustaining the next generation. These decisions may include planning to remain child-free, determining when to begin parenting, deciding on the number and spacing of children, and dealing with infertility. Considerations about adoption, foster care, parenting styles, and child-centred institutions and programs also fall within the scope of this dimension.

In the final analysis, these broad areas of personal growth and development that occur when most people are attending post-secondary institutions are intertwined with the overall quality of life. For this reason, the "new" definition of health presented here is based on the contribution health can make to the developmental tasks just discussed.

Key Term

high-risk health behaviour
A behavioural pattern, such as smoking, associated with a high risk of developing a chronic illness.

Health on the Web

Behaviour Change Activities

Following a Healthy Lifestyle

Students who take a personal health course usually want to improve their health behaviour. *Prevention* magazine offers an excellent general health Web site that addresses subjects such as health, weight loss and fitness, food, and community. The content varies, but it's always useful. Click on **www.prevention.com**, and choose a path that interests you.

Exploring Lifestyle Links

If you're seeking information on a multitude of lifestyle choices, this is the site for you. Topics include fitness, weight, exercise, food, nutrition, yoga, material arts, and sports clubs. Click on **www.wellness.com**, and choose Lifestyles to find links to each of these areas. Choose your favourite link and explore the topic in detail.[7]

HealthQuest Activities

www.mcgrawhill.ca/college/hahn

- Use the Wellboard to report your life score (number of years out of 114) and the score percentages for each of the six dimensions of health.
- Fill out the Wellboard using data from a fictional college or university student. On the first assessment screen, change the demographics to show how gender, ethnicity, age, marital status, and community affect average life expectancy.

THE ROLE OF HEALTH

Let's now consider a parallel role for health that complements the more traditional approaches. This role can be summarized in this way: The presence of health supports the activities that constitute your movement into, within, and through the areas of growth and development described. As a result, you feel increasing levels of personal competence, which is the basis for experiencing a meaningful sense of well-being.

THE MULTIPLE DIMENSIONS OF HEALTH

Your health comprises interacting, dynamic dimensions. By becoming familiar with these dimensions, you can recognize more easily what it is about your health that may or may not be helping you progress through the five developmental tasks. Because your health is dynamic, you can modify aspects of its dimensions to help you in your quest for well-being. A multidimensional concept of health (or **holistic health**) is a requirement for any definition of health that moves beyond the cure/prevention of illness and the postponement of death.

Your health is not static. The health you had yesterday no longer exists. The health you aspire to have next week or next year is not guaranteed. However, scientific evidence suggests that what you do today will help determine the quality of your future health. Let's briefly consider each of the six dimensions of health.

Physical Dimension

A number of physiological and structural characteristics—including your level of susceptibility to disease, body weight, visual ability, strength, coordination, level of endurance, and powers of recuperation—can help you participate in the experiences that form the basis of your growth and development. In certain situations the physical dimension of your health may be the most important. Perhaps this is why many authorities have traditionally equated health with the design and operation of the body and the absence of illness or a low level of risk for illness.

Emotional Dimension

Your emotional makeup can aid in your progress through the various growth areas. The emotional dimension of health includes the degree to which you are able to cope with stress, remain flexible, and compromise to resolve conflict. This dimension is most closely related to your feelings. How you feel about your family and friends, your life goals and ambitions, and your daily life situations is all tied to the emotional dimension of health.

Your growth and development can be associated with some vulnerability, which may lead to feelings of rejection and failure, reducing your overall productivity and satisfaction. People who consistently try to improve their emotional health appear to lead lives of greater enjoyment than those who let feelings of vulnerability overwhelm them or block their creativity. Specific techniques for improving your emotional health are presented in Chapter 2.

Social Dimension

Social ability is the third dimension of total health. Whether you identify it as social graces, skills, or insights, you probably have many strengths in this area. Because most of your growth and development has occurred in the presence of others, you can appreciate how this dimension of your health may become even more important in your future development.

The social abilities of many nontraditional-age students may already be firmly established. Entering a post-secondary institution may encourage them to develop new social skills that help them socialize with

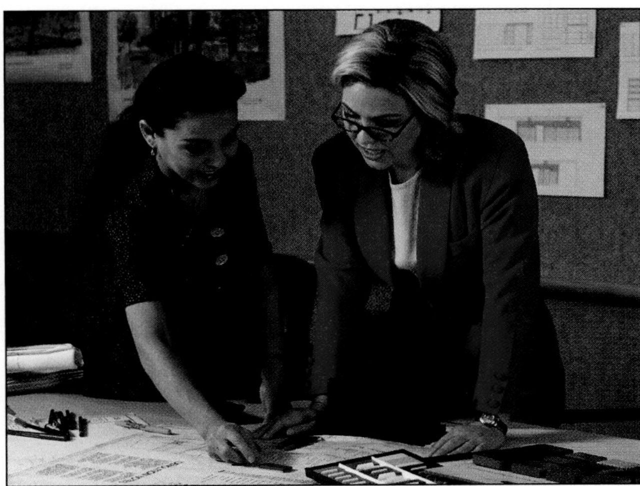

People who feel good about their work often have high self-esteem.

their traditional-age student colleagues. After being on campus for a while, nontraditional-age students often interact comfortably with traditional-age students in such diverse places as the classroom, the student centre, and the library. This type of interaction enhances the social dimension of health for both.

Intellectual Dimension

Your ability to process and act on information, clarify values and beliefs, and exercise your decision-making capacity is one of the most important aspects of total health. Coping skills, flexibility, or the knack of saying the right thing at the right time may not serve you as well as the ability to use information or understand a new idea. A refusal to grasp new information or undertake an analysis of your beliefs could hinder the degree of growth and development that your college or university experience can provide.

Spiritual Dimension

The fifth dimension of health is spiritual. Although you can include your religious beliefs and practices in this category, this discussion focuses on your relationship to other living things, the role of a spiritual direction in your life, the nature of human behaviour, and your willingness to serve others.

Many of today's students appear to be searching for a deeper understanding of the meaning of life. Although you may not feel uneasy about the nature of your spiritual beliefs, many students do feel anxious about the spiritual side of their lives. In fact, one explanation for the renewed interest in the spiritual dimension of health may stem from its value as a resource for lessening personal stress. The spiritual dimension is so significant that some health professionals believe it to be the actual core of wellness.

Exploring Your Spirituality
How Does Your Faith Affect Your Life?

Faith can include religious practice, but it can also be quite distinct from it. Faith is the most fundamental stage in the human quest for the meaning of life. It's a developing focus of the total person that gives purpose and meaning to life.

By the time people reach college or university age, their faith may have already placed them in uncomfortable situations. Taking seriously their responsibility for their own commitments, lifestyles, beliefs, and attitudes, they've had to make some difficult personal decisions. This demands objectivity and a certain amount of independence. It requires finding a balance between personal aspirations and a developing sense of service to others. Finally, the symbols and doctrines of faith must be translated into personalized spiritual concepts that become part of everyday living.

- Have you had any experiences that show you're growing in your faith?
- Do you consider yourself more spiritual or less spiritual than your friends or family members?
- What school-related experiences have affected the spiritual dimension of your health most powerfully?

Cultivating the spiritual side of your health may help you discover how you fit into this universe. You can enhance your spiritual health in a variety of ways, many of which involve opening yourself to new experiences with nature, art, body movement, or music. For many Canadians, the spiritual dimension of health is enhanced through an affiliation with an organized religion or belief system. For these people, the existence of a commonly shared doctrine describing the existence of God or an omnipotent Spirit, a familiar set of practices, and a sense of community with others helps provides meaningful answers to life's most profound questions (see the Exploring Your Spirituality box above). However, such religious affiliation is not essential to enjoying a meaningful spiritual life.

Occupational Dimension

The sixth dimension of health reflects the fact that employment satisfaction is directly related to health. When people feel good about their jobs, they tend to feel good about themselves and are more likely to have a healthier

Key Term

holistic health
A view of health in terms of its physical, emotional, social, intellectual, and spiritual makeup.

lifestyle. Usually, people have positive feelings about their employment situation if their jobs provide both external rewards (such as adequate salary and benefits) and internal rewards (such as positive social interactions and the opportunity for creative input).

Your future occupation will be linked to your future health status. Many colleges and universities have career counselling offices, where students can talk with professionals about career opportunities. Sometimes during career counselling, students undertake a series of psychological tests to help determine the kinds of jobs that match their personality profiles. Students can also learn about job opportunities in their major areas of study by talking with professors or from volunteer work, student employment or internships, and summer job experiences.

Wellness

Expanded perceptions of health are the basis for **wellness**. Recall that episodic health care, preventive medicine, and community health promotion are directly aligned with concerns over morbidity and mortality, while health promotion at the individual level is focused on aspects of appearance, weight management, body composition, and physical performance capabilities. Wellness differs from these kinds of health care because it has virtually no interest in morbidity and mortality.

Practitioners describe wellness as a process of extending information, counselling, assessment, and lifestyle modification strategies, leading to a desirable change in the recipients' overall lifestyle, or the adoption of a wellness lifestyle. Once adopted, the wellness lifestyle produces a sense of well-being (also called wellness) that in turn enables recipients to unlock their full potential.

This explanation of how wellness differs from episodic health care, preventive medicine, and health promotion does, on first hearing, seem progressive and clearly devoid of interest in morbidity and mortality concerns. But in practice, wellness programs are not all that different from other kinds of health care. Your authors have consistently noted that wellness programs, as carried out on college or university campuses, in local hospital wellness centres, and in corporate settings, routinely transmit familiar health-related information and engage in the same risk-reduction activities that characterize preventive medicine and health promotion. It is in the final aspect of wellness, the "unlocking of full potential," that wellness differs from other concepts of health. More than the absence of chronic illness, it involves achieving optimal health across all six of the dimensions of health discussed in the previous section.

A New Definition of Health

At the beginning of the chapter we asked you to consider a new way to view health—a view that would be far less centred in morbidity and mortality concerns than traditional concepts of health and even of wellness. The definition that we propose takes into account the differences between *what health is for* (its role) and *what health is* (its composition).

By combining the role of health with the composition of health, we offer a new definition of health that we believe is unique to this text:

> Health is a reflection of your ability to use the intrinsic and extrinsic resources related to each dimension of health to participate fully in the activities that contribute to your growth and development, with the goal of feeling a sense of well-being as you evaluate your progress through life.

In light of this definition, do not be surprised when your text asks whether you are resourceful (healthy) enough for the goals you wish to reach, or whether you are healthy enough to sustain a particular behavioural pattern that you have adopted, or whether you are experiencing the sense of well-being to which you aspire.

Key Term

wellness
The promotion and achievement of optimal health, including physical, emotional, social, spiritual, intellectual, and occupational well-being.

Taking Charge of Your Health

- Complete the Comprehensive Health Assessment on p. xx. Develop a plan to modify your behaviour in the areas in which you need improvement.
- Take part in a new spiritual activity, such as meditating, creating art or music, or appreciating nature.
- To promote the social dimension of your health, try to meet one new person each week during the semester.
- Choose one developmental task you would like to focus on, such as assuming responsibility, and plan the steps you can follow to progress in this area.
- Volunteer to be an assistant in a community service program, such as a literacy project or a preschool program.

SUMMARY

- Episodic medicine, preventive medicine, health promotion, and wellness have contributed to our traditional perceptions of health, which are based on morbidity and mortality and their consequences.
- Five important areas of growth and development await people ages 18 to 40, which increasingly characterizes today's post-secondary student population.
- A six-dimensional model of health is based on growth and development, and complements the traditional health models.
- Health is the ability to apply one's resources from the six dimensions to daily living, assuring growth, development, and a sense of well-being.

REVIEW QUESTIONS

1. What is the relationship between the term *episodic medicine* and our most familiar definition of health?
2. How are preventive medicine and health promotion similar? In what important way are they different?
3. What do the terms *morbidity* and *mortality* mean?
4. How does wellness differ from the other definitions of health discussed in this chapter?
5. What are the five areas of growth and development discussed in this text? How does each relate to the lives of people between ages 18 and 40?
6. What are the six dimensions of health? How do they relate to the composition of health as discussed in this text?
7. How does the term *multidimensional* apply to the concept of holistic health?

THINK ABOUT THIS...

- There is no perfect version of what an adult should be. From what you've heard other people say, what type of knowledge, attitudes, and activities characterize a successful, well-adjusted adult? What are your own intentions for adulthood in these areas?
- Few parents want their children to become so independent that all communication, particularly involving advice and various forms of support, would cease. If you are a traditional-age student, how do you think your family perceives your future level of independence? If you are a nontraditional-age student and parent, how have you fostered independence in your children while retaining important ties to them?
- Envision yourself in a conversation with the person who is soon to become your life partner. You are talking about the role of parenting in your partnership. What would you say about the number of children, the spacing between children, and the specific approach to rearing children that would be acceptable to you? If you should decide to be child-free, what would you say to others (including your future partner) if they suggest that your decision is based on selfishness or lack of self-confidence?
- A good friend shares with you his concerns about the possibility of never marrying (or being in a life partnership). Sensing that these concerns are genuine, and therefore extremely important, what would you tell your friend about the intimacy that can exist in other types of relationships?

REFERENCES

1. *Toward a healthy future: second report on the health of Canadians*, Charlottetown, P.E.I, Federal, Provincial and Territorial Advisory Committee on Population Health for the Meeting of the Ministers of Health, 1999.
2. Prochaska JO, Velicer WF: The transtheoretical model of health behavior change. *American Journal of Health Promotion.* 12:38–48, 1994.
3. Norcross JC, Prochaska JO: Using the stages of change. *Harvard Mental Health Letter.* 18(11):507, 2002.
4. Prochaska JO, Norcross JC, Clemente CC: *Changing for good.* William Morrow and Company, 1994.
5. Statistics Canada: Deaths, *The Daily*, **www.statscan.ca/Daily/English/040927/d040927a.htm**, September 27, 2004.
6. *The Ottawa charter for health promotion, 1986*, World Health Organization and Health and Welfare Canada, 1986.
7. Capacchione L: *The creative journal: the art of finding yourself* ed 2, New Page Books, 2001.

SUGGESTED READINGS

Angier N: *Woman: an intimate geography*, Boston, 1999, Houghton-Mifflin.

From unending praise to almost total rejection, this book elicits differing opinions about its blending of information from the biological sciences, cultural anthropology, evolutionary psychology, mythology, history, and other academic fields to explore the subject of being a woman. Even the author's writing style has been praised and criticized. You'll have to read it for yourself and see what you think.

Brown C: *Afterwards, you're a genius: faith, medicine, and the metaphysics of healing*, New York, 1998, Penguin.

In this highly regarded book, the author, who is a journalist, recounts his personal journey into the complex world where rational Western medicine, alternative medicine, and New Age healing interface. You're likely to find the author's uniquely personal and humorous writing style appealing, even if you question some of his conclusions.

Viorst J: *You're officially a grown-up: the graduate's guide to freedom, responsibility, happiness, personal hygiene, and the conquest of fear*, New York, 1999, Simon & Schuster.

This book is from the author of *Alexander and the Terrible, Horrible, No Good, Very Bad Day*. It's an everything-you-need-to-know guide to leaving adolescence and entering the world of adults. This witty book makes a great gift for the college or university graduate, regardless of age.

Focus on

THE DIVERSITY OF TODAY'S POST-SECONDARY STUDENTS

It's the fall of 1970, and you're about to meet a student in your first-year health class named Joe. Joe is an 18-year-old white man who graduated from high school last summer in the top half of his class. He lives in residence. Because his tuition is being paid by his parents, he can devote himself to his studies and college life on a full-time basis. When Joe looks around his health class, he sees some women and a few minorities and older students, but most of the students are much like himself. Joe is a typical student.

Flash forward to today. When you look around your health classroom, what kinds of students do you see? Students like Joe are probably still there, but they don't make up the overwhelming majority of the student body. The many changes in North American society that have taken place over the last 30 years are reflected in today's colleges and universities. Currently, slightly more women than men are graduating from university and college. As more older people find that they need better skills, more training, or a university degree or college diploma to keep their present jobs or find new ones, the average age of post-secondary students has risen. Also, schools are increasing their efforts in actively recruiting minority students.

Causes behind the Changes

Why are these changes occurring? Several factors seem to be affecting enrolment. Clearly, the changing climate of the economy has influenced enrolment. Corporate trends toward a more streamlined workforce and the gradual shift to a service-oriented marketplace have caused many workers to seek training for new careers or additional training for their current jobs. As a result, people who never thought they would see the inside of a classroom again are drawn back to school.

In response to the economic changes just described, colleges and universities have become more accessible in recent years. The trend toward open admissions, especially at community colleges, has opened the doors of higher education to those who otherwise might be held back by low high school grades or low test scores. Colleges are attempting to meet the needs of these new students with remedial courses and special programs designed to prepare them to meet strong academic standards.

Social changes have also played an important role in the changing demographics on college campuses. The Civil Rights movement of the 1950s and 1960s was instrumental in making post-secondary education available to minorities, and minority enrollment has increased as overall awareness of civil rights becomes more entrenched in society. Students with various physical disabilities are also finding it easier to obtain a college or university education.

As higher education has become more accessible, an attitude change about going to college has occurred. The feeling that everyone should continue to pursue education after high school is now more prevalent. Unfortunately, this emphasis on higher education has produced a cost to many important skilled trades, such as tool- and dye-making and construction. Students who might have once entered apprentice programs in these areas now feel compelled to seek a college or university degree.

Practical Implications of Diversity on Campus

With the rise of new populations on campuses, many practical changes have taken place to reflect the needs and interests of those students. For example, most colleges and universities now offer developmental education programs for students who need skill enhancement in reading, writing, and mathematics. Flexibility in the timing of course offerings is designed to accommodate the employment and parenting demands of nontraditional-age students. Many institutions also provide preschool centres for the children of parents who would otherwise find attendance more difficult or even impossible.

The post-secondary student population is also changing in terms of increased numbers of individuals of different racial backgrounds, ethnic groups, and national origin. In response to these developments, a wider range of courses in areas such as history, literature, fine arts, music, drama, and political science is reflected in course catalogues. Faculty composition is also diversifying; however, in some cases, the pool of qualified applicants is small in relation to demand. Campus libraries have expanded the diversity of their collections to accommodate the changing campus population. Likewise, campus bookstores offer a wider range of reading and musical selections. The increasing diversity of today's student bodies has also influenced the number and types of extracurricular offerings. Culturally diverse student associations, student political organizations, honour societies, and interest-based groups such as dance troupes are evident on many campuses. Greater accessibility to the Internet has brought even the most isolated campuses into the growing diversity that characterizes the population as a whole.

Changing Campuses and the Study of Health

Why mention the many changes taking place on campuses in a health text? Because of increasing diversity, students who are studying health (and most other disciplines) need to be aware of issues that affect students of different backgrounds. For example, many people are unaware of the fact that most pharmaceutical research is performed on men and then generalized to apply to women. This is a potentially dangerous practice because women are at greater risk for adverse drug reactions. Another example is the use of complementary (alternative) medical practitioners. Native Canadians view health care as a holistic, rather than a symptom-based, process. They are more likely to respond to a healer who looks at both the physical and spiritual person, than to a physician, who focuses only on the body. Knowledge of these and other related cultural health care issues will help students understand all members of our culturally diverse society.

Bringing cultural awareness into the health classroom introduces students to concepts they might not otherwise be exposed to. During your college or university career, you will encounter students from a variety of backgrounds. They may be young or old, rich or poor, from a rural or urban environment, or from an ethnic group different from yours. Just as your culture has its own unique health concerns, every other culture also has its own set of health concerns, and you need to be aware of them. *Focus on Health* will attempt to address the needs of students from different cultural backgrounds.

Part One

Chapter 2

Achieving Psychological Wellness

Chapter Objectives

Upon completing this chapter, you will be able to:

- Define the term *self-esteem* and describe how it applies to you.
- Describe the characteristics of psychologically healthy people.
- Define the term *emotional health* and explain how it relates to psychological health.
- Describe how humour can improve psychological health.
- Explain Maslow's hierarchy of needs and how it can apply to your daily activities.
- Describe strategies to enhance communication skills.
- Describe mood disorders, including the difference between having "the blues" and clinical depression.
- Describe anxiety disorders.
- Describe the characteristics of individuals who have developed their psychological wellness most fully.

Online Learning Centre Resources

www.mcgrawhill.ca/college/hahn

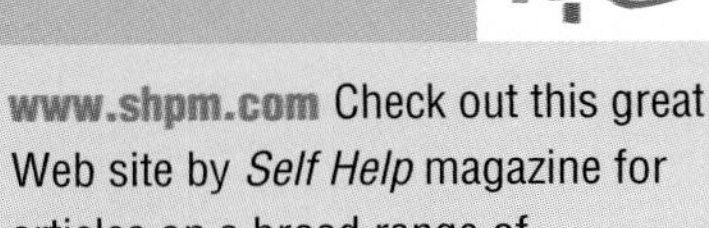

Log on to our Online Learning Centre (OLC) for access to Web links for study and exploration of health topics. Here are some examples of what you'll find:

- **www.cpa.ca** Click here for a link to the Canadian Psychological Association and information on mental disorders, treatment, and careers in psychology in Canada.
- **www.shpm.com** Check out this great Web site by *Self Help* magazine for articles on a broad range of emotional health topics.
- **www.suicideinfo.ca** Visit this site for information and resources on suicide and suicidal behaviour in Canada.

Media Pulse

Self-Help Books—Helpful or Hazardous?

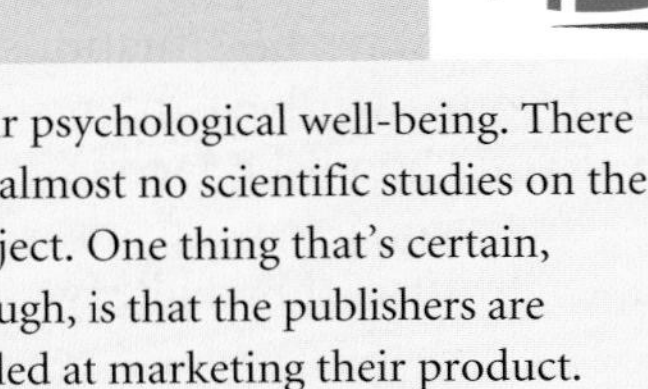

North Americans purchase thousands of self-help books each day. These books give them access to information that was once limited to a much smaller segment of the population, mainly professionals. There are hundreds of titles that focus on improving your psychological well-being. They offer advice on intimate relationships, coping with stress, gender-related issues, and building self-esteem. Many of these books have accompanying audiotapes, computer programs, and workbooks to complement the books' content. Workbooks that let readers chart their progress in changing their behaviour (by following the book's advice) are especially popular.

It's difficult to measure how effective self-help books are in assisting people to maintain or regain their psychological well-being. There are almost no scientific studies on the subject. One thing that's certain, though, is that the publishers are skilled at marketing their product. They know that the book titles need to be appealing; for example, *Awaken the Giant Within: How to Take Immediate Control of Your Mental, Emotional, and Financial Destiny* (by Anthony Robbins); and *Alter: A Simple Path to Emotional Wellness* (by Judy Curley). They also feature glowing summaries, such as this one for *Emotional Blackmail: When the People in Your Life Use Fear, Obligation, and Guilt to Manipulate You:*

> Susan Forward knows what pushes our hot buttons. Just as John Gray illuminates the communications gap between the sexes in *Men Are From Mars,*

Media Pulse *continued*

> *Women Are From Venus*, and Harriet Lerner describes an intricate dynamic in *The Dance of Anger*, so Susan Forward presents the anatomy of a relationship damaged by manipulation, and gives readers an arsenal of tools to fight back.

Publishers also highlight reviews by people who have read the book and tried its strategies. Here's one "reader's review" for the same book:

> An absolute MUST READ for everyone! Susan's book is fantastic. The information is priceless. I was trapped in a fog for many years, and after reading this book, my eyes opened WIDE. Now, I not only see how others manipulate with emotions, but also how I've manipulated myself! This should be a part of the infamous "Manual" we should get when we're born.

With this type of strong marketing and no objective way to measure how effective self-help books are, how can we judge their usefulness? The American Psychological Association (APA) says the answer is clear—we can't. After reviewing the limited research done on the subject, the APA presented these conclusions:

- Some self-help books on psychological wellness do appear to be helpful, based on anecdotal reports (reports based on personal experience, such as the one above), but why this should be so is unclear.
- There appears to be little relationship between the academic credentials of the authors and the effectiveness of their books, again based on anecdotal reports of helpfulness.
- There appears to be little relationship between successful clinically based approaches to enhancing psychological well-being and books designed to depict how to use these approaches in a nonclinical setting, such as the home or with friends or coworkers.

What all this means to you, the reader, is that you're truly on your own when browsing through self-help books at your favourite bookstore or checking out titles on the Internet. Does the author have good credentials and experience in his or her field? Is he or she affiliated with a respected university or organization? Of course, that's not everything—and certainly not a guarantee. But it's a good way to start.

People who are emotionally healthy have a high level of self-esteem. For them, social interaction is comfortable and rewarding. Adequate self-esteem is so important that it is sometimes equated with psychological wellness. But don't expect to feel personally fulfilled by everything. There will always be situations in which you must act against your own best interests for the sake of others. And if you should be faced with a serious health problem, your strong self-esteem will help you, but it won't completely offset this challenge.

CHARACTERISTICS OF A PSYCHOLOGICALLY WELL PERSON

A psychologically well person is one who is capable of using resources from each of the six dimensions of health (see Chapter 1) to feel good about life and other people. A more specific yardstick for measuring emotional health comes from the American National Mental Health Association. This group describes emotionally well people as having three fundamental characteristics:[1]

- They feel comfortable about themselves. They are not overwhelmed by their own feelings, and they can take many of life's disappointments in stride. They experience the full range of human emotions (for example, fear, anger, love, jealousy, guilt, and joy) but are not overcome by them.
- They interact well with other people. They are comfortable with others and are able to give and receive love. They are concerned about others' well-being and have relationships that are satisfying and lasting.
- They are able to meet the demands of life. Emotionally healthy people respond appropriately to their problems, accept responsibility, plan ahead without fearing the future, and are able to establish reachable goals.

The Canadian Mental Health Association (CMHA) believes mental health means striking a balance in all aspects of your life.[2] At times, you may tip the balance too much in one direction and have to find your footing again. Your personal balance will be unique, and your challenge will be to stay mentally healthy by keeping that balance.

It's important to realize that emotionally well people are not perfect. At times, they experience stress, frustration, self-doubt, failure, and rejection. What distinguishes the emotionally well person is resilience—the ability to recapture a sense of psychological wellness within a reasonable time after encountering a difficult situation.

EMOTIONAL AND PSYCHOLOGICAL WELLNESS

Is there a difference between emotional and psychological wellness? Many people don't think so. They believe that both reflect the absence of emotional illness and psychopathological conditions. However, other people think that emotional health refers specifically to the feelings people have in response to changes in their environment. These feelings, such as anger, jealousy, joy, disappointment, compassion, and sympathy, are familiar, healthy emotions. Responses to change vary from one person to the next and reflect each person's values. Emotionally healthy people feel good about their responses. Those who are less emotionally well feel negative about their responses.

In contrast to emotional health, some people think that psychological health refers more broadly to the development and functioning of a wide array of mental abilities, such as language, memory, perception, and awareness. For example, a person who believes he is being followed by government agents has faulty perception, so he would be considered not psychologically healthy. People who are psychologically healthy deal rationally with the world, have a fully functional personality, and resolve conflicts constructively. Finally, the psychophysical (mind-body) interface of the psychologically healthy person is sound.

Normal Range of Emotions

Do you know people who seem to be "up" all the time? These people appear to be confident, happy, and full of good feelings 24 hours a day. Although some people are like that, they are truly the exceptions. For most people, emotions are more like a roller-coaster ride. Sometimes they feel good about themselves and others, but other times nothing seems to go right. This is normal and healthy. Life has its ups and downs, and the concept of the "normal range of emotions" reflects these changes.

Self-Esteem

The key to overall psychological wellness is self-esteem. When people have positive self-esteem, they feel comfortable in social situations and with their own thoughts and feelings. They get along with others, cope in stressful situations, and make contributions when they work with others. Strong self-esteem may offset self-defeating or self-destructive behaviour problems. For example, a young woman who is slightly overweight but has high self-esteem would be unlikely to go on an unhealthy crash diet to conform to the currently fashionable thin body image. As you will see when you complete the Personal Assessment on p. 35, people with high levels of self-esteem find a comfortable balance between their idealized self and where they actually are.

Health on the Web
Behaviour Change Activities

Get a Grip on Depression

The bad news: Only a small percentage of depressed people ever seek help. The good news: Those who do enjoy a high rate of success with appropriate treatment. Visit **www.canmat.org** for further information on depression.

Expressing creativity helps people improve their self-esteem.

For some people, lack of self-esteem is understandable. Growing up in a dysfunctional household, being influenced by excessive feelings of guilt, and failing in early undertakings can all damage feelings of self-worth.

The foundation of positive self-esteem can be traced to childhood.[3] Interactions that young children experience can create powerful messages about their self-worth. Warm and supportive physical and emotional contact, communication that emphasizes talking "with" rather than "to" the child, and gradual loosening of control so that more and more decisions are made by the child tell children that they are competent and valued. Children's emerging self-esteem, then, is strongly influenced by their parents' behaviour. Children from less supportive or overly protective home environments will eventually seek positive feedback from other sources.

As important as parents and others (including peers) are to the development of self-esteem in children, people eventually become responsible for enhancing their own self-esteem. The extent to which people wish to nurture their self-esteem varies. However, many want to take an active role in developing a more solid sense of self-worth.

Hardiness

Hardiness and self-esteem work together to ensure psychological wellness.[4] Hardiness exists when a person consistently shows three important traits. First, hardy people possess a high level of *commitment* to something or someone; this commitment is the basis for their value orientation and sense of purpose in life. Maintaining this sense of commitment provides structure and direction, even in the face of a wide variety of stressors (see Chapter 3). Second, a sense of *control* characterizes hardy people. By possessing the ability to orchestrate the events in their lives, hardy people reduce their chance of feeling helpless and vulnerable when change is imposed from outside. Third, hardy people welcome *challenge*. They have the ability to take control of change and shape it to enhance their personal growth and fulfillment.

Hardiness may be more common among some types of people than others. Nevertheless, a high level of hardiness can be developed by focusing on signals from the body, assessing and responding to previous stressors, and engaging in activities that strengthen commitment, control, and challenge.

CHALLENGES TO PSYCHOLOGICAL WELLNESS

In spite of their best efforts to be hardy and resilient, many people have a less than optimal level of psychological wellness. Depression is the most common and one of the most treatable of these dysfunctional emotional states. Loneliness, shyness, and thoughts of suicide are also challenges to high-level psychological wellness. Although this chapter focuses on psychological well-being rather than emotional illness, it's important to examine these problem conditions. At some time during our lives, most of us will either have emotional problems ourselves or know someone who is experiencing them.

Depression

Depression is an emotional state characterized by feelings of sadness, melancholy, dejection, worthlessness, emptiness, and hopelessness that are inappropriate and out of proportion to reality.[5] The common symptoms of depression are listed in the Star Box below. One key indicator of depression is the long-term presence of some of these symptoms. Everyone feels down or blue at times, but depression is characterized by a chronic state of feeling low (see the Changing for the Better box on p. 23).

Common Symptoms of Depression

Any of the following may be indications of depression:

- Persistent sad moods
- Feelings of hopelessness or pessimism
- Loss of interest or pleasure in ordinary activities, including sex
- Sleep and eating disorders
- Restlessness, irritability, or fatigue
- Difficulty concentrating, remembering, or making decisions
- Thoughts of death or suicide
- Persistent physical symptoms or pains that do not respond to treatment

At any given time almost three million Canadians suffer from depression, but less than one-third of them seek help.[6] People with depression commonly have a number of compounding problems, including family problems and difficulty with social relationships. Depression is a common factor related to most suicides.

Types of depression

According to mental health experts, there are two main types of depression. When depression develops after a period of difficulty, such as a divorce or loss of a job, it is called *secondary* or *reactive depression*. However, when depression begins for no apparent reason, it is called *primary depression* and is caused by changes in brain chemistry. When taken in combination, these two forms of depression are incapacitating enough to be classified as *major depression*. The duration and depth of major depression is in contrast to a condition characterized by chronic periods of "blueness" that is clinically labelled as *dysthymia*. Both forms of major depression can be successfully treated through a combination of approaches, and recovery within two years is not uncommon, although never assured.

Today, the most effective treatments for major depression are psychotherapy and antidepressant medications. The psychotherapy model of choice is usually a form of cognitive-based therapy (CBT), in which the depressed person learns how to recognize and deal with life situations in a constructive fashion. Drug therapy typically involves one or more of four classes of antidepressive medications: monoamine oxidase (MAO) inhibitors, tricyclic antidepressants, selective serotonin reuptake inhibitors (SSRIs) such as Prozac, and the new serotonin/norepinephrine reuptake inhibitors such as Serzone and Effexor.[7] Research indicates that both psychotherapy and antidepressants can be effective when used alone or in combination. This contrasts with the heavy reliance on antidepressive medication alone favoured during the past decade.[8]

Only a small percentage (about 33%) of depressed people ever seek help.[9] This is unfortunate in light of the high rate of successful treatment. The Changing for the Better box on p. 23 lists several resources for people with depression.

Some people try to treat their depression by taking over-the-counter substances such as St. John's wort. This popular form of self-treatment should be viewed with caution and should be used only after consultation with your physician (see Star Box on p. 24). Exercise and activity level also play a significant role in alleviating and insulating people from depression. Again it seems that the endorphin levels and effects on brain chemistry and hormonal levels are part of the explanation for why this is a powerful antidote for depression.

Changing *for the Better*

Taking the First Step in Fighting Depression

Making the transition to university has been very tough for me. I feel down a lot, and I'm starting to think I'll never get rid of this feeling. Where do I go for help?

- Seek help from your university health centre, personal physician, or community health centre.
- Try your university mental health counselling and treatment programs.
- Family and social service agencies can identify mental health specialists.
- Check the telephone book for private psychologists or psychiatric clinics.
- Talk with a trusted professor.
- Contact one of the organizations listed below.

Canadian Mental Health Association
8 King St. E., Suite 810
Toronto, ON M5C 1B5
Tel: (416) 484-7750 Fax: (416) 484-4617
Email: info@cmha.ca
Web site: **www.cmha.ca**

Centre for Addiction and Mental Health
33 Russell Street
Toronto, ON M5S 2S1
Tel: 1-800-463-6273 in Ontario or (416) 595-6111
Email: public_affairs@camh.net
Web site: **www.camh.net**

Canadian Psychological Association
141 Laurier Ave. W., Suite 702
Ottawa, ON K1P 5J3
Tel: 1-888-472-0657 or (613) 237-2144
Email: cpa@cpa.ca
Web site: **www.cpa.ca**

For additional information on mental health, disorders, online diagnostic tools, research information, resources, and links, check out this site provided by Canadian psychiatrist Dr. Phillip Long:

Internet Mental Health
www.mentalhealth.com

Electroconvulsive Therapy (ECT) as Another Treatment for Depression

Electroconvulsive therapy (ECT) is another form of treatment for depression. While ECT had fallen out of favour in the past 25 years (due in part to depictions of it in the film *One Flew over the Cuckoo's Nest*), it has recently regained popularity. The procedure involves delivering a 90-volt burst of electricity, equal to the electricity in a 40-watt light bulb, to the brain for about a minute, causing a grand mal seizure. The patient is under anesthesia and receives muscle relaxants prior to administering the shock, and the heart rate and oxygen level are constantly monitored during the treatment. Most patients receive three ECT treatments each week, for a total of six to twelve sessions. Proponents of ECT claim that shock treatments produce positive treatment effects for depression when no other antidepressant or treatment regime has worked. Critics of ECT say that it causes brain damage and memory loss, and that the decrease in depressive symptoms is only temporary.[10] Although ECT has been used for the past 60 years, no one knows exactly how it works or why it alleviates depression.

Loneliness

Many depressed people display signs of loneliness, but loneliness is not always associated with depression. People are said to be lonely if they want close personal relationships but cannot establish them. It's possible to feel isolated and friendless even when you are around many people every day. In fact, loneliness is common among post-secondary students.

The difference between "being alone" and "feeling lonely" is important. Many people enjoy being alone occasionally to relax, exercise, read, enjoy music, or just think. These people can appreciate being alone, but they can also interact comfortably with others when they wish. However, when being alone or isolated is not enjoyable and seeking close relationships is very difficult, loneliness can produce serious feelings of rejection.

One unfortunate aspect of loneliness is that it tends to continue in people year after year unless they actively try to change it. Chronically lonely people frequently cope with their loneliness by becoming consumed by their occupations or by adopting habit-forming behaviours that increase their sense of loneliness (such as drinking alcohol).

Fortunately, there are successful techniques to help most lonely people. Counselling can help them change how they think about themselves when they interact with others. Another technique involves teaching people important social skills, such as starting a conversation, taking social risks, and introducing themselves. Through social skills training, people can also learn how to talk comfortably on the telephone, give and receive compliments, and enhance their appearance. If you need help in this area, contact your campus counselling centre or health centre.

Healing from Depression Naturally

One of the most popular reasons Canadians turn to the use of complementary medicine is for the treatment of depression.[11] Treatments such as herbal remedies, massage therapy, the healing touch, and acupuncture, once called "alternative medicine," are now labelled "complementary." This term is used because these treatments are used to complement traditional medicine, not to replace it.

There exists a great variety of such treatments, which are increasingly popular alternatives to traditional medical approaches. During a 1996 psychiatry symposium on alternative medicine, Dr. Jacques Bradwejn explained that 20% of people suffering from depression sought complementary treatments. He wasn't just talking about St. John's wort, an herbal remedy sometimes used to treat mild depression.

Alternative therapies that are not conventional treatments can be used to treat illness, and in some cases have good results. However, these results must be viewed with caution. Dr. Sagar Parikh, head of the Bipolar Unit at the Centre for Addiction and Mental Health in Toronto, says that some studies measuring the effect of exercise and acupuncture on depression may not be applying DSM-IV (*Diagnostic and Statistical Manual of Mental Disorders, 4th edition*) standards. The alternative evaluation methods may not be rigorous enough, says Dr. Parikh.[12] Also, Health Canada has warned physicians that St. John's wort could seriously alter or diminish the effectiveness of prescription medications.[13]

Benefits of complementary therapies are often reported and should not be discounted. Yet people should be encouraged not to abandon conventional methods that in the past have proven helpful. The use of nonsynthetic or "natural" remedies should be reported to and monitored by a physician.[14] In randomized trials, the use of St. John's wort to treat mild to moderate depression was found to be more effective than a placebo, as reported by the *British Medical Journal*.

Although we do not know exactly how St. John's wort works, we do know that it does have side effects. Consumers should also be aware that Canadian health authorities do not regulate the purity of medicinal ingredients in herbal remedies. There is a great variation in active ingredients in at least 10 brands, indicating overall unreliability in such over-the-counter herbal products. Wampole Canada Inc., in a study of 10 brands, showed that only three brands contained 0.3% of the necessary active ingredient, *hypericin*.[15]

Because of this lack of regulation of natural health products, a new Office of Natural Products is being established by Health Canada.[16] This new office will provide Canadian consumers with the assurance of safety, while enhancing consumer access to a full range of health products.

Shyness

Is loneliness the result of an inability to interact comfortably with others, something brought about by shyness? If so, why are some people so shy? Some argue that shyness is a genetic part of a person's temperament. They believe that shy people do not want to be shy, have not been conditioned to avoid contact with others, and have not had unpleasant experiences with others. Instead, they are genetically programmed to feel uncomfortable with other people. So shy people cope by avoiding such situations. Even if shyness is a genetic trait, social skills counselling and training can help those who are shy. Today, clinicians label shyness as *social anxiety*. When identified as a component of "type D" personality, shyness may play a role in the progression of some forms of cardiovascular disease.[17]

Suicide

Among the university-aged population, suicide is the third leading cause of death (accidents and homicide are first and second, respectively). In Canada a total of 3681 people committed suicide in 1997, down 6.6% from the previous year. In the last decade, the number of suicides in Canada has fluctuated between a low of 3379 in 1990 and a high of 3970 in 1995.

What separates the potentially suicidal person from the nonsuicidal person is the degree of despair and depression the person feels and the person's ability to cope with it. Suicidal people tend to become overwhelmed by a range of destructive emotions, including anxiety, anger, loneliness, loss of self-esteem, and hopelessness. They may believe that death is the only solution to all of their problems.

The majority of suicidal people have depressive disorders and feel helpless and powerless over their lives. They say things like "I just want the pain to stop" and don't see any other options available to them. There are some risk factors associated with suicidal behaviour such as having:

- Little to no support system
- Made previous suicide attempts
- A family history of mental illness, including substance abuse
- A family history of suicide
- Problems with drugs or alcohol
- Possession of a firearm
- Exposure to suicidal behaviour of others, including through the media

Some college and university students have committed suicide in a mistaken attempt to resolve academic failure, relationship difficulties, or problems of unemployment. This "solution" is tragic for them and for their families and friends.

Suicide prevention

Many communities currently recognize the need to provide or expand suicide prevention services. Most suicide prevention centres operate 24-hour hotlines and are staffed through volunteer agencies, mental health centres, public health departments, or hospitals. Staff members have extensive training in the counselling skills required to deal with suicidal people. Phone numbers for these services can be found in the telephone directory.

It is critically important to be alert for signs suggesting suicidal tendencies in the people you know. A family member, friend, or residence hall neighbour should be guided toward professional intervention if signs of suicidal intentions begin to cluster in a short time. Any combination of changes in appetite, sleep patterns, concentration, and routine activities should be noted. In addition, increases in agitation, social withdrawal, feelings of hopelessness and self-reproach, and guilt are also cause for concern. A person who is openly talking about or planning a suicide; giving away prized possessions, suggesting that he or she is no longer loved and supported by others, or experiencing extreme humiliation should be called to the attention of intervention experts immediately.

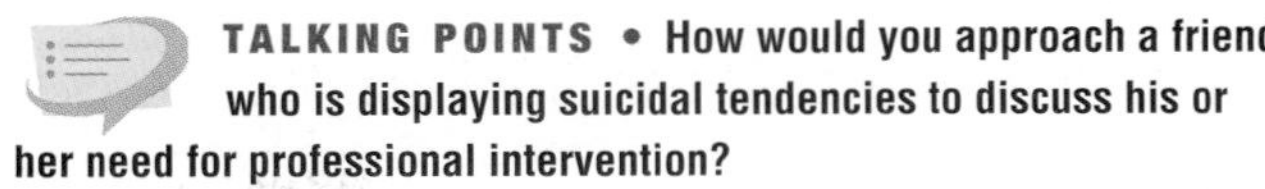

TALKING POINTS • How would you approach a friend who is displaying suicidal tendencies to discuss his or her need for professional intervention?

ANXIETY DISORDERS

While everyone tends to feel nervous or worry about something at some point in their lives, people with anxiety disorders feel anxious most, if not all, of the time. They also feel out of control and powerless to alleviate their anxiety, and tend to worry about becoming anxious, so their anxiety causes them even greater anxiety. Anxiety is related to fear and is part of daily life. Some anxiety can even be helpful and motivating at times. Anxiety is a physiological, adaptive response to danger or potential threat and can enhance performance and keep us out of harm's way. In Chapter 3, we will discuss the flight or fight response and how the stress response is related to anxiety. Anxiety disorders are differentiated from daily stress because the stress is

- Intense, often debilitating; people sometimes think they are going to die
- Long-lasting, persisting after the danger or stressful event has passed
- Dysfunctional, causing significant interference in life

Anxiety disorders include **generalized anxiety disorder (GAD)**, **obsessive-compulsive disorder (OCD)**, post-traumatic stress disorder, **panic disorder**, and phobias such as the **social phobia**. Anxiety disorders

The Do's and Don'ts of Suicide Intervention

Don't ...

1. **Avoid talking about suicide or dance around the topic.** Talking about suicide doesn't upset people more. In fact, often people who are thinking about killing themselves say it is a relief to talk about it and it helps them to let go of this idea, not pursue it further.
2. **Be judgmental or argumentative.** Now is not the time to debate the morality of suicide—you will lose the debate and possibly the person.
3. **Assume that the person is not serious.** Saying "You're not serious" or "You don't mean that" may inadvertently encourage the person to show you how serious she or he truly is.
4. **Argue.** Telling a suicidal person that things aren't that bad, or that other people have it worse, can make them feel worse about themselves and guilty about their feelings of unhappiness.
5. **Promise not to tell anyone.** If you keep this promise and something happens to this person, how will you feel?

Do ...

1. **Remain calm.** Talk about the person's feelings of sadness and helplessness.
2. **Offer support and assistance.** Tell the person he or she is not alone.
3. **Encourage problem solving and taking positive steps.**
4. **Emphasize the temporary nature of the problem.** Suicide is a permanent solution to a temporary problem.
5. **Seek help and don't try to handle this problem on your own.** This might involve the person's family, religious advisor, friends, teachers, or a mental health agency.
6. **Make a no-suicide contract.** Ask the person to promise not to hurt or kill him- or herself.
7. **If possible, stay with the person until you can get further assistance.**

affect 12% of Canadians, approximately 16% of females and 9% of males.[18] There is a genetic component associated with developing an anxiety disorder as studies suggest that you are more likely to develop one if your parents have one. Certainly, environmental stressors and events can be instrumental in whether this predisposition is activated or not.

The treatment for anxiety disorders usually involves a combination of medication and counselling. There is some evidence that a deficiency in the neurotransmitter serotonin or a disturbance in metabolizing serotonin is associated with this condition and taking an antidepressant increases the serotonin levels in the brain. Individuals suffering from anxiety disorders can also benefit from learning stress management, relaxation, and ways of coping with the stress.[19] Exercise, good nutrition, and avoidance of stimulants such as caffeine can also be helpful in alleviating anxiety.

ENHANCING PSYCHOLOGICAL WELLNESS

Most people have the opportunity to function at an enhanced level of psychological well-being. This state is often achieved by improving certain skills and abilities, including improving verbal and nonverbal communication, learning to use humour effectively, developing better conflict-management skills, and taking a proactive approach to life. This section explores each of these facets of psychological well-being.

Improving Communication

Communication can be viewed in terms of your role as sender or receiver. In sending messages, you can enhance the effectiveness of your *verbal* communication in several ways. First, take time before speaking to understand what needs to be said. For example, does the audience/listener need information, encouragement, humour, or something else? Try to focus on the most important thoughts and ideas. Talk with, rather than at, listeners to encourage productive exchanges. Begin all verbal exchanges on a positive note, and maintain a positive environment. Use "minimal encouragers," such as short questions, to gain feedback. Avoid using slanted language, which can be destructive to communication. Recognize when other forms of communication, such as email messages or handwritten notes, would be better for transmitting information or ideas.

You also need to be a skilled listener. First, listen attentively in order to hear everything that is being said. Then listen selectively, filtering out information that is repetitious or unrelated to the main point. In a polite way, stop the speaker at certain points and ask him or her to repeat or rephrase the information. This technique helps you to understand what the speaker really means rather than focusing on your own responses.

Communication skills are also very important in your personal life, especially in your intimate relationships. An approach to improving your skills in this area is outlined in the Changing for the Better box on page 27.

Strengthening your *nonverbal* communication skills may also enhance your psychological well-being. One way to do this is by using facial expressions. For example, a smile usually opens lines of communication. Eye contact is also important, although staring is undesirable. Practise using effective eye contact by studying your facial expressions in the mirror. Keeping a comfortable distance from the people you are speaking to, wearing appropriate clothing, and maintaining good posture all contribute to effective communication.

Using Humour Effectively

Having a sense of humour is another important component of psychological health. Humour helps to put things in their proper perspective, alleviating tension and pain by releasing more endorphins in our bodies. In addition, laughter reduces stress,[20] boosts the immune system,[21] alleviates pain[22] stabilizes mood,[23] decreases anxiety,[24] enhances communication,[25] and inspires creativity.[26] The research suggests that we need to laugh 30 minutes total per 24-hour period to attain these benefits. This is an easy task for children who on average laugh 250 times a day but more challenging for adults who tend to only laugh 15 times a day.[27] Employers have been putting the benefits of laughter to good use to increase productivity in factories. Factories in India have created "laughing clubs" in which workers laugh together for 20 minutes a day, resulting in less absenteeism and better performance.[28]

Recognizing the humour in everyday situations and being able to laugh at yourself will make you feel better about yourself. People who build humour into their daily lives generally feel positive, and others enjoy being around them. Some researchers have suggested that recovery from an injury or illness is enhanced when patients maintain a sense of humour. In the medical field, *therapeutic humour* can be used effectively with other forms of therapy, as demonstrated in the 1999 film *Patch Adams.*

Improving Conflict-Management Skills

In spite of our best efforts to avoid it, conflict regularly occurs when people interact. In fact, it is the presence of conflict, and the change that arises from its resolution, that leads to growth. The ability to meet and resolve conflict reflects a mature state of psychological wellness. However, some forms of conflict resolution are more

Changing *for the Better*

Communication Counts in a Close Relationship

My partner and I have been living together for two years. We get along well most of the time, but when we try to talk about problems, we just can't connect. How do we learn to communicate better?

- Schedule the conversation so that you and the other person will be prepared for it.
- Choose a neutral setting to lessen the possibility of hostility.
- Set aside any preoccupations before starting the discussion.
- State your position clearly and nonaggressively.
- Keep your tone, manner of speaking, and body language respectful.
- Focus on the topic at hand.
- Be specific when you praise or criticize.
- Listen to what the other person is saying—not just the words but the feelings behind them.
- Avoid using trigger words that might turn a discussion into an argument.
- Suggest and ask for ideas about a course of action that will help resolve the problem.

If you follow these suggestions, you'll be taking into account the psychological well-being of the other person and yourself. This creates a sense of equality within the intimate relationship. Since both of you will be aware of this fact, you'll begin on a positive note.

effective than others. The following discussion describes different approaches to conflict resolution.

Many people believe that a *hostile aggressive* approach to conflict resolution, in which the parties involved use force to win, is the least emotionally mature way of resolving differences. For example, attacking others for simply disagreeing shows both hostility and aggression. Whether the weapon used is a loud voice or a physical blow, this approach usually leads to more and deeper conflict.

Submission is another unacceptable technique for resolving conflict. When one person involved in the conflict gives in, the disagreement may appear to have been resolved. Yet the accommodating party generally remains angry. The conflict is merely driven temporarily out of sight and is likely to reappear later in a more intense form. Ask yourself, for example, "How long would I be willing to do only what others want, rather than what I would enjoy doing, before I became angry and resentful?"

Another emotionally immature approach to conflict resolution is *withdrawal*. Simply walking out of a room to avoid further disagreement is an example of this method. This approach may calm the atmosphere, but it rarely leads to a true and constructive resolution of the conflict. Withdrawal can be constructive if it provides time for one or both people to rethink the conflict situation and return to it later, using a more constructive approach.

One positive conflict resolution approach is *persuasion*. In this method, one or both parties use words to explain their reasons for the position they are taking. Pointing out the advantages of pursuing one course of action versus another is an example of persuasion. The idea is to make a convincing presentation, so that the other party involved will be motivated to resolve the conflict—by accepting the position being advanced. If all parties involved are given an opportunity to have the floor, this approach to conflict resolution can be constructive.

Perhaps the most mature conflict resolution technique is *dialogue*. In this approach, a verbal exchange of facts, opinions, and perceptions takes place so that the pros and cons of each of the positions being advanced can be weighed. The goal is to reach an acceptable compromise that all parties involved have helped to formulate. An example of this approach is the lengthy negotiation process that comes before the signing of peace accords

Key Terms

generalized anxiety disorder (GAD)
An anxiety disorder that involves experiencing intense and nonspecific anxiety for at least six months, in which the intensity and frequency of worry is excessive and out of proportion to the situation.

obsessive-compulsive disorder (OCD)
An anxiety disorder characterized by obsessions—intrusive thoughts, images, or impulses causing a great deal of distress—and compulsions—repetitive behaviours aimed at reducing anxiety or stress that is associated with the obsessive thoughts.

panic disorder
An anxiety disorder characterized by panic attacks, in which individuals experience severe physical symptoms. These episodes can seemingly occur "out of the blue" or because of some trigger, and can last for a few minutes or for hours.

social phobia
A phobia characterized by feelings of extreme dread and embarrassment in situations in which public speaking or social interaction is involved.

between nations. When dialogue is used, often there are no losers in the traditional sense. Instead, the compromise position allows all parties to contribute to a healthier relationship.

Taking a Proactive Approach to Life

In addition to the approaches already discussed, the plan that follows is intended to give you even greater control in enhancing your self-esteem. A key to psychological wellness is the ability to control the outcomes of your experiences and thus learn about your own emotional resources. Figure 2–1 shows a four-step process that continues throughout life: constructing perceptions of yourself, accepting these perceptions, undertaking new experiences, and reframing your perceptions based on new information. With some thought and practice, this process can be undertaken regularly by most people.

Constructing mental pictures

Actively taking charge of your emotional growth begins with constructing a mental picture of what you're like. Use the most recent and accurate information you have about yourself—what is important to you, your values, and your competencies.

To construct this mental picture, set aside a period of uninterrupted quiet time for reflection. Even in the midst of a busy schedule, most people can find several moments to complete a task that is important.

Before proceeding to the second step, you also need to construct mental pictures about yourself in relation to *other people and material objects*, including your residence and school or work environment, to clarify these relationships.

For example, after graduating from university with a degree in fine arts, Allison moved to a large city to become a jewelry designer. Two years later, her small business was thriving and she was living in a spacious loft apartment with room for her studio. Still, Allison felt that something was missing. She constructed a mental picture in which she saw herself as a resourceful, creative, independent person who was comfortable in her new surroundings. However, Allison realized that she wanted a partner to share her success and her life.

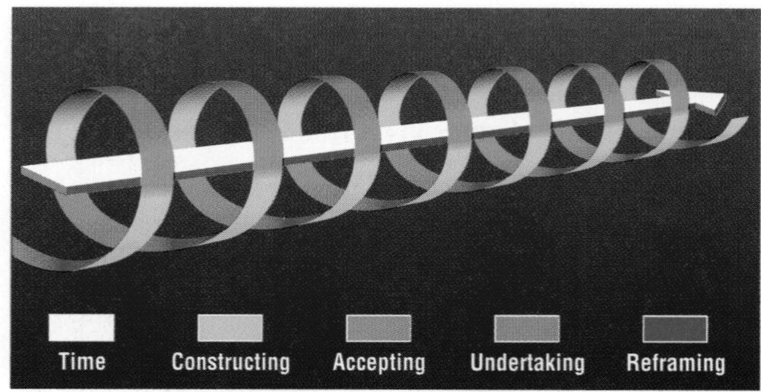

Figure 2–1 If you visualize the growth of the emotional dimension of health as a four-step process, you will see that continued emotional growth occurs in cycles throughout your life.

Accepting mental pictures

The second step of the plan involves an *acceptance* of these perceptions. This implies a willingness to honour the truthfulness of the perceptions you have formed about yourself and other people. For example, Allison should acknowledge her professional success and her artistic ability, but she must also accept the fact that she has been unable to establish the long-term romantic relationship she wants.

Like the first step, the second one requires time and commitment. Controlling emotional development is rarely a passive process. You must be willing to be *introspective* (inwardly reflective) about yourself and the world around you.

Learning from Our Diversity

Students Find Their Differences Rewarding

On most post-secondary campuses today, students encounter classmates with different backgrounds in terms of race, ethnicity, sexual orientation, and age. In addition, since the Canadian Human Rights Act was passed in 1985, students with disabilities are increasingly represented on many campuses. This changing student population makes the campus the perfect place to prepare yourself for the growing diversity in the larger community and throughout the world.

Although some students strongly resist diversity, most find that interacting with people who are different from themselves can be rewarding. Still, there's a tendency for students from diverse backgrounds or with special needs to form their own organizations and sign up for certain programs. That creates a situation in which both inclusion and isolation exist. Isolation becomes a challenge for the entire student community—to nurture respect for the diversity that's so important in today's society.

Every student is unique. Some students are willing to step outside their individual comfort zones and celebrate the diversity that surrounds them. For them, the college or university years can be a time of accelerated personal growth that prepares them to interact socially and work effectively with others throughout life.

Changing *for the Better*

Fostering Your Emotional Growth

As a 32-year-old college student, I feel as though I'm being pulled in too many different directions. Sometimes I think I'm losing my sense of self or wonder if I ever had one. What can I do to help myself grow emotionally?

Emotional growth requires two things from you—knowledge about yourself and willingness to undertake new activities and experiences and learn from them. People who actively promote their psychological health take steps toward this end. For example, many keep journals to record the events of the day. More important, they note how they felt about these events and how they managed any associated stress. Others join support groups, which allow them to interact empathetically (sharing their feelings and experiences) with others. Such groups create a sense of community that enriches the psychological health of all involved.

Many people find that counselling helps them maintain or re-establish a sense of psychological health. Growth-enhancing skills can be developed in individual or group counselling sessions, with a variety of effective counselling strategies used. As a college or university student, you have access to counselling services that are both dependable and affordable. Contacting the campus health centre or psychological services centre for referral may be the first step in improving your psychological health.

Undertaking new experiences

To mature emotionally, you must progress beyond the first two steps of the plan and test your newly formed perceptions. This *testing* is accomplished by *undertaking a new experience* or by re-experiencing something in a different way.

New experiences do not necessarily require high levels of risk, foreign travel, or money (see Learning from Our Diversity on page 28). They may be no more "new" than deciding to move from the dorm into an apartment, to change from one shift at work to another, or to pursue new friendships. The experience itself is not the goal; rather, it's a means of collecting information about yourself, others, and the objects that form your material world.

For instance, Allison volunteered to teach art therapy classes to chronically ill patients at a local hospital. This work was enjoyable and fulfilling for her, and she formed friendships with a few of the other hospital volunteers. Allison also met and began dating Mark, a staff physical therapist.

Reframing mental pictures

When you have completed the first three steps in the plan, the new information about yourself, others, and objects becomes the most current source of information. Regardless of the type of new experience you have undertaken and its outcome, you are now in a position to modify the initial perceptions constructed during the first step. Then you will have new insights, knowledge, and perspectives.

Allison reframed her mental pictures in light of the changes that had taken place in her life. Her volunteer work gave her a renewed appreciation for art. Also, she now saw herself as part of a circle of friends and as a partner in a long-term relationship with Mark. With her proactive approach to life, Allison had created challenges for herself that allowed her to change and grow.

If you are a parent, you also need to consider the challenge of fostering the emotional growth of your child.

REFLECTIONS OF PSYCHOLOGICAL WELLNESS

What characterizes people who have developed their psychological wellness most fully? The following discussion suggests three areas in which psychological wellness is evident. These include (1) movement toward fulfilling the highest level of need (as defined by Maslow), (2) development of a mature level of faith, and (3) expression of creativity in the context of a world that often restricts creative expression.

Maslow's Hierarchy of Needs

One of the most familiar ideas in developmental psychology is Abraham Maslow's model of need fulfillment. Maslow views emotional growth in terms of inner needs and motivation. He lists motivational requirements in the following order: physiological needs, safety needs, belonging and love needs, esteem needs, and **self-actualization** needs (Figure 2-2).[29] Maslow distinguishes between the lower *deficiency needs* and the higher *being needs*. People do not seek the higher needs until the lower demands have been reasonably satisfied. Accordingly, people who are hungry, feel unsafe, or have few friends will be highly unlikely to have high self-esteem until their lower needs have been met.

Key Term

self-actualization
The highest level of personality development; self-actualized people recognize their roles in life and use personal strengths to reach their fullest potential.

The people who are emotionally healthiest and most effective are those whose lives embody *being values*, such as truth, beauty, goodness, faith, wholeness, and love. Maslow labels these as "Theory Z" people, or **transcenders**. Self-actualization, the highest level of self-development, is clearly evident in the personality of transcenders, who are described as follows:[30]

- Transcenders have more peak or creative experiences and naturally speak the language of being values.
- Transcenders are more responsive to beauty, are more holistic in their perceptions of humanity and the cosmos, adjust well to conflict situations, and work more wholeheartedly toward goals and purposes.
- Transcenders are innovators who are attracted to mystery and the unknown and see themselves as people who live according to transcendent values, such as unconditional acceptance, love, honesty, and forgiveness.
- Transcenders tend to fuse work and play. They are less attracted by the rewards of money and objects and more motivated by the satisfaction of being and service values.
- Transcenders are more likely to accept others with an unconditional positive regard, and they tend to be more oriented toward spiritual reality.

From these descriptions, it's clear that there is a strong connection between transcenders and people with positive self-esteem.

Spiritual or Faith Development

A fully developed sense of self-esteem may involve accepting yourself as a person of **faith**. Many older adults say that they believe in something (such as the universal truths of beauty, honesty, and love) or someone greater than themselves and that this belief brings them great comfort and a sense of support. Many report that because of their personal level of faith, they do not fear death; they know that their lives have had meaning within the context of their deeply held beliefs. Such people would urge younger people to search for the strength and the direction that faith provides.[31]

As a resource for the spiritual dimension of health, faith provides a basis on which a belief system can mature and an expanding awareness of life's meaning can be fostered. Faith also gives meaning (or additional meaning) to your vocation (your life's work) and helps you better understand the consequences of your vocational efforts. For example, a post-secondary student might choose to major in education instead of marketing because he or she would find greater spiritual fulfillment in teaching than in business. In addition, faith in something (or someone) influences many of the experiences that you will seek throughout life and tempers your emotional response to these experiences.[32] The questions posed in Exploring Your Spirituality (p. 31) will help you consider how your faith affects your own life.

In nearly all cultures, faith and its accompanying belief system provide individuals and groups with rituals

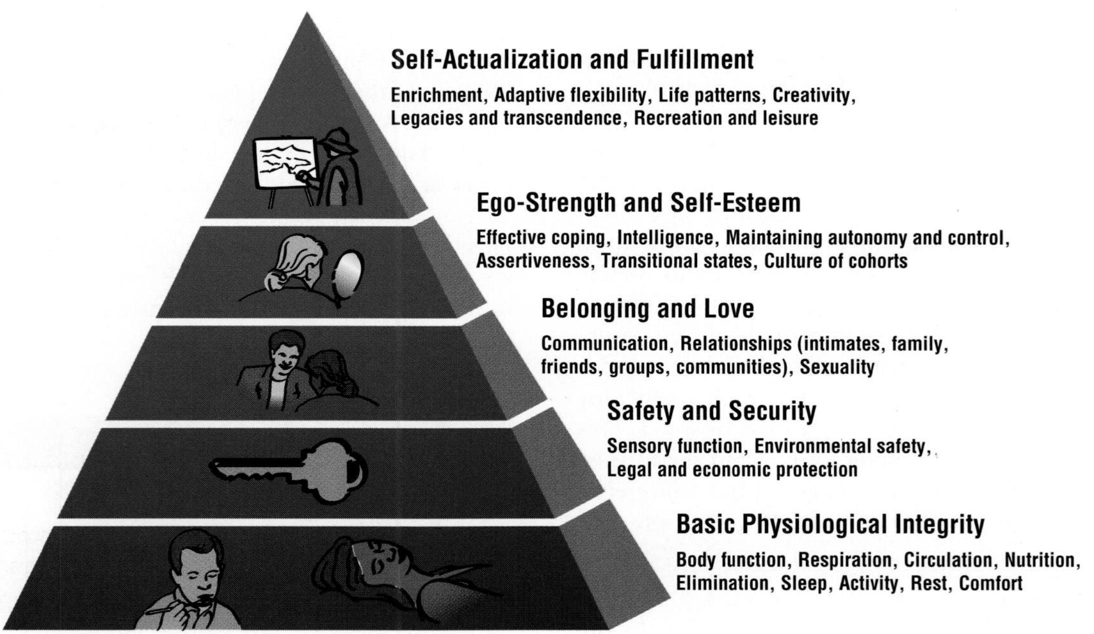

Figure 2–2 Maslow's hierarchy of needs.

Exploring Your Spirituality

Solitude: Time to Reflect, Regroup, Renew

Have you taken a moment today to be quiet and just be with yourself? Time alone can help you step away from a busy, fragmented world and draw inward for renewal. It provides an opportunity to reflect and to have new and deeper observations. Having strengthened awareness of yourself in both mind and body allows you to experience the fullness of the moment, even to feel in sync with the universe.

Solitude can also help you establish your identity, clarify what's important to you, and strengthen your independence. Because most of our time is spent living with, caring for, or responding to others, it is only when we are alone that we have the opportunity to fully emerge and become ourselves.

Any time you take for this meditation will be restorative. You may start with just five minutes every morning. You will need a place where you feel comfortable to be alone with your own thoughts, whether it be at the kitchen table, in bed, in the bath, at a coffee shop, in the library, or in the garden. Go for a walk, listen to music, weed the garden, write a letter to a friend, paint, read a poem, or just be still and concentrate on your breathing. All of these are solitary actions that, in the end, reconnect you to a life force and to others. Pretty soon you may feel that your time of solitude is more energizing than sleep! When you are faced with a difficult project, a household disaster, or something more serious, such as sickness or death, these reflective moments will give you mental and spiritual renewal.

It's not selfish to carve out whatever time you need alone to refresh yourself. By claiming solitude regularly, you're reconnecting to your inner self. This nourished spirit is what you can share with others, whether family, friends, coworkers, or strangers. Through your appreciation of a deep, rich, inner reality, you will feel rapture in the mystery and gift of just *being* here.

and practices that foster a sense of community—"a community of faith." In turn, the community nurtures the emotional stability, confidence, and sense of competence needed for living life fully.[33]

Key Terms

transcenders
Self-actualized people who have achieved a quality of being ordinarily associated with higher levels of spiritual growth.

faith
The purposes and meaning that underlie an individual's hopes and dreams.

Spending leisure time with others helps you become self-actualized.

Taking Charge of Your Health

- Assess your psychological wellness by considering the characteristics described on pp. 29–30.
- Think about what your self-esteem is like.
- If you are shy, make a special effort to join in a peer group activity that you find interesting.
- Try a new experience to discover new dimensions of your emotional makeup.
- Use dialogue to reach a compromise when you are in a conflict situation.
- Learn to be more proactive in your life by following the four-step process outlined on pp. 28–29.

SUMMARY

- Emotionally well people feel comfortable about themselves and other people and are able to meet the demands of life.
- *Emotional wellness* refers specifically to one's feelings in response to change, whereas *psychological wellness* refers more broadly to the adequate development and proper functioning of mental abilities.
- Emotions are not always constant; people experience a normal range of emotions.
- A sense of self-esteem may be the essence of emotional maturity.
- Hardiness reflects the existence of confidence and commitment and an ability to build on challenge.
- Depression can be recognized by the presence of characteristic symptoms.
- Loneliness results from the absence of adequate human contact.
- Shyness may be a basic component of temperament, yet social skills counselling can help shy people learn to interact more comfortably with others.
- Suicide represents an extreme and ineffective attempt to cope with life's problems.
- Anxiety disorders are long lasting, are often debilitating, and have the potential to significantly affect one's life.
- Effective verbal and nonverbal communication skills can be learned and used to enhance psychological well-being.
- Humour can contribute to psychological wellness and well-being.
- Conflict-management skills include a variety of approaches, some of which are more effective than others.
- A four-step plan can be used to foster greater emotional growth and enhanced psychological wellness.
- According to Maslow, the ability to meet basic human needs establishes a basis for pursuing higher emotional needs.
- People who possess a mature faith recognize the existence of guiding values in their lives.

REVIEW QUESTIONS

1. What are the characteristics of an emotionally healthy person?
2. How is psychological health related to but different from emotional health?
3. What is meant by the "normal range of emotions"?
4. Define self-esteem. List strategies that can be used to improve self-esteem.
5. What are three characteristics of hardy people?
6. What is depression, and what are the behavioural patterns of depressed people? How do major depression and dysthymia differ? How do the terms *primary* and *secondary* relate to major depression?
7. What is the important component missing in the lives of lonely people? What skills can such people learn to ease their sense of loneliness?
8. On the basis of current understanding, what is the most likely origin of shyness? What personality type includes shyness as one of its recognizable components?
9. What behavioural characteristics indicate a suicidal tendency? How should someone who observes these traits in another person respond?
10. What are the differentiating characteristics between general anxiety disorders and daily stress?
11. What are several characteristics of effective verbal communication?
12. What nonverbal cues encourage positive communication? What nonverbal cues detract from positive interpersonal communication?
13. What message is given to others by those who allow humour to be a part of their social interaction?
14. Which techniques are the more effective approaches to conflict management? Which are less effective?
15. Identify and explain the four components of the cyclic process that will help you enhance your emotional growth.
16. In what order are human needs encountered as one moves toward self-actualization?
17. What aspects of life are brought into focus as the spiritual dimension of health matures?

THINK ABOUT THIS ...

- How close do you come to meeting the characteristics of an emotionally healthy person?
- Are you ready to undertake a new experience? What kind of experience will it be?
- Why is it not a good idea to take life too seriously?
- How proactive are you in enhancing the emotional dimension of your health?

REFERENCES

1. *Mental health and you*, 1999, National Mental Health Association.
2. *Mental health for life*, 1993, Canadian Mental Health Association. **www.cmha.ca/english/store/mh_pamphlets/mh_pamphlet_01.pdf**
3. Berne P, Savary L: *Building self-esteem in children*, 1996, Crossroad Publishing Company.
4. Maddi S, Kobasa S: *The hardy executive: health under stress*, 1984, Irwin Professional Publishing.
5. *Mosby's medical, nursing, and allied health directory*, ed 5, 1997, Mosby.
6. The Clarke Institute of Psychiatry: *Facts about depression and other mood disorders*, Centre for Addiction and Mental Health. **www2.camh.net/clarkepages/about_illnesses/depression_facts.html**
7. *Physicians' desk reference*, ed 53, 1999, Medical Economics Data.
8. DeRubeis R et al: Medications versus cognitive behavior therapy for severely depressed outpatients: meta-analysis of four randomized comparisons, *Am J Psychiatry* 156(7):1007–1013, 1999.
9. Ibid.
10. Study puts spotlight on electroshock therapy, *USA Today*, March 13, 2001.
11. Centre for Addiction and Mental Health: Healing from depression naturally, *The Journal of Addiction and Health*, 2(6), 2001.
12. Ibid.
13. Wharry S: Health Canada sounds warning over St. John's wort, *Canadian Medical Association Journal*, 162(12):1723, 2000.
14. Healing from depression naturally.
15. Habib M: Report points to poor-quality herbal products, *The Canadian Press*, March 15, 1999. **www.canoe.ca/Health9903/16_alternative.html**
16. *Welcome to Natural Health Products Directorate*, Health Canada, June 26, 2002. **www.hc-sc.gc.ca/hpb/onhp/welcome_e.html**
17. Denollet J, Brutsaert D: Personality, disease severity, and the risk of long-term cardiac events in patients with decreased ejection fraction after myocardial infarction, *Circulation* 97(2):167–173, 1998.
18. Health Canada. *A report on mental illnesses in Canada*. Ottawa, Canada, 2002.
19. Borne E: *The anxiety and phobia workbook*, Oakland, CA. New Harbinger Publications Inc., 1995.
20. Castro B, Eshleman J, Shearer R: Using humor to reduce stress and improve relationships, *Seminar Nurse Management* 7(2), 90–92, 1999.
21. Berk LS, et al: Immune system changes during humor associated laughter, *Clinical Research* 39, 124a, 1991.
22. Cogan R, et al: Effects of laughter and relaxation on discomfort thresholds, *Journal of Behavioral Medicine*, 139–144, 1987.
23. Martin RA and Lefcourt HM: Sense of humor as a moderator between stressors and moods, *Journal of Personality and Social Psychology*, 45, 1313–1324, 1983.
24. Nezu A, Nezu C, and Blissett S: Sense of humor as a moderator of the relationship between stressful events and psychological distress, *Journal of Personality and Social Psychology* 54, 520–525, 1988.
25. Miller J: Jokes and joking: A serious laughing matter, in Durant J and Miller J, eds: *Laughing matters: a serious look at humor*. Longman Scientific and Technical, 1988, Essex England.
26. Lefcourt HM and Martin RA: *Humor and life stress: antidote to adversity*, Springer-Verlag, 1986, New York.
27. Kuhn C: *Humor techniques for health care professionals.* Presentation at Ball Memorial Hospital, April 22, 1998.
28. Nair M: A Documentary: "*The laughing clubs of India*," 2001.
29. Maslow A: *The farthest reaches of human nature*, 1983, Peter Smith.
30. Ibid.
31. Hemenway J, editor: *Assessing spiritual needs: a guide for care-givers*, 1993, Augsburg.
32. Fowler J: *Faith development and pastoral care*, 1987, Fortress Press.
33. *Assessing spiritual needs.*

SUGGESTED READINGS

Forward S: *Emotional blackmail: when the people in your life use fear, obligation, and guilt to manipulate you*, 1998, HarperCollins.

Is it possible for you to allow others, even those you love, to take control of your life? Susan Forward believes that this happens frequently. She claims that it is often done in a way that erodes your psychological well-being and deteriorates your health in all its dimensions. This book explores the techniques and consequences of being emotionally blackmailed by someone very close to you.

Gersten D, Dossey L: *Are you getting enlightened or losing your mind: how to master everyday and extraordinary spiritual experiences*, 1998, Three Rivers Publishing.

Where is the fine line between profound psychological disorders, such as schizophrenia, and the equally unfamiliar and uncomfortable spiritual experiences that some report? Are near-death experiences, out-of-body experiences, visitation by angels, and cases of spontaneous healing the products of spiritual connectedness, or are they illnesses to be diagnosed and treated? Dennis Gersten, M.D., a practising psychiatrist, helps the reader distinguish between dysfunction and spiritual transformation.

Gurley J: *Alter: a simple path to emotional wellness*, 1998, Footprint Press.

The author of this book believes that just as a computer can access incredible stores of information, you can tap into vast stores of self-knowledge through your unconscious mind. The idea is to use a "rub plate" to free the mind from the disturbing chatter, stress, anxiety, and emotional blinders that block access to our own store of personal information.

Name ______________________________ **Date** ______________

Personal Assessment

How Does My Self-Concept Compare with My Idealized Self?

Below is a list of 15 personal attributes, each portrayed on a 9-point continuum. Mark with an X where you think you rank on each attribute. Try to be candid and accurate; these marks will collectively describe a portion of your sense of self-concept. When you are finished with the task, go back and circle where you *wish* you could be on each dimension. These marks describe your idealized self. Finally, in the spaces on the right, indicate the difference between your self-concept and your idealized self for each attribute.

Decisive — Indecisive ____
9 8 7 6 5 4 3 2 1

Anxious — Relaxed ____
9 8 7 6 5 4 3 2 1

Easily influenced — Independent thinker ____
9 8 7 6 5 4 3 2 1

Very intelligent — Less intelligent ____
9 8 7 6 5 4 3 2 1

In good physical shape — In poor physical shape ____
9 8 7 6 5 4 3 2 1

Undependable — Dependable ____
9 8 7 6 5 4 3 2 1

Deceitful — Honest ____
9 8 7 6 5 4 3 2 1

A leader — A follower ____
9 8 7 6 5 4 3 2 1

Unambitious — Ambitious ____
9 8 7 6 5 4 3 2 1

Self-confident — Insecure ____
9 8 7 6 5 4 3 2 1

Conservative — Adventurous ____
9 8 7 6 5 4 3 2 1

Extroverted — Introverted ____
9 8 7 6 5 4 3 2 1

Physically attractive — Physically unattractive ____
9 8 7 6 5 4 3 2 1

Lazy — Hardworking ____
9 8 7 6 5 4 3 2 1

Funny — Little sense of humour ____
9 8 7 6 5 4 3 2 1

To Carry This Further ...

1. Overall, how would you describe the discrepancy between your self-concept and your self-ideal (large, moderate, small, large on only a few dimensions)?

2. How do sizable gaps for any of your attributes affect your sense of self-esteem?

3. Do you think that any of the gaps exist because you have had others' ideals imposed on you or because you have thoughtlessly accepted others' ideals?

4. Identify several attributes that you realistically believe can be changed to narrow the gap between your self-concept and your self-ideal and, thus, foster a well-developed sense of self-esteem.

Focus on

LENDING A HELPING HAND: BECOME A VOLUNTEER

"We ourselves feel that what we are doing is just a drop in the ocean. But the ocean would be less because of that missing drop."
—Mother Teresa

Every day, Canadians of all ages volunteer their skills, energy, and time to nonprofit and charitable organizations. In doing so, they play a vital role in improving the lives of others as well as their communities. The National Survey on Giving, Volunteering, and Participating (NSGVP) reported that Canadians contributed a total of 1 billion hours of volunteer time in the year 2000, equivalent to 549 000 full-time, year-round jobs. These volunteers served in a vast range of activities including canvassing and other fundraising, coaching children, assisting the elderly, teaching adult literacy, serving on boards and committees, and advocating on important issues.[1]

Canadians traditionally have expended their time, talents, and energy in support of others more freely than have the citizens of many other highly industrialized nations. Recent examples of this admirable Canadian response were the cleanup efforts following devastating tornadoes in Winnipeg, assistance to those affected by the massive damage inflicted by the ice storm in Quebec and eastern Ontario, and contributions and support to New Yorkers following the World Trade Center bombings. Less visible are the thousands of Canadians involved in volunteer programs in other countries.

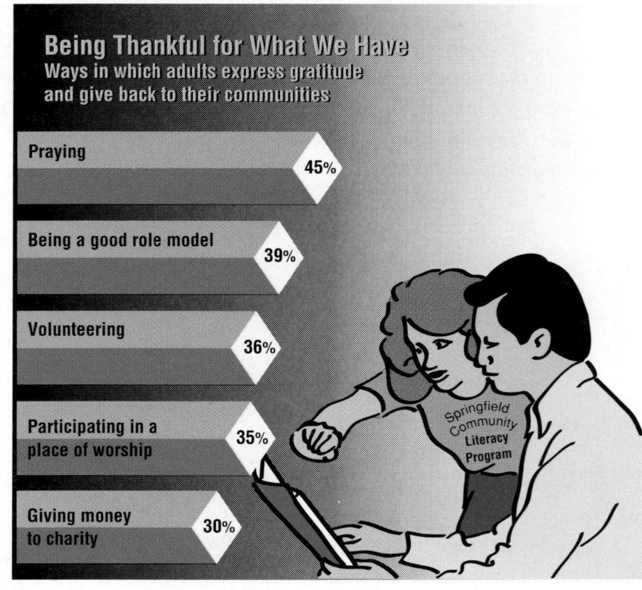

Many of us have been fortunate enough not to experience poverty, serious illness, or lack of education. Do you think it's important to express gratitude by giving something back to your community?

Helping Others and Improving Yourself

Although volunteer services benefit those in need, volunteering is also good for the volunteer. It provides companionship, friendship, and fellowship in working toward a common goal. Volunteer service may allow us to use skills and talents that we normally don't use in our daily jobs. It encourages us to branch out, learn new things, and become well rounded. The decision to become a volunteer fosters decision making and expands the scope of the volunteer's self-directed behaviour. Most important, volunteering brings people of diverse backgrounds together, gives those being served a greater sense of self-worth, and raises the aspirations of all involved.

Why Canadians Volunteer

The 2000 NSGVP revealed that Canadians volunteer for many different reasons. Believing in the cause supported by the organization was the most frequently reported reason for helping out. Other important reasons included wanting to put personal skills and experience to use, having been personally affected by the cause the organization supports, and seeing volunteering as an opportunity to explore one's own strengths.

Today, the importance of volunteering, referred to as *service learning*, is reflected in the fact that many colleges, universities, and high schools are requiring its inclusion in the curricula.[2,3] Students who have participated in volunteer programs appear to profit in terms of their academic performance, perhaps because of the time management skills and discipline involved. They also report an increased sense of concern for the well-being of others and a greater ability to respond empathetically, as well as sympathetically, to people in need.

More than three-quarters of Canadians aged 15 to 24 who were surveyed for the 2000 NSGVP felt that volunteering would help them get a job. Many of those who already had paid employment felt that volunteering gave them an opportunity to learn skills that could be applied directly to their jobs.

Employers are in fact beginning to notice—and value—the inclusion of volunteering on the transcripts of recent graduates. It is important to note, however, that volunteering is not necessarily highly regarded by employers unless it leads to skill development that is relevant to the organization.[4] Some members of the academic community question the appropriateness of requiring students to volunteer. Perhaps offering opportunities for students to volunteer (for credit) and to develop job-related skills is a good reason to include it in the curricula. Volunteering broadens the volunteer's world and sharpens his or her focus, enhancing both occupational performance and psychological well-being.

Ways to Volunteer

Become a CUSO Co-operant
One interesting way students can volunteer is to become involved with Canadian University Services Overseas (CUSO). The common thread between the CUSO partner organizations, volunteers, and staff is a commitment to global social justice. CUSO works with people striving for freedom, self-determination, gender and racial equality, and cultural survival. Co-operants advance this work by providing strategic, technical, and professional support to partner organizations in Africa, Asia, Latin America, the Caribbean, and the South Pacific.

Of course, this is just one way to volunteer. No matter what your interests, abilities, or time commitments are, there is much that you, as a post-secondary student, can do. Just a few of the areas where volunteer opportunities may exist are

AIDS
Arts/cultural enrichment
Business assistance
Citizenship
Civic affairs
Consumer service/legal rights
Day care/Head Start
Disaster response/emergency preparedness
Drug abuse/alcoholism
Education
Employment
Health issues
Law enforcement/crime prevention
Literacy
Mental health
Nutrition
Physical environment
Psychosocial support services
Recreation and sports
Teen pregnancy prevention
Parenting
Transportation and safety
Animal welfare
Women's crisis centres

Some specific Canadian volunteer organizations include Canada World Youth, Canadian Crossroads International, Youth Challenge International, and Katimavik, to name a few.

Volunteer Canada Snapshot
Since 1977, Volunteer Canada has been well known for its efforts in supporting the volunteer work of Canadians at the community level. This national agency supports civic participation through a variety of projects and programs. Volunteer Canada plays an important leadership role in the Canadian volunteer movement. Information and assistance is available on Volunteer Canada's Web site for all people who would like to be part of a volunteer organization. Agencies that may have trouble finding volunteer help are now able to do so online. Likewise, volunteers are able to find information on associations or agencies that they may wish to be part of as volunteers. The Volunteer Exchange is an excellent tool for connecting potential volunteers to agencies seeking volunteer help. Visit the Web site at **www.volunteer.ca**

For Discussion

Do you currently volunteer? Why or why not? If you decided to become a volunteer, what areas of work would interest you most? Can you think of a volunteer who has touched your life? How do you feel about compulsory service as a component in college, university, and high school curricula?

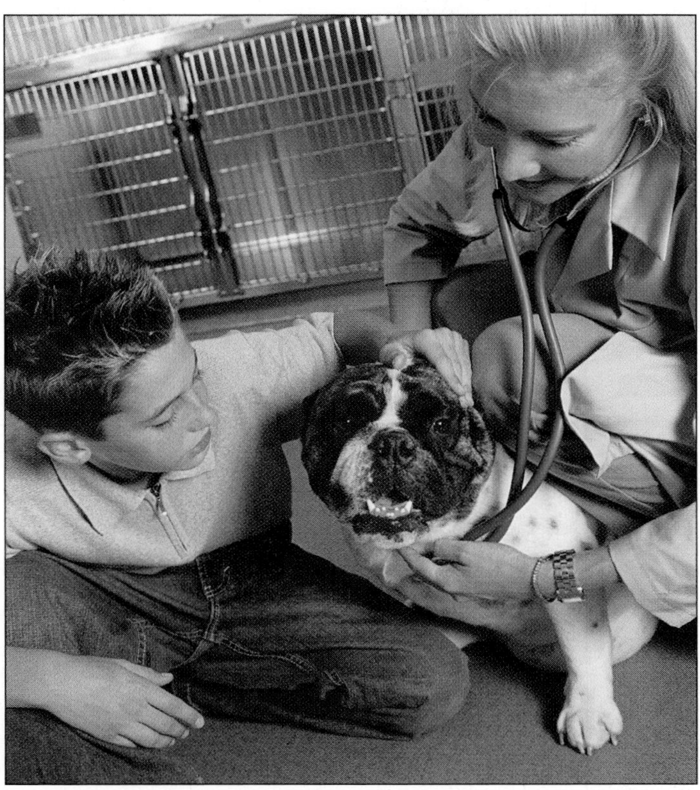

One way to volunteer is to work with the SPCA (The Society for the Prevention of Cruelty to Animals) to help abandoned animals find new homes.

Should time spent volunteering be counted as a contribution for income tax purposes (as a monetary contribution to a nonprofit agency would)?

References

1. Hall M, McKeown L, Roberts K: *2000 National Survey on Giving, Volunteering and Participating*, Statistics Canada, catalogue no. 71-542-XIE, 2001.
2. Sax L, Justin A: The benefits of service: evidence from undergraduates, *Educational Record*, Summer/Fall: 25–33, 1997.
3. Calderon J: Making a difference: service-learning as an activism catalyst and community builder, *American Association for Higher Education Bulletin* 52(1): 7–9, 1999.
4. Larry Beck: Personal interview with Larry Beck, Associate Director, Career Services, Ball State University, September 27, 1999.

InfoLinks

www.voe-reb.org
www.cuso.org

Chapter **3**

Managing Stress

Chapter Objectives

Upon completing this chapter, you will be able to

- Define stress, the stress response, and chronic stress.
- Describe the flight-or-fight response.
- Discuss the general adaptation syndrome including the three stages of stress: the alarm, resistance, and exhaustion stages.
- Discuss some of the types of student stress explored in this chapter.
- Describe various stress-management techniques.

Online Learning Centre Resources

www.mcgrawhill.ca/college/hahn

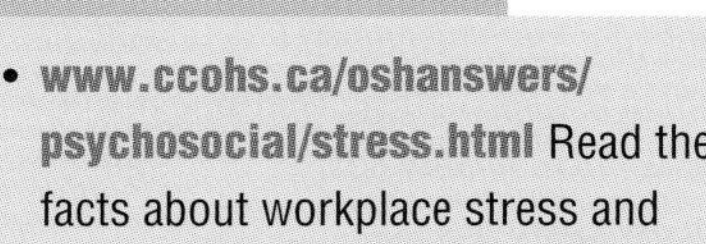

Log on to our Online Learning Centre (OLC) for access to Web links for study and exploration of health topics. Here are some examples of what you'll find:

- **www.optimumhealth.ca** Get information on recognizing stress, take a self-test for determining your stress level, and learn stress-management techniques.
- **www.ccohs.ca/oshanswers/psychosocial/stress.html** Read the facts about workplace stress and what you can do about it.
- **www.cyberpsych.com/stress.html** Don't miss *Reality Check: 20 Questions to Screw Your Head on Straight.*

Media Pulse

New Technology, New Stresses

Over the past 30 years, the technology explosion has created a massive volume of information and a faster pace of life in the workplace, in the classroom, and at home. Advances in technology offer many advantages, including saving time and increasing convenience. Would you want to go back to a world without email, voicemail, the Internet, and cell phones? Probably not. Yet these technologies also produce stressors.

Email: Correspondence of all types is increasingly being sent via computer. People who rarely exchanged written correspondence are now dropping lines via email. At the office, a worker may arrive in the morning and find a long list of electronic correspondence that needs to be answered. Forwarded memos and messages, sent for informational purposes, may not require a reply, but they still need to be read and sometimes require action.

Voicemail: Sometimes it's hard to ignore the blinking light on the phone. It's a constant reminder that you've missed a call and need to respond to it. To make that light stop blinking, you must listen to the message.

Automated Voice Message System: Many phone calls that we now make—to companies, community agencies, and even some homes—produce a familiar menu of choices. After listening to several choices, such as "For your current balance, press 3," you might like to wait for the final choice, "To speak to a company representative, please remain on the line." These automated services generate feelings ranging from annoyance to anger.

Media Pulse *continued*

For the caller who wants to talk to a knowledgeable person about an important question or concern, listening to the entire menu and waiting to talk to a "real" person can be stressful.

Junk Mail: Much of today's mail is unsolicited and unwanted, such as an application for a credit card, a request for financial support, or a clothing catalogue. A pile of junk mail may be the first stressor you encounter at the end of a stress-filled day at school or work. It's something that needs to be dealt with, if only sorted through and thrown away.

Fax Machines: Faxing is fast, convenient, and inexpensive. It can also be stressful, such as when the fax number is unknown and can't be located or the line is constantly busy. Poor print quality, especially for graphics, can also produce frustration. Also, the "urgent" message on a fax suggests that an immediate reply is expected.

Call Waiting: Some people find call waiting to be irritating. First, their phone conversation is interrupted so that the person they are speaking to can check to see who the other caller is. The first caller needs to wait until the conversation can be resumed or is told that he or she will be called back later. This juggling of call priorities creates stress for both parties—the called party may feel the need to talk to both callers, and the original caller may be annoyed if his or her call becomes a lower priority than the new call.

PDAs: For many busy people, it's convenient to carry a small electronic appointment book that interfaces with their personal computer. But when a person's schedule is recorded in a device that can be easily damaged or incapacitated (e.g., when power supplies run low), this information can be lost in an instant.

Pagers and Cell Phones: With electronic pagers and cell phones becoming so common, many people—employees, clients, and children—find themselves on call virtually all the time. The increasing pressure to keep in touch makes it more difficult to get away from it all. Even the enjoyment of watching a movie in a theatre or dining in a quiet restaurant is often interrupted by the beeping of pagers and ringing of cell phones. Some people consider these interruptions necessary; others think they are simply annoying and intrusive.

Listservs: As valuable and informative as listservs can be, the amount of sharing on a single topic can become overwhelming as membership grows. Even the process of disaffiliating from the service can be complicated and stressful.

Internet: The Internet literally puts a world of information at your fingertips. But this can be somewhat daunting. Suddenly you realize just how much information is out there. How can you get the right information? How is it that your computer searches through 25 000 sites without capturing the particular information you need? Why must you wait so long for pages to load? Why does your ISP always seem to be overloaded when you want to log on?

Clearly, these new technologies offer many advantages. But, like the technologies that preceded them, they create new stresses. Accepting that fact and developing a technology-friendly attitude will keep your stress level down as you make the new technology work for you.

Change is a part of daily living. Each person, institution, and situation in your environment holds the potential for change, which sometimes seems threatening. Taking control of this change or adjusting to it can be challenging, stimulating, and rewarding—contributing to your sense of well-being. But if you handle change poorly, stress can result, producing unpleasant experiences and the potential for harm to your health.

STRESS AND STRESSORS

On your university or college campus, you probably hear people talking about how much **stress** they feel. Certainly, for both traditional-age and nontraditional-age students, the demands of school, work, marriage, and parenting can produce feelings of distress that detract from wellness. Students with disabilities face these and additional stressors (see Learning from Our Diversity on p. 41).

Although you've experienced stress, you may not understand what it is and how it works. Hans Selye, a Canadian and the originator of stress theory, described stress as "the nonspecific response of the body to any demand made on it."[1] Stress can be viewed as a physical and emotional response that occurs when people are exposed to change. The events that produce stress are called **stressors**. Stressors are the cause, and stress is the effect.

Variation in Response to Stressors

Because individuals are unique, what is a stressor for one person might not be a stressor for another. For example, if the bookstore is out of a text that you need for an upcoming assignment, you'll be affected by this situation; however, someone who already has the book will not. If you need to find a babysitter for your child because of an unexpected school closing, you'll have to deal with this problem; for many of your classmates (without children), this would not be an issue. Therefore some

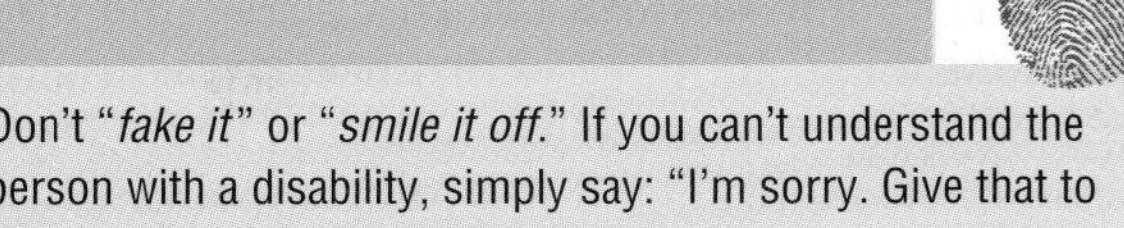

Learning from Our Diversity

Communicating with Students Who Have a Disability

For many university or college students, interacting with classmates who have a disability is uncomfortable and stressful. The students with the disability feel this discomfort, and it is a source of stress for them. They are also dealing with the demands of school in the context of their unique disability.

What approach could be taken to minimize the discomfort for all parties involved? The following list contains some suggestions:

- Remember that everyone is a *person first.* In addition, that person may have a disability. Think in terms of a student with a learning disability, not a learning-disabled student.
- Always make *eye contact* with the person. This simple courtesy is very important in assuring the individual with a disability that he or she is a part of your educational experience.
- *Talk with* the person with the disability rather than with the accompanying attendant or assistant.
- Keep in mind that the person in the attendant/assistant role may know only certain aspects of the individual with a disability.
- Don't "*fake it*" or "*smile it off.*" If you can't understand the person with a disability, simply say: "I'm sorry. Give that to me one more time."
- If verbal communication is very difficult or simply ineffective, *do what it takes* to interact with the person with a disability. For example, sit down at the computer and write a note.
- If you think that the person with a disability needs assistance, just ask: "*May I assist you?*" The worst that can happen is that the person might say no. If the person says yes, he or she might tell you how you can help.
- *Don't generalize* from a single negative and stressful experience about interacting with someone with a disability. Expect no more or no less from that person than you would from your able-bodied classmates.

A good source of information on disabilities for Canadian students and professionals is the Web site at **www.abilityinfo.com**.

people are always more *distressed* than others. This variation results from the unique information that each person applies in making decisions about certain situations. When people refer to "stress," they commonly mean the stress associated with fear, anger, anxiety, and uncertainty regarding changing events.

Stress can usually be categorized as *acute* (associated with a single isolated event, such as a car accident), *episodic* (related to a particular series of events, such as taking examinations), or *chronic* (such as being a parent of young children).

Positive or negative stressors

Stressors produce the same generalized physical response whether an individual views the stressor as good or bad. Poor academic performance, loss of a friend, or being the only minority student on the dorm floor can cause stress, just as giving birth, receiving a promotion, or starting a new romance can be stressors. In each case, the effect on the body's physical systems is similar.

Selye coined the word **eustress** to mean positive stress. Stressors that produce eustress can enhance longevity, productivity, and life satisfaction. Examples include the mild stress that helps you stay alert during a midterm examination, the anticipation you feel on the first day of a new job, and the exhilaration you experience while exercising. Some suggest that a personality type, type R (risk takers), may "require" the regular occurrence of high-risk activities as positive stressors. Recent research suggests that this risk-taking behaviour may be caused by a genetic predisposition.[2]

Selye calls harmful, unpleasant stress **distress**. If distress is not controlled, it can result in physical and emotional disruption, illness, and even death.

Stress and Disease

If the effects of a stressor are not minimized or resolved, the human body becomes exhausted, and an emotional and physical breakdown results. Depending on the

Key Terms

stress
The physiological and psychological state of disruption caused by the presence of an unanticipated, disruptive, or stimulating event.

stressors
Factors or events, real or imagined, that elicit a state of stress.

eustress
Stress that enhances the quality of life.

distress
Stress that diminishes the quality of life; commonly associated with disease, illness, and maladaptation.

strength of the stressor and the resistance of the person, this breakdown may occur quickly or may extend over many years, leading to stress-related diseases and disorders. Among the major diseases that have some origin in unresolved stress are hypertension, stroke, heart disease, depression, alcoholism, and gastrointestinal disorders. Other stress-related disorders are migraine headaches, allergies, asthma, anxiety, insomnia, impotence, and menstrual irregularities. Cigarette smoking, overeating or undereating, and underactivity are partly related to unresolved stress. Even the immune system, which protects the body from infection and disease, may be weakened by stress.[3]

POST-SECONDARY EDUCATION STRESSORS

For some people who have not attempted university or college work, the idea that post-secondary education is stressful may seem strange. After all, aren't these supposed to be the "best years" of your life? Yet students know that their experience is serious because it is preparing them for life and their career. For the part-time nontraditional-age student who comes to campus at night and returns to work, family, and community responsibilities during the day, classes can be especially stressful. (To find out how stressed you are, see the Personal Assessment on p. 54.)

In college and university settings, stressors can arise from a variety of areas, including the following:

- School policies that seem to make going to school too complicated, such as the inconvenient scheduling of classes and the restrictions on parking
- Expectations of faculty regarding various course requirements, such as attendance, out-of-class participation, and the type of examinations given by a particular instructor
- Difficulty in qualifying for loans or other forms of financial assistance and the need to work to afford school
- Personal goals that become unachievable, such as making an athletic team, earning a desired grade point average, or graduating with honours
- Uncertainties about previously held beliefs, including those related to religion, sexual abstinence, and politics
- Interpersonal relationships and decisions regarding interracial or interfaith dating, changing roommates, or being older than other students
- Availability of a job, acceptance into graduate or professional school, and the approach of real-world responsibilities
- Family expectations about whether school is being taken seriously enough, friends will be made, or money will be used wisely

Education is not a passive process. It demands your active participation and effort. At times, the post-secondary education experience may demand more than you believe you can give. Not surprisingly, it frequently becomes the source of many stressors.

Day-to-day living presents stressors that also must be confronted and resolved. Although different from stressors associated with higher education, life-centred stressors hold the same potential for causing physical and emotional distress and challenges to an individual's well-being. For advice on coping with stress in the workplace, read the Focus On article on p. 56.

FLIGHT-OR-FIGHT RESPONSE

Our response to stress involves many physiological changes that are collectively called the **flight-or-fight response**. In situations in which you must react immediately to danger, it is advisable to either fight off the danger or flee. For example, you are walking back from class at night, thinking about all the studying you need to do and you begin to cross the street. Suddenly, out of nowhere, you see a car coming right at you. Since your best response is probably not to fight the car, you run as fast as you can to the other side of the road. In that split second, when you see the car careening quickly toward you, your muscles tense, your heart beats faster, your adrenaline pumps faster and is released at higher levels into your bloodstream, your breathing becomes more shallow and rapid, and your pupils dilate to see the car better.

This is the flight-or-fight response. Again, all of these changes are very adaptive and helpful to your survival in getting out of harm's way. In the above example, when you get to the other side of the road and realize that you are okay, your body begins to relax and return to its normal state. You take a deep breath, expressing a big sigh of relief. Your muscles may feel weaker than usual, your breathing may become deeper and heavier than is typical, and you may feel shaky as your body goes from extreme arousal to relaxing very quickly. Figure 3–1[4] depicts these changes from your normal state to an arousal state to a very relaxed state then back to normal.

GENERALIZED PHYSIOLOGICAL RESPONSE TO STRESSORS

Once you're under the influence of a stressor, your body responds in certain predictable ways. For example, if you're asked to stand in front of a group and talk, you may find that your heart rate increases, your throat becomes dry, your palms sweat, and you feel dizzy or light-headed. You may even feel nauseous. You would have similar feelings if you were told that you had lost your job or that

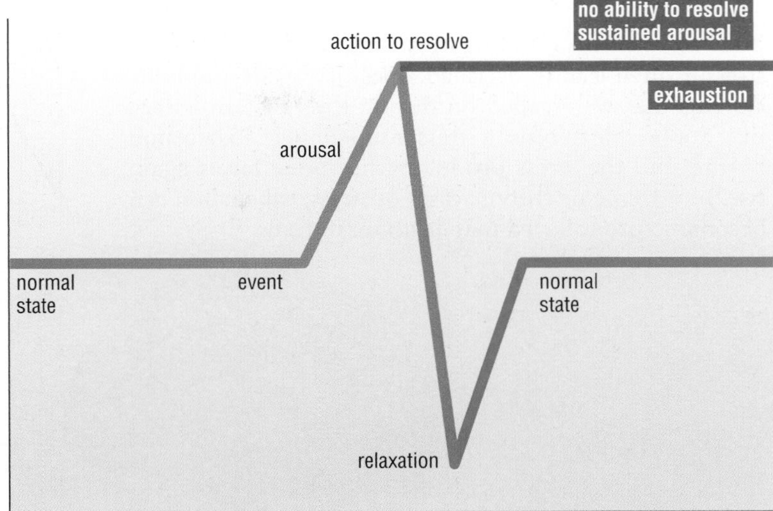

Figure 3–1 There is a tremendous difference in how long your body remains at a high level of physiological arousal depending upon how quickly and effectively you act to resolve the stress.

your spouse wanted a divorce. These different stressors all elicit certain common physical reactions.

Selye described the typical physical response to a stressor in his **general adaptation syndrome** model. He stated that the human body moves through three stages when confronted by stressors: alarm reaction, resistance, and exhaustion.

Alarm Reaction Stage

Once exposed to any event that is perceived as threatening or dangerous, the body immediately prepares for difficulty, entering what Selye called the **alarm stage**. These involuntary changes, described in Figure 3–2, are controlled by the hormonal and nervous system, and trigger the flight-or-fight response. For example, you realize that the final exam you thought was today was actually scheduled for yesterday. You may begin to experience fear, panic, anxiety, anger, depression, and restlessness.[5]

Resistance Stage

The resistance stage reflects the body's attempt to reestablish its internal balance, or *homeostasis*. The high level of energy seen in the initial alarm stage cannot be maintained very long. So the body attempts to reduce the intensity of the initial response to a more manageable level. This is accomplished by reducing the production of adrenocorticotropic hormone (ACTH) (see Figure 3–2), allowing *specificity of adaptation* to occur. Specific organ systems, such as the cardiovascular and digestive systems, become the focus of the body's response.[6]

The alarm stage gives way to the less damaging resistance stage, because of effective coping or because the status of the stressor changes. As control over the stressful situation is gained, homeostasis becomes reestablished in movement toward full recovery. When the *recovery stage* is complete, the body has returned to its prestressed state and there is minimal evidence of the stressor's existence.[7]

If the resistance stage is prolonged, the body may show clinical signs of the demands made on it by the continuing presence of stressors. At such times the person may begin to display the **psychogenic** and **psychosomatic** disorders associated with chronic stress. (See the Changing for the Better box on p. 46, which lists different types of headaches, some of which are worsened by stress.)

Key Terms

flight-or-fight response
The reaction to a stressor by confrontation or avoidance (sometimes called the flight, fight, fright, or folly [or 4F] response).

general adaptation syndrome
A sequenced physiological response to the presence of a stressor; the alarm, resistance, recovery, and exhaustion stages of the stress response.

alarm stage
The first stage of the stress response involving physiological, involuntary changes that are controlled by the hormonal and nervous system; the flight-or-fight response is activated in this stage.

psychogenic
Pertaining to mind-induced (emotional) changes in physical function, without evidence of structural change to body tissues.

psychosomatic
Pertaining to mind-induced (emotional) changes in both physical function and the normal structure of body tissues.

Exhaustion Stage

Body adjustments resulting from long-term exposure to a stressor often lead to overload. Specific organs and body systems that were called on during the resistance stage may not be able to resist a stressor indefinitely. Exhaustion results, and the stress-producing hormone levels again rise. In extreme or chronic cases of stress, exhaustion can become so pronounced that death may occur.

THE STRESS RESPONSE

Why could something as familiar as a telephone ringing late at night cause a person to feel fear and near-panic? Why is it that your hands sweat, your muscles tense, and your appetite leaves as you wait in the hallway outside the classroom where your final examination is to be held? Is the "cotton-mouth" feeling described by athletes

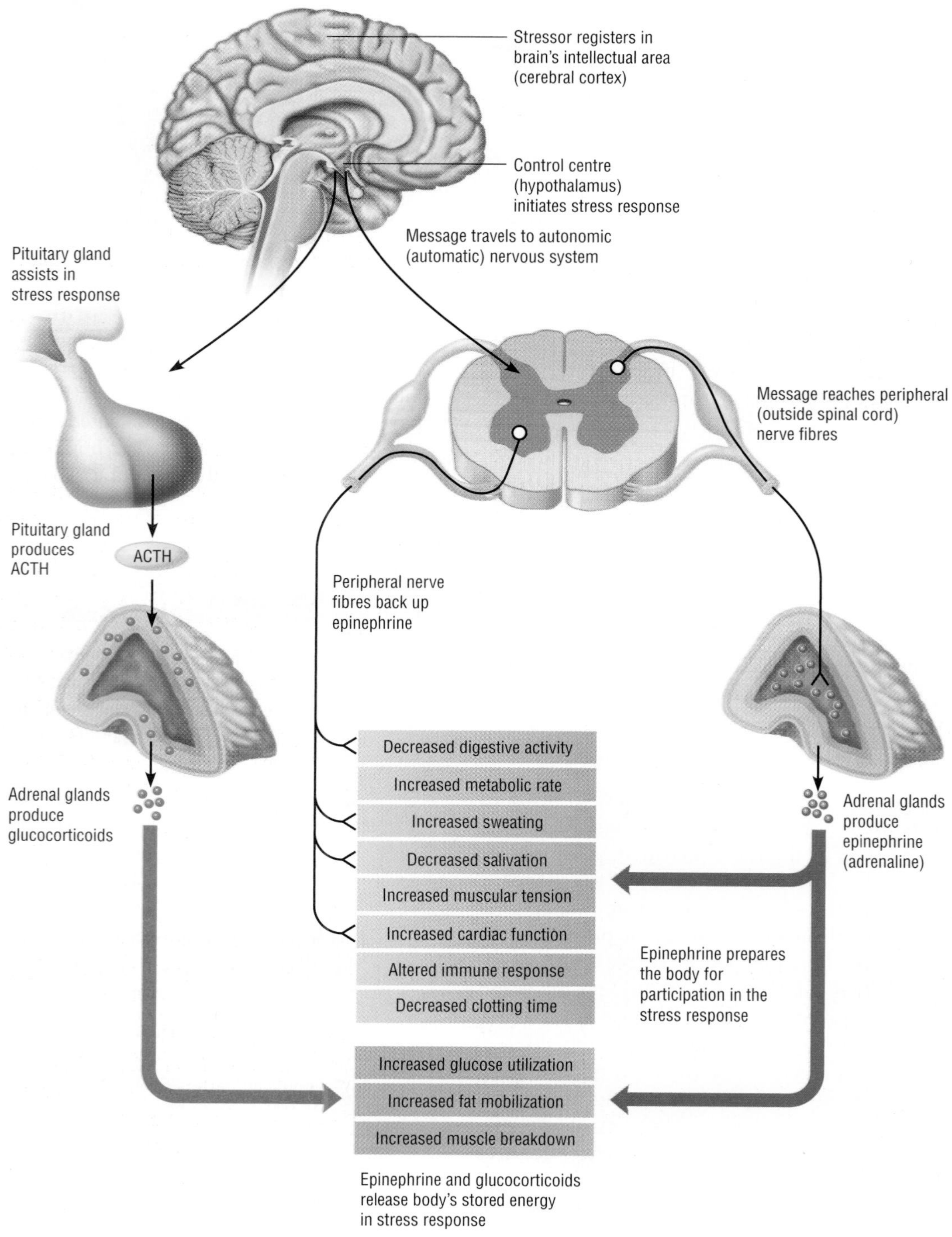
Stressor registers in brain's intellectual area (cerebral cortex)
Control centre (hypothalamus) initiates stress response
Message travels to autonomic (automatic) nervous system
Pituitary gland assists in stress response
Message reaches peripheral (outside spinal cord) nerve fibres
Pituitary gland produces ACTH
ACTH
Peripheral nerve fibres back up epinephrine
Adrenal glands produce glucocorticoids
Adrenal glands produce epinephrine (adrenaline)
Decreased digestive activity
Increased metabolic rate
Increased sweating
Decreased salivation
Increased muscular tension
Increased cardiac function
Altered immune response
Decreased clotting time
Epinephrine prepares the body for participation in the stress response
Increased glucose utilization
Increased fat mobilization
Increased muscle breakdown
Epinephrine and glucocorticoids release body's stored energy in stress response

Figure 3-2 The stress response: physiological reactions to a stressor.

a valuable aid to performance? The answers are simple and based on the body's primitive interpretation of reality. The body is looking for energy because it believes that all change is threatening and can be confronted by running, fighting, scaring away the "adversary", or engaging it in sexual activity (the flight, fight, fright, or folly response). For these responses, the body simply needs energy for physical activity.[8]

Stressors

For a state of stress to exist, a person must first be confronted by change, real or imagined. Any change holds the potential for becoming a stressor and stimulating the stress response (Figure 3–2).

THE COSTS AND BENEFITS OF STRESS

Stress can be costly, taking a toll on our physical and mental health as well as our finances.

Constant arousal and increased levels of adrenaline in your system will eventually wear down your body's immunological system. As this occurs, you will be less able to cope with stress, and so it takes less and less to cause a stress reaction. When you are chronically stressed, it takes very little to frustrate you and you feel easily irritated and stressed at the smallest thing. Your body is both psychologically as well as physically less able to cope with stress. This can cause your immune system to become compromised, and you may become ill more easily. It may also take longer for you to recover from illness. There are a variety of medical problems associated with stress, such as cardiovascular problems, gastrointestinal problems, sleep disorders, sexual dysfunction, infertility, and allergies.[9]

While too much stress can have a negative impact and cause some serious health problems, a moderate level of stress is positive and beneficial. Stress can be very motivating and energizing. Without some stress, many of us may not get much accomplished in our day or even get out of bed! Look at the diagram in Figure 3–3.[10] What do you notice? Too little and too much stress is not helpful. When you are not stressed at all, you can be apathetic and lethargic. When you are too stressed, you are paralyzed with fear, like deer in the headlights. This is referred to as the **Yerkes-Dodson Law**, which shows a bell-shaped curve demonstrating that there is an optimal level of stress for peak performance. This holds true for any type of performance, from academic or work activities to music or athletics.[11] Recognizing your appropriate level of stress for your ideal performance level is important in reaching your potential.

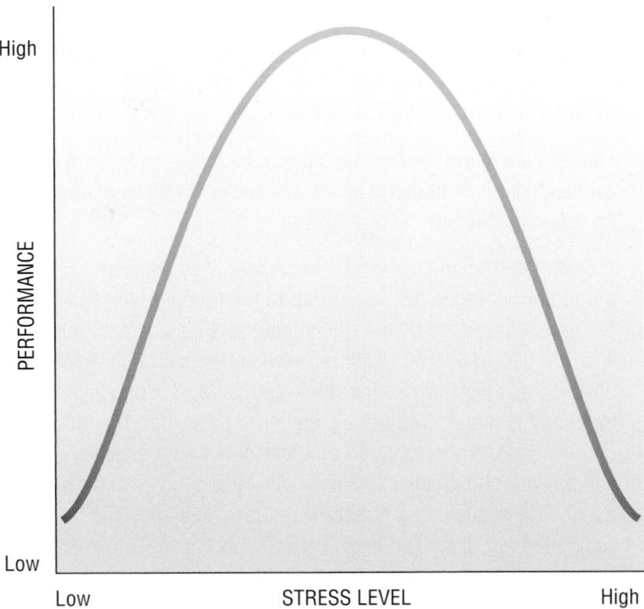

Figure 3–3 The Yerkes-Dodson Law Too little or too much stress is not helpful, but a moderate level of stress encourages peak performance.

PSYCHONEUROIMMUNOLOGY

Clinical observation and laboratory studies show that the emotional component of stress (e.g., anxiety and depression) and the disruption of social support systems contribute to the weakening of the immune response and the development of some illnesses. For example, high levels of stress can predispose individuals to the development of colds; when immunizations are given during periods of stress, they may be less effective than if given when stress is not a factor. What is not known, however, is which mechanisms stressors use in altering immune system function. Are the nervous system components and the endocrine components of the stress response both influenced by a single stressor?

Or is a combination of stressors necessary for seeing clinical evidence of immune system depression? In

Key Term

Yerkes-Dodson Law
A bell-shaped curve demonstrating that there is an optimal level of stress for peak performance; this law states that too little and too much stress is not helpful, while a moderate amount of stress is positive and beneficial.

Changing *for the Better*

When Do Headaches Need Attention?

I never used to get headaches, but now I seem to have them a lot, especially around midterm and exam weeks. Is this something to be concerned about?

An estimated 45 million North Americans have frequent, bothersome headaches. According to the Migraine Association of Canada, there are over 4 million adult Canadians (one in five) and 200 000 to 300 000 children who suffer from migraine headaches. Migraine occurs most often among people aged 20 to 50 and is considered to be an inherited disorder. If you have chronic headache symptoms or symptoms that are especially painful, you should seek medical help. Headaches can have many causes, including stress. The three most common categories are described here. For more headache information, visit **www.headache-help.org**.

Tension

Description

A dull, constricting pain centred in the hatband region. Pain may be on both sides of the head and extend down the neck to the shoulders. Produced by stress, eye strain, muscle tension, sinus congestion, temporomandibular joint dysfunction, nasal congestion, or caffeine withdrawal.

Treatment
Nonnarcotic pain relievers, muscle relaxants, relaxation exercises, massage.

Prevention
Preventive relaxation exercises, certain antidepressant medications.

Migraine

Description

Throbbing pain on one side of the head, usually preceded by visual disturbances. Sensitivity to lights and sounds; nausea and dizziness. More common in women. Can last from a few hours to two days.

Treatment
Three oral prescription medications (Imitrex, Maxalt, and Zomig) are now available. Imitrex is available as a nasal spray. An over-the-counter medication, Excedrin Extra Strength, is effective for many.

Prevention
Avoidance of certain foods, including red wines, other alcoholic beverages, ripened cheeses, chocolate, cured meats, and monosodium glutamate (MSG). In some cases, prescription medications are recommended.

Cluster

Description

Focused, intense pain near one eye, often producing a red and teary eye and a runny nose. Headaches occur daily for weeks or months. They mainly affect men and last up to two hours.

Treatment
Oxygen and/or ergot compounds during the headache.

Prevention
Avoidance of alcohol; nitrite-containing foods; and various prescription medications, including antidepressants, steroids, ergotlike compounds, or heart-regulating drugs.

addition, it is not clear whether studies done with immune cells removed from the body reflect what actually occurs in the body and whether studies done with animals can be applied to humans.

Despite these limitations, theoretical explanations for a strong relationship between stress and immune system function exist. Experts in the field of **psychoneuroimmunology** are aggressively pursuing clinical studies to clarify which pathways are involved and which forms of management, including social support, can be used to support the immune system during periods of stress.[12]

Personality Traits

Can personality play a role in making people more or less prone to stress? If so, what outlook on life is considered to be the most stress producing? The answer to the latter question has changed over the past three decades.

The initial, and still widely recognized, theory describing personality's role in fostering stress was that of type A and type B personalities, developed by cardiologists Friedman and Rosenman. In this model, time dependence (hurry sickness) was related to high levels of stress and, eventually, to heart disease.

Today, the concept of time dependence as the most influential personality trait associated with high levels of stress has given way to concern over high levels of *anger* and *cynicism*. Anger is the intense feeling of rage and fury that accompanies an event or a change. Some people always seem to be angry, and the resulting stress on the body is detrimental to both their physical and emotional health. In fact, an association between stress-induced anger and cardiovascular disease, as well as visceral obesity and insulin resistance syndrome (associated with type 2 diabetes mellitus), is well established.[13]

Closely related to anger is cynicism, the second personality trait that fosters high levels of stress. This trait is associated with deeply held dislike and distrust of others and their ideas. Cynics have nothing good to say about others. They are, perhaps, profoundly angry about their relationships with others and can express this feeling only by being very critical. Like anger, cynicism places the body under chronic stress and erodes the physical and emotional well-being of the person.[14] The only effective treatment for chronically angry or cynical people may be either a profoundly moving personal experience that truly changes their outlook on life, such as the birth of a child, or counselling that helps them identify the reasons underlying their negative outlook.

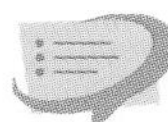

TALKING POINTS • How would you speak honestly with a friend who seems chronically angry and cynical?

Time Management

For many university and college students, the most significant problem with being a student is everything that interferes with academics, including campus activities, athletics, employment, relationships, parenting, and relaxation time. Ultimately, the problem becomes an issue of priorities and time management so that academic demands can be met. Without question, *effective time management* is at the heart of balancing the demands of the college experience. The Personal Assessment on p. 55 will assist you in determining how you are currently using your time.

Procrastination is the purposeful, though sometimes unrecognized, putting off of important tasks, often at the time they *should* be done. It expresses itself in a variety of ways. For example, some students put off working on important course assignments until the very last minute, leaving little time to meet the deadline (or do a good job). Others establish timetables for several projects but don't leave enough time for doing quality work. Some students place the responsibility for their work on others, for example, by not starting to write a paper until they can bounce their ideas off others (whose expertise they believe is needed). A final example of procrastination occurs when students blame others for interfering with their ability to stay on task. This approach is seen when students blame their school for having restricted library hours, their residence hall friends for not respecting their privacy, and their employers for extending opportunities to work extra hours. The motivations to procrastinate are subtle. They include anxiety or fear that the required work will not be done well (regardless of time) and a general sense of apathy.

Procrastination is sometimes fostered by the tendency to spend too much valuable time engaged in *maintenance tasks*, such as organizing materials on your desk, taking a nap, or going to lunch or dinner. The rationalization is that these things are a necessary part of getting ready for the work to be done. In contrast, *progress tasks* move you into your academic work, such as reviewing notes prior to the next class meeting, running database searches, and visiting professors for clarification of assignments. Although time consuming, progress tasks are valuable in terms of efficient use of time and quality of work.

Specific techniques can be used to structure your time in ways that enhance academic progress. The following list reflects one approach to time management taken by many successful post-secondary students:

1. *Investigate time use.* Make a time/activity log for one week. Include descriptive entries for each half-hour period of the day to see where and how you are using time. Then analyze the log to identify how you misuse time (e.g., procrastination, overuse of maintenance tasks).
2. *Organize activities.* Next, divide the day into blocks so that related activities can be scheduled together. Clearly identify the blocks for your major areas of responsibility, such as academics, employment, recreation, family activities, and socializing.
3. *Establish a time schedule.* For each block of activities, determine the amount of time you can assign to each block. Then, within that block, fill in the amount of time to be allotted to each specific activity. For example, on a particular day three hours may be assigned to review and refine class notes, with one hour given to a particular course and 40 minutes each to three other courses.
4. *Privatize time.* State your intentions about doing serious and time-consuming schoolwork. Post a "Do Not Disturb" sign on your door. Leave the social atmosphere of your home, residence hall room, or apartment to work in a public area. Libraries, empty classrooms, and some coffee shops make excellent work environments for many students.

Review and modify this process to fit your requirements. Time management is not impossible for most students. In fact, it is an effective approach used by the more successful (and busier) students on the typical university or college campus.

Test Anxiety

As examination time approaches, *test anxiety* may appear. For some students, the days and hours before major examinations are filled with real, but generalized, feelings

Key Term

psychoneuroimmunology
A newly emerging field of human biology and clinical medicine that studies the functional interfaces among the mind, nervous system, and immune system.

of discomfort because they think that they will not perform well. Often, this situation is the result of poor time management. Those students who know that they will experience test anxiety may be prompted to use time-management strategies to reduce this problem. If this approach doesn't work for you, and you still feel test anxiety, contact your campus psychological services centre. Most schools offer group sessions that explore methods of preparing for and taking examinations at no expense to students.

TALKING POINTS • How would you explain to a classmate that he is spending too much time on maintenance tasks before an important test and not enough time on progress tasks?

COPING: REACTING TO STRESSORS

It is no longer socially acceptable to escape stressors through negative dependency behaviour, withdrawal, or aggressiveness. Currently, the emphasis is on lifestyle-management techniques, such as time management, that are not only effective but also supportive of overall health, social relationships, and the environment.

Stress-Management Techniques

Experts in stress management have proposed several effective techniques for coping with stress. Each of these techniques is described in the material that follows, with specific instructions provided for some. You will not know whether a particular coping approach is effective for you until you study the technique and use it for an adequate time.

It is strongly advised that you enlist the assistance of qualified health professionals in each of the specified activities below in order to fully benefit from the experience, as well as to prevent injury.

Self-hypnosis

Techniques designed to increase awareness, induce mental relaxation, and enhance self-directedness are taught by trained professionals to people who can be hypnotized. These techniques, which can be learned in one lesson, are self-administered in daily sessions lasting from 10 to 20 minutes. Beware of unqualified practitioners, who frequently sell their services through newspaper advertisements. Contact professional organizations, such as psychological or psychiatric societies, for a list of qualified therapists.

The relaxation response

The "relaxation response," a technique developed by Herbert Benson, M.D., is a method of learning to quiet the body and the mind. The relaxation technique centres on exhalation and allowing the body to relax while sitting in a comfortable position. It can be learned in a single session but requires a commitment to practice. Effective for many people, the technique is described in Dr. Benson's book *The Relaxation Response.*[15]

Progressive muscle relaxation

Pioneered by the work of Edmund Johnson (author of *You Must Relax*),[16] progressive muscle relaxation (PMR) is a procedure in which each of several muscle groups is systematically contracted and relaxed. The theory is that by learning to recognize the difference between contracted and relaxed muscles, you can purposely place certain muscles into a controlled state of stress-reducing relaxation.

PMR is based on the appropriate use of positioning, breathing, and concentration. The position of choice is lying on the floor, with the hands at the sides and the palms facing upward. Once a comfortable position has been assumed, alternating periods of inhalation and exhalation are begun. During inhalation, the muscles are contracted. During exhalation, the muscle groups are relaxed. Concentration is focused on the "feelings" of relaxation that accompany the release of tension during each exhalation. Once mastered, the basics can be done in almost any setting, including in a moving car, at a desk, and in a college classroom. Depending on a person's level of expertise, contractions last from a maximum of 100 seconds to a minimum of 5 seconds. The face, jaw, neck, shoulders, upper chest, hands and

HealthQuest Activities
www.mcgrawhill.ca/college/hahn

HQ

- The *How Stressed Are You?* activity in the Stress Management and Mental Health Module lets you look at several areas of your life (including money, school, relationships, and health) and identify stress caused by various events and daily hassles. You can also rate your perceived stress level for each area. Use this feature to find out which area or areas generate the highest levels of stress for you.
- The *CyberStress* activity in the Stress Management and Mental Health Module simulates a stress-filled day. Use it to assess your reactions to daily stressors. Choose the scenario that most closely matches your own. For example, if you work and go to school, you should check both of these choices on the preferences screen. As you are presented with stressful situations, choose the reaction that is closest to how you would react. At the feedback screen, print the screen showing your score. Then evaluate your experience by answering the questions in the *What Do You Think?* section.

forearms, abdomen, lower back, buttocks, thighs, calves, and feet are tightened and then relaxed progressively. To the extent possible, each muscle group within the area is included.

Quieting

Quieting involves using a set of specific responses, such as striving for a positive mental state, an "inner smile," and a deep exhalation, with the tongue and shoulders relaxed, as soon as the onset of stress is noted. This technique can be practised at any time and is easily learned. Its main advantage is that it produces an immediate feeling of "being on top of" the stress. The technique can be learned by reading *QR: The Quieting Reflex*, by Charles Stroebel, M.D., Ph.D.[17]

Yoga

An ancient exercise program for the mind and body, yoga can be learned from a qualified instructor in 1 to 13 months. It is practised daily in a quiet setting in sessions lasting 15 to 45 minutes. Yoga can alter specific physiological functions, enhance flexibility, and free the mind from worry. Many good yoga books, classes, and videotapes are available.

Diaphragmatic breathing

A coping technique that combines elements of relaxation and quieting is diaphragmatic breathing. Aspects of this practice are seen in the Lamaze approach to childbirth, yoga, and tai chi. Although no single explanation for its effectiveness can be given, when practised regularly, diaphragmatic breathing produces relaxation that buffers the powerful stress response. A three-component approach to the practice of diaphragmatic breathing is described below:

1. *Assume a comfortable position.* Lie on the floor with arms by your sides, eyes closed, back straight. Begin breathing from the diaphragm, rather than by lifting the chest.
2. *Concentrate.* The ability to concentrate is important. It is most easily mastered by following the pathway of air as it enters the body and flows deeply into the lower levels of the lungs, followed by the rising of the stomach as the air leaves the lungs. Each ventilation can be fragmented into four distinct steps: (1) take air into your lungs through the nose and mouth, (2) pause slightly before exhaling, (3) release the air to flow out via the path from which it entered, and (4) pause slightly after exhalation before repeating step 1.
3. *Visualize.* Diaphragmatic breathing promotes relaxation most fully when it is practised in conjunction with visualization. What is visualized varies from person to person, but many feel that envisioning the air (or clouds) entering the body with each breath, travelling down the path taken by the air, and leaving through the nostrils is very effective. Extending the image of the air flowing throughout the entire body (energy breathing), rather than only into the lungs, is even more effective.

Once mastered, diaphragmatic breathing quiets the body. Experienced users of this technique can temporarily lower their breathing from a typical rate of 14 to 18 breaths per minute to as few as 4 breaths per minute. With this technique, the entire nervous system is slowed, in direct opposition to its role in the stress response.

Transcendental meditation

Transcendental meditation (TM) allows the mind to transcend thought effortlessly when the person recites a mantra, or a personal word, twice daily for 20 minutes. It is a seven-step program taught by trained professionals. TM centres are listed in the telephone directory under Transcendental Meditation.

Biofeedback

Biofeedback is a system for monitoring and controlling specific physiological functions, such as heart rate, respiratory rate, and body temperature. Training with an experienced instructor and appropriate monitoring instruments requires weekly sessions that last one hour or longer over 12 or more weeks. When used with other tension-reduction techniques, biofeedback provides reinforcement of stress-reduction goals. For more information, visit Mind-Body Medicine Canada at **www.mindbodycan.com**.

Exercise

Various movement activities are intended to reduce stress, expend energy, promote relaxation, provide enjoyment through social contact, and produce biological opiates. Running, jogging, lap swimming, walking, rope skipping, cycling, stair climbing, and aerobic dancing are all excellent ways to burn the energy produced by the stress response. Equipment needs, facilities, and required skills vary. Three to four sessions per week lasting a half-hour per session are sufficient for most people. Health and fitness clubs also offer exercise programs.

Art, dance, and poetry therapy

As an aid to emotional, physical, and spiritual health, the arts can be used to enhance an individual's sense of well-being. Qualified professional therapists in these fields work one on one or in group sessions. Although the methods used may vary, the idea is to foster a sense of peace through the art form and a focus for the troubled person's thoughts and energy during times of illness or stress.

Exploring Your Spirituality

Journaling: Self-Help for Stress

Feeling anxious about your college or university experience? Trying to put past events in perspective? Want to record your experiences? Focused, regular writing—journaling—is growing in popularity as a way to approach these issues.

Writing in a journal each day slows your pace. You sit and reflect. You connect with an experience by recalling details you may have forgotten, then write them down. For 15 to 30 minutes a day, you pause to make sense of your life.

Journaling generally gets easier the more you do it, so start by writing about nonthreatening topics. Try this: Each day, ask yourself a simple question, and then write the answer in your journal. As you gain experience, you may want to tackle more difficult issues.

Here are some journaling tips. Use an easy-to-carry spiral-bound notebook with a thick cover, so you can write anywhere. Or you may want to set aside a regular time and place so you won't be disturbed. Once you start writing, keep your pen moving continuously. Don't go back to correct spelling or punctuation. That will only slow you down and distract you from your thoughts, which are more important than perfect writing. Give yourself permission not to have to share your journal with others as this may inhibit your writing, making it less honest and open.

One powerful form of journaling is therapeutic, or healing, journaling, in which the individual writes about a traumatic event for 15 to 30 minutes a day, on three or four consecutive days. Studies by James W. Pennebaker, M.D. and colleagues noted lowered blood pressure and heart rates in healthy people who wrote about their innermost feelings for 20 minutes on three consecutive days.

Therapeutic writing can be very difficult and should be approached with caution. In particular, if you have been under medical treatment, check with your health care professional before you begin a therapeutic journaling program. If you write about private events, you can shred or burn your pages. Be aware of not just writing about negative events or emotions. Don't allow this to be a journal about "how I messed up today."

Want to know more about journaling? Personal Journaling Magazine (**www.journalingmagazine.com**) is a good place to start. You'll find that journaling takes many forms, including memoirs, dream journals, chronicles of daily life, and "blogging."

In college or university, most of the things you write, such as papers and reports, are assigned and judged by an instructor. But when you write in a journal, it's for yourself—no judgments, no grades.

Tired of being stressed out all the time? Want to clear out the cobwebs in your head? Take out paper and pen and embark on one of the most exciting trips you'll ever take—the journey into yourself.

Regular physical activity reduces stress and promotes relaxation.

A Realistic Perspective on Stress and Life

It's important to approach life with a tough-minded optimism based on hope and anticipation and understand that life will never be free of stress. To develop this type of realistic approach to today's fast-paced, demanding lifestyle, use the following guidelines:[18]

- *Don't be surprised by trouble.* Anticipate problems, and see yourself as a problem solver.
- *Search for solutions.* Act on a partial solution, even when a complete solution seems distant.
- *Take control of your own future.* Set out to accomplish all of your goals. Don't view yourself as a victim of circumstances.
- *Move away from negative thought patterns.* Don't extend or generalize difficulties from one area into another.
- *Rehearse success.* Don't disregard the possibility of failure. Instead, focus on the things that are necessary and possible to ensure success.
- *Accept the unchangeable.* The direction your life takes is only partly the result of your own doing. Cope as effectively as possible with the events over which you have no direct control.

- *Live each day well.* Combine activity, contemplation, and a sense of cheerfulness with the many things that must be done each day. Celebrate special occasions.
- *Act on your capacity for growth.* Undertake new experiences, and extract from them new information about your interests and abilities.
- *Allow for renewal.* Make time for yourself. Take advantage of opportunities to pursue new and fulfilling relationships. Foster growth of your spiritual nature.
- *Tolerate mistakes.* Both you and others will make mistakes. Recognize that these can cause anger or frustration, and learn to avoid feelings of hostility.

With a realistic and positive outlook on life, you'll need less coping time to live a satisfying and productive life. Change in all aspects of life is inevitable. With good health, change should be anticipated, nurtured, and incorporated into your maturing sense of well-being.

Taking Charge of Your Health

- Analyze your past successes in resolving stressful situations, noting the resources that were helpful to you.
- Prioritize your daily goals in a list that you can accomplish, allowing time for recreational activities.
- Counteract a tendency to procrastinate by setting up imaginary (early) deadlines for assignments and rewarding yourself when you meet those dates.
- Add a new physical activity, such as an intramural team sport, to your daily schedule.
- Replace a damaging coping technique that you currently use, such as smoking, with an effective alternative, such as diaphragmatic breathing or yoga.
- List the positive aspects of your life, and make them the focus of your everyday thoughts.
- Explore the stress-reduction services that are available in your community, both on and off campus.

SUMMARY

- Stress is the physiological and emotional response to the presence of a stressor. Stressors are events that generate the stress response.
- Distress and eustress reflect similar physiological responses but different emotional interpretations.
- Uncontrolled stress can lead to a variety of illnesses. Since the effects of stress are cumulative, stress-related health problems can develop slowly.
- The college or university experience can generate stressors from several different areas, including finances, classroom requirements, and personal expectations.
- In today's world, even the media, which deliver information to us, can cause as much or more stress than the messages they deliver.
- The general adaptation syndrome consists of three distinct stages: alarm, resistance, and exhaustion. Ideally, exhaustion from excessive stress will not occur and recovery will follow.
- An intricate interplay involving the brain, the nervous system, and the endocrine system results in a series of physiological changes that prepare the body to respond to stressors.
- The stress response mobilizes energy for the flight-or-fight response.
- Stress that is chronic in nature can generate both psychogenic and psychosomatic conditions.
- Yerkes-Dodson Law refers to a bell-shaped curve demonstrating that there is an optimal level of stress for peak performance. This law states that too little and too much stress is not helpful, while a moderate level of stress is positive and beneficial.
- Experts in psychoneuroimmunology are gaining insight into the mechanisms through which the mind influences the nervous system and the effectiveness of the immune system.
- Chronic feelings of anger and cynicism can be central to the development of stress.
- Ineffective time management may be the single most powerful stressor influencing post-secondary students. To overcome this problem, effective time-management techniques can be learned.
- A variety of coping techniques can be easily learned and used to reduce stress.
- Therapeutic techniques such as art, dance, and poetry therapy may aid in stress reduction by enhancing the spiritual dimension of health.
- An optimistic outlook on life may protect some people from the potentially damaging effects of stressors. A less stressful life also enhances health and fosters a greater sense of well-being.

REVIEW QUESTIONS

1. What is the difference between stress and stressors?
2. How do distress and eustress differ? In what way are they similar?
3. Which familiar health conditions are often attributed to chronic unresolved stress? To what extent are the effects of stress cumulative?
4. Describe the flight-or-fight response.
5. How does the college or university experience contribute to the stress level of students?
6. In what predictable manner does the stress response unfold? What is the role of the endocrine system? What are the principal energy stores used during the stress response? What is the role of epinephrine and the glucocorticoids in relationship to the energy needs associated with the stress response?
7. Describe the Yerkes-Dodson Law.
8. What is psychoneuroimmunology? To date, what has research found in regard to immune function and the occurrence of stress?
9. How do anger and cynicism contribute to stress? How do type R people use the stress response?
10. What coping techniques have proved helpful when used on a regular basis? How do various modern technologies contribute to the high levels of stress reported by many North Americans?
11. What are some techniques for improving time management? What is the difference between a maintenance task and a progress task?
12. What traits characterize the optimistic lifestyle?

THINK ABOUT THIS ...

- Can you remember a stressful experience you had recently in which your body responses clearly followed the pattern of Selye's general adaptation syndrome?
- If the body's response to stressors is similar for distress and eustress, how do we learn to distinguish between the two?
- What is a realistic perception about the potentially stressful nature of life?
- Which dimension of your health do you most frequently rely on when confronted with a stressful situation?
- What strategies would you recommend to a friend who is struggling to cope with stress? Why?

REFERENCES

1. Selye H: *Stress without distress*, 1975, New American Library.
2. Benjamin J et al: Population and familial association between the D4 dopamine receptor gene and measures of novelty seeking, *Nature Genetics*, 12(1):81–84, 1996.
3. DeGucht V, Fischler B, Demanet C: Immune dysfunction associated with chronic professional stress in nurses, *Psychiatry Res*, 85(1):105–111, 1999.
4. Selye H: *The stress of life*, 1976, New York: The McGraw-Hill Co.
5. Ibid.
6. *Stress without distress.*
7. Ibid.
8. Saladin K: *Anatomy and physiology: the unity of form and function*, 1998, McGraw-Hill.
9. Girdano DA, Everly GS, Dusek DE: *Controlling stress and tension*. 1996, Allyn & Bacon.
10. Hebb, DO: Drive and the CNS (central nervous system). *Psychological Review* 62(4) 243–254, 1955.
11. Benson H and Allen R: How much stress is too much? *Harvard Business Review*, September/October, 1980.
12. Elenkov I et al: Stress, corticotropin-releasing hormone, glucocorticoids, and the immune/inflammation response: acute and chronic effects, *Ann NY Acad Sci*, 866:1–11, discussion 11–13, 1999.
13. Keltikangas-Jarvinen L et al: Vital exhaustion, anger expression, and pituitary and adrenocortical hormones: implications for the insulin resistance syndrome, *Arterioscler Thromb Casc Biol*, 16(2):275–280, 1996.
14. Almada S et al: Neuroticism and cynicism and risk of death in middle-aged men: the Western Electric study, *Psychosom Med*, 53(2):165–175, 1991.
15. Benson H (with MZ Klipper): *The relaxation response*, 1990, Mass Marketing Paperback.
16. Jacobson E: *You must relax*, 1991, National Foundation for Progressive Relaxation.
17. Stroebel C: *QR: the quieting reflex*, 1983, Berkley.
18. McGinnis L: *The power of optimism*, 1990, Harper & Row.

SUGGESTED READINGS

Burke L: *Seven steps to stress-free teaching: a stress prevention planning guide for teachers*, 1999, Educators' Lighthouse.
In this book, an experienced teacher shares her step-by-step approach to reducing the stress of classroom teaching. Included are specific techniques to use for classroom management, time management, and parental pressure. The author also addresses aspects of the personal life of teachers and how they can be structured to avoid conflict with professional responsibilities. If you're an education major, you'll find this book helpful in planning your career as a classroom teacher.

Jevne R, Williams D: *When dreams don't work: professional caregivers and burnout*, 1998, Baywood Publishing Company.
In this book, the term *caregivers* is broadened to include a wide array of social service fields, such as teaching, social work, law enforcement, and other public service–centred occupations. Special attention is given to the motivations of people who enter these fields and to the emotional, social, and spiritual forces that precipitate the burnout they often experience. If you're considering a career in one of the helping professions, you may find this book a valuable source of information.

Mayer J: *Time management for dummies*, ed 2, 1999, IDG Books Worldwide.
The author, a recognized authority in the field of time management, focuses on areas such as organizing work space, establishing a daily planning process, efficient use of the telephone and other electronic equipment, setting goals, and making time for family activities.

1,001 perfectly legal ways to get exactly what you want, when you want it, every time, 1999, FC&A Publishing.
Sometimes the lack of a detail or certain obscure information makes daily life more stressful than it needs to be. This book supplies such information on topics ranging from financial management and child rearing to pet care. It promises readers that they will have more money in their pockets, more time and fun in their lives, and less stress after reading this book.

Making Headlines

An astounding 91% of Canadians say maintaining mental health is very important, yet few Canadians are willing to admit receiving treatment.

A national survey, conducted by Compas Research for the Canadian Mental Health Association (CMHA) determined that an overwhelming majority of Canadians say that maintaining their mental health is "very important." This is one of the highest "intense opinion" scores that Compas has ever recorded.

Woman are especially apt to feel that maintaining mental health is very important, 95% versus 88% for men, while Canadians 18 to 24 years of age were the least likely to feel that this is important (77% versus 91% of Canadians as a whole).

Surprisingly, despite these statistics, Canadians are feeling less comfortable about letting others know when they are receiving treatment or counselling for depression. Only 54% indicated that they might want a friend to know, compared to 69% in 1997. According to CMHA National President Bill Gaudette, "changing attitudes to mental illness continue to be our biggest challenge. Discrimination, ignorance and fear remain the enemies that we have to conquer."

The survey results also indicated that women are more willing than men to let friends know if they or one of their family members are getting counselling for depression. Sixty percent of women would definitely or probably want their friends to know, compared to only 40% of men.

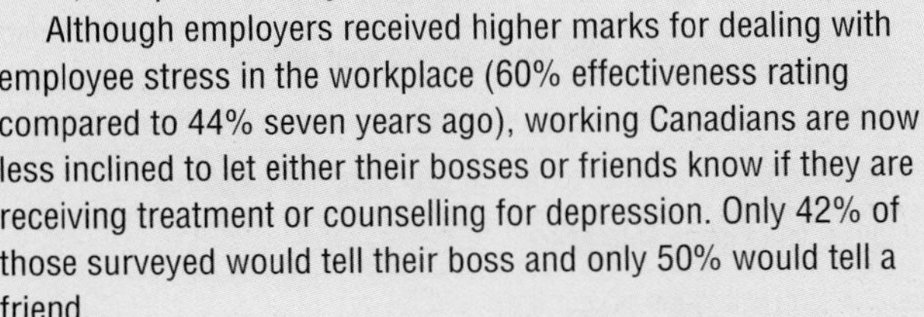

Although employers received higher marks for dealing with employee stress in the workplace (60% effectiveness rating compared to 44% seven years ago), working Canadians are now less inclined to let either their bosses or friends know if they are receiving treatment or counselling for depression. Only 42% of those surveyed would tell their boss and only 50% would tell a friend.

The national survey was commissioned by the Canadian Mental Health Association in 2001 to mark the 50th anniversary of Mental Health Week in Canada and as part of an ongoing study of changing attitudes toward mental health.

To help reduce the sense of isolation that people with mental illnesses often experience and to encourage people to speak freely about mental health issues, the CMHA is promoting the use of the new "Emerging into Light" symbol endorsed by the Canadian Alliance on Mental Illness and Health. Described as a symbol of recovery and resilience, the image was created by Jennifer Osborn, a talented young Canadian artist and consumer of mental health services. Rather than being a logo of any particular organization, the new symbol is being shared freely among individual Canadians who care about mental illness and health issues. Visit the CHHA Web site for information concerning stress and coping with stressors. (**www.cmha.ca**)

Name ______________________ **Date** __________

Personal Assessment

How Stressed Are You?

You must know how much stress you are under and what events are triggering your feelings of stress before you can begin to cope effectively. In the following stress test, developed by researchers at Carnegie Mellon University, you can obtain a rough measure of the level of stress you are under. The questions reflect some of the most familiar perceptions of people who are experiencing distress.

The higher your total score on this test, the higher your level of stress. In the general population, the average score for men was 12 and for women was 14.

Other stress assessments indicate that difficult or unexpected life events, such as the death of a family member, arrest and incarceration, the demands of school or work, a pregnancy (yours or your partner's), a serious illness or injury, and even marriage, are among the greatest sources of stress for most adults. How familiar are you with these events?

In the last month, how often have you felt	Never	Almost never	Sometimes	Fairly often	Very often
Upset because of something that happened unexpectedly?	0	1	2	3	4
Unable to control the important things in your life?	0	1	2	3	4
Nervous and "stressed"?	0	1	2	3	4
Unable to cope with all the things you had to do	0	1	2	3	4
Angered because of things that were beyond your control?	0	1	2	3	4
That difficulties were piling up so high that you could not overcome them?	0	1	2	3	4
Confident about your abilities to handle your personal problems?	4	3	2	1	0
That things were going your way?	4	3	2	1	0
Able to control irritations in your life?	4	3	2	1	0
That you were on top of things?	4	3	2	1	0

TOTAL SCORE: ______________

Name ______________________________ Date ______________

Personal Assessment

Do You Manage Your Time Effectively?

This assessment is designed to help you determine how you are spending your nonsleeping hours. With this information, you will be able to assess the effectiveness of your time management. In particular, you will be able to judge whether you are scheduling enough time for your academic responsibilities.

In one week, there are 168 hours available. You need six to eight hours of sleep per day. If six hours is used as a realistic figure for daily sleep, that makes 42 hours a week for sleep. So the remaining (nonsleeping) time for one week is 126 hours.

Directions: Calculate the number of hours per day that you spend in each of the activity categories listed on the right. Then multiply each figure by 7 to determine the number of hours spent weekly for each activity. Total these figures. Then subtract this total from 126. The result is the number of hours remaining for your classes and classwork.

1. Hours spent getting ready to begin the day _____ × 7 = _____
2. Hours spent "on the road" (going to and from class, work, and other locations) _____ × 7 = _____
3. Hours spent doing planned exercise _____ × 7 = _____
4. Hours spent eating (meals and snacks) _____ × 7 = _____
5. Hours spent watching television and DVDs _____ × 7 = _____
6. Hours spent on the Internet, excluding school-related assignments and research _____ × 7 = _____
7. Hours spent in extracurricular activities or employment _____ × 7 = _____
8. Hours spent "hanging out" with friends _____ × 7 = _____

TOTAL _____

After subtracting the total hours from 126, you will see how many hours are available for class attendance, research, writing, and test preparation. Are you showing signs of poor time management? Consider reassigning some of your time to different categories.

Focus on

MANAGING WORK-RELATED STRESS

When someone is introduced to you, the first thing you learn is the person's name. Next, you usually find out something about that person's occupation. Since North Americans identify people with the jobs they perform, our self-identity is linked to our occupations. As a result, anything that threatens our job or job performance can be a threat to our sense of personal worth.

Job stress is becoming a part of everyday life. In a 1999 study for *The Wirthin Report*, 67% of the respondents reported that their work was very stressful or moderately stressful. Only 10% said that their work was not stressful. If left unchecked, employment-related stress can have negative effects on our feelings of well-being and the structure and function of our bodies. The cardiovascular and immune systems are particularly vulnerable to work-related stress.[1,2]

Sources of Job Stress

Since work-related stress can be a significant problem, it is important to identify what specific things can cause stress in the workplace, such as the following:

- Conflicts with colleagues, supervisors, or workers under your supervision
- Changes in work routine
- Deadlines
- Too much (or too little) responsibility
- Lack of control over work methods and planning
- Long working hours
- Repetitive tasks
- Excessive or rhythmic noise
- Poor time management or organization
- Working with hazardous equipment or substances
- Threat of pay reduction or unemployment
- Lack of necessary resources

Nearly everyone has to deal with these issues at one time or another in the workplace. Although these stressors may vary from job to job, and individuals may react to them in different ways, they still produce an effect.

Job Stress among Older Workers

In general, older workers are hit hardest by job stress. Technological advances tend to cause more stress for them, especially for workers who have been performing a similar routine for a long time and are suddenly forced to assimilate new technology into their daily work.[3] Older workers are also prime targets for layoffs. As a result, some are leaving the workforce at an earlier age than expected. This situation may produce both financial and psychological stress.

Stress in the Modern Workplace

Throughout the last 25 years, corporate mergers and buyouts have eliminated entire companies and thousands of jobs, new technology has caused a drastic increase in the pace of work, and heightened competition has forced individual employees to take on much heavier workloads. All of this adds up to increased stress.

Technology

Today's workers must deal with stressors that are unique to our time. The most obvious is the drastic increase in workplace technology. Workers must be more knowledgeable about the new machines they use, and so re-education becomes necessary. Personal computers and computer networks, which are constantly increasing workplace efficiency and speed, also contribute to job stress. Getting more work done in a specified time means more profit for a company, but it also leads to the expectation that more work will continue to be accomplished in less time. Therefore the person working at the computer may be asked to perform more and more tasks in a workday. The increased productivity resulting from computer use can lead to the elimination of many jobs, since one worker may now be able to do the work that was once done by two or more people.

The computer may also contribute to physical problems. Constant work on a keyboard places excess stress on the fingers, hands, and wrists. This, in turn, may contribute to arthritic conditions or *carpal tunnel syndrome*. The simple act of sitting at the computer for extended periods with the body in a fixed position puts stress on the muscles and bones of the back, neck, and limbs.[4]

Problems caused by repetitive motions, unusual body postures, or holding static joint positions over extended periods are referred to as *repetitive strain injuries* (RSIs).[5] The risk of developing RSIs is increased during periods of emotional stress or deadline pressure.[6] RSIs can also develop because of improper placement of equipment (e.g., a keyboard). Company production goals based on quotas, such as counting workers' keystrokes, may influence employees to work through needed break periods to meet the expected work output.

Downsizing

The corporate practice of eliminating jobs to cut costs—downsizing—can contribute greatly to job stress.[7] This practice affects both rank-and-file workers and management; everyone is vulnerable. Often, cuts are made with little or no regard to an employee's years of service or experience (or senior employees are "let go" as a way of saving money). This lack of job security has been an important contributor to job stress over the last decade.

The fear of being unemployed and the difficult transition following unemployment causes workers and their families to develop a variety of stress-induced conditions, including anxiety and depression. These families also often display higher than normal rates of divorce and drug and alcohol abuse.

One extreme expression of the impact of work-related stress is death resulting from cardiovascular disease, particularly heart attack. As long ago as 1982, this trend was reported in the Swedish workforce.[8] Autopsies on these heart attack victims, some of whom were as young as 29, showed that no significant risk factors were present except for high levels of chemicals (e.g., epinephrine) that are released in response to stress. Other industrialized nations, including Canada and the United States, are observing signs of this trend in their workforces.

Competition

Although there are more than enough jobs being created to offset those lost through downsizing, many new jobs offer lower pay, fewer benefits, and less desirable working conditions. As a result, competition for good jobs is growing keener. A university education is no longer enough. More than 20 percent of adults hold at least a bachelor's degree, and over 40 percent of adults have some university or college experience. The most current statistics available (1994–1995 academic year) indicate that over 14 million students in the United States are currently enrolled at institutions of higher education.[9] In Canada in the academic year 1998–1999, universities enrolled 707 600 undergraduate students and 79 400 graduate students. At community colleges and related institutions, 409 848 students enrolled in full-time, post-secondary programs.[10] Workers whose jobs are cut are facing competition from new graduates, who will often work for less money, and from others who have been laid off. New graduates are competing with displaced workers, who usually have a wealth of work experience.

Reducing Work-Related Stress

Since work-related stress appears to be increasing in most professions, it is important to recognize the physical signs of stress and reduce job stress when possible. Here are a few things you can do to reduce the effects of work-related stress:

- *Recognize when stress is getting to you.* Be able to identify early warning signs that you may be under heavy stress. Emotional signs may include anxiety, lack of interest, and irritability. Mental fatigue, physical exhaustion, and frequent illness may be physical manifestations of stress. Know yourself well enough to recognize when stressors are affecting you.
- *Control your environment when you can.* Not every work situation can be controlled, but managing some situations can help reduce stress. Try not to schedule stressful work activities in succession. Break larger jobs down into smaller parts. Rearrange your work area to keep things fresh.
- *Know the things you cannot control and deal with them.* Becoming angry or obsessed over a situation you can't do anything about only increases your stress level. Developing a flexible attitude toward situations on the job that are not flexible is a healthy approach.
- *Take a break.* Schedule some down time to keep yourself refreshed. If your breaks are scheduled for you, don't use them to get extra work done. When performing repetitive tasks, step away from the task whenever you can. If you work at a computer terminal, get up occasionally and move around.
- *Get some exercise.* Physical activity can be healthy for the mind and the body. Exercise can actually increase energy levels and strengthen physical resistance to stress.
- *Make your workplace safe.* Take safety precautions when possible. If safety equipment is available, use it. Staying safe on the job can prevent stressful situations that may occur because of an injury, such as missed work, decreased productivity, and physical pain.

If you notice that stress on the job is affecting you physically or mentally, see your family doctor or a qualified mental health professional as soon as possible. Work-related stress does not have to become an overwhelming factor in your life. Managing stress is an important skill that all employees must learn to master. Set aside time to assess your problems and devise strategies to deal with your stressful situations.

References

1. McCann BS, Benjamin CA et al: Plasma lipid concentrations during episodic occupational stress, *Ann Behav Med*, 21(2):103–110, 1999.
2. DeGucht V, Fischler B, Demanet C: Immune dysfunction associated with chronic professional stress in nurses, *Psychiatry Res*, 85(1):105–111, 1999.
3. Reissman DB, Orris P et al: Downsizing role demands, and job stress, *J Occup Environ Med*, 41(4):289–293, 1999.
4. Tittiranonda P, Burastero S, Rempel D: Risk factors for musculoskeletal disorders among computer users, *Occup Med*, 14(1):17–38, 1999.
5. Nainzadeh N, Malantic-Lin A et al: Repetitive strain injury (cumulative trauma disorder): causes and treatment, *Mt Sinai J Med*, 66(3):192–196, 1999.
6. Alfredsson L, Karasek R, Theorell T: Myocardial infarction risk and psychosocial work environment: an analysis of the male Swedish working force, *Soc Sci Med*, 16(4):463–467, 1982.
7. Downsizing role demands.
8. Myocardial infarction risk.
9. US Bureau of the Census: *Statistical abstract of the United States: 1999*, 119th ed, 1999, Washington, DC.
10. Canadian Education Statistics Council: *Report of the pan Canadian education indicator program, 1999*, 1999.

Part Two

Chapter 4

Becoming Physically Fit

Chapter Objectives

After reading this chapter, you should be able to

- Explain why cardiorespiratory fitness is more important to health than other types of fitness, including muscular strength, muscular endurance, and flexibility.
- Describe the effects that regular aerobic exercise has on the heart, lungs, and circulatory system.
- Define aerobic energy production and anaerobic energy production.
- List and discuss the health concerns of midlife adults and elderly adults.
- Discuss the requirements of a suitable cardiorespiratory fitness program, including the mode of activity, frequency, intensity, duration, and resistance.
- Explain the role of the warm-up, conditioning, and cooldown in an exercise session.
- Explain the role exercise should play in pregnancy.
- Discuss the role of fluid replacement in exercise, including when one should consume fluids and the best types of fluids to consume.
- Discuss the contribution of sleep to overall wellness.

Online Learning Centre Resources

www.mcgrawhill.ca/college/hahn

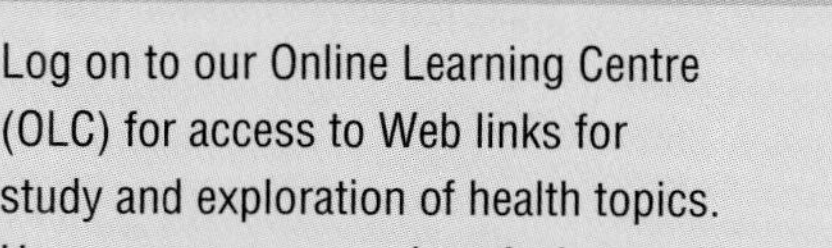

Log on to our Online Learning Centre (OLC) for access to Web links for study and exploration of health topics. Here are some examples of what you'll find:

- **www.primusweb.com/fitnesspartner** Use this jumpsite to find fitness information on topics ranging from nutrition to equipment.
- **www.netsweat.com** Click on this site for a fitness message board where you can post a question for discussion.

A guide to help you make wise choices about physical activity. Choices that will improve your health, help prevent disease, and allow you to get the most out of life

Get active your way ...

build physical activity into your daily life...
at home
at school
at work
at play
on the way
.... that's active living !

- **www.paguide.com** Find guidelines for a personal exercise program. Get active your way every day of your life.

Media Pulse

Magazines Feature Readers' Choice—Health News

In the past decade, popular magazines have initiated or greatly expanded their coverage of health issues. This is especially true for the magazines that cover national and international news. In fact, it is difficult to pick up a major news magazine (such as *Time, Newsweek,* or *Maclean's)* and *not* find one or two articles about health issues. Occasionally, these magazines have cover stories on topics such as fitness, obesity, smoking, prescription drugs, the environment, herbal supplements, growth and development, and sexuality.

Media Pulse *continued*

This inclusion of health issues did not come about without careful consideration by the media moguls. Readers have been routinely surveyed by publishers about their preferences for topics. Since readers have reported that they want more coverage of health issues, magazine publishers have complied.

Fortunately, the health editors and writers for these major publications generally do an excellent job of preparing their news reports. Most try to consult (and then quote) health researchers who are experts in their fields. Many reports in the popular news magazines present the results of health-related research that has been published in scientific journals or presented at professional meetings.

You, the consumer (reader), should be aware, however, that magazine articles may not give the most complete coverage of a health issue or may exaggerate the threat posed by certain diseases. Most health issues that are hot news items can be viewed from more than one perspective. Be inquisitive about finding out if there are conflicting views about stories that interest you. Find and read the original sources identified in the magazine article. Many of these original sources are available in your college or university library or on the Internet. If you have additional questions, ask professors, nutritionists, physical therapists, or physicians. Used in this way, magazine articles can provide an excellent first step in your quest to discover new information concerning your health.

TALKING POINTS • If you had a strong reaction to a news magazine's treatment of a certain health issue, would you consider writing a letter to the editor expressing your opinion?

PHYSICAL ACTIVITY

When your day begins early in the morning, then you go to class or work or immerse yourself in family activities, and your day does not end until after midnight, you must be physically fit to keep up the pace. Even a highly motivated college student must have a conditioned, rested body to maintain such a schedule. Yet despite understanding the importance of **physical activity**, many Canadians are not active enough (Figure 4–1).[1]

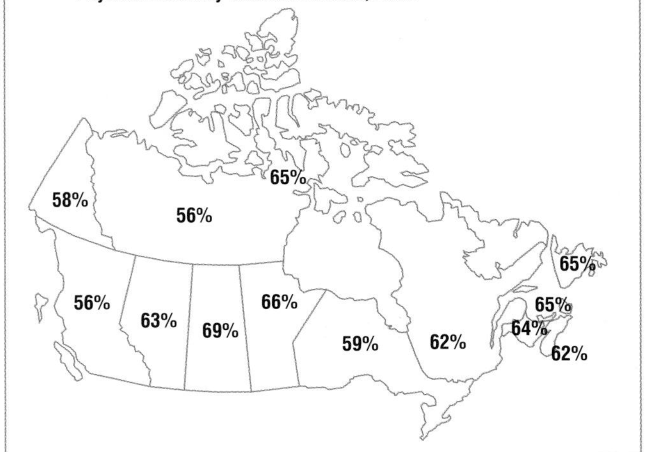

How Many Canadians Are Not Active Enough?
Physical inactivity levels in Canada, 2000

Figure 4–1 Physical inactivity remains pervasive in Canada, with 61% of adults aged 18 and older still considered insufficiently active for optimal health benefits in 2000, compared with 79% in 1981. While the physical inactivity rate is high in all regions of the country, it declines slightly as we move from Eastern to Western Canada.

More women (67%) than men (54%) are inactive. Physical inactivity levels also increase by age, with fewer 18- to 24-year-olds being inactive than adults in older age groups.

Fortunately, you don't have to be a top-notch athlete to enjoy the health benefits of physical activity. In fact, even a modest increase in your daily activity level can be rewarding. The health benefits of fitness can come from regular participation in moderate **exercise**, such as brisk walking or dancing[2] (see HealthQuest Activities, and the Changing for the Better box on p. 60).

COMPONENTS OF PHYSICAL FITNESS

Physical fitness is achieved when "the organic systems of the body are healthy and function efficiently so as to

Key Terms

physical activity
All leisure and nonleisure body movement produced by the skeletal muscles resulting in an increase in energy expenditure.

exercise
A form of leisure-time physical activity that is planned, structured, and repetitive. Its main objective is to improve or maintain physical fitness.

physical fitness
A set of attributes that are either health related or performance (or skill) related. Health-related fitness comprises those components of fitness that exhibit a relationship with health status. Performance/skill-related fitness involves those components of fitness that enable optimal work or sport performance.

Changing *for the Better*

The Many Benefits of Physical Activity

I'm probably not as active as I should be. What could I do to increase my activity level and generally feel better?

We know that being physically active provides benefits for all of us. Not being physically active is recognized by the Heart and Stroke Foundation of Canada as one of the four modifiable primary risk factors for coronary heart disease (along with high blood pressure, high blood cholesterol, and smoking). People are physically active for many reasons—play, work, competition, health, creativity, enjoying the outdoors, being with friends. There are also as many ways of being active as there are reasons for it. What we choose to do depends on our own abilities and desires. No matter what the reason or type of activity, physical activity can improve our well-being and quality of life. Well-being can also be enhanced by integrating physical activity with enjoyable healthy eating and positive self- and body image. Together, all three equal vitality. So take a fresh approach to living. Check out the vitality tips below!

Active Living

- Accumulate 30 minutes or more of moderate physical activity most days of the week.
- Take the stairs instead of an elevator.
- Get off the bus early and walk home.
- Join friends in a sport activity.
- Take the dog for a walk with the family.
- Follow a fitness program.

Healthy Eating

- Follow *Canada's Food Guide to Healthy Eating.*
- Enjoy a variety of foods.
- Emphasize cereals, breads, other grain products, vegetables, and fruit.
- Choose lower-fat dairy products, leaner meats, and foods prepared with little or no fat.
- Achieve and maintain a healthy body weight by enjoying regular physical activity and healthy eating.
- Limit salt, alcohol, and caffeine.
- Don't give up foods you enjoy—aim for moderation and variety.

Positive Self- and Body Image

- Accept who you are and how you look.
- Remember, a healthy weight range is one that is realistic for your own body makeup (body fat levels should neither be too high nor too low).
- Try a new challenge.
- Compliment yourself.
- Reflect positively on your abilities.
- Laugh a lot.
- Use *Canada's Physical Activity Guide to Healthy Active Living*

www.hc.sc.gc.ca/hppb/paguide

resist disease, to enable the fit person to engage in vigorous tasks and leisure activities, and to handle situations of emergency."[3] The following sections focus on cardiorespiratory endurance, muscular strength, muscular endurance, flexibility, and body composition.

Cardiorespiratory Endurance

If you were limited to improving only one area of your physical fitness, which would you choose—muscular strength, muscular endurance, or flexibility? Which would a dancer choose? Which would a marathon runner select? Which would an expert recommend?

HealthQuest Activities

www.mcgrawhill.ca/college/hahn

- The *How Fit Are You?* exercise in the Fitness Module will help you determine your current level of fitness in four major areas: cardiorespiratory capacity, muscular strength, flexibility, and body composition. Complete the series of questions about how much you exercise, what types of training you do, how intensely you exercise, and your body size. After you complete the questions, *HealthQuest* will give you feedback in each of the four areas mentioned above. Then develop an individual plan for improving or maintaining your current fitness level.
- The *Exercise Interest Inventory* in the Fitness Module allows you to rate your feelings about certain aspects of exercise. *HealthQuest* provides feedback about the activities and exercises you would most enjoy, based on your individual needs and preferences. First, write down the five fitness activities that you like best or those you participate in most often. After each one, indicate your motivation for engaging in that particular activity. For example, you could list "enjoyment," "habit," or "convenience." When you have completed the *Exercise Interest Inventory*, compare the two lists. Are there any surprises? What factors had you not considered to be influential in your choice of exercise?

Terry's Journey: The Marathon of Hope

Terry Fox was born in Winnipeg, Manitoba, but raised in Port Coquitlam, British Columbia, a community near Vancouver on Canada's west coast. An active teenager involved in many sports, Terry was only 18 years old when he was diagnosed with bone cancer and had his right leg amputated six inches above the knee in 1977.

The night before his operation, Terry read an article about an amputee who had competed in the New York Marathon. Indirectly, that story, along with Terry's observations of the intense suffering of cancer patients, set the stage for what would ultimately become the most important decision of his young life.

In 1980, Terry Fox inspired the nation by attempting to run across Canada on an artificial leg. He called this quest the Marathon of Hope. Its mission was to raise money and awareness for cancer research in Canada.

With little fanfare, Terry started his journey in St. John's, Newfoundland, on April 12, 1980. Although it was difficult to garner attention in the beginning, enthusiasm soon grew, and the money collected along his route began to mount. He ran 42 kilometres a day through Canada's Atlantic provinces, Quebec, and Ontario.

It was a journey that Canadians never forgot. However, on September 1st, after 143 days and 5373 kilometres, Terry was forced to stop his run outside Thunder Bay, Ontario, because the cancer had reappeared in his lungs. An entire nation was stunned and saddened. Terry passed away on June 28, 1981, at age 22.

The heroic Canadian was gone, but his legacy was just beginning. To date, $340 million worldwide has been raised for cancer research in Terry's name.

The experts, exercise physiologists, would probably say that another fitness dimension is even more important than those listed above. These research scientists regard improvement of your heart, lung, and blood vessel function as the key focal point of a physical fitness program. **Cardiorespiratory endurance** forms the foundation for whole-body fitness.

Cardiorespiratory endurance increases your capacity to sustain a given level of energy production for a prolonged period. Development of cardiorespiratory endurance helps your body to work longer and at greater levels of intensity.

Your body cannot always produce the energy it needs for long-term activity. Certain activities require performance at a level of intensity that will outstrip your cardiorespiratory system's ability to transport oxygen efficiently to contracting muscle fibres. When the oxygen demands of the muscles cannot be met, **oxygen debt** occurs. Any activity that continues beyond the point at which oxygen debt begins requires a form of energy production that does not depend on oxygen.

This oxygen-deprived form of energy production is called **anaerobic** (without oxygen) **energy production**,

Key Terms

cardiorespiratory endurance
The ability of the heart, lungs, and blood vessels to process and transport oxygen required by muscle cells so that they can contract over a period of time.

oxygen debt
The physical state that occurs when the body can no longer process and transport sufficient amounts of oxygen for continued muscle contraction.

anaerobic energy production
The body's means of energy production when the necessary amount of oxygen is not available.

the type that fuels many intense, short-duration activities. For example, rope climbing, weight lifting for strength, and sprinting are short-duration activities that quickly cause muscle fatigue; they are generally considered anaerobic activities.

Activities that are not generally associated with anaerobic energy production (walking, distance jogging, and bicycle touring) become anaerobic activities when they are either increased in intensity or continued for an extended period.

If you usually work or play at low intensity but for a long duration, you have developed an ability to maintain **aerobic** (with oxygen) **energy production**. As long as your body can meet its energy demands in this oxygen-rich mode, it will not convert to anaerobic energy production. Thus fatigue will not be an important factor in determining whether you can continue to participate. Marathon runners, serious joggers, distance swimmers, cyclists, and aerobic dancers can perform because of their highly developed aerobic fitness. The cardiorespiratory systems of these aerobically fit people take in, transport, and use oxygen in the most efficient manner possible.

Besides allowing you to participate in activities such as those mentioned, aerobic conditioning (cardiorespiratory endurance conditioning) may also provide certain structural and functional benefits that affect other dimensions of your life (see the Star Box on page 61). These recognized benefits (see the Star Box on this page) have received considerable documented support. Some data, for example, strongly suggest that aerobic fitness can increase life expectancy[4] and reduce the risk of developing cancer of the colon, heart, uterus, cervix, and ovaries.[5]

Muscular Strength

Muscular strength is essential for your body to accomplish work. Your ability to maintain posture, walk, lift, push, and pull are familiar examples of the constant demands you make on your muscles to maintain or increase their level of contraction. The stronger you are, the greater your ability to contract muscles and maintain a level of contraction sufficient to complete tasks.

Muscular strength can be improved best by training activities that use the **overload principle**. By overloading, or gradually increasing the resistance (load, object, or weight) your muscles must move, you can increase your muscular strength. The following three types of training exercises are based on the overload principle.

In **isometric** (meaning "same measure") **exercises**, the resistance is so great that your contracting muscles cannot move the resistant object at all. So your muscles contract against immovable objects, usually with increasingly greater efforts. Because of the difficulty of precisely evaluating the training effects, isometric exercises are not usually used as a primary means of developing muscular strength. These exercises can be dangerous for people with hypertension.

Progressive resistance exercises, also called *isotonic* or *same-tension* exercises, are currently the most popular type of strength-building exercises. Progressive resistance exercises include the use of traditional free weights (dumbbells and barbells), as well as Universal, Cybex, Body Master, and Nautilus machines. People who perform progressive resistance exercises use various muscle groups to move (or lift) specific fixed resistances or weights. Although during a given repetitive exercise the weight resistance remains the same, the muscular contraction effort required varies according to the joint angles in the range of motion. The greatest effort is required at the start and finish of the movement.

Isokinetic (meaning "same motion") **exercises** use mechanical devices that provide resistances that consistently overload muscles throughout the entire range of motion. The resistance will move only at a preset speed, regardless of the force applied to it. For the exercise to be effective, a user must apply maximal force.[6] Isokinetic training requires elaborate, expensive equipment.

Thus, the use of isokinetic equipment may be limited to certain athletic teams, diagnostic centres, or rehabilitation clinics. The most common isokinetic machines are Cybex, Orthotron, Biodex, Mini-Gym, and Exergenie.

Structural and Functional Benefits of Cardiorespiratory (Aerobic) Fitness

Aerobic fitness can help you do the following:

- Complete and enjoy your daily activities.
- Strengthen and increase the efficiency of your heart muscle.
- Increase the proportion of high-density lipoproteins in your blood.
- Increase the capillary network in your body.
- Improve **collateral circulation**.
- Control your weight.
- Stimulate bone growth.
- Cope with stressors.
- Ward off infections.
- Improve the efficiency of your other body systems.
- Bolster your self-esteem.
- Achieve self-directed fitness goals.
- Reduce negative dependence behaviour.
- Sleep better.
- Recover more quickly from common illnesses.
- Meet people with similar interests.
- Receive reduced insurance premiums.

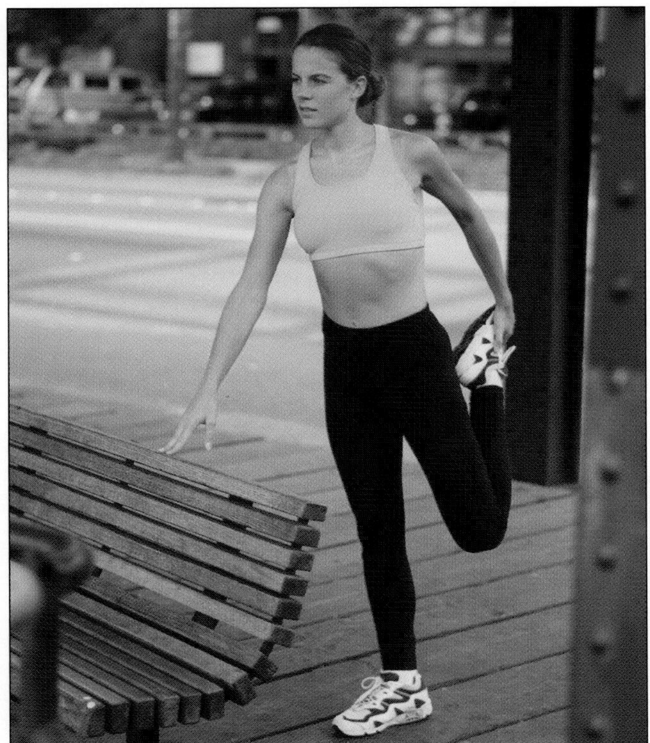

Stretching is important for flexibility and can be performed almost anywhere.

Which type of strength-building exercise (machines or free weights) is most effective? Take your choice, since all will help develop muscular strength. Some people prefer machines because they are simple to use, do not require stacking the weights, and are already balanced and less likely to drop and cause injury.

Other people prefer free weights because they encourage the user to work harder to maintain balance during the lift. In addition, free weights can be used in a greater variety of exercises than weight machines.

Muscular Endurance

Muscular endurance is a component of physical fitness associated with strength. When muscles contract and their individual muscle fibres shorten, energy is needed. Energy production requires that oxygen and nutrients be delivered by the circulatory system to the muscles. After these products are transformed into energy by individual muscle cells, the body must remove the potentially toxic waste by-products.

Amateur and professional athletes often wish to increase the endurance of specific muscle groups associated with their sports activities. This can be achieved by using exercises that gradually increase the number of repetitions of a given movement. However, muscular endurance is not the physiological equivalent of cardiorespiratory endurance. For example, a world-ranked distance runner with highly developed cardiorespiratory endurance and extensive muscular endurance of the legs may not have a corresponding level of muscular endurance of the abdominal muscles.

Flexibility

The ability of your joints to move through their natural range of motion is a measure of your **flexibility**. This fitness trait, like so many other aspects of structure and function, differs from point to point within your body and among different people. Not every joint in your body is equally flexible (by design), and over the course

Key Terms

aerobic energy production
The body's means of energy production when the respiratory and circulatory systems are able to process and transport a sufficient amount of oxygen to muscle cells.

muscular strength
The ability to contract skeletal muscles to engage in work; the force that a muscle can exert.

overload principle
The principle whereby a person gradually increases the resistance load that must be moved or lifted; this principle also applies to other types of fitness training.

isometric exercises
Muscular strength training exercises in which the resistance is so great that the object cannot be moved.

collateral circulation
The ability of nearby blood vessels to enlarge and carry additional blood around a blocked blood vessel.

progressive resistance exercises
Muscular strength training exercises in which traditional barbells and dumbbells with fixed resistances are used.

isokinetic exercises
Muscular strength training exercises in which machines are used to provide variable resistances throughout the full range of motion.

muscular endurance
The ability of a muscle or muscle group to function over time; supported by the respiratory and circulatory systems.

flexibility
The ability of joints to function through an intended range of motion.

Guidelines for Static Stretching

Take the following precautions to reduce the possibility of injury during stretching:

- Warm up using a slow jog or fast walk before stretching.
- Stretch only to the point at which you feel tightness or resistance to your stretching. Stretching should not be painful.
- Be sure to continue normal breathing during a stretch. Do *not* hold your breath.
- Use caution when stretching muscles that surround painful joints. Pain is an indication that something is wrong—it should not be ignored.

of time, use or disuse will alter the flexibility of a given joint. Certainly, gender, age, genetically determined body build, and current level of physical fitness will affect your flexibility.

Inability to move easily during physical activity can be a constant reminder that aging and inactivity are the foes of flexibility. Failure to use joints regularly will quickly result in a loss of elasticity in the connective tissue and shortening of muscles associated with the joints. Benefits of flexibility include improved balance, posture, and athletic performance as well as reduced risk of low back pain.

As seen in young gymnasts, flexibility can be highly developed and maintained with a program of activity that includes regular stretching. Stretching also helps reduce the risk of injury. Athletic trainers generally prefer **static stretching** to **ballistic stretching** for people who wish to improve their range of motion. Guidelines for static stretching are given in the Star Box above.

Body Composition

Body composition is the "makeup of the body in terms of muscle, bone, fat, and other elements."[7] Of particular interest to fitness experts are percentages of body fat and fat-free weight. Health experts are especially concerned about the large number of people in our society who are overweight and obese. Increasingly, cardiorespiratory fitness trainers are recognizing the importance of body composition and are including strength-training exercises to help reduce body fat. (See Chapter 6 for further information about body composition, health effects of obesity, and weight management.)

AGING PHYSICALLY

The period between 45 and 64 years of age brings with it a variety of subtle changes in the body's structure and function. When life is busy and the mind is active, these changes are generally not evident. Even when they become evident, they are not usually the source of profound concern. Your parents, older students in your class, and people with whom you will be working are, nevertheless, experiencing these changes.

- Decrease in bone mass and density
- Increase in vertebral compression
- Degenerative changes in joint cartilage
- Increase in adipose tissue—loss of lean body mass
- Decrease in capacity to engage in physical work
- Decrease in visual acuity
- Decrease in basal energy requirements
- Decrease in fertility
- Decrease in sexual function

For some midlife adults these health concerns can be quite threatening, especially for those who view aging with apprehension and fear. Some middle-aged people reject these physical changes and convince themselves they are sick. Indeed, *hypochondriasis* is much more common among midlife people than among young people.

Two medical conditions influenced by physical activity, osteoporosis and osteoarthritis, deserve careful examination and are discussed in the following sections.

Osteoporosis

Osteoporosis is a condition often seen in late middle-aged women. However, it is not fully understood why white menopausal women are so susceptible to the increase in calcium loss that leads to fracture of the hip, wrist, and vertebral column. Half of all women over the age of 50 will likely suffer an osteoporosis fracture.

The endocrine system plays a large role in the development of osteoporosis. At the time of menopause, a woman's ovaries begin a rapid decrease in the production of *estrogen*, one of two main hormones associated with the menstrual cycle. This lower level of estrogen may decrease the conversion of the precursors of vitamin D into the active form of vitamin D, the form necessary for absorbing calcium from the digestive tract. As a result, calcium may be drawn from the bones for use elsewhere in the body.

Premenopausal women have the opportunity to build and maintain a healthy skeleton through an appropriate intake of calcium. Current recommendations are for an intake of 1200 mg of calcium per day. Three to four daily servings of low-fat dairy products should provide sufficient calcium. Adequate vitamin D must also be in the diet because it aids in the absorption of calcium.

However, many women do not take in an adequate amount of calcium. Calcium supplements, again in combination with vitamin D, can be used to achieve recommended calcium levels. It is now known that calcium carbonate, a highly advertised form of calcium, is no

Cardiorespiratory fitness is essential for optimal heart, lung, and blood vessel function.

more easily absorbed by the body than are other forms of calcium salts.

In premenopausal women, calcium deposition in bone is facilitated by exercise, particularly exercise that involves movement of the extremities. Today, women are encouraged to consume at least the recommended servings from the milk group and engage in regular physical activity that involves the weight-bearing muscles of the legs, such as aerobics, jogging, or walking.

Postmenstrual women who are not elderly can markedly slow the resorption of calcium from their bones through the use of hormone replacement therapy (HRT). When combined with a daily intake of 1500 mg of calcium, vitamin D, and regular exercise, HRT almost eliminates calcium loss. Of course, women will need to work closely with their physicians in monitoring the use of HRT because of continuing concern over the role of HRT and the development of breast cancer.

Osteoarthritis

Arthritis is an umbrella term for more than 100 forms of joint inflammation. The most common form is **osteoarthritis**. It is likely that as we age, all of us will develop osteoarthritis to some degree. Often called "wear and tear" arthritis, osteoarthritis occurs primarily in the weight-bearing joints of the knee, hip, and spine. In this form of arthritis, joint damage can occur to bone ends, cartilaginous cushions, and related structures as the years of constant friction and stress accumulate.

The object of current management of osteoarthritis (and other forms) is not to cure the disease but rather to reduce discomfort, limit joint destruction, and maximize joint mobility. Aspirin and nonsteroidal anti-inflammatory agents are the drugs most frequently used to treat osteoarthritis.

It is now believed that osteoarthritis develops most commonly in people with a genetic predisposition for excessive damage to the weight-bearing joints. Thus the condition seems to "run in families." Further, studies comparing the occurrence of osteoarthritis in those who exercise and those who do not demonstrate that regular activity may decrease the likelihood of developing this form of arthritis.

DEVELOPING A CARDIORESPIRATORY FITNESS PROGRAM

For people of all ages, cardiorespiratory conditioning can be achieved through many activities. As long as the activity you choose places sufficient demand on the heart and lungs, improved fitness is possible. In addition to the familiar activities of swimming, running, cycling, and aerobic dance, many people today are participating in brisk walking, in-line skating, cross-country skiing, swimnastics, skating, rowing, and even weight training (often combined with some form of aerobic activity). Regardless of age or physical limitations (see Learning from Our Diversity, p. 67), you can select from a variety of enjoyable activities that will condition the cardiorespiratory system. Complete the Personal Assessment on p. 79 to determine your level of fitness.

Key Terms

static stretching
The slow lengthening of a muscle group to an extended stretch; followed by holding the extended position for a recommended period.

ballistic stretching
A "bouncing" form of stretching in which a muscle group is lengthened repetitively to produce multiple quick, forceful stretches.

osteoporosis
Loss of calcium from the bone, seen primarily in postmenopausal women.

osteoarthritis
Arthritis that develops with age; largely caused by weight bearing and deterioration of the joints.

Many people think that any kind of physical activity will produce cardiorespiratory fitness. Golf, bowling, hunting, fishing, and archery are considered to be forms of exercise. However, these activities would generally fail to produce positive changes in your cardiorespiratory and overall muscular fitness; they may enhance your health, be enjoyable, and produce some fatigue after lengthy participation, but they do not meet the fitness standards established by the American College of Sports Medicine (ACSM), the United States' premier professional organization of exercise physiologists and sport physicians.[8]

The ACSM's recommendations for achieving cardiorespiratory fitness were approved in 1998 and include six major areas: (1) mode of activity, (2) frequency of training, (3) intensity of training, (4) duration of training, (5) resistance training, and (6) flexibility training. These recommendations are summarized in the following sections. You may wish to compare your existing fitness program with these standards.

Mode of Activity

The ACSM recommends that the mode of activity be any continuous physical activity that uses large muscle groups and can be rhythmic and aerobic in nature. (The CCSM follows the ACSM guidelines.) Among the activities that generally meet this requirement are continuous swimming, cycling, aerobics, basketball, cross-country skiing, in-line skating, step training (bench aerobics), hiking, walking, rowing, stair climbing, dancing, and running. Recently, water exercise (water or aqua aerobics) has become a popular fitness mode, since it is especially effective for pregnant women and elderly, injured, or disabled people. (The Focus On article at the end of this chapter provides more information about exercise during pregnancy.)

Endurance games and activities, such as tennis, racquetball, and handball, are fine as long as you and your partner are skilled enough to keep the ball in play; walking after the ball will do very little for you. Riding a bicycle is a good activity if you keep pedalling. Coasting will do little to improve fitness. Softball and football are generally less than sufficient continuous activities—especially the way they are played by weekend athletes.

Regardless of which continuous activity you select, it should also be enjoyable. Running, for example, is not for everyone—despite what some accomplished runners say! Find an activity you enjoy. If you need others around you to have a good time, get a group of friends to join you. Vary your activities to keep from becoming bored. You might cycle in the summer, run in the fall, swim in the winter, and play racquetball in the spring. To help you maintain your fitness program, see the suggestions in the Changing for the Better box on p. 67.

Frequency of Training

Frequency of training refers to the number of times per week a person should exercise. The ACSM recommends three to five times per week. For most people, participation in fitness activities more than five times each week does not significantly improve their level of conditioning. Likewise, an average of only two workouts each week does not seem to produce a measurable improvement in cardiorespiratory conditioning. Thus, although you may have a lot of fun cycling twice each week, do not expect to see a significant improvement in your cardiorespiratory fitness level from doing so.

Intensity of Training

How much effort should you put into an activity? Should you run quickly, jog slowly, or swim at a comfortable pace? Must a person sweat profusely to become fit? These questions all refer to **intensity** of effort.

The ACSM recommends that healthy adults exercise at an intensity level of between 65% and 90% of their maximum heart rate (calculated by subtracting your age from 220). This level of intensity is called the **target heart rate (THR)**. This rate refers to the minimum number of times your heart needs to contract (beat) each minute to have a positive effect on your heart, lungs, and blood vessels. This improvement is called the *training effect*. Intensity of activity below the THR will be insufficient to make a significant improvement in your fitness level.

Although intensity below the THR will still help you expend calories and thus lose weight, it will probably do little to make you more aerobically fit. On the other hand, intensity that is significantly above your THR will probably cause you to become so fatigued that you will be forced to stop the activity before the training effect can be achieved. For persons who are quite unfit, the 1998 ACSM recommendations permit intensity levels as low as 55%.

Choosing a particular THR between 65% and 90% of your maximum heart rate depends on your initial level of fitness. If you are already in relatively good physical shape, you might want to start exercising at 75% of your maximum heart rate. A well-conditioned person might select a higher THR for his or her intensity level, whereas a person with a low fitness level will still be able to achieve a training effect at a lower THR of 55% of maximum.

In the example in the Star Box on p. 68, the younger person would need to participate in a continuous activity for an extended period while working at a THR of 160 beats per minute. The older person would need to function at a THR of 117 beats per minute to achieve a positive training effect.

Learning from Our Diversity

The Birth of the Special Olympics in Canada

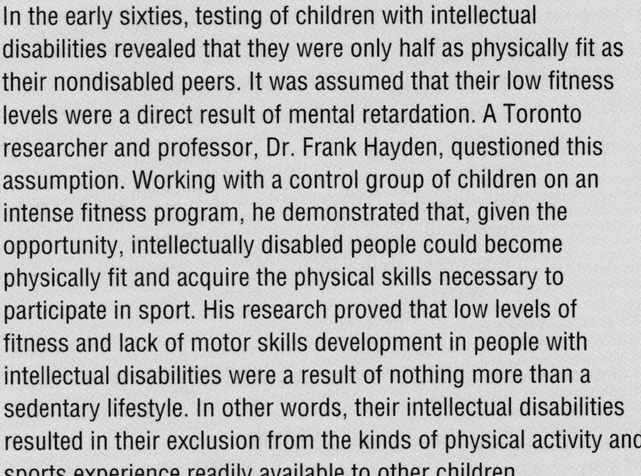

In the early sixties, testing of children with intellectual disabilities revealed that they were only half as physically fit as their nondisabled peers. It was assumed that their low fitness levels were a direct result of mental retardation. A Toronto researcher and professor, Dr. Frank Hayden, questioned this assumption. Working with a control group of children on an intense fitness program, he demonstrated that, given the opportunity, intellectually disabled people could become physically fit and acquire the physical skills necessary to participate in sport. His research proved that low levels of fitness and lack of motor skills development in people with intellectual disabilities were a result of nothing more than a sedentary lifestyle. In other words, their intellectual disabilities resulted in their exclusion from the kinds of physical activity and sports experience readily available to other children.

Inspired by his discoveries, Dr. Hayden began searching for ways to develop a national sports program for intellectually disabled people. It was a goal he eventually achieved, albeit not in Canada. His work came to the attention of Eunice Kennedy Shriver and the Kennedy Foundation in Washington, D.C., and led to the creation of the Special Olympics. The first sports competitions organized under the Special Olympics banner were held at Soldiers's Field in Chicago in 1968. To ensure that Canada was represented, Dr. Hayden called on an old friend, Harry "Red" Foster.

The late Red Foster was an outstanding sportsman, a famous broadcaster, a successful businessman, and a humanitarian whose tireless work on behalf of people with intellectual disabilities had already brought him international acclaim. Inspired by his mother's devotion to his younger brother, who was both blind and mentally disabled, Mr. Foster began early in his career to devote much of his time, energy, and wealth to addressing the problems faced by individuals with intellectual disabilities and their families.

Accompanying a floor hockey team from Toronto to those first Games in Chicago, Red was quick to see in the Special Olympics a further opportunity to enhance the lives of intellectually disabled Canadians. Upon returning to Canada he set about laying the foundation for the Special Olympics movement. The following summer, 1969, the first Canadian Special Olympics event was held in Toronto. From that modest beginning, the Special Olympics movement quickly spread across the country and grew into the national sports organization it is today.

Determining your heart rate is not a complicated procedure. Find a location on your body where an artery passes near the surface of the skin. Pulse rates are difficult to determine by touching veins, which are more superficial than arteries. Two easily accessible sites for determining heart rate are the *carotid artery* (one on either side of the windpipe at the front of your neck) and the *radial artery* (on the inside of your wrist, just above the base of the thumb).

You should practise placing the front surface of your index and middle fingertips at either of these locations and feeling for a pulse. Once you have found a regular pulse, look at the second hand of a watch. Count the number of beats you feel in a 10-second period. Multiply this number by 6. This number is your heart rate. With a little practice, you can become very proficient at determining your heart rate.

Changing *for the Better*

How to Stick to Your Exercise Program

I know that working out is important, but with a full load of classes and my activities, I don't have either the time or the energy. I just can't seem to stick with any routine I start. How can I make exercise part of my life?

- Fit your program into your daily lifestyle.
- Exercise with your friends.
- Incorporate music into your activity.
- Vary your activities frequently; crosstrain.
- Reward yourself when you reach a fitness goal.
- Avoid a complicated exercise program; keep it simple.
- Measure your improvement by keeping a log or diary.
- Take some time off to rest and recuperate.
- Keep in mind how important physical activity is to your life and health.

Key Terms

frequency
The number of times per week one should exercise to achieve a training effect.

intensity
The level of effort put into an activity.

target heart rate (THR)
The number of times per minute the heart must contract to produce a training effect.

Duration of Training

The ACSM recommends that the **duration** of training be between 20 and 60 minutes of continuous or intermittent aerobic activity. Intermittent activity can be accumulated in 10-minute segments throughout the day. This is especially helpful for persons who cannot take a single large chunk of time during the day to devote to an exercise program.

For most healthy adults however, the ACSM recommends moderate-intensity activity levels with longer duration times, perhaps 30 minutes to an hour. For healthy adults who train at higher intensity levels, the duration of training will likely be shorter, perhaps 20 minutes or more.[9] Adults who are unfit or have an existing medical condition should check with their fitness instructor or physician to determine an appropriate duration of training.

Resistance Training

Recognizing the important fact that overall body fitness includes muscular fitness, the ACSM recommends resistance training in its current standards. The ACSM suggests participation in strength training of moderate intensity two or three times a week. This training should help develop and maintain a healthy body composition—one with an emphasis on lean body mass. The goal of resistance training is not to improve cardiorespiratory endurance but to improve overall muscle strength and endurance. For the average person, resistance training with heavy weights is not recommended because it can induce a sudden and dangerous increase in blood pressure. See the Changing for the Better box on p. 69 for safety precautions to observe during strength training.

The resistance training recommended by the ACSM includes one set of 8 to 12 repetitions of 8 to 10 different exercises. These exercises should be geared to the body's major muscle groups (legs, arms, shoulders, trunk, and back) and should not focus on just one or two body areas. Progressive resistance (isotonic) or isokinetic exercises are recommended (see pp. 62–63). For the average person, resistance training activities should be done at a moderate to slow speed, use the full range of motion, and not impair normal breathing. With just one set recommended for each exercise, resistance training is not very time consuming. The ACSM, however, indicates that multiple sets could provide greater benefits, if time is available.

Flexibility Training

To develop and maintain a healthy range of motion for the body's joints, the ACSM suggests that flexibility exercises be included in one's overall fitness program. These exercises should stretch the major muscle groups of the body and be undertaken a minimum of two to three times per week. Stretching should be done according to safe and appropriate techniques. (See the Star box on p. 64.)

What's Your Target Heart Rate?

The target heart rate (THR) is the recommended rate for increasing cardiorespiratory endurance. To maintain a training effect, you must sustain activity at your THR. To calculate your THR, subtract your age from 220 (the maximum heart rate) and multiply by .60 to .90. Here are two examples:

For a 20-year-old person who wants a THR of 80% of maximum
Maximum heart rate: 220 – 20 = 200
200 × .80 = 160
THR = 160 beats per minute

For a 40-year-old person who wants a THR of 65% of maximum
Maximum heart rate: 220 – 40 = 180
180 × .65 = 117
THR = 117 beats per minute

Warm-up, Conditioning, Cooldown

Each training session consists of three basic parts: the warm-up, the workout, and the cooldown.[10] The warm-up should last 10 to 15 minutes. During this period, you should begin slow, gradual, comfortable movements related to the upcoming activity, such as walking or slow jogging. All body segments and muscle groups should be exercised as you gradually increase your heart rate. Near the end of the warm-up period, the major muscle groups should be stretched. This preparation helps protect you from muscle strains and joint sprains.

The warm-up is a fine time to socialize. Furthermore, you can mentally prepare yourself for your activity or think about the beauty of the morning sky, the changing colours of the leaves, or the friends you will meet later in the day. Mental warm-ups can be as beneficial for you psychologically as physical warm-ups are physiologically.

The second part of the training session is the conditioning, the part of the session that involves improving muscular strength and endurance, cardiorespiratory endurance, and flexibility. Workouts can be tailor-made, but they should follow the ACSM guidelines discussed earlier in this chapter.

The third important part of each fitness session, the cooldown, consists of a 5- to 10-minute session of relaxing exercises, such as slow jogging, walking, and stretching. This activity allows your body to cool and return to a resting state. A cooldown period helps reduce muscle soreness.

Changing *for the Better*

Considering Strength Training? Think Safety ...

I'm a 22-year-old college student thinking about starting a strength-training program. What kinds of safety precautions should I take?

- Warm up appropriately.
- Use proper lifting techniques.
- Always have a spotter if you are using free weights.
- Do not hold your breath during a lift.
- Avoid single lifts of very heavy weights.
- Before using a machine (such as Nautilus, Universal, or Cybex), be certain you know how to use it correctly.
- Seek advice for training programs from properly licensed or certified experts.
- Work within your limitations; avoid showing off.

Strength training helps you develop and maintain a healthy body composition.

Exercise for Older Adults

An exercise program designed for younger adults may be inappropriate for older people, particularly those over age 50. Special attention must be paid to matching the program to the interests and abilities of the participants. The goals of the program should include both social interaction and physical conditioning.

Older adults, especially those with a personal or family history of heart problems, should have a physical examination before starting a fitness program. This examination should include a stress cardiogram, a blood pressure check, and an evaluation of joint functioning. Participants should learn how to monitor their own cardiorespiratory status during exercise.

Well-designed fitness programs for older adults will include activities that begin slowly, are monitored frequently, and are geared to the enjoyment of the participants.[11] The professional staff coordinating the program should be familiar with the signs of distress (excessively elevated heart rate, nausea, breathing difficulty, pallor, and pain) and must be able to perform CPR. Warm-up and cooldown periods should be included. Activities to increase flexibility are beneficial in the beginning and ending segments of the program. Participants should wear comfortable clothing and appropriate shoes and should be mentally prepared to enjoy the activities.

A program designed for older adults will largely conform to the ACSM criteria specified in this chapter. However, except for certain very fit older adults (such as runners and triathletes), the THR should not exceed 120 beats per minute. Also, because of possible joint, muscular, or skeletal problems, certain activities may have to be done in a sitting position. Pain or discomfort should be reported immediately to the fitness instructor.

Fortunately, properly screened older adults will rarely have health emergencies during a well-monitored fitness program. Of course, for some older adults, individual fitness activities may be more enjoyable than supervised group activities. Either choice offers important benefits.

Low Back Pain

A common occurrence among adults is the sudden onset of low back pain. Each year, 10 million adults develop this condition, which can be so uncomfortable that they miss work, lose sleep, and generally feel incapable of engaging in daily activities. Eighty percent of all adults who have this condition will experience these effects two to three times per year.

Although low back pain can reflect serious health problems, most low back pain is caused by mechanical (postural) problems. As unpleasant as low back pain is, the problem usually corrects itself within a week or two. The services of a physician, physical therapist, or chiropractor are not generally required after an initial visit.

By engaging in regular exercise, such as swimming, walking, and bicycling, and by paying attention to your back during bending, lifting, and sitting, you can minimize the occurrence of this uncomfortable and incapacitating condition. Commercial fitness centres and campus recreational programs are starting to offer specific exercise classes geared to muscular improvement in the lower back and abdominal areas.

Key Term

duration
The length of time one needs to exercise at the THR to produce a training effect.

Well-designed fitness programs are beneficial to older adults.

FITNESS QUESTIONS AND ANSWERS

Along with the six necessary elements to include in your fitness program, you should consider many additional issues when you start a fitness program.

Should I See My Doctor Before I Get Started?

This issue has probably kept thousands of people from ever beginning a fitness program. The hassle and expense of getting a comprehensive physical examination is an excellent excuse for people who are not completely sold on the idea of exercise. A complete examination, including *blood analysis, stress test, cardiogram, serum lipid analysis,* and *body fat analysis,* is a valuable tool for developing some baseline physical data for your medical record.

Is this examination really necessary? Most exercise physiologists do not think so. The value of these measurements as safety predictors is questioned by many professionals. A good rule of thumb to follow is to undergo a physical examination if (1) you have an existing medical condition (for example, diabetes, obesity, hypertension, heart abnormalities, or arthritis), (2) you are a man over age 40 or a woman over age 50,[12] or (3) you smoke. (See the Star Box below for a questionnaire to help you determine if you need to see a physician before starting your fitness program. See also the Health on the Web box on p. 72.)

TALKING POINTS • If your screening tests indicate that you cannot start a vigorous fitness program, are you prepared to ask your doctor about alternative activities?

The Physical Activity Readiness Questionnaire (PAR-Q)

Becoming more active is very safe for most people, but if you're in doubt, please complete the questionnaire below. Some people should check with their doctor before they start becoming much more physically active. Start by answering the seven questions below. If you are between the ages of 15 and 69, the PAR-Q will tell you if you should check with your doctor before you start. If you are over 69 years of age, and are not used to being very active, definitely check with your doctor first.

1. Has your doctor ever said that you have a heart condition and that you should do only physical activity recommended by a doctor?
2. Do you feel pain in your chest when you do physical activity?
3. In the past month, have you had chest pain when you were not doing physical activity?
4. Do you lose your balance because of dizziness or do you ever lose consciousness?
5. Do you have a bone or joint problem that could be made worse by a change in your physical activity?
6. Is your doctor currently prescribing drugs (for example, water pills) for your blood pressure or heart condition?
7. Do you know of any other reason you should not do physical activity?

If you answered "yes" to one or more questions, talk with your doctor before you start becoming much more physically active. If you answered "no" to all questions, you can be reasonably sure that you can start becoming more physically active right now. Be sure to start slowly and progress gradually—this is the safest and easiest way to go.

Delay becoming much more active if

- You are not feeling well because of a temporary illness such as a cold or a fever—wait until you feel better.
- You are or may be pregnant—talk to your doctor before you start becoming much more active.

Note: If your health changes so that you then answer "yes" to any of the above questions, ask for advice from your fitness or health professional.

Canada's Man In Motion: The Rick Hansen Story

Rick Hansen was born on August 26, 1957, in Port Alberni and grew up in Williams Lake, British Columbia. As an athletic, carefree teenager, he loved sports and particularly enjoyed fishing. While returning home from an afternoon's fishing with a friend in 1973, the truck in which they were riding went out of control and crashed. That day, doctors told Rick that he was a paraplegic, and that he would never walk again. He was 15 years old.

Rick saw his situation as a challenge to overcome. He persevered through rehabilitation, and returned home to graduate from high school. He refocused his athletic abilities to master wheelchair sports and was the first student with a physical disability to graduate in Physical Education from the University of British Columbia. He became an elite wheelchair athlete, winning 19 international wheelchair marathons, including three world championships, and competing for Canada in the 1984 Olympics in Los Angeles.

In 1985, motivated by his athletic success and a desire to make a difference in the way people with disabilities were perceived, he embarked on the record-setting Man In Motion World Tour. Along the way, he inspired others to pursue their own dreams, raised the world's awareness of the potential of people with disabilities, raised $26 million for spinal cord injury research, rehabilitation, and wheelchair sport, and became a testament to the remarkable potential of the human spirit. He became a Canadian hero.

Today, Rick is the founder, President, and CEO of the Rick Hansen Man In Motion Foundation. To date, the Rick Hansen Man In Motion Foundation has made an impact of over $158 million for spinal cord injury.

As an inspiring speaker, Rick is in demand by many organizations to share his remarkable story and to inspire others to make a difference. He spends time in schools, committed to being a positive role model to children, remains dedicated to finding a cure for spinal cord injury, and has co-authored two books: *Rick Hansen: Man In Motion* and *Going the Distance: Seven Steps to Personal Change*. See **www.rickhansen.com**

How Beneficial Is Aerobic Dance Exercise?

One of the most popular fitness approaches is aerobic exercise, including aerobic dancing. Many organizations sponsor classes in this form of continuous dancing and movement. The rise in popularity of televised and video-taped aerobic exercise programs reflects the enthusiasm for this form of exercise. Because extravagant claims are often made about the value of these programs, the wise consumer should observe at least one session of the activity before enrolling. Discover for yourself whether the program meets the criteria outlined earlier in this chapter: mode of activity, frequency, intensity, duration, resistance training, and flexibility training.

Forms of dancing are fast becoming some of the most popular aerobic exercises. Popularized by rap music, hip-hop music, and the growth of vigorous dancing in music videos, these forms of dancing provide an excellent way of having fun and developing cardiorespiratory fitness. Have you experienced the exhilaration that results from an hour or two of dancing?

What Are Low-Impact Aerobic Activities?

Because long-term participation in some aerobic activities (for example, jogging, running, aerobic dancing, and rope skipping) may damage the hip, knee, and ankle joints, many fitness experts promote low-impact aerobic activities. Low-impact aerobic dancing, water aerobics, bench aerobics, Pilates, yoga, kick-boxing and brisk walking are examples of this kind of fitness activity. Participants still conform to the principal components of a cardiorespiratory fitness program. THR levels are the same as in high-impact aerobic activities.

The main difference between low-impact and high-impact aerobic activities is the use of the legs. Low-impact aerobics do not require having both feet off the ground at the same time. Thus weight transfer does not occur with the forcefulness seen in traditional high-impact aerobic activities. In addition, low-impact activities may include exaggerated arm movements and the use of hand or wrist weights. All of these variations are designed to increase the heart rate to the THR without damaging the joints of the lower extremities. Low-impact aerobics are excellent for people of all ages, and they may be especially beneficial to older adults.

Health on the Web

Behaviour-Change Activities

Do You Have What It Takes to Become Fit?

If you're like many students, you'd like to look in the mirror and see the kind of body that's glorified in the media: toned, trim, buff. Whatever you call it, fitness takes work and commitment. Do you have what it takes? Check out your fitness and physical activity IQ at **www.readersdigest.ca/mag/2000/08/living_exercise_quiz.html** and answer the questions. You can check your progress by visiting the site regularly and retaking the test. Good luck!

Do You Know the Facts about Fitness?

When it comes to fitness, most of us think we're pretty well informed. To check your fitness IQ, go to **www.hc-sc.gc.ca/hppb/paguide/quiz/question1.html**. Each time you answer a multiple-choice question, you'll find out whether or not you gave the correct response. How fitness savvy are you?

Do You Need an Exercise Rx?

Should you see your doctor before you begin a fitness program? If you're between the ages of 15 and 69, the PAR-Q assessment can help you decide whether this is necessary. Go to **www.csep.ca/pdfs/par-q.pdf** and answer the items on the questionnaire. Then submit your responses, and you'll receive a recommendation based on your personal profile. What did you learn?

In-line skating is one of the fastest-growing participant fitness activities. This low-impact activity has cardiorespiratory and muscular benefits similar to those of running without the pounding effect that running can produce. In-line skating requires important safety equipment: sturdy skates, knee and elbow pads, wrist supports, and a helmet.

Other aerobic activities require proper equipment as well. When selecting an athletic shoe, take the time to shop at specialty shoe stores and try the many varieties of shoes available in today's market. Selections vary from shoes for hiking, aerobics, cross-training, walking, and running to indoor and outdoor court shoes. Good advice on the best shoe for your needs is often readily available from trained sales clerks.

What Is the Most Effective Means of Fluid Replacement During Exercise?

Despite all the advertising hype associated with commercial fluid replacement products, for an average person involved in typical fitness activities, water is still the best fluid replacement. The availability and cost are unbeatable. However, when activity is prolonged and intense, commercial sports drinks may be preferable to water because they contain electrolytes (which replace lost sodium and potassium) and carbohydrates (which replace depleted energy stores). However, the carbohydrates in sports drinks are actually simple forms of sugar. Thus sports drinks tend to be high in calories, just like regular soft drinks. Regardless of the drink you choose, exercise physiologists recommend that you drink fluids before and at frequent intervals throughout the activity.

What Effect Does Alcohol Have on Sport Performance?

It probably comes as no surprise that alcohol use is generally detrimental to sport performance. Alcohol consumption, especially excessive intake the evening before a performance, consistently decreases the level of performance. Many research studies have documented the negative effects of alcohol on activities involving speed, strength, power, and endurance.[13]

Lowered performance appears to be related to a variety of factors, including impaired judgment, reduced coordination, depressed heart function, liver interference, and dehydration. Understandably, sports federations within the International Olympic Committee (IOC) have banned the use of alcohol in conjunction with sports competition.

Only in the sports of precision shooting (pistol shooting, riflery, and archery) have studies shown that low-level alcohol use may improve performance, by reducing the shooter's anxiety and permitting steady hand movements. However, alcohol use has also been banned from these sports.[14] Weapons and alcohol do not mix.

What Are the Risks and Benefits of Androstenedione?

Androstenedione ("andro") and creatine have recently received much attention for their use as possible **ergogenic aids**. Ergogenic aids are supplements taken to improve athletic performance.[15] Andro is a steroidlike precursor to the male hormone testosterone. When taken into the body, andro stimulates the body to produce more of its natural testosterone. Increased levels of testosterone help a person build lean muscle mass and recover from injury more quickly.

Andro's primary use as an ergogenic aid is to build muscle tissue, improve overall body strengh, and boost performance, especially in anaerobic sports. Andro is banned by Canadian Intercollegiate Sport (CIS), the National Football League (NFL), the National Collegiate Athletic Association (NCAA), the Canadian Olympic Academy (COA) and the Canadian Centre for Ethics in Sport. The health concerns that most physicians attribute to andro are similar to those of anabolic steroids.

St. Louis Cardinal baseball player Mark McGwire's admitted use of andro put this supplement in the national spotlight in the summer of 1998. That was the season when McGwire rocked the baseball world by surpassing Roger Maris's home run record by hitting 70 home runs. It is interesting, though, that during the 1999 baseball season McGwire opted to stop using andro but still managed to hit nearly 70 home runs.

What Are the Risks and Benefits of Creatine?

Creatine is an amino acid found in meat, poultry, and fish. In a person's body, creatine is produced naturally in the liver, pancreas, and kidneys. Typically, people get one to two grams of creatine each day from their food intake.[16] As an ergogenic aid, creatine performs its work in the muscles, where it helps restore the compound adenosine triphosphate (ATP). ATP provides quick energy for muscle contractions. It also helps to reduce the lactic acid buildup that occurs during physical exertion. This buildup causes a burning sensation that limits the amount of intense activity one can perform.

Early studies suggest that creatine can help athletes in anaerobic sports, which require short, explosive bursts of energy. However, the increase in performance has been small, the long-term health impacts are unknown, studies have been restricted to highly trained subjects (not recreational athletes), and damage to kidneys is possible with high dosages. Users are cautioned to consume ample amounts of water to prevent cramping and dehydration.

All in all, creatine is unlikely to prove as potentially dangerous as androstenedione. If additional studies should indicate that creatine can consistently improve performance, this substance might be banned by many sports federations. At the time of this writing, the safest, most prudent recommendation is for athletes to spend their time and energy improving their training programs rather than looking for a solution in a bottle.

How Worthwhile Are Commercial Health and Fitness Clubs?

The health and fitness club business is booming. Fitness clubs offer activities ranging from free weights to weight machines to step walking to general aerobics. Some clubs have saunas and whirlpools and lots of frills. Others have course offerings that include wellness, smoking cessation, stress management, time management, dance, and yoga. The atmosphere at most clubs is friendly, and people are encouraged to have a good time while working out.

If your purpose in joining a fitness club is to improve your cardiorespiratory fitness, measure the program offered by the club against the ACSM standards. If your primary purpose is to meet people and have fun, request a trial membership for a month or so to see whether you like the environment.

Before signing a contract at a health club or spa, do some careful questioning. Find out when the business was established, ask about the qualifications of the employees, contact some members for their observations, and request a thorough tour of the facilities. You might even consult your local Better Business Bureau for additional information. Finally, make certain that you read and understand every word of the contract.

What Is Cross-Training?

Cross-training is the use of more than one aerobic activity to achieve cardiorespiratory fitness. For example, runners may use swimming, cycling, or rowing periodically to replace running in their training routines. Cross-training allows certain muscle groups to rest and injuries to heal. Also, cross-training provides a refreshing change of pace for the participant. You will probably enjoy your fitness program more if you vary the activities.

What Are Steroids and Why Do Some Athletes Use Them?

Steroids are drugs that can be legally prescribed by physicians for a variety of health conditions, including certain forms of anemia, inadequate growth patterns, and chronic debilitating diseases. Steroids can also be prescribed to aid recovery from surgery or burns. **Anabolic steroids** are drugs that function like the male sex hormone testosterone. They can be taken orally or by injection.

Anabolic steroids are used by athletes who hope to gain weight, muscular size and strength, power, endurance, and aggressiveness. Over the last few decades,

Key Term

ergogenic aids
Supplements that are taken to improve athletic performance.

anabolic steroids
Drugs that function like testosterone to produce increases in weight, strength, endurance, and aggression.

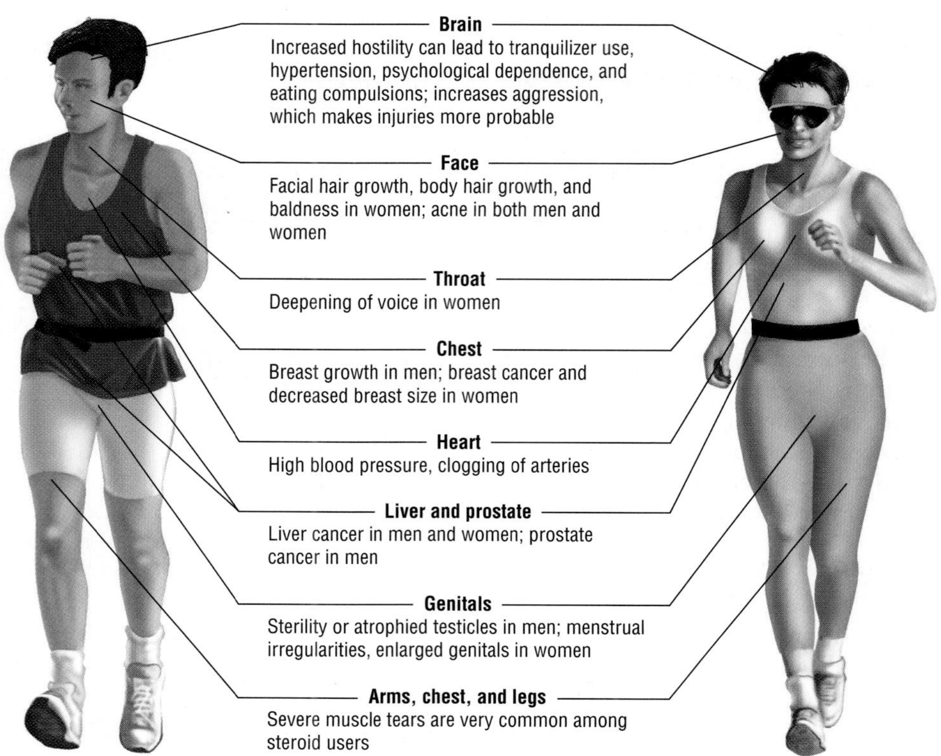

Brain
Increased hostility can lead to tranquilizer use, hypertension, psychological dependence, and eating compulsions; increases aggression, which makes injuries more probable
Face
Facial hair growth, body hair growth, and baldness in women; acne in both men and women
Throat
Deepening of voice in women
Chest
Breast growth in men; breast cancer and decreased breast size in women
Heart
High blood pressure, clogging of arteries
Liver and prostate
Liver cancer in men and women; prostate cancer in men
Genitals
Sterility or atrophied testicles in men; menstrual irregularities, enlarged genitals in women
Arms, chest, and legs
Severe muscle tears are very common among steroid users

Figure 4–2 Adverse effects of steroids on various parts of the body.

many bodybuilders, weightlifters, track athletes, and football players have chosen to ignore the serious health risks posed by illegal steroid use.

The use of steroids is highly dangerous because of serious, life-threatening side effects and adverse reactions. These effects include heart problems, certain forms of cancer, liver complications, and even psychological disturbances. The side effects on female steroid users are as dangerous as those on men. Figure 4–2 shows the adverse effects of steroid use.

Steroid users have developed a terminology of their own. Anabolic steroids are called "roids" or "juice." "Roid rage" is an aggressive, psychotic response to chronic steroid use. "Stacking" is a term that describes the use of multiple steroids at the same time.

Most organizations that control athletic competition (for example, Canadian Intercollegiate Sport, the NFL, and the IOC) have banned steroids and test athletes for illegal use.

Are Today's Children Physically Fit?

Major research studies published during the last 10 years have indicated that North American children and teenagers lead very sedentary lives. Children ages 5 to 17 score extremely poorly in the areas of strength, flexibility, and cardiorespiratory endurance. In many cases, parents are in better shape than their children.

Over half of children and youth aged 5 to 17 are not active enough for optimal growth and development. For the purposes of this analysis, the term "active enough" is equivalent to an energy expenditure of at least eight kilocalories per kilogram of body weight per day (KKD). For example, a half-hour of martial arts plus walking for a total of at least one hour throughout the day would be sufficient activity for a child.

Girls are less active than boys: 38% of girls and 48% of boys are considered active enough for optimal health benefits. This sex difference appears in both grade-school children and teenagers. For children aged 5 to 12, 44% of girls versus 53% of boys are considered active enough. Similarly, 30% of adolescent girls and 40% of adolescent boys are considered sufficiently active.

This information presents a challenge to educators and parents to emphasize the need for strenuous play activity. Television watching and parental inactivity were implicated as major reasons in these studies. For students reading this text who are parents or grandparents of young children, what can you do to encourage more physical activity and less sedentary activity?

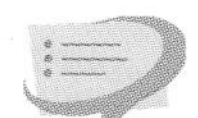

TALKING POINTS • What can you do to encourage children to become more active participants in physical activities?

Table 4–1 Common Injuries Associated with Physical Activity

Injury	Condition
Achilles tendinitis	A chronic tendinitis of the "heel cord," or muscle tendon, located on the back of the lower leg just above the heel. It may result from any activity that involves forcefully pushing off with the foot and ankle, such as in running and jumping. This inflammation involves swelling, warmth, tenderness to touch, and pain during walking and especially running.
Ankle sprains	Stretching or tearing of one or several ligaments that provide stability to the ankle joint. Ligaments on the outside or lateral side of the ankle are more commonly injured by rolling the sole of the foot downward and toward the inside. Pain is intense immediately after injury, followed by considerable swelling, tenderness, loss of joint motion, and some discolouration over a 24- to 48-hour period.
Groin pull	A muscle strain that occurs in the muscles located on the inside of the upper thigh just below the pubic area and that results from either an overstretch of the muscle or from a contraction of the muscle that meets excessive resistance. Pain will be produced by flexing the hip and leg across the body or by stretching the muscles in a groin-stretch position.
Hamstring pull	A strain of the muscles on the back of the upper thigh that most often occurs while sprinting. In most cases, severe pain is caused simply by walking or by any movement that involves knee flexion or stretch of the hamstring muscle. Some swelling, tenderness to touch, and possibly some discolouration extending down the back of the leg may occur in severe strains.
Patellofemoral knee pain	Nonspecific pain occurring around the knee, particularly the front part of the knee, or in the kneecap (patella). Pain can result from many causes, including improper movement of the kneecap in knee flexion and extension; tendinitis of the tendon just below the kneecap, which is caused by repetitive jumping; bursitis (swelling) either above or below the kneecap; and osteoarthritis (joint surface degeneration) between the kneecap and thigh bone. It may involve inflammation with swelling, tenderness, warmth, and pain associated with movement.
Quadriceps contusion "charley horse"	A deep bruise of the muscles in the front part of the thigh caused by a forceful impact that results in severe pain, swelling, discolouration, and difficulty flexing the knee or extending the hip. Without adequate rest and protection from additional trauma, small calcium deposits may develop in the muscle.
Shin splints	A catch-all term used to refer to any pain that occurs in the front part of the lower leg or shin, most often caused by excessive running on hard surfaces. Pain is usually caused by strain of the muscles that move the ankle and foot at their attachment points in the shin. It is usually worse during activity. In more severe cases it may be caused by stress fractures of the long bones in the lower leg, with the pain being worse after activity is stopped.
Shoulder impingement	Chronic irritation and inflammation of muscle tendons and a bursa underneath the tip of the shoulder, which results from repeated forceful overhead motions of the shoulder, such as in swimming, throwing, spiking a volleyball, or serving a tennis ball. Pain is felt when the arm is extended across the body above shoulder level.
Tennis elbow	Chronic irritation and inflammation of the lateral or outside surface of the arm just above the elbow at the attachment of the muscles that extend the wrist and fingers. It results from any activity that requires forceful extension of the wrist. Typically occurs in tennis players who are using faulty techniques hitting backhand ground strokes. Pain is felt above the elbow after forcefully extending the wrist against resistance or applying pressure over the muscle attachment above the elbow.

How Does Sleep Contribute to Overall Fitness?

Although sleep may seem to be the opposite of exercise, it is an important adjunct to a well-planned exercise program. Sleep is so vital to health that people who are unable to sleep sufficiently (those with insomnia) or who are deprived of sleep experience deterioration in every dimension of their health. Fortunately, exercise is frequently associated with improvement in sleeping.

The value of sleep is apparent in a variety of positive changes in the body. Dreaming is thought to play an important role in supporting the emotional dimension of health. Problem-solving scenarios that occur during dreams seem to afford some carryover value in actual coping experiences. A variety of changes in physiological functioning, particularly a deceleration of the cardiovascular system, occur while you sleep. The feeling of being well rested is an expression of the mental and physiological rejuvenation you feel after a good night's sleep.

The amount of sleep needed varies among people. In fact, for any person, sleep needs vary according to activity level and overall state of health. As we age, the need for sleep appears to decrease from the six to eight hours young adults require. Elderly people routinely sleep less than they did when they were younger. This decrease may be offset by the short naps older people often take during

What Are the Common Exercise Danger Signs?

- A delay of over one hour in your body's return to a fully relaxed, comfortable state after exercise.
- A change in sleep patterns.
- Any noticeable breathing difficulties or chest pains. Exercising at your THR should not initiate these problems. If these effects occur, consult a physician.
- Persistent joint or muscle pain. Any lingering joint or muscle pain might signal a problem. Seek the help of an athletic trainer, a physical therapist, or your physician.
- Unusual changes in urine composition or output. Marked colour change in your urine could signal possible kidney or bladder difficulties. Drink plenty of water before, during, and after you participate in your activity.
- Anything unusual that you notice after starting your fitness program. Examples are headaches, nosebleeds, fainting, numbness in an extremity, and hemorrhoids.

the day. For all people, however, periods of relaxation, daydreaming, and even an occasional afternoon nap promote electrical activity patterns that help regenerate the mind and body.

How Do I Handle Common Injuries That May Be Caused by My Fitness Activities?

For the most part, emergency care for injuries that pertain to the bones or muscles should follow the RICE acronym.[17] Depending on the type and severity of the injury, the importance of rest (R), ice (I) or cold application, compression (C), and elevation (E) cannot be overstated. Each type of injury identified in Table 4–1 has a particular RICE protocol to follow. Any significant injury should be reported to your campus student health centre, an athletic trainer, a physical therapist, or a physician. See the Star Box on this page for exercise danger signs you should be aware of.

What Is the Female Athlete Triad?

In the early 1990s, the American College of Sports Medicine identified a three-part syndrome of disordered eating, **amenorrhea** (lack of menstruation), and osteoporosis as the female athlete triad.[18] The conditions of this syndrome appear independently in many women, but among female athletes they appear together. The female athlete triad is most likely to be found in athletes whose sport activities emphasize appearance (for example, diving, ice skating, or gymnastics).

Parents, coaches, athletic trainers, and teammates should be watchful for signs of the female athlete triad. This syndrome has associated medical risks, including inadequate fuel supply for activities, inadequate iron intake, reduced cognitive function, altered hormone levels, reduced mental health, early onset of menopause, increased likelihood of skeletal trauma, altered blood fat profiles, and increased vulnerability to heart disease.[19] Vitally important is an early referral to a physician who is knowledgeable about the female athlete triad. The physician will likely coordinate efforts with a psychologist, a nutritionist, or an athletic trainer to improve the health of the athlete and prevent recurrences.

Key Term

amenorrhea
Cessation or lack of menstrual periods.

Taking Charge of Your Health

- Assess your level of fitness by completing the Personal Assessment Test on p. 79.
- Start a daily stretching program based on the guidelines in this chapter.
- Implement or maintain a cardiorespiratory fitness program that uses the most recent American College of Sports Medicine recommendations.
- Seek advice on your athletic shoes to determine their appropriateness for the fitness activities you do.
- Monitor your physical activities for potential danger signs indicating that you should consult an athletic trainer, physical therapist, or physician.
- For two weeks, keep track of the amount of sleep you are getting. Determine whether this is enough sleep, and make adjustments accordingly.

SUMMARY

- Physical fitness allows one to avoid illness, perform routine activities, and respond to emergencies.
- The health benefits of exercise can be achieved through regular moderate exercise.
- Fitness is composed of five components: cardiorespiratory endurance, muscular strength, muscular endurance, flexibility, and body composition.
- The American College of Sports Medicine's program for cardiorespiratory fitness has six components: mode of activity, frequency of training, intensity of training, duration of training, resistance training, and flexibility training.
- The target heart rate refers to the number of times per minute the heart must contract to produce a training effect.
- Training sessions should take place in three phases: warm-up, workout, and cooldown.
- Fitness experts are concerned about the lack of fitness in today's youth.
- Dancing, step aerobics, and in-line skating are currently popular aerobic activities.
- Post-secondary students who are interested in fitness should understand the important topics of steroid use, cross-training, fluid replacement, the female athlete triad, and proper sleep.

REVIEW QUESTIONS

1. Identify the five components of fitness described in this chapter. How does each component relate to physical fitness?
2. What is the difference between anaerobic and aerobic energy production? What types of activities are associated with anaerobic energy production? With aerobic energy production?
3. List some of the benefits of aerobic fitness.
4. Describe the various methods used to promote muscular strength. How do "andro" and creatine differ?
5. What does the principle of overload mean in regard to fitness training programs?
6. Identify the ACSM's six components of an effective cardiorespiratory fitness program. Explain the important aspects of each component.
7. Under what circumstances should you see a physician before starting a physical fitness program?
8. Identify and describe the three parts of a training session.
9. Describe some of the negative consequences of anabolic steroid use.
10. How does adequate sleep help improve one's fitness?

THINK ABOUT THIS ...

- What are your attitudes toward physical fitness? Do you participate in a regular physical fitness program? Why or why not?
- Does your present level of fitness allow you to effectively carry out the activities your schedule demands? Are there things that you would like to do but cannot because of your current level of fitness?
- Describe your level of fitness, taking into consideration cardiorespiratory endurance, strength, and flexibility.
- After determining your own target heart rate, calculate the THR for a parent or older friend. Talk to these people about starting their own fitness programs. Be ready to help with encouragement and accurate information. They may look to you as a role model for their own health.
- Design a physical fitness plan for yourself, taking into consideration all of the dimensions of body structure and function and the five components of an effective fitness program described in this chapter. What are the chances that you will continue this program after you graduate?

REFERENCES

1. Canada Fitness and Lifestyle Research Institute: *2002 Physical activity monitor*, **www.cflri.ca/cflri/pa/surveys/2002survey/2002survey.html**, October 10, 2005.
2. American College of Sports Medicine: Position stand on the recommended quantity and quality of exercise for developing and maintaining cardiorespiratory and muscular fitness and flexibility in healthy adults, *Med Sci Sports Exerc* 30(6):975–991, 1998.

3. American Heart Association, Councils on Clinical Cardiology and Nutrition, Physical Activity and Metabolism: Exercise and physical activity in the prevention and treatment of atherosclerotic cardiovascular disease. *Circulation*; 107:3109, 2003.
4. Fit, fitter, fittest, *Harvard Medical School Health Letter* 15(4):2, 1990.
5. Simon HB: Can you run away from cancer? *Harvard Medical School Health Letter* 17(5):5–7, 1992.
6. Exercise and physical activity.
7. Ibid.
8. Position stand.
9. Ibid.
10. Exercise and physical activity.
11. An exercise prescription for older people, *Harvard Heart Letter* 8(10):1–4, 1998.
12. American College of Sports Medicine. *Guidelines for exercise testing and prescription.* ed. 6, 2000, Lippincott, Williams, and Wilkins.
13. Williams MH: Alcohol and sport performance, *Sports Science Exchange* 4(40):1–4, 1992.
14. Ibid.
15. The creatine craze, *UC Berkeley Wellness Letter* 14(3):6, 1998.
16. Ibid.
17. Arnheim DD, Prentice WE: *Essentials of athletic training,* 1999, McGraw-Hill.
18. Stevens WC, Brey RA, Harris JE, Fowlkes-Godek S: The dangerous trio: a case study approach to the female athletic triad, *Athletic Therapy Today,* 2(2):30–36, 1997.
19. Ibid.

SUGGESTED READINGS

Cooper KH: *Antioxidant revolution,* 1997, Thomas Nelson Inc.

This book, written by Dr. Kenneth H. Cooper (the "father of aerobics"), examines the benefits of antioxidant supplementation combined with aerobic exercise. Cooper contends that vitamin C, vitamin E, beta-carotene, and other antioxidants strengthen the body's tissues by counteracting the effects of unstable oxygen molecules.

Fitness Magazine (editor) with K Andes: *The complete book of fitness: mind, body, spirit,* 1999, Three Rivers Press.

Written in an easy-to-read style, this book is a primer on fitness. It's an encyclopedia-like reference organized into four major sections: strength training, cardiovascular training, diet and nutrition, and wellness. You can use this book to customize a fitness program for your lifestyle, present fitness level, and body type.

Fitness Magazine (editor) with G Graves: *Pregnancy fitness,* 1999, Three Rivers Press.

This book provides the fitness information every expectant mother needs as she progresses through her pregnancy. It is based on the premise that exercise will help a woman have a healthier pregnancy, an easier delivery, and a faster postpartum recovery. *Pregnancy Fitness* is effectively illustrated and designed for women of every fitness level.

Kaehler K (with CK Olson): *Real-world fitness,* 1999, Golden Books Publishing Co.

Kathy Kaehler is a well-recognized fitness instructor. She works with many celebrities, appears regularly on the *Today* show, and has made several fitness videos. The author describes ways to become fit with exercises that can be done in the home or dorm room. Kaehler is a good motivator and a firm believer in the cumulative effect of short sessions of exercise.

Prentice WE: *Fitness and wellness for life,* 1999, McGraw-Hill.

This highly recommended, comprehensive text covers all aspects of fitness and wellness. It provides particularly well-written coverage of strength training and stretching activities. The author's unique background as a scholar, athletic trainer, and physical therapist strengthens the credibility of the book.

Name ______________________ Date __________

Personal Assessment

What Is Your Level of Fitness?

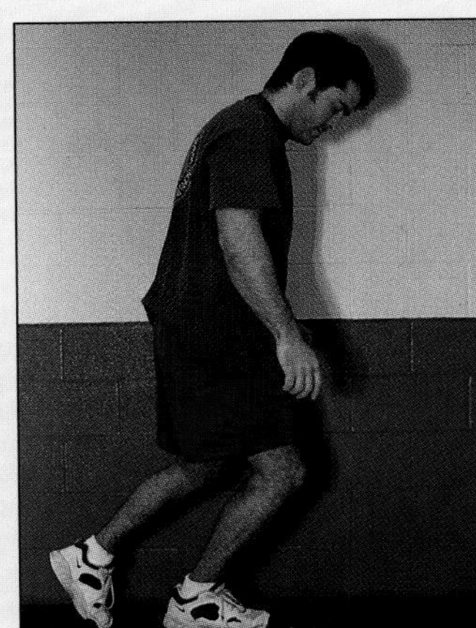

You can determine your level of fitness in 30 minutes or less by completing this short group of tests based on the National Fitness Test developed by the President's Council on Physical Fitness and Sports. If you are over 40 years old or have chronic medical disorders such as diabetes or obesity, check with your physician before taking this or any other fitness test. You will need another person to monitor your test and keep time.

Three-Minute Step Test

Aerobic capacity. Equipment: 30 cm bench, crate, block, or stepladder; stopwatch. Procedure: face bench. Complete 24 full steps (both feet on the bench, both feet on the ground) per minute for 3 minutes. After finishing, sit down, have your partner find your pulse within 5 seconds, and take your pulse for 1 minute. Your score is your pulse rate for 1 full minute.

Scoring standards (heart rate for 1 minute)

Age	18–29		30–39		40–49		50–59		60+	
Gender	F	M	F	M	F	M	F	M	F	M
Excellent	<80	<75	<84	<78	<88	<80	<92	<85	<95	<90
Good	80–110	75–100	84–115	78–109	88–118	80–112	92–123	85–115	95–127	90–118
Average	>110	>100	>115	>109	>118	>112	>123	>115	>127	>118

Sit and Reach

Hamstring flexibility. Equipment: metre stick; tape. Between your legs, tape the metre stick to the floor. Sit with legs straight and heels about 12 cm apart, heels even with the 40 cm mark on the yardstick. While in a sitting position, slowly stretch forward as far as possible. Your score is the number of centimetres reached.

Scoring standards (centimetres)

Age	18–29		30–39		40–49		50–59		60+	
Gender	F	M	F	M	F	M	F	M	F	M
Excellent	>56	>53	>56	>53	>53	>51	>51	>48	>51	>48
Good	43–56	33–53	43–56	33–53	38–53	33–51	36–51	30–48	36–51	30–48
Average	<43	<33	<43	<33	<38	<33	<36	<30	<36	<30

Arm Hang

Upper body strength. Equipment: horizontal bar (high enough to prevent your feet from touching the floor); stopwatch. Procedure: hang with straight arms, palms facing forward. Start watch when subject is in position. Stop when subject lets go. Your score is the number of minutes and seconds spent hanging.

Scoring standards (heart rate for 1 minute)

Age	18–29		30–39		40–49		50–59		60+	
Gender	F	M	F	M	F	M	F	M	F	M
Excellent	>1:30	>2:00	>1:20	>1:50	>1:10	>1:35	>1:00	>1:20	>:50	>1:10
Good	:46–1:30	1:00–2:00	:40–1:20	:50–1:50	:30–1:10	:45–1:35	:30–1:00	:35–1:20	:21–:50	:30–1:10
Average	<:46	<1:00	<:40	<:50	<:30	<:45	<:30	<:35	<:21	<:30

Name ______________________________ **Date** ____________

Personal Assessment *continued*

Curl-Ups

Abdominal and low back strength. Equipment: stopwatch. Procedure: Lie flat on upper back, knees bent, shoulders touching the floor, arms extended above your thighs or by your sides, palms down. Bend knees so that the feet are flat and 30 cm from the buttocks. Curl up by lifting head and shoulders off the floor, sliding hands forward above your thighs or the floor. Curl down and repeat. Your score is the number of curl-ups in 1 minute.

Scoring standards (number in 1 minute)

Age	18–29		30–39		40–49		50–59		60+	
Gender	F	M	F	M	F	M	F	M	F	M
Excellent	>45	>50	>40	>45	>35	>40	>30	>35	>25	>30
Good	25–45	30–50	20–40	22–45	16–35	21–40	12–30	18–35	11–25	15–30
Average	<25	<30	<20	<22	<16	<21	<12	<18	<11	<15

Push-Ups

Upper body strength. Equipment: stopwatch. Assume a front-leaning position. Lower your body until chest touches the floor. Raise and repeat for 1 minute. Your score is the number of push-ups completed in 1 minute.

Scoring standards (number in 1 minute)

Age	18–29	30–39	40–49	50–59	60+
Excellent	>50	>45	>40	>35	>30
Good	25–50	22–45	19–40	15–35	10–30
Average	<25	<22	<19	<15	<10

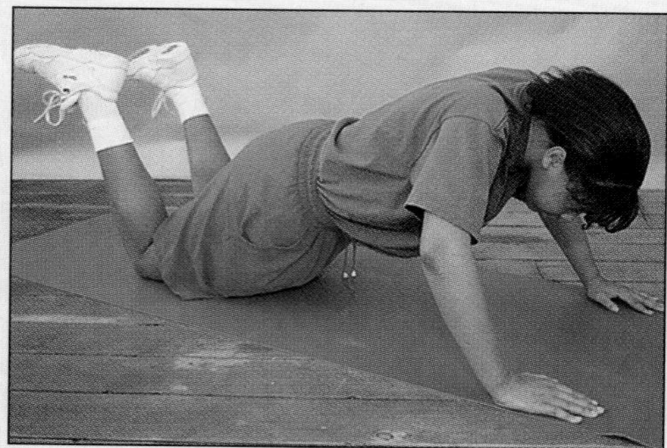

Modified Push-Ups

Upper body strength. Equipment: stopwatch. Assume a front-leaning position with knees bent up, hands under shoulders. Lower your chest to the floor, raise, and repeat. Your score is the number of push-ups completed in 1 minute.

Scoring standards (number in 1 minute)

Age	18–29	30–39	40–49	50–59	60+
Excellent	>45	>40	>35	>30	>25
Good	17–45	12–40	8–35	6–30	5–25
Average	<17	<12	<8	<6	<5

To Carry This Further ...

Note your areas of strengths and weaknesses. To improve your fitness, become involved in a fitness program that reflects the concepts discussed in this chapter. Talking with fitness experts on your campus might be a good first step.

Focus on

STAYING FIT DURING PREGNANCY

Like many other attitudes, our thinking on fitness during pregnancy has changed in recent years.[1] No longer is a pregnant woman treated as fragile. These days a doctor is likely to advise against a sedentary lifestyle for a healthy pregnant woman. Exercise during pregnancy can increase a woman's muscle strength, making delivery of the baby easier and faster. Exercise can also help control her weight, making it easier to get back to normal weight after delivery. The baby may benefit from the mother's exercise program as well.

Exercise is especially beneficial to pregnant women.

Importance of Exercise for Pregnant Women

Exercise in general is beneficial to the human body, and it is even more important for pregnant women to exercise regularly.[2] During pregnancy a woman's entire body undergoes many physical changes. Muscles are stretched, joints are loosened, and tissues are subjected to stress. If a woman is in good physiological condition, she is more likely to handle these changes with few complications.[3] The baby may also benefit: studies have shown that women who exercise during pregnancy tend to give birth to healthier babies.[4]

Types of Exercise

The types of exercises a woman should perform during pregnancy will vary with the individual and with the stage of pregnancy. General exercises that increase overall fitness and stamina should be practised, as well as exercises that strengthen specific muscle groups. Muscles of the pelvic floor, for example, should be exercised regularly, since these muscles will be supporting most of the extra weight of the baby. The pelvic floor muscles are involved with control of the bladder and rectum and with controlling increases in pressure within the abdominal cavity resulting from pushing during labour.[5] General exercises for the pelvic floor muscles include Kegel exercises. These exercises involve the contraction of pelvic floor muscles, and they can be performed by squeezing and then relaxing the anal sphincter.[6] These exercises work on the sphincters (rings of muscle) that control the openings of the urethra and anus.

The abdominal muscles are responsible for supporting the load of the growing fetus in the front of the mother's body. They are also used for pushing during delivery. These muscles must be kept in good shape so they can adequately support the increased weight.[7] Muscles involved in maintaining good posture, such as the back and leg muscles, should also be exercised. Efficient breathing should be practised as well.

A variety of exercises is available, including walking, swimming, stretching, and strengthening exercises.[8] Yoga and tai chi are also good forms of exercise for pregnant women. The muscles of the pelvic floor, abdomen, and back are especially subject to stress and strain during pregnancy and delivery, so certain exercises can also be performed to strengthen these muscles. Exercises can also be performed to speed recovery after delivery.[9] Such postpartum exercises can be started in some cases within 24 hours after delivery. Exercises can even be started before conception if a pregnancy is anticipated.

Hydrotherapy is becoming a popular option for expectant mothers. Exercising in the water helps reduce stress on joints. Water also provides more resistance than air, so muscles get a better workout. No special equipment is needed, but various props such as weights or fans can be used to increase resistance. Immersion in water has also been shown to decrease blood pressure, reduce heart rate, and reduce tissue swelling in pregnant women.[10] Exercising in water may also reduce the risk for pregnant women of getting overheated or tired. The water must not be too warm, however, since water that is too hot (around 97.8 F or above) may damage the nervous system and brain of the fetus.[11]

Risks to the Fetus

Although exercise during pregnancy has definite advantages, there are some drawbacks that must be considered as well. Studies suggest that exercise can be harmful to the fetus in some cases. Women who undergo exercise for long periods may experience a prolonged increase in core body temperature (a condition called *hyperthermia*), which may in turn increase the body temperature of the fetus. It is thought that such increases in fetal temperature may in turn put the baby at risk for congenital malformations. It has been shown that fever-induced hyperthermia is related to congenital malformation in many mammals, and recent studies suggest that this may be true for humans as well.[12] If fever from illness can increase the expectant mother's core temperature enough to produce malformations in the fetus, then it is possible that an increase in the mother's core temperature resulting from prolonged exercise may have similar effects. Fortunately, exercise over short periods 15 minutes or less) is not likely to raise the mother's core temperature enough to cause problems.[13]

Exercising Safely

If the expectant mother exercised regularly before becoming pregnant, she may have to alter her exercise routine. Intense, high-impact workouts should be avoided in favour of moderate exercise, since very intense workouts may reduce blood flow to the fetus and deprive it of nutrients. Sports that involve sudden stops, such as basketball or tennis, should be avoided, and certain strenuous sports may eventually result in birth complications.[14] Exercises that involve lying on the back should not be performed after the first trimester of pregnancy, since they may reduce blood flow to the mother's heart and the heart of the fetus. Deep knee bends, sit-ups, and toe touches should be avoided, as well as downhill skiing, rock climbing, and horseback riding.[15] Exercises should be chosen that minimize the risk of injury to the fetus and the mother. Because of the changes in the mother's weight distribution during the course of pregnancy, she should be especially aware of balance during workouts. Exercises that may put her at risk of losing her balance and falling should be avoided, especially during the last trimester.[16]

Once safety factors have been accounted for, the healthy pregnant woman still has an array of options to choose from for her exercise routine. As with any workout program, she should consult her physician before beginning. Her obstetrician can tell her which exercises will be most beneficial and can also give tips to reduce potential injury to her and her baby. The obstetrician can give the expectant mother guidelines concerning safe levels of exertion and duration times of exercise as well.

For Discussion

Do you think exercise during pregnancy is a good idea or not? Do the benefits outweigh the risks?

References

1. Kaehler K, Tivers C: *Primetime pregnancy: the proven program for staying in shape before and after your baby is born*, 1997, Contemporary Books.
2. Marti J, Hine A: *The alternative health and medicine encyclopedia*, 1995, Gale.
3. Noble E: *Essential exercises for the childbearing year*, 1982, Houghton Mifflin.
4. *The alternative health and medicine encyclopedia.*
5. *Essential exercises.*
6. Ibid.
7. Ibid.
8. *The alternative health and medicine encyclopedia.*
9. Parr R, Rudnitsky DA: *Rob Parr's post-pregnancy workout*, 1997, Berkeley Publishing Group.
10. Cefalo RC, Moos M-K: *Preconceptional health care: a practical guide*, 1995, Mosby.
11. *The alternative health and medicine encyclopedia.*
12. *Preconceptional health care.*
13. Ibid.
14. *The alternative health and medicine encyclopedia.*
15. Williams, RD: Healthy pregnancy, healthy baby, *FDA Consumer* 33(2):18–23, 1999.
16. *The alternative health and medicine encyclopedia.*

Chapter **5**

Understanding Nutrition and Diet

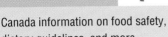

Chapter Objectives

After reading this chapter, you should be able to

- Name and describe the seven types of nutrients.
- Describe saturated fats and explain their effects on the human body.
- Define complete protein foods and incomplete protein foods, and give examples of each.
- Describe three processes that vitamins help perform in the body.
- Discuss the roles of minerals and water in the body.
- Describe the benefits of soluble and insoluble fibre.
- Describe *Canada's Food Guide to Healthy Eating* and the number of recommended servings for each food group.
- Describe food-borne illnesses and strategies for preventing them.
- Name three types of vegetarian diets and describe the advantages and disadvantages of each.

Online Learning Centre Resources

www.mcgrawhill.ca/college/hahn

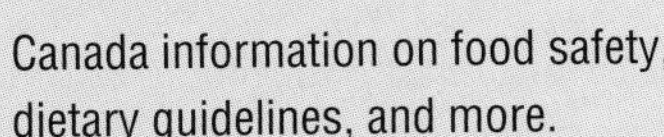

Log on to our Online Learning Centre (OLC) for access to Web links for study and exploration of health topics. Here are some examples of what you'll find:

- **www.hc-sc.gc.ca/food-aliment** Check out this site to find Health Canada information on food safety, dietary guidelines, and more.
- **www.dietitians.ca** Look at this site for nutritious recipes, a nutrition quiz, and a quick tool for assessing your diet, body weight, and physical activity.

Media Pulse

The Truth About Food Addiction

There is a lot of debate about whether we can be addicted to food. Certainly some chocolate lovers will tell you that they are "chocoholics," and must have their dose of daily chocolate or suffer miserably. But even though there may be a psychological dependence or issue with food (as we'll discuss in Chapter 6 on weight management), there is no evidence that people can become physiologically addicted to particular foods. Yet many popular diets—including Overeaters Anonymous, Sugar Busters, and the Carbohydrate Addicts Diet among others—are based on the premise that we can become addicted to food in the same way that we can become addicted to alcohol or drugs. What is the truth about food addiction?

Diet programs that are based upon an addiction model lack sufficient scientific support for their claims. These diets suggest that there is a biological craving for carbohydrates—especially white flour and refined sugar—and that we need more and more of these foods in order to satisfy this craving. But it is important to recognize the difference between a physiological need and psychological craving. A craving is based on your thoughts and feelings, while hunger is a biological or physiological process. While individuals with eating disorders or problems with compulsive overeating may experience psychological cravings, their cravings are not physiologically based. Indeed, there are some similarities between overeating and substance abuse—such as obsessively thinking about the food or drug, having periods of fasting and bingeing, and experiencing problems in day-to-day functioning—but this is where the likeness ends. Because, while even an addict can live without alcohol or drugs, nobody can abstain from food. We don't build up

Media Pulse *continued*

tolerance to certain foods, nor do we go through physiological withdrawal when abstaining from certain foods similar to what is seen with drug or alcohol withdrawal and physical dependence.

A number of popular diets are predicated on the idea that one can be addicted to sugar or carbohydrates because of the insulin reaction that occurs in the body when one eats any food. The glycemic index measures how much a food provokes the body to release insulin into the blood, causing the body to convert blood sugar (glucose) into fat. A high level of insulin speeds up the conversion too quickly and the blood sugar level plummets, causing individuals to feel light-headed, tired, and hungry. The higher the glycemic index, the faster the insulin response.

Diets based on the addiction model (such as The Atkins' Diet, Sugar Busters, the Carbohydrate Addict's Diet, or The Zone diet) are based upon the theory that people who are addicted to carbohydrates are "insulin resistant," and have an insulin imbalance in which their bodies produce too much insulin, causing them to feel constantly hungry which in turn causes them to overeat. Foods high in sugar, corn syrup, and complex carbohydrates like potatoes and carrots have a high glycemic index, and this is the reason the food addiction diets suggest avoiding carbohydrates.

The premise behind these diets is problematic for a number of reasons. First, they fail to take into consideration that when these foods are eaten in combination with other foods, such as eating carrots or potatoes with meat, this insulin response is not provoked. Second, these diets treat all carbohydrates the same, but we know this is not the case. Simple carbohydrates such as refined sugar provoke an insulin release into the blood, but complex carbohydrates such as whole grains, fruits, and vegetables do not, even though they too have a high glycemic index. Also problematic is these diets' reliance on high-fat, high-cholesterol meals that put you at risk for heart disease, colon cancer, and ketosis.

The best way to keep your insulin levels stable is to follow *Canada's Food Guide to Healthy Eating* and avoid sugary foods and drinks. So don't be fooled by diets based on the myth of food addiction!

Sources: Hall R. *The Unofficial Guide to Smart Nutrition.* Foster City, CA: IDG Books Worldwide International, 2000; Poston W and Haddock C. *Food as a Drug.* New York: The Haworth Press, 2000.

From the prenatal period throughout life, sound dietary practices are needed to maintain high-level health. Food provides the body with the **nutrients** required to produce energy, repair damaged tissue, promote tissue growth, and regulate physiological processes.

Physiologically, these nutrients—carbohydrates, fats, protein, vitamins, minerals, dietary fibre, and water—are essential, that is, they must be consumed in adequate quantities on a regular basis. In addition, the production, preparation, serving, and sharing of food enriches our lives in other ways (see Exploring Your Spirituality on p. 85).

TYPES AND SOURCES OF NUTRIENTS

Let's discuss the familiar nutrients first: carbohydrates, fats, and proteins. These three nutrients provide our bodies with **calories**.* Calories are used quickly by our bodies in energy metabolism, or they are stored in the form of glycogen or fat. The other nutrient groups, which are not sources of energy for the body, will be discussed later.

*The term "calorie" is used here to mean kilocalorie (kcal), which is the accepted scientific expression of the energy value of a food. The SI system uses the term "**joule**."

Carbohydrates

Carbohydrates are various combinations of sugar units, or saccharides. The body uses carbohydrates primarily for energy. Each gram of carbohydrate contains 4 calories. Since the average person requires approximately 2000 calories per day and about 60% of our calories come from carbohydrates, roughly 1200 calories per day should come from carbohydrates.[1]

Carbohydrates occur in three forms, depending on the number of saccharide (sugar) units that make up the molecule. Those that contain only one saccharide unit are classified as *monosaccharides* (glucose, or blood sugar), those with two units are *disaccharides* (sucrose, or table sugar), and those with more than two units are *polysaccharides* (starches).

In 2000 Canadian consumers each drank 113 L of soft drinks (up 15% over the decade).[2,3] In contrast, milk intake fell to 62 L annually per Canadian. This represents a 9% decrease over the decade.[4] The frequent consumption of soft drinks and other products that are abundant sources of the types of carbohydrates that are rapidly taken up into the bloodstream has been implicated in the development of obesity, type 2 diabetes, and cardiovascular disease. While there is more research needed in this area, it is advisable to choose your carbohydrates from less refined sources such as whole grains, fruit, vegetables, **legumes**, and nuts. These foods not only provide healthy

Exploring Your Spirituality

Mealtime—A Chance to Share and Bond

Food is important to your physical well-being—for energy, growth, repair, and regulation of your body and its function. But it's also important to the well-being of your spirit. The sharing of food nourishes our spiritual sense of community. This happens through the type of foods selected, the method of preparation, the uniqueness of presentation, and the people involved. From a spiritual perspective, the sharing of food can be a highly satisfying activity.

No closer sense of community exists than in the family. When food is shared in the company of those who care about us in the deepest and most personal ways, we experience a sense of value and well-being that is rarely found elsewhere. The simple act of being together and engaged in a familiar and comfortable practice is reassuring. It reminds us that we are valued in this setting. Meals that involve the extended family, especially dinners for special occasions or important holidays, are particularly rewarding.

Food is often at the centre of the celebration of special occasions. Weddings, birthdays, anniversaries, graduations, promotions, retirements, and funerals take on a special meaning when people come together to share food and drink. From the first birthday cake through the retirement dinner to the lunch provided by neighbours after the funeral of a loved one, food reminds us that these events are benchmarks in our passage through life.

Whether it's an unexpected gift certificate for your favourite restaurant, your favourite dinner prepared at home, an invitation to order anything you'd like from a menu, or a catered banquet, food is often used to recognize a special achievement. This reminds us—in a spiritually uplifting way—that people value us and have chosen to be a part of our success story.

Friends are among the most important resources we have in our quest for self-validation. The sharing of food provides an opportunity for us to have important and meaningful exchanges with our friends. It's also a way of introducing new friends into our lives. New and valuable friendships begin in residence hall dining rooms, on outdoor benches shared on a pleasant autumn day, at a restaurant when someone is invited to join a group at their table, and at picnics with coworkers. Without food, these opportunities might not exist.

Finally, food is the focus of many religious practices and observations. It may be a symbol in a religious service, a means of expressing religious values, or a way of unifying the congregation in times of joy and sorrow.

forms of carbohydrate (that is, starches and fibres), but also contain a vast array of essential nutrients.

Much of the sugar we consume is hidden. For example, it is an ingredient in foods such as ketchup, salad dressings, cured meat products, and canned vegetables and fruits. High-fructose corn syrup, often found in these items, is a highly concentrated sugar solution.

Starches are complex carbohydrates composed of long chains of sugar units. Starches are among the most important sources of dietary carbohydrates. Starches are found primarily in grains, legumes, vegetables, and fruit. Eating foods that have not been highly processed and are abundant in starches is nutritionally beneficial because most also contain much-needed vitamins, minerals, plant protein, and water. Many types of ethnic foods are high in carbohydrates and quite nutritious (see Learning from Our Diversity on page 86).

Fats

Fats (lipids) are an important nutrient in our diets. They provide a concentrated form of energy (9 calories per gram). Fat also helps give some food its pleasing taste, or **palatability**. Fats carry the fat-soluble vitamins A, D, E, and K. Without fat, these vitamins would quickly pass through the body. Fat also insulates our bodies to help us retain heat and provides a protective cushion for our internal organs and bones.

Key Terms

nutrients
Elements in foods that are required for the energy, growth, and repair of tissues and regulation of body processes.

calories
Units of heat (energy); specifically, one kcalorie (kilocalorie) equals the amount of heat required to raise the temperature of 1 kilogram of water by 1°C.
1 kilocalorie (kcal) = 1 calorie (Cal) = 1000 calories (cal)

joule
The System International (SI) unit for measuring the energy value of foods.
1 kilocalorie (kcal) = 4.2 kilojoules (kj)

carbohydrates
Chemical compounds composed of sugar units; the body's primary source of energy.

legumes
Include dried beans, dried peas, lentils, chick peas (garbanzo beans), and peanuts.

palatability
Pleasing to the palate.

Learning from Our Diversity

Do You Eat Real Ethnic Food?

The typical diets in many other countries tend to contain more high-carbohydrate foods and fewer foods high in animal fats than the common North American diet. Moreover, when ethnic foods are prepared in Canada and the United States, especially in restaurants, they are often "Americanized" by inclusion of larger portions of meat and cheese, and addition of extra sauces. The examples below describe some traditional, high-carbohydrate ethnic foods and their higher-fat Americanized versions. Which version of these ethnic foods do you tend to eat?

Chinese

- *Traditional:* Large bowl of steamed rice with small amounts of stir-fried vegetables, meats, and sauces as condiments.
- *Americanized:* Several stir-fried or batter-fried entrees in sauces, with a small bowl of fried rice on the side.

Japanese

- *Traditional:* Large bowl of steamed rice with broth-based soups containing rice noodles, vegetables, and small amounts of meat.
- *Americanized:* Tempura (batter-fried vegetables and shrimp), teriyaki chicken, oriental chicken salad with oil-based dressing.

Italian

- *Traditional:* Large mound of pasta with tomato-based sauce containing small amounts of meat or meatballs on the side; pizza with an extra-thick crust and a mere sprinkle of tomato sauce, herbs, and cheese.
- *Americanized:* Less pasta, more creamy sauces, and more meat; pizza with a thick crust, pepperoni, sausage, olives, and extra cheese.

Mexican

- *Traditional:* Mostly rice, beans, warmed tortillas, and lots of hot salsa and chiles.
- *Americanized:* Crispy fried tortillas, extra ground beef, added cheese, sour cream, and guacamole (avocado dip).

German

- *Traditional:* Large portions of potatoes, rye and whole-grain breads, stew with dumplings, and sauerkraut.
- *Americanized:* Fewer potatoes and less bread, more sausage and cheese.

Middle Eastern

- *Traditional:* Pita bread (round bread), pilaf (rice dish), hummus (chick pea dip), shaved slices of seasoned meat, diced vegetables, and yogurt-based sauces, all seasoned with garlic.
- *Americanized:* Meat kebobs, salads drenched in olive oil, less bread and pilaf.

Dietary sources of fat are often difficult to identify. The visible fats in our diet, such as butter, salad oils, and the layer of fat on some cuts of meat, represent only about 40% of the fat we consume. Most of the fat we eat is hidden in food.

At the grocery store, the fat content of some foods is expressed as a percentage of the product's weight. For example, the different types of milk available include skim milk (no fat), 1% and 2% milk, and whole milk (3% to 4%). The labelling of other dairy products such as yogurt indicates their percentage of fat as "% M.F." (milk fat).

The current recommendation is that no more than 25% to 30% of our calories come from fat (see the Star Box on p. 87). Complete the Personal Assessment on p. 105 to see whether you eat too many fatty foods. If so, the Changing for the Better box on p. 87 offers tips for reducing the amount of fat in your diet. Children under two years of age, however, need a certain amount of fat in their diets for growth.[5] Check with your doctor before restricting the amount of fat in a young child's diet.

All dietary fat is made up of a combination of three forms of fat: saturated, monounsaturated, and polyunsaturated, based on chemical composition. Paying attention to the amount of each type of fat in our diet is important because of the known link to heart disease (see Chapter 10). **Saturated fats**, including those found in animal sources and vegetable oils to which hydrogen has been added (hydrogenated), resulting in *trans-fatty acids*, need to be carefully limited in a healthy diet. Concern over the presence of trans-fatty acids (an altered form of a normal vegetable oil molecule) is associated with changes to the cell membrane, including those cells lining the artery wall. Among the changes being suggested is an increase in calcium deposits.[6] This could result in a rough surface, leading to plaque formation (see Chapter 10).

Concern over the presence of trans-fatty acids in margarines, snack foods, fast foods, and other commercial products is growing, and some have proposed changes to food labels that would indicate the presence of these acids and their relationship to cardiovascular disease. The amount of trans-fatty acids in the diet can be reduced by avoiding foods that contain hydrogenated plant oils.

How Much Fat Is Enough?

Is it a good idea to restrict your fat intake to less than 30% of total calories? Controversy over this question stems from an article that appeared in the *Journal of the American Medical Association* in 1997.[7] Researchers reported that men who had high cholesterol levels, a known risk factor for cardiovascular disease, showed an unexpected decline in levels of high-density lipoprotein (HDL) cholesterol, the so-called good cholesterol (thought to favour heart health), when fat intake was restricted. The researchers recommended caution in lowering fat intake too much.

Critics of the report contend that the researchers failed to consider the improved structural appearance of the arteries of people who restrict their fat intake to as little as 10% of total calories. More research needs to be done on this topic, including an assessment of artery wall changes.

Tropical oils

Although all cooking oils (and fats such as butter, lard, margarine, and shortening) have the same number of calories by weight (9 calories per gram), some oils contain high percentages of saturated fats. All oils and fats contain varying percentages of saturated, monounsaturated, and polyunsaturated fats. However, the tropical oils—coconut, palm, and palm kernel—contain much higher percentages of saturated fats than do other cooking oils. Coconut oil, for example, is 92% saturated fat. Tropical oils can still be found in some brands of snack foods, crackers, cookies, nondairy creamers, and breakfast cereals, although they have been removed from most national brands. Do you check for tropical oils on the ingredients labels of the foods you select?

Cholesterol

A high blood level of **cholesterol** may be a risk factor for the development of cardiovascular disease (see Chapter 10). Cholesterol is necessary in all animal tissue and is manufactured by our bodies. Evidence suggests that increased intake of saturated fats may increase serum (blood) cholesterol levels.[8] But the relationship between intake of dietary cholesterol and serum cholesterol levels remains unclear. However, most doctors still recommend that people restrict their dietary intake of cholesterol to 300 mg or less per day, reduce total fat and saturated fat intake, and exercise regularly. High-cholesterol foods include whole milk, shellfish, animal fat, and egg yolks. Only foods of animal origin contain cholesterol.

One of the first **functional foods** to appear in the Canadian marketplace was a margarine-type spread containing plant sterols, also known as **phytosterols**. In carefully controlled clinical studies in Finland, a similar product, when consumed on a regular basis, was shown to lower total cholesterol by 10% and the low-density lipoprotein (LDL) fraction by 15% (see Chapter 10). Health Canada has warned consumers that this product has not been officially approved for use by the general public and should not be used by children, pregnant women, those who are at risk for hemorrhagic stroke, or those people on cholesterol-lowering medication.

Changing *for the Better*

Tips for Reducing the Fat Content of Meals

Now that I'm sharing an apartment with friends, I'm eating more fatty foods than ever. How can I keep the fat content of my diet down?

- Become familiar with today's food labels, and use the information provided to reduce the fat content of your meals.
- When eating out, don't order foods with cream-based sauces, such as fettuccine alfredo.
- Trim all visible fat from meat—both within the cut and along the edges.
- Remove the skin from poultry.
- Roast or broil meat—this allows fat to drip off the meat.
- Layer vegetables over baked potatoes to reduce any tendency to add butter, margarine, or sour cream.
- Request salad dressing and other condiments on the side so that you can control the amount you use.
- Eat more vegetables, fruits, and breads in place of meats and cheeses.
- Use jelly and apple butter in place of butter and margarine on toast, bread, and bagels.

Key Terms

saturated fats
Fats that are difficult for the body to use; they are in solid form at room temperature; primarily animal fats.

cholesterol
A primary form of fat found in the blood; lipid material manufactured within the body and derived from dietary sources.

functional foods
Foods capable of contributing to the improvement/prevention of specific health problems.

phytosterol
A lipid-like material (sterol) found in plants.

Low-fat foods

The fat-free, low-fat, and reduced-fat food items that have appeared in stores and restaurants in recent years reflect our growing concern about how dietary fats are related to many health problems. Nutritionists believe, however, that this trend could weaken as the fast-food industry puts less emphasis on low-fat items. Consumers seem to favour good taste and large servings over the long-term health benefits of weight maintenance and reduced incidence of heart disease. It's important to remember that low-fat foods may be high in calories and therefore would not offer any significant benefit with respect to weight loss.

Proteins

Proteins are found in every living cell. They are composed of chains of **amino acids**. Of the 20 naturally occurring amino acids, the body can synthesize all but *nine essential amino acids** from the foods we eat. A food that contains all nine essential amino acids is called a *complete protein* food. Examples are animal products, including milk, meat, fish, cheese, and eggs. A food source that does not contain all nine essential amino acids is called an *incomplete protein* food. Vegetables, grains, and legumes are principal sources of incomplete protein. Soy beans and soy bean curd (tofu) are, however, sources of complete protein. For some people, such as vegans (see p. 99), with limited access to animal-based food sources, and those who have significantly limited their meat, egg, and dairy product consumption, it is important to understand that essential amino acids can be obtained from incomplete protein sources. This requires the daily selection of a variety of plant foods to ensure that all of the essential amino acids will be available for the body to synthesize its own proteins. Children and others with higher protein requirements should select their plant protein sources in combinations that will provide these essential amino acids at the same meal, as shown in the following list:

- Sunflower seeds/green peas
- Navy beans/barley
- Green peas/corn
- Red beans/rice
- Sesame seeds/soybeans
- Black-eyed peas/rice and peanuts
- Green peas/rice
- Corn/pinto beans

When even one essential amino acid is missing from the diet, a deficiency can develop.

Protein primarily promotes growth and maintenance of body tissue. However, when caloric intake falls, protein is broken down and converted into glucose. This loss of protein can impede growth and repair of tissue. Protein also is a primary component of enzyme and hormone structure. It helps maintain the *acid-base balance* of our bodies and is a source of energy (4 calories per gram consumed). Nutritionists recommend that 12% to 15% of our caloric intake be from protein, emphasizing that of plant origin.

Vitamins

Vitamins are organic compounds that are required in small amounts for normal growth, reproduction, and maintenance of health. Vitamins differ from carbohydrates, fats, and proteins because they do not provide calories or serve as structural elements for our bodies. Vitamins are often *coenzymes*. By facilitating the action of **enzymes**, vitamins help initiate a wide variety of body responses, including energy production, use of minerals, and growth of healthy tissue.

Vitamins can be classified as *water soluble* (capable of being dissolved in water) or *fat soluble* (capable of being dissolved in fat or lipid tissue). Water-soluble vitamins include the B-complex vitamins and vitamin C. In most cases any excess consumption of these water-soluble vitamins results in their being eliminated from the body in the urine. The fat-soluble vitamins are vitamins A, D, E, and K. Excessive intake of these vitamins causes them to be stored in the body in the lipid-storing tissues. It is therefore possible to consume and retain toxic amounts of these vitamins, particularly vitamins A and D.

Because water-soluble vitamins dissolve quickly in water, it's important not to lose them during the preparation of fresh fruits and vegetables. One method is not to overcook fresh vegetables. The longer vegetables are steamed or boiled, the more water-soluble vitamins will be lost. Some people save the water in which vegetables were boiled or steamed and use it for drinking or cooking.

To ensure adequate vitamin intake, a good approach is to eat a variety of foods. Unless there are special circumstances, such as pregnancy, lactation, infancy, or an existing health problem, nearly everyone who eats a reasonably well-rounded diet consumes enough vitamins to prevent deficiencies.

TALKING POINTS • What would you say to someone who is following a low-carbohydrate/high-fat weight-loss diet to help that person see the nutritional weaknesses of the diet?

Unfortunately, not all people eat a balanced diet based on a variety of foods. Recent studies suggest that a

*Eight additional compounds are sometimes classified as amino acids, so some nutritionists believe that there are more than 20 amino acids.

somewhat higher intake of vitamins A, C, and E for adults might reduce the risk of developing cancer or atherosclerosis, and result in depressed levels of high-density lipoprotein (HDL) cholesterol; however, several unanswered questions remain, including the amounts needed for effectiveness.[9]

Consuming an adequate amount of folic acid before and during pregnancy has been shown to reduce the incidence of birth defects. To ensure adequate folic acid intake (400 micrograms/day), in 1998 Health Canada began to require that bread and cereal products be supplemented with folic acid. Taking a daily multivitamin before and during pregnancy would easily provide the remaining amount of folic acid necessary to promote fetal neural tube closure (thus preventing spina bifida). Folic acid is also considered important in the prevention of cardiovascular disease.[10]

Minerals

Nearly 5% of the body is composed of inorganic materials, the *minerals*. Minerals function primarily as structural elements (in teeth, muscles, hemoglobin, and hormones). They are also critical in the regulation of body processes, including muscle contraction, heart function, blood clotting, protein synthesis, and red blood cell formation. Approximately 21 minerals have been recognized as essential for good health.

Major minerals are those that exist in relatively high amounts in our body tissues. Examples are calcium, phosphorus, sulfur, sodium, potassium, and magnesium. Examples of **trace elements**, minerals seen in relatively small amounts in body tissues, include zinc, iron, copper, selenium, and iodine. Trace elements are required in very small quantities, but they are essential for good health. As with vitamins, the safest, most appropriate way to prevent a mineral deficiency is to eat a balanced diet. However, calcium, a major mineral, can be difficult to obtain in adequate amounts if the diet does not emphasize milk or dairy products, and so may be taken as a supplement to help prevent osteoporosis.

Water

Water may well be our most essential nutrient, since without water most of us would die from the effects of **dehydration** in less than one week. We could survive for weeks or even years without some of the essential minerals and vitamins, but not without water. More than half our body weight comes from water. Water provides the medium for nutrient and waste transport, controls body temperature, and functions in nearly all of our body's biochemical reactions.

Most people seldom think about the importance of an adequate intake of water and fluids. Adults require about six to ten glasses a day, depending on their activity level and environment. People who drink beverages that tend to dehydrate the body (tea, coffee, and alcohol) should increase their water consumption. Needed fluids are also obtained from fruits, vegetables, juices, milk, and other noncaffeinated beverages. One other interesting note about water: dentists are increasingly concerned about the abnormally high number of dental caries (cavities) seen in children who have consumed bottled water rather than fluoridated tap water.[11]

Fibre

Although not considered a nutrient by definition, **fibre** is an important component of sound nutrition. Fibre consists of plant material that is not digested but moves through the digestive tract and out of the body. Grain products, legumes, fruits, and vegetables all provide us with dietary fibre.

Fibre can be classified into two large groups on the basis of water solubility. *Insoluble* fibres are those that can absorb water in the intestinal tract. By absorbing water, the insoluble fibres give the stool bulk and decrease the time it takes the stool to move through the digestive tract. In contrast, *soluble* fibre turns to a "gel" in the intestinal tract and binds to liver bile, which is made from the body's cholesterol. Thus the soluble fibres may be valuable in removing cholesterol, which lowers blood cholesterol levels. Also, foods that are high in soluble fibre contribute to keeping the blood sugar level low and reduce the risk of colon cancer.

Key Terms

proteins
Compounds composed of chains of amino acids; the primary components of muscle and connective tissue.

amino acids
The chief components of protein; can be manufactured by the body or obtained from dietary sources.

vitamins
Organic compounds that facilitate the action of enzymes.

enzymes
Organic substances that control the rate of physiological reactions but are not themselves altered in the process.

trace elements
Minerals present in very small amounts in the body; micronutrient elements.

dehydration
The abnormal depletion of fluids from the body; severe dehydration can be fatal.

fibre
Plant material that cannot be digested; found in cereal grains, legumes, nuts, fruits, and vegetables.

Food Guides in Canada

Canada's Food Guide to Healthy Eating is the primary food guide utilized by Canadians. However, alternative guidelines are employed by specific cultural groups or those with specific dietary preferences. Examples of such guides include the Northwest Territories Food Guide (which complements the traditions and customs of Aboriginals—see **www.nwtheadstart.org/comp_nutrition_food_guide.htm** for more information) and the Vegetarian Food Guide Rainbow at **www.dietitians.ca**.

Although earlier studies were contradictory regarding the effectiveness of soluble fibre in lowering cholesterol levels, now it appears that oat bran can lower cholesterol levels by five to six points in people whose initial cholesterol levels are moderately high. To accomplish this reduction, a daily consumption of oat bran equal to a large bowl of cold oat bran cereal or three or more packs of instant oatmeal would be necessary. Oatmeal can also be eaten as a cooked cereal or used in other foods, such as hamburgers, pancakes, or meatloaf.

THE FOOD GROUPS

The most effective way to take in adequate amounts of nutrients is to eat a **balanced diet**—one that includes a wide variety of foods from different food groups. *Canada's Food Guide to Healthy Eating* outlines four groups for which recommendations have been established and an additional group ("Other Foods") for which no specific recommendations exist (Figures 5–1[12] and 5–2[13]). Table 5–1[14] shows the adult recommended dietary allowances (RDAs) and adequate intakes. To determine whether you are eating a healthy diet balanced with choices from each food group, complete the Personal Assessment on p. 107.

Fruits and Vegetables

Five to ten servings from the fruit and vegetable group are recommended for an adult. An important function of this group is to provide vitamin A, vitamin C, complex carbohydrates, and fibre. Foods to emphasize in this group are dark-green, yellow, and orange vegetables and fruit. **Cruciferous vegetables**, such as broccoli, cabbage, brussels sprouts, and cauliflower, may be especially important in the prevention of certain forms of cancer.[15]

Milk, Yogurt, and Cheese

This group contributes two primary nutritional benefits: high-quality protein and calcium (required for bone and tooth development). Foods included in this group are milk, yogurt, cheese, ice cream, and fortifed soy or cereal beverages. The adult recommendation is 500 mL to 1L of milk or two to four equivalent servings from this group each day. Premenopausal women should consume three to four daily servings from this group to provide maximal protection from osteoporosis.

Meat, Poultry, Fish, Legumes, Eggs, and Nuts

It is essential to make daily selections from the protein-rich group because of our daily need for protein, iron, and the B vitamins. Meats include all red meat (beef, pork, and game), fish, and poultry. Non-meat choices include eggs, cheese, legumes, and peanut butter. The current recommendation for adults is two to three servings of 50 to 100 g of meat, fish, or poultry, or alternative per day.

The fat content of meat varies considerably. Some forms of meat yield only 1% fat, but others may be as high as 40% fat. Poultry and fish are usually significantly lower in overall fat than red meat. The higher the grade of red meat, the more fat will be marbled throughout the muscle fibre and thus the higher will be its caloric value.

Bread, Cereal, Rice, and Pasta

The nutritional benefit from this group lies in its contribution of B-complex vitamins and energy to our diets. Five to twelve servings daily from this group are recommended with an emphasis on whole-grain breads or cereals.

Fats, Oils, and Sweets

Where do such items as butter, candy, soft drinks, cookies, chips, and doughnuts fit into this food group pattern? They are included under the label "Other Foods." Most of these items contribute little to healthy nutrition. In general, they provide additional calories (generally from fat and/or sugar) and may contain large amounts of salt. Therefore they should be consumed in moderation. It is important to remember that cookies, crackers, and desserts that are called "fat free" or "low fat" may be high in sugar and calories. Many of these foods are known collectively as *junk foods* because of their low **nutrient density**.

FAST FOODS

Fast foods are convenience foods that are usually prepared in walk-in or drive-through restaurants. They deliver a high percentage of their calories from fat, often associated with their method of preparation (e.g., frying in saturated fat). **Fat density** is a serious limitation of fast foods (see Table 5–2[16]). In comparison with the recommended standard (25% to 30% of total calories from fat), 40% to 50% of the calories in fast foods come from fats. Although many fast-food restaurants are now using

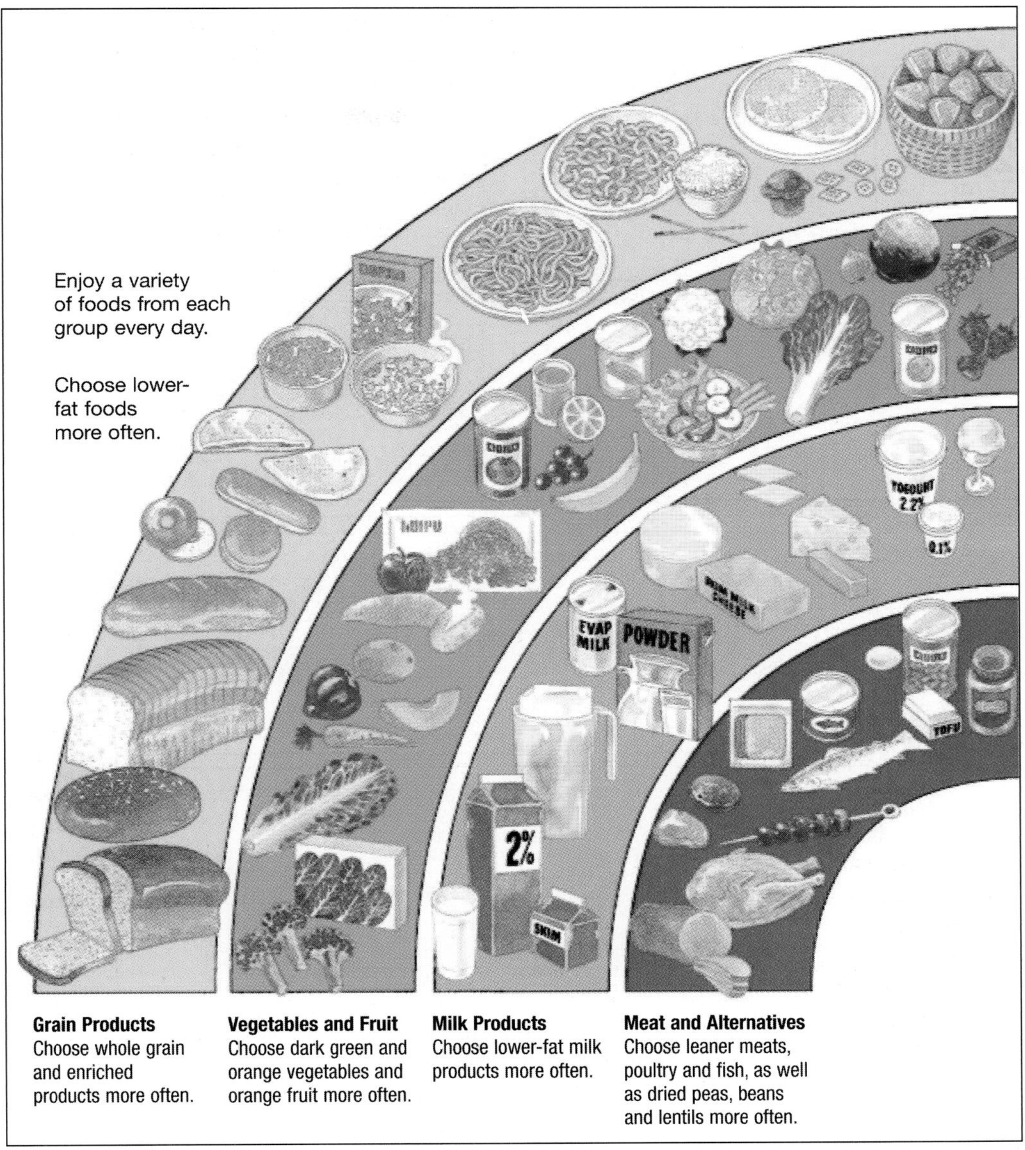
Enjoy a variety of foods from each group every day.
Choose lower-fat foods more often.
EVAP MILK
POWDER
2%
SKIM
YOGOURT 2.2%
0.1%
TOFU
Grain Products
Choose whole grain and enriched products more often.
Vegetables and Fruit
Choose dark green and orange vegetables and orange fruit more often.
Milk Products
Choose lower-fat milk products more often.
Meat and Alternatives
Choose leaner meats, poultry and fish, as well as dried peas, beans and lentils more often.

Figure 5–1 *Canada's Food Guide to Healthy Eating.*

vegetable oil instead of animal fat for frying (to reduce cholesterol levels), this change has not lowered the fat density of these foods. One average fast-food meal supplies over one-half the amount of fat needed in a day. In addition, fast foods are often high in sugar and salt.

During the early 1990s, the fast-food industry made an effort to offer alternatives to its fat-dense menu items by offering pasta, whole-wheat rolls, and lighter dressing. Unfortunately, this limited effort has nearly disappeared because many customers prefer large serving sizes (at low cost) and fat-dense foods. Today, supersize burgers, packing nearly 1000 calories each, and two-for-one pizzas are popular choices among 18- to 35-year-old customers. For more healthy options, see Table 5–3.[17]

Key Terms

balanced diet
A diet featuring daily food selections from each of the food groups of *Canada's Food Guide to Healthy Eating.*

cruciferous vegetables
Vegetables, such as broccoli, whose plants have flowers with four leaves in the pattern of a cross.

nutrient density
The nutritional quality of food, relative to its energy value; a food that is abundant in nutrients yet low in calories has a high nutrient density.

fat density
The percentage of a food's total calories that are derived from fat; above 30% is considered to be a high fat density.

Canada's Food Guide to Healthy Eating for People Four Years and Over

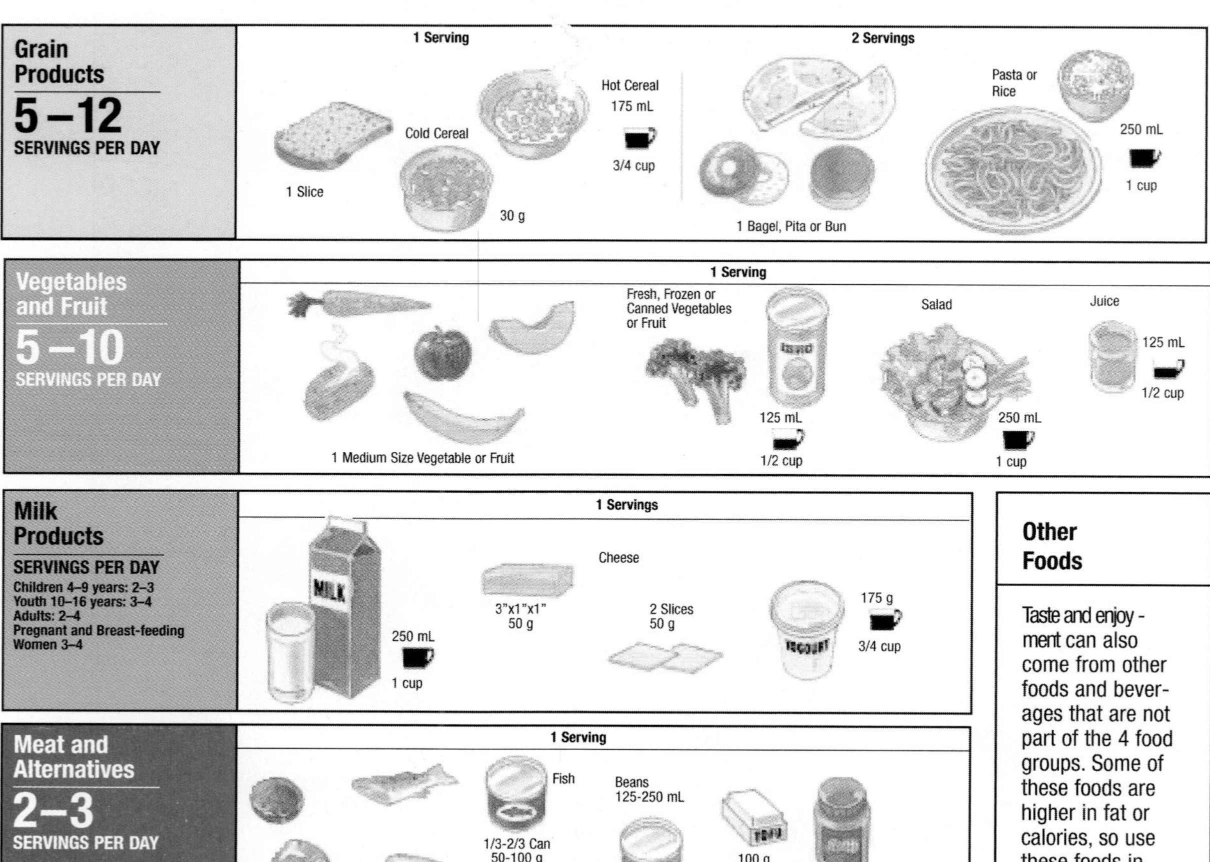

Figure 5–2 Different people need different amounts of food. The amount of food you need every day from the four food groups and other foods depends on your age, body size, activity level, whether you are male or female, and if you are pregnant or breast-feeding. That's why the *Food Guide* gives a lower and higher number of servings for each food group. For example, young children can choose the lower number of servings, while male teenagers can go to the higher number. Most other people can choose servings somewhere in between.

PHYTOCHEMICALS

Certain physiologically active components are believed to deactivate carcinogens or function as antioxidants. Among these are the carotenoids (from green vegetables), polyphenols (from onions and garlic), indoles (from cruciferous vegetables), and the allyl sulfides (from garlic, chives, and onions). These *phytochemicals* (naturally occurring substances found in plants) may be important agents in reducing the risk of cancer and heart disease in people who consume a large quantity of fruits, vegetables, and other plant-based foods such as whole grains and legumes. At this time, however, all of the mechanisms through which the various phytochemicals reduce the risk of disease are not fully understood.[18] Although it is generally agreed that these foods are important in planning food selections, no precise recommendations regarding the amounts of various phytochemical-rich plants have been made.

FUNCTIONAL FOODS

At the forefront of healthy nutrition is the identification and development of foods intended to affect a particular health problem or to improve the functional capability of the body. Functional foods contain not only recognized nutrients but also new or enhanced elements that impart medicine-like properties to the food. Alternative labels also exist for various subclasses of functional foods, such as *nutraceuticals*, or food elements that may be packaged in forms appearing more like medications (for example, pills or capsules), and *probiotics*, or foods that improve the microbial flora that reside within the human digestive tract.[19]

Table 5–1 Adult Recommended Dietary Allowances and Adequate Intakes

Life stage Group	Vitamin A (µg/d)[a]	Vitamin C (mg/d)	Vitamin D (µg/d)[b,c]	Vitamin E (mg/d)[d]	Thiamin (mg/d)	Riboflavin (mg/d)	Niacin (mg/d)[e]	Vitamin B_6 (mg/d)	Folate (µg/d)[f]	Vitamin B_{12} (µg/d)
Males										
9–13 y	600	45	5*	11	0.9	0.9	12	1.0	300	1.8
14–18 y	900	75	5*	15	1.2	1.3	16	1.3	400	2.4
19–30 y	900	90	5*	15	1.2	1.3	16	1.3	400	2.4
31–50 y	900	90	5*	15	1.2	1.3	16	1.3	400	2.4
51–70 y	900	90	10*	15	1.2	1.3	16	1.7	400	2.4
>70 y	900	90	15*	15	1.2	1.3	16	1.7	400	2.4
Females										
9–13 y	600	45	5*	11	0.9	0.9	12	1.0	300	1.8
14–18 y	700	65	5*	15	1.0	1.0	14	1.2	400[g]	2.4
19–30 y	700	75	5*	15	1.1	1.1	14	1.3	400[g]	2.4
31–50 y	700	75	5*	15	1.1	1.1	14	1.3	400[g]	2.4
51–70 y	700	75	10*	15	1.1	1.1	14	1.5	400	2.4
>70 y	700	75	15*	15	1.1	1.1	14	1.5	400	2.4

Life stage Group	Calcium (mg/d)	Iron (mg/d)	Magnesium (mg/d)	Zinc (mg/d)
Males				
9–13 y	1300*	8	240	8
14–18 y	1300*	11	410	11
19–30 y	1000*	8	400	11
31–50 y	1000*	8	420	11
51–70 y	1200*	8	420	11
>70 y	1200*	8	420	11
Females				
9–13 y	1300*	8	240	8
14–18 y	1300*	15	360	9
19–30 y	1000*	18	310	8
31–50 y	1000*	18	320	8
51–70 y	1200*	8	320	8
>70 y	1200*	8	320	8

NOTE: This table (taken from the DRI reports, see **www.nap.edu**) presents Recommended Dietary Allowances (RDAs) in **bold type** and Adequate Intakes (AIs) in ordinary type followed by an asterisk (*). RDAs and AIs may both be used as goals for individual intake. RDAs are set to meet the needs of almost all (97 to 98 percent) individuals in a group. The AI for the life stages and gender groups presented in this table is believed to cover needs of all individuals in the group, but lack of data or uncertainty in the data prevent being able to specify with confidence the percentage of individuals covered by this intake.

[a]As retinol activity equivalents (RAEs). 1 RAE = 1 µg retinol, 12 µg β-carotene, 24 µg α-carotene, or 24 µg β-cryptoxanthin. To calculate RAEs from REs of provitamin A carotenoids in foods, divide the REs by 2. For preformed vitamin A in foods or supplements and for provitamin A carotenoids in supplements, 1 RE = 1 RAE.

[b]cholecalciferol. 1 µg cholecalciferol = 40 IU vitamin D.

[c]In the absence of adequate exposure to sunlight.

[d]As α-tocopherol.

[e]As niacin equivalents (NE). 1 mg of niacin = 60 mg of tryptophan.

[f]As dietary folate equivalents (DFE). 1 DFE = 1 µg food folate = 0.6 µg of folic acid from fortified food or as a supplement consumed with food = 0.5 g of a supplement taken on an empty stomach.

[g]In view of evidence linking folate intake with neural tube defects in the fetus, it is recommended that all women capable of becoming pregnant consume 400 µg from supplements or fortified foods in addition to intake of food folate from a varied diet.

Examples of functional foods include garlic (believed to lower cholesterol), olive oil (thought to prevent heart disease), foods high in dietary fibre (which prevent constipation and lower cholesterol), and foods rich in calcium (which prevent osteoporosis). In addition, foods that contain high levels of vitamins A, C, and E—primarily fruits and vegetables—and provide the body with natural sources of antioxidants are functional foods.

Other functional foods are those that contain or are enriched with folic acid. These vitamin B–family foods aid in the prevention of spina bifida and other neural tube defects and the prevention of heart disease. Foods that are rich in selenium are sometimes categorized as functional foods because of selenium's potential as an agent in cancer prevention. Health Canada is introducing new labelling regulations that permit the inclusion of specific **health claims** on foods. These optional claims are highly regulated to ensure that only health claims that are supported by sound science are permitted and the food making a health claim really deserves to do so.

Key Term

health claims
Regulated statements attesting to a food's contribution to the improvement/prevention of specific health problems.

Table 5–2 Fast Food: Fast, Convenient, Affordable—But Fattening

Menu Item	Calories	Calories from Fat	% Calories from Fat
Burgers			
McDonald's Hamburger	260	81	31%
Wendy's Jr. Hamburger	270	90	33%
McDonald's Cheeseburger	320	117	38%
Wendy's Jr. Cheeseburger	320	117	38%
Wendy's Plain Single Hamburger	360	144	39%
Burger King Cheeseburger	380	171	45%
Wendy's Jr. Bacon Cheeseburger	380	171	45%
McDonald's Quarter Pounder	420	189	45%
Wendy's Plain Double Hamburger	560	261	46%
McDonald's Big Mac	560	279	50%
McDonald's Quarter Pounder w/Cheese	530	270	51%
Burger King Double Cheeseburger	600	324	53%
Burger King Whopper	640	351	55%
Burger King Whopper with Cheese	730	414	56%
Burger King Double Whopper	870	504	57%
Chicken Sandwiches			
McDonald's Plain Grilled Chicken Deluxe	300	45	15%
Wendy's Grilled Chicken Sandwich	310	72	23%
Wendy's Breaded Chicken Sandwich	440	162	36%
KFC Original Recipe Chicken Sandwich	497	198	40%
McDonald's Crispy Chicken Deluxe	500	225	44%
Burger King Broiler	550	261	47%
Burger King Chicken Sandwich	710	387	55%

Menu Item	Calories	Calories from Fat	% Calories from Fat
Sub Sandwiches (6")			
Subway Veggie Delite	237	27	11%
Subway Turkey Breast	289	36	12%
Subway Steak & Cheese	398	90	23%
Subway Cold Cut Trio	378	117	31%
Subway Meatball	419	144	34%
Subway Tuna	542	288	53%
French Fries			
Dairy Queen Large	390	162	41%
McDonald's Super Size	540	234	43%
McDonald's Small	210	90	43%
Wendy's Biggie	460	207	43%
McDonald's Large	450	198	44%
Wendy's Small	260	117	46%
Burger King Medium	370	180	49%
Tacos, Burritos, Pitas (and related items)			
Taco Bell Bean Burrito	380	108	29%
Taco Bell Steak Soft Taco	200	63	30%
Wendy's Chicken Caesar Pita	490	153	33%
Taco Bell Gordita Fiesta (steak)	270	90	33%
Wendy's Garden Veggie Pita	390	135	36%
Taco Bell Burrito Supreme	440	162	39%
Wendy's Classic Greek Pita	430	171	40%
Taco Bell Beef Burrito Supreme	520	207	40%
Taco Bell Steak Fajita Wrap	460	189	41%
Taco Bell Gordita Santa Fe (beef)	380	180	47%
Taco Bell Taco Supreme	220	117	55%
Taco Bell BLT Soft Taco	340	207	62%

One category of functional foods being researched is vegetables that are genetically engineered to produce a specific biological element that is important to human health. An example is tomatoes that are particularly high in lycopene, a potent antioxidant. Another example, as described earlier, is a new type of margarine that can lower the level of and change the properties of blood cholesterol. Food technologists are interested in expanding the functional food family to include a greater array of health-enhancing food items.

FOOD SAFETY

A consumer poll conducted in 2001 reported that 74% of Canadians are concerned about the safety of their food.[20] Those most troubled looked to the food-processing industry, restaurants and other food service outlets, and the farm as the objects of their concern. To better address the concerns of the Canadian public, the federal government has coordinated its programs to regulate food safety through the development of the Canadian Food Inspection Agency (CFIA).

One of the CFIA's greatest challenges has been that of controlling food-borne bacteria. Health Canada estimates that every year between 1 and 2 million people experience food-borne illness and about 30 die from it. Many factors have contributed to the fact that Canadians now have a greater risk of exposure to these pathogens than they did 20 years ago. Our demand for fresh fruit and vegetables year round means that during much of the year our produce is grown in countries that may not follow the same standards of production that are set in Canada and the United States. Disease-causing bacteria can be deposited on the food from fertilization with raw sewage, the unwashed hands of field workers, flies in holding and shipping areas, and unclean water—whether the food was produced at home or abroad. As consumers, we are less likely than ever before to cook our fruit and vegetables and so are missing the single most effective means of eliminating such bacteria from these foods.

How can you protect yourself? It can be as simple as thoroughly washing all your fruit and vegetables before preparing or eating them. Washing your hands, utensils, and surfaces with hot soapy water or a mild bleach solution

Table 5–3 Making Better Fast-Food Choices

Fast-food meals can be high in calories, fat, cholesterol, and sodium. But it is still possible to eat fast food occasionally and follow a sensible diet. Take a look at how a few sample meals stack up against each other, and against the recommended daily intake for calories (2000–2700 per day), fat (no more than 50–80 g), cholesterol (no more than 300 mg), and sodium (no more than 1100–3300 mg).

	Poor Choice	Sensible Choice
Burger (McDonald's)	Quarter-pound burger with cheese, large fries, 500 mL pop *1166 calories* *51 g fat* *95 mg cholesterol* *1450 mg sodium*	Hamburger, small fries, 500 mL diet pop *481 calories* *19 g fat* *30 mg cholesterol* *664 mg sodium*
Pizza (Domino's)	4 slices sausage and mushroom pizza, 500 mL pop *1000 calories* *28 g fat* *62 mg cholesterol* *2302 mg sodium*	3 slices cheese pizza, 500 mL diet pop *516 calories* *15 g fat* *29 mg cholesterol* *1470 mg sodium*
Chicken (KFC)	2 pieces fried chicken (breast and wing), buttermilk biscuit, mashed potatoes with gravy, corn-on-the-cob, 500 mL pop *1232 calories* *57 g fat* *157 mg cholesterol* *2276 mg sodium*	1 piece fried chicken (wing), mashed potatoes with gravy, cole slaw, 500 mL diet pop *373 calories* *19 g fat* *46 mg cholesterol* *943 mg sodium*
Taco (Taco Bell)	Taco salad, 500 mL pop *1057 calories* *55 g fat* *80 mg cholesterol* *1620 mg sodium*	3 light tacos, 500 mL diet pop *420 calories* *15 g fat* *60 mg cholesterol* *840 mg sodium*

especially after handling raw meat is also important. Keep your raw meats and poultry away from other foods during storage and preparation, and avoid transferring bacteria from one to the other by using the same knife, plate, or cutting board. Refrigerate or freeze your perishables and cooked foods within two hours. A good rule of thumb is to keep hot foods hot and cold foods cold. Bacteria flourish at temperatures in the middle range.

For further information on food safety, visit the Canadian Partnership for Consumer Food Safety Education Web site at **www.canfightbac.org/english/indexe.shtml** and the Canadian Food Inspection Agency Web site at **www.inspection.gc.ca/english/index/fssae.shtml**. See the Changing for the Better box on p. 97 for Do's and Don'ts for Food Safety.

FOOD LABELS

A number of consumer studies have shown that Canadians would like to see more information regarding the nutritional quality of their food printed on the food packaging.[21,22] While all food labels must list the product ingredients in descending order, in the past there have been no regulations that mandated identification of the nutrient content of foods. This request from shoppers has led Health Canada to introduce new nutrition labelling regulations that require food manufacturers to include nutrient content information on virtually all packaged products (see Figure 5–3). Every label identifies how much of each of a standard list of nutrients is contained in a serving of the food. In addition, the label indicates the percentage of the recommended daily intake (or Daily Value) of each nutrient provided by that serving. This enables the Canadian public to compare products for their relative contributions of some important nutrients and, in doing so, make better informed decisions in the marketplace. For more information on Health Canada's food labelling regulations, check the Health Canada Web site at **www.hc-sc.gc.ca/hppb/nutrition/labels/index.html**.

SUPPLEMENTS

Canadians are rapidly assuming greater responsibility for their own health, as well as exploring alternatives to the traditional medical system. Over 50% of the population now consumes vitamins and mineral supplements or other natural health products such as herbal preparations. Health Canada established the Natural Health Products

Changing *for the Better*

Milk Fat—Less Is More

I've been drinking whole milk for years, and I enjoy it. Would changing to one of the lower-fat types really make a health difference?

The next time you're grocery shopping, choose milk that's one level lower in fat than the kind you usually buy. Then, if you still have some of the high-fat milk left, ask someone to give you a blind taste test. If you can't distinguish between the two, try switching to the lower-fat form. You'll not only reduce your exposure to saturated fat but also cut down on calories.

Milk's New Names

Old Name	Possible New Names	Total Fat [per cup] Grams	% Daily Value	Calories per cup
Milk	Milk	8.0 g	12%	150
Low-fat 2% milk	Reduced fat or less fat milk	4.7 g	7%	122
Not on the market	Light milk	4.0 g or less	6% or less	116 or less
Low-fat 1% milk	Low-fat milk	2.6 g	4%	102
Skim milk	Fat-free, skim, zero-fat; no-fat or nonfat milk	less than 0.5 g	0%	80

As you can see from the information above, the names assigned to various types of milk have recently undergone a big change.

Directorate in 1999 to oversee the regulation of this type of product. This directorate established the Natural Health Products Regulations effective January 1, 2004. According to the Regulations, natural health products (NHPs) include the following: herbal remedies, vitamins, minerals, homeopathic medicines, and traditional medicines (e.g., Traditional Chinese Medicines). The regulations for NHPs that are deemed safe for self-care and do not require a prescription can be sold as over-the-counter merchandise. The role of the Natural Health Products Directorate is to ensure that NHPs are safe and effective for Canadian consumers. For further information concerning this directorate and its regulations, in addition to the implementation processes for the regulations, go to **www.hc-sc.gc.ca/ahc-asc/branch-dirgen/hpfb-dgpsa/nhpd-dpsn/index_e.html.**

The nutrient information is based on a specified quantity of food.
This number is the actual amount of the nutrient in the specified quantity of food.
The Nutrition Facts box includes this list of calories and 13 nutrients even if the amount is zero. Adding other nutrients to this list is optional.
The % Daily Value gives a context to the actual amount. It indicates if there is a lot or a little of the nutrient in the specified quantity of food.
Nutrition Facts
Per 1 cup (264 g)
Amount | % Daily Value
Calories 260
Fat 13 g 20%
Saturated Fat 3 g + Trans Fat 2 g 25%
Cholesterol 30 mg
Sodium 660 mg 28%
Carbohydrate 31 g 10%
Fibre 0 g 0%
Sugars 5 g
Protein 5 g
Vitamin A 4% • Vitamin C 2%
Calcium 15% • Iron 4%

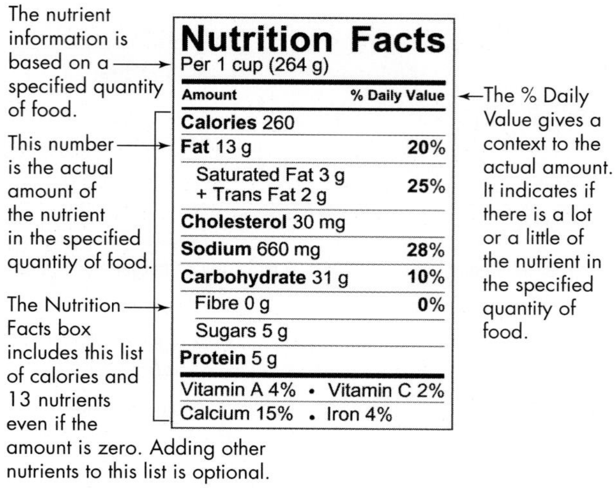

Figure 5–3 The Nutrition Facts box. Consumers reading labels and comparing products are able to use the Nutrition Facts box to make informed choices.

In the United States, the Food and Drug Administration (FDA) is a few steps ahead of Health Canada in regulating this type of product, and has taken a somewhat different position. In that country, nutrient supplements, herbal medications, and some hormone-like products are all identified as *dietary supplements*, even though many resemble drugs in their purposes and potencies. By the new U.S. regulations, dietary supplements now must be deemed safe for human use on the basis of information supplied to the FDA by the manufacturers. In addition, the labels on these products cannot make a direct claim, with the exception of calcium and folic acid supplements, that they can cure or prevent illnesses. However, other materials with such claims may be displayed close to the dietary supplements themselves or on the manufacturer's Web page. Further, the labels on dietary supplements must remind consumers that the FDA has not required these products to undergo the rigorous research required of prescription medications and so the FDA cannot attest to their effectiveness. Beyond this, consumers are left to themselves to decide whether to purchase and use dietary supplements.

Easily accessible to anyone, natural health products and dietary supplements can be purchased in grocery stores, drugstores, and discount stores, through mail-order catalogues, and over the Internet. Because of the great demand for these products, major pharmaceutical companies are now entering the dietary supplement field. Whether this trend leads to the development of more effective products or to a greater effort on the part of Health Canada and the FDA to demand proof of effectiveness remains to be seen. By definition, supplements are not foods, but simply "supplements." Therefore, they should never be seen as substitutes for a balanced diet.

Changing *for the Better*

Do's and Don'ts for Food Safety [23]

I keep reading about food poisoning and food contamination in restaurants and even from home-cooked meals. Is there any way to lessen my chances of contracting food poisoning?

The following are some do's and don'ts for food safety:

1. Don't thaw food on the countertop—keep it in a covered container in the refrigerator or thaw it out in the microwave.
2. Don't leave food out of the refrigerator for longer than two hours.
3. Don't use wooden cutting boards with deep grooves or knife scars.
4. Don't marinate food at room temperature—marinate in the refrigerator.
5. Do put groceries away as soon as you get home and don't make other stops first.
6. Do use two different plates for raw and grilled meat.
7. Do use different spoons to stir and taste the food.
8. Do refrigerate leftovers from restaurants immediately.
9. Do use different knives to cut raw meat and chop vegetables.
10. Do store food in an airtight container. Don't store food in open cans or on uncovered dishes.
11. Do wash fresh fruits and vegetables, even if you are throwing away the rind or peels, as cutting through the produce can carry bacteria from the outside surface to the inside of the produce.
12. Do rinse poultry and seafood in cold water.

TALKING POINTS • Several of your friends take multiple dietary supplements on a daily basis. What potential disadvantages of this practice would you point out to them?

TECHNOLOGICAL DEVELOPMENTS IN THE FOOD INDUSTRY

Technological advances in food production and processing have done much to assure that the food we eat is fresh and safe. Yet there is growing concern that certain recent developments may also produce harmful effects on humans. For example, irradiation of foods, genetic engineering of foods, and the use of growth-enhancement agents for food animals are currently at the centre of increasing controversy.

Irradiation of Food

Since the 1990s, numerous recalls of meat and meat products have been necessary because of bacterial contamination. As a result, the meat industry has been investigating irradiation as a way to significantly reduce this problem. Current estimates are that nearly 99% of all bacteria in both processed and fresh meat could be killed by exposure to radiation.

Opponents of this approach argue that the damaging effect that radiation has on the structure of all cells, both microorganisms and the muscle cells of meat, might alter the meat in some harmful way.

Genetically Modified Foods

The success of North American agriculture, in terms of food quality and marketability, has been based on the ability to genetically alter food sources to improve yield, reduce production costs, and introduce new food characteristics. Recent advances in gene technology such as gene cloning, gene splicing, and plant transformation have enabled scientists to produce an array of food crops bearing characteristics that improve yield, marketability, and even nutritional quality. The term *genetically modified foods* is used to describe these new discoveries.

It has been stated by many consumers and scientists alike that changes are being introduced faster than scientists can fully evaluate the effects of these changes. For example, the genetic makeup of plant seeds and animals is being modified while scientists are still trying to determine whether human and environmental health will be affected over extended periods. Concerned individuals and agencies in North America and abroad are calling for more extensive longitudinal research into safety issues.

Canadians have stated that they want labelling of genetically modified foods.[24] Health Canada requires labelling of foods modified by biotechnology only if there is a change with implications for health or safety (for example, from allergens) or a significant change in nutrition or composition. It does permit voluntary labelling of products, stating they do not contain genetically modified foods, on the condition that the claim is truthful and not misleading.

Hormones in Dairy and Meat Production

The use of powerful growth stimulants and antibiotics by Canadian and U.S. meat producers has already resulted in international political disagreements. In Europe, the import of North American meat products is being restricted because of safety concerns. In Canada, concern has been expressed in the *Canadian Medical Association Journal* over the potential for agricultural antimicrobial agents, used to enhance animal growth, to induce antibiotic-resistant varieties of microbes that cause diseases in humans.[25]

In contrast, the growth hormone recombinant bovine somatotrophin, or rBST, which is used in the United States to enhance the milk productivity of cows, has not been approved for use in Canada. After nine

Table 5–3 Recommended Dietary Changes to Reduce the Risk of Diseases and Their Complications

Change in Diet	Reduce Fats	Control Calories	Increase Starch* and Fibre	Reduce Sodium	Control Alcohol
Reduce risk of					
Heart disease	✓	✓		✓	
Cancer	✓	✓	✓		✓
Stroke	✓	✓		✓	✓
Diabetes	✓	✓	✓		
Gastrointestinal disease†	✓	✓	✓		✓

*Starch refers to less-refined carbohydrates provided by fruits, vegetables, legumes, and whole-grain products.

†Primarily gallbladder disease (fat), diverticular disease (fibre), and cirrhosis (alcohol).

years of comprehensive review, Health Canada concluded in 1999 that while rBST posed no significant risk to human health, it presented an unacceptable risk to the health and safety of dairy cows.

GUIDELINES FOR DIETARY HEALTH

While *Canada's Food Guide to Healthy Eating* (see Figures 5–1 and 5–2) outlines in a simple format how consumers can obtain all the essential nutrients through a balanced diet, Health Canada recognizes that Canadians need further practical dietary advice toward the prevention of chronic diseases such as heart disease, cancers, and type 2 diabetes. In 1990, *Canada's Guidelines for Healthy Eating* were developed to provide positive, action-oriented messages for the average consumer. These are shown in the Star Box on this page. Table 5–3 shows how healthy dietary changes can lead to reduced chances of developing certain major diseases. Notice that a reduction in fat and better control of caloric intake are important factors in reducing the likelihood of chronic illness.

Canada's Guidelines for Healthy Eating

- Enjoy a variety of foods.
- Emphasize cereals, breads, other grain products, vegetables, and fruits.
- Choose lower-fat dairy products, leaner meats, and foods prepared with little or no fat.
- Achieve and maintain a healthy body weight by enjoying regular activity and healthy eating.
- Limit salt, alcohol, and caffeine.

Almost all Canadians could make changes that would bring them closer to meeting these guidelines. The Changing for the Better box on p. 99 presents recommendations for making healthy food choices. For more nutrition information about the foods you eat, visit the Virtual Kitchen developed by the Dieticians of Canada at **www.dietitians.ca/english/frames.html**.

VEGETARIAN DIETS

During the post-secondary years, many students follow some kind of nontraditional diet. Vegetarian diets, weight-reduction diets, and overreliance on fast foods represent some of these nontraditional dietary approaches. Most nutritionists believe that these diets do not need to be discontinued or avoided; instead, they should be undertaken with care and insight because of their potential nutritional limitations.

A *vegetarian diet* relies on plant sources for all or most of the nutrients needed by the body. This approach includes a range of diets from those that allow some animal sources of nutrients to those that exclude animal sources and are also restrictive in terms of plant sources. Three types of vegetarian diets, beginning with the least restrictive, are summarized below. Go to **www.dietitians.ca** for a Vegetarian Food Guide Rainbow.

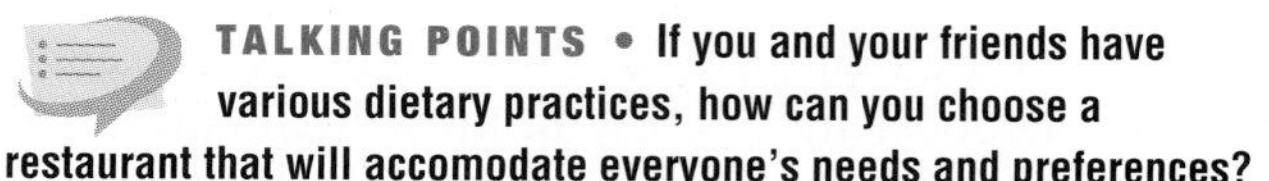
TALKING POINTS • If you and your friends have various dietary practices, how can you choose a restaurant that will accomodate everyone's needs and preferences?

Ovolactovegetarian Diet

Depending on the particular pattern of consuming eggs (*ovo*) and milk (*lacto*) or using one but not the other, an **ovolactovegetarian diet** can be a very sound approach to

Changing *for the Better*

Ways to Improve Your Nutritional Health

Two of my relatives had heart attacks in middle age. I'm only in my 20s, but I know I've got to do what I can now to lower my risk for heart disease. Where do I start?

It's very likely that you can improve your dietary health and reduce the risk of developing heart disease and cancer by implementing the following practices.

Eat More High-Fibre Foods

- Choose dried beans, peas, and lentils more often.
- Eat whole-grain breads, cereals, and low-fat crackers.
- Eat more vegetables—raw and cooked.
- Eat whole fruit in place of drinking fruit juice.
- Try other high-fibre foods, such as oat bran, barley, brown rice, or wild rice.

Eat Less Sugar

- Avoid regular soft drinks. One 355 mL can has nine teaspoons of sugar!
- Avoid eating table sugar, honey, syrup, jam, jelly, candy, pastries, fruit canned in syrup, regular gelatin desserts, cake with icing, pie, and other sweets.
- Choose fresh fruit or fruit canned in natural juice or water.
- If desired, use sweeteners that don't have any calories, such as saccharin or aspartame, instead of sugar.

Use Less Salt

- Reduce the amount of salt you use in cooking.
- Try not to salt your food at the table.
- Eat fewer high-salt foods, such as canned soups, ham, sauerkraut, hot dogs, pickles, and foods that taste salty.
- Eat fewer convenience and fast foods.

Eat Less Fat

- Eat smaller servings of meat. Eat fish and poultry more often. Choose lean cuts of red meat.
- Prepare all meats by roasting, baking, or broiling. Trim off all fat. Be careful of added sauces or gravy. Remove skin from poultry.
- Avoid fried foods. Avoid adding fat when cooking.
- Eat fewer high-fat foods, such as deli meats, bacon, sausages, hot dogs, doughnuts, cookies, snack foods, french fries, and pies.
- Drink skim or low-fat milk.
- Eat less ice cream, cheese, sour cream, cream, whole milk, and other high-fat dairy products.

healthy eating for adults. Ovolactovegetarian diets provide the body with the essential amino acids and typically limit the high intake of fats involved in more conventional diets. The exclusion of meat as a protein source usually lowers the total fat intake, and the consumption of milk or eggs allows an adequate amount of fat to remain in the diet. The consistent use of vegetable products as the primary source of nutrients complies with the current dietary recommendations for an increase in overall carbohydrates, complex carbohydrates, and fibre.

Lactovegetarian Diet

People who include dairy products in their diet but no other animal products, including eggs, are *lactovegetarians*. As with the ovolactovegetarian diet, there is little risk associated with this dietary pattern as long as foods included in the diet come from a wide variety of choices.

Vegan Diet

A **vegan diet** is one in which not only meat but also other animal products, including milk, cheese, and eggs, are not part of the diet. When compared with the ovolactovegetarian diet, the vegan diet requires greater nutritional knowledge and planning to avoid malnourishment.

When plants are the body's only source of nutrients, some difficulties can arise. The novice vegan needs to be particularly alert for these problems. One potential difficulty is obtaining all the essential amino acids. Since a single plant source does not contain all the essential amino acids, the vegan must learn to consistently eat a wide variety of foods each day including nuts, grains, seeds, and legumes. This diet probably should not be used by children, pregnant women, and **lactating** mothers.

Key Terms

ovolactovegetarian diet
A diet that excludes all meat but does include the consumption of eggs and dairy products.

vegan diet
A vegetarian diet that excludes all animal products, including eggs and dairy products.

lactating
Breastfeeding, nursing.

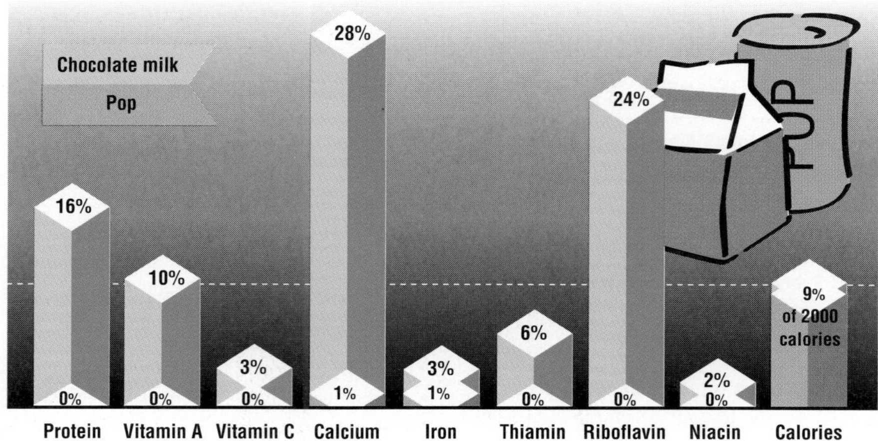

Figure 5–4 A comparison of the nutrient density of chocolate milk with that of a soft drink. The bars that represent protein, vitamin A, calcium, and riboflavin in chocolate milk are all taller than the calorie bar, showing that chocolate milk is nutrient dense for these nutrients. All of the nutrient bars for the soft drink are shorter than the calorie bar, illustrating that pop has a low nutrient density relative to the number of calories it supplies.

In addition, the vegan could have some difficulty in maintaining the necessary intake of vitamin B_{12}, iron, zinc, and calcium. Vitamin D deficiencies also can occur.

Because of the potential nutritional limitations of the vegan diet, many nutritionists do not recommend it unless professional guidance is available. This diet should be followed only for reasons related to ecological, philosophical, or animal rights beliefs, since the total exclusion of animal products seems to accomplish little—from a nutritional point of view—that cannot be accomplished through ovolactovegetarianism. Clearly, the ovolactovegetarian diet is much less likely to lead to malnutrition than is the vegan diet. Many people have now adopted semivegetarian diets, in which meat consumption is significantly reduced but not eliminated.

NUTRIENT DENSITY

For many post-secondary students, the issue of nutrient density may prompt certain dietary adjustments. The *nutrient density* of a food relates to its ability to supply proportionally more of the recommended dietary allowance (RDA) for select vitamins and minerals than for daily calorie requirements. Foods with a high nutrient density are better choices than those that supply only *empty calories* (Figure 5–4). For example, a bag of potato chips or a bottle of beer has a much lower nutrient density than either a serving of lightly steamed mixed vegetables or a 100 g serving of broiled skinless chicken breast. Choosing foods with a high nutrient density is especially important for people who are trying to limit their caloric intake.

NUTRITION AND THE OLDER ADULT

Nutritional needs change as adults age. Age-related changes to the structure and function of the body are primarily responsible for such altered nutritional requirements. These changes can involve the teeth, salivary glands, taste buds, oral muscles, gastric acid production, and peristaltic action. In addition, chronic constipation resulting from changes in gastrointestinal tract function can decrease the older adult's interest in eating.

The progressive lowering of the body's basal metabolism is another factor that will eventually influence the dietary patterns of older adults. As energy requirements fall, the body gradually senses the need for less food. In addition a tendency to decrease activity levels also occurs with aging. Because of this decreased need for calories, nutrient density—the nutritional value of food relative to calories supplied—is an important consideration for elderly people.

Psychosocial factors also alter the role of food in the lives of many older adults. Social isolation, depression, chronic alcohol consumption, loss of income, transportation limitations, and housing are lifestyle factors that can lessen the ease and enjoyment associated with the preparation and consumption of food. Consequently, a person's food intake might decrease.

INTERNATIONAL NUTRITIONAL CONCERNS

Nutritional concerns in Canada and the United States are centred on overnutrition, including fat density and excessive caloric intake. In contrast, in many areas of the world the main concern is the limited quantity and quality of food. Reasons for these problems are many, including the weather, the availability of arable land, religious practices, political unrest, war, social infrastructure, and material and technical shortages. Underlying nearly all of these factors, however, is unabated population growth.

To increase the availability of food to countries whose demand for food outweighs their ability to produce it, a number of steps have been suggested, including the following:

- Increase the yield of land currently under cultivation.
- Increase the amount of land under cultivation.
- Increase animal production on land not suitable for cultivation.
- Use water (seas, lakes, and ponds) more efficiently for the production of food.
- Develop unconventional foods through the application of technology.
- Improve nutritional practices through education.

Little progress is being made despite impressive technological breakthroughs in agriculture and food technology (such as "miracle" rice, disease-resistant high-yield corn, and soybean-enhanced infant foods), the efforts of governmental programs, and the support of the Food and Agricultural Organization of the United Nations.

The Canadian International Development Agency (CIDA) has played a major role in providing vitamin A supplements to some of the 100 million children worldwide who are suffering from a deficiency of this nutrient. Through CIDA, Canada has also been active in developing programs aimed at fortifying local foods with vitamin A. However, in developing nations, where fertility rates are two to four times higher than those of Canada and the United States, annual food production needs to increase between 2.7% and 3.9% to keep up with population needs. If population growth and food production are not altered in these countries, basic needs will continue to be unmet.

Taking Charge of Your Health

- Analyze your food intake for one week using the Personal Assessments on pp. 105–107.
- Develop a plan to modify your food intake patterns to make them agree with recommended guidelines.
- Explore ways in which you can balance the need for healthful meals with having an occasional fast-food meal.
- Practise judging portion sizes accurately.
- Experiment with alternative dietary patterns, such as semivegetarianism or ovolactovegetarianism.
- List any dietary supplements you take on a regular basis, and discuss this practice with your physician to determine whether they are necessary for your good health.
- Limit your intake of convenience foods, particularly those that are high in sugar and saturated fat.

SUMMARY

- Carbohydrates, fat, and protein supply the body with calories.
- Carbohydrates differ on the basis of their molecular makeup, with sugars being the least complex and starches the most complex.
- Fat is important for nutritional health beyond serving as the body's primary means of storage of excess calories.
- Saturated fats, including trans-fatty acids, should be carefully limited because of their association with chronic diseases.
- Protein supplies the body with amino acids needed to construct its own protein.
- When few foods of animal origin are consumed, a wide variety of incomplete protein sources must be eaten to provide complete protein in the diet.
- Vitamins serve as catalysts for body responses and are found in water-soluble and fat-soluble forms.
- The use of vitamin supplements is sometimes warranted, but extensive use of food supplements can be dangerous.
- Minerals are incorporated into various tissues of the body and participate in regulatory functions within the body.
- An adequate amount of water and other fluids is required by the body daily and is obtained from a variety of food sources, including beverages.
- Fibre is undigestible plant material and has two forms, water soluble and water insoluble.
- Foods are currently classified into four groups and recommendations regarding the needed number of daily servings have been given for these.
- Different people require different amounts of food.
- Fat-free or low-fat foods can be more calorie-dense than presumed by consumers.
- Fast foods should play only a limited role in a person's diet because of their low nutrient density and their high levels of fat, sugar, and sodium.

- Phytochemicals, capable of protecting the body from carcinogens or free radicals, are now being identified in many types of vegetables, fruit, legumes, and herbs.
- Functional foods are capable of assisting in the prevention of specific health conditions.
- The Natural Health Products Directorate, established by Health Canada, is responsible for ensuring that natural health products are safe and effective for Canadian consumers.
- Controversy exists about the application of new food technologies such as irradiation, genetic engineering, and the use of growth stimulants.
- Current dietary recommendations focus on the role of fat, saturated fat, starch, and sodium in health and disease.
- Ovolactovegetarianism, lactovegetarianism, and veganism are different forms of vegetarianism.
- Nutrient density plays an important role in the management of caloric intake for people of all ages, particularly older adults.
- A variety of factors contribute to malnourishment in many areas of the world.

REVIEW QUESTIONS

1. Which nutrients supply the body with calories?
2. How do sugars differ structurally from starches?
3. What is the function of fat in nutritional health besides serving as the body's primary means of storage for excess calories? What is the basis of our current concern about saturated fats, cholesterol, and trans-fatty acids?
4. What is the principal role of protein in the body? How can complete protein be obtained by people who eat few or no animal products?
5. Which vitamins are water soluble and which are fat soluble? What is the current perception regarding the need for vitamin supplementation? Which vitamins are regarded as antioxidants?
6. What functions do minerals have in the body? What is a trace element?
7. What are the two principal forms of fibre, and how does each contribute to health?
8. How many glasses of water per day are currently recommended?
9. What method of grouping foods is now used?
10. Explain why *Canada's Food Guide to Healthy Eating* provides a range of servings for each food group.
11. What are the current dietary recommendations regarding fat and saturated fat intake?
12. How can fat-free or low-fat foods be both low in nutritional density and high in caloric density?
13. What are functional foods, and how are they different from dietary supplements?

THINK ABOUT THIS ...

- Is it more economical to buy a generic brand of cereal and take a generic multivitamin than to buy a highly supplemented but more expensive brand-name cereal?
- What nutrients are missing from your diet?
- Do your roles in parenting, employment, school, or home management compromise your ability to eat healthy?
- Analyze your diet in terms of the recommendations made by *Canada's Food Guide to Healthy Eating* and *Canada's Guidelines for Healthy Eating.*
- Consider your own dietary practices and those of your friends. Are you/they following sound nutritional guidelines?
- Would you say that you live to eat or eat to live?
- What are the most immediate changes that need to be made in your diet?
- In your opinion, what is the role of diet in both the cause and prevention of chronic disease? Are we currently too concerned about the role of food in preventing disease and enhancing health?

REFERENCES

1. Wardlaw GM: *Perspective in nutrition*, ed 4, 1999, McGraw-Hill.
2. Statistics Canada: Per-capita food consumption 1999. *The Daily*. June 15, 2000. **www.statcan.ca/Daily/English/000615/d000615b.htm**
3. Statistics Canada: *Per capita consumption of major food groups*, **www.statcan.ca/english/Pgdb/famil102c.htm**, August 3, 2004.
4. Statistics *Canada: Food consumption highlights*, **www.statcan.ca/english/ads/23F0001XCB/highlight.htm**, August 3, 2004.

5. American Academy of Pediatrics Committee on Nutrition: Cholesterol in children, *Pediatrics* 101:114–117, 1998.
6. Kummerow FA, Zhou Q, Mahfouz MM: Effect of trans-fatty acids on calcium influx into human arterial endothelial cells, *Am J Clin Nutr* 70(5):832–838, 1999.
7. Noop RH et al: Long-term cholesterol-lowering effects of four fat-restricted diets in hypercholesterolemic and combined hyperlipidemic men: the dietary alternatives study, *JAMA*, 278(18):1509–1515, 1997.
8. U.S. Department of Health and Human Services: *The surgeon general's report on nutrition and health*, DHHS Pub No 88-50210, 1988, U.S. Government Printing Office.
9. Greenberg ER, Sporn MB: Antioxidant vitamins, cancer, and cardiovascular disease, *N Engl J Med* 334(18):1189–1190, 1996 [accompanied by three "Comment on" responses].
10. Jacques PF et al: The effect of folic acid fortification on plasma folate and total homocysteine concentrations, *N Engl J Med* 340(19):1449–1454, 1999.
11. *Children, water, and fluoride: AAPD parent information*, American Academy of Pediatric Dentistry. **www.aapd.org/parents/fluoride.html**
12. Health Canada: *Canada's Food Guide to Healthy Eating*, **www.hc-sc.gc.ca/fn-an/food-guide-aliment/fg_rainbow-arc_en_ciel_ga_e.html**, October 7, 2005.
13. Ibid.
14. Copyright 2001 by the National Academy of Sciences. All rights reserved.
15. American Cancer Society: *Cancer facts and figures—1999*, 1999, The Association.
16. Modified from Hegarty V: *Decisions in nutrition*, St. Louis, 1988, Mosby, 132–33.
17. Adapted from *Fast food facts* from the office of the Minnesota Attorney General. **www.olen.com/food/book.html**
18. Waladkhani AR, Clemens MR: Effect of dietary phytochemicals on cancer, *Int J Mol Med* 1(4): 747–753, 1998.
19. Fransworth ER: What we are trying to do? *Medicinal Food News* 1(1):1–6, 1999. **www.medicinalfoodnews.com/vol01/issue1.html**
20. Ipsos-Reid: Canadians and food safety, [poll], public release date October 9, 2001. **www.ipsos-reid.com/media/dsp_displaypr_cdn.cfm?id_to_view=1324**
21. *Nutrition labelling: perceptions and preferences of Canadians*, 1999, National Institute of Nutrition.
22. *Voluntary labelling of foods from biotechnology: report on a qualitative study among consumers*, 1999, National Institute of Nutrition. **www.inspection.gc.ca/english/ppc/biotech/labeti/ninintroe.shtml**
23. Duyff R: American Dietetic Association complete food and nutrition guide, ed 2, Hoboken, NJ, 2002, John Wiley & Sons.
24. *Voluntary labelling of goods from biotechnology*.
25. McGeer AJ: Agricultural antibiotics and resistance in human pathogens: villain or scapegoat? *Canadian Medical Association Journal* 159:1119–20, 1998.

SUGGESTED READINGS

Callaghan B, Roblin L: *Dietitians of Canada great food fast*, 2000, Robert Rose Inc.

This recipe book approaches cooking with the knowledge that most Canadians have little time to plan and prepare nutritious meals. Besides an array of tempting recipes, the book offers Timesaver Tips, Quick Food Facts, Nutrient Analyses, and simple ways to check up on your day's intake using the "Complete the Rainbow/Complete the Meal" section. Produced by the Dietitians of Canada, this is a reliable source of information and practical tips on good nutrition.

Duyff R: *The American Dietetic Association's complete food and nutrition guide*, 1998, John Wiley & Sons.

This 600-page book blends nutritional theory with advice about the day-to-day need for a varied and balanced diet. It's written in a very understandable style. Using the newest nutritional recommendations as a basis, the author strongly supports adherence to the current USDA-recommended Food Pyramid. Because of this, however, the book will not appeal to readers interested in alternative diets, such as the currently popular low-carbohydrate/high-fat diets.

Kraus B: *Calories and carbohydrates*, ed 13, 1999, Signet.

For whatever reason readers—lay and professional alike—want to know about the caloric and carbohydrate composition of individual food items. This book is the time-honoured standard. The author presents information about more than 8550 food items, including familiar North American food choices, such as pizza, fast-food items, and various snack foods. Special attention is given to portion size, an aspect of sound nutritional practice that has proven difficult to master, particularly when today's food industry promotes foods in large amounts.

Margen S: *Wellness encyclopedia of food and nutrition*, 1999, Rebus.

The author, a retired professor from the University of California, Berkeley, and an editor of that institution's highly regarded *Wellness Letter*, takes readers through the theory and practices of healthy eating. Included are topics as diverse as food selection in the supermarket; the preparation, serving, and storage of food; and the role of diet in the cause and prevention of several health problems. Information pertaining to over 500 separate food items, listed in alphabetical order, is visually supported through the use of over 80 colour photographs. This book is very highly regarded by nutritionists for both its content and presentation.

Making Headlines

A major British study investigating the effect of supplemental antioxidant nutrients has revealed that, in people at high risk of vascular disease, vitamin supplementation does not produce any significant reductions in the five-year risk of heart attack or stroke. The Heart Protection Study (HPS) followed 20 536 adults in the United Kingdom aged 40 to 80 years with coronary disease and other occlusive arterial disease in a double-blind, placebo-controlled intervention trial. Vitamin supplementation of 600 mg vitamin E, 250 mg vitamin C, and 20 mg beta-carotene daily did not produce any significant reductions in the five-year risk of heart attack, stroke, cancer, or other major health outcomes.

Name ________________________ **Date** ____________

Personal Assessment

Do You Have Fatty Habits?

Fat has earned a bad reputation because of the health problems to which it contributes when we eat too much of it. The questionnaire below will help you think about the amounts and types of fat that you generally eat. For each general type of food or food habit, circle the response category that is most typical for you. If you never or almost never eat any items of a particular food type, just skip that type.

Food Type/Habit	High Fat	Medium Fat	Low Fat
Chicken	Fried with the skin	Baked, broiled, or barbecued with the skin	Baked, broiled, or barbecued without the skin
Fat present on meats	Usually eat	Sometimes eat	Never eat
Fat used in cooking	Butter, lard, bacon grease, chicken fat	Margarine, oil	Nonstick cooking spray or no fat used
Additions to rice, bread, potatoes, vegetables, etc.	Butter, lard, bacon grease, chicken fat, coconut oil, cream cheese, margarine, oil, peanut butter		Butter-flavoured granules or no fat used
Pizza toppings	Sausage, pepperoni, extra cheese, combination	Ham	Vegetable
Sandwich spreads	Mayonnaise or mayonnaise-type dressing	Light mayonnaise, oil and vinegar	Mustard, fat-free mayonnaise
Milk and milk products (e.g., yogurt)	Whole milk and whole-milk products	2% milk and milk products	Skim milk and milk products
Sandwich side orders	Chips, potato salad, macaroni salad with creamy dressing	Coleslaw, pasta salad with clear dressing	Vegetable sticks, pretzels, pickle
Salad dressings	Blue cheese, Ranch, Thousand Island, other creamy type	Oil and vinegar, clear-base dressing	Oil-free dressing, lemon juice, flavoured vinegar
Typical meat portion eaten	150–225 g (5–8 oz) or more	110–140 g (3–5 oz)	55–85 g (2–3 oz)
Sandwich fillings	Beef or pork hot dogs, salami, bologna, pepperoni, cheese, tuna, or chicken salad	Turkey hot dogs, lower-fat luncheon meats such as ham and corned beef, peanut butter, hummus (chickpea paste)	Veggie dogs, very lean meats such as roast beef, turkey, lean ham
Ground meats	Ground meats (about 30% fat)	Regular or medium ground beef, ground pork, and ground turkey (23%–30% fat)	Lean and extra lean ground beef, ground pork and ground turkey (10% to 17% fat)
Deep-fried foods (e.g., french fries, onion rings, fish sticks or chicken fingers, egg rolls, tempura)	Eat every day	Eat once a week	Eat once a month or never

Personal Assessment *continued*

Food Type/Habit	High Fat	Medium Fat	Low Fat
Bread for sandwiches	Croissant	Scone	Whole wheat, French bread, tortilla, pita or pocket bread, bagel, sourdough,or English muffin
Cheeses	Cheddar, Swiss, provolone, American, processed, soft cheeses such as brie	Part-skim mozzarella, part-skim ricotta, low-fat and reduced-fat cheeses	Nonfat cheeses, nonfat cottage cheese, no cheese
Frozen desserts	Premium or regular ice cream	Ice milk or low-fat frozen yogurt	Sherbet, Italian water ice, nonfat frozen yogurt
Coffee lighteners	Cream, liquid or powdered creamer	Whole milk	Low-fat or skim milk
Snacks	Chips, pies, cheese and crackers, nuts, doughnuts, microwave popcorn, chocolate, granola bars	Muffins, toaster pastries, unbuttered commercial popcorn	Pretzels, vegetable sticks, fresh or dried fruit, air-popped popcorn, bread sticks, jelly beans, hard candy
Cookies	Chocolate coated, chocolate chip, peanut butter, filled sandwich type	Oatmeal	Ginger snaps, vanilla wafers, graham crackers, animal crackers, fruit newtons
SCORING:	(_______ × 2) +	(_______ × 1) +	(_______ × 0) =
			TOTAL SCORE _______

Once you have completed the questionnaire count the number of circles in each column and calculate your score as follows: multiply the number of choices in the left-hand (high fat) column by 2 and multiply the number of choices in the middle by 1. Any number of choices in the right-hand column will equal 0.

Less than 10 = Excellent fat habits
10 to 20 = Good fat habits
20 to 30 = Need to trim some fat
Over 30 = Very high-fat diet

If your score is 20 or above, try to substitute more foods from the middle (medium-fat) column or, better still, the right (low-fat) column for foods in the left-hand (high-fat) column.

Name ______________________________ **Date** ____________

Personal Assessment

Rate Your Plate

Take a closer look at yourself—your current food decisions and your lifestyle. Think about your typical eating pattern and food decisions.

Do You ...

	Usually	Sometimes	Never
Consider nutrition when you make food choices?	❑	❑	❑
Try to eat regular meals (including breakfast), rather than skip or skimp on some?	❑	❑	❑
Choose nutritious snacks?	❑	❑	❑
Try to eat a variety of foods?	❑	❑	❑
Include new-to-you foods in meals and snacks?	❑	❑	❑
Try to balance your energy (calorie) intake with your physical activity?	❑	❑	❑

Now for the Details

Do You ...

	Usually	Sometimes	Never
Eat at least 5 servings* of grain products daily?	❑	❑	❑
Eat at least 5 servings* of vegetables and fruit daily?	❑	❑	❑
Consume at least 2 servings* (3 for women) of milk, yogurt, or cheese daily?	❑	❑	❑
Go easy on higher-fat foods?	❑	❑	❑
Go easy on sweets?	❑	❑	❑
Drink 8 or more cups of fluids daily?	❑	❑	❑
Limit alcoholic beverages (no more than 1 daily for a woman or 2 for a man)?	❑	❑	❑

*Serving sizes vary depending on the food and food group. Refer back to Figure 5–2 for sample serving sizes.

Score Yourself

Usually = 2 points
Sometimes = 1 point
Never = 0 points

If you scored ...

24 or more points—Healthful eating seems to be your fitness habit already. Still, look for ways to stick to a healthful eating plan—and to make a "good thing" even better.

16 to 23 points—You're on track. A few easy changes could help you make your overall eating plan healthier.

9 to 15 points—Sometimes you eat smart—but not often enough to be your "fitness best."

0 to 8 points—For your good health, you're wise to rethink your overall eating style. Take it gradually—step by step!

Whatever your score, make moves for healthful eating. Gradually turn your "nevers" into "sometimes" and your "sometimes" into "usually."

Adapted from *The American Dietetic Association's Monthly Nutrition Companion: 31 Days to a Healthier Lifestyle*, Chronimed Publishing, 1997.

Focus on

MEAT SAFETY: IS IT SAFE TO EAT CANADIAN BEEF?

Because we don't have all the answers about diseases like mad cow, it's impossible to issue a guarantee about the safety of Canada's meat supply. However, most leading experts and politicians have maintained that the risk to Canadians has always been extremely low.

Federal and provincial agencies designed the meat inspection process to err on the side of caution. But, the system isn't infallible—a fact made evident in the investigation into the possible distribution of "deadstock" by an Ontario company, Aylmer Meat Packers.

Deadstock are animals that have died before slaughter, sometimes from illness. The potential of spreading illnesses, including mad cow disease, makes selling or processing meat from dead animals for human consumption illegal.

Scientists believe people develop the human version of bovine spongiform encephalopathy (BSE) when they eat meat from infected animals. Speaking about the initial case of BSE in Alberta, the Canadian Food Inspection Agency said: "Given that the cattle get the disease by eating contaminated feed and there is a feed ban in place, the probability of having more infected animals is very low."

In a statement on its web site on May 21, 2003, the CFIA said, "…we have no reason, at this point, to believe that there is a risk to human health." The agency was referring to the fact that no meat from the infected cow had entered the human food chain.

"I believe most sincerely that the beef products that we put on the market are safe," said then-Alberta Agriculture Minister Shirley McClellan.

"I think we should not be worried," Dr. Neil Cashman of the Centre for Research on Neurodegenerative Diseases at the University of Toronto told CBC News. "It is estimated two million infected cattle went into the human food chain in the United Kingdom alone in the '80s and '90s... This has to date only affected 130 people. That's tragic, of course, but if you compare the number of people affected with two million infected cattle, then you look at Canada's single isolated case or at most a few isolated cases, the risk looks minimal."

During the height of the BSE crisis in the U.K. and Europe in 1992, some consumers avoided British beef and beef products altogether. Others chose cuts with a lower chance of being contaminated, until beef on the bone was eventually banned outright. The British beef industry has still not recovered. There were 510 animals diagnosed with the disease in Britain in 2002. There were 36,680 cases in 1992.

Here is some basic information issued by the National Center for Infectious Disease and Health Canada about ways to avoid BSE:

- The best available scientific evidence indicates that whole cuts of meat without the bone, such as steaks and roast, provide a lower level of risk of potential BSE contamination than do processed products such as sausages, burgers or patés.
- Higher-risk items also include any other food products such as minced meats that might contain brain or spinal cord parts, since these are considered to have the highest concentration of prions (the disease-causing agent) in infected cattle and therefore carry the highest potential risk of transmission.
- BSE is unlike many other food-borne pathogens in that it cannot be killed simply by cooking the infected meat.
- Milk and milk products from cows are not believed to pose any risk for transmitting the BSE agent.

The Inspection Process

All animals are inspected within 24 hours before slaughter. If they are considered fit, they go to the kill floor with other inspected livestock. After the slaughter, the entire carcass is examined again (with particular attention to internal organs). If the inspector has any concerns, a veterinarian is consulted who will pass, condemn or hold the carcass for further testing.

Source: CBC News Online, *Indepth: mad cow,* **www.cbc.ca/news/background/madcow/meatsafety.html**, August 19, 2005.

Chapter **6**

Maintaining a Healthy Weight

Chapter Objectives

After reading this chapter, you should be able to

- Describe the role of the media and entertainment industry in defining the ideal body image.
- Define overweight and obesity.
- Discuss how effective body mass index, skin-fold measurements, hydrostatic weighing, and appearance are as methods of assessing body weight.
- Discuss the origins of obesity.
- Describe the body's use of food in activity requirements, in basal metabolism, and in the thermic effect.
- Discuss the primary types of weight-management techniques including dietary alterations, surgical interventions, medications, weight-loss programs, and physical activity.
- Define anorexia nervosa, bulimia nervosa, binge-eating disorder, chewing and spitting food syndrome, and night-time eating syndrome.
- Discuss the at-risk groups for eating disorders.
- Discuss ways of treating eating disorders.

Online Learning Centre Resources

www.mcgrawhill.ca/college/hahn

Log on to our Online Learning Centre (OLC) for access to Web links for study and exploration of health topics. Here are some examples of what you'll find:

- **www.dietitians.ca/english/frames.html** The Dietitians of Canada Web site includes a Healthy Body Quiz, a BMI (body mass index) calculator, and Top Ten Tips for healthy weight, lowering your fat intake, and eating a fibre-packed diet.
- **www.mirror-mirror.org/eatdis.htm** Look here for a wealth of information on eating disorders—signs and symptoms, complications, and getting help.
- **www.caloriecontrol.org** Have fun counting calories on this delightfully interactive site.
- **www.canadian-health-network.ca** This site provides considerable information about healthy eating.

Media Pulse

TV Zooms in on Body Image

What's on TV tonight? A minute of channel surfing tells you that it's bodies—bodies conditioned through athletics or dance, bodies hardened through training (and drug enhancement), and bodies thinned to anorexic proportions to show off fashions. Tune in to the cable medical channel and watch a liposuction procedure being done to remove unsightly fat. Or choose a documentary that details, with technical accuracy and human compassion, the struggles experienced by some obese people as they try to lose weight. It's all there—from the sensational to the educational.

Commercials for weight-loss programs and products are common on television. But you need to look carefully for the small-print disclaimers that say "results may vary widely." Ads for new prescription medications for weight loss are designed to prompt viewers to ask their doctors about these aids. It's only at the end of such ads that the long list of possible side effects and the caution that these drugs are intended for the most obese people are quickly flashed on the screen.

Prime-time sitcoms send powerful messages about thinness, obesity, and muscularity through their characters and story lines. The women characters on *The OC* and

Media Pulse *continued*

Desperate Housewives, for example, are all thin. For many teenage girls and young women, the message is that they should try to look like these characters on TV.

Critics of TV programming are asking some important questions. How reliable is the medical information we're getting? Can a 30-second feature give a balanced view of the dangers and benefits of a new drug? Is learning about liposuction on TV a good basis for deciding to have that procedure yourself? If the actors on *Desperate Housewives* look good on TV (which "adds pounds"), are they much too thin in real life? What do you think?

Obesity is a serious health concern. Recent data have indicated that 33% of adult Canadians are overweight, while 15% of adult Canadians are obese.[1] Moreover, close to 45% of Canadians are abdominally obese. In this condition, it is the location of the fat that imparts high risks for ischemic heart disease, stroke, high blood pressure, and type 2 diabetes.[2] In a society that has an abundance of high-quality food and a wide variety of labour-saving devices, being overweight is almost the rule rather than the exception.

When the body is supplied with more energy than it can use, the result is an excess of energy (or a **positive caloric balance**) stored in the form of fat. This continuous buildup of fat can eventually lead to obesity.

Few experts question the dangers to health and wellness from obesity.[3] Among the health problems caused by or complicated by obesity are increased surgical risk, hypertension, various forms of heart disease, stroke, type 2 diabetes mellitus,[4] several forms of cancer, deterioration of joints, complications during pregnancy, gallbladder disease, and an overall increased risk of mortality. Obesity is so closely associated with these chronic conditions that medical experts now recommend that obesity itself be defined and treated as a chronic disease.

BODY IMAGE AND SELF-CONCEPT

Although physicians focus on obesity, in our image-conscious society, being overweight is also a problem. The media tell people that being overweight is undesirable and that they should conform to certain ideal body images (such as being tall, thin, and "cut" with muscular definition). For example, the average actress and model is thinner than 95% of the female population and weighs 23% less than the average woman. Today's lean but muscular version of perfection is a very demanding standard for both women and men to meet (see Exploring Your Spirituality on p. 113).

People may become dissatisfied and concerned about their inability to achieve these ideals. The scope of this dissatisfaction is evident in a study of over 800 women, which revealed that nearly half were unhappy with their weight, muscle tone, hips, thighs, buttocks, and legs.[5] When this type of dissatisfaction exists, people begin to question their attractiveness. For some, their self-concept changes and their self-esteem declines. Growing older lessens, but does not eliminate, this dissatisfaction.

In comparison with being overweight, little media attention has been paid to being underweight. However, the body image problems experienced by some extremely thin people can be equally distressing.

MALNUTRITION

Imbalances between the body's need for nutrients and intake of nutrients may result in malnutrition. Malnutrition includes both undernutrition and overnutrition.[6] (See Table 6–1 for problems associated with body weight.)

OVERWEIGHT AND OBESITY DEFINED

What's the difference between overweight and obesity? Nutritionists have traditionally said that obesity is present when fat accumulation produces a body weight that is more than 20% above an ideal or **desirable weight**. People are said to be overweight if their weight is between 1% and 19% above their desirable weight. As weight increases above the 20% level, the label *obese* is routinely applied. An exception is excessive weight caused by extreme muscularity, such as that of many football players.

The term *obesity* requires further refinement. When people are between 20% and 40% above desirable weight, they are described as having *mild obesity* (about 90% of all obese people). Excessive weight in the range of 41% to 99% above desirable weight is defined as *moderate obesity* (9%). Weight of 100% or more above desirable weight is defined as *severe, gross,* or *morbid obesity* (<1%).

Central, or abdominal, fat is lipid that is stored in and around the body's organs or viscera. It behaves quite differently from other body fat, such as that under the skin or around the hips, in that it promotes a state of insulin resistance in the body. This condition, in turn, raises blood lipid levels, increases blood pressure, and encourages the development of chronic conditions such as hypertension and atherosclerosis. Men more typically carry their fat in the abdominal region, which partially

Table 6–1 Some Health Problems Associated with Body Weight

Overweight and obesity	Underweight*
Type 2 diabetes	Undernutrition
Dyslipidemia	Osteoporosis
Hypertension	Infertility
Coronary heart disease	Impaired immunocompetence
Gallbladder disease	
Obstructive sleep apnea	
Certain cancers	

* May include an eating disorder or other underlying illness.

explains their higher risk for cardiovascular disease. Following menopause, women also tend to develop abdominal fat stores instead of the hip and thigh fat they typically carry in their younger years.

Some clinicians and laymen continue to use standard height-weight tables to determine when weight is excessive and to classify obesity as mild, moderate, or severe. However, more precise techniques to determine health risk associated with body fatness are currently available. The *Canadian Medical Association Journal* (CMAJ) Web site has compiled links to articles published in CMAJ within the past four years concerning obesity (e.g., cost of obesity; the Canadian obesity epidemic, childhood obesity), in addition to links to other useful resources on the Internet. For this relevant information, go to **www.cmaj.ca/misc/obesity/index.shtml**.

DETERMINING HEALTHY WEIGHT AND FAT DISTRIBUTION

Some of the techniques used to determine overweight and obesity are common and are routinely used by the general public. Others are expensive and of limited availability.

Height-Weight Tables

Height and weight tables were originally developed to assist people in determining the relationship between their weight and desirable standards. Nearly every version of these tables has come under criticism for not considering variables such as gender, age, frame size, and body composition. Some versions were thought to be too rigorous in establishing cutoff points for desirable or ideal weight, and others were deemed too generous. Although still available, these tables are being gradually replaced by other assessment techniques.

Table 6–2 Body Mass Index

Classification	BMI Category (kg/m^2)	Risk of Developing health problems
Underweight	< 18.5	Increased
Normal Weight	18.5–24.9	Least
Overweight	25.0–29.9	Increased
Obese		
Class I	30.0–4.9	High
Class II	35.0–39.9	Very high
Class III	> 40.0	Extremely high

Note: For persons 65 years and older the "normal" range may begin slightly above BMI 18.5 and extend into the "overweight" range.

- The BMI (weight (kg)/height $(m)^2$) is not a direct measure of body fat but it is the most widely investigated and most useful indicator, to date, of health risk associated with under and overweight.

The Body Mass Index

Health Canada's *Canadian Guidelines for Body Weight Classification in Adults* uses **body mass index** (see Table 6–2[7]) to assess health risk. Individuals under the age of 18, in addition to pregnant and lactating women, are not classified using this system. Body mass index is determined by dividing weight (in kilograms) by the square of height (in metres). The BMI only roughly approximates body fatness levels; however, it is a useful indicator of health risk associated with either insufficient or excessive body weight. Table 6–2[8] shows the BMI ranges associated with both risk and good health. It is important to note that the classification system may underestimate or overestimate health risk for certain groups, namely adults with very lean or muscular bodies, certain ethnic/racial groups, young adults who have not completed growing, and seniors (65+). (See **www.hc-sc.gc.ca/fnan/nutrition/weights-poids/guide-ld-adult/qa-qr-prof_e.html** for more information).

Key Terms

positive caloric balance
Caloric intake greater than caloric expenditure.

desirable weight
The weight range deemed appropriate for people of a specific gender, age, and frame size.

body mass index (BMI)
A numerical expression of body weight based on height and weight.

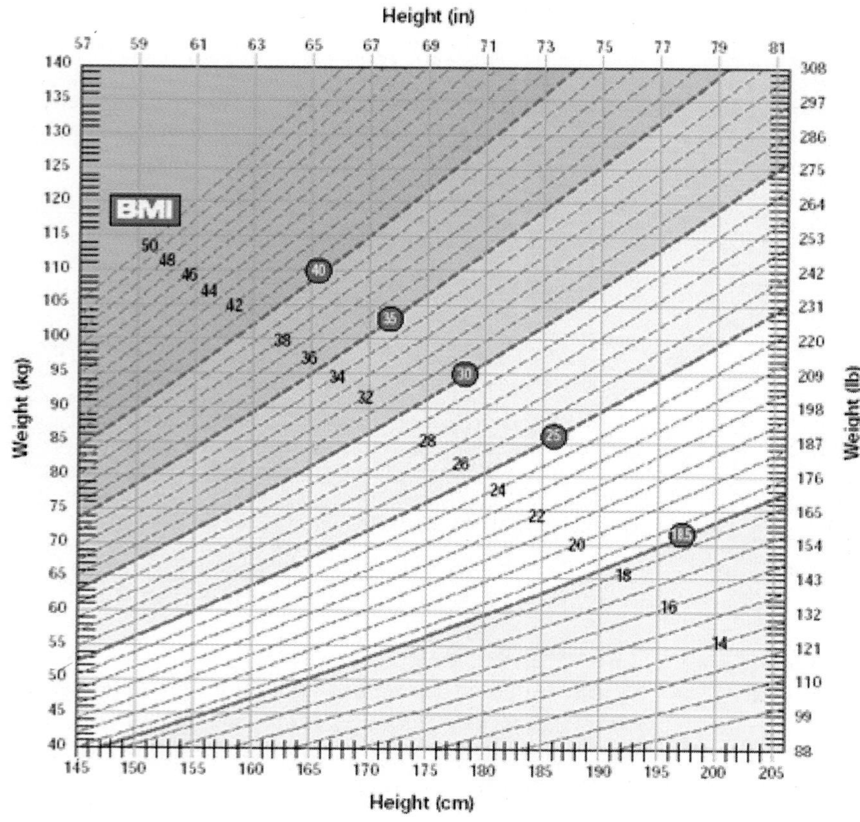

For a quick determination of BMI (kg/m^2), use a straight edge to help locate the point on the chart where height (in or cm) and weight (lb or kg) intersect. **Read the number on the dashed line closest to this point.** For example, an individual who weighs 69 kg and is 173 cm tall has a BMI of approximately 23.

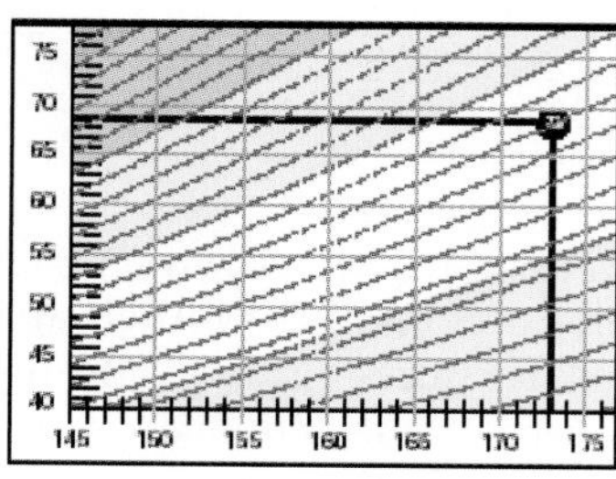

Figure 6–1 Body Mass index (BMI) Nomogram

Another method of determining whether the BMI is in a healthy range is to use a nomogram, such as that shown in Figure 6–1.[9] Like the BMI, the nomogram requires information about both height and weight. Health Canada suggests that factors other than height and weight (e.g., level of fitness, lifestyle practices, presence/absence of other conditions increasing one's risk of health) should also be considered when determining an individual's health risk classification.

TALKING POINTS • If a friend or close family member were dangerously overweight or obese, how would you express your concern?

Body Fat Distribution

You can determine whether you have excessive abdominal fat by converting two body measurements, the waist and the hip circumferences, into a waist-to-hip ratio (WHR). To make a WHR determination, follow these steps:

1. Measure around your waist near your navel while you stand relaxed (not pulling in your stomach).
2. Measure around your hips, over the buttocks where the hips are largest.
3. Divide the waist measurement by the hip measurement.

Lower risk is associated with a WHR of less than 0.8 for women and less than 1.0 in men. Higher health risk is associated with WHR measures above these. For example, a man with a waist circumference of 40 cm and a hip circumference of 36 cm has a WHR of 1.1, which suggests that he is carrying excessive central or abdominal body fat. An even simpler and equally accurate indicator of health risk is measuring waist circumference only. Waists of more than 1 m in men and 0.9 m in women point to higher risk.

People with a BMI value of 25.0 or above along with a WHR or waist circumference above the ideal are those in greatest need of losing body fat.

Body Composition

A variety of methods for determining the different proportions of the body that are made up of fat and lean weight are now in use. The most accurate of these are expensive and available only in clinics and laboratories. These include computer tomography scans (CT), dual electron absorptiometry (DEXA), and magnetic

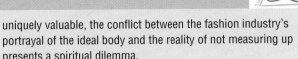

Exploring Your Spirituality
Want to Be Fashion-Model Thin?

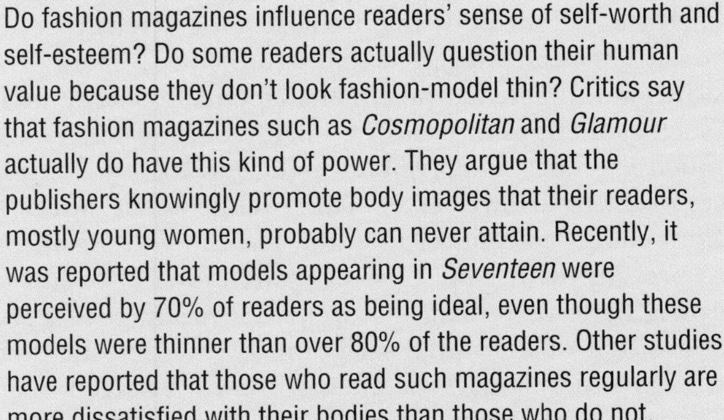

Do fashion magazines influence readers' sense of self-worth and self-esteem? Do some readers actually question their human value because they don't look fashion-model thin? Critics say that fashion magazines such as *Cosmopolitan* and *Glamour* actually do have this kind of power. They argue that the publishers knowingly promote body images that their readers, mostly young women, probably can never attain. Recently, it was reported that models appearing in *Seventeen* were perceived by 70% of readers as being ideal, even though these models were thinner than over 80% of the readers. Other studies have reported that those who read such magazines regularly are more dissatisfied with their bodies than those who do not.

The disparity between ideal body image and reality can affect an individual's spiritual health—at least among vulnerable adolescents and young adults. For those who believe that all people should love and respect themselves because they are created in the image of a higher being or that each person is uniquely valuable, the conflict between the fashion industry's portrayal of the ideal body and the reality of not measuring up presents a spiritual dilemma.

One response is to try to conform to the unrealistic ideal through strict dieting or purging. But at what price? What happens if you continue to fail—after more time spent in the weight room, tougher calorie restriction, or an expensive surgical procedure? How would you feel about yourself then?

An alternative approach is to search within yourself for other types of self-validation, such as undiscovered interests and untapped capabilities. Or you can look outward, into the real world, where you can make a positive difference by giving your talent, time, support, and personal faith to others. If you choose one of these approaches, the power of the fashion magazine will fade. By drawing on your deepest spiritual resources, you can put these images into perspective and strengthen your feelings of self-worth and self-esteem.

resonance imaging (MRI). Less expensive methods such as **electrical impedance** and infared light transmission are more widely available but may not give true measures of body composition.

Skinfold Measurements

Skinfold measurements are a relatively precise and inexpensive indicator of body composition. In this assessment procedure, constant-pressure **calipers** are used to measure the thickness of the layer of fat beneath the skin's surface, the *subcutaneous fat layer*. These measurements are taken at key places on the body. Through the use of specific formulas, skinfold measurements can be used to calculate the percentage of body fat. The percent body fat value can also be used in determining desirable weight.

Young adult men normally have a body fat percentage of 10% to 15%. The normal range for young adult women is 20% to 25%.[10] When a man's body fat is higher than 20% and a woman's body fat is above 30%, they are considered to be obese. The higher percentage of fat typically found in women is related to preparation for pregnancy and breastfeeding.

Hydrostatic Weighing

Hydrostatic (underwater) *weighing* is another precise method of determining the relative amounts of fat and lean body mass that make up body weight. A person's percentage of body fat is determined by comparing the underwater weight with the body weight out of water. The need for expensive facilities (a tank or pool) and experienced technicians make the availability and cost of this procedure limited to small-scale application, such as a large research university or teaching hospital.

HealthQuest Activities
www.mcgrawhill.ca/college/hahn

- The *Stages of Change* activity in the Nutrition and Weight Control Module 3 assesses your readiness to follow a diet containing appropriate levels of fats, carbohydrates, and proteins. It outlines concrete steps you can take to maintain healthy intake levels of these nutrients. The feedback for this activity is provided separately for each of these three dietary areas. You may address all three areas or choose among them. Develop a strategy for overcoming unhealthful eating habits and keep an ongoing account of your progress. Record your mood, activity level, schedule, and any other factors that may affect your eating behaviour. Then write down several ways to lessen the effects of such events on your eating behaviour.

Key Terms

electrical impedance
Method to test for the percentage of body fat using resistance to the flow of electrical current.

calipers
A device used to measure the thickness of a skinfold, from which percentage of body fat can be calculated.

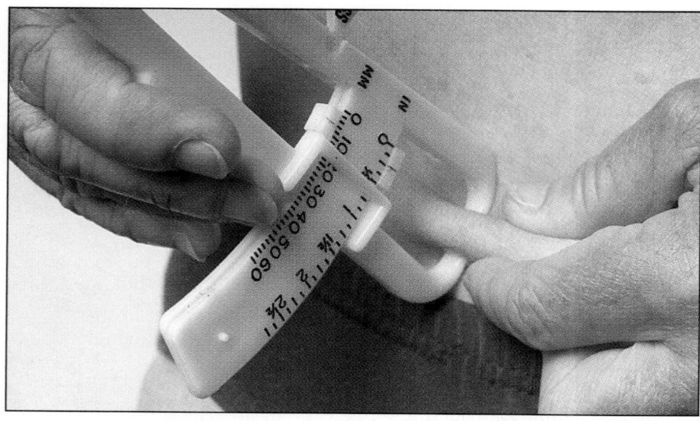

Body fat determination using skinfold calipers. Skinfold measurements are used in equations that calculate body fat density and percentage of body fat.

ORIGINS OF OBESITY

Experts continue to investigate the origins of obesity. Many theories focus on factors within the individual and from the environment. If the definitive causes of obesity are ever identified, they will probably have a complex basis that includes strong genetic and **neurophysiological** factors.

A great deal remains unknown about the causes of obesity. However, some basic explanations can be made about why some people gain weight easily.

Appetite Centres

In the early 20th century, the growing prevalence of obesity led researchers to speculate about the body's ability (or inability) to recognize feelings of hunger, as well as to note feelings of satiety, or fullness. By the 1940s, research directed toward finding the body's "appetite centre(s)" showed that both the hunger and satiety centres were located in the thalamic and hypothalamic areas of the brain. Subsequent research indicated that these centres controlled food intake by monitoring the levels of various materials in the blood, particularly glucose and various amino acids. They also recognized hormonal signals coming from endocrine glands and nervous stimuli arising both from within and outside the body. These signals informed the centres about the need to adjust eating behaviour. Most recent investigations have focused on how a hormone called leptin controls both appetite and physical activity in response to the level of fat in the body's fat cells.

Set Point Theory

The **set point** theory focuses on the central nervous system's ability or inability to fine-tune appetite and energy expenditure. Central to this theory is the contention that the control centres of the brain are programmed with an awareness of the body's most physiologically desirable weight. When functioning properly, the centres act as thermostats to adjust appetite and energy expenditure up or down to accommodate an excessive or inadequate caloric intake. By burning more energy or storing excessive energy as fat, the body maintains its best weight.

It has been suggested that if the body's energy (fat) stores are threatened by either inadequate energy intake (such as dieting) or excessive energy output (such as too much exercise), it prevents weight loss by adjusting the set point to a lower level. This change keeps stored fat from being depleted. In addition, according to this theory, to prevent further episodes of "starvation," once normal eating patterns return, lost weight is regained to a level above that of the initial set point. Every time the dieter tries to lose weight, he or she will "yo-yo" between weight loss and weight gain.

One mechanism by which the body may be controlling its energy expenditures and stores is **adaptive thermogenesis**, possibly accomplished through the actions of brown fat and other fat cells. Unlike white fat cells, which are designed to store excess calories as triglycerides, brown fat cells can convert stored fat into heat, which subsequently dissipates from the body. These brown fat cells are particularly prominent in infants; they may constitute as much as 6% of the infant's total body weight[11] and are thought to augment its underdeveloped temperature regulation system. As children age, however, the brown fat stores become less prominent. It may be that some adults lose the ability to disperse excess calories as heat, enabling their white fat cells to begin to store large quantities of surplus energy as fat. Most recently, a gene has been identified whose protein may relate to the functioning of brown fat.[12]

Genetic Basis of Obesity

Throughout the last half of the 20th century, the issue of faulty genetic mechanisms has been the focus of weight management, including obesity. In fact, today it is estimated that between 30% and 70% of obesity can be attributed to genetic causes.[13]

The initial clues to how inherited tendencies are involved in obesity resulted from the study of identical twins who, having been reared apart, demonstrated very similar body weights when reunited as adults. Today about 30 genetic markers for obesity have been identified.[14] These genes, when normally configured, communicate important information about hunger, satiety, and physical movement, allowing dietary intake, caloric expenditure, and fat storage to occur in a way that sustains healthy weight. When faulty genes are present, either through inheritance or mutation, people are predisposed to gain excessive weight when caloric intake exceeds caloric expenditure.

Central to the genetic theory of obesity is the recent discovery of faulty genes involved in the production and recognition of the protein leptin, which is critical in terminating food consumption and influencing energy expenditure. Leptin levels were first found to be in low in mice genetically bred for obesity, and so researchers were able to reverse obesity in these mice by injecting leptin. Most recently, small, carefully controlled studies involving the injection of leptin into obese humans produced modest weight loss.[15] Researchers remain optimistic that eventually leptin (or some related hormone) can be delivered to the brain in amounts sufficient to stimulate additional weight loss.[16]

While genetics may be an underlying factor associated with obesity, it is important to recognize that the environment must be permissive of gene expression. This means that whatever your genetic inheritance, it is still the balance of lifestyle factors affecting energy consumption and energy expenditure that determines whether obesity will develop.

TALKING POINTS • How would you advise a friend who complains that she is failing at another diet?

Infant and Adult Eating Patterns

Obesity can be categorized according to eating patterns. Two general feeding patterns are related to two forms of obesity: hypercellular obesity and hypertrophic obesity.

The first of these patterns involves infant feeding. Many researchers believe that the number of fat cells a person has will be determined during the first two years of life. Babies who are overfed will develop a greater number of fat cells than babies who receive a balanced diet of appropriate, infant-sized portions. Overfed babies, especially those with a family history of obesity, will tend to develop **hypercellular obesity**. When these children reach adulthood, they will have extra fat cells.

Late childhood and adolescence are also times when excessive weight gain may result in the formation of additional fat cells. For adults, substantial weight gain can also stimulate an increase in the number of fat cells and thus foster hypercellular obesity.

A second type of obesity with its origin in eating patterns is called **hypertrophic obesity**. It is related to a long-term positive caloric balance during adulthood. Over a period of years, existing fat cells increase in size to accommodate excess calorie intake.

Hypertrophic obesity is generally associated with excessive fat around the waist and is thought to contribute to conditions such as diabetes mellitus (type 2), high levels of fat in the blood, high blood pressure, and heart disease. In our society, hypertrophic obesity shows itself during middle age—a time when physical activity generally declines but food intake remains the same.

Endocrine Influence

For many years, people believed that obesity was the result of glandular problems. Often the thyroid gland was said to be underactive, preventing the person from burning up calories. Until recently it was believed that only a few obese people have an endocrine dysfunction that would cause obesity. Today, however, renewed interest in thyroid dysfunction is appearing.

Decreasing Basal Metabolic Rate

The body's requirement for energy to maintain basic physiological processes falls steadily with age. This change reflects the loss of muscle tissue that occurs as both men and women age. On a short-term basis, little adjustment needs to be made to maintain weight. However, if adjustments are not made, weight gain can become a problem over time. A gradual decrease in food intake combined with an increase in exercise can be effective in preventing the gradual onset of obesity.

Family Dietary Practices

Food preferences and eating practices are strongly influenced by the family. In some families lessons about eating are taught as though they were from a nutrition textbook. Other families encourage unhealthy food choices, which can lead to a lifetime of malnourishment, including obesity. For example, between-meal snacking on high-sugar or high-fat foods, large serving sizes, multiple servings, and high-calorie meals are poor lessons taught by some families.

Key Terms

neurophysiological
Pertaining to nervous system functioning; processes through which the body senses and responds to its internal and external environments.

set point
A genetically programmed range of body weight beyond which a person finds it difficult to gain or lose additional weight.

adaptive thermogenesis
Physiological response of the body to adjust its metabolic rate to the presence of food.

hypercellular obesity
A form of obesity seen in people who possess an abnormally large number of fat cells.

hypertrophic (high per TROH fick) obesity
A form of obesity in which fat cells are enlarged but not excessive in number.

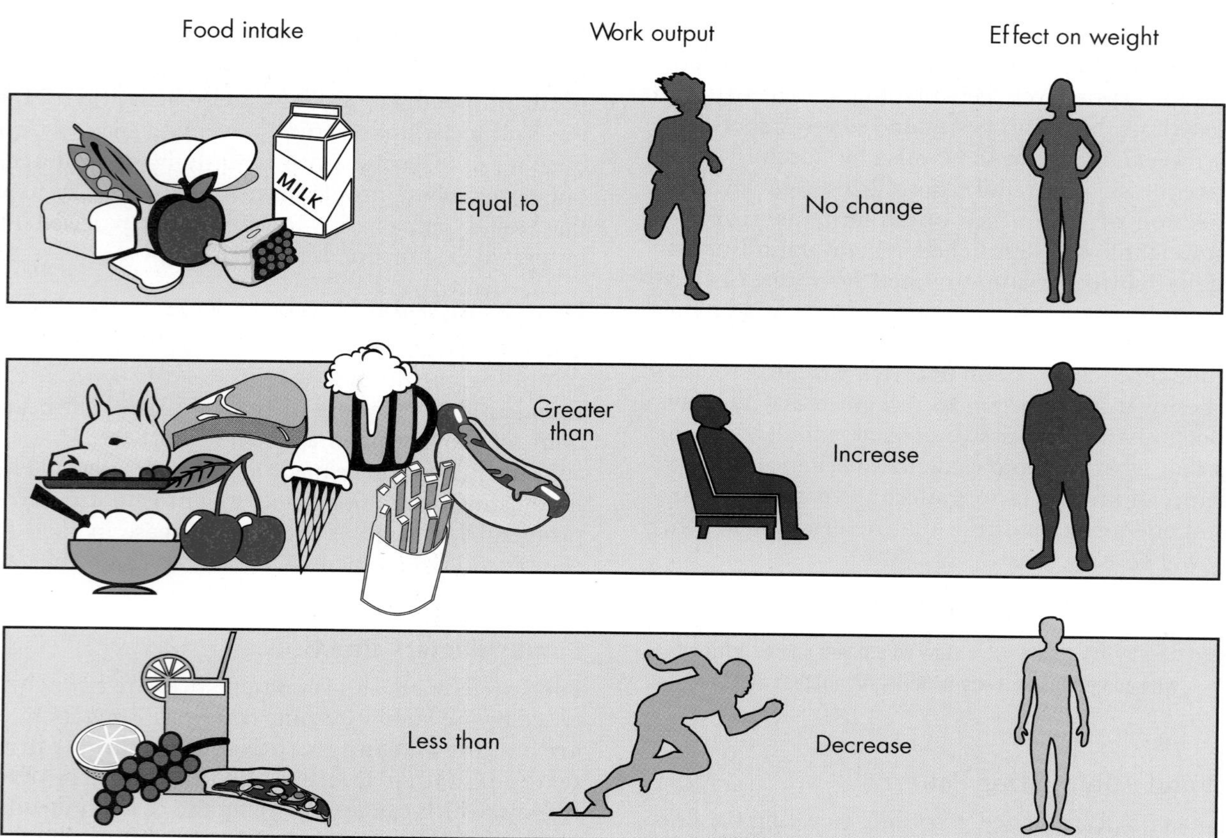

Figure 6–2 Caloric balance: energy input equals energy output, some of which comes from physical activity.

Inactivity

When weight-management experts are asked to identify the single most important reason for obesity in today's society, they point to inactivity. People of all ages tend to do less and therefore burn fewer calories than their ancestors did only a few generations ago. Automation in the workplace, labour-saving devices in the home, the inactivity associated with watching television, and a general dislike of exercise are a few of the reasons for this inactivity. Most important, however, is the sedentary lifestyle of many of today's children. Researchers believe that aggressive restrictions on television, videos, and video game use, as well as prohibiting snacking or meal eating while watching TV, may be necessary to halt their slide into lifelong obesity.[17]

CALORIC BALANCE

Any calories consumed in excess of those that are used by the body are converted to fat. We gain weight when our energy input is greater than our energy output. On the other hand, we lose weight when our energy output is greater than our energy input (Figure 6–2). Weight remains constant when caloric input and output are identical. In such situations, our bodies are said to be in *caloric balance*. To learn how you can reach and maintain caloric balance, complete the Personal Assessment on p. 132.

ENERGY NEEDS OF THE BODY

What are our energy needs? How many calories should we consume (or burn) to achieve a healthy weight? Although there are rough estimates for college-aged men (2500 to 3300 calories daily) and women (approximately 2500 calories daily), we all vary in our specific energy needs. These needs are based on three factors: (1) activity requirements, (2) basal metabolic rate (also referred to as resting energy expenditure, or REE), and (3) the thermic effect of food.

Activity Requirements

Each person's caloric *activity requirements* vary directly according to the amount of her or his daily physical activity. For example, sedentary office workers require a smaller daily caloric intake than construction workers, lumberjacks, or farm workers do.

Physical activity that occurs outside the workplace also increases caloric needs. Sedentary office workers

Health on the Web

Behaviour Change Activities

Are You Ready to Lose?

After reading this chapter, you're aware that obesity is a serious health concern. If you've tried to shed some pounds, you're familiar with the challenge this goal presents. The Mayo Clinic contends that a person must be ready for the challenge of losing weight. (see **www.mayoclinic.com/invoke.cfm?id=NU00266** for an article, including a series of questions, entitled "Are You Ready to Lose Weight?)

Check out Your BMI

It is also important to know if you really do need to lose weight. Go to the Dietitians of Canada Web site at **www.dietitians.ca/english/frames/html** to learn about body mass index (BMI). The site provides you with a link to calculate your BMI.

How Much Exercise Are You Getting?

The Dietitians of Canada Healthy Body Quiz also gives you an opportunity to explore the amount of exercise you get. Complete the Physical Activity Quiz and click on the Feedback button for information on how you're doing. Don't forget to look at the Top Ten Activity Tips.

may be quite active in their recreational pursuits. Active employees may spend their off hours lounging in front of the TV. It's important to closely examine the total amount of work or activity an individual engages in to accurately estimate that person's caloric requirements. Physical activity uses 20% to 40% of caloric intake. See Table 6–3 for a breakdown of caloric expenditures for various recreational pursuits.

TALKING POINTS • A good friend is clearly underweight. She is trying, with little success, to gain weight by increasing her food consumption. What suggestions would you give to help her?

Basal Metabolism

Of the three factors that determine energy needs, basal metabolism uses the highest proportion (50% to 70%) of the total calories required by each person. Expressed as a **basal metabolic rate (BMR)**, basal metabolism reflects the minimum amount of energy the body requires to carry on its vital functions, such as blood circulation and glandular activity. When a person is totally relaxed or sleeping, these vital body functions constitute the majority of the body's energy requirements.

Basal metabolism changes as people age. For both males and females, the BMR is relatively high at birth and continues to increase until the age of 2. Except for a slight rise at puberty, the BMR will then gradually decline throughout life.[18] If people fail to recognize that their BMR decreases as they grow older (2% per decade), they might also fail to adjust their food intake and activity level accordingly. Thus they will gradually put on unwanted pounds as they grow older.

Thermic Effect of Food

Formerly called the *specific dynamic action* of food, or *dietary thermogenesis*, the thermic effect of food represents the energy our bodies require for the digestion, absorption, and transportation of food. This energy breaks the electrochemical bonds that hold complex food molecules together, resulting in smaller nutrient units that can be distributed throughout the body. This energy requirement is in addition to activity needs and basal metabolic needs. The thermic effect of food is estimated to represent about 10% of total energy needs.

Pregnancy

During a normal pregnancy, about 75 000 additional calories are required to support the development of the fetus and the formation of maternal supportive tissues and to fuel the mother's BMR. In addition, the typical pregnant woman will develop about 4 extra kg (about 9 lbs) of fat tissue to be used as an energy source during breastfeeding. In total, the typical woman, under competent medical supervision, gives birth having gained, on average, about 13 kg (28 lbs) (normally ranging from 9 to 15 kg, or 19.8 to 33 lbs).[19]

After the birth of the baby, the woman will ideally have a weight gain of only 1 to 1.5 kg (2 to 3 lbs) over her prepregnancy weight. This small amount of additional weight will normally be lost by the end of the sixth to eighth month after childbirth.

Key Term

basal (BAY sal) metabolic rate (BMR)
The amount of energy (in calories) one's body requires to maintain basic functions.

Table 6–3 Kcalories Expended During Physical Activity

To determine the number of kcalories you have spent in an hour of activity, simply multiply the kcal/hour/kg column by your weight (in kilograms). For example, after an hour of basketball, a 60 kg person will have expended 499 kcalories; a 70 kg person, 582 kcalories; and an 80 kg person, 666 kcalories.*

Activity	kcal/hour/kg	Activity	kcal/hour/kg
Archery	3.83	Marching (rapid)	8.45
Basketball	8.32	Painting (outside)	4.62
Baseball	4.09	Playing music (sitting)	2.38
Boxing (sparring)	8.32	Racquetball	8.58
Canoeing (leisure)	2.64	Running (cross-country)	9.77
Climbing hills (no load)	7.26	Running	
Cleaning	3.56	11 min 30 sec per mile*	8.05
Cooking	2.64	9 min per mile	11.62
Cycling		8 min per mile	12.41
8.9 km/h	3.83	7 min per mile	13.73
15.1 km/h	5.94	6 min per mile	15.05
Racing	10.16	5 min 30 sec per mile	17.29
Dance (modern)	5.02	Scrubbing floors	6.60
Eating (sitting)	1.32	Sailing	2.64
Field hockey	8.05	Skiing	
Fishing	3.70	Cross-country	9.75
Football	7.92	Snow, downhill	8.45
Gardening		Water	6.86
Digging	7.52	Skating (moderate)	5.02
Mowing	6.73	Soccer	7.79
Raking	3.17	Squash	12.67
Golf	5.15	Swimming	
Gymnastics	3.96	Backstroke	10.16
Handball	8.32	Breaststroke	9.79
Hiking	5.54	Free, fast	9.37
Horseback riding		Free, slow	7.66
Galloping	8.18	Butterfly	10.30
Trotting	6.60	Table tennis	4.09
Walking	2.15	Tennis	6.60
Ice hockey	12.54	Volleyball	2.90
Jogging	9.13	Walking (normal pace)	4.75
Judo	11.75	Weight training	4.18
Knitting (sewing)	1.32	Wrestling	11.22
Lacrosse	12.54	Writing (sitting)	1.72

*One mile equals 1.6 km.

*A kilocalorie is a unit of heat required to raise the temperature of 1kg of water by 1°C at atmospheric pressure.

In spite of the modest (and short-term) additional weight a woman carries in the first few months following giving birth, some women may assume that pregnancy is a significant contributor to adult obesity. Although excessive weight gain does occur during pregnancy for some women, early competent medical management, emphasizing sound nutritional practices and regular physical activity, should largely eliminate this concern. In fact, after a well-managed pregnancy, some women weigh less than when they became pregnant. However, weight loss should not be a goal of pregnancy.

TALKING POINTS • A friend confides in you that she would like to have a child but does not want to become pregnant because she fears gaining weight. How would you respond?

Lifetime Weight Control

Obesity and frequent fluctuation in weight are thought to be associated with higher levels of morbidity and mortality, so it is highly desirable to maintain your weight and body composition at or near optimum levels. Although this may be a difficult goal to achieve, it is not unrealistic when begun early in life and from a starting point at or near optimum levels. The following are some keys to success:

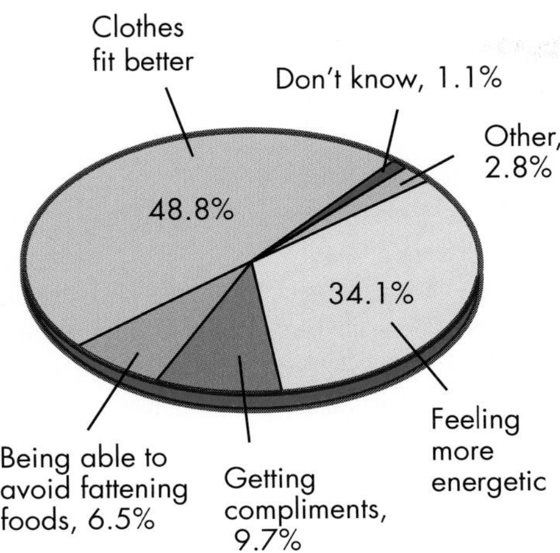

Figure 6–3 How do people measure success when it comes to losing weight? Most say better-fitting clothes or dropping a size is the best indicator that their diet is working.

- *Exercise.* Caloric expenditure through regular exercise, including cardiovascular exercise and strength training, is a key to maintaining optimum weight and body composition (see Chapter 4).
- *Dietary Modification.* Plan meals around foods that are low in total fat and saturated fat and high in complex carbohydrates, such as fruit, vegetables, legumes, and whole grains. This is an important approach to maintaining your optimum weight and body composition (see Chapter 5).
- *Lifestyle Support.* In addition to committing yourself to a lifestyle that features regular physical activity and careful food choices, build a support system that will nurture your efforts. Inform your family, friends, classmates, and coworkers that you intend to rely on them for support and encouragement.
- *Problem Solving.* Re-evaluate your current approaches to dealing with stressors. Replace any reliance on food as a coping mechanism with nonfood options, such as exercise or talking with friends or family members.
- *Redefinition of Health.* Think about health and wellness in terms of proactivity (see Chapter 2) and involvement, rather than simply focusing on not becoming sick or incapacitated.

If you have an acceptable weight and body composition at this time, these suggested lifestyle choices will make a significant contribution to preventing a weight problem later.

WEIGHT-MANAGEMENT TECHNIQUES

If you're already overweight, you may need to take specific measures to reduce your weight that are different

Changing *for the Better*

Tips for Losing Weight Successfully

I've tried all kinds of diets, and nothing seems to work for me. I have to lose weight, but I can't face another failure. What should I do?

- Keep a log of the times, settings, reasons, and feelings associated with your eating.
- Set realistic long-term goals (for example, loss of 0.5 kg a week instead of 2 kg per week).
- Don't completely deprive yourself of enjoyable foods (occasionally reward yourself with a small treat).
- Realize that the sacrifices you're making are important for your health and happiness.
- Eat slowly. It takes about 20 minutes for your brain to recognize satiety signals from your body.
- Put more physical activity into your daily routine (take stairs instead of elevators or park in the distant part of a parking lot, for example).
- Reward yourself when you reach your goals (with new clothes, sporting equipment, a vacation).
- Share your commitment to weight loss with your family and friends so that they can support your efforts.
- Keep careful records of your daily food consumption and weekly weight change.
- Be prepared to deal with occasional plateaus and setbacks in your quest for weight loss (see Figure 6–4).
- Remember that low-fat, low–saturated fat, and high–complex carbohydrate meals in combination with regular physical activity are the basis for these strategies.
- Eat only until you are satisfied.

from the total lifestyle approach just described. Once you reach a more healthy weight and body composition, maintaining that status will depend on adopting the lifestyle changes described on pp. 118–119. Figure 6–3 depicts ways, other than scale weight, through which people define whether their weight-loss program has been successful.

Fat loss occurs when the amount of energy taken into the body is less than that demanded by the body for maintenance and activity. A number of approaches to weight loss can be pursued. Complete the Personal Assessment on p. 133 to determine whether you are a candidate for weight loss.

Dietary Alterations

A diet that reduces caloric intake is the most common approach to weight loss. The choice of foods and the amount of food are the two factors that distinguish the wide range of diets currently available. It's important to

Learning from Our Diversity

Pyramid Power—Mediterranean Style

In Chapter 5 we explored the components of *Canada's Food Guide to Healthy Eating*, which is designed to help Canadians make healthy food choices in appropriate quantities. As you'll recall, we're encouraged to enjoy relatively more servings of bread, cereal, rice, pasta, fruits, and vegetables, while eating fewer servings of meat and dairy products.

Did you know that there are other food guide plans that point the way to nutritious food selections that are essential to successful weight control? One of these is the Mediterranean Pyramid, and some nutritionists believe it offers the best diet for good health (see the illustration below). Like *Canada's Food Guide,* the Mediterranean Pyramid emphasizes a diet based on grains, fruits, and vegetables. The Mediterranean Pyramid recommends eating red meat just a few times a month and allows generous amounts of olive oil. *Canada's Food Guide* recommends two to four servings of meat or meat alternates a day and suggests choosing low-fat foods whenever possible. Another important difference between these two food guides is that the Mediterranean Pyramid calls for limited consumption of alcohol, which may reduce the risk of coronary heart disease; Canada's Food Guide makes no such recommendation.

Here are some of the other reasons many nutritionists advocate a diet based on Mediterranean favourites:

Greens: Dark leafy greens are rich in antioxidant vitamins and phytochemicals, which may help guard against cancer and heart disease, and possibly prevent damage to the eyes. Greens are also excellent sources of calcium, iron, and the B vitamin folic acid, which research shows can reduce the risk of neural tube (spinal cord) defects in fetuses. Folic acid may also reduce the risk of heart disease and stroke.

Legumes: Like dark leafy greens, legumes such as garbanzo beans (chick peas), cannellini beans, and red kidney beans are rich in folic acid and iron. What's more, they're high in protein, making them low-fat, no-cholesterol alternatives to meat. And they're great sources of soluble fibre, which can help reduce levels of blood cholesterol.

Garlic: Also shown to be effective in lowering blood cholesterol even when eaten in small quantities, garlic is a traditional staple of Mediterranean cuisine that adds flavour without contributing either fat or sugar.

Olive oil: For centuries, olive oil has been the fat of choice in Mediterranean cooking. Unlike butter and lard, animal products that are loaded with saturated fat, olive oil is a monounsaturated fat, which some studies suggest may reduce the risk of atherosclerosis.

Do you know any students of Mediterranean descent, such as those of Italian, Greek, or Turkish ancestry, who follow a diet based on the Mediterranean Pyramid? If so, what foods do they typically eat? Using the pyramid structure, make a diagram of your current food choices, with those you consume the most at the bottom and those you eat least at the top. How close is your diet to that recommended by *Canada's Food Guide*? The Mediterranean Pyramid?

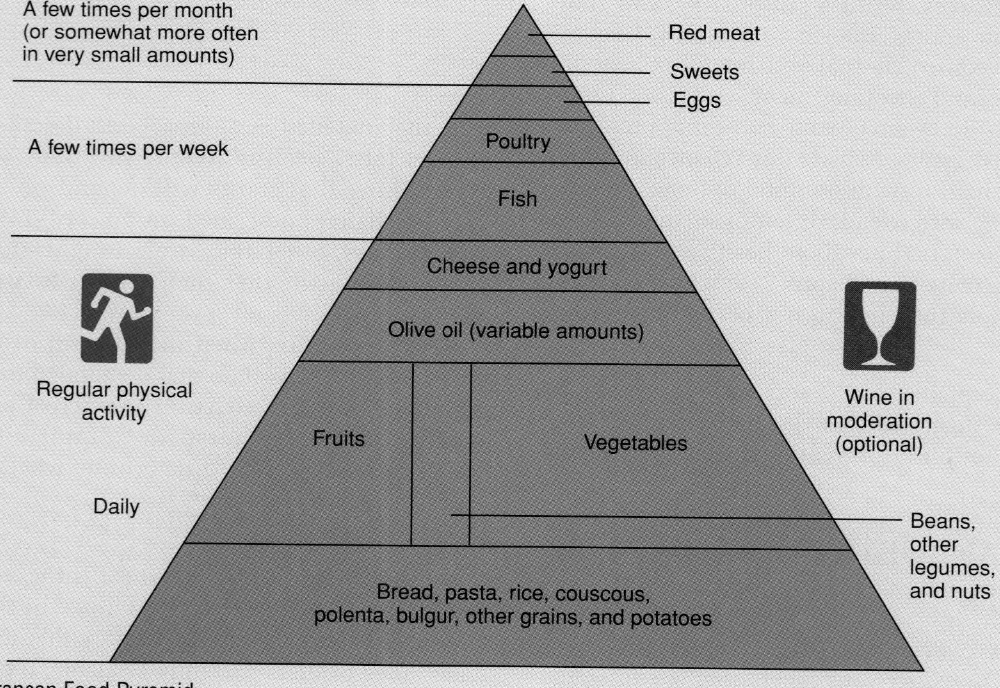

The Mediterranean Food Pyramid.

note, however, that dieting alone usually does not result in long-term weight loss. In fact, whether individuals manage their diets by themselves or follow a recognized weight-loss program, most dieters regain at least two-thirds of the weight they lost within two years of the initial loss. A study of successful dieters conducted by the U.S. National Weight Control Registry demonstrated that people in this select group relied on balanced diets and exercise, rather than restrictive diets and medication, to lose weight and maintain that loss[20] (see Changing for the Better, on p. 119).

Balanced diets supported by portion control

For nutritional health, a logical approach to weight loss and subsequent weight maintenance is to establish a nutritionally sound balanced diet (low in fat, especially saturated fat, and high in complex carbohydrates) that controls portions. Most people have difficulty controlling portion sizes. The labels of many packaged foods provide nutrition information for a single serving, yet the package often contains two or more servings of the food. In addition, restaurants, especially those offering fast food, rarely serve reasonable portion sizes, preferring to heap food on the plate or "supersize" a meal to give the customer a sense of value for money.[21] A balanced diet/portion control approach to weight loss is nutritionally sound and offers some probability of success.

Fad diets

Many people use fad diets in an attempt to lose weight quickly. These popular diets are often promoted in best-selling books written by people who claim to be nutrition experts (see Changing for the Better on p. 123). With few exceptions, these approaches are both ineffective and potentially unhealthy. In addition, some involve significant expense. A brief assessment of a variety of popular diet plans is presented in Table 6–4.

High-protein/low-carbohydrate diets

Currently, the most popular diets are those that reduce carbohydrate intake to an extremely low level while permitting an almost unlimited consumption of protein (in particular, meat), with its accompanying moderately high to high fat content. As indicated in Table 6–4, these diets, such as *Dr. Atkin's New Diet Revolution*, *Mastering the Zone*, and *Sugar Busters*, involve potential problems, particularly if followed for long periods. However, they may generate an impressive initial weight loss.

The central theory underlying these diets is the "short-circuiting" of insulin's role as a facilitator of fat storage when the body has to deal with excessive levels of glucose. This situation occurs easily in sedentary people who consume foods that are high in carbohydrates, particularly simple sugars. When the carbohydrate intake is greatly reduced, the insulin response is also reduced. In addition, as noted in Chapter 5, the body does not consider dietary protein to be a preferred source of calories; thus the body turns to stored fat as fuel for muscular activity. When fat becomes the principal source of calories, as happens in these diets, metabolic waste products are produced that acidify the body. Additionally, the need to metabolize large amounts of dietary protein produces a strain on the kidneys and an accompanying loss of water. The overall effect of the diet is similar to the metabolic state of people with undiagnosed or poorly managed diabetes. Unfortunately, the fat content of the diet will eventually resupply the body with calories that were initially obtained by breaking down the fat stores.

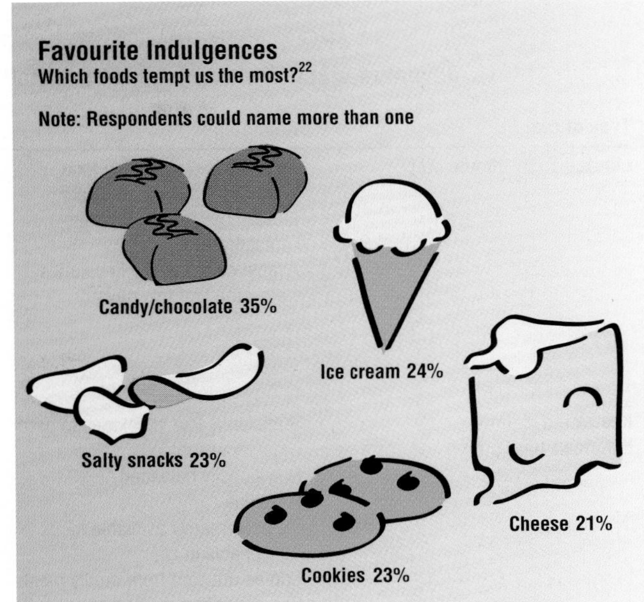

Figure 6–4 Late-night kitchen raids and too many daytime snacks can compromise a healthy diet. Which foods are the most difficult for you to resist?

Controlled fasting

In cases of extreme obesity, some patients are placed on a complete fast in a hospital setting. The patient is maintained on only water, electrolytes, and vitamins. Weight loss is profound because the body is quickly forced to begin **catabolism** of its fat and muscle tissues. Sodium loss, a negative nitrogen balance, and potassium loss are particular concerns.

Key Term

catabolism
The metabolic process of breaking down tissue for the purpose of converting it into energy.

Table 6–4 Advantages and Disadvantages of Selected Diets

Type of Diet	Advantages	Disadvantages	Examples
Limited-food-choice diet	Reduces the number of food choices made by the users Limited opportunity to make mistakes Almost certainly low in calories after the first few days	Deficient in many nutrients, depending on the foods allowed Monotonous—difficult to adhere to Eating out and eating socially are difficult Does not retrain dieters in acceptable eating habits Low long-term success rates No scientific basis for the diets	Banana and milk diet Fitonics for Life Diet Kempner rice diet The New Beverly Hills Diet Fit for Life
Restricted-calorie, balanced food plan	Sufficiently low in calories to permit steady weight loss Nutritionally balanced Palatable Includes readily available foods Reasonable in cost Can be adapted from family meals Permits eating out and social eating Promotes a new set of eating habits May employ a point system	Does not appeal to people who want a "unique diet" Does not produce immediate and large weight losses	Weight Watchers Diet Take Off Pounds Sensibly (TOPS) Overeaters Anonymous Jenny Craig
Fasting starvation diet	Rapid initial loss	Nutrient deficient Danger of ketosis >60% loss is muscle <40% loss is fat Low long-term success rate	ZIP Diet 5-Day Miracle Diet
High-carbohydrate diet	Emphasizes grains, fruits, and vegetables High in bulk Low in cholesterol	Limits milk, meat Nutritionally very inadequate for calcium, iron, and protein	Quick Weight Loss Diet Pritikin Diet Hilton Head Metabolism Diet
High-protein, low-carbohydrate diet Usually includes all the meat, fish, poultry, and eggs you can eat Occasionally permits milk and cheese in limited amounts Prohibits fruits, vegetables, and any bread or cereal products	Rapid initial weight loss because of diuretic effect Very little hunger	Too low in carbohydrates Deficient in many nutrients—vitamin C, vitamin A (unless eggs are included), calcium, and several trace elements High in saturated fat, cholesterol, and total fat Extreme diets of this type could cause death Impossible to adhere to these diets long enough to lose any appreciable amount of weight Dangerous for people with kidney disease Weight lost, which is largely water, is rapidly regained Expensive Unpalatable after first few days Difficult for dieter to eat out Unattractive side effects (e.g., bad breath) May require potassium and calcium supplements	Dr. Stillman's Quick Weight Loss Diet Calories Don't Count by Dr. Taller Dr. Atkin's New Diet Revolution Scarsdale Diet Air Force Diet The Carbohydrate Addict's Life Span Program Mastering the Zone Diet The Carbohydrate Addict's Diet Sugar Busters Protein Power Get Skinny on Fabulous Food (with modifications)

Continued

Table 6–4 Advantages and Disadvantages of Selected Diets

Type of Diet	Advantages	Disadvantages	Examples
Low-calorie, high-protein supplement diet Usually a premeasured powder to be reconstituted with water or a prepared liquid formula	Rapid initial weight loss Easy to prepare—already measured Palatable for first few days Usually fortified to provide recommended amount of micronutrients Must be labelled if >50% protein	Usually prescribed at dangerously low calorie intake of 300 to 500 calories Overpriced Low in fibre and bulk—constipating in short amount of time	Metracal Diet Cambridge Diet Liquid Protein Diet Last Chance Diet Oxford Diet Genesis New Direction
High-fibre, low-calorie diets	High satiety value Provide bulk	Irritating to the lower colon Decreases absorption of trace elements, especially iron Nutritionally deficient Low in protein	Pritikin Diet F Diet Zen Macrobiotic Diet
Protein-sparing modified fats <50% protein: 400 Cal	Safe under supervision High-quality protein Minimizes loss of lean body mass	Decreases BMR Monotonous Expensive	Optifast Medifast
Premeasured food plans	Provides prescribed portion sizes—little chance of too small or too large a portion Total food programs Some provide adequate calories (1200) Nutritionally balanced or supplemented	Expensive Does not retrain dieters in acceptable eating habits Precludes eating out or social eating Often low in bulk Monotonous Low long-term success rates	Nutri-System Carnation Plan

Today, some people regularly practise unsupervised modified fasting for short periods. Solid foods are removed from the diet for a number of days. Fruit juice, water, protein supplements, and vitamins are used to minimize the risks associated with total fasting. However, unsupervised short-term fasting that is done too frequently can be dangerous and is not generally recommended.

Commercial weight-reduction programs

In virtually every area of the country, at least one version of the popular commercial weight-reduction programs, such as TOPS (Take Off Pounds Sensibly), Jenny Craig, and Weight Watchers, can be found. These programs generally feature a format consisting of (1) a well-balanced diet emphasizing portion control and low-fat, low–saturated fat, and high–complex carbohydrate foods, (2) realistic weight loss goals to be attained over a reasonable period of time, (3) encouragement from supportive leaders and fellow group members, (4) emphasis on regular physical activity, and (5) a weight-management program (follow-up program). The Changing for the Better box on p. 124 presents some guidelines for choosing a commercial weight-loss program.

In theory, these programs offer an opportunity to lose weight for people who cannot or will not participate

Changing *for the Better*

Choosing a Diet Plan

I've been trying to find a good diet plan, but I'm confused by all the promotional materials. How can I recognize a sensible approach to weight loss?

- Make sure the program incorporates a balanced diet, an exercise program, and behaviour modification.
- Beware of inflexible plans, such as those that require you to eat certain foods on certain days.
- Avoid plans that allow fewer than 1200 kcalories a day, the minimum needed to get essential nutrients.
- Make sure the recommended rate of weight loss does not exceed 1 kg per week.
- Avoid programs that promote vitamins, pills, shots, gimmicks, gadgets, or brand-name diet foods.
- Look for a statement of approval by a reputable nutrition expert or institution.
- Beware of diets that promise fast, easy, or effortless weight loss or "a new secret formula."
- Choose a plan that teaches you how to keep the weight off once you've lost it.

Changing for the Better

Choosing the Right Weight-Loss Program

Dieting on my own isn't working for me. I need the guidance and support of a structured program. What things should I be cautious about in choosing a plan?

When checking out commercial weight-loss programs, avoid any program that

- Is not led by qualified specialists, including a registered dietitian
- Promises or encourages quick weight loss
- Does not require a pre-enrolment physical examination
- Does not warn clients of the risk of developing health problems related to weight loss, such as ketosis and diabetes-related complications
- Claims that an unusually high percentage of its clients are successful in achieving and maintaining weight loss
- Requires you to buy its products, such as foods or nutritional supplements
- Does not encourage lifestyle changes, including an exercise program
- Does not provide follow-up support after you reach your weight-loss goal

in an activity program. But their effectiveness is very limited. In fact, the limited success of these programs and the difficulty that people have in attending meetings have resulted in falling enrolment and the development of home-based programs, such as hospital-based wellness programs and YMCA and YWCA programs. All these programs are costly when compared with self-directed approaches, especially when the program markets its own food products.

Diet and physical activity

Most Canadians attempting to lose weight fail to include a physical activity component in their dietary approach. Recent research strongly encourages 150 minutes or more of increased activity per week to maximize success in losing weight and maintaining that loss.[23] Additionally, using home exercise equipment may be an important part of the success of programs that incorporate a structured short-term exercise activity.[24]

Physical Intervention

A second approach to weight loss involves techniques and products designed to alter basic eating patterns. Some are self-selected and self-applied, and others must be administered in an institutional setting by highly trained professionals.

Hunger- and satiety-influencing products

Many overweight people want to lessen their desire to eat or develop a stronger sense of when they have eaten enough. Today, many dieters are confused about the safety of pharmaceutical approaches to weight loss, including both over-the-counter (OTC) and prescription drugs.

Ephedrine has been linked to heart attacks and strokes and should not be used, either alone or in combination with caffeine or other stimulants for the purposes of increased energy, body building, or weight loss.

Some prescription medications have been shown to produce serious side effects. Two such medications, phentermine and fenfluramine, have been prescribed for patients who wanted to lose weight. Both drugs affect levels of serotonin, the neurotransmitter associated with satiety. This popular combination, referred to as *phen-fen*, gradually raised concern among health experts because of the side effects it produced in people with angina, glaucoma, and high blood pressure. In addition, reports began to surface that some patients had developed a rare but lethal condition called *pulmonary hypertension*. In 1999, sale of these drugs was discontinued in Canada.

Health Canada has since approved another serotonin-specific obesity drug, *sibutramine* (MERIDIA). Sibutramine functions as a serotonin reuptake inhibitor, as did fenfluramine, thus enhancing satiety. Unlike fenfluramine, however, sibutramine does not cause excessive production of serotonin in other areas of the nervous system. In addition, sibutramine retards the reuptake of norepinephrine, a second neurotransmitter that influences eating behaviour. When used in its approved form, sibutramine appears to have few serious side effects.[25] However, Health Canada advises that certain individuals should not take MERIDIA, such as individuals who experience arrhythmias, have experienced a prior heart attack, have congestive heart failure, have a diagnosis of depression, are pregnant or breastfeeding, or are under the age of 18 or over the age of 65. For more information go to Health Canada's Web site: **www.hc-sc.gc.ca/english/protection/warnings/2002/2002_21ebk.htm.**

A non-serotonin-influencing drug, *orlistat* (Xenical), has recently been approved. Unlike the serotonin-specific drugs, orlistat reduces fat absorption in the small intestine by about 30%. The drug is intended for use among people who are 20% or more above ideal weight. It could cause a 10% loss of body weight when accompanied by some dietary restriction. Some concern exists about the lack of absorption of fat-soluble vitamins among people taking the drug. Additionally, anal leakage may accompany the drug's use, particularly following meals with high fat content.

Surgical Measures

When a person is morbidly obese and weight loss is imperative, surgical intervention may be considered. A *gastric resection* is a major operation in which a portion of the small intestine is bypassed in an attempt to decrease the body's ability to absorb nutrients. Although this procedure can produce a major weight loss, it is associated with many unpleasant side effects (including diarrhea and liver damage) and various nutritional deficiencies.

Gastroplasty (stomach stapling) is a surgical procedure that involves sealing off a sizable portion of the stomach with surgical staples. The resulting reduced capacity of the stomach decreases the amount of food that can be processed at any one time. Patients feel full more quickly after eating a small meal. This procedure is reversible but carries the general risks associated with surgery and involves the expense of a major surgical procedure.

Liposuction

Another form of surgical fat reduction is *liposuction*, or *lipoplasty*. In this procedure, a physician inserts a small tube through the skin and vacuum aspirates away fat cells. This method is generally used for stubborn, localized pockets of fat and is usually appropriate for people under the age of 40.

Liposuction is basically a cosmetic procedure. Infection, pain and discomfort, bruising, swelling, discoloration, abscesses, and unattractive changes in body contours are possible outcomes of liposuction. Therefore, people considering this procedure should carefully investigate all its aspects, including the training and experience of the surgeon, to determine whether it is appropriate for them.

EATING DISORDERS

Some people have medically identifiable, potentially serious difficulties with body image, body weight, and food selection. Among these disorders are two that are frequently seen among university and college students—anorexia nervosa and bulimia. In addition, compulsive exercising, compulsive eating, and disorders involving anorexic and/or bulimic practices are also found in these populations. These topics are included in this chapter because most eating disorders begin with dieting. However, most eating disorders also involve inappropriate food choices and deep emotional needs (discussed in Chapters 2 and 5).

Anorexia Nervosa

A young woman, competitive and perfectionistic by nature, determines that her weight (and appearance) is unacceptable. Believing that she would feel better about herself if she lost some weight, she begins to disregard her appetite, and her food consumption virtually ceases. This young woman may be seen by her friends as active and intelligent, and simply dieting and exercising with an unusual degree of commitment. Eventually, however, they observe that her food consumption has nearly stopped. Her weight loss has continued beyond the point that is pleasing—at least to others. Still, her activity level remains high. When questioned about her weight loss, she says that she still needs to lose more weight.

This person is suffering from a medical condition called **anorexia nervosa** (see the Star Box on p. 126). This self-induced starvation is life threatening in 5% to 20% of cases. The stunning amount of weight that some anorexic people lose—up to 50% of their body weight—eventually leads to failure of the heart, lungs, and kidneys.

Although this condition involves a weight-loss orientation, experts believe that the anorexic person is attempting to meet a much deeper need for control. Specifically, in a family setting where much is expected of the individual but little opportunity for self-directed behaviour is provided, control over the body becomes a need-fulfilling tool. Eventually, a normal body image is lost, and the condition progresses as described above. Fortunately, psychological intervention in combination with medical and dietary support can return the anorexic person to a more healthy pattern of eating. The anorexic person needs professional help. If you observe this condition in a friend, it is vital to secure immediate assistance for this person. A good place to start would be your student health services.

Bulimia Nervosa

Bulimia nervosa is an eating disorder that involves gorging oneself with food. People who practise a pattern of massive eating followed by **purging** are said to suffer from *bulimarexia*, or *bulimia nervosa* (see the Star Box on page 126). Most often, however, the term *bulimia* is used to describe this binge–purge pattern. As with-anorexia nervosa, most people with bulimia are young women, although the incidence in men is growing.

Key Terms

anorexia nervosa
A disorder of emotional origin in which appetite and hunger are suppressed and marked weight loss occurs.

bulimia nervosa
A disorder of emotional origin in which binge eating patterns are established; usually accompanied by purging.

purging
Using vomiting or laxatives to remove undigested food from the body.

Recognizing Anorexia Nervosa and Bulimia

The American Psychological Association and the Canadian Mental Health Association use the following diagnostic criteria to identify anorexia nervosa and bulimia:[26]

Anorexia Nervosa

- 15% or more below desirable weight
- Fear of weight gain
- Altered body image
- Three or more missed menstrual periods; in young adolescents, no onset of menstruation

Bulimia

- Binge eating two or more times a week for three months
- A lack of control over bingeing
- Purging
- Concern about body image

Characteristic symptoms include the following. However, it is unlikely that all the symptoms will be evident in any one individual.

Anorexia Nervosa

- Looks thin and keeps getting thinner
- Feels overweight despite significant weight loss
- Skips meals, cuts food into small pieces, moves food around plate to appear to have eaten
- Loss of menstrual periods
- Wears "layered look" in an attempt to disguise weight loss
- Loss of hair from the head
- Growth of fine hair (lanugo) on face, arms, and chest
- Extreme sensitivity to cold
- Extreme preoccupation with body weight

Bulimia

- Bathroom use immediately after eating
- Inconspicuous eating
- Excessive time (and money) spent food shopping
- Shopping for food at several stores rather than one store
- Menstrual irregularities
- Excessive constipation
- Swollen and/or infected salivary glands, sore throat
- Bursting blood vessels in the eyes
- Damaged teeth and gums
- Dehydration and kidney dysfunction
- Eating beyond point of being full

People with bulimia lose or maintain weight not because they stop eating but because they eat and then purge their digestive system by vomiting or using laxatives. They may gorge themselves with food (up to 10 000 calories in a sitting) and then disappear, only to return later seemingly unaffected by the amount of food they ate. In all likelihood, they have regurgitated the food. In the mid-1980s, medical experts estimated that as many as 19% of 18- to 22-year-old women developed all the principal symptoms of bulimia. However, when all of the criteria mentioned in the Star Box above are applied, rather than simply reporting "experience" with bulimia-associated behaviour, the percentage drops to less than 2%.

In addition to the binge–purge disorder, people who binge but do not purge also suffer from an eating disorder. Whether called *bulimia*, "eating disorder not otherwise specified," or *binge-eating disorder*, this practice also requires intervention and effective treatment.

Binge-Eating Disorder/Compulsive Eating

Binge-eating disorder, sometimes referred to as compulsive eating, is characterized by the consumption of large amounts of food over a short time period, often to the point of feeling uncomfortably full. Bingers often eat when they are not physically hungry. Purging (e.g., vomiting, laxatives, fasting, etc.) does not occur after the uncontrollable eating binges, and this lack of purging is one of the factors that differentiates this condition from bulimia. During the binge-eating episode, individuals tend to feel out of control. This lack of control is eventually replaced by feelings of remorse, distress, depression, self-loathing, body-hatred, and shame. Binge eating allows individuals to *temporarily* cope with or block out stressors they do want to experience. In other words, the individuals are driven to eat and to experience the emotional comfort that the food provides at that moment. A few of the signs and symptoms of binge-eating disorder include hiding food, weight gain and fluctuations in weight, low self-esteem, anxiety, experimenting with many different diets, a history of diet failures, secretive eating patterns, avoiding social situations when food will be present, and feeling disgusted with oneself. The treatment of this disorder involves interventions similar to bulimia nervosa.[27] For more information on binge eating disorders, go to **www.mirror-mirror.org/binge.htm**.[28]

Chewing and Spitting out Food Syndrome

Chewing and spitting out one's food without swallowing it has also been used as a method for weight loss or weight management. This is a common eating disorder and falls within the "Eating Disorder Not Otherwise Specified" diagnosis. It differs from bulimia nervosa and researchers contend that chewing and spitting out food without swallowing may indicate a more severe eating disorder.[29]

Resources for Anorexia Nervosa and Bulimia Treatment

Local Resources

- College or university health centres
- College or university counselling centres
- Comprehensive mental health centres
- Crisis intervention centres
- Mental health associations

Organizations and Self-Help Groups

Bulimia Anorexia Nervosa Association
2109 Ottawa Street, Windsor, ON, N8Y 1R8
Tel: (519) 969-2112
Fax: (519) 969-0227

National Institute of Mental Health
Eating Disorders Information Page
www.nimh.nih.gov/publicat/eatingdisorders.cfm

The National Eating Disorder Information Centre
EST-421, 200 Elizabeth Street, Toronto, ON, M5G 2C4
Tel: (416) 340-4156 Fax: (416) 340-4736
Toll-free: 1-866-NEDIC-20 (1-866-633-4220)
Email: nedic@uhn.on.ca
www.nedic.ca

Eating Disorders; Mirror Mirror
This site includes a list of provincial and national organizations associated with eating disorders.
www.mirror-mirror.org/eatdis.htm

(U.S.) National Eating Disorders Association
www.NationalEatingDisorders.org

Health Canada
www.hc-sc.gc.ca

Table 6–5 Possible Physical/Medical Complications Resulting from Eating Disorders

Anorexia Nervosa

- Fatigue and lack of energy
- Skin problems
- Depression
- Cardiac arrest and death
- Shortness of breath
- Hair loss
- Dehydration
- Bloating and constipation
- Loss of menstruation
- Dizziness
- Infertility
- Osteoporosis
- Anemia
- Irregular heartbeat
- Headaches

Bulimia Nervosa

- Fatigue and lack of energy
- Erosion of teeth enamel
- Depression
- Headaches
- Dizziness
- Kidney and liver damage
- Chronic sore throat
- Shortness of breath
- Anemia
- Irregular heartbeat
- Cardiac arrest and death
- Chest pains
- Hair loss
- Dehydration
- Loss of menstruation and irregular menstruation

Compulsive Eating

- Arthritis
- Varicose veins
- Sleep deprivation
- Weight gain
- Fatigue
- Mobility problems
- Cardiac arrest and death
- Sciatica
- Embolism
- Toxemia during pregnancy
- Hypertension
- Heart ailments
- Diabetes
- Shortness of breath

Note: this is not an exhaustive list.

Night Eating Syndrome

Night eating syndrome has not yet been formally defined as an eating disorder. The signs and symptoms of this syndrome include eating more than half of one's daily food intake after dinner and before breakfast, feeling tense, anxious, and guilty while eating, difficulty falling or staying asleep at night, and having little to no appetite in the morning. Unlike binge eating, night eating involves eating throughout the evening hours rather than in short episodes. It is important to note that there is a strong preference for carbohydrates among night eaters. Some researchers speculate that night eating may be an unconscious attempt to self-medicate mood problems because eating carbohydrates can trigger the brain to produce so-called "feel good" neurochemicals. Research is underway in examining the underlying causes of this syndrome and developing subsequent treatment interventions. It seems likely that a combination of biological, genetic, and psychological factors contribute to this problem.

Treatment for Eating Disorders

The treatment of eating disorders is complex and demanding although essential to prevent possible complications (see Table 6–5).[30] The physical care for a person with advanced anorexia nervosa usually begins with hospitalization to stabilize the physical deterioration associated with starvation. Stomach tubes and intravenous feedings are sometimes necessary, particularly when the patient will not (or cannot) eat. In addition, drugs used to treat depression, obsessive-compulsive disorder, and anxiety are often prescribed. Behaviour modification, including eating contracts, is used; as is psychotherapy (in both individual and group formats). Nutritional and family counselling complete the therapy.

Treatment for bulimia involves individual, family, and nutritional counselling. Unlike treatment for anorexia, however, the treatment does not involve hospitalization as often. The Star Box on p. 127 lists resources for people with eating disorders.

Although eating disorders are clinical realities to the physicians and psychologists who treat affected patients and can be described with detachment, they are very personal matters to the patients and families involved. Effective treatment must take place within the supportive environment of concerned and knowledgeable friends and family members.

TALKING POINTS • You suspect that a close friend at school is anorexic but has hidden her physical condition from her family by going home infrequently and skillfully layering her clothing. Do you have an obligation to talk to your friend's family about her condition? If so, how would you approach the subject?

UNDERWEIGHT AND UNDERNOURISHED

For some young adults, the lack of adequate body weight is a serious concern. Particularly for those who have inherited an ectomorphic body build (tall, narrow shoulders and hips with a tendency to thinness), attempts to gain weight are routinely undertaken, often with limited success. These people would likely fall into a BMI range (see p. 111) of 18.5 and 16 and be from 10% to 20% below normal on a standard height-weight table.[31] If these people are to be successful in gaining weight, they must find an effective way to take in more calories than they burn.

Nutritionists believe that the healthiest way to gain weight is to increase the intake of calorie-dense food, such as dried fruits, peanut butter, bananas, nuts, granola, lean meats, and cheeses made from low-fat milk. These foods should be consumed later in a meal so that the onset of satiety that quickly follows eating fat-rich foods does not occur. The current recommendation is to eat three calorie-dense meals of moderate size per day, interspersed with two or three substantial snacks. Using *Canada's Food Guide to Healthy Eating* (see Chapter 5, p. 91) as a guide, underweight people should eat the highest number of recommended servings for each group.

A second component of weight gain for those who are underweight is ensuring at least eight hours of sleep each night and the curtailment of excessive physical activity. By carefully reducing their activity level, they can prevent the "burning up" of calories that can be used for development of body fat and muscle. However, activity should not be restricted to the point that cardiovascular conditioning declines or enjoyable activities are no longer done. See Chapter 4 to review the female athlete triad and its relationship to underweight.

A final consideration for healthy weight gain is an exercise program that uses weight-training activities intended to increase muscle mass. As detailed in Chapter 4, the use of anabolic drugs has no role in healthy weight gain.

For those who cannot gain weight, even by using these approaches, a medical evaluation may offer an explanation. If no medical reason can be found, the person must begin to accept the reality of his or her unique body type. The Focus On article on p. 134 further explores the problems of being underweight.

When individuals fall below 80% of their desirable weight on standard height-weight tables and display BMI rates from 16 to 10, it is highly probable that they are not only underweight but, more important, *undernourished*.[32] This condition suggests clinically significant deficiencies in both the quantity of food being consumed and its nutritional value. Whether the undernourishment is associated with anorexia nervosa, other medical conditions characterized by weight loss (such as irritable bowel diseases), or poverty or famine, affected people are in danger of death from starvation.

Taking Charge of Your Health

- Investigate the resources available on your campus that you could use to determine your healthy weight and body composition profile.
- Evaluate your eating behaviours to find out if you are using food to cope with stress. If you are, develop a plan to use nonfood options, such as exercise or interaction with friends or family members, to deal with stress.
- Formulate a realistic set of goals for altering your weight and body composition in a time frame that allows you to do so in a healthy way.
- Establish a daily schedule that lets you make any necessary dietary and physical activity adjustments.
- Keep a daily journal of your weight-management efforts.
- Monitor your progress toward meeting your weight-management goals.

SUMMARY

- There are many health problems associated with body weight.
- Overweight and obesity are the most common forms of malnutrition in Canada and the United States.
- Obesity results from an abnormal accumulation of fat.
- The health implications of moderate to severe obesity are clear, but the seriousness of mild obesity or overweight is questioned by some.
- Body image and self-concept can be adversely influenced by obesity.
- Obesity and overweight can be defined in a variety of ways and determined by different methods.
- Maintaining a healthy body weight is desirable because central–body cavity obesity is associated with a variety of serious health problems.
- Theories regarding the cause of obesity focus on factors from within the individual and from the environment.
- Many complex theories exist regarding the role of appetite centres, set point, thermogenesis, inheritance, body type, infant feeding patterns, aging, family dietary patterns, and activity patterns.
- Caloric balance influences weight gain, loss, and maintenance.
- The body's energy needs arise from three areas: activity, basal metabolic rate, and the thermic effect of food.
- If well managed, pregnancy should not contribute to excessive weight gain.
- Weight loss can be attempted through dieting, which is the restriction of food intake.
- A combination approach involving low-fat, low–saturated fat, high–complex carbohydrate food, portion-controlled dieting, and exercise may be the most effective way to lose weight.
- Surgical intervention may be required in cases of extreme obesity.
- Although many people can lose some weight through dieting, very few can maintain that weight loss, unless they also exercise.
- The use of certain prescription medications in various combinations caused serious heart valve damage and other dangerous side effects, leading to removal of these drugs from the market.
- Serious eating disorders usually begin with dieting but are often sustained in an attempt to meet deeper needs.
- Binge-eating disorder, chewing and spitting out food syndrome, and night-eating syndrome are less common forms of eating disorders.
- Underweight is a condition that may be resolved through consuming calorie-dense foods and restricting caloric expenditure.

REVIEW QUESTIONS

1. Why are obesity and overweight considered to be forms of malnutrition and potentially serious health problems?
2. How are obesity and overweight defined? Why is it possible to be overweight without being overfat? What is the set point?
3. In what ways can obesity be determined? What is desirable weight? What is body mass index? What is waist-to-hip ratio? Why is central-body cavity obesity of concern to physicians?
4. Describe the function of each of the following in causing obesity: heredity, set point, infant feeding patterns, pregnancy, aging, inactivity, and family eating patterns.
5. What is caloric balance? What are the body's three areas of energy needs? How does aging influence caloric balance? How is exercise involved in both weight loss and long-term weight maintenance?
6. What is the role of surgery, fasting, and fad diets?

7. How effective is dieting in terms of both immediate success and later weight maintenance?
8. What two techniques are used in a combination approach to weight loss? How should this program be structured to ensure the highest level of success?
9. What are the two principal eating disorders found among post-secondary students? How do they differ? What is binge-eating disorder? What differentiates bulimia nervosa from binge-eating disorder? How are eating disorders treated?

THINK ABOUT THIS ...

- What are your attitudes toward people with weight-control problems? Why do you feel this way?
- Do you believe that being underweight is as psychologically traumatic as being overweight? What issues would both groups face? (Hint: health; society)
- If you have a weight problem, explain why you have a responsibility to yourself and to society to reduce your weight.
- What do you see as your responsibility in dealing with a friend or family member who is displaying signs of an eating disorder?

REFERENCES

1. Statistics Canada: Canadian community health survey, *The Daily*, **www.statcan.ca/Daily/English/040615/d040615b.htm**, August 11, 2004.
2. Macdonald SM, Reeder BA, Chen Y, Depres J-P: Obesity in Canada: a descriptive analysis, *Can Med Assoc J* 157: s39–s45, 1997.
3. Crowley LV: *Introduction to human disease*, ed 4, 1996, Jones & Bartlett.
4. Must A et al: The disease burden associated with overweight and obesity, *JAMA* 282(16):1523–1539, 1999.
5. Cash T, Henry P: Women's body images: the results of national survey in the U.S.A., *Sex Roles: A Journal of Research* 33(1–2):19–29, 1995.
6. *The Merck Manual of Diagnosis and Therapy;* **www.merck.com/mrkshared/mmanual/section1/chapter2/2a.jsp**, August 11, 2004.
7. Adopted from WHO *Obesity: preventing and managing the global epidemic: report of a WHO consultation on obesity*, 2000.
8. Health Canada: Canadian guidelines for body weight classification in adults: quick reference tool for professionals, **www.hc-sc.gc.ca/hpfb-dgpsa/onpp-bppn/cg_quick_reference_e.pdf**, August 11, 2004.
9. Health Canada: Canadian guidelines for body weight classification in adults: quick reference tool for professionals, **www.hc-sc.gc.ca/fn-an/nutrition/weights-poids/guide-1d-adult/cg_quick_ref-1dc_rapide_ref_e.html**, August 11, 2004.
10. National Task Force on the Prevention and Treatment of Obesity: Weight cycling, *JAMA* 272(15):1196–1202, 1994.
11. Saladin KS: *Anatomy and physiology: the unity of form and function*, 1998, McGraw-Hill.
12. Fleury C, Neverova M, Collins S: Uncoupling protein 2 gene, *Nat Genet* 15:269–272, 1997.
13. Yanovski JA, Yanovski SZ: Recent advances in basic obesity research, *JAMA* 282(16):1504–1506, 1999.
14. Ibid.
15. Heymsfield SB et al: Recombinant leptin for weight loss in obese and lean adults: a randomized, controlled, dose-escalation trial, *JAMA* 282(16):1568–1575, 1999.
16. Fujioka K, Patane J, Lau D: CSF leptin levels after exogenous administration of recombinant methionyl human leptin (research letter), *JAMA* 282(16):1517–1518, 1999.
17. Robinson TN: Reducing children's television viewing to prevent obesity: a randomized controlled trial, *JAMA* 282(16):1561–1570, 1999.
18. Ganong WF: *Review of medical physiology*, ed 18, 1997, Appleton & Lange.
19. Thorsdottir I, Birgisdottir BE: Different weight gain in women of normal weight before pregnancy: postpartum weight and birth weight, *Obstet Gynecol* 92(3):377–383, 1998.
20. What it takes to take off weight (and keep it off), *Tufts University Health and Nutrition Letter* 15(4):4–5, January, 1998.
21. Hill JO, Peters JC: Environmental contributions to the obesity epidemic, *Science* 280(5368):1371–1374, 1998.
22. Opinion Research Corp. for Simply Lite Foods.
23. Serdula MK et al: Prevalence of attempting weight loss and strategies for controlling weight, *JAMA* 282(16):1353–1358, 1999.
24. Jakicic JM et al: Effects of intermittent exercise and use of home exercise equipment on adherence, weight loss, and fitness in overweight women, *JAMA* 282(16):1554–1559, 1999.
25. Center for Drug Evaluation and Research: *FDA announces withdrawal of fenfluramine and dexfenfluramine*, News Release # P97-32, September 15, 1997, U.S. Food and Drug Administration.
26. Canadian Mental Health Association. **www.cmha.ca**, August 15, 2005.

27. Fact sheet: binge eating disorder, **www.sheenasplace.org/quickfacts/bingeeating.html**, August 12, 2004.
28. Binge eating disorder, **www.mirror-mirror.org/binge.htm**, August 12, 2004.
29. *Update:* Chewing and spitting out food.
30. Adapted from **www.mirror-mirror.org**, June 2005.
31. *Eating Disorders Review,* July/August 2002.
32. Ferro-Luzzi A, James WP: Adult malnutrition: simple assessment techniques for use in emergencies, *Br J Nutr* 75(1):3–10, 1996.

SUGGESTED READINGS

Mellin L: *The solution: six winning ways to permanent weight loss*, 1998, Regan Books.

This book has been praised by many who have tried diet books only to experience failure. The author takes her readers deep inside to the underlying emotional needs that have been routinely dulled (but not met) by compulsive eating. Presented in a workbook format, this book helps readers move toward more nurturing relationships with themselves and others.

Price DS: *Healing the hungry self: the diet-free solution to lifelong weight management*, 1998, Plume.

Disturbances in the physical, emotional, mental, and spiritual selves that constitute each person are described as the basis of flawed relationships with food. The author, drawing on her expertise in the treatment of eating disorders, uses a workbook format to bring readers into contact with these selves in order to better understand each, thus enhancing their self-esteem and altering their relationship with food.

Toews J, Parton N: *Never say diet!* 1998, Key Porter Books.

The Canadian authors of this book and a companion planner, *Never say diet! Seven days a week*, are a registered dietitian and a well-known journalist. Together they have produced two fact- and fun-filled guides to why diets don't work for permanent weight loss, and how you can eat to get and stay healthy.

Name ______________________________ **Date** ____________

Personal Assessment

How Many Calories Do You Need?

Resting Energy Requirement (RER)

Women

3–10 years 22.5 × weight (kg) + 499
10–18 years 12.2 × weight (kg) + 746
18–30 years 14.7 × weight (kg) + 496
30–60 years 8.7 × weight (kg) + 829
>60 years 10.5 × weight (kg) + 596

Men

3–10 years 22.7 × weight (kg) + 495
10–18 years 17.5 × weight (kg) + 651
18–30 years 15.3 × weight (kg) + 679
30–60 years 11.6 × weight (kg) + 879
>60 years 13.5 × weight (kg) + 487

Activity Energy Requirement (AER)

At bed rest: 1.20
Low activity (walking): 1.30
Average activity: 1.50–1.75
High activity: 2.0

Instructions: Calculate your resting energy requirement based on your sex, age, and weight. Then multiply your RER by your AER to determine how many calories you need each day to maintain your weight.

Example: Woman
24 years
120 lbs = 54.5 kg
High activity
(REE) × (AER) = Total Energy Requirement
14.7 × 54.5 (kg) + 496 × 2.0 = 2594 calories/day

Note: 1 kg = 2.2 lbs.

Data from *Energy and protein requirements: report of a joint FAO/WHO/UNU expert consultation.* Technical Report Series 724. World Health Organization, 1985; Zeam FJ: *Clinical nutrition and dietetics*, 1991, Macmillan.

Name ______________________________ **Date** ____________

Personal Assessment

Is It Time for a Weight-Loss Program?

Before undertaking a program, it is important to look at your past experiences and feelings about weight loss. Perhaps in doing so, you might decide that you would do better with other alternatives besides dieting.

Answer each of the following items with a "True" or "False" as it applies to you.

_______ 1. I am frustrated about my inability to stick to a diet.
_______ 2. I have less self-control than most dieters.
_______ 3. Most of the times I try to lose weight I lose control and go off my diet.
_______ 4. When I try to develop a habit of regular exercise, something always interferes and I stop.
_______ 5. Exercise seems to be an ordeal to me.
_______ 6. I often feel tired during the day.
_______ 7. My weight has gone up and down several times when I go on and off diets.
_______ 8. My body seems to be getting thicker in the middle over the years.
_______ 9. My weight seems to be increasing over the years.
_______ 10. I find myself thinking about food more than I should.
_______ 11. I find myself thinking about my weight all through the day.
_______ 12. I feel there is probably no hope for my weight problem.
_______ 13. Sometimes I lose control and really binge on food.
_______ 14. I use food to make myself feel better when I am angry, nervous, or depressed.
_______ 15. Some people reject me as a friend because I am too heavy.
_______ 16. My social life is limited because of my weight.
_______ 17. My sex life is limited because of my weight.
_______ 18. Other people think I am unattractive because of my weight.
_______ 19. I put a lot of effort into choosing clothes that tend to cover up my weight problem.

To Carry This Further

For those items that you answered as true, consider these recommendations:

Items 1, 2, and 3: Rather than going on a diet, why not try to reduce your fat intake by avoiding fried food and foods with added fat? Eat more low-fat foods, and ensure that your dairy products are low fat and your meats are lean.

Items 4, 5, and 6: You need a gradual but regular exercise program. Check around your community, and identify a reputable program that has a proven success rate in helping others who have had a weight problem.

Items 7, 8, and 9: These items indicate the development of a weight problem that could truly be damaging your health. These are reasons for being serious about weight loss that go beyond appearance.

Items 10, 11, 12, 13, and 14: You may be into "living to eat" rather than "eating to live." Now is the time to give serious thought to what is important in your life, other than appearance-related needs.

Items 15, 16, and 17: Work at forming new relationships. Seek out people who are capable of looking beyond your physical appearance for those attributes that they will find to be attractive in you.

Items 18 and 19: As for 15 to 17, assess your current relationships. Put your efforts into relationships with people who seem capable of looking "into" you, rather than only "at" you.

Focus on

DYING YOUNG

Andrea Smeltzer was a vibrant and promising young woman, an exemplary student with a passion for life that made an impression on everyone she knew.

But in June, the 19-year-old became a sobering statistic. A Napa resident for most of her life, Andrea spent a year living abroad in Spain and was fluent in the language by the time she graduated from Vintage High School in 1997.

At the prestigious Pitzer College, where she was an active presence on campus, she managed to complete her undergraduate degree in international studies by the end of her sophomore year. After college, she hoped to use her degree to work with humanitarian agencies like Amnesty International. "She experienced more in life than many people do. But I used to say to her, 'Please slow down, you'll have nothing left at 30. It'll all be done,'" recalled her mother, Doris Smeltzer. "Maybe she knew."

On June 16, after a thirteen-month struggle with bulimia, Andrea died in her sleep when an electrolyte imbalance caused her heart to fail.

The public's perception of eating disorders—once thought to be the domain of adolescent girls and supermodels—is changing, thanks to recent high-profile incidents like the 1997 death of the San Francisco ballerina whose heart failure was linked with an eating disorder, and Princess Diana's often publicized struggle with bulimia.

For those who knew her, Andrea's death put yet another new face on the disease: that of a young, successful college woman with everything to live for.

Disorders Not Unique

Andrea's experience, although tragic, is not unique. It is estimated that as many as 25 percent of college-aged women deal with disordered eating habits of some kind, if not necessarily full-blown anorexia or bulimia, according to Carla Jackson, a health educator at Pitzer.

"It often develops in college because college is a big transition time: a lot of things are new, there are added responsibilities and expectations that people put on themselves," said Jackson. "They control their eating to be able to control one aspect of their lives."

There is no way to pinpoint exactly what happened to trigger the eating disorder in Andrea. Most likely it was a complex combination of factors and circumstances that ultimately became overwhelming.

Both of her parents had struggled with life-threatening illnesses when she was younger, and the trauma made its mark on Andrea.

In college, she balanced her rigorous academic demands against a legion of other commitments on campus, from hosting tours to mentoring other students. At the same time, she was charting new territory in her personal life in a turbulent relationship with her first boyfriend.

Andrea's mother doesn't underestimate the role that unrealistic standards of beauty, inundating society through television, movie screens and fashion magazines, played in her daughter's illness.

Robin Lasser, who struggled successfully to overcome an eating disorder of her own, agrees. Lasser is a San Jose State University professor who recently collaborated on an exhibit called "Eating Disorders in a Disordered Culture" that drew nationwide attention to the issue.

"Our culture says that in addition to everything else, being intelligent, funny and athletic, women must also be perfect-looking. Of course the standards of beauty are impossible to achieve," said Lasser.

How to Fight It

As awareness of the severity of the problem moves into the public's consciousness, a wealth of treatment programs and organizations have been established to combat eating disorders, many of them on college campuses.

Colleges, including the one that Andrea attended, often have health education outreach and counseling services specifically designed to target the issues surrounding eating disorders.

When Andrea developed an eating disorder in May of 1998, she did all the things that were supposed to save her life. She called her family the day after she threw up for the first time and told them what had happened. She sought professional help from both a nutritionist and a counselor, often for several sessions a week, and spent hours reading books and surfing the Internet to find out everything she could about the disease.

"Andrea knew eating disorders inside, outside, backwards, forwards," her mother said. "She could quote you line and verse. But knowledge does not equate with behavioral change. That is why just informing people is not enough. Just being educated is not enough. Because Andrea knew."

Despite the breadth of resources available to her, and her own commitment to healing, neither knowledge nor treatment was enough to save Andrea.

She is not alone. Although the majority of those who seek treatment do recover, 20 percent never experience any improvement at all, and between two and three percent eventually die from their condition, according to Anorexia Nervosa and Related Eating Disorders, Inc., an organization devoted to educating the public.

Statistics like these are precisely why many experts say that even comprehensive treatment programs aren't enough.

Consequently, many advocate prevention strategies that range from educating about body issues to attacking the social pressures that contribute to the development of eating disorders.

"Educators should introduce the topic in elementary school and middle school so that it is not such a shameful thing to discuss. Early intervention is essential so that the problem can be cured way before it becomes clinical," said Adriana Schoenberg, a nurse practitioner and member of the eating disorder team at the University of California at Berkeley Health Center. "Clinical people, especially pediatricians, should be trained to detect the symptoms."

While the benefits of programs that emphasize self-esteem building seem indisputable, some experts caution that educational programs that provide graphic details about the disease may backfire.

"Education is important, but not necessarily all the gory details like bingeing and purging," said Andrea James, a counselor for the Rader program, an eating disorder treatment center located in Los Angeles. "Kids could pick up dangerous tools and adopt them to cope with their problems."

Society's Pressure

Even the most optimistic admit that one of the most significant contributors to the development of eating disorders—the social emphasis on unattainable standards of weight and beauty—isn't likely to disappear anytime soon.

That doesn't mean that people have to accept without question the messages that are fed to them through the ever-expanding outlets of the media, according to Holly Hoff, the program director at Eating Disorders Awareness & Prevention, Inc.

"Watch for messages that don't represent diversity of body shape or a healthy ideal of weight," suggested Hoff. "Challenge these messages by writing a letter, or just tearing up a magazine picture or talking back to your TV when they don't project a positive image."

Doris Smeltzer wants people to understand exactly why challenging these attitudes and messages, which are often so deeply ingrained, is so important. Because someone who looks healthy and vital can die without warning. Because an electrolyte imbalance can happen in a matter of hours. Because getting help doesn't guarantee recovery.

Spreading the Word

Andrea can no longer speak for herself, but her mother intends to make sure that her voice is still heard. Doris Smeltzer is organizing a collection of Andrea's prose and poetry for publication. She has spoken at two memorial services for Andrea, and plans to speak out about her daughter's struggle on college campuses and disordered eating conventions in the future.

Andrea intended to use her talents to touch the lives of others and make a difference in the world—lofty goals, but in light of everything she had already accomplished, perhaps not so far-fetched. If her story can help keep even one life from being extinguished by the disease, Doris Smeltzer is convinced that it isn't too late to fulfill those ambitions.

"I think that my goal now in the new life that I have—because my life has been forever altered—is to spread her story," Andrea's mother says. "I want people to know that the best thing in the world to do is to prevent that first time so that it doesn't start, because curing an eating disorder is so incredibly difficult and complicated."

Source: Bryant B, Krupp S: Bulimia robs Napa teen of promising life, *Napa Register* **www.andreasvoice.org/article.htm**, August 19, 2005.

Part Three

Chapter 7

Making Decisions about Drug Use

Chapter Objectives

After reading this chapter, you should be able to

- Describe the effects of drugs on the central nervous system.
- Discuss drug addiction and the three common aspects of the addiction.
- Describe the physical and psychological dependence one develops when addicted to drugs.
- List the risks of combining drugs and dosages.
- List and describe the six classifications of psychoactive drugs, giving examples of each.
- List the serious side effects of non-prescription Ritalin use.
- List the short- and long-term effects of marijuana use.
- List the risks of combining drugs and dosages.
- Discuss the issue of drug testing.
- Identify the important aspects of drug-treatment programs.

Online Learning Centre Resources

www.mcgrawhill.ca/college/hahn

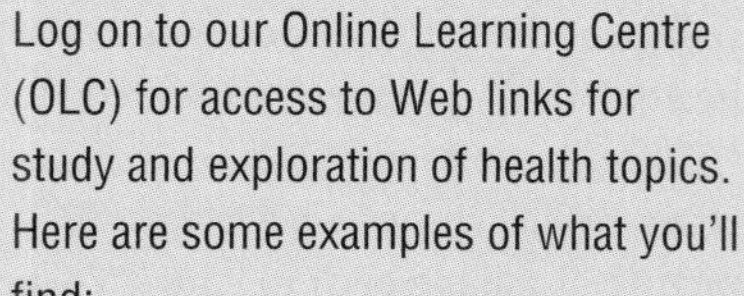

Log on to our Online Learning Centre (OLC) for access to Web links for study and exploration of health topics. Here are some examples of what you'll find:

- **www.doorway.org** Look here for prevention, education, intervention, and recovery information, and find dozens of links to other sources.
- **www.edc.org** Click on Alcohol and Other Drug News for up-to-the-minute information, and check out *Students* for lots of other good stuff.
- **www.habitsmart.com** Take the self-scoring alcohol checkup here if you're curious about your drinking habits.

Media Pulse

Do Media Scare Tactics Keep People from Using Drugs?

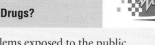

The media has tried to frighten people in many ways to keep them away from unhealthy behaviours. The classic film *Reefer Madness* was intended to scare people in the 1940s and 1950s from experimenting with marijuana. Recent films such as *Traffic* show the reality of illicit drug use in North America today. The late Frank Zappa, founder of the alternative music group the Mothers of Invention, warned young people in the early 1970s not to use stimulants (speed) because doing so would cause them "to turn out like your parents," a frightening thought for many counterculture youth. In the past few decades, many celebrities' drug addictions have become public knowledge and received much media attention. Matthew Perry and Drew Barrymore are recent examples of celebrities who have had their problems exposed to the public through media attention.

Posters produced by both government and private health agencies have depicted cigarette smokers as filthy, wrinkled old men and women. Many of these posters are eye catching in an almost humorous way. They grab the observer's attention and send the clear message that "this could happen to you." Advertisements for drug and alcohol rehabilitation facilities have shown alcoholics drowning in a sea of alcohol, drug users being confronted by their families, and employees caught by a drug screening test. The message is that miserable life situations can be changed if people are willing to get help.

It's difficult to measure the effectiveness of these approaches to drug prevention. Many people recall

Media Pulse *continued*

these media presentations, so they do make an impression. But, given the many variables involved in drug-taking behaviour—family influence, inherited predispositions, life events and situations, drug availability, and peer influence—it's impossible to pinpoint the influence of a single media event. These scare tactics seem to be especially effective among people who have already made the decision not to use drugs. They remind these people how dangerous it is to use drugs. For people who are thinking about starting drug use, these messages may be beneficial, since they portray drug use in a negative light.

For hard-core drug users, though, it's unlikely that scare tactics will be effective. These people tend to lead chaotic lives, may never see the ads, and often remain in denial about their addiction. Nonusers and individuals leaning away from drug use are more likely to be influenced by this approach. Despite the fact that these ad campaigns are highly visible and costly, they seem to have only limited influence in drug prevention.

SOCIETY'S RESPONSE TO DRUG USE

Most adults see drug abuse as a clear danger to society. This position has been supported by the development of community, school, provincial, and national organizations directed toward the reduction of illegal drug use. These organizations have included such diverse groups as Alcoholics Anonymous, Mothers Against Drunk Driving (MADD), Narcotics Anonymous, and Health Canada. Certain groups have concentrated their efforts on education, others on enforcement, and still others on the development of laws and public policy. Health Canada's Office of Cannabis Medical Access coordinates and administers the new regulatory approach permitting individuals to access marijuana (*cannabis*) for medical purposes. The Office also coordinates other Health Canada initiatives related to marijuana, including research on the safety and effectiveness of marijuana used for therapeutic purposes, and the establishment of a reliable Canadian source of medical research–grade marijuana.

The personal and social issues related to drug abuse are very complex. Innovative solutions continue to be devised. Some believe that only through early childhood education will people learn alternatives to drug use. Starting drug education in the preschool years may have a more positive effect than waiting until the upper elementary or junior high school years. Recently, the focus on reducing young people's exposure to **gateway drugs** (especially tobacco, alcohol, and marijuana) may help slow the move to other addictive drugs. Some people advocate harsher penalties for drug use and drug trafficking, including heavier fines and longer prison terms.

Others support legalizing all drugs and making governmental agencies responsible for drug regulation and control, as is the case with alcohol. Advocates of this position believe that drug-related crime and violence would virtually cease once the demand for illegal products is reduced. Sound arguments can be made on both sides of this issue. What's your opinion?

TALKING POINTS • Two addictive drugs, alcohol and tobacco, can be used legally. How would you explain to a friend why these addictive substances are legal, while others are not?

Key Term

gateway drug
An easily obtainable legal or illegal drug that represents a user's first experience with a mind-altering drug.

Learning from Our Diversity

Athletes Speak out against Drug Use

In the past decade, many public figures have been cautioning youth about the dangers of drug abuse. Politicians, rock stars, and actors have gone public with their antidrug messages. Some of them have admitted to having had drug-abuse problems in their own lives. Their personal accounts have probably influenced some drug abusers to curtail their drug-taking behaviours and seek professional help.

World-class athletes have also taken a public stance against drugs. The message to youth is that it's possible to achieve remarkable athletic success through hard work, personal sacrifice, and determination. The athletes headlining such campaigns come from a variety of sports, so it's likely that their message reaches a wide range of young people.

Can you recall other antidrug messages delivered by famous athletes or their families?

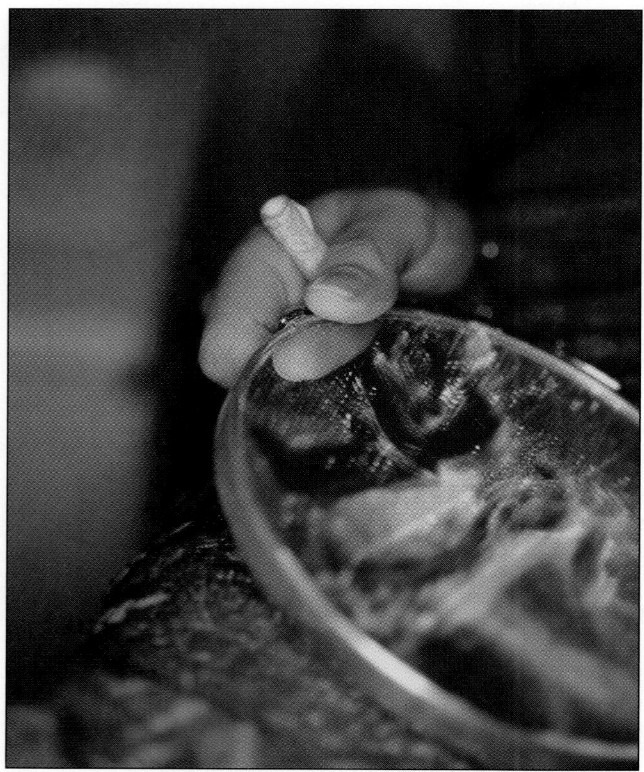

Drug abuse of all types remains a significant problem in the 21st century.

ADDICTIVE BEHAVIOUR

Experts in human behaviour view drug use and abuse as just one of the many forms of addictive behaviour. Such behaviour includes addictions to shopping, eating, gambling, sex, television, video games, and work, as well as to alcohol or other drugs.

TALKING POINTS • How would you tell a friend that her video game playing is becoming an addiction that needs to be controlled?

The Process of Addiction

The process of developing an addiction has been a much-studied topic. Three common aspects of addictive behaviour are exposure, compulsion, and loss of control.

Exposure

An addiction can begin after a person is exposed to a drug (such as alcohol) or a behaviour (such as gambling) that he or she finds pleasurable. Perhaps this drug or behaviour temporarily replaces an unpleasant feeling or sensation. This initial pleasure gradually, or in some cases quickly, becomes a focal point in the person's life.

Compulsion

Increasingly, the person spends more energy, time, and money pursuing the drug use or behaviour. At this point in the addictive process, the person can be said to have a compulsion for the drug or behaviour. Frequently, repeated exposure to the drug or behaviour continues despite negative consequences, such as the gradual loss of family and friends, unpleasant physical symptoms resulting from taking a drug, or problems at work.

During the compulsion phase, a person's normal life often degenerates while she or he searches for increased pleasures from the drug or the behaviour. An addicted person's family life, circle of friends, work, or study patterns become less important than the search for more and better "highs." The development of tolerance and withdrawal are distinct possibilities. (These terms are discussed later in the chapter.)

Why some people develop compulsions and others do not is difficult to pinpoint, but addiction might be influenced by genetic makeup, family dynamics, physiological processes, personality type, peer groups, and available resources for help.

Loss of control

Over time, the search for highs changes to a desire to avoid the effects of withdrawal from the drug or behaviour. Addicted people lose their ability to control their behaviour. Despite overwhelming negative consequences (for example, deterioration of health, alienation of family and friends, or loss of all financial resources), addicted people continue to behave in ways that make their lives worse. The person addicted to alcohol continues to drink heavily, the person addicted to shopping continues to run up heavy debts, and the person addicted to food continues to eat indiscriminately. This behaviour reflects a loss of control over one's life. Frequently, a person has addictions to more than one drug or behaviour.

Intervention and Treatment

The good news for people with addictions is that help is available. Within the last two decades, much attention has been focused on intervention and treatment for addictive behaviour. Many people with addictions can be helped through programs offered by the organizations listed in the Changing for the Better box on p. 139. These programs often include inpatient or outpatient treatment, family counselling, and long-term aftercare counselling.

It is common for people in aftercare treatment for addictive behaviour to belong to a self-help support group, such as Alcoholics Anonymous, Gamblers Anonymous, or Sex Addicts Anonymous. These groups are often listed in the phone book or in the classified section of the newspaper.

Changing *for the Better*

Finding Help for Drug Abuse

I have a friend who may need help for drug and alcohol abuse, and another who is addicted to cigarettes. Where can I find information about addictions and treatment options?

The Lung Association
3 Raymond Street, Suite 300
Ottawa, ON K1R 1A3
Tel: (613) 569-6411
Fax: (613) 569-8860
www.lung.ca/ca

Canadian Centre on Substance Abuse
75 Albert Street, Suite 300
Ottawa, ON K1P 5E7
Tel: (613) 235-4048
Fax: (613) 235-8101
www.ccsa.ca

MADD Canada
2010 Winston Park Drive, Suite 500
Oakville, ON L6H 5R7
Tel: (905) 829-8805
Toll-free: 1-800-665-6233
Fax: (905) 829-8860
www.madd.ca

Centre for Addiction and Mental Health
33 Russell Street
Toronto, ON M5S 2S1
Tel: (416) 535-8501
www.camh.net

Canadian Centre for Ethics in Sport
2197 Riverside Drive, Suite 202
Ottawa, ON K1H 7X3
Tel: (613) 521-3340
Fax: (613) 521-3134
www.cces.ca

Non-Smokers' Rights Association
720 Spadina Avenue, Suite 221
Toronto, ON M5S 2T9
Tel: (416) 928-2900
Fax: (416) 928-1860
www.nsra-adnf.ca

Physicians for a Smoke-Free Canada
1226A Wellington Street
Ottawa, ON K1Y 3A1
Tel: (613) 233-4878
Fax: (613) 233-7797
www.smoke-free.ca

DRUG TERMINOLOGY

Before discussing drug behaviour, it's important to become familiar with some basic terminology. Much of this terminology originates from the field of *pharmacology*, or the study of the interaction of chemical agents with living material.

What does the word *drug* mean? Each of us may have different ideas about what a drug is. Although a number of definitions are available, we will consider a drug to be "any substance, natural or artificial, other than food, that by its chemical or physical nature alters structure or function in the living organism."[1] Included in this broad definition is a variety of psychoactive drugs, medicines, and substances that many people do not usually consider to be drugs.

Psychoactive drugs alter the user's feelings, behaviour, perceptions, or moods. This group includes stimulants, depressants, hallucinogens, opiates, and inhalants. (The Changing for the Better box on p. 140 suggests ways to improve your mood without resorting to drug use.) Medicines function to heal unhealthy tissue. They are also used to ease pain, prevent illness, and diagnose health conditions. Although some psychoactive drugs are used for medical reasons, as in the case of tranquilizers and some narcotics, the most commonly prescribed medicines are antibiotics, hormone replacement drugs, sulfa drugs, diuretics, oral contraceptives, and cardiovascular drugs. Legal substances not usually considered to be drugs (but that certainly are drugs) include caffeine, tobacco, alcohol, aspirin, and other over-the-counter (OTC) preparations. These substances are used so commonly in our society that they are rarely perceived as true drugs.

For organizational reasons, this chapter primarily deals with psychoactive drugs. Alcohol is covered in Chapter 8. The effects of tobacco are discussed in Chapter 9. Prescription and OTC drugs and medicines are explored further in Chapter 15. Anabolic steroids, drugs used primarily for increasing muscle growth, are discussed in Chapter 4.

Routes of Administration

Drugs generally enter the body through one of four methods: ingestion, injection, inhalation, and absorption. *Ingestion*, or oral administration, is the entry of drugs through the mouth and into the digestive tract. *Injection* refers to the use of a needle to insert a drug into the body. With *inhalation*, the drug enters the body through the lungs. *Absorption* refers to the administration of a drug through the skin or mucous membranes.

Key Terms

psychoactive drug
Any substance capable of altering feelings, moods, or perceptions.

Changing *for the Better*

Improving Your Mood Without Drugs

It's tempting to reach for a pill when I feel down, but I don't want to get into the habit. What can I do to improve my mood without drugs?

Talk with a trusted friend. Confide your feelings to a close, trusted friend or family member. By opening up to another person, you'll gain insights into how you can get beyond your negative feelings without resorting to drug use.

Get moving. Go for a walk, ride your bike, or swim a few laps. Physical activity is a natural way to enhance your mood. Nearly every college or university provides recreation programs such as aerobics, swimming, dancing, or weight lifting.

Give yourself a break. If you're tired, take a quick power nap. If you're overworked, set aside some personal time—just for yourself. Read, watch TV, surf the Net, or phone an old friend. Decide what you like to do, and then do it. You'll return to your responsibilities with renewed enthusiasm.

Do volunteer work. One way to feel good is to help others. Teach reading to adults, become a Big Brother or Big Sister, work in a soup kitchen, or drive a van for elderly people in your community.

Re-examine your spiritual health. Many people find comfort by making connections to their spiritual life. Through activities such as meditation, spiritual reflection, and renewal of faith, people often gain reassurance and a sense of calmness.

Restructure your daily activities. If you have one hectic day after another but feel as though you're not accomplishing anything, try reorganizing your daily activities. Experiment with new patterns. Plan to get sufficient sleep, eat regular meals, and set aside specific times for work, family activities, and pleasure. Find out what works best for you.

Seek professional guidance. If you've tried these strategies but your mood still isn't improving, consider seeking professional help. This important first step is up to you. Visit your college or university health centre or counselling centre, and talk with people who are trained to help you learn how to become a happier person.

Dependence

Psychoactive drugs have a strong potential for the development of **dependence**. When users take a psychoactive drug, the patterns of nervous system function are altered. If these altered functions provide perceived benefits for the user, the drug use may continue, perhaps at increasingly larger dosages. If persistent use continues, the user can develop a dependence on the drug. Pharmacologists have identified two types of dependences: physical and psychological.

A person can be said to have developed a *physical dependence* when the body cells have become reliant on a drug. Continued use of the drug is then required because body tissues have adapted to its presence.[2] The person's body needs the drug to maintain homeostasis, or dynamic balance. If the drug is not taken or is suddenly withdrawn, the user develops a characteristic **withdrawal illness**. The symptoms of withdrawal reflect the attempt by the body's cells to regain normality without the drug. Withdrawal symptoms are always unpleasant (ranging from mild to severe irritability, depression, nervousness, digestive difficulties, and abdominal pain) and can be life threatening, as in the case of abrupt withdrawal from barbiturates or alcohol. In this chapter the term *addiction* is used interchangeably with physical dependence.

Continued use of most drugs can lead to **tolerance**. Tolerance is an acquired reaction to a drug in which continued intake of the same dose has diminishing effects.[3] The user needs larger doses of the drug to receive previously felt sensations. The continued use of depressants, including alcohol, and opiates can cause users to quickly develop a tolerance to the drug.

For example, fourth-year university students who have engaged in four years of beer drinking usually recognize that their bodies have developed a degree of tolerance to alcohol. Many such students can vividly recall the initial and subsequent sensations they felt after drinking. For example, five beers consumed during a first-year social gathering might well have resulted in inebriation, but if these same students continued to drink beer regularly for four years, five beers would probably fail to produce the response they experienced then. Seven or eight beers might be needed to produce such a response. Clearly, these students have developed a tolerance to alcohol.

TALKING POINTS • Some of your friends have started making a contest of beer drinking. How would you tell them you think this is dangerous without sounding preachy?

Tolerance developed for one drug may carry over to another drug within the same general category. This phenomenon is known as **cross-tolerance**. The heavy abuser of alcohol, for example, might require a larger dose of a preoperative sedative to become relaxed before surgery than the average person would. The tolerance to alcohol "crosses over" to the other depressant drugs.

A person who possesses a strong desire to continue using a particular drug is said to have developed a *psychological dependence*. People who are psychologically dependent on a drug believe that they need to consume the drug to maintain a sense of well-being. (The Exploring Your Spirituality box on this page shows how some people have a strong dependence on drugs for social situations.) They crave the drug for emotional reasons despite having persistent or recurrent physical, social, psychological, or occupational problems caused or worsened by the drug use. Abrupt withdrawal from a drug by such a person would not trigger the full-blown withdrawal illness, although some unpleasant symptoms of withdrawal might be felt. The term *habituation* is often used interchangeably with psychological dependence.

Drugs whose continued use can quickly lead to both physical and psychological dependence are the depressants (barbiturates, tranquilizers, and alcohol), narcotics (the opiates, which are derivatives of the Oriental poppy: heroin, morphine, and codeine), and synthetic narcotics (Demerol and methadone). Drugs whose continued use can lead to various degrees of psychological dependence and occasionally to significant (but not life-threatening) physical dependence in some users are the stimulants (amphetamines, caffeine, and cocaine), hallucinogens

Key Terms

dependence
General term that refers to the need to continue using a drug for psychological and/or physical reasons.

withdrawal illness
Uncomfortable, perhaps toxic response of the body as it attempts to maintain homeostasis in the absence of a drug; also called *abstinence syndrome.*

tolerance
An acquired reaction to a drug; continued intake of the same dose has diminished results.

cross-tolerance
Transfer of tolerance from one drug to another within the same general category.

Exploring Your Spirituality

Making Social Connections without Drugs

According to many college and university drug counsellors, students who undergo drug counselling often say that they started (or continued) to use drugs because they felt inadequate in social situations. These students believed that they were not attractive, talented, wealthy, or socially skilled enough to start and maintain relationships. In a dating situation, the drug allowed them to be more relaxed and less conscious of their perceived shortcomings. Then, if they did something foolish while socializing, they had an instant excuse—the drug made them act inappropriately.

What are some drug-free strategies you can use to enhance your social relationships? Start by finding people and activities that are free of drug use. Contrary to popular opinion, most students do not use illegal drugs. More students than ever are supportive of a drug-free lifestyle. So it shouldn't be difficult to find individuals and groups who will be a good match for you. Be aware of all the people around you. Don't get locked into one group too quickly. Keep your options open.

As you explore your inner self and try to connect with people at a deeper level, also consider these approaches:

Be true to yourself. Most people like someone who is genuine, so try to be the person you know yourself to be. Don't present a false image of yourself to others.

Be a good listener. One sure way to discourage a growing relationship is to talk more than you listen. Show others that you're interested in them by hearing what they have to say. Let the other person be the centre of attention, at least early in the relationship. By listening carefully, you can evaluate the person or group better and see if you're a good fit.

Be open to new people and ideas. It's good to have firm opinions and ideas, but it's also important to be open to new people and ideas. Take the attitude that the next person you meet or the next group you interact with may change your life forever. Don't limit yourself to a particular group of people or friends. Flexibility can be a real asset to your social life.

Be willing to laugh at yourself. Most surveys indicate that people rate humour as an important quality in people they want to date. Try to find humour in everyday situations. Focusing on the lighter side will make things easier for you and the people around you. Most importantly—be willing to laugh at yourself sometimes.

Be prepared for setbacks. One sign of social maturity is to recognize that setbacks can happen. Don't be defeated by them. Sometimes it's best for everyone involved when things don't work out. You'll always have another opportunity. Focus on the attitude that things will get better. Don't give in to the idea that drugs will make up for an unsatisfying social life. Seek professional help if things do not improve after a reasonable time.

(LSD, peyote, mescaline, and marijuana), and inhalants (glues, gases, and petroleum products).

Drug Misuse and Abuse

So far in this chapter we have used the term *use* (or *user*) in association with the taking of psychoactive drugs. At this point, however, it is important to define *use* and to introduce the terms *misuse* and *abuse*.[4] By doing so, we can more accurately describe the ways in which drugs are used.

The term *use* is all-encompassing and describes drug taking in the most general way. For example, Canadians use drugs of many types. The term *use* can also refer more narrowly to misuse and abuse.

The term **misuse** refers to the inappropriate use of legal drugs intended to be used as medications. Misuse may occur when a patient misunderstands the directions for use of a prescription or OTC drug or when a patient shares a prescription with a friend or family member for whom the drug was not prescribed. Misuse also occurs when a patient takes the prescription or OTC drug for a purpose or condition other than that for which it was intended or at a dosage other than that recommended.

The term **abuse** applies to any use of an illegal drug or any use of a legal drug when it is detrimental to health and well-being. The costs of drug abuse to the individual are extensive and include absenteeism and underachievement, loss of job, marital instability, loss of self-esteem, serious illnesses, and even death. The Changing for the Better box on p. 143 suggests strategies for coping with family and work stress that can keep you in control of your life and away from drug abuse.

EFFECTS OF DRUGS ON THE CENTRAL NERVOUS SYSTEM

To better understand the disruption caused by the actions of psychoactive drugs, a general knowledge of the normal functioning of the nervous system's basic unit, the **neuron**, is required.

First, stimuli from the internal or external environment are received by the appropriate sensory receptor, perhaps an organ such as an eye or an ear. Once sensed, these stimuli are converted into electrical impulses. These impulses are then directed along the neuron's **dendrite**, through the cell body, and along the **axon** toward the *synaptic junction* near an adjacent neuron. On arrival at the **synapse**, the electrical impulses stimulate the production and release of chemical messengers called *neurotransmitters*.[5] These neurotransmitters transmit the electrical impulses from one neuron to the dendrites of adjoining neurons. Thus neurons function in a coordinated fashion to send information to the brain for interpretation and to relay appropriate response commands outward to the tissues of the body.

The role of neurotransmitters is critically important to the relay of information within the system. A substance that has the ability to alter some aspect of transmitter function has the potential to seriously disrupt the otherwise normally functioning system. Psychoactive drugs are capable of exerting these disruptive influences on the neurotransmitters. Drugs "work" by changing the way neurotransmitters work, often by blocking the production of a neurotransmitter or forcing the continued release of a neurotransmitter (see Figure 7–1).

DRUG CLASSIFICATIONS

Drugs can be categorized according to the nature of their physiological effects. Most psychoactive drugs fall into one of six general categories: stimulants, depressants, hallucinogens, cannabis, narcotics, and inhalants (see Table 7–1).

Stimulants

In general, **stimulants** excite or increase the activity of the central nervous system (CNS). Also called "uppers," stimulants alert the CNS by increasing heart rate, blood pressure, and the rate of brain function. Users feel uplifted and less fatigued. Examples of stimulant drugs include caffeine, amphetamines, and cocaine. Most stimulants produce psychological dependence and tolerance relatively quickly, but they are unlikely to produce significant physical dependence when judged by life-threatening withdrawal symptoms. The important exception is cocaine, which seems to be capable of producing psychological dependence and withdrawal so powerful that continued use of the drug is inevitable in some users.

Caffeine

Caffeine, the tasteless drug found in chocolate, some soft drinks, coffee, tea, some aspirin products, and OTC "stay-awake" pills, is a relatively harmless stimulant when consumed in moderate amounts. Many coffee drinkers believe that they cannot start the day successfully without the benefit of a cup or two of coffee in the morning.

For the average healthy adult, moderate consumption of caffeine is unlikely to pose any serious health threat. However, excessive consumption (equivalent to 10 or more cups of coffee daily) could lead to anxiety, diarrhea, restlessness, delayed onset of sleep or frequent awakening, headache, and heart palpitations. Pregnant and breastfeeding women are advised to consume caffeine sparingly.

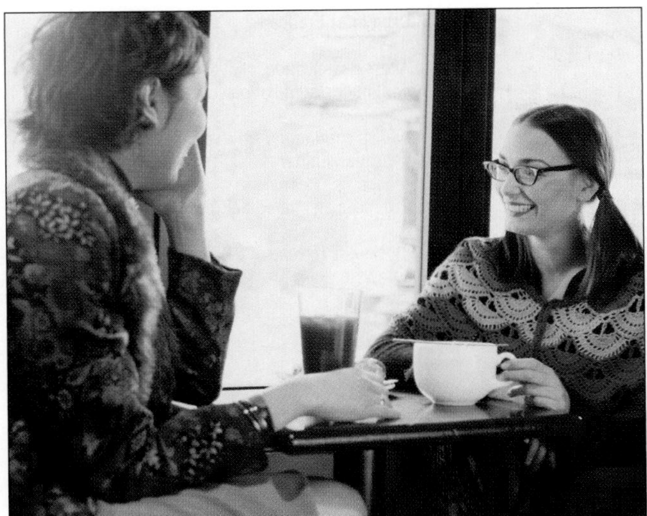

Coffee shops have become popular places to relax, work, or spend time with friends.

Changing *for the Better*

Coping with Family and Work Stress

Sometimes the pressures of being a student, a family member, a parent, and an employee are too much, and I wonder how I'll get through the day. How can I stay healthy and drug-free?

- *Keep the lines of communication open.* Work to communicate effectively with your friends, family members, and employers.
- *Recognize that trying to escape through drug use only makes situations worse.* Realize that using drugs in stressful situations only masks the underlying problems you face.
- *Discuss your concerns with a trusted friend.* Sometimes the person who knows you and your situation best can offer helpful guidance and support during difficult times.
- *Remember that you are a role model to your children.* Because young children look to their parents for guidance, your ability to cope without drugs during stressful times will send an important message to your children.
- *Seek professional help as soon as possible.* Many agencies and support groups are ready to help people who are having personal difficulties with family or work situations. Most large employers have Employee Assistance Programs that can be valuable resources. A campus counselling centre or a local mental health association is another good source of assistance. It's up to you, though, to make the decision to seek these services. Don't hesitate to help yourself.

Amphetamines

Amphetamines produce increased activity and mood elevation in almost all users. Amphetamines include several closely related compounds: amphetamine, dextroamphetamine, and methamphetamine. These compounds do not have any natural sources and are completely manufactured in the laboratory. Medical use of amphetamines is limited primarily to the treatment of obesity, **narcolepsy**, and **attention deficit hyperactivity disorder** (ADHD).

Amphetamines can be ingested, injected, or snorted (inhaled). At low to moderate doses, amphetamines elevate mood and increase alertness and feelings of energy by stimulating receptor sites for two naturally occurring neurotransmitters. They also slow the activity of the stomach and intestine and decrease hunger. In the 1960s

Key Terms

misuse
Inappropriate use of legal drugs intended to be medications.

abuse
Any use of a legal or illegal drug in a way that is detrimental to health.

neuron (NOOR on)
A nerve cell.

dendrite (DEN drite)
The portion of a neuron that receives electrical stimuli from adjacent neurons; neurons typically have several such branches or extensions.

axon
The portion of a neuron that conducts electrical impulses to the dendrites of adjacent neurons; neurons typically have one axon.

synapse (sinn APS)
The location at which an electrical impulse from one neuron is transmitted to an adjacent neuron; also referred to as a *synaptic junction.*

stimulants
Psychoactive drugs that stimulate the function of the central nervous system.

narcolepsy (nar co LEP see)
A sleep disorder in which a person has a recurrent, overwhelming, and uncontrollable desire to sleep.

attention deficit hyperactivity disorder (ADHD)
Above-normal rate of physical movement; often accompanied by an inability to concentrate well on a specified task; also called *hyperactivity.*

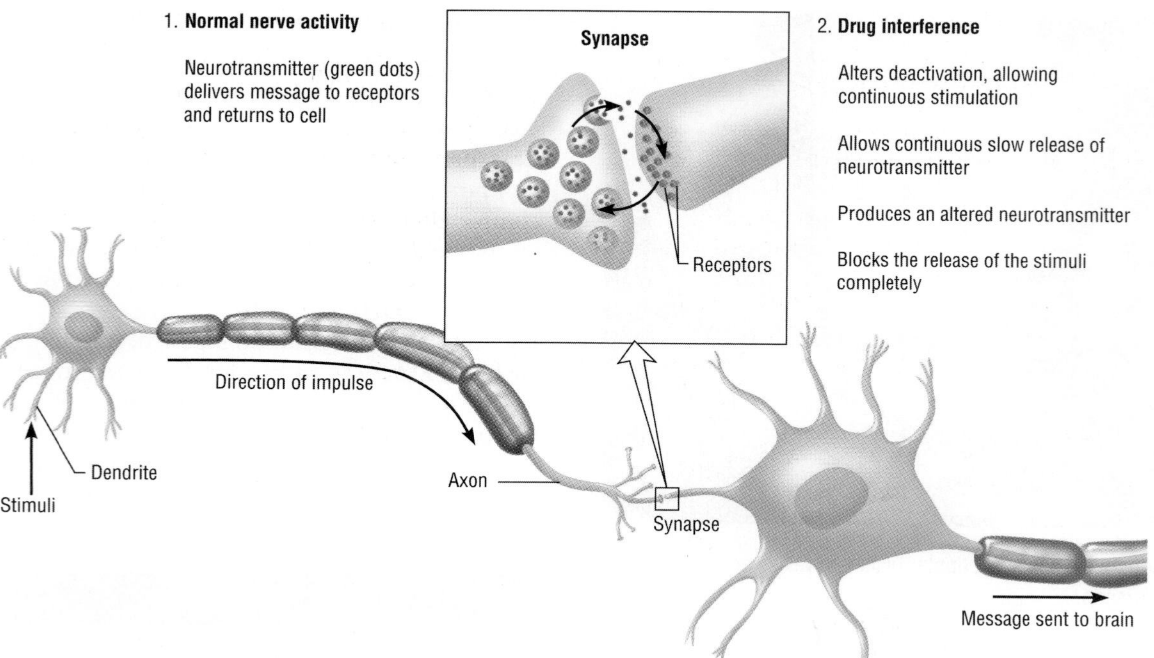

Figure 7–1 This illustration depicts the disruption caused by the action of psychoactive drugs on the central nervous system. Neurotransmitters are chemical messengers that transfer electrical impulses across the synapses between nerve cells. Psychoactive drugs interrupt this process, thus disrupting the coordinating functioning of the nervous system.

Health on the Web

Behaviour Change Activities

Test Your Substance Abuse Savvy

How much do you know about the effects of various kinds of substance abuse? Find out by going to **www.oasas.state.ny.us/pio/prev-qz3.htm** and taking the quiz you'll find there. Did you learn anything that surprised you?

Cocaine: Are You at Risk?

First-time cocaine users usually rave about the incredible thrill of their first "hit." As with many other drugs, however, the more one uses cocaine, the more is needed to reach the same level of euphoria achieved with the previous dose. Whether you've ever used this highly addictive substance, considered trying it, or never given it a thought, you'll gain some valuable insights by visiting the Cocaine Anonymous Web site at **www.ca.org** and completing the Self-Test for Cocaine Addiction.

Intervention—Helping Someone You Love

Do you believe someone close to you—friend, relative, roommate—has a substance abuse problem? If so, you should know that there's a caring, nonjudgmental way to confront that person and encourage him or her to get help. It's called intervention, and it involves following some very specific steps. To find out more about interventions, go to **www.intervention.net** and click on the pages under About Interventions. Did you find this information helpful? In what ways?

and 1970s, in fact, amphetamines were commonly prescribed for dieters. Later, when it was discovered that the appetite-suppression effect of amphetamines lasted only a few weeks, most physicians stopped prescribing them. At high doses, amphetamines can increase heart rate and blood pressure to dangerous levels. As amphetamines are eliminated from the body, the user becomes tired.

When chronically abused, amphetamines produce rapid tolerance and strong psychological dependence. Other effects of chronic use include impotence and episodes of psychosis. When use is discontinued, periods of depression may develop.

Today the abuse of amphetamines is a more pressing concern than it has been in the recent past. Underlying this sharp increase in abuse is methamphetamine. Known by a variety of names and forms, including "crystal meth," "crank," "ice," "crystal," "meth," "speed," and "zip," methamphetamine is produced in illegal home laboratories.

Table 7–1 Psychoactive Drug Categories

Drugs	Trade or Common Names	Medicinal Uses	Possible Effects
Stimulants			
Cocaine	Coke, crack, gin, girlfriend, girl, double bubble, California cornflakes, caballo, bouncing powder, flake, snow	Local anesthetic	Increased alertness, excitation, euphoria, increased pulse rate and blood pressure, insomnia, loss of appetite
Amphetamines	Biphetamine, Delcobese, Desoxyn, Dexedrine, mediatric, methamphetamine (ice), black Mollies, aimies, amps, bam, beans, benz	Hyperactivity, narcolepsy, weight control	
Phendimetrazine	Prelu-2		
Methylphenidate	Ritalin, Methidate		
Other stimulants	Adipex, Bacarate, Cylert, Didrex, Ionamin, Plegine, PreSate, Sanorex, Tenuate, ephedra		
Depressants			
Chloral hydrate	Noctec, Somnos	Hypnotic	Slurred speech, disorientation, drunken behaviour without odour of alcohol
Barbiturates	Amobarbital, Butisol, phenobarbital, phenoxbarbital, secobarbital, Tuinal, blockbusters, black bombers	Anesthetic, anticonvulsant, sedative, hypnotic	
Glutethimide	Doriden	Sedative, hypnotic	
Methaqualone	Optimil, Parest, Quaalude, Somnafec, Sopor	Sedative, hypnotic	
Benzodiazepines	Ativan, Azene, Clonopin, Dalmane, diazepam, Librium, Serax, Tranxene, Valium, Verstran	Antianxiety, anticonvulsant, sedative, hypnotic	
Gammahydroxybutyrate	GHB, liquid ecstasy, easy lay	None	Seizures, vomiting, coma
Other depressants	Equanil, Miltown, Noludar, Placidyl, Valmid	Antianxiety, sedative	
Hallucinogens			
LSD	Acid, microdot, brown dot, cap, California sunshine, brown bomber	None	Delusions and hallucinations, poor perception of time and distance
Mescaline and peyote	Mesc, buttons, cactus, chief	None	
Amphetamine variants (designer drugs)	2,5-DMA, DOM, DOP, MDA, MDMA, PMA, STP, TMA, clarity, chocolate chips, booty juice	None	
Phencyclidine	Angel dust, hog, PCP, AD, boat, black whack, amoeba, angel hair, angel smoke	Veterinary anesthetic	
Phencyclidine analogs	PCE, PCPy, TCP	None	Euphoria, relaxed inhibitions, increased appetite, disorientation
Other hallucinogens	Bufotenin, DMT, DET, ibogaine, psilocybin, psilocyn	None	

continued

Crystal Meth. Crystal meth, or ice, is among the most recent and dangerous forms of methamphetamine. Crystal meth is a very pure form of methamphetamine that looks like rock candy. When smoked, the effects are felt in about seven seconds as a wave of intense physical and psychological exhilaration. This effect lasts for several hours (much longer than the effects of crack) until the user becomes physically exhausted. Chronic use leads to nutritional difficulties, weight loss, reduced resistance to infection, and damage to the liver, lungs, and kidneys. Psychological dependence is quickly established. Withdrawal causes acute depression and fatigue but not significant physical discomfort.

Table 7–1 Psychoactive Drug Categories

Drugs	Trade or Common Names	Medicinal Uses	Possible Effects
Cannabis			
Marijuana	Acapulco gold, black Bart, black mote, blue sage, bobo, butterflowers, cannabis-T, cess, cheeba, grass, pot, sinsemilla, Thai sticks, weed	Under investigation	Euphoria, relaxed inhibitions, increased appetite, disoriented behaviour
Tetrahydrocannabinol	THC	Under investigation	
Hashish	Hash	None	
Hashish oil	Hash oil	None	
Narcotics			
Opium	Dover's powder, paregoric, Parapectolin, cruz, Chinese tobacco, China	Analgesic, antidiarrheal	Euphoria, drowsiness, respiratory depression, contricted pupils, nausea
Morphine	Morphine, Pectoal syrup, emsel, first line	Analgesic, antitussive	
Codeine	Codeine, Empirin compound with codeine, Robitussin A-C	Analgesic, antitussive	
Heroin	Diacetylmorphine, horse, smack, courage pills, dead on arrival (DOA)	Under investigation	
Hydromorphone	Dilaudid	Analgesic	Intoxication, excitation, disorientation, aggression, hallucination
Meperidine (pethidine)	Demerol, Pethadol	Analgesic	
Methadone	Dolophine, Methadone, Methadose	Analgesic, heroin substitute	
Other narcotics			
Inhalants	Darvon, Dromoran, Fentanyl, LAAM, Leitine, Levo-Dromoran, Percodan, Tussionex, Talwin, Lomotil, Oxyconclone	Analgesic, antidiarrheal, antitussive	
Anesthetic gases	Aerosols, petroleum products, solvents	Surgical anesthetic	
Vasodilators (amyl nitrite, butyl nitrite)	Aerosols, petroleum products, solvents	None	Intoxication, excitation, disorientation, aggression, hallucination, variable effects

Note: Since 1997, illicit drugs in Canada have come under Bill C-38, the Controlled Drugs and Substances Act.

Ephedra. Health professionals are warning people about the dangers of using any over-the-counter herbal supplement containing ephedra. Also known as *ma huang*, ephedra is an amphetamine-like drug that can be especially dangerous for people with hypertension or other cardiovascular disease. Currently, ephedra is used in many over-the-counter decongestants and asthma drugs. However, in these products, warning labels indicate possible harmful side effects and drug interactions. In herbal products that contain ephedra, some of which are promoted as weight-control aids, these warnings are not required.[6]

Ritalin. One prescription stimulant drug that has surged in popularity in recent years is Ritalin. This drug is typically prescribed to children and adolescents to help them focus attention if they are hyperactive or have difficulty concentrating. Some abusers use MPH for its stimulant effects: alertness, increased focus, euphoria, and appetite suppressant properties.

Ritalin is also known as "vitamin R," "R-ball," and the "smart drug." It costs between 50 cents and $5 per pill.

Tablets are taken orally, crushed into a powder and snorted, or dissolved in water and injected.

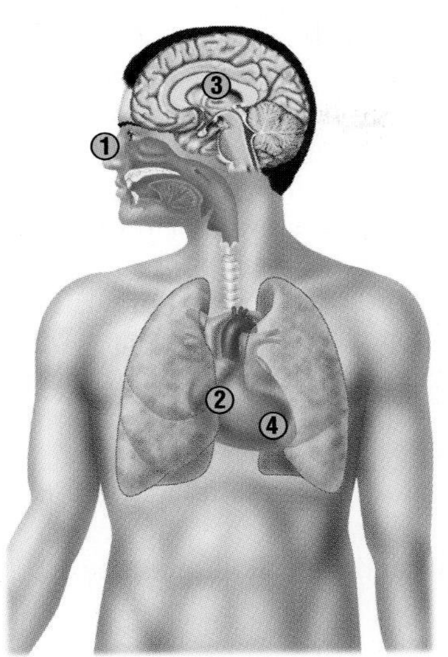

1. **The nose:** as cocaine is snorted, nasal vessels immediately constrict and prohibit about 40% of the drug from entering the body. The remaining 60% enters the bloodstream.

2. **The heart:** electrical impulses that regulate rhythmic pumping are impaired. Beating becomes irregular (arrhythmia). The heart can no longer supply itself with enough oxygenated blood.

3. **The brain:** dopamine and norepinephrine are released into the brain, producing a feeling of euphoria and confidence. Electrical signals to the heart are distorted, heart rate and pulse increase. A seizure may occur, causing coma and breathing stoppage.

4. **The heart:** blood circulation is out of control. The heart may simply flutter and stop, or it can be pumping so little oxygenated blood to the brain that the brain dies and the heart stops beating.

Figure 7–2 Cocaine's effects on the body.

Complications from injection are common since the fillers in MPH are not water soluble and can block small blood vessels, causing damage to the lungs and retina.

Side effects of Ritalin include

- Inability to fall or stay asleep
- Nervousness
- Loss of appetite
- Headache
- Increased blood pressure
- Increased heart rate
- Abdominal pain
- Abnormal heartbeat
- Abnormal muscular movements
- Chest pain
- Dizziness
- Seizures
- Psychosis
- Stroke[7]

Cocaine

Cocaine, perhaps the strongest of the stimulant drugs, has received much media attention. It is the primary psychoactive substance found in the leaves of the South American coca plant. The effects of cocaine last only briefly—from 5 to 30 minutes (Figure 7–2). Regardless of the form in which it is consumed, cocaine produces an immediate, near-orgasmic "rush," or feeling of exhilaration. This euphoria is quickly followed by a period of marked depression. Used only occasionally as a topical anesthetic, cocaine is usually inhaled (snorted), injected, or smoked (as *freebase* or *crack*). There is overwhelming scientific evidence that users quickly develop a strong psychological dependence to cocaine. There is considerable evidence that physical dependence also rapidly develops. However, physical dependence on cocaine does not lead to death upon withdrawal.

Freebasing. Freebasing and the use of crack cocaine are the most recent techniques for maximizing the psychoactive effects of the drug. Freebasing first requires that the common form of powdered cocaine (cocaine hydrochloride) be chemically altered (alkalized). This altered form is then dissolved in a solvent, such as ether or benzene. This liquid solution is heated to evaporate the solvent. The heating process leaves the freebase cocaine in a powder form that can then be smoked, often through a water pipe. Because of the large surface area of the lungs, smoking cocaine facilitates fast absorption into the bloodstream.

One danger of freebasing cocaine is the risk related to the solvents used. Ether is a highly volatile solvent capable of exploding and causing serious burns. Benzene is a known carcinogen associated with the development of leukemia. Clearly, neither solvent can be used without increasing the level of risk normally associated with cocaine use. This method of making smokeable cocaine led to a new epidemic of cocaine use, smoking crack.

Crack. In contrast to freebase cocaine, crack is made by combining cocaine hydrochloride with common baking soda. When this pastelike mixture is allowed to dry, a small rocklike crystalline material remains. This crack is heated in the bowl of a small pipe, and the vapours are inhaled into the lungs. Some crack users spend hundreds of dollars a day to maintain their habit.

The effect of crack is almost instantaneous. Within 10 seconds after inhalation, cocaine reaches the CNS and

Intravenous injection of cocaine results in an almost immediate high for the user.

influences the action of several neurotransmitters at specific sites in the brain. As with the use of other forms of cocaine, convulsions, seizures, respiratory distress, and cardiac failure have been reported with this sudden, extensive stimulation of the nervous system.

Within about six minutes, the stimulating effect of crack becomes completely expended, and users frequently become depressed. Dependence develops within a few weeks, since users consume more crack in response to the short duration of stimulation and rapid onset of depression.

Intravenous administration has been the preferred route for cocaine users who are also regular users of heroin and other injectable drugs. Intravenous injection results in an almost immediate high, which lasts about 10 minutes. A speedball is the injectable mixture of heroin and cocaine (or methamphetamine).[8]

Depressants

Depressants (or sedatives) sedate the user, slowing CNS function. Drugs included in this category are alcohol (see Chapter 8), barbiturates, and tranquilizers. Depressants produce tolerance in abusers, as well as strong psychological and physical dependence.

Barbiturates

Barbiturates are the so-called sleeping compounds that function by enhancing the effect of inhibitory neurotransmitters. They depress the CNS to the point where the user drops off to sleep or, as is the case with surgical anesthetics, the patient becomes anesthetized. Medically, barbiturates are used in widely varied dosages as anesthetics and for treatment of anxiety, insomnia, and epilepsy.[9] Regular use of a barbiturate quickly produces tolerance—eventually such a high dose is required that the user still feels the effects of the drug throughout the next morning. Some abusers then begin to alternate barbiturates with stimulants, producing a vicious cycle of dependence. Other misusers combine alcohol and barbiturates or tranquilizers, inadvertently producing toxic or even lethal results. Abrupt withdrawal from barbiturate use frequently produces a withdrawal syndrome that can involve seizures, delusions, hallucinations, and even death.

Methaqualone (Quaalude, "ludes," Sopor) was developed as a sedative that would not have the dependence properties of other barbiturates. Although this did not happen, Quaaludes were occasionally prescribed for anxious patients. Today, compounds resembling Quaaludes are manufactured in home laboratories and sold illegally so that they can be combined with small amounts of alcohol for an inexpensive, drunklike effect.

Tranquilizers

Tranquilizers are depressants that are intended to reduce anxiety and to relax people who are having problems managing stress. They are not specifically designed to produce sleep but rather to help people cope during their waking hours. Such tranquilizers are termed *minor tranquilizers*, of which diazepam (Valium) and chlordiazepoxide (Librium) may be the most commonly prescribed examples. Unfortunately, some people become addicted to these and other prescription drugs (see the Focus On article on prescription drug abuse, on p. 160).

Some tranquilizers are further designed to control hospitalized psychotic patients who may be suicidal or who are potential threats to others. These *major tranquilizers* subdue people physically but permit them to remain conscious. Their use is generally limited to institutional settings. All tranquilizers can produce physical and psychological dependence and tolerance. For more information on tranquilizers that are being used to subdue women for the purposes of involuntary sex, see the Star Box on p. 149.

Hallucinogens

As the name suggests, hallucinogenic drugs produce hallucinations—perceived distortions of reality. Also known as *psychedelic* drugs or *phantasticants*, **hallucinogens** reached their height of popularity during the 1960s. At that time, young people were encouraged to use hallucinogenic drugs to "expand the mind," "reach an altered state," or "discover reality." Not all of the reality distortions, or "trips," were pleasant. Many users reported "bummers," or trips during which they perceived negative, frightening distortions.

Hallucinogenic drugs include laboratory-produced lysergic acid diethylamide (LSD), mescaline (from the peyote cactus plant), and psilocybin (from a particular genus of mushroom). Consumption of hallucinogens

Facts on Rohypnol, the "Date Rape Drug"

Reports from the United States indicate serious concern regarding the drug *flunitrazepam*, more commonly known by its trade name, Rohypnol. Its use is increasing on campuses in Canada; the escalation of its popularity elsewhere in North America, as well as in Europe and Asia, serves as a warning.

Some facts on this substance ...

What Is Rohypnol?

- A benzodiazepine, or sedative, with approximately 10 times the potency of diazepam (Valium)
- Street names: roofies, roachies, LaRoche, forget pill, whities, ropes, pappas, ro-shays, robinal
- The tablets manufactured in Mexico (the source for most of the U.S. supply) are round, white, and slightly smaller than an aspirin. The manufacturer's markings are similar to those found on other pills, including Rivotril and Valium.

Is It Legal?

- Rohypnol cannot be prescribed or sold legally in Canada; however, it can be brought into the country in limited amounts if prescribed by a foreign physician. It cannot be prescribed, sold, or legally imported into the United States (importation was banned in March 1996).
- In March 1995, this drug became the first benzodiazepine to be moved to Schedule III* by the World Health Organization, requiring more thorough record keeping on its distribution.

Why the Concern?

- The first reports of Rohypnol abuse in the United States surfaced in 1993 in southern Florida (Proceedings of the Community Epidemiology Workgroup, National Institute on Drug Abuse, June 1993); since then cases have been reported to the Drug Enforcement Agency (DEA) in 32 states and Puerto Rico.
- Anecdotal reports indicate Rohypnol use is growing among high school students in the South, where it is seen as a cheap high. Continued use can result in addiction.
- Adverse effects can include loss of memory, impaired judgment, dizziness, and prolonged periods of blackout. Although a sedative, Rohypnol can induce aggressive behaviour.
- This drug has been associated with date rape in cases in which it was added to a woman's drink without her knowledge, for the purpose of reducing resistance. It is odourless, colourless, and tasteless when added to either alcoholic or nonalcoholic beverages.
- Use is also reported by poly-drug users, among whom Rohypnol is used as a secondary drug.

Symptoms

- Effects felt within 20 to 30 minutes of ingestion, with the strongest effects felt within one to two hours
- Effects are dose-related
- Impairment of judgment
- Potential loss of motor control, i.e., staggering gait
- Amnesia, or loss of memory
- Drowsiness, unconsciousness if large dose used

What Is Being Done?

- Hoffman LaRoche** has developed a new formulation of the drug that causes drinks to change colour and to appear murky when Rohypnol is present. The new drug still needs to be approved for use by all countries.

GHB ("g," "liquid ecstasy") and ketamine ("K," "Special K," "Cat") are additional depressants that are being used as date rape drugs. These drugs should serve as a reminder to all partygoers to keep an extremely careful watch over any drink in their possession.

* Schedule III of the Controlled Drugs and Substances Act, 1996, lists by name the amphetamines controlled by the act. For a detailed list of substances covered by Schedule III, go to **http://laws.justice.gc.ca/en/C-38.8**.

** An international pharmaceutical company.

TALKING POINTS • How can you protect yourself and your friends from becoming victims of Rohypnol and date rape?

seems to produce not physical dependence but mild levels of psychological dependence. The development of tolerance is questionable. *Synesthesia*, a sensation in which users report hearing a colour, smelling music, or touching a taste, is sometimes produced with hallucinogen use.

The long-term effects of hallucinogenic drug use are not fully understood. Questions about genetic abnormalities in offspring, fertility, sex drive and performance, and the development of personality disorders

Key Term

hallucinogens
Psychoactive drugs capable of producing hallucinations (distortions of reality).

have not been fully answered. One phenomenon that has been identified and documented is the development of *flashbacks*—the unpredictable return to a psychedelic trip that occurred months or even years earlier. Flashbacks are thought to result from the accumulation of a drug within body cells.

LSD

The most well-known hallucinogen is lysergic acid diethylamide. LSD ("acid") is a drug that helped define the counterculture movement of the 1960s. During the 1970s and the 1980s, this drug lost considerable popularity. However, LSD is making a comeback, with some studies showing that about 1 in 10 high school students and 1 in 20 post-secondary students in the United States have experimented with LSD. Fear of cocaine and other powerful drugs, boredom, low cost, and an attempt to revisit the culture of the 1960s are thought to have increased LSD's attractiveness to today's young people.

LSD is manufactured in home laboratories and frequently distributed in blotter paper decorated with cartoon characters. Users place the paper on their tongue or chew the paper to ingest the drug. LSD can produce a psychedelic (mind-viewing) effect that includes altered perception of shapes, images, time, sound, and body form. Synesthesia is common to LSD users. Ingested in doses known as "hits," LSD produces a six- to nine-hour experience.

Although the hits today are about half as powerful as those in the 1960s, users still tend to develop high tolerance to LSD. Physical dependence does not occur. Not all LSD trips are pleasant. Hallucinations produced from LSD can be frightening and dangerous. Users can injure or kill themselves accidentally during a bad trip. Dangerous side effects include panic attacks, flashbacks, and occasional prolonged psychosis.

Designer drugs

In recent years, chemists who produce many of the illicit drugs in home laboratories have designed versions of drugs listed in the **Controlled Drugs and Substances Act 1996, c. 19**. Designer drugs are said to produce effects similar to their controlled drug counterparts.

People who use designer drugs do so at great risk because the manufacturing of these drugs is unregulated. The neurophysiological effect of these homemade drugs can be quite dangerous. So far, a synthetic heroin product (MPPP) and several amphetamine derivatives with hallucinogenic properties have been designed for the unwary drug consumer.

DOM (STP), MDA (the "love drug"), and "ecstasy" ("MDMA" or "XTC") are examples of amphetamine-derivative, hallucinogenic designer drugs. These drugs produce mild LSD-like hallucinogenic experiences, positive feelings, and enhanced alertness. They also have a number of potentially dangerous effects. Experts are particularly concerned that ecstasy can produce strong psychological dependence and can deplete serotonin, an important excitatory neurotransmitter associated with a state of alertness. Permanent brain damage is possible.

Rolling a joint. Smoking a joint is one method of ingesting marijuana.

Phencyclidine

Phencyclidine (PCP, "angel dust") has been classified variously as a hallucinogen, a stimulant, a depressant, and an anesthetic. PCP was studied for years during the 1950s and 1960s and was found to be an unsuitable animal and human anesthetic. PCP is an extremely unpredictable drug. Easily manufactured in home laboratories in tablet or powder form, PCP can be injected, inhaled, taken orally, or smoked. The effects vary. Some users report mild euphoria, although most report bizarre perceptions, paranoid feelings, and aggressive behaviour. PCP overdose may cause convulsions, cardiovascular collapse, and damage to the brain's respiratory centre.

In a number of cases the aggressive behaviour caused by PCP has led users to commit brutal crimes against both friends and innocent strangers. PCP accumulates in cells and may stimulate bizarre behaviour months after initial use.

Cannabis

Cannabis (marijuana) has been labelled a mild hallucinogen for a number of years. However, most experts now consider it to be a drug category in itself. Marijuana produces mild effects like those of stimulants and depressants. The implication of marijuana in a large number of traffic fatalities makes this drug one whose consumption should be carefully considered. Marijuana is a wild plant (*Cannabis sativa*) whose fibres were once used in the manufacture of hemp rope. When the leafy material and small stems are dried and crushed, users can smoke the

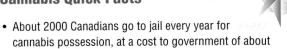

Cannabis Quick Facts[11]

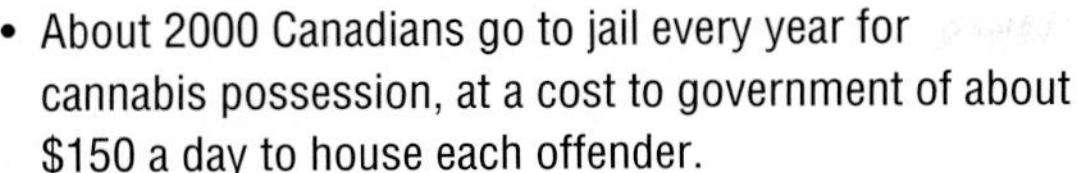

- About 2000 Canadians go to jail every year for cannabis possession, at a cost to government of about $150 a day to house each offender.
- In a Toronto study, 92% of those found guilty of cannabis possession were still using the drug a year later.
- Less than 1% of cannabis users are detected by law enforcement agencies in Canada every year.
- In 2000, the prevalence of past-year cannabis use among Toronto adults was 14%.
- The 2001 school survey found that cannabis use among students remains steady at 23%.
- High levels of marijuana use raise concerns with respect to driving under the influence of this drug.
- Frequency of cannabis use has increased across the country in the past decade.
- Cannabis is the most widely used illicit drug in Canada.
- Despite Canadian governments' recent acceptance of the use of marijuana to treat certain medical conditions under highly controlled circumstances, marijuana remains an illegal drug governed by provisions of the Canadian Controlled Drug and Substances Act, Schedule II.
- The *Controlled Drugs and Substance Act* (CDSA) provides that a person charged with simple possession of 30 g or less of cannabis or 1 g or less of cannabis resin may be prosecuted summarily to a maximum term of six months' imprisonment, a maximum fine of $1 000, or both. The CDSA applies to both adults and youth.

The Marihuana Medical Access Regulations, governing possession and production of cannabis for medical purposes, came into force. The program administers the Regulations including a clear decision-making framework whereby authorizations to possess and licences to cultivate marijuana may be approved.

TALKING POINTS • How does legalization of cannabis possession differ from decriminalization?

mixture in rolled cigarettes ("joints"), cigars ("blunts"), or pipes. The resins collected from scraping the flowering tops of the plant yield a marijuana product called *hashish*, or *hash*, commonly smoked in a pipe.

The potency of marijuana's hallucinogenic effect is determined by the percentage of the active ingredient tetrahydrocannabinol (THC) present in the product. Based on the analysis of samples from drug seizures and street buys, the concentration of THC averages about 3.5% for marijuana, 7% to 9% for higher-quality marijuana (sinsemilla), 8% to 14% for hashish, and as high as 50% for hash oil.

THC is a fat-soluble substance and thus is absorbed and retained in fat tissues within the body. Before being excreted, THC can remain in the body for up to a month. With the sophistication of today's drug tests, trace **metabolites** of THC can be detected for up to 30 days after consumption in the urine of chronic users of high doses of marijuana.[10] It is possible that the THC that comes from passive inhalation of high doses (for example, during an indoor rock concert) can also be detected for a short time after exposure.

Once marijuana is consumed, its effects vary from person to person. Being "high" or "stoned" or "wrecked" means different things to different people. Many people report heightened sensitivity to music, cravings for particular foods, and a relaxed mood. There is consensus that marijuana's behavioural effects include four probabilities: (1) users must learn to recognize what a marijuana high is like, (2) marijuana impairs short-term memory, (3) users overestimate the passage of time, and (4) users lose the ability to maintain attention to a task.

The long-term effects of marijuana use are still being studied. Chronic abuse may lead to an **amotivational syndrome** in some people. The irritating effects of marijuana smoke on lung tissue are more pronounced than those of cigarette smoke, and some of the over 400 chemicals in marijuana are now linked to lung cancer development. In fact, one of the most potent carcinogens, benzopyrene, is found in higher levels in marijuana smoke than in tobacco smoke. Marijuana smokers tend to inhale deeply and hold the smoke in the lungs for longperiods. It is likely that at some point the lungs of chronic marijuana smokers will be damaged.

Long-term marijuana use is also associated with damage to the immune system and to the male and female reproductive systems and with an increase in

Key Term

Controlled Drugs and Substances Act 1996, c. 19
The Canadian legislation that lists the drugs controlled by law in Canada stating that "Except as authorized under the regulations, no person shall possess a substance included in Schedule I, II, or III," and "No person shall seek or obtain a substance included in Schedule I, II, III or IV, or an authorization to obtain a substance included in Schedule I, II, III or IV."

metabolite
A breakdown product of a drug.

amotivational syndrome
Behavioural pattern characterized by lack of interest in productive activities.

HealthQuest Activities
www.mcgrawhill.ca/college/hahn

Drug abuse can occur with illegal drugs or with OTC or prescription drugs. Complete the wellness activity *Drugs: Are You at Risk?* in the Other Drugs Module to raise your awareness of the many decisions you make about drugs. What is your overall risk score? Do you think the score is accurate? Do you think your score reflects campuswide drug use? What are the causes of drug abuse, and what can be done to prevent it?

birth defects in babies born to mothers who smoke marijuana. Chronic marijuana use lowers testosterone levels in men, but the effect of this change is not known. The effect of long-term marijuana use on a variety of types of sexual behaviour is also not fully understood.

Because the drug can distort perceptions and thus perceptual ability (especially when combined with alcohol), its use by automobile drivers clearly jeopardizes the lives of many innocent people.

The only medical uses for marijuana are to relieve the nausea caused by chemotherapy, to improve the appetite in AIDS patients, and to ease the pressure that builds up in the eyes of glaucoma patients. However, a variety of other drugs, many of which are nearly as effective, are also used for these purposes.

Narcotics

The **narcotics** are among the most dependence-producing drugs. Medically, narcotics are used to relieve pain and induce sleep. On the basis of origin, narcotics can be subgrouped into the natural, quasisynthetic, and synthetic narcotics.

Natural narcotics

Naturally occurring substances derived from the Oriental poppy plant include opium (the primary psychoactive substance extracted from the Oriental poppy), morphine (the primary active ingredient in opium), and thebaine (a compound not used as a drug). Morphine and related compounds have medical use as analgesics in the treatment of mild to severe pain.

Quasisynthetic narcotics

Quasisynthetic narcotics are compounds created by chemically altering morphine. These laboratory-produced drugs are intended to be used as analgesics, but their benefits are largely outweighed by a high dependence rate and a great risk of toxicity. The best known of the quasisynthetic narcotics is heroin. Although heroin is a fast-acting and very effective analgesic, it is extremely addictive. Once injected into a vein or "skin-popped" (injected beneath the skin surface), heroin produces dreamlike euphoria and, like all narcotics, strong physical and psychological dependence and tolerance.

As with the use of all other injectable illegal drugs, the practice of sharing needles increases the likelihood of transmission of various communicable diseases, including HIV (see Chapter 11). Abrupt withdrawal from heroin use is rarely fatal, but the discomfort during **cold turkey** withdrawal is reported to be overwhelming. The use of heroin has increased during the last decade. The purity of heroin has improved while the price has dropped. Cocaine abusers may use heroin to "come down" from the high associated with cocaine.

Synthetic narcotics

Meperidine (Demerol) and propoxyphene (Darvon), common postsurgical painkillers, and methadone, the drug prescribed during the rehabilitation of heroin addicts, are *synthetic narcotics*. These opiate-like drugs are manufactured in medical laboratories. They are not natural narcotics or quasisynthetic narcotics because they do not originate from the Oriental poppy plant. Like true narcotics, however, these drugs can rapidly induce physical dependence. One important criticism of methadone rehabilitation programs is that in some cases, they merely shift the addiction from heroin to methadone. Oxycodone is a time-released legal prescription drug used to treat individuals with moderate to severe pain. Classified as a narcotic drug, oxycodone is an addictive controlled substance with an addiction potential similar to morphine.[12]

When crushed and chewed or inhaled through the nose, injected, or swallowed, the oxycodone will be released and absorbed rapidly, producing a heroin-like effect euphoria. For this reason it is often referred to as "hillbilly heroin."

A long-acting tablet marketed under the brand name Oxycontin is formulated to release oxycodone over a long period of time. When oxycodone-based drugs are used as prescribed, dependency is not likely. Misuse and abuse of this drug, similar to other opioids, leads to tolerance and dependence requiring higher and more frequent doses. Health Canada is aware of the increasing concern about the abundance of oxycodone-based prescription drugs in Canada, and in particular Atlantic Canada and is taking steps to address issues associated with abuse of oxycodone-based products.[13]

Inhalants

Inhalants are a class of drugs that includes a variety of volatile (quickly evaporating) compounds that generally produce unpredictable, drunklike effects in users. Users of inhalants may also have some delusions and hallucinations. Some users may become quite aggressive. Drugs in this category include anesthetic gases (chloroform, nitrous oxide, and ether), vasodilators (amyl nitrite and butyl nitrite), petroleum products and commercial solvents (gasoline, kerosene, plastic cement, glue, typewriter correction fluid, paint, and paint thinner), and certain aerosols (found in some propelled spray products, fertilizers, and insecticides).

Most of the danger in using inhalants lies in the damaging, sometimes fatal effects on the respiratory system. Furthermore, users may unknowingly place themselves in dangerous situations because of the drunk-like hallucinogenic effects. Aggressive behaviour may also make users a threat to themselves and others.

Key Terms

narcotics
Opiates; psychoactive drugs derived from the Oriental poppy plant; narcotics relieve pain and induce sleep.

cold turkey
Immediate, total discontinuation of use of a drug; associated withdrawal discomfort.

inhalants
Psychoactive drugs that enter the body through inhalation.

Human Rights Issues of Drug Testing

Everyone in Canada has rights to some degree, and drug testing is no exception. In September 2000 the Ontario Human Rights Commission released a Policy on Drug and Alcohol Testing in the workplace. The points below are from this policy. In effect, drug and alcohol testing is becoming a widespread health and safety tool in drug-free workplaces and fitness-for-duty programs throughout Canada for increasing safety, productivity, and wellness at work.

When considering drug testing in the workplace, the following questions should be considered by employers, where applicable:

1. Is there an objective basis for believing that job performance would be impaired by drug or alcohol dependency? In other words, is there a rational connection between testing and job performance?
2. In respect of a specific employee, is there an objective basis for believing that unscheduled or recurring absences from work, or habitual lateness to work, or inappropriate or erratic behaviour at work are related to alcoholism or drug addiction/dependency? These factors could demonstrate a basis for "for cause" or "post incident" testing, provided there is a reasonable basis for the conclusions drawn.
3. Is there an objective basis to believe that the degree, nature, scope, and probability of risk caused by alcohol or drug abuse or dependency will adversely affect the safety of coworkers or members of the public?

Pre-Employment Testing for Drug and Alcohol Used as Part of an Employment-Related Medical Examination

- Cannot be performed at the screening stages, only after conditional offer of employment has been extended.
- Limited to determining an individual's ability to perform the essential duties of a job.

Employer should notify job applicants of this requirement at the time an offer of employment is made.

On-the-Job Testing

- On-the-job testing should be administered only where a link has been established between impairment and performance of job functions, such as in the case of employees who are in safety-sensitive positions.
- Competent handling of test results.
- Confidentiality of test results.
- Review of results with employees by a Medical Review Officer (Medical Doctor).
- There should be an objective basis for testing—in other words, a basis for believing that job performance would be adversely affected by a drug or alcohol dependency.

"For cause" and "post incident" testing for either alcohol or drugs may be acceptable in specific circumstances. Following accidents or reports of dangerous behaviour, for example, an employer will have a legitimate interest in assessing whether the employee in question had consumed substances that are psychoactive and that may have contributed to the incident. The results of the assessment may provide an explanation of the cause of the accident. Such testing should be conducted only as part of a larger assessment of drug or alcohol abuse.

Further, the Canadian Human Rights Commission Policy on Alcohol and Drug Testing (2002) prohibits discrimination based upon disability and perceived disability.

Employers who randomly test or pre-screen their workers for drug and alcohol may be at risk for breaking the law. The following types of testing are not acceptable under the Commission Policy.

- Pre-employment drug testing
- Pre-employment alcohol testing
- Random drug testing
- Random alcohol testing of employees in non-safety-sensitive positions[14]

COMBINATION DRUG EFFECTS

Drugs taken in various combinations and dosages can alter and perhaps intensify effects.

A **synergistic drug effect** is a dangerous consequence of taking different drugs in the same general category at the same time. The combination exaggerates each individual drug's effects. For example, the combined use of alcohol and tranquilizers produces a synergistic effect greater than the total effect of each of the two drugs taken separately. In this instance a much-amplified, perhaps fatal, sedation will occur. In a simplistic sense, "one plus one equals four or five."

When taken at or near the same time, drug combinations produce a variety of effects. Drug combinations have additive, potentiating, or antagonistic effects. When two or more drugs are taken and the result is merely a combined total effect of each drug, the result is an **additive effect**. The sum of the effects is not exaggerated. In a sense, "one plus one plus one equals three."

When one drug intensifies the action of a second drug, the first drug is said to have a **potentiated effect** on the second drug. One popular drug-taking practice during the 1970s was the consumption of Quaaludes and beer. Quaaludes potentiated the inhibition-releasing, sedative effects of alcohol. This particular drug combination produced an inexpensive but potentially fatal drunklike euphoria in the user.

An **antagonistic effect** is an opposite effect one drug has on another drug. One drug may be able to reduce or offset another drug's influence on the body. Knowledge of this principle has been useful in the medical treatment of certain drug overdoses, as in the use of tranquilizers to relieve the effects of LSD or other hallucinogenic drugs.

DRUG TESTING

Society's response to concern over drug use includes the development and growing use of drug tests. Most of the specimens come from corporations that screen employees for commonly abused drugs. Among these are amphetamines, barbiturates, benzodiazepines (the chemical bases for prescription tranquilizers such as Valium and Librium), cannabinoids (THC, hashish, and marijuana), methaqualone, opiates (heroin, codeine, and morphine), and PCP. With the exception of marijuana, most traces of these drugs are eliminated by the body within a few days after use. However, marijuana can remain detectable for weeks after use.

How accurate are the results of drug testing? At typical cutoff standards, drug tests will likely identify 90% of recent drug users. This means that about 10% of recent users will pass undetected. (These 10% are considered false negatives.) Nonusers whose drug tests indicate drug use (false positives) are quite rare. (Follow-up tests on these false positives would nearly always show negative results.) Human errors are probably more responsible than technical errors for inaccuracies in drug tests.

Recently, scientists have been refining procedures that use hair samples to detect the presence of drugs. These procedures seem to hold much promise, although certain technical obstacles remain. Watch for refinements in hair-sample drug testing in the near future.

Most Fortune 500 companies, the armed forces, various government agencies, and nearly all athletic organizations have already implemented mandatory drug testing. Corporate substance-abuse policies are being developed, with careful attention to legal and ethical issues.

Do you think that the possibility of having to take a drug test would have any effect on college students' use of drugs? For a consideration of some of the human rights issues surrounding drug testing, see the Star Box on page 153.

CAMPUS AND COMMUNITY SUPPORT SERVICES FOR DRUG DEPENDENCE

Students who have drug problems and realize they need help might select assistance based on the services available on campus or in the surrounding community.

One approach to convince drug-dependent people to enter treatment programs is the use of *confrontation*. People who live or work with chemically dependent people are being encouraged to confront them directly about their addiction. Direct confrontation helps chemically dependent people realize the effect their behaviour has on others. Once chemically dependent people realize that others will no longer tolerate their behaviour, the likelihood of their entering treatment programs increases significantly. Although effective, this approach is very stressful for family members and friends, and requires the assistance of professionals in the field of chemical dependence. These professionals can be contacted at a drug treatment centre in your area.

Treatment

Comprehensive drug treatment programs are available in very few college or university health centres. College settings for drug-dependence programs are more commonly found in the university counselling centre. At such a centre the emphasis will probably be not on the medical management of dependence but on the behavioural dimensions of drug abuse. Trained counsellors and psychologists who specialize in chemical dependence counselling will work with students to (1) analyze their particular concerns, (2) establish constructive ways to cope

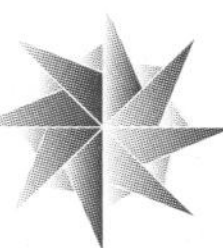

How Much of a Problem Is Drug Use in Canada?

Like alcohol abuse, drug abuse plays a large part in health and social problems in Canada. While the economic costs are not as high as they are with alcohol, drug abuse still takes its toll.

In the late 1990s illicit (illegal) drugs cost the Canadian economy about $1.4 billion per year. This is a small fraction of the total costs of substance abuse. Including tobacco and alcohol, the total cost of substance abuse is about $18.5 billion per year.

The largest economic costs of substance abuse are for

- People missing work because of accidents
- Disease
- People dying
- Direct health care
- Police and other types of law enforcement

Fortunately for most Canadians, drug treatment programs are available under Canada's Health Insurance Plan. As well, drug treatment programs that are administered by college and universities for students, faculty, and staff usually require no fees.

Canada's Strategy

Canada's current strategy on drugs includes alcohol. The long-term goal is to reduce the harm from alcohol and other drugs to individuals, families, and communities. The Government of Canada believes that there are five main ways to do this:

- Reduce the demand for drugs.
- Reduce drug-related death and disease.
- Make substance abuse information, treatment, and prevention better and easier to get.
- Make it harder to find illegal drugs, and harder to make money selling them.
- Reduce the costs of substance abuse to Canadian society.

The *Canadian Addiction Survey (CAS) 2004* has recently been completed to assess how Canadians use alcohol and drugs. The results are available at **www.hc-sc.gc.ca/dhp-mps/substan/alc-can/overview-apercu/index-e.html**.

with stress, and (3) search for alternative ways to achieve new "highs" (see the Personal Assessment on p. 159).

TALKING POINTS • Do you think that confronting a friend about her marijuana use would prompt her to get help?

Medical treatment for the management of drug problems may need to be obtained through the services of a community treatment facility administered by a local health department, community mental health centre, private clinic, or local hospital. Treatment may be on an inpatient or outpatient basis. Medical management might include detoxification, treatment of secondary health complications and nutritional deficiences, and therapeutic counselling for chemical dependence.

Some communities have voluntary health agencies that deliver services and treatment programs for drug-dependent people. Check your telephone book for listings of drug-treatment facilities. Some communities have drug hotlines that offer advice for people with questions about drugs. (See the Changing for the Better box on p. 139 for a list of anti–drug abuse organizations and hotline numbers.)

Key Terms

synergistic drug effect (sin er JIST ick)
Heightened, exaggerated effect produced by the concurrent use of two or more drugs in the same general category.

additive effect
The combined (but not exaggerated) effect produced by the concurrent use of two or more drugs.

potentiated (poe TEN she ay ted) effect
Phenomenon whereby the use of one drug intensifies the effect of a second drug.

antagonistic effect
Effect produced when one drug reduces or offsets the effects of a second drug.

Taking Charge of Your Health

- Assess your knowledge of drug use by completing the Personal Assessment on page 158.
- Calculate the amount of caffeine you consume daily. If you're drinking more than three cups of caffeinated beverages per day, develop a plan to reduce your overall intake.
- Prepare a plan of action to use if someone you know needs professional assistance with a drug problem.
- Identify five activities that can provide you with a drug-free high.
- Analyze your drug use patterns (if any), and assess the likelihood that you might fail a pre-employment drug test.
- Assess your lifestyle for addictive behaviors that do not involve drugs, such as overexercising or watching too much TV. Develop a plan to moderate these activities and achieve more balance in your life.

SUMMARY

- Drug abuse and misuse has a devastating effect on society.
- Society's response to drug abuse has been widely varied and has included education, enforcement, treatment, testing, and the search for drug-free ways to achieve highs.
- Drug use, drug abuse, tolerance, and dependence are important terms to understand.
- A drug affects the CNS by altering neurotransmitter activity on the neuron.
- Drugs can be placed into six categories: stimulants, depressants, hallucinogens, cannabis, narcotics, and inhalants.
- Drugs enter the body through ingestion, injection, inhalation, or absorption.
- Combination drug effects include synergistic, additive, potentiated, and antagonistic effects.
- Drug testing is becoming increasingly common in our society.

REVIEW QUESTIONS

1. How is the term *drug* defined in this chapter? What are psychoactive drugs? How do medicines differ from drugs?
2. Explain what *dependence* means. Identify and explain the two types of dependence.
3. Define the word *tolerance*. What does *cross-tolerance* mean? Give an example of cross-tolerance.
4. Differentiate between drug misuse and drug abuse.
5. Define the four routes of administration. Select one drug for each of the ways drugs enter the body.
6. Describe how neurotransmitters work.
7. List the six general categories of drugs. For each category, give several examples of drugs and explain their effects on the user. What are designer drugs?
8. What is the active ingredient in marijuana? What are its common effects on the user? What are the long-term effects of marijuana use?
9. Explain the terms *synergistic effect*, *additive effect*, *potentiated effect*, and *antagonistic effect*.
10. How accurate is drug testing?

REFERENCES

1. Ray O, Ksir C: *Drugs, society, and human behaviour*, ed 8, 1999, McGraw-Hill.
2. Pinger RR, Payne WA, Hahn DB, Hahn EJ: *Drugs: issues for today*, ed 3, 1998, McGraw-Hill.
3. Ibid.
4. *Drugs, society.*
5. Shier D, Butler J, Lewis R: *Essentials of anatomy and physiology*, ed 6, 1998, McGraw-Hill.
6. Avoid an herbal supplement containing ephedra, *UC Berkeley Wellness Letter*, 16(1):8, 1999.
7. *Cool Nurse: Ritalin abuse*, **www.coolnurse.com/ritalin.htm**
8. *Drugs: Issues.*
9. *Drugs, society.*
10. Ibid.
11. Canadian Centre on Substance Abuse: *Cannabis FAQs*, March 2003, **www.ccsa.ca**
12. Health Canada: *Misuse and abuse of oxycodone-based prescription drugs*, July 2004. **www.hc-sc.gc.ca/ahc-asc/media/nr-cp/2004/2004_oxycodone_e.html**
13. Bonnell K: *Health Canada examining oxycodone prescription abuse on East Coast*, **www.medbroadcast.com**, June 23, 2004.
14. Canadian Human Rights Commission Legislation & Policies **www.chrc-ccdp.ca/legislation_policies/alcohol_drug_testing-en.asp?pm=1**, August 22, 2005.

SUGGESTED READINGS

Breggin PR, Cohen D: *Your drug may be your problem: how and when to stop taking psychiatric drugs,* 1999, Perseus Books.

The authors of this book (an M.D. and a Ph.D.) contend that many people currently using psychiatric drugs, including Prozac and lithium-based medications, might be better off without them. They argue that the side effects of these drugs are dangerous enough, but the drugs also tend to reduce the users' abilities to solve their own difficulties. Much of the book is devoted to showing users how to gradually wean themselves from their medications. This book is controversial, so before starting its recommended program, consult with your physician.

Drummond EH: *Benzo blues: overcoming anxiety without tranquilizers,* 1998, Plume.

Drummond is a physician who believes that too many people are addicted to benzodiazepines ("benzos"), tranquilizers that are frequently prescribed for chronic anxiety. He believes that the problems created by dependence on these tranquilizers can overshadow the original basis for the chronic anxiety. Drummond's approach is to carefully move away from the benzodiazepines and address the core problems. He shows how this can be done successfully.

Marlatt GA: *Harm reduction: pragmatic strategies for managing high-risk behaviours*, 1998, Guilford Press.

This book does an excellent job of discussing harm reduction, the latest approach to treatment of addictions. Instead of focusing on abstinence from high-risk behaviours, harm reduction emphasizes careful management of high-risk activities so that a safe outcome is likely. The author discusses various public health issues, including HIV prevention, in light of this new approach.

West JW: *The Betty Ford Center book of answers: help for those struggling with substance abuse and the people who love them*, New York, 1997, Pocket Books.

This book is written by the former director of the Betty Ford Center, one of the leading alcohol- and drug-treatment centres in the United States. This authoritative source provides answers to many of the most frequently asked questions about treatment and recovery. It offers comprehensive coverage of drug abuse issues for addicts and their families.

Name ______________________ Date __________ Section __________

Personal Assessment

Test Your Drug Awareness

1. What is the most commonly used drug in North America?
   (*a*) Heroin
   (*b*) Cocaine
   (*c*) Alcohol
   (*d*) Marijuana

2. Name the three drugs most commonly used by children.
   (*a*) Alcohol, tobacco, and marijuana
   (*b*) Cocaine, crack, alcohol
   (*c*) Heroin, inhalants, marijuana

3. Which drug is associated with the most teenage deaths?
   (*a*) Heroin
   (*b*) Cocaine
   (*c*) Alcohol
   (*d*) Marijuana

4. By the eighth grade, how many kids have tried at least one inhalant?
   (*a*) One in one hundred
   (*b*) One in fifty
   (*c*) One in twenty-five
   (*d*) One in five
   (*e*) One in two

5. Crack is a particularly dangerous drug because it is
   (*a*) Cheap
   (*b*) Readily available
   (*c*) Highly addictive
   (*d*) All of the above

6. Fumes from which of the following can be inhaled to produce a high?
   (*a*) Spray paint
   (*b*) Model glue
   (*c*) Nail polish remover
   (*d*) Whipped cream canisters
   (*e*) All of the above

7. People who have not used alcohol and other drugs before their 20th birthday:
   (*a*) Have no risk of becoming chemically dependent.
   (*b*) Are less likely to develop a drinking problem or use illicit drugs.
   (*c*) Have an increased risk of becoming chemically dependent.

8. A speedball is a combination of which two drugs?
   (*a*) Cocaine and heroin
   (*b*) PCP and LSD
   (*c*) Valium and alcohol
   (*d*) Amphetamines and barbiturates

9. Methamphetamines are dangerous because use can cause
   (*a*) Anxiety/nervousness/irritability
   (*b*) Paranoia/psychosis
   (*c*) Loss of appetite/malnutrition/anorexia nervosa
   (*d*) Hallucinations
   (*e*) Aggressive behaviour
   (*f*) All of the above

10. How is marijuana harmful?
    (*a*) It hinders the user's short-term memory.
    (*b*) Students may find it hard to study and learn while under the influence of marijuana.
    (*c*) It affects timing and coordination.
    (*d*) All of the above

Source: *A parent's guide to prevention*, U.S. Department of Education.

Answers to Personal Assessment

1. c
2. a
3. c
4. d
5. d
6. e
7. b
8. a
9. f
10. d

Name ______________________________ **Date** ____________

Personal Assessment

Getting a Drug-Free High

Experts agree that drug use provides only short-term, ineffective, and often destructive solutions to problems. We hope that you have found (or will find) innovative, invigorating drug-free experiences that make your life more exciting. Circle the number for each activity that reflects your intention to try that activity. Use the following guide:

1 No intention of trying this activity
2 Intend to try this within two years
3 Intend to try this within six months
4 Already tried this activity
5 Regularly engage in this activity

1. Learn to juggle	1	2	3	4	5
2. Go backpacking	1	2	3	4	5
3. Complete a marathon race	1	2	3	4	5
4. Start a vegetable garden	1	2	3	4	5
5. Ride in a hot air balloon	1	2	3	4	5
6. Snow ski or water ski	1	2	3	4	5
7. Donate blood	1	2	3	4	5
8. Go river rafting	1	2	3	4	5
9. Learn to play a musical instrument	1	2	3	4	5
10. Cycle 100 kilometres	1	2	3	4	5
11. Go skydiving	1	2	3	4	5
12. Go rockclimbing	1	2	3	4	5
13. Play a role in a theatre production	1	2	3	4	5
14. Build a piece of furniture	1	2	3	4	5
15. Solicit funds for a worthy cause	1	2	3	4	5
16. Learn to swim	1	2	3	4	5
17. Overhaul a car engine	1	2	3	4	5
18. Compose a song	1	2	3	4	5
19. Travel to a foreign country	1	2	3	4	5
20. Write the first chapter of a book	1	2	3	4	5

TOTAL POINTS ____________________

Interpretation

61–100 You participate in many challenging experiences.
41–60 You are willing to try some challenging new experiences.
20–40 You take few of the challenging risks described here.

To Carry This Further

Looking at your point total, were you surprised at the degree to which you are aware of alternative activities? What are your top five activities, and can you understand their importance? What activities would you add to this list?

Focus on

PRESCRIPTION DRUG ABUSE

Lucy, a 35-year-old mother of two, seems like a typical suburban homemaker. She attends church regularly, belongs to the PTA, and volunteers at the local women's shelter. Her husband is a well-respected businessman, and her children are honour students at the local high school. Life seems perfect for Lucy and her family, at least on the outside. But Lucy has a secret that few outside her family know about.

Lucy's children and husband regularly come home to a disorderly household, finding Lucy passed out somewhere in the house or on the back porch. Lucy's mood swings are unpredictable. One day she is a loving, devoted wife and mother; the next, she talks rapidly and endlessly to whomever she can get to listen; sometimes, her speech slurs and she seems incoherent. All this usually occurs whenever a stressful or unpleasant situation comes up in her life with which she cannot cope. Lucy's family never knows what to expect from one day to the next. The children have moved in and out of the home to live with their grandparents dozens of times over the past several years, and Lucy's husband has threatened her with divorce. Lucy has been to inpatient detoxification programs three times, only to "fall off the wagon" whenever a stressful event occurs.

You would probably guess that Lucy is an alcoholic or an illegal drug addict; however, Lucy's drugs of choice are all legal and all readily available to her from any one of a number of reputable physicians she visits. She uses a combination of drugs that range from sedatives to tranquilizers to antidepressants. Lucy is a prescription drug addict. Her suppliers are unwitting physicians who have no idea that she is seeing other doctors.

The reported numbers on the abuse of prescription drugs are alarming.[1] It is estimated that up to 50% of all prescriptions are used incorrectly.[2,3]

Prescription drugs fall into the following categories:

- *Opioids.* These drugs are narcotics typically prescribed to relieve acute or chronic pain. Common prescription drugs include Demerol, Darvocet, Vicodin, and drugs with codeine.
- *Stimulants.* These drugs affect the central nervous system and increase mental alertness, decrease fatigue, and produce a sense of well-being. They are usually prescribed for appetite suppression, attention deficit disorder, and narcolepsy. Common prescription drugs include Dexedrine, Ritalin, Fastin, and Cyclert.
- *Sedatives.* These drugs depress the central nervous system and are frequently used to treat anxiety, panic disorder, and insomnia. Some are dispensed for either daytime or nighttime use. Common prescription drugs include Xanax, Valium, Ativan, Dalmane, and Ambien.

Under certain conditions, nearly anybody could abuse a prescription drug, but there are particular groups of people who are at high risk for prescription drug abuse. People with a family history of depression, smokers, and excessive drinkers are more likely to become addicted to prescription drugs, as are those with a history of abusing illegal drugs. Stress from traumatic experiences can also make a person more likely to abuse prescription drugs, and people who are hyperactive, obese, or who suffer from chronic pain are also at risk. Health care professionals are considered to be a high-risk group,[4,5,6] and older people have a greater tendency to abuse prescription drugs.[7]

A patient can become physiologically dependent on a drug, which is considered to be a more manageable condition than addiction. Physiological dependence, involving the body's adaptation to a drug over time, is considered a temporary, benign condition. Physiological dependence is usually treated by gradual reductions in use of the drug, and although there may be withdrawal symptoms during this period, there is not normally a relapse afterward. The gradual reduction in dosage can be handled with medical supervision, and the patient does not normally need to enter a substance abuse program. Addiction involves a continued need to use a drug for psychological effects or mood alteration, and the patient goes to great lengths to obtain the drug even if its effects become harmful. Addiction is considered a chronic, complex problem and is usually handled with specific chemical dependence treatment.[8]

Abuse is often caused or continued because of deliberate deception on the part of the patient, but misuse of a prescription drug can start innocently enough. A patient may be receiving several prescriptions that have the same effect, or a patient may have several doctors prescribing the same medication. Prescription drugs may react with each other and cause effects other than those intended. Sometimes communication problems between patient and physician cause errors in prescription dispensation. The patient may unintentionally use the prescription incorrectly. One of these situations or a combination of factors can start prescription drug abuse.[9] Often a single prescription drug, such as a painkiller or sedative, is enough to start the process of dependence.

Older people are considered at high risk for prescription drug abuse for several reasons. The process of aging or the transition to retirement can leave a person with symptoms of depression or anxiety, and illnesses can also increase as a person gets older. Many people see multiple doctors as they get older and thus may wind up getting several prescriptions for the same drug under different brand names without realizing it. Sometimes physicians give older patients the same dosages as younger patients. However, body functions slow and change with age, and when this occurs, the duration and intensity of drug effects can change as well.[10] Such conditions can increase the risk of drug abuse among the elderly.

If addiction starts, older people may then resort to the same tactics as any prescription drug addict. They may begin to "doctor-hop" (moving from one doctor to the next without informing the doctors) to get multiple prescriptions, or they may go to an emergency room to get a quick fix of a particular drug. Patients may also hoard pills or swap pills with friends to cut costs and ensure availability of their drug of choice. In the United States, it is estimated that two million older adults are at risk of addiction or are addicted to tranquilizers or sleeping pills.[11]

Health care professionals are also at high risk for prescription drug abuse. Physicians are five times more likely than the general population to take sedatives or tranquilizers without another doctor's supervision. The high stress of the job and the availability of drugs are both believed to be contributing factors to abuse among health care professionals. However, studies suggest that those physicians who are psychologically sound had little problem handling the stress of their jobs and generally resisted the temptation of readily available drugs. Those physicians considered to have psychological problems were more likely to be abusers.[12]

Effects of Abuse

As abuse of a drug continues, the tolerance of the body to that drug increases, which can lead to stronger self-dosing. As use increases, the detoxification process can become more difficult. In some cases, people refuse to believe they are addicted, and older people who are isolated from others do not even realize they are hooked.[13] Physicians may inadvertently promote the abuse by failing or refusing to acknowledge the signs of addiction in a patient.

If a person admits he or she has a problem with a drug, the recovery process can begin, but trying to kick the habit without professional help may make things worse. If the person tries to cut back or stop use of the drug, withdrawal symptoms may occur. These symptoms include pain, nausea, sleeplessness, nervousness, irritability, hallucinations, and confusion, and can be quite severe. Sometimes other underlying psychological problems (for example, depression) must also be dealt with to prevent a relapse.[14] In short, recovery from prescription drug abuse becomes as difficult as recovery from abuse of illegal drugs. For these reasons, professional help is usually necessary for a full recovery from prescription drug abuse.

If you or someone you know is abusing prescription drugs, help is available. Many hospitals that sponsor detoxification programs for alcoholics and illegal drug addicts also have programs for individuals who are addicted to prescription drugs. After detoxification the individual will need to continue recovery through a program such as Alcoholics Anonymous (the principles used for recovery from alcoholism are also applicable to recovery from drug addiction) or Narcotics Anonymous. These organizations can be found in the phone book.

If the addicted person has family or close friends who are being seriously affected by addiction issues, those people may want to try Al-Anon, Alateen, or Adult Children of Alcoholics support groups. Finally, individual or family counselling may be of value in helping to sort out emotional issues that lie behind the addiction. A certified addictions counsellor may be the most helpful person to an addict, or the family may choose a psychiatrist, psychologist, or social worker who has knowledge of addiction issues.

Although prescription drug addicts will always be "recovering" rather than "recovered," they can still lead relatively normal lives with proper physical and psychological treatment. However, there are no quick fixes or easy answers. Recovery is an ongoing process for both the addict and his or her family.

For Discussion

Do you know of anyone who has intentionally abused prescription drugs? Have you ever taken a prescription drug in a different way than it was prescribed? Have you ever taken someone else's prescription drug? If so, why did you do it? Can you think of a case where use of another person's prescription drug can be justified?

References

1. Colvin R: *Prescription drug abuse: the hidden epidemic*, 1995, Addicus Books.
2. Ibid.
3. Colvin R: I tried to be my brother's keeper: one family's battle with prescription drug abuse, *Family Circle*, 108(13), Sep 19, 1995.
4. Ibid.
5. Vaillant GE: Physician, cherish thyself: the hazards of self prescribing, *JAMA* 267(17), 1992.
6. Dabney D, Heffington TR: The pharmacy profession's reaction to substance abuse among pharmacists: the process and consequences of medicalization, *Journal of Drug Issues* 26(4), Fall 1996.
7. Tackleman K. Older but not wiser to addiction. More seniors are getting hooked on prescription drugs as a way to deal with anxieties of old age. *USA Today*. 24 July 2001.
8. *Prescription drug abuse.*
9. Older but not wiser.
10. Ibid.
11. Ibid.
12. Physician, cherish thyself.
13. Older but not wiser.
14. Ibid.

Chapter **8**

Taking Control of Alcohol Use

Chapter Objectives

After reading this chapter, you should be able to

- Describe the prevalence of drinking on college campuses.
- Describe the physiological effects of alcohol and how these effects differ by gender.
- List the symptoms and first aid procedures for acute alcohol intoxication.
- Explain how alcohol use plays a role in accidents, crime, and suicide.
- List the major organizations that support responsible drinking.
- Describe problem drinking and alcoholism.
- Define codependence and describe how it damages the alcoholic and codependent.
- Explain how denial and enabling can prolong problem drinking.
- List the common traits of adult children of alcoholics.

Online Learning Centre Resources

www.mcgrawhill.ca/college/hahn

Log on to our Online Learning Centre (OLC) for access to Web links for study and exploration of health topics. Here are some examples of what you'll find:

- **http://notes.camh.net/efeed.nsf/feedback** Assess your alcohol use with this interactive feedback form.
- **www.aa.org** Log on to the homepage of the best known of all alcohol abuse treatment programs, Alcoholics Anonymous.
- **www.niaaa.nih.gov** Check out this indexed site for the U.S. National Institutes of Health publications and databases, frequently asked questions, and more.
- **www2.camh.net** Get the facts on alcohol at this Web site provided by the Addiction Research Foundation.

Media Pulse

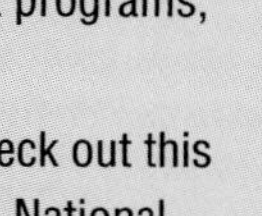

Binge Controversy

Do campaigns that focus on the problem of student binge drinking actually encourage students to drink to excess?

A debate has been brewing among various groups devoted to the study and control of alcohol problems among students. Recently the issues have played out in the pages of the *Chronicle for Higher Education*, a U.S. weekly.

The Inter-Association Task Force on Alcohol and other Substance Abuse Issues, an American alcohol education organization, wants the term "binge drinking" banned from media coverage of the student drinking patterns. It claims that the definition of binge drinking as five drinks for men and four drinks for women is too low and artificially inflates the number of students who have alcohol problems on campus.

In addition, the association says campaigns that use scare tactics about the perils of binge drinking actually encourage students to binge drink. Graphic posters showing a student throwing up in a toilet bowl or carnage from an alcohol-induced accident lead students to believe that binge drinking is the norm, everybody does it, and that to fit in, they should binge, too, they say.

The task force preaches the "social norms" approach to educate students and influence their behaviour to drink responsibly. "The social norms model spreads the message that most students drink responsibly and that drinking to excess is not normal. That influences students to drink less," says Fran

Media Pulse *continued*

Wdowczyk, executive director of the Student Life Education Company, the parent company of BACCHUS Canada, which supports the social norms model.

In a recent article in the *Chronicle of Higher Education*, Henry Wechsler, director of College Alcohol Studies at the Harvard University School of Public Health, stands by the definition and on the focus of binge drinking. "We are dumbfounded that some people in the field of higher education think that convening to abolish the "b-word" will solve the problem," he writes.

Dr. Wechsler says that his group's research shows that men who have five or more drinks in a row at least once in a two-week period, or women who have four or more drinks in a row, are at significantly greater risk of having any of 12 alcohol-related problems than those who drink less. The problems include vandalism, fights, injuries, drunken driving, and getting into trouble with the police, and they are at the heart of the five–four measure of binge drinking.

While some institutions report that the social norms approach is curbing excessive drinking on their campus, Dr. Wechsler says his studies find that students most often underestimate, rather than overestimate, the amount other students drink.

The push for zero-tolerance laws, the tightening of standards for determining legal intoxication, and the growing influence of national groups concerned with alcohol misuse show that our society is more sensitive than ever to the growing misuse of alcohol.

People are concerned about the consequences of drunk driving, alcohol-related crime, and lowered job productivity. National data indicate that per capita alcohol consumption has gradually dropped in the United States and Canada since the early 1980s.[1] Alcohol use remains the preferred form of drug use for most adults (including college and university students) but, as a society, we are increasingly uncomfortable with the ease with which alcohol can be misused.

Throughout the 1980s and 1990s, alcohol sales per person declined. In 1996 and 1997, sales expressed in terms of absolute alcohol increased to 7.6 litres per person from 7.4 litres per person in 1995–96. This was the first increase in alcohol sales per person since the 1980s.[2]

CHOOSING TO DRINK

Clearly, people drink alcoholic beverages for many different reasons. Most people drink alcohol because it is an effective, affordable, and legal substance for altering the brain's chemistry. As **inhibitions** are removed by the influence of alcohol, behaviour that is generally held in check is expressed (Figure 8–1).[3] At least temporarily, drinkers become a different version of themselves—more outgoing, relaxed, and adventuresome. If alcohol did not make these changes in people, it would not be consumed as much. Do you agree or disagree?

ALCOHOL USE PATTERNS

You cannot watch television, listen to the radio, or read a newspaper without being encouraged to buy a particular brand of beer, wine, or liquor. The advertisements create a warm aura about the nature of alcohol use. The implications are clear: alcohol use will bring you good times, handsome men or seductive women, exotic settings, and a chance to forget the hassles of hard work and study.

With the many pressures to drink, it's not surprising that most adults drink alcoholic beverages. Two-thirds of all North American adults are classified as drinkers. Yet one in three adults does not drink. In the college environment, where surveys indicate that 85% to 90% of all students drink, it's difficult for many students to imagine that every third adult is an abstainer. Although many students assume that drinking is a natural part of their social life, others are making alternative choices (see Exploring Your Spirituality box on p. 166). To see how your drinking habits compare to those of the rest of Canadians, see the Star Box on p. 165.

Alcohol-consumption figures are reported in many different ways, depending on the researchers' criteria. Various sources support the contention that about one-third of adults 18 years of age and older are abstainers, about one-third are light drinkers, and one-third are moderate-to-heavy drinkers. As a single category, heavy drinkers make up about 10% of the adult drinking population. Students who drink in college or university tend to classify themselves as light-to-moderate drinkers. It comes as a shock to students, though, when they read the criteria for each drinking classification. According to the combination of quantity of alcohol consumed per occasion and the frequency of drinking, these criteria are established as shown in Table 8–1.

TALKING POINTS • **How would you go about telling a friend that you think he or she has a drinking problem?**

Key Term

inhibitions
Inner controls that prevent a person from engaging in certain types of behaviour.

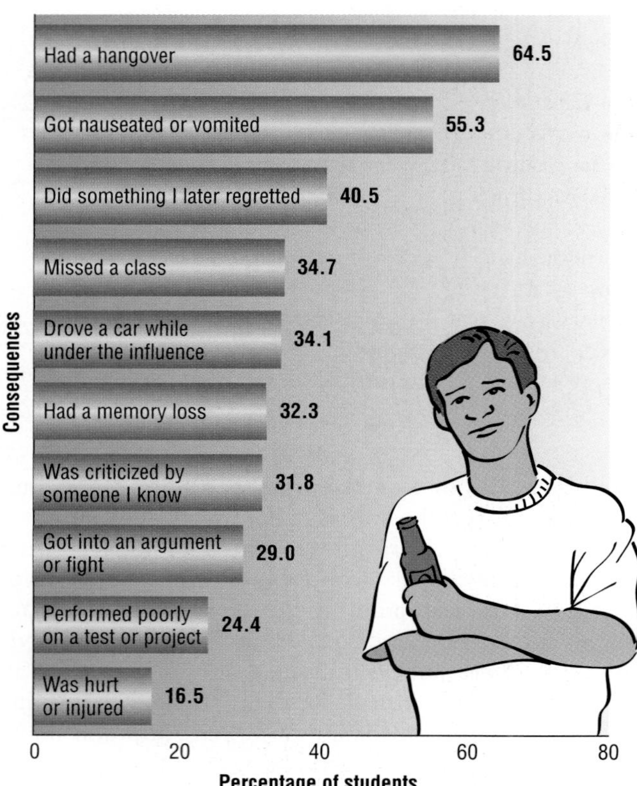

Figure 8–1 Presented above are the percentage of students who experienced negative consequences due to drinking within a given year. (*Occurred at least once in past year; year 2001 statistics from national sample of over 54 444 undergraduates from 131 colleges in the United States.)

Table 8–1 Criteria for Drinking Classifications

Classification	Alcohol-Related Behaviour
Abstainers	Do not drink or drink less often than once a year
Infrequent drinkers	Drink once a month at most and drink small amounts per typical drinking occasion
Light drinkers	Drink once a month at most and drink medium amounts per typical drinking occasion, or drink no more than three to four times a month and drink small amounts per typical drinking occasion
Moderate drinkers	Drink at least once a week and small amounts per typical drinking occasion or three to four times a month and medium amounts per typical drinking occasion or no more than once a month and large amounts per typical drinking occasion
Moderate/heavy drinkers	Drink at least once a week and medium amounts per typical drinking occasion or three to four times a month and large amounts per typical drinking occasion
Heavy drinkers	Drink at least once a week and large amounts per typical drinking occasion

NOTE: Small amounts = One drink or less per drinking occasion
Medium amounts = Two to four drinks per drinking occasion
Large amounts = Five or more drinks per drinking occasion (binge drinking)
Drink = 341 mL (12 fluid oz) of beer, 142 mL (5 fluid oz) of wine, or 43 mL (1.5 fluid oz) of distilled spirits

Moderate Drinking Redefined

Alcohol Alert, a publication of the U.S. National Institute on Alcohol Abuse and Alcoholism (NIAAA), and the Canadian Centre for Addiction and Mental Health (CAMH) indicate that moderate drinking can be defined as no more than two drinks each day for most men and one drink each day for women.[4,5] The Canadian Centre on Substance Abuse defines moderation, or "low-risk drinking guidelines" as follows: "Healthy adults who choose to drink should limit alcohol consumption to 2 or fewer standard drinks per day, with consumption not exceeding 14 standard drinks a week for men and 9 standard drinks per week for women."[6] These cutoff levels are based on the amount of alcohol that can be consumed without causing problems, either for the drinker or society. (The gender difference is due primarily to the higher percentage of body fat in women and to the lower amount of an essential stomach enzyme in women.) Elderly people are limited to no more than one drink each day, again due to a higher percentage of body fat.

These consumption levels are applicable to most people. Indeed, people who plan to drive, women who are pregnant, people recovering from alcohol addiction, people under the legal drinking age, people taking medications, and those with existing medical concerns should not consume alcohol. Additionally, although some studies have shown that low levels of alcohol consumption may have minor psychological and cardiovascular benefits, the NIAAA and the CAMH do not advise nondrinkers to start drinking.

Binge Drinking

Alcohol abuse by college and university students usually takes place through *binge drinking*. This practice refers to the consumption of five drinks in a row, at least once during the previous two-week period.[7] Students who fit the category of "heavy drinkers" rarely consume small amounts of alcohol each day but instead binge on alcohol one or two nights a week. Some students in our classes openly admit that they plan to "get really drunk" on the weekend. They plan to binge drink.

TALKING POINTS • Do you consider it your responsibility to tell a friend that he or she is binge drinking and to explain how dangerous it can be?

Evaluate Your Drinking[8]

1 What was your drinking like during a typical week in the past year?

List roughly how many drinks you have on each day of a typical week and add up the total:

Monday
Tuesday
Wednesday
Thursday
Friday
Saturday
Sunday
TOTAL

Be sure to estimate the number of "standard" drinks you usually have (it is important when you compare your drinking to other Canadians). Each of the drinks on the chart below has the same amount of alcohol and will all affect you in the same way.

One standard drink is

341 mL (12 oz.) beer (5% alcohol)	=	142 mL (5 oz.) wine (10–12% alcohol)	=	85 mL (3 oz.) fortified wine (16–18% alcohol)	=	43 mL (1.5 oz.) liquor (40% alcohol) (43 mL overproof liquor is about two standard drinks)

2 Now compare your weekly total to that of other Canadians

How does your weekly average compare? Look at the pie charts below to find where your drinking fits with the rest of the adult population. For example, if you are a male who drinks 15 standard drinks per week, you drink more alcohol than 94% of the other men in Canada do.

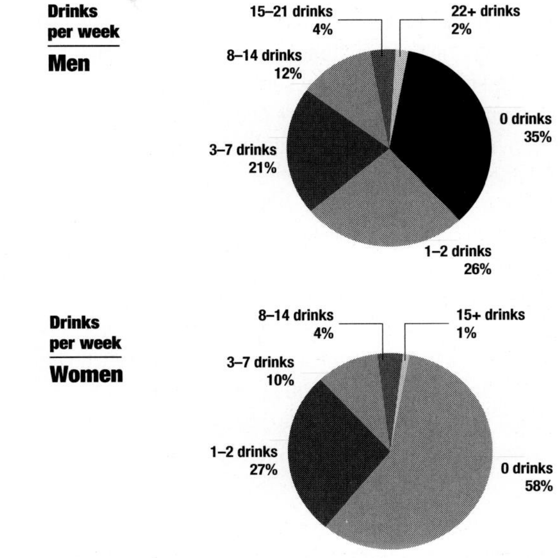

3 Risky drinking

A recent national survey looked at how much people drank in a week and how their drinking affected different areas of their lives. People were asked about their physical health, outlook on life, friends/social life, relationships with their spouses or partners and children, home life, financial position and work or studies. Not surprisingly, the results showed that the more people drank in a week, the greater the chance that the drinking was affecting more and more areas of their lives.

How likely are you to have problems as a result of your drinking? Look at the chart below to see where you fit.

Chance of negative consequences related to number of drinks per week

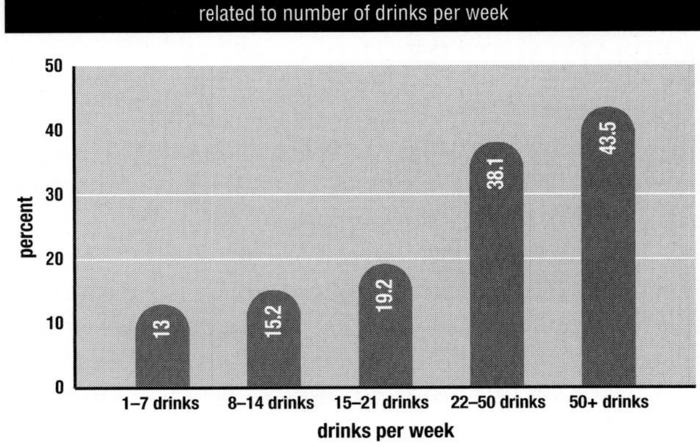

4 Your choices about drinking

Are you concerned about your drinking? Take a look at the options below to see if there is anything you would like to do right now. It is your choice.

- My drinking is fine for now. I will continue to watch how much I drink.
- I will think about changing my drinking. Did you know that 75% of people change their drinking on their own?
- I will reduce my drinking to a low-risk level. This means I will drink no more than two drinks a day, with a weekly maximum of 14 drinks for men and nine drinks for women. Most people watch their drinking—they put limits on how much, when, and where they drink. To avoid intoxication, they drink slowly, waiting at least one hour between drinks. They have food and nonalcoholic drinks along with alcohol. They have at least one or two days a week without any alcohol. And they don't drive or operate heavy equipment after drinking. Women who are pregnant, trying to conceive, or breastfeeding are encouraged not to consume any alcohol.
- I will contact the Drug and Alcohol Registry of Treatment (DART) to find out about other programs and groups that can help me or someone whom I am concerned about. (Call toll free 1-800-565-8603.)

Exploring Your Spirituality
What's a Social Life without Alcohol?

When was the last time you went to a get-together where alcoholic drinks weren't served? It's probably been years. Socia lizing and drinking are connected in our consciousness in many ways. For instance, it's Friday night after a hard week and your friends ask you to join them for a beer. Why not? It'll be fun. Or you're invited to a party and want to bring something. How about a bottle of wine? That's easy and always appreciated.

Associating drinking with fun is something that many people, including post-secondary students, do. For various reasons, though, some students are choosing to plan their fun around activities that don't involve drinking. Instead of going to a bar for a beer, they find a coffee shop and have a latté. Or they order a soft drink with their pizza. Others have discovered that they can get something that tastes great and is actually healthy at a juice bar.

What happens, though, when you go to a party and everyone else seems to be drinking? Choose something nonalcoholic—club soda, juice, a soft drink, or water. (You probably won't be the only one doing this.) If someone gives you trouble about your choice, be firm. Just say that's what you want. You don't need to explain. And you don't have to say "yes" to be nice.

But maybe you want to drink at a party because it loosens you up and makes it easier to talk to people. How will you start a conversation without a drink to relax you? Think about how you talk easily and naturally with the people in your drama group or one of your favourite classes. You've got things in common, so it's easier to do. When you meet someone new at a party, look for common interests. You may feel self-conscious at first. But soon you'll forget about the fact that he or she is a stranger because you'll be involved in what you're talking about. Without that drink, you'll actually be more yourself.

Some students are making the commitment to be active instead of sitting around and drinking. They're going backpacking, joining a cycling group, taking an exercise class, or playing a team sport. What they're discovering is that it feels good—physically and mentally. They're socializing, doing something they enjoy, and getting in better shape. Think about something you've always wanted to try, and get going on it.

Making the choice to have fun without alcohol doesn't mean cutting yourself off from your friends. (If they're real friends, they'll respect your choice.) It's all about deciding what's right for you and making a commitment to that choice.

Two-thirds of North American adults, including most of those in this nightclub, are classified as drinkers. Only one-third choose to abstain from alcohol.

Binge drinking can be dangerous. Drunk driving, physical violence, property destruction, date rape, police arrest, lowered academic performance, and even death are all closely associated with binge drinking.[9] The direct correlation between the amount of alcohol consumed and lowered academic performance is clear. Frequently, the social costs of binge drinking are very high, especially when intoxicated people demonstrate their level of immaturity. How common is binge drinking on your campus?

In response to the personal dangers and campus trauma associated with binge drinking, colleges and universities are fighting back. Some schools are conducting local alcohol education campaigns that feature innovative posters and materials displayed on campus.

For many students who drink, the post-secondary years are a time when they will drink more heavily than at any other time in their life (Figure 8–2).[10] Some will suffer serious consequences as a result (Figure 8–1). These years will also mark the entry into a lifetime of problem drinking for some.

THE NATURE OF ALCOHOLIC BEVERAGES

Alcohol (also known as *ethyl alcohol or ethanol*) is the principal product of **fermentation**. In this process, yeast cells act on the sugar content of fruits and grains to produce alcohol and carbon dioxide.

The alcohol concentration in distilled beverages (such as whiskey, gin, rum, and vodka) is expressed by the term *proof*, a number that is twice the percentage of alcohol by volume in a beverage. Thus 70% of the fluid in a bottle of 140 proof gin is pure alcohol. Most proofs in distilled beverages range from 80 to 160. The familiar pure *grain alcohol* that is often added to fruit punches and similar beverages has a proof of almost 200 (see Table 8–2).

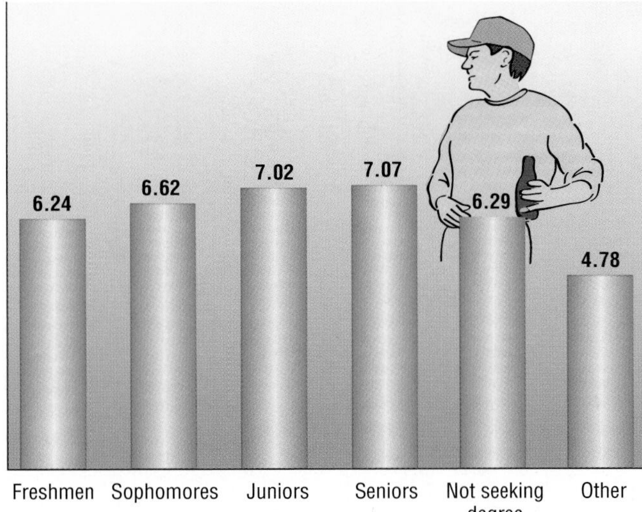

Figure 8–2 Average number of alcoholic drinks consumed by college drinkers (year 2001 statistics from international sample of over 54 444 undergraduates from 131 colleges in the United States).

The nutritional value of alcohol is extremely limited. Alcoholic beverages produced today through modern processing methods contain nothing but empty calories—about 100 calories per 30 mL (1 fluid oz) of 100-proof distilled spirits and about 150 calories for each 341 mL (12 oz) bottle or can of beer.[11] Clearly, alcohol consumption is a significant contributor to the additional pounds of fat that many post-secondary students accumulate. Pure alcohol contains only simple carbohydrates; it has no vitamins and minerals and no fats or protein.

"Light" beer and low-calorie wines have been introduced in response to concerns about the number of calories that alcoholic beverages provide. They are not low-alcohol beverages but merely low-calorie beverages. Only beverages marked "low alcohol" contain a lower concentration of alcohol than the usual beverages of that type.

The popular new ice beers actually contain a higher percentage of alcohol than other types of beer. This is due to a production process that chills the fermented mixture sufficiently to allow ice crystals to form. When the ice crystals are removed, the beer contains a higher percentage of alcohol than it had before.

Canadian Students' Drinking Habits Compared to American Students'[12]

The first national comparison of college students' drinking habits in the United States and Canada finds that while more Canadian students drink, American students drink more heavily.

Table 8–2 Categories of Alcoholic Beverages*

Alcoholic Beverage	Alcohol Content (%)†	Normal Measure
Beer		
Ale	5	341 mL (12 oz) bottle
Ice beer	5.5	341 mL (12 oz) bottle
Malt liquor	7	341 mL (12 oz) bottle
Light beer	4	341 mL (12 oz) bottle
Regular beer	4	341 mL (12 oz) bottle
Low-alcohol beer	1.5	341 mL (12 oz) bottle
Wine		
Fortified: port, sherry, muscatel, etc.	18	85 mL (3 oz) glass
Natural: red/white	12	85 mL (3 oz) glass
Champagne	12	114 mL (4 oz) glass
Wine cooler	6	341 mL (12 oz) bottle
Cider (Hard)	10	170 mL (6 oz) glass
Liqueurs		
Strong: sweet, syrupy	40	28 mL (1 oz) glass
Medium: fruit brandies	25	57 mL (2 oz) glass
Distilled Spirits		
Brandy, cognac, rum, scotch, vodka, whiskey	45	28 mL (1 oz) glass
Mixed Drinks and Cocktails		
Strong martini, manhattan	30	100 mL (3 1/2 oz) glass
Medium: old-fashioned, daiquiri, Alexander	15	114 mL (4 oz) glass
Light: highball, sweet and sour mixes, tonics	7	227 mL (8 oz) glass

*In all major alcoholic beverages—beer, table wines, cocktail and dessert wines, liqueurs and cordials, and distilled spirits—the significant ingredient is identical: alcohol. The typical drink, 14 mL (half an ounce) of pure alcohol, is provided by a shot of spirits, a glass of fortified wine, a larger glass of table wine, or a bottle of beer.

†In addition, these beverages contain other chemical constituents. Some come from the original grains, grapes, or other fruits; others are produced during the chemical processes of fermentation, distillation, and storage. Some are added as flavouring or colouring. These nonalcohol substances contribute to the effects of certain beverages either by directly affecting the body or by affecting the rates at which alcohol is absorbed into the blood.

Key Term

fermentation

A chemical process whereby plant products are converted into alcohol by the action of yeast cells on carbohydrate materials.

The study is based on the 1999 College Alcohol Study, conducted by the Harvard School of Public Health and the 1998 Canadian Campus Survey, conducted by the Centre for Addiction and Mental Health, based out of Toronto. Findings compare the responses of 12 344 American and 6729 Canadian randomly selected students under 25 years of age.

The prevalence of lifetime alcohol use (92% vs. 86%) and past-year alcohol use (87% vs. 81%) is significantly higher among Canadian than U.S. students.

However, when compared to Canadian students, American students had higher rates of heavy alcohol use (Harvard School of Public Health College Alcohol Survey defines "heavy alcohol use" as consuming 5 or more drinks in a row for males, 4 or more for females) in the past year (41% vs. 35%) and past week (54% vs. 42%).

American male students are also more likely to engage in heavy alcohol use than American female students. Gender difference is not significant in heavy alcohol use among Canadian students. In Canada and the United States, students living at home with their parents are less likely to be heavy drinkers (26% vs. 18%) than students who live on campus (41% vs. 35%). Living with parents reduced heavy drinking more among American students than Canadian students.

Heavy alcohol use is more prevalent among underage students (43% vs. 35%) than legal-aged students (29% vs. 30%) in Canada and the United States. The drinking age in Canada is 18 or 19 years of age (depending on the province). The drinking age in the United States is 21 years of age. However, in both countries heavy alcohol use is more prevalent among students age 20 or less.

For college students who report first drunkenness before the age of 16 in both countries, heavy alcohol use is more prevalent.

THE PHYSIOLOGICAL EFFECTS OF ALCOHOL

First and foremost, alcohol is classified as a drug—a very strong CNS depressant. The primary depressant effect of alcohol occurs in the brain and spinal cord. Many people think of alcohol as a stimulant because of the way most users feel after consuming a serving or two of a drink. Any temporary sensations of jubilation, boldness, or relief are attributable to alcohol's ability as a depressant drug to release personal inhibitions and provide temporary relief from tension.

Factors That Influence the Absorption of Alcohol

The **absorption** of alcohol is influenced by several factors, most of which can be controlled by the individual. These factors include the following:

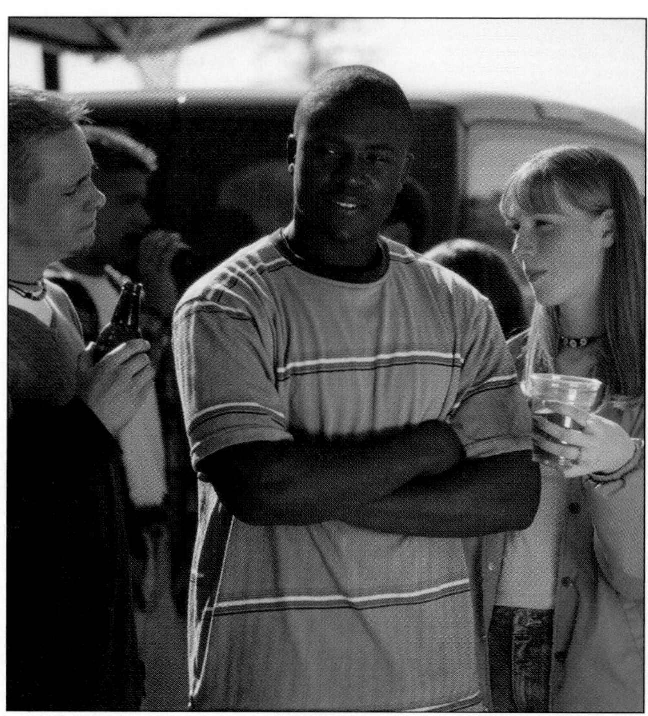

Mature adults know how to enjoy alcohol responsibly and understand how to decline alcohol use when they don't want to drink.

- *Strength of the Beverage.* The stronger the beverage, the greater the amount of alcohol that will accumulate within the digestive tract.
- *Number of Drinks Consumed.* As more drinks are consumed, more alcohol is absorbed.
- *Speed of Consumption.* If consumed rapidly, even relatively few drinks will result in a large concentration gradient that will lead to high blood alcohol concentration.
- *Presence of Food.* Food can compete with alcohol for absorption into the bloodstream, slowing the absorption of alcohol. When alcohol absorption is slowed, the alcohol already in the bloodstream can be removed. Slow absorption favours better control of blood alcohol concentration.
- *Body Chemistry.* Each person has an individual pattern of physiological functioning that may affect the ability to process alcohol. For example, in some conditions, such as that marked by "dumping syndrome," the stomach empties more rapidly than is normal, and alcohol seems to be absorbed more quickly. The emptying time may be either slowed or quickened by anger, fear, stress, nausea, and the condition of the stomach tissues.
- *Gender.* A significant study published in the *New England Journal of Medicine* reported that women produce much less alcohol dehydrogenase than men do.[13] This enzyme is responsible for breaking down alcohol in the

HealthQuest Activities

www.mcgrawhill.ca/college/hahn

The *Truth or Consequences Exploration,* found in the Alcohol Module, simulates an evening out on the town. The activity prompts you to make a variety of choices throughout the evening that may influence whether or how much you drink. The choice to drink alcohol comes up often. HealthQuest will then provide feedback on the outcome of the evening. Complete all of the scenarios, making different kinds of choices each time. Does the outcome of the evening reflect the drinking behaviour you entered? Were these the results you expected?

stomach. As a result, women absorb about 30% more alcohol into the bloodstream than men, despite an identical number of drinks and equal body weight.

Three other reasons help explain why women tend to absorb alcohol more quickly than men of the same body weight: (1) Women have proportionately more body fat than men. Since alcohol is not very fat soluble, it enters the bloodstream relatively quickly. (2) Women's bodies have proportionately less water than men's bodies of equal weight. Thus alcohol consumed does not become as diluted as in men. (3) Alcohol absorption is influenced by a woman's menstrual cycle. Alcohol is more quickly absorbed during the premenstrual phase of a woman's cycle. Also, there is evidence that women using birth control pills absorb alcohol faster than usual.[14]

With the exception of a person's body chemistry and gender, all factors that influence absorption can be moderated by the alcohol user.

Blood Alcohol Concentration

A person's **blood alcohol concentration (BAC)** rises when alcohol is consumed faster than it can be removed (oxidized) by the liver. A fairly predictable sequence of events takes place when a person drinks alcohol at a rate faster than one drink every hour. When the BAC reaches 0.05%, initial measurable changes in mood and behaviour take place. Inhibitions and everyday tensions appear to be released, while judgment and critical thinking are somewhat impaired. This BAC would be achieved by a 73 kg (160 lbs) person consuming about two drinks in an hour.

At a level of 0.10% (one part alcohol to 1000 parts blood), the drinker typically loses significant motor coordination. Voluntary motor function becomes quite clumsy. At this BAC, a drinker is legally intoxicated and thus incapable of safely operating a vehicle. Although physiological changes associated with this BAC do occur, certain users do not feel intoxicated or do not outwardly appear to be impaired.

As the BAC rises from 0.20% to 0.50%, the health risk of acute alcohol intoxication increases rapidly. A BAC of 0.20% is characterized by the loud, boisterous, obnoxious drunk person who staggers. A 0.30% BAC produces further depression and stuporous behaviour, and the drinker becomes so confused that he or she may not be capable of understanding anything. The 0.40% or 0.50% BAC produces unconsciousness. At this level, a person can die, since the brain centres that control body temperature, heartbeat, and breathing may be virtually shut down.

An important factor influencing the BAC is the individual's blood volume. The larger the person, the greater the amount of blood into which alcohol can be distributed. Conversely, the smaller person has less blood into which alcohol can be distributed, and as a result, a higher BAC will develop. Small, young, and immature high school students place themselves at serious risk when they consume alcohol. Older siblings and peers should be aware of this danger and refuse to assist them in obtaining alcohol under age.[15]

Sobering Up

Alcohol is removed from the bloodstream principally through the process of **oxidation**. Oxidation occurs at a constant rate (about 7 to 9 mL or ¼ to ⅓ oz of pure alcohol per hour) that cannot be appreciably altered. Since each typical drink of beer, wine, or distilled spirits contains about 14 mL or ½ oz of pure alcohol, it takes about two hours for the body to fully oxidize one typical alcoholic drink.[16]

Although people may try to sober up by drinking hot coffee, taking cold showers, or exercising, the oxidation rate of alcohol is unaffected by these measures. Thus far there is no commercial product that can help people achieve sobriety. Passage of time remains the only effective remedy for diminishing alcohol's effects.

Key Terms

absorption
The passage of nutrients or alcohol through the walls of the stomach or intestinal tract into the bloodstream.

blood alcohol concentration (BAC)
The percentage of alcohol in a measured quantity of blood; BACs can be determined directly through the analysis of a blood sample or indirectly through the analysis of exhaled air.

oxidation
The process that removes alcohol from the bloodstream.

First Aid for Acute Alcohol Intoxication

Not everyone who goes to sleep, passes out, or becomes unconscious after drinking has a high BAC. People who are already sleepy, have not eaten well, are sick, or are bored may drink a little alcohol and quickly fall asleep. However, people who drink heavily in a rather short time may be setting themselves up for an extremely unpleasant, toxic, potentially life-threatening experience because of their high BAC.

Although responsible drinking will prevent **acute alcohol intoxication** (poisoning), it will never be a reality for everyone. As a caring adult, what should you know about this health emergency that may help you save a life—perhaps even a friend's life?

The first real danger signs to recognize are the typical signs of **shock**. By the time these signs are evident, a drinker will already be unconscious. He or she will not be able to be aroused from a deep stupor. The person will probably have a weak, rapid pulse (over 100 beats per minute). The skin will be cool and damp, and breathing will be increased to once every three or four seconds. These breaths may be shallow or deep but will certainly occur in an irregular pattern. Skin will be pale or bluish. (In the case of a person with dark skin, these colour changes will be more evident in the fingernail beds or in the mucous membranes inside the mouth or under the eyelids.) Whenever any of these signs is present, seek emergency medical help immediately (see the Changing for the Better box on this page for a summary of these signs).

Involuntary regurgitation (vomiting) can be another potentially life-threatening emergency for a person who has drunk too much alcohol. When a drinker has consumed more alcohol than the liver can oxidize, the pyloric valve at the base of the stomach tends to close. Additional alcohol remains in the stomach. This alcohol irritates the lining of the stomach so much that involuntary muscle contractions force the stomach contents to flow back through the esophagus. By removing alcohol from the stomach, vomiting may be a life-saving mechanism for conscious drinkers.

An unconscious drinker who vomits may be lying in such a position that the airway becomes obstructed by the vomitus. This person is at great risk of dying from **asphyxiation**. As a first-aid measure, unconscious drinkers should always be rolled onto their sides to minimize the chance of airway obstruction. If you are with someone who is vomiting, make certain that his or her head is positioned lower than the rest of the body. This position minimizes the chance that vomitus will obstruct the air passages.

It is also important to keep a close watch on anyone who passes out from heavy drinking. Party-goers sometimes make the mistake of carrying these people to bed and then forgetting about them. Monitoring the physical condition of anyone who becomes unconscious from heavy drinking is crucial because of the risk of death. Observe the person at regular intervals until he or she appears to be clearly out of danger. This may mean an evening of interrupted sleep for you, but you could save a friend's life. Are you aware of any recent alcohol-related deaths among Canadian college or university students?

Changing *for the Better*

Are You Ready for an Alcohol-Related Emergency?

How can I recognize and cope with an acute alcohol emergency?

When you find a person who has been drinking heavily, look for these signs:

- Cannot be aroused
- Has a weak, rapid pulse
- Has an unusual or irregular breathing pattern
- Has cool (possibly damp), pale, or bluish skin

Immediately call for emergency help (call 911). Follow their directions. Position the unconscious person on his or her side to avoid choking in case vomiting occurs.

ALCOHOL-RELATED HEALTH PROBLEMS

The relationship of chronic alcohol use to the structure and function of the body is reasonably well understood. Heavy alcohol use causes a variety of changes to the body that lead to an increase in morbidity and mortality. Figure 8–3 describes these changes.

Research clearly shows that chronic alcohol use also damages the immune system and the nervous system. Thus chronic users are at high risk for a variety of infections and neurological complications.[17] Addition

Key Terms

acute alcohol intoxication
A potentially fatal elevation of the BAC, often resulting from heavy, rapid consumption of alcohol.

shock
Profound collapse of many vital body functions; evident during acute alcohol intoxication and other health emergencies.

asphyxiation
Death resulting from lack of oxygen to the brain.

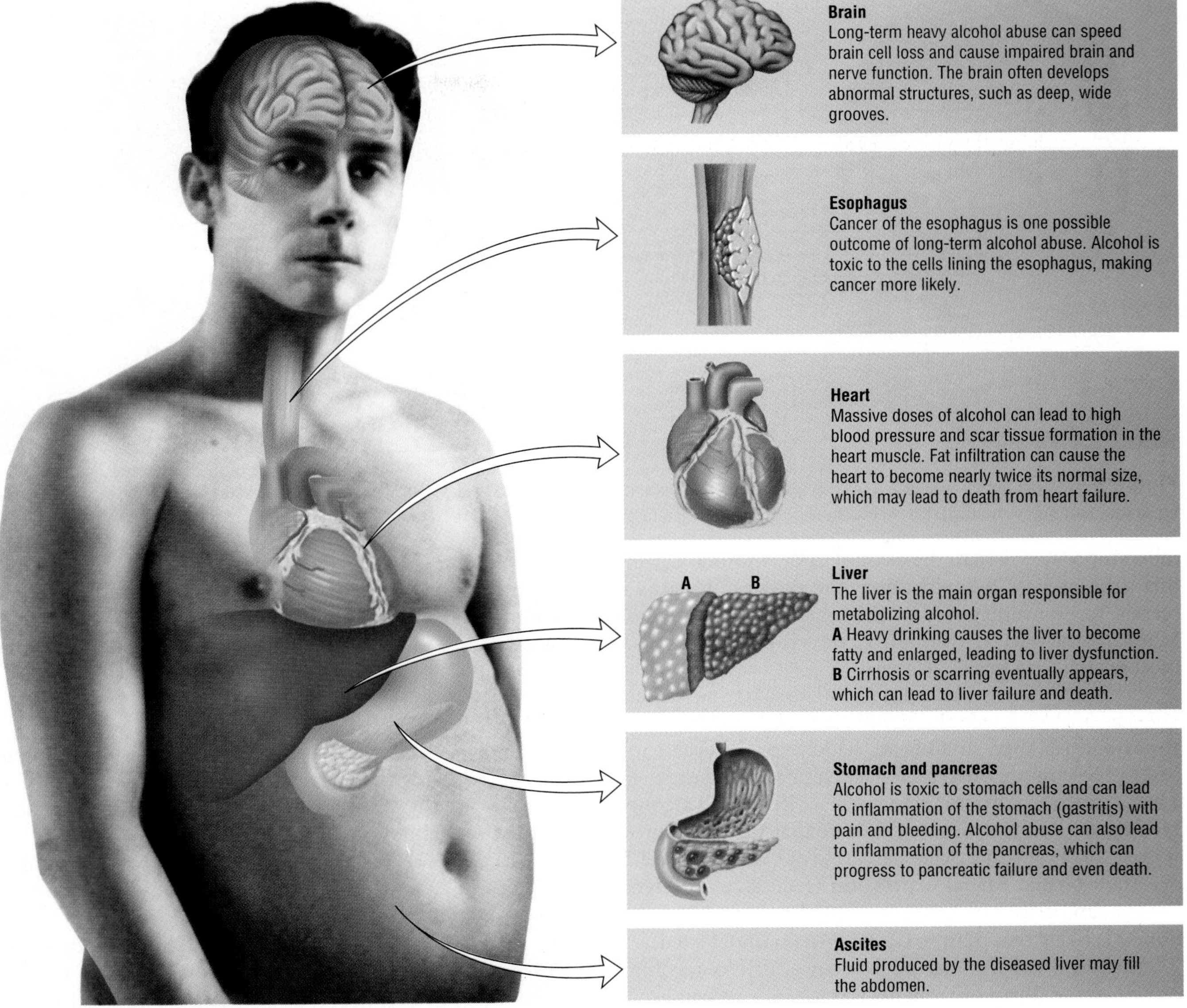

Brain
Long-term heavy alcohol abuse can speed brain cell loss and cause impaired brain and nerve function. The brain often develops abnormal structures, such as deep, wide grooves.
Esophagus
Cancer of the esophagus is one possible outcome of long-term alcohol abuse. Alcohol is toxic to the cells lining the esophagus, making cancer more likely.
Heart
Massive doses of alcohol can lead to high blood pressure and scar tissue formation in the heart muscle. Fat infiltration can cause the heart to become nearly twice its normal size, which may lead to death from heart failure.
A
B
Liver
The liver is the main organ responsible for metabolizing alcohol.
A Heavy drinking causes the liver to become fatty and enlarged, leading to liver dysfunction.
B Cirrhosis or scarring eventually appears, which can lead to liver failure and death.
Stomach and pancreas
Alcohol is toxic to stomach cells and can lead to inflammation of the stomach (gastritis) with pain and bleeding. Alcohol abuse can also lead to inflammation of the pancreas, which can progress to pancreatic failure and even death.
Ascites
Fluid produced by the diseased liver may fill the abdomen.

Figure 8–3 Effects of alcohol use on the body. The mind-altering effects of alcohol begin soon after it enters the bloodstream. Within minutes, alcohol numbs nerve cells in the brain. The heart muscle strains to cope with alcohol's depressive action. If drinking continues, the rising BAC causes impaired speech, vision, balance, and judgment. With an extremely high BAC, respiratory failure is possible. Over time, alcohol abuse increases the risk for certain forms of heart disease and cancer and makes liver and pancreas failure more likely.

ally, many alcoholics suffer from malnutrition, in part because they do not consume a variety of foods. With the deterioration of the liver, stomach, and pancreas, chronic heavy drinkers also have poor absorption and metabolism of many nutrients.

Fetal Alcohol Syndrome and Fetal Alcohol Effects

A growing body of scientific evidence indicates that alcohol use by pregnant women can result in birth defects in unborn children. When alcohol crosses the **placenta**, it enters the fetal bloodstream in a concentration equal to that in the mother's bloodstream. Because of the under developed nature of the fetal liver, this alcohol is oxidized

Key Term

placenta

The structure through which nutrients, metabolic wastes, and drugs (including alcohol) pass from the bloodstream of the mother into the bloodstream of the developing fetus.

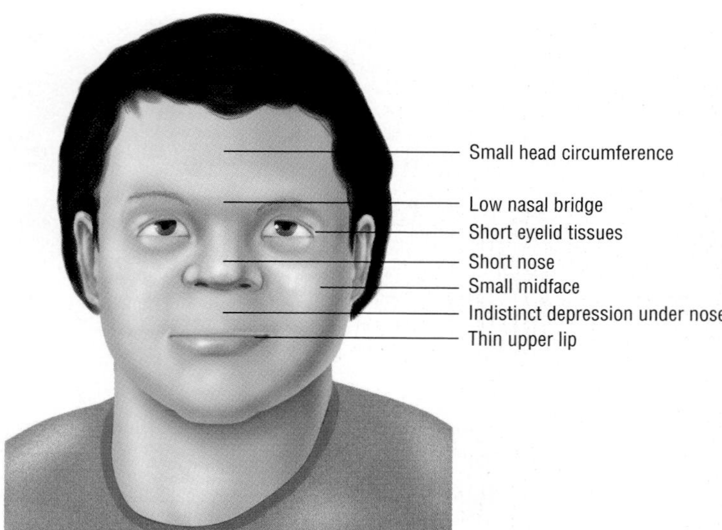

Figure 8–4 Fetal alcohol syndrome. The facial features shown are characteristic of affected children. Additional abnormalities in the brain and other internal organs accompany fetal alcohol syndrome but are not obvious in the child's appearance.

much more slowly than the alcohol in the mother. During this time of slow detoxification, the developing fetus is certain to be overexposed to the toxic effects of alcohol. Mental retardation frequently develops in babies of mothers who are heavy drinkers.

This exposure has additional disastrous consequences for the developing fetus. Low birth weight, facial abnormalities (e.g., small head, widely spaced eyes), and heart problems are often seen in such infants (Figure 8-4). This combination of effects is called **fetal alcohol syndrome**. Recent estimates indicate that the full expression of this syndrome occurs at a rate of between 1 and 3 per 1000 births. Partial expression (fetal alcohol effects [FAE]) can be seen in 3 to 9 per 1000 live births. In addition, it is likely that many cases of FAE go undetected.

Is there a safe limit to the number of drinks a woman can consume during pregnancy? Since no one can accurately predict the effect of drinking even small amounts of alcohol during pregnancy, the wisest plan is to avoid alcohol altogether.

Because of the critical growth and development that occur during the first months of fetal life, women who have any reason to suspect they are pregnant should stop all alcohol consumption. Furthermore, women who are planning to become pregnant and women who are not practising effective contraception must also consider keeping their alcohol use to a minimum.

ALCOHOL-RELATED SOCIAL PROBLEMS

Alcohol abuse is related to a variety of social problems. These problems affect the quality of interpersonal relationships, employment stability, and the financial security of both the individual and the family. Clearly, alcohol's negative social consequences lower our quality of life. In financial terms the annual cost of alcohol abuse and dependence in Canada has been estimated at more than $7.5 billion.

Unintentional Injuries

One major alcohol-related social problem is the unintentional injuries that result from its abuse or misuse. Injuries are the leading cause of death among Canadians throughout childhood to 40 years of age.[18]

In 2001 2778 people were killed in motor vehicle crashes in Canada. Thirty-five percent of these deaths were attributed to the abuse of alcohol.[19]

It is estimated that in 2001 about 356 000 individuals were injured in motor vehicle crashes. MADD Canada estimates that 71 563 individuals were injured due to impaired driving. This is about 195 people injured per day because of drunk driving. The cost of impaired driving in Canada has two figures. One is the real dollar model, which says the cost is $1.8 billion. The other model considers social costs (willingness to pay costs) and therefore is a lot higher at $10.8 billion.[20]

Causes of injury vary by age

The causes of severe injury vary with age. In 1999–2000 for people between the ages of 20 and 34, motor vehicle collisions accounted for 60% of all severe injuries. Only 12% of hospital admissions in this age group were due to falls. In contrast, 58% of severe injuries in people 65 and older were due to falls. Motor vehicle collisions accounted for only 31% of injuries in this age group. The leading cause of severe injury for people under 20 and those between 35 and 64 years of age was motor vehicle

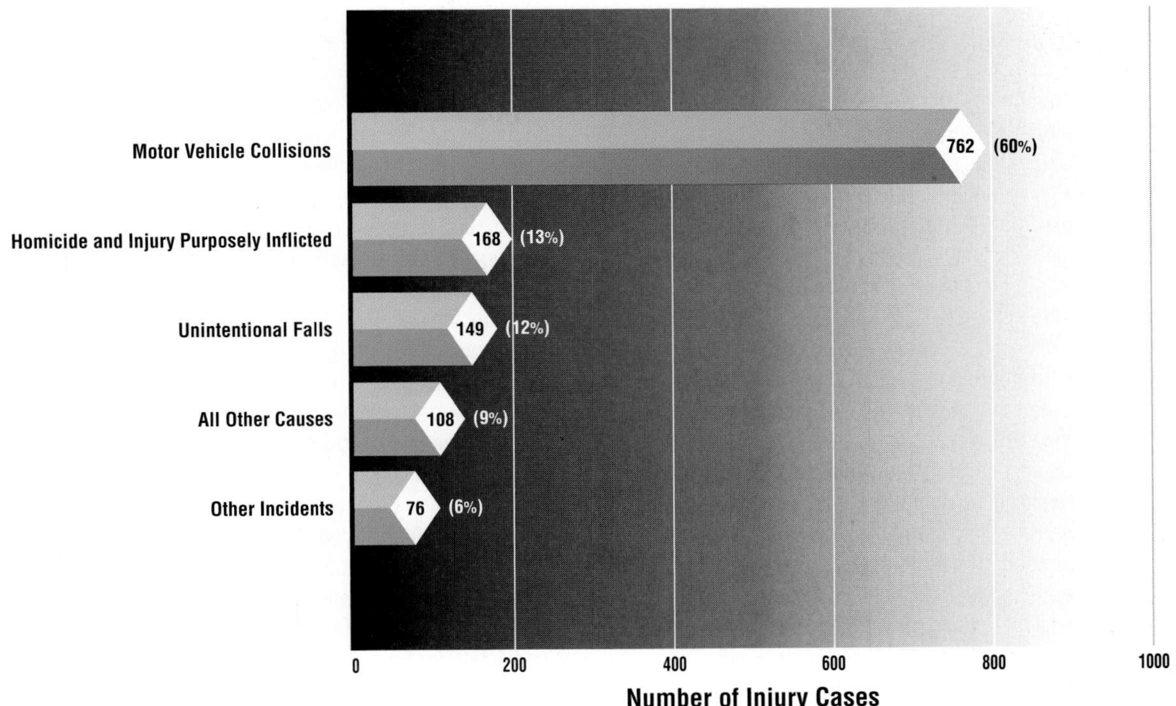

Figure 8–5 Causes of major injury—cases aged 20 to 34 years, 1999–2000.

collisions, accounting for 52% and 46% (respectively) of all severe injuries (see Figure 8–5).[21] If 35% of deaths caused by motor vehicle accidents in Canada are attributed to alcohol, it is reasonable to assume that at least this percentage of the severe injuries sustained in motor vehicle accidents by those under 20 and those between 35 and 60 are also caused by alcohol, and are therefore preventable.

Prevention of Unintentional Injury

Many Canadians do not see the risk in their everyday lives. However, if they are unable to see the risk, they cannot take measures to mitigate risk and possibly prevent injury or death.

The problem stems in part from our misuse of the word "accident." Injuries sustained in falls or motor vehicle crashes involving alcohol are not seen as the result of predictable events but rather the result of "accidents" or "acts of fate." Yet, when someone suffers from heart disease, for example, high cholesterol and smoking are identified as the predictable causes. It is time to acknowledge that alcohol-related injuries are predictable and preventable. Investing in injury prevention can save money and lives. Canadians do not need to spend $8.7 billion to treat nearly 2 million injuries that largely could have been prevented in the first place.[22] We need to be aware of the dangers of alcohol abuse and misuse, and take measures to prevent the tragic injuries that so often accompany them.

Prevention of motor vehicle collisions caused by drinking and driving can be greatly reduced through a national campaign against drunk driving. By implementing strategies such as designated drivers; **zero tolerance laws**; bartenders educated to recognize intoxicated customers; off-duty police officers as observers in bars; police road blocks, mechanical devices placed in cars to prevent intoxicated drivers from starting their cars; and early and repeated education on the hazards of drinking and driving, we may be able to reduce these horrible collisions. By implementing a prevention strategy based upon driving sober, we may ensure fewer hospitalizations, fewer injuries treated outside the hospital, and fewer injuries leading to permanent disability or death.

Key Terms

fetal alcohol syndrome
Characteristic birth defects noted in the children of some women who consume alcohol during their pregnancies.

zero tolerance laws
Laws that severely restrict the right to operate motor vehicles for drinkers who have been convicted of driving under any influence.

Getting Arrested for Drinking and Driving: The Aftermath

Many college and university students will admit to having driven a car after drinking alcohol. Some will even admit that they have left a party after drinking and then driven to another location, but could not remember actually driving the car. This behaviour reflects an alcoholic blackout. These are dangerous activities for the driver, the passengers, and anyone else on (or near) the road. The potential human costs of injury or death are staggering. However, for people who get arrested, a different drama will unfold—the aftermath of an arrest for drinking and driving.

Although laws vary from province to province, here is the general sequence of events: If you are driving a car and are stopped by a police officer who suspects you may have been driving under the influence of alcohol, you will first be asked to show your driver's licence and proof of your car's registration and insurance. You may be asked to get out of your car and undergo a field test for sobriety. This test could include tests of motor coordination, such as walking in a line in a heel-to-toe fashion. You may even be given an alcohol breath test on the spot.

If you appear to fail the field test, you could be arrested, frisked, and taken to the local jail. There you will likely be fingerprinted and photographed. A more precise blood alcohol test may be given. You will either spend some hours in jail (until your BAC is lowered) or be immediately released.

A date for your court appearance will be set. You will be required to face a judge and answer the charges against you. By this time, you probably will have hired an attorney to help you in this process. If you are convicted or decide to plead guilty to charges of "driving under the influence (DUI)" and this is your first offence, a typical scenario will follow. You will receive a minimum fine and be required to pay court costs. You may be required to attend alcohol education classes and be placed on a driving prohibition for a year.

You will likely lose points on your driver's licence and have an official police and court record. The total cost for a simple, first-time conviction can easily reach $1000 or more, depending on fines and legal fees.

The preceding discussion applies to a first offence. However, if you are arrested and charged with a second offence, the process changes radically. You will be arrested and put in jail for 14 days. Almost certainly, you will need an attorney to assist you through a lengthy court process. If you are ultimately convicted, you are likely to pay a heavy fine and spend time in jail or prison. After a criminal trial, injured people can also pursue a civil suit against you. A civil suit can be quite expensive and time consuming. Indeed, the repercussions of a criminal DUI conviction will last for years and will have a significant impact on you, your family, and the lives of others.

A conviction for impaired driving or refusal to provide a breath sample means the loss of your driver's licence for at least one year, and a criminal record that could hurt your employment possibilities and restrict your ability to travel outside Canada. Your motor vehicle insurance premiums will skyrocket and be very costly for five years because you are now a high-risk driver, which exacts high premiums. Figure 8–6 shows the BACs associated with the number of drinks consumed in a two-hour period.

Unfortunately, people who drink and drive fail to consider the aftermath of their behaviour until it is too late.

Crime and Violence

Have you noticed that most of the violent behaviour and vandalism on your campus is related to alcohol use? The connection of alcohol to crime has a long history. Prison populations have large percentages of alcohol abusers and alcoholics: People who commit crimes are more likely to have alcohol problems than are people in the general population. This is especially true for young criminals. Furthermore, alcohol use has been reported in 67% of all homicides, with the victim, the perpetrator, or both found to have been drinking. In rape situations, rapists are intoxicated 50% of the time and victims 30% of the time.[23]

Because of research methodological problems, pinpointing alcohol's connection to family violence is difficult.[24] However, it seems clear that among a large number of families, alcohol is associated with violence and other harmful behaviour, including physical abuse, child abuse, psychological abuse, and abandonment.[25] The Focus On article on p. 186 explores the link between alcohol and violence.

Suicide

Alcohol use has been related to large percentages of suicides. Half of all suicides are committed by alcoholics. Between 35% and 40% of the suicides committed by nonalcoholics are alcohol related. Also, alcohol use is associated with impulsive suicides rather than with premeditated ones. Drinking is also connected with more violent and lethal means of suicide, such as the use of firearms.[26]

For many of these social problems, alcohol use impairs critical judgment and allows a person's behaviour to quickly become reckless, antisocial, and deadly. Because most of us wish to minimize problems associated with alcohol use, acting responsibly when we host a party is a first step in this direction.

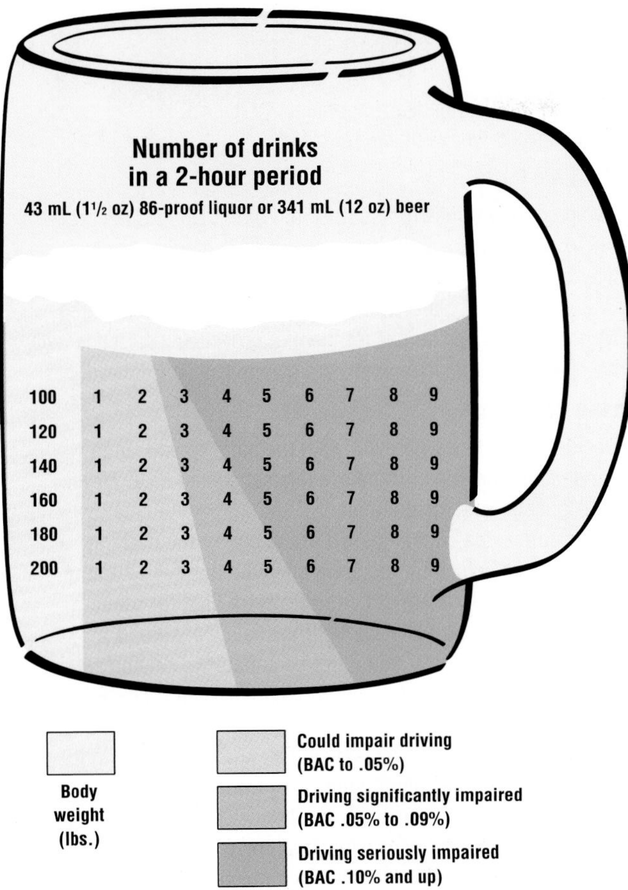

Number of drinks
in a 2-hour period
43 mL (1½ oz) 86-proof liquor or 341 mL (12 oz) beer
100 1 2 3 4 5 6 7 8 9
120 1 2 3 4 5 6 7 8 9
140 1 2 3 4 5 6 7 8 9
160 1 2 3 4 5 6 7 8 9
180 1 2 3 4 5 6 7 8 9
200 1 2 3 4 5 6 7 8 9
Body weight (lbs.)
Could impair driving (BAC to .05%)
Driving significantly impaired (BAC .05% to .09%)
Driving seriously impaired (BAC .10% and up)

Figure 8–6 In Canada, a BAC of .08% constitutes legal intoxication. However, lower BACs can impair functioning enough to cause a serious accident.

HOSTING A PARTY RESPONSIBLY

Some people might say that no party is totally safe when alcohol is served. These people are probably right, considering the possibility of unexpected **drug synergism**, overconsumption, and the consequences of released inhibitions. Fortunately, an awareness of the value of responsible party hosting seems to be growing among college and university communities. The impetus for this awareness has come from various sources, including respect for an individual's right to choose not to drink alcohol, the growing recognition that many automobile accidents are alcohol related, and the legal threats posed by **host negligence**.

Responsibly hosting parties at which alcohol is served is becoming a trend, especially among university and college-educated young adults. The Alberta Alcohol and Drug Abuse Commission has generated a list of guidelines for hosting a social event at which alcoholic beverages are served.[27] The list includes the recommendations shown in the Changing for the Better box on p. 176.

In addition, using a **designated driver** is an important component of responsible alcohol use. By planning to abstain from alcohol or to carefully limit their own alcohol consumption, designated drivers are able to safely transport friends who have been drinking. Have you noticed an increased use of designated drivers in your community? Would you be willing to be a designated driver?

TALKING POINTS • You've heard some of your friends joking about others using the designated-driver approach. How would you introduce this practice in a way that would be acceptable to them?

ORGANIZATIONS THAT SUPPORT RESPONSIBLE DRINKING

The serious consequences of the irresponsible use of alcohol have led to the formation of a number of concerned-citizen groups. Although each organization has a unique approach, all attempt to deal objectively with two indisputable facts: Alcohol use is part of our society, and irresponsible alcohol use can be deadly.

Mothers Against Drunk Driving

Mothers Against Drunk Driving (MADD) is a network of over 600 local chapters in the United States and Canada. This organization attempts to educate people about alcohol's effects on driving and to influence legislation and enforcement of laws related to drunk drivers. For more information about MADD, visit its Web site at **www.MADD.org**.

Students Against Destructive Decisions

Many students have known the acronym SADD to stand for the youth group Students Against Driving Drunk. Recently, the group has restructured itself to expand beyond drunk driving to include other high-risk activities

Key Terms

drug synergism (SIN er jism)
Enhancement of a drug's effect as a result of the presence of additional drugs within the system.

host negligence
A legal term that reflects the failure of a host to provide reasonable care and safety for people visiting the host's residence or business.

designated driver
A person who abstains from or carefully limits alcohol consumption to be able to safely transport other people who have been drinking.

Changing *for the Better*

Responsible Hosting

I like giving parties, but I worry about how much my friends might drink. How can I ensure that everyone will have a good time but that no one will get hurt?

Hosting a party can be a lot of fun. It also comes with some responsibilities. Here are some ideas to help you and your guests enjoy the party from start to finish.

Planning the Party

- Being a good host means providing something for everyone, not just those who want to drink alcohol. If you're serving punch, provide two choices—one with alcohol and one without alcohol—and label them.
- Also provide your guests with soft drinks and coffee or tea. You could also consider having a party where no alcohol is served; people can have fun without relying on alcohol.
- If you are serving mixed drinks, have measures (jiggers) beside the bottles so that the bartenders or guests don't rely on guesswork.
- Make sure you serve food, as it helps to slow the absorption of alcohol into the body—high-protein snacks such as meat, nuts, or cheese are especially good choices. Consider serving a meal instead of just snack food.
- Plan other activities such as games and dancing. Don't let drinking become the only reason for a party.
- Remember, if one of your guests causes a motor vehicle accident after drinking at your party, you could be found partially liable for any damage they do to themselves or others.
- Planning ahead means anticipating what might go wrong as well as what might go right. A good idea might be to have a spare bed or sofa for a guest who drinks too much and can't drive home. Or, make arrangements to have a designated driver available for guests.

During the Party

- Avoid serving drinks too soon or too often. Don't push drinks on someone who would prefer not to have alcohol or would like to stop after a few drinks.
- Watch the snack plates to make sure they stay well stocked.
- Mixing your guests' drinks for them or providing a bartender will help you make sure that no one will overdo it on individual drinks.

As the Party Ends

- Decide in advance when you want the party to end. Stop serving alcohol one hour before this scheduled time. Never offer guests "one for the road."
- Serve coffee, tea, and a dessert at the end of the evening. Coffee won't help sober up someone who has gone beyond his or her limit, but it will give some extra time for other guests to metabolize the alcohol they have consumed.
- If guests look like they might not be capable of driving safely, it's your responsibility to do something about it. Serving coffee is not the answer—this will produce only a wide-awake drunk. You could ask a guest who has not been drinking to drive the intoxicated person home, or offer a ride yourself, providing you aren't impaired. If intoxicated guests insist on driving, take their keys away and call them a taxi. If these options aren't acceptable, show your guests to the spare bedroom or sofa.
- Entertaining is an art, but it is also a responsibility. Your duties as host extend to being aware of the alcohol consumption of your guests. In doing so, you will make sure that everyone has a great time—from beginning to end.

that are detrimental to youth, such as underage drinking, drug use, drugged driving, and failure to use seat belts. Founded in 1981, this organization now has millions of members in thousands of chapters throughout the country. Remaining central to the drunk driving aspect of SADD is the "Contract for Life," a pact that encourages students and parents to provide safe transportation for each other if either is unable to drive safely after consuming alcohol. This contract also stipulates that no discussions about the incident are to be started until both can talk in a calm and caring manner. For more information about SADD, visit its Web site at **www.saddonline.com**.

TALKING POINTS • How would you approach asking your parents or friends to join you in signing a "Contract for Life"?

BACCHUS Post-Secondary Peer Education Network

BACCHUS (Boost Alcohol Consciousness Concerning the Health of University Students) began in 1975 as an alcohol-awareness organization at the University of Florida. Run by student volunteers, this organization promoted responsible drinking among university students who chose to drink. It was not an anti-alcohol group, but a "harm reduction" group. Over the years, hundreds of chapters were formed on campuses across North America. BACCHUS Canada is the oldest alcohol-awareness movement in North America, and is the longest established division within The Student Education Company. It is committed to the education, training, and support of post-secondary students across Canada, with regards to healthy lifestyles and responsible decision making. BACCHUS has national programs and conferences focused on educating youth about responsible use of alcohol. Go to **www.studentlifeeducation.com/about_bacchus. html**.

With the broadening of the original BACCHUS organization has come an expansion of the health issues this group addresses. Originally, the focus was on alcohol abuse and prevention. Now BACCHUS confronts a variety of student health and safety issues. For additional information about this organization, check out its Web site at **www.bacchusgamma.org**. For information on the history of BACCHUS in Canada, log on to **www.studentlifeeducation.com**.

Other Approaches

Other responsible approaches to alcohol use are surfacing nearly every day. Many university student functions are now conducted without the use of alcohol, and growing numbers of activities are alcohol free.

Another encouraging sign on many campuses is the increasing number of alcohol-use task forces. Although each of these groups has its own focus and title, many are meeting to discuss alcohol-related concerns on their particular campus. These task forces often try to formulate detailed, comprehensive policies for alcohol use across the entire campus community. Membership on these committees often includes students (on-campus and off-campus, graduate and undergraduate), faculty and staff members, academic administrators, residence hall advisors, university police, health centre personnel, alumni, and local citizens. Does your campus have such a committee?

Progressive Stages of Alcohol Dependence

Early

- Escape drinking
- Binge drinking
- Guilt feelings
- Sneaking drinks
- Difficulty stopping once drinking has begun
- Increased tolerance
- Preoccupation with drinking
- Occasional blackouts

Middle

- Loss of control
- Self-hate
- Impaired social relationships
- Changes in drinking patterns (more frequent binge drinking)
- Temporary sobriety
- Morning drinking
- Dietary neglect
- Increased blackouts

Late

- Prolonged binges
- Alcohol used to control withdrawal symptoms
- Alcohol psychosis
- Nutritional disease
- Frequent blackouts

PROBLEM DRINKING AND ALCOHOLISM

Problem Drinking

At times the line separating **problem drinking** from alcoholism is difficult to distinguish (see the Star Box above). There may be no true line, with the exception that an alcoholic is unable to stop drinking. Problem drinking is a pattern of alcohol use in which a drinker's behaviour creates personal difficulties or difficulties for other people. What are some of these behaviours? Examples might be drinking to avoid life stressors, going to work intoxicated, drinking and driving, becoming injured or injuring others while drinking, solitary drinking, morning drinking, an occasional **blackout**, high-risk sexual activity, and being told by others that you drink too much. For college and university students, two clear indications of problem drinking are missing classes and lowered academic performance caused by alcohol involvement. The Changing for the Better box on p. 178 offers suggestions that can help you keep drinking under control.

Problem drinkers are not always heavy drinkers; they might not be daily or even weekly drinkers. Unlike alcoholics, problem drinkers do not need to drink to maintain "normal" body functions. However, when they do drink, they (and others around them) experience problems—sometimes with tragic consequences. It's not surprising that problem drinkers are more likely than other drinkers to eventually develop alcoholism. Are there people around you who show signs of problem drinking?

Key Terms

problem drinking
An alcohol-use pattern in which a drinker's behaviour creates personal difficulties or difficulties for other people.

blackout
A temporary state of amnesia experienced by a drinker; an inability to remember events that occurred during a period of alcohol use.

Changing *for the Better*

Cool, Calm, and Collected: Keeping Your Drinking under Control

I've watched some of my friends do crazy things while drinking too much at a party. What things should I focus on to avoid overdoing it at parties?

- Do not drink before a party.
- Avoid drinking when you are anxious, angry, or depressed.
- Measure the liquor you put in mixed drinks (use only 28 to 43 mL or 1 to 1½ oz).
- Eat ample amounts of food and drink lots of water before and during the time you are drinking.
- Avoid salty foods that may make you drink more than you had planned.
- Drink slowly.
- Do not participate in drinking games.
- Do not drive after drinking; use a designated, nondrinking driver.
- Consume only a predetermined number of drinks.
- Stop alcohol consumption at a predetermined hour.

Alcoholism

In the early 1990s a revised definition of **alcoholism** was established by a joint committee of experts on alcohol dependence.[28] This committee defined alcoholism as follows:

> Alcoholism is a primary, chronic disease with genetic, psychosocial, and environmental factors influencing its development and manifestations. The disease is often progressive and fatal. It is characterized by impaired control over drinking, preoccupation with the drug alcohol, use of alcohol despite adverse consequences, and distortions in thinking, most notably denial. Each of these symptoms may be continuous or periodic.

This definition incorporates much of the knowledge gained from addiction research during the last two decades. It is well recognized that alcoholics do not drink for the pleasurable effects of alcohol but to escape being sober. For alcoholics, being sober is stressful.

Unlike problem drinking, alcoholism involves a physical addiction to alcohol. For the true alcoholic, when the body is deprived of alcohol, physical and mental withdrawal symptoms become evident. These withdrawal symptoms can be life threatening.

Uncontrollable shaking can progress to nausea, vomiting, hallucinations, shock, and cardiac and pulmonary arrest. Uncontrollable shaking combined with irrational hallucinations is called *delirium tremens* (DT), an occasional manifestation of alcohol withdrawal.

The complex reasons for the physical and emotional dependence of alcoholism have not been fully explained. Why, when more than 100 million adults in North America use alcohol without becoming dependent on it, are 10 million or more others unable to control its use?

Could alcoholism be an inherited disease? Studies in humans and animals have provided strong evidence that genetics plays a role in some cases of alcoholism. Two forms of alcoholism are thought to be inherited: type I and type II. Type I is thought to take years to develop and may not surface until midlife. Type II is a more severe form and appears to be passed primarily from fathers to sons. This form of alcoholism frequently begins earlier in a person's life and may even start in adolescence.

Genetics may also help protect some Asians from developing alcoholism. About half of all Asians produce low levels of an important enzyme that helps metabolize alcohol. These people cannot tolerate even small amounts of alcohol. Genetic factors pertaining to the absorption rates of alcohol in the intestinal tract have been hypothesized to predispose some of North America's Aboriginal peoples to alcoholism. It is likely that more research will be undertaken concerning the role of genetic factors in all forms of chemical dependence.

The role of personality traits as conditioning factors in the development of alcoholism has received considerable attention. Factors ranging from unusually low self-esteem to an antisocial personality have been implicated. Additional factors making people susceptible to alcoholism may include excessive reliance on denial, hypervigilance, compulsiveness, and chronic levels of anxiety. Always complicating the study of personality traits is the uncertainty of whether the personality profile is a predisposing factor (perhaps from inheritance) or is caused by alcoholism.

Codependence

Within the last decade, a new term has been used to describe the relationship between drug-dependent people and those around them—**codependence**. This term implies a kind of dual addiction. The alcoholic and the person close to the alcoholic are both addicted, one to alcohol and the other to the alcoholic. People who are codependent often find themselves denying the addiction and enabling the alcohol-dependent person.

Unfortunately, this kind of behaviour damages both the alcoholic and the codependent. The alcoholic's intervention and treatment may be delayed for a considerable time. Codependent people often pay a heavy price as well. They often become drug or alcohol dependent themselves, or they may suffer a variety of psychological consequences related to guilt, loss of self-esteem, depression, and anxiety. Codependents may be at increased risk for physical and sexual abuse.

Researchers continue to explore this dimension of alcoholism. Many students have found some of the resources identified in this chapter to be especially helpful.

Denial and Enabling

Problem drinkers and alcoholics frequently use the psychological defence mechanism of *denial* to maintain their drinking behaviour. By convincing themselves that their lives are not affected by their drinking, problem drinkers and alcoholics are able to maintain their drinking patterns. A person's denial is an unconscious process that is apparent only to rational observers.

Formerly, it was up to alcoholics to admit that their denial was no longer effective before they could be admitted to a treatment program. This is not the case today. Currently, family members, friends, or coworkers of alcohol-dependent people are encouraged to intervene and force an alcohol-dependent person into treatment.

TALKING POINTS • One of your professors is a known alcoholic. You wonder why no one has persuaded her to seek treatment. Would you intervene in any way to make that happen? If so, how?

During treatment, it is important for chemically dependent people to break through the security of denial and admit that alcohol controls their lives. This process is demanding and often time consuming, but it is necessary for recovery.

For family and friends of chemically dependent people, denial is part of a process known as **enabling**. In this process, people close to the problem drinker or alcoholic inadvertently support drinking behaviour by denying that a problem really exists. Enablers unconsciously make excuses for the drinker, try to keep the drinker's work and family life intact, and in effect make the continued abuse of alcohol possible. For example, students enable problem drinkers when they clean up a drinker's messy room, lie to professors about a student's class absences, and provide class notes or other assistance to a drinker who can't keep up academically.

Alcohol counsellors contend that enablers are an alcoholic's worst enemy because they can significantly delay the onset of effective therapy. Do you know of a situation in which you or others have enabled a person with an alcohol problem?

Alcoholism and the Family

Considerable disruption occurs in the families of alcoholics, not only from the consequences of the drinking behaviour (such as violence, illness, and unemployment), but also because of the uncertainty of the family's role in causing and prolonging the situation. Family members often begin to adopt a variety of new roles that will allow them to cope with the presence of the alcoholic in the family. Among the more commonly seen roles are the family hero, the lost child, the family mascot, and the scapegoat.[29] Unless family members receive appropriate counselling, these roles may remain intact for a lifetime.

Once an alcoholic's therapy has begun, family members are encouraged to participate in many aspects of the recovery. This participation will also help them understand how they are affected by alcoholism. If therapy and aftercare include participation in Alcoholics Anonymous (AA), family members will be encouraged to become affiliated with related support groups.

Helping the Alcoholic: Rehabilitation and Recovery

Once an alcoholic realizes that alcoholism is not a form of moral weakness but rather a clearly defined illness, the chances for recovery are remarkably good. It is estimated that as many as two-thirds of alcoholics can recover. Recovery is especially enhanced when the addicted person has a good emotional support system, including concerned family members, friends, and employer. When this support system is not well established, the alcoholic's chances for recovery are considerably lower.

AA is a voluntary support group of recovering alcoholics who meet regularly to help each other get and stay sober. Over 51 000 groups exist in the United States, another 5000 in Canada, and nearly 40 000 more worldwide.[30] AA encourages alcoholics to admit their lack of power over alcohol and to turn their lives over to a higher power (although the organization is nonsectarian). Members of AA are encouraged not to be judgmental about the behaviour of other members. They support anyone with a problem caused by alcohol.

Key Terms

alcoholism
A primary, chronic disease with genetic, psychosocial, and environmental factors influencing its development and manifestations.

codependence
An unhealthy relationship in which one person is addicted to alcohol or another drug and a person close to him or her is "addicted" to the alcoholic or drug user.

enabling
Inadvertently supporting a drinker's behaviour by denying that a problem exists.

Al-Anon and Alateen are parallel organizations that give support to people who live with alcoholics. Al-Anon is geared toward spouses and other relatives, and Alateen focuses on children of alcoholics. There are 28 000 Al-Anon groups and 3000 Alateen groups worldwide. Both organizations help members realize that they are not alone and that successful adjustments can be made to nearly every alcoholic-related situation. AA, Al-Anon, and Alateen chapter organizations are usually listed in the telephone book or in the classified sections of local newspapers. You can locate Al-Anon and Alateen on the Web at **www.al-anon.alateen.org**.

For people who feel uncomfortable with the concept that their lives are controlled by a higher power, *secular recovery programs* are becoming popular. These programs maintain that sobriety comes from within the alcoholic. Secular programs strongly emphasize self-reliance, self-determination, and rational thinking about one's drinking. Secular Organizations for Sobriety (SOS) is a good example of a secular recovery program that has branches in Canada.

Common Traits of Adult Children of Alcoholics

Adult children of alcoholics may:

- Have difficulty identifying normal behaviour
- Have difficulty following a project from beginning to end
- Lie when it would be just as easy to tell the truth
- Judge themselves without mercy
- Have difficulty having fun
- Take themselves very seriously
- Have difficulty with intimate relationships
- Overreact to changes over which they have no control
- Constantly seek approval and affirmation
- Feel that they are different from other people
- Be super-responsible or super-irresponsible
- Be extremely loyal, even in the face of evidence that the loyalty is undeserved
- Tend to lock themselves into a course of action without considering the consequences

Drugs to Treat Alcoholism

Could there be a medical cure for alcoholism? For nearly 50 years, the only prescription drug physicians could use to help drinkers stop drinking was Antabuse. Antabuse would cause drinkers to become extremely nauseated whenever they used alcohol.

In 1995 the U.S. Food and Drug Administration approved the drug naltrexone (Revia), which works by reducing the craving for alcohol and the pleasurable sensations felt when drinking. Revia is also available in Canada. Combining naltrexone with conventional behaviour modification has shown promising results. Additionally, the use of antidepressants by some alcoholics has been especially helpful during treatment.

CURRENT ALCOHOL CONCERNS

Adult Children of Alcoholic Parents

In recent years a new dimension of alcoholism has been identified—the unusually high prevalence of alcoholism among adult children of alcoholics (ACOAs). It is estimated that these children are about four times more likely to develop alcoholism than children whose parents are not alcoholics. Even the ACOAs who do not become alcoholics may have a difficult time adjusting to everyday living. Janet Geringer Woititz, author of the best-selling book *Adult Children of Alcoholics*,[31] describes 13 traits that most ACOAs exhibit to some degree (see the Star Box above).

In response to this concern, support groups have been formed to help prevent the adult sons and daughters of alcoholics from developing the condition that afflicted their parents (see the Star Box on p. 181). If a stronger link for an inherited genetic predisposition to alcoholism is found, these groups may play an even greater role in the prevention of alcoholism.

Women and Alcohol

For decades, women have consumed less alcohol and had fewer alcohol-related problems than men. At present, evidence is mounting that more women are choosing to drink and that some subgroups of women, especially young women, are drinking more heavily. An increased number of admissions of women to treatment centres may also reflect that alcohol consumption among women is on the rise.[32] Special approaches for women to use for staying sober are discussed in the Learning from Our Diversity box on p. 181.

Studies indicate that currently there are almost as many female as male alcoholics. However, there appear to be differences between men and women when it comes to alcohol abuse: (1) More women than men can point to a specific triggering event (such as a divorce, death of a spouse, a career change, or children leaving home) that started them drinking heavily. (2) Alcoholism among women often starts later and progresses more quickly than alcoholism among men. (3) Women tend to be prescribed more mood-altering drugs than men, so women face greater risk of drug interaction or cross-tolerance. (4) Nonalcoholic men tend to divorce their alcoholic spouses nine times more often than nonalcoholic women divorce their alcoholic spouses. Thus alcoholic women are not as likely to have a family support system to aid them in their recovery attempts. (5) Female alcoholics do not tend to receive as much social support

Resources for Adult Children of Alcoholics

Experts agree that adult children of alcoholics who believe they have come to terms with their feelings sometimes face lingering problems. It can prove worthwhile to seek help if you experience the following:

- Difficulty in identifying your needs
- Persistent anger or sadness
- Inability to enjoy your successes
- Willingness to tolerate inappropriate behaviour
- Continual fear of losing control

Here are some support groups to contact for more information:

Al-Anon Family Group Headquarters
Capital Corporate Centre
9 Antares Drive, Suite 245
Ottawa, ON K2E 7V5
Tel: (613) 723-8484
Fax: (613) 723-0151
www.Al-Anon.Alateen.org

Adult Children of Alcoholics
World Service Organization, Inc.
P.O. Box 3216
Torrance, CA 90510
www.adultchildren.org

The Awareness Center
Resources for Adult Children of Alcoholics
(Web site of Dr. Janet Woititz)
www.drjan.com

Learning from Our Diversity

Staying Sober: New Pathways for Women

Since 1935, when it was founded by two white, American, male alcoholics, Alcoholics Anonymous has expanded to encompass millions of members in virtually every region of the world who strive to achieve and maintain sobriety by adhering to AA's well-known 12-step program of recovery. With its strong spiritual orientation emphasizing the acknowledgement of a "higher power," AA offers safety, comfort, and structure to people of all ages and backgrounds, and both sexes. For decades, women as well as men have made AA the cornerstone of their efforts to get sober and stay sober.

Not all women, however, are comfortable with AA's focus on Christian spirituality and the perceived masculine orientation of its chief text, *Alcoholics Anonymous* (familiarly known as the "Big Book"), and other program literature. These women place an equally high value on sober living as do AA adherents, but they prefer to pursue that goal in other settings. In recent years, alternatives to AA have emerged that offer peer group acceptance and support for recovering alcoholic women, but do so in a nonspiritual, nonsexist context.

One such group, Women for Sobriety, is a mutual aid organization for women with alcohol problems that was founded in 1975 by Dr. Jean Kirkpatrick. The WFS program focuses on improving self-esteem; members achieve sobriety by taking responsibility for their actions and by learning not to dwell on negative thoughts. Another alternative, Rational Recovery, is open to both men and women. RR, which is based on the theories of psychologist Albert Ellis's Rational Emotive Therapy, also uses a cognitive, nonspiritual approach that fosters cohesiveness and provides the emotional support sought by people who seek to gain and maintain sobriety.

Particularly for "marginalized" alcoholic women such as lesbians, racial and ethnic minorities, and those of non-Christian religious backgrounds, alcoholism-treatment professionals increasingly are being encouraged to present the full range of support-group options, including but not emphasizing the approach of Alcoholics Anonymous.

If you were seeking help to achieve and maintain sobriety, would you be more inclined to attend a program based on spirituality, or one that offers a rational, cognitive approach? Why?[33, 34, 35]

as men in their treatment and recovery. (6) Unmarried, divorced, or single-parent women tend to have significant economic problems that may make entry into a treatment program especially difficult. (7) Women seem to be more susceptible than men to medical complications resulting from heavy drinking.[36] In light of the generally recognized educational, occupational, and social gains made by women during the last two decades, it will be interesting to see whether these male-female differences continue. What's your best guess?

Alcohol Advertising

Every few years, careful observers can see subtle changes in the ways the alcoholic beverage industry markets its products. Recently, the marketing push appears to be directed toward minorities (through advertisements for malt liquor and fortified wines), women (through wine and wine cooler ads), and youth (through trendy, young adult-oriented commercials and Web sites).

On college and university campuses, aggressive alcohol campaigns have used rock stars, beach party scenes, athletic event sponsorships, and colourful newspaper supplements as vehicles to encourage the purchase of alcohol. Critics claim that most of the collegiate advertising is directed at the "below age 21" crowd and that the prevention messages are not strong enough to offset the potential health damage to this population. How do you feel about alcohol advertising on your campus? If you're a nontraditional-age student, do you find the advertising campaigns amusing or potentially dangerous?

Taking Charge of Your Health

- Determine whether you are affected by someone's drinking by doing the Personal Assessment on p. 185.
- Prepare for a possible alcohol-related emergency by reviewing the signs listed in the Changing for the Better box on p. 170.
- Learn how to host a party responsibly by reading the Changing for the Better box on p. 176.
- If you think that you are a problem drinker or an alcoholic, join a support group to get help.
- Enter into a "Contract for Life" with your parents or closest friends, a pact that says that you will provide safe transportation for each other if either of you is unable to drive safely after consuming alcohol.
- Make a commitment to responsible alcohol use by joining a campus group that works toward this goal.

SUMMARY

- Alcohol is the drug of choice among post-secondary students and the rest of Canadian society.
- Many factors affect the rate of absorption of alcohol into the bloodstream.
- As BAC rises, predictable depressant effects take place.
- People with acute alcohol intoxication must receive first-aid care immediately.
- The health effects of chronic alcohol abuse are quite serious.
- Problem drinking reflects an alcohol use pattern in which a drinker's behaviour creates personal difficulties or problems for others.
- Alcoholism is a primary, chronic disease with a variety of possible causes and characteristics.
- Denial, enabling, codependence, ACOAs, and alcohol advertising are current issues related to alcohol abuse in Canada.
- Recovery and rehabilitation programs can be effective in helping alcoholics become sober.
- Antabuse, naltrexone, and antidepressants are drugs prescribed by physicians to help alcoholics in treatment.

REVIEW QUESTIONS

1. What percentage of North American adults consume alcohol? Approximately what percentage of adults are classified as abstainers? What percentage of post-secondary students drink?
2. What is binge drinking?
3. What is meant by the term *proof*?
4. What is the nutritional value of alcohol? How do "light" and low-alcohol beverages compare?
5. Identify and explain the various factors that influence the absorption of alcohol. Why is it important to be aware of these factors?
6. What is BAC? Describe the general sequence of physiological events that takes place when a person drinks alcohol at a rate faster than the liver can oxidize it.
7. What are the signs and symptoms of acute alcohol intoxication? What are the first-aid steps you should take to help a person with this problem?
8. Describe the characteristics of fetal alcohol syndrome and fetal alcohol effects.
9. Explain the differences between problem drinking and alcoholism.
10. What is codependence? What roles do denial and enabling play in alcoholism?

11. What are some common traits of ACOAs?
12. What unique alcohol-related problems exist for women?
13. Describe the activities undertaken by SADD, MADD, and BACCHUS, and by AA, Al-Anon, and Alateen.

THINK ABOUT THIS ...

- How much is your decision to drink or not drink influenced by those around you?
- This chapter refers to data indicating that over one-third of college and university drinkers can be considered heavy drinkers. Do you think this is true at your school?
- What role should men play in the prevention of fetal alcohol syndrome?
- Do you believe it is your responsibility to make sure friends do not drink and drive?
- Do you think your drinking pattern will change when you graduate?

REFERENCES

1. U.S. Department of Health and Human Services: *Alcohol and health: tenth special report to the U.S. Congress*, NIH Pub No 00-1583, 2000, U.S. Government Printing Office.
2. *Canadian Profile 1999: Alcohol*, 1999, Canadian Centre on Substance Abuse, **www.ccsa.ca/Profile/cp99alc.htm**.
3. Core Institute. 2001 statistics on alcohol and other drug use on American college campuses, **www.sic.edu.departments/ coreinst/public/html/recent.html**, June 16, 2003.
4. U.S. Department of Health and Human Services: *NIAAA alcohol alert: moderate drinking*, No. 16 (PH 315), April 1992, U.S. Government Printing Office.
5. Alcohol and your health: it's a question of balance, *Low risk drinking guidelines*, 1997, Toronto's Addiction Research Foundation.
6. Drinking and you, **www.drinkingandyou.com/site/can/moder.htm**, August 22, 2005.
7. U.S. Department of Health and Human Services: *NIAAA alcohol alert: college drinking*, No. 29 (PH 357), July 1995, U.S. Government Printing Office.
8. Centre for Addiction and Mental Health: Evaluate your drinking, **www.camh.net/publications/evaluate_your_drinking.html**.
9. *How much of a problem is alcohol use in Canada*? 1999, Canadian Centre on Substance Abuse.
10. Core Institute: 2001 statistics on alcohol and other drug use on American college campuses (online), **www.siu.edu/departments/ coreinst/public_html/recent.html**. June 16, 2003.
11. Kinney J: *Loosening the grip: a handbook of alcohol information*, ed 6, 1998, McGraw-Hill.
12. Meichun K et al, More Canadian students drink but American students drink more: comparing college alcohol use in two countries, *Addition* 97: 1583–1592, 2003.
13. Frezza M et al: High blood alcohol levels in women: role of decreased gastric alcohol dehydrogenase, activity and first-pass metabolism, *N Engl J Med 322*(4), 95–99, 1990.
14. *Loosening the grip.*
15. Aldaf EM, Paglia A, Beitchman JH: *The mental health and well-being of Ontario students, 1991–2001: findings from the OSDUS*, 2002, Canadian Centre for Addiction and Mental Health.
16. Ray O, Ksir C: *Drugs, society and human behavior*, ed 8, 1999, McGraw-Hill.
17. *Alcohol and health.*
18. Health Canada: *Safety and injury.* **www.hc-sc.gc.ca/english/lifestyles/injury.html**.
19. Health Canada: Healthy living safety and injury, **www.hc-sc.gc.ca/index_e.html**, August 22, 2005.
20. MADD Canada: The magnitude of the alcohol/drug-related crash problem in Canada overview, **www.madd.ca/english/research/magnitudememo.html**, August 22, 2005.
21. Canadian Institute for Health Information: *Motor vehicle collisions: most frequent causes of severe injuries*, CIHI. **www.hc-sc.gc.ca/hpb/lcdc/publicat/pcd97/mrt_mf_e.html**.
22. Health Canada: *The economic burden of unintentional injury*, Child Injury Division. **www.hc-sc.gc.ca/hpb/lcdc/brch/injury/unintent**.
23. *NIAAA alcohol alert.*
24. *Alcohol and health.*
25. *NIAAA alcohol alert.*
26. Ibid.
27. Alberta Alcohol and Drug Abuse Commission: *ABC fact sheet: being a good host.* **http://corp.aadac.com/alcohol/factsheets/good_host.asp**.
28. Morse RM et al: The definition of alcoholism, *JAMA* 268(8): 1012–1014, 1992.
29. *NIAAA alcohol alert.*
30. Web site information, **www.alcoholicsanonymous.org**, November 24, 1999.
31. Woititz, JG: *Adult children of alcoholics*, 1990, Health Communications, Inc.
32. *NIAAA alcohol alert.*
33. Galanter M et al: Rational recovery: alternative to AA for addiction? *American Journal of Drug and Alcohol Abuse*, 19: 499, 1993.

34. Hall J: Lesbians' participation in Alcoholics Anonymous: experience of social, personal, and political tensions. *Contemporary Drug Problems,* 23(1): 113. Spring 1996.

35. Kaskutas L: A road less traveled: choosing the "Women for Sobriety" program. *Journal of Drug Issues,* 26(1): 77, Winter 1996.

36. *NIAAA alcohol alert.*

SUGGESTED READINGS

Beattie M: *Playing it by heart: taking care of yourself no matter what,* 1999, Hazelden Education Information.
This book is a follow-up to the author's highly successful *Codependent no more: how to stop controlling others and start caring for yourself.* Melody Beattie shows how to keep focused on yourself as you move between being afraid to trust someone and being absorbed in another's life. The author shows people in recovery that their lives may be challenging but that balance and healing are possible.

Dick B, Seiberling JF: *The Akron genesis of Alcoholics Anonymous,* Newton revised ed, 1998, Paradise Research Publications.
This book traces the fascinating beginning of Alcoholics Anonymous at the Akron, Ohio, home of Dr. Bob Smith, in 1935. The development of the AA spiritual principles is discussed, as well as the activities undertaken in the early meetings of AA in homes and hospitals. The important role of the wives of the early AA members is traced.

Kettelhack G: *First-year sobriety: when all that changes is everything,* 1998, Hazelden Information Education.
This book is an excellent guide for coping with all the changes that take place during the first year of an alcoholic's sobriety. Interacting with family and friends on new levels is one of the many new experiences sober people face during the first year. Additional changes, such as those that occur at work, are also discussed. How to use newly acquired free time effectively is also explored in this book.

Nuwer H: *The wrongs of passage: fraternities, sororities, hazing and binge drinking,* 1999, Indiana University Press.
Binge drinking remains a cornerstone of various Greek activities and rituals, despite the public image displayed by fraternities and sororities. In his serious, critical exploration of the Greek system that exists on many American college campuses, Nuwer builds on his 1990 book *Broken pledges: the deadly rite of hazing.* He discusses the continuing problems experienced by young students as they try to fit in with older brothers and sisters. Nuwer places some of the blame on college administrators who fail to acknowledge the continuing problems with alcohol.

Name ______________________________ **Date** ______________

Personal Assessment

Are You Troubled by Someone's Drinking?

The following questions are designed to help you decide whether you are affected by someone's drinking and could benefit from a program such as Al-Anon. Record your number of yes and no responses in the boxes at the end of the questionnaire.

	Yes	No
1. Do you worry about how much someone else drinks?	____	____
2. Do you have money problems because of someone else's drinking?	____	____
3. Do you tell lies to cover up for someone else's drinking?	____	____
4. Do you feel that if the drinker loved you, he or she would stop drinking to please you?	____	____
5. Do you blame the drinker's behaviour on his or her companions?	____	____
6. Are plans frequently upset or meals delayed because of the drinker?	____	____
7. Do you make threats, such as: "If you don't stop drinking, I'll leave you?"	____	____
8. Do you secretly try to smell the drinker's breath?	____	____
9. Are you afraid to upset someone for fear it will set off a drinking bout?	____	____
10. Have you been hurt or embarrassed by a drinker's behaviour?	____	____
11. Are holidays and gatherings spoiled because of the drinking?	____	____
12. Have you considered calling the police for help in fear of abuse?	____	____
13. Do you search for hidden alcohol?	____	____
14. Do you often ride in a car with a driver who has been drinking?	____	____
15. Have you refused social invitations out of fear or anxiety that the drinker will cause a scene?	____	____

	Yes	No
16. Do you sometimes feel like a failure when you think of the lengths to which you have gone to control the drinker?	____	____
17. Do you think that if the drinker stopped drinking, your other problems would be solved?	____	____
18. Do you ever threaten to hurt yourself to scare the drinker?	____	____
19. Do you feel angry, confused, or depressed most of the time?	____	____
20. Do you feel there is no one who understands your problems?	____	____
TOTAL	____	____

Interpretation

If you answered yes to three or more of these questions, Al-Anon or Alateen may be able to help. You can contact Al-Anon or Alateen by looking in your local telephone directory or by writing to Al-Anon Family Group Headquarters, Inc., 1600 Corporate Landing Parkway, Virginia Beach, VA 23454-5617, or log on to **www.al-anon-alateen.org**.

To Carry This Further ...

Sometimes the decision to seek help from a support group is a difficult one. If you answered yes to any of the questions above, spend a few moments reflecting on your responses. How long have you been experiencing problems because of someone else's drinking? How would sharing your feelings with others—people who have dealt with very similar problems—help you cope with your own situation? Knowing you're not alone can often be a great relief; it's up to you to take the first step.

Focus on

ALCOHOL AND VIOLENCE: A DANGEROUS LINK

Drinking and driving is by far the largest criminal cause of injury in Canada.[1] About 3000 people per year die in motor vehicle crashes. Of that total, 35% are attributed to alcohol.[2] In recent years, there has been an increase in public service messages to raise awareness about driving under the influence of alcohol. In fact, the massive campaign against drinking and driving has been quite successful in reducing the number of drunk-driving accidents and fatalities. However, people may think that as long as a person doesn't get behind the wheel, it's okay to drink. But there are other potential dangers to the abuse of alcohol. One particular problem that perhaps has not been stressed enough in the media is the link between alcohol use and violent crime.[3]

Obviously, not everyone who drinks becomes violent, but in many violent crimes at least one person involved has been drinking. Perhaps alcohol by itself is not enough to cause violence, but use of alcohol may be one of several factors that act in combination to cause violent behaviour in some instances.[4] In the early 1990s in Canada more than half of the people accused of murder had used some kind of substance (alcohol, drugs, or a combination of both) beforehand.[5]

Alcohol and Types of Violent Crime

The risk of a person's perpetrating a violent event is higher among heavy drinkers than light drinkers. Heavy drinkers are also at higher risk of being victims of violent crime and are also more likely to inflict and to receive violent injuries.[6] A Johns Hopkins University study shows that being a victim of sexual abuse or assault is also linked to high rates of alcohol use.[7]

Alcohol plays a significant role in various types of violent crime. Substantial numbers of sexual-assault victims and offenders were drinking before their crime occurred. Alcohol use is present in over half of all domestic violence cases, and frequency of drunkenness for husbands appears to be associated with spouse abuse.[8] One study estimated that incidences of spouse abuse were almost 15 times higher for households where husbands were described as often drunk as opposed to never drunk. And drinking may also increase the risk of becoming a robbery victim.[9,10]

Campus Crime and the Effects of Alcohol

Of particular interest to college and university students are the data linking campus crimes to alcohol use. A *USA Today* study of 13 000 students suggests that as many as four out of five campus crimes committed by students are related to alcohol or drug use or both. The attitudes of students may be a contributing factor to alcohol abuse on campus; 85% of freshmen in the survey condoned binge drinking (defined in this study as over five drinks in a continuous period). Victims of violent crime on campus generally reported heavier drinking habits than nonvictims,[11] and this parallels data from the general population.[12] When sexual assaults and rapes were reported, both the perpetrator and the victim had typically been drinking.[13]

Most researchers in the field are certain that alcohol plays a role in violence against women on college and university campuses. For example, the Canadian National Survey found a relationship between the number of times a week that men went out drinking and the likelihood that they would admit to being physical or sexual abusers of women on campus.[14]

Impact of Alcohol on Violent Behaviour

So why is alcohol a contributing factor in violent crime? Alcohol acts as a depressant, which can reduce reaction time, impair coordination, and cloud judgment. Such impairment could decrease the chances of avoiding personal injury once a physical altercation begins. Alcohol also decreases inhibitions and may increase aggressive behaviour. It also may increase the likelihood of inflicting or receiving a severe injury during a violent act and has been shown to increase the severity of injuries obtained in violent acts. Alcohol impairs cognitive abilities and may increase the chances for miscommunication or misinterpretation during verbal conflicts.[15,16] The fact that many drinkers do not exhibit violent behaviour suggests that individual differences in brain chemistry may promote aggressive behaviours in some people but not others.[17]

What You Can Do

Although alcohol alone may not cause violence, when alcohol is introduced into a situation that has the potential to become violent, it can increase the chances that violence will occur. As the number of drunk drivers on the road has decreased, so has the number of drunk-driving accidents and fatalities. It seems logical to assume that if alcohol is kept out of the hands of people who are predisposed to violence, the number of alcohol-related crimes may also decrease.[18] This is not always possible, but it is possible for you to use good common sense when you are drinking or if you are with people who are drinking. Try to avoid potentially violent situations, and avoid people drinking around you who are acting in a reckless or violent manner. Drink in moderation, and help your companions recognize when they have had too much. Perhaps you or one of your companions can remain sober (a "designated thinker") to help avoid potentially dangerous situations and stay safe while partying.

For Discussion ...

Have you ever encountered an angry drinker? Is there a safe way to handle a person who is drunk and intending to do harm to someone? If you have ever been drunk, do you feel that you could have controlled your actions in a confrontation while you were drunk?

References

1. *Facts about alcohol*, 1991, Addiction Research Foundation. **www2.camh.net/arfpages/isd/pim/alcohol.html**.
2. Health Canada: *Leading causes of death in Canada*, 1997. **www.hc-sc.gc.ca/hpb/lcdc/publicat/pcd97/mrt_mf_e.html**.
3. Quigley BM, Corbett AB, and Tedeschi JT: Desired image of power, alcohol expectancies, and alcohol-related aggression, *Psychology of Addictive Behaviours*, 16 (4), 318–324, 2002.
4. Messerschmidt PM: Epidemiology of alcohol-related violence, *Alcohol Health and Research World*, 17(2), 1993.
5. *How much of a problem is drug use in Canada*? 1999, Canadian Health Network. **www.canadian-health-network.ca/faq-faq/substance_use_addictions-toxicomanie/2e.html**.
6. Cherpitel CJ: What emergency room studies reveal about alcohol involvement in violence-related injuries, *Alcohol Health and Research World*, 17(2), 1993.
7. Violence, drugs, alcohol spur decline of youth health across U.S., study says, *Jet*, 88(7), June 26, 1995.
8. Epidemiology.
9. Ibid.
10. Statistics Canada: Types of violence experienced by sex of victim, Canada, 1999, *Family violence in Canada: a statistical profile*, catalogue no. 85-224-X18, 1999, Canadian Centre for Justice Statistics.
11. Siegel D: What is behind the growth of violence on college campuses? *USA Today Magazine*, 122(2588), May 1994.
12. Epidemiology.
13. What is behind the growth of violence on college campuses?
14. De Keseredy WL, Schwartz M: *Women abuse on campus: results from the National Survey*, 1998, Sage.
15. Epidemiology.
16. What emergency rooms studies reveal.
17. U.S. Department of Health and Human Services: *NIAAA alcohol alert: alcohol, violence, and aggression*, No. 38-1997, October 1997, U.S. Government Printing Office.
18. Smart GL, Moore TM, Kahler CW, and Ramsey SE: Substance abuse and relationship violence among men court-referred to batterers' intervention programs. *Substance Abuse*, 24 (2), 107-122, 2003.

Chapter **9**

Rejecting Tobacco Use

Chapter Objectives

After reading this chapter, you should be able to

- Examine smoking rates among Canadians.
- Identify techniques used by the tobacco industry to encourage people to smoke.
- Critically evaluate tobacco advertisements to determine what audience particular ads target, and what messages they send to consumers.
- Administer the ten-item Hooked on Nicotine Checklist (HONC) to friends who smoke to determine the existence and depth of dependence.
- Explain the bolus theory, the adrenocorticotropic hormone (ACTH) theory, and the self-medication theory of nicotine addiction.
- Explain the particulate phase and the gaseous phase of tobacco smoke and identify the primary components of each.
- Describe the relationship between smoking and cardiovascular disease.
- Trace the role of smoking in the development of respiratory-tract cancer.
- Identify smoking-cessation aids, including various nicotine-delivery techniques, and describe steps that smokers can take to reduce or eliminate their use of tobacco.
- Explain the dangers of secondhand smoke and develop steps to reduce your exposure to it.

Online Learning Centre Resources

www.mcgrawhill.ca/college/hahn

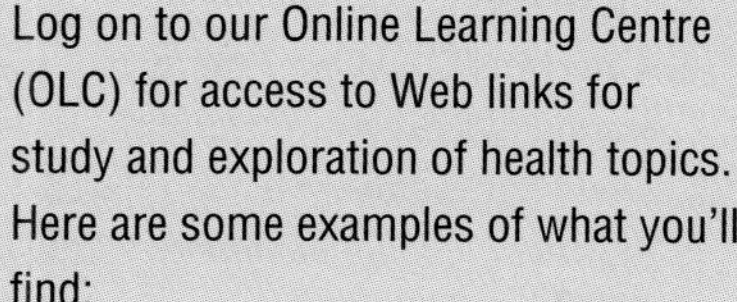

Log on to our Online Learning Centre (OLC) for access to Web links for study and exploration of health topics. Here are some examples of what you'll find:

- **www.healthservices.gov.bc.ca/ttdr** Check out this site, which provides information concerning the additives and ingredients in cigarettes.
- **www.cdc.gov/tobacco** Read all about it here: smoking kills more people than AIDS, alcohol, drug abuse, car crashes, murders, suicides, and fires—combined.
- **www.quitnet.org** Surf this Web site for help in quitting, including an online support group.
- **www.smoke-free.ca** Recent information from Physicians for a Smoke-Free Canada.

Media Pulse

Struggle to Get Hollywood to Butt Out Rages On

Now although the movie industry has denied it, a new study says that films showing actors smoking are contributing to the number of people who are choosing to light up.

The study, conducted by researchers at the University of California at San Diego, says girls are most susceptible to emulating people they admire on screen. Researchers found that if a star smokes, her female fans are twice as likely to do the same.

Film producers, though, have come up with an oft-repeated retort. They say they're simply reflecting society. Some people don't buy that.

"I've been to L.A. a million times, I've been to New York. You can't smoke in these restaurants, yet the characters are always smoking. I mean, you can't do that," film critic Jim Gordon says.

That reality leaves antismoking activists frustrated—particularly in Canada, where people are watching more movies than ever before.

"It gives children especially a false impression of what's normal, what's acceptable," says Verda Peters of the Canadian Lung Association.

A television host for MTV says it's marketers who are to blame. As the number of smokers declines, tobacco companies try to target teens.

"You want to make it look cool," Brian Adler said. "Give the Olsen twins a cigarette. Okay, they're successful, they're famous. People like to be like them, let's smoke a cigarette."

Hollywood and the tobacco industry deny there's any relationship between them. Meanwhile, people concerned with excessive smoking in films have started a movement. They say if there's too much smoking in a film, it should get an "R" rating.[1]

Today, the evidence linking tobacco use to impaired health is beyond serious challenge.[2] The regular user of tobacco products, particularly cigarettes, is more likely to become sick, remain sick for extended periods, and die prematurely than is a nonuser. It is estimated that tobacco use, cigarette smoking in particular, resulted in two million deaths between 1986 and 2000. In Canada, 45 000 Canadians die from smoking each year and the number is still growing. Smoking is responsible for one in five deaths annually, five times the number of deaths caused by car accidents, suicides, drug abuse, murder, and AIDS combined. Of the 45 000 people who die each year, 29 000 are men, 16 000 are women, and 100 are infants. Cigarettes are the leading cause of preventable death in North America.[3] Therefore, any contention made by the tobacco industry that tobacco use is not dangerous is groundless and ignores the growing weight of scientific evidence.

TOBACCO USE IN CANADIAN SOCIETY

Results from the Canadian Tobacco Use Monitoring Survey collected in 2003 estimated that 5.1 million Canadians smoke. This figure represents approximately 20% of the population of individuals over the age of 15, a minor decrease from the previous year (21%). Men (22%) still out-puff women (18%), except in the 15 to 19 category, where 19% of teenage girls smoke compared to 16% of boys. It is important to note that smoking trends indicate that fewer Canadians are smoking than previous years. In 1985, daily smokers smoked an average of 20.6 cigarettes per day. In 2003, smokers reported consuming 15.7 cigarettes per day. Further, 60% of smokers indicated that they used "light" or "mild" cigarettes.[4]

The situation in the United States is similar. Cigarette smoking among adults 18 years of age and older is currently at 22.5% and remains relatively constant. Men are more likely to smoke (25.2%) than women (20.0%). Smoking rates among men have fallen steadily since 1964, but rates among women increased until the early 1990s, when they began a gradual decline.

How much do you know about cigarette smoking? Find out by completing the Personal Assessment on p. 210. Figure 9–1[5] shows the trends in the prevalence of current smokers in Canada.

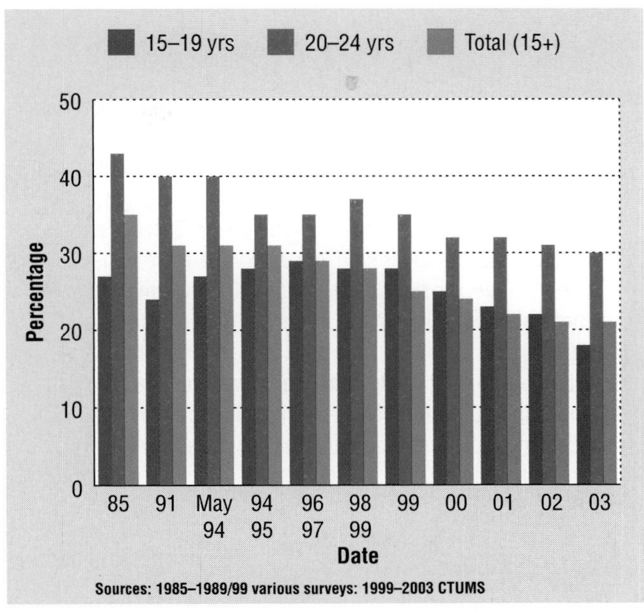

Figure 9–1 Trends in the Prevalence of Current Smokers (February–December 2003)

Advertising Approaches

In the face of an overall decline in cigarette smoking and overwhelming evidence that tobacco products are life threatening, the tobacco industry has tried to maintain the loyalty of its consumers. It accomplished this through continuous product development, skilled marketing, aggressive political lobbying, and diversification. These techniques included:

- Shrink-wrapping three-packs of brand-name cigarettes and selling them for the price of two or offering mail-in rebate coupons, making the products more affordable to young and low-income buyers
- Continued marketing of generic brands under the label of "value brands"
- Lowering the price of brand-name cigarettes to compete with value brands
- Carefully targeting advertising, particularly to women, minorities, and less-educated young adults
- Directing advertisements to youths (while simultaneously supporting public policy statements to control minors' access to cigarettes)
- Increased marketing of tobacco products overseas, where health restrictions are less forceful
- Acquiring non–tobacco related companies (corporate diversification) to minimize the loss of revenues from decreased sales of tobacco products
- Marshalling tobacco users into a "grassroots" effort to counter the growing political power of antismoking groups

Tobacco and Diseases of the Oral Cavity

Inhaling tobacco smoke in any form, whether from cigarettes, cigars, or pipes, places the oral cavity and mouth at risk for disease. Exposure to tobacco smoke in the form of cigarettes increases the likelihood of dying from oral and pharyngeal cancer by sixfold compared to a nonsmoker. There is a twofold increase of risk for cigar smokers as compared to nonsmokers.

The tongue, the floor of the mouth, and the gingiva are all possible sites for cancers. It was estimated in 1996 that approximately 700 Canadians died as a result of smoking-attributable lip, oral cavity, and pharyngeal cancers. The risk of oral cancers (with tobacco-specific nitrosamines being the suspected carcinogenic agents) also increases with the use of chewing tobacco.

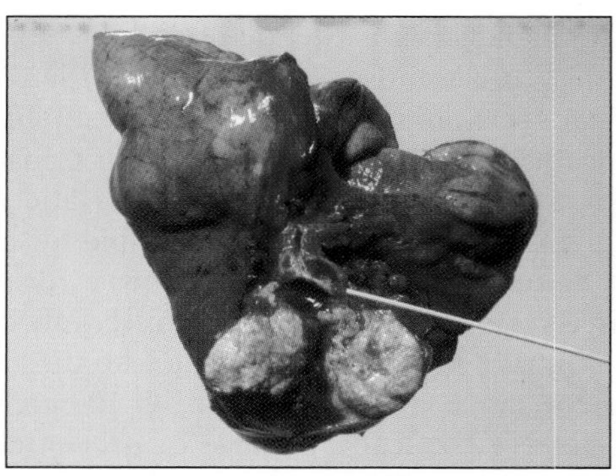

Graphic images, like this diseased lung, are becoming commonplace in advertising to discourage smoking.

Clearly, the tobacco industry remains healthy and its products remain life threatening to both smokers and nonsmokers.

The Tobacco Industry under Fire

How much has the tobacco industry known about the addictive and life-shortening nature of its products, particularly cigarettes? The protective wall of denial built by the tobacco industry crumbled in November 1998, when 46 U.S. states joined four other states that had settled with the tobacco industry earlier. The tobacco industry agreed to pay $246 billion (over 25 years) to reimburse the states for Medicaid expenditures associated with treating smoking-related illnesses; to stop advertisements intended to influence tobacco use by children; and to fund antismoking education program development and implementation. In turn, the states agreed not to initiate further class-action lawsuits against the tobacco industry.

Currently, the evidence linking tobacco use to impaired health is beyond challenge. In fact, it has been admitted by the tobacco industry via internal documents released by the Liggett Tobacco Company. These documents (totalling 11 million pages) detail activities by the tobacco industry to disprove, mask, and deny its own knowledge that nicotine is addictive and that cigarette smoking causes cancer and chronic obstructive lung disease and increases the risk of developing cardiovascular disease. The documents also revealed that concerted marketing efforts were directed toward children and young adolescents to influence them to smoke.

Since the now outdated Tobacco Restraint Act of 1908, Canada has tried to regulate tobacco products. Various pieces of legislation have been proposed, passed, and challenged during the government's fight to address the health problems associated with the use of tobacco. Attempts to access relevant information regarding tobacco manufacture, sale, labelling and promotion, and the impact of tobacco on the health of Canadians is ongoing.

Canada is recognized for having taken an early and continuing international leadership role in combatting smoking and in regulating the use, sale, marketing, and labelling of tobacco products. Under the Tobacco Products Control Act, many regulations governing the sale and control of tobacco products in Canada have been legislated. These include regulations on the sale of tobacco to young persons.

The Tobacco Act of 1997 regulates the "manufacture, sale, labelling and promotion of tobacco products" in Canada. The act, a legislative response to the Canadian public health concern of smoking, includes protecting Canadian youth from the effects of smoking by restricting their access to tobacco products. For complete details of this act visit the Canadian Department of Justice Web site: **http://laws.justice.gc.ca/en/T-11.5**.

In addition to the regulation of the sale of tobacco to young persons, other regulations include bans on advertising and mandatory health warning labels on packaging. Under the new Tobacco Products Information Regulations, graphic health warning messages were made mandatory in December 2000 on Canada's best-selling cigarette brands. As of June 2001, all other tobacco products were required to display warning messages. These precedent-setting regulations are a vital part of the government's tobacco-control strategy. See the Star Box on p. 191 for more information on tobacco. Visit Health Canada's Web site (**www.hc-sc.gc.ca/ahc-asc/media/nr-cp/1999/1999_07bk3_e.html**) to view images that appear on cigarette packages.

Thanks, But No Cigar

For those cigar smokers who will apparently continue, and for those of you who might be increasingly interested in this form of tobacco use, consider the following information:

- *Secondhand (sidestream) cigar smoke is more poisonous than secondhand cigarette smoke.* The smoke from one cigar equals that of three cigarettes. Carbon monoxide emissions from one cigar are 30 times higher than for one cigarette.
- *Cigar smoking can cause cancer of the larynx (voice box), mouth, esophagus, and lungs.* Cancer death rates for cigar smokers are 34% higher than for nonsmokers.
- *Ninety-nine percent of cigar smokers have atypical cells found in the larynx.* These cells are the first step toward malignancy (cancer).
- *Cigar smokers are three to five times more likely to die of lung cancer than are nonsmokers.*
- *Cigar smokers have five times the risk of emphysema compared to nonsmokers.*
- *Nicotine does not have to be inhaled to damage the heart and blood vessels.* It is absorbed into the bloodstream through the mucous membranes of the mouth. Nicotine increases the heart rate and constricts the blood vessels, which reduces blood flow to the heart.

Pipe and Cigar Smoking

Many people believe that pipe or cigar smoking is a safe alternative to cigarette smoking. However, this is not the case. All forms of tobacco pose health threats.

When compared with cigarette smokers, pipe and cigar smokers have cancer of the mouth, throat, larynx (voice box), and esophagus at the same frequency. Cigarette smokers are more likely than pipe and cigar smokers to have lung cancer, chronic obstructive lung disease (COLD), and heart disease. However, the incidence of respiratory disease and heart disease in pipe and cigar smokers is still greater than that of nonusers of tobacco.[6]

TOBACCO USE AND THE DEVELOPMENT OF DEPENDENCE

Dependence can imply both a physical and a psychological relationship. With cigarettes, *physical dependence* or *addiction*, with its associated *tolerance*, *withdrawal*, and **titration**, is strongly developed by nearly one-half of all smokers. Most of the remaining population of smokers will experience lesser degrees of physical dependence. The difference in the extent of addiction may reflect a genetic tendency.[7] *Psychological dependence* or *habituation*, with its accompanying psychological *compulsion* and *indulgence*, is frequently seen.

Compulsion is a strong emotional desire to continue tobacco use despite restrictions on smoking and awareness of the health risks. The user is "compelled" to engage in uninterrupted tobacco use by the fear of the unpleasant physical, emotional, and social effects that result from discontinuing its use. In compulsion, indulgence is seen as "rewarding" oneself for aligning with a particular group or behaviour pattern. Indulgence is made possible by the reward systems built around tobacco use.

To the great benefit of the tobacco industry, dependence on tobacco is easily established. Many experts believe that physical dependence on tobacco is far more easily established than is dependence on alcohol, cocaine (other than crack), or heroin. Of all people who experiment with cigarettes, 85% develop some type of dependent relationship. This potential for dependence, including addiction, has prompted the U.S. FDA to request that tobacco products be defined as drug delivery systems, which would allow the FDA to regulate their availability.

A small percentage of smokers, known as "chippers," can smoke a few cigarettes on a daily basis without becoming dependent. Experts believe that these people have a defective gene that increases the toxic effect of nicotine. Because they enjoy smoking less, chippers smoke fewer cigarettes less frequently than regular smokers. They may be true "social smokers." Many inexperienced smokers also consider themselves "social smokers," yet can fail to realize that a few months of occasional smoking can lead to a lifetime of dependency.

Physiological Factors

The establishment and maintenance of physical **dependence** or addiction is less than fully understood. Most experts, however, believe that for a specific individual,

Key Term

titration
Particular level of a drug within the body; adjusting the level of nicotine by adjusting the rate of smoking.

dependence
General term that refers to the need to continue using a drug for psychological and/or physical reasons.

Health on the Web

Get Set to Quit

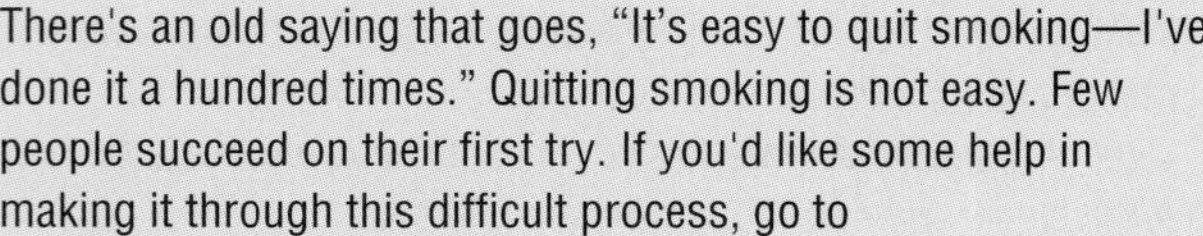

There's an old saying that goes, "It's easy to quit smoking—I've done it a hundred times." Quitting smoking is not easy. Few people succeed on their first try. If you'd like some help in making it through this difficult process, go to **www.hc-sc.gc.ca/hl-vs/tobac-tabac/quit-cesser/now-maintenant/road-voie/step-etape08_e.html**. The site offers information pertaining to the stages of quitting, quitting tips, and methods of quitting, to name a few.

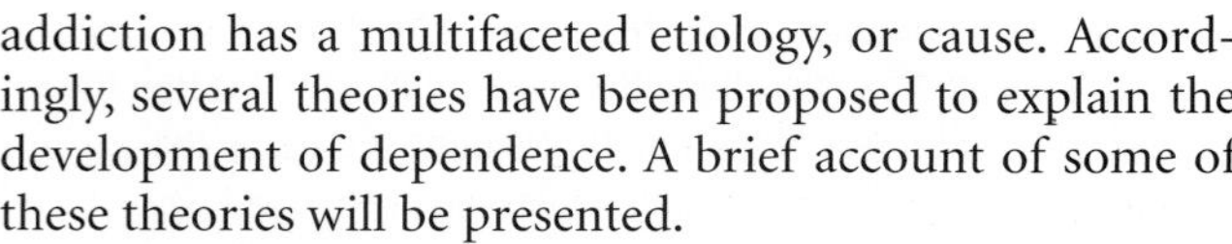

addiction has a multifaceted etiology, or cause. Accordingly, several theories have been proposed to explain the development of dependence. A brief account of some of these theories will be presented.

In the **bolus theory** of nicotine addiction, one of the oldest and most general theories of addiction, each inhalation of smoke releases into the blood a concentrated quantity of nicotine (a ball or bolus) that reaches the brain and results in a period of neurohormonal excitement. The smoker perceives this period of stimulation as pleasurable but, unfortunately, short lived. Accordingly, the smoker attempts to reestablish this pleasurable feeling by again inhaling and sending another bolus of nicotine on its way to the brain. Several hundred puffs per day quickly establish the schedule necessary to maintain the desired effect.

Nicotine may stimulate the release of adrenocorticotropic hormone (ACTH) from the pituitary gland (see Chapter 3). In response to ACTH, beta endorphins (naturally occurring opiate-like chemicals) are produced in specific areas of the brain, leading to mild feelings of euphoria. This stresslike response mechanism involving ACTH may also account for the increased energy expenditure seen in smokers and thus their tendency to maintain lower body weight than nonsmokers.

When these physiological responses are viewed collectively, nicotine may be seen as biochemically influencing brain activity by enhancing the extent and strength of various forms of "communication" between different brain areas. If this is the case, once the smoker is addicted, the functioning of that person's nervous system is greatly altered in comparison with that of a nonsmoker.

Another explanation, called *self-medication*, suggests that nicotine, through the effects of mood-enhancing neurotransmitters, may allow smokers to "treat" feelings of tiredness and lack of motivation. In other words, a smoke lifts the spirits, if only briefly. Eventually, however, smokers become dependent on tobacco as a "medication" to make them feel better. Because tobacco is a legal drug, it becomes preferred over equally effective illegal drugs such as cocaine and stimulants.

For most smokers, the smoking behaviour is eventually adjusted to maintain titration and prevent the discomfort of withdrawal. The desire not to experience withdrawal becomes as important as the arousal produced by nicotine.

Nicotine as an Addictive Drug

A great deal of interest and controversy arose regarding information about the addictive nature of nicotine contained in documents released by people once inside the tobacco industry. Among these issues were the extent to which the tobacco industry was aware of the addictive nature of nicotine and the appropriateness of studies conducted by the tobacco industry to determine whether young children would become future smokers. Further issues include allegations that the tobacco industry adjusted the pH levels of smokeless tobacco brands to alter nicotine levels and that research was conducted by the industry regarding nicotine enhancement of tobacco products.[8] Many people believe that since tobacco companies knew of the dangers of smoking and still encouraged nicotine addiction, they should compensate smokers or their families for losses resulting from smoking-related illnesses. As a result, hundreds of lawsuits have been filed.

Although these issues are far from resolved, the FDA and various other health organizations remain convinced that tobacco products are, in fact, drug delivery systems intended to deliver a powerfully addictive drug, nicotine. However, since it was determined in 2000 by the U.S. Supreme Court that the FDA lacked the authority to regulate the availability of tobacco products, they will continue to be sold as they are now, with tobacco itself under the jurisdiction of the U.S. Department of Agriculture. This situation is very different from what now exists in Canada because of the laws we have in place regarding the sale, use, and marketing of tobacco products. See the Learning from Our Diversity box on page 193 for another approach toward countering the acceptance of tobacco.

TALKING POINTS • A smoker says that she does not consider smoking to be a form of drug use. She becomes angry at the suggestion that cigarettes are part of a drug delivery system. How would you respond to her position?

Learning from Our Diversity

World No-Tobacco Day Seeks Support from Athletes and Artists

Sports and smoking seem to make strange bedfellows—but not in the world of advertising. For decades, cigarette manufacturers have worked hand-in-glove with professional athletes and teams, exchanging huge sums of money for endorsements of tobacco products or for the promotion and sponsorship of major sporting events. Although cigarette advertising has been banned from American television for nearly 30 years, the cozy connections continue, with perhaps the most notable example being the women's tennis tournament sponsored by Virginia Slims cigarettes (whose slogan, "You've come a long way, baby," resonated with women of a generation ago but is increasingly quoted in tones ranging from irony to contempt).

A step in the opposite direction is World No-Tobacco Day, promoted annually since 1988 by the World Health Organization (WHO), a unit of the United Nations. On a designated day each year, WHO urges tobacco users to abstain for at least that day—and, ideally, for good. WHO says the annual observance of World No-Tobacco Day (in Canada we recognize this day as Weedless Wednesday, a part of National Non-Smoking Week[9]) "is a unique opportunity to mobilize athletes, artists, and the media, as well as the public in general, in support of the objective of promoting a society and a way of life where tobacco use is no longer an accepted norm."

In sponsoring World No-Tobacco Day, WHO has focused on smoking in public places, on public transportation, in the workplace, and in medical facilities. A recent campaign escalated the stop-smoking effort with a theme of "United Nations and Specialized Agencies against Tobacco," with the aim of sharply reducing tobacco use worldwide.

As noted earlier, tobacco interests continue to promote many sporting events, as well as some cultural events. As far as sports are concerned, however, WHO officials see reason for encouragement in the recent smoke-free history of the Olympic Games. Beginning with the 1988 Winter Games in Calgary, all Olympic Games—both summer and winter—have been smoke free.

While a major cigarette manufacturer congratulates its (female) customers on having "come a long way, baby," the World Health Organization is strongly conveying the message that you'll go a lot farther if you don't smoke.

Which tactic do you think is most likely to reduce the rate of tobacco use worldwide: legal bans and restrictions, campaigns of persuasion like World No-Tobacco Day, or a combination of these two approaches?

For years, ill and dying smokers (and their survivors) have been suing tobacco companies, without success, for damages resulting from tobacco-induced illnesses. The success for the industry in countering these suits has been built around the contention that before 1964, they were unaware of any suspected dangers, and that since 1966, they have warned smokers of the dangers they face when using cigarettes. Smokers were found to be responsible for their own poor judgment, and the tobacco companies were judged to be free of liability because of their compliance with mandates to warn smokers.

With the release of the tobacco industry's internal documents and the successful settlement between 48 of the 50 states in the United States for Medicaid reimbursement, however, it is anticipated that individual smokers will be increasingly able to use the same documents to bring successful suits against the tobacco industry. It is notable that, increasingly, these suits are taking the form of class-action suits involving hundreds of deceased or former smokers.

Psychosocial Factors

Behavioural scientists suggest that dependence on tobacco can also be explained by psychosocial factors. Both research and general observation support many of the powerful influences these factors have on the beginning smoker.

Modelling

Because tobacco use is a learned behaviour, it is reasonable to accept that *modelling* acts as a stimulus to experimental smoking. Modelling suggests that susceptible people smoke to emulate, or model, their behaviour after smokers whom they admire or with whom they share other types of social or emotional bonds. Particularly for young adolescents (ages 14 to 17), smoking behaviour correlates with the smoking behaviour of slightly older peers and very young adults (ages 18 to 22), older siblings, and, to some degree, parents. Is it possible that the very young and attractive models used in tobacco (and beer) advertisements are seen by young adolescents as being closer to their own age than they really are?

Key Term

bolus theory
A theory of nicotine addiction based on the body's response to the bolus (ball) of nicotine delivered to the brain with each inhalation of cigarette smoke.

Modelling is particularly evident when smoking is a central factor in peer group formation and association; it can lead to a shared behavioural pattern that differentiates the group from others and from adults. When risk-taking behaviour and disregard for authority are common to the group, smoking becomes the behavioural pattern that most consistently identifies and bonds the group. Particularly for those young people who lack self-directedness or the ability to resist peer pressure, initial membership in a tobacco-using peer group may become inescapable.

When adolescents have lower levels of self-esteem and are searching for a way to improve their self-image, a role model who smokes is often seen as tough, sociable, and sexually attractive. The last two traits have been played up by the tobacco industry in its carefully crafted advertisements.

Manipulation

Tobacco use may meet the beginning smoker's need to physically manipulate something and provide the manipulative tool necessary to offset boredom, feelings of depression, or social immaturity. Taking out a cigarette or filling a pipe adds a measure of structure and control to situations in which people might otherwise feel somewhat ill at ease. The cigarette becomes a readily available and dependable "friend" to turn to in stressful moments.

Susceptibility to advertising

The images of the smoker's world portrayed in tobacco advertisements can be attractive. For adolescents, women, minorities, and other carefully targeted groups of adults, the tobacco industry associates a better life with the use of its products. Young and potential users are told that using tobacco products offers a sense of power, liberation, affluence, sophistication, and adult status. The message is that smoking will let them achieve things that most people must work a long time to gain.

Despite the satisfaction of their psychological needs through tobacco use, approximately 90% of adult smokers have, on at least one occasion, expressed a desire to quit, and 80% have actually attempted to become nonsmokers.

TOBACCO: THE SOURCE OF PHYSIOLOGICALLY ACTIVE COMPOUNDS

When burned, the tobacco in cigarettes, cigars, and pipe mixtures is a source of an array of physiologically active chemicals, many of which are closely linked to significant changes in normal body structure and function. With each puff of smoke the body is exposed to over 4000 chemical compounds, hundreds of which are known to be physiologically active, toxic, and carcinogenic. The 70 000-plus puffs taken in annually by the one-pack-a-day cigarette smoker result in a regularly occurring environment that makes the most polluted urban environment seem clean in comparison.

Cigarette, cigar, and pipe smoke can be described on the basis of two phases or components: the particulate phase and the gaseous phase. The **particulate phase** includes nicotine, water, and a variety of powerful chemical compounds known collectively as *tar*. Tar includes phenol, cresol, pyrene, DDT, and a benzene-ring group of compounds that includes benzo[*a*]pyrene. As tar is drawn down the airway, the larger particles settle along its length, while the smaller particles reach the alveoli, or small saclike ends of the airway, where air comes in close association with the bloodstream. Most carcinogenic (cancer-causing) compounds are found within the tar.

The **gaseous phase** of tobacco smoke, like the particulate phase, is composed of a variety of physiologically active compounds, including carbon monoxide, carbon dioxide, ammonia, hydrogen cyanide, isoprene, acetaldehyde, and acetone. At least 43 of these compounds have been determined to be carcinogenic and dozens more may be co-carcinogens.[10] *Carbon monoxide* is the most damaging compound found in this component of tobacco smoke. Its effects are discussed below.

Nicotine

Nicotine is a powerful psychotropic (psychoactive) chemical agent found in the particulate phase of tobacco smoke. When drawn into the lungs, about one-quarter of the nicotine in the inhaled smoke passes into the circulation and into the brain within 10 seconds of inhalation. *Nicotine receptors* within the brain are activated and produce a variety of responses, most of which are stimulating (see the discussion of nicotine addiction on pp. 191–193). High levels of nicotine, however, depress the CNS and result in the relaxation associated with heavy smoking.

The remaining nicotine absorbed into the blood travels throughout the body to nicotinic receptors located in a variety of tissues. Among the currently understood additional effects of nicotine are the reduction of intestinal activity, the release of epinephrine from the adrenal glands, the release of **norepinephrine** from peripheral nerves, an increase in heart rate, the constriction of peripheral blood vessels, and the dilation of airways within the respiratory system.

Nicotine that enters the body by routes other than inhalation produces similar effects but at a much slower rate. Smokeless tobacco, for example, reaches its fullest physiological effect by the end of 20 minutes, nicotine-containing gum within 30 minutes, and transdermal nicotine patches within several hours.

Table 9–1 Selected Established and Suspected Health Effects of Cigarette Smoking[12]

	Category of Condition	Established and Suspected Effects
1	Lung Disease	Lung cancer, chronic obstructive lung disease; increased severity of asthma; increased risk of developing various respiratory infections
2	Cancer Risk	Esophageal, laryngeal, oral, bladder, kidney, stomach, pancreatic, vulvar, cervical, and colorectal cancers
3	Heart Disease	Coronary heart disease; angina pectoris; heart attack; repeat heart attack; arrhythmia; aortic aneurysm; cardiomyopathy
4	Peripheral Vascular Disease	Pain and discomfort in the legs and feet resulting from restricted blood flow into the extremities
5	Skin Changes	Wrinkling; fingernail discoloration; psoriasis; palmoplantar pustulosis
6	Surgical Risk	Need for more anesthesia; increased risk of postsurgical respiratory infection; increased need for supplemental oxygen following surgery; delayed wound healing
7	Orthopedic Problems	Disc degeneration; less successful back surgery; musculoskeletal injury; delayed fracture healing
8	Rheumatologic Conditions	Osteoporosis and osteoarthritis
9	Environmental Tobacco Smoke and Pediatric Illnesses	Infections of the lower respiratory tract; more severe asthma; middle ear infections; Crohn's disease and ulcerative colitis; sudden infant death syndrome; impaired delivery of oxygen to body tissues
10	Complications in Obstetrics and Gynecology	Infertility; miscarriage; fetal growth retardation; prematurity; stillbirth; transmission of HIV to the fetus from the infected biological mother; birth defects; intellectual impairment of offspring; sudden infant death syndrome; earlier menopause
11	Male Infertility and Sexuality Dysfunctions	Decreased sperm motility; decreased sperm density; impotence
12	Neurological Disorders	Transient ischemic attack; stroke; worsened multiple sclerosis
13	Brain and Behaviour	Depression
14	Abnormalities of the Ears, Nose, and Throat	Snoring and hearing loss
15	Eyes	Cataracts; complications from Graves' disease; macular degeneration; optic neuropathy
16	Oral Health	Periodontal disease
17	Endocrine System	Increased metabolic rate; blood-sugar abnormalities; increased waist-to-hip ratio; redistribution of body fat
18	Gastrointestinal Diseases	Stomach and duodenal ulcers; Crohn's disease
19	Immune System	Impaired humoral and cell-mediated immunity
20	Emergency Medicine	Injuries from fires caused by smoking; occupational injuries

Carbon Monoxide

Burning tobacco forms **carbon monoxide (CO)** gas. Carbon monoxide is one of the most harmful components of tobacco smoke.

Carbon monoxide is a colourless, odourless, tasteless gas that possesses a very strong physiological attraction for hemoglobin, the oxygen-carrying component of each red blood cell. When carbon monoxide is inhaled, it quickly bonds with hemoglobin and forms a new compound, *carboxyhemoglobin*. In this form, hemoglobin is unable to transport oxygen to the tissues and cells where it is needed.

The presence of excessive levels of carboxyhemoglobin in the blood of smokers leads to shortness of breath and lowered endurance. Brain function may be reduced, reactions and judgment are dulled, and cardiovascular function is impaired. Fetuses are especially at risk for this oxygen deprivation because fetal development is so critically dependent on a sufficient oxygen supply from the mother.

Key Terms

particulate phase
Portion of the tobacco smoke composed of small suspended particles.

gaseous phase
Portion of tobacco smoke containing carbon monoxide and many other physiologically active gaseous compounds.

norepinephrine
Adrenaline-like chemical produced within the nervous system.

carbon monoxide (CO)
Chemical compound that can "inactivate" red blood cells.

ILLNESS, PREMATURE DEATH, AND TOBACCO USE

For people who begin tobacco use as adolescents or young adults, smoke heavily, and continue to smoke, the likelihood of premature death is virtually ensured. Two-pack-a-day cigarette smokers can expect to die seven to eight years earlier than their nonsmoking counterparts. Only deaths not related to smoking, which can afflict both smokers and nonsmokers alike, such as automobile accidents, keep the difference at this level rather than much higher. Not only will smokers, as a group, die sooner, but they also will probably experience painful, debilitating illnesses for an extended time (see Table 9–1).

Cardiovascular Disease

Cardiovascular disease is the leading cause of death among all adults, accounting for 945 836 deaths annually in the United States.[11] Statistics Canada reported that 74 824 cardiovascular disease deaths occurred in Canada in 2001.[12] Tobacco use, and cigarette smoking in particular, is clearly one of the major factors contributing to this cause. So important is tobacco use as a contributing factor in deaths from heart disease that cigarette smokers double the risk of experiencing a **myocardial infraction** and increase their risk of **sudden cardiac death** by two to four times. Fully one-third of all cardiovascular disease can be traced to cigarette smoking. The relationship between tobacco use and cardiovascular disease is centred on two major components of tobacco smoke: nicotine and carbon monoxide.

Nicotine and cardiovascular disease

The influence of nicotine on the cardiovascular system occurs when it stimulates the nervous system to release norepinephrine. This powerful stimulant increases the rate at which the heart contracts. The extent to which this is dangerous depends in part on the ability of the heart's own blood supply system to provide blood to the working heart muscle.

In addition to its influence on heart rate, nicotine is also a powerful constrictor of blood vessels throughout the body. As vessels constrict, the pressure within them increases. Recent research shows that nonreversible atherosclerotic damage to major arteries also occurs with smoking.[13]

Nicotine also increases blood **platelet adhesiveness**. *Platelets* are the component of blood that causes it to clot, or coagulate, after an injury. Nicotine makes these platelets more likely to adhere to one another, or "clump," which can cause blood clots to develop in the arteries. Heart attacks occur when clots form within the coronary arteries (see Chapter 10) or are transported to the heart from other areas of the body.

In addition to other influences on the cardiovascular system, nicotine possesses the ability to decrease the proportion of high-density lipoproteins (HDLs) and to increase the proportion of low-density lipoproteins (LDLs) and very low density lipoproteins that make up the body's blood cholesterol. (See Chapter 10 for further information about cholesterol's role in cardiovascular disease.)

Carbon monoxide and cardiovascular disease

Carbon monoxide, a second substance contributed by tobacco, influences the type and extent of cardiovascular disease found among tobacco users. Carbon monoxide interferes with oxygen transport within the circulatory system.

As described previously, carbon monoxide is a component of the gaseous phase of tobacco smoke and readily attaches to the hemoglobin of the red blood cells. Once attached, carbon monoxide makes the red blood cell permanently weaker in its ability to transport oxygen. These red blood cells remain relatively useless during the remainder of their 120-day life. Levels of carboxyhemoglobin in heavy smokers are associated with significant increases in the incidence of heart attack.

When a person has impaired oxygen-transporting abilities, physical exertion becomes increasingly demanding on both the heart and the lungs. The cardiovascular system will attempt to respond to the body's demand for oxygen, but these responses are themselves impaired as a result of the influence of nicotine on the cardiovascular system. If tobacco does create the good life, as advertisers claim, it also decreases the smoker's ability to participate actively in that life.

Cancer

Despite the toxic chemicals contained in cigarettes, not all smokers develop cancer. Perhaps the extent to which the body's cancer suppressor genes are influenced by carcinogenic substances in tobacco smoke puts some smokers at greater risk for tobacco-related cancer than others.

Recall that tobacco smoke has both a gaseous phase and a particulate phase. The particulate phase contains the tar fragment of tobacco smoke. This rich chemical environment contains over 4000 known chemical compounds, hundreds of which are possible carcinogens, or co-carcinogens.

In the normally functioning respiratory system, particulate matter suspended in the inhaled air settles on the tissues lining the airways and is trapped in **mucus** produced by specialized *goblet cells* (Figure 9–2). This mucus, with its trapped impurities, is continuously swept upward by the beating action of hairlike **cilia** of the cells lining the air passages. On reaching the throat, this mucus is swallowed and eventually removed through the digestive system.

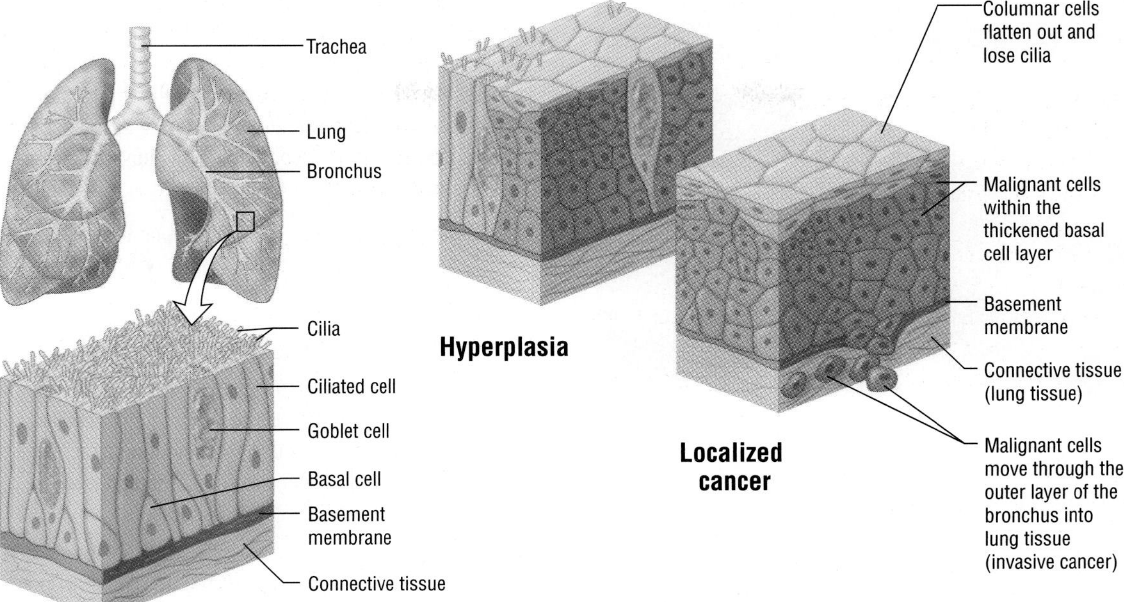

Figure 9–2 Tissue changes associated with bronchogenic carcinoma (lung cancer).

When tobacco smoke is drawn into the respiratory system, however, its rapidly dropping temperature allows the particulate matter to accumulate. This brown, sticky tar contains compounds known to harm the ciliated cells, goblet cells, and the *basal cells* of the respiratory lining. As the damage from smoking increases, the cilia become less effective in sweeping mucus upward to the throat. When cilia can no longer clean the airway, tar accumulates on the surfaces and brings carcinogenic compounds into direct contact with the tissues of the airway.

At the same time that the sweeping action of the lining cells is being slowed, substances in the tar are stimulating the goblet cells to increase the amount of mucus they normally produce. The "smoker's cough" is an attempt to remove this excess mucus.

With prolonged exposure to the carcinogenic materials in tar, predictable changes will begin to occur within the respiratory system's *basal cell layer*. The basal cells begin to display changes characteristic of all cancer cells (Figure 9–2). When a person stops smoking, these cells do not repair themselves as quickly as once thought.[14]

By the time lung cancer is usually diagnosed, its development is so advanced that the chance for recovery is very poor. Only 14% of all lung cancer victims survive for five years or more after diagnosis.[15] Most die in an agonizing way.

Cancerous activity in other areas of the respiratory system, including the *larynx*, and the oral cavity (mouth) follows a similar course. With oral cancer, carcinogens found in the smoke and in the saliva are involved in the cancerous changes. Tobacco users, such as pipe smokers, cigar smokers, and users of smokeless tobacco, have a very high rate of cancer of the mouth, tongue, and voice box.

Key Terms

myocardial infarction
Heart attack; the death of heart muscle caused by a blockage in one of the coronary arteries.

sudden cardiac death
Immediate death caused by a sudden change in the rhythm of the heart.

platelet adhesiveness
Tendency of platelets to clump together, thus enhancing the speed at which the blood clots.

mucus
Clear, sticky material produced by specialized cells within the mucous membranes of the body; mucus traps much of the suspended particulate matter within tobacco smoke.

cilia
Small, hairlike structures that extend from cells that line the air passages.

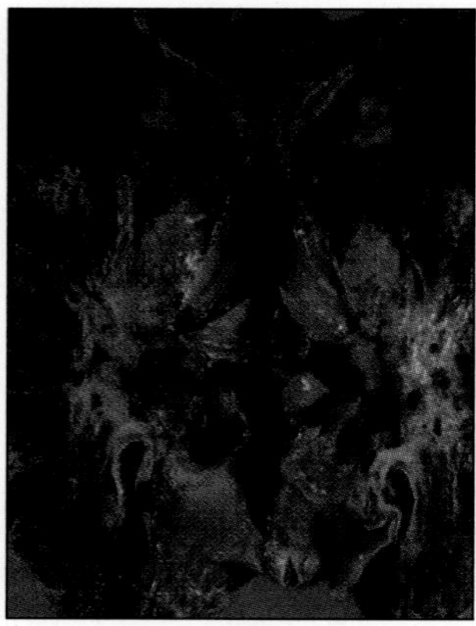
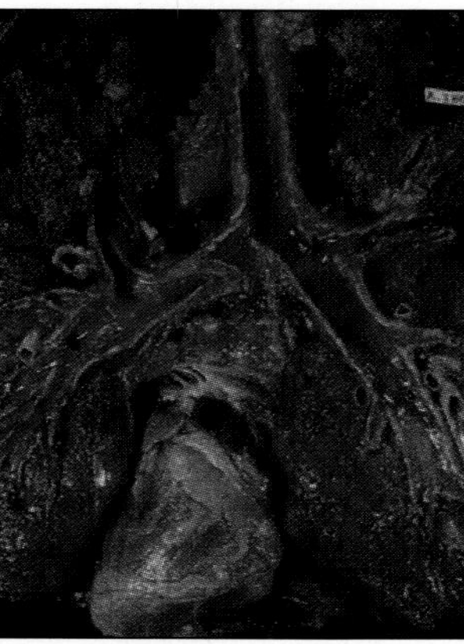

A healthy lung (right) vs. the lung of a smoker (left).

In addition to drawing smoke into the lungs, tobacco users swallow saliva that contains an array of chemical compounds from tobacco. As this saliva is swallowed, carcinogens are absorbed into the circulatory system and transported to all areas of the body. The filtering of the blood by the liver, kidneys, and bladder may account for the higher than normal levels of cancer in these organs among smokers.

Chronic Obstructive Lung Disease

Chronic obstructive lung disease (COLD) is a **chronic disorder** in which air flow in and out of the lungs becomes progressively limited. COLD is a disease state that comprises two separate but related diseases: **chronic bronchitis** and **pulmonary emphysema**.

With chronic bronchitis, excess mucus is produced in response to the effects of smoking on airway tissue, and the walls of the bronchi become inflamed and infected. This produces a characteristic narrowing of the air passages. Breathing becomes difficult, and activity can be severely restricted. People who stop smoking can reverse chronic bronchitis.

For post-secondary students who have only recently begun smoking, the chronic nature of bronchitis may not yet be in place. However, it is important to realize that the now occasional episodes of airway inflammation and congestion will occur on a more regular basis, and eventually the foundation for COLD will be established.

Pulmonary emphysema causes damage to the tiny air sacs of the lungs, the **alveoli**, that cannot be reversed. Chest pressure builds when air becomes trapped by narrowed air passages (chronic bronchitis), and the thin-walled sacs rupture. Emphysema patients often develop a "barrel chest" as they lose the ability to exhale fully. You have most likely seen people with this condition in shopping malls and other locations as they walk slowly, carrying or pulling their portable oxygen tanks.

Quick Facts on Cigarette Smoking

This year Health Canada estimates that more than 45 000 Canadians will die prematurely because of tobacco use. More than 1000 of these individuals will be nonsmokers.[16]

- Cigarette smoking is the predominant cause of lung cancer, accounting for 85% of all new cases of lung cancer in Canada.
- During their lifetime, 1 in 11 men will develop lung cancer and 1 in 12 will die from this condition. Lung cancer is by far the leading cause of cancer deaths in Canadian men.
- For women, 1 in 21 will develop lung cancer, and 1 in 22 will die from this disease, making lung cancer the most likely cause of cancer death in Canadian women.

More than 10 million North Americans have COLD. It is responsible for a greater limitation of physical activity than any other disease, including heart disease.[17] COLD patients tend to die a very unpleasant, prolonged death, often from a general collapse of normal cardiorespiratory function that results in *congestive heart failure* (see Chapter 10).

Additional Health Concerns

In addition to the serious health problems stemming from tobacco use already described, other health-related changes that are routinely seen include a generally poor state of nutrition, the gradual loss of the sense of smell, and premature wrinkling of the skin. Tobacco users are also more likely to experience strokes (a potentially fatal condition), lose bone mass leading to osteoporosis, experience more back pain and muscle injury, and find that fractures heal more slowly. Further, smokers who have surgery spend more time in the recovery room. Although not perceived as a "health problem" by people who continue smoking to control their weight, smoking does appear to minimize weight gain. In studies using male identical twins, the siblings who smoked were about 2.5 kg to 3.5 kg (6 to 8 pounds) lighter than their nonsmoking siblings.[18] See the Star Box on this page for more facts on cigarette smoking in Canada.

SMOKING AND REPRODUCTION

In all of its dimensions the reproductive process is impaired by the use of tobacco, particularly cigarette smoking. Problems can be found in association with infertility, problem pregnancy, breastfeeding, and the health of the newborn.

Infertility

Recent research indicates that cigarette smoking by both men and women can reduce levels of fertility. Among men, smoking adversely affects sperm motility and shape and can also inhibit sperm production. Among women, lower levels of estrogen (a hormone necessary for uterine wall development), a reduced ability to conceive, and a somewhat earlier onset of menopause appear to be related to cigarette smoking.

Problem Pregnancy

The harmful effects of tobacco smoke on the course of pregnancy are principally the result of the carbon monoxide and nicotine to which the mother and her fetus are exposed. Carbon monoxide is carried to the placenta, where it "locks up" fetal hemoglobin. As a result of this exposure to carbon monoxide, the fetus is deprived of normal oxygen transport, leading to a condition called *hypoxia*, or the abnormally low level of oxygen in tissues throughout the body.

Nicotine also exerts its influence on the developing fetus. Thermographs of the placenta and fetus show signs of marked constriction of blood vessels within a few seconds after inhalation by the mother. This constriction further reduces oxygen supplies. In addition, nicotine stimulates the mother's stress response, placing the mother and fetus under the potentially harmful influence of elevated epinephrine and corticoid levels (see Chapter 3). Any fetus exposed to all of these agents is more likely to be miscarried or stillborn.[19] Children born to mothers who smoked during pregnancy often have low birth weights. Additionally, NNK (4-(methylnitro samino)-1-(3-pyridyl)-L butanone) can cross the placental barrier, exposing the developing fetus to one of the most powerful carcinogenic agents in tobacco smoke.[20]

Breastfeeding

Women who smoke while they breastfeed their infants will continue to expose their children to the harmful effects of tobacco smoke. Women who stop smoking during pregnancy should be encouraged to remain nonsmokers or to continue to refrain from smoking while they are breastfeeding.

Health Problems among Infants

Babies born to women who smoked during pregnancy will, on average, be shorter and have a lower birth weight than children born to nonsmoking mothers. During the earliest months of life, babies born to mothers who smoke experience an elevated rate of death caused by *sudden infant death syndrome* (SIDS). Statistics also show that these infants are more likely to develop chronic respiratory problems, be hospitalized, and have poorer overall health during their early years of life. Additionally, children exposed to the influences of tobacco prenatally may hold a greater chance of developing *attention deficit hyperactivity disorder* (ADHD) and may have an increased risk of antisocial behaviour extending into adulthood.[21]

Parenting, in the sense of assuming responsibility for the well-being of a child, begins before birth, especially in the case of smoking. A pregnant woman who continues to smoke is disregarding the well-being of the child she is carrying. Other family members, friends, and coworkers who subject pregnant women to cigarette, pipe, or cigar smoke are, in a sense, contributing a measure of their own disregard for the health of the next generation. For more information concerning second-hand smoke and children's health, go to the Web site established by Physicians for a Smoke-Free Canada: **www.smoke-free.ca/factsheets**.

ORAL CONTRACEPTIVES AND TOBACCO USE

Women who smoke and use oral contraceptives, particularly after age 35, are placing themselves at a much greater risk of experiencing a fatal cardiovascular accident (heart attack, stroke, or **embolism**) than oral contraceptive users who do not smoke. This risk of cardiovascular complications increases further for oral contraceptive users 40 years of age or older. Women who both smoke and use oral contraceptives are four times more likely to die from myocardial infarction (heart attack) than are women who only smoke. Because of this adverse relationship, *it is strongly recommended that women who smoke should not use oral contraceptives.*

Key Terms

chronic disorder
Condition that develops and progresses slowly over an extended period of time.

chronic bronchitis
Persistent inflammation and infection of the smaller airways within the lung.

pulmonary emphysema
Irreversible disease process in which the alveoli are destroyed.

alveoli
Thin, saclike terminal ends of the airways; the sites at which gases are exchanged between the blood and inhaled air.

embolism
Potentially fatal condition in which a circulating blood clot lodges itself in a smaller vessel.

SMOKELESS TOBACCO USE

As the term implies, smokeless tobacco is not burned; rather, it is placed into the mouth. Once in place, the physiologically active nicotine and other soluble compounds are absorbed through the mucous membranes and into the blood. Within a few minutes, chewing tobacco and snuff generate blood levels of nicotine in amounts equivalent to those seen in cigarette smokers.

Chewing tobacco is taken from its foil pouch, formed into a small ball (called a "wad," "chaw," or "chew"), and placed into the mouth. Once in place, the ball of tobacco is sucked and occasionally chewed but not swallowed. Some users develop great skill at spitting the copious dark brown liquid residue into an empty coffee can, out a car window, or on the sidewalk.

Snuff, a more finely shredded smokeless tobacco product, is marketed in small, round cans. Snuff is formed into a small mass (or "quid"). The quid is "dipped," or placed between the jaw and the cheek; the user sucks the quid and spits out the brown liquid.

Although smokeless tobacco would seem to free the tobacco user from many of the risks associated with smoking, chewing and dipping have their own substantial risks. The presence of *leukoplakia* (white spots) and *erythroplakia* (red spots) on the tissues of the mouth indicate precancerous changes (see the Changing for the Better box on this page). In addition, an increase in **peridontal disease** (the pulling away of the gum from the teeth and later tooth loss), the abrasive damage to the enamel of the teeth, and the high concentration of sugar in processed tobacco all contribute to health problems seen among users of smokeless tobacco.

In addition to the damage done to the tissues of the mouth, the need to process the inadvertently swallowed saliva that contains dissolved carcinogens places both the digestive and urinary systems at risk of cancer.

In the opinion of health experts, the use of smokeless tobacco and its potential for life-threatening disease is currently at the place cigarette smoking was 45 years ago. Consequently, television advertisement has been banned, and one of the following warnings appears on every package of smokeless tobacco:

WARNING: THIS PRODUCT MAY CAUSE MOUTH CANCER.
WARNING: THIS PRODUCT MAY CAUSE GUM DISEASE AND TOOTH LOSS.
WARNING: THIS PRODUCT IS NOT A SAFE ALTERNATIVE TO CIGARETTE SMOKING.

Clearly, smokeless tobacco is a dangerous product. There is little doubt that continued use of tobacco can result in serious health problems.

Changing *for the Better*

Early Detection of Oral Cancer

I started using smokeless tobacco a few years ago, thinking it was safe. Recently, I read an article about it that was frightening. What are the real danger signs?

If you have any of the following signs, see your dentist or physician immediately:

- Lumps in the jaw or neck area
- Colour changes or lumps inside the lips
- White, smooth, or scaly patches in the mouth or on the neck, lips, or tongue
- A red spot or sore on the lips or gums or inside the mouth that does not heal in two weeks
- Repeated bleeding in the mouth
- Difficulty or abnormality in speaking or swallowing

THE RISKS OF INVOLUNTARY (PASSIVE) SMOKING

The smoke generated by the burning of tobacco can be classified as either **mainstream smoke** (the smoke inhaled and then exhaled by the smoker) or **sidestream smoke** (the smoke that comes from the burning end of the cigarette, pipe, or cigar). When either form of tobacco smoke is diluted and stays within a common source of air, it is referred to as **environmental tobacco smoke**. All three forms of tobacco smoke lead to *involuntary smoking* and can present health problems for both nonsmokers and smokers. As discussed in Exploring Your Spirituality (p. 201), the effects that smoking produces on others are not only physical but also psychological and social.

Surprisingly, mainstream smoke makes up only 15% of our exposure to involuntary smoking. This is because much of the nicotine, carbon monoxide, and particulate matter are retained within the active smokers.

TALKING POINTS • Your 13-year-old brother inadvertently leaves a tin of smokeless tobacco on the desk in his room and you see it. Would you say anything to him about it? If so, what?

Sidestream smoke is responsible for 85% of our involuntary smoke exposure. Because it is not filtered by the tobacco, the filter, or the smoker's lungs, sidestream smoke contains more free nicotine and produces higher

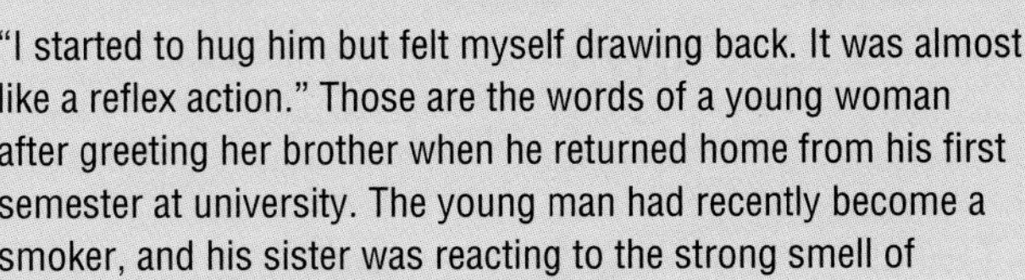

Exploring Your Spirituality

The Hidden Price Tag of Smoking

"I started to hug him but felt myself drawing back. It was almost like a reflex action." Those are the words of a young woman after greeting her brother when he returned home from his first semester at university. The young man had recently become a smoker, and his sister was reacting to the strong smell of smoke in his clothes and hair.

Dramatic as it may sound, smoking does set up barriers between people. First, there's the health issue. Some nonsmokers are adamant about not wanting people they care about to smoke. They also want to protect their children from this danger. And they certainly don't want to breathe in smoke themselves. So, at a family gathering, a smoker may want to have a cigarette after dinner, in the living room with everyone else. But the nonsmokers say no—go outside if you want to smoke. In the process, a birthday dinner or a special holiday is marred by this disagreement.

Whether the person is a family member or a friend, it's difficult to feel close to someone who's doing something you disapprove of—such as smoking. But, from the smoker's point of view, it's hard to feel good about someone who acts superior and doesn't accept you as you are. What do children think about all this? If smoking is bad, as a little girl constantly hears at school and at home, why does her favourite uncle smoke?

The physical toll that smoking takes is apparent when the smoker finds himself sitting on the sidelines. A young man wants to play basketball with his buddies, but the last time he tried, he had a coughing fit—very embarrassing. A young woman meets some new people, and they ask her to join them for an "easy hike." Well, easy for them. She needs a break after only 10 minutes and sees what looks like pity in her friends' eyes.

On the job, smoking has gone the way of the three-martini lunch. It's just not politically correct. In fact, many companies have a no-smoking policy. Or smoking is allowed in designated areas only. Ever drive by a big factory or office building and see a group of people standing outside, perhaps huddled under umbrellas? They're not organizing a strike—they're having a smoke (and being reminded of their high school days). Once again, the smoker feels isolated. Just as in the family group, the smoker feels the judgment of others—only now it's her boss or secretary who's frowning.

The price of smoking is hard to measure. The damage to the smoker's health is beyond dispute. But the spiritual and psychological costs are also real. How does it feel to always be the outsider? The unaccepted? Why does the smoker have to take the chance of missing an exciting play in the stadium to go smoke a cigarette? Or feel the resentment of others at work because he leaves to take a smoking break every hour? It's easy for nonsmokers to say: "Just quit." Smokers know it's not that simple. Many who have stopped smoking—often after several attempts—say that they thought about more than their health in deciding to quit. They thought about many situations—involving family, outdoor activities, and work—before they threw away the pack and said: "That was my last cigarette."

yields of both carbon dioxide and carbon monoxide. Much to the detriment of nonsmokers, sidestream smoke has 20 to 100 times the quantity of highly carcinogenic substances (*N-nitrosamines*) that mainstream smoke has.

Current scientific opinion suggests that smokers and nonsmokers are exposed to very much the same smoke when tobacco is used within a common airspace. The important difference is the quantity of smoke inhaled by smokers and nonsmokers. It is likely that for each pack of cigarettes smoked by a smoker, nonsmokers who must share a common air supply with the smokers will involuntarily smoke the equivalent of three to five cigarettes per day. Because of the small size of the particles produced by burning tobacco, environmental tobacco smoke cannot be completely removed from an indoor site by even the most effective ventilation system.

Environmental tobacco smoke is associated with lung cancer, asthma, low birth weight babies, eye irritation, headaches, and coughs in nonsmokers. Most recently, genetic mutations have been found in the newborn children of women exposed to involuntary smoke during pregnancy.[22]

For these reasons, provincial, municipal, and private-sector initiatives to restrict smoking have been

Key Terms

periodontal disease
Destruction of soft tissue and bone that surround the teeth.

mainstream smoke
Smoke inhaled and then exhaled by a smoker.

sidestream smoke
Smoke that comes from the burning end of a cigarette, pipe, or cigar.

environmental tobacco smoke
Tobacco smoke that is diluted and stays within a common source of air.

Changing *for the Better*

Getting off Tobacco

I started smoking at parties to feel more relaxed. Now I smoke at least a pack a day, and I'm afraid I'm hooked for life. How do I get myself off tobacco?

The suggestions below, many of which are recommended by the Canadian Cancer Society, will help you make a concerted effort to stop smoking. Are you ready to try?

- Realize how much more independent you could be if you quit smoking. Few smokers can say that they are fully self-directed when they can barely function without their cigarettes.
- Think of one sentence that expresses your personal reason for wanting to quit smoking. Repeat the sentence to yourself often.
- Observe nonsmokers. Note that they are not missing out on anything by not smoking. Recognize that the price you will pay for no longer smoking is not as high as it might have first appeared.
- Pick a quit day, sometime within the next two weeks. Plan either to stop cold turkey or to cut down gradually.
- Plan ahead for how you will handle tough times in your first few days off cigarettes.
- Stock up on low-calorie or no-calorie snacks.
- On your quit day, drink a lot of water and keep busy.
- Limit your contact with other cigarette smokers. Keep in mind that once you quit, smokers won't go out of their way to assist you in your efforts.
- Stay clear, as much as possible, of the locations and activities that are now associated with your smoking. Old habits are hard to break, but you don't need to be constantly reminded of them.
- Establish a series of rewards that you will give yourself as you progress through your smoking-cessation program.
- Call the Canadian Cancer Society for more information about quitting: self-help, how-to's, and group sessions in your community.
- Check out Health Canada's new interactive smoking-cessation Web site; it will lend support to those Canadians who are trying to quit as well as those who are considering it. The Web site is found at **www.infotobacco.com**.

A less effective alternative to total cessation is to reduce your exposure to tobacco. This can be accomplished through one or more of the following approaches:

- Reduce the consumption of your present high-tar and high-nicotine brand by smoking fewer cigarettes, inhaling less often and less deeply, and smoking the cigarette only halfway down.
- Switch to a low-tar and low-nicotine brand of cigarette. Be careful, though, not to compensate for this change by smoking more cigarettes or by inhaling more deeply and frequently. Instead, try to reduce the number of cigarettes you smoke and the depth and number of inhalations. Smoke only a limited portion of each cigarette.
- Switch to a smokeless form of tobacco, but be prepared for the potential problems that were discussed on p. 200.

introduced. Most buildings in which people work, study, play, reside, eat, or shop now have some smoking restrictions if not complete bans. In Canada smoking is restricted entirely during air travel.

Involuntary smoking poses serious threats to nonsmokers within residential settings. Spouses and children of smokers are at greatest risk from involuntary smoking. Scientific studies suggest that nonsmokers married to smokers are three times more likely to experience heart attacks than nonsmoking spouses of nonsmokers, and they have a 30% greater risk of lung cancer than nonsmoking spouses of nonsmokers.

The children of parents who smoke are twice as likely as children of nonsmoking parents to experience bronchitis or pneumonia during the first year of life. In addition, throughout childhood, these children will experience more wheezing, coughing, and sputum production than children whose parents do not smoke. Also, they will have a higher incidence of middle ear infection.[23] Of course, the impact on children who have two parents who smoke is greater than on children who have only one parent who smokes.

NONTOBACCO SOURCES OF NICOTINE

Regardless of whether they are intended as aids to smoking cessation or only supplemental forms of nicotine for use when smoking is not permitted, numerous new forms of nicotine delivery systems have appeared in the marketplace. An area of growing concerns is, of course, that these nontobacco delivery sources of nicotine could provide introductory exposure to nicotine, at a tragically early age, for the next generation of nicotine-dependent youth. Included among these nontobacco sources of nicotine are multiple flavours of nicotine suckers, nicotine-flavoured gum, nicotine straws, nicotine-enhanced water (Nico Water), inhalers, sprays, drops, lozenges, and transdermal patches.

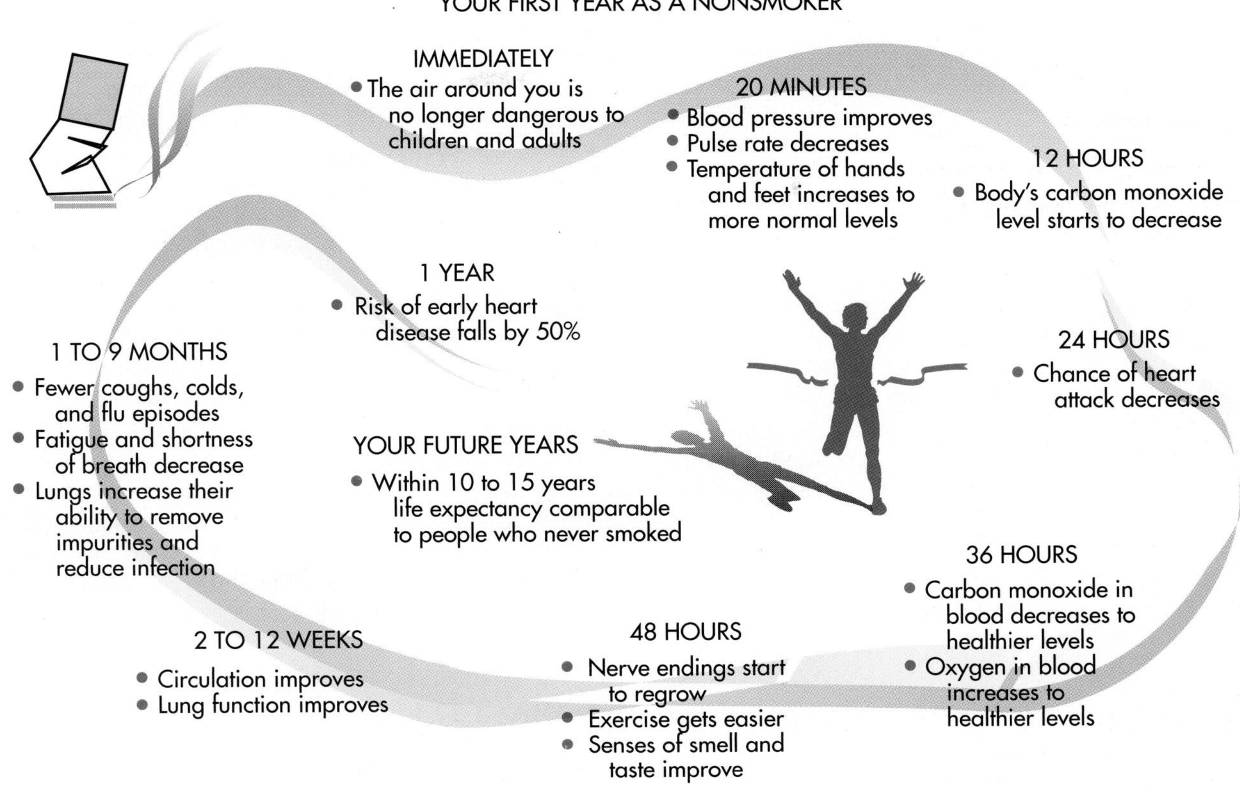
YOUR FIRST YEAR AS A NONSMOKER
IMMEDIATELY
• The air around you is no longer dangerous to children and adults
20 MINUTES
• Blood pressure improves
• Pulse rate decreases
• Temperature of hands and feet increases to more normal levels
12 HOURS
• Body's carbon monoxide level starts to decrease
24 HOURS
• Chance of heart attack decreases
36 HOURS
• Carbon monoxide in blood decreases to healthier levels
• Oxygen in blood increases to healthier levels
48 HOURS
• Nerve endings start to regrow
• Exercise gets easier
• Senses of smell and taste improve
2 TO 12 WEEKS
• Circulation improves
• Lung function improves
1 TO 9 MONTHS
• Fewer coughs, colds, and flu episodes
• Fatigue and shortness of breath decrease
• Lungs increase their ability to remove impurities and reduce infection
1 YEAR
• Risk of early heart disease falls by 50%
YOUR FUTURE YEARS
• Within 10 to 15 years life expectancy comparable to people who never smoked

Figure 9–3 The health benefits of quitting smoking begin immediately and become more significant the longer you stay smoke free.

STOPPING WHAT YOU STARTED

As in the case of weight reduction, there are several ways to attempt to stop smoking. Among these are the *cold turkey* approach, a gradual reduction in cigarette use, organized smoking-cessation programs, and the use of medically prescribed and OTC drug treatment. For those who fear the discomfort of going cold turkey, a more gradual approach can be attempted. The Changing for the Better box on page 202 provides several suggestions for quitting smoking or cutting down on tobacco consumption until stopping totally is possible.

Although it is far from easy to stop smoking, most of the 1.3 million people who quit smoking each year do so by throwing away their cigarettes and going cold turkey. After days, weeks, or even months of discomfort, the body will eventually function more effectively (Figure 9–3). Respiratory capacity will return, the ability to taste will return, and, if undertaken soon enough, tissues of the airways will begin returning to a more normal appearance. On a less pleasant note, it may take years before the mental pictures of "smoking pleasures" have faded. For most, some weight will be gained (about 2.5 to 3.5 kg, or 6 to 8 lbs), but this represents a minimal health risk in comparison with the benefits of not smoking. The Changing for the Better box on p. 204 offers tips for avoiding weight gain when you quit smoking.

Many group-based smoking-cessation programs are available. These programs are usually operated by hospitals, universities, health departments, voluntary health agencies, private physicians, and even local churches. Perhaps the best that can be said is that the better programs will have limited success—a 20% to 50% success rate as measured over one year—and the remainder will have even poorer levels of success.

Two approaches for weaning smokers from cigarettes to a nontobacco source of nicotine dependency are nicotine-containing chewing gum (Nicorette) and the transdermal nicotine patches (Nicoderm, Habitrol, Prostep) that allow nicotine to slowly diffuse through the skin surface into the body. The chewing gum has been on the market for a number of years and, when used correctly along with smoking-cessation counselling, has demonstrated a success rate of 40% or more. Correct use of nicotine-containing chewing gum requires an immediate cessation of smoking, a determination of the initial dosage (4 mg or 2 mg of nicotine per piece), the manner of chewing each piece (rate of chewing and the avoidance of certain foods or beverages), the number of pieces to be chewed each day (usually 9 to 12), and the

Changing *for the Better*

Avoiding Weight Gain When You Stop Smoking

I tried to quit smoking once, but I gained weight immediately. How can I avoid this problem next time?

For many smokers, particularly women, an important plus for smoking is weight management. To them, the risks associated with tobacco use are offset by cigarettes' ability to curb their appetite so they can restrict their caloric intake. This fear of weight gain frequently prevents them from seriously trying to stop smoking or lets them lapse back into cigarette use easily.

This fear is well founded. Most people who quit smoking do gain weight during the 10 years after they stop. The amount of weight gain is usually greater than that seen in people who continue smoking or who have never smoked. Still, this weight gain is relatively small and only slightly greater than that experienced by age-mates who smoke or have never smoked. Certainly, the weight gained is a minimal health risk compared with the risks associated with continued smoking.

Success in minimizing weight gain after smoking is centred in two areas: (1) the ability to manage the smoking urges associated with the first several months of being a former smoker without resorting to eating and (2) the willingness to adopt healthy eating and exercise behaviours.

People who are attempting to quit smoking should recognize that smoking urges are powerful but temporary, usually lasting only about two minutes. During these periods of intense desire for a cigarette, coping activities such as taking a short walk, drinking water or a diet beverage, or talking with a coworker or family member can be used to distract the mind from a cigarette until the urge has passed. If you must eat during these times, choose healthy low-calorie snacks, such as apple slices.

To minimize weight gain (or actually lose weight) in the years after stopping smoking, it's important to make a commitment to a serious wellness-oriented lifestyle involving both exercise and diet. Specific information about adult fitness and sound nutrition can be found in Chapters 4 and 5, respectively.

individual manner of withdrawal from chewing the gum after two to three months of its use. A nonprescription version of Nicorette is available.

In comparison with nicotine-containing chewing gum, the more recently developed transdermal nicotine patches appear to be somewhat less effective than the chewing gum but easier to use. The transdermal nicotine patches, such as Nicoderm, can now be obtained in OTC versions. For these transdermal patches, which come in three dosages, a determination must be made about the appropriate initial dosage, the length of time at that dosage and lower dosages, and the manner of withdrawal after the usual 8 to 12 weeks of patch wearing. Nicotine-replacement therapies using inhalation and nasal sprays have been approved by the U.S. FDA. These systems, available by prescription, should prove very effective because of the large surface area of the lungs, which allows rapid absorption of nicotine into the blood.

To aid smoking-cessation efforts, nicotine replacement products can be used alone or with other therapies. Zyban and Wellbutrin (bupropion) are antidepressant medications that increase the production of dopamine, a neurotransmitter. Dopamine production declines when a smoker quits, creating the craving to smoke. When combined, nicotine patches and a sustained-release antidepressant are a substantially more effective approach to smoking cessation than the nicotine patch used alone. An anti-depressant used alone was, however, nearly as effective as the combination.[24]

TOBACCO USE: A QUESTION OF RIGHTS

Consider these two simple questions about the issues of smokers' vs. nonsmokers' rights:

- To what extent should smokers be allowed to pollute the air and endanger the health of nonsmokers?
- To what extent should nonsmokers be allowed to restrict the personal freedom of smokers, particularly since tobacco products are sold legally?

At this time, answers to these questions are only partially available, but one trend is developing: the tobacco user is being forced to give ground to the nonsmoker. Today, in fact, it is becoming more a matter of when the smoker will be allowed to smoke rather than a matter of when smoking will be restricted. Increasingly, smoking is tolerated less and less. The health concerns of the majority are prevailing over the dependence needs of the minority. See the Focus On article on p. 213 for a fuller explanation of this topic.

IMPROVING COMMUNICATION BETWEEN SMOKERS AND NONSMOKERS

Exchanges between smokers and nonsmokers are sometimes strained, and in many cases, friendships are damaged beyond repair. As you have probably observed, roommates are changed, dates are refused, and memberships in groups are withheld or rejected because of the opposing rights of these two groups.

Recognizing that social skill development is an important task for young adults, the following simple considerations or approaches for smokers can reduce some conflict currently associated with smoking.

If you smoke:

- Ask whether smoking would bother others near you.
- When in a neutral setting, seek physical space where you can smoke and in a reasonable way not interfere with nonsmokers' comfort.
- Accept the validity of the nonsmoker's statement that your smoke causes everything and everyone to smell.
- Respect stated prohibitions against smoking.
- If a nonsmoker requests that you refrain from smoking, respond with courtesy, regardless of whether you intend to comply.
- Practise "civil smoking" by applying a measure of restraint when you recognize that smoking is offensive to others. In particular, respect the aesthetics that should accompany any act of smoking—ashes on dinner plates and cigarette butts in flower pots are not appreciated by others.

The suggestions above can become skills for the social dimension of your health that can be applied to other social conflicts. Remember that as a smoker, you are part of a statistical minority living in a society that often makes decisions and resolves conflict based on majority rule.

For those of you who are nonsmokers, the following approaches can make you more sensitive and skilled in dealing with smoking behaviour:

- Attempt to develop a feeling for or sensitivity to the power of the dependence that smokers have on their cigarettes.
- Accept the reality of the smoker's sensory insensitivity—an insensitivity that is so profound that the odours you complain about are not even recognized by the smoker.
- When in a neutral setting, allow smokers their fair share of physical space in which to smoke. As long as the host does not object to smoking, you as a guest do not have the right to infringe on a person's right to smoke.
- When asking a person to not smoke, use a manner that reflects social consideration and skill. State your request clearly, and accept a refusal gracefully.
- Respond with honesty to inquiries from the smoker as to whether the smoke is bothering you.

If you are contemplating smoking, consider carefully whether the social isolation that appears to be more and more common for smokers will be offset by the benefits you might receive from cigarettes. Finding satisfaction through social contact may be one of the most important dimensions in a productive and rewarding adult life.

Taking Charge of Your Health

- Commit yourself to establishing a smoke-free environment in the places where you live, work, study, and recreate.
- Support friends and acquaintances who are trying to become smoke free.
- Support legislative efforts, at all levels of government, to reduce your exposure to environmental tobacco smoke.
- Be civil toward tobacco users but respond assertively if they infringe on smoke-free spaces.
- Support agencies and organizations committed to reducing tobacco use among young people through education and intervention.

SUMMARY

- Only about one-quarter of Canadian adults smoke.
- The incidence of adolescent and young-adult smoking increased in recent years but is now levelling off.
- A successful class-action suit in the United States exposed the strategies of the tobacco industry and required it to compensate states for Medicaid expenses.
- Dependence, including addiction and habituation, is established quickly through tobacco use.
- Nicotine is the addictive agent in tobacco whose level in tobacco products can be modified.
- Modelling, self-reward, and self-medication play important roles in the development of tobacco dependence.
- The federal government has proposed a broadly based program intended to reduce the use of cigarettes by adolescents.

- Tobacco smoke can be divided into gaseous and particulate phases. Each phase has its unique chemical composition.
- Nicotine, carbon monoxide, and phenol have damaging effects on various body tissues. Several hundred carcinogenic agents are found in tobacco smoke.
- Nicotine has predictable effects on the function of the cardiovascular system when used at relatively low doses.
- Most forms of cancer are worsened by tobacco use. Lung cancer progresses in a predictable fashion.
- Chronic obstructive lung disease (COLD) is a likely consequence of long-term cigarette smoking, with early symptoms appearing shortly after beginning regular smoking.
- Smoking alters normal structure and function of the body, as seen in premature wrinkling, diminished ability to smell, and bone loss leading to osteoporosis.
- Several areas of reproductive health are negatively influenced by tobacco use. Cigarette smoking and long-term use of oral contraceptives are not compatible.
- Smokeless tobacco carries its own health risks, including oral cancer.
- Involuntary smoke carries with it a wide variety of threats to the spouse, children, and coworkers of the smoker.
- Stopping smoking can be undertaken in any one of several ways.
- Smoking-cessation therapies are available in a variety of forms, including nicotine gum, transdermal patches, nicotine inhalation devices, and effective antidepressants.
- Both smokers and nonsmokers have certain rights regarding the use of tobacco. Effective communication can be established between smokers and nonsmokers.

REVIEW QUESTIONS

1. What percentage of the Canadian adult population smokes? In what direction has change been occurring? What is the current direction of the adolescent smoking rate? What factors may account for this newly observed trend?
2. In what way do modelling and advertising explain the development of emotional dependency on tobacco? How do self-esteem, self-image, and self-directedness relate to tobacco use?
3. What was the outcome of the massive class-action suit in the United States brought against the tobacco industry by state governments in an attempt to recoup Medicaid funds? What is the current status of the Canadian government's attempt to further control the tobacco industry?
4. In comparison to cigarettes, what health risks are associated with pipe and cigar smoking?
5. What are the principal components of the gaseous and particulate phases of tobacco smoke?
6. What are the specific influences of nicotine and carbon monoxide on the normal function of the body?
7. In what ways does cigarette smoking contribute to cardiovascular disease? What effect does nicotine have on the cardiovascular system?
8. To what extent is tobacco use a factor in cancer? What specific airway tissues are involved in lung cancer?
9. What is the traditional progression of chronic obstructive lung disease? In what ways does tobacco use impair reproductive health?
10. In what ways is smokeless tobacco equal to smoking in the development of serious health concerns?
11. What is involuntary smoking? Why is there growing concern about the effects of passive smoke on spouses, children, and coworkers?
12. What is the most effective way to stop smoking? What is the average weight gain after stopping smoking? How effective are other approaches to stopping smoking? What are the principal nicotine replacement systems in use today? What are the Canadian government's latest guidelines for successful smoking cessation?
13. What rights do smokers and nonsmokers have in public places? How can communication be enhanced between smokers and nonsmokers?

THINK ABOUT THIS ...

- Why has the current generation of post-secondary students apparently chosen to disregard the tobacco-related risks understood by earlier generations of students and graduates?
- If you saw a minor being sold cigarettes, would you feel comfortable mentioning your concern to the merchant?
- If you are among the minority of North Americans (including college and university students) who smoke, do you understand why you will be most likely to die sooner than your classmates if you continue to smoke?
- If you are a smoker, do you understand why some people may feel unappreciative of your presence?

REFERENCES

1. **www.ctv.ca/servlet/ArticleNews/print/CTVNews/1088969628153_84378828/?hub=Entertainment&subhub=PrintStory**, October 2004.
2. Health Canada: The facts about tobacco: Health effects of smoking, **www.hc-sc.gc.ca/ahc-asc/media/nr-cp/2003/2003_89bk3_e.html**, August 22, 2005.
3. Physicians for a Smoke-Free Canada: *Health Canada national clearinghouse on tobacco and health*, Canadian Centre for Substance Abuse. **www.smokefree.ca**
4. Ibid.
5. Health Canada: Canadian tobacco use monitoring survey (CTUMS): summary of results for wave 1 (February to June) of 2003, **www.hc-sc.gc.ca/hl-vs/pubs/tobac-tabac/ctums-esutc-2004/supplement2004_e.html**, August 22, 2005.
6. Satcher D: Cigars and public health, *N Engl J Med* 340(23):1829–1831, 1999.
7. Lerman C et al: Evidence suggesting the role of specific genetic factors in cigarette smoking, *Health Psychol* 18(1):14–20, 1999.
8. Henningfield JE, Radzius A, Cone EJ: Estimation of available nicotine of six smokeless tobacco products, *Tobacco Control* 4:57–61, 1995.
9. *Health Canada marks Weedless Wednesday with variety of initiatives*, Health Canada News Release, January 17, 2001. **www.hc-sc.gc.ca/english/media/releases/2001/2001_05e.htm**.
10. Centers for Disease Control: The surgeon general's 1989 report on reducing the health consequences of smoking: 25 years of progress (executive summary), *MMWR* 38 (suppl 5)2:1, 1989.
11. American Heart Association: *Heart disease and stroke statistics—2003 update.* 2002.
12. Heart and Stroke Foundation: cardiovascular deaths, **www.heartandstroke.on.ca**.
13. Howard G et al: 1989. Cigarette smoking and progression of atherosclerosis, *JAMA* 279(2):119–124, 1998.
14. Wistuba I et al: Molecular damage in the bronchial epithelium of smokers, *J Natl Cancer Inst* 89(18):1366–1373, 1997.
15. *Cancer facts & figures–2001*, 2001, American Cancer Association.
16. Health Canada: The facts: preventing youth smoking, **www.hc-sc.gc.ca/ahc-asc/media/nr-cp/2003/2003_89bk3_e.html**, August 22, 2005.
17. Crowley LV: *Introduction to human disease*, ed 4, 1996, Jones & Bartlett.
18. Eisen S et al: The impact of cigarette and alcohol consumption on weight and obesity: an analysis of 1911 monozygotic twin pairs, *Arch Intern Med* 153(21):2457–2463, 1993.
19. Mills JL: Cocaine, smoking, and spontaneous abortion, *N Engl J Med* 340(5):380–381, 1999.
20. Lackmann GM et al: Metabolites of a tobacco-specific carcinogen in urine from newborns, *J Natl Cancer Inst* 91(5):459–465, 1999.
21. Fergusson DM: Prenatal smoking and antisocial behavior, *Arch Gen Psychiatry* 56(3):223–224, 1999.
22. Finette BA et al: Gene mutations with characteristic deletions in cord blood T lymphocytes associated with passive maternal exposure to tobacco smoke, *Nat Med* 4(10):1144–1151, 1998.
23. Adair-Bischoff CE, Sauve RS: Environmental tobacco smoke and middle ear disease in preschool-age children, *Arch Pediatr Adolesc Med* 152(2):127–133, 1998.
24. Jorenby DE et al: A controlled trial of sustained-release bupropion, a nicotine patch, or both for smoking cessation, *N Engl J Med* 340(9):685–691, 1999.

SUGGESTED READINGS

Gebhardt J: *The enlightened smoker's guide to quitting*, 1998, Element Books.

A smoking-cessation program must be tailored to the smoking history of the person attempting to quit. Using a seven-step approach, the author discusses individualizing these components for participants in order to enhance their chance for success. The approach described is frequently used by programs approved by the American Cancer Society.

Hirschfelder AB: *Kick butts: a kid's guide to a tobacco-free America*, 1998, Silver Burdett Press.

The decision to smoke is often made at a surprisingly early age, well before the behaviour begins. The author skillfully focuses the information and activities of her book to the children she wants to reach. Her account of the last 100 years of tobacco use is informative to all readers, but the activities described in the latter portion of the book are well suited to young children and will be well received by them. This book is recommended for both parents and teachers.

Orey M: *Assuming the risk: the mavericks, the lawyers, and the whistle-blowers who beat big tobacco*, 1999, Little, Brown & Company.
Michael Orey, a legal journalist for a major national newspaper, uses his expertise and objectivity to describe the tobacco industry's reversal of fortune within the judicial system. Beginning with an obscure 1987 lawsuit on behalf of a poor Mississippi labourer who died of lung cancer and ending with the massive class-action suit brought by the states seeking Medicaid compensation, this is the complete account of how the seemingly impenetrable defences of the tobacco industry were finally bridged.

Tate C: *Cigarette wars: the triumph of the "the little white slaver,"* 1999, Oxford University Press.
This book tells the story of how the cigarette went from being the evil "coffin nail" at the turn of the century to the widely used symbol of personal independence and internationally recognized Americana by mid-century. All the principal players, both against and for the birth and adoption of this "child of the twentieth century," are discussed. This book lays an excellent foundation for Orey's book, described above.

Making Headlines

Banning the Butt: Global Antismoking Efforts

Day by day, smoking is becoming a thing of the past in Canada. The number of smokers declines every year, going hand in hand with an increase in efforts by government and health activists to tighten up restrictions on the sale and use of tobacco.

Smoking has been banned from most offices for some time, but the bans are now extending to bars, restaurants and other public places. Some cities have banned smoking outright, shutting down separate smoking rooms altogether.

Canada is considered to be among those countries at the forefront of anti-smoking legislation, but the rest of the world is beginning to catch up. Here's a sampler of homegrown and global anti-smoking measures:

Efforts in Canada

- Ontario has passed a province-wide ban on smoking in workplaces and all indoor public areas, including designated smoking rooms. The ban would effectively prohibit smoking in all indoor areas except people's homes or temporary accommodations such as hotel rooms. It would also ban smoking in work vehicles, and prominent displays of tobacco products in stores. It is scheduled to come into effect in June 2006.
- On Jan. 19, 2005, the Supreme Court of Canada rules that Saskatchewan can reinstate a law requiring store owners to keep tobacco products out of sight, the so-called "shower curtain law."
- On Jan. 1, 2005, all public places in Saskatoon, including outdoor seating areas and veterans' clubs, go smoke-free. Smokers can be fined up to $10,000 for lighting up. Fines against businesses can go as high as $25,000.
- On Oct. 1, 2004, the governments of New Brunswick and Manitoba institute province-wide smoking bans in all public areas. Restaurants and bars will no longer be able to have smoking sections or glassed-in smoking areas.
- As of June 1, 2004, Toronto requires all bars, pool halls, bingo halls, casinos and racetracks to be smoke-free. Fines range from $205 to $5,000. A 2001 bylaw banned smoking in all restaurants, dinner theatres and bowling centres, except in designated smoking rooms. A plan to outlaw designated smoking rooms in Toronto by 2005 was sent back to city council for review.
- On May 1, 2004, the Worker's Compensation Board for the Northwest Territories and Nunavut bans smoking in all enclosed businesses and work sites in both territories. The ban includes bars. It takes precedence over and goes further than the law passed by Nunavut's legislature six months earlier, which banned smoking in all public places—and would have been extended to bars, within two years. The ban hits a region with the highest smoking rates in the country.
- On Sept. 1, 2003, authorities in Winnipeg begin enforcing a smoking ban in all public places, starting on Sept. 1, 2003. The ban was to have gone into effect July 1, 2003, but the city agreed to a two-month grace period to get inspectors ready to enforce the ban in provincial casinos.
- A province-wide smoking ban goes into effect in P.E.I. on June 1, 2003, banning smoking in any public place or workplace, except in specially ventilated smoking rooms.
- On April 1, 2003, a law goes into effect in Alberta in which people under age 18 who are caught smoking or in possession of tobacco products can not only have their cigarettes seized by police, but also can be fined up to $100.
- On Jan. 1, 2003, the Northwestern (Ontario) Health Unit bans smoking in all public places and private businesses. Intended to be one of the toughest anti-smoking bylaws anywhere, penalties range from $5,000 to $25,000 a day.

- On Jan. 1, 2003, Nova Scotia bans smoking in many public places, including taxicabs, bowling alleys and schoolyards. In bars and restaurants, smoking is restricted to an enclosed room that's separately ventilated and available only to adults. Police can also seize tobacco from people under age 19. In earlier legislation, Nova Scotia banned smoking in prison.
- On Dec. 31, 2002, Saskatchewan passes a law forcing bingo parlours, bars, casinos, restaurants and bowling alleys to designate 40 per cent of space as non-smoking. The requirement increases to 60 per cent by 2004.
- Anti-smoking bylaws in Winnipeg and St. John's, Nfld., go into effect on Jan. 1, 2002. They ban smoking in any indoor location where minors are present. Some coffee shops and restaurants get around the new rules by banning children.
- The City of Ottawa bans smoking in all workplaces and public spaces, with no allowance for designated smoking rooms, effective Aug. 1, 2001. Victoria, B.C., and Waterloo, Ont., have similar bans.
- On May 22, 2001, the City of Edmonton bans smoking in all public places where children are served, except for lounges.
- In Quebec, it is against the law to sell tobacco by mail order, over the internet, on school grounds or in a health-care, social services or child-care facility.
- Ontario prohibits tobacco sales at hospitals, psychiatric facilities, nursing homes, long-term care facilities and charitable institutions.

Quick Facts

In 2000–2001, just over 6 million Canadians over 15, or 24 per cent, were smokers compared to 31 per cent in 1994, and 38 per cent two decades ago.

Of Canadian women over age 12, 19.4 per cent smoked in 2000–2001. That's down from 26 per cent in 1994.

Among Canadian men over age 12, 23.5 per cent were smokers. That's down from 32 per cent in 1994.

Nunavut has a higher smoking rate than any other province or territory. There, 48 per cent of the population smokes, which is more than double the national average of 21.5 per cent. About two-thirds of territory's aboriginal children aged 15–17 smoke, while almost one of four children aged 10–14 smoke.

Efforts around the World

- On Feb. 7, 2005, Cuba banned smoking in public places, except for designated smoking areas in restaurants. It also banned sales of cigarettes to children under 16 and at stores within 100 metres of a school. Four in 10 Cubans smoke.
- Italy introduced legislation on Jan. 10, 2005, to ban smoking in public places. It was originally expected to take effect Dec. 31, 2004, but legislators decided to allow smokers to light up on New Year's. Restaurant and bar owners are upset that they will be required to report their customers if they break the law.
- The Himalayan kingdom of Bhutan in December 2004 became the first country in the world to ban all tobacco sales and smoking in public.
- In March 2004, Ireland becomes the first country to institute a total ban on smoking in all workplaces, including the country's more than 10,000 pubs.
- On March 1, 2003, a law in New York City goes into effect that bans smoking in bars and restaurants with few exceptions, such as parts of outdoor cafes, existing cigar bars, and owner-operated private clubs.
- In May 2001, the European Union gives its final approval to legislation that would ban the use of the terms "light" and "mild" for advertising cigarettes, and allow for graphic pictures of diseased lungs and hearts on cigarette packs.
- In March 2001, Israel bans smoking in all public places including hospitals, shopping malls and restaurants. Separate smoking rooms with ventilation may be permitted in some cases.
- In April 2001, Egypt enacts a ban on cigarette advertising on state-run television. At the time, the government already restricted smoking in government buildings and airports.
- Also in April 2001, health officials from eight Asian countries—Indonesia, Thailand, India, Bangladesh, Myanmar, Nepal, Bhutan and Sri Lanka—agree to support a proposal to totally ban cigarette advertising.
- In February 2001, Russia's Duma gives preliminary approval to bills banning tobacco ads in print media, on street billboards and in public transportation. They were already banned from television.

Restaurants and bars invariably predict sales will plummet once a smoking ban is put in place. In Ireland, a month after the ban went into effect, the government's Office of Tobacco Control reported that 97 per cent of inspected pubs and restaurants were complying with the law. It also cited two studies which suggested that the number of non-smokers visiting pubs and bars had increased, while the number of smokers doing so had remained the same. A day later, the main bar owners' association cited a study of its own. It suggested sales had fallen 12 to 15 per cent. But Ireland's restaurant association reported sales were about the same as they were a year earlier.

Source: CBC News Online: In-depth smoking, **www.cbc.ca/news/background/smoking/smokingbans.html**, July 8, 2005.

Personal Assessment

How Much Do You Know about Cigarette Smoking?

Are the following assumptions about smoking true or false? Take your best guess, and then read the answer to the right of each statement.

Assumption		**Discussion**
1. There are now safe cigarettes on the market.	F	Depending on the brand, some cigarettes contain less tar and nicotine; none are safe, however.
2. A small number of cigarettes can be smoked without risk.	F	Even a low level of smoking exposes the body to harmful substances in tobacco smoke.
3. Most early changes in the body resulting from cigarette smoking are temporary.	T	Some changes, however, cannot be reversed—particularly changes associated with emphysema.
4. Filters provide a measure of safety to cigarette smokers.	T	However, the protection is far from adequate.
5. Low-tar, low-nicotine cigarettes are safer than high-tar, high-nicotine brands.	T	Many people, however, smoke low-tar, low-nicotine cigarettes in a manner that makes them just as dangerous as stronger cigarettes.
6. Mentholated cigarettes are better for the smoker than are nonmentholated brands.	F	Menthol simply makes cigarette smoke feel cooler. The smoke contains all of the harmful agents found in the smoke from regular cigarettes.
7. It has been scientifically proven that cigarette smoking causes cancer.	T	Particularly lung cancer and cancers of the larynx, esophagus, oral cavity, and urinary bladder.
8. No specific agent capable of causing cancer has ever been identified in the tobacco used in smokeless tobacco.	F	Unfortunately, smokeless tobacco is no safer than the tobacco that is burned. The user of smokeless tobacco swallows much of what the smoker inhales.
9. The cure rate for lung cancer is so good that no one should fear developing this form of cancer.	F	Approximately 14% of people who have lung cancer will live the five years required to meet the medical definition of "cured."
10. Smoking is not harmful as long as the smoke is not inhaled.	F	Because of the toxic material in smoke, even its contact with the tissue of the oral cavity introduces a measure of risk in this form of cigarette use.
11. The "smoker's cough" reflects underlying damage to the tissue of the airways.	T	The cough occurs in response to an inability to clear the airway of mucus as a result of changes in the cells that normally keep the air passages clear.
12. Cigarette smoking does not appear to be associated with damage to the heart and blood vessels.	F	Cigarette smoking is in fact the single most important risk factor in the development of cardiovascular disease.
13. Because of the design of the placenta, smoking does not present a major risk to the developing fetus.	F	Children born to women who smoked during pregnancy show a variety of health impairments, including smaller birth size, premature birth, and more illnesses during the first year of life. Smoking women also have more stillbirths than nonsmokers.
14. Women who smoke cigarettes and use an oral contraceptive should decide which they wish to continue because there is a risk in using both together.	T	Women over 35 years of age, in particular, are at risk of experiencing serious heart disease should they continue using both cigarettes and an oral contraceptive.

Personal Assessment *continued*

Assumption		**Discussion**
15. Air pollution is a greater risk to our respiratory health than is cigarette smoking.	F	Although air pollution does expose the body to potentially serious problems, the risk is considerably less than that associated with smoking.
16. Addiction, in the sense of physical addiction, is found in conjunction with cigarette smoking.	T	Dependence, including true physical addiction, is widely recognized in cigarette smokers.
17. Among the best "teachers" a young smoker has are his or her parents.	T	There is a strong correlation between cigarette smoking of parents and the subsequent smoking of their children. Parents who do not want their children to smoke should not smoke.
18. Nonsmoking and higher levels of education are directly related.	T	The higher one's level of education, the less likely one is to smoke.
19. About as many women smoke cigarettes as do men.	T	Although in the past, more men smoked than did women, the gap is narrowing.
20. Fortunately, for those who now smoke, stopping is relatively easy.	F	Unfortunately, relatively few smokers can quit. The best advice is never to begin smoking.

To Carry This Further ...

Were you surprised at the number of items that you answered correctly? In what areas did you hold misconceptions regarding cigarette smoking? Do you think that most university students are as knowledgeable as you?

Where do you see the general public in terms of its understanding of cigarette smoking? How can the health care community do a better job in educating the public about tobacco use?

Personal Assessment *continued*

A Simple Dependency Test Regarding Your Relationships with Cigarettes

To nonsmokers it must seem that smokers would realize the existence of their dependency on cigarettes; however, such might not be the case. The Hooked On Nicotine Checklist (HONC) appearing below is a simple way to determine whether a cigarette-based dependency exists. If you are a smoker, answer each question asked by the HONC in an honest manner. When completed, give careful consideration to your findings. If you are a nonsmoker, ask a smoker to complete the HONC and share responses to each item with you. In the latter case, a good discussion could ensue.

Nicotine Addiction's 10 Warning Signs

HONC—Hooked On Nicotine Checklist

1.	Have you ever tried to quit but couldn't?
2.	Do you smoke now because it is really hard to quit?
3.	Have you ever felt like you were addicted to tobacco?
4.	Do you ever have strong cravings to smoke?
5.	Have you ever felt like you really needed a cigarette?
6.	Is it hard to keep from smoking in places where you are not supposed to, like school?
In answering the last four questions, when you tried to stop smoking, or when you have not used tobacco for a while ...	
7.	Did you find it hard to concentrate?
8.	Did you feel more irritable?
9.	Did you feel a strong need or urge to smoke?
10.	Did you feel nervous, restless, or anxious because you couldn't smoke?

Answering "yes" to any one of the above ten questions indicates that you may already be hooked on nicotine and are chemically dependent. Think about it! Your "yes" answer is your own honest self-assessment that you have already lost the freedom and ability to simply and effortlessly walk away. Two-thirds of all teens who you see smoking regularly will spend their entire life as slaves to nicotine. If you HONC we'll help—www.WhyQuit.com

Source: HONC—(Hooked on Nicotine Checklist), Tobacco Control, Sept. 2002 Dr. JR Difranza, Development of symptoms of tobacco dependency in youths. Reliability study of HONC factors—July 2002
Created by www.WhyQuit.com—Join us for motivation, education and support!

Focus on

SMOKERS vs. NONSMOKERS: A QUESTION OF RIGHTS

A quiet battle is being waged in North America over smoking, an activity that was once universally accepted. Regulations restricting smoking now affect stores, restaurants, offices, and public buildings. It is difficult these days to find a place of business where smoking is totally unrestricted. Some of these restrictions are put in place by law or municipal ordinances; some are placed voluntarily by business management. However, it is clear that the voices of nonsmokers, long silent and largely ignored by society, are finally being heard and are behind the recent increase in restrictions on smoking.

Changing Attitudes

For decades, people smoked whenever and wherever they wished. Smoking was glamorized in the movies, on television, and in print throughout most of the 20th century. Famous athletes and movie stars were found in cigarette advertisements. Some ads even promoted the "health benefits" of smoking. Although a few people felt that smoking was dangerous, their voices had little effect on society's acceptance of tobacco use. Gradually, these attitudes began to change. As data from medical studies began to accumulate on the dangers of tobacco, antismoking advocates started to achieve some victories in society and in public policy.

Restrictions on Tobacco Use

In the 1980s, restrictions on smoking greatly increased. In 1987, smoking was banned on all U.S. domestic airplane flights of less than two hours;[1] now this ban includes all domestic flights. A growing number of federal, provincial, and municipal laws curtailing or banning smoking in places of business have been enacted. Many businesses that were not forced by law to restrict smoking did so anyway, citing public sentiment in favour of such regulations.

As a result of these restrictions, smoking areas in places of business are shrinking in size or are being eliminated. Congregations of smokers outside office buildings have become a common sight. Some smokers have taken the changes in stride. Others have cut back on smoking or have quit altogether. Many, however, are not happy about having to go outside in all kinds of weather to smoke. They feel ostracized and are speaking out against what they perceive as an outright attack on their personal freedoms.

The Prosmoker Defence

Smokers have started to become organized on a worldwide level and within individual communities and workplaces. They are clearly worried that this trend of restricting tobacco use will not stop until smoking is eliminated everywhere and the use of tobacco becomes illegal.

Groups such as the British-based Freedom Organisation for the Right to Enjoy Smoking Tobacco (FOREST) have actively pushed smokers' rights and have espoused the "benefits" of smoking.[2] They cite controversial scientific studies demonstrating that smokers are less likely to develop Alzheimer's disease and Parkinson's disease and that teen acne is "almost exclusively" a nonsmokers' affliction.

Smokers are also worried about how their smoking activities are perceived by employers and insurers. Companies are growing less tolerant of unhealthy activities by their employees, since they must pay increased insurance costs for treatment. Many smokers fear that insurance companies will begin to refuse treatment to smokers who continue to smoke.

The worst-case scenario for smokers is that their smoking will even be restricted at home. "What if the government starts keeping us from having kids because we smoke?" worries "Earl," a two-pack-a-day smoker. "I've heard tell that we could have our kids taken away because we smoke at home. Do we have to step outside of our own homes to smoke?"[3]

Fighting for Clean Air

Many nonsmokers are just as adamant about their position, saying that smokers have been subjecting them to cancer-causing agents for decades and that the restrictions are long overdue. They are tired of having smoke blown in their faces in public. Antismoking activists find the "individual freedom" argument of smokers objectionable. "What about my right to breathe?" asks "Stan," an office worker who is subjected to smoke from nearby cubicles. "The management, most of whom smoke, have decided that since we don't deal directly with the public, smoking is okay," he complains.[4]

Many nonsmoking activists feel that it is in the public's best interest to restrict exposure to tobacco smoke and cut back on overall tobacco use. They are angered not only because they have to be exposed to smoke, but also because a good portion of their insurance premiums is going toward health care costs from smoking. As the data accumulate on the hazards of smoking, many nonsmokers are becoming concerned about their exposure to secondhand smoke. They are also worried about the addictive properties of nicotine and are concerned that their children may get hooked.

Even without the health problems posed by tobacco smoke, many nonsmokers feel that smoking should be curtailed simply because of its unpleasant smell. Since smoking is not a self-contained activity, smoke diffuses far away from the smoker, often offending people metres away. "What good does it do to seat a nonsmoker next to the smoking section in a restaurant?" notes "Irina," an antismoking activist.[5] "The smoke just drifts over anyway. It stinks, and not just during the meal. It gets into your clothes and hair and stays with you all day. Why must we tolerate smoke?"

For information about the negative effects of smoking visit **www.smoke-free.ca**. This national health organization (Physicians for a Smoke-Free Canada—PSC) was developed in 1985 with one goal: "the reduction of tobacco-caused ilness through reduced smoking and reduced exposure to second-hand smoke." This site provides a wealth of support for the rights of nonsmokers.

What the Future May Hold

Such arguments may open the door to more restrictions on smoking, a possibility that makes smokers' rights advocates angry. Many are convinced that antismoking forces want nothing less than a total ban on tobacco use—or at least want these bans to be used more aggressively. This might occur, according to smokers' rights advocates, by allowing the courts to use smoking as a factor in determining child custody cases or in defining parental smoking as a form of child endangerment.

Antismoking advocates do not see these regulations as restrictions on individual freedom. They view them as a means of liberation from decades of exposure to smoke with little or no form of legal recourse. Many nonsmokers feel that they should not be forced to breathe in smoke simply because someone wants to light up. Advocates for these regulations claim that tobacco-related illnesses increase health care costs for everyone. They also complain that their tax dollars are being used to subsidize the tobacco industry—in effect, they are paying to be exposed to the smoke of others.

Since smoking, by its very nature, is not a self-contained activity, conflicts are bound to happen. Perhaps some acceptable middle ground can be reached between smokers and nonsmokers, both in law and in society.

For Discussion ...

Have you ever asked someone not to smoke near you or been asked not to smoke around someone? Should taxpayers be responsible for taking on the burden of those being treated for smoking-related diseases? Are the individual freedoms of smokers being infringed on by smoking regulations? Are the individual freedoms of nonsmokers being violated by smokers? Is smoking at home around your children a form of child endangerment?

References

1. The tyranny of the majority, *The Economist* 313:7626, 1989.
2. Platt S: Ashes to ashes, *New Statesman and Society* 7(289), Feb 11, 1994.
3. Anonymous: Personal communication, January 1996.
4. Anonymous: Personal communication, June 1996.
5. Anonymous: Personal communication, March 1996.

Part Four

Chapter 10

Reducing Your Risk for Chronic Disease

Chapter Objectives

After reading this chapter, you should be able to

- Describe the prevalence of cardiovascular disease compared to other diseases.
- List the cardiovascular disease risk factors and distinguish between those that can vs. those that cannot be modified.
- Explain how each of the modifiable cardiovascular disease risk factors can be changed.
- Explain the signs of a heart attack and the recommended action that should be taken.
- Explain how coronary heart disease is diagnosed and treated.
- Explain the recommendations for prevention and treatment of hypertension.
- Distinguish between the different types of stroke.
- Describe different types of cancers and specific early-detection methods for each.
- List diagnosis tools and treatments for different types of cancer.
- Offer several lifestyle choices that effectively reduce your risk for cancer.
- Describe diabetes and diabetes treatments.

Online Learning Centre Resources

www.mcgrawhill.ca/college/hahn

Log on to our Online Learning Centre (OLC) for access to Web links for study and exploration of health topics. Here are some examples of what you'll find:

- **www.cancer.ca** This site offers links to provincial branches of the Canadian Cancer Society, along with answers to frequently asked questions about cancer. You can also find annual lists of cancer statistics.
- **www.hc-sc.gc.ca/english/ahc_asc** Search "diabetes" and learn all about Health Canada's Diabetes Strategy and find out more about your own risk for this increasingly common condition by visiting the Health Canada Web pages.
- **www.heartandstroke.ca** Find hundreds of topics related to cardiovascular health and disease, including prevention, nutrition, smoking cessation, and other lifestyle considerations.

Media Pulse

Support Is Just a Click Away

Health support groups are composed of people who come together to help each other through the demands of a chronic health condition. These groups have traditionally been organized by institutions in the local health care community, such as hospitals; by the provincial and local affiliates of national organizations, such as the Canadian Cancer Society; or by citizens who have the same chronic condition. Increasingly common today, however, are support groups whose members are connected, not by physical proximity, but by the Internet.

Health self-help groups on the Internet develop in one of two ways. The first occurs when a brick-and-mortar organization, such as a national agency or health care institution, develops a support group for its homepage. The second occurs when a person with the condition (or a family member of that person) organizes an online group.

You can find a health support group simply by surfing the Internet. Or you can be referred to a site by a health care professional. You can also go to the homepage of a medical institution or a national agency to find out if it provides a support group link.

Learning from Our Diversity

Prevention of Chronic Disease Begins in Childhood

Youth is one aspect of diversity that is sometimes overlooked. Yet age is important, especially when adults have influence over children's health behaviour. Many adults never seriously consider that their health behaviours are imitated by the children around them. When adults care little about their own health, they can also be contributing to serious health consequences in young people. Nowhere is this age diversity issue more pronounced than in the area of cardiovascular health.

For many aspects of wellness, preventive behaviours are often best learned in childhood, when they can be repeated and reinforced by family members and caregivers. This is especially true for preventive actions concerning heart disease. Although many problems related to heart disease appear at midlife and later, the roots of heart disease start early in life.

The most serious childhood health behaviours associated with heart disease are poor dietary practices, lack of physical activity, and cigarette smoking. Unfortunately, the current state of health for North America's youth shows severe deficiencies in all three areas. Children's diets lack nutrient density and remain far too high in overall fat. Teenage children are becoming increasingly overweight and obese. Studies consistently show a decline in the amount of physical activity by today's youth, since television and video games have become the after-school companions for many children. In addition, cigarette smoking continues to rise among schoolchildren, especially teenagers.

These unhealthy behaviours are laying the foundation for coronary artery disease, hypertension, cancer, and type 2 diabetes in the future. The focus should be on health measures in childhood that prevent cardiovascular problems and cancers rather than treatment of older, already affected people. Parents must make efforts to encourage children to eat more nutritiously and be physically active. Adults should discourage cigarette use by young people. Perhaps the best approach for adults is to set a good example by adopting healthy behaviours themselves. Following *Canada's Food Guide to Healthy Eating* (see Chapter 5) and exercising regularly are excellent strategies that can be started early in life.

Unlike the acute infectious diseases we will explore in Chapter 11, another group of diseases is responsible for the majority of illness and death in developed countries. This group includes the chronic conditions of cardiovascular diseases, cancers, and diabetes. What makes them **chronic** is both the extent of their progression before they are detected (before signs and symptoms appear), and their duration once diagnosed. There is strong evidence that these major chronic diseases begin their development in early adulthood, if not sooner, yet they may not become evident as clinical diseases until middle or old age. Once diagnosed, it is often impossible to completely cure these diseases, as can be done with most infectious diseases. Instead, they are amenable to clinical and lifestyle management, or secondary and tertiary prevention, which aim to keep these conditions from worsening. These conditions, often called "lifestyle" diseases because many of the risk factors associated with their development, such as smoking, inactivity, and poor dietary choices, are felt by some to be within the control of the individual.

CARDIOVASCULAR DISEASE

If you're a traditional-age post-secondary student, you may have a difficult time realizing the importance of **cardiovascular** health. Unless you were born with a heart problem, it's easy to think that cardiovascular damage will not occur until you reach your 50s or 60s. During your young adult years, you're much more likely to be concerned about cancer and sexually transmitted diseases.

Yet autopsy reports on teenagers and young adults who have died in accidents are now showing that relatively high percentages of young people have developed changes consistent with coronary artery disease; that is, fatty deposits have already formed in their coronary arteries. (See the Learning from Our Diversity box above to discover why these changes have occurred.) Since the foundation for future heart problems starts early in life, cardiovascular health is a very important topic for all college and university students.

Even though mortality rates have been in decline for the past 30 years, heart disease continues to be the number one killer of both Canadians and Americans.

PREVALENCE OF CARDIOVASCULAR DISEASE

Cardiovascular diseases are directly related to over one-third of all deaths in Canada. Heart disease and stroke killed nearly 79 000 Canadians in 1999.[1] In fact, cardiovascular disease is our nation's number one "killer". It is therefore not surprising that 8 in 10 Canadians possess one risk factor for cardiovascular disease, while 11% have 3+ risk factors (see Table 10–1).[2] Cardiovascular diseases cost the Canadian economy an estimated $18.5 billion each year.

Table 10–1 Heart and Stroke Foundation Fact Sheet— Risk Factors for Cardiovascular Disease (CVD), by Province

Province or Territory	Smoking[1] (%)	Inactivity[2] (%)	Overweight[2] (%)	Inadequate Fruit and Vegetable Consumption[2] (%)	High Blood Pressure[2] (%)	Diabetes[2] (%)
Nunavut		52.4	55.5	68.4	7.7	2.0
Northwest Territories		55.4	56.8	74	9.6	3.3
Yukon		36	46.2	61.7	10.1	3.8
British Columbia	14	43.7	42.6	61.7	13.0	4.4
Alberta	21	48	49.3	66.8	12.0	3.9
Saskatchewan	21	52.5	54	69.7	14.6	4.6
Manitoba	21	55.8	52.5	69.3	15.5	4.5
Ontario	16	53.9	48.2	62.1	14.9	4.8
Quebec	20	58.5	43.7	57.7	14.2	4.6
New Brunswick	22	61.6	55.8	68.7	16.5	5.8
Nova Scotia	21	53.3	55.5	67.1	18.6	5.8
Prince Edward Island	22	56.4	57.6	65.4	16.2	5.6
Newfoundland	22	59.6	60.2	70.4	17.7	6.7
Canada	**18**	**53.5**	**47.5**	**62.4**	**14.4**	**4.7**

[1] Health Canada. Canadian Tobacco Use Monitoring Survey (CTUMS).

[2] Statistics Canada. National Population Health Survey (NPHS); Canadian Community Health Survey (CCHS).

Table 10–1 Risk Factors for Cardiovascular Disease (CVD), by Province

NORMAL CARDIOVASCULAR FUNCTION

The cardiovascular or circulatory system uses a muscular pump to send a complex fluid on a continuous trip through a closed system of tubes. The pump is the heart, the fluid is blood, and the closed system of tubes is the network of blood vessels.

The Vascular System

The term *vascular system* refers to the body's blood vessels. Although we might be familiar with the arteries (vessels that carry blood away from the heart) and the veins (vessels that carry blood toward the heart), arterioles, capillaries, and venules are also included in the vascular system. Arterioles are the farther, small-diameter extensions of arteries. These arterioles lead eventually to capillaries, the smallest extensions of the vascular system. At the capillary level, exchanges of oxygen, food, and waste occur between cells and the blood.

Once the blood leaves the capillaries and begins its return to the heart, it drains into small veins, or venules. The blood in the venules flows into increasingly larger vessels called *veins.* Blood pressure is highest in arteries and lowest in veins, especially the largest veins, which empty into the right atrium of the heart.

The Heart

The heart is a four-chambered pump designed to create the pressure required to circulate blood throughout the body (see Figure 10–1).

For the heart muscle to function well, it must be supplied with adequate amounts of oxygen. The two main **coronary arteries** (and their numerous branches) accomplish this. These arteries are located outside the heart. If the coronary arteries are diseased and not functioning well, a heart attack is possible.

Key Terms

chronic
Develops slowly and persists for a long period of time.

cardiovascular
Pertaining to the heart (cardio) and blood vessels (vascular).

coronary arteries
Vessels that supply oxygenated blood to heart muscle tissues.

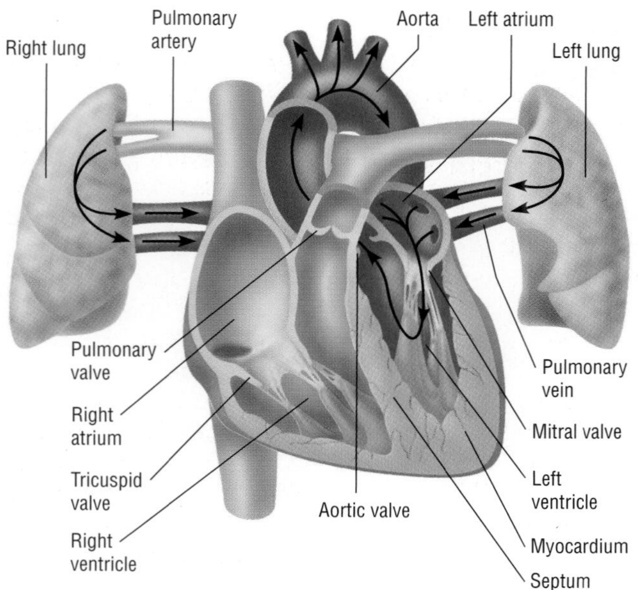

Figure 10–1 The heart functions like a complex double pump. The right side of the heart pumps deoxygenated blood to the lungs. The left side of the heart pumps oxygenated blood through the aorta to all parts of the body. Note the thickness of the walls of the ventricles. These are the primary pumping chambers.

Blood

The average-sized adult has approximately 6 L of blood in his or her circulatory system. The functions of blood, which are performed continuously, are similar to the overall functions of the circulatory system and include the following:

- Transportation of nutrients, oxygen, wastes, hormones, and enzymes
- Regulation of water content of body cells and fluids
- Buffering to help maintain appropriate pH balance of body fluids
- Regulation of body temperature; the water component in the blood absorbs heat and transfers it
- Prevention of blood loss; by coagulating or clotting, the blood can alter its form to prevent blood loss through injured vessels
- Protection against toxins and microorganisms, accomplished by chemical substances called *antibodies* and specialized cellular elements circulating in the bloodstream

CARDIOVASCULAR DISEASE RISK FACTORS

As you have just read, the heart and blood vessels are among the most important structures in the human body. The best time to start protecting and improving your cardiovascular system is early in life, when lifestyle patterns are developed and reinforced (see Learning from Our Diversity, p. 216). Of course, it's impossible to move backward through time, so the second best time to start protecting your heart is today. Improvements in certain lifestyle activities can pay significant dividends as your life unfolds.

All people can protect and enhance their heart health by examining the 11 cardiovascular risk factors related to various forms of heart disease. A *cardiovascular risk factor* is an attribute that a person has or is exposed to that increases the likelihood that he or she will develop some form of heart disease. The first three risk factors are ones you will be unable to change. An additional six risk factors are ones you can change. There is also one final group of risk factors that are thought to be contributing factors to heart disease.

Risk Factors That Cannot Be Changed

The three risk factors that you cannot change are increasing age, male gender, and heredity.[3] However, your knowledge that they might be an influence in your life should encourage you to make a more serious commitment to the risk factors you can change.

Increasing age

Heart diseases tend to develop gradually over the course of one's life. Although we may know of a few people who experienced a heart attack in their 30s or 40s, most of the serious consequences of heart disease are evident in later decades. For example, approximately 85% of people who die from heart diseases are age 65 and older.[4]

Male gender

Young women have lower rates of heart disease than young men. Yet when women move through menopause (typically in their 50s), their rates of heart disease are similar to those of men. It is thought that women are somewhat more protected from heart disease than men because of their natural production of the hormone estrogen during their fertile years.

Heredity

Like increasing age and male gender, heredity cannot be changed. By the luck of the draw, some people are born into families in which heart disease has never been a serious problem; others are born into families in which heart disease is quite prevalent. In this latter case, children are said to have a genetic predisposition (tendency) to develop heart disease as they grow and develop throughout their lives. These people have every reason to be highly motivated to reduce the risk factors they can control.

Race is also a consideration related to heart disease. African Americans have moderately high blood pressure at rates twice that of whites and severe hypertension at rates three times higher than whites. Hypertension significantly increases the risk of both heart disease and stroke; however, it can be controlled through a variety of methods. It is especially important for African Americans to take advantage of every opportunity to have their blood pressure measured so that preventive actions can be started immediately if necessary.

Risk Factors That Can Be Changed

There are six cardiovascular risk factors that are influenced largely by our lifestyle choices. These risk factors are cigarette and tobacco smoke, physical inactivity, high blood lipid levels, high blood pressure, diabetes mellitus, and obesity and overweight. Healthy behaviour changes you make for these "big six" risk factors can help you protect and enhance your cardiovascular system.

Tobacco use

Although the other five controllable risk factors are important, this one may be the most critical risk factor. Smokers have a heart attack risk that is over twice that of nonsmokers. Smoking cigarettes is the major risk factor associated with sudden cardiac death.

Cigarette or tobacco smoke also adversely affects nonsmokers who are exposed to environmental tobacco smoke. Studies suggest that the risk of death caused by heart disease is increased about 30% in people exposed to secondhand smoke in the home. Because of the health threat to nonsmokers, restrictions on indoor smoking in public areas and business settings are increasing tremendously in every part of the country.

For years, it was believed that if you had smoked for many years, it was pointless to try to quit; the damage to one's health could never be reversed. However, data now indicate that by quitting smoking, regardless of how long or how much you have smoked, your risk of heart disease declines rapidly. For people who have smoked a pack or less of cigarettes per day, within three years after quitting smoking, their heart disease risk is virtually the same as those who never smoked.

This news is exciting and should encourage people to quit smoking, regardless of how long they have smoked. Of course, if you have started to smoke recently, the healthy approach would be to quit now—before the nicotine controls your life and damages your heart. (For additional information about the health effects of tobacco, see Chapter 9.)

TALKING POINTS • A friend complains of not being able to quit smoking after several serious attempts. How could you direct this person toward a new approach?

Physical inactivity

Lack of exercise is a significant risk factor for heart disease. Regular aerobic exercise (discussed in Chapter 4) helps strengthen the heart muscle, maintain healthy blood vessels, and improve the ability of the vascular system to transfer blood and oxygen to all parts of the body. Additionally, physical activity helps lower overall blood cholesterol levels for most people, encourages weight loss and retention of lean muscle mass, and allows people to moderate the stress in their lives.

With all the benefits of physical activity, it amazes health professionals that so few North Americans participate in regular exercise. Some people feel that they don't have enough time or that they must work out strenuously. However, you'll recall from Chapter 4 that only 20 to 60 minutes of moderate aerobic activity three to five times each week is recommended. This is not a large price to pay for a lifetime of cardiovascular health. Find a partner and get started!

If you are middle-aged or older and have been inactive, consult with a physician before starting an exercise program. Also, if you have any known health condition that could be aggravated by physical activity, check with a physician first.

TALKING POINTS • You've started exercising many times by yourself, but you can't seem to stick to it. How would you convince a new friend that you can help each other get started on regular physical activity and keep it up?

High blood lipid levels

The third controllable risk factor for heart disease is high blood lipid levels. Generally speaking, the higher the blood lipid level, the greater the risk for heart disease, especially when combined with other important risk factors.

High blood pressure

The fourth of the "big six" cardiovascular risk factors is high blood pressure, or *hypertension*. You will soon be reading more about hypertension, but for now, suffice it to say that high blood pressure can seriously damage a person's heart and blood vessels. High blood pressure causes the heart to work much harder, eventually causing the heart to enlarge and weaken. It increases the chances for stroke, heart attack, congestive heart failure, and kidney disease.

When high blood pressure is present along with other risk factors, the risk for stroke or heart attack is increased tremendously. Yet this "silent killer" is easy to monitor and can be effectively controlled using a variety of approaches. This is the positive message about high blood pressure.

Women and Heart Disease

Is heart disease mainly a problem for men? NO. In fact, data indicate that 53% of all cardiovascular disease deaths occur in women.

For many years, it was thought that men were at much greater risk than women for the development of cardiovascular problems. Today it is known that young men are more prone to heart disease than young women, but once women reach menopause (usually in their early to middle 50s), their rates of heart-related problems quickly equal those of men.

The protective mechanism for young women seems to be the female hormone estrogen. Estrogen appears to help women maintain a beneficial profile of blood fats. When the production of estrogen is severely reduced at menopause, this protective factor no longer exists. Prescribing estrogen replacement therapy (ERT) was a common practice by many physicians in treating a number of factors in postmenopausal women. One of the benefits of ERT was considered to be prevention of cardiovascular diseases. However, in 2002 a major clinical research trial was stopped due to the finding that more women on ERT were experiencing heart attacks and strokes. ERT should not be used for the purpose of preventing cardiovascular diseases. Certainly, ERT may still be utilized for other purposes (i.e., relief of menopausal symptoms or osteoporosis prevention).[5] Women who are prescribed ERT need to be aware of the increased risk for cardiovascular disease in evaluating its value. Certainly, much more research is underway that may influence the use of ERT in the future. Women should discuss the risks and benefits of ERT with their physicians.

Young women should not rely solely on naturally produced estrogen to prevent heart disease. The general recommendations for maintaining heart health—good diet, adequate physical activity, monitoring blood pressure and cholesterol levels, controlling weight, avoiding smoking, and managing stress—will benefit women at every stage of life.[6]

Diabetes mellitus

Diabetes mellitus (discussed in greater detail on pp. 237–238) is a debilitating chronic disease that has a significant effect on the human body. In addition to increasing the risk of developing kidney disease, blindness, and nerve damage, diabetes increases the likelihood of developing heart and blood vessel diseases. Over 80% of people with diabetes die of some type of heart or blood vessel disease. The cardiovascular damage is associated with chronic high levels of blood lipids and blood glucose. With weight management, exercise, dietary changes, and drug therapy, diabetes can be relatively well controlled in most people. Even with careful management of this disease, diabetic patients are susceptible to eventual heart and blood vessel damage.

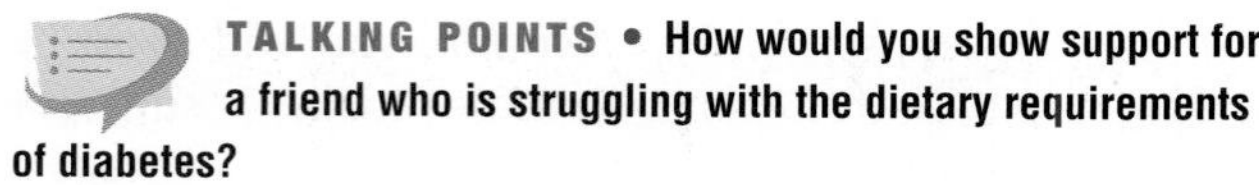

TALKING POINTS • How would you show support for a friend who is struggling with the dietary requirements of diabetes?

Obesity and overweight

Even if they have no other risk factors, obese people are more likely than nonobese people to develop heart disease and stroke. Obesity, especially in the abdomen, places considerable strain on the heart, and it tends to influence both blood pressure and blood lipid levels. Also, obesity tends to trigger type 2 diabetes in predisposed people. The importance of maintaining body weight within a desirable range minimizes the chance of obesity ever happening. To accomplish this, you need to make a commitment to a reasonably sound diet and an active lifestyle.

TALKING POINTS • How could you tactfully bring up a friend's weight problem to show concern for his or her health?

Contributing Risk Factors

The traditional risk factors just described account for about one-half of cardiovascular diseases; however, other risk factors include high blood levels of a natural chemical called *homocysteine*, bacteria originating in the oral cavity, individual response to stress, sex hormones, birth control pills, and drinking too much alcohol. Unresolved stress can encourage negative health dependencies (for example, smoking, poor dietary practices, underactivity) that lead to changes in blood fat profiles, blood pressure, and heart workload. Female sex hormones tend to protect women from cardiovascular disease until they reach menopause, but male hormones do the opposite. Birth control pills can increase the risk of blood clots and heart attack, although the risk is small unless the woman also smokes and is over age 35. The consumption of too much alcohol can cause elevated blood pressure and heart failure, and lead to stroke, although moderate drinking (no more than one drink per day for women and two drinks per day for men) is associated with lower risk of heart disease.[7]

FORMS OF CARDIOVASCULAR DISEASE

There are six major forms of cardiovascular disease (CVD): coronary heart disease, hypertension, stroke, congenital heart disease, rheumatic heart disease (damage to the heart from a streptococcal infection as a result of rheumatic fever), and congestive heart failure (the inability of the heart to pump out all the blood that returns to it, leading to dangerous fluid build up in the veins.) A person may have just one of these diseases or a combination of them at the same time. Each form exists in varying degrees of severity. All are capable of causing secondary damage to other body organs and systems. In this chapter, we will be examining the first three of these conditions. Visit the Heart and Stroke Foundation of Canada's Web site to obtain further information about all forms of cardiovascular disease: **www.heartandstroke.ca**.

Coronary Heart Disease

This form of cardiovascular disease, also known as *coronary artery disease*, involves damage to the vessels that supply blood to the heart muscle. The bulk of this blood is supplied by the coronary arteries. Any damage to these important vessels can cause a reduction of blood (and its vital oxygen and nutrients) to specific areas of heart muscle. The ultimate result of inadequate blood supply is usually a heart attack.

Atherosclerosis

The principal cause for the development of coronary heart disease is atherosclerosis (Figure 10–2). **Atherosclerosis** produces a narrowing of the coronary arteries. This narrowing stems from the long-term buildup of fatty deposits, called *plaque*, on the inner walls of the arteries. This buildup reduces the blood supply to specific portions of the heart. Some arteries of the heart can become so blocked (occluded) that all blood supply is stopped. Heart muscle tissue begins to die when it is deprived of oxygen and nutrients. This damage is known as myocardial infarction. In lay terms, this event is called a *heart attack*. Atherosclerosis can also lead to a heart attack if a plaque breaks open and triggers the formation of blood clots (thrombi), which can suddenly block the artery.

Cholesterol and lipoproteins. For many years, scientists have known that atherosclerosis is a complicated disease that has many causes. Some of these causes are not well understood, but others are clearly understood. *Cholesterol*, a soft, fatlike material, is manufactured in the liver and small intestine and is necessary in the formation of sex hormones, cell membranes, bile salts, and nerve fibres. Elevated levels of serum cholesterol (4.7 mmol/L or more for adults) are associated with an increased risk for developing atherosclerosis.[8]

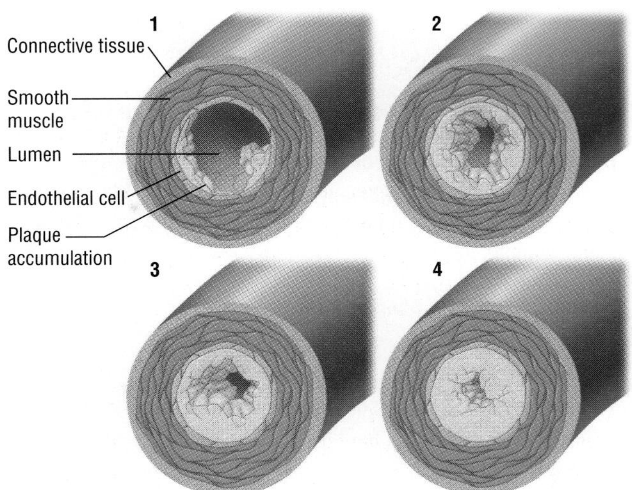

Figure 10–2 Progression of atherosclerosis. This diagram shows how plaque deposits gradually accumulate to narrow the lumen (interior space) of an artery. Although enlarged here, coronary arteries are only as wide as a pencil lead.

Initially, most people can help lower their serum cholesterol level by adopting three lifestyle changes: lowering their intake of saturated fats, lowering their caloric intake to a level that does not exceed body requirements, and increasing exercise. By carefully following such a plan, people with elevated serum cholesterol levels typically are able to reduce them. However, lifestyle changes such as these do not affect people equally; some will experience greater reductions than others. Some will not respond at all to dietary changes and may need to take cholesterol-lowering medications and increase their physical activity.

Cholesterol is attached to structures called lipoproteins. Lipoproteins are particles that circulate in the blood and transport lipids (including cholesterol). Two major classes of lipoproteins exist: **low-density lipoproteins (LDLs)** and **high-density lipoproteins (HDLs)**. A person's total cholesterol level is chiefly determined by the amount of the LDLs and HDLs in a measured sample of blood.

Key Terms

atherosclerosis
Buildup of plaque on the inner walls of arteries.

low-density lipoprotein (LDL)
The type of lipoprotein that transports the largest amount of cholesterol in the bloodstream; high levels of LDL are related to heart disease.

high-density lipoprotein (HDL)
The type of lipoprotein that transports cholesterol from the bloodstream to the liver, where it is eventually removed from the body; high levels of HDL are related to a reduction in heart disease.

Changing *for the Better*

Recognizing Signs of a Heart Attack and Taking Action

I was walking by the track field and saw a runner in distress. I froze and watched as someone else ran to his aid. How could I tell whether or not this person was having a heart attack? What action should I have taken?

Warning Signs of a Heart Attack

- Uncomfortable pressure, fullness, squeezing, or pain in the centre of your chest lasting two minutes or longer
- Pain spreading to your shoulders, neck, or arms
- Severe pain, dizziness, fainting, sweating, nausea, or shortness of breath

Not all of these warning signs occur with every heart attack. If some start to occur, don't wait. Get help immediately!

How to Prepare for an Emergency

- Find out which hospitals in your area have 24-hour emergency cardiac care.
- Determine (in advance) the hospital or medical facility that is nearest your home and office, and tell your family and friends to call this facility in an emergency.
- Keep a list of emergency rescue service numbers next to your telephone and in your pocket, wallet, or purse.

What to Do in an Emergency

- If you have chest discomfort that lasts for two minutes or more, call the emergency rescue service (911).
- If you can get to a hospital faster by going yourself and not waiting for an ambulance, have someone drive you there.

How to Be a Heart Saver

- If you are with someone experiencing the signs of a heart attack and the warning signs last for two minutes or longer, act immediately.
- Expect denial. It is normal for someone with chest discomfort to deny the possibility of something as serious as a heart attack. Don't take "no" for an answer. Insist on taking prompt action.
- Call the emergency rescue service (911), or get to the nearest hospital emergency room that offers 24-hour emergency cardiac care.
- Give CPR (mouth-to-mouth breathing and chest compression) or use an AED (automated external defibrillator) if it is necessary and if you are properly trained.

It has been determined that high levels of LDL are a significant promoter of atherosclerosis. This makes sense because LDLs carry the greatest percentage of cholesterol in the bloodstream. LDLs are more likely to deposit excess cholesterol into the artery walls. This contributes to plaque formation.

For this reason, LDLs are often called the "bad cholesterol." High LDL levels are determined partially by inheritance, but they are also clearly associated with smoking, poor dietary patterns, obesity, and lack of exercise.

On the other hand, high levels of HDLs are related to a decrease in the development of atherosclerosis. HDLs are thought to transport cholesterol out of the bloodstream. Thus HDLs have been called the "good cholesterol." Certain lifestyle alterations, such as quitting smoking, reducing obesity, increasing physical activity, decreasing overall dietary fat intake, and replacing saturated fats with monosaturated fats help many people increase their level of HDLs.

Reducing total serum cholesterol levels is a significant step in reducing the risk of death from coronary heart disease. For people with elevated cholesterol levels, a 1% reduction in serum cholesterol level yields about a 2% reduction in the risk of death from heart disease.

Angina pectoris. When coronary arteries become narrowed, chest pain, or *angina pectoris,* is often felt. This pain results from a reduced supply of oxygen to heart muscle tissue. Usually, angina is felt when the patient becomes stressed or exercises too strenuously. Angina reportedly can range from a feeling of mild indigestion to a severe viselike pressure in the chest. The pain may extend from the centre of the chest to the arms and even up to the jaw. Generally, the more severe the blockage, the more pain is felt.

Some cardiac patients relieve angina with the drug *nitroglycerin*, a powerful blood vessel dilator. This prescription drug, available in slow-release transdermal patches or small pills that are placed under the patient's tongue, causes the coronary arteries to dilate and allow a greater flow of blood into heart muscle tissue.

Emergency response to heart crises

Heart attacks are not always fatal. The consequences of any heart attack depend on the location of the damage to the heart, the extent to which heart muscle is damaged, and the speed with which adequate circulation is restored. Injury to the ventricles may very well prove fatal unless medical countermeasures are immediately undertaken. The recognition of heart attack is critically important. The Changing for Better Box on this page explains how to recognize the signs of a heart attack and what to do next.

HealthQuest Activities
www.mcgrawhill.ca/college/hahn

- The *Heart Attack Risk* and *What Is Your CAD Risk?* activities in the Cardiovascular Health Module allow you to assess your risk for cardiovascular disease. In the first of these activities, *Heart Attack Risk*, answer the questions about your health history, behavioural practices, and knowledge about heart disease. *HealthQuest* will then provide the correct answers and point out any health risks indicated by your responses. In the *Cardiovascular Exploration* section, fill out all of the items, and then click on the "Get Results" button to find out your overall risk. You can get more specific feedback on each risk factor by clicking on the Tutorial link in this section.

Hypertension

Just as a car's water pump recirculates water and maintains water pressure, your heart recirculates blood and maintains blood pressure. When the heart contracts, blood is forced through your arteries and veins. Your blood pressure is a measure of the force that your circulating blood exerts against the interior walls of your arteries and veins.

Blood pressure is measured with a *sphygmomanometer*. This instrument is attached to an arm-cuff device that can be inflated to stop the flow of blood temporarily in the brachial artery. A physician, nurse, or technician using a stethoscope will listen for blood flow while the pressure in the cuff is released. Two pressure measurements will be recorded: the **systolic pressure** is the blood pressure against the vessel walls when the heart contracts, and the **diastolic pressure** is the blood pressure against the vessel walls when the heart relaxes (between heartbeats). Expressed in millimetres of mercury displaced on the sphygmomanometer, blood pressure is recorded in the form of a fraction, for example, 115/82. Because blood pressure drops when the heart relaxes, the diastolic pressure is always lower than the systolic pressure.

TALKING POINTS • You're having a regular physical examination, and your doctor remarks that your blood pressure puts you in the category of "borderline hypertension." What questions would you ask about managing this condition?

Hypertension refers to a consistently elevated blood pressure. Generally, concern about a young adult's high blood pressure begins when he or she has a systolic reading of 140 or above or a diastolic reading of 90 or above. Approximately 1 in 5 Canadian adults are estimated to have hypertension.[9]

Although the reasons for 90% to 95% of the cases of hypertension are not known, the health risks produced by uncontrolled hypertension are clearly understood. Throughout the body, hypertension makes arteries and arterioles become less elastic and thus incapable of dilating under a heavy workload. Brittle, calcified blood vessels can burst unexpectedly and produce serious strokes (brain accidents), kidney failure (renal accidents), or eye damage (**retinal hemorrhage**). Furthermore, it appears that blood and fat clots are more easily formed and dislodged in a vascular system affected by hypertension. Thus hypertension can be a cause of heart attacks. Clearly, hypertension is a potential killer.

Ironically, despite its deadly nature, hypertension is referred to as "the silent killer" because people with hypertension often are not aware that they have the condition. They cannot feel the sensation of high blood pressure. The condition does not produce dizziness, headaches, or memory loss unless one is experiencing a medical crisis. It is estimated that nearly one-third of the people who have hypertension do not realize they have it.[10] Many who are aware of their hypertension do little to control it. Only a small percentage (34%) of people who have hypertension control it adequately, generally through dietary measures, physical activity, relaxation training, and drug therapy.

Hypertension is a controllable disease, yet if therapy is stopped, the condition returns. As a responsible adult, use every opportunity you can to measure your blood pressure on a regular basis.

Prevention and treatment

Weight reduction, physical activity, moderation in alcohol use, increasing fruit and vegetable intake, and moderate sodium restriction are often used to reduce hypertension. For overweight or obese people, a reduction in body weight may produce a significant drop in blood pressure. Physical activity helps lower blood pressure by expending calories (which leads to weight loss) and improving overall circulation. Reducing alcohol consumption to less than about 60 mL (2 oz) daily helps reduce blood pressure in some people.

Key Terms

systolic pressure
Blood pressure against blood vessel walls when the heart contracts.

diastolic pressure
Blood pressure against blood vessel walls when the heart relaxes.

retinal hemorrhage
Uncontrolled bleeding from arteries within the eye's retina.

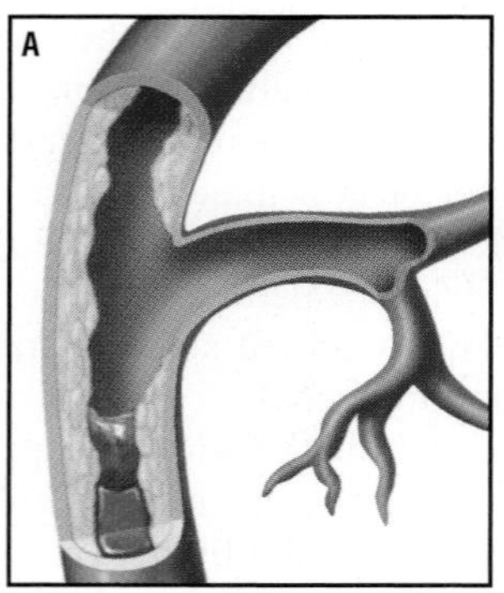

Thrombus
A clot that forms within a narrowed section of a blood vessel and remains at its place of origin.

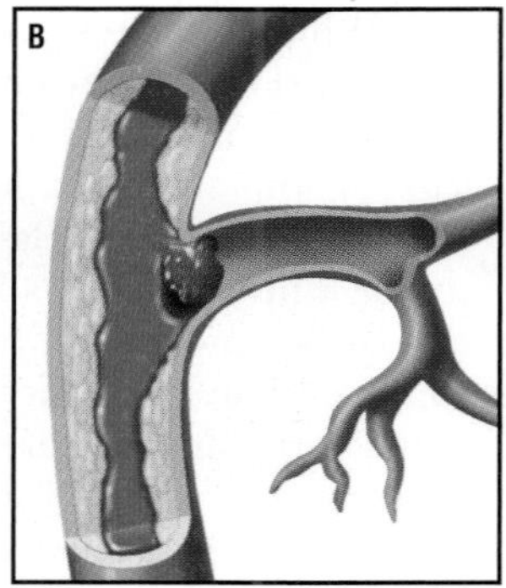

Embolus
A clot that moves through the circulatory system and becomes lodged at a narrowed point within a vessel.

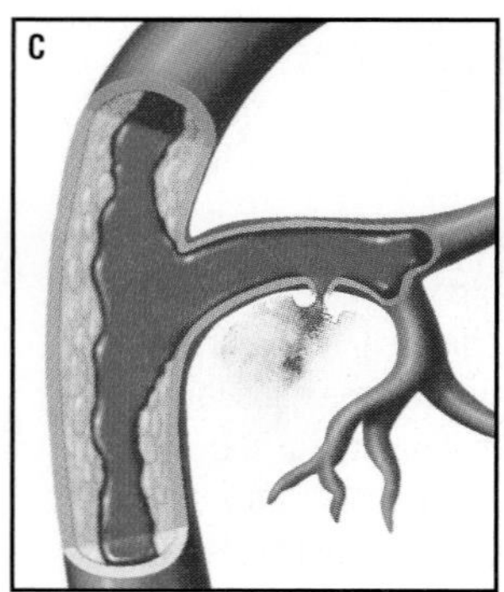

Hemorrhage
The sudden bursting of a blood vessel.

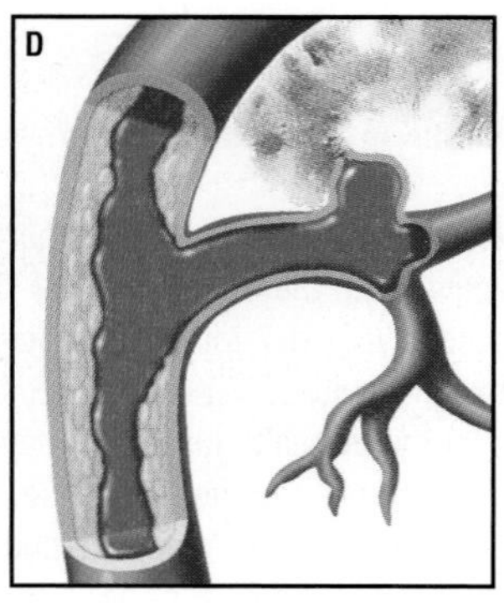

Aneurysm
A sac formed when a section of a blood vessel thins and balloons; the weakened wall of the sac can burst, or rupture, as shown here.

Figure 10–3 Causes of stroke.

The restriction of sodium (salt) in the diet also helps some people reduce hypertension. Interestingly, this strategy is effective only for those who are **salt sensitive**—estimated to be about 25% of the population. Reducing salt intake would have little effect on the blood pressure of the rest of the population. Nevertheless, since our daily intake of salt vastly exceeds our need for salt, the general recommendation to curb salt intake still makes good sense.

Many of the stress-reduction activities discussed in Chapter 3 are receiving increased attention in the struggle to reduce hypertension. In recent years, behavioural scientists have reported the success of meditation, biofeedback, controlled breathing, and muscle-relaxation exercises in reducing hypertension. Look for further research findings in these areas in the years to come.

There are literally dozens of drugs available for use by people with hypertension. Unfortunately, many patients refuse to take their medication on a consistent basis, probably because of the mistaken notion that "you must feel sick to be sick."

Stroke

Stroke is a general term for a wide variety of crises (sometimes called *cerebrovascular accidents* [CVAs] or brain attacks) that result from blood vessel damage in the brain. Just as the heart muscle needs an adequate blood supply, so does the brain. Any disturbance in the proper supply of oxygen and nutrients to the brain can pose a threat.

Perhaps the most common form of stroke results from the blockage of a cerebral (brain) artery. Similar to coronary occlusions, **cerebrovascular occlusions** can be started by a clot that forms within an artery, called a *thrombus*, or by a clot that travels from another part of the body to the brain, called an *embolus* (Figure 10–3, *A* and *B*). The resultant accidents (cerebral thrombosis or cerebral embolism) cause between 70% and 80% of all strokes. The portion of the brain deprived of oxygen and nutrients can literally die.

A third type of stroke can result from an artery that bursts to produce a crisis called *cerebral hemorrhage* (Figure 10–3, *C*). Damaged, brittle arteries can be especially susceptible to bursting when a person has hypertension.

A fourth form of stroke is a *cerebral aneurysm*. An aneurysm is a ballooning or outpouching on a weakened area of an artery (Figure 10–3, *D*). Their development is not fully understood, although there seems to be a relationship between aneurysms and hypertension. When a cerebral aneurysm bursts, a stroke results. See the Changing for the Better box on page 225 to learn the warning signs of stroke.

Managing Heart Health

The Health Heart Kit, developed by Health Canada and the Heart and Stroke Foundation of Canada, provides interactive and detailed information about controlling risk factors for, and consequently reducing, risk of heart disease. Visit **www.phac-aspc.gc.ca/ccdpc-cpcmc/hhk-tcs/english/ index_e.htm** to start reducing your risk of heart disease.

CANCER IN CANADA

It is estimated that in 2004, 145 000 new cases of cancer will be diagnosed and 68 300 Canadians will die of this disease.[11] Among men, mortality rates for all cancers combined have been in slow decline since 1988, largely as a result of earlier drops in smoking prevalence among Canadian males. Canadian women have seen a steady

Changing *for the Better*

Recognizing Warning Signs of Stroke

My father died of a stroke a few years ago, and ever since then I've had a fear that I might be alone with someone who experiences a stroke. How would I recognize the signs of a stroke?

Although many stroke victims have little advance warning of an impending crisis, there are some warning signals of stroke that should be recognized. Everyone is encouraged to be aware of the following signs:

- Sudden, temporary weakness or numbness of the face, arm, and leg on one side of the body
- Temporary loss of speech or trouble in speaking or understanding speech
- Temporary dimness or loss of vision, particularly in one eye
- Unexplained dizziness, unsteadiness, or sudden falls

Many severe strokes are preceded by "little strokes," warning signals like the above, experienced days, weeks, or months before the more severe event. Prompt medical or surgical attention to these symptoms may prevent a fatal or disabling stroke from occurring.

reduction in all-cancer mortality since the 1970s, with the exception of deaths from lung cancer. These deaths currently remain more than four times higher than they were in 1971. This reflects the increase in tobacco use among women.

CANCER: A PROBLEM OF CELL REGULATION

Just as a corporation depends on competent individuals to staff its various departments, the body depends on its basic units of function—the cells. Cells band together as tissues, such as muscle tissue, to perform a prescribed function. Tissues in turn join to form organs, such as the heart, and organs are assembled into the body's several organ systems, such as the cardiovascular system. This is the "corporate structure" of the body.

If individuals and cells are the basic units of function for their respective organizations, the failure of either to perform in a prescribed, dependable manner can erode the overall organization to the extent that it might not be able to continue. Cancer, the second leading cause of death among adults, reflects cell dysfunction in its most extreme form.[12] In cancer the normal behaviour of cells ceases.

HealthQuest Activities

www.mcgrawhill.ca/college/hahn

- The wellness activity *Cancer: What's Your Risk?*, found in the Cancer Module, allows you to examine how your family history, personal health history, occupation, environment, and behaviour affect your risk of developing cancer. *HealthQuest* will estimate whether you are at decreased, average, or above-average risk of developing several kinds of cancer. Complete the self-assessment and then gather more information about the cancers for which you are at increased risk.

Cell Regulation

Most of the tissues of the body lose cells over time. This continual loss requires that replacement cells be brought forward from areas of young and less specialized cells. The process of *specialization* required to turn the less specialized cells into mature cells is carefully controlled by genes within the cells. Upon becoming specialized, these newest cells copy, or *replicate*, themselves. These two processes are carefully monitored by the cells' **regulatory genes**. Failure to regulate specialization and replication results in abnormal, or cancerous, cells.

Cells also have genes designed to repair mistakes in the copying of genetic material (the basis of replication) and genes to suppress the growth of abnormal cells if they occur. Thus *repair genes* and *suppressor genes*, such as the *p53* gene, join regulatory genes to prevent the development of abnormal cells.[13] If these genes fail to function properly and malignant (cancerous) cells develop, the immune system (see Chapter 11) will, ideally, recognize their presence and remove them before a clinical (diagnosable) case of cancer can develop.

Key Terms

salt sensitive
Term used to describe people whose bodies overreact to the presence of sodium by retaining fluid, thus experiencing an increase in blood pressure.

cerebrovascular occlusion
Blockages to arteries supplying blood to the cerebral cortex of the brain; strokes.

regulatory genes
Genes within the cell that control cellular replication, or doubling.

Because specialization, replication, repair, and suppressor genes can become cancer-causing genes, or **oncogenes**, when they do not work properly, these four types of genes can also be referred to as **protooncogenes**, or potential oncogenes.[14] The failure of tumour suppressor genes to regulate the formation of abnormal cells is now thought to be a critical factor in the development of cancer. In addition to the *p53* gene, other specific genes have been associated with certain types of breast cancer, ovarian cancer, colon cancer, and prostate cancer.[15] In the future, scientists may discover that virtually all cancers have genetic predispositions or specific oncogenes associated with their development.

Oncogene Formation

All cells have protooncogenes. But what changes normal cancer-preventing genes so that they become cancer-causing genes? Three mechanisms—genetic mutations, viral infections, and carcinogens—have received much attention.

Genetic mutations develop when dividing cells miscopy genetic information. If the gene that is miscopied is a protooncogene, the oncogene that results will stimulate the formation of cancerous cells. A variety of factors, including aging, free radical formation, radiation, and an array of carcinogens, are associated with the miscopying of the complex genetic information that comprises the genes found within the cell, including those intended to prevent cancer.

In both animals and humans, *cancer-producing viruses*, such as the leukemia virus in cats and the human immunodeficiency (HIV) virus, herpes virus, and human papillomavirus (HPV) in humans (see Chapter 11), have been identified. These viruses seek out cells of a particular type, such as those of the immune system, and alter their genetic material to convert these cells into virus-producing cells. In the process, they change the makeup of one or more of the regulatory genes, converting these protooncogenes into oncogenes. Once converted into oncogenes, the altered genes are passed on through cell division.

A third possible explanation for the conversion of protooncogenes into oncogenes is the presence of environmental agents known as *carcinogens*. Over an extended period, carcinogens, such as chemicals found in tobacco smoke, polluted air and water, toxic wastes, and the high fat content of foods, may convert protooncogenes into oncogenes. These carcinogens may work alone or in combination (*co-carcinogens*). Thus people might develop lung cancer only if they are exposed to the right combination of carcinogens over an extended period.

Our understanding of the role of genes in the development of cancer is expanding rapidly. In conjunction with the **Human Genome Project** and the *Cancer Genome Anatomy Project (CGAP)*,[16] the scientific community has now identified over 160 oncogenes, tumour suppressor protooncogenes, and other genetic markers for human cancers.[17] Among the most familiar to the public are the *p16* oncogene for lung cancer, the *BRCA1* and *BRCA2* tumour-suppressor genes for breast cancer and ovarian cancer, and the *MSH2* and *MSH1* genes for colon cancer. As geneticists continue to discover additional genetic links to cancer, the possibility of some form of "gene-repair" technology or a "gene chip" to aid screening becomes a possibility in the war against cancer.

The Cancerous Cell

In comparison with their noncancerous cousins, cancer cells are both similar and dissimilar in how they function. It is the dissimilar aspects that usually make them unpredictable and more difficult to manage.

One unique aspect of cancerous cells is their infinite life expectancy. It appears that cancerous cells can produce an enzyme, *telomerase*, that blocks the biological clock that tells normal cells that it's time to die.[18] In spite of this ability to live forever, cancer cells do not necessarily divide more quickly than normal cells. In fact, they can divide at the same rate or even at a slower rate.[19]

Because cancerous cells do not possess the *contact inhibition* (a control mechanism that influences the number of cells that can occupy a particular space) of normal cells, they can accumulate and eventually alter the structure of a body organ or break through its wall into neighbouring areas (invasion). Also, the absence of *cellular cohesiveness* (a property seen in normal cells that "keeps them at home") allows cancer cells to spread through the circulatory or lymphatic system to distant points via **metastasis** (Figure 10–4). A final unique characteristic of cancerous cells is their ability to command extra blood supply to meet their metabolic needs and provide additional routes for metastasis. This *angiogenesis potential* of cancer cells makes them extremely hardy in comparison with noncancerous cells, although progress against this capability is being made. Avastin was the first angiogenesis inhibitor to market, in 2004.[20]

Benign Tumours

Noncancerous, or **benign**, tumours can also form in the body. These tumours are usually enclosed by a fibrous membrane and do not spread from their point of origin as cancerous tumours can. Benign tumours are dangerous, however, when they crowd out normal tissue within a confined space.

Types of Cancer and Their Locations

Cancers are named on the basis of the type of tissues where they occur. The following classifications are used by physicians to describe malignancies to the layperson:

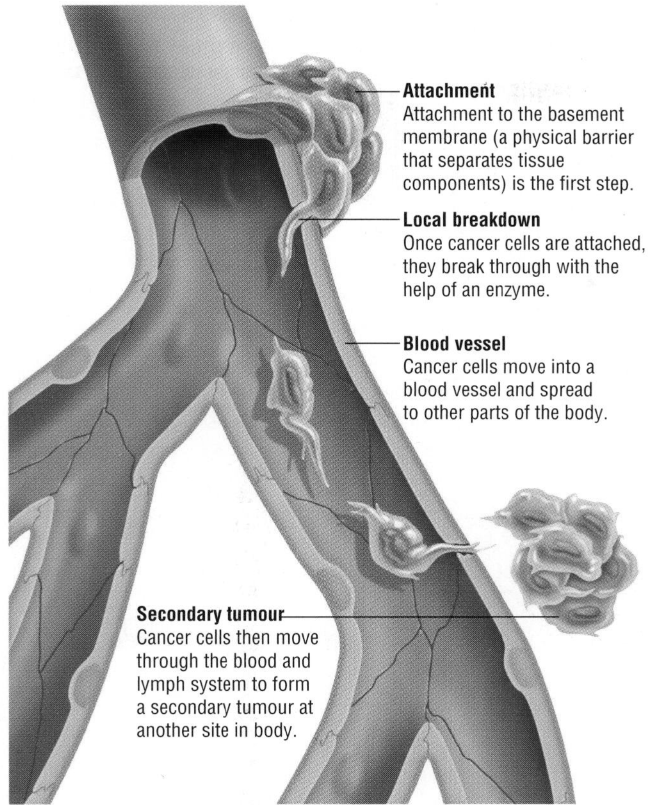

Attachment
Attachment to the basement membrane (a physical barrier that separates tissue components) is the first step.
Local breakdown
Once cancer cells are attached, they break through with the help of an enzyme.
Blood vessel
Cancer cells move into a blood vessel and spread to other parts of the body.
Secondary tumour
Cancer cells then move through the blood and lymph system to form a secondary tumour at another site in body.

Figure 10–4 How cancer spreads. Locomotion (movement) is essential to the process of metastasis (spread of cancer). Scientists have identified a protein that causes cancer cells to grow arms, or pseudopodia, enabling them to move to other parts of the body.

- *Carcinoma.* Found most frequently in the skin, nose, mouth, throat, stomach, intestinal tract, glands, nerves, breasts, urinary and genital structures, lungs, kidneys, and liver; approximately 85% of all malignant tumours are classified as carcinomas
- *Sarcoma.* Formed in the connective tissues of the body; bone, cartilage, and tendons are the sites of sarcoma development; only 2% of all malignancies are of this type
- *Melanoma.* Arises from the melanin-containing cells of skin; found most often in individuals who have had extensive sun exposure, particularly a deep, penetrating sunburn; although once rare, the amount of this cancer has increased markedly in recent years; remains among the most deadly forms of cancer
- *Neuroblastoma.* Originates in the immature cells found within the central nervous system; neuroblastomas are rare; usually found in children
- *Adenocarcinoma.* Derived from cells of the endocrine glands
- *Hepatoma.* Originates in cells of the liver; although not thought to be directly caused by alcohol use, hepatomas are more frequently seen in individuals who have experienced **sclerotic changes** in the liver
- *Leukemia.* Found in cells of the blood and blood-forming tissues; characterized by abnormal, immature white blood cell formation; multiple forms found in children and adults
- *Lymphoma.* Arises in cells of the lymphatic tissues or other immune system tissues; includes lymphosarcomas and Hodgkin's disease, characterized by abnormal white cell production and decreased resistance

Figure 10–5[21] presents information about the incidence of cancer and the deaths from cancer at various sites in both men and women.

CANCER AT SELECTED SITES IN THE BODY

A second, more familiar way to describe cancer is according to the organ (or tissue) site where it occurs. The following discussion focuses on some of these familiar sites. Regular screening procedures can lead to early identification of cancer at these sites (see the Changing for the Better box on p. 229).

Lung

Lung cancer is one of the most lethal forms of cancer. Primarily because its symptoms first appear when the disease is at an advanced stage, only 15% of all lung cancer victims survive five years beyond diagnosis.[22] By the time victims are sufficiently concerned about their persistent cough, blood-streaked sputum, and chest pain, it is often too late for treatment to be effective.

Key Terms

oncogenes
Genes that are believed to activate the development of cancer.

protooncogenes
Normal regulatory genes that may become oncogenes.

Human Genome Project
International quest by geneticists to identify the location and composition of every gene within the human cell.

metastasis
The spread of cancerous cells from their site of origin to other areas of the body.

benign
Noncancerous; tumours that do not spread.

sclerotic changes
Thickening or hardening of tissues.

Men	Incidence	Deaths
Lung	11 900	10 700
Kidney	2600	950
Stomach	1800	1150
Pancreas	1600	1600
Colon/rectum	10 400	4500
Bladder	3700	1150
Prostate	20 100	4200
Leukemia	2300	1300
Testis	820	35

Women	Incidence	Deaths
Lung	9800	8200
Breast	21 200	5200
Stomach	1000	750
Pancreas	1700	1700
Colon/rectum	8800	3900
Ovary	2300	1550
Uterus	3800	700
Leukemia	1650	930
Cervix	1350	410

Figure 10–5 These 2004 estimates of cancer incidence and deaths reveal some significant similarities between men and women. Note that lung cancer is the leading cause of cancer deaths for both genders.

Chemotherapy is a treatment for many types of cancer.

Every week, on average, 417 Canadians are diagnosed with lung cancer, and 363 die from it.[23] Smokers account for 87% of all reported cases of lung cancer, and lung cancer causes 30% of all cancer deaths. Environmental agents, such as radon, asbestos, and air pollutants, contribute to a lesser degree in the development of lung cancer.

According to the World Health Organization, the incidence of lung cancer has risen 200% for women, paralleling their increased smoking. Currently, lung cancer exceeds breast cancer as the leading cause of cancer deaths in women. The incidence of lung cancer has shown an encouraging decline in men while their use of tobacco is decreasing.

Breast

Surpassed only by lung cancer, breast cancer is the second leading cause of death from cancer in women. During a woman's lifetime, her chances of developing breast cancer are 1 in 9, though only 1 in 27 dies from it.[24] As they age, women are increasingly at risk for developing breast cancer. Early detection is the key to complete recovery. In fact, 97% of women who discover their breast cancer before it has spread will survive more than five years.[25]

Although all women and men are at some risk for developing breast cancer, women whose menstrual periods began when they were young and for whom menopause was late (longer exposure to higher estrogen levels), women who had no children (high risk seen later in life) or had their first child later in life (nursing helps lower risk, however), and women with a family history of breast cancer are at greater risk.[26] Also, women whose diets are high in saturated fats and who have excessive fat in the waist area are more likely to develop breast cancer, although the exact role of dietary fats remains contested. Alcohol consumption, use of an oral contraceptive, and use of hormone replacement therapy (HRT) still foster controversy regarding their influence in women's risk for developing breast cancer. Environmental pollutants and regional influences are also being investigated as causative factors in the development of breast cancer.[27] In the latter case, lifestyle differences may account for different breast cancer rates from region to region.

Changing *for the Better*

Canadian Cancer Society's Guidelines for Early Detection and Screening for Cancer

Cancer runs in my family—on both sides. What cancer screening test should each family member get, and when?

Test or Procedure	Sex	Age	Guidelines for Early Detection and Screening
Breast Self-Examination	Female	Adult women —emphasis on women 40 and over	The need to do a monthly Breast Self-Examination becomes more important with age, especially after age 40. The best time to check your breasts is 7 to 10 days after you start your period. If you are not having periods each month, mark a special day of the month on your calendar. Report any changes to your doctor.
Clinical breast examination	Female	All women	By a doctor or trained health professional at least every two years.
Mammography	Female	50 to 69	Every two years if you are between the ages of 50 and 69. Women under 50 or over age 69 should check with their doctor about mammograms.
		High Risk*	Individualized plan of surveillance as outlined by your doctor. *High-risk groups include first-degree relative (mother, daughter, sister) with breast cancer, family history of cancer.
Pap test/Pelvic examination	Female		You need a Pap test once you become sexually active at any age, and even if you don't have sex anymore. Pap testing is performed every one to three years depending on the screening guidelines in each province.
Digital rectal examination	Female/Male	Age 50 and over	Every year, starting at age 50. Digital rectal examination can be helpful to detect cancers of both the rectum and the prostate.
		High Risk*	**Colorectal Cancer:** Individualized plan of surveillance as outlined by your doctor. *High-risk groups include those with chronic ulcerative colitis, other bowel disorders, previous colorectal cancer, benign polyps, and a strong family history of colorectal cancer. **Prostate Cancer:** Men in high-risk groups, such as African-Canadian men, and those with a strong family history of prostate cancer may wish to discuss the need for testing at a younger age.
PSA Test (Prostate Specific Antigen)	Male	Age 50 and over	Men over 50 should discuss the potential benefits and risks of early detection using PSA and digital rectal examination with their doctor. Men in high-risk groups, such as African-Canadian men and those with a strong family history of prostate cancer, may wish to discuss the need for testing at a younger age.
Skin examination	Female/Male	All ages	Regular skin examination; report any changes to your doctor.
Testicular self-examination	Male	All men 15 and over	Monthly testicular self-examination is an early detection measure. This is best done monthly after a warm bath or shower, when the scrotal sac is relaxed. Report any changes to your doctor.

The Canadian Cancer Society's guidelines for early detection of breast cancer can be found in the Changing for the Better box on this page. These include physical examination by a trained health care professional and mammography for women over the age of 50 years. Breast Self-Examination (BSE) continues to be recommended by the CCS; however, a 2001 report by the Canadian Task Force on Preventive Health Care stated "there is fair evidence of no benefit, and good evidence of harm" associated with BSE instruction. The harm refers to increases in physician visits for benign breast lesion evaluations, in addition to elevated rates of benign biopsies.[28] Be sure to discuss any concerns you have regarding your breast health with a health care professional.

Regardless of age, each woman has a unique risk profile. Therefore, the recommendation of her physician should be given careful consideration.

Regardless of the detection method, if a lump is found, a breast biopsy can determine what the lump is. If the lump is cancerous, treatment is highly effective if the cancer is found in an early stage. Since many choices exist about the type of surgery used to remove the cancer, women should seek a second opinion.

Today, for the first time, the potential for preventing breast cancer may be at hand—with a family of drugs that block the influence of estrogen on abnormal breast

Changing *for the Better*

Breast Self-Examination

I've never felt confident about doing a breast self-exam. What is the proper technique?

The following explains how to do a breast self-examination:

1. In the shower: Examine your breasts during a bath or shower; hands glide more easily over wet skin. With your fingers flat, move gently over every part of each breast. Use right hand to examine left breast, left hand for right breast. Check for any lump, hard knot, or thickening. This self-examination should be done monthly, preferably 7 to 10 days after the end of the menstrual period.
2. Before a mirror: Inspect your breasts with arms at your sides. Next, raise your arms high overhead. Look for any changes in contour of each breast, a swelling, dimpling of skin, changes in the nipple. Then rest palms on hips, and press down firmly to flex your chest muscles. Left and right breast will not exactly match—few women's breasts do.
3. Lying down: To examine your right breast, put a pillow or folded towel under your right shoulder. Place right hand behind your head—this distributes breast tissue more evenly on the chest. With left hand, fingers flat, press gently in small circular motions around an imaginary clock face. Begin at outermost top of your right breast for 12 o'clock, then move to 1 o'clock, and so on around the circle back to 12 o'clock. A ridge of firm tissue in the lower curve of each breast is normal. Then move in an inch toward the nipple; keep circling to examine every part of your breast, including the nipple. This requires at least three more circles. Now slowly repeat the procedure on your left breast with a pillow under your left shoulder and left hand behind head. Notice how your breast structure feels. Finally, squeeze the nipple of each breast gently between thumb and index finger. Any discharge, clear or bloody, should be reported to your doctor immediately.

Breast cancer can occur in men too. Therefore this examination should be performed monthly by men. Regular inspection shows what is normal for you and will give you confidence in your examination.

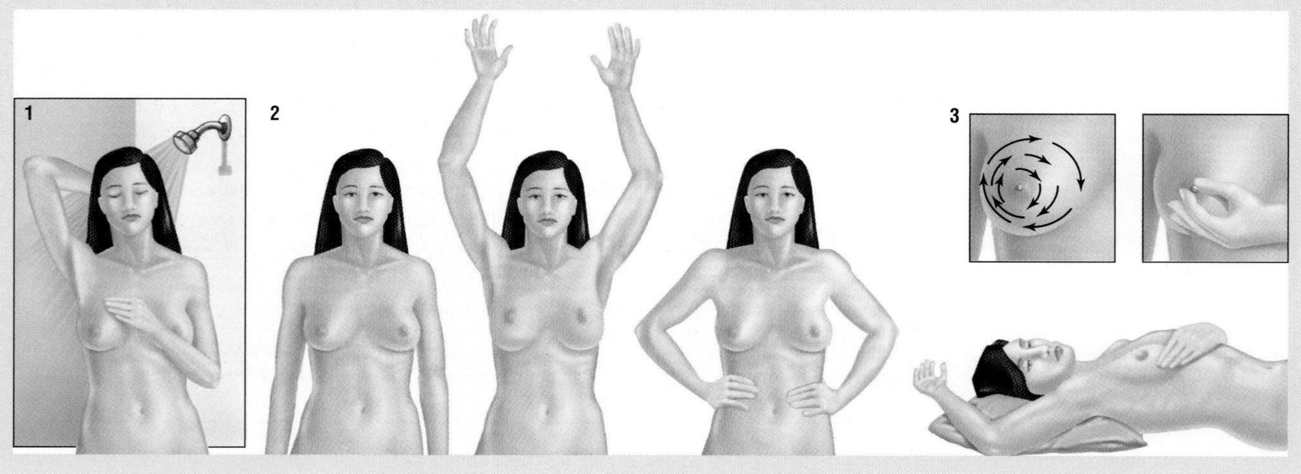

cells. These *selective estrogen-receptor modulators* (SERMs) are now available to women who are at high risk for breast cancer. Tamoxifen, the best studied SERM, has recently been joined by Raloxifene as an approved preventive agent. Additionally, at least two other SERMs are in or nearly in the marketplace.[29] The SERMs also hold promise as effective agents in the prevention of osteoporosis and cardiovascular disease.

Uterus

In 2004, approximately 5150 new cases of cancer of the body of the uterus were anticipated in Canada. Included in this figure were 3800 cases of cancer of the uterine lining (endometrial cancer) and 1350 cases of cancer of the uterine neck (cervical cancer).[30] Fortunately, the death rate from uterine cancer has dropped greatly since 1950, largely because of the use of the **Pap test**. This test looks for precancerous changes in the cells taken from the cervix.

The importance of women having a Pap test for cervical cancer on a routine basis cannot be overemphasized. Without screening, a 20-year-old of average risk has a 250 in 10 000 chance of getting cervical cancer and a 118 in 10 000 chance of dying from it. With screening, a 20-year-old of average risk has a 35 in 10 000 chance of getting this form of cancer and only an 11 in 10 000 chance of dying from it. The Pap test is not perfect, however; about 7% of the tests will miss finding abnormal changes.[31] Further, not all women whose test results are abnormal receive adequate follow-up care, nor do they have subsequent Pap tests on a regular enough basis.

In addition to changes discovered by a Pap test, symptoms suggesting cancer of the uterus include abnormal bleeding between periods. The Canada Cancer Society states that there is no single cause of cervical or uterine cancer. However, some of the more notable risk factors for cervical cancer include early age of first intercourse, multiple sexual partners, a sexual partner who has had multiple partners, and HPV infections. Risk factors for uterine cancer include advanced age, obesity, childlessness, late age for menopause onset, prolonged use of medications containing estrogen, and taking the drug tamoxifen. It is important to note that some women will develop cervical or uterine cancer without any of these risk factors.

TALKING POINTS • Three risk factors are associated with HPV-induced cervical cancer: early age of first sexual intercourse, higher-than-average number of partners, and lack of protection against sexually transmitted diseases (e.g., condoms). How would you introduce this topic to a teenage daughter, sister, or niece?

Ovary

In 2004, it was estimated that 2300 new cases of ovarian cancer would be identified and 1550 Canadian women would die.[32] Most cases of ovarian cancer develop in women who are older than 40 and who have not had children or began menstruation at an early age. The highest rate is in women over 60. The incidence of ovarian cancer is greatest among women who have had a relatively longer exposure to hormones during their menstrual cycles.[33] The inheritance of the *BRCA1* tumour suppressor gene mutation and, particularly, the *BRCA2* mutation, increases the risk of developing ovarian cancer.

Because of its vague symptoms, ovarian cancer has been referred to as a *silent* cancer. Digestive disturbances, gas, and stomach distention are often its only symptoms.

Prostate

The prostate gland is a walnut-size gland located near the base of the penis. It surrounds the neck of the bladder and the urethra. Cancer of the prostate is the third most common form of cancer in men and a leading cause of death from cancer in older men. On the basis of current statistics, approximately 1 out of 8 men will develop this form of cancer. Men with a family history of prostate cancer are at greater risk of developing this form of cancer than men without this family history. Additionally, a link between prostate cancer and dietary patterns, such as excessive red meat and dairy product consumption, has been suggested. African American men also have a higher risk of developing prostate cancer.

Symptoms of Prostate Disease

- Difficulty in urinating
- Frequent urination, particularly at night
- Continued wetness for a short time after urination
- Blood in the urine
- Low back pain
- Ache in upper thighs

The symptoms of prostate disease, including prostate cancer, are listed in the Star Box above. If these symptoms appear, particularly in men 50 years of age and older, it is important to consult a physician. Screening for prostate cancer should begin by age 50. It involves an annual rectal examination and the prostate-specific antigen (PSA) blood test. This test has been joined by a more sensitive version that can identify the "free" antigen most closely associated with prostate cancer, thus cutting down on false positives and the extensive use of biopsies. In addition, an ultrasound rectal examination is used in men whose PSA scores are abnormally high.

Traditionally, prostate cancer has been treated through surgery or the use of radiation and chemotherapy, with a survival rate of 100% when diagnosed early and 93% overall.[34] Because this type of cancer grows slowly, it is increasingly likely that men whose cancer is very localized and whose life expectancy is less than 10 years at the time of diagnosis will not receive treatment but rather will be closely monitored for any progression in the cancer.[35]

Testicle

Cancer of the testicle is among the least common forms of cancer; however, it represents the most common solid tumour in men between the ages of 20 and 34 years. Testicular cancer has a tendency to run in families and is more common in African American men whose testicles were undescended during childhood. The incidence of this cancer has been increasing in recent years. However,

Key Term

Pap test
A cancer screening procedure in which cells are removed from the cervix and examined for precancerous changes.

Changing *for the Better*

Testicular Self-Examination

I feel unsure about how to perform a testicular self-exam. What is the correct method?

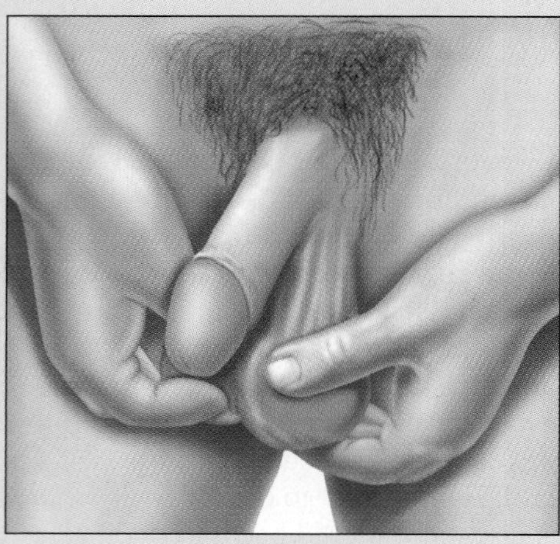

Your best hope for early detection of testicular cancer is a simple three-minute monthly self-examination. The following explains how to do a testicular self-examination. The best time is after a warm bath or shower, when the scrotal skin is most relaxed.

1. Roll each testicle gently between the thumb and fingers of both hands.
2. If you find any hard lumps or nodules, you should see your doctor promptly. They may not be malignant, but only your doctor can make the diagnosis.

After a thorough physical examination, your doctor may perform certain X-ray studies to make the most accurate diagnosis possible.

Monthly testicular self-examinations are as important for men as breast self-examinations are for women.

no single explanation can be given for this increase. Factors such as a difficult pregnancy, elevated temperature in the groin, or mumps may be involved. However, testicular cancer may develop in men who do not possess any of these risk factors. The incidence of this cancer has increased by 100% since 1930, and a corresponding drop in sperm count has been seen. Agricultural pesticide toxicity may be involved in both of these changes.

Symptoms of cancer of the testicles include a small, painless lump on the side of the testicle, a swollen or enlarged testicle, or heaviness or a dragging sensation in the groin or scrotum. The importance of testicular self-examination, as well as early diagnosis and prompt treatment, cannot be overemphasized for men in the at-risk age group of 20 to 34 years. The Changing for the Better box above explains how to perform a testicular self-examination.

Colon and Rectum

Cancer of the colon and rectum (colorectal cancer) has a combined incidence and death rate second only to that of lung cancer. Two types of tumours, carcinoma and lymphoma, can be found in both the colon and rectum. Fortunately, when diagnosed in a localized state, colorectal cancer has a relatively high survival rate of 90% through the first five years.[36] Underlying the development of colorectal cancer are at least two important risk factors: genetic susceptibility and dietary patterns. Genes have recently been discovered that lead to familial colon cancer and familial polyposis (abnormal tissue growth that occurs before formation of cancer) and are believed to be responsible for the tendency for colon and rectal cancer to run in families.[37] These forms of cancer may be higher in people whose diets are both high in saturated fat from red meat and low in fruits and vegetables, which contain antioxidant vitamins and fibre. Also, an association between colorectal cancer and smoking has been identified, suggesting that carcinogens may be ingested or may pass into the digestive system from the bloodstream.

Symptoms associated with colon and rectal cancers include bleeding from the rectum, blood in the stool, or a change in bowel habits.

There is evidence that the development of colorectal cancer may be prevented or slowed through regular exercise and through the regular use of aspirin.[38] The treatment of colorectal cancer involves surgery combined with the use of chemotherapy drugs. A *colostomy* is required in 15% of the cases of colon and rectal cancer.

Skin

Thanks largely to a desire for a fashionable tan, too many teens and adults are spending more time in the sun (and in tanning booths) than their skin can tolerate. As a result, skin cancer, once common only among those people who worked in the sun, is occurring with alarming frequency. Severe sunburning during childhood and chronic sun exposure during adolescence and younger adulthood are responsible for these increases in skin cancer. The reduction of ultraviolet protection caused by environmental pollutants depleting the earth's ozone layer is also believed to be raising the incidence of this form of cancer.

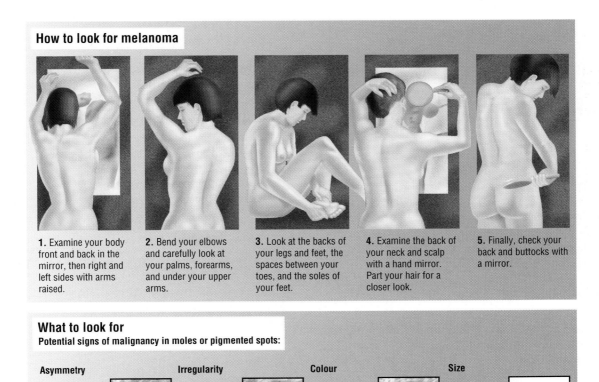

How to look for melanoma

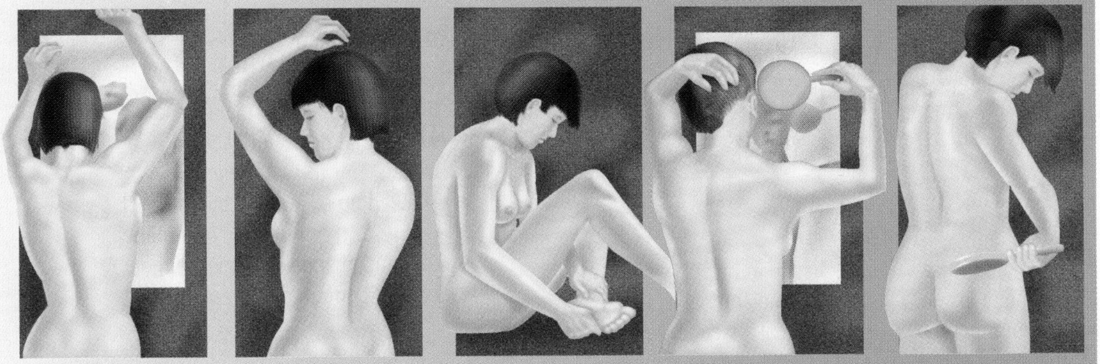

1. Examine your body front and back in the mirror, then right and left sides with arms raised.

2. Bend your elbows and carefully look at your palms, forearms, and under your upper arms.

3. Look at the backs of your legs and feet, the spaces between your toes, and the soles of your feet.

4. Examine the back of your neck and scalp with a hand mirror. Part your hair for a closer look.

5. Finally, check your back and buttocks with a mirror.

What to look for
Potential signs of malignancy in moles or pigmented spots:

Asymmetry
One half unlike the other half

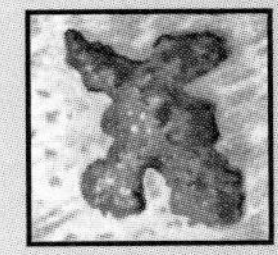

Irregularity
Border irregular or poorly defined

Colour
Colour varies from one area to another; shades of tan, brown, or black

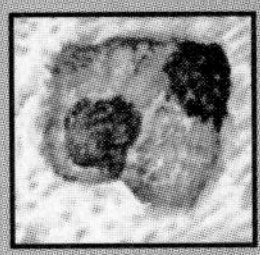

Size
Diameter larger than 6 mm, as a rule (diameter of a pencil eraser)

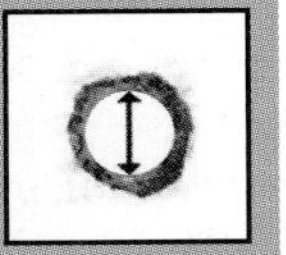

Although many doctors do not emphasize this point enough, the key to the successful treatment of skin cancer lies in early detection. In the case of basal cell or squamous cell cancer, the development of a pale, waxlike, pearly nodule or red, scaly patch may be the first symptom. For others, skin cancer may be noticed as a gradual change in the appearance of an already existing skin mole. If such a change is noted, a physician should be contacted. Melanoma usually begins as a small molelike growth that increases progressively in size, changes colour, ulcerates, and bleeds easily. For help in detecting melanoma, the American Cancer Society recommends using the guidelines below:

A is for **a**symmetry
B is for **b**order irregularity
C is for **c**olour (change)
D is for a **d**iameter greater than 6 mm
E is for **e**levation (raised margins)

The photographs on the next page show a mole that would be considered harmless and one that clearly demonstrates the ABCDE characteristics just described. Again, it is important to be observant and not fail to recognize the changing status of a mole or other skin lesion. The illustration above depicts the steps to take in making a regular inspection of the skin.

When nonmelanoma skin cancer is found, an almost 100% cure rate can be expected. Treatment of these skin cancers can involve surgical removal, destruction through burning or freezing, or X-ray therapy. When the more serious melanomas are found in an early stage, a high cure rate is accomplished using the same techniques. However, when malignant melanomas are more advanced, extensive surgery and chemotherapy become necessary, and recovery is rare.

Prevention of skin cancer should be a high priority for people who enjoy the sun or must work outdoors. The use of sunscreen is of great importance. In addition, parents can help their children prevent skin cancer later in life by restricting their outdoor play from 11:00 AM to 2:00 PM, requiring them to wear hats that shade their faces, and applying a sunscreen with SPF 15 regardless of a child's skin tone.

THE DIAGNOSIS OF CANCER

Is cancer survivable? The answer is, of course, yes. The chances for survival (defined as living without

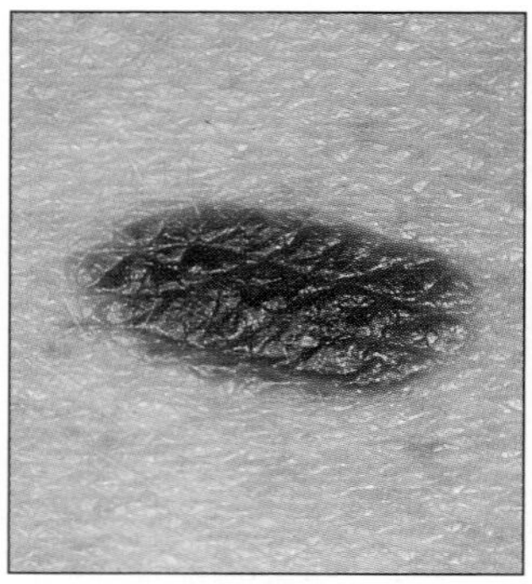

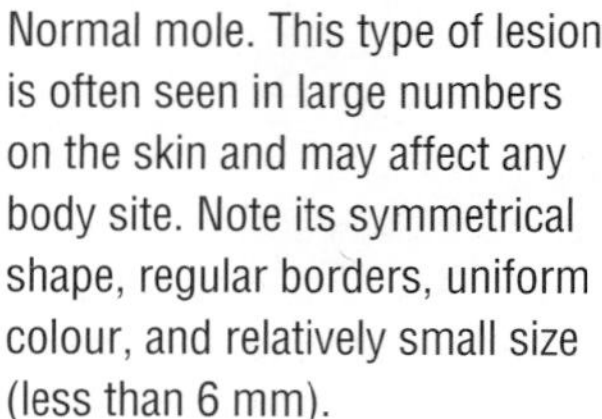

Normal mole. This type of lesion is often seen in large numbers on the skin and may affect any body site. Note its symmetrical shape, regular borders, uniform colour, and relatively small size (less than 6 mm).

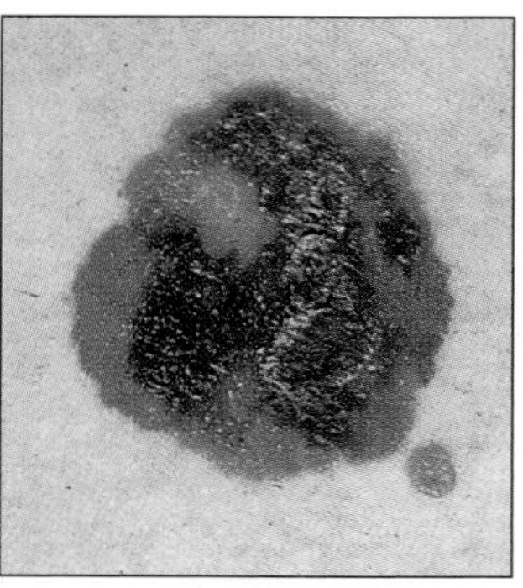

Malignant melanoma. Note its asymmetrical shape, irregular borders, uneven colour, and relatively large size (about 2 cm).

Cancer's Seven Warning Signs

Listed below are the seven warning signs of cancer, which the acronym CAUTION will help you remember:

1. **C**hange in bowel or bladder habits
2. **A** sore that does not heal
3. **U**nusual bleeding or discharge
4. **T**hickening or lump in breast or elsewhere
5. **I**ndigestion or difficulty in swallowing
6. **O**bvious change in a wart or mole
7. **N**agging cough or hoarseness

If you have a warning sign that persists for more than five days, see your doctor!

reoccurrence at least five years after diagnosis) depend greatly on the promptness of diagnosis and treatment. Thus the chances for recovery from cancer are best when cancer is detected early. The familiar "cancer's seven warning signals" can serve as a basis for early detection (see the Star Box on this page). Also, unexplained weight loss can be a signal for the presence of a malignancy. Weight loss, however, is not usually an early indicator of cancer. Persistent headaches and vision changes should be evaluated by a physician.

In addition to the recognition of danger signals, undergoing regularly scheduled screening for malignancy-related changes is important. A monthly breast self-examination for all women over the age of 20 is recommended. For men, monthly testicular self-examinations are strongly recommended. Step-by-step procedures for both of these self-examinations are provided in the Changing for the Better boxes on pp. 230 and 232. The remaining screening procedures require the services of a medical practitioner.

Treatment

In today's approach to cancer treatment, proven therapies and promising new experimental approaches are often combined. The traditional therapies are surgery, radiation, and chemotherapy. Used independently or in combination, they form the backbone of our increasingly successful efforts in treating cancer. Newer, more experimental therapies are also being used on a limited basis.

Surgery

Surgical removal of tissue suspected to contain cancerous cells is the oldest approach to cancer therapy. When undertaken early in the course of the disease, surgery is particularly suited for cancers of the skin, gastrointestinal tract, breast, uterus, cervix, prostate gland, and testicle. Minimal procedures are undertaken whenever possible, and radiation or chemotherapy is often used with surgery to ensure maximum effectiveness.

Radiation

Radiation is capable of killing cancer cells by altering their genetic material during cell division. Since neighbouring cells also divide, they are exposed to the damaging effects of radiation as well. However, by carefully planning the length of exposure and time of treatment and by focusing the radiation with precision, damage to noncancerous cells can be held to a minimum.

Chemotherapy

The important advances in successful cancer treatment can be attributed to advances in chemotherapy, including new drugs and the more effective combination of new drugs and familiar chemotherapeutic agents. Most often, these drugs work by destroying cancer cells' ability to use important materials or carry out cell division in a normal manner. Because chemotherapy influences cell division, it will influence noncancerous cells that divide frequently. Among the cells most susceptible to this influence are those that make up bone marrow, the lining of the intestinal tract, and the hair follicles. People who are undergoing chemotherapy often have side effects directly related to these changes—immune system suppression, diarrhea, and hair loss.

Anti-Cancer Drugs

Although many chemotherapy agents have been in use for decades and new ones are being developed, there is an array of anti-cancer drugs that do not fit into the traditional five classes of chemotherapy agents. More than 350 drugs are now in various stages of development and clinical trials, and many of them should be widely

Resources from the Home Front

Although we typically envision the treatment and management of cancer as being conducted in or near the confines of a medical centre, certain aspects of our personal "war on cancer" can be conducted from home.

Social Support

One particularly useful component in managing the pain and discomfort often associated with cancer is social involvement and the support of family, friends, and coworkers. Studies now suggest that many cancer victims who maintain active involvement in the community and who maintain contact with other people demonstrate less pain and discomfort than those who cannot or choose not to be so involved. Unknown at this time, however, is whether less than average amounts of pain and discomfort have allowed these people to remain involved, or whether their decision to remain connected has helped lessen their level of discomfort.

Music Therapy

Another potential home-front aid in dealing with cancer is music therapy. Using the professional expertise of a certified music therapist, cancer victims have been helped in reducing their level of discomfort by listening to carefully selected music recorded for their use. The home offers a wonderful environment in which musical selections can be enjoyed at little or no cost.

Stress Management

A final area of low-tech assistance for improving the long-term management of cancer is the use of stress management to enhance the function of the immune system. Experts in the field of psychoneuroimmunology (PNI) have contended, on the basis of both animal and human subject research and anecdotal reports, that reduction of stress enhances immune system function. Accordingly, oncological treatment plans increasingly involve stress management instruction that can be routinely used in the home and community.

available in the next 10 years. Perhaps the most familiar to the general public are the **anti-angiogenesis** drugs, which "starve" tumours by restricting their blood supply, and Herceptin, which may prevent the development of breast cancer in some people.

Immunotherapy

Immunotherapy is the use of a variety of substances to trigger a person's own immune system to attack cancer cells or prevent them from becoming activated. Among these new forms of immunotherapy are the use of interferon, monoclonal antibodies, interleukin-2, tumour necrosis factor (TNF), and certain bone marrow growth regulators. The use of immature blood cells taken from human embryos to "reprogram" the immune system (after normal blood cells are destroyed by massive doses of radiation) is one of the newer forms of immunotherapy. These products are being manufactured using genetic engineering technology.

RISK REDUCTION

Risk reduction refers to reducing your individual risk of developing cancer. Your risk of cancer can be increased or decreased by the lifestyle behaviours you select and by your surrounding environment. The Canadian Cancer Society contends that "low risk does not mean that you won't get cancer, it means that the chances of getting it are small. High risk means that your chances may be higher, but it does not mean that you will develop cancer."[39] As with cardiovascular disease, some of the risk factors for cancer cannot be changed (e.g., age, heredity). However, the following factors, which could make you vulnerable to cancer, can be controlled or at least recognized.

- *Know your family history.* You are the recipient of the genetic strengths and weaknesses of your biological parents and your more distant relatives. If cancer is prevalent in your family medical history, you cannot afford to disregard this fact. It may be appropriate for you to be screened for certain types of cancer more often or at a younger age.
- *Select your occupation carefully.* Because of recently discovered relationships between cancer and occupations that bring employees into contact with carcinogenic agents, you must be aware of risks with certain job selections and assignments. Worksites associated with frequent contact with pesticides, strong solvents, volatile hydocarbons, and airborne fibres could pay well but also shorten life.
- *Do not use tobacco products.* You may want to review Chapter 9 on the overwhelming evidence linking all forms of tobacco use (including smokeless tobacco) to the development of cancer. Smoking is so detrimental to health that it is considered the number one preventable cause of death.
- *Follow a sound diet.* The Changing for the Better box on p. 236 provides general guidelines on eating to reduce your cancer risk. In addition, review Chapter 5 for information regarding dietary practices and the incidence of

Key Term

anti-angiogenesis
Drug-based therapy that prevents cancerous tumours from developing an enriching blood supply.

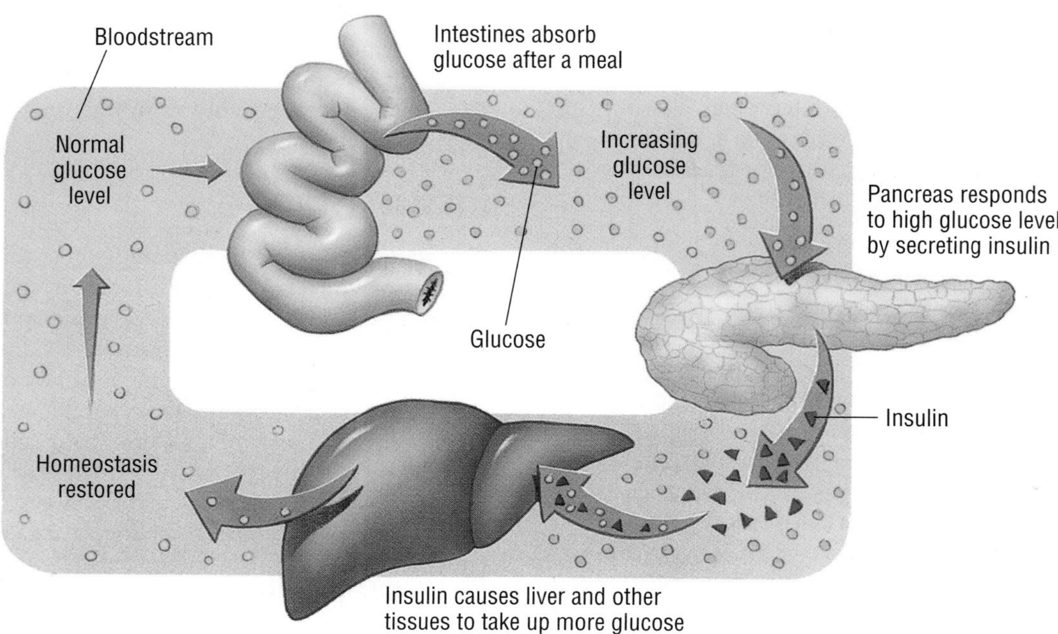
Bloodstream
Intestines absorb glucose after a meal
Normal glucose level
Increasing glucose level
Pancreas responds to high glucose level by secreting insulin
Glucose
Insulin
Homeostasis restored
Insulin causes liver and other tissues to take up more glucose

Figure 10–6 The secretion of insulin is regulated by a mechanism that tends to reverse any deviation from normal. Thus an increase in blood glucose level triggers secretion of insulin. Since insulin promotes glucose uptake by cells, blood glucose level is restored to its lower, normal level.

various diseases, including cancer. That chapter also discusses the role of fruits and vegetables known to be sources of cancer-preventing phytochemicals.

- *Control your body weight.* Particularly for women, obesity is related to a higher incidence of cancer of the uterus, ovary, and breast. Maintaining a desirable body weight could improve overall health and lead to more successful management of cancer if it develops.
- *Exercise regularly.* Chapter 4 discusses in detail the importance of regular, moderate exercise to all aspects of health, including reducing the risk of chronic illnesses. Moderate exercise increases the body's ability to deliver oxygen to its tissues and increases protection from cancer-enhancing free radicals formed during incomplete oxidation of nutrients. Moderate exercise also stimulates the production of enzymes that remove free radicals.
- *Limit your exposure to sun.* It is important to heed this message, even if you enjoy many outdoor activities. Particularly for people with light complexions, the radiation received through chronic exposure to the sun may foster the development of skin cancer.
- *Consume alcohol in moderation—if at all.* Heavier users of alcohol experience an increased prevalence of several types of cancer, including cancer of the oral cavity, larynx, and esophagus. It should be noted, however, that moderate alcohol consumption is now believed to be a positive factor in prevention of cardiovascular disease. Drinking lightly (see Chapter 8) is therefore recommended for persons who already enjoy alcoholic beverages, but abstinence is equally acceptable for those who do not. Living a healthy life and developing policies that protect the health of individuals can help prevent an estimated 50% of cancers. Go to the Canadian Cancer Society's Web Site to explore in further detail cancer risk-reduction strategies: **www.cancer.ca**.

Changing *for the Better*

Dietary Tips for Reducing Cancer Risk

I've heard that the food you eat can be important for reducing your cancer risk. What sorts of things should I avoid? What should I be eating more of?

The Canadian Cancer Society recommends the following dietary tips to help reduce the risk of getting cancer:

- Eat 5 to 10 servings of vegetables and fruit a day.
- Eat a diet rich in fibre.
- Adopt a lower-fat diet.
- Drink less alcohol.
- Limit the amount of meats you eat that are preserved in salt.
- Limit the amount of smoked meat you eat.
- Avoid charring or deep-browning your food.
- Include more of vitamins E, C, A, and beta carotene in your diet by eating a variety of vegetables, fruits, and whole-grain products.

Differences between Types of Diabetes Mellitus

Type 1

(These symptoms usually develop rapidly.)

- Extreme hunger
- Extreme thirst
- Frequent urination
- Extreme weight loss
- Irritability
- Weakness and fatigue
- Nausea and vomiting

Type 2

(These symptoms usually develop gradually.)

- Any of the symptoms for insulin-dependent diabetes
- Blurred vision or a change in sight
- Itchy skin
- Tingling or numbness in the limbs

If you notice these symptoms occurring, bring them to the attention of your physician.

Tips for Healthy Eating

Eat three regular meals a day no more than six hours apart.
Here's Why: Eating at regular times helps your body control blood glucose levels.

Limit sugars and sweets like sugar, regular pop, desserts, candy, jam, and honey.
Here's Why: The more sugar you eat, the higher your blood glucose will be.

Limit the amount of high-fat food you eat like fried foods, chips, and pastries.
Here's Why: High-fat foods may cause weight gain. A healthy weight helps control blood glucose levels.

Eat more high-fibre foods.
Here's Why: High-fibre foods may help you feel full and may lower blood glucose and cholesterol levels.

Drink water if you are thirsty.
Here's Why: Drinking regular pop and fruit juice will raise your blood glucose.

Add physical activity to your life.
Here's Why: Regular physical activity will improve your blood glucose management.[41]

Visit the Canadian Diabetes Association Web site to obtain more detailed information about managing Type 2 Diabetes: **www.diabetes.ca/Section_About/type2.asp#eating**.

DIABETES MELLITUS

Diabetes mellitus is not a single condition but rather two metabolic disorders with important similarities and differences. About two million Canadians have diabetes. Over 90% of these individuals have what is now known as type 2 diabetes mellitus.

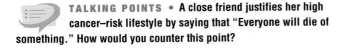

TALKING POINTS • A close friend justifies her high cancer–risk lifestyle by saying that "Everyone will die of something." How would you counter this point?

Type 2 diabetes mellitus

In people who do not have diabetes mellitus the body's need for energy is met through the "burning" of glucose (blood sugar) within the cells. Glucose is absorbed from the digestive tract and carried to the cells by the blood system. Passage of glucose into the cell is achieved through a transport system that moves the glucose molecule across the cell's membrane. Activation of this glucose transport mechanism requires the presence of the hormone insulin (Figure 10–6). Specific receptor sites for **insulin** can be found on the cell membrane. In addition to its role in the transport of glucose into sensitive cells, insulin is required for the conversion of glucose into glycogen in the liver and the formation of fatty acids in adipose cells. Insulin is produced in the cells of the islets of Langerhans in the pancreas. The release of insulin from the pancreas corresponds to the changing levels of glucose within the blood.[40]

In adults with a **genetic predisposition** for developing type 2 diabetes mellitus, a trigger mechanism (most likely central obesity) begins a process through which the body cells become increasingly less sensitive to the presence of insulin, although a normal (or slightly greater than normal) amount of insulin is produced by the pancreas. The growing ineffectiveness of insulin in getting glucose into cells results in the buildup of glucose in the blood. Elevated levels of glucose lead to *hyperglycemia*, a hallmark symptom of non-insulin-dependent diabetes mellitus.

Key Terms

insulin
A pancreatic hormone required by the body for the effective metabolism of glucose (blood sugar).

genetic predisposition
An inherited tendency to develop a disease process if necessary environmental factors exist.

In response to this buildup, the kidneys begin the process of filtering glucose from the blood. Excess glucose then spills over into the urine. This removal of glucose in the urine demands large amounts of water, a process called *diuresis*, a second important symptom of adult-onset diabetes. Increased thirst, a third symptom of developing diabetes, results in response to the movement of fluid from extracellular spaces into the circulatory system to maintain homeostasis.

For many adults with diabetes, dietary modification (with an emphasis on monitoring total carbohydrate intake, not just sugar) and regular exercise is the only treatment required to maintain an acceptable level of glucose use. Weight loss will improve the condition by "releasing" more insulin receptors, and exercise increases the actual number of receptor sites. With better insulin recognition, the affected person can return to a more normal state of functioning. See the Star Box on p. 237 for tips on healthy eating.

For people whose condition is more advanced, dietary modification and weight loss are not sufficient, and a hypoglycemia agent must be used. These can help improve insulin recognition. For those who require insulin by injection or another delivery method, management of the condition becomes much more demanding. Diabetes pills don't work for everyone. Only a patient and his or her doctor can determine if they are appropriate. Pills are never used in type 1 diabetes or during pregnancy.

In addition to genetic predisposition and obesity, unresolved stress appears to be involved in the development of hyperglycemic states. Although stress alone probably cannot produce a diabetic condition, it is likely that stress can create a series of endocrine changes that can lead to a state of hyperglycemia.

Diabetes can cause serious damage to several important structures within the body. The rate and extent to which people with diabetes develop these changes can be markedly influenced by the nature of their condition and their compliance with its management requirements. For those who already have diabetes, an understanding of the condition and a commitment to its management are important elements in living with diabetes mellitus. However, for the thousands of Canadians who are thought to be "borderline" diabetics and not yet diagnosed, the need to be "discovered" is a growing concern. Accordingly, initial blood glucose testing should ideally begin during young adulthood (by age 25), rather than at middle age, when it typically begins.

Type 1 diabetes mellitus

A second type of diabetes mellitus is type 1 diabetes. The onset of this condition generally occurs before age 35, most often during childhood. In contrast to type 2 diabetes, in which insulin is produced but is ineffective because of insensitivity, in type 1 diabetes the body does not produce insulin at all. Destruction of the insulin-producing cells of the pancreas by the person's immune system (possibly in combination with a genetic predisposition) accounts for this sudden and irreversible loss of insulin production.[42]

Common Complications of Diabetes

- Cataract formation
- Glaucoma
- Blindness
- Dental caries
- Stillbirths/miscarriages
- Neonatal deaths
- Congenital defects
- Cardiovascular disease
- Kidney disease
- Gangrene
- Impotence

In most ways the two forms of diabetes are similar, with the important exception that insulin-dependent diabetes mellitus requires the use of insulin from an outside source. Today this insulin is obtained either from animals or through genetically engineered bacteria. It is taken by injection (one to four times per day), through the use of an insulin pump that provides a constant supply of insulin to the body, by transdermal patch, or through nasal inhalation. As noted earlier, an insulin pill will probably be perfected within the next few years.[43] The use of a glucometer, a highly accurate device for measuring the amount of glucose in the blood, allows for sound management of this condition and a life expectancy that is essentially normal. With both forms of diabetes mellitus, sound dietary practice, weight management, planned activity, and control of stress are important for keeping blood glucose levels within normal ranges. Without good management of diabetes mellitus, several serious problems can result, including blindness, gangrene of the extremities, kidney disease, and heart attack. These and other common complications of diabetes are listed in the Star Box above. People who cannot establish good control are likely to live a shorter life than those who can.

Taking Charge of Your Health

- Complete the Personal Assessment on p. 242 to determine your risk for chronic disease.
- Review *Canada's Food Guide to Healthy Eating* in Chapter 5, and make changes to your diet so that it is more "heart healthy and cancer protective."
- Begin or continue an aerobic exercise program that is appropriate for your current fitness level.
- Stay attuned to media reports about chronic conditions so that you can make informed choices.

SUMMARY

- Cardiovascular disorders are responsible for more disabilities and deaths than any other disease.
- A cardiovascular risk factor is an attribute that a person has or is exposed to that increases the likelihood of heart disease.
- The "big six" risk factors are tobacco use, physical inactivity, high blood lipid levels, high blood pressure, diabetes mellitus, and obesity and overweight. These are controllable risk factors.
- Increasing age, male gender, race, and heredity are risk factors that cannot be controlled.
- Other possible contributing risk factors to heart disease are emerging with new research.
- Cancer is a condition reflecting the body's inability to control the growth and specialization of cells.
- Genes that control replication, specialization, repair, and suppression of abnormal activity hold the potential of becoming oncogenes and thus can be considered protooncogenes.
- Cancer cells demonstrate a variety of interesting characteristics in comparison with normal cells of the same type. Benign tumours, made up of noncancerous cells, can present serious health problems.
- Cancer can be described on the basis of the type of tissue in which it has its origin—carcinoma, sarcoma, melanoma, etc.
- Cancer can be described on the basis of its location within the body—lung, breast, prostate, etc.
- Cigarette smoking and having a genetic predisposition are both related to the development of lung cancer.
- Breast cancer demonstrates clear familial patterns that suggest a genetic predisposition. Mammograms are recommended as an important component of breast cancer identification. Important options should be considered before the treatment of breast cancer.
- Regular use of Pap tests is related to the early detection of uterine (cervical) cancer. Ovarian cancer is often "silent" in its presentation of symptoms.
- The PSA test improves the ability to diagnose prostate cancer.
- Regular self-examination of the testicles leads to early detection of testicular cancer.
- Colon and rectal cancers have strong familial links and are possibly related to diets high in fat and low in fruits and vegetables.
- Skin cancer prevention requires protection from excessive sun exposure.
- Your risk of cancer can be increased or decreased by the lifestyle behaviours you select and by your surrounding environment.
- Diabetes mellitus, in both of its forms, is a chronic condition in which the body is unable to use glucose in the normal manner.

REVIEW QUESTIONS

1. Define cardiovascular risk factor. What relationship do risk factors have to cardiovascular disease?
2. Identify those risk factors for cardiovascular disease that cannot be changed. Identify those risk factors that can be changed. Identify the risk factors that can be contributing factors.
3. What are the six major forms of cardiovascular disease? For cardiovascular disease, angina, and hypertension, describe what the disease is, its cause (if known), and its treatment.
4. Describe how high-density lipoproteins differ from low-density lipoproteins.
5. What problems does atherosclerosis produce?
6. Why is hypertension referred to as "the silent killer"?
7. What are the warning signals of stroke?
8. What is the relationship between regulatory genes and tumour suppressor genes in the development of cancer? Why are regulatory genes called both protooncogenes and oncogenes?
9. What are some of the major types of cancer, based on the tissue in which they have their origin?

10. What are the principal factors that contribute to the development of lung cancer? Of breast cancer?
11. When should regular use of mammography begin, and which women should begin using it earliest?
12. How does the PSA test contribute to the early detection of prostate cancer?
13. What signs indicate the possibility that a skin lesion has become cancerous?
14. What important information can be obtained with the use of Pap tests?
15. Differentiate between the risk factors for cervical and uterine cancer.
16. What are the steps for effective self-examination of the breasts and testicles?
17. Why is ovarian cancer described as a "silent" cancer?
18. What are the conventional treatments most often used in the treatment of cancer?
19. How do type 1 and type 2 diabetes mellitus differ? To what extent are they similar conditions?

THINK ABOUT THIS ...

- Have you ever considered your potential for developing heart disease?
- In the last week, what have you done to improve your cardiovascular system?
- When was the last time you had your blood pressure checked? What were the readings?
- Are you comfortable talking with your relatives about their possible risk factors for cardiovascular disease?
- Do you believe you could cope with a significant health problem at this time in your life?
- Do you know anyone who has or has had cancer? How did cancer affect that person's life?
- How regularly do you perform breast or testicular self-examination?
- If you were diagnosed as having a terminal illness, how willing would you be to serve as a subject in a research project that tested a potentially toxic experimental drug?
- Which conditions in this chapter are you likely to develop, and which are you not likely to develop?

REFERENCES

1. Heart and Stroke Foundation of Canada: *General information—incidence of cardiovascular disease.* **www.heartandstroke.ca**
2. Heart and Stroke Foundation of Canada. The growing burden of heart disease and stroke in Canada, 2003, 2003, Ottawa, Canada.
3. American Heart Association: **www.americanheart.org Heart_and_Stroke_A_Z_Guide.html**, December 6, 1999.
4. American Heart Association: *1999 Heart and stroke statistical update,* 1998, The Association.
5. American Heart Association: **www.americanheart.org/presenter.jhtml?identifier54536**, July 21, 2003.
6. Ibid.
7. American Heart Association: *Heart and stroke statistical update, 2004,* 2004.
8. *1999 Heart and stroke statistical update.*
9. Heart and Stroke Foundation of Canada: **www.heartandstroke.ca/Page.asp?PageID=33&ArticleID=434&Src=stroke&From=SubCategory**, August 22, 2005.
10. American Heart Association, December 6, 1999.
11. Canadian Cancer Society: General Cancer Stats, **www.cancer.ca/ccs/internet/standard/0,3182,3172_14423__langId-en,00.html**, August 22, 2005.
12. Songer J, oncologist: Personal interview, December 1999.
13. Ibid.
14. Ibid.
15. Ibid.
16. A library of hope: the Cancer Genome Anatomy Project, *Cancer Smart* 4(3):6–7, 1998.
17. *CGAP tumor suppressor and oncogene directory,* December 13, 1999. **www.ncbi.nlm.nih.gov/CGAP/cgaptso.cig**
18. Program cell death: natural cancer suppression, *Cancer Smart* 4(2):6–7, 1998.
19. Songer: Personal interview.
20. Drugdevelopment-technology.com: *Avastin,* **www.drugdevelopment-technology.com/avastin**, August 22, 2005
21. National Cancer Institute of Canada: *Canadian cancer statistics.* 2004.
22. American Cancer Society, *Cancer facts and figures: 2003,* 2003, The Society.
23. Canadian Cancer Society: Stats at a glance, **www.cancer.ca/ccs/internet/standard/0,3182,3172_14411__langId-en,00.html**, August 22, 2005.
24. Ibid.
25. *Cancer facts and figures, 2003.*
26. Sidransky D, Stix G: Advances in cancer detection, *Scientific American* 275(3):104–106, 1996.
27. Blat WJ, McLaughlin JK: Geographic patterns of breast cancer among American women, *J Natl Cancer Inst* 87(24):1819–1820, 1995.
28. Baxter N: Preventive health care, 2001 update: should women be routinely taught breast self-examination to screen for breast cancer? *CMAJ* 164(13):1837–46, 2001.

29. Estrogen and breast cancer: fighting fire with fire, *Cancer Smart* 4(4):4–5, 1998.
30. *Canadian cancer statistics.*
31. Janerich DT et al: The screening histories of women with invasive cervical cancer, Connecticut, *Am J Public Health* 85(6):791–794, 1995.
32. *Canadian cancer statistics.*
33. Schildkraut JM, Berchiuck A: Relationship between life-time ovulatory cycles and overexpression of mutant p53 in epithelial ovarian cancer, *J Natl Cancer Inst* 89(13):932–938, 1997.
34. *Cancer facts and figures, 2003.*
35. Albertsen PC et al: Competing risk analysis of men aged 55 to 74 years at diagnosis managed conservatively for clinically localized prostate cancer, *JAMA* 280(11):975–980, 1998.
36. *Cancer facts and figures, 2003.*
37. Peterson SK et al: Familial colorectal cancer in Ashkenazim due to a hypermutable tract in APC, *Nat Genet* 17(1):79–83, 1997.
38. Giocannucci E et al: Aspirin and the risk of colorectal cancer in women, *N Engl J Med* 332(14):609–614, 1995.
39. Canadian Cancer Society Web site at **www.cancer.ca**, August 22, 2005.
40. Saladin KS: *Anatomy and physiology: the unity of form and function*, 1998, McGraw-Hill.
41. Canadian Diabetes Association: Healthy eating, **www.diabetes.ca/Section_About/type2.asp#eating**, August 22, 2005.
42. *Anatomy and physiology.*
43. Gura T: New lead found to a possible "insulin pill," *Science* 284(5416):866, 1999.

SUGGESTED READINGS

Burkman K: *The stroke recovery book: a guide for patients and families*, 1998, Addicus Books.

For the half million people annually who have strokes, this short reference book is a valuable guide for both patients and their families. Written by a physician, this book provides easy-to-understand answers to many of the questions about stroke. The various types of strokes, their causes, and treatments are explained. The author describes how strokes affect both body functioning and mental processes, including emotions and cognitive processes.

Josephson R: *The HeartSmart™ Shopper*, 1999, Douglas and McIntyre Ltd.

This book is designed to help anyone bewildered by all the food choices on supermarket shelves or whose busy schedules limit the time they have to devote to wise food choices. It is a practical, step-by-step guide to healthy supermarket (and corner store) choices both for well Canadians and those who are affected by heart disease.

Lindsay A: *Lighthearted Everyday Cooking*, 1991, Macmillan Canada.

This book of recipes and heart-healthy nutrition information is one of a series published in association with the Heart and Stroke Foundation of Canada. Each offers a broad range of exciting recipes with nutrient information on each, as well as menu suggestions and other valuable tips.

Meyer B, Davidson AI, Zorda R (editors): *Diabetes mellitus: diagnosis and treatment*, ed 4, 1998, W.B. Saunders Company.

Although directed primarily at health care professionals, this highly regarded book, in its fourth edition, has also been well received by lay people. Using the latest scientific research as the book's technical core, four contributing authors provide additional information for patient management of both type 1 and type 2 diabetes. Topics include fasting before special diagnostic procedures, foot-care management, and criteria for making subtle insulin adjustments. In addition to clinicians and persons with diabetes mellitus, this is an excellent book for caregivers.

Piver MS, Wilder G, Bull J: *Gilda's disease: sharing personal experiences and a medical perspective on ovarian cancer*, 1998, Bantam Doubleday Dell Publishing.

For those who remember Gilda Radner's death from ovarian cancer in 1989, a moving new dimension, her husband's deeply personal relationship with his wife and her disease, is added to the story. The addition of medical perspectives by Steven Piver, M.D., regarding ovarian cancer and the various treatment options makes this book an important resource for individuals interested in the "silent killer."

Name ______________________ **Date** ____________

Personal Assessment

What Is Your Risk for Chronic Disease?

Cholesterol

Your serum cholesterol level (mmol/L) is

0	4.91 or below
+ 2	4.93 to 5.94
+ 6	5.97 to 7.47
+12	7.49 to 8.24
+16	Over 8.27

Your HDL cholesterol (mmol/L) is

− 2	Over 1.55
0	1.16 to 1.55
+ 2	0.90 to 1.15
+ 6	0.75 to 0.88
+12	0.59 to 0.74
+16	Below 0.59

Smoking

You smoke now or have in the past

0 Never smoked, or quit more than five years ago
+ 1 Quit two to four years ago
+ 3 Quit about one year ago
+ 6 Quit during the past year

You now smoke

+ 9 ½ to 1 pack a day
+12 1 to 2 packs a day
+15 More than 2 packs a day

The quality of the air you breathe is

0 Unpolluted by smoke, exhaust, or industry at home and at work
+ 2 Live **or** work with smokers in unpolluted area
+ 4 Live **and** work with smokers in unpolluted area
+ 6 Live or work with smokers **and** live or work in air-polluted area
+ 8 Live **and** work with smokers **and** live and work in air-polluted area

Blood Pressure

Your blood pressure is

0 120/75 or below
+ 2 120/75 to 140/85
+ 6 140/85 to 150/90
+ 8 150/90 to 175/100
+10 175/100 to 190/110
+12 190/110 or above

Exercise

Your exercise habits are

0 Exercise vigorously 4 or 5 times a week
+ 2 Exercise moderately 4 or 5 times a week
+ 4 Exercise only on weekends
+ 6 Exercise occasionally
+ 8 Little or no exercise

Body Mass Index

Your body mass index is

0 BMI between 19 and 24
+ 1 BMI between 24 and 26
+ 2 BMI between 27 and 30
+ 3 BMI between 31 and 35
+ 4 BMI over 35

Stress

You feel overstressed

0 Rarely at work or at home
+ 3 Somewhat at home but not at work
+ 5 Somewhat at work but not at home
+ 7 Somewhat at work **and** at home
+ 9 Usually at work **or** at home
+12 Usually at work **and** at home

Diabetes

Your diabetic history is

0 Blood sugar always normal
+ 2 Blood glucose slightly high (prediabetic) or slightly low (hypoglycemic)
+ 4 Diabetic beginning after age 40 requiring strict dietary or insulin control
+ 5 Diabetic beginning before age 30 requiring strict dietary or insulin control

Alcohol

You drink alcoholic beverages

0 Never or only socially, about once or twice a month, or only one 142 mL (5 oz) glass of wine or 341 mL (12 oz) glass of beer or 43 mL (1½ oz) of hard liquor about 5 times a week
+ 2 Two to three 142 mL (5 oz) glasses of wine or 341 mL (12 oz) glasses of beer or 43 mL (1½ oz) cocktails about 5 times a week
+ 4 More than three 43 mL (1½ oz) cocktails or more than three 142 mL (5 oz) glasses of wine or 341 mL (12 oz) glasses of beer almost every day

Name ______________________________ **Date** ____________

Personal Assessment *continued*

Diet

On a daily basis you eat:

0	Eight or more servings of fruit and vegetables
+ 1	5 to 7 servings of fruit and vegetables
+ 3	3 or 4 servings of fruit and vegetables
+ 5	1 or 2 servings of fruit and vegetables
+ 7	One or fewer servings of fruit or vegetables

Interpretation

Add all sources and check below

0 to 21: Low risk. Excellent family history and lifestyle habits.

22 to 53: Moderate risk. Family history or lifestyle habits put you at some risk. You might lower your risks if you change any poor habits.

54 to 79: High risk. Habits and family history indicate high risk of major chronic diseases. Change your habits now.

Above 79: Very high risk. Family history and a lifetime of poor habits put you at very high risk of major chronic diseases. Eliminate as many of the risk factors as you can.

To Carry This Further ...

Were you surprised with your score on this assessment? What were your most significant risk factors? Do you plan to make any changes in your lifestyle to reduce your chronic disease risks? Why or why not?

The above are broad questions that look at risk factors for the chronic diseases discussed in this chapter. For more specific risk assessments of cancers, diabetes, heart disease, osteoporosis, and stroke, go to The Harvard Centre for Cancer Prevention Web site at **www.yourcancerrisk.harvard.edu**.

Focus on

MANAGING CHRONIC PAIN

Carlotta loved to spend her spare time puttering around in her flower garden. Every weekend, she would work outside for hours—tilling soil, putting in new plants, pruning, and landscaping. One Saturday afternoon as she was lifting some railroad ties to create a new border for her plants, she heard a loud popping noise and felt a sharp pain in her lower back. She tried aspirin, bed rest, massage, and heat, but the pain was still excruciating after two weeks. She went to see her doctor, who prescribed pain medication and a brief course of physical therapy, but the pain persisted. Finally, after nearly a year passed with no relief, her doctor recommended back surgery. Carlotta spent almost three months recovering from the surgery, after which she hoped to lead a normal, pain-free life.

Unfortunately, Carlotta's pain persists today, almost two years since her initial injury. Carlotta suffers from chronic pain, a type of pain that persists beyond the expected healing time. Chronic pain differs from most other kinds of pain, such as pain resulting from a headache, a fall, or surgery. According to the Canadian Pain Society, chronic pain is difficult to treat because it doesn't respond to normal pain treatments. Also, some of the usual signs that accompany acute pain, such as sweating, increased heart rate, and dilated pupils, are not present in individuals with chronic pain.[1]

Causes of Chronic Pain

Chronic pain occurs as the result of one of three primary causes. In some patients, it is linked to injuries to the central or peripheral nervous systems, according to John D. Loeser, M.D., director of the Multidisciplinary Pain Center at the University of Washington School of Medicine.[2] In these patients, no tissue damage ever occurred in the part of their body that hurts. Whenever the nervous system heals itself, the functions of the nerve cells lost in the injury are not restored. As a result, the patient's neurological functions are impaired. This type of pain can occur as a result of limb amputation, shingles, diabetes, or surgery.

A second cause of chronic pain is linked to degenerative changes in joints. In these cases, tissue damage has not healed properly. Patients have both inflammation of the joints and chronic degenerative problems.[3] This cause of pain is often involved in diseases such as arthritis and lupus.

The third "cause" of pain is the catch-all category: "no known pathological mechanism."[4] Doctors are unsure why these patients are having pain. The one criterion used to place a patient in this category is whether the patient's pain complaints exceed the physician's expectations based on the illness or injury the patient has suffered.

Conditions Associated with Chronic Pain

Several types of conditions are commonly associated with sufferers of chronic pain, but the most common one is the headache. Up to 57% of men and 76% of women in the adolescent and young adult age groups experience recurrent headaches. The National Headache Foundation in the United States estimates that 45 million Americans suffer from chronic headaches. The four most common types of headaches associated with chronic pain are tension headaches, migraines, cluster headaches, and sinus headaches.[5]

Four out of five Americans experience back pain at some point in their lives. The problem usually resolves itself. However, it is estimated that more than 11 million Americans have back pain that is severe enough to cause impairment. This cause of chronic pain is particularly troublesome because of its economic impact on society. Based on all analyses of possible cost factors, back pain costs American society anywhere from US$75 billion to US$100 billion annually.[6]

Another debilitating condition commonly associated with chronic pain is arthritis. More than 35 million Americans have a form of this disease. Two principal types of arthritis exist. *Osteoarthritis* is the breaking down of the cartilage found at the ends of the long bones. Weight-bearing and frequently used joints are the areas most commonly affected. *Rheumatoid arthritis* is an autoimmune disorder in which the patient's own immune system produces antibodies that attack the tissues in the joints of the body. Symptoms of both types include stiffness and swelling of the joints.

Cancer and Chronic Pain

Although cancer is often associated with chronic pain, pain experts put it in a class by itself. Chronic cancer pain is complex because the pain can occur as a result of bone invasion, tumours compressing nerves, tumours affecting internal organs, obstruction of blood vessels, surgery, chemotherapy, or radiation treatment.[7]

Effects of Chronic Pain

Because chronic pain is such a disruptive, ongoing phenomenon, it can affect most aspects of an individual's life. For example, because of chronic pain many people find it difficult to continue their usual recreational pursuits, such as running, bicycling, and gardening. Also, tasks of daily living, such as dressing oneself and preparing meals, can become difficult or impossible to do without assistance.

The devastation of losing a job is another potential effect of suffering with chronic pain. Because the pain is so invasive and persistent, it affects a person's ability to concentrate, perform essential job duties, or even go to work. The time spent away from work to attend therapy sessions or to visit a physician can become an issue in performance evaluations and may affect a person's ability to keep his or her job.

Sleep disorders are a third potential effect of chronic pain. Sleep disorders can come about in two ways. Either a patient is unable to sleep because of the pain, or the individual becomes dependent on a pain or sleep medication that disrupts the sleep cycle. As sleep deprivation increases, the person's emotional outlook becomes increasingly fragile, interpersonal relationships may begin to show signs of strain, and the probability of accidents increases.

Serious psychological problems can also result from chronic pain. Depression is one of the most common problems. As the individual becomes increasingly impaired by the chronic pain, a lack of motivation sets in. As the level of depression deepens, job performance deteriorates, contact with other people is lessened, and, eventually, a sense of isolation takes over. Fortunately, the depressive aspects of chronic pain can be controlled through a combination of antidepressive medication and psychological intervention.

The final significant side effect of chronic pain is potential damage to the immune system. This effect can be particularly troublesome in patients whose chronic pain is the result of cancer. Studies have shown that pain can suppress the immune system, causing cancer patients to have difficulty recovering.[8] Since this problem can have fatal results, it is especially important for cancer patients to have prompt and effective treatment of their pain.

Methods of Managing Chronic Pain

Although chronic pain has several negative side effects, many of them can be controlled. Most pain specialists recommend a multidisciplinary management approach that involves a combination of methods to achieve the most relief.

One of the most common and effective methods of achieving relief of chronic pain is the use of opioid drugs. These drugs have been proven to provide quick relief of pain, particularly among cancer patients and headache sufferers. However, physicians are often reluctant to prescribe these drugs for several reasons. First, doctors are afraid that if they are perceived as prescribing too many opioids, they could be reported to the medical board and ultimately lose their licences. Second, society in general disapproves of prescribing narcotics because of the fear of addiction and the idea that all narcotics are "bad," despite their potential for pain relief. Finally, medical personnel tend to underestimate the amount of pain that patients suffer. Most people who suffer severe pain and request narcotics will not become addicts. Yet some medical personnel who work with pain sufferers have the mindset that people with chronic pain do not hurt as badly as they claim to.

For chronic headache sufferers, several other types of drugs also offer hope. For example, the antidepressant Deseryl has been found effective in persons who have trouble sleeping for any of several reasons, including the chronic pain of headaches.[9]

Other drugs that provide relief include beta-blockers, calcium channel blockers, and anticonvulsants. Doctors may try several combinations of these drugs to see which one will most effectively relieve headache symptoms, with the eventual goal of removing as many medications as possible from the patient's daily regimen.[10]

For patients with arthritis, two classes of drugs appear to offer the most relief. The first type is known as *nonsteroidal anti-inflammatory drugs*, or *NSAIDs*. The most well-known of these drugs are Advil, Nuprin, Naprosyn, and Anaprox. New to this class of NSAIDSs are two highly effective medications that provide pain relief with greatly reduced gastric irritation. These medications, Vioxx and Celebrex, block pain from the joints without affecting the enzymes that protect the sensitive linings of the stomach and intestinal tract.[11] Recently, however, some researchers have questioned this protective capacity.[12] One advantage is that these drugs provide relief within two hours. A second type of anti-arthritic medicine is known as *slow-acting antirheumatic drugs*, or *SAARDs*. These drugs provide time-released, long-lasting relief.

Surgery is another option for managing chronic pain. This method is most effective in helping patients with cancer. Surgery may also become necessary for the arthritis pain sufferer. Replacement of cartilage or an affected joint will often help a sufferer lead a more normal, less painful life. Surprisingly, however, surgery is generally not an effective option for back pain sufferers.

Because the mind is such a powerful instrument of healing, pain specialists often recommend that patients undertake psychological methods of pain relief in conjunction with traditional methods. For example, many headache specialists recommend biofeedback techniques so that patients can learn to control their responses to pain. Pain specialists also recommended deep-breathing exercises and meditation techniques to promote relaxation.

Physical methods of managing pain can add another dimension to chronic pain management. One time-tested method of relief is massage. Other helpful treatments include nerve blocks to the affected area, physical therapy, and exercises as prescribed by a physical therapist or physician. Finally, a patient can make some lifestyle changes to lessen the pain. Eating regularly, getting plenty of rest, and reducing caffeine intake have all been found to be particularly helpful to headache sufferers. This approach may also help others afflicted with chronic pain.

Although there is still no cure for chronic pain, it can be managed successfully with the help of trained personnel from a variety of fields. However, chronic pain sufferers must be vocal and persistent to get the help they desperately need. Doctors and patients alike must realize that chronic pain is not "all in the patient's head" but a real, treatable condition.

For Discussion ...

Have you ever known someone who suffered (or still suffers) from chronic pain? What were your feelings about this person and his or her pain? If you suffered from chronic pain, what treatments do you think would be the best for you? Would you be willing to try nonconventional therapies like the ones described in this article, or would you be more comfortable with traditional methods of therapy? Why?

References

1. Cowles J: *Pain relief!—how to say "no" to acute, chronic, and cancer pain*, 1993, Master Media.
2. Ibid.
3. Ibid.
4. Ibid.
5. Marcus NJ, Arbeiter JS (contributor): *Freedom from pain: the breakthrough method of pain relief based on the New York Pain Treatment Program at Lenox Hill Hospital*, 1995, Fireside.
6. *Pain relief.*
7. Ibid.
8. Buterbaugh L: Breaking through cancer pain barriers, *Medical World*, Oct 15, p 10, 1993.
9. *Physicians' desk reference 2000*, 1999, Medical Economics Data.
10. Brooks PM: Clincal management of rheumatoid arthritis, *Lancet* (341): 8840, 1993.
11. *Physician's desk reference.*
12. Josefson D: COX 2 inhibitors can affect the stomach lining, *BMJ* 391: 1518, 1999.

Chapter **11**

Preventing Infectious Diseases

Chapter Objectives

Upon completing this chapter, you should be able to

- Describe the movement of a cold virus through each link in the chain of infectious disease.
- Explain why individuals with HIV/AIDS do not generally progress beyond the clinical stage of their disease.
- Develop and then implement a plan to protect (or enhance) your immune system.
- Assess your own immunization status, and make arrangements for any additional immunizations such as flu shots.
- Understand and describe the importance of frequent hand washing, particularly during the cold and flu season.
- Recognize the importance of testing dead birds found on campus or in your neighbourhood for the presence of the West Nile virus.
- Identify those forms of hepatitis that are potentially sexually transmitted, in comparison to those that are not.
- Take proper precautions to protect yourself from HIV/AIDS and other sexually transmitted diseases.

Online Learning Centre Resources

www.mcgrawhill.ca/college/hahn

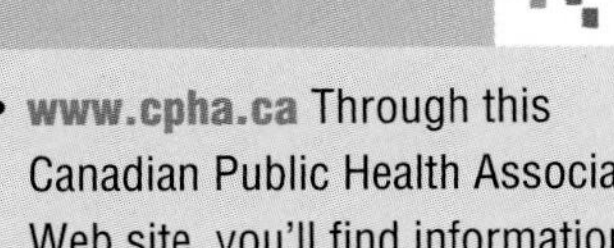

Log on to our Online Learning Centre (OLC) for access to Web links for study and exploration of health topics. Here are some examples of what you'll find:

- **www.phac-aspc.gc.ca/about_apropos/index.html** This new Public Health Agency Web site focuses on chronic and infectious disease.
- **www.cdc.gov** Visit this U.S. Centers for Disease Control Web site for the single best group of links covering infectious diseases.
- **www.cpha.ca** Through this Canadian Public Health Association Web site, you'll find information on immunization, HIV/AIDS, and other public health initiatives aimed at controlling infectious diseases.
- **www.aidsida.com** This new site is part of the Canadian government's initiative to educate Canadians about their risk for HIV/AIDS.
- **www.ashastd.org** Find answers to frequently asked questions about sexually transmitted infections (STIs).

Media Pulse

From Fear to Hope—AIDS in the News

In the early days of news coverage about AIDS, magazines like *Time* and *Newsweek* ran articles called "The AIDS Epidemic," "Epidemic of Fear," "Plague Mentality," "Fear of Sex," "The Growing Threat," "A Spreading Scourge," "The New Untouchables," "AIDS Spreading Panic Worldwide," "A Grim Race Against the Clock," and "The Lost Generation." The titles reflected fear of the unknown, a new killer disease.

When the case of Kimberley Bergalis broke into the news in 1991, a routine visit to the dentist was suddenly fraught with risk. Bergalis was the first American to die of AIDS after being infected by her dentist, Dr. David Acer. Four of Acer's other patients became infected with AIDS—all traced back to Acer. The public's reaction was near-hysteria. *Time* ran an article called "Should You Worry About Getting AIDS from Your Dentist?" People started asking their dentists (and other doctors) about their use of sterile precautions and even whether they had been tested for HIV.

By 1996, when the "cocktail" approach to AIDS treatment started showing remarkably good results, Magic Johnson was on the cover of both *Time* and *Newsweek* the same week. After more than four years of retirement from pro basketball—and

Media Pulse *continued*

the announcement that he had tested positive for HIV—he was back in the game. The secret to his survival? New drug treatments, a healthy diet, regular exercise, support from family and friends, and a positive attitude.

By the late 1990s, many news articles reflected a more hopeful tone: "Living Longer with AIDS," "Hope with an Asterisk," "Are Some People Immune?" and "What—I'm Gonna Live?" Doctors, too, are feeling more positive about the disease. As one AIDS specialist said: "I go to work feeling like there's something I can do for my patients."

For people with HIV/AIDS in the most highly developed countries the future holds different things. For some, who can't afford or tolerate the new drugs, it's still a matter of waiting to die. Others feel that they've been given a second chance. They can think about having relationships again—something many put on hold when they learned they were HIV positive. They can make plans for what they want to do with the rest of their lives—however long that may be.

Most people with HIV/AIDS are buying time—hoping for the big breakthrough, the cure for AIDS. They're trying new drug treatments, hoping that one treatment won't disqualify them from the next one. They're watching TV news, reading the newspapers, and using the Internet with greater attention. Will protease-inhibiting drugs be the answer? Are the even newer antiviral medications the breakthrough hoped for? Is a vaccine on the horizon?

Today, the media are calling our attention to yet other aspects of the AIDS pandemic. For the more developed countries, the failure of younger gays and bisexuals to protect themselves from exposure to HIV has led to a reversal in the progress made over the last 20 years. In ways all too familiar to public health professionals, a younger generation can too easily forget the progress against disease and premature death made by those who came before, and in doing so, unravel the threads of progress.

Increasingly, media attention has also been focused on the plight of the millions of HIV/AIDS victims in developing countries, particularly in Africa and areas of Asia. Television increasingly exposes the suffering in countries where diagnosis is inadequately undertaken and, once done, virtually no effective treatment exists for those infected. Beyond the suffering and limited hope for those infected, the media has also publicized the plights of the tens of thousands of orphaned children in these areas whose parents have died from AIDS. Our federal government and pharmaceutical industry has been exposed to this suffering as well, and initial responses are being mustered.

Sources: Gayle HD. Curbing the global AIDS epidemic. *N Engl J Med* 348(18):1802–1805, 2003. Klausner RD, et al. Medicine, The need for a global HIV vaccine enterprise. *Science* 300(5628):2036–2039, 2003.

INFECTIOUS DISEASES IN THE 2000s

In the 1900s, infectious diseases were the leading cause of death. These deaths resulted from exposure to organisms that produced diseases such as smallpox, tuberculosis (TB), influenza, whooping cough (pertussis), typhoid, diphtheria, and tetanus. However, by midcentury, improvements in public sanitation, the widespread use of antibiotic drugs as a treatment method, and vaccinations as preventive therapy had considerably reduced the number of people who died from infectious diseases.

Today, we have a new respect for infectious diseases. AIDS continues to threaten millions of people in many areas of the world. We are witnessing the resurgence of TB. We recognize the role of pelvic infections in infertility. We also know that failure to fully immunize children, particularly in developing countries, has laid the groundwork for a return of whooping cough, polio, and other serious childhood diseases.

New dimensions of infectious disease have recently come to our attention. These include the appearance of extremely virulent viruses, such as the Ebola virus in Zaire, which is fatal to 75% of the people who contract it and for which there is no immunization or understanding of its transmission; the increasing resistance of bacteria such as *Staphylococcus aureus*, *Enterococcus*, and *Mycobacterium* (which causes TB) to antibiotics because of overuse, improper use, and biological "redesign" of the organisms themselves; the role of a bacterium (*Helicobacter pylori*) in the development of gastric ulcers; and, finally, the growing concern over transmission of infectious organisms through contaminated food, improper preparation of food, and contamination of water. The development of new antibiotics and more cautious use of current ones represent an encouraging trend.

INFECTIOUS DISEASE TRANSMISSION

Infectious diseases can generally be transferred from person to person, although that transfer is not always direct. These diseases can be especially dangerous because of their ability to spread to large numbers of people, producing *epidemics*, in which a large number of people are infected within a specific geographical area, such as a

Table 11–1 Pathogens and Common Infectious Diseases

Pathogen	Description	Representative Disease Processes
Viruses	Smallest common pathogens; nonliving particles of genetic material (DNA) surrounded by a protein coat	Rubeola, mumps, chicken pox, rubella, influenza, warts, colds, oral and genital herpes, shingles, AIDS, genital warts
Prion	A protein particle that lacks DNA and is believed to be infectious to animals, including humans	Creutzfeldt-Jakob disease, scrapie, mad cow disease
Bacteria	One-celled microorganisms with sturdy, well-defined cell walls; three distinctive forms: spherical (cocci), rod shaped (bacilli), and spiral shaped (spirilla)	Tetanus, strep throat, scarlet fever, gonorrhea, syphilis, chlamydia, toxic shock syndrome, Legionnaires' disease, bacterial pneumonia, meningitis, diphtheria, food poisoning, Lyme disease
Fungi	Plantlike microorganisms; moulds and yeasts	Athlete's foot, ringworm, histoplasmosis, San Joaquin Valley fever, candidiasis
Protozoa	Simplest animal form, generally one-celled organisms	Malaria, amoebic dysentery, trichomoniasis, vaginitis
Rickettsia	Viruslike organisms that require a host's living cells for growth and replication	Typhus, Rocky Mountain spotted fever, rickettsialpox
Parasitic worms	Many-celled organisms; represented by tapeworms, leeches, and roundworms	Dirofilariasis (dog heartworm), elephantiasis, onchocerciasis

region of the country, or *pandemics*, in which an infectious disease crosses national borders and infects millions of people worldwide.

The sections that follow explain the process of disease transmission and the stages of infection.

Pathogens

For a disease to be transferred, a person must come into contact with the disease-producing agent, or **pathogen**, such as a virus, bacterium, or fungus. When pathogens enter our bodies, they are sometimes able to resist body defence systems, flourish, and produce an illness. This is commonly called an *infection*. Because of their small size, pathogens are sometimes referred to as *microorganisms*, *microbes*, or *germs*. Table 11–1 describes the more familiar infectious disease agents and some of the illnesses they produce.

Chain of Infection

The transmission of a pathogenic agent through the various links in the chain of infection (Figure 11–1) forms the basis for an understanding of how diseases spread. However, not every pathogenic agent will move all the way through the chain of infection because various links in the chain can be broken. Therefore, the presence of a pathogen creates only the potential for a disease.

Agent

The first link in the chain of infection is the disease-causing **agent**. Although some agents are very **virulent** and cause serious infectious illnesses such as HIV, which causes AIDS, others produce far less serious infections, such as the common cold. Through mutation (change), some pathogenic agents, particularly viruses, become more virulent than they once were.

Reservoir

Infectious agents must have the support and protection of a favourable environment to survive. This environment forms the second link in the chain of infection and is referred to as the *reservoir*. In many common infectious diseases, the reservoirs in which the pathogenic organisms live are the bodies of already infected people. Here the agents thrive before being spread to others. These infected people are the **hosts** for particular disease agents.

For other infectious diseases, the reservoirs in which the agents are maintained are the bodies of animals. Rabies

Key Terms

pathogen
Disease-causing agent.

agent
Causal pathogen of a particular disease.

virulent (veer yuh lent)
Capable of causing disease.

host
An infected person capable of infecting others.

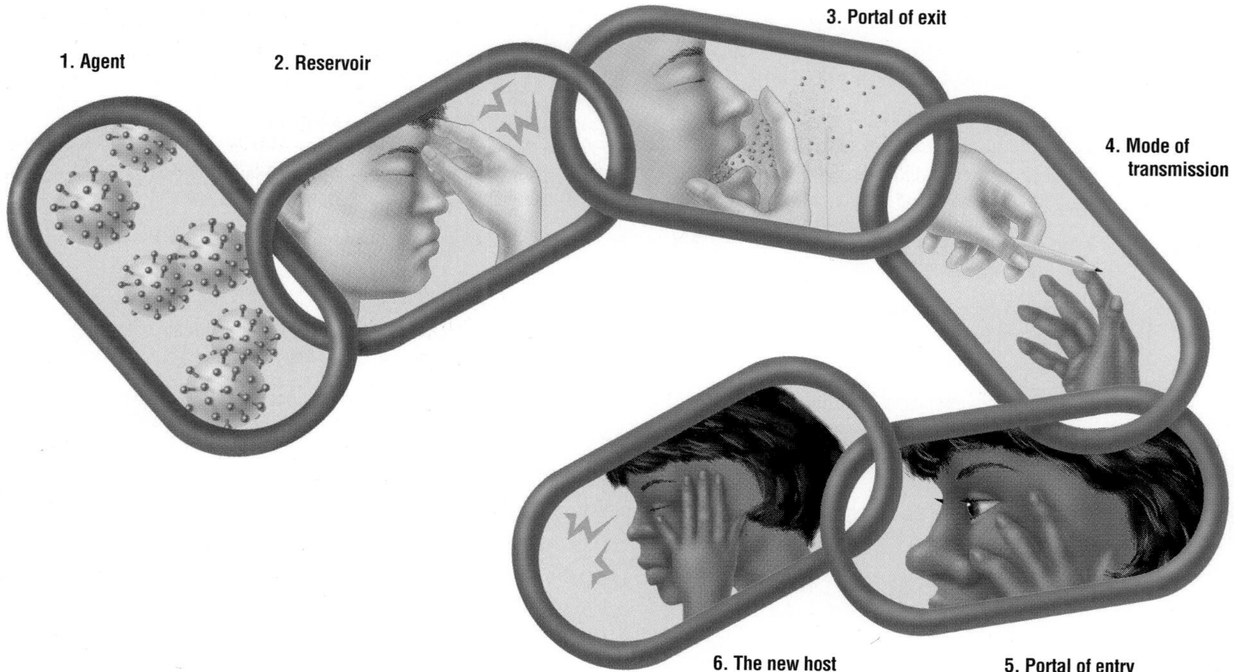

Figure 11–1 The six links in the chain of infection. The example above shows a rhinovirus, which causes the common cold, being passed from one person to another. I, The *agent* (pathogen) is a rhinovirus; 2, The *reservoir* is the infected person; 3, The *portal of exit* is the respiratory system (coughing); 4, The *mode of transmission* is indirect hand contact; 5, The *portal of entry* is the mucous membranes of the uninfected person's eye; 6, The virus now has a *new host.*

is among the most familiar of the animal-reservoir diseases. Affected animals will not always be sick or show symptoms similar to those of an infected person.

The third type of reservoir in which disease-causing agents can reside is a nonliving environment, such as the soil. (The spores of the tetanus bacterium can survive in soil for up to 50 years, entering the human body in a puncture wound.) Warm and moist locker room floors are another example of this environment because the fungi that cause ringworm and jock itch can survive there.

Portal of exit

For pathogenic agents to cause diseases and illnesses in others, they must leave their reservoirs. The third link in the chain of infection is the portal of exit, or the point where agents leave their reservoirs.

In infectious diseases that involve human reservoirs, the principal portals of exit are familiar—the digestive system, the urinary system, the respiratory system, the reproductive system, and the blood.

Mode of transmission

The fourth link in the chain of infection is the mode of transmission, or the way that pathogens are passed from reservoirs to susceptible hosts. Two principal methods are *direct transmission* and *indirect transmission.*

Three types of direct transmission are observed in human-to-human transmission. These include *contact* between body surfaces (such as kissing, touching, and sexual intercourse), *droplet spread* (inhalation of contaminated air droplets), and *fecal-oral spread* (feces on the hands are brought into contact with the mouth).

Indirect transmission occurs between infected and uninfected people when infectious agents travel by means of nonhuman materials. Vehicles of transmission include *inanimate objects*, such as water, food items, soil, towels, clothing, and eating utensils.

A second method of indirect transmission of infectious agents occurs in conjunction with vectors. The term *vector* is related to living things, such as insects, birds, and other animals that carry diseases from human to human. An example of a vector is the deer tick that transmits Lyme disease.

Airborne indirect transmission involves the *inhalation* (breathing in) of infected particles that have been suspended in an air source for an extended period. Unlike droplet transmission, in which both infected and uninfected people must be in close physical proximity, noninfected people can become infected through airborne transmission by sharing air with infected people who were in the same room hours earlier. Viral infections such as German measles may be spread in this manner.

Portal of entry

The fifth link in the chain of infection is the portal of entry. As with the portals of exit, there are three primary portals of entry for pathogenic agents to enter the bodies of uninfected people. These are the digestive system, the respiratory system, and the reproductive system. In addition, a break in the skin provides another portal of entry. In most infectious conditions the portals of entry are within the same system as the portals of exit. In the case of HIV, however, cross-system transmission occurs. Oral and anal sex allow for infectious agents to pass between the warm, moist tissues of the reproductive system and those of the digestive system.

The new host

In theory, all people are at risk for contracting infectious diseases and so can be considered as susceptible hosts. In practice, however, factors such as overall health, acquired immunity, health care services, and health-related behaviour can influence a person's susceptibility to infectious diseases.

Stages of Infection

When a new host is assaulted by a pathogenic agent, a reasonably predictable sequence of events takes place. That is, the disease moves through five rather distinctive stages.[1] You may be able to recognize these stages of infection each time you catch a cold.

1. *The Incubation Stage.* This stage lasts from the time a pathogen enters your body until it multiplies enough to produce signs and symptoms of the disease. The length of this stage can vary from a few hours to many months, depending on the virulence of the organisms, the concentration of organisms, the host's (your) level of immune responsiveness, and other health problems you may have. This stage has been called a *silent stage*. Transmission of the pathogen to a new host is possible but not probable during this stage: a host may be infected during this stage but not infectious. HIV infection is an exception to this rule.
2. *The Prodromal Stage.* The incubation stage is followed by a short period during which you may experience a variety of general signs and symptoms, including watery eyes, runny nose, slight fever, and overall tiredness. These symptoms are nonspecific and may not be strong enough to force you to rest. During this stage the pathogenic agent continues to multiply. Now you (the host) can transfer pathogens to a new host. In fact, because the activity level of the host is generally not restricted and you may still feel well, some believe that this stage is as infective as is the clinical or acute stage. Self-imposed isolation should be practised during this stage to protect others. Again, HIV infection is different in regard to this stage.
3. *The Clinical Stage.* This stage, also called the *acme* or *acute stage*, is often the most unpleasant stage for you, the host. At this time the disease reaches its highest point of development. All of the clinical (observable) signs and symptoms for the particular disease can be seen or analyzed by appropriate laboratory tests. The likelihood of transmitting the disease to others is highest during this peak stage; all of our available defence mechanisms are in the process of resisting further damage from the pathogen.
4. *The Decline Stage.* During this stage, you experience the first signs of recovery. The infection is ending or, in some cases, being reduced to a subclinical level. Relapse may occur if you overextend yourself. In HIV and AIDS, this is almost always the last stage before death.
5. *The Recovery Stage.* Also called the *convalescence stage*, this stage is characterized by apparent recovery from the invading agent. Disease transmission during this stage is possible but not probable. Until your overall health has been strengthened, you may be especially susceptible to another (perhaps different) disease pathogen. Fortunately, after the recovery stage, further susceptibility to the pathogenic agent should be reduced because of the body's buildup of immunity. Such immunity is not always permanent; for example, many sexually transmitted infections can be contracted repeatedly.

Later in the chapter HIV/AIDS will be discussed. However, prior to that time, it may be helpful to state that this critically important pandemic infectious disease does not easily fit into the five-stage model of infectious diseases just presented. In individuals infected with HIV there is an initial asymptomatic *incubation stage*, followed by a *prodromal stage* characterized by generalized signs of immune system inadequacy. However, once the level of specific protective cells of the immune system declines to the point that the body cannot be protected from opportunistic diseases, and the label AIDS is assigned, the five-stage model becomes less easily applied.

BODY DEFENCES: MECHANICAL AND CELLULAR IMMUNE SYSTEMS

Much as a military installation is protected by a series of defensive alignments, so too is the body. These defenses can be classified as mechanical or cellular (Figure 11–2). *Mechanical defences* are first-line defences. They physically separate the internal body from the external environment. Examples are the skin, the mucous membranes that line the respiratory and gastrointestinal tracts, earwax, the

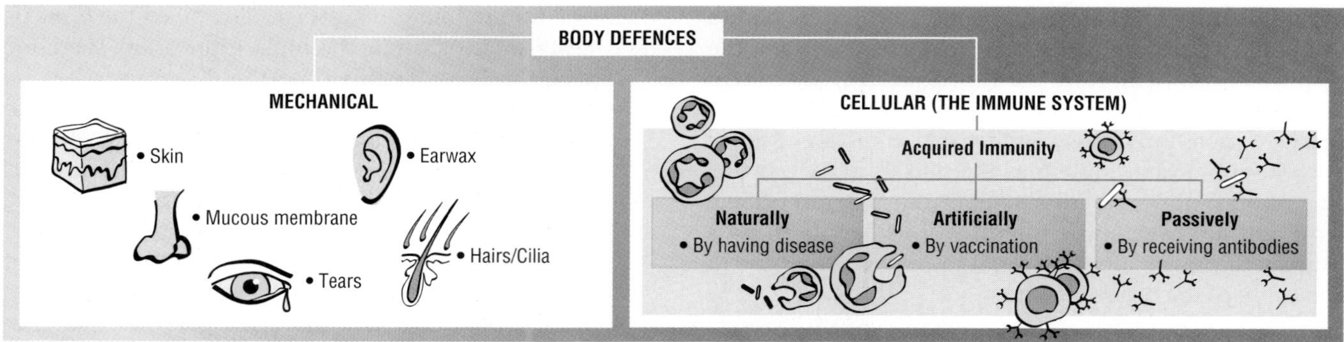

Figure 11–2 The body has a variety of defences against invading organisms. Mechanical defences are the first means of protection, since they separate the internal body from the external environment. Cellular defences include chemicals and specialized cells that provide immunity to subsequent infections.

tiny hairs and cilia that filter incoming air, and even tears. These defenses serve primarily as a shield against foreign materials that may contain pathogenic agents. They can, however, be disarmed, as happens when tobacco smoke kills the cilia that protect the airway, resulting in chronic bronchitis, or when contact lenses decrease tearing, leading to irritation and eye infection.

The second component of the body's protective defences is the *cellular* system or, more commonly, the **immune system**. In comparison with the mechanical defences, this cell-based component is far more specific. Its primary purpose is to eliminate microorganisms, foreign proteins, and cells foreign to the body. A wellness-oriented lifestyle, including sound nutrition, effective stress management, and regular exercise, strengthens this important division of the immune system. The microorganism, foreign proteins, or abnormal cells whose presence activates this cellular component are identified collectively as *antigens*.[2]

Divisions of the Immune System

Closer examination of the immune system, or cellular defences, reveals two separate but highly cooperative groups of cells. One group of cells has its origins in the fetal thymus gland. It produces *T cell–mediated immunity*, or simply cell-mediated immunity. The second group of cells consists of the B cells (bursa of Fabricius), which are the working units of *humoral immunity*.[3] Cellular elements of both cell-mediated and humoral immunity are found in the bloodstream, the lymphatic tissues of the body, and the fluid that surrounds body cells.

Although you were born with the structural elements of both cell-mediated and humoral immunity, for you to develop an immune response, the components of these cellular systems had to encounter and successfully defend against specific antigens. Once this occurred, your immune system was primed to respond quickly and effectively if the same antigens were encountered again. This confrontation resulted in the development of a state of **acquired immunity (AI)**. As seen in Figure 11–2, the development of AI can occur in different ways.

- **Naturally acquired immunity (NAI)** occurs when the body is exposed to infectious agents. When you catch an infectious disease, you fight the infection and in the process may become immune (protected) from developing that illness again.
- **Artificially acquired immunity (AAI)** occurs when your body is exposed to weakened or killed infectious agents introduced through vaccination or immunization. As in NAI, the body engages the infectious agents and remembers how to fight the same battle again. A Routine Immunization Schedule for children from birth through 16 years is available from the Canadian Immunization Awareness Program at **www.phac-aspc.gc.ca/im/ptimprog-progimpt/table-1_e.html**. Adults with questions about their immunization status or required immunizations for travel abroad should consult their primary care physicians.
- **Passively acquired immunity (PAI)** results when antibodies are introduced into the body. These antibodies, for a variety of specific infections, are produced outside the body (either in animals or by the genetic manipulation of microorganisms). When introduced into the human body, they provide immediate protection until a more natural form of immunity can be developed.

Collectively, these three forms of immunity can provide important protection against infectious disease.

IMMUNIZATIONS

Although the incidence of several childhood communicable diseases is at or near the lowest level ever, the risk of a resurgence of diseases such as measles, polio, diphtheria, and rubella is very real. This possible upturn in childhood infectious diseases could be prevented if parents ensured that their children were fully immunized. Overall, about 90% of children receive all necessary immunizations. There are regional variations in the level of immunization, and some racial/ethnic groups are below this overall level.

Currently, vaccines against several potentially serious infectious conditions are available and should be given. These include the following:

- *Diphtheria:* a potentially fatal illness that leads to inflammation of the membranes that line the throat, swollen lymph nodes, and heart and kidney failure
- *Whooping Cough:* a bacterial infection of the airways and lungs that results in deep, noisy breathing and coughing
- *Hepatitis B:* a viral infection that can be transmitted sexually or through the exchange of blood or body fluids and causes serious liver damage
- *Haemophilus Influenzae Type B:* a bacterial infection that can damage the heart and brain, resulting in meningitis, and can also produce profound hearing loss
- *Tetanus:* a fatal infection caused by bacteria found in the soil that damages the central nervous system
- *Rubella (German measles):* a viral infection of the upper respiratory tract that can cause damage to a developing fetus when the mother contracts the infection during the first trimester of pregnancy
- *Measles (red measles):* a highly contagious viral infection leading to a rash, high fever, and upper respiratory tract symptoms
- *Polio:* a viral infection capable of causing paralysis of the large muscles of the extremities
- *Mumps:* a viral infection of the salivary glands
- *Chicken Pox:* a varicella zoster virus spread by airborne droplets leading to a sore throat, rash, and fluid-filled blisters
- *Pneumoccal Infection:* A bacterium capable of causing infections, including pneumonia, heart, kidney, and middle ear infection.

Parents of a newborn should take their infant to their family care physician, pediatrician, or well-baby clinic (operated by community health departments) to begin the immunization schedule. The development of new vaccines and the evaluation of currently used vaccines are ongoing processes for preventing infectious diseases in this country.

THE IMMUNE RESPONSE

Fully understanding the function of the immune system requires a substantial understanding of human biology and is beyond the scope of this text. Figure 11–3 presents a simplified view of the immune response.

When antigens (whether microorganisms, foreign substances, or abnormal cells) are discovered within the body, various types of white blood cells confront and destroy some of these antigens. Principal among these blood cells are the *macrophages* (very large white blood cells) that begin ingesting antigens as they are encountered. In conjunction with this "eating" of antigens, macrophages display segments of the antigen's unique protein coat on their outer surface. Now in the form of macrophage/antigen complexes, macrophages transport their captured antigen identifiers to awaiting helper T cells whose recognition of the antigen will initiate the full expression of the cell-mediated immune response. This involves the specialization of "basic" T cells into four specialized forms: helper T cells, killer T cells, suppressor T cells, and memory T cells.

Once helper T cells have been derived from the "parent" T cells by the presence of the macrophage/antigen complex, they notify a second component of cellular immunity, the killer T cells. Killer T cells produce powerful chemical messengers that activate specific white blood cells that destroy antigens through the production of caustic chemicals called cytotoxins, or "cellpoisons." In addition to the helper T cells' activation of killer T cells, helper T cells also play a critical role in the activation of B cells, principal players in the expression of humoral immunity.

Activation of the humoral immunity component of the overall immune response involves the helper T cells' ability to construct a working relationship between themselves, the macrophage/antigen complexes (mentioned earlier), and the small B cells. Once these three elements have been constituted into working units, the B cells are transformed into a new version of themselves

Key Terms

immune system
System of cellular elements that protects the body from invading pathogens and foreign materials.

acquired immunity (AI)
The "arming" of the immune system through its intial exposure to an antigen.

naturally acquired immunity (NAI)
Type of acquired immunity resulting from the body's response to naturally occurring pathogens.

artificially acquired immunity (AAI)
Type of acquired immunity resulting from the body's response to pathogens introduced into the body through immunizations.

passively acquired immunity (PAI)
Temporary immunity achieved by providing antibodies to a person exposed to a particular pathogen.

Learning from Our Diversity

Infectious Disease: A Challenge for Older Adults

It's not always easy for young adults in excellent health to recover quickly and completely from some infectious diseases. Later in life the recovery often becomes much more difficult and in some cases impossible. For a variety of reasons older adults do not respond to infectious conditions with the same resiliency as they once did.

Central to this issue is the gradual degradation of the immune system over time. For reasons not fully understood, the immune system loses both its ability to recognize the presence of pathogens that have entered the body and its ability to mount an effective response against them. Particularly important in this regard are the decreased prevalence of active immune system cells and the inability of existing immune cells to respond effectively. Whether this reduced level of immune protection is a "programmed" aspect of aging (all human life does end at some point in time) or whether it reflects a process that is preventable (perhaps through lifestyle modifications) remains hotly debated. Perhaps no group of older adults is at greater risk because of a compromised immune system than are those with AIDS. People over age 50 with this immune system– destroying disease have a decreased ability to resist all infectious conditions, even when their HIV levels are suppressed through drug therapy.

In addition to the normal aging of their immune systems, older adults are generally afflicted with a variety of chronic conditions. The presence of multiple chronic illnesses (known as comorbidity) places the body under great stress, which also undermines the immune system. The combined effects of these conditions result in damage to different organ systems of the body—most importantly, the cardiovascular system, the respiratory system, and the renal system. Any time these systems are compromised by the effects of illness, either chronic or acute, the body becomes particularly vulnerable to infectious agents that routinely exist in our environment.

Compounding this situation is the inability of many older adults to understand the potential seriousness of infections at this stage of their lives. They may even have a false sense of confidence that their bodies are just as "good" at warding off infections as they once were. In addition, a lack of social support, isolation from health care facilities, and the inability to afford expensive prescription medication together make important medical care less available at a time when it could be effective.

When these factors are combined, as they are for many older adults, serious and even fatal infectious conditions become a reality. Therefore, anyone who is responsible for the health and well-being of older individuals needs to understand their susceptibility to infectious conditions and recognize the fact that timely and competent care is of critical importance.

called *plasma cells*. Plasma cells then utilize the information about the antigen's identity to produce massive numbers of "locks" called **antibodies**. Upon release from the plasma cells, these antibodies then circulate throughout the body and "lock-up" or capture free antigens in the form of *antigen/antibody complexes*.[4] The "captured" antigens are now highly susceptible to a variety of white blood cells that ingest or chemically destroy these infectious agents.

To assure that the initial response to the presence of the antigen can be appropriately controlled, a third group of T cells, the suppressor T cells, have been formed by the initial activation of parent T cells. These suppressor T cells monitor the outcome of the humoral response (antibody formation) and when comfortable with the number of antibodies produced, turn off further plasma cell activity. The fourth group of specialized T cells, the memory T cells, record this initial recognition-based game plan for fighting the original antigen invasion so that any subsequent similar antigen appearance will be quickly mounted.

An additional group of cells that operate independently from the T cell/B cell interplay just described are the natural killer (NK) cells. These immune cells continuously patrol the blood and intracellular fluids looking for abnormal cells, including cancer cells and viral-infected cells. When these are found, the NK cells attack them with destructive cytotoxins in a process called *lysing*.[5]

Clearly, without a normal immune system employing both cellular and humoral elements, we would quickly fall victim to serious and life-shortening infections and malignancies. As you will see later, this is exactly what occurs in many people infected with HIV (see the Learning from Our Diversity box above).

Emerging medical technology holds promise for repairing damaged immune systems. In a current form of treatment, *adult stem cells* are harvested from nondiseased tissues of a person's body or from a biologically related family member and used to replace damaged or diseased cells within the immune system.[6,7] A second form of immune system repair involves harvesting *cord blood (stem) cells* taken from the umbilical cord blood collected and "banked" at birth. After careful matching, these cells can be transplanted into a recipient in anticipation that they will specialize into the cell type needed by the damaged or diseased immune system.[8] It is important to note that considerable controversy now

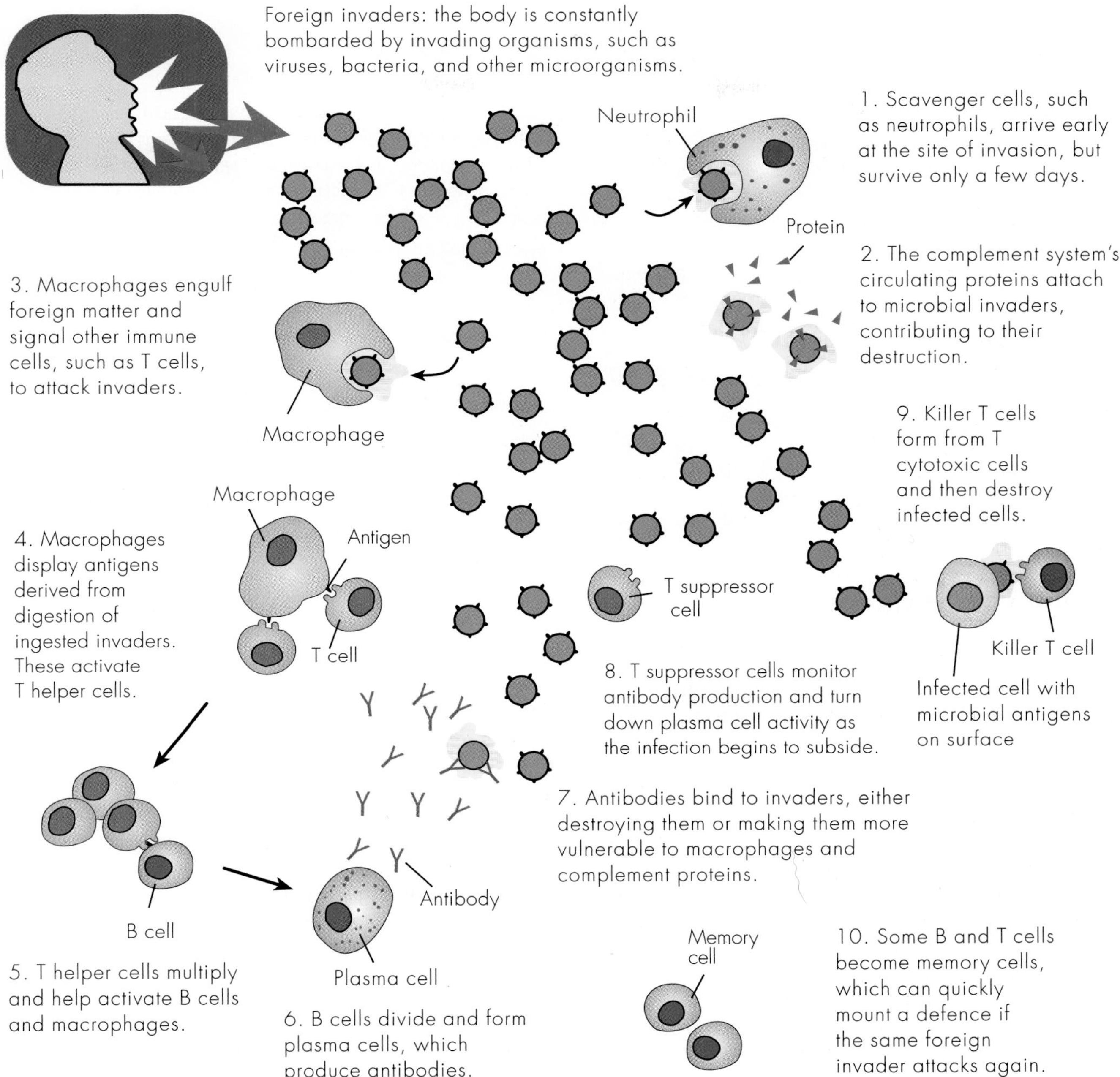

Foreign invaders: the body is constantly bombarded by invading organisms, such as viruses, bacteria, and other microorganisms.
Neutrophil
1. Scavenger cells, such as neutrophils, arrive early at the site of invasion, but survive only a few days.
Protein
2. The complement system's circulating proteins attach to microbial invaders, contributing to their destruction.
3. Macrophages engulf foreign matter and signal other immune cells, such as T cells, to attack invaders.
Macrophage
9. Killer T cells form from T cytotoxic cells and then destroy infected cells.
Macrophage
Antigen
4. Macrophages display antigens derived from digestion of ingested invaders. These activate T helper cells.
T cell
T suppressor cell
Killer T cell
Infected cell with microbial antigens on surface
8. T suppressor cells monitor antibody production and turn down plasma cell activity as the infection begins to subside.
7. Antibodies bind to invaders, either destroying them or making them more vulnerable to macrophages and complement proteins.
Antibody
B cell
Plasma cell
Memory cell
5. T helper cells multiply and help activate B cells and macrophages.
6. B cells divide and form plasma cells, which produce antibodies.
10. Some B and T cells become memory cells, which can quickly mount a defence if the same foreign invader attacks again.

Figure 11–3 Biological warfare. The body commands an army of defenders to reduce the danger of infection and guard against repeat infections. Antigens are the ultimate targets of all immune responses.

surrounds the use of stem cells obtained from embryonic or fetal tissue sources. Stem cell research in Canada is governed and restricted by Bill C-13. Even though these are considered in the United States to be the "best" stem cells, restrictions by the federal government (and several states) on their collection and use have forced clinicians to use stem cells from the sources mentioned earlier, as well as from cadavers.[9,10]

Key Term

antibodies
Chemical compounds produced by the body's immune system to destroy antigens and their toxins

Health on the Web

Behaviour Change Activities

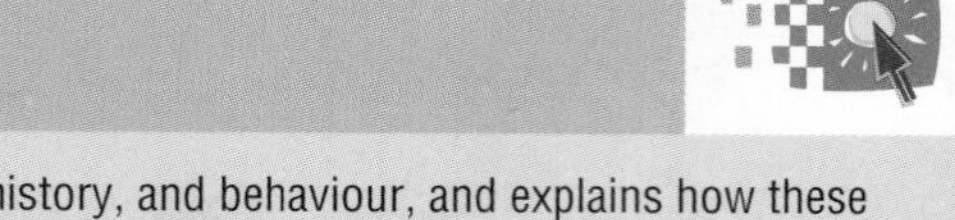

The "Truth" About STIs

Preventing and treating sexually transmitted infections is a top health priority for Canada, and the entire world. Your best defence against STIs is knowing the facts about them and understanding what places you at risk for contracting them. Go to **www.mayoclinic.com/programsandtools/morequizzes.cfm** and scroll down to "STD Quiz: Are You Taking Proper Preventive Steps?" This 10-question quiz is an anonymous service provided only for educational purposes. Absolutely no information about you is collected when you answer the questions, and you're the only person who can view the results, which are deleted forever when your browser session ends.

Create Your Own Risk Profile

Using the same Web site as in Activity 1, calculate your risk of contracting a sexually transmitted infection. Select *Risk Profiler.* This feature accepts your answers to questions about your age, gender, sexual history, and behaviour, and explains how these factors create your own personal risk profile. After each question, the meter shows you the relative risk based on your answer. When you've answered all the questions, click on the "Generate Report" button. You may want to print out the report for future reference.

Are You Cool About Colds?

Almost everyone gets a cold sooner or later, but although colds are one of the most common infections in existence, there's a lot of misunderstanding about what causes colds and what works—and what doesn't—in preventing and treating them. Go to **http://blueprint.bluecrossmn.com/article/quizzes/117807** and take the quiz Do You Know How to Stop a Cold? Answer the nine questions you'll find. How much did you know about colds?

CAUSES AND MANAGEMENT OF SELECTED INFECTIOUS DISEASES

This section focuses on some of the common infectious diseases and some that, although less common, are serious. This information provides reference points you can use to judge your own disease susceptibility.

The Common Cold

The common cold, an acute upper respiratory tract infection, is humankind's supreme infectious disease. Also known as **acute rhinitis**, this highly contagious viral infection can be caused by any of the nearly 200 known rhinoviruses. Colds are particularly common during periods when people spend time in crowded indoor environments, such as classrooms.

The signs and symptoms of a cold are fairly predictable. Runny nose, watery eyes, general aches and pains, a listless feeling, and a slight fever may all accompany a cold in its early stages. Eventually the nasal passages swell, and the inflammation may spread to the throat. Stuffy nose, sore throat, and coughing may follow. The senses of taste and smell are blocked, and the appetite declines.

With the onset of symptoms, management of a cold should begin promptly. After a few days, most of the cold's symptoms subside. In the meantime, you should isolate yourself from others, drink plenty of fluids, eat moderately, and rest. Keep in mind that antibiotics are effective only against bacterial infections—not viral infections such as colds.

Management of a cold can be aided by using some of the many OTC cold remedies. These remedies will not cure your cold but may lessen the discomfort associated with it. Nasal decongestants, expectorants, cough syrups, and aspirin or acetaminophen can all provide some temporary relief. Use of some of these products for more than a few days is not recommended, however, since a rebound effect may occur.

If a cold appears to become more persistent—as evidenced by prolonged chills, noticeable fever above 39.4°C (103°F), chest heaviness or aches, shortness of breath, coughing up rust-coloured mucus, or persistent sore throat or hoarseness—contact a physician. Also, it is now recognized that a certain virus associated with the common cold can result in a rare form of potentially serious heart dysfunction. Therefore, if you are not feeling back to normal after having had a cold for two to four weeks, you should contact a physician.[11]

Preventing colds is almost impossible. Since colds are now thought to be transmitted most readily by hand contact, frequent handwashing and the use of tissues are recommended.

Influenza

Influenza is also an acute, contagious disease caused by viruses. Some influenza outbreaks have produced widespread death, as seen in the influenza pandemics of 1889 to 1890, 1918 to 1919, and 1957. In Canada, between 500 and 1500 people die annually from the flu or its complications. The viral strains that produce this infectious disease have the potential for more severe complications

Washing your hands often is the best way to prevent the common cold.

than the viral strains that produce the common cold. The viral strain for a particular form of influenza enters the body through the respiratory tract. After brief incubation and prodromal stages, the host develops signs and symptoms not just in the upper respiratory tract but throughout the entire body. These symptoms include fever, chills, cough, sore throat, headache, gastrointestinal disturbances, and muscular pain. Physicians may recommend only aspirin, fluids, and rest. Parents are reminded not to give aspirin to children because of the danger of Reye's syndrome. Reye's syndrome is an aspirin-enhanced complication of influenza in which central nervous system changes can occur, including brain swelling. For a person seeking a quicker resolution to the debilitating symptoms of flu, four antiviral medications are currently available; two are intended for influenza virus type A and two for both virus types A and B. Specific recommendations regarding use of these prescription medications, including age limitations, also exist.[12]

Most young adults can cope with the milder strains of influenza that appear each winter or spring. However, pregnant women and older people—especially older people with additional health complications, such as heart disease, kidney disease, emphysema, and chronic bronchitis—are not as capable of handling this viral attack. People who regularly come into contact with the general public, such as teachers, should also consider annual flu shots.

Today approximately 70 million North Americans receive annual flu shots. In past years, these annual immunizations, tailored to work against the flu viruses anticipated for the coming flu season, were principally received by adults over 50 years of age and others with special needs. During the flu epidemic of 2003/2004, younger adults moved into the recipient population. Today, extending flu shots to include all children 6 to 23 months of age and youth between 6 months to 18 years of age who are residing with adults at greatest risk for contracting influenza due to illness or occupational exposure is recommended.

In recent years, several antiviral medications have been developed to reduce the duration of flu symptoms. A newly developed oral medication (Tamiflu) has shown the ability to reduce the degree of viral activity within the body and reduce associated symptoms of the flu when administered immediately before and immediately after exposure to a particular flu virus.[13] Another recently developed medication, (Relenza) delivered by nasal inhalation, has shown a protective effect during the course of a single flu season in much the same way that the injectable flu vaccines do.[14] The most effective defence against catching the flu is getting a flu vaccination annually in October or November. The vaccine generally takes effect about two weeks after immunization, and protection usually lasts for six months. All flu vaccines must be accurately formulated to match the viruses expected to be prevalent during an upcoming flu season. (See Table 11–2 for a comparison of influenza with the common cold.)

Tuberculosis

The rate of tuberculosis (TB) in Canada, which steadily declined after World War II, has levelled off and remained constant in the last decade or two. About 10% of the Canadian population, or about three million people, are carriers of TB. Yet, only 2000 Canadians develop "active" tuberculosis disease each year. People who are in reasonably good health usually have strong enough immune systems to keep it in check, and so will not become ill even though they are carriers.[15]

Worldwide, however, multiple drug-resistant TB strains are starting to emerge, largely due to poor or incomplete antibiotic treatment carried out in less developed countries. To date, the new strains are rare in

Key Term

acute rhinitis
The common cold; the sudden onset of nasal inflammation.

Table 11–2 Is It a Cold or the Flu?

	Cold	Flu
Symptoms		
Fever	Rare	Characteristic, high—38.9°–40°C (102°–104° + F); lasts 3–4 days
Headache	Rare	Prominent
General aches, pains	Slight	Usual; often severe
Fatigue, weakness	Quite mild	Can last up to 2–3 weeks
Extreme exhaustion	Never	Early and prominent
Stuffy nose	Common	Sometimes
Sneezing	Usual	Sometimes
Sore throat	Common	Sometimes
Chest discomfort, cough	Mild to moderate, hacking cough	Common, can become severe
Complications	Sinus congestion, earache	Pneumonia, bronchitis; can be life threatening
Prevention	Avoidance of infected people	Annual vaccination; amantadine or rimantadine (antiviral drugs)
Treatment	Temporary relief	Amantadine or rimantadine within 24–48 hours after onset of symptoms

Canada; however, with globalization it is difficult to predict what will unfold in the future.

TB kills up to three million people worldwide every year, more than any other infectious disease.[16]

Because TB is spread through coughing, the disease thrives in crowded places, where infected people are in constant contact with others. Prisons, hospitals, public housing units, and student residence halls are places where close day-to-day contact occurs. In such settings a single infected person can spread the TB agents to many others.

When healthy people are exposed to TB agents, their immune systems generally are able to contain the bacteria to prevent the development of symptoms and to reduce the likelihood of infecting others. However, when the immune system is damaged, such as in the elderly, the malnourished, and those who are infected with HIV, the disease can become established and may eventually be transmitted to other people at risk.

Multiple drug–resistant (MDR) TB has been reported as 2% of all TB cases. Increasingly prevalent in this country, MDR TB is the result of patients' inability to follow their physicians' instructions when initially treated (for various reasons), inadequate treatment by physicians, and increased exposure of HIV-infected people to TB. Only 50% of people with this form of TB can be cured.

Health officials are again requesting that TB testing programs be implemented. They are also recommending that those infected, once identified, be isolated and closely supervised during the entire six to eight months of treatment required for complete recovery. New diagnostic tests have been developed and should result in more prompt treatment and effective control of the transmission of the disease.

Until recently the skin prick test was used to determine the presence of TB. A dose of tuberculin was placed under the surface of the skin of the arm. After several days if a bump developed of a certain size, it was an indication the person had TB. A new blood test called ELISPOT (enzyme-linked immunospot) is the first diagnostic test that uses the immune systems T-cells to determine TB infection. The test is simple and quick with results available the morning after the test was taken. The test will make detection of the disease known long before those infected have symptoms and become contagious. Early detection is one way to start to eliminate such a devastating infectious disease.[17]

Pneumonia

Pneumonia is a general term used for a variety of infectious respiratory conditions. Bacterial, viral, fungal, rickettsial, mycoplasmal, and parasitic forms of pneumonia exist.[18] However, bacterial pneumonia is the most common form. It is often seen in conjunction with other illnesses that weaken the body's immune system. This is why even healthy young people should consider colds and flu as potentially serious and treat them properly. In fact, pneumonia is so common in the frail elderly that it is often the specific condition causing death. *Pneumocystis carinii* pneumonia, a parasitic form, is of great importance today, since it is a principal opportunistic infection associated with the diagnosis of AIDS in HIV-infected people.

Among older adults with a history of chronic obstructive lung disease, cardiovascular disease, diabetes, or alcoholism, a midwinter form of pneumonia known as *acute community-acquired pneumonia* is often a serious health problem.[19] The sudden onset of chills, chest pain, and a cough producing sputum are characteristics of this condition. Additionally, a symptom-free form of pneumonia known as *walking pneumonia* is also commonly seen in adults and can become serious without warning. Individuals with any of these illnesses should be watched carefully during the high-risk season of the year and provided with effective treatment if symptoms develop.

As the number of older North Americans grows, recommendations regarding immunization against pneumococcal pneumonia have been established and vaccination programs undertaken. Today, these recommendations encourage vaccination beginning at 50 years of age. The cost-effectiveness of pneumonia immunizations for older adults, and particularly for minority older adults, is well established.[20]

The first known drug-resistant strains of pneumonia have been identified in North America. As a result, some experts are calling for an even more comprehensive vaccination plan for older adults.

Mononucleosis

Of all the common infectious diseases that a student can contract, **mononucleosis** **("mono")** can force a lengthy period of bed rest during a semester or quarter when it can least be afforded. Other common diseases that are likely to affect you can be managed with minimal amounts of disruption. However, the overall weakness and fatigue seen in many people with mono sometimes require one or two months of rest and recuperation.

Mono is a viral infection in which the body produces an excessive number of mononuclear leukocytes (a type of white blood cell). After uncertain, perhaps lengthy, incubation and prodromal stages, the acute symptoms of mono can appear, including weakness, headache, low-grade fever, swollen lymph glands (especially in the neck), and sore throat. Mental fatigue and depression are sometimes reported as side effects of mononucleosis. Usually after the acute symptoms disappear, the weakness and fatigue remain—perhaps for a few months. Mono is diagnosed on the basis of characteristic symptoms. Also, a blood smear can be used to determine the prevalence of abnormal white blood cells. In addition, an antibody test can detect activity of the immune system that is characteristic of the illness.

Since mononucleosis is caused by a virus (Epstein-Barr virus), antibiotic therapy is not recommended. Treatment most often includes bed rest and the use of OTC remedies for fever (aspirin or acetaminophen) and sore throat (lozenges). In extreme cases, corticosteroid drugs can be used. Appropriate fluid intake and a well-balanced diet are also important in the recovery stages of mono. Fortunately, the body tends to develop NAI to the mono virus, so subsequent infections of mono are unusual.

For years, mono has been labelled the "kissing disease"; however, mono is not highly contagious and is known to be spread by direct transmission in ways other than kissing. No vaccine has been developed to confer AAI for mononucleosis. The best preventive measures include the steps that you can take to increase your resistance to most infectious diseases: (1) eat a well-balanced diet, (2) exercise regularly, (3) sleep sufficiently, (4) use health care services appropriately, (5) live in a reasonably healthy environment, and (6) avoid direct contact with infected people.

Chronic Fatigue Syndrome

Perhaps the most perplexing "infectious" condition seen by physicians is **chronic fatigue syndrome (CFS)**. First identified in 1985, this mononucleosis-like condition is most commonly seen in women in their 30s and 40s. People with CFS, many of whom are busy professional people, report flu-like symptoms, including severe exhaustion, fatigue, headaches, muscle aches, fever, inability to concentrate, allergies, intolerance to exercise, and depression. Examinations done on the first people with CFS revealed antibodies to the Epstein-Barr virus. Thus it was assumed to be an infectious viral disease (and initially called *chronic Epstein-Barr syndrome*).

Since its first appearance, the condition has received a great deal of attention regarding its exact nature. Today, opinions vary widely as to whether the condition is a specific viral infection, a condition involving both viral infections and nonviral components, or some other disorder.[21]

In recent years it has been noted that another chronic condition, fibromyalgia, appears in a manner similar to CFS. As in CFS, the person with fibromyalgia demonstrates fatigue, inefficient sleep patterns, localized areas of tenderness and pain, morning stiffness, and headaches. The onset of this condition, like that of CFS, can follow periods of stress, infectious disease, physical trauma such as falls, thyroid dysfunction, or appear in conjunction with a connective tissue disorder.[22] Therefore some clinicians believe that the two conditions might be very closely related,[23] drawing on an explanation based on immune system involvement.

Regardless of its cause or causes, CFS is extremely unpleasant for its victims. Certainly, those experiencing the symptoms over an extended time need to be seen by a physician experienced in dealing with CFS.

Measles

Previously thought to be only a childhood disease, *red measles* (also called **rubeola** or *common measles*) has

Key Terms

mononucleosis ("mono")
Viral infection characterized by weakness, fatigue, swollen glands, sore throat, and low-grade fever.

chronic fatigue syndrome (CFS)
Illness that causes severe exhaustion, fatigue, aches, and depression; mostly affects women in their 30s and 40s.

rubeola (roo BE oh luh)
Red or common measles.

Exploring Your Spirituality

Living with an Infectious Disease—Life Is Not Over, Just Different

A chronic infectious disease can wear down your body and your spirit. First, you've got to deal with the pain, fatigue, and medicinal side effects associated with the condition. But you also need to learn to adapt everything—your routine, your relationships, and your work—to the illness. As the quality of your life changes dramatically, you may feel depressed, frustrated, and alone. What is the best way to handle the different aspects of your life as you learn to cope with a long-term illness such as chronic fatigue syndrome, hepatitis, or HIV? Will it ever be possible to enjoy a full life again?

Your workplace may present the first big challenge. Since your energy level will be decreased by your illness, you may have trouble completing tasks on time and handling your normal workload. Your allotted sick time and vacation days may be used up quickly for doctor's appointments, hospitalizations, and those days when you are simply too exhausted to go to work. Your coworkers and your supervisor may discriminate against you in subtle ways, making you feel that you're not doing your fair share. The best way to handle these challenges is to maintain a positive and friendly attitude, carefully manage your time off, promote open communication with your employer, and do your best to produce quality work even when you're not feeling well.

Your intimate relationships may also be strained. Your partner may not understand the new limits your illness places on your activities, especially if you were very active before. The best approach is open and honest communication. Try to dispel (or come to terms with) any fears your partner may have about your illness. Take all necessary precautions to avoid infecting your partner if the disease is transmissible. Also, reassure your partner that you're taking these precautions so that he or she won't become ill. Make a point of including your partner in your daily routines. Keep him or her informed of all doctor's appointments, procedures you must undergo, and any news of progress or setbacks. Share your feelings as a way of reducing anxiety for both of you. Create adaptations so that you can still enjoy a romantic relationship. Make the most of your time together, and find new ways to enjoy each other's company.

If you have children, they will also be affected by your illness. Young children may not understand why you can't take them for a sled ride when you feel sick or why you can't go to a school play because of a doctor's appointment. It's best to let children know that their fears and anxieties are valid and that you want them to share them with you. Tell them about your prognosis, taking care not to make any false promises of recovery if that is not expected. Spend time with each child—helping with homework, reading a story, or doing light chores around the house. Always allow the child to ask questions.

From your home to your workplace, your life will change along with your condition. As you adapt to your new situation, it is important to

- *Be your own best friend.* Eat well, exercise as much as you can, rest when you need to, and follow the treatments prescribed by your physician.
- *Know and understand your limits.* Don't feel guilty about not doing things you used to do before you got sick. Instead, set goals and handle responsibilities as your condition allows.
- *Find new things to do for fun.* This is a good time to start a new hobby that's relaxing. You can also make adaptations so that you can continue activities you've always enjoyed. Maybe you can't run three miles a day, but an after-dinner walk might be a pleasant substitute.
- *Communicate openly with others.* Share your feelings respectfully, and allow others around you to share theirs. Together, you can calm your fears, instill hope in each other, and foster a sense of belonging.
- *Remain positive.* Remember, life is not over—just different. Look forward to the good days, when you feel well, and take advantage of them. Create new ways to fulfill your needs and desires. Remain positive about the future and your treatment. New discoveries do occur, and treatments are always evolving. However, be realistic about your situation. Joining a support group may be one of the best things you can do for yourself.

What you learn about yourself throughout your illness may surprise you. You may discover a strength of spirit you never knew you had. Some days may be very hard, but somehow you get through them. You may see life in a new way—slowing down and taking pleasure in a job well done, enjoying friendships more, listening to your inner voice, spending time with your children, taking a second look at nature, and being thankful for today and tomorrow.

recently been seen in large numbers on some North American college campuses. Red measles is the highly contagious type of measles characterized by a short-lived, relatively high fever (39.4° to 40°C or 103° to 104°F) and a whole-body red spotty rash that lasts about a week. The other type of measles, German measles (**rubella**, or three-day measles), is a much milder form that can be devastating to unborn babies in the first trimester. In fact, the vaccine was developed primarily to protect susceptible pregnant women. In the unborn baby rubella can cause congenital rubella syndrome (CRS), which can lead to miscarriage, stillbirth, and severe birth defects for newborn babies of mothers who contracted this disease during pregnancy. Highly successful vaccines are now available for both varieties of measles and are usually given in the same injection. Women should receive these vaccinations before they become pregnant.

The outbreak of red measles among post-secondary students during the early 1990s points to the fact that our society mistakenly believes that most infectious diseases have now been eliminated. Public health experts now realize that those who contracted the disease either had never been vaccinated or had been vaccinated with a killed-variety vaccine used before 1969. Only students who had already had red measles as children or who had been vaccinated with a live virus were guaranteed full immunity against the red measles virus. Nontraditional-age post-secondary students in particular should attempt to determine whether their immunization status is based on use of the older, less effective vaccine.

Bacterial Meningitis

Over the last few years, a formerly infrequently seen, but potentially fatal infectious disease, meningococcal meningitis, has appeared on university and college campuses as well as in some high schools, suggesting that students are currently at greater risk of contracting the disease than other groups. Particularly interesting is the fact that among students, the risk of contracting this infection on campus appears to be highest for those students living in residence halls, suggesting that close living quarters, as well as smoking and alcohol consumption, favours transmission of the bacteria.

Meningococcal meningitis is a bacterial infection of the thin membranous coverings of the brain. In its earliest stages, this disease can easily be confused with the flu. Symptoms usually include a high fever, severe headache, stiff neck, nausea with vomiting, extreme tiredness, and the formation of a progressive rash. For about 10% of people who develop this condition, the infection is fatal, often within 24 hours. Therefore, the mere presence of the symptoms described above signals the need for immediate medical evaluation. If done promptly, treatment is highly effective. Vaccines are available for immunization against bacterial meningitis.

Toxic Shock Syndrome

Toxic shock syndrome (TSS), first reported in 1978, made front-page headlines in 1980, when it was reported by the Centers for Disease Control (CDC) in Atlanta that there was a connection between TSS and the presence of a specific bacterial agent (*Staphylococcus aureus*) in the vagina and the use of tampons.

Superabsorbent varieties of tampons apparently can irritate the vaginal lining three times more quickly than regular tampons. This vaginal irritation is enhanced when the tampons remain in the vagina for a long time (over five hours). Once this irritation has begun, the staphylococcal bacteria (which are commonly present in the vagina) have relatively easy access to the bloodstream. Proliferation of these bacteria in the circulatory system and their resultant toxins produce TSS. Left untreated, the victim can die—usually as a result of cardiovascular failure. Currently, only about 5% of women diagnosed as having TSS die from the condition.

Although the extent of this disease is still quite limited (only about 3 to 6 cases per 100 000 women per year) and the mortality figures are low (comparable with those in women who use oral contraceptives), women should show reasonable caution in using tampons. Recommendations are that (1) tampons should not be the sole form of sanitary protection used, and (2) tampons should not be in place for too long. Women should change tampons every few hours and intermittently use sanitary napkins. Tampons should not be used during sleep.

The incidence of TSS has dropped significantly since the early 1980s. Possible reasons for this decrease are the removal of some superabsorbent tampons from the market and the standardization of the labels for junior, super, and super-plus tampons that began in 1990.

Hepatitis

Hepatitis is an inflammatory process of the liver that can be caused by several viruses. Types A, B (once called non-A), C (once called non-B), D, and E have been recognized. Hepatitis can also be caused indirectly from abuse of alcohol and other drugs. General symptoms of hepatitis include fever, nausea, loss of appetite, abdominal pain, and jaundice (yellowing of the skin and eyes).

Type A hepatitis is often associated with consuming fecal-contaminated water or food, such as raw shellfish. Poor sanitation, particularly in the handling of food and diaper-changing activities has produced outbreaks in child care centres. Canadian health authorities report between 1000 and 3000 cases of hepatitis A each year; however, the disease is frequently asymptomatic, so the actual incidence is considerably higher.[24]

Key Terms

rubella
German or three-day measles.

toxic shock syndrome (TSS)
Potentially fatal condition resulting from the proliferation of certain bacteria in the vagina that enter the general blood circulation

TALKING POINTS • You've noticed that one of your restaurant coworkers doesn't wash her hands after using the restroom. Would you say something to her about this or notify the manager?

Type B hepatitis (HBV) is spread in various ways, including sexual contact, intravenous drug use, tattooing, and medical and dental procedures. In Canada, there are about 20 000 new cases each year, largely among young adults.[25] Chronic HBV infection has been associated with liver cirrhosis and liver cancer. An effective immunization for hepatitis B is now available. Although usually given during childhood, it should be seriously considered for a wide array of people, including all health care professionals (physicians, dentists, nurses, laboratory technicians, dental assistants, athletic trainers, etc.), food service workers, day care centre staff, social workers, police officers, teachers, and college and university students.

Type C hepatitis is contracted in ways similar to type B (sexual contact, tainted blood, and shared needles). Only 30% of the 210 000 to 275 000 Canadians currently infected with hepatitis C know they have the virus.[26] There is no vaccine for the disease.

The newly identified *type D* (delta) hepatitis is very difficult to treat. It is found almost exclusively in people already suffering from type B hepatitis. This virus, like type B hepatitis and HIV, makes unprotected sexual contact, including oral and anal sex, very risky. *Type E* hepatitis, associated with water contamination, is rarely seen in this country, except in people returning from affected areas of the world.

Sudden Acute Respiratory Syndrome (SARS)

In February 2003, the world became aware of a previously unknown respiratory disease, initially thought to be a form of pneumonia. This disease, characterized by high fever 38.5°C (100.4+°F), chills, headaches and, a few days later a dry cough, was, in fact, a new viral disease, Sudden Acute Respiratory Syndrome (SARS). First reported in Hanoi, then in Singapore, mainland China, and other Asian countries, the disease quickly presented in Europe and North America. In actuality, the disease had first appeared in a rural area of China, during the fall of 2002, but the Chinese government had apparently chosen not to disseminate this information.

The first SARS cases in Canada were identified in March 2003 in people returning from Hong Kong. All subsequent cases could be traced to close contacts with these original cases or to other travellers who had been in Asia.[27]

With the rapid spread of SARS, the World Health Organization, CDC, and Health Canada issued travel advisories against unnecessary travel to several areas and cities of Asia, as well as to Toronto. At the same time, scientists isolated the virus responsible for the respiratory disease and identified it as a member of the coronavirus family—a viral family with links to upper respiratory infection (colds). This particular virus, however, apparently entered the human germ pool in conjunction with the eating of civet cats—a delicacy in China—again demonstrating that many infectious conditions in humans have their origins in other animals—**zoonosis**.

With news of the SARS outbreak, the international scientific community began a cooperative effort to understand the disease's human-to-human transmission. It was quickly determined that the virus was transmitted by respiratory droplets. It was further determined that the frail, the elderly, and the young were at greatest risk, as well as persons in direct contact with symptomatic persons (family members and hospital staff). Soon thereafter, a diagnostic test was developed and treatment protocols became more focused and effective. These developments, in combination with concerted public health measures regarding the recognition of symptoms and curtailment of transmission opportunities, led to a rapid decline of reported new cases. On June 5, 2003, the World Health Organization declared that SARS had peaked and was subsiding in all infected areas.[28] By the WHO-defined end of the pandemic, August 15, 2003, worldwide 8422 had been infected and 916 had died.[29] Clearly, in terms of a potentially pandemic disease, the global village had been condensed in size by international travel and commerce.

Lyme Disease

Lyme disease is an infectious disease that is becoming increasingly common in eastern Canada and eastern, southeastern, upper midwestern, and West Coast states. This bacterial disease results when infected deer ticks, usually in the nymph (immature) stage, attach to the skin and inject the infectious agent as they feed on a host's blood. Deer ticks become infected by feeding on infected white-tailed deer or white-footed mice.

The symptoms of Lyme disease vary but typically appear within 30 days as small red bumps surrounded by a circular red rash at the site of bites. The red rash, traditionally described as being "bulls eye" in shape, with a whitish centre, may also be circular with redness throughout. Flulike symptoms may accompany this phase I stage, including chills, headaches, muscle and joint aches, and low-grade fever. A phase II stage develops in about 20% of infected people. This phase may produce disorders of the nervous system or heart. Those who remain untreated even to this stage can develop a phase III stage, which can include chronic arthritis, lasting up to two years. Fortunately, Lyme disease can be treated with antibiotics.[30] Unfortunately, however, no immunity develops, so infection can recur. Because some physicians order tests and begin antibiotic therapy too quickly, however, the basis of concern should be the appearance of phase I symptoms, not simply having been bitten by a tick. Lyme disease may be more difficult to diagnose in children than in adults.

Hantavirus Pulmonary Syndrome

Since 1993 a small but rapidly growing number of people have been dying of extreme pulmonary distress caused by the leakage of plasma into the lungs. In the initial cases, the people lived in the U.S. Southwest, had been well until they began developing flulike symptoms over one or two days, then quickly experienced difficulty breathing, and died only hours later. Epidemiologists quickly suspected a viral agent such as the hantavirus, known to exist in Asia and, to a lesser degree, in Europe.

Today hantavirus pulmonary syndrome has been reported in areas beyond the Southwest, including most of the western states and some of the eastern states. The common denominator in all these areas is the presence of deer mice. We now know that this common rodent serves as the reservoir for the virus. In fact, so common is the mouse that in 2000 the National Park Service began warning hikers, campers, and off-road bikers that hantavirus probably existed in every national park and that caution should be taken to avoid high-risk sites.

Because there is no vaccine for hantavirus pulmonary syndrome, people who are likely to be exposed to the infected excrement of deer mice should seek early evaluation of flulike symptoms.

West Nile Virus

This vector-borne infectious virus is transmitted from a reservoir, most often birds, by mosquitoes that in turn infect humans.[31] Human-to-human transmission (via mosquitoes) apparently does not occur. West Nile virus infection involves flulike symptoms, including fever, headache, muscle ache, fatigue, and joint pain. In young children, individuals with immune systems weakened by HIV, and older adults, West Nile virus infection may involve encephalitis, a potentially fatal inflammation of the brain that closely resembles St. Louis encephalitis. Physicians recommend that any unusual neurological symptoms be considered as a possible West Nile infection. The West Nile virus deaths that have occurred since the infection's initial appearance in 1999 have been the result of encephalitis.

In an attempt to determine the extent of the West Nile virus range, public health officials throughout the eastern United States and Canada have tested mosquitoes, sentinel chickens, crows, other birds, cows, and other animals, including humans. Additionally, mosquito habitats are being treated in an attempt to reduce the vector population. Public service announcements focusing on protection against mosquito bites are routinely made in high-risk areas. It is important to test dead birds to determine if they are carriers. A test to accurately screen for infected blood has been developed, as has a new diagnostic test, developed in Australia, that significantly reduced the time needed to obtain confirmation of the West Nile virus.

AIDS

AIDS is rapidly becoming the most devastating infectious disease of modern times. On the basis of current data, since the initial reporting of the disease in 1981 through to the end of 2004, 40 million people worldwide had become infected with HIV/AIDS; there were 5 million new cases per year by 2001. Since the beginning of the epidemic more than 24 million people have died from this disease.[32]

Globally, HIV/AIDS has tragic human and socioeconomic impact. Children are robbed of their parents, men and women lose their loved ones, and those with the disease face huge economic costs, stigma, and discrimination. HIV is preventable but yet the numbers of people infected worldwide continue to grow. In sub-Saharan Africa, two-thirds of all HIV positive people live where care treatment and support are almost nonexistent.[33]

In Canada, an estimated 56 000 Canadians are living with HIV/AIDS in 2004. While the overall infection rate has remained steady, Canada sees about 2500 new cases a year.[34]

The economic cost of HIV/AIDS is considerable, not only through the loss of productive years of life, but in hospital care, and out-of pocket expenses for medications. The monthly cost of approximately $1500 for virus-controlling drugs can be impoverishing, sometimes leading a person with HIV to abandon treatment (with the associated risk of producing drug-resistant strains) and/or compromise on other health-maintaining choices such as good nutrition.

Key Terms

zoonosis
The transmission of diseases from animals to humans.

Lyme disease
A bacterial infection transmitted by deer ticks.

Cause of AIDS

AIDS is the disease caused by HIV, a virus that attacks the helper T cells of the immune system. When HIV attacks helper T cells, people lose the ability to fight off a variety of infections that would normally be easily controlled. Because these infections develop while people are vulnerable, they are collectively called *opportunistic infections*. HIV-infected (HIV+) patients become increasingly vulnerable to infection by bacteria, protozoa, fungi, and several viruses. A variety of malignancies also develop during this period of immune-system vulnerability.

HIV+ with AIDS was originally diagnosed based on the presence of specific conditions. Among these were *Pneumocystis carinii* pneumonia and Kaposi's sarcoma, a rare but deadly form of skin cancer. Gradually, experts recognized that additional conditions were associated with advancing deterioration of the immune system and thus added them to the list of AIDS conditions. This list now includes almost 30 definitive conditions, with more conditions being added as they become apparent. Among the conditions found on the current version of the list are toxoplasmosis within the brain, cytomegalovirus retinitis with loss of vision, lymphoma involving the brain, recurrent salmonella blood infections, and a wasting syndrome that includes invasive cervical cancer in women, recurrent pneumonia, and recurrent tuberculosis. Today, however, experts tend to assign the label of HIV1 with AIDS to HIV-infected people when their level of helper T cells drops below 250 cells per cubic mm of blood, regardless of whether specific conditions are present.

Spread of HIV

HIV cannot be contracted easily in comparison to other infectious conditions such as colds, flu, and some childhood infections that can spread quickly within a classroom or office complex. The chances of contracting HIV through casual contact with HIV-infected people at work, school, or home are extremely low or nonexistent. HIV is known to be spread only by direct sexual contact involving the exchange of bodily fluids (including blood, semen, and vaginal secretions), the sharing of hypodermic needles, transfusion of infected blood or blood products, and perinatal transmission (from an infected mother to a fetus or newborn baby). For HIV to be transmitted, it must enter the bloodstream of the noninfected person, such as through needles or tears in body tissues lining the rectum, mouth, or reproductive system. Current research also indicates that HIV is not transmitted by sweat, saliva, tears, or urine, although the virus may be found in very low concentrations in these fluids. The virus cannot enter the body through the gastrointestinal system because digestive enzymes destroy the virus. An exception to this generalization, however, might exist, as studies conducted in Africa indicate that transmission can occur in conjunction with breast feeding infants.[35] A second exception involves the transmission of HIV between infected individuals and their uninfected sexual partners during episodes of unprotected oral sex when the uninfected individuals have evident gingivitis and bleeding gums.[36]

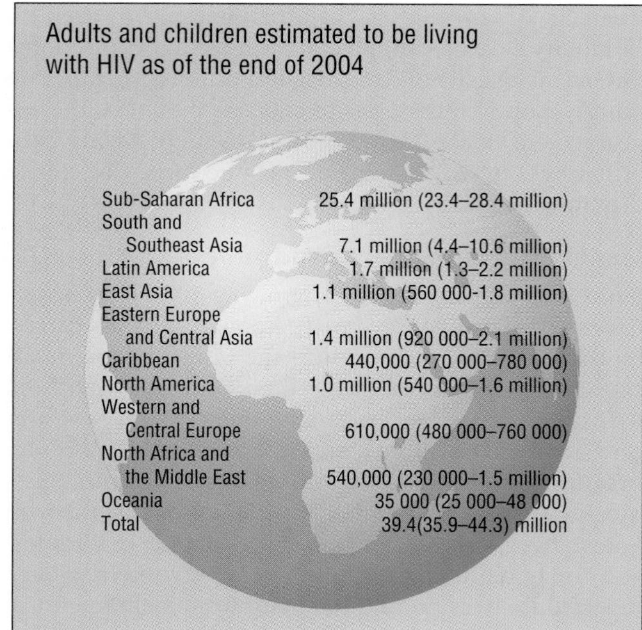

Adults and children estimated to be living with HIV as of the end of 2004
Sub-Saharan Africa 25.4 million (23.4–28.4 million)
South and Southeast Asia 7.1 million (4.4–10.6 million)
Latin America 1.7 million (1.3–2.2 million)
East Asia 1.1 million (560 000-1.8 million)
Eastern Europe and Central Asia 1.4 million (920 000–2.1 million)
Caribbean 440,000 (270 000–780 000)
North America 1.0 million (540 000–1.6 million)
Western and Central Europe 610,000 (480 000–760 000)
North Africa and the Middle East 540,000 (230 000–1.5 million)
Oceania 35 000 (25 000–48 000)
Total 39.4(35.9–44.3) million

Figure 11–4 For every person counted in these statistics, there is a face and a story. What are you doing to protect yourself from HIV/AIDS?

Women are at much greater risk than men of contracting HIV through heterosexual activity because of the higher concentration of lymphocytes in semen (± 10 million lymphocytes/tsp.) than in vaginal secretions (± 1 200 000 lymphocytes/tsp).[37] This susceptibility is seen in part by the increasing percentage of women with AIDS who were infected through heterosexual contact—from 8% in 1981, to 19% in 1993, and 36% in 2001.[38] Women under age 25 contract the virus principally through heterosexual contact. Figure 11–4[39] shows the estimated number of cases of HIV worldwide.

Signs and Symptoms of HIV Infection

Most people infected with HIV initially feel well and have no symptoms (that is, they are asymptomatic). Experts generally consider the *incubation stage* for HIV infection to be 6 months to 10 or more years, with the average approximately 6 years. Despite the long period between infection and the first clinical observation of damage to the immune system, antibodies to HIV may appear within several weeks to three months of contracting the virus. Of course, relatively few people are tested for HIV infection at any time during the incubation period. Thus infected people could remain asymptomatic

Each panel of the AIDS quilt is crafted by loved ones in memory of a family member or friend who has died. People with HIV/AIDS are living longer, and researchers are working hard to find a cure.

(currently described as HIV+ without symptoms) and be carriers of HIV for years before they experience signs of illness sufficient to warrant a physical examination.

Without symptoms of immune-system deterioration or AIDS-testing results, sexually active people need to redefine the meaning of monogamy. Couples must now account for the sexual partners they have both had over the past 10 years. Unfortunately, people do this so infrequently that some observers are labelling today's young adults "a generation in jeopardy."

Most people infected with HIV, in the absence of early screening and prophylactic drug treatment, eventually develop signs and symptoms of a more advanced stage of the disease. These signs and symptoms include tiredness, fever, loss of appetite and weight, diarrhea, night sweats, and swollen glands (usually in the neck, armpits, and groin). At this point, they are said to be HIV+ with symptoms. (See Table 11–3.)

Given sufficient time, perhaps as long as 15 years, most infected people without prophylactic drug treatment will move beyond HIV with symptoms into the *acute stage*. At this point, the label HIV+ with AIDS is applied, either on the basis of clinically defined conditions or more likely on the basis of a helper T cell count below 250 per cubic mm of blood. A normal helper T cell range is 800 to 1000. The efficacy of treatment is based in part on improvements in the T cell count over time.

A small percentage of infected people can suppress the infection and have survived for over two decades without developing AIDS, but experts do not fully understand this ability (possibly attributing it to a suppressor compound formed by specific immune system cells).

Diagnosis of HIV Infection

HIV infection is diagnosed through a clinical examination, laboratory tests for accompanying infections, and an initial screening test. Should the initial screening test produce a negative result, persons at risk for infection should be rescreened in three to six months. For individuals reluctant to present themselves for screening in a clinical setting, home screening tests are also available. Regardless, once initial screening has been undertaken, to eliminate the small chance of a false positive having occurred, more sensitive tests can be administered, including the enzyme-linked immunosorbent assay (ELISA) and Western blot test. Although expensive and not completely reliable, more recently developed tests are now available. One of these tests identifies the existence of viral mutations known to be drug resistant,[40] while another helps determine whether a particular drug will function in suppressing the contracted viral strain. This information helps physicians structure treatment protocols.

Treatment of HIV and AIDS

There is no cure for HIV infection and the resultant AIDS. It is critically important, however, that treatment begin upon diagnosis. Current treatment uses a combination of drugs drawn principally from two distinct groups: the *reverse-transcriptase* inhibitors and the *protease inhibitors.*

The reverse-transcriptase inhibitors block (or inhibit) the action of reverse transcriptase, an enzyme the virus requires to replicate itself within the host's infected T helper cells. Currently a combination of two of the many available reverse-transcriptase inhibitors is used to formulate a portion of the drug "cocktail" employed in treating HIV infection.

Introduction of the protease inhibitors, in combination with the reverse-transcriptase inhibitors, has revolutionized the treatment of HIV infection. These drugs inhibit the ability of the virus to undertake the replication process. In most treatment protocols, one protease inhibitor is combined with two reverse-transcriptase inhibitors to complete the drug cocktail.

Protease inhibitors have revolutionized AIDS care, reducing HIV to undetectable levels in thousands of people. The number of deaths from AIDS has decreased dramatically. However, people should not consider this improvement to mean that the emergency is over. In fact, when the drug cocktail therapy described above is discontinued, viral loads frequently move back toward pretreatment levels. This suggests the existence of well-protected sequestered (hidden) viruses within other tissues of the body.

In addition to reverse-transcriptase inhibitors and protease inhibitors, three types of medications, including two entry inhibitors, two co-receptor inhibitors, and two

Table 11–3 The Spectrum of HIV Infection

	HIV+ Without Symptoms (Asymptomatic)	HIV+ With Symptoms	HIV+ With AIDS
External signs	No symptoms Looks well	Fever Night sweats Swollen lymph glands Weight loss Diarrhea Minor infections Fatigue	Kaposi's sarcoma *Pneumocystis carinii* pneumonia and/or other predetermined illnesses Neurological disorders One or more of an additional 25 + diagnosable conditions or a T4 helper cell count below 200 per cubic mm
Incubation	Invasion of virus to 10 years	Several months to 10 or more years	Several months to 10–12 or more years
Internal level of infection	Antibodies are produced Immune system remains intact Positive antibody test	Antibodies are produced Immune system weakened Positive antibody test	Immune system deficient Positive antibody test
Infectious?	Yes	Yes	Yes

Changing *for the Better*

Reducing Your Risk of Contracting HIV

I've had only one partner in the past, but now I'm starting to date others with whom I may become sexually active. What should I do to protect myself from HIV and sexually transmitted infections?

It is important to keep in mind that sexual partners may not reveal their true sexual history or drug habits. If you are sexually active, you can lower your risk of infection with HIV and STIs by adopting the following safer sex practices.

- Learn the sexual history and HIV status of your sex partner.
- Limit your sexual partners by practising abstinence or by maintaining long-term monogamous relationships.
- Always use condoms correctly and consistently.
- Avoid contact with body fluids, feces, and semen.
- Curtail use of drugs that impair good judgment.
- Never share hypodermic needles.
- Refrain from sex with known injectable drug abusers.*
- Avoid sex with HIV-infected patients, those with signs and symptoms of AIDS, and the partners of high-risk individuals.*
- Get regular tests for STIs.
- Do not engage in unprotected anal intercourse.

How easy will it be to adopt these behaviours? How real is your risk of becoming HIV-positive?

*Current studies indicate that the elimination of high-risk people as sexual partners is the single most effective safer sex practice that can be implemented.

fusion inhibitors, have been developed to further enhance the battle against HIV/AIDS.[41] Now, newer and even more potent "cocktails" are developed by combining both older and new medication. The treatment is deemed highly active antiretroviral therapy, or *HAART*. HAART has proven highly effective in extending the life of many persons with HIV/AIDS by significantly reducing the level of HIV (viral load) in the body. Decision as to what a given patients' HAART will consist of is determined by factors such as the viral load data and the presence of preexisting conditions.

In the final analysis, however, as effective as HAART is in improving the length and quality of life for people with HIV/AIDS, mortality concerns remain, and life expectancy is compromised. The inability of people with AIDS to move into and through the *decline stage* and on to the *recovery stage* reflects the relationship between the disease and the immune system itself. Although drug cocktails stabilize the downward movement of the helper T cell count for an extended period, the viral load moves rapidly upward when drugs are discontinued. Additionally, drug therapy is demanding on the overall body, opportunistic infections continue to develop, and pre-existing conditions, such as incipient cardiovascular disease, may often worsen.[42]

In addition to the antiviral drugs, physicians also have a variety of medications to treat the symptoms associated with various infections and malignancies that make up AIDS. These drugs, of course, cannot reverse HIV status or cure AIDS.

Researchers continue to search for vaccines to prevent HIV infection. One large-scale clinical trial involving a vaccine is now completed. The vaccine, AIDSVAX, that employed two genetically altered AIDS virus types (North American and European strains), did not, however, result in the anticipated level of protection. It did, however, provide a slightly higher level of protection for blacks and Asian than for whites.[43] The FDA has advised the manufacturer that it will certify the vaccine for sale, if the level of protection can reach 30%.

The reality of HIV/AIDS in Africa and Asia is only now being recognized worldwide. With an estimated 29.4 million infected people in sub-Saharan Africa and an additional 6.0 million infected people in Southeast Asia, the need for a vaccine specific to the viral strains of these areas is growing rapidly.[44] In late 2000, a radically new and relatively inexpensive vaccine using segments of HIV DNA attached to salmonella bacteria underwent its initial human trials in Uganda. Should this innovative approach prove safe and effective, then progress can be made in quelling the potential catastrophe that is taking form on these two continents. Conversely, in the absence of a vaccine (and the inability to effectively treat those currently infected), it is projected that African life expectancy will drop to 29 years and that more than 29 million orphans will need care. Similar consequences would be expected in areas of Asia.

Prevention of HIV Infection

Can HIV infection be prevented? The answer is a definite yes. HIV infection rates on college and university campuses are considered low (approximately 0.2%), but students can be at risk. Every person can take several steps to reduce the risk of contracting and transmitting HIV. All of these steps require understanding one's behaviour and the methods by which HIV can be transmitted. Some appropriate steps for college-aged people are abstinence, safer sex, sobriety, and communication with potential sexual partners. To ensure the greatest protection from HIV, one should abstain from sexual activity.

TALKING POINTS • You're dating someone you like very much, and you think you might become sexually involved soon. How would you ask that person about his or her HIV status?

Sexually Transmitted Infections

Sexually transmitted infections (STIs) were once referred to as venereal diseases (for Venus, the Roman goddess of love). Today the term *venereal disease* has been replaced by the broader term *sexually transmitted infection*. The current emphasis is on the successful prevention and treatment of STIs rather than on the ethics of sexuality (Figure 11–5).[45] The following points about STIs should be remembered: (1) more than one STI can exist in a person at a given point in time; (2) the symptoms of STIs can vary over time and from person to person; (3) little

Figure 11–5 Average number of sexual partners men and women have had since age 18. The fewer the number of partners you've had, the lower your risk of contracting HIV or an STI.

immunity is developed for STIs; and (4) STIs can predispose people to additional health problems, including infertility, birth defects in their children, cancer, and long-term disability. Additionally, the risk of HIV infection is higher when sexual partners are also infected with STIs.

This section focuses on the STIs most frequently diagnosed among post-secondary students (chlamydia, gonorrhea, human papillomavirus infection, herpes simplex, syphilis, and pubic lice). A short section follows, covering common vaginal infections, some of which may occur without sexual contact. Completing the Personal Assessment on p. 276 will help you determine your own risk of contracting an STI. Also, refer to the Changing for the Better box on p. 266 for safer sex practices.

Chlamydia (nonspecific urethritis)

Chlamydia is considered the most prevalent STI in Canada and the United States today and reported cases continue to rise. Chlamydia infections occur an estimated 5 times more frequently than gonorrhea and up to 10 times more frequently than syphilis. From January to June 2004, more than 29 000 cases of chlamydia were reported to Health Canada.[46]

Key Terms

sexually transmitted infections (STIs)
Infectious diseases that are spread primarily through intimate sexual contact.

chlamydia
The most prevalent sexually transmitted disease. Caused by a nongonococcal bacterium.

Because of the high prevalence of chlamydia in sexually active adolescents, they should be screened for chlamydia twice a year, even in the absence of symptoms. Because chlamydia frequently accompanies gonorrheal infections, a dual therapy is often appropriate when gonorrhea is found. Sexually active people in the 20- to 24-year age range should also be considered for routine screening, particularly if they have a history of multiple sex partners and have not practised a form of barrier contraception.[47]

Chlamydia trachomatis is the bacterial agent that causes the chlamydia infection. Chlamydia is the most common cause of nonspecific urethritis (NSU). NSU refers to infections of the **urethra** and surrounding tissues that are not caused by the bacterium responsible for gonorrhea. Only when a culture for suspected gonorrhea proves negative do clinicians diagnose NSU, usually by calling it *chlamydia*. About 80% of men with chlamydia describe gonorrhea-like signs and symptoms, including painful urination and a whitish pus discharge from the penis. As in gonorrheal infections and many other STDs, most women report no overt signs or symptoms. A few women might exhibit a mild urethral discharge, painful urination, and swelling of vulval tissues. Whereas oral forms of penicillin are used in the treatment of gonococcal infections, oral tetracycline or doxycycline is prescribed for chlamydia and other NSUs.

As with all STIs, both sexual partners should receive treatment to avoid the ping-pong effect: the back-and-forth reinfection that occurs among couples when only one partner receives treatment. Furthermore, as with other STIs, having chlamydia does not effectively confer immunity.

Unresolved chlamydia can lead to the same negative health consequences that result from untreated gonorrheal infections. In men the pathogens can invade and damage the deeper reproductive structures (prostate gland, seminal vesicles, and Cowper's glands). Sterility can result. The pathogens can spread further and produce joint problems (arthritis) and heart complications (damaged heart valves, blood vessels, and heart muscle tissue).

In women the pathogens enter the body through the urethra or the cervical area. If not properly treated, the invasion can reach the deeper pelvic structures, producing a syndrome called **pelvic inflammatory disease (PID)**. The inner uterine wall (endometrium), the fallopian tubes, and any surrounding structures may be attacked to produce this painful syndrome. A variety of further complications can result, including sterility and **peritonitis**. Infected women can transmit a chlamydia infection to the eyes and lungs of newborns during a vaginal birth. For both men and women the early detection of chlamydia and other NSUs is of paramount concern.

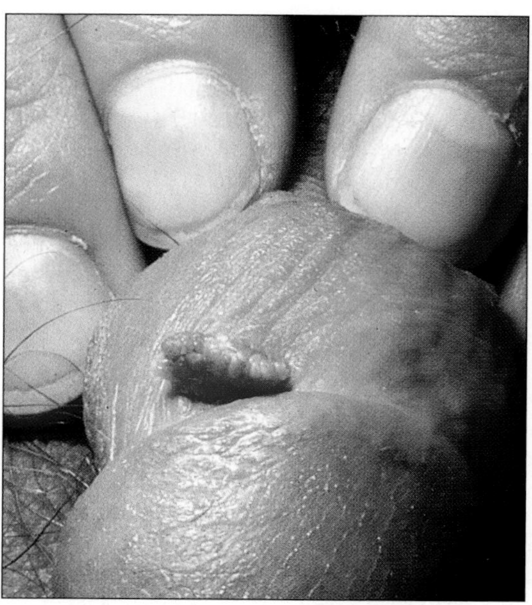

A human papillomavirus infection (genital warts).

Human papillomavirus

Human papillomavirus (HPV) infections are generally asymptomatic, and so the exact extent of the disease is unknown. A study of a group of sexually active college women found HPV infection in approximately 20% of the women. HPV-related changes to the cells of the cervix are found in nearly 5% of the Pap smears taken from women under age 30. It is currently believed that for women, risk factors for HPV infection include (1) sexual activity before age 20, (2) intercourse with three or more partners before age 35, and (3) intercourse with a partner who has had three or more partners.[48] The extent of HPV infection in men is even less clearly known, but it is likely widespread.

The concern about HPV infections is centred on the ability of some of the more than 50 forms of the virus to foster precancerous changes in the cervix. In addition, HPV is associated with the development of genital warts (condyloma acuminata). These pinkish-white lesions may be found in raised clusters that resemble tiny heads of cauliflower (see the photograph above). Found most commonly on the penis, scrotum, labia, cervix, and around the anus, genital warts are the most common symptomatic viral STI in this country. Although most genital wart colonies are small, they may become very large and block the anus or birth canal during pregnancy.

Treatment for HPV, including genital warts, may include burning, freezing, removal with a CO_2 laser, or the use of various medications. Regardless of treatment, however, return of the viral colonies will most likely occur. Condom use should be encouraged in an attempt to prevent transmission of HPV.

Changing *for the Better*

Talking with Your Partner about Herpes

My girlfriend told me she has herpes and said she's "taking care of everything." What can I do to get things out in the open?

Although herpes rarely has serious consequences, the lesions are infectious and tend to reappear. It is important to talk openly with your partner about this sexually transmitted disease. Here are some tips to make things easier:

- *Educate yourself.*
  Be aware that herpes is rarely dangerous.
  Learn when the disease is most contagious (during the eruption and blister stage), and that herpes can be spread even during the non-eruption, non-blister periods—traditionally defined as safe periods.
- *Choose the right time to talk.*
  Discuss herpes with your partner only after you have gotten to know each other.
- *Listen to your partner.*
  Be prepared to answer any questions that he or she may have.
- *Together, put things in perspective.*
  Keep a positive outlook.
  Remember that you are not alone.
  Be aware that using a condom and abstaining from coitus during the most infectious period can prevent transmission of the disease.
  Although there is no known cure, research continues on an antiviral drug.
  Join a local support group together.

Gonorrhea

Another extremely common STI, gonorrhea is caused by a bacterium (*Neisseria gonorrhoeae*). In men this bacterial agent can produce a milky-white discharge from the penis, accompanied by painful urination. About 80% of men who contract gonorrhea report varying degrees of these symptoms. This figure is approximately reversed for women: only about 20% of women are symptomatic and thus report varying degrees of frequent, painful urination, with a slimy yellow-green discharge from the vagina or urethra. Oral sex with an infected partner can produce a gonorrheal infection of the throat (pharyngeal gonorrhea). Gonorrhea can also be transmitted to the rectal areas of both men and women.[49] From January to June 2004, 4013 cases of gonorrhea were reported to Health Canada.[50] In light of the asymptomatic (showing no symptoms) nature of the disease in women, the roughly equal number of reported cases for men and women suggests a high level of self-referral by women, regular preventive reproductive health care by women, and cooperative case finding on the part of both men and women.

Diagnosis of gonorrhea is made by culturing the bacteria. Antibiotic treatment regimens include use of penicillin, tetracycline, ampicillin, or other drugs. Some strains of gonorrhea (penicillin-resistant strains) are much more difficult to treat than others.

Testing for gonorrhea is included as a part of prenatal care so that infections in mothers can be treated before birth. If the birth canal is infected, newborns can easily contract the infection in the mucous membranes of the eye.

Herpes simplex

Public health officials think that the sexually transmitted genital herpes virus infection rivals chlamydia as the most prevalent STI. Recent studies show that about 20% of the adult population is infected with genital herpes virus, although most people are asymptomatic for genital herpes.[51] Herpes is really a family of over 50 viruses, some of which produce recognized diseases in humans (chicken pox, **shingles**, mononucleosis, and others). One subgroup called *herpes simplex 1 virus* (HSV-1) produces an infection called *labial herpes* (oral or lip herpes). Labial herpes produces common fever blisters or cold sores seen around the lips and oral cavity. Herpes *simplex*

Key Terms

urethra (yoo REE thra)
Passageway through which urine leaves the urinary bladder

pelvic inflammatory disease (PID)
Acute or chronic infection of the peritoneum or lining of the abdominopelvic cavity; associated with a variety of symptoms and a potential cause of sterility.

peritonitis (pare it ton EYE tis)
Inflammation of the peritoneum or lining of the abdominopelvic cavity.

human papillomavirus (HPV)
Sexually transmitted virus capable of causing precancerous changes in the cervix; causative agent for genital warts.

shingles
Viral infection affecting the nerve endings of the skin.

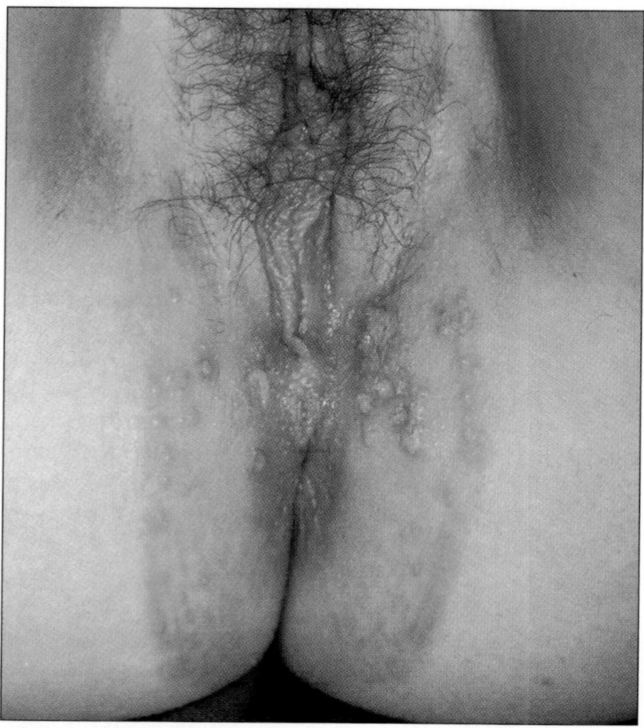

A severe herpes infection.

2 virus (HSV-2) is a different strain that produces similar clumps of blisterlike lesions in the genital region. Laypeople have referred to this second type of herpes as the STI type, although both types produce identical clinical pictures. Both forms can exist at either site. Oral-genital sexual practices have resulted in genital herpes cases now being caused by HSV-1.

Herpes appears as a single sore or as a small cluster of blisterlike sores (see the photograph above). These sores burn, itch, and (for some) become quite painful. The infected person might also report swollen lymph glands, muscular aches and pains, and fever. Some patients feel weak and sleepy when blisters are present. The lesions may last from a few days to a few weeks. A week is the average time for active viral shedding; then the blisters begin scabbing, and new skin is formed.

Herpes is an interesting virus for several reasons. It can lie dormant for extended periods. However, for reasons not well understood but perhaps related to stress, diet, or overall health, the viral particles can be stimulated to travel along the nerve pathways to the skin and then create an active infection. Thus herpes can be considered a recurrent infection. Fortunately for most people, recurrent infections are less severe than the initial episode and do not last as long. Herpes is also interesting because, unlike most STIs, no treatment method has been successful at killing the virus. Recommended treatment for an initial outbreak of herpes calls for the use of one of three medications. These medications are taken orally, multiple times each day, for 7 to 10 days. Since these medications only temporarily suppress the infection process, some clinicians choose to treat each recurrence, but others prefer to use medications on a continuing basis in an attempt to suppress recurrences.[52] There are also some medications that may provide symptomatic relief. Diagnosis of genital herpes is almost always made by a clinical examination.

The best prevention against ever getting a herpes infection is to avoid all direct contact with a person who has an active infection. Do not kiss someone with a fever blister—or let them kiss you (or your children) if they have an active lesion. Do not share drinking glasses or eating utensils. Check your partner's genitals. Do not have intimate sexual contact with someone who displays the blisterlike clusters or rash. (Condoms are only marginally helpful and cannot protect against lesions on the female vulva or the lower abdominal area of men). Be careful not to infect yourself by touching a blister and then touching any other part of your body. The Changing for the Better box on p. 269 provides helpful advice for talking to your partner if you have genital herpes.

Newborn babies are especially susceptible to the virus if they come into contact with an active lesion during the birth process. Newborns have not developed the defence capabilities to resist the invasion. They can quickly develop a systemic general infection (neonatal herpes) that is often fatal or local infections that produce permanent brain damage or blindness. Most of these possible problems can be prevented through proper prenatal care. If there is any chance that the viral particles may be present at birth, a cesarean delivery can be performed, although this is less commonly done today than in the past.

Syphilis

Like gonorrhea, syphilis is caused by a bacterium (*Treponema pallidum*) and is transmitted almost exclusively by sexual intercourse. The incidence of syphilis is far lower than gonorrhea. Only 598 cases were reported to Health Canada from January to June 2004.[53]

Unlike other STIs, syphilis is characterized by a progression through a series of stages that unfold over several decades. Following an incubation period of 10 to 90 days, the *primary stage* of syphilis is characterized by the formation of a small, raised, painless sore called a *chancre.* In 90% of women and 50% of men, this highly infectious lesion is not easily identified, and so treatment is generally not received. Even in the absence of treatment, however, the chancre will heal in four to five weeks, marking the end of this stage.

Following an asymptomatic period of several weeks, the *secondary stage* of the disease appears. In this extremely contagious stage, the bacteria have become systemically distributed and may result in a variety of symptoms, including a generalized body rash, a sore throat, bone and joint soreness, or a patchy loss of hair. A blood test (VDRL) will be positive, and treatment can be effectively administered. If the disease is untreated, this stage will subside within two to six weeks. It is during this stage that syphilis is easily transmitted by a pregnant woman to her fetus. Congenital syphilis often results in a stillbirth or an infant born with a variety of life-threatening complications. Early treatment of a pregnant women can prevent this.

After the secondary stage has subsided, an extended *latency period* develops, lasting from many months to many years. During this stage there are no visible signs of the illness, and infected persons are noninfectious because the bacteria have become sequestered, only to reappear many years later.

The *late stage* of syphilis generally occurs two or more decades following the initial infection. In this terminal stage of the disease, soft rubbery tumours can be found on the body, either in ulcerated or partially healed states. In addition to this skin damage, extensive damage to the brain, heart and circulatory system, and eyes has also occurred. At this stage, treatment is at best only partially effective and death generally ensues.

In all stages of the disease, including the latency period, treatment involves the use of antibiotics. When treatment is begun during the later stages of syphilis, damage being done to the body can be stopped, but any damage that has already occurred is unlikely to be reversed.

Pubic lice

Three types of lice infect humans: the head louse, the body louse, and the pubic louse all feed on the blood of the host. Except for the relatively uncommon body louse, these tiny insects do not carry diseases. They are, however, quite annoying.

Pubic lice, also called *crabs*, attach themselves to the base of the pubic hairs, where they live and attach their eggs (nits). These eggs move into a larval stage after one week; after two more weeks, they develop into mature adult crab lice.

People usually notice they have a pubic lice infestation when they are confronted with intense itching in the genital region. Both prescription and OTC creams, lotions, and shampoos are extremely effective in killing both the lice and their eggs.

Lice are not transmitted exclusively through sexual contact, but also by contact with bedsheets and clothes that may be contaminated. If you develop a pubic lice infestation, you will have to treat yourself, your clothes, your sheets, and your furniture.

Vaginal infections

Two common pathogens produce uncomfortable vaginal infections in women. The first is the yeast or fungus *Candida (Monilia) albicans*, often called thrush. This organism, commonly found in the vagina, seems to multiply rapidly when some unusual stressor (pregnancy, use of the birth control pill or antibiotics, diabetes) affects a woman's body. This infection, now called *vulvovaginal candidiasis (VVC)*,[54] is signaled by a white or cream-coloured vaginal discharge that resembles cottage cheese. Vaginal itching and vulvar swelling are also commonly reported. Current treatment is based on the use of one of several prescription and OTC drugs.

Nonprescription products offer effective home treatment. You should consult a physician before using these products for the first time. (Men rarely report this infection, although some may report mildly painful urination or a barely noticeable discharge at the urethral opening or beneath the foreskin of the penis.)

The protozoan *Trichomonas vaginalis* also produces a vaginal infection. This parasite can be transmitted through sexual intercourse or by contact with contaminated (often damp) objects, such as towels, or toilet seats, that may contain some vaginal discharge. In women, this infection, called *trichomoniasis*, or "trich," produces a foamy, yellow-green, foul-smelling discharge that may be accompanied by itching, swelling, and painful urination. Although topically applied treatments with limited effectiveness are available, only one highly effective oral medication is currently on the market.[55] Men infrequently contract trichomoniasis but may harbour the organisms without realizing it. They also should be treated to minimize reinfection of partners.

The vagina is warm, dark, and moist, an ideal breeding environment for a variety of organisms. Unfortunately, some commercial products seem to increase the incidence of vaginal infections. Among these are tight pantyhose (without cotton panels), which tend to increase the vaginal temperature, and commercial vaginal douches, which can alter the acidity of the vagina. Both of these products might promote infections. Women are advised to wipe from front to back after every bowel movement to reduce the opportunity of direct transmission of pathogenic agents from the rectum to the vagina. Although difficult to do in many cases, avoiding public restrooms is also a good practice. If you notice any unusual discharge from the vagina, you should report this to your physician.

Cystitis and urethritis

Cystitis, an infection of the urinary bladder, and *urethritis*, an infection of the urethra, occasionally can be caused by a sexually transmitted organism. Such infections can also be traced to the organisms that cause vaginitis and organisms found in the intestinal tract. A culture is required to identify the specific pathogen associated with a particular case of cystitis or urethritis. The symptoms are pain when urinating, the need to urinate frequently, a dull aching pain above the pubic bone, and the passing of blood-streaked urine.

Physicians can easily treat cystitis and urethritis with antibiotics when the specific organism has been identified. In fact, newer medications can be effective in a single dose.

If cystitis or urethritis is left untreated, the infectious agent could move upward in the urinary system and infect the ureters and kidneys. These upper urinary tract infections are more serious and require more extensive evaluation and aggressive treatment. Therefore, you should obtain medical care immediately if symptoms are noticed.

Preventing cystitis and urethritis depends partly on the source of the infectious agent. You can generally reduce the incidence of infection by urinating completely (to fully empty the bladder) and by drinking ample fluids to flush the urinary tract. It has also been recognized that compounds found in cranberry juice may be helpful in reducing urinary tract infections.[56]

Taking Charge of Your Health

- Since microorganisms develop resistance to antibiotics, continue taking all such medications until gone, even when the symptoms of the infection have subsided.
- Check your current immunization status to make sure you are protected against preventable infectious diseases.
- If you are a parent, take your children to receive their recommended immunizations as necessary.
- Because of the possibility of contracting HIV/AIDS and sexually transmitted infections, incorporate disease prevention into all your sexual activities.
- Use the Personal Assessment on p. 276 to determine your risk of contracting a sexually transmitted infection.
- If you have ever engaged in high-risk sexual behaviour, get tested for HIV.

SUMMARY

- Progress has been made in reducing the incidence of some forms of infectious disease, but other infectious conditions are becoming more prevalent.
- A variety of pathogenic agents are responsible for infectious conditions.
- A chain of infection with six links characterizes every infectious condition.
- Infectious conditions progress through five distinct stages.
- Immunity can be acquired through both natural and artificial means. Immunization should be received on a regularly scheduled basis.
- The immune system's response to infection relies on cellular and humoral elements.
- The common cold and influenza display many similar symptoms but differ in terms of infectious agents, incubation period, prevention, and treatment.
- Tuberculosis and pneumonia are potentially fatal infections of the respiratory system.
- Mononucleosis and chronic fatigue syndrome are infections that result in chronic tiredness.
- Fibromyalgia is a chronic condition that may be similar in some ways to chronic fatigue syndrome.
- Measles is a childhood infection that can be harmful when contracted during adulthood.
- Bacterial meningitis is of growing concern on university and college campuses.
- Hepatitis B (serum hepatitis) is a blood-borne infectious condition that can lead to serious liver damage. Hepatitis A, C, D, and E also exist.
- HIV/AIDS is a widespread, incurable viral disease transmitted through sexual activity, intravenous drug use, and the use of infected blood products; across the placenta during pregnancy; and in breast milk.
- The definitive definition of AIDS can be based on the presence of specific conditions or the diminished number of helper T cells.
- Effective treatment of HIV and AIDS is considerably improved but still not capable of resulting in a cure, and prevention through the use of an effective vaccine is nonexistent.
- A variety of sexually transmitted conditions exists, many of which do not produce symptoms in most infected women and many infected men.
- Safer sex practices can reduce the risk of contracting STIs.

REVIEW QUESTIONS

1. What are the agents responsible for the most familiar infectious conditions?
2. What are the six links that form the chain of infection?
3. What are the five stages that characterize the progression of infectious conditions?
4. What are the two principal components of the immune system, and how do they cooperate to protect the body from infectious agents and abnormal cells?
5. How are the common cold and influenza similar? How do they differ in terms of causative agents, incubation period, prevention, and treatment?
6. What symptoms make mononucleosis, chronic fatigue syndrome, and fibromyalgia similar? What aspects of each are different?
7. What is the relationship between bacterial meningitis and living patterns on campus?
8. How is hepatitis B transmitted? How do forms A, C, D, and E compare with hepatitis B?
9. How is HIV transmitted? To what extent is the treatment of HIV/AIDS effective? What is meant by the term *safer sex*?
10. What specific infectious diseases could be classified as being STIs?
11. Why are women more often asymptomatic for STIs than men?
12. To what extent and in what manner can STI transmission be prevented?

THINK ABOUT THIS ...

- How do you feel when a classmate or coworker comes to class or work ill? Is it fair to expose you to his or her illness?
- Which infectious disease have you had in the recent past? What impact did this infection have on your day-to-day activities?
- What diseases have you been immunized against?
- How do you feel about parents who do not have their children immunized?
- What would your initial reaction be if you found out that someone close to you had a sexually transmitted infection?

REFERENCES

1. Hamann B: *Disease: identification, prevention and control*, ed 2, 2001, McGraw-Hill.
2. Ibid.
3. Saladom KS: *Anatomy and physiology: unity of form and function*, 1998, McGraw-Hill.
4. Vander A, Sherman J, and Luciano D. *Human physiology: the mechanisms of body function*. McGraw-Hill, 2004.
5. Ibid.
6. Korbling M, Estrov Z, Champlin R. Adult stem cells and tissue repair. *Bone Marrow Transplant* 32 Suppl 1:S23–24, 2003.
7. Burt RK, Traynor AE. SLE—hematopoietic stem cell transplantation for systemic lupus erythematosus. *Arthritis Res Ther* 5(5):207–209, 2003.
8. Ooi J, et al. Unrelated cord blood transplantation for adult patients with de novo acute myeloid leukemia. *Blood* August 21, 2003 (Epub).
9. Latkovic MS. The morality of human embryonic stem cell research and President Bush's decision: how should Catholics think about such things? *Linacre Q* 69(4):289–315, 2002.
10. Gershon D. Complex political, ethical and legal issues surround research on human embryonic stem cells. *Nature* 422(6934):928–929, 2003.
11. Pauschinger M et al: Detection of adenoviral genome in the myocardium of adult patients with idiopathic left ventricular dysfunction, *JAMA* 99(10):1348–1354, 1999.
12. Prevention and control of influenza, recommendations of the Advisory Committee on Immunization Practices (ACIP). *MMWR* 52, RR-08, 2003.
13. Hayden FG et al: Use of the oral neuraminidase inhibitor oseltamivir in experimental human influenza: randomized controlled trials for prevention and treatment, *JAMA* 282(13):1240–1246, 1999.
14. Nichol KL et al: Effectiveness of live, attenuated intranasal influenza virus vaccine in healthy, working adults: a randomized controlled trial, *JAMA* 282(2):137–144, 1999.
15. Health Canada: **www.hc-sc.gc.ca/english/iyh/diseases/tuberculosis.html**
16. CBC News: New TB test could trounce disease, **www. cbc.ca /stories/2003/04/04/Consumers/TB_test_030404**, April 2003.
17. Ibid.
18. Mandell GL, Bennett JE, Dolin R: *Principles and practice of infectious disease*, ed 5, 1999, Churchill Livingstone.
19. Ibid.
20. Sisk JE, et al. Cost-effectiveness of vaccination against invasive pneumococcal disease among people 50

through 64 years of age: role of comorbid conditions and race. *Ann Intern Med* 1389(12):960–968, 2003.
21. National Institute of Allergy and Infectious Diseases (NIAID): *Chronic fatigue syndrome—etiological theories*, 1999. **www.niaid.nih.gov/publication/cfs/etio.htm**
22. *Fibromyalgia basics: symptoms, treatments and research*, 1999. **www.fmnetnews.com/pages/basic.html**
23. *Diagnostic criteria for fibromyalgia and CFS*, 1999. **www.fmnetnews.com/pages/criteria.html**
24. Wu J, Zou S, Giulivi A: Viral hepatitis and emerging bloodborne pathogens in Canada: hepatitis A and its control, *Canada Communicable Disease Report,* Vol 27S3 September 2001, Health Canada. **www.hc-sc.gc.ca/pphb-dgspsp/publicat/ccdr-rmtc/01vol27/27s3/27s3d_e.html**
25. Wu J, Zou S, Giulivi A: Viral hepatitis and emerging bloodborne pathogens in Canada: hepatitis B in Canada, *Canada Communicable Disease Report* Vol 27S3 September 2001, Health Canada. **www.hc-sc.gc.ca/pphb-dgspsp/publicat/ccdr-rmtc/01vol27/27s3/27s3e_e.html**
26. Health Canada: *It's your health: hepatitis C.* **www.hc-sc.gc.ca/english/iyh/diseases/hepc.html**
27. Health Canada: It's your health. Ottawa, Canada, 2004.
28. *WHO: SARS outbreak "over the peak" around the world, including China.* Intelihealth: *Health News* (The Associated Press), June 5, 2003.
29. Summary table of SARS cases by country, 1 November 2002–7 August 2003. World Health Organization. August 15, 2003. **www.who.int/entity/crs/sars/country/en/country2003_08_15.pdf**
30. Nowakowski J, et al. Long-term follow-up with culture-confirmed Lyme disease. *Am J Med* 115(2):91–96, 2003.
31. Hamann B. *Disease identification, prevention, and control*, ed. 2 McGraw-Hill, 2001.
32. Public Health Agency of Canada: *HIV and AIDS in Canada—surveillance report to December 31, 2004.* **www.phac-aspc.gc.ca/publicat/aids-sida/index.html**, April 2005.
33. Ibid.
34. Ibid.
35. Ogundele MO, Coulter JB. HIV transmission through breastfeeding: Problems and prevention. *AnnTrop Paediatr* 23(2):91–106, 2003.
36. Edwards S, Crane C. Oral sex and the transmission of viral STIs. *JAMA* 74(1):6–10, 1998.
37. Cox FD. *The aids booklet*, ed. 6 McGraw-Hill, 2000.
38. HIV/AIDS Surveillance Report.
39. UNAIDS and World Health Organization: *Global estimates for adults and children, end 2004.* **www.unaids.org/wad2004/EPIupdate2004_html_en/Epi04_13_en.htm**, October 17, 2005.
40. Hirsh, MS et al: *Antiretroviral drug resistance testing in adult HIV-1 infection: recommendations of an International AIDS society*—USA panel.
41. Gulick RM (Presentor). *Current status of new antiretroviral drugs in development*. Topics in HIV Medicine. International AIDS Society-USA. Washington, DC, May 2002.
42. Hui D. HIV protease inhibitors and atherosclerosis. *J Clin Invest* 111(3):317–318, 2003.
43. HIV gp120 vaccine—VaxGen: AIDSVAX, AIDSVAX B/B, AIDSVAX B/E, HIV gp120 vaccine—Genentech, HIV gp120 vaccine AIDSVAX—VaxGen, HIV vaccine AIDSVAX-VaxGen. Drug R.D. 4(4):249–243, 2003.
44. Global estimates of the HIV/AIDS epidemic, as of end 2002. December 2002. **www.avert.org/worldstats.htm**
45. Michael RT, Gagnon JH, Lauman EO, Kolata G: Sex in America: a definitive study, Warner, 1994.
46. Health Canada, Centre for Infectious Disease Prevention and Control: Reported cases and rates of notifiable STI from January 1 to June 30, 2004, **www.phac-aspc.gc.ca/std-mts/stdcases-casmts/index.html**, March 14, 2005.
47. Centers for Disease Control: Sexually transmitted diseases treatment guidelines 2002. *MMWRSI*: (No. RR-6), 2002
48. Hatcher R et al: *Contraceptive technology: 1998*, ed 17, 1998, Irvington.
49. Health Canada: *Reported gonorrhea cases and rates in Canada by age group and sex, 1980–2000*, STD Data Tables, Population and Public Health Branch. **www.hc-sc.gc.ca/pphb-dgspsp/std-mts/stddata0701/tab2-1_e.html**
50. Health Canada, Centre for Infectious Disease Prevention and Control: Reported cases and rates of notifiable STI from January 1 to June 30, 2004, **www.phac-aspc.gc.ca/std-mts/stdcases-casmts/index.html**, March 14, 2005.
51. Flemming DT et al: Herpes simplex virus type 2 in the United States, 1976–1994, *N Engl J Med* 337(16):1105–1111, 1997.
52. 1998 Guidelines for treatment of sexually transmitted diseases, *MMWR* (suppl) 1997 Jan; 47(RR-1):1–16.
53. Health Canada, Centre for Infectious Disease Prevention and Control: Reported cases and rates of notifiable STI from January 1 to June 30, 2004, **www.phac-aspc.gc.ca/std-mts/stdcases-casmts/index.html**, March 14, 2005.
54. 1998 Guidelines.
55. Ibid.
56. Howell AB et al: Inhibition of the adherence of P-fimbriated *Escherichia coli* to uroepithelial-cell surfaces by proanthocyanidin extracts from cranberries, *N Engl J Med* 339(15):1085–1086, 1998.

SUGGESTED READINGS

Farrell J: *Invisible enemies: stories of infectious disease*, 1998, Farrar, Straus & Giroux.

The book's author, Jeanette Farrell, literally tells the story of seven of the most important and interesting infectious diseases, including leprosy, the plague, cholera, and smallpox. Her narrative style carries the younger reader through the epidemiological backroads that lead to a fuller understanding of how these diseases were discovered, how they are treated, what is currently being learned about each one, and what the outcome of treatment is most likely to be. This book would be an excellent addition to the science education major's professional library.

Homes F et al: *Sexually transmitted diseases*, ed 3, 1999, McGraw-Hill.

This book is a valuable resource for people who need to know about STIs from the widest range of perspectives, including microbiological, clinical, legal, and social. It is intended for professionals who work in the fields of STI care and prevention, although it would be an equally good resource for students majoring in public health.

Marr L: *Sexually transmitted disease: a physician tells you what you need to know*, 1998, The Johns Hopkins University Press.

Here is a simple, understandable, and helpful source of information about the cause, treatment, and prevention of subsequent infections. It is presented by a physician who is experienced in the treatment of infectious conditions. The author addresses the many myths about STI transmission and treatment.

Turkington C: *Hepatitis C: the silent killer*. 1998, Contemporary Books.

The intended audience for this book is people who have recently been diagnosed with hepatitis C and their loved ones. The author clearly presents current information about the cause, treatment, and management of this viral infection of the liver.

Making Headlines

AIDS death hits Mandela family

Nelson Mandela, who has devoted much of his life after leaving South Africa's presidency to a campaign against AIDS, said Thursday that his 54-year old son Makgatho had died of the ailment in a Johannesburg clinic.

Makgatho L. Mandela had been seriously ill for more than a month, but the nature of his ailment had not been made public before his death Thursday morning. At a news conference a few hours later in Johannesburg, the elder Mandela, 86, said that he was revealing the cause of his son's death to focus more public attention on AIDS, which is still a taboo topic among many South Africans.

"I announce that my son has died of AIDS," he said. "Let us give publicity to HIV-AIDS and not hide it, because the only way to make it appear like a normal illness like TB, like cancer, is always to come out and say somebody has died because of HIV-AIDS, and people will stop regarding it as something extraordinary."

Mandela issued the statement surrounded by his family, including his daughter, Makaziwe, and his grandchildren.

Since leaving office, Mandela has been the country's most prominent voice calling for greater action against HIV, the disease that causes AIDS, and he has said that as president he failed to recognize the seriousness of the epidemic.

"I have been saying this for the past years even before I even suspected a member of my family has AIDS," he said Thursday.

The United Nations has estimated that about five million South Africans, including more than one in five adults, have AIDS or have been infected with HIV. But families usually attribute deaths from the disease to other causes.

Mandela challenged that practice on a number of fronts, suggesting that openess is actually the way to greater dignity.

Makgatho Mandela was Mandela's only surviving son; another son died in an auto accident in 1969, shortly after Mandela began 27 years of imprisonment as punishment for anti-apartheid activities.

Makgotho Mandela and his sister, Makaziwe, were the only surviving children of Nelson Mandela's first marriage, to Evelyn Mase, who died last May at 82.

Makgotha Mandela worked as an insurance underwriter before earning a law degree in 1997 and being admitted to the South African bar in 2000 and becoming counsel to a major bank. He also was an executive of a South African health-care company.

Makgatho Mandela's wife Zondi died of pneumonia in 2003 at age 46. He is survived by three daughters.

Source: Wines, M: AIDS death hits Mandela family, *The Chronicle Herald*, January 7, 2005.

Name ______________________ **Date** __________

Personal Assessment

What Is Your Risk of Contracting a Sexually Transmitted Infection?

A variety of factors interact to determine your risk of contracting a sexually transmitted infection (STI). This inventory is intended to provide you with an estimate of your level of risk.

Circle the number of each row that best characterizes you. Enter that number on the line at the end of the row (points). After assigning yourself a number in each row, total the number appearing in the points column. Your total points will allow you to interpret your risk for contracting an STI.

						Points
Age						
1 0–9	3 10–14	4 15–19	5 20–29	3 30–34	2 35+	____
Sexual History						
0 Never engage in sex	1 One sex partner	2 More than one sex partner but never more than one at a time	4 Two to five sex partners	6 Five to ten sex partners	8 Ten or more sex partners	____
Sexual Attitudes						
0 Will not engage in nonmarital sex	1 Premarital sex is okay if it is with future spouse	8 Any kind of premarital sex is okay	1 Extramarital sex is not for me	7 Extramarital sex is okay	8 Believe in complete sexual freedom	____
Attitudes toward Contraception						
1 Would use condom to prevent pregnancy	1 Would use condom to prevent STIs	6 Would never use a condom	5 Would use the birth control pill	4 Would use other contraceptive measure	8 Would not use anything	____
Attitudes toward STI						
3 Am not sexually active so I do not worry	3 Would be able to talk about STI with my partner	4 Would check an infection to be sure	6 Would be afraid to check out an infection	6 Can't even talk about an infection	6 STIs are no problem—easily cured	____
					YOUR TOTAL POINTS	____

Interpretation

5–8 Your risk is well below average
9–13 Your risk is below average
14–17 Your risk is at or near average
18–21 Your risk is moderately high
22+ Your risk is high

To Carry This Further . . .

Having taken this Personal Assessment, were you surprised at your level of risk? What is the primary reason for this level? How concerned are you and your classmates and friends about contracting an STI?

Focus on

THE CHANGING PICTURE OF INFECTIOUS DISEASE

Just a generation ago, many scientists believed we were wiping out infectious disease. Armed with improved sanitation, better hygiene practices, antibiotics, and pesticides, humankind had malaria, cholera, and tuberculosis (TB) on the run and smallpox and polio well on the way to extinction. In fact, infectious diseases were in decline until 1980, but as we enter the next century, the tide is turning. Ebola, HIV, Marburg virus, Lassa fever, Legionnaires' disease, hantavirus, and hepatitis C are but a few of the more than 30 new pathogens researchers have identified in the last few decades.

Previously unknown microbes have been evolving for thousands of years in animals and insects. They become threatening to humans only when conditions are right for transmission of the diseases from animals, including insects, to us, through zoonosis.

Recent Global Epidemics

The Ebola virus struck in the African countries of Zaire and Sudan in 1976, and again in Sudan in 1979. In 1995 Ebola revisited Zaire, but in Gabon in 1996 it was recognized and stopped before it could take hold. In October 2000, Ebola reappeared in Uganda after not being reported in Africa for several years. The source of Ebola in nature is unclear. Monkeys do become infected but die quickly, as do humans. To be an effective reservoir or source of disease, an animal must be able to tolerate the disease organism and therefore remain active and alive for a longer time in which the virus can be spread. For example, monkeys may be the source of human immunodeficiency virus (HIV) because they harbour a similar virus, simian immunodeficiency virus (SIV), but don't become sick. Of course, HIV/AIDS is a dangerous virus, but Ebola is more infective and runs a shorter disease course. As one author put it, "Ebola does in ten days what it takes AIDS ten years to accomplish."[1] This is terrible for the nine out of ten people infected with Ebola who die in a matter of days, but ironically by making its victims so sick so quickly, Ebola limits its own spread. Being deathly ill limits the social interactions of carriers.

Many other diseases also pose threats.[2] After a heat wave in 1988, mosquitos carrying dengue (pronounced "ding-ee") spread through Mexico. In 1991 an epidemic of cholera in South America killed 5000 of the 500 000 people infected. A record year for infectious disease occurred in 1993, possibly set into effect by weather patterns associated with El Niño, which warmed the waters in the tropical Pacific. A year later, epidemic bubonic plague swept through India. In the summer of 1996, a dengue outbreak began in Latin America. By the time it ended, 140 000 people from Argentina to Texas had been infected, and 4000 of those infected had died.[3]

Occurrence of New Infectious Diseases in the United States and Elsewhere

As the 1996 dengue outbreak illustrates, infectious disease is not just a problem for developing countries. In 1989 an airborne strain of Ebola, which fortunately was not dangerous to humans, was brought to Virginia in Philippine crab-eating monkeys that were to be distributed to research labs across the United States.

Hantavirus became an American problem in 1993. Following an extremely rainy year that was good for vegetation, the rodent population exploded in the Four Corners area of New Mexico, Arizona, Colorado, and Utah. The rodent population spread hantavirus to 16 states. This virus killed half of the 94 people it infected.[4] More recently, the first case of hantavirus transmission between humans occurred in Argentina. Apparently eighteen people, including five physicians, contracted the disease after having contact with sick patients.

The 1994 earthquake in Southern California provided more evidence to support the theory that new infectious diseases can spread to humans during environmental disturbances. The earthquake exposed a soil fungus that infected 200 people and killed 3.

Today zoonosis-related infections seem even more common as the American public becomes increasingly familiar with conditions such as Lyme disease, West Nile virus infections, SARS, and Monkey Pox. Even more recently, potential zoonotic infectious agents have been identified, such as bacterial pathogens in fish raised through aquaculture (rainbow trout in Italy),[5] avian (bird) influenza in China,[6] and flying squirrel–associated typhus in this country.[7] Of course, the relationship of these latter infections to the greater North American public remains to be seen.

Leading the Fight for Public Health

The United States leads the international health community with its premier monitoring and response services provided by the Centers for Disease Control and Prevention (CDC).[8] Of course, international cooperation is vital, but we have seen why disease vigilance is in our own interest as well. To move from the reactive system now in place to a predictive one, some specific goals must be met.

A global network of epidemiological field stations should be established to detect and characterize outbreaks early, both in North America and abroad. Insect carriers of disease need to be managed in a variety of ways, including but not solely relying on pesticides. Further, insecticides and pesticides must be developed that are both effective and environmentally safe. Safe food and water must be made available to everyone, and new antibiotics and vaccines need to be developed. These goals are hard to achieve, particularly in the face of episodes of armed conflict within and between countries, growing religious intolerance that becomes transformed into national disputes, and a global economy that continues to separate the affluent developed countries from those far less developed and affluent.

Having entered a new millennium, Americans may encounter the threat of emerging diseases associated with biological weapons and regional armed conflict. This threat looms even larger when one realizes that some countries view these disease organisms as agents of war and are capable of using them as such. With about a dozen countries in possession or pursuit of biological weapons arsenals, the understanding of deadly pathogens becomes a matter of national security as well as global health. Interestingly in this regard, the principal reason that the United States military personnel gave in 2000 for not re-enlisting in the armed forces was their fear of receiving the required Anthrax vaccine developed for use by American forces in order to protect personnel from Anthrax-based biological warfare.

For Discussion ...

In your view, what is the most important step we can take to fight infectious disease? Do you think the United States does more than its share in monitoring these diseases? What kinds of precautions might prevent zoonosis infections from taking hold in North America? Do you know anyone who works in the public health field? If so, what does he or she do?

1. Monastersky R: Health in the hot zone. *Science News* 1996; 149(14):218–219.
2. Gubler DJ: Resurgent vector-borne diseases as a global health problem. *Emerg Infect Dis* 1998; 4(3):442–450.
3. Health in the hot zone.
4. Anon: Climate creates a hot zone. *Environment* 1996; 37(10):27.
5. Ghittino C, et al: Emerging pathologies in aquaculture: effects on production and food safety. *Vet Res Common.* 2003 Sep; 27 Suppl 1:471–479.
6. Sims LD, et al: Avian influenza in Hong Kong 1997–2002. *Avian Dis.* 2003; 47(3 Suppl):832–838.
7. Reynolds MG, et al: Flying squirrel-associated typhus, United States. *Emerg Infect Dis.* 2003 Oct; 9(10):1341–1343.
8. Preventing emerging infectious diseases: a strategy for the 21st century: overview of the updated plan. *MMWR* (suppl) 1998; 47(15):1–14.

InfoLinks

www.who.Int
www.cdc.gov/ncidod

Part Five

Chapter 12
Sexuality and Relationships

Chapter Objectives

After reading this chapter, you will be able to

- Explain the genetic basis and gonadal basis of sexuality.
- Describe the psychosocial basis of sexuality, including gender identity, gender preference, gender adoption, and initial adult gender identification.
- Define androgyny and discuss its role in our society.
- Explain the components of the male and female reproductive systems.
- Trace the menstrual cycle and identify the hormones that control the cycle.
- Identify the four stages of the human sexual response pattern.
- Discuss the refractory period and how it affects male sexual performance.
- Discuss the impact of aging on both male and female sexual performance.
- Define the three categories of sexual orientation.
- Identify and discuss a few of the various lifestyles and relationships presented in this chapter.

Online Learning Centre Resources
www.mcgrawhill.ca/college/hahn

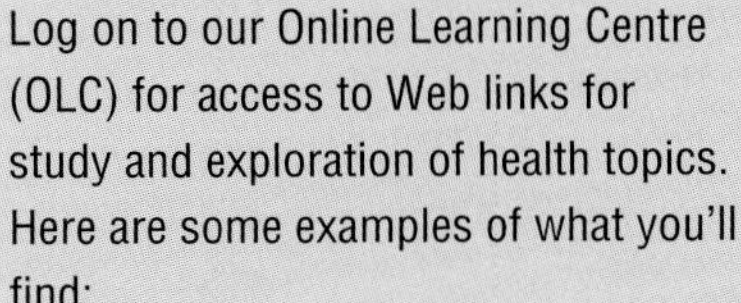

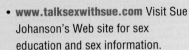

Log on to our Online Learning Centre (OLC) for access to Web links for study and exploration of health topics. Here are some examples of what you'll find:

- **www.indiana.edu/~kinsey** Study the findings of the Kinsey Institute for Research in Sex, Gender, and Reproduction.
- **www.positive.org/JustSayYes/contents.html** Take an online tour here, through the most important topics for teens who are sexually active or just thinking about it.
- **www.talksexwithsue.com** Visit Sue Johanson's Web site for sex education and sex information.
- **www.egale.ca** Advances equality and justice for lesbian, gay, and bisexual and transgendered people and their families in Canada.
- **www.pflag.ca** Parents, Families, and Friends of Lesbians and Gays.

Media Pulse
WTN's *Sunday Night Sex Show*

Where do many of today's young adults go for information about relationships and sex? Many young reviewers have been captivated by the one-hour show on WTN's television network called the *Sunday Night Sex Show*. This is a call-in program hosted by Sue Johanson, a straight-talking grandmother and registered nurse who has been talking to Canadians for close to 30 years.

The host takes calls from viewers that may involve any issue related to sex and relationships: sexual performance, sexually transmitted diseases, drugs and sex, dating, intimacy, starting and ending relationships, and sexual identity. No question is too bizarre or naive. She provides relevant, factual information in a clear, concise, nonjudgmental, and humorous way to help the callers.

The result is a show that provides generally excellent information about sex and relationships. However, the *Sunday Night Sex Show* is not for everyone. The show is geared toward young adults who have an interest in explicit topics. Sexually conservative viewers will probably quickly change the channel. Launched in 1995, *Sunday Night Sex Show* consistently draws a large audience of both women and men, proving that sex is as popular as ever.

Media Pulse *continued*

Call Sue toll free on Sunday nights between 11:00 PM and 12:00 AM ET at 1-888-393-TALK (8255) or for responses to questions you'd like to ask Sue, send a self-addressed, stamped envelope to: "Dear Sue" c/o *Sunday Night Sex Show*, 800-1255 Bay Street, Toronto, ON, M5R 2A9.

Currently, we have reached an understanding of both the biological and psychosocial factors that contribute to the complex expression of our **sexuality**. As a society, we are now inclined to view human behaviour in terms of a complex script written on the basis of both biology and conditioning. Reflecting this understanding is how we use the words "male" or "female" to refer to the biological roots of our sexuality and the words "man" or "woman" to refer to the psychosocial roots of our sexuality. This chapter explores human sexuality as it relates to the dynamic interplay of the biological and psychosocial bases that form your **masculinity** or **femininity**.

BIOLOGICAL BASES OF HUMAN SEXUALITY

Within a few seconds after the birth of a baby, someone—a doctor, nurse, or parent—emphatically labels the child: "It's a boy," or "It's a girl." For the parents and society as a whole, the child's **biological sexuality** is being displayed and identified. Another female or male enters the world.

Genetic Basis

At the moment of conception, a Y-bearing or an X-bearing sperm cell joins with the X-bearing ovum to establish the true basis of biological sexuality.[1] A fertilized ovum with sex chromosomes XX is biologically female, and a fertilized ovum bearing the XY sex chromosomes is biologically male. Genetics forms the most basic level of an individual's biological sexuality.

Gonadal Basis

The gonadal basis for biological sexuality refers to the growing embryo's development of **gonads**. Male embryos develop testes about the seventh week after conception, and female embryos develop ovaries about the twelfth week after conception.

Structural Development

The development of male or female reproductive structures is initially determined by the presence or absence of hormones produced by the developing testes—androgens and the müllerian inhibiting substance (MIS). With these hormones present, the male embryo starts to develop male reproductive structures (penis, scrotum, vas deferens, seminal vesicles, prostate gland, and Cowper's glands).

Because the female embryo is not exposed to these male hormones, it develops the characteristic female reproductive structures: the uterus, fallopian tubes, vagina, labia, and clitoris.

Biological Sexuality and the Childhood Years

The growth and development of the child in terms of reproductive organs and physiological processes have traditionally been thought to be "latent" during the childhood years. However, a gradual degree of growth occurs in both girls and boys. The reproductive organs, however, will undergo more greatly accelerated growth at the onset of **puberty** and will achieve their adult size and capabilities shortly.

Puberty

The entry into puberty is a gradual maturing process for young girls and boys. For young girls, the onset of menstruation, called **menarche**, usually occurs around age 13 but may come somewhat earlier or later.[2] Early menstrual cycles tend to be **anovulatory**. Menarche is usually preceded by a growth spurt that includes the budding of breasts and the growth of pubic and underarm hair.

Young males follow a similar pattern of maturation, including a growth spurt followed by a gradual sexual maturity. However, this process takes place about two years later than in young females. Genital enlargement, underarm and pubic hair growth, and a lowering of the voice commonly occur. The male's first ejaculation is generally experienced by the age of 14, most commonly through **nocturnal emission** or masturbation. For many young boys, fully mature sperm do not develop until about age 15.

Reproductive capability gradually declines over the course of the adult years. In the woman, however, the onset of **menopause** signals a more definite turning off of the reproductive system than is the case for the male adult. By the early to mid-50s, virtually all women have entered a postmenopausal period, but for men, relatively high-level **spermatogenesis** may continue for a decade or two.

The story of sexual maturation and reproductive maturity cannot, however, be solely focused on the changes that take place in the body. The psychosocial processes that accompany the biological changes are also important.

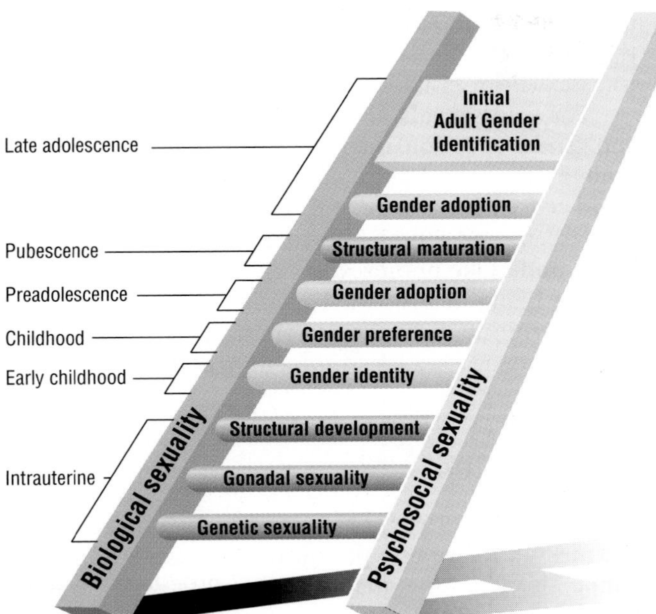

Figure 12–1 Our sexuality develops through biological and psychosocial stages.

PSYCHOSOCIAL BASES OF HUMAN SEXUALITY

If growth and development of our sexuality were to be visualized as a stepladder (Figure 12–1), one vertical rail of the ladder would represent our biological sexuality. The rungs would represent the sequential unfolding of the genetic, gonadal, and structural components.

Because humans, more than any other life form, can rise above a life centred on reproduction, a second dimension (or rail) to our sexuality exists—our **psychosocial sexuality**. The reason we possess the ability to be more than reproductive beings is a question for the theologian or philosopher. We are considerably more complex than the functions determined by biology. The process that transforms a male into a man and a female into a woman begins at birth and continues to influence us through the course of our lives.

Gender Identity

Although expectant parents may prefer to have a child of one **gender** over the other, they know that this matter is determined when the child is conceived. External genitals "cast the die," and femininity or masculinity is traditionally reinforced by the parents and society in general. By age 18 months, typical children have both the language and the insight to correctly identify their gender. They have established a **gender identity**.[3] The first rung rising from the psychosocial rail of the ladder has been climbed.

Gender Preference

During the preschool years, children receive the second component of the *scripting* required for the full development of psychosocial sexuality—the preference for the gender to which they have been assigned. The process through which **gender preference** is transmitted to the child is a less subtle form of the practices observed during the gender identity period (the first 18 months). Many parents begin to control the child's exposure to experiences traditionally reserved for children of the opposite gender. This is particularly true for boys; parents may stop play activities they perceive as being too feminine.

Key Terms

sexuality
The quality of being sexual; can be viewed from many biological and psychosocial perspectives.

masculinity
Behavioural expressions traditionally observed in males.

femininity
Behavioural expressions traditionally observed in females.

biological sexuality
Male and female aspects of sexuality.

gonads
Male or female sex glands; testes produce sperm and ovaries produce eggs.

puberty
Achievement of reproductive ability.

menarche (muh nar key)
Time of a female's first menstrual cycle.

anovulatory (an oh vyu luh tory)
Not ovulating.

nocturnal emission
Ejaculation that occurs during sleep; "wet dream."

menopause
Decline and eventual cessation of hormone production by the female reproductive system.

spermatogenesis (sper mat oh jen uh sis)
Process of sperm production.

psychosocial sexuality
Masculine and feminine aspects of sexuality.

gender
General term reflecting a biological basis of sexuality; the male gender or the female gender.

gender identity
Recognition of one's gender.

gender preference
Emotional and intellectual acceptance of one's own gender.

With the increasing importance of competitive sports for women, many of the skills and experiences once reserved for boys are now being fostered in young girls. What effect, if any, this movement will have on the speed at which gender preference is reached is a topic for further research.*

Gender Adoption

The process of reaching an initial adult gender identification requires a considerable period of time. The specific knowledge, attitudes, and behaviour characteristic of adults must be observed, analyzed, and practised. The process of acquiring and personalizing these "insights" about how men and women think, feel, and act is reflected by the term **gender adoption**, the first and third rungs below the initial adult gender identification rail of the ladder in Figure 12–1.

In addition to developing a personalized version of an adult sexual identity, it is important that the child—and particularly the adolescent—construct a *gender schema* for a member of the opposite gender. Clearly, the world of adulthood, involving intimacy, parenting, and employment, will require that men know women and women know men. Gender adoption provides an opportunity to begin to assemble this equally valuable "picture" of what the other gender is like.

Initial Adult Gender Identification

By the time young people have climbed all of the rungs of the sexuality ladder, they have arrived at the chronological point in the life cycle when they need to construct an initial adult **gender identification**. You might notice that this label seems similar to the terminology used to describe one of the developmental tasks being used in this textbook. In fact, the task of forming an initial adult identity is closely related to developing an initial adult image of oneself as a man or a woman. Although most of us currently support the concept of "person" in many gender-neutral contexts (for some very valid reasons), we still must identify ourselves as either a man or a woman.

Transsexualism

Students are often intrigued by a sexual variance that is first noticed during one or two of the psychosocial stages just discussed. Transsexualism is a sexual variance of the most profound nature because it represents a complete rejection by an individual of his or her biological sexuality. The male transsexual believes that he is female and thus desires to be the woman that he knows he is. The female transsexual believes that she is male and wants to become the man that she knows she should be. Psychiatrists, sex therapists, and transsexuals do not view transsexualism as a homosexual orientation.

For transsexuals, the periods of gender preference and gender adoption are perplexing as they attempt, with limited success, to resolve the conflict between what their mind tells them is true and what their body displays. Adolescent and young adult transsexuals often cross-dress, undertake homosexual relationships (which they view as being heterosexual relationships), experiment with hormone replacement therapy, and sometimes actively pursue a **sex reassignment operation**.

ANDROGYNY: SHARING THE PLUSES

Over the last 25 years our society has increasingly accepted an image of a person who possesses both masculine and feminine qualities. This accepted image has taken years to develop because our society traditionally has reinforced rigid masculine roles for men and rigid feminine roles for women.

In the past, from the time a child was born, we assigned and reinforced only those roles and traits that were thought to be directly related to his or her biological gender. Boys were not allowed to cry, play with dolls, or help in the kitchen. Girls were not encouraged to become involved in sports; they were told to learn to sew, cook, and babysit. Men were encouraged to be strong, expressive, dominant, aggressive, and career oriented, and women were encouraged to be weak, shy, submissive, passive, and home oriented.

These traditional biases have resulted in some interesting phenomena related to career opportunities. Women were denied jobs requiring above-average physical strength; admittance into professional schools requiring high intellectual capacities, such as law, medicine, and business; and entry into most levels of military participation. Likewise, men were not encouraged to enter traditionally feminine careers, such as nursing, clerical work, and elementary school teaching.

For a variety of reasons, the traditional picture has changed. **Androgyny**, or the blending of both feminine and masculine qualities, is more clearly evident in our society now than ever before. Today it is more acceptable to see men involved in raising children (including changing diapers) and doing routine housework. It is also more acceptable to see women entering the workplace in jobs traditionally managed by men and participating in sports traditionally played by men. Men are not scoffed at when they are seen crying after a touching movie. Women are not laughed at when they choose to assert themselves. The disposal of numerous sexual stereotypes has probably benefited our society immensely by relieving

*If you want to test the existence of gender preference, ask a group of first- or second-grade boys or girls if they would be happier being a member of the opposite gender. Be prepared for some frank replies.

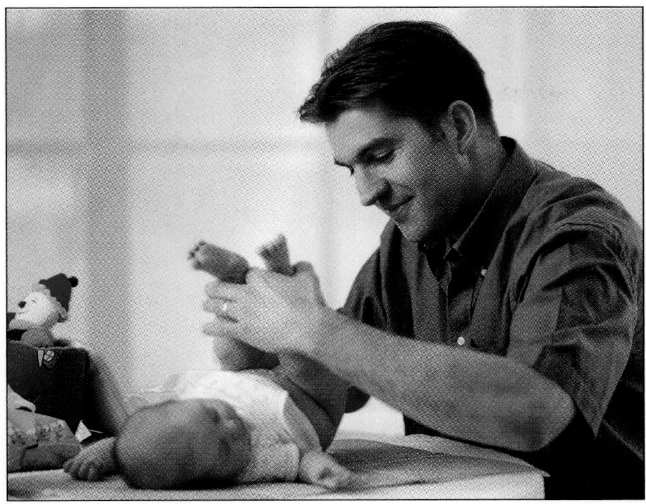

Just as women have broken into traditionally male careers, many men have taken on jobs and tasks that were once considered women's exclusive domain.

people of the pressure to be 100% "womanly" or 100% "macho."

Research data suggest that androgynous people are more flexible, have greater self-esteem, and show more social skills and motivation to achieve.[4] This should encourage you to be unafraid to break the gender role stereotype.

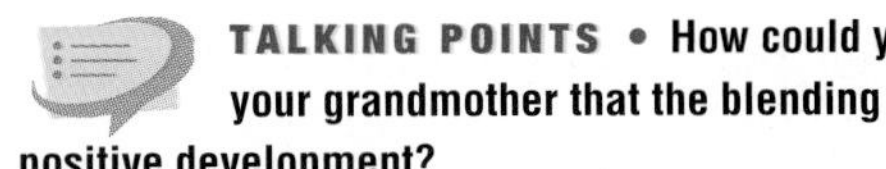

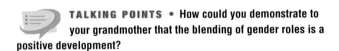

TALKING POINTS • How could you demonstrate to your grandmother that the blending of gender roles is a positive development?

REPRODUCTIVE SYSTEMS

The most familiar aspects of biological sexuality are the structures that compose the reproductive systems. Each structure contributes to the reproductive process in unique ways. Thus, with these structures, males have the ability to impregnate. Females have the ability to become pregnant, give birth, and nourish infants through breastfeeding. Many of these structures are also associated with nonreproductive sexual behaviour.

Male Reproductive System

The male reproductive system consists of external structures of genitals (the penis and scrotum) and internal structures (the testes, various passageways or ducts, seminal vesicles, the prostate gland, and the Cowper's glands) (Figure 12–2, *A*). The *testes* (also called *gonads* or *testicles*) are two egg-shaped bodies that lie within a saclike structure called the *scrotum*. During most of the fetal development, the testes lie within the abdominal cavity. They descend into the scrotum during the last two months of fetal life. The testes are housed in the scrotum because a temperature lower than the body core temperature is required for adequate sperm development. The walls of the scrotum are composed of contractile tissue and can draw the testes closer to the body during cold temperatures (and sexual arousal) and relax during warm temperatures. Scrotal contraction and relaxation allow a constant, productive temperature to be maintained in the testes.

Each testis contains an intricate network of structures called *seminiferous tubules* (Figure 12–2, *B*). Within these 300 or so seminiferous tubules, the process of sperm production (spermatogenesis) takes place. Sperm cell development starts at about age 11 in boys and is influenced by the release of the hormone **ICSH (interstitial cell-stimulating hormone)** from the pituitary gland. ICSH does primarily what its name suggests: it stimulates specific cells (called *interstitial cells*) within the testes to begin producing the male sex hormone *testosterone*. Testosterone in turn is primarily responsible for the gradual development of the male secondary sex characteristics at the onset of puberty. By the time a boy is approximately 15 years old, sufficient levels of testosterone exist so that the testes become capable of full spermatogenesis.

Before the age of about 15, most of the sperm cells produced in the testes are incapable of fertilization. The production of fully mature sperm (*spermatozoa*) is triggered by another hormone secreted by the brain's pituitary gland—**FSH (follicle-stimulating hormone)**.

Key Terms

gender adoption
Lengthy process of learning the behaviour that is traditional for one's gender.

gender identification
Achievement of a personally satisfying interpretation of one's masculinity or femininity.

sex reassignment operation
Surgical procedure designed to remove the external genitalia and replace them with genitalia appropriate to the opposite gender.

androgyny (an DROJ en ee)
The blending of both masculine and feminine qualities.

ICSH (interstitial [in ter stish ul] cell-stimulating hormone)
A gonadotropic hormone of the male required for the production of testosterone.

FSH (follicle-stimulating hormone)
A gonadotropic hormone required for initial development of ova (in the female) and sperm (in the male).

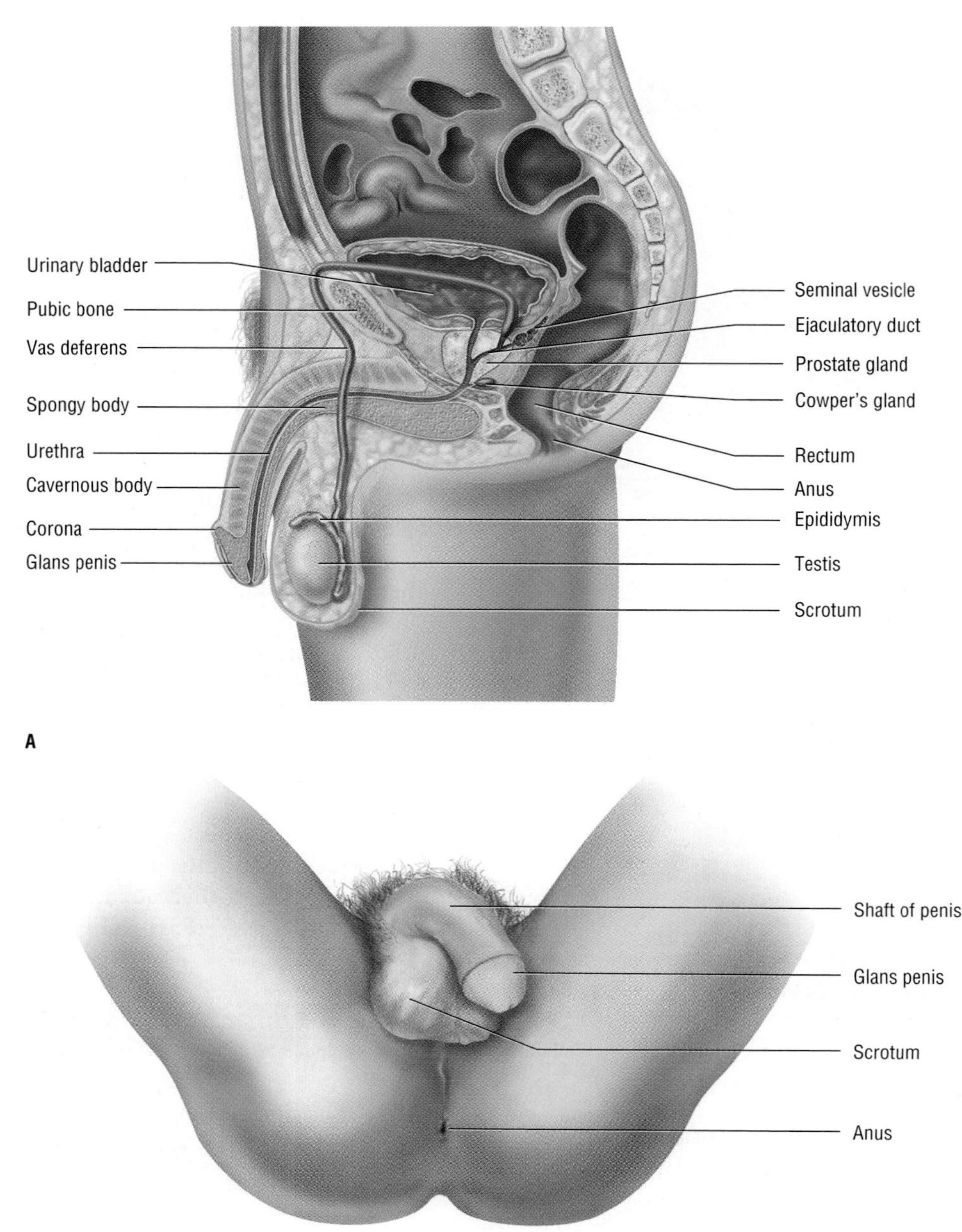

Figure 12–2 The male reproductive system. **A**, Side view, **B**, Front view.

FSH influences the seminiferous tubules to begin producing spermatozoa that are capable of fertilization.

Spermatogenesis takes place around the clock, with hundreds of millions of sperm cells produced daily. The sperm cells do not stay in the seminiferous tubules but rather are transferred through a system of ducts that lead into the *epididymis*. The epididymis is a tubular coil that attaches to the back side of each testicle. These collecting structures house the maturing sperm cells for two to three weeks. During this period the sperm finally become capable of motion, but they remain inactive until they mix with the secretions from the accessory glands (the seminal vesicles, prostate gland, and Cowper's glands).

Each epididymis leads into an 18-inch passageway known as the *vas deferens* (plural: *vasa deferentia*). Sperm, moved along by the action of hairlike projections called *cilia*, can also remain in the vas deferens for an extended time without losing their ability to fertilize an egg.

Each vas deferens extends into the abdominal cavity, where it meets with a *seminal vesicle*—the first of the three accessory structures or glands. Each seminal vesicle contributes a clear, alkaline fluid that nourishes the

Health on the Web

Behaviour Change Activities

Rate Your Relationship

Our relationships with others are an essential aspect of our health. Relationships offer us the opportunity to fulfill our need both to love and to be loved. Go to **www.psychtests.com** and complete the Relationship Satisfaction Test. This inventory is designed to evaluate various aspects of your interaction with another person, rather than to impart value judgments about how a relationship is supposed to work. Complete the inventory, then click on the "submit" button to view your results. Any surprises?

sperm cells with fructose and permits the sperm cells to be suspended in a movable medium. The fusion of a vas deferens with the seminal vesicle results in the formation of a passageway called the *ejaculatory duct*. Each ejaculatory duct is only about 2 cm long and empties into the final passageway for the sperm—the urethra.

This juncture takes place in an area surrounded by the second accessory gland—the *prostate gland*. The prostate gland secretes a milky fluid containing a variety of substances, including proteins, cholesterol, citric acid, calcium, buffering salts, and various enzymes. The prostate secretions further nourish the sperm cells and also raise the pH level, making the mixture quite alkaline. This alkalinity permits the sperm to have greater longevity as they are transported during ejaculation through the urethra, out of the penis, and into the highly acidic vagina.

The third accessory glands, the Cowper's glands, serve primarily to lubricate the urethra with a clear, viscous mucus. These paired glands empty their small amounts of pre-ejaculatory fluid during the plateau stage (the state of arousal immediately before orgasm) of the sexual response cycle. Alkaline in nature, this fluid also neutralizes the acidic level of the urethra. It is hypothesized that viable sperm cells can be suspended in this fluid and can enter the female reproductive tract before full ejaculation by the male.[5] This may account for many of the failures of the "withdrawal" method of contraception.

The sperm cells, when combined with secretions from the seminal vesicles and the prostate gland, form a sticky substance called **semen**. Interestingly, the microscopic sperm actually makes up less than 5% of the seminal fluid discharged at ejaculation. The paired seminal vesicles contribute about 60% of the semen volume, and the prostate gland adds about 30%.[6] Thus the fear of some men that a **vasectomy** will destroy their ability to ejaculate is completely unfounded (see Chapter 13).

During *emission* (the gathering of semen in the upper part of the urethra), a sphincter muscle at the base of the bladder contracts and inhibits semen from being pushed into the bladder and urine from being deposited into the urethra.[7] Thus semen and urine rarely intermingle, even though they leave the body through the same passageway.

Ejaculation takes place when the semen is forced out of the penis through the urethral opening. The involuntary, rhythmic muscle contractions that control ejaculation result in a series of pleasurable sensations known as *orgasm*.

The urethra lies on the underside of the penis and extends through one of three cylindrical chambers of erectile tissue (two cavernous bodies and one spongy body). Each of these three chambers provides the vascular space required for sufficient erection of the penis. When a male becomes sexually aroused, these areas become congested with blood (*vasocongestion*). After ejaculation or when a male is no longer sexually stimulated, these chambers release the blood into the general circulation and the penis returns to a **flaccid** state.

The *shaft* of the penis is covered by a thin layer of skin that is an extension of the skin that covers the scrotum. This loose layer of skin is sensitive to sexual stimulation and extends over the head of the penis, except in males who have been circumcised. The *glans* (or head) of the penis is the most sexually sensitive (to tactile stimulation) part of the male body. Nerve receptor sites are especially prominent along the *corona* (the ridge of the glans) and the *frenulum* (the thin tissue at the base of the glans).

Female Reproductive System

The external structures (genitals) of the female reproductive system consist of the mons pubis, labia majora, labia minora, clitoris, and vestibule (Figure 12–3). Collectively these structures form the *vulva* or vulval area. The *mons pubis* is the fatty covering over the pubic bone.

Key Terms

semen
Secretion containing sperm and nutrients discharged from the urethra at ejaculation.

vasectomy
Surgical procedure in which the vasa deferentia are cut to prevent the passage of sperm from the testicles; the most common form of male sterilization.

flaccid (fla sid)
Nonerect; the state of erectile tissue when vasocongestion is not occurring.

The mons pubis (or mons veneris, "mound of Venus") is covered by pubic hair and is quite sensitive to sexual stimulation. The *labia majora* are large longitudinal folds of skin that cover the entrance to the vagina, whereas the *labia minora* are the smaller longitudinal skin folds that lie within the labia majora. These hairless skin folds of the labia minora join at the top to form the *prepuce*. The prepuce covers the glans of the *clitoris*, which is the most sexually sensitive part of the female body.

A rather direct analogy can be made between the penis and the clitoris. In terms of the tactile sensitivity, both structures are the most sensitive parts of the male and female genitals. Both contain a glans and a shaft (although the clitoral shaft is beneath the skin surface). Both organs are composed of erectile tissue that can become engorged with blood. Both are covered by skin folds (the clitoral prepuce of the female and the foreskin of the male), and both structures can collect **smegma** beneath these tissue folds.[8]

The *vestibule* is the region enclosed by the labia minora. Evident here are the urethral opening and the entrance to the vagina (or vaginal orifice). Also located at the vaginal opening are the *Bartholin's glands*, which secrete a minute amount of lubricating fluid during sexual excitement.

The *hymen* is a thin layer of tissue that stretches across the opening of the vagina. Once thought to be the only indication of virginity, the intact hymen rarely covers the vaginal opening entirely. Openings in the hymen are necessary for the discharge of menstrual fluid and vaginal secretions. Many hymens are stretched or torn to full opening by adolescent physical activity or by the insertion of tampons. In women whose hymens are not fully ruptured, the first act of sexual intercourse will generally accomplish this. Pain may accompany first intercourse in females with relatively intact hymens.

The internal reproductive structures of the female include the vagina, uterus, fallopian tubes, and ovaries. The *vagina* is the structure that accepts the penis during sexual intercourse. Normally the walls of the vagina are collapsed, except during sexual stimulation, when the vaginal walls widen and elongate to accommodate the erect penis. Only the outer third of the vagina is especially sensitive to sexual stimulation. In this location, vaginal tissues swell considerably to form the **orgasmic platform**. This platform constricts the vaginal opening and in effect "grips" the penis (or other inserted object)—regardless of its size.[9] So the belief that a woman receives considerably more sexual pleasure from men with large penises is not supported from an anatomical standpoint.

The *uterus* (or *womb*) is approximately the size and shape of a small pear. This highly muscular organ is capable of undergoing a wide range of physical changes, as evidenced by its enlargement during pregnancy, its contraction during menstruation and labour, and its movement during the orgasmic phase of the female sexual response cycle. The primary function of the uterus is to provide a suitable environment for the possible implantation of a fertilized ovum, or egg. This implantation, should it occur, will take place in the innermost lining of the uterus—the *endometrium*. In the mature female, the endometrium undergoes cyclic changes as it prepares a new lining on a near-monthly basis.

The lower third of the uterus is called the *cervix*. The cervix extends slightly into the vagina. Sperm can enter the uterus through the cervical opening, or *cervical os*. Mucous glands in the cervix secrete a fluid that is the consistency of egg white near the time of ovulation. Mucus of this consistency apparently facilitates sperm passage into the uterus and deeper structures. However, cervical mucus is much thicker during certain points in the menstrual cycle (when pregnancy is improbable) and during pregnancy (to protect against bacterial agents and other substances that are especially dangerous to the developing fetus).

The upper two-thirds of the uterus is called the *corpus*, or *body*. This is where implantation of the fertilized ovum generally takes place. The upper portion of the uterus opens into two *fallopian tubes*, or *oviducts*, each about 10 cm long. The fallopian tubes are each directed toward an *ovary*. They serve as a passageway for the ovum in its week-long voyage toward the uterus. Usually, conception takes place in the upper third of the fallopian tubes.

The ovaries are analogous to the testes in the male. Their function is to produce the ovum, or egg. Usually, one ovary produces and releases just one egg each month. Approximately the size and shape of an unshelled almond, an ovary produces viable ova in the process known as *oogenesis*. The ovaries also produce the female sex hormones through the efforts of specific structures within the ovaries. These hormones play multiple roles in the development of female secondary sex characteristics, but their primary function is to prepare the endometrium of the uterus for possible implantation of a fertilized ovum. In the average healthy female, this preparation takes place about 13 times a year for a period of about 35 years. At menopause, the ovaries shrink considerably and stop nearly all hormonal production.

Menstrual cycle

Each month or so, the inner wall of the uterus prepares for a possible pregnancy. When a pregnancy does not occur (as is the case throughout most months of a woman's fertile years), this lining must be released and a new one prepared. The breakdown of this endometrial wall and the resultant discharge of blood and endometrial tissue is known as *menstruation* (or *menses*) (Figure

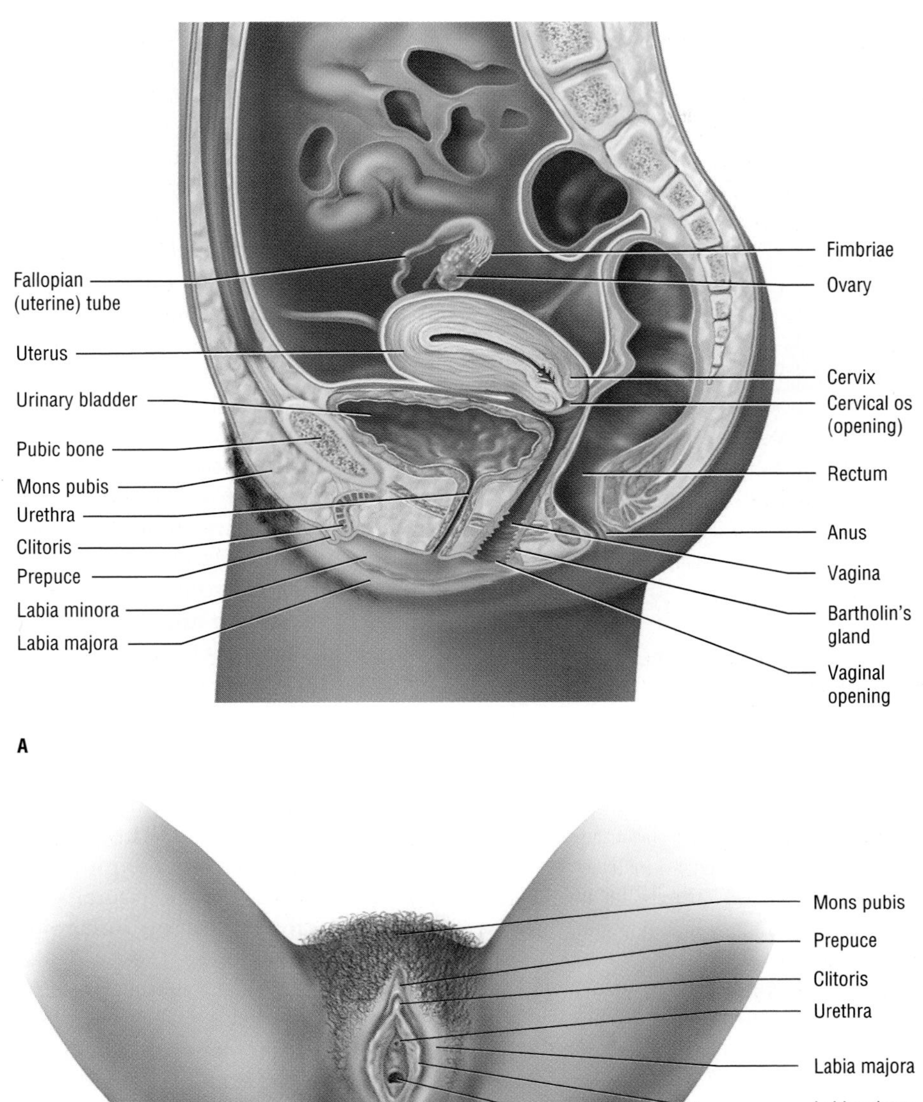

Figure 12–3 The female reproductive system. **A**, Side view, **B**, Front view.

12–4). The cyclic timing of menstruation is governed by hormones released from two sources: the pituitary gland and the ovaries.

Girls generally have their first menstrual cycle, the onset of which is called *menarche*, sometime between 12 and 14 years of age. Body weight, nutrition, heredity, and overall health are factors related to menarche. After a girl first menstruates, she may be anovulatory for a year or

Key Terms

smegma
Cellular discharge that can accumulate beneath the clitoral hood and the foreskin of an uncircumcised penis.

orgasmic platform
Expanded outer third of the vagina that grips the penis during the plateau phase of the sexual response pattern.

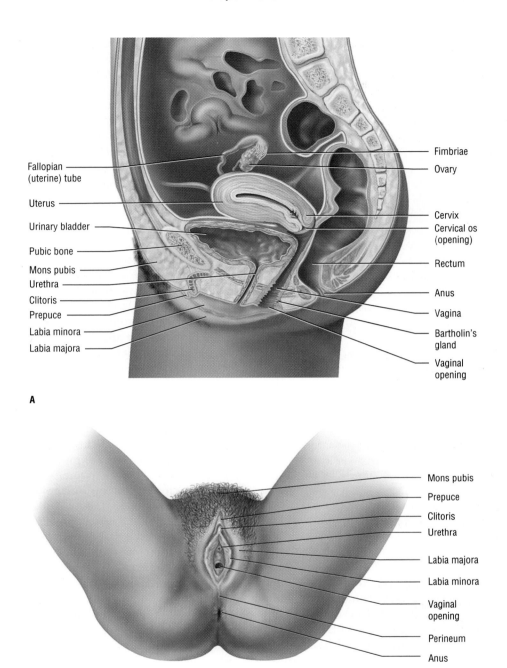

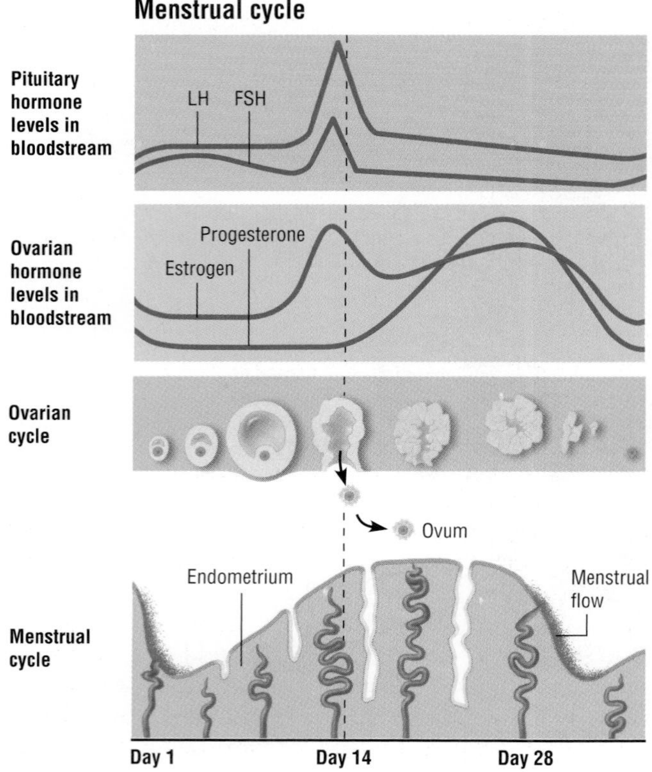

Figure 12–4 The menstrual cycle involves the development and release of an ovum, supported by hormones from the pituitary, and the buildup of the endometrium, supported by hormones from the ovary, for the purpose of establishing a pregnancy.

longer before a viable ovum is released during her cycle. This cyclic activity will continue until about age 45 to 55.

This text refers to a menstrual cycle that lasts 28 days. However, few women display perfect 28-day cycles. Most women fluctuate by a few days to a week around this 28-day pattern, and some women vary greatly from this cycle.

Your knowledge about the menstrual cycle is critical for your understanding of pregnancy, contraception, menopause, and issues related to the overall health and comfort of women (see the Star Box on p. 289 for a discussion of endometriosis). Although at first this cycle may sound like a complicated process, each segment of the cycle can be studied separately for better understanding.

The menstrual cycle can be thought of as occurring in three segments or phases: the menstrual phase (lasting about one week), the proliferative phase (also lasting about one week), and the secretory phase (lasting about two weeks). Day 1 of this cycle starts with the first day of bleeding, or menstrual flow.

The *menstrual phase* signals the woman that a pregnancy has not taken place and that her uterine lining is being sloughed off. During a five- to seven-day period, a woman will discharge about ¼ to ½ cup of blood and tissue. (Only about 30 mm or 1 oz of the menstrual flow is actual blood.) The menstrual flow is heaviest during the first days of this phase. Since the muscular uterus must contract to accomplish this tissue removal, some women have uncomfortable cramping during menstruation. Most women, however, report more pain and discomfort during the few days before the first day of bleeding. (See the discussion of premenstrual syndrome [PMS] on p. 289.)

Modern methods of absorbing menstrual flow include the use of internal tampons and external pads. Caution must be exercised by the users of tampons to prevent the possibility of toxic shock syndrome (TSS) (see Chapter 11). Since menstrual flow is a positive sign of good health, women are encouraged to be normally active during menstruation.

The *proliferative phase* or preovulation phase of the menstrual cycle starts about the time menstruation stops. Lasting about one week, this phase is first influenced by the release of FSH from the pituitary gland. FSH circulates in the bloodstream and directs the ovaries to start the process of maturing approximately 20 primary ovarian *follicles*. Thousands of primary egg follicles are present in each ovary at birth. These follicles resemble shells that house immature ova. As these follicles ripen under FSH influence, they release the hormone estrogen. Estrogen's primary function is to direct the endometrium to start the development of a thick, highly vascular wall. As the estrogen levels increase, the pituitary gland's secretion of FSH is reduced. Now the pituitary gland prepares for the surge of the **luteinizing hormone (LH)** required to accomplish ovulation.[10]

In the days immediately preceding ovulation, one of the primary follicles (called the *graafian follicle*) matures fully. The other primary follicles degenerate and are absorbed by the body. The graafian follicle moves toward the surface of the ovary. When LH is released in massive quantities on about day 14, the graafian follicle bursts to release the fully mature ovum. The release of the ovum is **ovulation**. Regardless of the overall length of a woman's cycle, ovulation occurs 14 days before her first day of menstrual flow.

The ovum is quickly captured by the fingerlike projections (*fimbriae*) of the fallopian tubes. In the upper third of the fallopian tubes, the ovum is capable of being fertilized in a 24- to 36-hour period. If the ovum is not fertilized by a sperm cell, it will begin to degenerate and eventually will be absorbed by the body.

After ovulation, the *secretory phase* or postovulation phase of the menstrual cycle starts when the remnants of the graafian follicle restructure themselves into a **corpus luteum**. The corpus luteum remains inside the ovary, secreting estrogen and a fourth hormone called *progesterone*. Progesterone, which literally means "for pregnancy," continues to direct the endometrial buildup. If pregnancy

Endometriosis

Endometriosis is a condition in which endometrial tissue that normally lines the uterus is found growing within the pelvic cavity. Because the tissue remains sensitive to circulating hormones, it is the source of pain and discomfort during the latter half of the menstrual cycle. Endometriosis is most commonly found in younger women and is sometimes related to infertility in women with severe cases.

In addition to painful cramping before and during menstruation, the symptoms of endometriosis include low back pain, pain during intercourse, painful bowel movements, heavy menstrual flow, and difficulty becoming pregnant.

Treatment of endometriosis largely depends on its extent. Drugs to suppress ovulation, including birth control pills, may be helpful in mild cases. For more severe cases, surgical removal of the tissue or a hysterectomy may be necessary. For some women, endometriosis is suppressed during pregnancy and does not return after pregnancy.[11]

occurs, the corpus luteum monitors progesterone and estrogen levels throughout the pregnancy. If pregnancy does not occur, high levels of progesterone signal the pituitary gland to stop the release of LH and the corpus luteum starts to degenerate on about day 24. When estrogen and progesterone levels diminish significantly by day 28, the endometrium is discharged from the uterus and out the vagina. The secretory phase ends, and the menstrual phase begins. The cycle is then complete.

PMS. PMS is characterized by psychological symptoms, such as depression, lethargy, irritability, and aggressiveness, or somatic symptoms, such as headache, backache, asthma, and acne, that recur in the same phase of each menstrual cycle, followed by a symptom-free phase in each cycle. Some of the more frequently reported symptoms of PMS include tension, tender breasts, fainting, fatigue, abdominal cramps, and weight gain.

The cause of PMS appears to be hormonal. Perhaps a woman's body is insensitive to a normal level of progesterone, or her ovaries fail to produce a normal amount of progesterone. These reasons seem plausible because PMS types of symptoms do not occur during pregnancy, during which natural progesterone levels are very high, and because women with PMS seem to feel much better after receiving high doses of natural progesterone in suppository form. When using oral contraceptives that supply synthetic progesterone at normal levels, many women report relief from some symptoms of PMS. However, the effectiveness of the most frequently used form of treatment, progesterone suppositories, is now being questioned.

Until the effectiveness of progesterone has been fully researched, it is unlikely that the medical community will deal with PMS through any approach other than a relatively conservative treatment of symptoms through the use of *analgesic drugs* (including *prostaglandin inhibitors*), diuretic drugs, dietary modifications (including restriction of caffeine and salt), vitamin B_6 therapy, exercise, and stress-reduction exercises. The exact nature of PMS has been further complicated by the classification of severe PMS as a mental disturbance by some segments of the American Psychiatric Association.

Fibrocystic breast condition. In some women, particularly those who have never been pregnant, stimulation of the breast tissues by estrogen and progesterone during the menstrual cycle results in an unusually high degree of secretory activity by the cells lining the ducts. The fluid released by the secretory lining finds its way into the fibrous connective tissue areas in the lower half of the breast, where in pocketlike cysts the fluid presses against neighbouring tissues. In many women, excessive secretory activity produces a fibrocystic breast condition characterized by swollen, firm or hardened, tender breast tissue before menstruation.

Women who experience a more extensive fibrocystic condition can be treated with drugs that have a "calming" effect on progesterone production. In addition, occasional draining of the fluid-filled cysts can bring relief.

Menopause

For the vast majority of women in their late 40s through their mid-50s, a gradual decline in reproductive system function, called *menopause*, occurs. Menopause is a normal physiological process, not a disease process. It can, however, become a health concern for some women who have unpleasant side effects resulting from this natural stoppage of ovum production and menstruation.

Key Terms

luteinizing (loo ten eye zing) hormone (LH)
A gonadotropic hormone of the female required for fullest development and release of ova; ovulating hormone.

ovulation
The release of a mature egg from the ovary.

corpus luteum (kore pus loo tee um)
Cellular remnant of the graafian follicle after the release of an ovum.

As ovarian function and hormone production diminish, a period of adjustment must be made by the hypothalamus, ovaries, uterus, and other estrogen-sensitive tissues. The extent of menopause as a health problem is determined by the degree to which **hot flashes**, vaginal wall dryness, depression and melancholy, breast changes, and the uncertainty of fertility are experienced.

In comparison with past generations, today's midlife women are much less likely to find menopause to be a negative experience. The end of fertility, combined with children leaving the home, makes the middle years a period of personal rediscovery for many women.

For women who are troubled by the changes brought about by menopause, physicians may prescribe **hormone replacement therapy (HRT)**. Women are advised to use the smallest effective dose of HRT to treat menopause symptoms for the shortest possible time.

HUMAN SEXUAL RESPONSE PATTERN

Although history has many written and visual accounts of the human's ability to be sexually aroused, it was not until the pioneering work of Masters and Johnson[12] that the events associated with arousal were clinically documented. Five questions posed by these researchers gave direction to a series of studies involving the scientific evaluation of human sexual response:

Do the Sexual Responses of Males and Females Have a Predictable Pattern?

The answer to the first question posed by the researchers was an emphatic yes. A predictable sexual response pattern was identified;[13] it consists of an initial **excitement stage**, a **plateau stage**, an **orgasmic stage**, and a **resolution stage**. Each stage involves predictable changes in the structural characteristics and physiological function of reproductive and nonreproductive organs in both the male and the female. These changes are shown in Figure 12–5.

Is the Sexual Response Pattern Stimuli-Specific?

The research of Masters and Johnson[14] clearly established a "no" answer to the second question concerning stimuli specificity. Their findings demonstrated that numerous senses can supply the stimuli necessary for initiating the sexual response pattern. Although touching activities might initiate arousal in most people and maximize it for the vast majority of people, in both males and females, sight, smell, sound, and *vicariously formed stimuli* can also stimulate the same sexual arousal patterns.

Sexual Performance Difficulties and Therapies

Despite the predictability of the human sexual response pattern, many people find that at some point in their lives, they are no longer capable of responding sexually. The inability of a person to perform adequately is identified as a sexual difficulty or dysfunction. Sexual difficulties can have a negative influence on a person's sense of sexual satisfaction and on a partner's satisfaction. Fortunately, most sexual difficulties can be resolved through strategies that use individual, couple, or group counselling. Many sexual performance difficulties stem from psychogenic (originating in the mind) factors. The most widely publicized breakthrough in treatments for erectile dysfunction in men was the drug Viagra, approved for use in Canada in 1999.

What Differences Occur in the Sexual Response Pattern?

Differences between males and females

Several differences are observable when the sexual response patterns of males and females are compared:

- With the exception of some later adolescent males, the vast majority of males are not multiorgasmic. The **refractory phase** of the resolution stage prevents most males from experiencing more than one orgasm in a short period, even when sufficient stimulation is available.
- Females possess a **multiorgasmic capacity**. Masters and Johnson[15] found that as many as 10% to 30% of all female adults routinely experience multiple orgasms.
- Although they possess multiorgasmic potential, about 10% of all female adults are *anorgasmic*—that is, they have never experienced an orgasm.[16] For many anorgasmic females, orgasms can first be experienced when masturbation, rather than **coitus**, provides the stimulation.
- When measured during coitus, males reach orgasm far more quickly than do females. However, when masturbation is the source of stimulation, females reach orgasm as quickly as do males.[17]

More important than any of the differences pointed out is the finding that the sexual response patterns of males and females are far more alike than they are different. Not only do males and females experience the four basic stages of the response pattern, but they also have similar responses in specific areas, including the **erection** and *tumescence* of sexual structures; the appearance of a **sex flush**; the increase in cardiac output, blood pressure, and respiratory rate; and the occurrence of *rhythmic pelvic thrusting.*[18]

Differences among subjects within a same-gender group

When a group of subjects of the same gender was studied in an attempt to answer questions about similarities and differences in the sexual response pattern, Masters and Johnson noted considerable variation. Even when variables such as age, race, education, and general health were held constant, the extent and duration of virtually every stage of the response pattern varied.

Differences within the same individual

For a given person the nature of the sexual response pattern does not remain constant, even when observed over a relatively short period. A variety of internal and external factors can alter this pattern. The aging process, changes in general health status, levels of stress, altered environmental settings, use of alcohol and other drugs, and behavioural changes in a sexual partner can cause one's own sexual response pattern to change from one sexual experience to another. Sexual performance difficulties and therapies are briefly discussed in the Star Box on p. 290.

What Are the Basic Physiological Mechanisms Underlying the Sexual Response Pattern?

The basic mechanisms in the fourth question posed by Masters and Johnson are now well recognized. One factor, *vasocongestion*, or the retention of blood or fluid within a particular tissue, is critically important in the development of physiological changes that promote the sexual response pattern.[19] The presence of erectile tissue underlies the changes that can be noted in the penis, breasts, and scrotum of the male and the clitoris, breasts, and labia minora of the female.

A second mechanism now recognized as necessary for the development of the sexual response pattern is that of *myotonia*, or the buildup of *neuromuscular tonus* within a variety of body structures.[20] At the end of the plateau stage of the response pattern, a sudden release of the accumulated neuromuscular tension gives rise to the rhythmic muscular contractions and pleasurable muscular spasms that constitute orgasm, as well as ejaculation in the male.

What Role Is Played by Specific Organs and Organ Systems within the Sexual Response Pattern?

The fifth question posed by Masters and Johnson, which concerns the role played by specific organs and organ systems during each stage of the response pattern, can be readily answered by referring to the material presented in Figure 12–5. As you study this figure, remember that direct stimulation of the penis and either direct or indirect stimulation of the clitoris are the principal avenues toward orgasm. Also, intercourse represents only one activity that can lead to orgasmic pleasure.[21]

Key Terms

hot flashes
Temporary feelings of warmth experienced by women during and after menopause, caused by blood vessel dilation.

hormone replacement therapy (HRT)
Medically administered estrogen and progestin to replace hormones lost as the result of menopause.

excitement stage
Initial arousal stage of the sexual response pattern.

plateau stage
Second stage of the sexual response pattern; a levelling off of arousal immediately before orgasm.

orgasmic stage
Third stage of the sexual response pattern; the stage during which neuromuscular tension is released.

resolution stage
Fourth stage of the sexual response pattern; the return of the body to a pre-excitement state.

refractory phase
That portion of the male's resolution stage during which sexual arousal cannot occur.

multiorgasmic capacity
Potential to have several orgasms within a single period of sexual arousal.

coitus (co ih tus)
Penile-vaginal intercourse.

erection
The engorgement of erectile tissue with blood; characteristic of the penis, clitoris, nipples, labia minora, and scrotum.

sex flush
The reddish skin response that results from increasing sexual arousal.

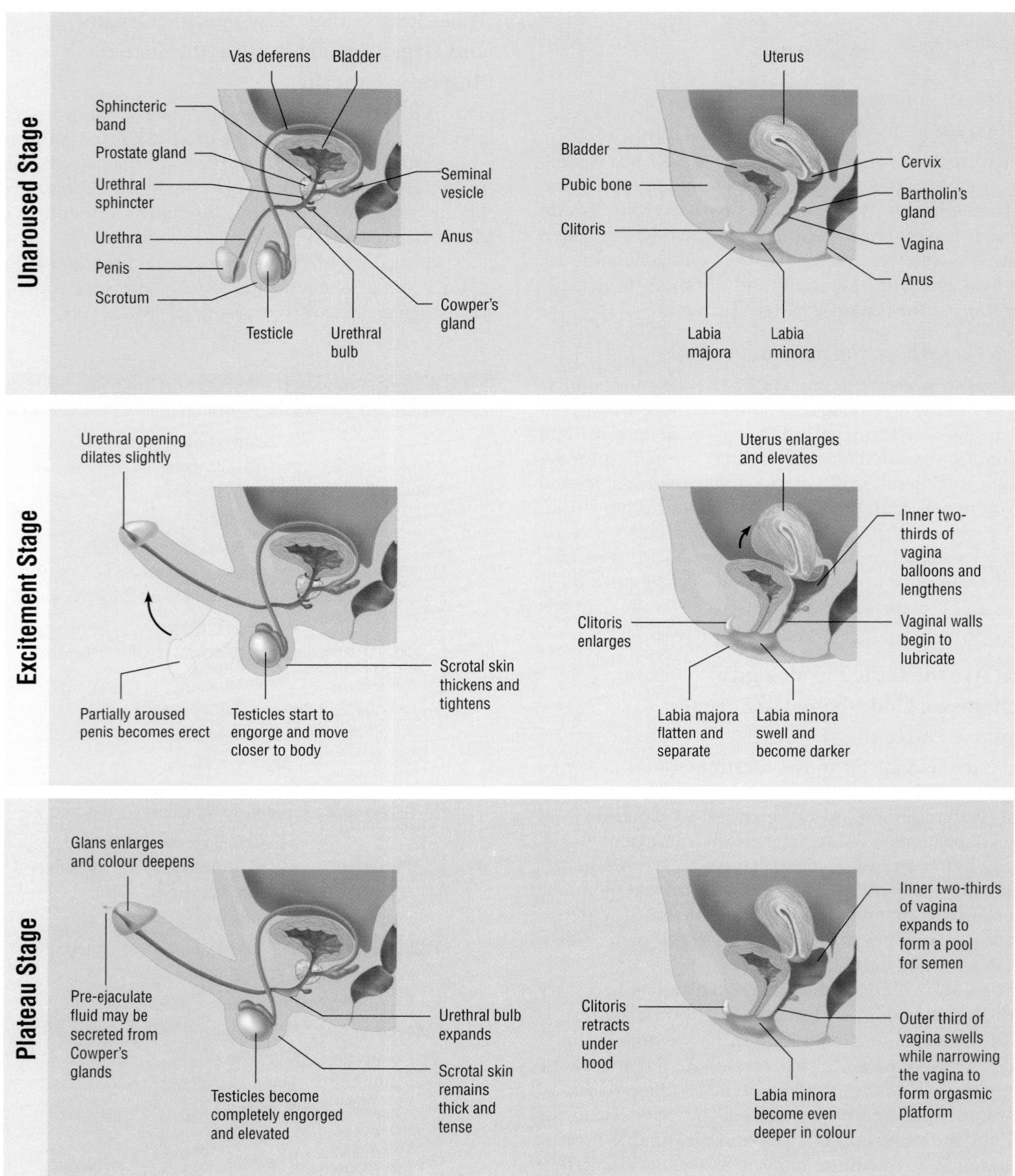

Figure 12–5 The sexual response pattern in men and women.

Orgasmic Stage

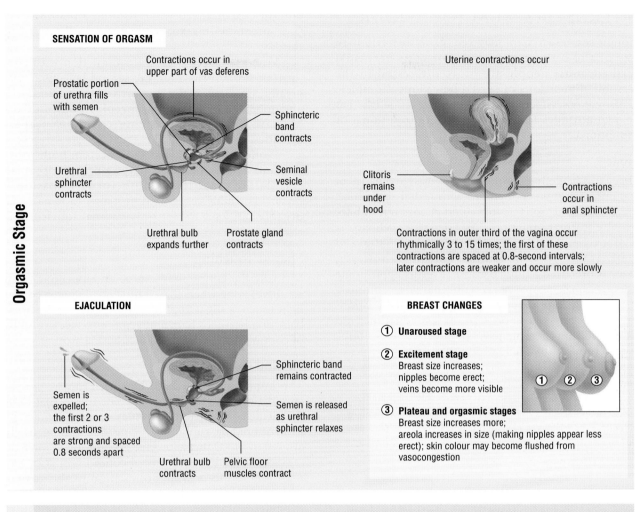

SENSATION OF ORGASM

Contractions occur in upper part of vas deferens

Prostatic portion of urethra fills with semen

Sphincteric band contracts

Urethral sphincter contracts

Seminal vesicle contracts

Urethral bulb expands further

Prostate gland contracts

Uterine contractions occur

Clitoris remains under hood

Contractions occur in anal sphincter

Contractions in outer third of the vagina occur rhythmically 3 to 15 times; the first of these contractions are spaced at 0.8-second intervals; later contractions are weaker and occur more slowly

EJACULATION

Semen is expelled; the first 2 or 3 contractions are strong and spaced 0.8 seconds apart

Sphincteric band remains contracted

Semen is released as urethral sphincter relaxes

Urethral bulb contracts

Pelvic floor muscles contract

BREAST CHANGES

① **Unaroused stage**

② **Excitement stage**
Breast size increases; nipples become erect; veins become more visible

③ **Plateau and orgasmic stages**
Breast size increases more; areola increases in size (making nipples appear less erect); skin colour may become flushed from vasocongestion

① ② ③

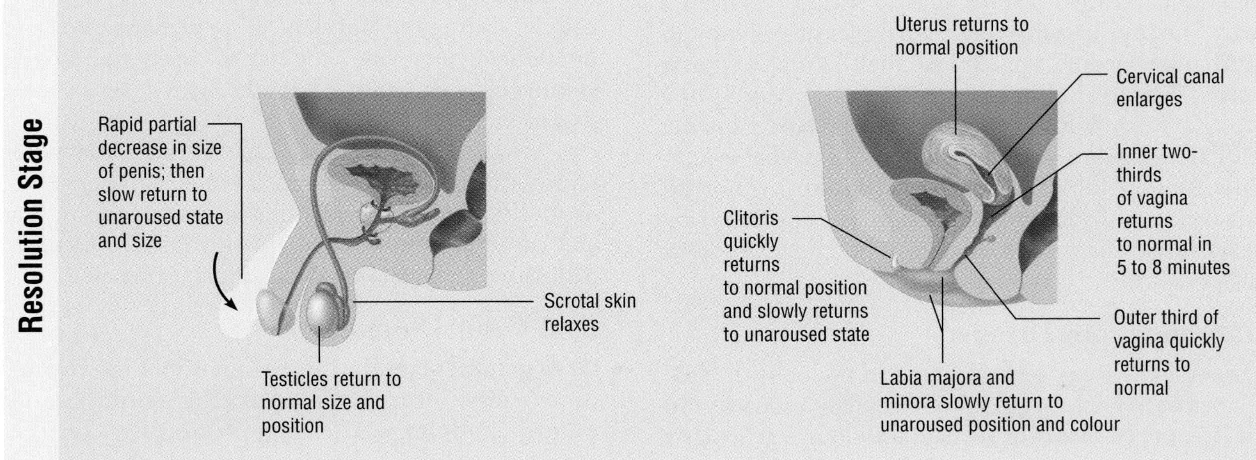

Figure 12–5 Continued.

PATTERNS OF SEXUAL BEHAVIOUR

Although sex researchers may see sexual behaviour in terms of the human sexual response pattern just described, most people are more interested in the observable dimensions of sexual behaviour. Complete the Personal Assessment on p. 305 to determine whether your own attitudes toward sexuality are traditional or nontraditional.

Celibacy

Celibacy can be defined as the self-imposed avoidance of sexual intimacy. It is synonymous with sexual abstinence. There are many reasons people could choose not to have a sexually intimate relationship. For some, celibacy is part of a religious doctrine. Others might be afraid of sexually transmitted infections. For most, however, celibacy is preferred simply because it seems appropriate for them. Celibate people can certainly have deep, intimate relationships with other people—just not sexual relationships. Celibacy may be short term or last a lifetime, and no identified physical or psychological complications appear to result from a celibate lifestyle.

TALKING POINTS • You have decided to remain celibate until you're ready to make a lifetime commitment to someone. How would you explain this to the person you are now dating?

Masturbation

Throughout recorded history, **masturbation** has been a primary method of achieving sexual pleasure. Through masturbation, people can explore their sexual response patterns. Traditionally, some societies and religious groups have condemned this behaviour based on the belief that intercourse is the only "right" sexual behaviour. With sufficient lubrication, masturbation cannot do physical harm. Today masturbation is considered by most sex therapists and researchers to be a normal source of self-pleasure.

Fantasy and Erotic Dreams

The brain is the most sensual organ in the body. In fact, many sexuality experts classify **sexual fantasies** and **erotic dreams** as forms of sexual behaviour. Particularly for people whose verbal ability is highly developed, the ability to create imaginary scenes enriches other forms of sexual behaviour.

Sexual fantasies are generally found in association with some second type of sexual behaviour. When occurring before intercourse or masturbation, fantasies prepare a person for the behaviour that will follow. As an example, fantasies experienced while reading a book may focus your attention on sexual activity that will occur later in the day.

When fantasies occur in conjunction with another form of sexual behaviour, the second behaviour may be greatly enhanced by the supportive fantasy. Both women and men fantasize during foreplay and intercourse. Masturbation and fantasizing are often inseparable activities.

Erotic dreams occur during sleep in both men and women. The association between these dreams and ejaculation resulting in a nocturnal emission (wet dream) is readily recognized in males. In females, erotic dreams can lead to not only vaginal lubrication but also orgasm.

Shared Touching

Virtually the entire body can be an erogenous (sexually sensitive) zone when shared touching is involved. A soft, light touch, a slight application of pressure, the brushing back of a partner's hair, and gentle massage are all forms of communication that heighten sexual arousal.

Genital Contact

Two important uses can be identified for the practice of stimulating a partner's genitals. The first is that of being the tactile component of **foreplay**. Genital contact, in the form of holding, rubbing, stroking, or caressing, heightens arousal to a level that allows for progression to intercourse.

The second role of genital contact is that of *mutual masturbation* to *orgasm*. Stimulation of the genitals so that both partners have orgasm is a form of sexual behaviour practised by many people, as well as some couples during the late stage of a pregnancy. For couples not desiring pregnancy, the risk of conception is virtually eliminated when this becomes the form of sexual intimacy practised.

As is the case of other aspects of intimacy, genital stimulation is best enhanced when partners can talk about their needs, expectations, and reservations. Practice and communication can shape this form of contact into a pleasure-giving approach to sexual intimacy.

Oral-Genital Stimulation

Oral-genital stimulation brings together two of the body's most erogenous areas: the genitalia and the mouth. Couples who engage in oral sex consistently report that this form of intimacy is highly satisfactory. Some people have experimented with oral sex and found it unacceptable, and some have never experienced this form of sexual intimacy. Some couples prefer not to participate in oral sex because they consider it immoral (according to religious doctrine), illegal (which it is in some states in the United States), or unhygienic (because of a partner's unclean genitals). Some couples may refrain because of the mistaken belief that oral sex is a homosexual practice. Regardless of the reason, a person who does not consider oral sex to be pleasurable should not be coerced into this behaviour.

Because oral-genital stimulation can involve an exchange of body fluids, the risk of disease transmission is real. Small tears of mouth or genital tissue may allow transmission of disease-causing pathogens. Only couples who are absolutely certain that they are free from all sexually transmitted infections (including HIV infection) can practise unprotected oral sex. Couples in doubt should refrain from oral-genital sex or carefully use a condom (on the male) or a latex square to cover the female's vulval area. Increasingly, latex squares (dental dams) can be obtained from drug stores or pharmacies. (Dentists may also provide you with dental dams, or you can make your own latex square by cutting a condom into an appropriate shape, or you can use plastic kitchen wrap, which is not as effective as the latter two methods.)

Three basic forms of oral-genital stimulation are practised by both heterosexual and homosexual couples.[22] **Fellatio**, in which the penis is sucked, licked, or kissed by the partner, is the most common of the three. **Cunnilingus**, in which the vulva of the female is kissed, licked, or penetrated by the partner's tongue, is only slightly less frequently practised.

Mutual oral-genital stimulation, the third form of oral-genital stimulation, combines both fellatio and cunnilingus. When practised by a heterosexual couple, the female partner performs fellatio on her partner while her male partner performs cunnilingus on her. Homosexual couples can practise mutual fellatio or cunnilingus.

Intercourse

Sexual intercourse (coitus) refers to the act of inserting the penis into the vagina. Intercourse is the sexual behaviour that is most directly associated with **procreation**. For some, intercourse is the only natural and appropriate form of sexual intimacy.

The incidence and frequency of sexual intercourse is a much-studied topic. Information concerning the percentages of people who have engaged in intercourse is readily available in textbooks used in sexuality courses. Data concerning sexual intercourse among college and university students may be changing somewhat because of concerns about HIV infection and other STIs, but a reasonable estimate of the percentage of students reporting sexual intercourse is between 60% and 75%.

These percentages reflect two important concepts about the sexual activity of post-secondary students. The first is that a large majority of students is having intercourse. The second concept is that a sizeable percentage (25% to 40%) of students is choosing to refrain from intercourse. Indeed, the belief that "everyone is doing it" may be a bit shortsighted. From a public health standpoint, we believe it is important to provide accurate health information to protect those who choose to have intercourse and to actively support a person's right to choose not to have intercourse.

Couples need to share their expectations concerning sexual techniques and frequency of intercourse. Even the "performance" factors, such as depth of penetration, nature of body movements, tempo of activity, and timing of orgasm are of increasing importance to many couples. Issues concerning sexually transmitted diseases (including HIV infection) are also critically important for couples who are contemplating intercourse. These factors also need to be explored through open communication.

There are a variety of books (including textbooks) that provide written and visually explicit information on intercourse positions. Four basic positions for intercourse—male above, female above, side by side, and rear entry—offer relative advantages and disadvantages.

SEXUALITY AND AGING

Students are often curious about how aging affects sexuality. This is understandable because we live in a society that idolizes youth and demands performance. Many younger people become anxious about growing older because of what they think will happen to their ability to express their sexuality. Interestingly, young adults are willing to accept other physical changes of aging (such as the slowing down of basal metabolism, reduced lung capacity, and even wrinkles) but not those changes related to sexuality.

Key Terms

masturbation
Self-stimulation of the genitals.

sexual fantasies
Fantasies with sexual themes; sexual daydreams or imaginary events.

erotic dreams
Dreams whose content elicits a sexual response.

foreplay
Activities, often involving touching and caressing, that prepare individuals for sexual intercourse.

fellatio (feh lay she oh)
Oral stimulation of the penis.

cunnilingus (cun uh ling gus)
Oral stimulation of the vulva or clitoris.

procreation
Reproduction.

Exploring Your Spirituality

Coming out—Then What?

If you are openly gay, when you finally told your family and friends about your sexual orientation, a lot of things changed. But one thing probably stayed the same—you still feel like an outsider. Most of the couples holding hands on campus are young men and women. TV sitcoms are centred on heterosexual couples. They may include a gay character, but usually in a minor role. Popular magazines—through their ads, their features, their entire focus—are telling you how to be attractive to the opposite sex.

Being openly gay has probably made you wonder about some of the mixed messages you receive. The person who says it's OK that you're gay also seems to feel sorry for you—because you can't have a "normal" life and enjoy some of the things she does. Your mother makes remarks that suggest she still has hopes that someday you'll marry her best friend's son.

Feeling good about being gay in a straight world doesn't come easily. You've got to work at it. Start by finding support among your gay friends. Knowing that you're not alone is important—especially right after coming out. Realizing that other good, whole people are gay helps to reinforce your self-esteem. Joining a campus gay organization is good for ongoing support, but don't limit yourself to that group. To grow as an individual, you also need to interact with and be part of heterosexual society.

Focus on what you value about yourself. Are you creative? Someone who gets things accomplished? A dependable friend? Think about the contributions you make—to your family, school, friends, religious groups, and community. Remind yourself that you're a worthy person.

What do your friends appreciate about you? Do they value your advice? Like your sense of humour? Admire your courage? Think you're a strong leader?

Reinforcing the fact that you're a whole, worthy person is up to you. Listen to the "tapes" that are constantly playing in your head—both positive and negative. Edit out the negative thoughts, and turn up the volume on the positive ones. Take charge of what you think about yourself, rather than accepting what others think you are or should be.

TALKING POINTS • How would you react if a close family member told you that he or she was gay? How could you be supportive or at least communicate your feelings without anger or criticism?

Most of the research in this area suggests that older people are quite capable of performing sexually. As with other aspects of aging, certain anatomical and physiological changes will be evident, but these changes do not necessarily reduce the ability to enjoy sexual activity.[23] Most experts in sexuality report that many older people remain interested in sexual activity. Furthermore, those who are exposed to regular sexual activity throughout a lifetime report being most satisfied with their sex lives as older adults.

As people age, the likelihood of alterations in the male and female sexual response cycles increases. In postmenopausal women, vaginal lubrication commonly begins more slowly, and the amount of lubrication usually diminishes. However, clitoral sensitivity and nipple erection remain the same as in earlier years. The female capacity for multiple orgasms remains the same, although the number of contractions that occur at orgasm typically is reduced.

In the older man, physical changes are also evident. This is thought to be caused by the decrease in the production of testosterone between the ages of 20 and 60 years. After age 60 or so, testosterone levels remain relatively steady. Thus many men, despite a decrease in sperm production, remain fertile into their 80s. Older men typically take longer to achieve an erection (however, they are able to maintain their erection longer before ejaculation), have fewer muscular contractions at orgasm, and ejaculate less forcefully than they once did. The volume of seminal fluid ejaculated is typically less than in earlier years, and its consistency is somewhat thinner. The resolution phase is usually longer in older men. In spite of these gradual changes, some elderly men engage in sexual intercourse with the same frequency as do much younger men.

SEXUAL ORIENTATION

Sexual orientation refers to the direction in which people focus their sexual interests. People can focus their attention on opposite-gender partners, same-gender partners, or partners of both genders.

Heterosexuality

Heterosexuality (or heterosexual orientation) refers to an attraction to opposite-gender partners. (*Heteros* is a Greek word that means "the other.") Throughout the world, this is the most common sexual orientation. For reasons related to species survival, heterosexuality has its most basic roots in the biological dimension of human sexuality. Beyond its biological roots, heterosexuality has significant cultural and religious support in virtually every country in the world. Most societies expect men to be attracted to women and women to be attracted to men. Worldwide, laws related to marriage, living arrangements, health benefits, child rearing, financial matters, sexual behaviour, and inheritance generally support relationships that are heterosexual in nature.

Homosexuality

Homosexuality (or homosexual orientation) refers to an attraction to same-gender partners. The term *homosexuality* comes from the Greek word *homos*, meaning "same." The word *homosexuality* may be used with regard to males or females. Thus we use the terms *homosexual males* and *homosexual females*. Frequently the word *gay* is used to refer to homosexual orientation in both males and females. *Lesbianism* is also used to refer to the sexual attraction between females.

The distinctions among the three categories of sexual orientation are much less clear than their definitions might suggest. Most people probably fall somewhere along a continuum between exclusive heterosexuality and exclusive homosexuality. In 1948, Kinsey presented just such a continuum.[24]

Why does a given individual have a particular orientation? There is no simple answer to this question. (Post-secondary human sexuality textbooks devote entire chapters to this topic.) In the mid-1990s, some research pointed to differences in the sizes of certain brain structures as a possible biological basis for homosexuality. However, for sexual orientation in general, no one theory has emerged that fully explains this developmental process. Regardless of the cause, however, reversal to heterosexuality generally does not occur. Furthermore, most homosexuals report that no single event "triggered" their homosexuality. Many homosexuals also indicate that they knew their orientations were "different" from other children as far back as their prepuberty years. See Exploring Your Spirituality on p. 296 for insight into some of the issues that homosexuals often need to face.

The extent of homosexuality in our society is a debatable issue. Clearly, gathering valid information of this kind is difficult. The extent of homosexual orientation is probably much greater than many heterosexuals realize. Furthermore, many people refuse to reveal their homosexuality and thus prefer to remain "in the closet."

Although operational definitions of homosexuality may vary from researcher to researcher, Kinsey estimated that about 2% of American females and 4% of American males were exclusively homosexual.[25,26] There are no Canadian data on the percentage of homosexuals in the general population.[27] More recent estimates place the overall combined figure of homosexuals at about 10% of the population. Clearly the expression of same-gender attraction is not uncommon.

Bisexuality

People whose preference for sexual partners includes both genders are referred to as *bisexuals*. Bisexuals may fall into one of three groups: those who are (1) genuinely attracted to both genders, (2) homosexual but feel the need to behave heterosexually, or (3) aroused physically by the same gender but attracted emotionally to the opposite gender. Some people participate in a bisexual lifestyle for extended periods. Others move quickly to a more exclusive orientation. The size of the bisexual population is not accurately known.

A particularly pressing reason for learning more about the bisexual lifestyle is its relationship to the transmission of HIV infection. Except for intravenous drug users, bisexuals hold the greatest potential for extending HIV infection into the heterosexual population. Since the prevalence of bisexuality is unknown, the consistent use of safer-sex practices becomes more important than ever.

LOVE

Love may be one of the most elusive yet widely recognized concepts that describe some level of emotional attachment to another. Various forms of love include friendship, erotic, devotional, parental, and altruistic love. Two types of love are most closely associated with dating and mate selection: *passionate love* and *companionate love*.

Passionate love, also described as romantic love or **infatuation**, is a state of extreme absorption in another person. It is characterized by intense feelings of tenderness, elation, anxiety, sexual desire, and ecstasy. Often appearing early in a relationship, passionate love typically does not last very long. Passionate love is driven by the excitement of being closely involved with a person whose character is not fully known.

If a relationship progresses, passionate love is gradually replaced by companionate love. This type of love is less emotionally intense than passionate love. It is characterized by friendly affection and a deep attachment that is based on extensive familiarity with the partner. This love is enduring and capable of sustaining long-term, mutual growth. Central to companionate love are feelings of empathy for, support of, and tolerance of the partner. Complete the Personal Assessment on p. 306 to determine whether you and your partner are truly compatible.

Key Term

infatuation
A relatively temporary, intensely romantic attraction to another person.

Changing *for the Better*

Can You Improve Your Marriage?

Between working and taking classes, my wife and I both have heavy schedules. One thing that's not getting any attention is our relationship. What can we do to make our marriage better?

Few marital relationships are "perfect." All marriages are faced with occasional periods of strain or turmoil. Even marriages that do not exhibit major signs of distress can be improved, mostly through better communication. Marriage experts suggest that implementing some of these patterns can strengthen marriages:

- Problems that exist within the marriage should be brought into the open so that both partners are aware of the difficulties.
- Balance should exist between the needs and expectations of each partner. Decisions should be made jointly. Partners should support each other as best they can. When a partner's goals cannot be actively supported, he or she should at least receive moral support and encouragement.
- Realistic expectations should be established. Partners should negotiate areas in which disagreement exists. They should work together to determine the manner in which resources should be shared.
- Participating in marriage counselling and marriage encounter groups can be helpful.

A sense of permanence helps sustain a marriage over the course of time. If the partners are convinced that their relationship can withstand difficult times, then they are more likely to take the time to make needed changes. Couples can develop a sense of permanence by implementing some of the patterns described above.

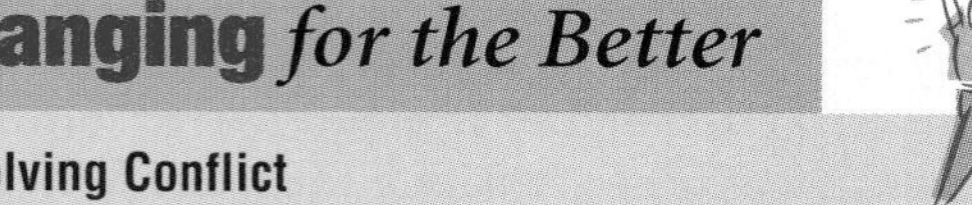

Resolving Conflict

Whenever I have a disagreement with my girlfriend, both of us say hurtful things and end up feeling bad. How can we resolve our conflicts in a positive way?

Here are some successful ways to manage conflict:

- Show mutual respect.
- Identify and resolve the real issue.
- Seek areas of agreement.
- Mutually participate in decision making.
- Be cooperative and specific.
- Focus on the present and future—not the past.
- Don't try to assign blame.
- Say what you are thinking and feeling.
- When talking, use sentences that begin with "I."
- Avoid using sentences that start with "you" or "why."
- Set a time limit for discussing problems.
- Accept responsibility.
- Schedule time together.
- Do not interrupt.
- Be a good listener.

RECOGNIZING UNHEALTHY RELATIONSHIPS

Clearly, not all dating relationships will continue. Many couples recognize when a partnership is nearing an end, and they reach a mutual decision to break off the relationship. This is a traditional, natural way for people to learn about their interactions with others. They simply decide to split up and move on.

However, sometimes people do not recognize or heed the warning signs of an unstable relationship, so they stay involved long after the risks outweigh the benefits. These warning signs include abusive behaviour, including both emotional and physical abuse (see Chapter 16). Another red flag is excessive jealousy about a partner's interactions with others. Sometimes excessive jealousy evolves into controlling behaviour, and one partner attempts to manage the daily activities of the other partner. By definition, controlling behaviour limits your creativity and freedom.

Other warning signs are dishonesty, irresponsibility, lack of patience, and any kind of drug abuse. We certainly do not want to see these qualities in those we have initially judged to be "nice people," even though these unappealing characteristics may be obvious to others. If you suspect that any of these problems may be undermining your relationship, talk about your concerns with one or two trusted friends, and seek the advice of a professional counsellor at your college or university. Try to realize that ending your relationship might be the best thing you could do for yourself.

TALKING POINTS • Your sister is in an unhealthy relationship but doesn't seem to see the warning signs. How could you alert her to the potential dangers?

Learning from Our Diversity
The Debate over Same-Sex Marriage

What is the definition of marriage? Must the marriage partners be a man and woman? Would same-sex marriages weaken our society?

Same-sex marriage would grant gays an array of legal and economic rights, including joint parental custody, insurance and health benefits, alimony and child support, inheritance of property, family leave, and a spouse's retirement benefits.

Same-sex unions have been debated for many years. Some North American clergy were presiding over gay "marriages" in the 1980s, and several hundred companies now offer benefits to same-sex partners of employees. Gay publications debated the subject in the 1950s. In *Same-Sex Unions in Premodern Europe*, the late John Boswell, a Yale University historian, suggested that ancient marriage ceremonies provide evidence that Greeks and medieval Christians celebrated same-sex relationships.

The Canadian federal government controls marriage laws for all of the provinces except Quebec. The provincial governments issue marriage certificates and record marriages. Marriage is restricted by the Federal Marriage Act to one man and one woman. During the late 1990s in Canada, the total number of adults wishing to retain special marriage rights for heterosexuals became a minority. Most provinces are proposing and passing various pieces of legislation concerning the rights of same-sex couples. Because there exists an apparent conflict among the Federal Marriage Act, some provincial marriage acts, and the Canadian Charter of Rights and Freedoms, gay couples are going to court. At the time of writing, there were three active court cases in Canada involving gay marriages: one each in Quebec, Ontario, and British Columbia.

Some observers predict that this will be the greatest gay rights debate in history. Where do you stand on this issue? Should gay partners be granted the same legal right to marriage as heterosexual couples? Or do you believe legal marriage should be limited to its traditional definition of a union between opposite-sex partners?

FRIENDSHIP

One of the exciting aspects of college or university life is that you will probably meet many new people. Some of these people will become your best friends. Because of your common experiences, it is likely that you will keep in contact with a few of these friends for a lifetime. Close attachments to other people can have an important influence on all of the dimensions of your health.

What is it that draws friends together? With the exception of physical intimacy, many of the same growth experiences seen in dating and mate selection are also seen in the development of friendships. Think about how you and your best friend developed the relationship you now have. You probably became friends when you shared similar interests and experiences. Your friendship progressed (and even faltered at times) through personal gains or losses. In all likelihood, you cared about each other and learned to share your deepest beliefs and feelings. Then, you cemented your friendship by transferring your beliefs into behaviour.

Throughout the development of a deep friendship, the qualities of trust, tolerance, empathy, and support must be demonstrated. Otherwise the friendship can fall apart. You may have noticed that the qualities seen in a friendship are very similar to the qualities noted in the description of companionate love. In both cases, people develop deep attachments through extensive familiarity and understanding.

INTIMACY

When most people hear the word **intimacy**, they immediately think about physical intimacy. They think about shared touching, kissing, and even intercourse. However, sexuality experts and family therapists prefer to view intimacy more broadly, as any close, mutual, verbal, or nonverbal behaviour within a relationship. In this sense, intimate behaviour can range from sharing deep feelings and experiences with a partner to sharing profound physical pleasures with a partner.

Intimacy is present in both love and friendship. You have likely shared intimate feelings with your closest friends, as well as with those you love. Intimacy helps us feel connected to others and allows us to feel the full measure of our own self-worth.

TALKING POINTS • Your teenage son equates intimacy with sex. How would you explain the emotional intimacy involved in marriage?

Key Term

intimacy
Any close, mutual, verbal, or nonverbal behaviour within a relationship.

Changing *for the Better*

Coping with a Breakup

My husband and I have been married for 10 years. Recently, he announced that he wants to be "free." There's no one else, he says. He just wants to leave. I'm angry, hurt, and sad. How can I get through this crisis?

The following tips suggest both alternatives to breakup and ways to cope with it.

- *Talk first.* Try to deal effectively and directly with the conflicts. The old theory said that it was good for a couple to fight. However, anger can cause more anger and even lead to violence. Freely venting anger is as likely to damage a relationship as to improve it. So, cool off first, then discuss issues fully and freely.
- *Obtain help.* The services of a *qualified* counsellor, psychologist, or psychiatrist may help a couple resolve their problems. Notice the emphasis on the word *qualified.* Some people who have little training or competence represent themselves as counsellors. For this reason a couple should insist on verifying the counsellor's training and licensing.
- *Trial separation.* Sometimes only a few weeks apart can convince a couple that it is far better to work together than to go it totally alone. It is generally better to establish the rules of such a trial quite firmly. Will the individuals see others? What are the responsibilities if children are involved? There should also be a time limit, perhaps a month or two, after which the partners reunite and discuss their situation again.
- *Allow time for grief and healing.* When a relationship ends, people are often tempted to immediately become as socially and sexually active as possible. This can be a way to express anger and relieve pain. But it can also cause frustration and despair. A better solution for many is to acknowledge the grief the breakup has caused and allow time for healing. Up to a year of continuing one's life and solidifying friendships typically helps the rejected partner establish a new equilibrium.

MARRIAGE

Just as there is no single best way for two people to move through dating and mate selection, marriage is also a variable undertaking. In marriage, two people join their lives in a way that affirms each as an individual and both as a legal pair. Some are able to resolve conflicts constructively (see the Changing for the Better box on Resolving Conflict, on p. 298). However, for a large percentage of couples, the demands of marriage are too rigorous, confining, and demanding. They will find resolution for their dissatisfaction through divorce or extramarital affairs. For most, though, marriage will be an experience that alternates periods of happiness, productivity, and admiration with periods of frustration, unhappiness, and disillusionment with the partner. Each of you who marries will find the experience unique in every regard. The Changing for the Better box on p. 298 presents some advice for improving marriage.

Currently, certain trends regarding marriage are evident. The most obvious of these is the age at first marriage. Today men are waiting longer than ever to marry. The average age at first marriage for men is 27 years.[28] In addition, these new husbands are better educated than in the past and are more likely to be established in their careers. Women are also waiting longer to get married and tend to be more educated and career oriented than they were in the past. Recent statistics indicate that the median age at first marriage for women is 25 years.[29]

Marriage still appeals to most adults. Currently, 76% of adults age 19 and older are either married, widowed, or divorced.[30] Thus only about one-quarter of today's adults have not married. Within the last decade, the percentage of adults who have decided not to marry has nearly doubled. Singlehood and other alternatives to marriage are discussed later in this chapter. See the Learning from Our Diversity box on p. 299 for a discussion of same-sex marriage.

DIVORCE

Marriages, like many other kinds of interpersonal relationships, can end. Today, marriages—relationships begun with the intent of permanence "until death do us part"—end through divorce nearly as frequently as they continue.

Why should approximately half of marital relationships be so likely to end? Unfortunately, marriage experts cannot provide one clear answer. Rather, they suggest that divorce is a reflection of unfulfilled expectations for marriage on the part of one or both partners, including the following:

- The belief that marriage will ease your need to deal with your own faults and that your failures can be shared by your partner
- The belief that marriage will change faults that you know exist in your partner
- The belief that the high level of romance of your dating and courtship period will be continued through marriage

- The belief that marriage can provide you with an arena for the development of your personal power, and that once married, you will not need to compromise with your partner
- The belief that your marital partner will be successful in meeting all of your needs

If these expectations seem to be ones you anticipate through marriage, then you may find that disappointments will abound. To varying degrees, marriage is a partnership that requires much cooperation and compromise. Marriage can be complicated. Because of the high expectations that many people hold for marriage, the termination of marriage can be an emotionally difficult process to undertake (see the Changing for the Better box on p. 300).

Concern is frequently voiced over the well-being of children whose parents divorce. Different factors, however, influence the extent to which divorce affects children. Included among these factors are the gender and age of the children, custody arrangements, financial support, and the remarriage of one or both parents. For many children, adjustments must be made to accept their new status as a member of a blended family.

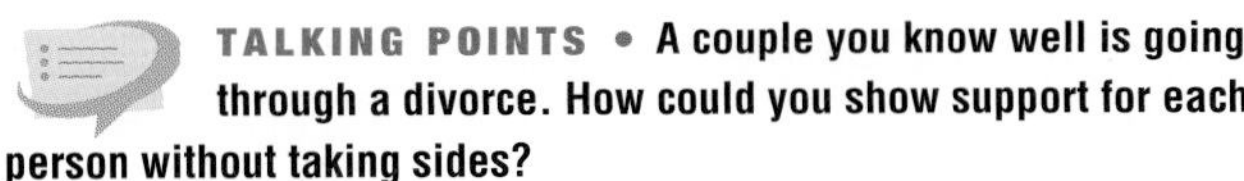

TALKING POINTS • A couple you know well is going through a divorce. How could you show support for each person without taking sides?

ALTERNATIVES TO MARRIAGE

Although the great majority of you have experienced or will experience marriage, alternatives to marriage certainly exist. This section briefly explores singlehood, cohabitation, and single parenthood.

Singlehood

An alternative to marriage for adults is *singlehood*. For many people, being single is a lifestyle that affords the potential for pursuing intimacy, if desired, and provides an uncluttered path for independence and self-directedness. Other people, however, are single because of divorce, separation, death, or the absence of an opportunity to establish a partnership. Both Canadian Census data and the U.S. Bureau of the Census data indicate that 37% of women and 35% of men over the age of 19 are currently single.[31,32]

Many different living arrangements are seen among singles. Some single people live alone and choose not to share a household. Other arrangements for singles include cohabitation, periodic cohabitation, singlehood during the week and cohabitation on the weekends or during vacations, or the *platonic* sharing of a household with others. For young adults, large percentages of single men and women live with their parents.

Like habitation arrangements, the sexual intimacy patterns of singles are individually tailored. Some singles practise celibacy, others pursue heterosexual or homosexual intimate relationships in a **monogamous** pattern, and others may have multiple partners. As in all interpersonal relationships, including marriage, the levels of commitment are as variable as the people involved.

Cohabitation

Cohabitation, or the sharing of living quarters by unmarried people, represents another alternative to marriage. Results from the 2001 General Social Survey revealed that 48% of Canadians that had never been married or had been previously married reported that they would consider living common-law in the future. Fifty-two percent of respondents felt that they could not.[33]

Although cohabitation may seem to imply a vision of sexual intimacy between male and female roommates, several forms of shared living arrangements can be viewed as cohabitation. For some couples, cohabitation is only a part-time arrangement for weekends, during summer vacation, or on a variable schedule. In addition, **platonic** cohabitation can exist when a couple shares living quarters but does so without establishing a sexual relationship. Close friends and people of retirement age might be included in a group called *cohabitants*.

Single Parenthood

Unmarried young women becoming single parents is a continuing reality in Canada. A new and significantly different form of single parenthood is, however, also a reality in this country: the planned entry into a single parenthood by older, better educated people, the vast majority of whom are women.

In contrast to the teenaged girl who becomes a single parent through an unwed pregnancy, the more mature woman who desires single parenting has usually planned carefully for the experience. She has explored several important concerns, including questions about how she will become pregnant (with or without the knowledge of

Key Terms

monogamous (mo nog a mus)
Paired relationship with one partner.

cohabitation
Sharing of a residence by two unrelated, unmarried people; living together.

platonic (pluh ton ick)
Close association between two people that does not include a sexual relationship.

a male partner or through artificial insemination), the need for a father figure for the child, the effect of single parenting on her social life, and its effect on her career development. Once these questions have been resolved, no legal barriers stand in the way of her becoming a single parent.

A very large number of women and a growing number of men are actively participating in single parenthood in conjunction with a divorce settlement or separation agreement involving sole or joint custody of children. In Canada, in 1996, single women headed 945 230 households with children under the age of 18. In contrast, single men headed 192 275 households with children under the age of 18.[34]

A few single parents have been awarded children through adoption. The likelihood of a single person's receiving a child this way is small, but more people have been successful recently in single-parent adoptions.

Taking Charge of Your Health

- Take the Personal Assessment on p. 305 to understand your sexual attitudes better.
- Use the Personal Assessment on p. 306 to find out how compatible you and your partner are.
- If being around someone whose sexual orientation is different from yours makes you feel uncomfortable, focus on getting to know that person better as an individual.
- If you are in an unhealthy relationship, take the first step toward getting out of it through professional counselling or group support.
- If you are in a sexual relationship, communicate your sexual needs to your partner clearly. Encourage him or her to do the same so that you will both have a satisfying sex life.
- Consider whether your lifetime plan will involve marriage, singlehood, or cohabitation. Evaluate your current situation in relation to that plan.

SUMMARY

- Biological and psychosocial factors contribute to the complex expression of our sexuality.
- The structural basis of sexuality begins as the male and female reproductive structures develop in the growing embryo and fetus. Structural sexuality changes as one moves through adolescence and later life.
- The psychosocial processes of gender identity, gender preference, and gender adoption form the basis for an initial adult gender identification.
- The male and female reproductive structures are external and internal. The complex functioning of these structures is controlled by hormones.
- The menstrual cycle's primary functions are to produce ova and to develop a supportive environment for the fetus in the uterus.
- The sexual response pattern consists of four stages: excitement, plateau, orgasm, and resolution.
- Many older people remain interested and active in sexual activities. Physiological changes may alter the way in which some older people perform sexually.
- Three sexual orientations are heterosexuality, homosexuality, and bisexuality.
- A variety of lifestyles and relationships exist in our society.
- A large majority of adults will marry at some time.
- Many marriages will end in divorce.
- Although most individuals marry at some time in their lives, alternatives to marriage exist, including singlehood, cohabitation, and single parenthood.

REVIEW QUESTIONS

1. Describe the following foundations of our biological sexuality: the genetic basis, the gonadal basis, and structural development.
2. Define and explain the following terms: gender identity, gender preference, gender adoption, initial adult gender identification, and transsexualism.
3. Identify the major components of the male and female reproductive systems. Trace the passageways for sperm and ova.
4. Explain the menstrual cycle. Identify and describe the four main hormones that control the menstrual cycle.
5. What similarities and differences exist between the sexual response patterns of males and females?
6. What is the refractory period?
7. How do myotonia and vasacongestion differ?
8. Explain the differences between heterosexuality, homosexuality, and bisexuality. How common are each of these sexual orientations in our society?

THINK ABOUT THIS ...

- How would you summarize your feelings about the changes in your body that took place during puberty?
- To what extent do you think that knowledge about the menstrual cycle will be pertinent to you as you move through adulthood? (This question is for BOTH men and women.)
- Do you think a celibate lifestyle is possible or practical in this new millennium? Why or why not?
- What are your estimates of the percentages of men and women at your college or university who have had sexual intercourse?
- In comparison with a decade ago, are heterosexuals generally more comfortable or less comfortable with homosexuals in our society? Support your answer with specific examples.

REFERENCES

1. Thibodeau GA: *The human body in health and disease*, ed 2, 1999, Mosby.
2. Hyde JS, DeLamater J: *Understanding human sexuality*, ed 7, 1999, McGraw-Hill.
3. Crooks R, Baur K: *Our sexuality*, ed 7, 1998, Brooks/Cole Publishing Co.
4. Ibid.
5. Ibid.
6. Thibodeau GA: *Structure and function of the body*, ed 10, 1999, Mosby.
7. Allgeier ER, Allgeier AR: *Sexual interactions*, ed 5, 2000, Houghton Mifflin.
8. *Our sexuality*.
9. Ibid.
10. Hatcher RA et al: *Contraceptive technology*, ed 17, 1998, Ardent Media, Inc.
11. *Your guide to endometriosis*, **www.my.webmd.com/content/article/46/2953_501.htm**. July 10, 2003.
12. Masters W, Johnson V: *Human sexual response*, 1966, Lippencott, Williams & Wilkins.
13. Ibid.
14. Ibid.
15. Ibid.
16. Ibid.
17. Ibid.
18. Ibid.
19. Ibid.
20. Ibid.
21. *Understanding human sexuality*.
22. *Sexual interactions*.
23. *Our sexuality*.
24. Kinsey AC, Pomeroy WB, Martin CE: *Sexual behavior in the human male*, reprint edition, 1998, Indiana University Press.
25. Ibid.
26. Kinsey AC et al: *Sexual behavior in the human female*, reprint edition, 1998, Indiana University Press.
27. Hyde J, DeLamater J, Byers J: *Understanding human sexuality*, Canadian ed, 2001, McGraw-Hill Ryerson.
28. U.S. Bureau of the Census: *Statistical abstract of the United States: 2000*, ed 120, 2000, U.S. Government Printing Office.
29. Statistics Canada: CANSIM 11, Table 051-0010, March 2002.
30. *Statistical abstract*, ed 120.
31. Ibid.
32. Statistics Canada: *Population by marital status and sex, 2001*. **www.statcan.ca/english/Pgdb/People/Families/famil01a.htm**
33. Statistics Canada: *Would you live common-law?* Autumn 2003, October 15, 2005.
34. Statistics Canada: *1996 census families in private households by family structure, 1991 and 1996 censuses.* **www.statcan.ca/english/Pgdb/People/Families/famil51a.htm**

SUGGESTED READINGS

Byington J, Bly RW, Eliaz I: *Natural alternatives to Viagra: how to recharge your sexual performance without surgery or prescription drugs*, 1999, Birch Lane Press.

The anti-impotence drug Viagra is not a wonder drug for all men. In fact, it can produce some uncomfortable, even dangerous, side effects for certain men. This book offers a variety of natural methods for coping with erectile problems. It is written in a manner that is easily understood by both men and women.

Dalton K, Holton W, Dalton K: *Once a month: understanding and treating PMS*, ed 6, 1999, Hunter House.

Researchers estimate that about 75% of women experience some conditions related to premenstrual syndrome. This book describes the most common symptoms of PMS, strategies for coping with these symptoms, and the effect of PMS on the development of osteoporosis.

Gittleman AL, Wright JV: *Before the change: taking charge of your perimenopause*, 1999, Harper.

Perimenopause, roughly the 10 years before menopause, can be a difficult time—emotionally and physically—for some women. This book is a do-it-yourself guide to coping with the symptoms of perimenopause without resorting to hormonal treatments. The symptoms of perimenopause are clearly identified, and a self-diagnosis quiz is included. A perimenopause diet is presented, as well as recommendations for the use of herbs, natural hormones, and vitamin and mineral supplementation.

Gottman JM, Silver N: *The seven principles for making marriage work*, 1999, Crown Publishing.

This book is written by a psychology professor who is the director of the Seattle Marital and Family Institute. Dr. Gottman combines his research findings with his experience as a marital therapist to help couples discover what really matters in a relationship. This book is helpful to married couples as well as to those contemplating marriage.

Hyde J, DeLamater J, Byers J: *Understanding human sexuality*, Canadian ed, 2001, McGraw-Hill Ryerson.

This timely and relevant text on human sexuality researches and explains the regional and multicultural diversity of Canadians' sexual behaviour. An excellent discussion on Canadian laws dealing with sexual assault, pornography, prostitution, and other issues of sexuality provides further important information in a Canadian context.

Making Headlines

Canadian Court Rules for Gay Teenager

In May 2002, the BBC News ran the following article:

In May 2002, a Superior Court judge in Ontario, Canada, ruled that a gay teenage student has the legal right to take his boyfriend to a Roman Catholic school's end-of-year dance. The school board had tried to bar the student from doing so because it argued that homosexuality was against Catholic teaching.

In his ruling, Justice Robert MacKinnon said the student, Marc Hall, was a Roman Catholic Canadian trying to be himself. The fact that he is gay should not deny him the right to attend a school function to celebrate the end of his high school career with his friends.

But the Roman Catholic Education Board in Oshawa, Ontario, east of Toronto, had argued that while it was not its policy to discriminate against gays and lesbians, it could not endorse what it calls a homosexual lifestyle. It pointed out that Mr. Hall could have attended a secular state school.

The student's lawyer said that the ruling showed that in Canada, Catholic schools would no longer be able to discriminate on the basis of sexual orientation when dealing with young people. The ruling was made just hours before the dance itself, which the school was not allowed to cancel.

Constitutionally, the case is thorny and could be appealed. Canada's *Charter of Rights and Freedoms* guarantees both religious freedom and strong individual rights. To complicate matters further, in the province of Ontario, Roman Catholic schools are publicly funded. Mr. Hall's legal battle has drawn high-profile support from politicians and TV stars. It has even earned him a cameo appearance on the North American version of the gay TV series *Queer as Folk*.

Name ______________________________ **Date** ____________

Personal Assessment

Sexual Attitudes: A Matter of Feelings

Respond to each of the following statements by selecting a numbered response (1–5) that most accurately reflects your feelings. Circle the number of your selection. At the end of the questionnaire, total these numbers for use in interpreting your responses.

1 Agree strongly
2 Agree moderately
3 Uncertain
4 Disagree moderately
5 Disagree strongly

Men and women have greater differences than they have similarities.	1	2	3	4	5
Homosexuality and bisexuality are immoral and unnatural.	1	2	3	4	5
Our society is too sexually oriented.	1	2	3	4	5
Pornography encourages sexual promiscuity.	1	2	3	4	5
Children know far too much about sex.	1	2	3	4	5
Education about sexuality is solely the responsibility of the family.	1	2	3	4	5
Dating begins far too early in our society.	1	2	3	4	5
Sexual intimacy before marriage leads to emotional stress and damage to one's reputation.	1	2	3	4	5
Sexual availability is far too frequently the reason that people marry.	1	2	3	4	5
Reproduction is the most important reason for sexual intimacy during marriage.	1	2	3	4	5
Modern families are too small.	1	2	3	4	5
Family planning clinics should not receive public funds.	1	2	3	4	5
Contraception is the woman's responsibility.	1	2	3	4	5
Abortion is the murder of an innocent child.	1	2	3	4	5
Marriage has been weakened by the changing role of women in society.	1	2	3	4	5
Divorce is an unacceptable means of resolving marital difficulties.	1	2	3	4	5
Extramarital sexual intimacy will destroy a marriage.	1	2	3	4	5
Sexual abuse of a child does not generally occur unless the child encourages the adult.	1	2	3	4	5
Provocative behaviour by the woman is a factor in almost every case of rape.	1	2	3	4	5
Reproduction is not a right but a privilege.	1	2	3	4	5

YOUR TOTAL POINTS ____________

Interpretation

20–34 points	A very traditional attitude toward sexuality
35–54 points	A moderately traditional attitude toward sexuality
55–65 points	A rather ambivalent attitude toward sexuality
66–85 points	A moderately nontraditional attitude toward sexuality
86–100 points	A very nontraditional attitude toward sexuality

To Carry This Further ...

Were you surprised at your results? Compare your results with those of a roommate or close friend. How do you think your parents would score on this assessment?

Name ______________________ **Date** ____________

Personal Assessment

How Compatible Are You?

This quiz will help test how compatible you and your partner's personalities are. You should each rate the truth of these 20 statements based on the following scale. Circle the number that reflects your feelings. Total your scores and check the interpretation following the quiz.

1 Never true
2 Sometimes true
3 Frequently true
4 Always true

We can communicate our innermost thoughts effectively.	1	2	3	4
We trust each other.	1	2	3	4
We agree on whose needs come first.	1	2	3	4
We have realistic expectations of each other and of ourselves.	1	2	3	4
Individual growth is important within our relationship.	1	2	3	4
We will go on as a couple even if one partner doesn't change his or her behaviour.	1	2	3	4
Our personal problems are discussed with each other first.	1	2	3	4
We both do our best to compromise.	1	2	3	4
We usually fight fairly.	1	2	3	4
We try not to be rigid or unyielding.	1	2	3	4
We keep any needs to be "perfect" in proper perspective.	1	2	3	4
We can balance desires to be sociable and the need to be alone.	1	2	3	4
We both make friends and keep them.	1	2	3	4
Neither of us stays down or up for long periods.	1	2	3	4
We can tolerate the other's mood without being affected by it.	1	2	3	4
We can deal with disappointment and disillusionment.	1	2	3	4
Both of us can tolerate failure.	1	2	3	4
We can both express anger appropriately.	1	2	3	4
We are both assertive when necessary.	1	2	3	4
We agree on how our personal surroundings are kept.	1	2	3	4

YOUR TOTAL POINTS ____________

Interpretation

20–35 points	You and your partner seem quite incompatible. Professional help may open your lines of communication.
36–55 points	You probably need more awareness and compromise.
56–70 points	You are highly compatible. However, be aware of the areas where you can improve.
71–80 points	Your relationship is very fulfilling.

To Carry This Further ...

Ask your partner to take this test too. You may have a one-sided view of a "perfect" relationship. Even if you scored high on this assessment, be aware of areas where you can still improve.

Focus on

SEX ON THE WEB

It's like a singles bar without the loud music. If you have a computer and a modem, you can gain access to the world's largest "meet market." From the comfort of your home, you can browse the Internet and meet people for conversation, friendship, romance, and even "sex" (such as it is in cyberspace). There is a cover charge, but you won't have to buy drinks to start up a conversation or get your toes smashed on the dance floor. You won't even have to worry about getting diseases (except for the occasional computer virus).

However, there are drawbacks when you enter this hangout. Can you be sure the person you're chatting with is all he or she seems to be? How can you be certain of a person's personality, age, or even his or her gender? And is there a safe way to meet a "cyberfriend" face to face? The Internet way of meeting people has its own built-in set of advantages—but inviting the world into your home has its dangers as well.

Today's Internet user can find a variety of potential conversation topics using a Web browser and typing in various keywords. As the Internet grows, so does the number of Web sites and USENET discussion groups. Some people see this expansion as a source of entertainment. They think that the Internet is a fun and interesting way to meet people who share their interests. Others think that the Internet allows pornographers, pedophiles, and other deviants to perpetuate their behaviour and prey on innocent children. Both groups are attempting to use the law either to keep the Internet as a haven for free speech or to clean it up and make it safer for children. This clash of ideals is creating a continual battle over the nature and character of the Internet.

Fun and Games on the Web

The world wide web is a large group of computer networks, both public and private, that connect millions of computer users in an estimated 150 countries. Over 70 000 private computer bulletin boards exist in North America alone, and private commercial networks such as Sympatico, Prodigy, America Online, and CompuServe provide millions of subscribers worldwide with access to the Internet.[1] Although the Internet contains information about all facets of life, the sexually oriented sites are proving to be the most popular areas among the general public. For example, alt.sex, a USENET discussion group where people can chat in real time with other users, is the most often visited site on the Internet.[2] Brian Reid, director of the Network Systems Laboratory at Digital Equipment Corporation, reports that between 180 000 and 500 000 users drop into this discussion group on a monthly basis.[3]

On Web sites, computer bulletin boards that usually include photographs, interested parties can find almost anything that conforms to their sexual desires. Many pictures of nude men and women that can be found at most adult-oriented video stores and booksellers can be downloaded (placed on a user's computer disk or printed on his or her own printer).[4] However, other types of less common sexual images are also available at Web sites, including explicit images that many people find objectionable.

The Positive Side of the Web

Despite the potentially offensive graphic images available online, the Internet does have several good points. One positive aspect is that people who are interested in meeting others can use the Internet as a sort of virtual pick-up bar without many of the unpleasant consequences. The Internet gives people the freedom either to be themselves without fear of repercussions or to adopt a totally new persona. Best of all, cybersex participants don't have to worry about looking their best during a virtual date.[5] Who you are (or who you pretend to be) becomes more important than what you look like in cyberspace chat rooms.

Sexually oriented Internet sites can also be positive in the sense that they sometimes inspire creative impulses and prevent people from engaging in destructive behaviour. Some sites house participatory novels in which users can immerse themselves and create new realities for themselves and other participants.[6] In this respect, these sites are similar to fantasy game pages that house activities such as Dungeons & Dragons. People are able to cast off their old identities and create exciting new personas that are able to engage in sexual practices that the users themselves would never attempt in real life. Thus the Internet becomes a harmless outlet for sexual fantasies: the ultimate safe sex.

A third plus to using the Internet to meet people is that occasionally, people who use it do fall in "virtual love," choose to meet face to face, and end up developing a relationship or even getting married.[7] Although this is a rare occurrence, the chance that it could happen is enough to keep some people involved with online romances in the hope of finding a perfect cybermate who will be as good in person.

Pitfalls of Online Sex

Although virtual sex has many points in its favour, there are also several negative aspects. One of the worst possible scenarios of online sex is discovering that

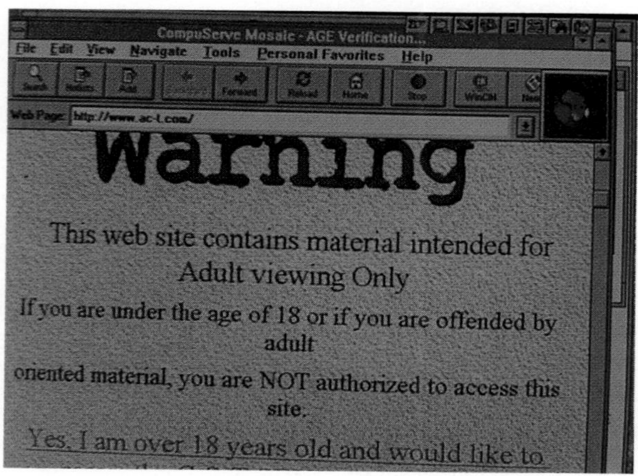

the person with whom you have been pursuing a virtual relationship is not who he or she claims to be. This pitfall is particularly dangerous when one of the parties in the relationship is a minor. In response to a recent online query, 130 female teenagers stated that they had posted erotic stories on a sexually oriented bulletin board and corresponded with adult men. In the stories, the teenagers pretended to be adults. Several of the teenagers also admitted that they had scheduled face-to-face meetings with these adult men without telling anyone.[8] Although none of the teenagers reported any negative consequences as a result of these meetings, the potential for danger was most certainly present.

A second drawback to online sex is the considerable cost. Although chat rooms are sometimes free and Web sites have "visitor's passes" that allow sneak previews, most of the hard-core sexual activity can be very expensive. Some chat rooms charge as much as $12 an hour for a conversation.[9] To get to the more explicit photographs and participatory novels on the Internet, a member's fee is required, which ranges anywhere from $19.95 for six months to $129.95 for a year. These fees are generally paid by credit card online. A digital video camera, which is necessary to create real-time pictures to transmit through a personal computer, costs at least $100.[10] Upgrades to computer memory and equipment to handle more technologically advanced transmissions such as video clips can also be costly, running into the thousands of dollars.

A third potential problem is cybersex addiction. Some people become so involved with virtual reality that they find themselves uninterested in the real world. A librarian at a large college recently reported that many college students have to be asked to log off the library's computers that have Internet connections. These students ignore library policy that limits their Internet use to 30 minutes. One student had to be threatened by campus police; he was logged onto a sexually oriented chat room for almost four hours. In another case at the same college a library employee was disciplined after he was caught downloading sexually explicit material.[11] As a result of these incidents the college now blocks many sexually explicit sites and has disabled its computers' ability to download any material.

Avoiding Sex on the Internet

With all the publicity and notoriety surrounding sexually oriented Internet sites, many concerned parents want to ensure that their children do not have access to sexual material through their personal computers. Other people are offended by cybersex and do not want it coming into their homes for religious or moral reasons. For these people, several options exist. Parents can subscribe to an online service that blocks potentially offensive sites. CompuServe, one of the largest online providers, suspended 200 sex discussion groups in response to German authorities' contention that the groups violated German obscenity laws.[12] Also, AOL and Prodigy have mechanisms available on their services to block access to areas that most parents would consider inappropriate for their children.[13] These mechanisms are available free of charge with subscription to the services.

A second option is to purchase a program that will block out undesirable material. One such program, Surf-watch, will automatically block access to 1000 sites and will let you screen all user groups, Web sites, and other electronic avenues. The cost of this program is $49.95 plus a $5.95 monthly service fee. Other types of blocker programs include NetNanny, which lets parents monitor everything that passes through their computer, and Time's Up, which lets parents set up time limits and appropriate times for their children to use the computer.[14]

A third, decidedly low-tech option is the most obvious and also the most overlooked. Parents should watch what their children are doing while they are online and monitor all activities, perhaps by making computer use a family activity.[15] As columnist Michael J. Miller points out, much of the fear that children will accidentally stumble onto a sexually oriented site is unfounded. Unlike broadcast media, on the Internet, you must enter a specific address or follow a specific link to reach a sexually oriented site. Parents who watch their kids will know exactly where the kids go during an online jaunt. Additionally, parents should teach their children some basic safety information such as to never to give out their real name, address, or telephone number to people they meet online. Children should understand that even though they may have online friends, these people are really strangers whom they know little about.[16–20]

The Telecommunications Competition and Deregulation Act

In February 1996, U.S. President Clinton signed into law the Telecommunications Competition and Deregulation Act, a law that contains a provision called the Telecommunications Decency Act to block indecency online. Anyone caught transmitting obscene, lewd, or indecent communications by any electronic means could be fined as much as U.S. $100 000 and sent to prison for as long as two years.[21, 22, 23]

In Canada, telecommunication is governed by the Canadian Radio and Television Commission (CRTC). The Criminal Code of Canada contains measures to protect children against indecency. Bill C-15A contains new provisions to counter sexual exploitation of children on the Internet. Section 163.1 of the Criminal Code prohibits the production, distribution, and possession of child pornography; Bill C-15A, clauses 11(2) and (3), amends section 163.1 to ensure these criminal prohibitions extend to analogous conduct in an Internet context. The code also makes it an offence to communicate via a "computer system" with a person under a certain age for the purpose of facilitating the commission of certain sexual offences in relation to children or child abduction.[24]

Civil libertarians in Canada and the United States and users of sexually oriented Internet sites oppose these laws because of freedom of speech and believe that this freedom should include the Internet. They also believe that the laws as written are too broad and confusing; they could be interpreted as banning any use of profanity or nudity online, including news reports, legal documents, literature, and even the Bible.[25, 26, 27]

Some parents and religious groups, on the other hand, are applauding these new acts. They feel they give them more control over what kinds of materials are coming into their homes. They believe that legislation is necessary to protect children from being exposed to pornography online.

A line has been drawn in the sand regarding sex on the Internet. Supporters of the new laws are joining organizations that work to defend traditional values and fight against increased pornography. Meanwhile, Web search engines such as Yahoo protested the American legislation by turning their Web pages to black with white lettering for 48 hours to demonstrate "virtual mourning," and the American Civil Liberties Union filed a federal court complaint to block enforcement of the law.[28]

Using the Internet for sexual purposes can have both positive and negative consequences; therefore, people who do so should weigh all factors involved before they decide to enter the world of cybersex. Parents should be especially careful about what they allow to come into their homes via the personal computer. Although blocking methods and the new federal laws provide some protection from sexually oriented material, it is ultimately the individual's responsibility to choose and to monitor what types of information come up while surfing the Internet.

For Discussion ...

Have you or has someone you know ever explored sexually oriented Web sites on the Internet? If so, was it a positive or a negative experience? Would you be willing to meet a virtual friend face to face? Why or why not? Do you support the clauses referring to the Internet in Bill C-15? Why or why not?

References

1. Lewis PH: Despite a new plan for cooling it off, cybersex stays hot, *New York Times*, p A1, March 26, 1995.
2. Nashawatz C: Where the wild things are: anonymous sex is back, *Entertainment Weekly*, Sept 23, 1994.
3. Levy S, Stone B: No place for kids: a parents' guide to sex on the Net, *Newsweek*, July 3, 1995.
4. Despite a new plan.
5. Van der Leur G: Twilight zone of the id, *Time*, 145(12), p 36, Special Issue, Spring 1995.
6. Machure B: MUDs and MUSHes and MOOs, *PC Magazine*, p 10, April 30, 1995.
7. Twilight zone.
8. Bennahan DS: Lolitas on-line, *Harper's Bazaar*, p 3406, Sept 1995.
9. Twilight zone.
10. Miller MJ: Cybersex shock, *PC Magazine*, Oct 10, 1995.
11. Anonymous: Personal communication, March 23, 1996.
12. Mezer M: A bad dream comes true in cyberspace, *Newsweek*, p 2, Jan 8, 1996.
13. No place for kids.
14. Cybersex shock.
15. No place for kids.
16. Ibid.
17. Twilight zone.
18. MUDs and Mustles.
19. Lolitas on-line.
20. Cybersex shock.
21. Despite a new plan.
22. A bad dream comes true.
23. Wagner M: Tempers flare over web censorship, *Computerworld*, Feb 12, 1996.
24. Bill C-15: Criminal Code Law Amendment Act, 2001 (L5-404E).
25. Tempers flare.
26. Makin, K: Child porn case spurs intense arguments, *The Globe & Mail*, January 19, 2000.
27. Department of Justice Canada: Highlights of the Omnibus Bill, *Backgrounder*, 2001. **http://canada.justice.gc.ca/en/news/nr/2001/doc_26058.html**
28. Tempers flare.

Chapter 13
Managing Your Fertility

Chapter Objectives

After reading this chapter, you should be able to

- Explain the difference between the terms *birth control* and *contraception.*
- Define the theoretical effectiveness and the use effectiveness of contraceptive methods and why they differ.
- Discuss the advantages and disadvantages of each form of birth control.
- Identify the many ways in which contraceptive hormones can be delivered to females.
- Identify the circumstances under which emergency contraception might be used.
- Identify and explain the procedures that produce male and female sterilization.
- Identify physiological obstacles and aids to fertilization.
- Describe the events that take place during each of the three stages of labour.
- Identify and explain the four procedures available through assisted reproductive technologies (ART).

Online Learning Centre Resources

www.mcgrawhill.ca/college/hahn

Log on to our Online Learning Centre (OLC) for access to Web links for study and exploration of health topics. Here are some examples of what you'll find:

- **www.ppfc.ca** Check here for family planning, contraception, abortion, and counselling services information.
- **www.naral.org** Visit this site for a pro-choice point of view about abortion.
- **www.lifesite.net** Look here for a different point of view—includes information on alternatives to abortion and the politics of the pro-life movement.

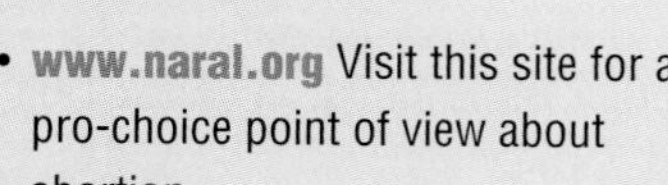

Media Pulse

Information Online—Birth Control and Sexuality

The Internet offers resources for locating information about contraception, birth control, and related topics. Planned Parenthood Federation of Canada provides one of the most comprehensive sites at **www.ppfc.ca**. Here you can find a wide selection of pamphlets, books, newsletters, and videotapes, as well as links to other Web sites.

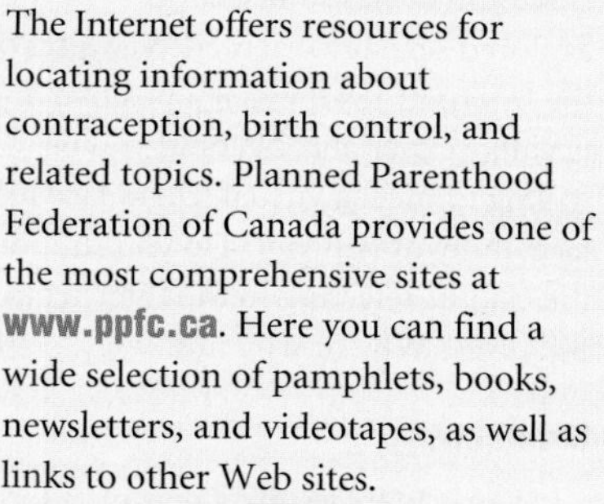

If you're looking for birth control information, click on Planned Parenthood's "Frequently Asked Questions," "Hot Issues," "Resources," and "Links." Some of the frequently asked questions are

- Am I pregnant?
- What can I do if I am pregnant?
- Do I have a sexually transmitted infection?
- What are the laws in my province about teens' access to abortion services and birth control?
- How can I get access to birth control?

Answers follow each of these questions. Planned Parenthood believes that when people are empowered with knowledge, they are better able to make sound decisions about their health and sexuality.

The "Hot Issues" option at Planned Parenthood's Web site provides various reports on specific topics, such as abortion, birth control, family planning, sexually transmitted diseases, and teen pregnancy and abortion.

Three additional online sites offer reliable information about sexuality and reproductive choices. The first is the Alan Guttmacher Institute Web site at **www.agi-usa.org**. This institute is dedicated to protecting the reproductive choices of

Media Pulse *continued*

women and men throughout the world. It fulfills its mission by disseminating information and the results of scientific research on the subject. The Guttmacher Institute's menu of options includes abortion, law and public policy, pregnancy and birth, prevention and contraception, sexual behaviour, and sexually transmitted diseases and youth.

A Canadian Web site devoted to sexuality education information is **www.sexualityandu.ca**. This site provides reliable information on topics varying from sexually transmitted infections (STIs) to contraceptive choices.

The Sex Information and Education Council of Canada is a nonprofit organization dedicated to developing, collecting, and disseminating information about sexuality. SIECCAN's Web site is at **www.sieccan.org**. This organization promotes comprehensive sexuality education and advocates the right of individuals to make responsible sexual choices. SIECCAN publishes and distributes thousands of pamphlets, booklets, and bibliographies each year to professionals and the general public.

If you wish to search for information about certain sexuality topics from a pro-life perspective, you might wish to examine the Web site for Pro-life Canada Index at **www.webhart.net/vandee/prolife.shtml**. This site provides links to information related to abortion alternatives, crisis pregnancy centres, pro-life news, and pro-life groups online.

How you decide to control your **fertility** will have an important effect on your future. Your understanding of information and issues related to fertility control will help you make responsible decisions in this complex area.

For traditional-age students, these decisions may be fast approaching (see Exploring Your Spirituality on p. 312 for a discussion of decision making about sex and the spiritual dimension of sexuality). Frequently, nontraditional-age students are parents who have had experiences that make them useful resources for other students in the class.

BIRTH CONTROL VS. CONTRACEPTION

Any discussion about the control of your fertility should start with an explanation of the subtle differences between the terms **birth control** and **contraception**. Although many people use the words interchangeably, they reflect different perspectives about fertility control. *Birth control* is an umbrella term that refers to all of the procedures you might use to prevent the birth of a child. Birth control includes all available contraceptive measures, as well as sterilization, use of the intrauterine device (IUD), and abortion procedures.

Contraception is a much more specific term for any procedure used to prevent the fertilization of an ovum. Contraceptive measures vary widely in the mechanisms they use to accomplish this task. They also vary considerably in their method of use and their rate of success in preventing conception. A few examples of contraceptive methods are the use of condoms, oral contraceptives, spermicides, and diaphragms.

Beyond the numerous methods mentioned, certain forms of sexual behaviour not involving intercourse could be considered forms of contraception. For example, mutual masturbation by couples virtually eliminates the possibility of pregnancy. This practice, as well as additional forms of sexual expression other than intercourse (such as kissing, touching, and massage), has been given the generic term *outercourse*. Not only does **outercourse** protect against unplanned pregnancy, it may also significantly reduce the transmission of sexually transmitted infection (STIs), including HIV infection.

THEORETICAL EFFECTIVENESS VS. USE EFFECTIVENESS

People considering the use of a contraceptive method need to understand the difference between the two effectiveness rates given for each form of contraception. *Theoretical effectiveness* is a measure of a contraceptive method's ability to prevent a pregnancy when the method is used precisely as directed during every act of intercourse. *Use effectiveness*, however, refers to the effectiveness of a method in preventing conception when used by the general public. Use effectiveness rates take into account factors that lower effectiveness below that

Key Terms

fertility
The ability to reproduce.

birth control
All of the methods and procedures that can prevent the birth of a child.

contraception
Any method or procedure that prevents fertilization.

outercourse
Sexual activity that does not involve intercourse.

Exploring Your Spirituality

There's More to Sex than You Thought ...

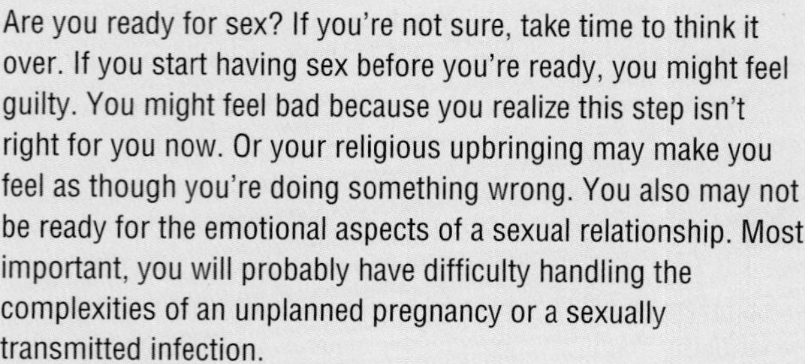

Are you ready for sex? If you're not sure, take time to think it over. If you start having sex before you're ready, you might feel guilty. You might feel bad because you realize this step isn't right for you now. Or your religious upbringing may make you feel as though you're doing something wrong. You also may not be ready for the emotional aspects of a sexual relationship. Most important, you will probably have difficulty handling the complexities of an unplanned pregnancy or a sexually transmitted infection.

If you do feel ready for sex, you still have a choice. Sex may be OK for you now. It may be personally fulfilling, something that enhances your self-esteem. Alternatively, you can choose to abstain from sex until later—another way of enhancing your self-esteem. You'll feel empowered by making the decision for yourself, rather than doing what is expected. Being strong enough to say "no" can also make you feel good about yourself. For some, making this decison may reflect a renewed commitment to spiritual or religious concerns.

If you're married, sex is a good way of connecting as a couple. It's something that the two of you alone share. It's a time to give special attention to each other—taking a break from the kids, your jobs, and your other responsibilities. It's a way of saying: "This relationship is important—it's something I value."

Going through a pregnancy together is another opportunity for closeness. From the moment you know that you're going to be parents, you're connected in a new way. Your focus becomes the expected child. You'll watch the fetus grow on ultrasound, go to parenting and Lamaze classes together, visit the doctor together, mark the various milestones, and share new emotions. When your child is born, you'll be connected as never before.

Whether you're thinking about starting to have sex, making the decision to wait, or examining the sexual life you have now, you can't ignore the possibilities and the consequences. Is the time right for you? Are you doing this for yourself or for someone else? What do you think you will gain from waiting? Do you expect your future partner to also have made the decision to wait? What do you expect to get from a sexual relationship—pleasure, intimacy, love? What do you expect to give? Do you want an emotional commitment? Do you view sex and love as inseparable? Do you understand how sex can enhance your spirituality? Taking time to consider these questions can make you feel good about yourself—no matter what you decide.

based on "perfect" use. Failure to follow proper instructions, illness of the user, forgetfulness, physician (or pharmacist) error, and a subconscious desire to experience risk or even pregnancy are a few of the factors that can lower the effectiveness of even the most theoretically effective contraceptive technique.

Effectiveness rates are often expressed in terms of the percentage of women users of childbearing age who do not become pregnant while using the method for one year. In Canada the Pearl Index is used, referring to the failure rate for 100 women using the method for one year. For some methods the theoretical- and use-effectiveness rates are vastly different; the theoretical rate is always higher than the use rate. Table 13–1 presents data concerning effectiveness rates, advantages, and disadvantages of many birth control methods.

SELECTING YOUR CONTRACEPTIVE METHOD

In this section, we discuss some of the many factors that should be important to you as you consider selecting a contraceptive method. Remember that no method possesses equally high marks in all of the following areas. It is important that you and your partner select a contraceptive method that is both acceptable and effective, as determined by your unique needs and expectations. Completing the Personal Assessment on p. 338 will help you make this decision.

For a contraceptive method to be acceptable to those who wish to exercise a large measure of control over their fertility, the following should be given careful consideration:

- *It should be safe.* The contraceptive approach you select should not pose a significant health risk for you or your partner.
- *It should be effective.* Your approach must have a high success rate in preventing pregnancy.
- *It should be reliable.* The form you select must be able to be used over and over again with consistent success.
- *It should be reversible.* Couples who eventually want to have a family should select a method that can be reversed.
- *It should be affordable.* The cost of a particular method must fit comfortably into a couple's budget.
- *It should be easy to use.* Complicated instructions or procedures can make a method difficult to use effectively.
- *It should not interfere with sexual expression.* An ideal contraceptive fits in comfortably with a couple's intimate sexual behaviour.

TALKING POINTS • The method of birth control your partner prefers doesn't allow for spontaneous sex. How would you explain that this decreases your enjoyment?

Table 13–1 Effectiveness Rates of Birth Control for 100 Women During One Year of Use

Method	Estimated Effectiveness: Theoretical	Estimated Effectiveness: Use	Advantages	Disadvantages
No method (chance)	15%	15%	Inexpensive	Totally ineffective
Withdrawal	96%	81%	No supplies or advance preparation needed; no side effects; men share responsibility for family planning	Interferes with coitus; very difficult to use effectively; women must trust men to withdraw as orgasm approaches
Periodic abstinence Calendar Basal body temperature Cervical mucus method Symptothermal	91%–99%	75%	No supplies needed; no side effects; men share responsibility for family planning; women learn about their bodies	Difficult to use, especially if menstrual cycles are irregular, as is common in young women; abstinence may be necessary for long periods; lengthy instruction and ongoing counselling may be needed
Cervical cap (no prior births)	91%	80%	No health risks; helps protect against some STIs and cervical cancer	Limited availability
Spermicide (gel, foam, suppository, film)	94%	80%	No health risks; helps protect against some STIs; can be used with condoms to increase effectiveness considerably	Must be inserted 5 to 30 minutes before coitus; effective for only 30 to 60 minutes; some women may find them awkward or embarrassing to use
Diaphragm with spermicide	94%	80%	No health risks; helps protect against some STIs and cervical cancer	Must be inserted with jelly or foam before every act of coitus and left in place for at least 6 hours after coitus; must be fitted by health care personnel; some women may find it awkward or embarrassing to use; may be inconvenient to clean, store, and carry
Male condom Male condom with spermicide	97% 99%	86% 95%	Easy to use; inexpensive and easy to obtain; no health risks; very effective protection against some STIs; men share responsibility for family planning	Must be put on just before coitus; some men and women complain of decreased sensation
Female condom	95%	79%	Relatively easy to use; no prescription required; polyurethane is stronger than latex; provides some STI protection; silicone-based lubrication provided; useful when male will not use a condom	Contraceptive effectiveness and STI protection not as high as with male condom; couples may be unfamiliar with a device that extends outside the vagina; more expensive than male condoms
IUCD Nova-T (Copper) Mirena (Progestin)	 99%+ 98%	 95% 98%	Easy to use; highly effective in preventing pregnancy; does not interfere with coitus; repeated action not needed; depending on the device, can be effective for up to 10 years	May increase risk of pelvic inflammatory disease (PID) and infertility in women with more than one sexual partner; not usually recommended for women who have never had a child; must be inserted by health care personnel; may cause heavy bleeding and pain in some women
Combined pill (Estrogen-progestin) (Progesterone-only pill)	99%+ 99%	95% 95%	Easy to use; highly effective in preventing pregnancy; does not interfere with coitus; regulates menstrual cycle; reduces heavy bleeding and menstrual pain; helps protect against ovarian and endometrial cancer	Must be taken every day; requires medical examination and prescription; minor side effects such as nausea or menstrual spotting; possibility of circulatory problems, such as blood clotting, strokes, and hypertension, in a small percentage of users
Depo-Provera (3 month)	99%+	95%	Easy to use; highly effective for an extended period; continued use prevents menstruation	Requires supervision by a physician; administered by injection; some women experience irregular menstrual spotting and weight gain in early months of use
Subdermal implants	99%+	99%+	Highly effective for 5-year period; helps prevent anemia and regulates menstrual cycle	Requires minor surgery; some women experience irregular menstrual spotting and difficult removal
Tubal ligation	99%+	99%+	Permanent; removes fear of pregnancy	Surgery-related risks; generally considered irreversible
Vasectomy	99%+	99%+	Permanent; removes fear of pregnancy	Generally considered irreversible
Contraceptive ring (estrogen-progestin)	99%+	n/a	Easy to use after learning how to insert; remains in place for 3 weeks	Like other hormonal methods, does not protect against STIs; requires a physician's prescription; possibility of CV problems in a small percentage of users
Contraceptive patch	99%+	n/a	Easy to apply; must be changed weekly for 3 weeks	Like other hormonal methods, does not protect against STIs; requires a physician's prescription; possibility of CV problems in a small percentage of users

Health on the Web

Behaviour Change Activities

Making Informed Choices

In this chapter you will learn about a number of birth control methods. You also can find a vast amount of information about birth control on the Internet. An excellent resource is the Planned Parenthood Web site at **www.ppfc.ca**. Planned Parenthood believes in the right of each individual to manage his or her fertility, regardless of income, marital status, race, ethnicity, sexual orientation, age, national origin, or residence. To assist people in making reproductive decisions, Planned Parenthood provides information on contraceptive choices throughout the lifespan. Take time to read about the different methods available and consider how well each would work for you if you are sexually active. In addition, consider Planned Parenthood's position on reproductive rights. Do you agree or disagree with this position? Explain your answer.

Questions About Sexual Health? Go Ask Alice!

No matter what our age or experience, most of us from time to time have questions about sexuality or sexual health. *Go Ask Alice* is an interactive question-and-answer service offered by the Health Education and Wellness Program of the Columbia University Health Service. The service was established to help students make choices that will enhance their health and happiness and the well-being of their partners. Go to **www.alice.columbia.edu/index.html**. Click on *Go Ask Alice*, then choose "Sexual Health." Now select from the list of questions other post-secondary students have asked about birth control, or submit your own question.

Calculate the Due Date

During pregnancy, a series of complex yet coordinated changes occur in the female body. Go to **www.mydr.com.au/tools/pregnancy.asp** to obtain an interactive due date calculator. Use the calculator to identify the milestones during a pregnancy.

CURRENT BIRTH CONTROL METHODS

Withdrawal

Withdrawal, or **coitus interruptus**, is the contraceptive practice in which the erect penis is removed from the vagina just before ejaculation of semen. Theoretically this procedure prevents sperm from entering the deeper structures of the female reproductive system. The use effectiveness of this method, however, reflects how unsuccessful this method is in practice (see Table 13–1)[1].

There is strong evidence to suggest that the clear pre-ejaculate fluid that helps neutralize and lubricate the male urethra can contain *viable* (capable of fertilization) sperm.[2] This sperm can be deposited near the cervical opening before withdrawal of the penis. This phenomenon may in part explain the relatively low effectiveness of this method. Furthermore, withdrawal does not protect users from the transmission of STIs.

Periodic Abstinence

There are four approaches included in the birth control strategy called **periodic abstinence**: (1) the calendar method, (2) the basal body temperature (BBT) method, (3) the Billings cervical mucus method, and (4) the symptothermal method.[3] All four methods attempt to determine the time a woman ovulates. Figure 13–1 shows a day-to-day fertility calendar used to estimate fertile periods. Most research indicates that an ovum is viable for only about 24 to 36 hours after its release from the ovary. (Once inside the female reproductive tract, some sperm can survive up to a week.)

When a woman can accurately determine when she ovulates, she must refrain from intercourse long enough for the ovum to begin to disintegrate. Of course, for couples trying to become pregnant, their goal will be to find the most fertile days that unprotected intercourse could produce a pregnancy.

Fertility awareness, *rhythm*, *natural birth control*, and *natural family planning* are terms interchangeable with periodic abstinence. Remember that periodic abstinence methods *do not* provide protection against the spread of STIs and HIV infection.

Periodic abstinence is the only acceptable method endorsed by the Roman Catholic Church. For some people who have deep concerns for the spiritual dimensions of their health, the selection of a contraceptive method other than periodic abstinence may indicate a serious compromise of beliefs.

Key Terms

withdrawal (coitus interruptus)
A contraceptive practice in which the erect penis is removed from the vagina before ejaculation.

periodic abstinence
Birth control methods that rely on a couple's avoidance of intercourse during the ovulatory phase of a woman's menstrual cycle; also called *fertility awareness* or *natural family planning.*

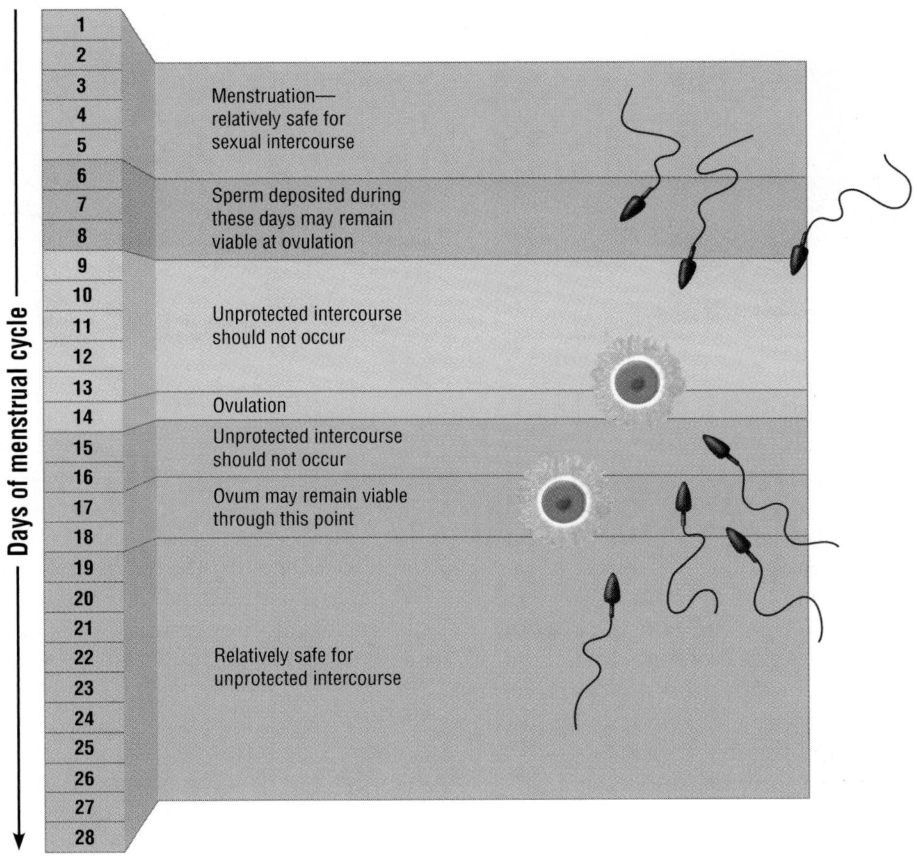

Figure 13–1 Periodic abstinence (fertility awareness or natural family planning) can combine use of the calendar, basal body temperature measurements, and Billings mucus techniques to identify the fertile period. Remember that most women's cycles are not consistently perfect 28-day cycles, as shown in most illustrations.

The **calendar method** requires close examination of a woman's menstrual cycle for at least eight cycles. Records are kept of the length (in days) of each cycle. *A cycle* is defined as the number of days from the first day of menstral flow in one cycle to the first day of menstral flow in the next cycle.

To determine the days she should abstain from intercourse, a woman should subtract 18 from her shortest cycle; this is the first day she should abstain from intercourse in an upcoming cycle. Then she should subtract 11 from her longest cycle; this is the last day she must abstain from intercourse in an upcoming cycle.

The *basal body temperature method* requires a woman (for about three or four successive months) to take her body temperature every morning before she rises from bed. A finely calibrated thermometer, available in many drugstores, is used for this purpose.[4] The theory behind this method is that a distinct correlation exists between body temperature and the process of ovulation. Just before ovulation, the body temperature supposedly dips and then rises about 0.2°C to 0.4°C (0.5° to 1.0° F) for the rest of the cycle. The woman is instructed to refrain from intercourse during the interval when the temperature change takes place.

Drawbacks of this procedure include the need for consistent, accurate readings and the realization that all women's bodies are different. Some women may not fit the temperature pattern projection because of biochemical differences in their bodies. Also, body temperatures can fluctuate because of a wide variety of illnesses and physical stressors.

The *Billings cervical mucus method* is another periodic abstinence technique. Generally used with other periodic abstinence techniques, this method requires a woman to evaluate the daily mucus discharge from her cervix. Users of this method become familiar with the changes in both appearance (from clear to cloudy) and consistency (from watery to thick) of their cervical

Key Term

calendar method
A form of periodic abstinence in which the variable lengths of a woman's menstrual cycle are used to calculate her fertile period.

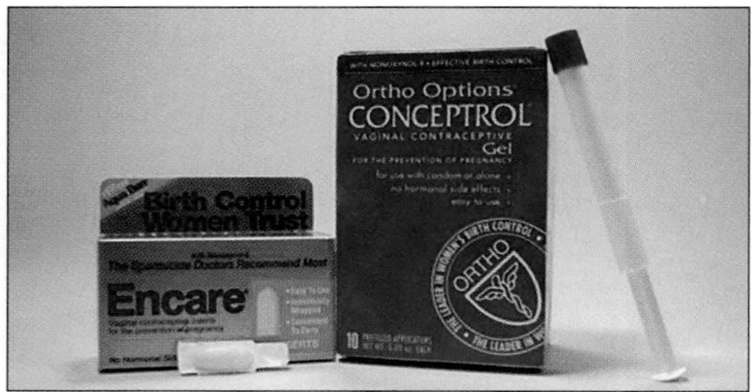

Vaginal spermicide.

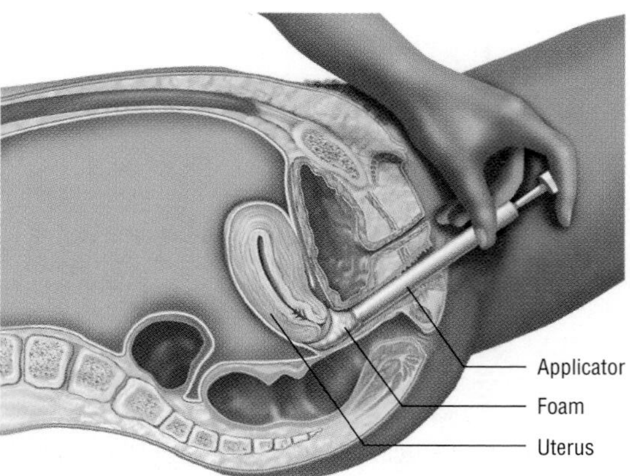

Figure 13–2 Spermicidal foams, gels, and suppositories are placed deep into the vagina in the region of the cervix no longer than 30 minutes before intercourse.

mucus throughout their cycles. Women are taught that the unsafe days are when the mucus becomes clear and is the consistency of raw egg whites. Such a technique of ovulation determination must be learned from a physician or family planning professional.

The *symptothermal method* of periodic abstinence combines the use of the BBT method and the cervical mucus method. Couples using the symptothermal method are already using a calendar to chart the woman's body changes. Thus some family planning professionals consider the symptothermal method a combination of all of the periodic abstinence approaches.

Vaginal Spermicides

Spermicides are agents that are capable of killing sperm. Although they are not recommended as the primary form of fertility control, spermicidal agents are often recommended to be used with other forms of birth control. Alone, **spermicides** offer a reasonable amount of contraceptive protection for the woman who is sexually active on an *infrequent* basis. Spermicides containing nonoxynol-9 do not provide reliable protection against STIs and HIV infection.

Modern spermicides are safe, reasonably effective, reversible forms of contraception that can be obtained without a physician's prescription; they can be purchased in most drugstores and in many supermarkets. Like condoms, spermicides are relatively inexpensive. When used together, spermicides and condoms provide a high degree of contraceptive protection and disease prevention.

Spermicides, which are available in foam, cream, gel suppository, or film form, are made of water-soluble bases with a spermicidal chemical incorporated in the base. The base material is designed to liquefy at body temperature and distribute the spermicidal component in an even layer over the tissues of the upper vagina (Figure 13–2). The Star Box on p. 317 describes a unique film spermicide.

Spermicides are not specific to sperm cells; they also attack other cells and thus may provide the woman with some additional protection against many STIs and *pelvic inflammatory disease* (PID). However, when used alone, spermicides do not provide sufficient protection against most pathogens, including the HIV virus.

Condoms

Coloured or natural, smooth or textured, straight or shaped, plain or reservoir-tipped, dry or lubricated—the condom is approaching an art form. This is perhaps an exaggeration. Still, the familiar **condom** remains a safe, effective, reversible contraceptive device.

For couples who are highly motivated in their desire to prevent a pregnancy, the effectiveness of a condom can approach that of an oral contraceptive—especially if condom use is combined with a spermicide. (Many lubricated condoms now also contain a spermicide.) For couples who are less motivated or who use condoms on an irregular basis, the condom can be considerably less effective. This readily available and inexpensive method of contraception requires responsible use if it is to achieve a high level of effectiveness (see the Changing for the Better box on p. 318).

The condom offers a measure of protection against STIs. For both the man and the woman, chlamydial infections, gonorrhea, HIV infection, and other STIs are less likely to be acquired when the condom is used. When combined with a spermicide containing nonoxynol-9, condoms may become even more effective against the spread of STIs. Although advertisements suggest that condoms provide protection against the transmission of genital herpes, users of condoms must remember that this protection is limited to the penis and vagina—not to the surrounding genital region, where significant numbers of lesions are found. Like other barrier methods of contraception, the condom is a reasonable choice for couples who are motivated in their desire to prevent a

Vaginal Contraceptive Film

A unique spermicide delivery system developed in England is vaginal contraceptive film (VCF). Vaginal contraceptive film is a sheet containing nonoxynol-9 that is inserted into the vagina and placed over the cervical opening. Shortly after insertion the VCF dissolves into a gel-like material that clings to the cervical opening. The VCF can be inserted up to an hour before intercourse. Over the course of several hours, the material will be washed from the vagina in the normal vaginal secretions.

This spermicide is a nonprescription form of contraception that is as effective as other spermicidal foams and jellies. Like other spermicidal agents, VCF may help in minimizing the risk of some STIs and PID but when used alone does not provide reliable protection against all pathogens, including HIV.

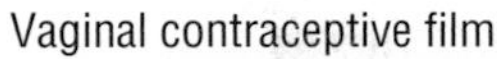

Vaginal contraceptive film.

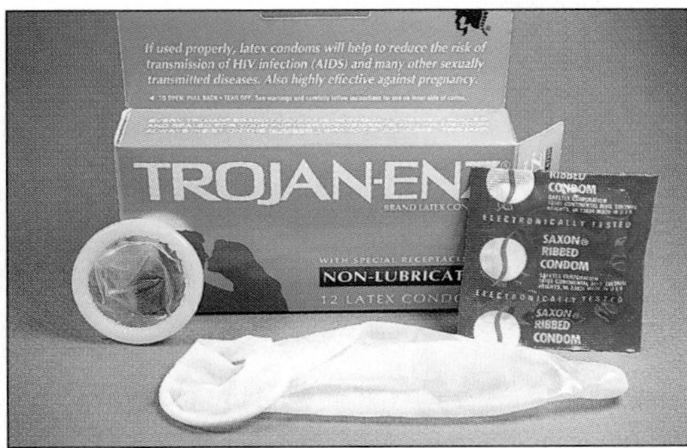

Condoms.

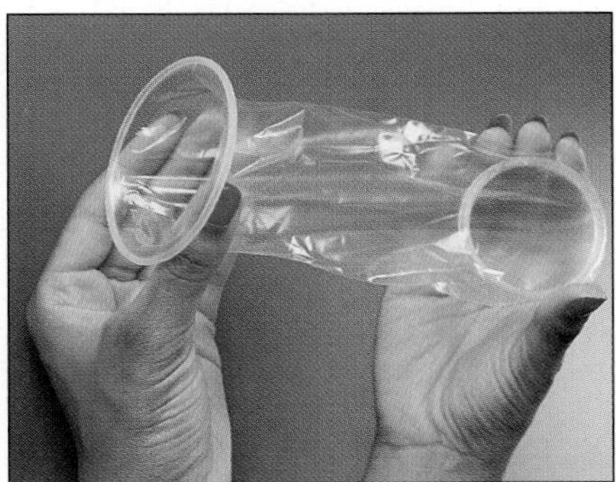

Female condom.

pregnancy and who are willing to assume the level of responsibility required.

Both Health Canada and the FDA have approved two types of polyurethane condoms. The Avanti male condom (Durex Consumer Products) and the Reality female condom (Female Health Company) are available as OTC one-time-use condoms.[5,6] These condoms are good alternatives for people who have an allergic sensitivity to latex. Also, they are thinner and stronger than latex condoms and can be used with oil-based lubricants. Currently, these condoms are believed to provide protection against STIs that is comparable to that of latex condoms, but definitive studies have not yet been completed.

The Reality female condom is a soft, loose-fitting polyurethane sheath containing two polyurethane rings (see photo). Reality is inserted like a diaphragm to line the inner walls of the vagina. The larger ring remains outside the vagina, and the external portion of the condom provides some protection to the labia and the base of the penis. Reality is coated on the inside with a silicone-based lubricant. Additional lubricant is provided for the outside of the sheath. This lubricant does not contain a spermicide. Female and male condoms should not be used together since they might adhere to each other and cause slippage or displacement.[7] The contraceptive effectiveness of the female condom is not as high as that of the male condom. However, as people become more familiar with using the female condom, its effectiveness may increase.

Key Term

spermicides
Chemicals capable of killing sperm.

condom
A latex or polyurethane shield designed to cover the erect penis and retain semen on ejaculation; "rubber" or "safe."

Changing *for the Better*

Maximizing the Effectiveness of Condoms

Putting on a condom seems so easy. Is there anything else I need to know about condom use?

These simple directions for using condoms correctly, in combination with your motivation and commitment to regular use, should provide you with reasonable protection:

- Keep a supply of condoms at hand. Condoms should be stored in a cool, dry place so that they are readily available at the time of intercourse. Condoms that are stored in wallets or automobile glove compartments may not be in satisfactory condition when they are used. Avoid temperature extremes. Check the condom package for the expiration date.
- Do not test a condom by inflating or stretching it. Handle it gently and keep it away from sharp fingernails.
- For maximum effectiveness, put the condom on before genital contact. Either the man or the woman can put the condom in place. Early application is particularly important in the prevention of STIs. Early application also lessens the possibility of the release of pre-ejaculate fluid into the vagina.
- Unroll the condom on the erect penis. For those using a condom without a reservoir tip, leave a 1 cm space to catch the ejaculate. To leave this space, pinch the tip of the condom as you roll it on the erect penis. Do not leave any air in the tip of the condom (Figure 13–3).
- Lubricate the condom if this has not already been done by the manufacturer. When doing this, be certain to use a water-soluble lubricant and not a petroleum-based product such as petroleum jelly. Petroleum can deteriorate the latex material. Other oil-based lubricants, such as mineral oil, baby oil, vegetable oil, shortening, and certain hand lotions, can quickly damage a condom. Use water-based lubricants only!

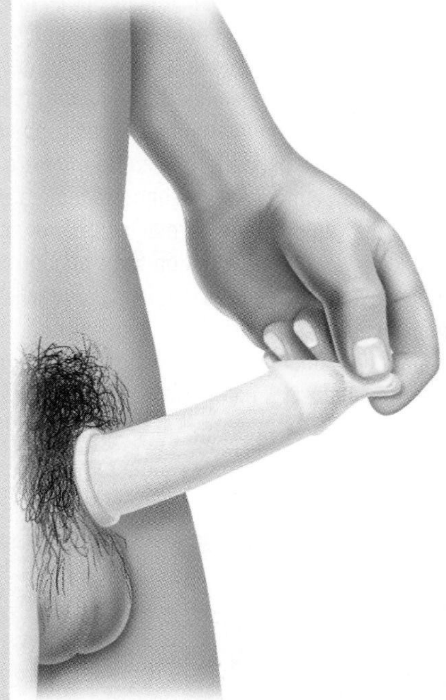

Figure 13–3 Pinch the end of the condom to leave 1 cm of space at the tip.

- After ejaculation, be certain that the condom does not become dislodged from the penis. Hold the rim of the condom firmly against the base of the penis during withdrawal. Do not allow the penis to become flaccid (soft) while still in the vagina.
- Inspect the condom for tears before throwing it away. If the condom is damaged in some way, immediately insert a spermicidal agent into the vagina.

Diaphragm

The **diaphragm** is a soft rubber cup with a springlike metal rim that, when properly fitted and correctly inserted by the user, rests in the top of the vagina. In its proper position the diaphragm covers the cervical opening (Figure 13–4). During intercourse the diaphragm stays in place quite well and cannot usually be felt by either the man or the woman.

The diaphragm is always used with a spermicidal cream or jelly. The diaphragm should be covered with an adequate amount of spermicide inside the cup and around the rim. When used properly with a spermicide, the diaphragm is a relatively effective contraceptive, and when combined with the man's use of a condom, its effectiveness is even greater.

Diaphragms must always be fitted and prescribed by a physician. The cost of obtaining a diaphragm and keeping a supply of spermicide may be higher than that of other methods. Also, a high level of motivation to follow the instructions *exactly* is important.

Diaphragms and other vaginal barrier methods, such as the cervical cap, do not provide reliable protection against STIs and HIV infection. If you are concerned about possible infection, either avoid sexual activity or use a latex condom and spermicide in combination.

Cervical Cap

The **cervical cap** is a small, thimble-shaped device that fits over the entire cervix. Resembling a small diaphragm, the cervical cap is placed deeper than the diaphragm.

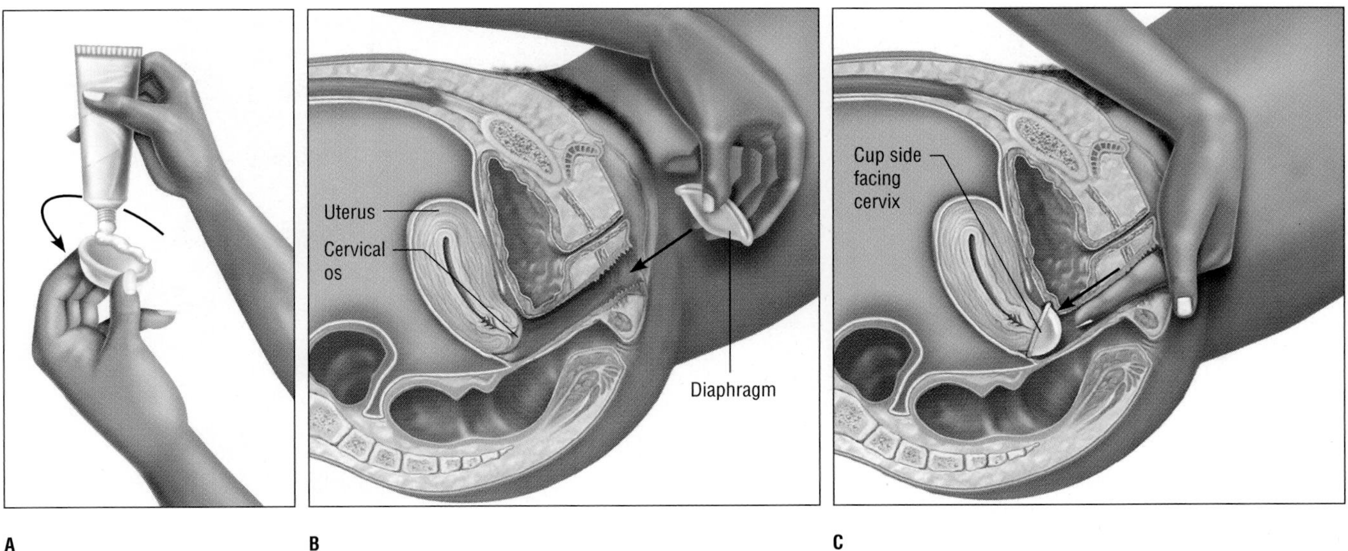

Figure 13–4 **A**, Spermicidal cream or jelly is placed into the diaphragm. **B**, The diaphragm is folded lengthwise and inserted into the vagina. **C**, The diaphragm is then placed against the cervix so that the cup portion with the spermicide is facing the cervix. The outline of the cervix should be felt through the central part of the diaphragm.

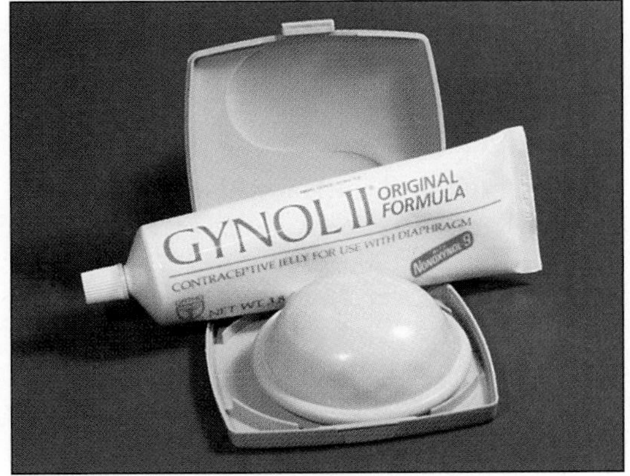

Diaphragm and contraceptive jelly.

Cervical cap.

The cap is held in place by suction rather than by pushing against anatomical structures (Figure 13–5). As with the diaphragm, a spermicide is used with the cervical cap. Thus it requires many of the same skills for insertion and care as does the diaphragm. The use effectiveness of the cervical cap appears to be approximately equal to that of the diaphragm. As with the diaphragm, the effectiveness of the cervical cap is much higher in women who have never had children. Cervical caps are distributed through physician prescription.

Contraceptive Sponge

The sponge is a small, pillow-shaped polyurethane device containing nonoxynol-9 spermicide. The sponge is dampened with tap water and inserted deep in the vagina to cover the cervical opening. This device provides contraceptive protection for up to 24 hours, regardless of the number of times intercourse occurs. After intercourse, the device must be left in place for at least six hours. Once removed, the sponge must be discarded. The sponge must not be left in place for longer than 24 to 30 hours because of the risk of toxic shock syndrome.[8]

Key Terms

diaphragm
A soft rubber cup designed to cover the cervix.

cervical cap
A small, thimble-shaped device designed to fit over the cervix.

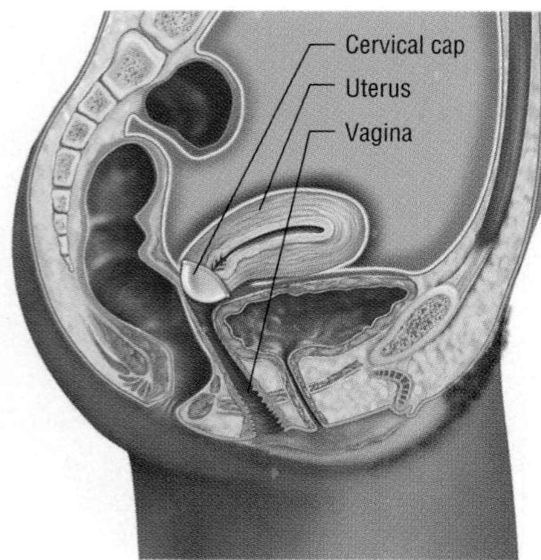

Figure 13–5 After the spermicidal cream or jelly is placed in the cervical cap, the cap is inserted into the vagina and placed against the cervix.

Used alone, the sponge does not provide reliable protection against STIs and HIV infection. In women who have not given birth to children, the contraceptive effectiveness of the sponge is similar to that of the diaphragm.

Intrauterine Contraceptive Device (IUCD)

There are two types of **intrauterine contraceptive devices (IUCDs)** available in Canada. The Nova-T is a copper-containing intrauterine device (IUCD) and the Mirena is a progestin- (Levonorgestrel) releasing intrauterine system (IUS). The copper-containing IUCD induces a foreign body reaction within the endometrium, is toxic to the sperm, and alters sperm motility. The progestin-releasing IUS interferes with endometrial development and cervical mucus production. Both IUCDs and IUSs are inserted into the uterine cavity. The contraceptive effect lasts for five years. Maximal contraceptive effect is achieved immediately. The Nova-T IUCD can also be inserted up to one week after an episode of unprotected intercourse as a means of emergency contraception. The IUCD is a highly effective form of contraception, with a Pearl Index of 0.2 (failure rate for 100 women using the method for one year).[9] Only a skilled physician can prescribe and insert an IUCD. As with many other forms of contraception, IUCDs do not offer protection against STIs or HIV infection.

As Table 13–1 indicates, IUCDs are very effective birth control devices, surpassed in effectiveness only by abstinence, sterilization, and oral (or implanted, or injected) contraceptives. Some women using IUCDs experience increased menstrual bleeding and cramping. Two uncommon but potentially serious side effects of IUCD use are uterine perforation (in which the IUCD imbeds itself into the uterine wall) and PID (which is a life-threatening infection of the abdominal cavity).

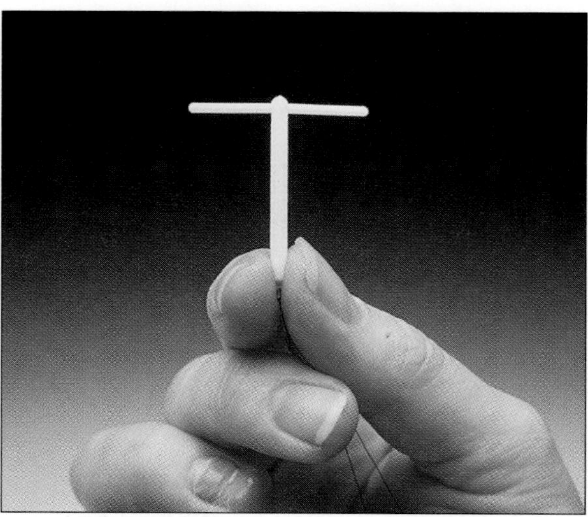

Progestasert IUCD.

A woman deciding whether to use an IUCD must discuss any concerns openly with her physician. The IUCD can be a very acceptable form of contraception, especially for women who are in their middle to late reproductive years, unable to take birth control pills, in a stable monogamous relationship, and not at risk for STIs.

Oral Contraceptives

Introduced in 1960, the **oral contraceptive pill** provides one of the highest effectiveness rates of any single reversible contraceptive method used today. "The pill" is the method of choice for over 16 million users in North America.[10] The oral contraceptive has become the most widely used method among Canadian women.

Use of the pill requires a physical examination by a physician and a prescription. Since oral contraceptives are available in a wide range of formulas, follow-up examinations are important to ensure that a woman is receiving an effective dosage with as few side effects as possible. Determining the right prescription for a particular woman may require a few consultations.

All oral contraceptives contain synthetic (laboratory-made) hormones. The *combined pill* uses both synthetic estrogen and synthetic progesterone in each of 21 pills. As with many forms of contraception, it must be emphatically stated that *oral contraceptives do not provide protection from the transmission of STIs or HIV infection.* Furthermore, the use of antibiotics lowers the pill's contraceptive effectiveness.

Oral contraceptives function in several ways. The estrogen in the pill tends to reduce ova development and ovulation. The progesterone in the pill helps reduce ovulation (by lowering the release of luteinizing hormone). The progesterone in the pill also causes the uterine wall to develop inadequately and helps thicken

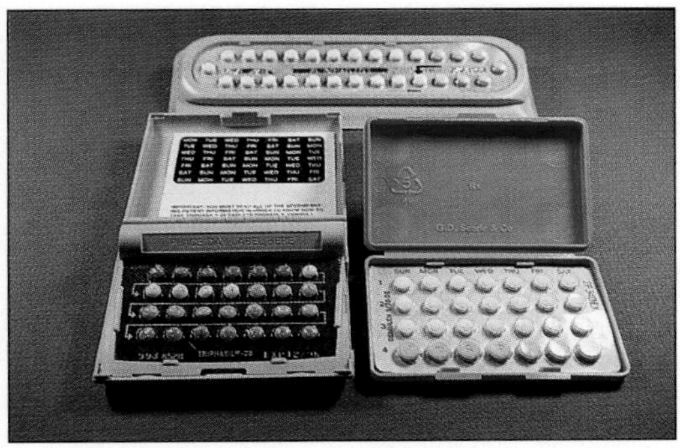

Oral contraceptives.

cervical mucus, thus making it difficult for sperm to enter the uterus.

The physical changes produced by the oral contraceptive provide some beneficial side effects in women. Since the synthetic hormones are taken for 21 days and then are followed by **placebo pills** or no pills for 7 days, the menstrual cycle becomes regulated. Even women who have irregular cycles immediately become "regular." Since the uterine lining is not developed to the extent seen in a nonuser, the uterus is not forced to contract with the same amount of vigor. Thus menstrual cramping is reduced, and the resultant menstrual flow is diminished. Research indicates that oral contraceptive use may provide protection against anemia, PID, noncancerous breast tumours, recurrent ovarian cysts, ectopic pregnancy, endometrial cancer, and ovarian cancer.[11]

The negative side effects of the oral contraceptive pill can be divided into two general categories: (1) unpleasant and (2) potentially dangerous. The unpleasant side effects generally subside within two or three months for most women. A number of women report some or many of the following symptoms:

- Tenderness in breast tissue
- Nausea
- Mild headaches
- Slight, irregular spotting
- Weight gain
- Fluctuations in sex drive
- Mild depression
- More frequent vaginal infections

TALKING POINTS • You've tried two different types of oral contraceptives and had unpleasant side effects with both. Your doctor says you should consider another birth control method, but you disagree. How could you talk to her about this in a matter-of-fact way?

The potentially dangerous side effects of the oral contraceptive pill are most often seen in the cardiovascular system. Blood clotting, strokes, hypertension, and heart attack all seem to be associated with the estrogen component of the combined pill. When compared with the risk to nonusers, the risk of dying from cardiovascular complications is only slightly increased among healthy young oral contraceptive users.

Additionally, the present consensus is that oral contraceptive users place themselves at slightly increased risk of developing breast cancer and cervical cancer.[12] However, it must be emphasized that this risk is quite small. Most health professionals agree that the risks related to pregnancy and childbirth are much greater than those associated with oral contraceptive use. Certainly, a woman who is contemplating the use of the pill must discuss all of the risks and benefits with her physician.

There are some **contraindications** for the use of oral contraceptives. If you have a history of blood clotting, migraine headaches, liver disease, a heart condition, high blood pressure, obesity, diabetes, epilepsy, or anemia, or if you have not established regular menstrual cycles, the pill probably should not be your contraceptive choice. A thorough health history is important before a woman starts to take the pill.

Two additional contraindications are receiving considerable attention by the medical community. Cigarette smoking and advancing age are highly associated with an increased risk of potentially serious side effects. Increasing numbers of physicians are not prescribing oral contraceptives for their patients who smoke. The risk of cardiovascular-related deaths is enhanced in women over age 35. The risk is even higher in female smokers over age 35.

For the vast majority of women, however, the pill, when properly prescribed, is safe and effective. Careful scrutiny of a woman's health history and careful follow-up

Key Terms

intrauterine contraceptive device (IUCD)
A small, plastic, medicated or unmedicated device that prevents continued pregnancy when inserted in the uterus.

oral contraceptive pill
A pill taken orally, composed of synthetic female hormones that prevent ovulation or implantation; "the pill."

placebo pills
Pills that contain no active ingredients.

contraindications
Factors that make the use of a drug inappropriate or dangerous for a particular person.

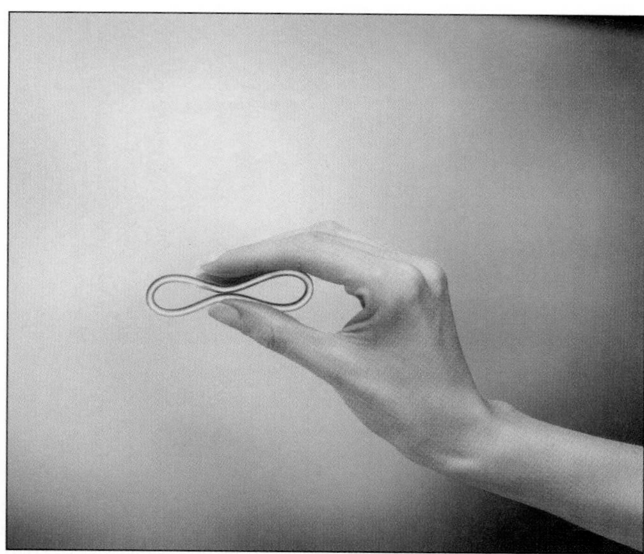

The NuvaRing contraceptive ring is a flexible ring that, when inserted into the vagina, delivers a low dose of hormones similar to those found in oral contraceptives.

examinations when a problem is suspected are essential elements that can provide a margin of safety. The ease of administration, the relatively low cost, and the effectiveness of the pill make it a sound choice for many women.

Progesterone-only pills (POPs)

Some women prefer not to use the combined oral contraceptive pill. To avoid some of the potentially serious side effects of the combined pill, some physicians are prescribing **progesterone-only pills (POPs)**. These oral contraceptives contain no estrogen—only low-dose progesterone. The POP seems to work by making an unsuitable environment for the transportation and implantation of the fertilized ovum. Endometrial suppression and thickening of the cervical mucus is the POP's primary mechanism of action. Ovulation is also inhibited in 60% of women taking the POP. The POP is taken daily and at the same time of day (within three hours) to ensure a reliable effect. The pills should be started on the first day of the menstrual cycle, and then daily (non-stop) thereafter. There is no pill-free interval. All 28 pills in a package contain active medication.[13] The effectiveness of the POP is slightly lower than that of the combined pill. Breakthrough bleeding and **ectopic pregnancy** are more common in POP users than in combined-pill users. POPs are also called minipills.

Emergency contraception

Emergency contraception is designed to prevent pregnancy after unprotected vaginal intercourse. This method is also called post-coital or "morning after" contraception. Emergency contraception is available in two forms: emergency hormonal contraception and the insertion of an IUCD. Canadian women are now able to ask for the morning-after pill, known as Plan B, without having to obtain a prescription from their doctor.

Emergency hormonal contraception involves the use of two doses of certain oral contraceptives.[14] The most commonly used oral contraceptives are the combined pills, which contain both synthetic estrogen and progesterone. The first dose of pills is taken within 72 hours of unprotected intercourse. A second dose is taken 12 hours later. If POPs are used for emergency contraception, the first dose must be taken within 48 to 72 hours after unprotected intercourse.

The insertion of an IUCD is a less commonly used, but highly effective, form of emergency contraception. To function as a contraceptive, however, the Nova-T IUCD must be inserted within seven days after unprotected intercourse.

Injectable Contraceptives

Injectable contraceptives provide an extremely high degree of effectiveness for a three-month period. The success rate for one such injectable contraceptive, *Depo-Provera*, is higher than 99%. For women who prefer not to take daily birth control pills or use the Norplant implants (see "Subdermal Implants"), Depo-Provera may be a good alternative.

New users of Depo-Provera report occasional breakthrough bleeding in the early months of use as the most common unpleasant side effect. Once the woman's body becomes adjusted to the presence of this drug, breakthrough bleeding is reduced considerably. After this point, the most commonly reported side effect is amenorrhea (the absence of periods). Many women

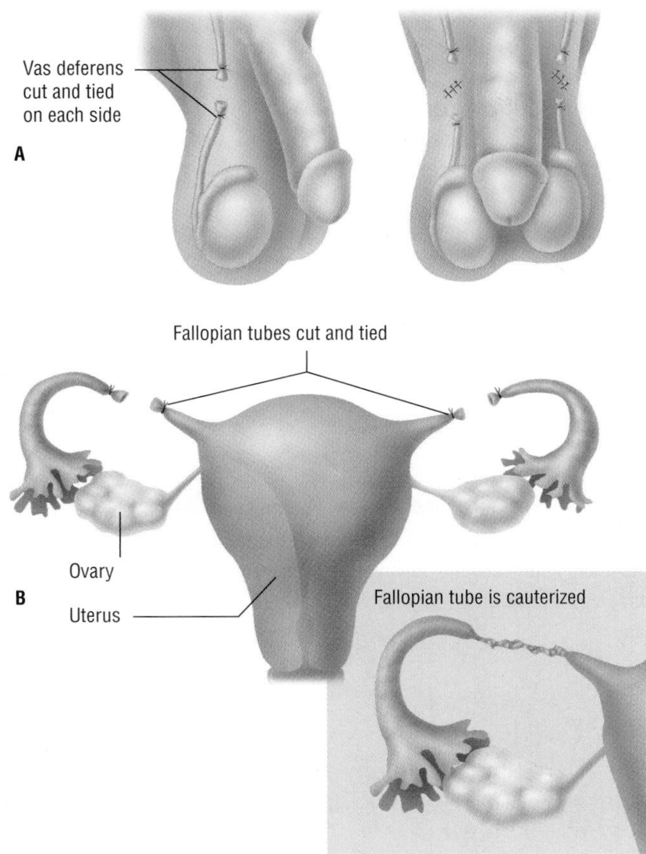

Figure 13–6 The most frequently used forms of male and female sterilization. **A**, Vasectomy. **B**, Tubal ligation.

consider amenorrhea to be a desirable effect of Depo-Provera use. Unlike users of oral contraceptives and subdermal implants, who return to fertility a few months after stopping their use, women who stop using Depo-Provera may experience infertility for a period of up to one year.[15]

The Contraceptive Ring

One of the newest contraceptives on the market is the vaginal **contraceptive ring** (NuvaRing). Available by prescription, NuvaRing is a thin polymer ring (5 cm in diameter and 0.3 cm thick) that contains synthetic estrogen and progestin. Users insert this device deep into the vagina where it remains for three weeks. At the end of the third week, the device is removed for a week and the woman has her period. The NuvaRing provides effective contraception (98–99% effective when used properly) for the entire four-week time frame.[16]

The ring functions in a manner similar to the oral contraceptive pill: it reduces the chances of ovulation and thickens cervical mucus. Women who use the ring cannot at the same time use cervical caps or diaphragms as a backup method. The contraceptive ring does not protect against sexually transmitted diseases, including the virus that causes HIV.

The Contraceptive Patch

The Ortho Evra **contraceptive patch** contains continuous levels of estrogen and progestin delivered from a 4.5 cm square patch that is applied weekly to one of four areas on the woman's body: the buttocks, abdomen, upper chest (front or back, excluding the breasts), or upper outer arm.[17] The patch remains attached even while a woman bathes, swims, or exercises. After three weeks of patches, the woman uses no patch for the fourth week, during which time the woman has her period. The patch functions in a manner similar to the oral contraceptive pill. Like all hormonal measures of contraception, the patch does not protect against sexually transmitted diseases, including the virus that causes HIV.

Subdermal Implants

This form of contraception, called Norplant, involves the use of six silicone rods filled with synthetic progesterone. Using a local anesthetic, the physician implants these rods just beneath the skin of the woman's upper or lower arm. The rods release low levels of the hormone for five years. An extremely effective contraceptive, with no responsibility beyond attendance for implant and removal, subdermal implants appear to produce minimal side effects. Irregular patterns of menstrual bleeding are the most common side effect. Sometimes the implanted rods are difficult to remove.

Sterilization

All of the contraceptive mechanisms or methods already discussed have one quality in common: they are reversible. Although microsurgical techniques are

Key Terms

progesterone-only pills (POPs)
Low-dose progesterone oral contraceptives.

ectopic pregnancy
A pregnancy in which the fertilized ovum implants at a site other than the uterus, typically in the fallopian tubes.

contraceptive ring
Thin, polymer contraceptive device containing estrogen and progestin; placed deep within the vagina for a three-week period.

contraceptive patch
Contraceptive skin patch containing estrogen and progestin; replaced each week for a three-week period.

providing medical breakthroughs, **sterilization** should generally be considered an irreversible procedure.[18]

When you decide to use sterilization, you will no longer be able to produce offspring. For this reason, couples considering sterilization procedures usually must undergo extensive discussions with a physician or family planning counsellor to identify their true feelings about this finality. People must be aware of the possible changes in self-concept they might have after sterilization. If you are a man who equates fertility with masculinity, you may have trouble accepting your new status as a sterile man. If you are a woman who equates motherhood with femininity, you might have adjustment problems after sterilization.

The male sterilization procedure is called a *vasectomy*. Accomplished with a local anesthetic in a physician's office, this 20- to 30-minute procedure consists of the surgical removal of a section of each vas deferens. After a small incision is made through the scrotum, the vas deferens is located and a small section is removed. The remaining ends are either tied or *cauterized* (Figure 13–6, *A*).

Immediately after a vasectomy, sperm may still be present in the vas deferens. A backup contraceptive is recommended until a physician microscopically examines a semen specimen. This examination usually occurs about six weeks after the surgery. After a vasectomy, men can still produce male sex hormones, get erections, have orgasms, and ejaculate. (Recall that sperm account for only a small portion of the semen.) Some men even report increased interest in sexual activity, since their chances of impregnating a woman are virtually nonexistent.

What happens to the process of spermatogenesis within each testicle? Sperm cells are still being produced, but they are destroyed by specialized white blood cells called *phagocytic leukocytes*.

The most common method of female sterilization is *tubal ligation*. During this procedure, the fallopian tubes are cut and the ends are tied. Some physicians cauterize the tube ends to ensure complete sealing (Figure 13–6, *B*). The fallopian tubes are usually reached through the abdominal wall. In a *minilaparotomy*, a small incision is made through the abdominal wall just below the navel. The resultant scar is quite small and is the basis for the term *band-aid surgery*.

Female sterilization requires about 20 to 30 minutes, with the patient under local or general anesthesia. The use of a *laparoscope* has made female sterilization much simpler than in the past. The laparoscope is a small tube equipped with mirrors and lights. Inserted through a single incision, the laparoscope locates the fallopian tubes before they are cut, tied, or cauterized. When a laparoscope is used through an abdominal incision, the procedure is called a *laparoscopy*.

Women who are sterilized still produce female hormones, ovulate, and menstruate. However, the ovum cannot move down the fallopian tube. Within a day of its release, the ovum will start to disintegrate and be absorbed by the body. Freed of the possibility of becoming pregnant, many sterilized women report an increase in sex drive and activity.

Two other procedures produce sterilization in women. *Ovariectomy* (the surgical removal of the ovaries) and *hysterectomy* (the surgical removal of the uterus) accomplish sterilization. However, these procedures are used to remove diseased (cancerous, cystic, or hemorrhaging) organs and are not considered primary sterilization techniques.

TALKING POINTS • You and your husband have children, and you'd like to stop taking the pill for health reasons. Your husband says you're pressuring him to have a vasectomy. How can you keep the dialogue going in a cooperative way?

New Developments in Contraception

Currently there are many new and exciting forms of contraception available in Canada, and more await approval. Following is a brief summary of some new developments.[19]

- *Lunelle*. A new injectable containing estrogen and progestin, which must be administered once a month in the doctor's office.
- *Mircette*. A new 0.02 mg oral contraceptive pill containing ethinyl and desogestrel. The active ingredient (0.01 mg ethinyl estradiol) extends into the placebo week with only two pill-free days.
- *Yasmin*. A new oral contraceptive pill containing ethinyl estradiol and drospirenone. This new progestin pill, because of its anti-mineralcorticoid properties, may slightly lower body weight as well as blood pressure.
- *Select*. This is a new oral contraceptive pill administered daily for 84 days at a time. There are only four withdrawal bleeds per year.

Abortion

Regardless of the circumstances under which pregnancy occurs, women may choose to terminate their pregnancies. No longer must women who do not want to be pregnant seek potentially dangerous, illegal abortions. On the basis of current technology and legality, women need never experience childbirth. The decision is theirs to make.

Abortion should never be considered a first-line, preferred form of fertility control. Rather, abortion is a final, last-chance undertaking. The decision to abort a fetus is a highly controversial, personal one—one that needs serious consideration by each woman.

In Canada, abortion was a Criminal Code offence from 1869 to 1969. Canadian women continued to have abortions during this period, but these illegal abortions were clandestine and usually unsafe. In 1969, a law was passed to regulate abortion under the Criminal Code. This law permitted a qualified medical practitioner to perform an abortion, if prior approval was obtained by a therapeutic abortion committee.[20]

A 1988 Supreme Court of Canada decision found this process unconstitutional. The 1969 law was rendered unenforceable and abortion was effectively decriminalized. As of 1998, a woman may obtain an abortion in a hospital or clinic in all provinces and territories in Canada, except Prince Edward Island. However, in most hospitals and clinics, the procedure is limited to a gestational age range that is specific to that facility.[21]

Abortion in Canada today is governed by the same legislation and medical standards as govern other medical procedures. There is no "abortion law" as such. Abortions are performed when a pregnant woman requests one from her doctor and a doctor grants her request.

To arrive at this point, there has been a long, difficult, and sometimes violent legal battle between pro-abortionists, led by people such as Dr. Henry Morgentaler, and anti-abortion, right-to-life groups throughout the country. The debate continues between those who wish to protect the rights of the unborn fetus and those who have worked to get easier access to abortion for Canadian women.

TALKING POINTS • You're unexpectedly pregnant, but abortion doesn't seem like a good choice for you. Your boyfriend, your family, and your friends all have strong but conflicting opinions about the situation. How can you show that you value their advice but still make it clear that the final decision needs to be yours alone?

First-trimester abortion procedures

Menstrual Extraction. Also referred to as *menstrual regulation*, *menstrual induction*, and *pre-emptive abortion*, menstrual extraction is a process carried out between the fourth and sixth week after the last menstrual period (or in the days immediately after the first missed menstrual period). This procedure is generally performed in a physician's office with a local anesthetic or *paracervical anesthetic* used. A small plastic *cannula* is inserted through the undilated cervical canal into the cavity of the uterus. Once the cannula is in position, a small amount of suction is applied by a hand-held syringe. By rotating and moving the cannula across the uterine wall, the physician can withdraw the endometrial tissue.

Vacuum Aspiration. Induced abortions undertaken during the sixth through ninth weeks of pregnancy are generally done through *vacuum aspiration* of the uterine contents. Vacuum aspiration is the most commonly performed abortion procedure. This procedure is similar in nature to menstrual extraction. Unlike menstrual extraction, however, vacuum aspiration may require **dilation** of the cervical canal and the use of a local anesthetic. In this more advanced stage of pregnancy, a larger cannula must be inserted into the uterine cavity. This process can be accomplished by using metal dilators of increasingly larger sizes to open the canal. After aspiration by an electric vacuum pump, the uterine wall may also be scraped to confirm complete removal of the uterine contents.

Dilation and Curettage (D & C). When a pregnancy is to be terminated during the ninth through fourteenth weeks, vacuum aspiration gives way to a somewhat similar procedure labelled **dilation and curettage**, or more familiarly, **D & C**. D & C usually requires a general anesthetic, not a local anesthetic.

Like vacuum aspiration, the D & C involves the gradual enlargement of the cervical canal through the insertion of increasingly larger metal dilators. When the cervix has been dilated to a size sufficient to allow for the passage of a *curette*, the removal of the endometrial tissue can begin. The curette is a metal instrument resembling a spoon, with a cup-shaped cutting surface on its end. As the curette is drawn across the uterine wall, the soft endometrial tissue and fetal parts are scraped from the wall of the uterus. (The D & C is also used in the medical management of certain health conditions of the uterine wall, such as irregular bleeding or the buildup of endometrial tissue.)

Key Terms

sterilization
Generally permanent birth control techniques that surgically disrupt the normal passage of ova or sperm.

abortion
Induced premature termination of pregnancy.

dilation
Gradual expansion of an opening or passageway, such as the cervix.

dilation and curettage (D & C)
A surgical procedure in which the cervical canal is dilated to allow the uterine wall to be scraped.

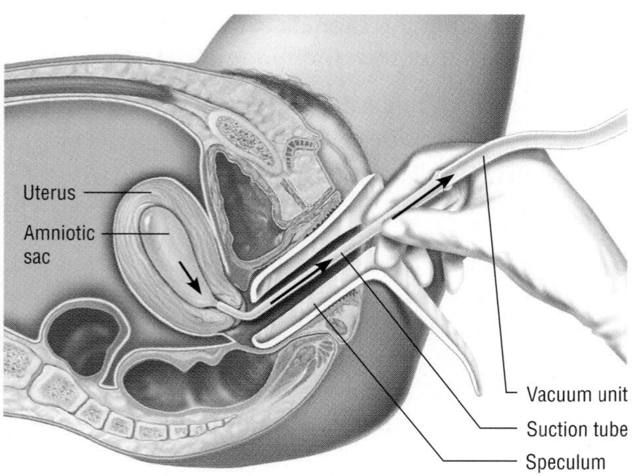

Figure 13–7 During dilation and evacuation, the cervix is dilated and the contents of the uterus are aspirated (removed by suction). This procedure is used to perform abortions up to 16 weeks' gestation.

As in the case of menstrual extraction, both vacuum aspiration and D & C are very safe procedures for the woman. The need to dilate the cervix more fully in a D & C increases the risk of cervical trauma and the possibility of perforation, but these risks are reported to be low. Bleeding, cramping, spotting, and infections present minimal controllable risks when procedures are done by experienced clinicians under clinical conditions.

Medical Abortion. Mifepristone and methotrexate are drugs that a woman can use under medical supervision to induce an abortion during the first trimester. Formally known as RU-486, mifepristone blocks the action of progesterone and causes the uterine lining, and any fertilized egg, to shed. This method of early abortion is widely used in France, Britain, Sweden, and China, and has recently become available in the United States, but is not as yet available in Canada.[22]

Under FDA guidelines in the United States, women must use mifepristone within 49 days of their first menstrual period. Women take three pills at the first visit to the doctor, and then return 48 hours later to take a second drug, misoprostol, which causes menstruation to occur, usually within five hours. A third visit to a physician is necessary to ensure that the woman is recovering well from the procedure and to conduct blood tests or an ultrasound exam to verify that the medical abortion was successful.[23]

Methotrexate is a drug used since the 1950s for cancer treatment. However, physicians sometimes use this drug to induce a first-term abortion. Typically, a woman receives an injection of methotrexate and, during a second office visit three to seven days later, receives prostaglandin. The fetal contents are expelled, usually within a day, but some methotrexate abortions take up to a week to occur. This is similar to the type of medical abortion conducted in Canada.[24]

If these and other new drugs continue to gain favour with women and their physicians, it is likely that more women will use physician's offices, rather than abortion clinics, for abortion services.

Second-trimester abortion procedures

When a woman's pregnancy continues beyond the fourteenth week of gestation, termination becomes a more difficult matter. The procedures at this stage are more complicated and take longer to complete. Complications are also more common. Fortunately, these procedures are becoming increasingly rare.

Dilation and Evacuation. Vacuum aspiration and D & C can be combined in a procedure called *dilation and evacuation (D & E)* during the earliest weeks of the second trimester (Figure 13–7). The use of D & E increases the likelihood of trauma and postprocedural complications, since larger instruments and greater dilation are required. After about 16 weeks, more intensive procedures will be required to terminate the late second-trimester pregnancy.

Hypertonic Saline Procedure. From the sixteenth week of gestation to the end of the second trimester, intrauterine injection of a strong salt solution into the amniotic sac is the procedure most frequently used. The administration of intrauterine **hypertonic saline solution** requires a skilled operator so that the needle used to introduce the salt solution enters the amniotic sac. Once the needle is in place, some amniotic fluid is withdrawn, allowing the saline solution to be injected.

Some physicians support the saline procedure by dilating the cervix with *laminaria* or another dilatory product and administering the hormone oxytocin to stimulate uterine contractions. The onset of uterine contractions will expel the dehydrated uterine contents within 24 to 36 hours.

Prostaglandin Procedure. The use of prostaglandin is the third type of abortion procedure used during the second trimester. Prostaglandins are hormonelike chemicals that have a variety of useful effects on human tissue. Produced naturally within the body, these substances influence the contractions of smooth muscle. Since the uterine wall is composed entirely of smooth muscle, it is particularly sensitive to the presence of prostaglandins. When prostaglandin is administered in sufficient quantity (through either a uterine intramuscular injection or a vaginal suppository), uterine contractions become strong enough to expel the fetal contents.

Third-trimester abortion procedures

If termination of a pregnancy is required in the latter weeks of the gestational period, a surgical procedure in which the fetus is removed (*hysterotomy*) or a procedure in which the entire uterus must be removed (*hysterectomy*) can be undertaken. These procedures are more complicated and involve longer hospitalization, major abdominal surgery, and an extended period of recovery.

Post-Abortion Syndrome

Some women who have an abortion may be faced with the consequence of psychological difficulties in the years that follow the abortion. The term **post-abortion syndrome** refers to "the suggested long-term negative psychological effects of abortion."[25] It is possible that these difficulties may arise soon after the abortion or may not surface until years later. The signs and symptoms of post-abortion syndrome are not unlike those of the more well-known post-traumatic stress disorder. (However, it should be noted that the American Psychiatric Association and other organizations do not recognize post-abortion syndrome as an identifiable illness.)

Women having post-abortion syndrome may experience some or all of the following effects: difficulties with personal relationships, substance abuse problems, nightmares, sexual difficulties, communication problems, damage to self-esteem, and, possibly, suicide.[26] These symptoms may range from mild to severe and may be lengthy in duration.

Fortunately, there are abortion follow-up services that can be helpful to women who believe they are suffering from the consequences of abortion. Individual and group counselling, as well as post-abortion support groups, can help women cope with difficult, complicated feelings. Look for these services through your medical care provider, or check your local phone book for helpful resources.

PREGNANCY

Pregnancy is a condition that requires a series of complex yet coordinated changes to occur in the female body. This discussion follows pregnancy from its beginning, at fertilization, to its conclusion, with labour and childbirth.

Physiological Obstacles and Aids to Fertilization

Many sexually active young people believe that they will become pregnant (or impregnate someone) only when they want to, despite their haphazard contraceptive practices. Because of this mistaken belief, many young people are not sold on the use of contraceptives. It is important for young adults to remember that from a species survival standpoint, our bodies were designed to promote pregnancy. It is estimated that about 85% of sexually active women of childbearing age will become pregnant within one year if they do not use some form of contraception.[27]

With regard to pregnancy, each act of intercourse can be considered a game of physiological odds. There are obstacles that may reduce a couple's chance of pregnancy, including the following:

Obstacles to fertilization

1. *The acidic level of the vagina is destructive to sperm.* The low pH of the vagina will kill sperm that fail to enter the uterus quickly.
2. *The cervical mucus is thick during most of the menstrual cycle.* Sperm movement into the uterus is more difficult, except during the few days surrounding ovulation.
3. *The sperm must locate the cervical opening.* The cervical opening is small compared with the rest of the surface area where sperm are deposited.
4. *Half of the sperm travel through the wrong fallopian tube.* Most commonly, only one ovum is released at ovulation. The two ovaries generally "take turns" each month. The sperm have no way of "knowing" which tube they should enter. Thus it is probable that half will travel through the wrong tube.
5. *The distance sperm must travel is relatively long compared with the tiny size of the sperm cells.* Microscopic sperm must travel about 18 or 20 cm (7 or 8 in.) once they are inside the female.
6. *The sperm's travel is relatively "upstream."* The anatomical positioning of the female reproductive structures necessitates an "uphill" movement by the sperm.
7. *The contoured folds of the tubal walls trap many sperm.* These folds make it difficult for sperm to locate the egg. Many sperm are trapped in this maze.

There are also a variety of aids that tend to help sperm and egg cells join. Some of these are listed below.

Aids to fertilization

1. *An astounding number of sperm are deposited during ejaculation.* Each ejaculation contains about a

Key Term

hypertonic saline solution
A salt solution with a concentration higher than that found in human fluids.

post-abortion syndrome
Long-term negative psychological effects of abortion experienced by some women.

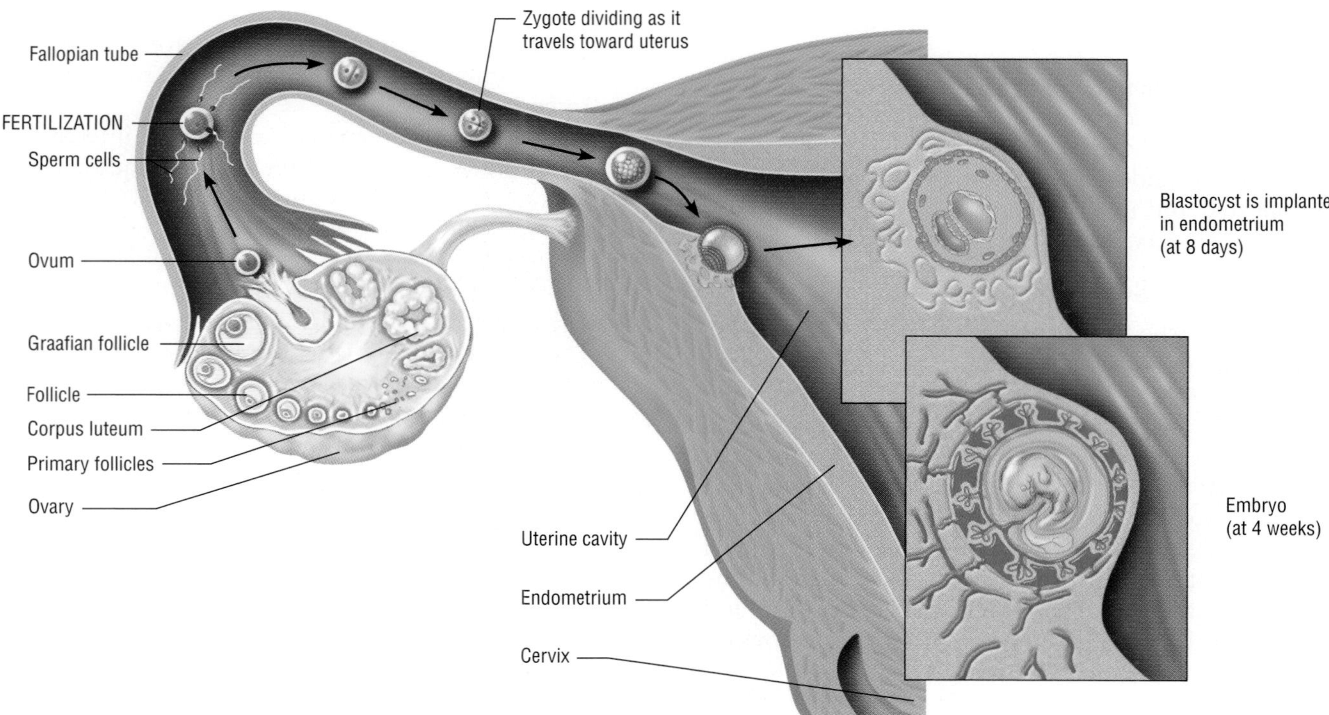

Figure 13–8 After its release from the follicle, the ovum begins its week-long journey down the fallopian tube. Fertilization generally occurs in the outermost third of the tube. Now fertilized, the ovum progresses toward the uterus, where it embeds itself in the endometrium. A pregnancy is established.

teaspoon of semen.[28] Within this quantity are between 200 and 500 million sperm cells. Even with large numbers of sperm killed in the vagina, millions are able to move to the deeper structures.

2. *Sperm are deposited near the cervical opening.* Penetration into the vagina by the penis allows for the sperm to be placed near the cervical opening.
3. *The male accessory glands help make the semen nonacidic.* The seminal vesicles, prostate gland, and Cowper's glands secrete fluids that provide an alkaline environment for the sperm. This environment helps protect sperm in the vagina until they can move into the deeper, more alkaline uterus and fallopian tubes.
4. *Uterine contractions aid sperm movement.* The rhythmic muscular contractions of the uterus tend to cause the sperm to move in the direction of the fallopian tubes.
5. *Sperm cells move rather quickly.* Despite their tiny size, sperm cells can move relatively quickly—just about 2 cm (1 in.) per hour. Powered by sugar solutions from the male accessory glands and the whiplike movements of their tails, sperm can reach the distant third of the fallopian tubes in less than eight hours as they swim in the direction of the descending ovum.

Health on the Web

Behaviour Change Activities

Selecting Your Contraceptive Method

People use birth control for many reasons. Career-minded men and women want to plan the timing and spacing of their children. Others want reliable birth control to ensure that they will never have children. Fear of contracting a sexually transmitted infection prompts some people to use particular forms of birth control. Go to **www.fhi.org/en/fp/nfp.html** and click on "Frequently Asked Questions about Contraception" for help in selecting a contraceptive method if you are or may become sexually active.

Exploring Parenting Issues

The *Pregnancy Today* Web site provides a panel of health advisors, including midwives, doctors, lactation consultants, nutritionists, and fitness consultants. These professionals are available at **www.pregnancytoday.com/experts** to answer your questions about pregnancy, childbirth, and the postpartum period. You can also read answers to questions posed by other visitors to the site.

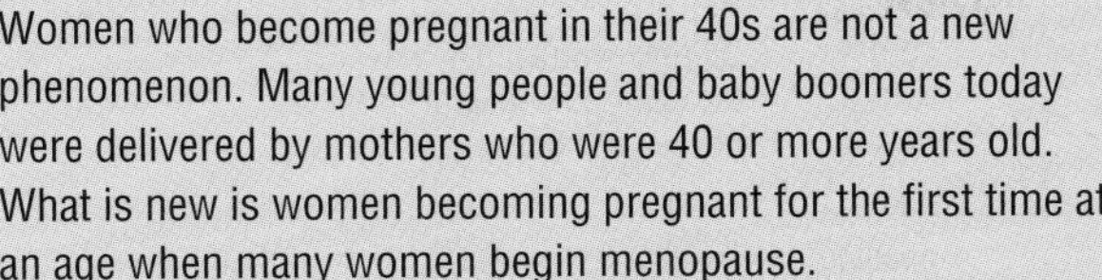

Learning from Our Diversity

Pregnancy and Parenting after 40

Women who become pregnant in their 40s are not a new phenomenon. Many young people and baby boomers today were delivered by mothers who were 40 or more years old. What is new is women becoming pregnant for the first time at an age when many women begin menopause.

The reasons are several. Some couples may have tried to conceive for years and only succeeded when in their 40s. Other women and couples delayed pregnancy in order to build their careers, travel, or become more financially secure. In addition, fertility technology, such as in vitro fertilization, microsurgery, and donor eggs or sperm have finally given many couples the baby they long wanted.

The trend of later childbearing began in the late 1970s, when better-educated baby-boom women began entering the workforce. For women 40 to 44, the rate of first babies increased from 0.3 to 1.4 per 1000, still a small percentage but a significant jump.[29]

The common belief that men can father babies well into middle age is supported not only by anecdotal evidence (such as Pierre Trudeau, former Prime Minister of Canada, and Larry King, of CNN's *Larry King Live*), but also recent research that shows that sperm function in older men does not differ significantly from that of younger men.[30]

Women traditionally were discouraged from becoming pregnant for the first time in their 40s because of the health risks to the mother and the risk of birth defects for the baby. It is true that women 40 and older suffer more complications during childbirth, and the risk of having a baby with Down syndrome or another genetic abnormality increases as a mother ages.[31]

The chances of having a cesarean delivery are about 40% higher than a younger woman's.[32] The number of women with gestational diabetes and high blood pressure is also higher. Many have more difficulty with labour and deliver babies that are underweight or premature. In addition, the risk of fetal death is higher in women over 35 years old.[33]

Women who want to have a baby should use this information to prevent problems, however, rather than let it discourage them from having a baby at all, researchers say.

Women who want to start families in their 40s should consider the following:

- Infertility can become a problem with age, but fertility drugs such as Clomid or treatments such as in vitro fertilization can help.
- The rate of miscarriage is higher among older women, so immediate prenatal care is vital.
- Early genetic testing can ease the fears about birth defects. Tests can reveal the presence of Down syndrome, Tay-Sachs disease, cystic fibrosis, and sickle-cell anemia.
- Cesarean sections are more common in older mothers.

On the plus side, another study recently reported that women who are able to give birth after age 40 (not including those who become pregnant through the use of fertility treatments) may be "slow to age" and live longer.[34] This can be good news to older moms who wonder whether they will have the energy to chase a toddler.

6. *Once inside the fallopian tubes, sperm can live for days.* Some sperm may be viable for up to a week after reaching the comfortable, nonacidic environment of the fallopian tubes. Most sperm, however, will survive an average of 48 to 72 hours. Thus they can "wait in the wings" for the moment an ovum is released from the ovary (Figure 13–8).
7. *The cervical mucus is thin and watery at the time of ovulation.* This mucus allows for better passage of sperm through the cervical opening when the ovum is most capable of being fertilized.

Learning from Our Diversity (above) discusses the particular issues related to pregnancy and parenting after age 40.

Signs of Pregnancy

Aside from pregnancy tests done in a professional laboratory, a woman can sometimes recognize early signs and symptoms. Signs of pregnancy have been divided into three categories:

Presumptive signs of pregnancy

- Missed period after unprotected intercourse the previous month
- Nausea on awakening (morning sickness)
- Increase in size and tenderness of breasts
- Darkening of the areolar tissue surrounding the nipples

Probable signs of pregnancy

- Increase in the frequency of urination (the growing uterus presses against the bladder)
- Increase in the size of the abdomen
- Cervix becomes softer by the sixth week (detected by a pelvic examination by clinician)
- Positive pregnancy test

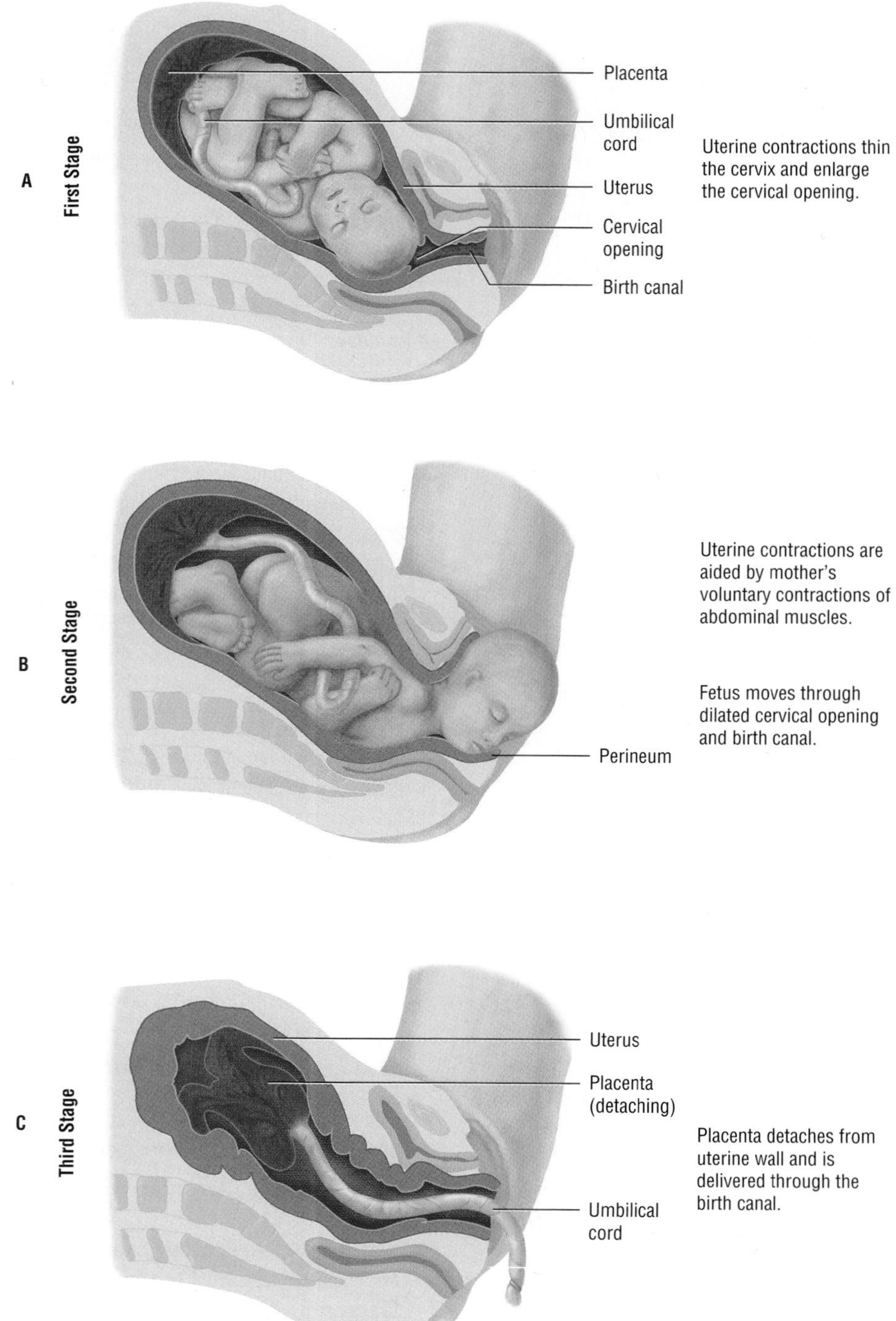
A
First Stage
Placenta
Umbilical cord
Uterus
Cervical opening
Birth canal
Uterine contractions thin the cervix and enlarge the cervical opening.
B
Second Stage
Uterine contractions are aided by mother's voluntary contractions of abdominal muscles.
Fetus moves through dilated cervical opening and birth canal.
Perineum
C
Third Stage
Uterus
Placenta (detaching)
Placenta detaches from uterine wall and is delivered through the birth canal.
Umbilical cord

Figure 13–9 Labour, or childbirth, is a three-stage process. During effacement and dilation, the first stage (**A**), the cervical canal is gradually opened by contractions of the uterine wall. The second stage (**B**), delivery of the fetus, encompasses the actual delivery of the fetus from the uterus and through the birth canal. The delivery of the placenta, the third stage (**C**), empties the uterus, thus completing the process of childbirth.

Learning from Our Diversity

What Is a Family?[35]

The Vanier Institute of the Family defines a family as any combination of two or more persons who are bound together over time by ties of mutual consent, birth and/or adoption, or placement and who together assume responsibility for variant combinations of some of the following:

- Physical maintenance and care of group members
- Addition of new members through procreation or adoption
- Socialization of children
- Social control of members
- Production, consumption, distribution of goods and services
- Affective nurturance—love

How Many Families Are There?

According to Statistics Canada's 2001 Census there are 8.4 million families* in Canada.

- 41% are married couples with children
- 29% are married couples without children
- 6% are common-law couples with children
- 8% are common-law couples without children
- 16% are lone-parent (83% of lone parents are female)

Lesbian and Gay Families.

Increasingly, gay and lesbian couples are creating families that include children. Legislation in some provinces, including British Columbia and Ontario, prohibits discrimination on the basis of sexual orientation in adoption, custody, or access decisions. This legislation recognizes the result of research on the effects on children living in a gay or lesbian family. Research consistently shows no difference between the children of lesbian and gay families and those in heterosexual families. See **www.adoption.ca/research.htm** for more information.

---

*Statistics Canada defines family as a now-married couple (with or without never-married sons and/or daughters of either or both spouses), a couple living common-law (again with or without never-married sons and/or daughters of either or both partners), or a lone parent of any marital status, with at least one never-married son or daughter living in the same dwelling.

Positive signs of pregnancy

- Determination of a fetal heartbeat
- Feeling of the fetus moving (quickening)
- Observation of fetus by ultrasound or optical viewers

Agents That Can Damage a Fetus

A large number of agents that come into contact with a pregnant woman can affect fetal development. Many of these (rubella and herpes viruses, tobacco smoke, alcohol, and virtually all other drugs) are discussed in other chapters of this text. The best advice for a pregnant woman is to maintain close contact with her caregiver during pregnancy and to consider carefully the ingestion of any OTC drug (including aspirin, caffeine, and antacids) that could harm the fetus.

It is also important for all women to avoid exposure to radiation during pregnancy. Such exposure, most commonly through excessive X-rays or radiation fallout from nuclear testing, can irreversibly damage fetal genetic structures.

CHILDBIRTH: THE LABOUR OF DELIVERY

Childbirth, or *parturition*, is one of the true peak life experiences for both men and women. Most of the time, childbirth is a wonderfully exciting venture into the unknown. For the parents, this intriguing experience can provide a stage for personal growth, maturity, and insight into a dynamic, complex world.

During the last few weeks of the third **trimester**, most fetuses will move deeper into the pelvic cavity in a process called *lightening*. During this movement, the fetus's body will rotate and the head will begin to engage more deeply into the mother's pelvic girdle. Many women will report that the baby has "dropped."

Another indication that parturition may be relatively near is the increased reporting of *Braxton Hicks contractions*. These uterine contractions, which are of mild intensity and often occur at irregular intervals, may be felt throughout a pregnancy. During the last few weeks of pregnancy (*gestation*), these mild contractions can occur more frequently and may cause a woman to feel as if she is going into labour (**false labour**).

Labour begins when uterine contractions become more intense and occur at regular intervals. The birth of a child can be divided into three stages: (1) effacement and dilation of the cervix, (2) delivery of the fetus, and

Key Terms

trimester
A three-month period; human pregnancies encompass three trimesters.

false labour
Conditions that resemble the start of true labour; may include irregular uterine contractions, pressure, and discomfort in the lower abdomen.

(3) delivery of the placenta (Figure 13–9). For a woman having her first child, the birth process lasts an average of 12 to 16 hours. The average length of labour for subsequent births is much shorter—from 4 to 10 hours on average. Labour is very unpredictable: labours that last between 1 and 24 hours occur daily at most hospitals.

Stage One: Effacement and Dilation of the Cervix

In the first stage of labour the uterine contractions attempt to thin (efface) the normally thick cervical walls and to enlarge (dilate) the cervical opening.[36] These contractions are directed by the release of prostaglandins and the hormone oxytocin into the circulating bloodstream.

The first stage of labour is often the longest. The cervical opening must thin and dilate to a diameter of 10 cm before the first stage of labour is considered complete. Often this stage begins with the dislodging of the cervical mucous plug. The subsequent *bloody show* (mucous plug and a small amount of blood) at the vaginal opening may indicate that effacement and dilation have begun. Another indication of labour's onset may be the bursting or tearing of the fetal amniotic sac. "Breaking the bag of waters" refers to this phenomenon, which happens in various measures in expectant women.

The pain of the uterine contractions becomes more intense as the woman moves through this first phase of labour. As the cervical opening effaces and dilates from 0 to 3 cm, many women report feeling happy, exhilarated, and confident. In the early phase of the first stage of labour, the contractions are relatively short (lasting from 15 to 60 seconds) and the intervals between contractions range from 20 minutes to 5 minutes as labour progresses. However, these rest intervals will become shorter and the contractions more forceful when the woman's uterus contracts to dilate 4 to 7 cm.

In this second phase of the first stage of labour, the contractions usually last about one minute each and the rest intervals drop from about five minutes to one minute over a period of five to nine hours.

The third phase of the first stage of labour is called *transition*. During transition, the uterus contracts to dilate the cervical opening to the full 10 cm required for safe passage of the fetus out of the uterus and into the birth canal (vagina). This period of labour is often the most painful part of the entire birth process. Fortunately, it is also the shortest phase of most labours. Lasting between 15 and 30 minutes, transition contractions often last 60 to 90 seconds each. The rest intervals between contractions are short and vary from 30 to 60 seconds.

An examination of the cervix by a nurse or physician will reveal whether full dilation of 10 cm has occurred. Until the full 10 cm dilation, women are cautioned not to "push" the fetus during the contractions. Special breathing and concentration techniques help many women cope with the first stage of labour.

Stage Two: Delivery of the Fetus

Once the mother's cervix is fully dilated, she enters the second stage of labour, the delivery of the fetus through the birth canal. Now the mother is encouraged to help push the fetus out (with her abdominal muscles) during each contraction. In this second stage the uterine contractions are less forceful than during the transition phase of the first stage and may last 60 seconds each, with a one- to three-minute rest interval.

This second stage may last up to two hours in first births. For subsequent births, this stage will usually be much shorter. When the baby's head is first seen at the vaginal opening, *crowning* is said to have taken place. Generally the back of the baby's head appears first. (Infants whose feet or buttocks are presented first are said to be delivered in a *breech position*.) Once the head is delivered, the baby's body rotates upward to let the shoulders come through. The rest of the body follows quite quickly. The second stage of labour ends when the fetus is fully expelled from the birth canal.

Stage Three: Delivery of the Placenta

Usually within 30 minutes after the fetus is delivered, the uterus will again initiate a series of contractions to expel the placenta (or *afterbirth*). The placenta is examined by the attending physician to ensure that it was completely expelled. Torn remnants of the placenta could lead to dangerous *hemorrhaging* by the mother. Often the physician will perform a manual examination of the uterus after the placenta has been delivered.

Once the placenta has been delivered, the uterus will continue with mild contractions to help control bleeding and start the gradual reduction of the uterus to its normal, nonpregnant size. This final aspect of the birth process is called **postpartum**. External abdominal massage of the lower abdomen seems to help the uterus contract, as does an infant's nursing at the mother's breast.

Cesarean Deliveries

A **cesarean delivery** (cesarean birth, C-section) is a procedure in which the fetus is surgically removed from the mother's uterus through the abdominal wall. This type of delivery, which is completed in up to an hour, can be performed with the mother having a regional or a general anesthetic. A cesarean delivery is necessary when either the health of the baby or the mother is at risk.

Although a cesarean delivery is considered major surgery, most mothers cope well with the delivery and postsurgical and postpartum discomfort. The hospital stay is usually a few days longer than for a vaginal delivery.

Where to Find Help for Infertility

Adoption Council of Canada
Bronson Centre 211 Bronson Ave.
Suite 210, Ottawa, ON K1R 6H5
Tel: 613-235-0344
Fax: 613-235-1728
acc@adoption.ca
www.adoption.ca

Canadian International
Adoption Services
297 Sheppard Ave. W., Suite 202
Toronto, ON, M2N 1N4
Tel: 416-250-0520
Fax: 416-352-5081
Info@AdoptionCanada.com
www.adoptioncanada.com

Infertility Network
160 Pickering St.
Toronto, ON, M4E 3J7
Tel: 416-691-3611
Fax: 416-690-8015
www.infertilitynetwork.org

Infertility Awareness
Association of Canada
2100 Marlowe Ave, Suite 39
Montreal, QC H4A 3L5
Tel: 514-484-2891
Fax: 514-484-0454
www.iaac.ca

Multiple Births Canada
PO Box 432
Wasaga Beach, ON, L9Z 1A4
Toll-Free (in Canada) 1-866-228-8824
Tel: 705-429-0901
Fax: 705-429-9809
office@multiplebirthscanada.org
www.multiplebirthscanada.org

INFERTILITY

Most traditional-age college and university students are interested in preventing pregnancy. However, increasing numbers of other people are trying to do just the opposite: they are trying to start a family (see the Learning from Our Diversity box on p. 331 concerning the changing definition of "family"). It is estimated that about one in six couples has a problem with *infertility*. These couples wish to become pregnant but are unable to do so.

Why do couples experience infertility? The reasons are about evenly balanced between men and women. About 10% of infertility has no detectable cause. The most common male complication is insufficient sperm production and delivery. A number of approaches can be used to increase sperm counts. Among the simple approaches are the application of periodic cold packs on the scrotum and the replacement of tight underwear with boxer shorts. When a structural problem reduces sperm production, surgery can be helpful. Opinion is divided about whether increased frequency of intercourse improves fertility. Most experts (fertility endocrinologists) suggest that couples have intercourse at least a couple of times in the week preceding ovulation.

Men can also collect (through masturbation) and save samples of their sperm to use in a procedure called *artificial insemination by partner*. Near the time of ovulation, the collected samples of sperm are then deposited near the woman's cervical opening. In the related procedure called *artificial insemination by donor*, the sperm of a donor are used. Donor semen is screened for the presence of pathogens, including the HIV virus.

Causes of infertility in women centre mostly on obstructions in the reproductive tract and the inability to ovulate. The obstructions sometimes result from tissue damage (scarring) caused by infections. Chlamydial and gonorrheal infections often produce fertility problems. In certain women the use of IUCDs has produced infections and PID; both of these increase the chances of infertility. Other possible causes of structural abnormalities include scar tissue from previous surgery, fibroid tumours, polyps, and endometriosis. A variety of microsurgical techniques may correct some of these complications.

One of the most recent innovative procedures involves the use of **transcervical balloon tuboplasty**. In this procedure, a series of balloon-tipped catheters are inserted through the uterus into the blocked fallopian tubes. Once inflated, these balloon catheters help open the scarred passageways.

Key Terms

postpartum
The period after the birth of a baby, during which the uterus returns to its prepregnancy size.

cesarean delivery
Surgical removal of fetus through the abdominal wall.

transcervical balloon tuboplasty
The use of inflatable balloon catheters to open blocked fallopian tubes; a procedure used for some women with fertility problems.

When a woman has ovulation difficulties, pinpointing the specific cause can be very difficult. Increasing age produces hormone fluctuations associated with lack of ovulation. Being significantly overweight or underweight also has a serious effect on fertility. However, in women of normal weight who are not approaching menopause, it appears that ovulation difficulties are caused by lack of synchronization between the hormones governing the menstrual cycle. Fertility drugs can help alter the menstrual cycle to produce ovulation. Clomiphene citrate (Clomid), in oral pill form, and injections of a mixture of LH and FSH taken from the urine of menopausal women (Pergonal) are the most common fertility drugs available. Both are capable of producing multiple ova at ovulation.

Assisted Reproduction Technologies (ART)

For couples who are unable to conceive after drug therapy, surgery, and artificial insemination, the use of *in vitro fertilization and embryo transfer (IVF-ET)* is another option. This method is sometimes referred to as the "test tube" procedure. Costing thousands of dollars per attempt, IVF-ET consists of surgically retrieving fertilizable ova from the woman and combining them in a glass dish with sperm. After several days, the fertilized ova are transferred into the uterus.

A newer test tube procedure is called *gamete intrafallopian transfer (GIFT)*. Similar to IVF-ET, this procedure involves depositing a mixture of retrieved eggs and sperm directly into the fallopian tubes.

Fertilized ova (zygotes) can also be transferred from a laboratory dish into the fallopian tubes in a procedure called *zygote intrafallopian transfer* (*ZIFT*). One advantage of this procedure is that the clinicians are certain that ova have been fertilized before the transfer to the fallopian tubes.

Surrogate Parenting

Surrogate parenting is another option although the legal and ethical issues surrounding this method of conception have not been fully resolved. Surrogate parenting exists in a number of forms. Typically, an infertile couple will make a contract with a woman (the surrogate parent), who will then be artificially inseminated with semen from the expectant father. In some instances the surrogate will receive an embryo from the donor parents. In some cases, women have served as surrogates for their close relatives. The surrogate will carry the fetus to term and return the newborn to the parents. Because of the concerns about true "ownership" of the baby, surrogate parenting may not be a particularly viable or legal option for many couples.

The process of coping with infertility problems can be an emotionally stressful experience for a couple. Hours of waiting in physicians' offices, having numerous examinations, scheduling intercourse, producing sperm samples, and undergoing surgical or drug treatments place multiple burdens on a couple. Knowing that other couples are able to conceive so effortlessly adds to the mental strain. Fortunately, support groups exist to assist couples with infertility problems. Some of these groups are listed in the Star Box on p. 333.

What can you do to reduce the chances of developing infertility problems? Certainly avoiding infections of the reproductive organs is one crucial factor. Barrier methods of contraception (condoms, diaphragm) with a spermicide reportedly cut the risk of developing infertility in half. The use of an IUCD should be carefully considered, and the risk from multiple partners should encourage responsible sexual activity. Men and women should be aware of the dangers from working around hazardous chemicals or consuming psychoactive drugs. Maintaining overall good health and having regular medical (and, for women, gynecological) checkups are also good ideas. Finally, since infertility is linked with advancing age, couples may not want to indefinitely delay having children.

Taking Charge of Your Health

- Use the Personal Assessment on p. 338 to help you determine which birth control method is best for you.
- Talk to your doctor about the health aspects of different types of birth control before making your decision.
- If the method of birth control you are currently using is unsatisfactory to you or your partner, explore other options.
- Reduce your risk of infertility by choosing a birth control method carefully, protecting yourself from infections of the reproductive organs, and maintaining good overall health.
- If you plan to have children, set a time frame that takes into account decreased fertility with advancing age.

SUMMARY

- *Birth control* refers to all of the procedures that can prevent the birth of a child.
- *Contraception* refers to any procedure that prevents fertilization.
- Each birth control method has both a theoretical-effectiveness rate and a use-effectiveness rate. For some contraceptive approaches, these rates are similar (such as hormonal methods), and for others the rates are very different (such as condoms, diaphragms, and periodic abstinence).
- Many factors should be considered when deciding which contraceptive is best for you.
- Sterilization (vasectomy and tubal ligation) is generally considered an irreversible procedure.
- Abortion procedures vary according to the stage of the pregnancy.
- There are numerous obstacles and aids to fertilization that influence the likelihood of pregnancy.
- Childbirth takes place in three distinct stages: effacement and dilation of the cervix, delivery of the fetus, and delivery of the placenta.
- Infertility is an important concern for some couples. Various technologies are improving infertile couples' chances of having children.

REVIEW QUESTIONS

1. Explain the difference between the terms *birth control* and *contraception*. Give examples of each.
2. Explain the difference between theoretical- and use-effectiveness rates. Which one is always higher? Why is it important to know the difference between these two rates?
3. Identify some of the factors that should be given careful consideration when selecting a contraceptive method. Explain each factor.
4. For each of the methods of birth control, explain how it works and its advantages and disadvantages.
5. How do progesterone-only pills differ from the combined oral contraceptive? What is a morning-after pill? How do subdermal implants (Norplant) differ from Depo-Provera? How does the contraceptive ring differ from the contraceptive patch?
6. Identify and describe the different abortion procedures that are used during each trimester of pregnancy. When is the safest time for an abortion?
7. What are some obstacles and aids to fertilization presented in this chapter? Can you think of others?
8. Identify and describe the events that occur during each of the three stages of childbirth. Approximately how long is each stage?
9. What can be done to reduce chances of infertility? Explain IVF-ET, GIFT, and ZIFT procedures.

THINK ABOUT THIS ...

- What factors would be most important to you in selecting an appropriate contraceptive method?
- Do you think post-secondary students understand that oral contraceptives do not protect against STIs or HIV infection?
- Under what circumstances, if any, do you believe abortion is acceptable? Unacceptable?
- Will you or your partner someday undergo sterilization? If so, which of you will have the surgery? Why?
- Can you identify locations at or near your school where professional family-planning services are available?
- What effects do you think starting parenthood at a later age has on the parent and on the child?
- How do you feel about a couple's choice not to have children?
- If a woman should not smoke, drink, or use other drugs during pregnancy, should these limitations also be placed on the father? Why or why not?
- To what extent should fathers participate in the birth experience?
- Do you plan to become a parent? If so, when?
- To what extent should men participate/take responsibility for birth control?

REFERENCES

1. Adapted from Hatcher RA et al: *Contraceptive technology,* 17th rev ed, 1998, Ardent Media, Inc.
2. Crooks R, Baur K: *Our sexuality*, ed 7, 1998, Brooks/Cole Publishing.
3. Hatcher RA et al: *Contraceptive technology*, ed 17, rev, 1998, Ardent Media, Inc.
4. Allgeier ER, Allgeier AR: *Sexual interactions*, ed 5, 2000, Houghton Mifflin.
5. *Contraceptive technology.*
6. Health Canada: *It's your health: condoms.* **www.hc-sc.gc.ca/english/iyh/products/condoms.html**
7. *Contraceptive technology.*

8. Ibid.
9. *How to choose the right contraception method with your patients.* **http://sexualityandu.ca/eng/includes/health/pdf/choosing_the_right_contraception.pdf**
10. *Contraceptive technology.*
11. Ibid.
12. Ibid.
13. Fifteen-year Canadian contraception trends, *The Canadian Journal of Human Sexuality,* vol. 8(3) Fall, 1999.
14. Planned Parenthood Federation of America: PPFA Web site, **www.plannedparenthood.org**. September 21, 2001.
15. *Contraceptive technology.*
16. Columbia University Health Education Program: *The NuvaRing—another birth control option,* **www.goaskalice.columbia.edu**, (November 11, 2002), September 10, 2003.
17. Ortho-McNeil Pharmaceutical: *The first birth control patch receives FDA approval* (press release November 20, 2001), **www.ortho-mcneil.com/news/archive/pr/news_evra.htm**, November 27, 2001.
18. *Sexual interactions.*
19. *How to choose the right contraception method.*
20. Trouton K, Dzakpasu S: Induced abortion, Canadian perinatal surveillance system fact sheets, Health Canada. **www.hc-sc.gc.ca/hpb/lcdc/brch/factshts/inabor_e.html**
21. Ibid.
22. Weibe E: Abortion induced with methotrexote and misoprostol, *Canadian Medical Association Journal* 154(2):165–170, 185–7, 1996.
23. Ibid.
24. Ibid.
25. Blonna R, Levitan J: *Healthy sexuality,* 2000, Morton Publishing Co.
26. Ibid.
27. *Contraceptive technology.*
28. Hyde JS, DeLamater JD: *Understanding human sexuality,* ed 6, 1997, McGraw-Hill.
29. Blackburn B: Moms starting families in 40s test odds, *USA Today,* September 24, 1977, 14A.
30. Haidl G, Jung A, Schill WB: Aging and sperm function, *Hum Reprod* 1996:11(3):558–560.
31. Moms starting families in 40s.
32. Later age pregnancy: Preparing for the happy, healthy event after 40, *Health Oasis,* Mayo Clinic, 1998. **www.mayohealth.org/mayo/9708/htm/aged_p.htm**
33. Fretts RC et al: Increased maternal age and risk of fetal death, *N Engl J Med* 1995:333(15):953–957.
34. Moms starting families in 40s.
35. Statistics Canada: 2001 Census, **www.statcan.ca/english/Pqdb/famil54a.htm**
36. *Understanding human sexuality.*

SUGGESTED READINGS

Boston Women's Health Book Collective: *Our bodies, our selves,* 2005, Touchstone.
This book explores sexual health, reproductive rights, community organizations, and the conditions that often limit women's access to quality health care.

Bullough VL, Bullough B: *Contraception: a guide to birth control methods,* ed 2, 1997, Prometheus Books.
Written for the general reader interested in knowing about a wide range of contraceptive options, this book contains information about the history of contraception and probable future developments in the field.

Cain, M: *The childless revolution: what it means to be childless today,* 2001, Perseus Publishing.
Cain's childless-by-happenstance category is a catchall of women whose other life choices ended up stopping them from having children; some didn't have children because of their spouses' attitudes, some because they had no spouse at all, and some because they waited too long and their biological clocks stopped ticking. Citing a 1993 *American Demographics* article that claims there will be a 44 percent increase in the number of childless couples by 2010, Cain asserts that despite that projected increase, society will still harshly criticize women without children as complete aberrations.

Maushart, S: *The mask of motherhood: how becoming a mother changes everything and why we pretend it doesn't,* 2000, Penguin Books.
The author (a nationally syndicated columnist in Australia and the mother of three children) explores the effect childbearing has upon women. In the process, she removes the veils of serenity and satisfaction to reveal what she holds to be the truth: the early years of motherhood are physically difficult and can be emotionally devastating.

Merkoff, H: *What to expect when you're expecting,* 2002, Workman.
This book addresses the many questions of expectant parents as they plan and experience a pregnancy.

Peoples D, Ferguson HR: *What to expect when you're experiencing infertility: how to cope with the emotional crisis and survive,* 2000, W.W. Norton & Co.
This book helps couples cope with one of the most difficult emotional, medical, and financial crises—infertility. Written in a question-and-answer format, the book offers practical advice about the uncertainties of infertility. It can help couples communicate more clearly and face the disappointments of miscarriages and failed treatments.

Runkle A: *In good conscience: a practical, emotional, and spiritual guide to deciding whether to have an abortion*, 1998, Jossey-Bass Publishers.

Cutting through the religious and political rhetoric surrounding abortion, this book presents solid information on the subject. Written in a compassionate tone, it is directed toward women who want to make this decision themselves.

Williams, J: *Unbending gender: why family and work conflict, and what to do about it*, 2000, Oxford University Press.

With special attention to the diversity of women's experience in terms of race and social class, this book challenges common assumptions about gender roles and women's choices concerning work, family, and career. Arguing that the liberal feminist ideal of full equality in the workforce and the anti-feminist call to full-time domesticity do not represent a satisfactory range of options, Williams, who is the co-director of the Gender, Work, and Family Project at the American University Law School, says that the time is ripe to acknowledge the "norm of parental care," and work to develop flexible employment policies that will mitigate the stresses of the work/family dilemma.

Name ______________________________ **Date** ____________

Personal Assessment

Which Birth Control Method Is Best for You?

To assess which birth control method is best for you, answer the following questions, and check the interpretation below.

Do I: *Yes* *No*

1. Need a contraceptive immediately?
2. Want a contraceptive that can be used completely independent of sexual relations?
3. Need a contraceptive only once in a great while?
4. Want something with no harmful side effects?
5. Want to avoid going to the doctor?
6. Want something that will help protect against sexually transmitted infections?
7. Have to be concerned about affordability?
8. Need to be virtually certain that pregnancy will not result?
9. Want to avoid pregnancy now but want to have a child sometime in the future?
10. Have any medical condition or lifestyle that may rule out some form of contraception?

Interpretation

If you have checked *Yes* to number:

1. Condoms and spermicides may be easily purchased without prescription in any pharmacy.
2. Sterilization, oral contraceptives, hormone implants or injections, cervical caps, and periodic abstinence techniques do not require that anything be done just before sexual relations.
3. Diaphragms, condoms, or spermicides can be used by people who have coitus only once in a while. Periodic abstinence techniques may also be appropriate but require a high degree of skill and motivation.
4. IUCDs should be carefully discussed with your physician. Sometimes the use of oral contraceptives or hormone products results in some minor discomfort and may have harmful side effects.
5. Condoms and spermicides do not require a prescription from a physician.
6. Condoms and, to a lesser extent, spermicides and the other barrier methods may help protect against some sexually transmitted infections. No method (except abstinence) can guarantee complete protection.
7. Be a wise consumer: check prices, ask pharmacists and physicians. Sterilization is permanent, but there is no additional expense for a lifetime.
8. Sterilization provides near certainty. Oral contraceptives, hormone implants or injections, or a diaphragm-condom-spermicide combination also give a high measure of reliable protection. Avoid periodic abstinence, withdrawal, and douche methods. Outercourse may be a good alternative.
9. Although it is sometimes possible to reverse sterilization, it requires surgery and is more complex than simply stopping use of any of the other methods.
10. Smokers and people with a history of blood clots should probably not use oral contraceptives or other hormone approaches. Some people have an allergic reaction to a specific spermicide and should experiment with another brand. Some women cannot be fitted with a diaphragm or cervical cap because of the position of the uterus. The woman and her health care provider will then need to select another suitable means of contraception.

To Carry This Further ...

There may be more than one method of birth control suitable for you. Always consider how a method you select can also help you avoid an STI. Study the methods suggested above, and consult Table 13–1 to determine what techniques may be most appropriate.

Focus on

SOCIOETHICAL IMPLICATIONS OF BIOTECHNOLOGY

Reproductive Technologies

In response to political pressure from Canadian women's organizations, the Royal Commission on New Reproductive Technologies was appointed in 1989 to consult the public and study the issue of new reproductive technologies.

In 1993, the Royal Commission on New Reproductive Technologies released its report. Through extensive studying of public and stakeholder preferences for new reproductive technologies, the Royal Commission concluded that

> New reproductive technologies possess a conceptual and practical integrity and distinctiveness. Their fundamental object is human reproduction, with all its distinct historical, social, and ethical implications ... More than any other aspect of health-related technology or service, the research and application of new reproductive technologies have significance beyond the individuals directly involved ... Public control over the development and use of new reproductive technologies is therefore necessary to safeguard a wide range of interests. Some relate directly to the health and well-being of the individuals involved. Others relate to the welfare of particular groups such as women, for whom reproduction has always had particular social, economic, and legal consequences.

The Commission adopted an Ethic of Care to determine the desirability of the consequences of new reproductive technologies. The Commission used an Ethic of Care that includes individual autonomy, equality, protection of the vulnerable, accountability, respect for human life and dignity, non-commercialization of reproduction (specific to RCNRT), appropriate use of resources, and balancing individual and collective interests as criteria for deciding the social benefits of new reproductive technologies.

Based on this ethic, the Commission made 293 recommendations which dealt with the prevention of infertility, the management of assisted reproduction, sex selection for nonmedical reasons, prenatal diagnosis techniques and gene therapy, judicial intervention in pregnancy and birth, and the use of fetal tissue. The Commission called on government to control the development of this technology: First, there is an urgent need for well-defined boundaries around the use of new reproductive technologies, so that unethical use of knowledge is not permitted. Second, within those boundaries, accountable regulation is needed to protect the interests of those involved, as well as those of society as a whole. Third, given the ongoing and, indeed, increasing pace of knowledge and development, a flexible and continuing response to evolving technologies that involves wide input from Canadians is an essential component of their responsible delivery.

The two key recommendations made by the Commission for managing the development of new reproductive technologies were made, not on medical or scientific grounds, but considering the impacts on the social status of women, children, and disabled people in society. First, the Commission recommended legislation that would ban research and application of several new technologies. Second, the Commission proposed that the federal government establish a regulatory and licensing agency. The National Reproductive Technologies Commission would be responsible for licensing, establishing standards, public information, and policy development.

Created under the Inquiries Act, the Royal Commission operated independently of government departments and agencies. Because of the Royal Commission on New Reproductive Technologies, Health Canada has taken a lead role in researching the socioethical implications of this technology and has made a concerted effort to develop policies that address these concerns. Health Canada has acted on these recommendations. In July 1995, the Government of Canada announced a voluntary moratorium on nine problematic new reproductive and genetic technologies. The moratorium was an interim measure pending legislation. The prohibitions legislation introduced in June 1996 bans

- Sex selection for non-medical purposes
- Buying and selling of eggs, sperm, and embryos
- Gene-line genetic alteration
- Maintaining an embryo in an artificial womb
- Cloning human embryos
- Creation of animal-human hybrids
- Retrieval of sperm and eggs from fetuses and cadavers for fertilization or implantation, or research involving the maturation of sperm or eggs outside the human body
- Commercial surrogacy arrangements
- Transfer of embryos between humans and other species
- The use of human sperm or eggs without informed consent of donors
- Research on human embryos later than 14 days after conception
- Creation of embryos for research purposes only
- The offer to provide or pay for prohibited services

Health Canada defends these prohibitions because these practices are inconsistent with the principles of human dignity and respect and the non-commercialization of reproduction.

Health Canada has moved forward with legislation to establish a regulatory structure with broad representation from the public. The regulatory agency would report directly to the minister of Health. It would be responsible for the development of standards for the use of reproductive materials in medical research and practice, for licensing to permit such activities, and for inspection to ensure compliance with these standards.

Health Canada has had success in managing the socioethical implications of new reproductive technologies. Health Canada recognized new reproductive technologies as distinct, undertook research to understand public preferences for its development, and created legislation to direct its applications. The new broad-based regulatory agency will provide a forum for the discussion and direction of the socioethical consequences of new reproductive technologies for Canada.

Source: Industry Canada: *Socioethical implications of biotechnology*. March 1997. **http://strategis.ic.gc.ca/pics/ca/socio_e.pdf**. Accessed October 25, 2005.

Chapter **14**

Aging and the End of Life

Chapter Objectives

After reading this chapter, you will be able to:

- Define aging.
- Explain changes associated with aging.
- Describe health conditions associated with aging.
- Explain the clinical determinants of death.
- Discuss the issue of euthanasia, including voluntary and involuntary euthanasia.
- Summarize the psychological stages that dying people often experience.
- Describe the guidelines for interacting with dying people.
- Describe the recommendations for talking with children about death.
- Discuss the challenges of coping with the death of a child, infant, or unborn child.
- Explain the concept of hospice care and describe its strategies.
- Describe some of the feelings that accompany grief over the death of a friend or loved one.
- Describe the common rituals of death practices in our society.

Online Learning Centre Resources

www.mcgrawhill.ca/college/hahn

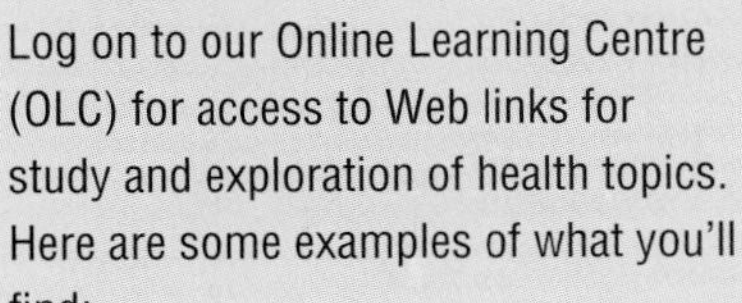

Log on to our Online Learning Centre (OLC) for access to Web links for study and exploration of health topics. Here are some examples of what you'll find:

- **www.canadian-health-network.ca/1seniors.html** The Canadian Health Network's page on seniors is a valuable source of information for and about Canadians over the age of 65. It features in-depth information on issues affecting the health of older Canadians as well as links to seniors' health resources from around the world. See also Health Canada's Web site for similar information: **www.hc-sc.gc.ca/jfy-spv/seniors-aines_e.html**
- **www.50plus.com** Go to the Web site for the Canadian Association of Retired Persons (CARP) for information of interest to people over the age of 50 (not just those who are retired), including health, politics, travel, and more.
- **www.bereavedfamilies.net** Bereaved Families Online is the Web site of the Bereaved Families of Ontario, a mutual aid society founded to support people who have lost an immediate family member. It is a welcoming site for people from across the country who find themselves in this situation.

Media Pulse

Portrayal of Older Adults in the Media

The next time you channel surf for a TV program, or go to a movie, or read a magazine, pay attention to the images of older people that you see—if you see any at all.

Contemporary society values youth, beauty, and vigour to the extent that it is rare to see people, or images of people, in the media who do not have these attributes. From the man who reads the news reports to the characters on popular family sitcoms, it is unusual to see anyone over the age of 50. When we are shown older adults, they are frequently characterized in a stereotypical way. Perhaps you've seen them portrayed as cantankerous, forgetful, or meddling in situation comedies, or in woeful need of medications in advertisements. It would be a challenge to identify any instances in which older adults are portrayed as athletic, fashionable, intellectual, or sexual. Yet these can be features of older adults, just as they can be of any other adult group. We become socialized by what we see on

Media Pulse *continued*

popular television shows and in magazines and advertisements. They communicate to us, in either a direct or an indirect manner, how various members of society act, who represents the norm, and which groups are not part of that norm. The exclusion or negative stereotyping of older adults is a type of ageism that appears to be common in the North American media.

Studies reaching back 20 years have indicated that on prime-time television, elderly characters are underrepresented relative to their proportion of the actual population.[1] When older adults do appear in the media, older male characters are portrayed more often and in a more positive light than older female characters.[2] Advertisers in both North America and the United Kingdom have been identified as not using older people to a representative extent in their advertising, and when they do, it is for a limited range of products that emphasize incapacity in old age.[3]

As the baby boom generation, those born between 1946 and 1966, moves toward senior citizen status, it is likely that this will change. Typically, the media, including magazines, movies, and television, target a specific age-centred audience—usually one that will be the purchasers of their sponsor's products. As a consumer group of significant size in North America, the baby boomers will be willing to pay for products and entertainment that speak to them. Have you seen any indication of this?

However, not all media venues portray these typical stereotypes of seniors. For example, Dove (**www.dove.com**) is responsible for conducting a campaign for real beauty with the premise that "real beauty comes in many shapes, sizes, and ages." The Campaign for Real Beauty calls into question society's stereotypical views on aging. (Also see **www.campaignforrealbeauty.com.**)

One goal of this chapter is to examine the process of human aging, in particular, the challenges associated with the aging process and how it can be a healthy and fulfilling phase of the human life span. A second goal is to help people realize that the reality of death can serve as a focal point for a more enjoyable, productive, and contributive life.

While we typically associate old age with dying, only 75% of deaths in Canada are among the elderly.[4] It is important, therefore, not to think of the elderly only in terms of imminent death, and likewise not to think of death only in terms of later life.

WHAT IS AGING?

We often think of aging as the process of growing old, although in strictly **chronological** terms, everyone from the newborn baby to the **centenarian** and beyond is aging. Aging can be defined as "a process or group of processes occurring in living organisms that with the passage of time lead to a loss of adaptability, functional impairment, and eventually death."[5] Although aging is not completely understood, we do know that it is an inevitable, universal, irreversible, and dynamic process. Aging is also a very individual experience. This experience involves physical, psychological, and social changes and adaptation that occurs throughout one's life.

Throughout history there has been much speculation about the causes of aging, often in hopes of finding a "cure" and ultimately the achievement of immortality. The Human Genome Project has given scientists more insight than ever before into the aging process, identifying at least 36 genes that drive **senescence** and perhaps another 200 that are involved in its fine-tuning.[6] A number of these genes tell the body to produce antioxidant enzymes, our natural protection against **free radicals**. These are harmful oxygen molecules that arise from the everyday conversion of food into energy, as well as from environmental pollutants, UV radiation, hormones, and tobacco use, among other causes. However, oxidative damage is only one of a number of possible causes of aging. Others include the linking of glucose with protein molecules, which ultimately changes the way these proteins behave as well as their function. These altered proteins appear as hardened arteries, cataracts, and sagging skin, among other changes typically associated with older age.

Scientists have looked to specific genetic conditions such as Hutchinson-Gilford syndrome or progeria to find some clues. In this condition, which affects 1 in 8 million births, a single gene mutation appears to be responsible for the premature and rapid aging of the appearance of very young children. While these children appear normal at birth, by the age of three they are already showing evidence of hair loss and greying, skin changes, and cardiovascular deterioration typical of someone 20 times their age. Remarkably, not all of the biological systems in these children are aging at this staggering rate. For example, they follow the same intellectual developmental track as other children their age. Down syndrome, a more common genetic defect that appears in approximately 1 in 700 births in Canada, also manifests signs of early aging, including the development of cardiovascular disease and Alzheimer's disease as early as age 20. These mutations result in significantly lower life expectancies than those of the general population. See the Learning from Our Diversity box on p. 343 for more information about life expectancies.

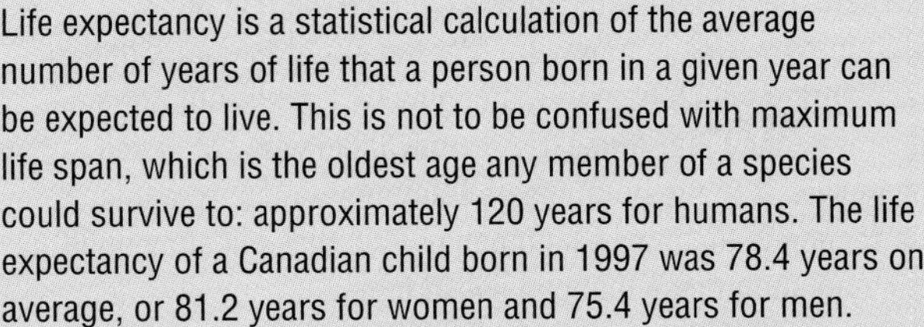

Learning from Our Diversity
Life Expectancy in Canada and around the World

Life expectancy is a statistical calculation of the average number of years of life that a person born in a given year can be expected to live. This is not to be confused with maximum life span, which is the oldest age any member of a species could survive to: approximately 120 years for humans. The life expectancy of a Canadian child born in 1997 was 78.4 years on average, or 81.2 years for women and 75.4 years for men.

Life expectancy at birth has risen dramatically in this country over the past century. This is mostly due to the decline in infectious disease and accident-related deaths in the first half of the 20th century, particularly among young people. Not all Canadians, however, can share this relatively recent expectation of such longevity. Among poorer Canadians, and especially within the urban Aboriginal population, average life expectancy is significantly lower than the national average.

Life expectancy across the planet has risen from 46 years in 1950 to 66 years in the late 1990s, and is expected to reach 76 years by 2050.[7] Much of this is by virtue of lowered infant mortality rates, safer childbirth (fewer deaths among mothers giving birth), and reduced overall fertility rates worldwide. Fewer births results in fewer infant deaths that would bring down the life expectancy average.

Not all countries are experiencing the global rise in life expectancy. Due to the epidemic of HIV-AIDS in sub-Saharan Africa over the past 10 years, life expectancy at birth has dropped for females to 46.3 years and for males to 44.8 years. Similarly, post-Soviet Russia witnessed a fall in its life expectancy brought about by dramatic downward shifts in social, economic, and health status of many citizens formerly supported by the communist system.

The World Health Organization (WHO) has recently begun collecting statistics on Healthy Life Expectancy (HALE), which is the "expected number of years to be lived in what might be termed the equivalent of full health."[8,9] It is calculated by subtracting years of ill health, which are weighted according to severity, from the overall life expectancy of a nation.

Japan holds the worldwide record for healthy life expectancy at 73.8 years, while Canada ranks 17th among 191 nations, ahead of the 28th-placed United States, with HALEs of 70.0 and 67.2 years respectively. These low levels for Canada and the United States are in part caused by the wide gap in income distribution between the rich and poor, leading to the particularly compromised health status of our Aboriginal peoples and other marginalized people. In addition, when compared to countries such as Greece, Sweden, and Australia, which rank above us, we tend to use more tobacco and exhibit other lifestyle behaviours that lead to chronic diseases that abbreviate our old age.[10]

The combination of rising life expectancies and falling fertility rates has led to what is called "population aging," whereby the average age of the Canadian population is getting progressively higher. Seniors, counted as those over the age of 65 years, are one of the fastest growing population groups in Canada. Currently, 13% of the Canadian population is older than 65 and when those born during the baby boom years from 1946 to 1966 start to enter their senior years in 2011, this segment of the population will also "boom." Statistics Canada has projected that by 2021 adults over the age of 65 will represent 19% of the population, and that by 2041 they will represent one-quarter of all Canadians.[11]

Whatever they are, the molecular changes happening at the level of aging cells are likely the same for everybody. How these changes add up to a person being physiologically and mentally older is quite variable; so much so that it is difficult to know what "normal" aging is. Almost all organs lose what is called functional or reserve capacity, leaving them less able to accommodate stresses or challenges to homeostasis or balance. Pathogenic organisms, chronic disease, accidents, medications, and psychological distress are examples of stresses that can more readily lead to morbidity, disability, and mortality in an older person than in a younger one. Much evidence, however, suggests that many of the features we interpret as decline and illness in old age are the results of disuse as much as they are the processes of senescence.

CHANGES ASSOCIATED WITH AGING

Renowned scholar in kinesiology and gerontology Waneen Spirduso articulates that "the first truth about aging is that everybody does it. The second truth is that

Key Terms

chronological
Measuring by time, for example years.

centenarian
Someone living to and beyond 100 years.

senescence
A gradual decline in the functional capacity of the body's systems, including an increased vulnerability to disease.

free radicals
Harmful oxygen molecules that can damage cells and their genetic material.

Osteoporosis

Osteoporosis is a condition characterized by extensive loss of bone mineral density, usually resulting in one or more fractures. The name comes from the porous appearance of the bone, a feature that makes it more vulnerable to fracture. Osteoporosis is not a new disease; archeologists have found evidence of osteoporosis in female skeletons dating from the Bronze Age. Until recently, this condition was considered an inevitable fact of aging for women because one-third of all women typically experienced fractures at some point in their old age.

As with many body tissues, bone is constantly replacing itself to enable growth and maintenance. Cells called *osteoclasts* are responsible for the breaking down of existing bone, while cells known as *osteoblasts* rebuild it. Throughout adulthood, the activity of these two types of cells is usually synchronized so that bone mass is maintained. In the fourth decade of life, osteoclasts appear to get slightly ahead of osteoblasts, and bone mass starts to decline in both men and women. The loss of estrogen, either through menopause or as a result of disordered eating at any age, enhances this imbalance between the breakdown and buildup of bone. Over time, certain bones become too weak to hold the weight of the body, so they fracture. You may have noticed elderly people who appear to be permanently bent over. This *kyphosis* is the result of osteoporotic crush fractures of the vertebrae in the spine. For a person with osteoporosis, falling can be an especially devastating event.

There are two obvious ways to reduce the risk of osteoporosis. One is to ensure that the skeleton enters the years during which osteopenia begins with sufficient bone mineral density that those losses inevitable with aging will not weaken it to the point where fractures are unavoidable. The second is to adopt health behaviours that will slow bone loss, and shun those that can speed it up.

Osteoporosis has been called a pediatric disease with geriatric consequences. This is because the most significant gains in bone strength can be achieved during the early teenage years of a person's life. This is the time during which diet and exercise must be optimal to affect maximum possible bone density gains. The skeleton you produce during this period is the one that will be supporting you in old age. Factors that will enhance your ability to produce a strong skeleton for life include a balanced diet that is abundant in calcium and vitamin D, regular physical activity that puts weight-bearing stress on your bones (such as running, jumping, and carrying weight), tobacco avoidance, and a healthy body weight (not being underweight or undertaking frequent diets to reduce body weight). These same behaviours can assist older women to slow bone loss and, in the case of tobacco avoidance, not hasten it.

For more information on osteoporosis, check out the Osteoporosis Society of Canada's Web site at **www.osteoporosis.ca**.

everybody does it differently."[12] For example, we can examine the rate of aging—the change in function of the body's systems and organs per a specified unit of time.

No two tissues or organ systems of the human body age at the same rate. Similarly, there is a large inter-individual difference in the rate of aging. Some students in their early university years may already be showing outward signs of aging such as a receding hairline or greying hair. Others may be experiencing internal changes such as arteriosclerosis or bone loss. Some of the changes that appear to be an inevitable part of aging can be slowed, but not halted, by healthy lifestyle choices. Alternatively, disease and accidents have the potential to change the rate of deterioration of organs and systems, and subsequently affect aging.

Changes in Body Composition

There are many changes in body composition associated with aging. Muscle tissue, for example, declines along with other lean tissues such as organ mass. Strength is the most obvious loss associated with aging (*sarcopenia*—the decrease in muscle mass), but this can be slowed and even reversed at very old ages by appropriate strength- training regimes.

Fat tissue tends to accumulate with age, though again, this is not inevitable if attention is paid to diet and exercise. However, the range of BMIs associated with good health among the elderly tends to be wider and higher than for younger people.

Bone loss, or *osteopenia*, starts in the fourth decade of life for both men and women. While exercise, diet, and for some women, hormone replacement therapy (HRT), can attenuate some of this loss, it is critical that both men and women arrive at middle age with their genetic potential for peak bone mass. The Star Box above takes a closer look at osteoporosis.

Skin exposed to UV light for a lifetime experiences photoaging, which is largely responsible for the wrinkled and dried texture of old people's skin. In addition, aging itself slows the replacement of skin cells, thins the skin layers, and makes it less elastic. Wound healing is significantly slower.

The thinning hair associated with age is caused by the follicles declining in diameter by about 20%, and strand losses being less efficiently replaced. Loss of pigment in the hair shafts leaves them colourless or grey in appearance over time.

The Cardiovascular System

Arteriosclerosis, or the hardening of the arteries, appears to be a normal consequence of aging, while *atherosclerosis,* or the buildup of fatty calcified plaques, is understood to be a disease process (atherosclerosis was discussed in detail in Chapter 10). Both conditions reduce the vessels' capacity to accommodate changes in the volume of blood, leading to hypertension. Chapter 10 outlines the pathologies that accompany the atherosclerotic process and hypertension. With age, the heart muscle loses elasticity and accumulates fat. The maximum heart rate that can be achieved during sustained exercise declines in direct association with age, though there are large individual differences. Declines in lung function caused by weakening muscles are slowed by regular exercise in middle and old age, as are many of the declines in this system.

The Renal and Urinary Systems

The size and weight of the kidneys decline with age, as does the number of operational glomerula (the structures that filter wastes out of the blood). As a result, renal function drops to about half of that for a young adult. This reduction of function can cause problems with drug disposal, nutrient retention, and blood pressure regulation. Bladder capacity may also be reduced by about 50% in older adults. Due to a combination of this and other problems that are often centred in the nervous system, between 10% and 30% of community-dwelling seniors and half of those living in care facilities are affected by urinary incontinence.[13]

The Gastrointestinal System

Some older people experience a diminished capacity to generate many of the digestive juices normally produced in the stomach. This can reduce their ability to absorb all the nutrients in their diet, necessitating more nutrient-dense dietary choices (see Chapter 5). Lack of exercise, low fluid intake, and low dietary fibre intakes often lead to constipation in older adults. This again is a condition felt by many to be normal in old age, but can be largely avoided or corrected by a healthy lifestyle.

The Senses and Nervous System

Age has a tendency to reduce the capacity to hear high-pitch sounds, such as whispers and ringing telephones. This condition is called *presbycusis.* A similarly named condition, *presbyopia* (*presby* means "elder"), is the aging-associated change in the eye that makes accommodation of the lens more difficult, often necessitating reading glasses from mid-life onward. The lenses of the eye also tend to become cloudy with cataracts. Some aspects of the sense of taste may decline such that older people tend to prefer greater concentrations of salt and sugar in their food. The nervous system as a whole works less rapidly as neurotransmitters and synapses (the junctions between two neurons) are altered by age. As a result, older people may experience slower reflexes and reaction times.

The Reproductive System

The female reproductive system undergoes a much more dramatic change with aging than does the male system. Around the age of 50, female production of estrogen and progesterone starts to decline rapidly. This process is known as *menopause* and results in the cessation of reproductive capacity. As the affected hormones have a vast array of functions in the body, many of which are still poorly understood, their loss can alter the way a woman looks, feels, and acts. In the male, there is a very gradual loss of testosterone over the middle years of life that can ultimately lead to what is now being labelled "andropause." While andropause may exert a gradual effect of lowering sperm count and may make impotence a more common occurrence, men are able to produce sufficient viable sperm for reproduction up to a very old age.

HEALTHY AGING

Physical and Mental Exercise

Physical activity has been highlighted throughout this text and in Chapter 4 as a critical factor in preventing many of the aspects of aging that are associated with both disease and disuse. For younger adults, appropriate levels of physical activity can reduce the risk for cardiovascular disease, osteoporosis, some cancers, hypertension, and type 2 diabetes in later years.[14] For those who are already elderly, exercise can assist in controlling chronic disease, preventing falls and depression, and gaining a sense of control and self-efficacy. Older adults who are physically active have better physical and mental health overall, and are less likely to need assistance with basic activities of living or to require nursing home care.[15]

Unfortunately, many older Canadians are not taking advantage of the array of benefits that physical activity has to offer. According to the 1996–1997 National Population Health Survey, only 29% of men and 19% of women over the age of 74 were physically active.[16] This may be due in part to the fact that these individuals grew up in a very different environment; one in which domestic, transportation, and labour force activities involved considerable physical movement. Exercise over and above this day-to-day activity was seldom necessary. In contrast, the contemporary work, transportation, and home environments offer us little opportunity for physical activity, so it has become necessary to add exercise, for its own sake, to our day. Additionally, Canadian studies have shown that many of today's older adults are misinformed about the risks associated with exercising in old age.[17] In fact, the risks of being inactive far outweigh those minimal hazards connected with exercising in even advanced old age.[18] For more information see Health Canada's *Physical Activity Guide for Older Adults*, which provides information promoting physical activity in the aging population: **www.phac-aspc.gc.ca/pau-uap/paguide/older/index.html**.

Just as muscle and bone will deteriorate rapidly in old age if you don't work them, the capacity of the brain has also been shown to decline with disuse. Rats kept in intellectually arousing environments that include complicated mazes and challenging tasks are able to learn better and stay smarter in old age than animals who have lived their lives in ordinary cages. So too with humans, those who have higher education and continue to stimulate their minds throughout life are significantly less likely to develop dementias associated with old age.

Falls

Falling results in substantial disability, morbidity, and mortality among seniors.[19] For example, falling is the leading cause of injury admissions to acute-care hospitals and in-hospital deaths.[20] Each year approximately one-third of seniors experience a fall,[21] although the majority of these falls do not lead to serious injury, hospitalization, or death.[22] However, many seniors will experience complications, which may include soft tissue injuries or fractures and impaired mobility resulting from injury, fear, a lack of self-confidence, or restricted ambulation. Falls may also often lead to serious psychological and social consequences for the elderly.[23]

Falling is a major problem in the elderly not only because of the high incidence, but the high susceptibility for injury. This susceptibility for injury is associated with a high prevalence of clinical disease (e.g., osteoporosis) and age-related changes (e.g., slowed reflexes) that make even a seemingly mild fall dangerous.

It is estimated that between one-third and one-half of falls can be attributed to environmental factors.[24] Pay attention to scatter rugs, footwear, telephone cords, stairs, and lighting within the home. Outside hazards include poor stair and railing design, slippery surfaces, uneven sidewalks, and the misuse or nonuse of walking aids. Some of the personal risk factors associated with falling can be reduced through well-designed exercise programs that emphasize strength and balance.

Osteoarthritis

Osteoarthritis (OA) is one of the most common disorders in elderly Canadians, with an estimated 80% of those over the age of 75 affected.[25] It is also the leading cause of disability in this group. OA is believed to be caused by wear and tear in the joints, which over time erodes the protective cartilage, leaving bone to grind against bone without its usual cushioning. Movement can become painful and joints tend to stiffen. Yet regular use of specific forms of exercise can reduce the stiffening and pain of OA.

Mental Health in Old Age

Aging can present a number of challenges to an older adult's mental health. Losses such as the deaths of friends and loved ones, declines in physical and mental capacity, and development of chronic diseases can add up over the later years. These can be compounded by the way in which our Western culture often views older people as marginal, useless, and potentially nuisance members of society. Depression is not believed to be any more common amongst the elderly than among younger adults, although between 30% and 40% of elderly living in institutions suffer to some degree from this condition.[26] The signs of depression in older adults are somewhat different from those you read about in Chapter 2. Depressed elderly people are more likely to complain about physical symptoms and memory disorders, and express anxiety and agitation.[27] As with many of the conditions associated with aging, health-promoting behaviours such as staying socially connected with others, getting sufficient sleep and exercise, and eating a balanced diet can go a long way to reduce the likelihood of developing depression in later years.[28]

Dementia

Approximately 8% of Canadians over the age of 65 and between one-quarter and one-third of those over the age of 85 have some form of dementia.[29] Most of these cases are Alzheimer's disease and vascular dementia, which is caused by small strokes or interruptions of the blood vessels supplying the brain. More than memory is lost with these conditions. Judgment and reasoning abilities deteriorate, and mood and behaviour changes. Risk factors associated with the development of Alzheimer's disease include low educational level, family history, head injury, and occupational exposure to glues, pesticides, and fertilizers.[30]

DYING IN TODAY'S SOCIETY

Since shortly after the turn of the 20th century, the manner in which people experience death in this society has changed significantly. Formerly, most people died in their own homes, surrounded by family and friends. Young children frequently lived in the same home with their aging grandparents and saw them grow older and eventually die. Death was seen as a natural extension of life. Children grew up with a keen sense of what death meant, both to the dying person and to the grieving survivors.

Times have indeed changed. Today approximately 70% of people die in hospitals, nursing homes, and extended care facilities, not in their own homes. The extended family is seldom at the bedside of the dying person.[31] Frequently, frantic efforts are made to keep a dying person from death. Although medical technology has improved our lives, some people believe that it has reduced our ability to die with dignity. Many are convinced that our way of dying has become more artificial and less civilized than it used to be. The trend toward palliative care may be a positive response to this high-tech manner of dying (see p. 350).

DEFINITIONS OF DEATH

Before many of the scientific advancements of the past 30 years, death was relatively easy to define. People were considered dead when a heartbeat could no longer be detected and when breathing ceased. Now, with the technological advancements made in medicine, especially emergency medicine, some patients who give every indication of being dead can be resuscitated. Critically ill people, even those in comas, can now be kept alive for years with many of their bodily functions maintained by medical devices, including feeding tubes and respirators.

Thus, death can be a very difficult concept to define.[32] Numerous professional associations and ad hoc interdisciplinary committees have struggled with this problem and have developed criteria by which to establish death. Some of these criteria have been adopted by various governments, although there is certainly no consensus definition of death that all jurisdictions embrace.

Clinical determinants of death refer to measures of bodily functions. Often judged by a physician, who can then sign a legal document called a *medical death certificate*, these clinical criteria include the following:

1. Lack of heartbeat and breathing.
2. Lack of central nervous system function, including all reflex activity and environmental responsiveness. Often this can be confirmed by an **electroencephalograph** reading. If there is no brain wave activity after an initial measurement and a second measurement after 24 hours, the person is said to have undergone *brain death*.
3. The presence of **rigor mortis**, indicating that body tissues and organs are no longer functioning at the cellular level. This is sometimes referred to as *cellular death*.

The *legal determinants* used by government officials are established by law and often adhere closely to the clinical determinants already listed. A person is not legally dead until a death certificate has been signed by a physician, **coroner**, or health department officer.

U.S. physician Dr. Jack Kevorkian has admitted to assisting in a number of suicides and was convicted of murder in 1999. How do you stand on the issue of physician-assisted suicide?

EUTHANASIA AND ASSISTED SUICIDE

Assisted suicide and euthanasia have been the focus of important legal cases in Canada. While suicide is not against the law in this country, knowingly assisting someone who is trying to commit suicide is a criminally indictable offence. In the early 1990s, Sue Rodriguez, a woman with amyotrophic lateral sclerosis (ALS or Lou Gehrig's Disease), went to the Supreme Court of Canada requesting the right to have assistance in ending her life. This was to be at a time of her own choosing, but when

Key Terms

electroencephalograph
An instrument that measures the electrical activity of the brain.

rigor mortis
Rigidity of the body that occurs after death.

coroner
An appointed legal official empowered to pronounce death and to determine the official cause of a suspicious or violent death.

her disabling and fatal disease would have made it impossible to commit suicide on her own. While she lost her case, Sue Rodriguez was helped to die in her home by an anonymous physician; an example of voluntary euthanasia. Involuntary euthanasia, sometimes called "mercy killing" is illustrated by the case of Robert Latimer, a Saskatchewan farmer who was found guilty of murdering his severely disabled daughter Tracy in order to relieve her of the extreme suffering she experienced on a daily basis. As she was mentally incapable of consenting, this was involuntary euthanasia. Even if she had been able to consent, her father's act would still have been an indictable offence under Canadian law.[33]

Refusing care, withholding care, or withdrawing life-support from a terminally ill person should not be confused with euthanasia or assisted suicide. Since the early 1980s in this country, a competent person has been able to refuse medical interventions, request that life support be withheld, or ask that medical devices that are sustaining life be withdrawn. These same orders can be expressed through the use of a living will or **advance directive**, a legal document prepared by an individual in the event that he or she at some point becomes incompetent to communicate requests for end-of life care (see the Star Box on this page). Similarly, physicians and other health care professionals in Canada are compelled neither to offer nor provide care that is considered futile.[34]

TALKING POINTS • You're having a class discussion on euthanasia. How would you argue different viewpoints —including euthansia as murder and euthansia as an act of mercy?

EMOTIONAL STAGES OF DYING

A process of self-adjustment has been observed in people who have a terminal illness. The stages in this process have helped form the basis for the modern movement of death education. An awareness of these stages may help you understand how people adjust to other important losses in their lives.

Perhaps the most widely recognized name in the area of death education is Dr. Elisabeth Kübler-Ross. As a psychiatrist working closely with terminally ill patients at the University of Chicago's Billings Hospital, Kübler-Ross was able to observe the emotional reactions of dying people. In her classic book *On Death and Dying*, Kübler-Ross summarized the psychological stages that dying people often experience.[35]

- *Denial.* This is the stage of disbelief. Patients refuse to believe that they actually will die. Denial can serve as a temporary defence mechanism and can allow patients the time to accept their prognosis on their own terms.

Advance Directives

Aging may be a time when the control of many aspects of one's life is taken over by others. One way many aging Canadians are ensuring they maintain control over many important aspects of their lives is through advance directives. These are legal documents that are completed with the help of a lawyer, when an individual is mentally competent. The advance directive usually names someone, or possibly a number of people, whom the individual has chosen to conduct his or her affairs in case of mental incompetency. Those chosen are often relatives or close friends, and usually have a good knowledge of the individual's values and wishes. Among the directives that can be stated are those for finances, business, health care, and end-of-life care. While these are legally binding in most jurisdictions, a directive cannot be made for either assisted suicide or involuntary euthanasia.

- *Anger.* A common emotional reaction after denial is anger. Patients can feel as if they have been cheated. By expressing anger, patients are able to vent some of their fears, jealousies, anxieties, and frustrations. Patients often direct their anger at relatives, physicians and nurses, religious symbols, and normally healthy people.
- *Bargaining.* Terminally ill people follow the anger stage with a stage characterized by bargaining. Patients who desperately want to avoid their inevitable deaths attempt to strike bargains—often with God or a church leader. Some people undergo religious conversions. The goal is to buy time by promising to repent for past sins, to restructure and rededicate their lives, or to make a large financial contribution to a religious cause.
- *Depression.* When patients realize that, at best, bargaining can only postpone their fate, they may begin an unpredictable period of depression. In a sense, terminally ill people are grieving for their own anticipated death. They may become quite withdrawn and refuse to visit with close relatives and friends. Prolonged periods of silence or crying are normal components of this stage and should not be discouraged.
- *Acceptance.* During the acceptance stage, patients fully realize that they are going to die. Acceptance ensures a relative sense of peace for most dying people. Anger, resentment, and depression are usually gone. Kübler-Ross describes this stage as one without much feeling. Patients feel neither happy nor sad. Many are calm and introspective and prefer to be left either alone or with a few close relatives or friends.

One or two additional points should be made about the psychological stages of dying. Just as each person's life is totally unique, so is each person's death. Unfolding deaths vary as much as do unfolding lives. Some people move through Kübler-Ross's stages of dying very predictably, but others do not. It is not uncommon for some dying people to avoid one or more of these stages entirely.

The second important point to be made about Kübler-Ross's stages of dying is that the family members or friends of dying people often pass through similar stages as they observe their loved ones dying. When informed that a close friend or relative is dying, many people will also experience varying degrees of denial, anger, bargaining, depression, and acceptance. Because of this, as caring people we need to recognize that the emotional needs of the living must be fulfilled in ways that do not differ appreciably from those of the dying.

TALKING POINTS • You and your brother are grieving over the recent death of your father in an auto crash. You're getting back to normal gradually, but your brother is in a serious depression—having trouble functioning at work and at home. How would you recommend professional counselling to your brother without making him feel worse?

INTERACTING WITH DYING PEOPLE

Facing the impending death of a friend, relative, or loved one is a difficult experience. If you have yet to go through this situation, be assured that, as you grow older, your opportunities will increase. This is part of the reality of living.

Most counsellors, physicians, nurses, and ministers who spend time with terminally ill people suggest that you display one quality when interacting with dying people: honesty. Just the thought of talking with a dying person may make you feel uncomfortable. (Most of us have had no training in this sort of thing.) Sometimes, to make ourselves feel less anxious or depressed, we may tend to deny that the person we are with is dying. Our words and nonverbal behaviour indicate that we prefer not to face the truth. Our words become stilted as we gloss over the facts and merely attempt to cheer up both our dying friend and ourselves. This behaviour is rarely beneficial or supportive—for either party.

As much as possible, we should attempt to be genuine and honest. We should not try to avoid crying if we feel the need to cry. At the same time, we can provide emotional support for dying people by allowing them to express their feelings openly. We should resist the temptation of trying to pull someone out of the denial, anger, or depression. We should not feel obliged to talk constantly and to fill long pauses with idle talk. Sometimes nonverbal communication, including touching, may be much more appreciated than mere talk. Since our interactions with dying people help fulfill our needs, we too should express our emotions and concerns as openly as possible.

TALKING WITH CHILDREN ABOUT DEATH

Because most children are curious about everything, it is not surprising that they are also fascinated by death. From a very young age, children are exposed to death through mass media (cartoons, pictures in newspapers and magazines, and news reports), adult conversations ("Aunt Emily died today," "Uncle Antonio is terminally ill"), and their discoveries (a dead bird, a crushed bug, a dead flower). The manner in which children learn about death will have an important effect on their ability to recognize and accept their own mortality and to cope with the deaths of others.

Psychologists encourage parents and older friends to avoid shielding children from or misleading children about the reality of death. Young children need to realize that death is not temporary and it is not like sleeping. Parents should make certain they understand children's questions about death before they give an answer. Most children want simple, direct answers to their questions, not long, detailed dissertations, which often confuse the issues. For example, when a four-year-old asks her father, "Why is Zev's dog dead?" an appropriate answer might be, "Because he got very, very sick and his heart stopped beating." Getting involved in a lengthy discussion about "doggy heaven" or the causes of specific canine diseases may not be necessary or appropriate.

Parents should answer questions when they arise and always respond with openness and honesty. In this way, young children can learn that death is a real part of life and that sad feelings are a normal part of accepting the death of a loved one.

TALKING POINTS • Your six-year-old child's favourite teacher has died of cancer, and she is having trouble accepting that her teacher is gone forever. How would you explain the reality of the situation in a positive way?

Key Term

advance directive
A legal document prepared by an individual in the event that he or she at some point becomes incompetent; advance directives can be used to communicate requests for end-of life care.

PALLIATIVE AND HOSPICE CARE FOR THE TERMINALLY ILL

The activities of acute-care hospitals revolve around helping people recover from illness and accidents. When recovery is no longer possible, a patient may have the choice of *palliative care*, either in the hospital, in a long-term care facility (such as a nursing home), in a **hospice**, or in the person's own home. Palliative care emphasizes the relief of pain and other symptoms, rather than treatment or cure. It ideally involves a multidisciplinary team of care providers who seek to meet the physical, emotional, and spiritual needs of the dying person, his or her family, caregivers, and other loved ones. The following strategies are typical of palliative care programs:

- *Pain Control.* Dying people are not usually treated for their terminal disease; they are provided with appropriate drugs to keep them free from pain, alert, and in control of their faculties. Drug dependence is of little concern, and patients can receive pain medication when they feel they need it.
- *Family Involvement.* Family members and friends are trained and encouraged to interact with the dying person and with each other. Family members often care for the dying person at home. If the hospice arrangement includes a hospice ward in a hospital or a separate building (also called a hospice), the family members have no restrictions on visitation.
- *Multidisciplinary Approach.* The hospice concept promotes a team approach.[36] Specially trained physicians, nurses, social workers, counsellors, and volunteers work with the patient and family to fulfill important needs. The needs of the family receive nearly the same priority as those of the patient.
- *Patient Decisions.* Contrary to most hospital approaches, hospice programs encourage patients to make their own decisions. The patient decides when to eat, sleep, go for a walk, and just be alone. By maintaining a personal schedule, the patient is more apt to feel in control of his or her life, even as that life is slipping away.

Another way in which palliative care differs from the traditional hospital approach concerns the care given to the survivors. Even after the death of the patient, the family receives a significant amount of follow-up counselling. Helping families with their grief is an important role for the pallative care team.

GRIEF AND THE RESOLUTION OF GRIEF

The emotional feelings that people experience after the death of a friend or relative are collectively called *grief. Mourning* is the process of experiencing these emotional feelings in a culturally defined manner. See the Star Box on p. 351 for more information about the grieving process. The expression of grief is seen as a valuable process that gradually permits people to detach themselves from the deceased. Expressing grief, then, is a sign of good health.

Although people experience grief in remarkably different ways, most people have some of the following sensations and emotions:

- *Physical Discomfort.* Shortly after the death of a loved one, grieving people display a rather similar pattern of physical discomfort. This discomfort is characterized by "sensations of somatic distress occurring in waves lasting from 20 minutes to an hour at a time, a feeling of tightness in the throat, choking with shortness of breath, need for sighing, and an empty feeling in the abdomen, lack of muscular power, and an intense subjective distress described as a tension or mental pain. The patient soon learns that these waves of discomfort can be precipitated by visits, by mentioning the deceased, and by receiving sympathy."[37]
- *Sense of Numbness.* Grieving people may feel as if they are numb or in a state of shock. They may deny the death of their loved one.
- *Feelings of Detachment from Others.* Grieving people see other people as being distant from them, perhaps because the others cannot feel the loss. A person in grief can feel very lonely. This is a common response.
- *Preoccupation with the Image of the Deceased.* The grieving person may not be able to complete daily tasks without constantly thinking about the deceased.
- *Guilt.* The survivor may be overwhelmed with guilt. Thoughts may centre on how the deceased was neglected or ignored. Sensitive survivors feel guilt merely because they are still alive. Indeed, guilt is a common emotion.
- *Hostility.* Survivors may express feelings of loss and remorse through hostility, which they direct at other family members, physicians, lawyers, and others.
- *Disruption in Daily Schedule.* Grieving people often find it difficult to complete daily routines. They can suffer from an anxious type of depression. Seemingly easy tasks take a great deal of effort. Initiation of new activities and relationships can be difficult. Social interaction skills can be lost.
- *Delayed Grief.* In some people, the typical pattern of grief can be delayed for weeks, months, and even years.

The grief process will continue until the bereaved person can establish new relationships, feel comfortable with others, and look back on the life of the deceased person with positive feelings (see the Changing for the Better box on p. 351). Although the duration of the grief resolution process will vary with the emotional

The Grieving Process

The grieving process consists of four phases, each of which is variable in length and unique in form to the individual. These phases are composed of the following:

1. *Internalization of the Deceased Person's Image.* By forming an idealized mental picture of the dead person, the grieving person is freed from dealing too quickly with the reality of the death.
2. *Intellectualization of the Death.* Mental processing of the death and the events leading up to its occurrence move the grieving person to a clear understanding that death has occurred.
3. *Emotional Reconciliation.* During this third and often delayed phase, the grieving person allows conflicting feelings and thoughts to be expressed and eventually reconciled with the reality of the death.
4. *Behavioural Reconciliation.* Finally, the grieving person is able to return comfortably to a life in which the death has been fully reconciled. Old routines are re-established and new patterns of living are adopted where necessary. The grieving person has largely recovered.

A mistake that might be made by the friends of a grieving person is encouraging a return to normal behaviour too quickly. When friends urge the grieving person to return to work right away, make new friends, or become involved in time-consuming projects, they may be preventing necessary grieving from occurring. It is not easy or desirable to forget about the fact that a spouse, friend, or child has recently died.

attachments one has to a deceased person, grief usually lasts from a few months to a year. Professional help should be sought when grieving is characterized by unresolved guilt, extreme hostility, physical illness, significant depression, and a lack of other meaningful relationships. Trained counsellors, physicians, and hospice workers can all play significant roles in helping people through grief. Exploring Your Spirituality (p. 352) shows how handling grief can vary greatly from one individual to another.

TALKING POINTS • The boyfriend of one of your best friends recently drowned. Your friend has withdrawn from her family and friends in her grief. How could you help her get professional counselling without making her family feel that you are interfering?

RITUALS OF DEATH

Our society has established a number of rituals associated with death that help the survivors accept the reality of death, ease the pain associated with the grief process, and provide a safe disposal of the body. Our rituals give us the chance to formalize our goodbyes to a person and to receive emotional support and strength from family members and friends. In recent years, more of our rituals seem to be celebrating the life of the deceased. In doing this, our rituals also reaffirm the value of their own lives.

Most of our funeral rituals take place in funeral homes, churches, and cemeteries. *Funeral homes* (or *mortuaries*) are business establishments that provide a variety of services to the families of dead people. The services are carried out by licensed funeral directors.

Changing *for the Better*

Helping the Bereaved

I know someone whose brother just died. I want to help without getting in the way at this difficult time. What's the best approach?

Leming and Dickinson[38] point out that the peak time of grief begins in the week after a loved one's funeral. Realizing that there is no one guaranteed formula for helping the bereaved, you can help by performing some or all of the following:

- Make few demands on the bereaved; allow him or her to grieve.
- Help with the household tasks.
- Recognize that the bereaved person may vent anguish and anger and that some of it may be directed at you.
- Recognize that the bereaved person has painful and difficult tasks to complete; mourning cannot be rushed or avoided.
- Do not be afraid to talk about the deceased person; this lets the bereaved know that you care for the deceased.
- Express your own genuine feelings of sadness, but avoid pity. Speak from the heart.
- Reassure bereaved people that the intensity of their emotions is very natural.
- Advise the bereaved to get additional help if you suspect continuing severe emotional or physical distress.
- Keep in regular contact with the bereaved; let him or her know you continue to care.

Key Term

hospice
A residence in which people with terminal illnesses and their loved ones can receive palliative care; hospice is also a philosophy of providing comprehensive palliative care to the dying.

Exploring Your Spirituality

Will I Ever Get over Losing My Friend?

The news that one of your close friends committed suicide came as a shock. Jack was a social guy who was liked by everyone. His girlfriend recently broke up with him, but he seemed to be taking it all right. He talked to you about the situation; he seemed disappointed but not despairing. He mentioned that he was still in touch with his former girlfriend and seemed glad about that.

That's why his suicide is so hard to comprehend. Were there warning signs you missed? If you had done more to support him during the breakup, would he still be here? Did you talk to him enough? Did you really listen to him? How could you be a good friend and not know that he was despondent? You feel guilty every time you think of Jack.

It's hard to come to terms with any death—even one that's expected, such as when the person is sick or old. But Jack was healthy and young, just about your age. That makes it harder to accept his death. Still, you need to come to terms with it—let yourself feel sad about it, reflect on your friendship with him, and, ultimately, get on with your own life. What can you do to cope?

- *Don't blame yourself.* If Jack was sending out signals for help, you were not alone in missing them. His whole network of family and friends did, too. Whatever your friend's mental state was at the time of his death, it was his decision to take his own life.
- *Talk about the problem.* You and your friends are all feeling sad and guilty, missing Jack, and confused about his death. So try to support one another. Take the time to listen to them and share your own feelings. Recognize that it's going to take time to deal with this death. Not facing it now will only delay the grieving process.
- *Take solace in your religious or spiritual beliefs.* Talk to your spiritual advisor, if you have one, about what you're going through. An objective listener can help you put your thoughts and feelings in perspective. Ask your religious group to add your friend's name (and his family's) to their remembrance list.
- *Do something positive.* Consider doing volunteer work for a suicide hotline in your community. You can't bring Jack back, but you may be able to help keep someone else from making the fatal choice he did.

Your friend's death could be a turning point for you. Examine your own life—how you're living now and what you hope to accomplish in the future. Start taking action on your lifetime goals. Show your love for others. Make a difference on campus and in your community. Make the world a better place for yourself and for others.

Rituals of death, such as this memorial service for the Canadian soldiers killed in Afghanistan, give those who are grieving a chance to receive emotional support from others.

Most funeral directors are responsible for preparing the bodies for viewing, filing death certificates, preparing obituary notices, establishing calling hours, assisting in the preparation and details of the funeral, casket selection, transportation to and from the cemetery, and family counselling. Many of these duties require directions based on decisions made by the bereaved family. Funeral choices can be made and pre-paid in advance of death, or in the days following death when family are often least able to think clearly about these important decisions. A full funeral can cost more than $5000 in Canada.[39] Significantly less expensive options include memorial services and cremation.

TALKING POINTS • How would you approach your parents to learn about their wishes concerning their own deaths, a subject they have never brought up?

Funeral Services

Funeral services vary according to religious preference and the emotional needs of the survivors. Although some services are held in religious institutions, many funeral services today take place in a funeral home, where a special room might serve as a chapel. Some services are held at the graveside. Families may also choose to have a simple *memorial service* at some time after the funeral. Completing the Personal Assessment on p. 358 will help you think about what kind of funeral arrangements you would prefer for yourself.

Organ Donation

Organ and tissue donation offers the opportunity to enhance someone else's life or possibly give them a second chance at living. Unfortunately, Canada's rate for organ donation is ranked in the bottom half among Westernized countries where organ transplants are completed. Currently in Canada there are more than 3500 waiting for an organ to be donated. Annually 150 die waiting for a donation that never occurs.[40] This gift can also help console the family of the deceased by giving them a sense that their loved one's death was not in vain.

Organs can be donated following a tragic and sudden "brain death," as long as heart and lung function is maintained by a ventilator so that vital organs can be kept alive for transplant. This cadaveric organ donation is the most typical source for organ transplants. Living donation, in which a kidney or part of a liver of a healthy living person is donated, is sometimes able to serve the same life-saving role as cadaveric donation.

Tissue donation is possible for almost everyone after death because a number of transplantable body tissues such as corneas, bones, muscles, and pancreatic and nerve cells can survive for a limited time without the use of a respirator, that is, a sudden "brain death" is not a prerequisite.

While the majority of Canadians support the idea of organ donation, only a fraction have discussed the idea of organ donation with a family member. In most parts of Canada, it is the families of the deceased that make the final decision on organ donation, most often in the difficult minutes following the sudden death of a loved one.

Canada's national organ and tissue donation Web site (**www.hc-sc.gc.ca/ahc-asc/media/nr-cp/2001/2001_36bk1_e.html**) offers the following steps to becoming an organ and tissue donor:

Step 1: Discuss organ and tissue donation with your family and let them know why this is important to you. Should you die suddenly from severe brain injury, your family may be approached about organ donation. Having discussed this with them will make it easier for them to know and respect your wishes in an emotionally difficult time.

Step 2: Ask your family to support your decision. Even if you have registered your intention to be an organ donor, doctors in most provinces will not likely go ahead with organ and tissue donation without your family's permission.

Step 3: Register your decision to become a donor. Check at the above URL for information on how to record your intention of being an organ and tissue donor in your province or territory.

Disposition of the Body

Bodies are disposed of in one of three ways. *Ground burial* has in the past been the most common method. About 75% of all bodies are placed in ground burial. The casket is almost always placed in a metal or concrete vault before being buried. The vault serves to further protect the body (a need only of the survivors) and to prevent collapse of ground because of the decaying of caskets. Use of a vault is required by most cemeteries.

A second type of disposition is *entombment*. Entombment refers to nonground burial, most often in structures called **mausoleums**. A mausoleum has a series of shelves where caskets can be sealed in vaultlike areas called *niches*. Entombment can also occur in the basements of buildings, especially in old, large churches. The bodies of famous church leaders are sometimes entombed in vaultlike spaces called **crypts**.

Cremation is a third type of body disposition. This method is rapidly increasing in popularity in Canada; it is used for as few as 3% of deaths in Newfoundland to as many as 68% in British Columbia.[41] Generally both the body and casket (or cardboard cremation box) are incinerated so that only the bone ash from the body remains. The body of an average adult produces about 2 to 4 kg (about 5 to 7 pounds) of bone ash. These ashes can then be placed in containers called urns, and then buried, entombed, or scattered. Cremation followed by a memorial service offers more flexibility and reduces the urgency that is often associated with traditional funeral and burial services.

Regardless of the rituals you select for the handling of your body (or the body of someone in your care), most educators are encouraging people to prearrange their plans. Before you die, you can save your survivors a lot of misery by putting your wishes in writing. *Funeral prearrangements* relieve the survivors of many of the details that must be handled at the time of your death. You can gather much of the information for your obituary notice and your wishes for the disposition of your body.

Key Terms

mausoleum (moz oh lee um)
An above-ground structure, which frequently resembles a small stone house, into which caskets can be placed for disposition.

crypts
Burial locations generally underneath churches.

Prearrangements can be made with a funeral director, family member, or attorney. Many individuals also prepay the costs of their funeral. By making arrangements in advance of need, you can enhance your own peace of mind. Currently about 30% to 40% of funerals are preplanned or prepaid or both. Interestingly, in the 1960s, nearly all funerals were planned by relatives at the time of a person's death.

PERSONAL PREPARATION FOR DEATH

This chapter is designed to help you discover some new perspectives about death and develop your own personal death awareness. Remember that the ultimate goal of death education is a positive one—to help you best use and enjoy your life. Becoming aware of the reality of your own mortality is a step in the right direction. Reading about the process of dying, grief resolution, and the rituals surrounding death can also help you imagine that someday you too will die.

There are some additional ways in which you can prepare for the reality of your own death. Preparing a will, purchasing a life insurance policy, making funeral prearrangements, preparing an advance directive, and considering an anatomical or organ donation are measures that help you prepare for your own death (The Star Box on p. 353 considers the question of organ donation). At the appropriate time, you might also wish to talk with family and friends about your own death. You may discover that an upbeat, positive discussion about death can help relieve some of your apprehensions and those of others around you.

Another suggestion to help you emotionally prepare for your own death is to prepare an *obituary notice* or **eulogy** for yourself. Include all the things you would like to have said about you and your life. Now compare your obituary notice and eulogy with the current direction your life seems to be taking. Are you doing the kinds of activities for which you want to be known? If so, great! If not, perhaps you will want to consider why your current direction does not reflect how you would like to be remembered. Should you make some changes to restructure your life's agenda in a more personally meaningful fashion?

Another suggestion to help make you aware of your own eventual death is to write your own **epitaph**. Before doing this, you might want to visit a cemetery. (Unfortunately, most of us visit cemeteries only when we are forced to.) Reading the epitaphs of others may help you develop your own epitaph.

Further awareness of your own death might come from attempting to answer these questions in writing (since this pushes you beyond mere thinking): (1) If I had only one day to live, how would I spend it? (2) What one thing would I like to accomplish before I die? (3) Once I am dead, what two or three things will people miss most about me? By answering these questions and accomplishing a few of the tasks suggested in this section, you will have a good start on accepting your own death and understanding the value of life itself.

Key Terms

eulogy
A composition or speech that praises someone; often delivered at a funeral or memorial service.

epitaph
An inscription on a grave marker or monument.

Taking Charge of Your Health

- Make a list of your three main lifetime goals, and begin taking steps toward reaching them.
- Talk to family members and friends about their thoughts on death to broaden your views on this subject.
- Review the steps in planning for organ donation, and make this commitment.
- Set up a realistic timetable for planning death-related issues, such as having a will drawn up and arranging for an advance medical directive.
- Begin a weekly journal for recording your thoughts on living and dying. Review your entries periodically to see how your opinions may change over time.
- Explore your current feelings about living and dying by answering the three important questions above.

SUMMARY

- Aging is an inevitable, universal, irreversible, and dynamic process.
- Disease and accidents have the potential to change the rate of deterioration of organs and systems.
- Personal death awareness encourages you to live a meaningful life.
- Death is determined primarily by clinical and legal factors.
- Euthanasia can be categorized as either voluntary or involuntary.
- Advance directives permit critically ill people (especially those who cannot communicate) to die with dignity.
- Denial, anger, bargaining, depression, and acceptance are the five classic psychological stages that dying people commonly experience, according to Kübler-Ross.
- Hospice care provides an alternative approach to dying for terminally ill people and their families.
- The expression of grief is a common experience that can be expected when a friend or relative dies. The grief process can vary in intensity and duration.
- Death in our society is associated with a number of rituals to help survivors cope with the loss of a loved one and to ensure proper disposal of the body.

REVIEW QUESTIONS

1. What is aging?
2. Why do individuals age at different rates?
3. How does the experience of dying today differ from that in the early 1900s?
4. Identify and explain the clinical and legal determinants of death and indicate who establishes each of them.
5. Explain the difference between voluntary and involuntary euthanasia.
6. Identify the five psychological stages that dying people tend to experience. Explain each stage.
7. Identify and explain the four strategies that form the basis of hospice care. What are the advantages of hospice care for the patient and the family?
8. Explain what is meant by the term *grief*. Identify and explain the sensations and emotions most people have when they experience grief. When does the grieving process end? How can adults cope with the death of a child? How can we assist grieving people?
9. What purposes do the rituals of death serve? What are the three ways in which bodies are disposed of?
10. What activities can we undertake to become better aware of our own mortality?

THINK ABOUT THIS ...

- When is a person old?
- Is aging a disease?
- How were issues related to death handled in your family when you were growing up?
- Will hospice care be an option you might choose someday?
- Have you or any of your relatives prepared an advance directive?
- At your death, would you want your organs or body tissue donated to help another person? Are there any organs you would prefer not to donate?
- If you found out you were going to die tomorrow, what would you do today?
- If it were determined that you were in a persistent vegetative state, would you want your life support to be disconnected?

REFERENCES

1. Chen MYT, Zhou N: The portrayal of older people in Canadian advertisements: regular vs. specialized magazines, in Marshall V, McPherson BD, editors: *Aging: Canadian perspectives*, Peterborough, ON, 1994, Broadview Press, 206–217.
2. Vasil J, Wass H: Portrayal of the elderly in the media: a literature review and implications for educational gerontologists, *Educational Gerontology* 19(1): 71–85, 1993.
3. Carrigan M, Szmigin I: Representations of old people in advertisements, *Journal of Market Research Society* 41(3):311–326, 1999.
4. National Advisory Council on Aging: *1999 and beyond: challenges of an aging Canadian society*, Minister of Public Works and Government Services Canada. Cat. H88-3/28-1999E, 1999.
5. Spirduso, WW: *Physical dimensions of aging*, 1995, Human Kinetics: Champaign Illinois, 6.

6. Brown K: How long have you got? *Scientific American Presents* 11(2): 9–15, 2000.
7. Brandstrader JR: From baby boom to geezer glut, *Scientific American Presents* 11(2): 23–25, 2000.
8. World Health Organization: *Annex Table 4—Healthy life expectancy (HALE) in all member states, estimates for 2000.* **www3.who.int/whosis/hale/hale.cfm?path=whosis, hale&language=english**
9. World Health Organization: *WHO issues new healthy life expectancy ranking, 2000.* **www.who.int/inf-pr-2000/en/pr2000-life.html**
10. *Annex Table 4.*
11. Health Canada: *Seniors.* **www.hc-sc.gc.ca/seniors-aines/pubs/factoids_2001/no04_e.htm.**
12. *Physical dimensions of aging.*
13. Hooyman N, Kiyak HA: *Social gerontology.* ed 5, Toronto, 1999, Allyn and Bacon.
14. Mazzeo RS, Cavanagh P, Evans WJ, Fiatarone M, Hagberg J, McAuley E, Startzell J: American College of Sports Medicine position statement on physical activity for older adults, *Medicine & Science in Sports & Exercise* 30(6):992–1008, 1998.
15. Active Living Coalition for Older Adults: *A blueprint for action for active living and older adults,*1999.
16. Ibid.
17. O'Brien Cousins S: *Exercise, aging and health: overcoming barriers to an active old age*, Philadelphia, Taylor & Francis, 1998.
18. Ibid.
19. Canadian Institute of Health Information, 2000, **www.cihi.ca**
20. Fletcher, PC: Falls: An issue among older women, *Stride: excellence in long-term care*, 2002, 6-11.
21. Josephson, KR, Fabacher, DA & Rubenstein, LZ: Home safety and fall prevention, *Clinics in Geriatric Medicine.* 7(4): 707-731.
22. Lilley, M, Arie, T, & Chilvers, CED: (1995). Accidents involving older people: A review of the literature, *Age and Ageing* 24: 346-365.
23. Tinetti, ME, Speechley, M, & Ginter, SF: Risk factors for falls among elderly persons living in the community, *The New England Journal of Medicine* 319(26): 1701-1707.
24. *1999 and beyond.*
25. Ibid.
26. Ibid.
27. Ibid.
28. Ibid.
29. Ibid.
30. Ibid.
31. Leming MR, Dickinson GE: *Understanding dying, death, and bereavement*, ed 5, 2001, Harcourt.
32. Kastenbaum RJ: *Death, society, and human experience*, ed 6, 1998, Allyn and Bacon.
33. Northcott HC, Wilson DM: *Dying and death in Canada*, Aurora, ON, 2001, Garamond Press.
34. Ibid.
35. Kübler-Ross E: *On death and dying*, reprint ed, 1997, Collier Books.
36. DeSpelder LA, Strickland AL: *The last dance: encountering death and dying*, ed 5, 1999, Mayfield.
37. Lindemann E: Symptomology and management of acute grief. In Fulton et al, editors: *Death and dying: challenge and change*, 1978, Addison-Wesley.
38. *Understanding dying.*
39. *Death and dying in Canada.*
40. Organ and Tissue: Canada's National Information Site, **www.hc-sc.gc.ca/english/organandtissue/index.html**, 2004.
41. Nault F, Ford D: An overview of deaths in Canada in 1992, *Health Reports* 6(2):287–294, 1994.

SUGGESTED READINGS

Albom, Mitch: *Tuesdays with Morrie*, 1997, Doubleday.
The story of the author's relationship with his former teacher, who is dying of ALS. During their weekly visits they discuss relationships, aging, and love.

Health Canada: *Canada's physical activity guide to healthy active living for older adults.*
Promotes active living among older adults by providing information on why physical activity is important, tips to increase physical activity, suggested activities, and sources of community support. Prepared in collaboration with the Canadian Society for Exercise Physiology and the Active Living Coalition of Older Adults. Cat. No. H39-429/1999-2E. To order, call (613) 941-3109 or go online at **www.phac-aspc.gc.ca/pau-uap/paguide/older/index.html**.

James JW, Friedman R: *The grief recovery handbook: the action program for moving beyond death, divorce, and other losses*, revised ed, 1998, HarperCollins.
This is a revised edition of a highly successful book that has helped people progress after a serious loss. Readers will come to realize that the passage of time alone rarely heals, but charting a specific course of action can provide a positive recovery. This book can help people rediscover joy in their lives.

Loving C: *My son, my sorrow: a mother's plea to Dr. Kevorkian*, 1998, New Horizon Press.
Carol Living's 27-year-old son begged her to help him die as he developed more and more serious complications from Lou Gehrig's disease. Confronting this dilemma, Loving turned to Dr. Kevorkian for assistance. This book illuminates one side of the debate about physician-assisted suicide.

National Advisory Council on Aging: *1999 and beyond: challenges of an aging Canadian society*, Minister of Public Works and Government Services Canada, 1999. Cat. H88-3/28-1999E.

This useful monograph provides a brief snapshot of the lives of Canadian seniors at the end of the 20th century. It also anticipates how the lives of older Canadians might change in the future. While health is a major focus, this document also examines diversity, abuse and neglect, housing, and transportation issues.

Spirduso WW, Francis KL, & MacRae PG: *Physical dimensions of aging*, ed 2, 2005, Human Kinetics.

This resource provides up-to-date information on aging, particularly focusing on physical aging and its effects on the other dimensions of health. Key areas addressed in this book include an introduction to aging, physical changes in structure capacity and endurance; motor co-ordination, motor control and skill, physical-psychosocial relationships; and physical performance and achievement.

Making Headlines

Stem cells are found in all animals, including humans. What sets them apart from other cells is their unique ability to reproduce themselves or turn into any of a host of specialized cells, such as those that make up an organ or body tissue. Stem cells have been receiving a lot of attention from Canadian news media lately for a number of reasons. Foremost, their potential to replace or repair degenerated tissues damaged by conditions such as Alzheimer's and Parkinson's diseases, diabetes, kidney failure, and heart disease has given rise to speculation that they might one day be a key to immortality. Another focus of media reports has been discussions, both international and in Canada, of the legal and ethical issues surrounding the use of stem cells for research and medical purposes. The ethical challenges are due to the fact that the stem cells believed to be most useful are those found in embryos, either created through *in vitro* fertilization or extracted from fetuses that have been therapeutically aborted. Editors and journalists are helping news consumers explore difficult issues such as whether human embryonic tissues (the results of an egg being fertilized by a sperm) should be deliberately generated for the purposes of "farming" stem cells rather than creating human life.

Name ______________________________ **Date** ______________

Personal Assessment

Planning Your Funeral

In line with this chapter's positive theme of the value of personal death awareness, here is a funeral service assessment that we frequently give to our health classes. This inventory can help you assess your reactions and thoughts about the funeral arrangements you would prefer for yourself.

After answering each of the following questions, you might wish to discuss your responses with a friend or close relative.

1. Have you ever considered how you would like your body to be handled after your death?
   ______ Yes ______ No

2. Have you already made funeral prearrangements for yourself?
   ______ Yes ______ No

3. Have you considered a specific funeral home or mortuary to handle your arrangements?
   ______ Yes ______ No

4. If you were to die today, which of the following would you prefer?
   ______ Ground burial
   ______ Cremation
   ______ Entombment
   ______ Donation to medical science

5. If you prefer to be cremated, what would you want done with your ashes?
   ______ Buried ______ Entombed
   ______ Scattered
   ______ Other; please specify ______________________

6. If your funeral plans involve a casket, which of the following ones would you prefer?
   ______ Plywood (cloth covered)
   ______ Hardwood (oak, cherry, mahogany, maple, etc.)
   ______ Steel (sealer or nonsealer type)
   ______ Stainless steel
   ______ Copper or bronze
   ______ Other; please specify ______________________

7. How important would a funeral service be for you?
   ______ Very important
   ______ Somewhat important
   ______ Somewhat unimportant
   ______ Very unimportant
   ______ No opinion

8. What kind of funeral service would you want for yourself?
   ______ No service at all
   ______ Visitation (calling hours) the day before the funeral service; funeral held at church or funeral home
   ______ Graveside service only (no visitation)
   ______ Memorial service (after body disposition)
   ______ Other; please specify ______________

9. How many people would you want to attend your funeral service or memorial service?
   ______ I do not want a funeral or memorial service
   ______ 1–10 people
   ______ 11–25 people
   ______ 26–50 people
   ______ Over 51 people
   ______ I do not care how many people attend

10. What format would you prefer at your funeral service or memorial service? Select any of the following that you would like.

	Yes	No
Religious music	______	______
Nonreligious music	______	______
Clergy present	______	______
Flower arrangements	______	______
Family member eulogy	______	______
Eulogy by friend(s)	______	______
Open casket	______	______
Religious format	______	______

Other; please specify ______________________

11. Using today's prices, how much would you expect to pay for your total funeral arrangements, including cemetery expenses (if applicable)?
    ______ Less than $4500
    ______ Between $4501 and $6000
    ______ Between $6001 and $7500
    ______ Between $7501 and $9000
    ______ Above $9000

To Carry This Further ...

Which items had you not thought about before? Were you surprised at the arrangements you selected? Will you share your responses with anyone else? If so, whom?

Focus on

DEATH OF AN INFANT OR UNBORN CHILD

Life is fragile at all stages but especially so during the prenatal and early formative years. Indeed, from conception through development, birth, infancy, and childhood, humans require an amazing amount of parental care and nurturing. Few other organisms are so dependent on others for their safety and well-being during the early months of life. Thus parents and children are tied together by a physical and emotional bond like no other. When that bond is severed by the tragic death of a young child, the pain and anguish the parents feel can be too much to bear. Getting through such a traumatic experience can be one of life's toughest challenges.[1]

Most pregnancies progress to full term and result in the birth of a healthy child. However, researchers now believe that about one-third of pregnancies end in miscarriage. Since the development of accurate home-pregnancy tests, many women are finding out early in the first trimester that they are pregnant. Thus, rather than mistaking the miscarriage for a late heavy menstrual period, more women are now aware that their pregnancy has ended. Most then go through the grieving process discussed here. In addition, other complications occur in a small number of cases. These problems can sometimes cause termination of the pregnancy (miscarriage or elective abortion), death of the baby during birth, or death during infancy. Though most people know that such things can happen, many feel that such tragedies happen only to others. When faced with the death or potential loss of a child, parents often find their belief system shaken and their faith tested.[2]

The Mourning Process

The process of grieving is different for each family. There are no set rules for getting over the loss of a child. There is no right way to mourn and no time limit for the mourning process. The first days, months, and years may seem meaningless, and parents may find themselves living day to day with no real purpose or focus.[3]

Despite the pain each individual in the family feels, care must be taken to preserve family unity. Each person must realize that other family members may grieve in different ways. Wives and husbands may grieve differently, and this can cause strain in their marriage. If one parent seems quiet or preoccupied, the other should not mistake this behaviour for a lack of emotion. Parents should also make sure that they do not ignore the feelings of other children in the family. Sometimes the mourning parents become wrapped up in their own grief and forget that the tragedy affects their other children as well. Siblings should be encouraged to discuss their feelings to help with their own grief and to reaffirm their importance within the family.[4]

The way a baby dies can affect the mourning process. Whether the child is lost before birth (miscarriage, abortion), during birth (stillbirth, trauma), or in infancy (sudden infant death syndrome [SIDS], accident, birth defect) can affect how the parents deal with the loss. It can also have an effect on how family and friends provide support for the parents.

Death of an Unborn Child

Miscarriage can be especially difficult to deal with for the woman involved. The baby has been lost within the mother's womb, and she may blame herself for the loss as a result. She may think that something she did (or did not do) has caused the miscarriage.[5,6] "One night just before I found out I was pregnant, I went out with friends and had a few beers," recalls Gabrielle, who had a miscarriage when she was 26.[7] "I didn't know I was pregnant. I was late with my period but didn't suspect I was pregnant until later. I can't help but wonder if the alcohol caused it (the miscarriage)." Consumption of alcohol or over-the-counter medications before a woman knows she is pregnant is a common cause of guilt after a miscarriage. An exact cause of a miscarriage may never be determined, and the woman needs to be reassured that she did not cause any abnormalities in the fetus.[8]

A miscarriage can be painful, embarrassing, and stressful for the woman. Physical symptoms may not occur when the baby dies but may be delayed for some time. Rosalinda became pregnant in the first month after she stopped taking her birth control pills. About three weeks into the pregnancy, "I found myself crying uncontrollably while driving home from work," she recalls. "Although I had no visible signs of miscarriage, I was sure something was wrong." Rosalinda had always been successful in other endeavours, but she started to fear that she would fail in her attempts to bring a baby into the world. "At 11 weeks my fears came true. We were on a much-needed vacation in Las Vegas. Two days of cramping turned into uncontrollable hemorrhaging." She and her husband wound up in the hotel lobby trying to get a cab to the hospital. "You can imagine my utter embarrassment as I'm holding a towel in front of me to hide the blood as my husband is haggling with the bellman to let us go to the front of the line."[9]

Sometimes parents find out about a potentially fatal or severely debilitating problem with the fetus before the child is born. In these situations the parents are faced with the choice of continuing the pregnancy or terminating it. Hearing such a diagnosis, taking in all available information, and reaching a decision can be a traumatic experience. Parents must weigh many factors when making this decision, including their spiritual beliefs, potential suffering of the baby (if the long-term prognosis is poor), effects on the family of having a child with special needs, and financial considerations. If a decision is made to terminate the pregnancy (or if a continued pregnancy may result in miscarriage or stillbirth), the couple must be prepared for the sadness and trauma of parting with their baby.

Death during the Birthing Process

In some instances, the parents know beforehand that the baby has a poor chance of surviving through birth, so they have a chance to prepare for this occurrence. For others, however, the baby's death is totally unexpected. Parents who thought they would be bringing home a healthy baby end up dealing with the devastation of losing their child. "The worst part was returning home," recalls Marcus, whose wife delivered a stillborn child after complications during birth. "The nursery was all set up ... that brought back all of the feelings we had initially experienced after the birth."[11]

In the past, babies with lethal birth defects were often quickly taken away from their mothers, but today many parents are being given the option of spending time holding and saying good-bye to their baby, and medical personnel are encouraged to accommodate the parents and support their wishes in this regard.[12]

Losing a Baby after He or She Is Born

Even after a baby is delivered, there are health risks. After her miscarriage, Gabrielle gave birth to a seemingly healthy daughter, only to lose her five months later. "She just stopped breathing," Gabrielle recalls. "We had all been asleep, and when we went in to check on her she wasn't moving or breathing. We tried to wake her ... she wasn't face down or anything like that. The doctors had no reason for it. They said it was SIDS."

The loss of a second child was devastating for Gabrielle, and it nearly ruined her marriage. "We were both very tense. We thought about trying again, but we felt jinxed. We fought a lot in the weeks after it happened." Gabrielle and her husband received counselling and eventually began to realize that they were not at fault for their tragic losses. They now have a healthy three-year-old daughter. "We got up the courage to try one more time, thank God," she says.[13]

Dealing with the Loss of a Baby

Support of family and friends is especially important when trying to recover from the death of a child. Friends and coworkers can help by acknowledging the death of the child and offering support.[14] Often people will not mention the baby because they feel that the parents will become upset by bringing up the subject, but not talking about the baby can cause pain for the parents.[15] Showing up in person (as opposed to just calling or sending a card) to offer support can also help.[16]

While the mother is still in the hospital, medical personnel should be made aware of what the mother has been through. Sometimes a mother who has lost her baby will remain in the maternity wing of the hospital. A discreet notice posted on the door of her room will alert personnel that the room's occupant has lost her child, thus preventing any unfortunate assumptions.[17]

Tactful language can also help prevent unpleasant feelings for the parents. If an unhealthy fetus were miscarried or had to be aborted, sometimes people try to rationalize the loss for the parents by saying it was "nature's way" of preventing the birth of an imperfect child.[18] Such comments are not only insensitive but also imply that the parents should be grateful that they lost the baby. Even seemingly innocent comments can cause pain in the wrong context. Rosalinda wondered why she had continued to gain weight for two months even though the doctor said the baby had probably died only three or four weeks into her pregnancy. "'It's probably just pizza,' my husband said. The doctor laughed and agreed." Rosalinda felt that her husband's attempt to lighten the situation was "probably the most insensitive statement I've ever heard him make ... my opinion of the doctor also dropped dramatically at that point."[19] She later underwent a D & C (dilation and curettage) but was asked to sign a form giving her permission for an abortion even though she had already miscarried. She was "deeply humiliated to have to sign this. Didn't they realize how much I had already been through?"

Often parents will want to hold on to the memory of the child. Such feelings are quite normal and do not mean that the parents are holding on to their grief or are neurotic.[20] Remembering the child can give a sense of meaning to parents' lives. Often parents will do something constructive to help them remember their baby and get over the death. Putting together a scrapbook, donating the baby's clothes and toys to charity, writing memoirs, or setting up a place for remembrance can help the family keep memories of the baby.[21,22,23]

Eventually the grief should lose its intensity. It may flare up again around "anniversaries" (the baby's due date or birthday, the day of the baby's death), but gradually things should become bearable. The family will be forever changed by the experience. The death of a child can cause the value system of the parents to change, and their spiritual beliefs may be shaken as well.[24] But if the parents receive support from medical staff, family, and friends, ultimately the devastation can be overcome.

For Discussion ...

What are the differences in dealing with losing a child before, during, or after he or she is born? If you were faced with the choice of giving birth to a child with severe birth defects or terminating the pregnancy, which would you choose? If your baby died, would you try again to have one?

References

1. DeSpelder LA, Strickland AL: *The last dance: encountering death and dying*, ed 5, 1999, Mayfield.
2. Hitchcock Pappas DJ, McCoy MC: Grief counseling. In Kuller JA et al, editors: *Prenatal diagnosis and reproductive genetics*, 1995, Mosby.
3. Cole D: When a child dies, *Parents' Magazine*, p. 3, March 1994.
4. Ibid.
5. Grief counseling.
6. Salmon DK: Coping with miscarriage, *Parents' Magazine*, p. 5, May 1991.
7. Anonymous: Personal communication, April 1996.
8. Grief counseling.
9. Anonymous: Personal communication, March 1996.
10. Coping with miscarriage.
11. Anonymous: Personal communication, Dec 1995.
12. Coping with miscarriage.
13. Personal communication, April 1996.
14. When a child dies.
15. Ibid.
16. Allison C: For Felicity, *Reader's Digest*, p. 199, Jan 1993.
17. Grief counseling.
18. For Felicity.
19. Coping with miscarriage.
20. When a child dies.
21. Ibid.
22. For Felicity.
23. Robb DB: Moving on, *Reader's Digest*, p. 223, Jan 1995.
24. When a child dies.

Part Six

Chapter 15

Becoming an Informed Health Care Consumer

Chapter Objectives

Upon completing this chapter, you should be able to

- Identify several sources of reliable health information available to Canadian consumers, and be able to discuss the health information you find through them with your health care provider.
- Explain the role of the primary care physician as it relates to diagnosis, treatment, screening, consultation, and prevention.
- Compare and contrast the medical training received by doctors of medicine with that received by complementary medicine practitioners.
- Describe the five principles of the Canada Health Act.
- Talk to friends and family about their level of satisfaction with their own health care coverage.
- Explain how new drugs gain Health Canada approval.

Online Learning Centre Resources

www.mcgrawhill.ca/college/hahn

Log on to our Online Learning Centre (OLC) for access to Web links for study and exploration of health topics. Here are some examples of what you'll find:

- **www.reutershealth.com** Check the validity of studies, research, treatment, and medicines, and look for valuable women's health information.
- **www.pitt.edu/~cbw/altm.html** Use this jumpsite for links to the latest information on complementary and alternative medicine.
- **www.quackwatch.com** Beware of quacks: this is the premiere site for evaluating health information.

Media Pulse

The Internet—Your New Health Superstore

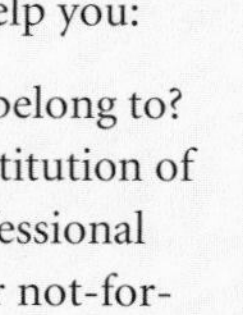

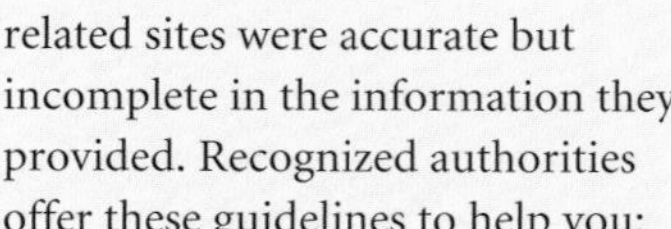

Each year, an estimated 60 million North Americans explore the Internet in search of information, products, and services related to their health. The majority, an estimated 53%, will search for information about specific conditions, such as cancer or hypertension. Smaller but still impressive percentages of people will look for information about dieting and nutrition, fitness, women's health, and pharmaceuticals.

The biggest challenge for you as a health consumer is determining the credibility of the information you find on the Internet. How can you know that this information (and accompanying products or services) is trustworthy, motivated by concern for your health and well-being rather than just by profit? A recent study found that the majority of health-related sites were accurate but incomplete in the information they provided. Recognized authorities offer these guidelines to help you:

- Who does the Web site belong to? Is it sponsored by an institution of higher education, a professional society, a government or not-for-profit agency, or a recognized pharmaceutical company? If not, who is responsible for the information? Remember, virtually anyone can develop a Web page and begin disseminating information.
- Is the information carefully referenced, showing sources such as government reports, professional journal articles, or respected reference publications? Are the references clearly documented and current? Is the Web page updated

Media Pulse *continued*

regularly? Does the information appear to agree with the titles of its own references?

- Does the content of the information seem to have a critical or negative bias toward a particular profession, institution, or treatment method? Is the information more discrediting of others than supportive of itself?
- Are "significant breakthroughs" promised in a way that suggests that only this source has the "ultimate answer" to certain problems? Does this answer involve throwing out your prescriptions, going against your physician's orders, or considering suicide as a way of escaping the pain and difficulties associated with your illness?

If you are skeptical about the credibility of any health care information you find online, submit the information to a respected health care professional or organization for assessment. If you and your physician find suspicious information or fraudulent health claims, report this to Health Canada at **www.hc-sc.gc.ca** or The Office of Consumer Affairs **http://strategis.gc.ca**. Today, most health care practitioners feel comfortable with well-informed patients. Many will welcome the chance to learn about your sources of information and share with you any concerns they might have about them.

Once you feel secure about distinguishing reliable and valid information from questionable or fraudulent information, you will be able to make better judgments and choices. Together, you and your health care provider can use that information in the management of your health care and in planning your approach to a healthier lifestyle.

Health care providers often evaluate you by criteria pertaining to their area of expertise. The nutritionist knows you by the food you eat. The physical fitness professional knows you by your body type and activity level. In the eyes of the expert in health care consumerism, you are the product of the health information you believe, the health-influencing services you use, and the products you consume. When your decisions about health information, services, and products are made after careful study and consideration, your health will probably be improved. However, when your decisions lack insight, your health, as well as your wallet, may suffer.

HEALTH INFORMATION

The Informed Consumer

To be an informed consumer, you need to learn about services and products that can influence your health. Practitioners, manufacturers, advertisers, and sales personnel use a variety of approaches to try to convince you to buy their products or use their services. Because your health is potentially at stake when you buy into these messages, being an informed consumer is important. Complete the Personal Assessment on p. 381 to rate your own skills as a health consumer.

Sources of Information

The sources of health information available to you are as diverse as the people you know, the publications you read, and the experts you see or hear. At present, no single agency or profession regulates the quantity or quality of the health information you receive. The section that follows takes a look at many different sources of information. You will quickly recognize that all are familiar and that some provide more accurate and honest information than others.

Family and friends

From a health care consumerism point of view, the accuracy of information provided by a friend or family member may be questionable. Too often the information provided by family and friends is based on common knowledge that is wrong. In addition, family members or friends may provide information they believe is in your best interest rather than giving factual information that may have a more negative effect on you.

Today more than ever, family and friends may provide health information as a part of their involvement in the pyramid sales of health products. Strong encouragement toward the use of a particular line of food supplements or vitamins could lead to a forceful sales pitch or even the offer of an opportunity to be a part of their sales team.

Advertisements and commercials

Many people spend a good portion of every day watching television, listening to the radio, and reading newspapers or magazines. Since many advertisements are health oriented, you shouldn't be surprised to learn that these are significant sources of information. Remember that the primary purpose of advertising is to sell products or services. Consider the currently popular "infomercials" in which a compensated studio audience watches a skillfully produced program designed to inform them about the benefits of a particular product or service.

Labels and directions

Federal law requires that many consumer product labels, including many kinds of food (see Chapter 5) and all medications, contain specific information. For example, when a prescription medication is dispensed by a pharmacist, a detailed information sheet describing the drug should be given along with the medication. This insert contains information about the medication's appropriate use, side effects, precautions and contraindications, and interactions with any other medications being used. In addition, it provides instruction for appropriate storage of the medications, as well as directions regarding missed doses.

Many health care providers and agencies provide consumers with detailed directions about their health problem. Generally, information from these sources is accurate, current, and provided with the health of the consumer in mind.

Folklore

Because it is often passed down from generation to generation, folklore about health is the primary source of health information for some people.

The truthfulness of health information obtained from family members, neighbours, and coworkers is difficult to evaluate. As a general rule, however, use caution concerning its scientific soundness. A blanket criticism is not warranted, however, since folk wisdom is on occasion supported by scientific evidence. Also, the emotional support provided by the suppliers of this information could be the best medicine for some people.

Testimonials

People feel strongly about sharing information that has been beneficial to them. The recommendations made by other people concerning a particular practitioner or health care product may at first appear to be nothing more than testimonials. Since they are frequently the basis for decision making by others, we assign a small measure of importance to them as sources of health information. However, the exaggerated testimonials that accompany the sales pitches of the medical quack or the "satisfied" customers appearing in advertisements and on commercials and infomercials should never be interpreted as valid endorsements.

Mass media

Health programming on television stations, lifestyle sections in newspapers, health care correspondents appearing on TV news shows, and a growing number of health/fitness magazines are examples of health information in the mass media.

Although health information is generally presented well, it is sometimes so brief or superficial that it is of limited use. However, the consumer who wants more complete coverage of a health topic can obtain it by combining sources. The mass media topics most frequently sought out by today's consumers include dietary supplements, nutrition, alternative health maintenance approaches (such as exercise), and cancer. At the same time, however, this information is often viewed as confusing.[1]

Practitioners

The health care consumer also receives much information from individual health practitioners and their professional associations. In fact, patient education is so clearly provided by today's health care practitioner that finding one who does not exchange some information with a patient would be unusual. Education enhances patient **compliance** with health care directives, which is important to the practitioner and the consumer.

An important development in the area of practitioner-provided information and patient education is the evolution of the hospital as an educational institution. Wellness centres, chemical dependence programs, sports medicine centres, and community-based outreach centres have become more common.

Online computer services

The development of computer technology has created new sources of health information. Today, more than 220 million North Americans use online services, and 65% of this group access the Web for health information.[2] Information delivered by experts from major medical centres and local hospitals is perceived by Web users as more accurate, timely, and objective than similar information provided by pharmaceutical companies or disease-oriented national agencies.[3]

Personal computer programs and DVDs featuring health information are important sources of information for some consumers.

Reference libraries

Even though a large percentage of households possess health reference material and health care professionals are dispensing more and more information to the consumer, public and university libraries continue to be much-used sources of health information. Reference librarians can be consulted, and audiovisual and printed materials can be checked out. More and more of these holdings are becoming available through home computer–based online services.

Consumer advocacy groups

A variety of nonprofit consumer advocacy groups patrol the health care marketplace, particularly in relation to services and products (see the Star Box on p. 366). These groups produce and send out information designed to aid the consumer in recognizing questionable services and products. Large, well-organized groups, such as The

Canadian Healthcare Association and The Consumers' Association of Canada, and smaller groups at the provincial and local levels champion the right of the consumer to receive valid and reliable information about health care products and services.

Federal government agencies such as The Canadian Human Rights Commission also play a role in advocacy. The Commission is responsible for ensuring that human rights are protected and does this by informing people about equality issues and by trying to make them more aware of how their actions may be discriminating against others (see the Learning from Our Diversity box on p. 367).

Voluntary health agencies

Volunteerism and the traditional approach to health care and health promotion are virtually inseparable. Few countries besides Canada and the United States boast so many national voluntary organizations, with provincial and local affiliates, dedicated to the enhancement of health through research, service, and public education. The Canadian Cancer Society, the Canadian Red Cross, and the Canadian Heart and Stroke Foundation are all voluntary (not-for-profit) health agencies. Consumers can, in fact, expect to find a voluntary health agency for virtually every health problem.

Government agencies

Government agencies are effective providers of information to the public. Through meetings and the release of information to the media, agencies such as Health Canada, the Ministry of Trade and Industry, Canada Post, and Environment Canada contribute to public awareness of health issues. Through labelling, advertising, and the distribution of information, government agencies also control the quality of information sent out to the buying public. Many government agencies, in particular Health Canada, regularly release research findings and recommendations about clinical practices, which in turn reach the consumer through clinical practitioners.

Despite their best intentions, federal health agencies are often less effective than the public deserves. A variety of factors, including inadequate staff, poor administration, and lobbying by special interest groups, prevent these federal agencies from enforcing the consumer protection legislation that exists. As a result, the public is left with a sense of false confidence regarding the consumer protection provided by the federal government.

Provincial governments also provide the public with health information. Provincial agencies are primary sources of information, particularly in the areas of public health and environmental protection.

Qualified health educators

Health educators work in a variety of settings and provide their services to diverse groups of individuals. Community health educators work with virtually all of the agencies mentioned above; patient educators function in primary care settings; and school health educators are found at all educational levels. Increasingly, health educators are being employed in a wide range of wellness-based programs in community, hospital, corporate, and school settings.

HEALTH CARE PROVIDERS

The types and sources of health information just discussed can contribute greatly to the decisions you make as an informed consumer. The choices you make about physicians and health services will reflect your commitment to remain healthy and your trust in specific people who are trained in keeping you healthy. Refer to the Changing for the Better box on p. 368 for tips on choosing a physician.

Physicians and Their Training

In every city and many smaller communities, the local telephone directory shows the many types of physicians engaged in the practice of medicine. These health care providers hold the academic degree of Doctor of Medicine (M.D.).

The training of medical physicians is a long process. Usually, four years of initial undergraduate preparation is required. There is strong emphasis on the sciences—biology, chemistry, mathematics, anatomy, and physiology. Many undergraduate schools have preprofessional courses of study for students interested in medical school.

Once accepted into professional schools, students generally spend four years or more in intensive training, which includes advanced study in the preclinical medical sciences and clinical practice. When this phase of training is completed, the students are awarded the M.D. degree. Next, they take a medical licence examination. Newly licensed physicians complete a residency at a hospital. During this period, physicians gain experience in various clinical areas and begin specialized programs. Residency programs vary in length from three to four years. At the conclusion of residency programs, board-eligible or board-certified status is granted.

Complementary (Alternative) Practitioners

Several forms of health care offer complementary or alternative approaches within the large health care market. Examples include chiropractic, acupuncture, reflexology,

Key Term

compliance
Willingness to follow the directions provided by another person, such as a physician.

Consumer Protection Agencies and Organizations

Federal Agencies
Health Canada
A.L. 0900C2
Ottawa, ON
K1A 0K9
Tel: 613-957-2991
Toll-free: 1-866-225-0709
www.hc-sc.gc.ca

Canadian Healthcare Association
17 York Street
Ottawa, ON
K1N 9J6
Tel: 613-241-8005
Fax: 613-241-5055
www.cha.ca

Canadian Food Inspection Agency
59 Camelot Drive
Ottawa, ON
K1A 0Y9
Tel: 613-225-2342
Fax: 613-228-4550
www.inspection.gc.ca/

Consumer Organizations
The Office of Consumer Affairs
235 Main Street, 9th Floor East
Ottawa, ON
K1A 0H5
Fax: 613-952-6927
http://strategis.ic.gc.ca/epic/internet/inoca-bc.nsf/en/home

Consumers' Association of Canada
436 Gilmore Street, 3rd floor
Ottawa, ON
K2P 0R8
Tel: 613-238-2533
Fax: 613-238-2538
www.consumer.ca

Professional Organizations
Canadian Medical Association
1867 Alta Vista Drive
Ottawa, ON
K1G 3Y6
Toll-free: 1-800-457-4205
Fax: 613-236-8864
www.cma.ca

Canadian Pharmaceutical Association
55 Metcalfe Street
Suite 1220
Ottawa, ON
K1P 6L5
Tel: 613-236-0455
Fax: 613-236-6756
www.canadapharma.org

homeopathy, naturopathy, herbalism, and ayurveda. Although the traditional medical community has long scoffed at these alternatives as ineffective and unscientific, many people use these forms of health care principally, not alternatively, and believe strongly that they are as effective as (or more effective than) traditional medicine.

Osteopathy

Osteopathy is a system of medical practice that combines the principles of **allopathy** with specific attention to the postural mechanics of the body. So far in Canada, unlike the United States, trained osteopathic professionals do not receive legal recognition for osteopathic manual practice. In the United States, osteopaths and allopaths can function as primary care physicians.[4]

Chiropractic

This system is based on manual manipulation of the spine to correct misalignments. Recent studies have shown that **chiropractic** treatment of some types of low-back pain can be more effective than conventional care. There are over 50 000 practitioners in North America; 5000 of them are in Canada. Chiropractic is the third-largest health profession, after medicine and dentistry. The Canadian Chiropractic Association was federally chartered in 1953. Chiropractic care is recognized by legislation in every province in Canada and in Yukon.[5]

Acupuncture

Acupuncture is, for North Americans, the most familiar component of the 3000-year-old Chinese medical system. This system is based on balancing the active and passive forces with the patient's body to strengthen the chi ("chee"), or life force. Acupuncturists place hair-thin needles at certain points in the body to stimulate the patient's chi.

Of all the Chinese therapies, acupuncture is the most widely accepted in the West. Researchers have produced persuasive evidence of acupuncture's effectiveness as an anesthetic and as an antidote to chronic pain, migraines, dysmenorrhea, and osteoarthritis.[6] In addition, some studies have found that acupuncture can help patients overcome addictions to alcohol, drugs, and tobacco. Conversely, research funded by the federal government shows that acupuncture is far more than a placebo but is not superior to standard pain management care.[7]

Reflexology

Reflexology uses principles similar to those of acupuncture but focuses on treating certain disorders through massage of the soles of the feet. In Canada, licensing for practitioners providing "holistic services" (that is, any modality used as a tool for therapeutic and wellness

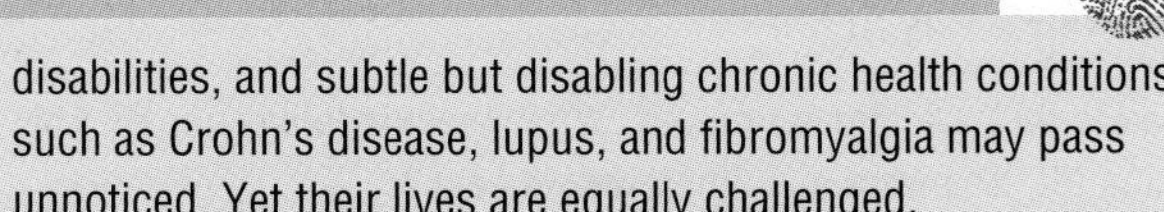

Learning from Our Diversity

Canadians with Disabilities—New Places to Go

A federal law designed to end discrimination on the basis of gender and race was enacted in Canada decades ago. This law, The Canadian Human Rights Act (1977), has done a great deal to level the playing field for people with disabilities, both on post-secondary campuses and in the larger community. On campuses today, it's common to see students whose obvious disabilities would have prevented them from attending college or university before this law was enacted. Students with cerebral palsy, spina bifida, spinal cord injuries, sensory impairments, and orthopedic disabilities share living quarters, lecture hall seats, and recreational facilities with their nondisabled classmates.

Equally important are those students whose disabilities are largely unobservable. Students with learning disabilities, mental disabilities, and subtle but disabling chronic health conditions such as Crohn's disease, lupus, and fibromyalgia may pass unnoticed. Yet their lives are equally challenged.

The Canadian Human Right Commission is responsible for making the act work. It does not suggest that preferential treatment be given to students with disabilities, nor does it allow students to be unaccountable for their behaviour. Instead, it seeks to create an environment—on campus and beyond—where people, regardless of disability, can learn new things, form meaningful relationships, and develop independence.

This act has the power to remove the physical and emotional barriers that can hinder a person with a disability from succeeding. It allows students with disabilities to go where everyone else can—and beyond.

Acupuncture has received increasing acceptance within the Western medical community.

purposes) varies from province to province. The profession supports the concept of self-regulation apart from the government.[8]

Homeopathy

Homeopathy uses infinitesimal doses of herbs, minerals, or even poisons to stimulate the body's curative powers. The theory on which homeopathy is based, called the *Law of Similars*, is that if large doses of a substance can cause a problem, tiny doses can trigger healing of that same problem. Historically, practitioners of homeopathy have argued that their homeopathic preparations are effective in treating hay fever, diarrhea, and various other conditions. To date, a single carefully controlled study comparing a homeopathic medication for an inner ear balance disorder (vertigo) has found it to be as effective as its histamine-based counterpart in conventional Western medicine.[9]

Key Terms

osteopathy (os tee OP ah thee)
System of medical practice that combines allopathic principles with specific attention to postural mechanics of the body.

allopathy (ah LOP ah thee)
System of medical practice in which specific remedies (often pharmaceutical agents) are used to produce effects different from those produced by a disease or injury.

chiropractic
Manipulation of the vertebral column to relieve pressure and cure illness.

acupuncture
Insertion of fine needles into the body to alter electroenergy fields and cure disease.

reflexology
Massage applied to specific areas of the feet to treat illness and disease in other areas of the body.

homeopathy (ho mee OP ah thee)
The use of minute doses of herbs or minerals to stimulate healing.

Changing *for the Better*

Choosing a Physician

I need to find a doctor for myself. What specific things should I be looking for, and what questions should I ask?

When choosing a physician, plan to obtain answers to the following questions during your initial visit:

- What is the physician's medical background, such as education, residencies, and specialty areas?
- What are the normal office hours? What should be done if help is needed outside normal office hours?
- What is included in a comprehensive physical examination?
- How does the physician feel about second and third opinions?
- Which hospitals is the physician affiliated with in your area?
- Is the physician comfortable referring patients to specialists when the complexity of a condition warrants their expertise?
- With which specialists is the physician associated?

Ask yourself the following questions after your visit:

- Was I comfortable with the physician's demeanour? Did I find communication with the physician to be understandable and reassuring? Were all my questions answered?
- Did the physician seem interested in having me as a patient?
- Are the physician's training and practice specialty in an area most closely associated with my present needs and concerns?
- Does the physician have staff privileges at a hospital of my preference?
- Did the physician take a complete medical history as a part of my initial visit? Was prevention, health promotion, or wellness addressed by the physician at any point during my visit?
- Did I at any point during my visit sense that the physician was unusually reluctant or anxious to try new medical procedures or medications?
- When the physician is unavailable, are any colleagues on call around the clock? Did I feel that telephone calls from me would be welcomed and responded to in a reasonable period?

If you have answered yes to most of these questions, you have found a physician with whom you should feel comfortable. If you have been using the services of a particular physician but are becoming dissatisfied, how could you resolve this dissatisfaction?

It's important to have a good relationship with the people who help keep us healthy.

Naturopathy

Proponents of **naturopathy** believe that when the mind and the body are in balance and receiving proper care, with a healthy diet, adequate rest, and minimal stress, the body's own vital forces are sufficient to fight off disease. Getting rid of an ailment is only the first step toward correcting the underlying imbalance that allowed the ailment to take hold, naturists believe. Correcting the imbalance might be as simple as rectifying a shortage of a particular nutrient or as complex as reducing overlong work hours, strengthening a weakened immune system, and identifying an inability to digest certain foods. Naturopathic medicine integrates natural healing therapies including botanical medicine, homeopathy, clinical nutrition, hydrotherapy, naturopathic manipulation, traditional Chinese medicine/acupuncture, and prevention and lifestyle counselling.[10]

Herbalism

Herbalism may be the world's oldest and most widely used healing form. Herbalists make herbal brews for treating a variety of ills, such as depression, anxiety, and hypertension. In some cases, scientific research supports the herbalists' beliefs. For example, several studies have found St. John's wort to be more effective than a placebo in alleviating mild depression.[11]

Ayurveda

Even older than Chinese medicine, India's **ayurveda** takes a preventive approach and focuses on the whole person. This system employs diet, tailored to the patient's constitutional type, or "dosha"; herbs; yoga and breathing exercises; meditation; massages; and purges, enemas, and aromatherapy. Research has shown ayurveda to be effective in treating rheumatoid arthritis, headaches, and chronic sinusitis.

If you'd like to consult a practitioner in one of the alternative disciplines but don't know where to start, see the Changing for the Better box on p. 370 for some tips on choosing a provider in alternative medicine.

Massotherapy

The idea of rubbing the body to make it feel better is as old as humankind. Trained therapists know how to find the knots of stress on a person's body and the best ways to work them out using their hands primarily but sometimes even the elbows. Many different techniques are used, but all follow a few basic rules. First and foremost **massotherapy** is a pain-relieving exercise, and even if treating a relatively painful area, some relief should be almost immediately perceptible. Following is a list of some massage therapies practised in Canada and elsewhere.

Types of Massage

- Acupressure
- Amma Therapy
- Californian
- Craniosacral Therapy
- Deep Tissue Massage
- Hydrotherapy
- Indian Head Massage
- Lymph Drainage
- Reflexology
- Rolfing
- Shiatsu
- Swedish Massage Therapy
- Thai Massage
- Trager Therapy
- Trigger Point Therapy
- Watsu[12]

For more Web links on this topic, go to the Online Learning Centre at **www.mcgrawhill.ca/college/hahn**.

Restricted-Practice Health Care Providers

Much of your health care is provided by medical physicians. However, you probably also use the services of various health care specialists who have advanced graduate-level training. Among these professionals are dentists, psychologists, podiatrists, and optometrists.

Dentists (Doctor of Dental Surgery, D.D.S.) are trained to deal with a wide range of diseases and impairments of the teeth and oral cavity. Dentists undergo undergraduate predental programs that emphasize the sciences, followed by four additional years of graduate study in dental school and, with increasing frequency, an internship program. Like medical physicians, dentists can also specialize by completing a postdoctoral master's degree in fields such as oral surgery, **orthodontics**, and **prosthodontics**. Dentists are also permitted to prescribe therapy programs (such as appliances for the treatment of temporomandibular joint dysfunction) and drugs that pertain to their practices (primarily analgesics and antibiotics).

Psychologists provide services related to an understanding of behaviour patterns or perceptions. The consumer should examine the credentials of a psychologist. Legitimate psychologists have received advanced graduate training (often leading to a Ph.D. or Ed.D. degree) in clinical, counselling, industrial, or educational psychology. Psychologists may have special interests and credentials from professional societies in individual, group, family, or marriage counselling. Some are certified as sex therapists.

Unlike psychiatrists, who are medical physicians, psychologists cannot prescribe or dispense drugs. They may refer to or consult with medical physicians about clients who might benefit from drug therapy.

Podiatrists are highly trained clinicians who practise podiatric medicine, or care of the feet (and ankles). Although not M.D.s, doctors of podiatric medicine treat

Key Terms

naturopathy (nay chur OP ah thee)
A system of treatment that avoids drugs and surgery and emphasizes the use of natural agents to correct underlying imbalances.

herbalism
An ancient form of healing in which herbal preparations are used to treat illness and disease.

ayurveda (ai yur vey da)
Traditional Indian medicine based on herbal remedies.

massotherapy
The therapeutic use of massage.

orthodontics
Dental specialty that focuses on the proper alignment of the teeth.

prosthodontics
Dental specialty that focuses on the construction and fitting of artificial appliances to replace missing teeth.

Changing *for the Better*

Choosing the Best Complementary Medical Practitioner for You

I'm interested in exploring complementary approaches to medicine, but I feel uncertain about how to proceed. What steps should I take?

Perhaps you are one of the millions of people who feel that their doctors don't encourage them to ask questions, don't seek their opinion about their medical condition, or don't take a thorough medical history. Perhaps you want advice on improving your health rather than just a quick diagnosis and prescription.

For whatever reasons, millions of North Americans are turning to complementary medical practitioners, such as doctors of naturopathy, Chinese medicine, or ayurveda. Unfortunately, the patient looking for these alternatives faces other problems: practitioners' training may be weak, they might not be licensed or covered by insurance, they may be hard to find, and they usually are not permitted to prescribe drugs unless they also happen to be medical doctors. This means that you must do some legwork to find a good provider who can meet your needs.

Consider the following tips for finding the practitioner who is right for you.

- *Don't forget the family doctor.* Family-practice medicine is enjoying a surge in Canada and the United States and many of these doctors tend to think holistically.
- *Find a doctor who believes in complementary therapies.* Your doctor's attitude toward the treatment can be just as important as your own.
- *Give the treatment time.* Complementary therapies encourage the body to do its own healing. This often takes time. Seek a doctor who is confident in your self-healing ability, so you won't become discouraged if it takes some time.
- *Request natural healing.* Natural healing tends to change the internal conditions so that pathogens are less likely to gain a foothold; conventional medicine seeks to destroy the pathogen. Natural healing searches for the causes of symptoms, while conventional medicine treats symptoms.
- *Know your disease.* Find books that describe your conditions and offer complementary as well as conventional treatments. This way you can discuss your treatment with your doctor and can create an effective treatment plan.
- *Treat yourself.* Don't overuse your health care provider, whether conventional or complementary. For many conditions, you can be your own best doctor; of course, persistent or severe symptoms should send you to the doctor.
- *Learn whether the treatment is covered by your extended health coverage plan.* Complementary treatments may be included under some plans but excluded by others. Check with your extended health coverage provider.
- *Talk to professional associations.* Most of the more established complementary fields have associations that can give you a list of providers. Use it as a start.
- *Get a brochure.* The doctor's literature can tell you a lot about his or her outlook and experience.
- *Interview the doctor.* Before making an appointment, talk with the doctor over the telephone. Then, in the doctor's office, take notes, even use a tape recorder, to make certain you understand. Watch for a doctor who is a good listener, a good communicator, and open-minded.

a wide variety of conditions related to the feet, including corns, bunions, warts, bone spurs, hammertoes, fractures, diabetes-related conditions, athletic injuries, and structural abnormalities. Podiatrists perform surgery, prescribe medications, and apply orthotics (supports or braces), splints, and corrective shoes for structural abnormalities of the feet.

Doctors of podiatric medicine follow an educational path similar to that taken by M.D.s, consisting of a four-year undergraduate preprofessional curriculum, four additional years of study in a podiatric medical school, and an optional residency of one or two years. Board-certified areas of specialization include surgery, orthopedics, and podiatric sports medicine. Hospital affiliation generally requires board certification in a specialized area.

Optometrists are defined as independent primary-care providers who specialize in the examination, diagnosis, treatment, management, and prevention of disease and disorders of the visual system, the eye, and associated structures. Optometrists require a minimum of five years of post-secondary education to obtain the Doctor of Optometry (O.D.) designation.

The main duties of the optometrist are examination of the human eye by any method other than surgery, to diagnose, treat, and/or refer for treatment any abnormal condition of the eye in cooperation with physicians and other health professionals; prescription, fitting, and application of glasses, contact lenses, or other devices; and prescription, supervision, and management of therapy for the improvement and monitoring of visual health.[13]

Opticians are technicians who manufacture and fit eyeglasses or contact lenses. They perform the important function of grinding lenses to the precise prescription designated by an optometrist or *ophthalmologist* (physicians who have specialized in vision care). To save money and time, many consumers take an optometrist's or ophthalmologist's prescription for glasses or contact lenses to optician-staffed retail stores that deal exclusively with eyewear products.

Nurse Professionals

Nurses constitute a large group of health professionals who practise in a variety of settings. Frequently, the responsibilities of nurses vary according to their academic preparation. Registered nurses in Canada (RNs) are academically prepared at two levels: (1) diploma and (2) degree. Both diploma and degree nurses must successfully complete licensing examinations before they can practise as RNs. Students in British Columbia, Alberta, Quebec, and the territories can choose a diploma or degree program to prepare for a career in nursing.[14] In all other provinces a baccalaureate degree in nursing is required to prepare for a career in nursing. The goal of the Canadian Nurse Association is for all nurses entering the profession to have a degree in nursing to meet the changing needs of the health care system.[15]

Some professional nurses continue their education and earn master's and doctoral degrees in nursing or other health fields. Some professional nurses specialize in a clinical area (such as pediatrics, gerontology, public health, or school health) and become certified as *nurse practitioners*. Working under the supervision of physicians, nurse practitioners perform many of the diagnostic and treatment procedures performed by physicians. The ability of these highly trained nurses to function at this level provides communities with additional primary care providers, as well as freeing physicians to deal with more complex cases. Many college and university health centres employ nurse practitioners because of their ability to deliver high-quality care at a low cost to the institution. Three provinces, Ontario, Alberta and Newfoundland, have passed legislation to support these roles for nurses. In the remainder of the provinces and territories nurses work within existing legislation. Nursing practice is regulated by legislation at the provincial level.[16]

Licensed practical nurses (LPNs) are trained in hospital-based programs ranging from 12 to 18 months. For example, the Nova Scotia Community College offers a 13-month program that includes 20 weeks of clinical placement plus a four-week internship program. Because of their brief training, LPNs' scope of practice is limited.

Allied Health Care Professionals

Our primary health care providers are supported by a large group of allied health care professionals, who often take the responsibility for highly technical services and procedures. Such professionals include respiratory and inhalation therapists, radiological technologists, nuclear medicine technologists, pathology technicians, general medical technologists, operating room technicians, emergency medical technicians, registered nurse midwives, physical therapists, occupational therapists, clinical social workers, family therapists, cardiac rehabilitation therapists, dental technicians, physician assistants, and dental hygienists. Depending on the particular field, the training for these specialty support areas can take from one to five years of post–high school study. Programs include hospital-based training leading to a diploma through associate, bachelor's, and master's degrees.

SELF-CARE

The emergence of the **self-care movement** suggests that many people are becoming more responsible for the maintenance of their health. They are developing the expertise to prevent or manage numerous types of illness, injuries, and conditions. They are learning to assess their health status and treat, monitor, and rehabilitate themselves in a way that was once thought possible only with the direct help of a physician or other health care specialist.

The benefits of this movement are that self-care can (1) lower health care costs, (2) be effective for particular conditions, (3) free physicians and other health care specialists to spend time with other patients, and (4) enhance interest in health activities.

Self-care is an appropriate alternative to professional care in three areas. First, self-care may be appropriate for certain acute conditions that have familiar symptoms and are of limited duration and seriousness. Common colds and flu, many home injuries, sore throats, and nonallergic insect bites are often easily managed with self-care.

A second area in which self-care might be appropriate is therapy. For example, many people are now administering injections for allergies and migraine headaches and continuing physical therapy programs in their homes. Asthma, diabetes, and hypertension are also conditions that can be managed or monitored with self-care.

A third area in which self-care has appropriate application is health promotion. Weight-loss programs, physical conditioning activities, and stress-reduction programs are particularly well suited to self-care.

Although self-care is sometimes appropriate, visiting a physician to obtain a diagnosis is often a wise choice. Additionally, some self-care skills should (or must) be first practised under the supervision of a health care professional before being implemented at home. In fact,

Key Term

self-care movement
Trend toward individuals taking increased responsibility for prevention or management of certain health conditions.

some conditions that can be managed on a daily basis, such as diabetes, require regular assessment by a physician to ensure that management criteria are being met on a consistent basis.

People interested in practising more self-care must be skilled consumers. The self-care marketplace is growing very rapidly and is expected to be a multibillion-dollar industry by the end of the decade. Equipment such as blood pressure–measuring instruments, stethoscopes, and screening kits for cholesterol, HIV, and pregnancy, as well as over-the-counter (OTC) drugs can represent significant investments. Clearly, your money, time, and willingness to develop expertise are important factors in this growing area of health care consumerism. See Exploring Your Spirituality, on p. 373, for a discussion of how taking charge of your own health can be an empowering experience.

HEALTH INSURANCE

Canada has a predominately publicly financed, privately delivered health care system known to Canadians as Medicare. It provides access to universal comprehensive insurance coverage for medically necessary hospital, in-patient, and out-patient physician services. Most doctors are private practitioners who work in independent or group practices, enjoy a high degree of autonomy, and are generally paid on a fee-for-service basis.

The federal government, the ten provinces, and the three territories have key roles to play in the health care system in Canada. The federal government is responsible for setting and administering national principles or standards for the health care system; assisting in the financing of provincial health care services through fiscal transfers; delivering direct health services to specific groups including veterans, Aboriginals, individuals living on reserves, military personnel, inmates at federal penitentiaries, and the Royal Canadian Mounted Police; and fulfilling other health-related functions such as health protection, disease prevention, and health promotion.

The provincial and territorial governments are responsible for managing and delivering health services; planning, financing, and evaluating the provision of hospital care; providing physical and allied care services; and managing some aspect of prescription and public health. Some health care services, like prescription drugs, dental care, vision care, physiotherapy, and private-duty nursing are not provided under Medicare, and provinces and territories may not provide these services. Individuals wanting insurance coverage for these items can purchase extended coverage health insurance from a private insurance company. Extended health coverage is often made available to individuals through their employers under group insurance plans.

The Canada Health Act

The Canadian health care system has evolved into its present form over five decades. In 1947 Saskatchewan was the first province to establish public universal health insurance, and 10 years later, the government of Canada passed legislation to allow the federal government to share in the cost of provincial hospital insurance plans. By 1972 all provinces and territorial plans had been extended to include doctors' services. In response to concerns about extra-billing by doctors and user fees levied by hospitals, Parliament passed the Canada Health Act in 1984 to discourage these practices and prevent the development of a two-tiered health care system.

The five principles of the Canada Health Act (CHA) are the cornerstone of the Canadian health care system. They are

1. *Public Administration*: the administration of the health care insurance plan must be carried out on a nonprofit basis by a public authority.
2. *Comprehensiveness*: all medically necessary services provided by hospitals and doctors must be insured.
3. *Universality*: all insured persons must be entitled to insurance coverage on uniform terms.
4. *Portability*: insured services must be maintained when an insured person travels outside Canada. However, insured services are covered at the Canadian provincial fee schedule, which may be much lower than the cost of a foreign service. Some services provided in foreign countries are not covered at all by provincial fee schedules.
5. *Accessibility*: reasonable access to medically necessary hospital and physician's services must not be impeded by financial or other barriers.

TALKING POINTS • In a conversation with your parents, you learn that their extended-coverage health insurance plan will not provide coverage for you after you turn 25, even though you'll still be a full-time student. How could you suggest an arrangement that would benefit both parties?

HEALTH-RELATED PRODUCTS

Prescription and OTC drugs constitute an important part of any discussion of health care products.

Prescription Drugs

Prescription drugs must be ordered for patients by a licensed practitioner. Because these compounds are legally controlled and may require special skills for their administration, access to these drugs takes place through a pharmacist.

Exploring Your Spirituality

Good Health—What's It Worth, Now and Later?

The average life expectancy for women in Canada today is 82.1 years. For men, it's 77.2 years. That's a dramatic change from just a few generations ago. Thanks to tremendous advances in medical science and technology, many people are enjoying healthy, happy, and spiritually fulfilling lives well into their final years.

But this longevity comes with a price tag. It means that making healthy choices every day—including a balanced diet, exercise, adequate rest, and opportunities for emotional and spiritual expression—takes on new importance. If you're going to live 10 "extra" years, what do you want to do with that time? Probably many of the things you're doing now, plus some different ones. Are you going to be able to meet the challenge healthwise?

Taking charge of your health right now, when you're young and healthy, can be one of the most empowering things you do. By consciously choosing a healthy lifestyle—limiting your intake of alcohol, avoiding drugs and cigarette smoking, and limiting your sexual partners—you are building the foundation for good health in your later years.

If you should ever have a serious health problem, you'll be better equipped to handle it if you're used to taking care of yourself. You'll feel comfortable being involved in your treatment decisions and doing whatever you can to control the quality of your life. You'll see your health crisis as a challenge you need to deal with, instead of viewing yourself as a helpless victim.

Taking charge of your own health—by being an informed health care consumer, by choosing a healthy lifestyle, and by fostering a positive attitude—brings a sense of peace. It's knowing that you're doing everything you can to take care of yourself. It's enhancing the quality of your life today and preparing for an active and rewarding tomorrow.

The rapid expansion of online pharmacies noted in 1999 is unlikely to influence the number of prescriptions filled. Instead, their presence is more likely to affect the sales of "brick and mortar" drugstore chains.

Research and development of new drugs

As consumers of prescription drugs, you may be curious about how drugs gain Health Canada approval for marketing. The rigour of this process may be why fewer than 416 new drugs were added to the list of approved drugs in the past 15 years.[17]

On a continuous basis, pharmaceutical companies are exploring the molecular structure of various chemical compounds in an attempt to discover important new compounds with desired types and levels of biological activity. Once these new compounds are identified, extensive in-house research with computer simulations and animal testing is required to determine whether clinical trials involving humans are warranted. These compounds are then passed on to Health Canada to undergo the evaluation process necessary to gain approval for further research with humans. Once a drug is approved for clinical trials, the pharmaceutical companies can secure a patent, which prevents the drug from being manufactured by other companies for the next 20 years. The innovative pharmaceutical industry and the federal government have a common goal: to ensure that Canadians have timely access to effective medicines; are never put at undue risk by medicines available to them; and are fully informed about the risks and benefits of those medicines. Before a drug can be marketed in Canada, data on its safety and efficacy must first be reviewed by Health Canada.[18]

The multi-million dollar price tag for bringing a new drug into the marketplace reflects this slow, careful process. If this 10 to 15-year process goes well, a pharmaceutical company will have 5 to 10 years of legally protected retail sales before generic versions of the drug can be offered by other companies.[19]

Generic versus brand-name drugs

When a new drug comes into the marketplace, it carries with it three names: its **chemical name,** its **generic name**, and its **brand name**. While the patent is in effect, no other drug with the same formulation can be sold. When the patent expires, other companies can manufacture a drug of chemical and therapeutic equivalence and market it under the brand-name drug's original generic name. Because extensive research and development are not necessary at this point, the production of generic drugs is far less costly than the initial development of the

Key Terms

chemical name
Name used to describe the molecular structure of a drug.

generic name
Common or nonproprietary name of a drug.

brand name
Specific patented name assigned to a drug by its manufacturer.

Drug Identification Number[20]

What is a DIN?

The Drug Identification Number (DIN) is the number located on the label of prescription and over-the-counter drug products that have been evaluated by the Therapeutic Products Directorate (TPD) and approved for sale in Canada.

When is a DIN issued?

Once a drug has been approved, the Therapeutic Products Directorate issues a DIN, which permits the manufacturer to market the drug in Canada. For drugs where there is minimal market history in Canada, there is a more stringent review and the drug is required to have a Notice of Compliance and a DIN in order to be marketed in Canada.

What purpose does a DIN serve?

A DIN lets the user know that the product has undergone and passed a review of its formulation, labelling and instructions for use. A drug product sold in Canada without a DIN is not in compliance with Canadian law. The DIN is also a tool to help in the follow-up of products on the market, recall of products, inspections, and quality monitoring.

Do DINs only appear on prescription drugs?

No. A DIN is assigned to all approved prescription and over-the-counter drugs.

Do medicinal herbs require a DIN?

Yes. If a manufacturer wants to sell a medicinal herb or market a herb with drug claims, the product requires a DIN.

Is there a significance or special meaning for the numbers in the DIN?

No. Numbers are assigned sequentially and have no particular meaning.

Can a product defined as a drug be sold without a DIN?

No. If a product defined as a drug under the Food and Drugs Act is sold without a DIN, it is not in compliance with Canadian law and regulatory action will be taken.

What is a GP?

The Therapeutic Programme no longer issues General Public (GP) numerical identifiers. They have now been replaced by DINs. Similar to DINs, GPs were used to identify proprietary medicines—products that may be purchased without prescriptions in any retail outlet. An example is fluoride toothpaste.

Do I need a DIN to sell a drug product in Canada?

Yes. If a product defined as a drug under the Food and Drugs Act is sold without a DIN, it is not in compliance with Canadian law.

brand-name drug. Pharmacists may substitute generic drugs for brand-name drugs, as long as the prescribing physician approves.

In the United States, the pharmaceutical industry is actively attempting to extend the patent protection on several of the most profitable drugs on the market because their period of protected sales is expiring.[21] In some cases the manufacturers have appealed directly to Congress for waivers to the current patent law, contending that they need additional time to recoup research and development costs. Other manufacturers have quietly "layered" additional patents onto their products to prevent manufacturers of generic versions from using the same shape or colour used in brand-name versions, even though the chemical formulations are no longer protected. In another approach, manufacturers of highly profitable brand-name drugs have offered to pay manufacturers of generic drugs to refrain from making generic versions of their products once the patent protection has expired.

TALKING POINTS • On a visit to your campus health centre, you get a prescription with "Do Not Substitute" indicated. You happen to know that a generic form is available and that generics often cost 40% to 70% less than brand-name drugs. How could you ask the physician why he or she specified that you should buy the name brand?

Over-the-Counter Drugs

When people are asked when they last took some form of medication, many say that they took aspirin, a cold pill, or a laxative that very morning. In making this decision, these individuals made a self-diagnosis, determined a course of self-treatment, self-administered that treatment, and freed a physician to serve people whose illnesses are more serious than theirs. None of this would have been possible without readily available, inexpensive, and effective OTC drugs.

In comparison with the 2500 prescription drugs available, there are as many as 300 000 different OTC products, routinely classified into 26 different families (see the Star Box on p. 375). Like prescription drugs, nonprescription drugs are regulated by Health Canada. However, for OTC drugs, the marketplace is a more powerful determinant of success.

In Canada the regulation of OTC drugs falls under the Food and Drugs Act. Once a product defined as a

Categories of Over-the-Counter (OTC) Products

- Antacids
- Antimicrobials
- Sedatives and sleep aids
- Analgesics
- Cold remedies and antitussives
- Antihistamines and allergy products
- Mouthwashes
- Topical analgesics
- Antirheumatics
- Hematinics
- Vitamins and minerals
- Antiperspirants
- Laxatives
- Dentrifices and dental products
- Sunburn treatments and preventives
- Contraceptive and vaginal products
- Stimulants
- Hemorrhoidals
- Antidiarrheals
- Dandruff and athlete's foot preparations

drug has been approved under the Food and Drugs Act, a Drug Identification Number (DIN) is issued by the Therapeutic Products Directorate, which permits the manufacturer to market the drug in Canada. A DIN lets the user know the product has undergone and passed a review of its formulation labelling and instructions for use. A DIN is assigned to all approved prescription and OTC drugs. Today in the United States, more than 600 products (containing over 56 active ingredients) that were once available only by prescription have FDA approval for OTC sale. As many as 25 additional such products reach the market each year.

There are no drug label standards in Canada. Requirements that products meet standards take several different forms. Some standards are mandatory legal requirements, others are industry standards developed on a voluntary basis, and some are purely market driven as a particular technology becomes the industry standard.

Like the proposed label shown in Figure 15–1, some Canadian labels reflect FDA and the Food and Drugs Act requirements. The labels must clearly state the type and quantity of active ingredients, alcohol content, side effects, instructions for appropriate use, warnings against inappropriate use, and risks of using the product with other drugs (polydrug use). Unsubstantiated claims must be carefully avoided in advertisements for these products.

Dietary Supplements

Currently, more than 60 million North Americans are using a vast array of vitamins, minerals, herbal products, hormones, and amino acids in their quest for improved health. Possible reasons for this trend include the following: baby boomers are now in middle age and have increasing concerns about illness and premature death; North Americans increasingly view traditional Western medicine as impersonal; some people are seeking an alternative to prescription medications; and many people want a greater sense of control over their bodies and health. These products are now subject to the "safe and effective" standards that OTC products must meet. Regulation of these products is the same as for prescription drugs. Natural health products, such as vitamins and mineral supplements and herbal products, are also regulated as drugs.

The traditional medical community is showing increasing interest in the potential health benefits of dietary supplements. A growing number of teaching hospitals are establishing departments of complementary medicine, and medical students are learning about the documented role (to the extent it is known) that dietary supplements can play in preventive medicine. Additionally, major international pharmaceutical companies are beginning to market dietary supplements. The reputations and resources of these companies are likely to generate extensive research into the efficacy of these products.

HEALTH CARE QUACKERY AND CONSUMER FRAUD

A person who earns money by marketing inaccurate health information, unreliable health care, or ineffective health products is called a fraud, quack, or charlatan. **Consumer fraud** flourished with the old-fashioned medicine shows of the late 1880s. Unfortunately, consumer fraud still flourishes (see the Focus On article on p. 382). Look no further than large city newspapers to see questionable advertisements for disease cures and weight-loss products. In health and illness, quacks have found the perfect avenues to realize maximum gain with minimum effort.

Key Term

consumer fraud
Marketing of unreliable and ineffective services, products, or information under the guise of curing disease or improving health; quackery.

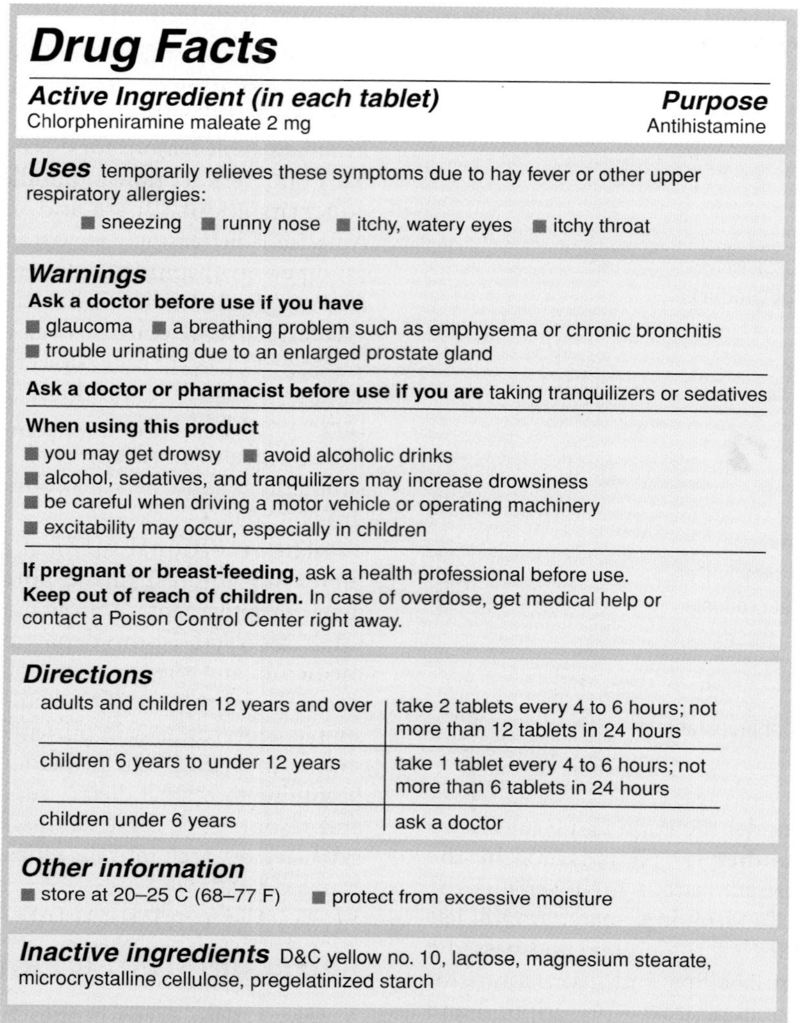

Drug Facts

Active Ingredient (in each tablet) — **Purpose**
Chlorpheniramine maleate 2 mg — Antihistamine

Uses temporarily relieves these symptoms due to hay fever or other upper respiratory allergies:
■ sneezing ■ runny nose ■ itchy, watery eyes ■ itchy throat

Warnings
Ask a doctor before use if you have
■ glaucoma ■ a breathing problem such as emphysema or chronic bronchitis
■ trouble urinating due to an enlarged prostate gland

Ask a doctor or pharmacist before use if you are taking tranquilizers or sedatives

When using this product
■ you may get drowsy ■ avoid alcoholic drinks
■ alcohol, sedatives, and tranquilizers may increase drowsiness
■ be careful when driving a motor vehicle or operating machinery
■ excitability may occur, especially in children

If pregnant or breast-feeding, ask a health professional before use.
Keep out of reach of children. In case of overdose, get medical help or contact a Poison Control Center right away.

Directions

adults and children 12 years and over	take 2 tablets every 4 to 6 hours; not more than 12 tablets in 24 hours
children 6 years to under 12 years	take 1 tablet every 4 to 6 hours; not more than 6 tablets in 24 hours
children under 6 years	ask a doctor

Other information
■ store at 20–25 C (68–77 F) ■ protect from excessive moisture

Inactive ingredients D&C yellow no. 10, lactose, magnesium stearate, microcrystalline cellulose, pregelatinized starch

Figure 15–1 There are no drug label standards in Canada.

When people are in poor health, they may be afraid of dying. So powerful is their desire to live and be relieved of their suffering that they may be especially vulnerable to promises of improved health and longer life. Even though many people have great faith in their physicians, they also would like to have access to experimental treatments or products touted as being superior to currently available therapies. When tempted with the promise of real help, people are sometimes willing to set aside traditional medical care. Of course, quacks recognize this vulnerability and present a variety of "reasons" to take their advice (see the Changing for the Better box on p. 377). Gullibility, blind faith, impatience, superstition, ignorance, or hostility toward professional expertise may eventually carry the day. In spite of the best efforts of agencies at all levels, no branch of government can protect consumers from their own errors of judgment that so easily play into the hands of quacks and charlatans.

Regardless of the specific motivation that leads people into consumer fraud, the outcome is frequently the same. First, the consumer suffers financial loss. The services or products provided are grossly overpriced, and the consumers have little recourse to help them recover their money. Second, the consumers often feel disappointed, guilty, and angered by their own carelessness as consumers. Far too frequently, consumer fraud may lead to unnecessary suffering.

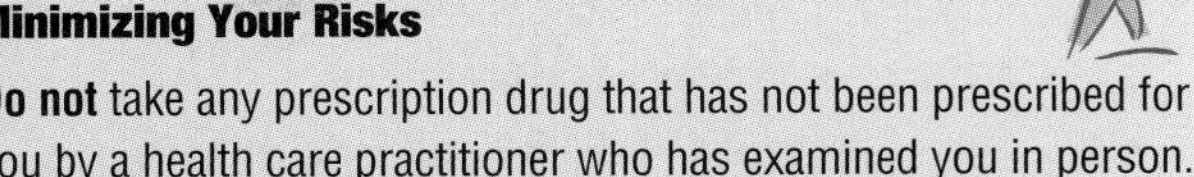

Changing *for the Better*

Buying Drugs over the Internet[22]

The Issue

If you buy drugs on line, you may be putting your health at serious risk. This is especially true if you order prescription drugs without having been examined in person by a health care practitioner.

Background

A simple Internet search will turn up hundreds of Web sites that sell drugs. Some Internet pharmacies are legitimate, but many offer products and services that are dangerous. Some sites sell drugs that are not approved for use in Canada because of safety concerns. Some sites take advantage of people desperate for relief by offering "miracle cures" for serious illnesses like cancer. Many offer prescription drugs based on answers to an online questionnaire. These sites tell you they will save you the "embarrassment" of talking to your doctor about certain prescription drugs, such as Viagra™, or drugs to prevent hair loss, or promote weight loss. What they do not tell you is that it is dangerous to take a prescription drug without being examined in person and monitored by a health care practitioner.

Risks Associated with Buying Drugs On Line

Buying drugs from Internet pharmacies that do not provide a street address and telephone number may pose serious health risks. You have no way of knowing where these companies are located, where they get their drugs, what is in the drugs, or how to reach them if there is a problem. If you order from Web sites, you may get counterfeit drugs with no active ingredients, drugs with the wrong ingredients, drugs with dangerous additives, or drugs past their expiry date. Even if these drugs do not harm you directly or immediately, your condition may get worse without effective treatment. If you order prescription drugs without being examined and monitored by a health care practitioner, you may be misdiagnosed, and miss the opportunity to get an appropriate treatment that would help you. You may also put yourself at risk for drug interactions, or harmful side effects that a qualified health professional could better foresee. Buying drugs on the Internet may also pose financial risks. In some cases, the product may not be shipped at all, or if it is shipped from another country, it could be stopped at the border by Canadian authorities.

The Status of Internet Pharmacy in Canada

A number of pharmacies in Canada have legitimate Web sites that offer a limited range of products and services, including information for consumers. The practice of pharmacy in Canada is regulated by the provinces, and any licensed pharmacy that offers Internet services must meet the standards of practice within its own province. If you have questions about whether an Internet pharmacy is legitimate, contact the licensing body in your province or territory.

Minimizing Your Risks

Do not take any prescription drug that has not been prescribed for you by a health care practitioner who has examined you in person.

Do tell your doctor and pharmacist about all of the health products you take, including vitamin and natural health products, as well as prescription and over-the-counter drugs. They need this information to assess and advise you about potential side effects and drug interactions.

If you decide to order drugs on line, **do not** do business with a Web site that

- Refuses to give you a street address, telephone number, and a way of contacting a pharmacist
- Offers prescription drugs without a prescription, or offers to issue a prescription based on answers to an online questionnaire
- Claims to have a "miracle cure" for any serious condition
- Sells drugs that do not have a DIN (see below) issued by Health Canada

Do make sure you are dealing with a Canadian-based Web site that is linked to a pharmacy that meets the regulatory requirements in your province/territory. Finally, if you have a question or complaint about therapeutic drug products purchased online, call Health Canada's toll-free hotline at 1-800-267-9675.

Health Canada's Role

Health Canada regulates therapeutic drugs in Canada through a rigorous licensing process, which includes an extensive pre-market review and ongoing post-market assessment of a drug's safety, effectiveness, and quality. As part of this process, Health Canada conducts risk/benefit assessments, monitors adverse reactions, and communicates information about risks to health professionals and the public. All drugs approved for sale in Canada have an eight-digit Drug Identification Number (DIN). The DIN assures you that Health Canada has assessed a drug, and considers it safe and effective when used as directed on the label. The DIN also provides a way to track adverse drug reactions.

Health Canada licenses and conducts regular inspections of companies that manufacture, import, and/or distribute drugs. In addition, Health Canada investigates complaints related to the sale or use of therapeutic drugs, including complaints about Web sites that sell drugs, and takes action where appropriate. Also, Health Canada works with the Canada Revenue Agency to control the illegal entry of prescription and over-the-counter drugs. Individual Canadians are allowed to import a three-month supply of therapeutic drugs, subject to a number of restrictions.

To learn more about the process for drug approvals in Canada, visit **www.cbdn.ca/english/ip_primer/Web/Graphics/DrugApprovalTimes.pdf**

For details about purchasing drugs on the Internet, see **www.hc-sc.gc.ca/iyh-vsv/med/internet_e.html**

For more information from the National Association of Pharmacy Regulatory Authorities about standards for Internet pharmacies in Canada, visit: **www.napra.org/docs/0/95/158/186.asp**

Taking Charge of Your Health

- Keep yourself well informed about current health issues and new developments in health care.
- Analyze the credibility of the health information you receive before putting it into practice.
- Select your health care providers by using a balanced set of criteria (see p. 368).
- Explore alternative forms of health care, and consider using them as a complement to traditional health care.
- In selecting an extended-coverage health care plan, compare various plans on the basis of several key factors, not simply cost.
- Assemble a complete personal/family health history as soon as possible. Be sure to include information from older family members.
- Comply with all directions regarding the appropriate use of prescription and OTC medications.

SUMMARY

- Sources of health information include family, friends, commercials, labels, and information supplied by health professionals.
- Physicians are Doctors of Medicine (M.D.s).
- Although alternative health care providers, including chiropractors, naturopaths, and acupuncturists, meet the health care needs of many people, systematic study of these forms of health care is only now underway.
- Restricted-practice health care providers play important roles in meeting the health and wellness needs of the public.
- Nursing at all levels is a critical health care profession.
- Self-care is often a viable approach to preventing illness and reducing the use of health care providers.
- Medicare is critical in our ability to afford modern health care services.
- The development of prescription medication is a long and expensive process for pharmaceutical manufacturers.
- More than 60 million North Americans use some type of dietary supplement. Government-sponsored research is underway to determine the efficacy of supplements in the treatment and prevention of illness.
- Critical health consumerism, including the avoidance of health quackery, requires careful use of health-related information, products, and services.

REVIEW QUESTIONS

1. Determine how you would test the accuracy of the health-related information you have received in your lifetime.
2. Identify and describe some sources of health-related information presented in this chapter. What factors should you consider when using these sources?
3. Point out the similarities between allopathic and osteopathic physicians. What is an alternative health care practitioner? Give examples of each type of alternative practitioner.
4. Describe the services that are provided by the following restricted-practice health care providers: dentists, psychologists, podiatrists, optometrists, and opticians. Identify several allied health care professionals.
5. In what ways is the trend toward self-care evident? What are some reasons for the popularity of this movement?
6. What is extended-coverage health insurance? Why might some Canadians wish to purchase it?
7. What do the chemical name, brand name, and generic name of a prescription drug represent?
8. In comparison with prescription medications and OTC products, what regulatory control does Health Canada exercise over dietary supplements?
9. What is health care quackery? What can a consumer do to avoid consumer fraud?

THINK ABOUT THIS ...

- How do you rate yourself as an informed consumer of health information, services, and products?
- Are there any types of providers mentioned in this chapter whom you would not choose to consult? Explain your answer.
- To what extent and in what ways have you engaged in self-care?
- Drugs are not generally covered by public health insurance plans, and some drugs are not covered by private plans. Under what circumstances do you think

that expensive medications should be prescribed for terminally ill patients?

- Is life insurance more important than extended-health insurance for young adults? Explain your answer.
- Why do you think it is difficult to get people to seek help for preventive care even though it is usually less expensive than treatment services?
- When you read a newspaper or magazine, do some health-related advertisements seem questionable to you?

REFERENCES

1. *Confusing health news*, Princeton Research Associates, 1999, Rodale Press.
2. Global Reach: Global Internet statistics, **www.glreach.com/globstats**, March 30, 2004.
3. *Trusted for on-line health*, MSB Associates, cyberdialogue/findsvp, February, 1999.
4. *History of osteopathy, osteopathy in Canada*, The Collège d'Études Ostéopathiques of Montreal and the Canadian College of Osteopathy. **www.osteopathy-canada.ca/history_of_osteopathy.htm**
5. *Chiropractic in Canada*, Canadian Chiropractic Association. **www.ccachiro.org**
6. NIH panel issues consensus statement on acupuncture (press release), Nov 5, 1997. **www.nih.gov/news/pr/nov97/od.or.htm**
7. Acupuncture effective for certain medical conditions, panel says, *CAM Newsletter*, January 1998. **nccam.nih.gov/nccam/cam/jan/1.htm**
8. *Metro Toronto (Ontario) bylaw—licensing requirements for reflexologists*, Ontario College of Reflexology. **www.ocr.edu/toronto.htm**
9. *Complementary and alternative medicine at the NIH*, National Institutes of Health, Office of Alternative Medicine 5(3):1, Fall 1998. **nccam.nih.gov/nccam/cam/1998/fall/full.html**
10. The Canadian Naturopathic Association (CAN) Web site. **www.naturopathicassoc.ca**
11. Verbach EU et al: Efficacy and tolerability of St. John's wort extract LI 160 versus imipramine in patients with severe depression episodes according to ICD-20, *Pharmacopsychiatry* 30 (suppl 2):81–85, 1997.
12. MontrealPlus.ca: Health matters, **http://english.montrealplus.ca/portal/feature/12475/massotherapy.jsp#top**, August 30, 2005.
13. The Canadian Association of Optometrists Web site. **www.opto.ca**
14. Canadian Nurses Association. **www.cna-nurses.ca/**
15. Canadian Nurses Association. *Why is nursing changing*? **www.cna-nurses.ca/pages/career/why_is_nrsg_edu_changing.htm**
16. Canadian Nurses Association. *Nurse practitioners in Canada*, **www.cna-nurses.ca/pages/career/nurse_practitioners_in_canada.htm**
17. Health Canada: Drug approval times, **www.cbdn.ca/english/ip_primer/Web/Graphics/DrugApprovalTimes.pdf**, July 2004.
18. *Drug approval times*, Rx&D™ Canada's Research-Based Pharmaceutical Companies Web site, Industry Publications Fact Sheets. **www.canadapharma.org/Industry_Publications/Fact_Sheets/sheet4_e.pdf**
19. Canada's Research-Based Pharmaceutical Companies: Information guide, **www.canadapharma.org/Industry_Publications/Information_Guide/english.pdf**, May 2003.
20. Health Canada: Drug identification number, **www.hc-sc.gc.ca/dhp-mps/index_e.html**, October 1, 2004.
21. Who's really raising drug prices? *Time* 153(9):46–48, March 8, 1999.
22. Health Canada: It's your health, **www.hc-sc.gc.ca/english/iyh/medical/internet.html**, August 30, 2005.

SUGGESTED READINGS

Molony D: *The American Association of Oriental Medicine's complete guide to Chinese herbal medicine: how to treat illness and maintain wellness with Chinese herbal medicine*, 1998, Berkeley Publishing.

This book reviews the 4000-year-old history of Chinese medicine and explains the underlying principles of using herbs to promote inner balance. The author also details the efficacy and methods of use of 170 herbs, alone and in combination. The book includes a list of conditions that can be safely and effectively treated with herbs, a helpful glossary of terms, and the location of reputable suppliers of medicinal herbs.

Rappaport K (ed): *Directory of schools for alternative and complementary health care*, 1998, Orxy Press.

For people who are interested in entering the field of complementary health care, this book offers help in finding acceptable programs in Canada and the United States. It presents a wide array of information, including names, locations, telephone and fax numbers, courses of study, admission requirements, costs, and accessibility to people with disabilities. Although the programs are not ranked, background information is provided for accreditation, certification of graduates, and professional associations. A glossary of alternative medical terms appears at the end of the book.

Making Headlines

In December 2004, Health Canada released an advisory about safety concerns regarding the group of drugs known as selective COX-2 inhibitor NSAIDs (non-steroidal anti-inflammatories). These include Vioxx (rofecoxib), which has been withdrawn from the market, Celebrex (celecoxib), Bextra (valdecoxib), and Mobicox (meloxicam), which are used in the treatment of symptoms of rheumatoid arthritis, osteoarthritis and primary dysmenorrhea (menstrual pain).

Accumulating evidence indicates that the use of selective COX-2 inhibitor NSAIDs, in certain individuals, is associated with an increased risk of heart attack or stroke when compared to placebo. The risk appears to increase with the total daily dose and the length of the treatment. However, given the available data, it is not possible to identify which patients would present a higher risk of heart attack and stroke.

Health Canada has requested additional safety information from the manufacturers of Celebrex®, BextraTM, Mobicox® and generic forms of meloxicam, and continues to review the safety profile of these drugs in order to fully consider what is presently known about the risks and benefits of these drugs when used according to their labelling.

Until further information from long-term clinical trials becomes available, one should consider that there is a strong possibility of an increased risk of cardiovascular events, including heart attack and stroke, when using selective COX-2 inhibitor NSAIDs (Celebrex®, Bextra™, Mobicox®, and all generic forms of meloxicam).

Patients should discuss the benefits and risks of treatment options with their physician, in light of the following information:

Vioxx® (rofecoxib)—Vioxx® was withdrawn on September 30, 2004, based on new safety information from a three-year, randomized double-blind clinical trial, called APPROVe, showing a possible increased risk of cardiovascular events. The APPROVe (Adenomatous Polyp Prevention on VIOXX) clinical trial was designed to assess the effectiveness of 25 mg Vioxx® in preventing the recurrence of colon polyps (abnormal tissue growth, which may or may not be cancerous). In the APPROVe trial, Vioxx® was compared to a placebo (sugar pill). Merck & Co withdrew Vioxx from the worldwide market after the study indicated an increased risk of serious cardiovascular events, such as heart attacks and strokes, after 18 months of continuous treatment.

Bextra™ (valdecoxib)—On December 10, 2004, Pfizer Inc. released new information about cardiovascular risks associated with Bextra™. In a study conducted by Pfizer, which included over 1,500 patients treated for acute pain after coronary artery bypass grafting (CABG), an increased risk of cardiovascular events was observed in patients treated with Bextra™ compared to placebo. These cardiovascular events included myocardial infarction (heart attack), cerebrovascular accident (stroke), deep vein thrombosis (blood clots in the leg), and pulmonary embolism (blood clot in the lung). The risk of these effects was observed to be greater with the intravenous form of the drug (approximately two percent of patients had such an adverse event), in comparison with the oral form of the drug (approximately 1 percent of patients), immediately following CABG surgery. About 0.5 percent of patients taking the placebo had an adverse cardiovascular event.

Celebrex® (celecoxib)—On December 17, 2004, the National Cancer Institute (NCI) in the United States announced that it had stopped a three-year Celebrex® study called Adenoma Prevention with Celecoxib (APC) due to an interim analysis showing a statistically significant increase in the risk of heart attack, stroke and cardiovascular death. Health Canada has withdrawn market authorization for the use of Celebrex® for the prevention of recurrence of Familial Adenomatous Polyposis, which is predictive of colorectal cancer. Celebrex® should not be taken for the prevention of recurrence of Familial Adenomatous Polyposis and patients should discuss alternative therapeutic options with their doctors.

Background on Selective COX-2 Inhibitor NSAIDs—Selective COX-2 inhibitor NSAIDs were first authorized for sale in Canada in 1999 based on data showing a better gastrointestinal safety profile than traditional (non-selective) NSAIDs (for example, ibuprofen). There was a need for new therapies because of the well-documented frequent and severe gastro-intestinal adverse events (for example ulcers and gastric haemorrhages) associated with the use of traditional (non-selective) NSAIDs. Also, a significant number of patients could not tolerate traditional (non-selective) NSAIDs because of stomach upset.

It should be noted that alternative therapies to selective COX-2 inhibitor NSAIDs also present risks. Therefore, patients should discuss with their physician all benefits and risks of selective COX-2 inhibitor NSAIDs versus alternative therapies, in order to determine the most appropriate treatment in their individual case.

Source: Health Canada: Advisory, **www.hc-sc.gc.ca/english/protection/warnings/2004/2004_69_e.html**, December 22, 2004.

Name ______________________ **Date** __________

Personal Assessment

Are You a Skilled Health Consumer?

Circle the selection that best describes your practice. Then total your points for an interpretation of your health consumer skills.

1 Never
2 Occasionally
3 Most of the time
4 All of the time

1. I read all warranties and then file them for safekeeping.
   1 2 3 4
2. I read labels for information pertaining to the nutritional quality of food.
   1 2 3 4
3. I practise comparative shopping and use unit pricing, when available.
   1 2 3 4
4. I read health-related advertisements in a critical and careful manner.
   1 2 3 4
5. I challenge all claims pertaining to secret cures or revolutionary new health devices.
   1 2 3 4
6. I engage in appropriate medical self-care screening procedures.
   1 2 3 4
7. I maintain a patient-provider relationship with a variety of health care providers.
   1 2 3 4
8. I inquire about the fees charged before using a health care provider's services.
   1 2 3 4
9. I maintain adequate extended health insurance coverage.
   1 2 3 4
10. I consult reputable medical self-care books before seeing a physician.
    1 2 3 4
11. I ask pertinent questions of health care providers when I am uncertain about the information I have received.
    1 2 3 4
12. I seek second opinions when the diagnosis of a condition or the recommended treatment seems questionable.
    1 2 3 4
13. I follow directions pertaining to the use of prescription drugs, including continuing their use for the entire period prescribed.
    1 2 3 4
14. I buy generic drugs when they are available.
    1 2 3 4
15. I follow directions pertaining to the use of OTC drugs.
    1 2 3 4
16. I maintain a well-supplied medicine cabinet.
    1 2 3 4

YOUR TOTAL POINTS

Interpretation

16–24 points	A very poorly skilled health consumer
25–40 points	An inadequately skilled health consumer
41–56 points	An adequately skilled health consumer
57–64 points	A highly skilled health consumer

To Carry This Further ...

Could you ever have been the victim of consumer fraud? What will you need to do to be a skilled consumer?

Focus on

FACT OR FICTION? USING HEALTH INFORMATION ON THE INTERNET

So you want to find some information on health. Maybe you have a paper due in this class. Maybe you need more information on a condition that you or a loved one has. Or maybe you simply want to take advantage of the latest information on fitness and nutrition to make healthy decisions. No matter what information you're looking for, you can probably find it on the Internet. But be wary as you search—a great deal of misinformation is also available, and it may be hard for you to separate health fact from health fiction.

You can be relatively certain that government sites and links such as the Health Canada Web site (**www.hc-sc.gc.ca**) contain reliable information. Be aware that information alone can't take the place of health care you may need. But it can make you an informed partner in your own health care. This site leads you to selected online publications, databases, Web sites, support and self-help groups, government agencies, and not-for-profit organizations that provide reliable health information to the public.[1]

Unfortunately, the government does not have the resources to filter out all false and misleading health care information that appears on the Internet. Many people mistakenly believe that advertising claims must be true or advertisers would not be allowed to continue making them. Not enough time, money, and regulators are available to assess the validity of each and every health claim. However, health care professionals and consumer advocates can give us the tools we need to determine the reliability of health information for ourselves.

Using health information from reliable Web sites can help you become an active participant in your own health care.

What Is Quackery and How Can You Spot It?

One prominent American consumer advocate is Stephen Barrett, a retired physician and nationally renowned author (with 45 books to his credit).[2] In 1969 he founded the Lehigh Valley Committee against Health Fraud, which recently changed its name to Quackwatch. Investigation of questionable claims, answering of inquiries, distribution of reliable publications, reporting of illegal marketing, and improvement of the overall quality of health information on the Internet are all tasks that this group takes on.

Quackery is more difficult to spot than most people think.[3] Fraud is deliberate deception and is more easily recognized and corrected. Quackery involves the use of methods that are not scientifically valid;[4] therefore, information purveyed by quacks cannot be scientifically confirmed or denied. This is where the problem arises. There is no way to separate the good from the bad or the harmful from the benign or helpful.

Anecdotes and Testimonials

Some alternative health care methods have been accepted by the scientific community, having met reliable criteria for safety and effectiveness; other methods are in the experimental stages. These methods are unproven but are based on plausible, rational principles and are undergoing responsible testing. But many other alternative health remedies are groundless and completely lack scientific rationale. Instead of scientific tests, people who promote these methods rely on anecdotes and testimonials to "prove" the effectiveness of their products. Much of the "success" of these products is due to the placebo effect; no cause-and-effect relationship has been established between use of the product and abatement of symptoms. People who use the remedies either get better coincidentally or think that their condition has improved simply because they're taking something for it.

Intelligent Consumer Behaviour

North Americans waste US$50 million to US$150 million per year on bogus mail-order health remedies.[5] Many of these products are now available on the Internet. You can avoid wasting your money in this way by not buying any of these products without medical advice from your physician or other health care professional. And don't be fooled by money-back guarantees; they're usually as phoney as the products that they back.

Be wary of characteristic quackery ploys. Purveyors of quackery may say that they care about you, but their care, even if it were sincere, can't make useless medicine work. These products are commonly touted as having no side effects. If this is true, then the product is too weak to have any effect at all. Quacks will encourage you to jump on the bandwagon of their time-tested remedy, as if popularity and market longevity are surrogates for effectiveness. When they do claim that their products are backed by scientific studies, these studies turn out to be untraceable, misinterpreted, irrelevant, nonexistent, or based on poorly designed research.

The costs of buying into health care quackery are more than financial. The psychological effects of disillusionment and the physical harm caused by the method itself or by abandoning more effective care are much worse.

HONcode Principles

Any reputable health information site on the Internet subscribes to the HONcode Principles. These principles are put forth and monitored by the Geneva-based Health On the Net Foundation and have arisen from input from webmasters and medical professionals in several countries.[6] According to these principles, any medical advice appearing at a site must meet the following requirements:

- It must be given by medically trained and qualified professionals unless a clear statement is made that the information comes from a nonmedically qualified individual or organization.
- The information must be intended to support, not replace, the physician-patient relationship.
- Data relating to individual patients and visitors to a medical Web site are confidential.
- Site information must have clear references to source data, and, where possible, specific links to that data.
- Claims related to the benefit or performance of a treatment, product, or service must be supported by appropriate, balanced evidence.
- The webmaster's e-mail address should be clearly displayed throughout the Web site.
- Commercial and noncommercial support and funding for the site should be clearly revealed.
- There must be a clear differentiation between advertising at the site and the original material created by the institution operating the site.

Be skeptical about any health information you find on the Internet that does not meet these criteria. Ask your physician whether the information is accurate, or move on to a more reliable site.

Assessing Health Care Information

The Internet is a valuable health care tool. Reliable information is supplied by government health agencies, research universities, hospitals, disease foundations, and other experts. However, not all health sites are reputable. As the saying goes, you can't believe everything you read, even if it's on the Internet. Anyone can create an online resource that looks professional. Ordinary people who believe they've been helped by a product, companies trying to sell products and services, and even cheats and quacks are all out there spouting their information. To protect yourself, you must be an informed consumer of information. To evaluate the credibility of an online source, ask yourself the following questions:[7]

1. Who is sponsoring the site?
2. Who manages this site?
3. What are the credentials of the sponsor and manager?
4. Who is the site's content intended for?
5. Do there appear to be any vested interests involving the site's sponsorship and management and the content of the site? (For example, is this a pharmaceutical manufacturer's site with content related to studies supported by the manufacturer?)
6. Is the information provided current and is the last updating posted on the site?
7. If opinionated statements are made, are they identified as such?

Although the Internet cannot and should not replace visits with a physician, reliable information obtained on the Net can make us more active partners in our own health care. It can help us to stay healthy and prevent disease. It can help us to ask our doctors the right questions and educate us so that we're not afraid to ask them. It can connect us to people who are experiencing the same things as we are. It can help us learn about our health, receive support from others, and make sound health care decisions based on fact—not fiction.

For Discussion ...

Which health sites have you visited on the Internet? Did you find them informative? reliable? fun? What could be done to improve the status of health information on the Internet?

References

1. Health Canada Web site. **www.hc-sc.gc.ca**
2. Rosen M: *Biography magazine interview of Dr. Stephen Barrett,* M.D., November 17, 1998. **www.quackwatch.com/10Bio/biography.html**
3. Barrett S: *Common misconceptions,* 1997. **www.quackwatch.com/01QuackeryRelatedTopics/miscon.html**
4. Barrett S: *Quackery: how should it be defined,* 1997. **www.quackwatch.com/quackdof.html**
5. Barrett S: *Mail-order quackery,* 1996. **www.com/01QuackeryRelatedTopics/mailquack.html**
6. *Health On the Net Foundation. HONcode principles,* 1997. **www.quackwatch.com/00AboutQuackwatch/honcode.html**
7. Miller L: How to diagnose good sites, *USA Today,* July 14, 1999, p 5D.

Chapter 16
Protecting Your Safety

Chapter Objectives

After studying this chapter, you should be able to

- Define the terms *intentional* and *unintentional injuries* and give three examples of each.
- Discuss the different types of domestic violence, including intimate partner violence, child maltreatment, and elder maltreatment.
- List some ways to reduce your risk of becoming a victim of violent crime in your home, in your car, or on campus.
- Explain the particular way guns contribute to violent crime statistics.
- List groups who are targets of hate crimes.
- If you are male, list five things you can do to avoid perpetrating a date rape; if you are female, list five things you can do to reduce your risk of becoming a date rape victim.
- List 10 things you can do to reduce your risk of becoming seriously injured in a motor vehicle crash.
- List 10 things you can do to prevent injuries from occurring in the home.
- Explain what identity theft is, and list several steps that you can take to protect yourself from it.

Online Learning Centre Resources

www.mcgrawhill.ca/college/hahn

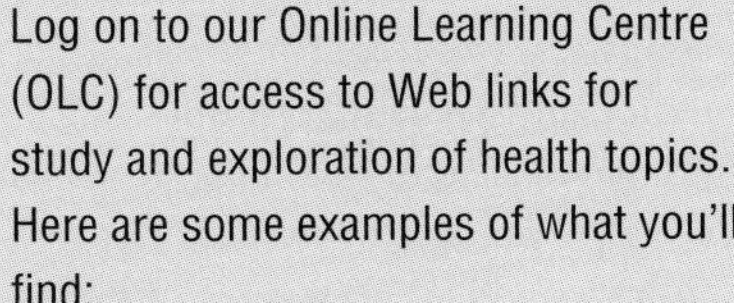

Log on to our Online Learning Centre (OLC) for access to Web links for study and exploration of health topics. Here are some examples of what you'll find:

- **www.youngdrivers.com** Read up on traffic safety issues, get tips for new drivers, and learn how to deal with road rage.
- **www.jointogether.org** Get the facts about substance abuse and gun violence from people who are working to solve these problems in their own communities.

Media Pulse

Terrorism on Television: The Tragedy of September 11—The World Trade Center Disaster

Where were you on the morning of September 11, 2001? How did you hear the news about the terror attacks on New York and Washington? The entire world stood stunned as TV cameras captured a passenger jet crashing into one of New York's twin towers, followed a few minutes later by a second plane that hit the second tower. Soon after, it was reported that a third plane had hit the Pentagon, and a fourth had crashed in a field in Pennsylvania.

Most of the day's horrors were captured by television cameras, as well as by a few film crews who happened to be filming in Manhattan that day. Viewers watched in horror as networks played and replayed footage of each plane hitting the World Trade Center, and of the fires that ensued; they saw office workers running for their lives and witnessed firefighters and other rescue workers going back into buildings that were clearly unsound to guide people out of the burning towers. And finally, they saw the two towers crumble to the ground.

For three full days the major TV networks suspended their regular programming to cover the disaster in depth. No commercials, no sitcoms, no soap operas, and no David Letterman or Jay Leno for days. When Letterman returned to the air, it wasn't to tell jokes but to have Dan Rather talk about the tragic events, and viewers saw the normally staunch newsman's eyes fill with tears. When *Saturday Night Live* featured New York Mayor Rudolph Giuliani, it was as a respected guest, not as a target for a spoof. By Saturday morning the

Media Pulse *continued*

cartoons were back—for the children. In fact, many networks geared toward children—most notably PBS—tailored their programming to offer them more comforting fare, and provided special public service announcements advising parents on how to help their children feel safe despite their own uncertainty.

In the weeks and months that followed, the media helped provide a sense of unity to a grieving nation. But the constant coverage of the tragedy and its aftermath—including footage of the attacks, and of rescue workers searching the rubble of Ground Zero for the bodies of their fallen comrades —took a toll on many people watching.

People lost sleep and felt depressed. Some worried about having to get on an airplane again. Young children had an especially difficult time—wondering why this happened and whether *they* would be victims of a terrorist attack. Some children touched buildings to make sure they were "safe" before going inside.

Today, Americans are acutely aware of the possibility of terror attacks on their soil. The international news media regularly report on anti-American sentiments in Middle Eastern countries. The Department of Homeland Security continually evaluates the national threat level, with a system ranging from Code Green (low) to Code Red (severe). When the national threat level was raised from Yellow (elevated) to Orange (heightened) in December 2003 and July 2005, it was major news. Many media outlets—especially the 24-hour news channels—report on the U.S.'s state of alert every day. Continual coverage of the War on Terror—first in Afghanistan and then in Iraq—only add to the concern for safety at home and abroad for all North Americans.

Do you worry about another attack? How closely do you follow media coverage of national and international terror issues? Are you aware of the United States' state of alert on any given day? Do you watch the news differently from the way you watched it before September 11, 2001?

As recently as 20 years ago, the suspicious disappearance of a school-aged child or the death of a bystander during a drive-by shooting was virtually unheard of. However, violent crimes are now committed so frequently in North America that it is difficult to watch a television news report or read a newspaper without seeing headlines announcing some heinous murder or other senseless act of violence, including terrorist attacks.

Although the overall crime rate has dropped in the last decade, domestic violence continues to be directed at women and children, and many people fear being a random victim of a homicide, robbery, or carjacking. Law enforcement officials contend that gang activities and hard-core drug involvement are significant factors related to continued violent behaviour in our society.

Although violence may seem to be focused in urban areas, no community is completely safe. Even people who live in small towns and rural areas now must lock their doors and remain vigilant about protecting their safety. Crime on college and university campuses remains a threat for all students. Complete the Personal Assessment on p. 406 to see whether you are adequately protecting your own safety.

INTENTIONAL INJURIES

Intentional injuries are injuries that are committed on purpose. Except for suicide (which is self-directed), intentional injuries reflect violence committed by one person acting against another person. Examples include homicide, robbery, rape, assault, child abuse, spouse abuse, and elder abuse.

In 2003, nearly 2.9 million crimes were committed against Canadian residents. Of these intentional crimes, 545 were homicides. About one-third involved the use of firearms, compared with about two-thirds of the homicides in the United States. Although violent crime rates are lower in Canada than in the United States, crime rates in both countries have followed similar trends during the last two decades. After peaking in 1991, both violent crime and property crime have generally declined with a slight rise again in 2003.[1]

Violent Crime

In recent years, many of our communities have become safer places to live, with fewer violent crimes such as homicides, assaults, and robberies. The rate of violent criminal incidents per capita had been decreasing throughout most of the 1990s, though in 2001, it remained 6% higher than in 1989. In 2002, the rate decreased in most major categories of violent crime, including attempted murder, assault, robbery and abduction. Altogether, violent crime comprised 13% of Criminal Code offences in 2002.

Violent crime rates vary significantly across the country. Although Quebec reported an increase in violent crime in 2002, it still had the lowest incidence of violent crime in the country—719 per 100,000. Nova Scotia's violent crime rate was the highest east of Ontario, with 1,099 reported incidents per 100,000, although rates remained generally higher in the western provinces. Manitoba's and Saskatchewan's rates of violent crime were the highest among the provinces with over 1,600 and 1,800 incidents per 100,000 people, respectively.

Safe Driving—It's Your Call[2]

Many of the 13 million wireless phones in Canada are used in motor vehicles. With a cell phone in the car you can call for help or report a dangerous situation; Canadians use wireless phones to call 9-1-1 over six million times annually. When you're stuck in traffic, calling to say you'll be late can reduce stress and make you less inclined to drive aggressively.

If you drive with a cell phone, avoid unnecessary calls and always make the driving task your top priority. Here are a few basic safety tips from the Canada Safety Council:

Keep your hands on the wheel—Buckle your seat-belt and place all ten fingers on the steering wheel. Wrap them firmly around it, positioned at "10 and 2 o'clock" and keep them there while you drive.

Keep your eyes on the road—Learn how to operate your phone without looking at it. Memorize the location of all the controls, so you can press the buttons you need without ever taking your eyes off the road.

Practise off-road—If your phone is new, practise using it and the voice mail while your car is stopped. Practice will make you feel more comfortable, and safe, using it when you are on the road.

Use a hands-free model—A hands-free unit lets you keep both hands on the wheel while you talk on the phone. Attach the microphone to the visor just above your line of vision, so you can keep your eyes on the road. You can then talk on the phone as if you were talking to a passenger.

Stay in your lane—Don't get so wrapped up in a conversation that you drift into the other lane. Pull into the right-hand lane while talking, so you only have to worry about traffic to the left.

Use speed dialing—Program frequently called numbers and your local emergency number into the speed dial feature of your phone for easy, one-touch dialing. When available, use auto answer or voice-activated dialing.

Never dial while driving—If you must dial manually, do so only when stopped. Pull off the road, or better yet have a passenger dial for you.

Take a message—Let your voice mail pick up your calls in tricky driving situations. It's easy to retrieve your messages later on.

Know when to stop talking—Keep conversations brief so you can concentrate on your driving. If a long discussion is required, if the topic is stressful or emotional, or if driving becomes hazardous, end your call and continue when you're not in traffic.

Keep the phone in its holder—Make sure your phone is securely in its holder when you are not using it. That way it won't pop out and distract you when you are driving.

Don't take notes while driving—If you need to take something down, use a tape recorder or pull off the road. If you have an electronic scratch pad on your phone, use it to record numbers while you are talking.

Be a wireless Samaritan—Wireless enables you to report crimes, life-threatening emergencies, collisions, or drunk drivers.

Drive defensively—Being in the right will not save you from a crash. You must be prepared for the unsafe actions of other motorists or for poor driving conditions.

The **homicide** rate—which includes first- and second-degree murder, manslaughter, and infanticide—has generally been declining since the mid-1970s. In 1999, the homicide rate hit its lowest level in 32 years, though it has increased slightly each year since then. In 2002, homicides, together with attempted murders, represented less than 0.4% of all reported violent incidents.

Fewer than 1 in 10 violent crimes in 2002 was a robbery. The rate of robberies has declined by 9% since 1999 and has generally been dropping since 1991. The use of firearms during the commission of a robbery has declined significantly in the last 20 years. In 2002, some 13% of all robberies were committed with a firearm, compared with 25% in 1988 and 37% in 1978.

Robberies were much more likely than all other violent crimes to involve youths aged from 12 to 17. In 2002, one-third of all those charged with robbery were youths, even though they accounted for only 15% of assaults and 9% of homicides.[3]

Domestic Violence

Domestic violence refers to criminal acts of violence committed within a home or homelike setting by people who have some type of relationship with the victim. This text will discuss three forms of domestic abuse: intimate partner abuse, child maltreatment, and elder abuse.

Key Terms

intentional injuries
Injuries that are purposely committed by a person.

homicide
The intentional killing of one person by another person.

Tie One On

Ribbons tie supporters to issues. For just about every cause or organization one can imagine there is an array of colourful ribbons available to tie or pin to your chest. Whether it is pink (calling for a cancer cure), white (for the prevention of violence against women), red (for AIDS awareness) or blue (honouring free speech online), ribbons can draw attention to a cause and offer comfort to victims and their families.

The use of ribbons dates back centuries. Virtually every culture and society has used ribbons in a show of allegiance and/or support, including black mourning bands worn on the arm, wreaths and bows at funerals, and red, white, and blue bunting during the French Revolution. During the Iranian–American hostage crises in 1979, people tied yellow ribbons everywhere. Some of the ribbon tying was inspired by Tony Orlando's song "Tie a Yellow Ribbon 'Round the Old Oak Tree." Yellow ribbons are now used widely in North America by the families and friends of missing people.

Wearing ribbons allows people to be advocates, promotes public awareness, advances a cause, and can be a simple sign of support and comfort. Ribbons can now range from the very serious to the very funny. For example, the serious purple ribbon stands for awareness of domestic violence, whereas the brown ribbon is worn tongue-in-cheek for the fight against decaffeinated coffee.

At present there are over 200 ribbons linked to causes or organizations, proof that ribbon popularity continues and is an ongoing part of our culture.

Rubber wristbands are the newest way to show support for a cause. Cyclist Lance Armstrong is credited with the wristbands' surge in popularity, due to his yellow Livestrong wristband, proceeds from which benefit cancer research.

Intimate partner abuse

Intimate partner abuse, or *spousal abuse*, the term used in Canada, refers to violence committed by a current or former spouse or boyfriend or girlfriend.[4] Intimate violence can include murder, rape, sexual assault, robbery, aggravated assault, and simple assault. Violent acts that constitute abuse range from a slap on the face to murder.

The 1999 Social Survey indicated that 226 000 (3%) women and 177 000 (2%) men with a current or former spouse were victims of violence by their partners in the past 12 months. The risk of being exposed to spousal violence is almost the same for men as for women. For most victims of spousal violence, common assault is the most common offence.[5]

Most homicides in Canada were committed by someone known to the victim. In 2003, 57 victims (14%) were killed by a stranger—the lowest number in more than 25 years. Half (51%) of all victims were killed by an acquaintance and one-third (34%) by a family member.[6]

The 139 victims killed by a family member represented a large decline from 182 in 2002 and the average of 172 over the previous decade. Most of the decline in family-related homicides was related to nonspousal killings committed by parents, grown children, siblings, and extended family members.[7]

The spousal homicide rate declined by 8% in 2003, with six fewer spouses killed. This rate has been gradually declining since the mid-1970s for both men and women. Of the 78 spousal homicides, 64 men killed their wives (including common-law, separated and divorced persons) and 14 women killed their husbands.[8]

Homicides involving other types of intimate partner relationships also dropped, from 17 in 2002 to 11 in 2003. These include homicides committed by boyfriends, girlfriends, and current or estranged partners.[9]

Women were much more likely than men to be killed by an intimate partner. Among all solved homicides of victims who were 15 years of age and older, almost two-thirds (64%) of females were killed by someone with whom they had an intimate relationship at one point in time compared with 7% of males. Males were far more likely to be killed by a casual acquaintance (31%), a stranger (19%), or a criminal associate (13%).[10]

One serious issue related to domestic violence is the vast underreporting of this crime to law enforcement authorities. The U.S. Department of Justice estimates that about half of the survivors of domestic violence do not report the crime to police. Too many survivors view these violent situations as private or personal matters and not actual crimes. Despite painful injuries, many survivors view the offences against them as minor.

It's easy to criticize the survivors of domestic violence for not reporting the crimes committed against them, but this may be unfair. Why do women stay in abusive relationships? Many women who are injured may fear being killed if they report the crime. They may also fear for the safety of their children. Women who receive economic support from an abuser may worry about being left with no financial resources.

However, help is available for victims of intimate abuse. Most communities have family support or domestic violence hotlines that abused people can call for help. (See the Star Box above for more information on ribbon campaigns for this and other causes.) Many have shelters where abused women and their children can seek safety while their cases are being handled by the police or court officials. If you are being abused or know of someone who is being injured by domestic violence, don't hesitate to use the services of these local hotlines or shelters.

TALKING POINTS • A close friend confides that her boyfriend sometimes "gets rough" with her. She's afraid to talk to him about it because she thinks that will make things worse. What immediate steps would you tell her to take?

Child maltreatment

Like intimate partner abuse, **child maltreatment** tends to be a silent crime. In 2002, children and youth under the age of 18 represented 23% of the population and, according to a subset of 94 police departments, they accounted for 61% of victims of sexual assault and 20% of all victims of physical assault.[11]

Girls represented 79% of victims of family-related sexual assaults reported to a subset of police departments. Rates of sexual offences were highest among girls between the ages of 11 and 14, with the highest rate at age 13 (165 per 100,000 females). Among boys, rates of family-related sexual assault were highest for those between the ages of 3 and 7. Rates of family-related physical assaults against girls and boys generally increased with age. The highest age-specific rate for girls was at age 17 (362 per 100,000 females) and the highest rate for boys was at age 15 (196 per 100,000 males).[12] Some children are survivors of repeated crimes, and since many survivors do not report these crimes, the actual incidence of child maltreatment is difficult to determine.

Children are abused in various ways.[13] Physical abuse reflects physical injury, such as bruises, burns, abrasions, cuts, and fractures of the bones and skull. Sexual abuse includes acts that lead to sexual gratification of the abuser. Examples include fondling, touching, and various acts involved in rape, sodomy, and incest. Child neglect is also a form of child abuse and includes an extreme failure to provide children with adequate clothing, food, shelter, and medical attention. A strong case can also be made for psychological abuse as a form of child abuse. Certainly, children are scarred by family members and others who routinely damage their psychological development. However, this form of abuse is especially difficult to identify and measure.

The most common form of child abuse is neglect.[14] The incidence of child neglect is approximately three times that of physical abuse and about seven times the incidence of child sexual abuse. Each form of abuse can have devastating consequences for the child—both short term and long term.

Research studies in child abuse reveal some noteworthy trends. Abused children are much more likely than nonabused children to grow up to be child abusers themselves. Abused children are also more likely to suffer from poor educational performance, increased health problems, and low levels of overall achievement. Recent research points out that abused children are significantly more likely than nonabused children to become involved in adult crime and violent criminal behaviour.[15]

It is beyond the scope of this book to discuss the complex problem of reducing child abuse. However, the violence directed against children can likely be lessened through a combination of early identification measures and violence prevention programs. Teachers, friends, relatives, social workers, counsellors, psychologists, police, and the court system must not hesitate to intervene as soon as child abuse is suspected. The later the intervention, the more likely that the abuse will have worsened. Once abuse has occurred, it is likely to happen again.

Today there is increased awareness that a person's vulnerability to abuse may be increased by factors such as dislocation, colonization, racism, sexism, homophobia, disability, poverty, and isolation. For example, in the past, many abused children were from marginalized groups in our society including, among others, children with disabilities, children from racial and ethnic minorities, Aboriginal children, and children living in poverty.[16]

Violence prevention programs can help parents and caregivers learn how to resolve conflicts, improve communication, cope with anger, improve parenting skills, and challenge the view of violence presented in movies and television. Such programs may help stop violence before it begins to damage the lives of young children.

Elder maltreatment

There are few statistics available on the abuse of elderly persons. A national study in 1990 indicated that 4% of elderly persons in private dwellings had experienced some form of abuse or neglect. The most common forms

Key Terms

intimate partner abuse
Violence committed against a person by her or his current or former spouse, boyfriend, or girlfriend.

child maltreatment
The act or failure to act by a parent or caretaker that results in abuse or neglect of a child or which places the child in imminent risk of serious harm.

Learning from Our Diversity

Violence against People with Disabilities

No one is totally free from the risk of senseless violence—not children, not adults, not students. Perhaps no group, however, is a more tragic target of violence than people with disabilities. Despite the protective efforts of laws, this group remains an easily victimized segment of the population.

Because of the high level of vulnerability of people with disabilities, advocacy groups are working to assist them, their caregivers, and the general population in reducing the risk of violence to this group. However, much can also be accomplished on an individual basis. You may be able to implement the following suggestions on your campus:

- Encourage your peers with disabilities to remain vigilant by staying tuned into their environment.
- Support your friends with disabilities in the challenges imposed by their limitations, particularly when they are in unfamiliar environments.
- Suggest that peers with disabilities carry or wear a personal alarm.
- Remind your friends with disabilities to inform others about their schedules, for example when they are leaving campus and when they are likely to return home.
- Encourage people with disabilities to seek the assistance of security personnel when leaving a campus building or shopping mall.
- Be an advocate for your friends with disabilities.

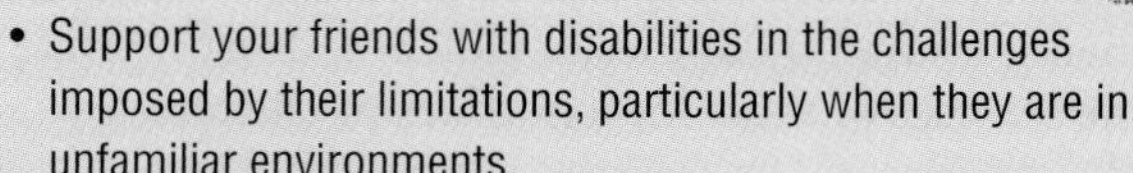

of maltreatment of elderly persons were financial and emotional. According to a 1999 victimization survey, seniors are much more likely to have experienced emotional or financial abuse (7%) than physical assault (1%) by a family member. Women over the age of 70, people who are socially or geographically isolated, and people with physical or mental health limitations have the highest risk of being victims of elder abuse.[17]

Analysis of police-reported family-related violence against older adults has found that rates have increased between 1998 and 2002. Rates against older females increased by 42% (from 38 to 54 victims per 100,000 females) while rates for older male victims increased by 30% (from 30 to 39 per 100,000 men) during this five-year period.[18]

Many elderly people are hit, kicked, attacked with knives, denied food and medical care, and have their pension cheques and vehicles stolen. Often, the abusers are the adult children of the victims. This problem reflects a combination of factors, particularly the stress of caring for failing older people by middle-aged children who may also be faced with the demands of dependent children and careers. In many cases, the middle-aged children were themselves abused, or there may be a chemical dependence problem. The alternative, institutionalization, is so expensive that it is often not an option for either the abused or the abusers.

Although protective services are available in most communities through welfare departments, elder abuse is frequently unseen and unreported. In many cases, the elderly people themselves are afraid to report their children's behaviour because of the fear of embarrassment that they were not good parents to their children. Regardless of the cause, however, elder abuse must be reported to the appropriate protective service so that intervention can occur.

One other group that is vulnerable to abuse is people with disabilities. See the Learning from Our Diversity box above for more information.

Gangs and Youth Violence

In the last 20 years, gangs and gang activities have been increasingly responsible for escalating violence and criminal activity. Before that time, gangs used fists, tire irons, and, occasionally, cheap handguns ("Saturday night specials"). Now, gang members don't hesitate to use AK-47s (semiautomatic military assault weapons) that have the potential to kill large groups of people in a few seconds.

Most, but not all, gangs arise from big city environments, where many socially alienated, economically disadvantaged young people live. Convinced that society has no significant role for them, gang members can receive support from an association of peers that has well-defined lines of authority. Rituals and membership initiation rites are important in gang socialization. Gangs often control particular territories within a city. Frequently, gangs are involved in criminal activities, drug trafficking, and robberies.

Youth violence is also spreading from the inner cities to the suburbs. Public health officials and law enforcement personnel claim that youth violence is growing in epidemic proportions.

Attempting to control gang and youth violence is expensive for communities. For every gang-related homicide, there are many nonfatal gang-related intentional injuries, so gang violence becomes an expensive health care proposition. Furthermore, gang and youth violence takes an enormous financial and human toll on law enforcement, judicial, and corrections departments. Reducing gang and youth violence is a daunting task.

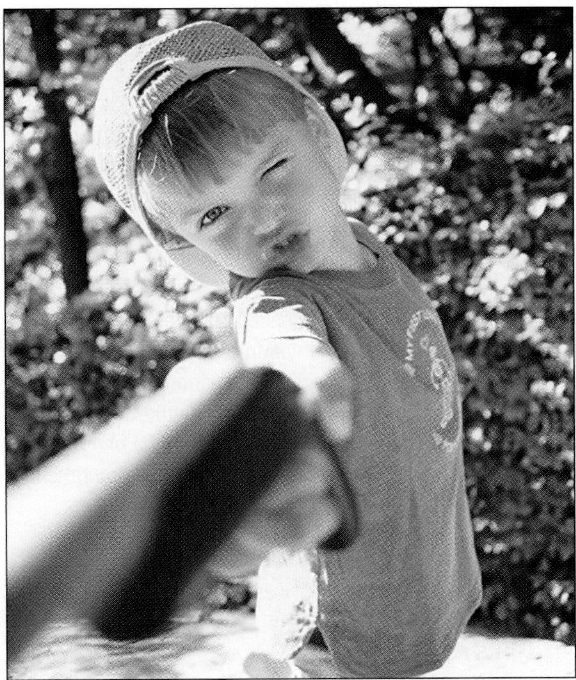

A child with a gun is a frightening image. Guns and ammunition should be stored separately in locked containers, and children should be taught that guns are not toys.

Gun Violence

The tragic effect of gun violence has already been touched on in this chapter. Guns are being used more than ever in our society and in other parts of the world. Gun violence is a leading killer of teenagers and young men, especially Black Canadian men, and the use of semiautomatic assault weapons by individuals and gang members continues. Accidental deaths of toddlers and young children from loaded handguns is another dimension of the violence attributable to guns in our society. In addition, guns are often used in **carjackings** (see the Changing for the Better box on this page).

The growing use of firearms has prompted the enactment of gun control laws in Canada. The Firearms Act and Regulation apply to any person (including visitors to Canada) and any business that owns, wants to acquire, or uses firearms. A licence is now required to possess or acquire a gun. Before a licence is issued, a safety check is carried out on the applicant. The new system links police databases with the new firearm registry system, which required all guns to be registered by January 1, 2003. New applicants for firearms must pass the Canadian Firearms Safety test. Mandatory minimum sentences of four years for violent crimes committed with a firearm are in force.[19]

Gun control activists want fewer guns manufactured and greater controls over the sale and possession of handguns. Gun supporters believe that such controls are not necessary and that people (criminals) are responsible for gun deaths, not simply the guns. This debate will certainly continue.

Changing *for the Better*

Preventing Carjacking

There have been several carjacking incidents in my area recently. What can I do to avoid this problem without carrying a gun?

In the last 10 years a new form of violence has reached the streets of North America. This crime is commonly called *carjacking.* Unlike auto theft, in which a car thief attempts to steal an unattended parked car, carjacking involves a thief's attempt to steal a car with a driver still behind the wheel.

Most carjacking attempts begin when a car is stopped at an intersection, usually at a traffic light. A carjacker will approach the driver and force him or her to give up the car. Resisting an armed carjacker can be extremely dangerous. Law enforcement officials offer the following tips to prevent carjacking:

- Drive only on well-lit and well-travelled streets, if possible.
- Always keep your doors locked when driving your car.
- Observe traffic that may be following you. If you think that something suspicious is happening, try to locate a police officer or a busy, populated area to seek help.
- If someone approaches your car and you cannot safely drive away, roll the window down only slightly and leave the car running and in gear. If the situation turns bad, use your wits and quickly flee the scene, either in the car or on foot. Remember: your life is worth more than your car.
- If another car taps the rear bumper of your car (a common carjacking manoeuvre to get you to exit your car) and you feel uncomfortable about getting out of your car, tell the other driver that you are driving to the police station to complete the accident report.

TALKING POINTS • **At a campus talk on carjacking, one student announced that he planned to carry a registered gun to protect himself. How would you respond to his position?**

Key Term

carjacking
A crime that involves a thief's attempt to steal a car while the owner is behind the wheel; carjackings are usually random, and unpredictable, and frequently involve handguns.

Violence Based on Sexual Orientation

Recent news reports indicate that violence based on sexual orientation continues to occur in Canada and the United States. Nowhere is this more clear than in the case of Matthew Shepard, an openly gay University of Wyoming freshman who was murdered in October 1998. Shepard was lured from a Laramie, Wyoming, bar by two young adult men posing as homosexuals. These men beat Shepard severely, stole $20 from him, and tied him to a fence post, where he was left to die. The men were later convicted of kidnapping and murder.

In December 2003 a 19-year-old who admitted he helped kill a man in Vancouver's Stanley Park in November 2001 was given the maximum sentence—three years in prison.

Aaron Webster was beaten to death by four young men armed with baseball bats and golf clubs—in an area of the park frequented by gay men.

The teen, who cannot been named because he was a juvenile at the time, had pleaded guilty to manslaughter.

The young man and some friends had been drinking when they went looking for gay men who cruised Stanley Park for sex.

The judge called the attack savage and cowardly and compared the teens to "thugs" who used to roam the streets of Nazi Germany.[20]

Crimes motivated by prejudice based on race, religion, colour, or national origin and sexual orientation have been added to the list in Canada's Bill C-36 Hate Crimes Prevention Act.

The public outcry following the death of Matthew Shepard indicates that much support exists for some version of a Hate Crimes Prevention Act in the United States, and the strengthening of already existing laws in Canada.

Bias and Hate Crimes

One sad aspect of any society is the way some segments of the majority treat certain people in the minority. Nowhere is this more obvious than in **bias and hate crimes**. These crimes are directed at individuals or groups of people solely because of a racial, ethnic, religious, or other difference attributed to these minorities. The targeted individuals are often verbally and physically attacked, their houses are spray painted with various slurs, and many are forced to move from one neighbourhood or community to another.

Typically, the offenders in bias or hate crimes are fringe elements of the larger society who believe that the mere presence of someone with a racial, ethnic, or religious difference is inherently bad for the community, region, or country. Examples in North America include skinheads, the Ku Klux Klan, and other white supremacist groups. (The case of Matthew Shepard [see the Star Box above] drew worldwide attention to hate crimes.)

Following the attack on the World Trade Center in New York on September 11, 2001, Canadians have called for a renewed commitment to the values of respect, equality, diversity, and fairness, and a strong condemnation of hate-motivated violence. Bill C-36, which received royal assent on December 18, 2001, contains legislation that addresses the root causes of hatred, reaffirms Canadian values, and ensures that Canada's respect for justice and diversity is reinforced. These measures include amendments regarding elections, hate propaganda, mischief motivated by bias or hate based on religion, and a prohibition against spreading hate messages telephonically.

Road Rage

Within the last 10 years, a phenomenon called "road rage" has been on the rise on the streets and highways of North America. This violence occurs when a driver becomes enraged at the driving behaviour of others—cutting off someone, driving too slowly, going through yellow lights and red lights, playing loud music, passing a long line of cars on the shoulder, playing "chicken" as two lanes merge into one. Toss in horn-honking, four-letter words, and hand gestures, and you have all the elements of the daily commute.

Sometimes road rage has deadly results. It's not unusual for road ragers to force other cars into accidents. Since some drivers carry guns, they may injure or kill other drivers. These tragedies usually are not premeditated. They often happen when a driver loses control under the pressure of a triggering incident.

There is no typical profile of a person who expresses road rage. Although road ragers are frequently young-adult, aggressive males, road rage can be displayed by anyone who drives and is stressed by time constraints, family problems, or job difficulties. One quick way to determine if you are prone to road rage is to tape record your voice while you're driving. If you hear yourself screaming and complaining, you could be considered an aggressive driver. You will need to find ways to calm yourself during your commute.

To avoid becoming a perpetrator or a victim of road rage, follow these recommendations:

- Avoid making hand gestures.
- Use your horn sparingly.
- Allow plenty of time to reach your destination.
- Imagine yourself being videotaped while driving.

Exploring Your Spirituality
Putting Fear in Perspective

Your elderly neighbour stays locked in her house all day, afraid to open the door to anyone. Too many hours of watching local TV news, you think. But it's not just older people who are living in fear. Parents, women, gays, and minorities are all looking over their shoulders.

Some parents who walked to school when they were children wouldn't think of letting their kids do that. What about child molesters and kidnappers? A young woman at a party guards her drink all night—afraid that someone might put a drug in it. She's afraid of being raped. The gay person who goes to his old neighbourhood to visit his grandmother feels uneasy. Is it his imagination, or are people looking at him in a threatening way? A man walking down the street hears a racial slur. Should he ignore it, or stop and say something?

All of these situations call for caution. If you're a parent, you need to be careful about your child's safety. But your child can walk to school—accompanied by you, another parent, or an older child. If you're a woman, you can keep an eye on your drink at a party without making that the focus of your attention. If you're a gay man who feels uncomfortable in an unfamiliar part of town, stay focused on where you're going. Walk quickly and confidently, without being intimidated. If you're being taunted, keep your dignity and remain calm.

Putting fear in perspective takes practice. First, stay reasonable. Recognize that acts of violence represent the extreme elements of society. There's a good reason you probably haven't met many (or any) murderers, robbers, or rapists. They make up a small segment of society. The people you usually encounter, who are basically good, represent the large majority. Second, be aware. Pay attention to what's going on around you. See things in a neutral way. If you do, you'll realize when an argument is about to turn into a fistfight or worse. Third, use common sense. Don't put yourself at risk, but don't stop living. You can't build your life around avoiding a potential act of violence. Fourth, trust your senses. If someone is walking too close to you and you feel uncomfortable, cross the street and go into a store. Last, practise what-if situations. For example, what would you do if you were in your car at a stoplight and someone held a gun up to your window? Considering your possible actions ahead of time, without dwelling on them, is one way of preparing yourself for real-life threats.

Living in fear is something that happens gradually—as fear takes control of a person's life. But that doesn't need to happen to you. You can take control of fear in a healthy, positive way—to build a life of rich experiences balanced by caution and good sense.

The stresses of home, work, and commuting, the anonymity of driving, and other factors can add up to road rage.

- Avoid blocking the passing lane.
- Avoid switching lanes without signalling.
- Use only one parking place.
- Avoid parking in a space for people with disabilities, unless you have a disability.
- Refrain from tailgating.
- Do not allow your door to hit the parked car next to you.
- If you drive slowly, pull over and let others pass.
- Avoid the unnecessary use of high-beam headlights.
- Do not talk on the phone while driving.
- Avoid making eye contact with aggressive drivers.
- Keep your music volume under control.

Always drive defensively. Assume that a difficult situation may get out of hand, so conduct yourself in a calm, courteous manner. It's better to swallow your pride and preserve your health than to risk unnecessary danger to yourself or other people on the road.

TALKING POINTS • You're in a car with a friend when another driver starts tailgating you very closely. Your friend (the driver) slows down to annoy the tailgater. How would you convince your friend that his action is dangerous?

Key Term

bias and hate crimes
Criminal acts directed at a person or group solely because of a specific characteristic, such as race, religion, ethnic background, or political belief.

Reducing Your Risk for Identity Theft[21]

The Office of the Privacy Commissioner of Canada makes the following suggestions to fight identity theft:

- Minimize the risk. Be careful about sharing personal information or letting it circulate freely.
- When you are asked to provide personal information, ask how it will be used, why it is needed, who will be sharing it and how it will be safeguarded.
- Give out no more than the minimum, and carry the least possible with you.
- Be particularly careful about your SIN; it is an important key to your identity, especially in credit reports and computer databases.
- Don't give your credit card number on the telephone, by electronic mail, or to a voice mailbox, unless you know the person with whom you're communicating or you initiated the communication yourself, and you know that the communication channel is secure.
- Take advantage of technologies that enhance your security and privacy when you use the Internet, such as digital signatures, data encryption, and "anonymizing" services.
- Pay attention to your billing cycle. If credit card or utility bills fail to arrive, contact the companies to ensure that they have not been illicitly redirected.
- Notify creditors immediately if your identification or credit cards are lost or stolen.
- Access your credit report from a credit reporting agency once a year to ensure it's accurate and doesn't include debts or activities you haven't authorized or incurred.
- Ask that your accounts require passwords before any inquiries or changes can be made, whenever possible.
- Choose difficult passwords—not your mother's maiden name. Memorise them, change them often. Don't write them down and leave them in your wallet, or some equally obvious place.
- Key in personal identification numbers privately when you use direct purchase terminals, bank machines, or telephones.
- Find out if your cardholder agreement offers protection from credit card fraud; you may be able to avoid taking on the identity thief's debts.
- Be careful what you throw out. Burn or shred personal financial information such as statements, credit card offers, receipts, insurance forms, etc. Insist that businesses you deal with do the same.

Stalking

In recent years the crime of stalking has received considerable attention. **Stalking** refers to an assailant's planned efforts to pursue an intended victim. Most stalkers are male. Many stalkers are excessively possessive or jealous and pursue people with whom they formerly had a relationship. Other stalkers pursue people with whom they have had only an imaginary relationship.

Stalkers often go to great lengths to locate their intended victims and frequently know their daily whereabouts. Although not all stalkers plan to batter or kill the person they are pursuing, their presence and potential for violence can create an extremely frightening environment for the intended victim and family. Some stalkers serve time in prison for their offence, waiting years to "get back at" their victims.

If you think you are or someone you know is being stalked, contact the police (or a local crisis intervention hotline) to report your case and follow their guidance. Be on the alert if someone from a past relationship suddenly reappears in your life or if someone seems to be irrationally jealous of you or overly obsessed with you. Report anyone who continues to pester or intimidate you with phone calls, notes or letters, e-mails, or unwanted gifts. Report people who persist in efforts to be with you after you have told them you don't want to see them. Until the situation is resolved, be alert for potentially threatening situations and keep in close touch with friends. Exploring Your Spirituality (p. 393) features the question of dealing with fear in our lives.

TALKING POINTS • You suspect that someone is stalking you, but your friends think you're being dramatic. How would you get objective advice on what to do?

Identity Theft

Identity theft has been on the rise since the early 1990s. Thieves use falsely obtained names, addresses, and social insurance numbers to open credit card accounts and bank accounts, purchase cell phone services, and secure loans to buy automobiles and other big-ticket items. They might even avoid paying taxes by working under false social insurance numbers, or use your identity for other purposes—if they are arrested, for example. Identity thefts can drain a person's bank account and ruin a credit rating before a person knows he or she has become a victim. Often the crime is not discovered until a person wants to make a major purchase—like a house or a car—which requires a credit check.

Health on the Web

Behaviour Change Activities

Get the Facts about Family Violence

In this chapter you learned about the alarming increase in reported incidence of family violence. The Federal Government, through Health Canada, maintains a Web site (the National Clearinghouse on Family Violence) dedicated to this phenomenon. Visit the Web site at www.phac-aspc.gc.ca/ncfv-cnivf/familyviolence/index.html and explore the wealth of resources available on this issue.

What Do You Know about Drunk Driving?

Most accidental deaths in Canada take place on our highways and streets. About 40% of fatal traffic accidents are alcohol related. What's more, the likelihood of being involved in a fatal collision is about eight times greater for a drunk driver than for a sober one. To find out how well informed you are about impaired driving, go to www.safety-council.org/quiz/drunkq.htm and take the Drunk Driving Quiz. How did you score?

First Aid Information

Unintentional injuries are very costly for our society, both from a financial standpoint and from the perspective of personal and family loss. Knowing basic first aid procedures may help save the life of someone who has suffered an injury. If you have not already done so, we encourage you to take a first aid course from the Canadian Red Cross. You can find out more by visiting the Canadian Red Cross First Aid Program Information Web site at www.redcross.ca.

Being aware of your surroundings when using an ATM is important for personal safety.

There are several steps that you can take to avoid becoming a victim of identity theft. The most important step involves ordering copies of your credit reports each year to make sure that there are no fraudulent accounts in your name. Other steps are outlined in the Star box on p. 394.

SEXUAL VICTIMIZATION

Ideally, sexual intimacy is a mutual, enjoyable form of communication between two people. Far too often, however, relationships are approached in an aggressive, hostile manner. These sexual aggressors always have a victim—someone who is physically or psychologically traumatized. *Sexual victimization* occurs in many forms and in a variety of settings. This section takes a brief look at sexual victimization as it occurs in rape and sexual assault, sexual abuse of children, sexual harassment, and the commercialization of sex.

Rape and Sexual Assault

As violence in our society increases, the incidence of rape and sexual assault correspondingly rises. The victims of these crimes fall into no single category. Victims of *rape* and *sexual assault* include young and old, male and female. They can be people with disabilities, prisoners, hospital patients, and students. We all are potential victims, and self-protection is critical. Read the Star Box on p. 397 concerning myths about rape.

Sometimes a personal assault begins as a physical assault that turns into a rape situation. Rape is generally considered a crime of sexual aggression in which the victim is forced to have sexual intercourse. Current thought about rape characterizes this behaviour as a violent act that happens to be carried out through sexual contact. (See the Changing for the Better boxes on p. 396 and p. 398 on rape awareness guidelines and help for the rape survivor.)

Key Terms

stalking
A crime involving an assailant's planned efforts to pursue an intended victim.

identity theft
A crime involving the fraudulent use of a person's name, social insurance number, credit line, or other personal financial or identifying information.

Changing *for the Better*

Avoiding Date Rape

I've heard that there are warning signs for date rape. What signs should I be alert for?

First, consider your partner's behaviours. Many, but not all, date rapists show one or more of the following behaviours: a disrespectful attitude toward you and others, lack of concern for your feelings, violence and hostility, obsessive jealousy, extreme competitiveness, a desire to dominate, and unnecessary physical roughness. Consider these behaviours as warning signs for possible problems in the future. Reevaluate your participation in the relationship.

Below are some specific ways both men and women can avoid a date rape situation:

Men

- *Know your sexual desires and limits.* Communicate them clearly. Be aware of social pressures. It's OK not to have sex.
- *Being turned down when you ask for sex is not a rejection of you personally.* Women who say no to sex are not rejecting the person; they are expressing their desire not to participate in a single act. Your desires may be beyond control, but your actions are within your control.
- *Accept the woman's decision.* "No" means "No." Don't read other meanings into the answer. Don't continue after you are told "No!"
- *Don't assume that just because a woman dresses in a sexy manner and flirts that she wants to have sexual intercourse.*
- *Don't assume that previous permission for sexual contact applies to the current situation.*
- *Avoid excessive use of alcohol and drugs.* Alcohol and other drugs interfere with clear thinking and effective communication.

Women

- *Know your sexual desires and limits.* Believe in your right to set those limits. If you are not sure, STOP and talk about it.
- *Communicate your limits clearly.* If someone starts to offend you, tell him so firmly and immediately. Polite approaches may be misunderstood or ignored. Say "No" when you mean "No."
- *Be assertive.* Often men interpret passivity as permission. Be direct and firm with someone who is sexually pressuring you.
- *Be aware that your nonverbal actions send a message.* If you dress in a sexy manner and flirt, some men may assume you want to have sex. This does not make your dress or behaviour wrong, but it is important to be aware of a possible misunderstanding.
- *Pay attention to what is happening around you.* Watch the nonverbal clues. Do not put yourself into vulnerable situations.
- *Trust your intuitions.* If you feel you are being pressured into unwanted sex, you probably are.
- *Avoid excessive use of alcohol and drugs.* Alcohol and other drugs interfere with clear thinking and effective communication.

Changing *for the Better*

Rape Awareness Guidelines

I don't want to live in fear, but I have a special concern about the potential for rape. What common-sense things should I be doing to avoid this possibility?

- Never forget that you could be a candidate for personal assault.
- Use approved campus security or escort services, especially at night.
- Think carefully about your patterns of movement to and from class or work. Alter your routes frequently.
- Walk briskly with a sense of purpose. Try not to walk alone at night.
- Dress so that the clothes you wear do not unnecessarily restrict your movement or make you more vulnerable.
- Always be aware of your surroundings. Look over your shoulder occasionally. Know where you are so that you won't get lost.
- Avoid getting into a car if you do not know the driver well.
- If you think you are being followed, look for a safe retreat. This might be a store, a fire or police station, or a group of people.
- Be especially cautious of first dates, blind dates, or people you meet at a party or bar who push to be alone with you.
- Let trusted friends know where you are and when you plan to return.
- Keep your car in good working order. Think beforehand how you would handle the situation should your car break down.
- Limit, and even avoid, alcohol to minimize the risk of rape.
- Trust your best instincts if you are assaulted. Each situation is different. Do what you can to protect your life.

Myths about Rape

Despite the fact that we are all potential victims, many of us do not fully understand how vulnerable we are. Rape, in particular, has associated with it a number of myths (false assumptions), including the following:

- *Women are raped by strangers.* In approximately half of all reported rapes, the victim has some prior acquaintance with the rapist. Increasingly, women are being raped by husbands, dating partners, and relatives.
- *Rapes almost always occur in dark alleys or deserted places.* The opposite is true. Most rapes occur in or very near the victim's residence.
- *Rapists are easily identified by their demeanour or psychological profile.* Most experts indicate that rapists do not differ significantly from nonrapists.
- *The incidence of rape is overreported.* Estimates are that only one in five rapes is reported.
- *Rape happens only to people in low socioeconomic classes.* Rape occurs in all socioeconomic classes. Each person, male or female, young or old, is a potential victim.
- *There is a standard way to escape from a potential rape situation.* Each rape situation is different. No one method to avoid rape can work in every potential rape situation. Because of this, we encourage personal health classes to invite speakers from a local rape prevention services bureau to discuss approaches to rape prevention.

Acquaintance and date rape

In recent years, closer attention has been paid to the sexual victimization that occurs during relationships. *Acquaintance rape* refers to forced sexual intercourse between individuals who know each other. *Date rape* is a form of acquaintance rape that involves forced sexual intercourse by a dating partner. Studies on a number of campuses suggest that about 20% of college and university women reported having experienced date rape. An even higher percentage of women report being kissed and touched against their will. Alcohol is frequently a significant contributing factor in these rape situations. (See Chapter 8 concerning alcohol's role in campus crime.) Some men have reported being psychologically coerced into intercourse by their female dating partners. In many cases the aggressive partner will display certain behaviours that can be categorized (see the Changing for the Better box on p. 396).

Psychologists believe that aside from the physical harm of date rape, a greater amount of emotional damage may occur. Such damage stems from the concept of broken trust. Date rape victims feel particularly violated because the perpetrator was not a stranger: it was someone they initially trusted, at least to some degree. Once that trust is broken, developing new relationships with other people becomes much more difficult for the date rape victim.

Nearly all victims of date rape seem to suffer from *post-traumatic stress syndrome.* They may have anxiety, sleeplessness, eating disorders, and nightmares. Guilt concerning their own behaviour, loss of self-esteem, and judgment of other people can be overwhelming, and the individual may require professional counselling. Because of the seriousness of these consequences, all students should be aware of the existence of date rape.

Date rape drugs

As you may recall from Chapter 7, Rohypnol, GHB (liquid ecstasy), and ketamine ("K," "Special K," "Cat") have joined alcohol as forms of date rape intoxicants. For their own safety, students must be vigilant about being duped into consuming substances that increase the likelihood of sexual assault and violence.

Sexual Abuse of Children

One of the most tragic forms of sexual victimization is the sexual abuse of children. Children are especially vulnerable to sexual abuse because of their dependent relationships with parents, relatives, and caregivers (such as babysitters, teachers, and neighbours). Often, children are unable to readily understand the difference between appropriate and inappropriate physical contact. Abuse may range from blatant physical manipulation, including fondling, to oral sex, sodomy, and intercourse.

Because of the subordinate role of children in relationships involving adults, sexually abusive practices often go unreported. Sexual abuse can leave emotional scars that make it difficult to establish meaningful relationships later in life. For this reason, it is especially important for people to pay close attention to any information shared by children that could indicate a potentially abusive situation.

Sexual Harassment

Sexual harassment consists of unwanted attention of a sexual nature that creates embarrassment or stress. Examples of sexual harassment include unwanted physical contact, excessive pressure for dates, sexually explicit humour, sexual innuendos or remarks, offers of job advancement based on sexual favours, and overt sexual assault. Unlike more overt forms of sexual victimization, sexual harassment may be applied in a subtle manner and can, in some cases, go unnoticed by coworkers and fellow students. Still, sexual harassment produces stress that cannot be resolved until the harasser is identified and forced to stop. Both men and women can be victims of sexual harassment.

Changing *for the Better*

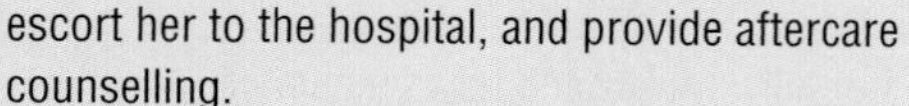

Help for the Rape Survivor

If I should be in a position to help someone who has been raped, what information do we both need to know?

- *Call the police immediately to report the assault.* Police can take you to the hospital and start gathering information that may help them apprehend the rapist. Fortunately, many police departments now use specially trained officers (many of whom are female) to work closely with rape victims during all stages of the investigation.
- If you do not want to contact the police immediately, *call a local rape crisis centre.* Generally operated on a 24-hour hotline basis, these centres have trained counsellors to help the survivor evaluate her options, contact the police, escort her to the hospital, and provide aftercare counselling.
- *Do not alter any potential evidence related to the rape.* Do not change your clothes, douche, take a bath, or rearrange the scene of the crime. Wait until all the evidence has been gathered.
- *Report all bruises, cuts, and scratches, even if they seem insignificant.* Report any information about the attack as completely and accurately as possible.
- *You will probably be given a thorough pelvic examination.* You may have to ask for STD tests and pregnancy tests.
- Although it is unusual for a rape victim's name to appear in the media, you might *request that the police withhold your name* as long as is legally possible.

Sexual harassment can occur in many settings, including employment and academic settings. On campus, harassment may be primarily in terms of the offer of sex for grades. If this occurs to you, think carefully about the situation and document the specific times, events, and places where the harassment took place. Consult your school's policy concerning harassment. Next, you could report these events to the appropriate administrative officer (perhaps the affirmative action officer, dean of academic affairs, or dean of students). You may also want to discuss the situation with a staff member of the university counselling centre.

If harassment occurs in the work environment, the victim should document the occurrences and report them to the appropriate management or personnel official. Reporting procedures will vary from setting to setting. Sexual harassment is a form of illegal sex discrimination and violates Part III of the Canada Labour Code.[22]

Most employers are well aware of their obligations to protect employees from sexual harassment and infringement of other human rights in the workplace. In Québec, the decision has been made to broaden the scope of the protection with a prohibition against psychological harassment—a first in any North American jurisdiction. As of June 1, 2004, the Québec government proclaimed new psychological harassment provisions of its labour standards law to be in force. Employers have raised many questions as to how the new provisions should be interpreted and the extent of their potential liability.[23]

In 1986 the U.S. Supreme Court ruled that the creation of a "hostile environment" in a work setting was sufficient evidence to support the claim of sexual harassment. This action served as an impetus for thousands of women to step forward with sexual harassment allegations. Additionally, some men are also filing sexual harassment lawsuits against female supervisors.

Not surprisingly, this rising number of complaints has served as a wake-up call for employers. From university settings to factory production lines to corporate board rooms, employers are scrambling to make certain that employees are fully aware of actions that could lead to a sexual harassment lawsuit. Sexual harassment workshops and educational seminars on harassment are now common and serve to educate both men and women about this complex problem.

Violence and the Commercialization of Sex

It is beyond the scope of this book to explore whether sexual violence can be related to society's exploitation or commercialization of sex. However, sexually related products and messages are intentionally placed before the public to try to sway consumer decisions. Do you believe that there could be a connection between commercial products, such as violent pornography in films and magazines, and violence against women? Does prostitution lead directly to violence? Do sexually explicit "900" phone numbers or Internet pornography cause an increase in violent acts? Can the sexual messages in beer commercials lead to acquaintance rape? What do you think?

UNINTENTIONAL INJURIES

Unintentional injuries are injuries that have occurred without anyone intending that any harm be done. Common examples include injuries resulting from car crashes, falls, fires, drownings, firearm accidents, recreational accidents, and residential accidents. Unintentional injuries are the third-greatest cause of death overall in Canada, responsible for approximately 9000 deaths per year. However, they remain the leading cause of death among Canadians aged 1 to 44.[24]

Who are injured? Children and youth: Injuries are the leading cause of death among Canadians throughout childhood and from 1 to 40 years of age. In 1996, unintentional injuries (such as automobile crashes, poisoning, and falls) accounted for almost 70% of injury-related deaths among children and youth. Seniors: The injury rate leading to death or hospitalization is higher for seniors than any other age group in Canada and is expected to grow as the Canadian population ages. The most common cause of injury among seniors is falls and in 1995, more than $980 million was spent to cover the cost of direct medical care to treat these falls.[25]

As mentioned, unintentional injuries are very expensive for our society, both from a financial standpoint and from a personal and family standpoint. Fortunately, to a large extent it is possible to avoid becoming a victim of an unintentional injury. By carefully considering the tips presented in the safety categories that follow, you will be protecting yourself from many preventable injuries.

Since this section of the chapter focuses on a selected number of safety categories, we encourage readers to consider some additional, related activities. For further information in the area of safety, consult a safety textbook (one of which is listed in the references for this chapter). Finally, we encourage you to take a first aid course from the Canadian Red Cross. Canadian Red Cross first aid courses incorporate a significant amount of safety prevention information along with the teaching of specific first aid skills.

Residential Safety

Many serious accidents and personal assaults occur in dorm rooms, apartments, and houses. As a responsible adult, you should make every reasonable effort to prevent these tragedies from happening. One good idea is to discuss some of the following points with your family or roommates and see what cooperative strategies you can implement:

- Fireproof your residence. Are all electrical appliances and heating and cooling systems in safe working order? Are flammable materials safely stored?
- Prepare a fire escape plan. Install smoke or heat detectors.
- Do not give personal information over the phone to a stranger.
- Use initials for first names on mailboxes and in phone books.
- Install a peephole and deadbolt locks on outside doors.
- If possible, avoid living in first-floor apartments. Change locks when moving to a new apartment or home.
- Put locks on all windows.
- Require repair people or delivery people to show valid identification.
- Do not use an elevator if it is occupied by someone who makes you feel uneasy.
- Be cautious around garages, laundry rooms, and driveways (especially at night). Use lighting for prevention of assault.

Recreational Safety

The thrills we get from risk taking are an essential part of our recreational endeavours. Sometimes we can get into serious accidents because we fail to consider important recreational safety information. Do some of the following recommendations apply to you?

- Always wear your automobile seat belt.
- Seek appropriate instruction for your intended activity. Few skill activities are as easy as they look.
- Make certain that your equipment is in excellent working order.
- Use safety gear specifically designed for the activity (e.g., cycling, in-line skating, or riding a scooter).
- Involve yourself gradually in an activity before attempting more complicated, dangerous skills.
- Remember that alcohol use greatly increases the likelihood that people will get hurt.
- Protect your eyes from serious injury.
- Learn to swim. Drowning occurs most frequently to people who never intended to be in the water.
- Obey the laws related to your recreational pursuits. Many laws are directly related to the safety of the participants.
- Be aware of weather conditions. Many outdoor activities turn to tragedy with sudden shifts in the weather. Always prepare yourself for the worst possible weather.

Firearm Safety

Each year about 550 Canadians are murdered with guns.[26] Many murders, about one-third, are committed with handguns. (Shotguns and rifles tend to be more cumbersome than handguns and thus are not as frequently used in murders, accidents, or suicides.) Over half of all murders result from quarrels and arguments between acquaintances or relatives. With many homeowners arming themselves with handguns for protection against intruders, it is not surprising that over half of all gun accidents occur in the home. Children are frequently involved in gun accidents, often

Key Term

unintentional injuries
Injuries that have occurred without anyone's intending that harm be done.

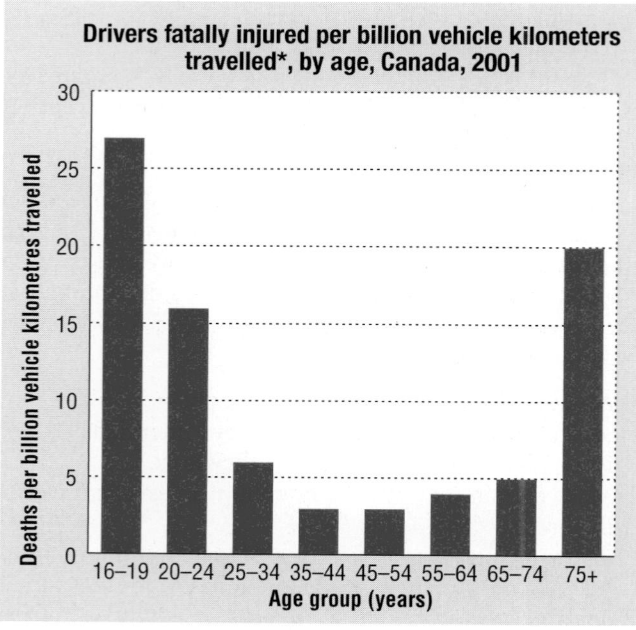

Canadian Motor Vehicle Traffic Collision Statistics: 2003

Fatalities and Injuries by Age Group

Age Group	Fatalities	Injuries
0–4	30	2866
5–14	78	12 397
15–19	327	27 757
20–24	353	29 304
25–34	419	40 053
35–44	449	38 266
45–54	396	30 080
55–64	228	17 150
65+	469	16 682
Not stated	29	7 705
Total	**2778**	**222 260**

Figure 16–1 Driving is a dangerous activity for those under age 25. What could be done to reduce the number of driving fatalities among this age group?

after they discover a gun they think is unloaded. Handgun owners are reminded to adhere to the following safety reminders:

- Make certain that you conform to the Canadian Firearms Act. Handguns with a barrel shorter than 105 mm are prohibited.
- Make certain that your gun is in good mechanical order.
- If you are a novice, enroll in a gun safety course.
- Consider every gun to be a loaded gun, even if someone tells you it is unloaded.
- Never point a gun at an unintended target.
- Keep your finger off the trigger until you are ready to shoot.
- When moving with a handgun, keep the barrel pointed down.
- Load and unload your gun carefully.
- Store your gun and ammunition safely in a locked container. Use a trigger lock on your gun when not in use.
- Take target practice only at approved ranges.
- Never play with guns at parties. Never handle a gun when intoxicated.
- Educate children about gun safety and the potential dangers of gun use. Children must never believe that a gun is a toy.

Motor Vehicle Safety

There are about 3000 accidental deaths per year on Canada's highways and streets. Young people are most likely to die from a motor vehicle accident (Figure 16–1).[27,28] In 2001, 2778 people died in motor vehicle crashes in Canada. Of that total, approximately 35% were attributed to alcohol.[29] According to Bever,[30] the following is a description of a prime candidate for such a death:

> ... a male, 15 to 24 years of age, driving on a two-lane, rural road between the hours of 10 PM and 2 AM on a Saturday night. If he has been drinking and is driving a subcompact car or motorcycle, the likelihood that he and his passengers will have a fatal accident is even more pronounced.

Motor vehicle accidents also cause disabling injuries. Concern for the prevention of motor vehicle accidents should be important for all students, regardless of age. With this thought in mind, we offer some important safety tips for motor vehicle operators:

- Make certain that you are familiar with the traffic laws in your province.
- Do not operate an automobile or motorcycle unless it is in good mechanical order. Regularly inspect your brakes, lights, and exhaust system.
- Do not exceed the speed limit. Observe all traffic signs.
- Always wear seat belts, even on short trips. Require your passengers to buckle up. Always keep small children in child restraints.
- Never drink and drive. Avoid horseplay inside a car.
- Be certain that you can hear the traffic outside your car. Keep the car's radio/music system at a reasonable decibel level.
- Give pedestrians the right-of-way.

Changing *for the Better*

Making Your Home Safe, Comfortable, and Secure

I take a common-sense approach to safety, but I worry sometimes that I haven't thought about something important. What's the basic checklist for different areas?

Entry

- Install a deadbolt lock on the front door and locks or bars on the windows.
- Add a peephole or small window in the front door.
- Trim bushes so burglars have no place to hide.
- Add lighting to the walkway and next to the front door.
- Get a large dog.

Bedroom and Nursery

- Install a smoke alarm and a carbon monoxide detector.
- Remove high threshold at doorway to avoid tripping.
- Humidifiers can be breeding grounds for bacteria; use them sparingly and follow the manufacturer's cleaning instructions.
- In the nursery, install pull-down shades or curtains instead of blinds with strings that could strangle a child.

Living Room

- Secure loose throw rugs or use ones with nonskid backing.
- Remove trailing wires where people walk.
- Cover unused electrical outlets if there are small children in the home.
- Provide additional lighting for reading, and install adjustable blinds to regulate glare.

Kitchen

- To avoid burns, move objects stored above the stove to another location.
- Install ceiling lighting and additional task lighting where food is prepared.
- Keep heavy objects on bottom shelves or countertops; store lightweight or seldom-used objects on top shelves.
- Promptly clean and store knives.
- Keep hot liquids such as coffee out of children's reach, and provide close supervision when the stove or other appliances are in use.
- To avoid food-borne illness, thoroughly clean surfaces that have come into contact with raw meat.

Bathroom

- A child can drown in standing water; keep the toilet lid down and the tub empty.
- Clean the shower, tub, sink, and toilet regularly to remove mold, mildew, and bacteria that can contribute to illness.
- Store medications in their original containers in a cool, dry place out of the reach of children.
- Add a bath mat or nonskid strips to the bottom of the tub.
- Add grab bars near the tub or shower and toilet, especially if there are elderly adults in the home.
- Keep a first-aid kit stocked with bandages, first-aid ointment, gauze, pain relievers, syrup of Ipecac, and isotonic eyewash; include phone numbers of your physician and a nearby emergency centre.

Stairway

- Add a handrail for support.
- Remove all obstacles or stored items from stairs and landing.
- Repair or replace flooring material that is in poor condition.
- Add a light switch at the top of the stairs.
- If there is an elderly person in the home, add a contrasting colour strip to the first and last steps to identify the change of level.

Fire Prevention Tips

- Install smoke detectors on every level of your home.
- Keep fire extinguishers handy in the kitchen, basement, and bedrooms.
- Have the chimney and fireplace cleaned by a professional when there is more than half a centimetre (¼ inch) of soot accumulation.
- Place space heaters at least 1 metre (3 feet) from beds, curtains, and other flammable objects.
- Don't overload electrical outlets, and position drapes so that they don't touch cords or outlets.
- Recycle or toss combustibles, such as newspapers, rags, old furniture, and chemicals.
- If you smoke, use caution with cigarettes and matches; never light up in bed.
- Plan escape routes and practise using them with your family.

- Drive defensively at all times. Do not challenge other drivers. Refrain from drag racing.
- Look carefully before changing lanes.
- Be especially careful at intersections and railroad crossings.
- Carry a well-maintained first aid kit that includes flares or other signal devices.
- Alter your driving behaviour during bad weather.
- Do not drive when you have not had enough sleep.

Home Accident Prevention for Children and the Elderly

Approximately 1 person in 10 is injured each year in a home accident. Children and the elderly spend significantly more hours each day in a home setting than do young adults and midlife people. It is especially important that accident prevention be given primary consideration for these groups (see the Changing for the Better box on p. 401). Here are some important tips to remember. Can you think of others?

For everyone

- Be certain that you have adequate insurance protection.
- Install smoke detectors appropriately.
- Keep stairways clear of toys and debris. Install railings.
- Maintain electrical and heating equipment.
- Make certain that inhabitants know how to get emergency help.

For children

- Know all the ways to prevent accidental poisoning.
- Use toys that are appropriate for the age of the child.
- Never leave young children unattended, especially infants.
- Keep any hazardous items (guns, poisons, etc.) locked up.
- Keep small children away from kitchen stoves.

For the elderly

- Protect from falls.
- Be certain that elderly people have a good understanding of the medications they may be taking. Know the side effects.
- Encourage elderly people to seek assistance when it comes to home repairs.
- Make certain that all door locks, lights, and safety equipment are in good working order.

Refer to p. 390 for additional information related to the protection of older adults.

CAMPUS SAFETY AND VIOLENCE PREVENTION

Although many of the topics in this chapter are unsettling, students and faculty must continue to lead normal lives in the campus environment despite potential threats to our health. The first step in being able to function adequately is knowing about these potential threats. You have read about these threats in this chapter; now you must think about how this information applies to your campus situation.

At one time the university campus was thought to be a safe haven from the real world. Now there is plenty of evidence to indicate that significant intentional and unintentional injuries can happen to anyone at any time on campus. The December 6, 1989, Montreal Massacre at l'École Polytechnique changed the face of Canadian campuses forever when 14 young women were tragically killed by a lone gunman because of their gender.

For this reason, you must make it a habit to think constructively about protecting your safety. In addition to the personal safety tips presented earlier in this chapter, remember to use the safety assistance resources available on your campus. One of these might be your use of university-approved escort services, especially in the evenings as you move from one campus location to another. Another resource is the campus security department (campus police). Typically, campus police have a 24-hour emergency phone number. If you think you need help, don't hesitate to call this number. Campus security departments frequently offer short seminars on safety topics to student organizations or residence hall groups. Your counselling centre on campus might also offer programs on rape prevention and personal protection.

Taking Charge of Your Health

- Use the Personal Assessment on p. 406 to determine how well you manage your own safety.
- Assess your behaviours and those of your dating partners for signs of potential date rape by reviewing the Changing for the Better box on p. 396.
- Check your residence for the safety strategies listed on p. 401. Make the necessary changes to correct any deficiences.
- Review the motor vehicle safety tips on pp. 400–401. If you need to make changes to your car or your driving, begin working on them at once.
- Check the recommendations for recreational safety on p. 399, and put them into practice. Be assertive about using these measures when you are participating in activities with others.
- Find out about the security services available on your campus, and take advantage of them. Post the 24-hour-help phone number in your room and carry it with you.

SUMMARY

- Everyone is a potential victim of violent crime.
- Domestic violence includes intimate partner abuse (or spousal abuse), child abuse, and elder abuse.
- Forms of child abuse include physical abuse, sexual abuse, and child neglect. Child neglect is the most common form.
- Youth violence is a serious social problem, and much of the violence is related to gang activities.
- Bias and hate crimes, crimes based on sexual orientation, and stalking are increasingly recognized as serious violent acts.
- Rape and sexual assault, acquaintance rape, date rape, and sexual harassment are forms of sexual victimization in which victims often are both physically and psychologically traumatized.
- Unintentional injuries are injuries that occur accidentally. The numbers of fatal and nonfatal unintentional injuries are exceedingly high.

REVIEW QUESTIONS

1. Identify some of the categories of intentional injuries. How many people are affected each year by intentional injuries?
2. Identify the three types of domestic violence discussed in the chapter.
3. What reasons might explain why so many people do not report domestic violence?
4. Aside from the immediate consequences of child abuse, what additional problems do many abused children face in the future?
5. Explain why gangs and gang activities have increased tremendously over the last 30 years. What effect do gangs have on a community?
6. List some examples of groups that are known to have committed bias or hate crimes.
7. Identify some general characteristics of a typical stalker.
8. Explain some of the myths associated with rape. How can date rape be prevented?
9. Identify some examples of behaviours that could be considered sexual harassment. Why are employers especially concerned about educating their employees about sexual harassment?
10. Identify some common examples of unintentional injuries. Point out three safety tips from each of the safety areas listed at the end of this chapter.
11. What steps can be taken to avoid "identity theft"?

THINK ABOUT THIS ...

- To what extent are you concerned about your personal safety? Are you comfortable with your level of concern? Or do you think you should be more or less concerned?
- Has there been any gun violence on your campus? Are you aware of any students carrying guns or other concealed weapons?
- Do you know of educational programs on your campus that have dealt with rape prevention or sexual harassment? Where can you go on your campus to seek help for crises related to these issues?
- Is there a particular place on your campus where you believe that your personal safety is threatened? If so, how do you cope with this threat?

REFERENCES

1. Statistics Canada: *Crimes by offences, provinces and territories*, 2003. **www.statcan.ca/english/Pgdb/State/Justice/legal02c.htm**
2. Canada Safety Council: Safe driving—it's your call, **www.safety-council.org/info/traffic/cellular.html**, May 2005.
3. Statistics Canada: Violent crime, **http://142.206.72.67/04/04b/04b_002a_e.htm**, January 13, 2004.
4. U.S. Department of Justice: *Murder by intimates declined 36 percent since 1976*, press release, March 16, 1998, p. 1.
5. Statistics Canada: *Family violence in Canada: a statistical profile 2002*, Canadian Centre for Justice Statistics. **www.statcan.ca/english/freepub/85-224-XIE/85-224-XIE00002.pdf**
6. Statistics Canada: *The Daily*, **www.statcan.ca/Daily/English/040929/d040929a.htm**, September 29, 2004.
7. Ibid.
8. Ibid.
9. Ibid.
10. Ibid.

11. Statistics Canada: Family violence in Canada—A statistical Profile, 2004, Canadian Centre for Justice Statistics, Catalogue 85-224-XIE, **www.phac-aspc.gc.ca/ncfv-cnivf/familyviolence/pdfs/85-224-XIE2004000.pdf**
12. Ibid.
13. Widom CS: The cycle of violence, *Research in brief*, National Institute of Justice, U.S. Department of Justice, U.S. Government Printing Office, 1992.
14. Ibid.
15. Ibid.
16. Department of Justice Canada: *Child abuse: a fact sheet from the Department of Justice Canada.* **http://canada.justice.gc.ca/en/ps/fm/childafs.html#factors**
17. McFadgen SD: *Family violence and personal safety*, Nova Scotia Advisory Council on the Status of Women, 2001.
18. Family violence in Canada.
19. Canadian Firearms Centre: *Highlights of* The Firearms Act. **www.cfc-ccaf.gc.ca/en/general_public/highlights/default.asp**
20. **http://vancouver.cbc.ca/regional/servlet/View?filename=bc _killing20031218**
21. Office of the Privacy Commissioner of Canada: Identity theft—what it is and what you can do about it, **www.privcom.gc.ca/fs-fi/02_05_d_10_e.asp**, April 1, 2004.
22. Human Resources Development Canada: *Pamphlet 12: sexual harrassment.* **http://info.load-otea.hrdc-drhc.gc.ca/publications/labour_standards/harassment.shtml**
23. Blakes, Cassels & Graydon: New prohibitions against psychological harassment in Quèbec, **www.blakes.com/english/publications/leb/Nov2004/NewProhibitions.asp**, November 2004.
24. Health Canada: **www.hc-sc.gc.ca/hl-vs/securit/index_e.html**, August 30, 2005.
25. Bever, DL: *Safety: a personal focus*, ed 4, 1996, Mosby.
26. **www.statcan.ca/Daily/English/040929/d040929a.htm**
27. Statistics Canada, Transport Canada: Traffic accident information database, Canadian vehicle survey 2001, **www.tc.gc.ca/roadsafety/stats/overview/2004/menu.htm**, August 22, 2005.
28. Transport Canada: Canadian motor vehicle traffic collision statistics, 2003, **www.tc.gc.ca/roadsafety/tp/tp3322/2003/page2.htm**, August 30, 2005.
29. Canadian Motor Vehicle Traffic Collision Statistics: 2001, **www.hc-sc.gc.ca/hl-vs/securit/index_e.html**
30. *Safety: a personal focus*

SUGGESTED READINGS

Brandenburg, JB: *Confronting sexual harassment: what schools and colleges can do*, 1997, Teachers College Press.
This book explains the origins and scope of the problem of sexual harassment on campus. The author discusses ways to develop policies and grievance procedures, examines legal issues, and suggests useful education programs and strategies.

Giggans PO, Levy B: *50 ways to a safer world: everyday actions you can take to prevent violence in neighborhoods, schools, and communities*, 1997, Seal Press Feminist Publications.
This handbook offers practical advice in an easy-to-read format. It suggests simple, logical ways to prevent violence in the home, on the streets, and in schools. Each of the 50 actions is clearly explained in this 144-page publication.

Goold GB: *First aid in the workplace: what to do in the first five minutes*, ed 2, 1998, Prentice-Hall.
This book covers all essential elements required by OSHA's current guidelines. It's designed for a six- to eight-hour first aid course for people with little or no first aid training. Presenting information clearly and concisely, it details basic first aid procedures for a number of injuries that can occur in the workplace. Photographs are used to illustrate specific skills.

Marques L, Carter L, Nelson M: *Child safety made easy*, 1998, Screamin' Mimi Publications.
Illustrated with cartoon characters, this humorous book presents hundreds of important safety tips for various people who care for small children. The writing style is straightforward, and explanations are concise. This book would be especially useful for first-time parents.

Making Headlines

Murders Down and Counterfeiting Up

For the first time in over a decade, the Canadian crime rate rose substantially in 2003. The rise was largely due to the increase in counterfeiting across the country. The number of property crimes and minor offences such as disturbing the peace also increased, but the violent crime rate stayed the same, and the number of murders was down from 2002.

Counterfeiting—There was a huge increase of 72 percent in counterfeiting crimes in 2003, bringing counterfeiting up to the sixth largest crime category in Canada. While some of this apparent increase in activity could be due to the improvement in the detection of counterfeit currency, the Bank of Canada's 2003 Annual Report reported double the number of counterfeit notes in circulation compared to the previous year.

Property Crime in Canada—The property crime rate in Canada, including residential and business break-ins and vehicle thefts, went up 4 percent in 2003. That was from a 20-year low the year before, so the rate is still more than 25 percent lower than it was a decade ago. Vehicle thefts were up about 5 percent across Canada, except for in Alberta where they went up 15 percent. Other provinces with large increases in vehicle thefts in 2003 were Saskatchewan, Newfoundland, New Brunswick, and Prince Edward Island.

Drug Crime in Canada—In 2003, the drug crime rate in Canada fell about 8 percent, dropping for the first time in a decade. A reduction in the rate of cannabis possession offences by 18 percent was the significant factor in the drop. The uncertainty from court rulings and the introduction of a bill to reform marijuana laws likely contributed to the reduction in the number of charges for marijuana possession laid by police in 2003.

British Columbia continues to be the province with the highest rate in drug crimes in Canada.

Source: Statistics Canada: *The Daily*, **www.statcan.ca/Daily/English/040728/d040728.pdf**, July 28, 2004.

Name ______________________________ **Date** ______________

Personal Assessment

How Well Do You Protect Your Safety?

This quiz will help you measure how well you manage your personal safety. For each item below, circle the number that reflects the frequency with which you do the safety activity. Then, add up your individual scores and check the interpretation at the end.

3 I regularly do this

2 I sometimes do this

1 I rarely do this

1. I am aware of my surroundings and do not get lost.
   3 2 1
2. I avoid locations in which my personal safety could be compromised.
   3 2 1
3. I intentionally vary my daily routine (such as walking patterns to and from class, parking places, and jogging or biking routes) so that my whereabouts are not always predictable.
   3 2 1
4. I walk across campus at night with other people.
   3 2 1
5. I am careful about disclosing personal information (address, phone number, social insurance number, my daily schedule, etc.) to people I do not know.
   3 2 1
6. I carefully monitor my alcohol intake at parties.
   3 2 1
7. I watch carefully for dangerous weather conditions and know how to respond if necessary.
   3 2 1
8. I do not keep a loaded gun in my home.
   3 2 1
9. I know how I would handle myself if I were to be assaulted.
   3 2 1
10. I maintain adequate insurance for my property.
    3 2 1
11. I keep emergency information numbers near my phone.
    3 2 1
12. I keep my first aid skills up to date.
    3 2 1
13. I use deadbolt locks on the doors of my home.
    3 2 1
14. I use the safety locks on the windows at home.
    3 2 1
15. I check the batteries used in my home smoke detector.
    3 2 1
16. I have installed a carbon monoxide detector in my home.
    3 2 1
17. I use adequate lighting in areas around my home and garage.
    3 2 1
18. I have the electrical, heating, and cooling equipment in my home inspected regularly for safety and efficiency.
    3 2 1
19. I use my car seat belt.
    3 2 1
20. I drive my car safely and defensively.
    3 2 1
21. I keep my car in good mechanical order.
    3 2 1
22. I keep my car doors locked.
    3 2 1
23. I have a plan of action if my car should break down while I am driving it.
    3 2 1
24. I use appropriate safety equipment, such as flotation devices, helmets, and elbow pads, in my recreational activities.
    3 2 1
25. I can swim well enough to save myself in most situations.
    3 2 1
26. I use suggestions for personal safety each day.
    3 2 1

TOTAL POINTS ________

Interpretation

Your total may mean that

72–78 points	You appear to carefully protect your personal safety.
65–71 points	You adequately protect many aspects of your personal safety.
58–64 points	You should consider improving some of your safety-related behaviours.
Below 58 points	You must consider improving some of your safety-related behaviours.

To Carry This Further ...

Although no one can be completely safe from personal injury or possible random violence, there are ways to minimize the risks to your safety. Scoring high on this assessment will not guarantee your safety, but your likelihood for injury should remain relatively low. Scoring low on this assessment should encourage you to consider ways to make your life more safe. Refer to the text and this assessment to provide you with useful suggestions to enhance your personal safety. Which safety tips will you use today?

Focus on

SAFETY AND SAFE USE OF CELLULAR PHONES

With the growing popularity of hand-held cellular phones (or cell phones), questions have been raised about the safety of being exposed to the radiofrequency (RF) energy they emit.

Background

The number of cell phone users in Canada has risen from 100,000 in 1987 to more than 9.5 million in 2001. This rapid expansion has raised health concerns about RF exposure, including alarming media reports that appear to link their long-term use to diseases such as brain cancer.

Cell phones are portable radio devices that transmit and receive signals from a network of fixed, low-power, base stations. The transmitting power of a cell phone varies, depending on the type of network and distance from the base station. The power generally increases as you move farther away from the nearest base station.

Prior to 1996, all cell phones in Canada were analog devices that operated in a lower cellular frequency band than that of the digital system, which was introduced in 1997. The electromagnetic energy given off by cell phones is a type of nonionizing radiation, similar to the radiation that occurs naturally in thunderstorms.

RF electromagnetic energy is used in radio communications and broadcasting, as well as in medical treatments and industrial heating. Unlike the ionizing radiation given off by X-ray machines, RF electromagnetic energy from cell phones and other devices cannot break chemical bonds. In other words, it is unlikely to damage your body's genetic material.

Health Risks from Cell Phones

The RF electromagnetic energy generated by cell phones can penetrate your body. The depth of penetration and the amount of energy you absorb depends on many factors, such as how close you hold the cell phone to your body and how strong the signal is. The important indication of RF exposure is the rate of energy absorbed in your body. This is called the "specific absorption rate" or SAR and it is measured in watts (unit of power) per kilogram. So far, there is currently no convincing evidence, from animal or human studies, that the energy from cell phones is enough to cause serious health effects, such as cancer, epileptic seizures, or sleep disorders. Some scientists have reported that cell phone use may cause changes in brain activity, reaction times, or the time it takes to fall asleep. But these findings have not yet been confirmed.

Cell phone use is, however, not entirely risk free. Studies have shown that

- Using cell phones while driving may increase the chance of traffic accidents.
- Cell phones may interfere with medical devices such as pacemakers, defibrillators, and hearing aids.
- Cell phones can also interfere with aircraft electronics.

Cell Phone Safety

Health Canada has published Safety Code 6—Limits of Human Exposure to Radiofrequency Electromagnetic Fields in the Frequency Range from 3 kHz to 300 GHz. This safety code is one of a series of guidelines Health Canada has produced on the safe use of devices that emit radiation. Safety Code 6 has been adopted by many organizations across Canada and referred to in a number of regulations, including the Canada Occupational Safety and Health Regulations. The limits given in Safety Code 6 were arrived at after looking at many scientific studies on the health effects of RF energy exposure. International exposure standards were also taken into account. For portable radio transmitters such as cell phones, the SAR limit for the general public is 1.6 watts per kilogram.

However, some studies claim that biological effects may occur at RF energy levels below the Safety Code 6 limits. These biological effects are not well established and their implications for human health need further study. Right now, there is no convincing scientific evidence to support lowering the limits. Health Canada is taking part in the International EMF Project, coordinated by the World Health Organization. The goals of this project are to verify reported biological effects from electromagnetic fields and to characterize any associated health risks to humans.

Department of Industry—Industry Canada licences radiocommunication equipment, approves where cell phone base stations are located, and conducts compliance assessments on both cell phones and base stations. This department has adopted Safety Code 6 in the licencing of radiocommunication equipment and facilities. Steps have been taken to ensure that all cell phones in Canada meet the exposure limits published in Safety Code 6.

Reducing Cell Phone Risks

There is no firm evidence to date that RF emissions from cell phones cause ill health. Only you can decide if you can live with the possibility of an unknown risk from cell phone use. If you are concerned, you can reduce your risk by limiting the length of your cell phone calls and using "hands-free" devices that keep cell phones away from your head and body. Also, because of the risk of traffic accidents, do not use your cell phone while driving.

Source: Health Canada: Safety and safe use of cell phones, **www.hc-sc.gc.ca/iyh-vsv/prod/cell_e.html**, August 9, 2005.

Chapter 17
The Environment and Your Health

Chapter Objectives

After reading this chapter, you should be able to

- Identify several environmental factors that can impact your personal health in either positive or adverse ways.
- Explain how your personal health is influenced by different environmental factors on several scales, including personal environment, the community and regional environment, and the global environment.
- Describe specific actions that you can take to minimize health risks associated with your personal environment—your home, your automobile, your workplace.
- Detail several specific actions that you can take to minimize environmental health risks at the community and regional level.
- Describe several global environmental health issues, and offer several actions that you might take to foster change.

Online Learning Centre Resources

www.mcgrawhill.ca/college/hahn

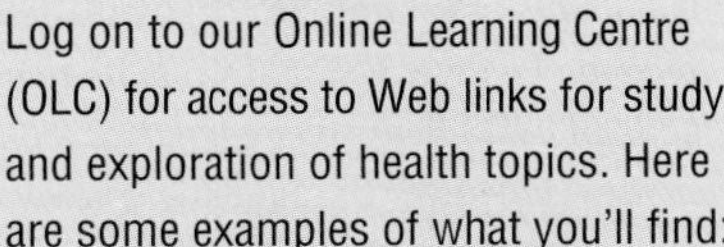

Log on to our Online Learning Centre (OLC) for access to Web links for study and exploration of health topics. Here are some examples of what you'll find:

- **www.sierraclub.ca** This site highlights the Sierra Club of Canada's activities related to matters of public policy and environmental awareness.
- **http://consumerinformation.ic.gc.ca** The Canadian Consumer Information Gateway Web site has a useful page on the environment that includes information and documents related to a vast range of environmental issues, both provincial and national.

- **www.davidsuzuki.org** The David Suzuki Foundation Web site explores the human impact on the environment, with an emphasis on finding solutions.
- **www.ec.gc.ca/envhome.html** Environment Canada's Internet resource for weather and environmental information, "The Green Lane" is designed to help Canadians exchange information and share knowledge for environmental decision making.

Media Pulse

Does Eco-Terrorism Really Work to Protect Our Environment?

According to its Web site, the Earth Liberation Front, or ELF, is an international underground organization that uses "direct action" (called eco-terrorism by others) in the form of economic sabotage to stop the destruction of the natural environment. Since 1997, the ELF in North America has caused over $100 million in damages to entities that profit from the destruction of life and the planet.

Many people are angered by the degradation of our shared natural environment, but is direct action/eco-terrorism ever justified in a democratic society? For some, the degradation or destruction of a local wetland, a forested mountaintop, or a local river or lake is a personal loss, like the death of an old friend. Many people are frustrated by the perception that well-funded corporate interests have bought out our democratic political system so that they can exploit our shared natural lands. Some wonder, "If the system is unfair, why not take direct action to right these wrongs?"

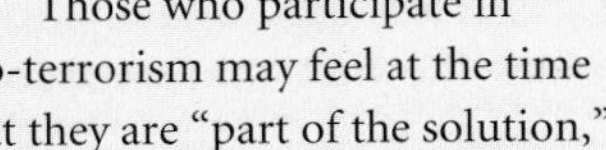

Those who participate in eco-terrorism may feel at the time that they are "part of the solution,"

Media Pulse *continued*

but are they really? To shift the course of the global human population toward a more ecologically sustainable path will require many changes, large and small, governmental and personal. Does eco-terrorism really change people's attitudes and behaviours toward protecting our environment? Will eco-terrorism stimulate governments toward more ecologically sound policies, or cause a societal backlash against all groups that work to protect the environment? Does direct action against environmental "bad guys" discourage their activities, or allow them to claim "victim" status that brings them assistance in proceeding with their destructive practices?

One likely motivation for ELF's acts of economic sabotage is to get environmental problems on the national agenda in order to make people more aware and motivated to act in the political process. Certainly, this strategy worked well for the civil rights movement. The TV pictures of peaceful black demonstrators being viciously attacked by white police officers and their dogs caused western nations to wake up to the problem of institutional racism. To date, the main results from actions by ELF are short-lived news stories that show damage to expensive SUVs and burned-out buildings. These news stories never show pictures of environmental damage associated with the manufacture of the SUVs or economic development of natural habitats. All the public sees is waste of resources in the burned hulks of automobiles, the vandalism of extremists. This does not seem to be a particularly effective way to draw public attention to environmental problems. Even worse, some anti-environment commentators use widely televised actions of ELF to discredit the entire environmental movement. Using the media to get environmental issues on the national agenda is a good thing only if it advances positive changes that provide real environmental protection.

Throughout this book we have read about areas of health over which people have significant control. For example, people select the foods they eat, how much alcohol they consume, and how they manage the stressors in their lives.

The study of the environment and its effect on health provides an interesting contrast to the daily control people have over their own health. Perhaps because of the natural processes of life and death and the vital function of the environment, we are inclined to think that we cannot make personal decisions concerning it. This is, however, changing. Barry Commoner is a professor of plant physiology and chairman of the Department of Botany at Washington University. He says, "The separation of the laws of nature among the different sciences is a human conceit; nature itself is an integrated whole."[1] Commoner lists the four laws of ecology:

1. Everything is connected to everything else.
2. Everything must go somewhere.
3. Nature knows best.
4. There is no such thing as a free lunch.[2]

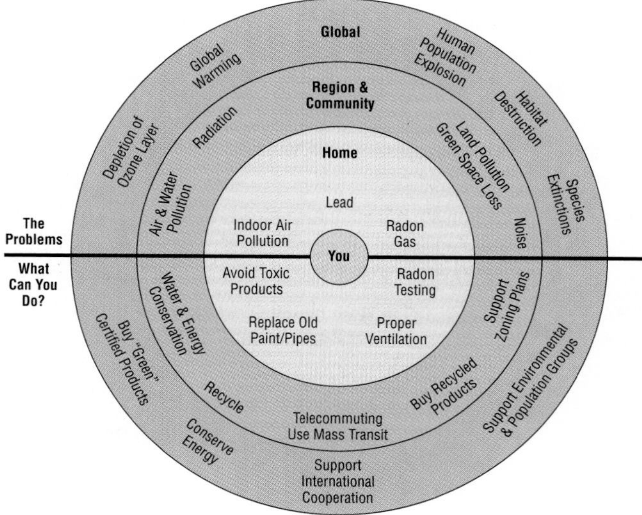

Figure 17–1 Spatial scales of environmental health risks and appropriate personal responses to environmental problems.

In comparison with the 1980s, when concerns about the environment focused on problems over which we had little direct responsibility or control (such as the ozone layer and nuclear accidents), the 1990s were characterized by a focus on the individual and the home. Issues such as the disposal of municipal waste; the recycling of glass, plastic, and aluminum; the venting of radon gas from basements, and the reduction of water use reflect the fact that people can act to support the environment (see Figure 17–1). The 21st century has heralded a more urgent awareness that countries and their citizens must think and act both globally and locally. The behaviours that are required of individuals will affect, ultimately, not only their own well-being, but that of their fellow humans, and of generations to come. Environmental health not only requires adjustments to individual behaviour, such as reducing the use of automobile transportation, but also obliges us to inform others of their impact on the environment, and to urge those making policy decisions on our behalf to consider environmental health in all legislation.

Environmental concerns also extend to developing countries. With the world population at 6 billion in 2001

The Kyoto Protocol

In late 1997, the world's industrialized countries met in Kyoto, Japan, to agree to legally binding targets for the reduction of their greenhouse gas emissions in an effort to slow global climate change. These modest targets were based on the reduction of total emissions to 5% below 1990 levels over the years between 2008 and 2012. While the initial agreement was struck in 1997, it took another four years of legal and political wrangling to work out how this commitment would operate. A variety of means by which nations could earn reduction "credits" included domestic emission reductions, investment in international reduction projects, purchasing the surplus from other countries' emission quotas, and protecting "sinks" such as forests and agricultural land that naturally absorb greenhouse gases. Following 2001, it then fell to each nation to determine how and if it would ratify or endorse the Kyoto Protocol. In March 2001, the world's largest emitter of greenhouse gases, the United States, withdrew from the Kyoto Protocol, citing that endorsement would damage the U.S. economy. Similar resistance has come from Canadian provinces for whom gas and oil production is an economic mainstay but Canada as a country supports Kyoto.

and moving toward 10.8 billion in 2060 (with the greatest rate of increase in less economically developed countries), the demands made on the environment are already substantial (see the Star Box on p. 413). As the continuing destruction of the tropical rain forests shows, the search for living space and natural resources continues unabated despite our knowing the experiences of those who damaged the environment in earlier decades. Complete the Personal Assessment on p. 431 to see if you're an environmentalist.

HUMAN POPULATION EXPLOSION

Many scientists warn that the human population is increasing at a rate that cannot be sustained by the resources of the Earth. Every year the world's population grows by about 78 million people, with 97% born into the poorest countries.[3] Consider the vast problems we face with the current population, including depletion of natural resources (freshwater, food, and oil), air and water pollution, conflict and political upheaval, starvation, and destruction of natural communities. Now imagine trying to solve these problems in the 21st century with twice as many people trying to make a living and raise a family on the same Earth.

The effects of the human population explosion on personal health depend on who you are and where you live. Many of the poorer nations of Asia, Africa, and

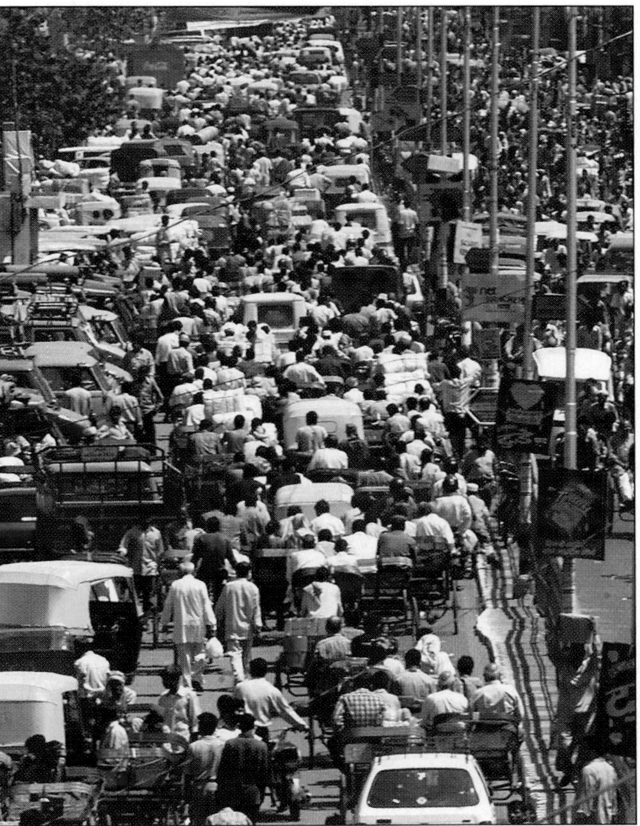

Overpopulation is often evident in large urban centres, as this typical street scene in New Delhi illustrates. The migration of people from surrounding rural areas into urban centres throughout the developing world can overload an already burdened infrastructure.

South America will not be able to feed their people; starvation and associated diseases will be major health problems for these populations. Growing populations in dry regions are exceeding their freshwater supply, and hundreds of millions of people must drink from contaminated water sources. Every year, 5 million children die from waterborne diarrhea diseases associated with unsanitary drinking water.[4] By 2025, 2.5 billion people may live in regions where available freshwater is insufficient to meet their needs.

In many extremely poor countries, hungry people will destroy most or all of the remaining natural communities (tropical rain forests, African savanna) in vain efforts to grow food on lands that are not suited for agriculture. Six hundred thousand square miles of forest were cut down worldwide in the 1990s. How much will remain in a world with 10 billion people? Overcultivation of farmlands has already degraded the fertility of a land area equivalent to that of the United States and Canada combined.[5] Hungry people on oceanic islands destroy their coral reefs by using dynamite or cyanide to catch

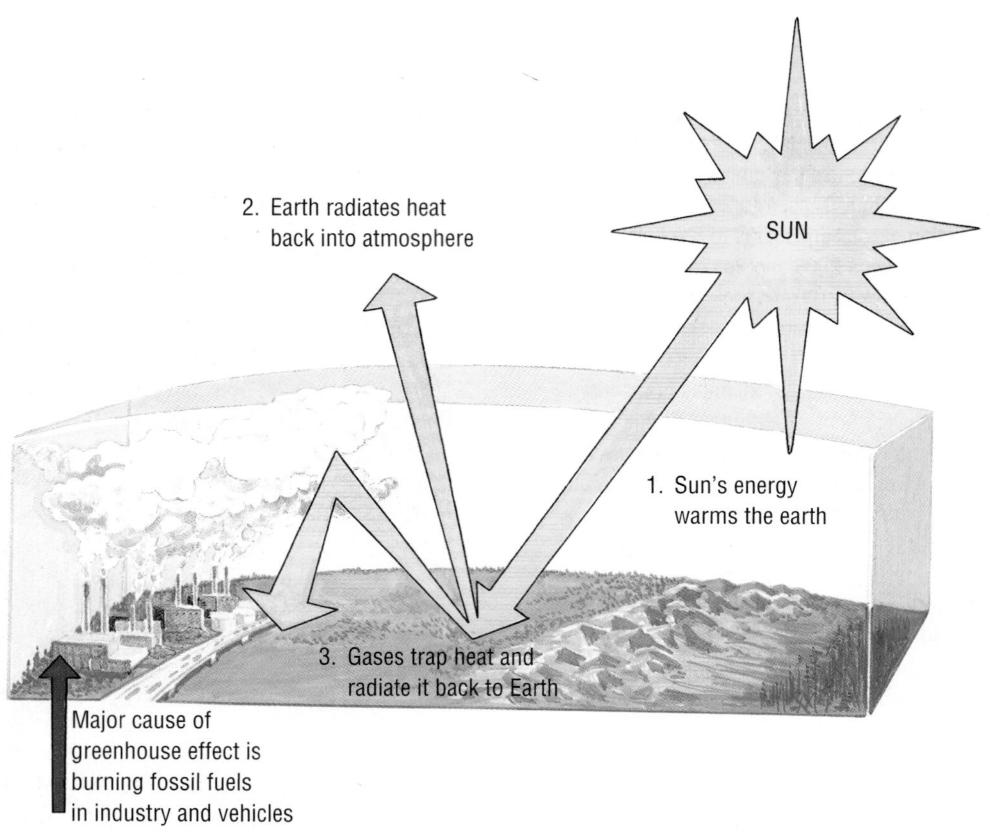
2. Earth radiates heat back into atmosphere
SUN
1. Sun's energy warms the earth
3. Gases trap heat and radiate it back to Earth
Major cause of greenhouse effect is burning fossil fuels in industry and vehicles

Figure 17–2 The greenhouse effect.

fish. In Africa hungry people hunt wild game for food, putting more species at risk of extinction.

Competition among nations for limited supplies of water and oil is often a root cause of political tensions, terrorism, and war. Political upheaval in the Middle East, terrorist attacks on U.S. targets, and the war in Iraq can be partially explained by competition for scarce resources (water, land, and oil). The genocide that killed hundreds of thousands in Rwanda in 1994–95 has been traced to inequitable distribution of land and associated hunger in some parts of that country.[6]

The solutions to the human population growth problem are simple in theory but often complex in their implementation. Basic population ecology theory states that the rate of population growth can be reduced if (1) women have fewer children over their lifetime, and (2) if they delay the start of their reproduction. A somewhat counterintuitive pattern is that population growth rate slows when infant survival rate is increased by better health care. Women choose to have fewer children if they are confident that the children they do have will survive.[7]

Simply providing education opportunities to girls can have major and long-lasting effects that act to reduce population growth. Girls who become educated delay having their first child; educated women have half the pregnancies of their uneducated sisters.[8] Educated women are more likely to be able to find employment outside the home. Working women usually have fewer children, and women with an independent income have a greater say about how many children they will have. Access to birth control information and affordable contraception is also needed to allow women to control their family size.

Unfortunately, these proactive initiatives are often held hostage to political and cultural controversies. The sad result is that human populations may ultimately be controlled by increased death rates associated with starvation, disease, and war, rather than reduced birth rates.

TALKING POINTS • Many citizens of the developing world feel that they should have the same rights as those in developed countries, to cut down forests and dam rivers for agriculture and commercial purposes. How would you explain to a group of such citizens that exploiting their forests and rivers this way will intensify the damage already done to the world's climate?

AIR POLLUTION

If you think that air pollution is a modern concern reflecting technology that has gone astray, keep in mind

The Ecological Footprint

The concept of the "ecological footprint" was developed by two Canadians, Mathis Wackernagel and William Rees, as a way of assessing the sustainability of populations.
It involves measuring the estimated "load" that a population imposes on nature and natural processes. Expressed as a "footprint," it represents the area of land that is required to sustain the current level of resource consumption and waste discharge by that population. This makes it easy to compare the environmental impact of countries across the world.

The earth has a surface area of 51 billion hectares, yet only 8.3 billion hectares are biologically productive land. The remaining area is either water, or unproductive land lacking in water or covered by either ice or unsuitable soil. If divided equally, each of the 6 billion people on earth has about 1.7 hectares of ecologically productive land to draw from for resources and waste disposal. Economically developed countries draw disproportionately from the earth's ecosystem; each of their citizens leaves an ecological footprint that is much greater than his or her fair share of 1.7 hectares.

The American footprint, for example, is 5.1 hectares. The Canadian footprint is 4.8 hectares. This is the total amount of land each Canadian requires for food, housing, transport, consumer goods, and services. Energy accounts for more than half of our footprint, at 2.9 hectares. The second largest component (at 1.1 hectares) is agriculture for food supply and consumer goods. Forestry takes up 0.6 hectares to supply the fibre for housing and consumer goods such as paper. Finally, the built environment takes up 0.2 hectares for housing and transport. Compare that to those people living in India, who only require 0.8 hectares each to sustain them.

If everyone worldwide lived like the average North American, we would require at least three Earths to provide all the necessary material and energy to maintain our current lifestyle. These sorts of analyses raise questions about the implications of economic expansionism as a remedy for poverty.

that the air is routinely polluted by nature. Sea salt, soil particles, ash, dust, soot, microbes, assorted trace elements, and plant pollens are consistently found in the air. These natural pollutants are part of our global ecosystem, and in most cases provide benefits to living organisms, including humans.

Pollution caused in part by humans also has a long history. From the fires that filled our ancestors' caves with choking smoke, through the "killer fogs" of 19th-century London, to the dust storms of the Great Depression, humans have contributed to air pollution. Today, its effects can be seen in countries throughout the world. The five countries that produce the most airborne gases that contribute to global warming are the United States, Russia, Japan, China, and Brazil. In 1997, these countries met with 161 other nations including Canada, in Kyoto, Japan, to formulate a global strategy for reducing greenhouse gases.[9] (See the Star Box on p. 411.)

Sources of Air Pollution

The sources of modern air **pollution** should be familiar. A leading source is the internal combustion engine. Cars, trucks, and buses contribute a variety of materials to the air, including carbon monoxide, carbon dioxide, and hydrocarbons. Industrial processes, domestic heating, refuse burning, and the use of pesticides and herbicides also contribute to our air pollution problem. In recent years the massive deforestation of the tropical rain forest in the Amazon River basin of South America has contributed significant amounts of gaseous and particulate pollutants to the air.

Gaseous pollutants

The pollutants dispersed into the air by the sources just identified are generally in the form of gases, including carbon dioxide and carbon monoxide. Carbon dioxide is the natural by-product of combustion and is produced whenever fuels are burned. Electricity production, car and truck emissions, and industry are the principal producers of carbon dioxide.

As first predicted over a decade ago, the progressive increase in carbon dioxide appears to have resulted in a **greenhouse effect** (Figure 17–2). This effect has caused a slight but progressive warming of the earth's surface. An increase of only 0.75°C over the past century, resulting from increased trapping of industrial gases, has resulted in a shift of the world's hydrologic cycles.[10] Today the atmosphere is more laden with moisture, and air circulation

Key Terms

pollution
The introduction into the biosphere of materials that, because of their quantity, chemical nature, or temperature, have a negative impact on the ecosystem or that cannot be readily absorbed by natural recycling processes.

greenhouse effect
Warming of the earth's surface that is produced when solar heat becomes trapped by layers of carbon dioxide and other gases.

El Niño and La Niña: Weather Siblings with a Stormy Disposition

During January and February 1998, many areas of Canada and the United States experienced unusual weather, including some of unprecedented severity. Ice storms struck in Ontario and Quebec and adjacent parts of the United States, leaving millions of households without electricity for weeks. Torrential rains fell along the California coast, causing devastating floods and mudslides. Elsewhere in the world, floods ravaged Peru, China, and Bangladesh, displacing 230 million people; drought nearly destroyed the wheat crop in Australia, and forest fires burned out of control over wide areas of Indonesia when monsoon rains would normally have been falling. These unusual weather events were caused by a global weather phenomenon known as El Niño.

El Niño is a massive weather pattern that develops in the mid-latitudes of the Pacific Ocean when high pressure in the eastern Pacific sends strong trade winds blowing westward. These winds in turn push a ridge of water toward the Asian coast. When the high pressure dissipates, the mass of water now in the western Pacific begins flowing eastward, forcing a layer of cool water (called a thermocline) downward, which increases the surface temperature of the ocean. As this surface layer of warm water reaches the continental shelf along the western edge of the Americas, warm currents are deflected northward, toward B.C. and Alaska, and southward, toward Chile. Warmed by the El Niño effect, eastward-blowing winds change the weather patterns across wide areas of North and South America.

Storms intensified by El Niño have caused flooding and mudslides in many parts of the world.

La Niña, the sister of El Niño, is a rebound effect that pushes the once–eastward moving ridge of water back toward the western Pacific, where a subsequent reversal will occur, resulting in a second El Niño.

The El Niño phenomenon has occurred periodically for thousands of years. However, the increasing frequency of this weather pattern suggests the influence of global warming. How has El Niño affected the weather in your part of the country?

patterns have shifted, leading to greater extremes in all aspects of weather. Weather events over the past decade offered clear examples of these extremes, including

- Hurricanes, such as Katrina, which destroyed much of New Orleans
- Torrential rains along the entire California coast, which caused flooding and mudslides
- Ice storms in Ontario and Quebec
- Record snow depths in the Maritimes and Newfoundland and Labrador
- Uncontrolled forest fires in Indonesia caused by the absence of monsoon rains
- Drought and massive brush fires in Australia
- Flooding in Peru
- **Tsunami** in South Asia

As a northern country, Canada is particularly affected by global warming. Low snowfalls are creating dust-bowl conditions on prairie farmland. Water levels in the St. Lawrence Seaway and Great Lakes are falling, and arctic habitats are disappearing. See the Star Box above for an explanation of *El Niño* and *La Niña* and their role in creating these unusual weather conditions.

Whether these trends will continue is, of course, uncertain. Current attempts to reduce hydrocarbon emissions could be effective enough to begin moderating the temperature increase noted during the past century.

Carbon monoxide is a colourless and odourless gas produced when fuels are burned incompletely. Also occurring in gaseous form are methane, from decaying vegetation; the terpenes, produced by trees; and benzene and benzo(a)pyrene, which may cause cancer when taken into the respiratory system.[11]

Nitrogen and sulfur compounds are pollutants produced by a variety of industrial processes, including the burning of high–sulfur content fuels, especially coal. When nitrogen and sulfur oxides combine with moisture in the atmosphere, they are converted to nitric and sulfuric acid. The resulting **acid rain**, acid snow, and acid fog are responsible, for example, for the destruction of aquatic life and vegetation.[12] Acid rain is currently threatening 15 000 lakes and forests in eastern Canada.

In urban areas located in cooler climates (or other cities during the winter months), sulfur oxides and particulate matter (from heating systems) combine with moisture to form a grayish haze, or **smog**. This *gray-air* *smog* contributes to respiratory problems that are common in these areas during the winter months. In warmer areas, or during the summer months in other areas, brown-air smog develops when hydrocarbons and particulate matter from automobile exhaust interact in the presence of sunlight.[13] This photochemical smog produces ozone. Ozone is highly reactive to the human respiratory system, plants, and materials such as rubber.

An environmental concern currently being studied is the destruction of the ultraviolet light–absorbing **ozone layer**.[14] Nitrous oxides and materials containing **chlorofluorocarbons (CFCs)** can destroy this protective ozone layer within the stratosphere. Nitrous oxides come from the burning of fossil fuels like coal and gasoline. CFCs are used in air conditioners, many fast-food containers, insulation materials, and solvents.

Although changes in the ozone layer have been recognized for over 15 years, the progress of deterioration is advancing in spite of international efforts to slow its pace. Annual satellite images taken over both poles show the seasonal widening of the ozone hole, while data accumulated over a number of years confirm that the earth's ozone layer is gradually thinning. If deterioration of the ozone layer continues, health dangers such as skin cancer, cataracts, snowblindness, and premature wrinkling of skin will continue to increase.

Particulate pollutants

There are many particulate pollutants, including both naturally occurring materials and particles derived from industrial processes, mining, agriculture, and, of course, tobacco smoke. Inhalation of particulate matter can cause potentially fatal respiratory diseases, including those caused by quartz dust, asbestos fibres, and cotton fibres.

Trace mineral elements, including lead, nickel, iron, zinc, copper, and magnesium, are also among the particles polluting the air. Chronic **lead toxicity** is among the most serious health problems associated with this form of air pollution, although significant progress has been made because of legislation requiring the use of nonleaded gasoline. However, even today, lead toxicity is disproportionately seen in children of low-income families, principally because of the lead-based paints found in older houses, heavy motor vehicle traffic on city streets, and the use of lead soldering in older plumbing systems. For these children, lower IQs, learning disabilities, attention deficit hyperactivity disorder, delinquency,[15] and hypertension[16] may result.

Temperature Inversions

On a normal sunny day, radiant energy from the sun warms the ground and the air immediately above it. As this warmed air rises, it carries pollutants upward and disperses them into a larger, cooler air mass above. Cool air sinking to replace the rising warmed air minimizes the concentration of pollutants.

On those occasions when high pressure settles over an area, warm air can be trapped immediately above the ground. Unable to rise, this trapped, warm, polluted air layer stagnates and produces a potentially health-threatening *subsidence inversion*.[17] (This is the inversion layer that meteorologists talk about on the evening news.)

A second form of thermal inversion, *radiation inversion*, is frequently seen during winter.[18] At this time of year, late-afternoon cooling of the ground causes a layer of cool air to develop under a higher, warmer layer of air. With the inability of the cool layer of air to rise, pollutants begin to accumulate near the ground and remain there until the next morning. Warming of the ground later in the morning restores the heating of the lower-level air and re-establishes the normal dispersal of pollutants.

Indoor Air Pollution

Not all air pollution occurs outside. Concern is growing over the health risks associated with indoor air pollution. Toxic materials, including cigarette smoke (see Chapter 9), asbestos, radon, formaldehyde, vinyl chloride, and cooking gases, can be found in buildings ranging from houses and apartments to huge office complexes and manufacturing plants.

Key Terms

tsunami
A sea wave of local or distant origin that results from large-scale seafloor displacements associated with large earthquakes, major submarine slides, or exploding volcanic islands.

acid rain
Rain that has a lower pH (i.e., is more acidic) than that normally associated with rain.

smog
Air pollution made up of a combination of smoke, photochemical compounds, and fog.

ozone layer
Layer of triatomic oxygen that surrounds the earth and filters much of the sun's radiation before it can reach the earth's surface.

chlorofluorocarbons (CFCs)
Gaseous chemical compounds that contain chlorine and fluorine.

lead toxicity
Blood lead level above 25 micrograms/decilitre.

Exploring Your Spirituality

Religious Perspectives on Human–Environment Relationships

Lynn White stated that the root of all the environmental problems today can be found in Judeo-Christian and Islamic scripture. According to scripture of these religious traditions, the purpose of all of creation was to meet the needs and uses of humankind. This established a dualism (human versus not human) that did not exist in earlier religions that perceived divinity in all of creation. White proposed that this dualism encourages exploitation and dominion over nature by humans, resulting in the many environmental problems facing us today.

Earth-based religions of many indigenous cultures of the world (pre-Christian Europe, Native American, African) believed that many or all aspects of the natural world were manifestations of one or more gods. Humans were perceived as being at the mercy of these powerful natural forces, and often performed religious rituals to gain favours or atone for sins against Nature. Many of these cultures appear to have lived in ecological balance with their environment. Whether this balance was the consequence of their religious beliefs, their small populations, their limited technologies, or the combination of these factors is unknown. Modern Earth-based religions (including Paganism, Wicca, Druidism, and Goddess religions) also worship the natural world as a manifestation of the energy of God or Creation. People who follow these religious traditions are often dedicated to protecting the environment.[19]

Traditional Hinduism also lacks the distinction between humankind as separate from the rest of Creation. Hindus believe that humans, gods, and nature are all parts of a single organic whole; God is present in all of Nature. Because divine forces sustain all life on Earth, Hindus believe they should live in harmony with Creation. Any abuse of Nature is considered a sacrilegious act. These traditional beliefs encourage Hindus to live in balance with their environment. However, in their efforts to develop a modern economic system in India, many Hindus have abandoned these traditional beliefs: in recent decades India has suffered from the same environmental degradation as many other developed nations.[20]

In the Islamic tradition, humankind is considered the most favoured of God's creation, and all the rest of Creation is deemed subservient to human needs and uses. However, Islamic tradition also holds that all living things in Nature are partners of humankind, deserving of respect and their own existence. Islamic tradition also stipulates that humankind should be good stewards of natural resources and should not pollute clean waters with their wastes. Muslims are encouraged to put the common good ahead of personal benefit, and to be moderate in consumption, including the use of natural resources.[21]

While the Judeo-Christian scripture has passages that could be seen as justifying environmentally destructive behaviour, it also has distinctly environment-friendly teachings. In the Judeo-Christian tradition, God created the heavens and Earth, the land and waters, the plants and animals, and humankind. At the end of each day of Creation, the Bible states that God saw each of his creations was "good." Some theologians interpret these statements to mean that the Creator valued all aspects of Creation, not just humankind. Several biblical passages invoke human responsibility to be "good stewards" over the other parts of Creation. However, other passages in the Bible are less environmentally friendly, including statements that humankind should "go forth and multiply" and "subdue the Earth." These passages are often cited by those who seek a religious basis to justify unchecked human population growth and environmental destruction in pursuit of human goals.

The National Religious Partnership for the Environment is an umbrella organization for Christians and Jews who believe that protecting the environment is a mandate well-founded in their scriptural traditions.[22] This association of religious congregations works to increase awareness of the environmental message in the Bible and Torah. A main objective of this association is to enhance the activity of its members in the political process in support of environmental protection. For people who are committed to protecting the environment and dedicated to their Judeo-Christian religion, this organization offers a community of like-minded people working toward similar goals.

Of all of the indoor air pollutants, none is of greater concern than *tobacco smoke*. Many provinces have legislated no-smoking laws in public buildings, including restaurants. The dangers of secondhand and mainstream tobacco smoke have been examined in Chapter 9.

Radon gas is a form of indoor air pollution whose role as a serious health risk is currently under investigation.[23] This radioactive gas enters buildings through a variety of routes (the water supply, block walls, slab joints, drains, even cracks in the floor) from underlying rock formations and stone building materials where it is found. Because radon gas can concentrate when air is stagnant, energy-efficient airtight homes, schoolrooms, and buildings are most affected. A national survey conducted over 20 years ago reported elevated levels of radon in some houses in Winnipeg and Regina as well as in a number of mining communities in Ontario and Saskatchewan. The levels found were not felt to pose an unacceptable risk to homeowners in these areas.[24] Radon buildup is a concern because of the relationship of radon exposure to the development of lung cancer.

Environmental tobacco smoke and radon gas join formaldehyde (from building material), vinyl chloride (from PVC plumbing), and other pollutants (including asbestos from insulation) to form the basis of the *sick building syndrome.*[25] For people with respiratory illnesses and immune system hypersensitivities, as well as the elderly, home or work sites could be less healthy than was once thought.

Health Implications

Because of the complex nature of many health problems, it is difficult to assess clearly the effects of air pollution on health. Age, gender, genetic predisposition, occupation, residency, and personal health practices complicate this assessment. Nevertheless, air pollution may severely affect health problems for elderly people, people who smoke or have respiratory conditions such as asthma, and people who must work in polluted air.

WATER POLLUTION

Although water is the most abundant chemical compound on the earth's surface, we are finding it increasingly difficult to maintain a plentiful and usable supply. Pollution, excessive use, and misuse are depriving people of the water they need to meet their typical needs (see Table 17–1).

As the stewards of 9% of the world's renewable fresh water supply, Canada is a water-rich nation. Yet, globally, Canadians are the second-highest users of water in their day-to-day lives, after the United States. Our high per capita water usage, coupled with other stressors such as population densification, puts pressure on Canada's fresh water resources. The 2000 tragedy of Walkerton, Ontario, where seven people died and thousands were made ill from drinking water polluted with a particular strain of the *E. coli* bacterium, is one example of the crisis this country could face if fresh water resources are not cared for. While we enjoy one of the highest standards of clean water in the world, in many areas, people cannot drink their local water without first boiling it, swim in their regional lakes, or eat the fish they catch from them.[26]

Yesterday's Pollution Problem

Like air pollution, water pollution is not solely a phenomenon of 20th-century overpopulation or unchecked technology. Throughout history, humans have routinely polluted surface and ground water, including their own drinking water supplies. Both urban and agricultural sewage, largely composed of human and animal intestinal pathogens such as *E. coli,* have caused disease and often death among those unfortunate enough to rely on this water for drinking.

Table 17–1 Home Water Use

Use	Litres
Washing car	400
Taking a bath	140
Washing clothes	125–250
Washing dishes	40–115
Brushing teeth	40–75
Shaving	40–75
Watering lawn	30/min
Taking a shower	
regular shower head	20/min
low-flow shower head	7/min
Flushing toilet	20–25
Leaky faucet	8/day

Today's Pollution Problem

Today, water sources are most often damaged by pollutants from agricultural, urban, and industrial sources. Most of these pollutants are either biological or chemical products, and many can be either removed from the water or brought within acceptable safety limits. For some pollutants, however, management technology has been only partially successful or is still being developed.

TALKING POINTS • You are concerned about the safety of your drinking water. What questions would you ask your municipal authorities?

Sources of Water Pollution

Water pollution is not the result of only one type of pollutant. In fact, many sources of water pollution exist.

Pathogens

Pathogenic agents, in the form of bacteria, viruses, and protozoa, enter the water supply through human and animal wastes. Communities with sewage treatment systems designed around a combined sanitary and storm system can, during heavy rain or snow melt, allow untreated sewage to rush through the processing plant.

Key Term

radon gas
A naturally occurring radioactive gas produced by the decay of uranium.

In addition, pathogenic organisms can enter the water supply when sewage is flushed from boats. Pathogenic agents are also introduced into the water supply from animal wastes at feed lots and at meat processing facilities.

During heavy rain, pathogens such as **coliform bacteria**, of which *E. coli* is the most common, may be washed into creeks, rivers, streams, lakes, or groundwater. When these are used as sources of drinking water—and the water is not treated or is inadequately treated—*E. coli* and other pathogens may end up in drinking water. In 2000, mismanagement of the Walkerton, Ontario, water treatment program resulted in unchecked contamination of the town's water supply by a particularly toxic strain of *E. coli.*

Municipalities are responsible for ensuring that their water is safe to drink. They do this by setting regulations for sewage and industrial outflow, as well as through treatment of water to meet national safety standards. Sewage treatment plants and public health laboratories routinely test for the presence of pathogenic agents.

Biological imbalances

Aquatic plants tend to thrive in water rich in nitrates and phosphates. This overabundance leads to **eutrophication**, which can render a stream, pond, or lake unusable.[27]

During hot, dry summers, aquatic plants die in large numbers. Since the decay of vegetation requires aerobic bacterial action, the biochemical oxygen demand will be high.[28] To satisfy the biochemical oxygen demand, much of the water's oxygen is used. When such a condition exits, fish may be killed in great numbers. **Putrefaction** of the dead fish not only further pollutes the water but also fouls the air.

Toxic substances

Of the pollutants found in today's surface water and groundwater supply, perhaps none are of greater concern than toxic chemical substances. These chemical toxins, including metals and hydrocarbons, are dangerous because when in the surface water, they have the ability to enter the food chain. When they do, their concentration per unit of weight increases with each life form in the chain. By the time humans consume the fish that have fed on the contaminated lower forms of aquatic life, the toxic chemicals have been concentrated to dangerous levels.[29] In groundwater supplies, of course, toxic substances are consumed directly by humans in drinking water.

Among the important toxic substances is mercury in the form of methyl mercury. Derived from industrial wastes, methyl mercury is ingested and concentrated by shellfish and other fish. When humans eat these fish regularly, mercury levels increase to the point that hemoglobin and central nervous system function can be seriously impaired.

A variety of other metals have also been found in North American rivers, lakes, and groundwater sources. In the surface water, arsenic, cadmium, copper, lead, and silver are all capable of entering the food chain. In many cases, only very low levels of these metals need to be taken into the body before damage to health becomes evident.

Of the wide variety of agricultural products currently used on Canadian and American farms, *pesticides* and *herbicides* are among the most toxic. Containing more than 1800 different chemical compounds, these agricultural products deliver a diverse array of chemicals to our water supplies, as well as directly on or in the food that people eat. The level of herbicides in the water supply rises particularly rapidly during the summer months.

Today there is mounting concern regarding pesticides and herbicides and the development of testicular cancer and drop in sperm production in men, leukemia in children, and breast cancer in women.[30]

Among the most serious of the toxic chemicals found in our water are the chlorinated hydrocarbons, including *DDT* (dichlorodiphenyltrichloroethane), *chlordane*, and *Kepone* (chlordecone). While DDT has been banned, it resists decay and continues to be found both in wildlife and human tissues in Canada. The **mutagenic, carcinogenic**, and **teratogenic** effects of these hydrocarbon products continue to receive careful study.

PCBs (polychlorinated biphenyls) are another group of hydrocarbons causing a great deal of concern because of their presence in the water supply[31] and in the food chain. For example, beluga whales in the St. Lawrence River have blood levels of PCBs (and pesticides) 10 times higher than belugas in the North. PCBs are, on the basis of their chemical structure, very stable, heat-resistant compounds that have been used extensively in transformers and electrical capacitors. In many areas of the country, discarded electrical equipment has broken open and released PCBs into the surrounding water supply. Environment Canada now sets strict limits on the amount of PCBs permitted for use in electrical equipment in this country. Tests are now being conducted at these dump sites to determine the extent of contamination of the underground water supply. In laboratory animals, PCBs produce liver and kidney damage, gastric and reproductive disorders, skin lesions, and tumours.[32] Studies on people who have been exposed to high levels of PCBs in drinking water are ongoing. It is now known that PCBs can concentrate in the fat that makes up breast tissue and that they have been found in women with breast cancer.

Other sources

Three additional types of pollution that affect our water are important, although their effect on human health is not fully understood. The pollution from these sources is

Reducing Risk of Waterborne Illness When You Travel Abroad

If you travel to other countries, especially developing countries in Asia, Africa, or South America, you should be aware that drinking water in many of these countries may be contaminated with biological pollutants. One report estimated that 30% of travellers contract some form of traveller's diarrhea during a typical one-week vacation abroad.[33] To minimize your risk, you should consider the following:

1. Drink only bottled water or soft drinks from a reputable source (read the label). Do not drink unpasteurized milk.
2. If you cannot find bottled drinks, boil, filter, or chemically treat with purification tablets any water you put in your mouth, including when you brush your teeth.
3. Avoid using ice, which is often made with unsafe tap water.
4. Eat only well-cooked foods, and avoid seafood, undercooked meat, and raw fruits or vegetables that you did not peel and wash. You are more likely to get sick from contaminated food than from water.[34]
5. As much as possible, keep flies away from your food. Open sewers are not uncommon in many underdeveloped countries. Flies lay their eggs in the sewers and then join you for lunch.
6. Check with your doctor to determine which immunizations against waterborne diseases you need for the countries you plan to visit.
7. In addition to these preventive measures, you should also bring over-the-counter diarrhea medicine (such as Imodium or Pepto Bismol) and ask your doctor for an antibiotic prescription (Ciprofloxacin), just in case.[35] Some authors suggest that taking Pepto Bismol (2 tablets or 2 liquid oz., four times per day) can reduce your risk of developing diarrhea by 60%.[36]

detrimental to aquatic life; alters the aesthetic value of our waterways; and reduces recreational use of our rivers, lakes, and shores.

Oil spills include not only the severe spills resulting from tanker accidents but also spills that occur on inland waters and those that result from the seeping of crude oil from the ground. Any kind of oil spill can foul our water. Fish, aquatic plants, seabirds, and beaches can be damaged by both surface-oil film and tar masses that float below the surface or roll along the ocean bottom. Less noticeable but potentially harmful to human health is the contamination of groundwater by inappropriately disposed of oil-based products or by gasoline leaking from underground storage tanks.

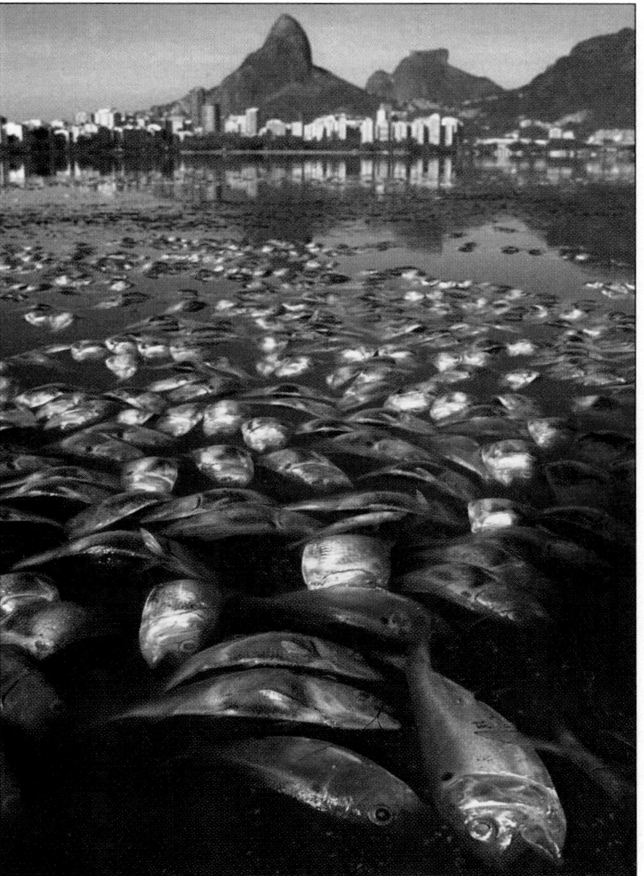

Water pollution can be an insidious force, wreaking havoc on ecosystems.

Key Terms

coliform bacteria
Intestinal tract bacteria whose presence in a water supply suggests contamination by human or animal waste.

eutrophication
Enrichment of a body of water with nutrients, which causes overabundant growth of plants.

putrefaction
Decomposition of organic matter.

mutagenic
Capable of promoting genetic alterations in cells.

carcinogenic
Related to the production of cancerous changes; property of environmental agents, including drugs, that may stimulate the development of cancerous changes within cells.

teratogenic
Capable of promoting birth defects.

Finding a viable solution to solid waste disposal is becoming increasingly difficult as the amount of garbage produced increases and the availability of land for disposal sites decreases.

Power plants that use water from lakes and rivers to cool their steam turbines cause *thermal pollution*. When this heated water is returned to its source, temperatures in the water may rise significantly. As temperatures increase, the oxygen-carrying capacity of the water decreases and the balance of aquatic life forms is altered. In water that is raised only 10° C (18° F), entire species of fish can disappear and aquatic plants can proliferate out of control.[37]

Finally, *sediments* in the form of sand, clay, and other soil constituents regularly reach waterway channels. Rivers, lakes, reservoirs, and oceans serve as settling basins for these sediments. If cleared land areas cannot be returned to vegetative cover, then dredging may be required to keep the waterway usable, although this is an expensive and relatively ineffective response.

Effects on Wetlands

The progressive loss of wetlands resulting from drainage and the dumping of debris is of great concern. With the loss of wetlands, the natural habitat for countless species of fish, shellfish, birds, and marine mammals is lost. Canada's wetlands are disappearing at an alarming rate. On a more positive note, concerted efforts to re-establish wetlands are occurring throughout the country. Unfortunately, at the same time, continued loss occurs in other areas.

Health Implications

When water becomes polluted, its quality falls below acceptable standards for its intended use, and some aspects of our health will be harmed (see the Star Box on p. 419). Polluted water is associated with disease and illness, but it also distresses us emotionally, limits our social activities, and challenges us intellectually and spiritually to become more active stewards of our environment.

LAND POLLUTION

Since we live, work, and play on land, it may be difficult to believe that land constitutes only about 30% of the earth's surface. The rest is, of course, water. When we consider the rivers, streams, marshes, and lakes found on our land surfaces, our land surface seems even smaller. Uninhabitable land areas, such as swamps, deserts, and

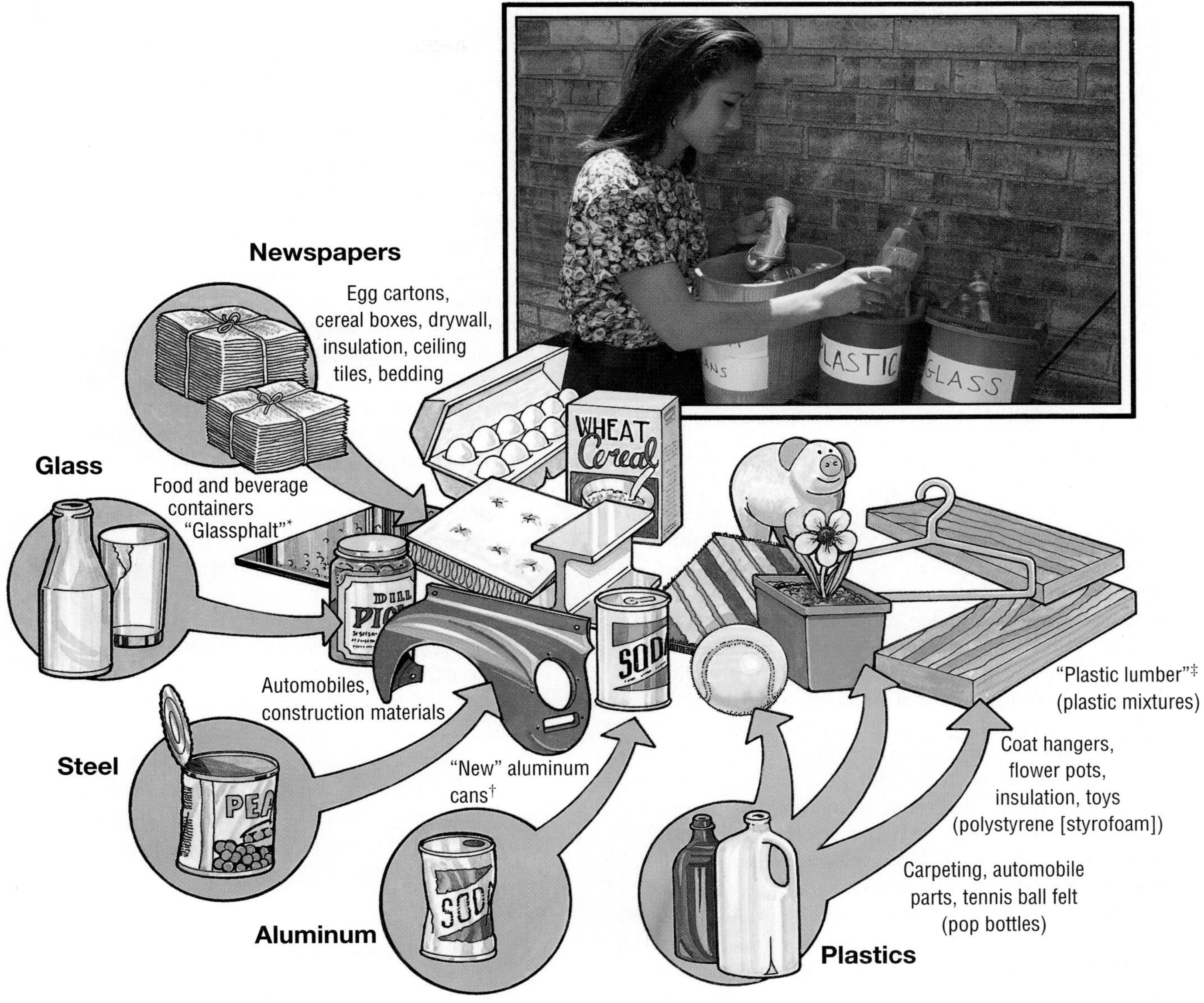

Figure 17–3 Many useful products can be made from recycled materials. The amount of material that is recycled depends on consumer demand for these products. Would you be willing to use an alternative product made from recycled components, such as a deck made of plastic lumber?

mountain ranges, further reduce the available land on which humans can live. Our land is a precious commodity —one that we have taken for granted.

The effects of our growing population on our limited land resources are becoming more evident. However, the greatest effect on our land comes from the products our society discards: *solid waste* products and *chemical waste* products.

Solid Waste

The garbage that is collected from our homes is composed of a wide variety of familiar materials. Each year, Canadians dispose of paper, newspaper, cardboard, clothing, yard waste, wood pallets, food waste, glass, metal, disposable tableware, plastics, and an endless variety of other types of solid waste. Agricultural, mining, and industrial wastes contribute even more to our solid waste problems. On a per capita basis, Canadians generate approximately 1000 kg of solid waste annually. Regardless of the source, solid waste requires some form of disposal. Traditionally, these forms have been taken:

- *Open Dumping*. Solid waste is compacted and dumped on a dump site. Open dumps are discouraged or illegal in many urban areas.
- *Sanitary Landfill*. Solid waste is compacted and buried in huge open pits. Each day, a layer of soil is pushed over the most recently dumped material to encourage decomposition, reduce unpleasant odours, and contain the material to keep it from being scattered.
- *Incineration*. Solid waste can be incinerated. A variety of types of incinerators exist, including cement kilns, boilers and furnaces, and commercial incinerators.
- *Ocean Dumping*. When near enough to the ocean, solid waste can also be collected, loaded into barges, and taken to offshore dump sites.

Open and ocean dumping have obvious implications for polluting the environment. Landfills use valuable land, but are also a significant source of greenhouse gases, and often contribute to groundwater contamination and air pollution. Modern incinerators, while superior to those of previous decades, still emit fine particulates, acid gases, carbon dioxide, and toxic chemicals.

Additionally, a large proportion of solid waste represents lost resources. To solve the problem of solid waste disposal, Canadians must be committed to reducing, reusing, and **recycling** waste to save resources and prevent contamination of the environment (see the Star Box on this page). It has been difficult to convince manufacturers and the public that many of our solid waste products should be recycled. Efforts to recycle glass, aluminum, paper, and plastic (see Figure 17–3) have not been fully adopted by society. The cost of recycling and a lack of markets for reclaimed materials often discourage municipalities and industries from practising more recycling. In jurisdictions committed to reducing solid waste, recycling and other programs have shown to be remarkably successful. For example, in British Columbia, waste recycling increased from 19% of waste generated in 1990 to 42% in 1998.[38]

TALKING POINTS • Your parents were raised in an era when recycling was not common. How would you convince them of the importance of recycling?

Chemical Waste

According to many environmental consumer group leaders, the quality of our lives is deteriorating, in part because of the unsafe disposal of hazardous chemicals from industrial and agricultural sources. Because it costs much more money to detoxify, recycle, and reuse toxic chemical products than to dump them, too many chemical companies have been more than willing to secretly and unlawfully bury their chemical wastes.

The Three R's of Controlling Solid Waste Disposal

As consumers and environmentally concerned citizens, we need to do more than control the disposal of solid waste so that it does not adversely influence our health and the health of our environment. We must prevent this waste from occurring in increasing quantities. To accomplish this goal, a commitment to reduce, reuse, and recycle must be made.

The first step in dealing with the problem of solid waste disposal is to find ways to *reduce* the use of materials that eventually pollute our environment. A concerned public willing to make do with less, such as the amount of packaging material used with small consumer products, is a positive step. As concerned citizens, we must all learn to *reuse* as much as possible. Glass milk bottles that can be used again by the dairy, as well as cloth diapers rather than the nondegradable disposable diapers, are examples of reuse at its best.

Finally, we must *recycle* as much material as possible. Recent experience has taught us that Canadians will recycle when a system for collecting material is in place. However, recycling will go only as far as the demand and a market for recycled materials exists.

When combined, the three R's of reduction, reuse, and recycling could significantly reduce our need to engage in the more expensive disposal of toxic wastes.

Pesticides

Since Rachel Carson wrote her now-classic book *Silent Spring* in 1962, the public has been aware of the potential dangers associated with the use of some **pesticides**. Although Carson's primary concern was with the pesticide DDT, a number of other hazardous pesticides have since been removed from the marketplace. Tighter controls established by the Canadian Environmental Protection Act have restricted the availability of other, less hazardous pesticides. Farmers contend they need to use effective poisons to save their crops from insect destruction. However, equal concern seems to be focused now on the effects of pesticides on food and water supplies, soil quality, animals, other insects, and humans.[39] Harmful agents such as pesticides can enter an **ecosystem** and affect the entire food chain.

Herbicides

Herbicides also contribute to the growing problem of water and soil pollution and to the contamination of the food chain. These weed-killing chemicals are sprayed on plants and incorporated into the soil through plowing but are not totally taken up by the plant tissues they are intended to kill. The extent to which herbicides cause illness in humans is not fully known, although the potential appears to be real.

RADIATION

We have lived in the nuclear age since the end of World War II. Today the hopes for nuclear energy lie primarily in its enormous potential to reduce our dependence on fossil fuels as energy sources. Also, nuclear energy can (and already does) improve our industrial and medical technology, as evidenced by an expanding use of radioactive materials in the diagnosis and treatment of various health disorders.

The two greatest concerns over nuclear energy are (1) the harmful health effects that come from day-to-day exposure to radiation and (2) the potential for a nuclear accident of regional or global consequences. A third concern, that of nuclear terrorism, also exists, but is beyond the scope of this text.

Fission, the decay of radioactive materials, produces not only a great amount of energy but also **ionizing radiation** in the form of radioactive particles. We are exposed to various forms of ionizing radiation daily through natural radiation, including ultraviolet radiation from the sun and natural radioactive mineral deposits, and synthetic radiation, including waste from nuclear reactors, industrial products, and X-ray examinations. Most of the exposures we get on a daily basis produce negligible health risks. Although it is clear that no kind of radiation exposure is good for you, safe levels of exposure are difficult to determine.

Health Effects of Radiation Exposure

The health effects of radiation exposure depend on many factors, including the duration, type, dose of exposure, and individual sensitivity. Clearly, heavy exposure (as in a severe nuclear accident) can produce **radiation sickness** or immediate death. Lesser exposure can be quite harmful as well. Of particular concern are the effects of radiation on egg and sperm production, embryonic development, and dangerous or irreversible changes to the eyes and skin. Cancer, particularly of the blood-forming tissue, is also a concern. From a health perspective, the message is clear: avoid any unnecessary exposure to radioactive materials. Make it a point to question the value of diagnostic X-ray examinations, especially routine dental and chest X-ray studies and mammograms. Routine X-ray studies have been discouraged by professional societies and consumer groups. Recent studies suggest that the risk is minimal for most people.[40]

Electromagnetic Radiation

What do waterbed heaters, electric razors, electric blankets, high-tension electrical transmission lines, and cellular telephones have in common? They all produce electromagnetic fields or electromagnetic waves, even more specifically, electromagnetic fields that come in close proximity to the body or pass very near your home, as in the case of transmission lines.

In recent years, concern has been voiced as to whether the electromagnetic fields generated by these familiar devices could cause cancer. Research using laboratory animals and studies comparing the incidence of cancer in people using these devices with those who do not have been far from conclusive. A recent study of 138 905 utility workers whose exposure to electromagnetic fields was in conjunction with power line sources did, however, show a higher than expected rate of death from brain cancer.[41] Therefore, in light of this study and until more research has been done regarding non-employment-related exposure, some care should be exercised in the use of appliances that generate radiation fields. For example, heaters for waterbeds should be turned on early to allow the bed to warm and then turned off once in the bed, cellular telephone calls should be kept short, and a morning shave should not last more than a few minutes.

Key Terms

recycling
Converting disposable items into reusable materials.

pesticide
Agent used to destroy insects and other pests.

ecosystem
An ecological unit made up of both animal and plant life that interact to produce a stable system.

ionizing radiation
Form of radiation capable of releasing electrons from atoms.

radiation sickness
Illness characterized by fatigue, nausea, weight loss, fever, bleeding from mouth and gums, hair loss, and immune deficiencies, resulting from overexposure to ionizing radiation.

The High-Tech Revolution and E-Waste

The much heralded high-tech revolution has a hidden dark side, mountains of accumulating obsolete electronic equipment that contain large amounts of toxic substances. During the period from 1997 to 2007, it is estimated that over 500 million computers must be disposed of. These computers will contain 6.2 billion pounds of plastic, 1.6 billion pounds of lead, 3 million pounds of cadmium, 1.9 million pounds of chromium, and 632 000 pounds of mercury. Lead, cadmium, chromium, and mercury are highly toxic metals, and can cause a wide range of severe health effects if they end up in the air, drinking water, or food supply.[42, 43]

Computers contain over 1000 different substances, many of which are toxic. This makes recycling a complex, labour-intensive process that can cost more than the value of the recycled materials. Only 6% of obsolete computers disposed of after 1998 were recycled. The remainder was deposited in landfills across the country. It is estimated that 70% of heavy metals such as lead and mercury going into U.S. landfills today come from electronic waste. Several states, including California and Massachusetts, have banned disposal of computer monitors in landfills to protect groundwater.[44] While recycling of computers is seen as the ideal solution to the problem of waste disposal, it is estimated that 50% to 80% of computers "recycled" before the year 2002 were actually shipped to poor Asian countries. Workers in these countries disassemble computers to recover useful materials for very low wages and with minimal or no protection from the toxic materials to which they are exposed. These countries have weak or poorly enforced environmental regulations, so materials that cannot be recycled are dumped into rivers or burned in open air pits. These practices expose the recycling workers and surrounding local populations to toxic substances.[45]

The practice of shipping toxic computer waste to underdeveloped countries is now banned by an international treaty, but the United States is the only developed nation that has not ratified this treaty. The "free market" justification for the practice of shipping toxic computer waste to underdeveloped countries is that this provides jobs and helps poor people. The question is whether or not it is moral to give poor people the choice between poverty or poisons.[46]

Given that the use of computers and electronics will only increase in the future, many argue that we must develop environmentally responsible computer recycling systems. Recently proposed legislation would require the Environmental Protection Agency to help set up computer recycling across the United States. The program would be funded by a fee of up to $10 on all retail sales of desktop and laptop PCs and computer monitors. The electronics industry favours charging consumers the fee when they return their old computers to the manufacturer rather than on new computers. Some computer manufacturers are already initiating computer take-back programs. However, development of a comprehensive national strategy for responsibly addressing the computer waste problem continues. Environment Canada, Natural Resources Canada, and Industry Canada are working together with manufacturers, provinces, territories, and other stakeholders to forge a national industry-led program to take back and properly recycle unwanted equipment.[47]

The other, and perhaps most important, approach to the computer waste problem is to develop electronic equipment that is less toxic and more easily recycled. This will require development of, and investment in, new technologies. In our free market system, this will happen only when the electronics manufacturers must share the cost of dealing with computer waste.

Nuclear Reactor Accidents and Waste Disposal

To generate the nuclear energy to produce electrical energy, more than 100 nuclear power plants have been constructed in North America. There are 14 nuclear power plants currently operating in Canada, 12 in Ontario, and one each in Quebec and New Brunswick. These nuclear power plants were designed to produce electrical energy in an efficient, economical, and safe manner. Much public criticism has been directed at these power plants, claiming that their safety and efficiency have not been documented.

Concern over the safety of nuclear power plants was heightened in this country and around the world when, on April 26, 1986, a **meltdown** occurred at the Chernobyl nuclear power plant in the former Soviet Union. Human error was responsible for creating a situation in which excessive heat was allowed to build up in the core of the nuclear reactor. The resultant explosion killed two people, hospitalized hundreds, and exposed hundreds of thousands of people to nuclear radiation. As a result of the Chernobyl accident, the Russian government had to resettle 200 000 people. Furthermore, a leading Soviet scientist estimated that 10 000 miners and soldiers died as a result of exposure to radiation received during cleanup operations after the accident.

The safe disposal of nuclear waste is an additional serious problem that also has not been fully solved. The by-products of nuclear fission remain radioactive for

Key Term

meltdown
The overheating and eventual melting of the uranium fuel rods in the core of a nuclear reactor.

Noise Pollution and Its Effects on Hearing

The loudness of sounds is measured in decibels (dB). Sound intensity is determined logarithmically, not arithmetically. Each increase of 10 dB produces a tenfold increase in sound intensity. Thus 30 dB has 10 times the intensity of 20 dB, and 40 dB has 100 times the intensity of 20 dB. Hearing damage depends on the dB level and the length of exposure. Presented below are dB ranges, common sources, and effects on hearing.

Decibel	Common sources	Effect on hearing
0	Lowest sound audible to human ear	—
30	Quiet library, soft whisper	—
40	Quiet office, study lounge, bedroom away from traffic	—
50	Light traffic at a distance, refrigerator, quiet conversation, gentle breeze	—
60	Air conditioner at 6 metres (20 feet), normal conversation, sewing machine	—
70	Busy traffic, noisy office or cafeteria	Annoying; may start to affect hearing if constant
80	Heavy city traffic, alarm clock at half a metre (2 feet), typical factory	Starts to affect hearing if exposed more than 8 hours
90	Truck traffic, noisy home appliances, shop tools, lawn mower	Temporary hearing loss can occur in less than 8 hours
100	Chain saw, pneumatic drill (jackhammer), loud motorcycle, or farm equipment	Unprotected exposure for 2 hours can produce serious damage to hearing
120	Rock band concert in front of speakers, sand blasting, loud thunderclap	Immediate danger threat
140	Shotgun blast, jet plane from 15 metres (50 feet)	Immediate pain threat; any length of exposure is dangerous
180	Rocket pad area during launch (without ear protection)	Immediate, irreversible, and inevitable hearing loss

Changing *for the Better*

Reducing Noise Pollution

I have enough stress in my life! How can I reduce the noise pollution around me?

Beyond giving your political support to legislation and enforcement policies designed to reduce environmental noise pollution, the following suggestions are a few of the recommended approaches:

- Limit your exposure to highly amplified music. The damage from occasional exposure to sound intensity between 110 and 120 decibels can be reversible. Daily exposure, however, will result in permanent hearing loss.
- Reduce the volume on your portable headsets. When others can hear the music coming through your headset while you are wearing it, you should probably turn down the volume.
- Wear ear plugs (wax or soft plastic) and sound-absorbing ear muffs when using firearms or operating loud machinery.
- Maintain your automobile, motorcycle, or lawn mower exhaust systems in good working order.
- Furnish your room, apartment, home, and office with sound-absorbing materials. Drapes, carpeting, and cork wall tiles are excellent for reducing both interior and exterior noises.
- Establish noise reduction as a criterion in selecting a site for your residence. Living near a highway or airport may prove to be less than desirable.

Since you are a person with a lifetime of hearing ahead, noise pollution reduction deserves your participation and your support.

Your Role in Creating a Sustainable Environment

As we search for solutions to complex environmental problems, we may have to make some difficult decisions. For example, will we attempt to feed the world's hungry people? Will we continue to protect endangered species of plants and animals? Will populations in some nations be forced to use contraception or sterilization? Will we strive more forcefully for nuclear disarmament? Can we commit ourselves to cleaning up all of our toxic waste sites? Answers to these complex questions about *stewardship* will probably be based not only on our knowledge but also on our moral predispositions.

Answers to these sorts of complex questions can come from recognizing the value of a *sustainable environment.* This environment will be developed only when individuals and groups are willing to do the following:

- Evaluate their environment.
- Become environmentally educated.
- Choose a simpler, less consumption-oriented lifestyle.
- Recognize the limitations of technology in solving problems.
- Become involved in environmental protection activities.
- Work with people on all sides of environmental issues.

These suggestions might sound abstract for a person confronted with a local environmental problem. However, each of these steps can be applied to a local situation with only limited modifications. How far do you think people are willing to go to make lifestyle changes that will improve the environment? What are you willing to do?

many years. Although the current method of disposing of these wastes is to bury them, eventual leakage into our environment is a serious risk.

Proponents of nuclear power maintain that not one person in Canada or the United States has died as the result of a power plant accident. They point to a spotless safety record and reiterate that our fossil fuel supply is limited. Supporters of the nuclear industry feel that a public commitment to establishing more nuclear reactors is important for the future of our country. Currently, nearly 13% of our electrical energy is generated by nuclear power.

NOISE POLLUTION

In much the same fashion that a weed is an unwanted plant and can ruin a lawn, noise is an unwanted sound that can be detrimental to our overall health. In some cases a sound that is desirable, such as music, can function like a true noise because of the intensity of the presentation. Regardless, today's world is characterized by sounds whose loudness and unrelenting presence are dangerous to our health. These intense sounds can reduce our hearing acuity, disrupt our emotional tranquility, infringe on our social interactiveness, and interrupt our concentration.

Noise-Induced Hearing Loss

Sound, or a wave of compressed air molecules moving in response to a pressure change, is characterized by two qualities—frequency and intensity. High intensity is primarily responsible for the loss of hearing experienced by many people living in noise-polluted environments. Intensity of sound exceeding 80 to 85 decibels (1200 to 4800 cycles-per-second frequency range) can cause hearing damage. The Star Box on p. 425 shows sound intensity associated with several common environmental sound sources.

The interpretation of a sound (hearing) is a sophisticated and sensitive physiological process involving the progressive conversion of acoustical energy to mechanical energy, then to hydraulic energy, and, finally, to electrochemical energy. Electrochemical energy is then transmitted by the acoustic nerve to the brain for interpretation. The destructive influence of exposure to sounds of high intensity lies in the destruction of special hair cells in the inner ear that are responsible for converting hydraulic energy into electrochemical energy. Loud music, jet engine noise, vehicular traffic, and a wide range of industrial noises can collapse these sensitive cells. Ironically, the cells that are damaged are those responsible for hearing the high-frequency sounds associated with normal conversation, not those that hear the damaging sound itself. Thus the environmental sources of noise rob you of your ability to hear sound of a far greater value—the sound of the unamplified human voice.

The damage just described is initially reversible. However, with continued exposure, the changes in the sensitive cells of the inner ear become permanent. The Changing for the Better Box on p. 425 suggests ways to reduce noise pollution.

Noise As a Stressor

In addition to the damaging effects of noise on hearing, the role of noise as a stressor has long been recognized. Indeed, the absence of noise (silence) and prolonged noise are both proven techniques to break the will of prisoners during war. Recently, however, attention has shifted to the role of noise in terms of the stress response, presented in Chapter 3. In people stressed by unrelenting noise, the elevated epinephrine levels contribute to hypertension and other stress-related health problems.

TALKING POINTS • Your roommates are unaware of the noise created by their stereo systems and computer games. How would you explain to them the effect this noise has on you?

IN SEARCH OF BALANCE

How often have you heard people yearn for a return to the "good old days"? They reminisce about times when people moved more slowly, cared more for their neighbours, and appreciated their natural resources. After listening to these nostalgic impressions, you could believe that our society was once almost idyllic—with little or no pollution, population concerns, or threats of nuclear accidents.

Certainly it is nice to dream, but it is doubtful that our advancing technology and exploding worldwide population will permit us to find such an ideal world. Instead, we need to focus on finding the appropriate balance between technological growth and environmental deterioration.

We must learn to think beyond the present. Each decision we make for the future should be considered in light of its influence on our environmental systems (see the Star Box on p. 426). If our decisions are based solely on financial gain or personal convenience, we will be committing a monumental disservice to our children and future generations.

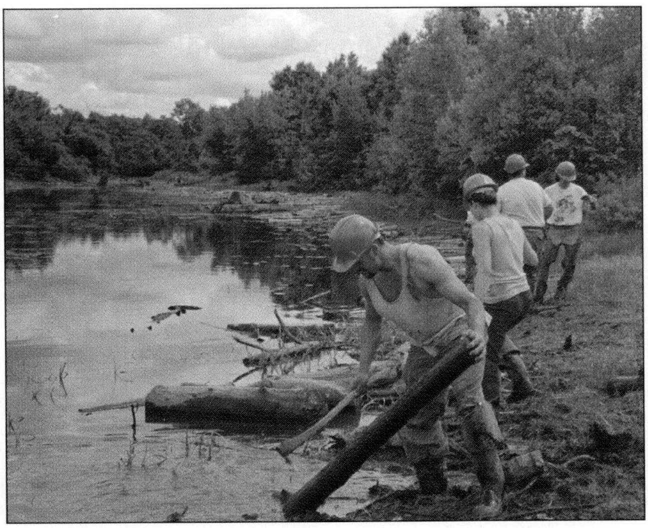

Tourism can often be an incentive for environmental cleanup efforts, as demonstrated by these individuals working to restore the natural beauty of a river in Quebec.

Taking Charge of Your Health

- Complete the Personal Assessment on p. 431 to determine if you're an environmentalist. You may be surprised at the many ways you as an individual can make a difference.
- Volunteer for an environmental cause you feel strongly about; it may be a tree-planting initiative, a public area cleanup, or beautifying your neighbourhood. If no organization exists, start one!
- Never underestimate the positive effect you can have on the environment, and don't become discouraged by the scope of some environmental problems. Your actions can inspire others to become active, concerned citizens.
- Become an example to your family as a waste watcher by reusing materials, composting organic waste, and recycling.
- Practise Earth Day—every day!

SUMMARY

- World population growth continues at an alarming rate, and wealthy nations leave an increasingly disproportionate global ecological footprint, resulting in increased environmental pressure and human suffering.
- Gases and solid pollutants contribute to air pollution and its associated health concerns.
- Worldwide increases in carbon dioxide production could result in a greenhouse effect, leading to climatic warming and extreme weather conditions.
- Acid rain, acid fog, and acid snow, as well as smog, result from the release of gaseous and particulate pollutants into the air.
- Deterioration of the ozone layer could result in exposure to high levels of ultraviolet radiation and serious health problems.
- Particulate matter, including fibres and trace mineral elements, are found in the air.
- Temperature inversions increase the seriousness of air pollution.
- Indoor air pollution is now recognized as a serious threat to health, particularly from radon gas, which can easily accumulate in modern houses.

- Water pollution results from a variety of causative agents, including toxic chemicals and pathogens from human and animal wastes.
- Increased levels of pesticides and herbicides can be found in both surface water and groundwater sources.
- Chlorine from a variety of sources, including PCBs, can also be found in both surface water and groundwater sources.
- Solid wastes are traditionally buried, dumped, or incinerated.
- Reduction, reuse, and recycling are important aspects of the prevention of environmental pollution.
- Toxic wastes from both industry and agriculture are serious sources of land pollution.
- As with water pollution, pesticides and herbicides have been found to pollute land.
- Radiation, including ultraviolet and ionizing radiation from nuclear power plants, could result in serious health problems.
- Electromagnetic radiation may be associated with severe health problems, including brain cancer.
- Noise pollution can lead to hearing loss, particularly the ability to hear the human voice.
- We must seek a balance between lifestyle and the health of the environment, not only for our generations but also for those who will follow.

REVIEW QUESTIONS

1. In what direction is the world population changing? What could be the consequences of this change on the environment? How can the rate of this change be moderated?
2. What is the greenhouse effect? How does deforestation influence this process? What is the anticipated consequence of the greenhouse effect?
3. How are acid rain, acid fog, and acid snow produced? What sort of damage is attributed to them? Where does it usually occur?
4. What is causing the deterioration of the ozone layer? What steps have been taken to slow this process? What are the consequences of ozone layer deterioration?
5. What are the major particulate pollutants in our air? What is the principal risk associated with lead as a pollutant? What specific diseases are associated with particulate material in our air?
6. How are gray-air smog and brown-air smog formed? When and where is one form more likely to be seen than the other?
7. What pollutants contribute to indoor air pollution? What risks are associated with radon gas?
8. What toxic chemicals are most often the sources of water pollution? What is the consequence of having too little oxygen dissolved in water? What is thermal pollution? How do pesticides and herbicides enter both our water supply and soil? What is the principal source of the chlorine found in water?
9. What are several forms of solid waste? How much solid waste do Canadians produce per year on a per capita basis?
10. How are solid wastes most often disposed of? Why are these techniques less than fully acceptable?
11. What are the three R's of better solid waste prevention?
12. What are the principal sources of radiation that are of concern today? Which are natural sources of radiation, and which are the result of human intervention? What familiar appliances may be sources of electromagnetic fields?
13. How does noise pollution result in hearing loss? What are the most common sources of noise pollution?
14. For whom is a balance between a modern lifestyle and a healthy environment important?

THINK ABOUT THIS ...

- To what extent do your driving habits contribute to air pollution?
- In what ways do your recreational activities contribute to water pollution?
- If land were very affordable, would you build a new house on land reclaimed from a toxic waste dump site?
- How close to a nuclear power plant would you feel comfortable living?
- Is your home protected from potential radon gas leaks?
- The environmental focus of the 1990s shifted from global concerns, such as the ozone layer, deforestation, and world population, to local concerns, such as recycling and indoor air pollution. Will it now be possible to "think globally while acting locally"?
- Would you be willing to spend more for a lightbulb designed to last 20 000 hours, use little energy, and last several years rather than a much less expensive incandescent bulb to reduce energy costs?
- Do you know where the energy supply to your school or home originates? Have you ever thought about ways to reduce your dependence on this energy source?

REFERENCES

1. Commoner B. *Science and survival*, Penguin, 1967.
2. Commoner B: *The closing circle: nature, man, and technology*, 1971.
3. The Population Institute. *Population matters*, **www.populationinstitiute.org**, August 30, 2005.
4. Ibid
5. Ibid
6. Gasana J: Remember Rwanda? *World Watch* 15(5): 24–33, 2002
7. *Population matters.*
8. Ibid
9. The Kyoto agreement: what now? *Scientific American Forum*, Dec 6, 1997.
10. Climatic Research Unit, University of East Anglia (England), as reported in *Newsweek*, Jan 22, 1996.
11. Arms K: *Environmental science*, ed 2, Fort Worth, TX, 1994, Saunders College Publishing.
12. Chiras D: *Environmental science: action for a sustainable future*, ed 4, Redwood City, CA, 1994, Benjamin-Cummings.
13. Ibid.
14. Kerr JB, McElroy CT: Evidence for large upward trends of ultraviolet-B radiation linked to ozone depletion, *Science* 262:1032–1034, 1993.
15. Needleman HL et al: Bone lead levels and delinquent behavior, *JAMA* 275(3):363–369, 1996.
16. Kim R et al: A longitudinal study of low-level lead exposure and impairment of renal function. The Normative Aging Study, *JAMA* 275(15):1177–1181, 1996.
17. *Environmental science.*
18. *Environmental science.*
19. Pagan and Earth-based Religions: **www.beliefnet.com/index/index_10015.html**
20. Adhopia A: *Hinduism promotes environmental protection*. 2001. **www.indianest.com/analysis/ 018.htm**
21. Alhilaly TH: *Islam and ecology*. 1993. **www.ummah.com/islam/taqwapalace/fitness/microcosm page2.html**
22. National Religious Partnership for the Environment: **www.nrpe.org**
23. Cole L: *Element of risk: the politics of radon*, New York, 1994, Oxford University Press.
24. Environment Canada: The state of Canada's environment, 1996, *State of the environment reports.* **www.ec.gc.ca/soer-ree/English/soer/1996Report/Doc/1-8-3-4-5-1.cfm**
25. Menzie R et al: The effect of varying levels of outdoor air supply on the symptoms of sick building syndrome, *N Engl J Med* 328(12):821–827, 1993.
26. Environment Canada: Greenline™. **www.ec.gc.ca/envhome.html**. Accessed April 2002.
27. Cunningham WP, Saigo B: *Environmental science: a global concern*, ed 4, Dubuque, IA 1997, WCB/McGraw-Hill.
28. Ibid.
29. Miller GT: *Living in the environment: an introduction to environmental science*, ed 7, Belmont, CA, 1992, International Thompson.
30. Leiss JK, Savitz DA: Home pesticide use and childhood cancer: a case-control study, *Am J Public Health* 85(2): 249–252, 1995.
31. *Living in the environment.*
32. Ibid.
33. Thornton J: The clinic: gut reaction: to fight traveler's diarrhea, pack the right drugs, *National Geographic Adventure,* March 2003: 34. For additional information on options to purify water while travelling: **www.sweet-h2o.com/sweetwater/faq.html**
34. Ibid.
35. Ibid.
36. Ibid.
37. *Environmental science.*
38. British Columbia Ministry of Environment: *Annual report* 1996, Lands and Parks. **wlapwww.gov.bc.ca/main/annrep/ar9596/ar_07.htm**
39. Kelce WR et al: Persistent DDT Metabolite p,p'=DDE is a potent androgen receptor antagonist, *Nature* 357(6532): 581–585, 1995.
40. Boice J et al: Diagnostic x-ray procedures and risk of leukemia, lymphoma, and multiple myelona, *JAMA* 265(10):1290, 1991.
41. Savitz DA, Loomis DP: Magnetic field exposure in relation to leukemia and brain cancer mortality among electric utility workers, *Am J Epidemiol* 141(2):123–128, 1995.
42. Puckett J, et al: *Exporting harm: the high-tech trashing of Asia.* The Basal Action Network and Silicon Valley Toxics Coalition, 2002.
43. U.S. Environmental Protection Agency: *WasteWise update: electronics reuse and recycling.* 2003. **www.epa.gov/wastewise/pubs/wwupda14.pdf**
44. *Exporting harm.*
45. Ibid.
46. Ibid.
47. Envirozine: Mounting concerns over electronic waste, **www.ec.gc.ca/envirozine/english/issues/33/print_version_e.cfm?page=feature1**, August 30, 2005.

SUGGESTED READINGS

Cooper A, Elerling D (illustrator): *Along the seashore*, Boulder, CO, 1997, Roberts Rinehart Publishing.
This is the perfect book for parents who want to introduce their four- to eight-year-old children to nature's ecosystem. Informative text and beautiful illustrations take them to a tidal pool filled with plants and animals. The book was produced in cooperation with the Denver Museum of Natural History.

Mabey N (ed): *Argument in the greenhouse: the international economics of controlling global warming*, New York, 1997, Routledge.
This book is for readers who are interested in the international causes of global warming. It examines the problem of using past and current models and evaluates abatement strategies designed to reduce the economic, political, and cultural need to burn fossil fuels.

Quintana D: *100 jobs in the environment*, Indianapolis, IN, 1997, Macmillan.
You may care about the environment so much that you want to dedicate your life to the cause, yet you also need to earn a living. The jobs described in this book offer the perfect solution. You may have already thought of becoming a wildlife biologist, a nature preserve manager, or a water pollution investigator, but have you considered becoming a windfarmer, an exotic animal nutritionist, or a nature photojournalist? These and many other exciting job opportunities are presented in this book.

Somerville RC: *The forgiving air: understanding environmental change*, Berkeley, CA, 1996, university of California Press.
The ozone hole, acid rain, and the greenhouse effect are among the many phenomena caused by human activities. Using authoritative, up-to-date scientific information, the author educates his readers so that they can participate in important decisions that affect the environment. This reader-friendly book uses historical anecdotes to illustrate contemporary environmental issues.

Suzuki D, McConnell A: *Sacred balance: rediscovering our place in nature*, David Suzuki Foundation and Greystone Books, 1997.
This book offers concrete suggestions for meeting our physical and spiritual needs while creating a way of life that is sustainable, fulfilling, and just.

Wackernagel M, Rees W: *Our ecological footprint: reducing human impact on the earth*, 1995, New Society Publishers.
Using the concept of the ecological footprint, these Canadian experts examine the natural resources required to sustain populations.

Name ______________________________ Date ____________

Personal Assessment

Are You an Environmentalist?

When asked, many people will say that they are an "environmentalist," including political leaders who are widely criticized for decisions perceived by others to be environmentally destructive. So what is an "environmentalist"? One definition of environmentalism is that it is an ideology that values and reveres Nature, and works to protect and preserve natural systems for both ethical reasons and because humankind depends on these systems for life. However, beyond this general statement environmentalists encompass a wide diversity of beliefs and practices. For some, their environmental beliefs are a form of religion, others function mainly in the political process, and some operate like terrorist groups that use violence to fight human economic development on behalf of Earth.[1] The wide diversity of beliefs and practices encompassed under "environmentalism" creates a situation where almost anyone could claim to be an environmentalist. Perhaps more useful criteria for determining if you are an environmentalist would be (1) your awareness of how various human activities create environmental health hazards or degrade natural systems; (2) your willingness to consider your own role in creating environmental problems; and (3) your willingness to act in ways that reduce your personal risk from environmental hazards and your contribution to the causes of these hazards. These three criteria define a hierarchy of commitment to environmental protection. First you have to know a problem exists. Then you have to recognize your own part in creating that problem. The last, and most difficult, step is that you must be willing to reduce or eliminate your contribution to environmental problems. Your answers to the following questions will help you think about where you really stand on protecting the environment for yourself, your community, and all the rest of life on Earth.

Awareness of Environmental Problems

1. Have you ever read the water quality assessment provided by the supplier of your drinking water?
2. If your drinking water is from a well, do you know about potential sources of contamination (landfills or other waste disposal sites, large agricultural areas, confined feedlot livestock operations) in your watershed?
3. If your drinking water supply is from a well, do you know if your water contains potentially harmful contaminants?
4. Do you know whether or not your community wastewater treatment system occasionally dumps raw sewage into the local river, lake, or ocean during high-rainfall events?
5. If you use a gas furnace or kerosene space heater, do you know whether or not these appliances are functioning properly so as to maximize energy efficiency and minimize risks from indoor air pollution?
6. Have you ever made a note of air pollution alerts or information about high ultraviolet radiation published in a local newspaper or presented on a local TV news program?
7. Have you ever searched for information on air, water, and land pollution in your community?
8. When you eat fish, are you aware of health advisories regarding contaminants in fish (e.g., mercury, PCBs) and recommendations that you limit the amount of the fish you consume?
9. When you purchase products, do you look at packaging materials for warnings that the product contains toxic chemicals?
10. When you listen to loud music, do you think about potential long-term damage to your hearing and the nuisance noise you create for your neighbors?
11. Do you know if your community (city, region, province) has a land-use management (zoning) plan?
12. When you see new economic developments (malls, superstores, warehouses, suburban housing developments) being constructed, do you wonder if wildlife habitat is being destroyed?
13. Do you know the proposed human causes of global warming and the potential consequences of this change in climate?
14. Do you know the causes and potential health effects of depletion of the stratospheric ozone layer?
15. Do you know the link between the wood you buy and species extinctions?

Willingness to Consider Your Personal Environmental Impact

16. When you think about having a family of your own, do you worry about contributing to a rapidly growing human population that is responsible for widespread environmental degradation?
17. When you think about purchasing a vehicle, do you consider fuel efficiency more important than "image" sold by advertisers?
18. When you consider purchasing any product, do you consider the resources used, and pollution created, to produce that product?
19. When you purchase an electric appliance or a gas-powered device, do you consider energy efficiency?

Name ______________________________ Date ____________

Personal Assessment *continued*

20. When planning to build a new home, do you consider how your choices regarding location and amount of land could contribute to loss of green space and natural habitat?
21. When you use or dispose of household, yard, and automotive chemicals and fluids, do you consider that you may be contributing to local water pollution?
22. When you hear about global warming, do you recognize that your own use of electricity and gas-powered vehicles contributes to this problem?
23. Did you know that if you vent your home or automotive air conditioning system coolant while performing do-it-yourself maintenance, you are contributing to the depletion of the stratospheric ozone layer?
24. When you purchase lumber, do you wonder if the wood you are buying was harvested using environmentally sound practices, or if critical wildlife habitats or wilderness was destroyed to produce the lumber?
25. Do you consider how your vote in elections can affect government policies that impact the environment?

Willingness to Alter Your Lifestyle to Protect Yourself and the Environment

26. Would you limit the number of your own children to one or two so as to reduce your contribution to the problem of global human population explosion?
27. When you purchase a vehicle, is energy efficiency your main concern?
28. Would you use mass transit to travel from home to work, if it is available, to reduce your contribution to local air pollution and need for paving more land to expand highways?
29. When you buy a home, would you seek to minimize the distance from work and schools to reduce gas consumption, minimize air pollution, and reduce demand for construction of new roads?
30. When you buy a home, would you look for a smaller, energy-efficient home to minimize your contribution to natural resource exploitation and pollution associated with energy consumption?
31. When you buy lighting, do you buy energy-efficient lightbulbs (compact fluorescent and LED) that are initially more expensive, but more efficient and less expensive over the long term?
32. When furnishing your home, would you seek out water-efficient toilets, faucets, and shower heads that conserve fresh-water and reduce demands on wastewater treatment systems?
33. Do you set the thermostat in your home to cooler temperatures in winter and warmer temperatures in summer to conserve energy?
34. Would you invest money and effort to better insulate your home so as to reduce energy needed for heating and cooling?
35. When buying food, would you be willing to pay more for organically grown foods that were produced without the use of pesticides and fertilizers that pollute the surrounding environment?
36. Would you buy locally grown foods to support farmers (and their green spaces) in your community and reduce energy spent on long-distance transport?
37. When purchasing wood products, would you buy more expensive wood that is certified to have been harvested using environmentally sound practices?
38. Would you be willing to have something less than the perfect lawn so that you avoid using fertilizers and pesticides that contaminate local waterways?
39. Would you limit your personal consumption of material goods to mainly those things you need, so as to reduce exploitation of natural resources?
40. When you dispose of household chemicals, automotive fluids, and spent batteries, do you make the extra effort to be sure they do not end up polluting the environment, like taking them to a Tox-Away Day location?
41. Do you make the effort to recycle paper, glass, plastic, and metals?
42. When you make purchases, do you look for products made from recycled materials (e.g., post-consumer recycled paper, "plastic wood," fleece clothing made from recycled plastic)?
43. Do you limit the noise that you produce (loud music, loud car or motorcycle engines, barking dogs) to reduce noise pollution in your neighborhood?
44. Do you contribute financial support to environmental groups that promote conservation and protection of natural resources through the legal and political systems?
45. When you consider candidates for public office, do you vote for the candidates who have strong records or position statements for environmental protection?

If the majority of your answers to questions 1 to 15 are "Yes," you are likely "environmentally aware." That is, you pay attention to news stories about environmental issues or have taken an environmental science course.

Name ______________________________ **Date** ______________

Personal Assessment *continued*

If most of your answers to questions 1 to 25 are "Yes," you are "environmentally conscious." That is, you are not only aware of the problems, but beginning to think about how these problems are related to your own lifestyle.

If the majority of your answers to questions 26 to 45 are "Yes," you are likely "environmentally active." That is, you are personally involved in efforts to address environmental problems through your own lifestyle choices and through the political process.

[1] Wikipedia (The Free Encyclopedia). **www.wikipedia.org/wiki/Environmentalism**

Focus on

TELECOMMUTING

Technological advances continue to astound and amaze. In recent years, many of the most promising advances have been made in the areas of computer technology and communications technology. Computers have improved to the point where processes that used to take hours now can be performed in seconds. Communications now allow contact to be established with virtually anyplace in the world within seconds. Such advances have allowed companies and individual employees to save money and valuable environmental resources by taking advantage of telecommuting.

Loosely defined, telecommuting means working at home by logging into your office computer system from your home computer. This growing trend could transform the way business is performed. Companies and employees could save millions of dollars in transportation costs, and the potential environmental benefits from energy conservation and pollution reduction are very appealing to society as a whole. Plane flights, cab rides, and twice-daily commutes could be replaced by a walk to the computer. But will the environmental benefits of telecommuting outweigh the potential costs? And could changes in the traditional office environment prove to be unmanageable for employees and employers?

How Telecommuting Can Change Everyday Life

Debbie is a stock trader, working for a Bay Street firm. She is on top of the daily trends of the stock market and gets market price updates as they happen. She stays in contact with her clients and buys and sells stock for them on a daily basis.

But you won't find Debbie on the trading floor.

She's in Winnipeg.

Debbie is one of a growing number of employees who have opted to telecommute to work. Debbie's situation demonstrates what is possible with telecommuting using today's technology. It also illustrates the savings that are possible when conventional travel is eliminated from the daily schedule, and it shows the potential social advantages that come from working at home.[1]

When her husband's job required a move to Winnipeg, Debbie tried the traditional commuting route, keeping a regular work-week schedule in Toronto and flying to Winnipeg on the weekends. The commute took its toll, and she eventually left her job. Then she got an offer from a Bay Street firm that was willing to help accommodate her in this unusual situation. She now has separate phone lines for a fax machine, voice mail, and a direct link to her Toronto office. She also obtains up-to-the-minute stock quotes through a real-time stock market quote service. This technology has enabled Debbie to avoid the hassles of commuting and the stress of the trading floor and has allowed her to enjoy life with her family while working.

This all sounds too good to be true. However, telecommuting has been hailed as the wave of the future in business, and its potential benefits have been touted in the popular press for several years. Nevertheless, although it may have its advantages, there are some problems that may occur if telecommuting gains widespread acceptance.

Environmental Advantages and Problems

Telecommuting may have advantages with regard to conservation of natural resources. A 1990 study by the Arthur D. Little environmental consulting firm showed that significant benefits could result if telecommuting and videoconferencing could be substituted for conventional transportation. If such substitutions accounted for 10% to 20% of the time spent working, shopping, conducting meetings, and sending data, a net yearly savings of up to US$23 billion could result. We could also conserve 13 million litres of gasoline per year and reduce yearly pollution production by 1.8 million tons.[2]

Telecommuting also reduces vehicular wear and tear and lowers energy requirements and costs incurred by driving.[3] It may also reduce traffic on the roads in general. In an effort to reduce vehicular traffic problems, the U.S. Environmental Protection Agency may force California and other heavily populated states to require more telecommuting. California businesses have already been trying to find ways to reduce the number of cars coming to and from work on a weekly basis. Carpooling is already encouraged in many big Canadian cities, where multiple-passenger cars are allowed sole access to "carpool only" lanes. But telecommuting has the potential to eliminate many cars altogether from the daily commuting process, which can be painfully slow and time consuming in large metropolitan areas. Businesses in California may also be required to install more fibre-optic networks and advanced teleconferencing equipment to reduce both local and long-range travel by employees.[4]

Home-based employees will also have the ability to make their home offices more environmentally sound than the typical office. Using a personal computer that saves energy is a start.[5] Plain-paper fax machines eliminate the need to make photocopies of faxed documents, and all waste paper, foam packing materials, and toner cartridges can be recycled as well. Home-based employees can also get an energy audit for their home office to help make it as waste-free as possible.[6]

Although there appear to be many environmental advantages to telecommuting, many potential drawbacks to widespread telecommuting have been noted. As workers find that they do not need to live near urban workplaces, many of these workers may move to more rural areas to enhance their quality of life. This trend is not new, but those people who have moved out of the inner city have at least moved to communities within a moderate drive from the city. Telecommuting allows an employee to live virtually anywhere, and some experts fear that many workers may flee not just the city but the suburbs as well. These rural areas may not have the infrastructure to handle a massive influx of new residents.[7] Urban areas may face decay as citizens (and possibly businesses) leave cities.[8] Forests and openland may be destroyed as population expands in rural areas.[9]

The Social Aspects of Telecommuting

The potential advantages of telecommuting are very appealing for the individual worker. The most obvious advantage is that the employee is freed from the stress of physically commuting to the office, thus being spared the aggravation and wasted time of driving or riding to and from work.[10] Up to 3.1 billion hours of personal time could be gained by substituting telecommuting for general work activities 10% to 20% of the time.[11] Staying at home can also give workers more free time and allow employees (in some cases) to adjust their work schedules to fit their lifestyles.[12] Schedules can be more easily altered to adjust to unexpected occurrences, such as illness of a family member.[13] More time at home can allow workers more quality time with their families and may help employees develop deeper emotional relationships with their families and friends. Having more people at or near home may foster greater community stability as well.[14]

The individual telecommuter may face some problems, however. Being at home more often (and being expected to work in a home setting) may place stress on family relationships.[15] Being away from an office setting may cause workers to feel isolated from other company employees,[16,17] and their social skills may suffer as a result of lack of contact with others. The loss of the office as a community and the sense of support from coworkers may also be felt. Employees may not be able to judge the importance of their work in relation to the goals of the company.[18–20]

Supervisors may also have difficulty in evaluating the work of their employees. A loss of company loyalty may also develop if workers spend more time networking with other telecommuters than with company people.[21] Because of the increase in technology, employees may find themselves on call at all hours instead of working a normal daily schedule. Employers may begin to expect workers to be available to work anytime and anywhere[22] through the use of pagers, cellular phones, and laptop computers.

The Future is Now

Ready or not, this new era of office employment is here. It is estimated that roughly half of all workers could be telecommuting in some form by the year 2006. Technological advances are also paving the way for increased telecommuting. The advent and growth of fibre-optic systems allow information to be transmitted much more quickly and efficiently. Thus high-powered personal computers can communicate with large mainframe computers at high speed with few problems. Differences between computer brands and data types are being overcome as well. The Integrated Services Digital Network can interface with other computers regardless of the type of computer used or the data transmitted.[23] For those employees who do not want to stay tied down to the house, laptop computers and fax transmission equipment now make it possible to send and receive information from nearly anywhere.

And, as Debbie will tell you, that includes her back porch.

For Discussion ...

After weighing the pros and cons, do you think telecommuting is beneficial to the environment? Why or why not? Do you think that you would enjoy a job where telecommuting is a mandatory part of your work schedule? What personal benefits could you get from telecommuting? What are the potential drawbacks?

References

1. 1. Young J: Sand, sun, mutual fund, *Forbes* 152(10), Oct 25, 1993.
2. Raven PH, Berg LR, Johnson GB: Telecommuting: good for the planet (Envirobrief), *Environment*, Philadelphia, 1995, Saunders.
3. Cunningham S: Communication networks: a dozen ways they'll change our lives, *The Futurist* 26(1), Jan–Feb 1992.
4. Keaver M: Technology sows some seeds for environmental protection, *PC Week* 6(17), May 1, 1989.
5. Townsend AK: Setting up your green home office, E 5(4), Aug 1994.
6. Ibid.
7. Information superhighway: an environmental menace, *USA Today Magazine* 124(2604), Sept 1995.
8. Communication networks.
9. Information superhighway.
10. Lundquist E: A Labor Day look at PCs; home work, *PC Week* 12(35), Sept 4, 1995.
11. Telecommuting.
12. A Labor Day look.
13. Sullivan N: Double whammy, *Home Office Computing* 12(5), May 1994.
14. Communication networks.
15. Ibid.
16. Ibid.
17. A Labor Day look.
18. Ibid.
19. Double whammy.
20. Connelly J: Let's hear it for the office, *Fortune* 131, Mar 6, 1995.
21. Ibid.
22. A Labor Day look.
23. Communication networks.

Exam Prep

Chapter 1

Charting a Plan for Behaviour Change

MULTIPLE CHOICE

1. What health strategy involves following specific eating plans or exercise programs?
   A. Health screenings
   B. Education activities
   C. Behaviour changes
   D. Regimentation
2. Why is it necessary to formulate an initial adult identity?
   A. To answer the question, "Who am I?"
   B. To have a productive and satisfying life
   C. To help you move through other stages of development
   D. All of the above
3. Which developmental task involves using your own resources to follow a particular path?
   A. Forming an initial adult identity
   B. Assuming responsibility
   C. Establishing independence
   D. Developing social skills
4. Which of the following statements is *false*?
   A. The deeper the emotional relationships a person has, the better.
   B. Maintaining and improving your health is an important responsibility.
   C. The need to interact socially will at times negatively influence your health.
   D. Development of social skills can enhance your independence from your family.
5. Which of the following is *not* a dimension of health?
   A. Transitional dimension of health
   B. Emotional dimension of health
   C. Holistic dimension of health
   D. Both A and C
6. Which dimension of health do some professionals believe to be the "core of wellness"?
   A. Emotional
   B. Spiritual
   C. Social
   D. Intellectual
7. Why is the occupational dimension of health important?
   A. Because you won't be happy unless you make a lot of money after graduation
   B. Because both external and internal rewards from work affect your happiness
   C. Because when people feel good about their work, they are more likely to live a healthier lifestyle
   D. Both B and C
8. Which of the following is a strategy for changing your behaviour?
   A. Make a personal contract to accomplish your goals.
   B. "Go it alone!" It is better not to involve family or friends.
   C. Don't reward yourself until you get to the final outcome.
   D. Don't let any obstacles occur or you will fail.

CRITICAL THINKING

1. What is health?

2. What is meant by the term *wellness*?

3. How does empowerment affect overall health and well-being?

4. Which dimensions of your health would you like to improve, and why?

5. How do you plan to successfully complete your developmental tasks?

Chapter **2**

Achieving Psychological Wellness

MULTIPLE CHOICE

1. Emotionally well people
   A. Experience the full range of human emotions but are not overcome by them.
   B. Are concerned only with their own well-being.
   C. Set goals that are far and above what they can realistically accomplish.
   D. Trust only those who have proven their worth.

2. What factors shape self-esteem?
   A. Warm and supportive physical contact
   B. Religious indoctrination leading to guilt
   C. Failure to be successful in early undertakings
   D. All of the above

3. What three traits show a person's hardiness?
   A. Success, direction, and ability
   B. Commitment, control, and challenge
   C. Commitment, self-control, and self-esteem
   D. None of the above

4. What type of depression may occur after the death of a spouse or some other period of difficulty?
   A. Primary depression
   B. Reactive depression
   C. Chemically induced depression
   D. None of the above

5. Which is the most mature form of conflict resolution?
   A. Dialogue
   B. Submission
   C. Persuasion
   D. Aggression

6. What is the first step toward taking a proactive approach to life?
   A. Undertaking new experiences
   B. Taking risks
   C. Accepting mental pictures
   D. None of the above

7. Which of the following are motivational needs defined by Maslow?
   A. Physiological needs
   B. Economic needs
   C. Sexual needs
   D. Material needs

8. Which of the following statements describes creative individuals?
   A. They are intuitive and open to new experiences.
   B. They are less interested in detail than in meaning and implications.
   C. They are flexible.
   D. All of the above

CRITICAL THINKING

1. What is meant by a "normal range of emotions"?

2. What are some ways to overcome feelings of loneliness and shyness?

3. What are the warning signs of suicide, and how should they be treated?

4. What is the four-step process that allows one to control the outcomes of experiences and learn about one's emotional resources?

5. How do faith and spirituality affect emotional well-being?

Chapter 3

Managing Stress

MULTIPLE CHOICE

1. An event that produces stress is called a
   A. Response
   B. Stressor
   C. Type B
   D. None of the above

2. Positive stress is called
   A. Eustress
   B. Distress
   C. Type R stress
   D. None of the above

3. Which of the following is *not* a stage in Selye's general adaptation syndrome model?
   A. Alarm reaction stage
   B. Relaxation stage
   C. Resistance stage
   D. Exhaustion stage

4. Which part of the body is responsible for the interconnection between the nervous system and the endocrine system?
   A. Hypothalamus
   B. Pituitary gland
   C. Adrenal gland
   D. None of the above

5. When the body perceives stress, a number of responses are brought about by the epinephrine (adrenaline) and corticoids released. Which of the following is an expected response?
   A. Decreased cardiac and pulmonary function
   B. Increased digestive activity
   C. Decreased fat use
   D. Altered immune system response

6. PMR, or progressive muscular relaxation, is
   A. A procedure of alternately contracting and relaxing muscle groups.
   B. A correct way of breathing, by relaxing the diaphragm.
   C. An Eastern relaxation technique that employs the use of a mantra.
   D. A form of self-hypnosis that costs between $250 to $400 to learn.

7. Which of the following diseases have some origin in unresolved stress?
   A. Irritable bowel syndrome
   B. Allergies
   C. Asthma
   D. All of the above

8. Which of the following personality traits fosters high levels of stress?
   A. Self-confidence and practicality
   B. Anger and cynicism
   C. Both A and B
   D. Neither A nor B

9. Stress is best described as
   A. Something completely beyond your control
   B. The leading cause of cynicism
   C. A physical and emotional response to change
   D. A realistic and positive outlook on life

10. What three areas of the body prepare the body to respond to stressors?
   A. Circulatory system, lymphatic system, and brain
   B. Brain, nervous system, and endocrine system
   C. Brain, muscular tissue, and nervous system
   D. Heart, lungs, and brain

CRITICAL THINKING

1. What is stress? Give an example of a stressful situation and how the person might feel.

2. Can stress be positive? Give an example.

3. What physiological reactions occur in the body because of stress?

4. How can repeated stress, if not dealt with properly, affect long-term health?

5. What are some healthy ways to deal with stress? Which would you choose to adopt, and why?

Chapter **4**

Becoming Physically Fit

MULTIPLE CHOICE

1. Which of the following is *not* a benefit of physical fitness?
   A. The person can engage in various tasks and leisure activities.
   B. Body systems function efficiently to resist disease.
   C. Body systems are healthy enough to respond to emergency (threatening) situations.
   D. All of the above are benefits.

2. Which of the following areas of physical fitness do exercise physiologists say is most important?
   A. Muscular strength
   B. Muscular endurance
   C. Cardiorespiratory endurance
   D. Flexibility

3. Anaerobic, or oxygen-deprived, energy production
   A. Is the result of low-intensity activity.
   B. Is the result of short-duration activities that quickly cause muscle fatigue.
   C. Is the result of activities such as walking, distance jogging, and bicycle touring.
   D. None of the above

4. Which of the following types of training exercises are based on the *overload principle*?
   A. Isometric exercises
   B. Progressive resistance exercises
   C. Isokinetic exercises
   D. All of the above

5. Of the following statements, which accurately describes flexibility?
   A. It is relatively the same throughout your body.
   B. Not every joint in your body is equally flexible.
   C. Nothing alters the flexibility of a particular joint.
   D. Gender and age do not affect flexibility.

6. The ability of a muscle group to continue to contract is a definition of which physical fitness component?
   A. Muscular strength
   B. Muscular endurance
   C. Agility
   D. Flexibility

7. The American College of Sports Medicine recommends six significant areas to consider for achievement of cardiorespiratory fitness. Which of these is *not* one of the areas?
   A. Mode of activity
   B. Frequency of training
   C. Intensity of training
   D. Popularity of activity

8. What is target heart rate (THR)?
   A. An intensity level of between 60% and 90% of maximum heart rate
   B. An intensity level of between 70% and 100% of maximum heart rate
   C. The maximum number of times your heart should contract each minute to give your respiratory system a work overload
   D. The rate at which you become so fatigued that you must stop exercising

9. What are the three basic parts of a good training session?
   A. Running, weightlifting, stretching
   B. Warm-up, workout, cooldown
   C. Warm-up, stretching, cooldown
   D. Mental warm-up, socialize, workout

10. Which of these is an abnormal sign to be aware of, during or after exercise?
    A. A delay of over one hour in your body's return to a fully relaxed, comfortable state after exercise
    B. Difficulty sleeping
    C. Noticeable breathing difficulties or chest pains
    D. All of the above

CRITICAL THINKING

1. What are the components of a well-designed fitness program for older adults?

2. How serious is low back pain, and what should a person do to alleviate or prevent it?

3. Explain what steps you would take to develop a cardiorespiratory fitness program, taking into account all six areas recommended by the American College of Sports Medicine.

4. Describe some of the newest trends in physical activity (such as inline skating, water exercise, or "hip-hop"). Which most appeals to you, and why?

5. Why is steroid use dangerous?

Chapter **5**

Understanding Nutrition and Diet

MULTIPLE CHOICE

1. What three nutrients provide the body with calories?
   A. Sugar, amino acids, and supplements
   B. Carbohydrates, fats, and proteins
   C. Tropical oils, food additives, and carbohydrates
   D. None of the above

2. Which of the following statements accurately describes carbohydrates?
   A. They occur in two forms only, depending on the number of proteins that make up the molecule.
   B. About 20% of our calories comes from carbohydrates.
   C. Carbohydrates are combinations of sugar units, or saccharides.
   D. Each gram of carbohydrate contains 400 calories.

3. Which of the following statements is *false*?
   A. Fats are important nutrients in our diets.
   B. Fats make it impossible for our bodies to absorb vitamins A, D, E, and K.
   C. Fat insulates our bodies, helping us retain heat.
   D. Most of the fat we eat is "hidden" in food.

4. What are vitamins?
   A. Inorganic materials necessary for tissue repair and disease prevention
   B. Pills that can be taken each morning to give the body energy all day
   C. Organic compounds that are required in small amounts for normal growth, reproduction, and maintenance of health
   D. Nutrients that provide more than half our body weight

5. Which of the following nutrients could the body not live without for over a week?
   A. Minerals
   B. Fibre
   C. Vitamins
   D. Water

6. Which of the following is a recommendation based on *Canada's Food Guide* ?
   A. Adults should eat two to four servings from the cereals and grains group each day.
   B. Three to five servings from the fruit and vegetable group each day are recommended for an adult.
   C. Adults should consume two to four servings from the milk, yogurt, and cheese group each day.
   D. All of the above

7. What are phytochemicals?
   A. Physiologically active components that function as antioxidants and may deactivate carcinogens
   B. The additives used in foods that preserve freshness or enhance flavour, colour, or texture
   C. The chemicals used to enrich breads and cereals
   D. None of the above

8. What kind of vegetarian eats milk products but not eggs?
   A. Ovolactovegetarian
   B. Macrobiotic vegetarian
   C. Lactovegetarian
   D. Vegan

9. Which of the following is a suggested step toward increasing the availability of food?
   A. Increase the yield of land under cultivation.
   B. Increase the amount of land under cultivation.
   C. Use water more efficiently for the production of food.
   D. All of the above

10. Foodborne diseases usually come from
   A. Pesticides and herbicides sprayed on crops
   B. Bacteria orginating from fertilizers, human handling, or contamination of raw foods from uncooked meat
   C. All of the above
   D. None of the above

CRITICAL THINKING

1. Based on your personal assessment of your current diet, are you getting all the nutrients you need? In which areas do you need to improve?

2. What role does cholesterol play in the diet?

3. Explain the difference between water-soluble and fat-soluble vitamins and the characteristics of each.

4. Would you consider becoming a vegetarian? Why or why not?

5. What is nutrient density? Why is it important to consider this concept when making food choices?

Chapter **6**

Maintaining a Healthy Weight

MULTIPLE CHOICE

1. Which weight measurement technique measures relative amounts of fat and lean body mass by comparing underwater weight with out-of-water weight?
   A. Skinfold measurements
   B. Body mass index (BMI)
   C. Electrical impedance
   D. Hydrostatic weighing

2. Which may be the simplest method of estimating a person's health risk related to excess body fat?
   A. Appearance
   B. Height-weight tables
   C. Body mass index (BMI)
   D. Waist-to-hip ratio

3. What influences obesity?
   A. Environment
   B. Genetics
   C. Both environment and genetics
   D. None of the above

4. Which area(s) within the hypothalamus tell the body when it should begin and end food consumption?
   A. Feeding and satiety centres
   B. Central nervous system (CNS)
   C. Thyroid and pituitary glands
   D. None of the above

5. Which of the following statements describes "brown fat"?
   A. These cells are prominent in infants.
   B. There is a renewed interest in the study of it.
   C. It burns calories as heat without generating energy units that are stored in fat cells.
   D. All of the above

6. Which of the following conditions are associated with excessive abdominal adiposity?
   A. Type 1 diabetes and gallbladder disease
   B. Cancers and HIV
   C. Hypertension, ischemic heart disease, and type 2 diabetes
   D. None of the above

7. What is hypercellular obesity?
   A. The increase of fat cells later in life as a result of being overfed in infancy or substantially gaining weight in childhood or adolescence
   B. When fat cells increase in size as a result of long-term positive caloric balance in adulthood
   C. Excessive fat around the waist, which can contribute to the onset of diabetes mellitus
   D. None of the above

8. What would most experts cite as the most important reason for the widespread problem of obesity?
   A. Family dietary practices
   B. Endocrine influence
   C. Infant feeding patterns
   D. None of the above

9. What is basal metabolic rate (BMR)?
   A. The rate of caloric intake to caloric output
   B. The minimum amount of energy the body requires to carry on all vital functions
   C. The rate of a food's thermic output
   D. None of the above

10. Which weight management technique involves the use of pharmaceuticals?
    A. Balanced diets supported by portion control
    B. Fad diets
    C. Hunger/satiety-influencing products
    D. Self-help weight reduction programs

CRITICAL THINKING

1. What factors influence your body image and self-concept?

2. What steps might you take to successfully control your weight throughout your lifetime?

3. Why is dieting alone not a good technique for achieving and maintaining weight loss?

4. What are reasons someone might develop anorexia nervosa or bulimia? How should a person be treated for these disorders?

5. What does it mean to exercise or eat compulsively?

Chapter **7**

Making Decisions about Drug Use

MULTIPLE CHOICE

1. Which of these is an aspect of addictive behaviour?
   A. Exposure
   B. Compulsion
   C. Loss of control
   D. All of the above

2. What kind of drugs alter the user's feelings, behaviours, or moods?
   A. Medicines
   B. Over-the-counter drugs
   C. Psychoactive drugs
   D. Steroids

3. Which type of dependence creates *full* withdrawal symptoms when the drug use is stopped?
   A. Psychological
   B. Physical
   C. Cross-tolerant
   D. None of the above

4. What are neurotransmitters?
   A. Chemical messengers that transmit electrical impulses
   B. Organic messengers that transmit the chemicals in drugs directly to the brain
   C. Hallucinogenic drugs that are currently popular with college and university students
   D. None of the above

5. How do drugs "work"?
   A. By blocking the production of a neurotransmitter
   B. By forcing the continued release of a neurotransmitter
   C. Either A or B
   D. Neither A nor B

6. Which type of psychoactive drug *excites* the activity of the central nervous system (CNS)?
   A. Inhalants
   B. Hallucinogens
   C. Narcotics
   D. None of the above

7. What is "crack"?
   A. Powdered cocaine that is alkalized in benzene or ether and smoked through a waterpipe
   B. A small, rocklike crystalline material made from cocaine hydrochloride and baking soda
   C. A white powder that is snorted in "lines" through a rolled dollar bill or tube
   D. A pure form of methamphetamine that looks like rock candy

8. Which type of psychoactive drug slows down the function of the central nervous system (CNS)?
   A. Inhalants
   B. Hallucinogens
   C. Cannabis
   D. Depressants

9. What is THC?
   A. A hallucinogen derived from the peyote cactus plant
   B. A drug popular in the 1960s
   C. The active ingredient in marijuana
   D. A new "designer" drug

10. Which drugs are among the most dependence producing?
    A. Inhalants
    B. Hallucinogens
    C. Depressants
    D. Narcotics

CRITICAL THINKING

1. What is the difference between drug misuse and drug abuse?

2. How has cocaine use affected poor urban areas?

3. What are possible long-term effects of marijuana use?

4. What is a synergistic effect, and why is it dangerous?

5. What do you think about the legalization of drugs and about drug testing?

Chapter **8**

Taking Control of Alcohol Use

MULTIPLE CHOICE

1. What is binge drinking?
   A. The practice of drinking and then purging
   B. A harmless activity popular among post-secondary students
   C. The practice of consuming five drinks in a row, at least once during the previous two-week period
   D. The practice of consuming two drinks in a row, at least once a day

2. What is the alcohol content of a bottle of 140-proof gin?
   A. 140% of the fluid in the bottle
   B. 70% of the fluid in the bottle
   C. 14% of the fluid in the bottle
   D. 1.4% of the fluid in the bottle

3. What type of drug is alcohol?
   A. Stimulant
   B. Hallucinogen
   C. Depressant
   D. Narcotic

4. What should be done with people who become unconscious resulting from alcohol consumption?
   A. They should be given a cold shower to wake them up.
   B. They should be made to drink coffee.
   C. They should be taken to bed and left undisturbed for several hours.
   D. They should be put on their side and monitored frequently.

5. Which of the following leading causes of accidental death has connections to alcohol use?
   A. Motor vehicle collisions
   B. Falls
   C. Drownings
   D. All of the above

6. Which of the following is a good guideline to follow for responsibly hosting a party?
   A. Make alcohol the primary entertainment, especially with a keg or other popular way to serve alcohol.
   B. Ridicule those who are too afraid to drink.
   C. If friends say they are just fine to drive home even though they have been drinking, let them go.
   D. None of the above

7. What is the main difference between problem drinking and alcoholism?
   A. Problem drinkers stay away from hard liquor.
   B. Alcoholics usually don't engage in binge drinking.
   C. Alcoholism involves a physical addiction to alcohol.
   D. Problem drinking is easier to detect.

CRITICAL THINKING

1. Why do people drink alcohol?

2. What physiological differences in women make them more susceptible to the effects of alcohol?

3. What are the possible effects of drinking alcohol while pregnant?

4. What role does alcohol use play in violent crime, family violence, and suicide?

5. Explain *denial*, *enabling*, and *codependence* as they occur with alcoholism.

Chapter **9**

Rejecting Tobacco Use

MULTIPLE CHOICE

1. Which factor most affects a person's decision to smoke?
   A. Gender
   B. Age
   C. Education
   D. Race

2. What are psychosocial factors of tobacco dependence?
   A. Manipulation
   B. Advertising
   C. Modelling
   D. Both A and C

3. The rate of smoking in the Canadian population is highest in which of the following groups?
   A. College graduates
   B. High school dropouts
   C. Teens under the age of 18
   D. Young adults between the ages of 18 and 24

4. Which phase of tobacco use includes nicotine, water, and a variety of powerful chemical compounds known collectively as *tar*?
   A. Active phase
   B. Particulate phase
   C. Gaseous phase
   D. Nicotine phase

5. What signals the beginning of lung cancer?
   A. Changes in the basal cell layer resulting from constant irritation by accumulating tar in the airways
   B. An inability to breathe normally
   C. A "smoker's cough"
   D. Mucus swept up to the throat by cilia, where it is swallowed and removed through the digestive system

6. What is COLD?
   A. Chronic obstructive lung disease
   B. A chronic disease in which air flow in and out of the lungs becomes progressively limited
   C. A disease state made up of chronic bronchitis and pulmonary emphysema
   D. All of the above

7. Which of the following statements is *false*?
   A. It is strongly recommended that women who smoke not use oral contraceptives.
   B. Chewing tobacco and snuff generate blood levels of nicotine in amounts equivalent to those seen in cigarette smokers.
   C. Contrary to some claims, secondhand smoke is not a serious health threat.
   D. Children of parents who smoke are twice as likely to develop bronchitis or pneumonia during the first year of life.

8. Which of the following statements is *true*?
   A. Chewing tobacco is a safe alternative to smoking.
   B. Sidestream smoke makes up only 15% of our exposure to involuntary smoking.
   C. Spouses of smokers may have a 30% greater risk of lung cancer.
   D. The only effective way to quit smoking is to go "cold turkey."

9. Which is more effective as a means of quitting smoking?
   A. Nicotine-containing chewing gum
   B. Transdermal patch
   C. Neither A nor B work
   D. Both A and B are equally effective

10. What is the main debate concerning smoking today?
    A. The validity of health warnings
    B. The rights of the nonsmoker vs. the rights of the smoker
    C. The rights of young adults to buy cigarettes
    D. None of the above

CRITICAL THINKING

1. What advertising tactics do tobacco companies use to offset the potential decline in sales from reports of health risks?

2. In what ways is tobacco addictive?

3. How does smoking adversely affect health?

4. Why should a pregnant or breastfeeding woman refrain from smoking?

5. Do you think smoking should continue to be banned from public places? Why or why not?

Chapter **10**

Reducing Your Risk for Chronic Disease

MULTIPLE CHOICE

1. What is the nation's number one killer?
   A. AIDS
   B. Lung disease
   C. Cancer
   D. Cardiovascular disease

2. Which of the following is a function of the blood?
   A. Regulation of water content of body cells and fluids
   B. Transportation of nutrients, oxygen, wastes, and hormones
   C. Buffering to help maintain appropriate pH balance
   D. All of the above

3. What are three cardiovascular risk factors that cannot be changed?
   A. Age, gender, body composition
   B. Heredity, weight, glandular production
   C. Age, heredity, and metabolism
   D. None of the above

4. Which disease predisposes people to developing heart disease?
   A. Cancer
   B. Epilepsy
   C. Diabetes
   D. Multiple sclerosis

5. Which form of cardiovascular disease involves damage to the vessels that supply blood to the heart muscle?
   A. Hypertension
   B. Stroke
   C. Coronary heart disease
   D. Congenital heart disease

6. What is hypertension?
   A. A consistently elevated blood pressure
   B. Stress on arterial walls resulting from plaque build-up
   C. The tendency for blood to clot
   D. Abnormally low blood pressure

7. What are protooncogenes?
   A. Genes that repair damaged cells
   B. Genes that suppress the immune system
   C. Genes that have the potential to become cancerous
   D. Abnormal genes

8. What is the Human Genome Project?
   A. The testing of new cancer-fighting drugs
   B. A scientific study of genes
   C. A secret military project that exposed World War II troops to carcinogens
   D. The study of cancer-producing viruses

9. Which type of cancer is found in cells of the blood and blood-forming tissues?
   A. Lymphoma
   B. Neuroblastoma
   C. Carcinoma
   D. Leukemia

10. Which is the most common site of the body to develop cancer in women?
    A. Breast
    B. Uterus
    C. Lung
    D. Skin

11. Which test greatly improves the chances of preventing cervical cancer?
    A. Mammography
    B. MRI
    C. Pap test
    D. Biopsy

CRITICAL THINKING

1. Do you exhibit any risk factors for cardiovascular disease? What steps can you take to change them, if they can be changed?

2. What is the difference between HDLs and LDLs?

3. What social and environmental factors contribute to the onset of cancer?

4. What steps can men and women take to prevent cancer or to detect the early stages of cancer?

5. What are the differences and similarities between type 1 and type 2 diabetes?

Chapter 11

Preventing Infectious Diseases

MULTIPLE CHOICE

1. What is a pathogen?
   A. A disease-causing agent
   B. A virus, bacterium, or fungus
   C. Neither A nor B
   D. Both A and B

2. What is the function of a reservoir in the chain of infection?
   A. To cause disease
   B. To offer a favourable environment in which an infectious agent can thrive
   C. To act as a portal of exit
   D. To transmit the agent from person to person

3. Which term describes insects, animals, or birds that carry diseases from human to human?
   A. Vectors
   B. Pathogens
   C. Reservoirs
   D. Agents

4. During which of the following stages of infection is the infected person *most* contagious?
   A. Prodromal stage
   B. Clinical stage
   C. Decline stage
   D. Incubation stage

5. Which type of immunity is the result of vaccination or immunization?
   A. Naturally acquired immunity
   B. Artificially acquired immunity
   C. Passively acquired immunity
   D. None of the above

6. Which viral infection has mental fatigue and depression as side effects?
   A. Influenza
   B. Common cold
   C. Mononucleosis
   D. Pneumonia

7. What is chronic fatigue syndrome (CFS)?
   A. A mononucleosis-like condition most commonly seen in women in their 30s and 40s
   B. A condition that may be linked to neurally mediated hypotension
   C. A condition that may be a psychological disorder
   D. All of the above

8. How is Lyme disease transmitted?
   A. Through droplet spread
   B. Through fecal-oral spread
   C. Through the deer tick nymph
   D. Through inhalation

9. Which sexually transmitted disease occurs as blister-like lesions on the genitals or lips?
   A. Herpes simplex
   B. Gonorrhea
   C. Syphilis
   D. Human papillomavirus

10. Of the following STIs, which has no cure?
    A. Vaginal infections
    B. Cystitis and urethritis
    C. Herpes simplex
    D. Gonorrhea

CRITICAL THINKING

1. What are the two main components to the body's protective defence? How do they work?

2. Why do the elderly and people with additional health complications need to take extra precautions to avoid contracting influenza?

3. Why should people pay close attention to their immunization history, especially college- and university-aged students?

4. What precautions should women take when using tampons to avoid toxic shock syndrome?

5. How is AIDS transmitted, and what precautions can be taken to avoid contracting it?

Chapter **12**

Sexuality and Relationships

MULTIPLE CHOICE

1. Which basis for biological sexuality refers to the growing embryo's development of gonads?
   A. Genetic
   B. Gonadal
   C. Structural
   D. None of the above

2. At which age are typical children able to correctly identify their gender?
   A. 4 years
   B. 2 years
   C. 18 months
   D. 6 months

3. What part of the testis produces sperm?
   A. Seminiferous tubules
   B. Scrotum
   C. Epididymis
   D. Interstitial cells

4. Which is the most sensitive part of the female body?
   A. Mons pubis
   B. Vagina
   C. Clitoris
   D. Prepuce

5. During which phase of the menstrual cycle does ovulation occur?
   A. Menstrual
   B. Proliferative
   C. Secretory
   D. None of the above

6. Which phase of the sexual response pattern prevents men from having multiple orgasms?
   A. Excitement
   B. Plateau
   C. Orgasmic
   D. Refractory

7. Which of the following statements is *not* true about celibacy?
   A. Celibate people may have intimate relationships without sex.
   B. It is defined as the self-imposed avoidance of sexual contact.
   C. Psychological complications often result from a celibate lifestyle.
   D. All are true.

8. Which type of love is enduring and capable of sustaining long-term mutual growth?
   A. Infatuation
   B. Passionate love
   C. Companionate love
   D. Devotional love

9. Which of the following statements is *not* true of cohabitation?
   A. It is an alternative to marriage.
   B. It can sometimes exist between people sharing a platonic relationship.
   C. Approximately half of all cohabitating couples will disband.
   D. Couples who cohabit are more likely to get married than those in a more traditional dating relationship.

CRITICAL THINKING

1. How do biological and psychosocial factors contribute to the complex expression of our sexuality?

2. How has a blending of feminine and masculine qualities benefitted society?

3. Why might the "withdrawal" method of contraception not work?

4. What changes, both physiological and psychological, might menopause create in a woman's life?

5. What effect does the aging process have on the sexual response pattern?

6. To provide yourself with reasonable protection, what simple directions should you follow for using condoms correctly?

Chapter **13**

Managing Your Fertility

MULTIPLE CHOICE

1. Which form of birth control *does not* prevent STIs?
   A. Withdrawal
   B. Calendar method
   C. IUCD
   D. All of the above

2. Which two forms of birth control, when used together, provide a high degree of contraceptive protection *and* disease control?
   A. IUCD and spermicides
   B. Spermicides and condoms
   C. Calendar method and spermicides
   D. Oral contraceptive and spermicides

3. Which of the following statements is *not* true of oral contraceptives?
   A. The use of antibiotics lowers their contraceptive effectiveness.
   B. They regulate a woman's menstrual cycle.
   C. The user may experience more frequent vaginal infections, weight gain, mild headaches, and mild depression.
   D. They are useful in the prevention of STIs.

4. What are progesterone-only pills?
   A. Smaller versions of the regular oral contraceptive that can be swallowed more easily
   B. The placebo pills taken between cycles
   C. Oral contraceptives that contain no estrogen—only low-dose progesterone
   D. Less expensive versions of the pill that are slightly less effective

5. What is Depo-Provera?
   A. An injectable contraceptive
   B. A subdermal implant contraceptive
   C. A type of diaphragm
   D. A brand of oral contraceptive

6. Which type of abortion is performed in the earliest stages of the first trimester?
   A. Menstrual extraction
   B. Dilation and curettage
   C. Dilation and evacuation
   D. Hypertonic saline procedure

7. What is Plan B?
   A. The "morning-after" pill
   B. The process of using prostaglandin to influence muscle contractions that expel uterine contents
   C. A hypertonic saline solution
   D. A drug that blocks the action of progesterone, thus producing an early abortion

8. The most common method of female sterilization is
   A. Vasectomy
   B. Tubal ligation
   C. Colpotomy
   D. Hysterectomy

9. Which of the following is an obstacle to pregnancy?
   A. 200 to 500 million sperm cells are deposited in each ejaculation.
   B. Sperm cells are capable of moving quickly.
   C. The acidic level of the vagina is destructive to sperm.
   D. Once inside the fallopian tubes, sperm can live for days.

10. Which type of artificial fertilization involves transferring fertilized ova from a laboratory dish into the fallopian tubes?
    A. In vitro fertilization and embryo transfer (IVF-ET)
    B. Gamete intrafallopian transfer (GIFT)
    C. Zygote intrafallopian transfer (ZIFT)
    D. Surrogate parenting

CRITICAL THINKING

1. What factors should you consider when choosing a method of birth control?

2. Which of the available methods of birth control would you be most likely to use, if you needed to?

3. What serious questions need to be considered before deciding to have children?

4. Describe the birth process from beginning to end.

Chapter **14**

Aging and the End of Life

MULTIPLE CHOICE

1. Which of the following is a criterion by which death may be determined?
   A. Lack of heartbeat and breathing
   B. Lack of central nervous system function
   C. Presence of rigor mortis
   D. All of the above
2. What does the physician's order "DNR" stand for?
   A. Death not recorded
   B. Do not resuscitate
   C. Do not release
   D. Do not recognize
3. Which psychological stage for dying people serves as the earliest temporary defence mechanism?
   A. Denial
   B. Anger
   C. Bargaining
   D. None of the above
4. Which of the following describes the appropriate way to act toward someone who is dying?
   A. Refrain from crying so as not to upset them.
   B. Remain optimistic even when there is no hope for recovery.
   C. Try to be genuine and honest.
   D. Try to distract the person from talking about death.
5. Which of the following is *not* a normal, healthy expression of grief over the loss of a loved one?
   A. Physical discomfort
   B. Sense of numbness
   C. Guilt
   D. Extreme hostility
6. Which of the following best describes life expectancy?
   A. The average number of years a person can expect to live
   B. The maximum number of years a human can live
   C. The number of years a person can expect to live free of disease or disability
   D. None of the above
7. Which of the following describes the condition known as presbycusis?
   A. The reduction of visual capacity associated with cataracts
   B. The weakening of bones commonly experienced by the elderly
   C. A condition of failing memory leading to dementia
   D. A loss of hearing of high-pitch sounds
8. In what ways can exercise improve the health of older adults?
   A. It can reduce the need for assistance in living or care in a nursing home.
   B. It can reduce the stiffening and pain of arthritis.
   C. It can improve mental health.
   D. All of the above
9. Alzheimer's disease and vascular dementias involve deterioration of which of the following?
   A. Memory
   B. Mood
   C. Judgment and reasoning
   D. All of the above
10. Which of the following are believed to intensify the aging process?
    A. Tobacco use
    B. UV irradiation
    C. Sleep
    D. A and B

CRITICAL THINKING

1. What are advance directives? Why would it be prudent to have completed these documents?

2. What risk factors for osteoporosis do you exhibit? How can you improve your lifestyle to reduce this risk?

3. What aspects of old age lead to depression? How does this differ from depression in younger adults?

4. How does palliative care differ from traditional hospital care with respect to care of the terminally ill?

5. In what ways do death rituals aid people in dealing with death?

Chapter **15**

Becoming an Informed Health Care Consumer

MULTIPLE CHOICE

1. Which of the following statements is *false*?
   A. The accuracy of health information from friends and family members may be questionable.
   B. The mass media routinely supply public service messages that give valuable health-related information.
   C. Never trust the labels and directions on prescription medication; it is usually misleading and intended to make you buy more of the product.
   D. Folk wisdom is on occasion supported by scientific evidence.

2. Federal health agencies are often less effective than the public deserves. Which of the following is *not* a reason for the lack of effectiveness?
   A. Inadequate staff
   B. Poor administration
   C. Interference by the medical community
   D. Lobbying by special interest groups

3. Which type of health care professional provides services relating to understanding behaviour patterns or perceptions but does not dispense drugs?
   A. Dentist
   B. Psychiatrist
   C. Podiatrist
   D. Psychologist

4. What does an optician do?
   A. Specializes in vision problems due to refractory errors
   B. Provides prescriptions for eyewear products
   C. Grinds lenses according to a precise prescription
   D. Specializes in vision care with a base in general medicine

5. What type of nursing position is helping to provide communities with additional primary care providers?
   A. Nurse practitioner
   B. Registered nurse
   C. Licensed practical nurse
   D. Technical nurse

6. The established amount that the insuree must pay before the insurer reimburses for services is
   A. Fixed indemnity
   B. Coinsurance
   C. Deductible
   D. Exclusion

7. Which of the following is a sign of quackery?
   A. Makes promises of quick, dramatic, painless, or drugless treatment
   B. Claims a product provides treatment for multiple illnesses
   C. States that the treatment is secret or not yet available in this country
   D. All of the above

CRITICAL THINKING

1. What are some pros and cons of obtaining health information from mass media?

2. What are some sources of health information available to you?

3. What are some alternative health care practices? Would you be willing to try them?

4. How can self-care benefit both individuals and the health care industry as a whole?

Chapter **16**

Protecting Your Safety

MULTIPLE CHOICE

1. The annual homicide rate in North America has ____________ over the past decade.
   A. Increased
   B. Stayed the same
   C. Declined
   D. None of the above

2. Who is most often a victim of intimate partner maltreatment?
   A. Prostitutes
   B. Teenage girls
   C. Spouses or former spouses of the assailant
   D. Men

3. Which form of child maltreatment occurs most frequently?
   A. Neglect
   B. Physical
   C. Psychological
   D. Sexual

4. Crimes directed at individuals or groups because of racial, ethnic, religious, or other differences are called
   A. Hate crimes
   B. Assault crimes
   C. Global crimes
   D. Difference crimes

5. Aside from the physical harm of rape, what other effects may occur?
   A. Post-traumatic stress syndrome
   B. Guilt
   C. Emotional damage resulting from "broken trust"
   D. All of the above

6. Which of the following constitutes sexual harassment?
   A. Excessive pressure for dates
   B. Sexually explicit humour
   C. Unwanted physical contact
   D. All of the above

7. Which of the following can help increase safety around your home?
   A. Make sure your name is spelled correctly in the phone book.
   B. Try to live in apartments on the first floor.
   C. Require repair people to show valid identification.
   D. Leave windows unlocked in case you need to escape in a hurry.

8. Over half of all murders result from
   A. Random crime
   B. Domestic abuse
   C. Arguments between acquaintances or relatives
   D. None of the above

9. Which of the following resources will help improve your safety on campus?
   A. University-approved escorts
   B. Campus security departments
   C. Campus counselling centre
   D. All of the above

CRITICAL THINKING

1. What factors may have contributed to a drop in North American homicide rates?

2. How should suspected child maltreatment be properly handled?

3. What is rape? What is acquaintance rape? What is date rape?

4. How can you increase your personal safety?

5. What steps can you take to protect children and the elderly?

Chapter **17**

The Environment and Your Health

MULTIPLE CHOICE

1. What has caused the greenhouse effect?
   A. A progressive increase in carbon dioxide in the atmosphere
   B. A hole in the ozone layer
   C. A slight warming of the earth's surface
   D. All of the above

2. What substances produce acid rain when they combine with moisture in the atmosphere?
   A. Coal and hydrogen
   B. Hydrocarbons and particulate matter
   C. Chlorofluorocarbons
   D. Nitrogen and sulfur

3. Which type of pollution disproportionately affects children of low-income families?
   A. Radon gas
   B. Lead
   C. Subsidence inversion
   D. Radiation inversion

4. What is eutrophication?
   A. A biological imbalance that causes fish to die in great numbers from lack of oxygen
   B. The overabundance of aquatic plants that results when water is rich in nitrates and phosphates
   C. Both A and B
   D. Neither A and B

5. Which of the following is the name of a hydrocarbon found in the water supply that has been linked to cancer?
   A. Chlorine
   B. PCB
   C. DDT
   D. EPA

6. Which of the following sources of water pollution comes from power plants?
   A. Oil spills
   B. Thermal pollution
   C. Sediments
   D. None of the above

7. Which of the following devices generates electromagnetic fields?
   A. Water bed heater
   B. Electric razor
   C. Cellular phone
   D. All of the above

8. The ecological footprint of a city or nation represents which of the following?
   A. The amount of pollution left after manufacturing over the course of a year
   B. The amount of forest required to absorb the CO_2 created by that region
   C. The area of land that is required to sustain the current level of resource consumption and waste discharge by that population
   D. The population of that city or nation

9. Which of the following best describes the Kyoto Protocol?
   A. The world's industrialized countries tentatively agreed to legally binding targets for the reduction of their greenhouse gas emissions in an effort to slow global climate change.
   B. Japan, the world's largest emitter of greenhouse gases, has withdrawn from this agreement.
   C. The Kyoto targets are dramatic, based on the reduction of total emissions to 50% below 1990 levels.
   D. All of the above.

10. Which of the following best describes the environmental impact of garbage landfills?
    A. They use valuable land.
    B. They are a significant source of greenhouse gases.
    C. They can contribute to groundwater contamination and air pollution.
    D. All of the above

CRITICAL THINKING

1. How do different types of air pollution adversely affect us?

2. Discuss the impact of climate change on your region, your province, Canada, and the world.

3. Where does your drinking water come from? How is it treated to ensure its safety?

4. What are some concerns related to nuclear energy?

5. Which of your own behaviours contribute to the pollution of your environment? Which of these behaviours are you willing to change to reduce your personal impact on the environment?

Glossary

A

abortion Induced premature termination of a pregnancy

absorption The passage of nutrients or alcohol through the walls of the stomach or intestinal tract into the bloodstream

abuse Any use of a legal or illegal drug that is detrimental to health

acid rain Rain that has a lower pH (i.e., is more acidic) than that normally associated with rain

acquired immunity (AI) The "arming" of the immune system through its initial exposure to an antigen

acupuncture Insertion of fine needles into the body to alter electroenergy fields and cure disease

acute alcohol intoxication A potentially fatal elevation of the BAC, often resulting from heavy, rapid consumption of alcohol

acute rhinitis The common cold; the sudden onset of nasal inflammation

adaptive thermogenesis Physiological response of the body to adjust its metabolic rate to the presence of food

additive effect The combined (but not exaggerated) effect produced by the concurrent use of two or more drugs

advance directive A legal document prepared by an individual in the event that he or she at some point becomes incompetent; advance directives can be used to communicate requests for end-of-life care

aerobic energy production The body's means of energy production when the respiratory and circulatory systems are able to process and transport a sufficient amount of oxygen to muscle cells

agent Causal pathogen of a particular disease

alarm stage The first stage of the stress response involving physiological, involuntary changes that are controlled by the hormonal and nervous system; the flight-or-fight response is activated in this stage

alcoholism A primary chronic disease with genetic, psychosocial, and environmental factors influencing its development and manifestations

allopathy System of medical practice in which specific remedies (often pharmaceutical agents) are used to produce effects different from those produced by a disease or injury

alveoli Thin, saclike terminal ends of the airways; the sites at which gases are exchanged between the blood and inhaled air

amenorrhea Cessation or lack of menstrual periods

amino acids The chief components of protein; can be manufactured by the body or obtained from dietary sources

amotivational syndrome Behavioural pattern characterized by lack of interest in productive activities

anabolic steroids Drugs that function like testosterone to produce increases in weight, strength, endurance, and aggression

anaerobic energy production The body's means of energy production when the necessary amount of oxygen is not available

androgyny The blending of both masculine and feminine qualities

anorexia nervosa A disorder of emotional origin in which appetite and hunger are suppressed and marked weight loss occurs

anovulatory Not ovulating

antagonistic effect Effect produced when one drug reduces or offsets the effects of a second drug

anti-angiogenesis Drug-based therapy that prevents cancerous tumours from developing an enriching blood supply

antibodies Chemical compounds produced by the body's immune system to destroy antigens and their toxins

artificially acquired immunity (AAI) Type of acquired immunity resulting from the body's response to pathogens introduced into the body through immunizations

asphyxiation Death resulting from lack of oxygen to the brain

atherosclerosis Buildup of plaque on the inner walls of arteries

attention deficit hyperactivity disorder (ADHD) Above-normal rate of physical movement; often accompanied by an inability to concentrate well on a specified task; also called *hyperactivity*

axon The portion of a neuron that conducts electrical impulses to the dendrites of adjacent neurons; neurons typically have one axon

ayurveda Traditional Indian medicine based on herbal remedies

B

balanced diet A diet featuring daily food selections from each of the food groups of *Canada's Food Guide to Healthy Eating*

ballistic stretching A "bouncing" form of stretching in which a muscle group is lengthened repetitively to produce multiple quick, forceful stretches

basal metabolic rate (BMR) The amount of energy (in calories) one's body requires to maintain basic functions

benign Noncancerous; tumours that do not spread

bias and hate crimes Criminal acts directed at a person or group solely because of a specific characteristic, such as race, religion, ethnic background, or political belief

biological sexuality Male and female aspects of sexuality

birth control All of the methods and procedures that can prevent the birth of a child

blackout A temporary state of amnesia experienced by a drinker; an inability to remember events that occur during a period of alcohol use

blood alcohol concentration (BAC) percentage of alcohol in a measured quantity of blood; BACs can be determined directly through the analysis of a blood sample or indirectly throuth the analysis of exhaled air

body mass index (BMI) A numerical expression of body weight based on height and weight

bolus theory A theory of nicotine addiction based on the body's response to the bolus (ball) of nicotine delivered to the brain with each inhalation of cigarette smoke

brand name Specific patented name assigned to a drug by its manufacturer

bulimia nervosa A disorder of emotional origin in which binge eating patterns are established; usually accompanied by purging

C

calendar method A form of periodic abstinance in which the variable lengths of a woman's menstrual cycle are used to calculate her fertile period

calipers A device used to measure the thickness of a skinfold from which percentage of body fat can be calculated

calories Units of heat (energy); specifically, 1 kcalorie (kilocalorie) equals the amount of heat required to raise the temperature of 1 kilogram of water by 1°C. 1 kilocalorie (kcal) = 1 Calorie (Cal) = 1000 calories (cal)

carbohydrates Chemical compounds composed of sugar units; the body's primary source of energy

carbon monoxide Chemical compound (CO) that can "inactivate" red blood cells

carcinogenic Related to the production of cancerous changes; property of environmental agents, including drugs, that may stimulate the development of cancerous changes within cells

cardiorespiratory endurance The ability of the heart, lungs, and blood vessels to process and transport oxygen required by muscle cells so they can contract over a period of time

cardiovascular Pertaining to the heart (cardio) and blood vessels (vascular)

carjacking A crime that involves a thief's attempt to steal a car while the owner is behind the wheel; carjackings are usually random, and unpredictable, and frequently involve handguns

catabolism The metabolic process of breaking down tissue for the purpose of converting it to energy

centenarian Someone living to and beyond 100 years

cerebrovascular occlusion Blockages to arteries supplying blood to the cerebral cortex of the brain; stroke

cervical cap A small, thimble-shaped device designed to fit over the cervix

cesarean delivery Surgical removal of fetus through the abdominal wall

chemical name Name used to describe the molecular structure of a drug

child maltreatment The act or failure to act by a parent or caretaker that results in abuse or neglect of a child or which places the child in imminent risk of serious harm

chiropractic Manipulation of the vertebral column to relieve pressure and cure illness

chlamydia The most prevalent sexually transmitted disease; caused by a nongonococcal bacterium

chlorofluorocarbons (CFCs) Gaseous chemical compounds that contain chlorine and fluorine

cholesterol primary form of fat found in the blood; lipid material manufactured within the body, and derived through dietary sources

chronic Develops slowly and persists for a long period of time

chronic bronchitis Persistent inflammation and infection of the smaller airways within the lungs

chronic disorder Condition that develops and progresses slowly over an extended period of time

chronic fatigue syndrome (CFS) Illness that causes severe exhaustion, fatigue, aches, and depression; mostly affects women in their 30s and 40s

chronological Measuring by time; for example years

cilia Small, hairlike structures that extend from cells that line the air passages

codependence An unhealthy relationship in which one person is addicted to alcohol or another drug and a person close to him or her is "addicted" to the alcoholic or drug user

cohabitation Sharing of a residence by two unrelated, unmarried people; living together

coitus Penile-vaginal intercourse

cold turkey Immediate, total discontinuation of use of a drug; associated withdrawal discomfort

coliform bacteria Intestinal tract bacteria whose presence in a water supply suggests contamination by human or animal waste

collateral circulation The ability of nearby blood vessels to enlarge and carry additional blood around a blocked blood vessel

compliance Willingness to follow the directions provided by another person, such as a physician

condom A latex or polyurethane shield designed to cover the erect penis and retain semen on ejaculation; "rubber" or "safe"

consumer fraud Marketing of unreliable and ineffective services, products, or information under the guise of curing disease or improving health; quackery

contraception Any method or procedure that prevents fertilization

contraceptive patch Contraceptive skin patch containing estrogen and progestin; replaced each week for a three-week period

contraceptive ring Thin, polymer contraceptive device containing estrogen and progestin; placed deep within the vagina for a three-week period

contraindications Factors that make the use of a drug inappropriate or dangerous for a particular person

Controlled Drugs and Substances Act 1996, c. 19 The Canadian legislation that lists the drugs controlled by law in Canada stating that "Except as authorized under the regulations, no person shall possess a substance included in Schedule I, II, or III," and "No person shall seek or obtain a substance included in Schedule I, II, III or IV, or an authorization to obtain a substance included in Schedule I, II, III or IV."

coronary arteries Vessels that supply oxygenated blood to heart muscle tissues

coroner An elected legal official empowered to pronounce death and to determine the official cause of a suspicious or violent death

corpus luteum Cellular remnant of the graafian follicle after the release of an ovum

cross-tolerance Transfer of tolerance from one drug to another within the same general category

cruciferous vegetables Vegetables, such as broccoli, that have flowers with four leaves in the pattern of a cross

crypts Burial locations generally underneath churches

cunnilingus Oral stimulation of the vulva or clitoris

D

dehydration The abnormal depletion of fluids from the body; severe dehydration can be fatal

dendrite The portion of a neuron that receives electrical stimuli from adjacent neurons; neurons typically have several such branches or extensions

dependence General term that refers to the need to continue using a drug for psychological and/or physical reasons

designated driver A person who abstains from or carefully limits alcohol consumption to be able to safely transport other people who have been drinking

desirable weight The weight range deemed appropriate for people of a specific gender, age, and frame size

diaphragm A soft rubber cup designed to cover the cervix

diastolic pressure Blood pressure against blood vessel walls when the heart relaxes

dilation Gradual expansion of an opening or passageway, such as the cervix

dilation and curettage (D & C) A surgical procedure in which the cervical canal is dilated to allow the uterine wall to be scraped

distress Stress that diminishes the quality of life; commonly associated with disease, illness, and maladaptation

drug synergism Enhancement of a drug's effect as a result of the presence of additional drugs within the system

duration The length of time one needs to exercise at the target heart rate to produce a training effect

E

ecosystem An ecological unit made up of both animal and plant life that interact to produce a stable system

ectopic pregnancy A pregnancy in which the fertilized ovum implants at a site other than the uterus, typically in the fallopian tubes

electrical impedance Method to test the percentage of body fat using resistance to the flow of electrical current

electroencephalograph An instrument that measures the electrical activity of the brain

embolism Potentially fatal condition in which a circulating blood clot lodges itself in a smaller vessel

enabling Inadvertently supporting a drinker's behaviour by denying that a problem exists

environmental tobacco smoke Tobacco smoke that is diluted and stays within a common source of air

enzymes Organic substances that control the rate of physiological reactions but are not themselves altered in the process

epitaph An inscription on a grave marker or monument

erection The engorgement of erectile tissue with blood; characteristic of the penis, clitoris, nipples, labia minora, and scrotum

ergogenic aids Supplements that are taken to improve athletic performance

erotic dreams Dreams whose content elicits a sexual response

eulogy A composition or speech that praises someone; often delivered at a funeral or memorial service

eustress Stress that enhances the quality of life

eutrophication Enrichment of a body of water with nutrients, which causes overabundant growth of plants

excitement stage Initial arousal stage of the sexual response pattern

exercise A form of leisure-time physical activity that is planned, structured, and repetitive; its main objective is to improve or maintain physical fitness

F

faith The purposes and meaning that underlie an individual's hopes and dreams

false labour Conditions that resemble the start of true labour; may include irregular uterine contractions, pressure, and discomfort in the lower abdomen

fat density The percentage of a food's total calories that are derived from fat; above 30% is considered to be a high fat density

fellatio Oral stimulation of the penis

femininity Behavioural expressions traditionally observed in females

fermentation A chemical process whereby plant products are converted into alcohol by the action of yeast cells on carbohydrate materials

fertility The ability to reproduce

fetal alcohol syndrome Characteristic birth defects noted in the children of some women who consume alcohol during their pregnancies

fibre Plant material that cannot be digested; found in cereal, grains, legumes, nuts, fruits, and vegetables

flaccid Nonerect; the state of erectile tissue when vasocongestion is not occurring

flexibility The ability of joints to function through an intended range of motion

flight-or-fight response The reaction to a stressor by confrontation or avoidance (sometimes called the fight, fright, flight, or folly [or 4F] response)

foreplay Activities, often involving touching and caressing, that prepare individuals for sexual intercourse

free radicals Harmful oxygen molecules that can damage cells and their genetic material

frequency The number of times per week one should exercise to achieve a training effect

FSH (follicle-stimulating hormone) A gonadotropic hormone required for initial development of ova (in the female) and sperm (in the male)

functional foods Foods capable of contributing to the improvement/prevention of specific health problems

G

gaseous phase Portion of tobacco smoke containing carbon monoxide and many other physiologically active gaseous compounds

gateway drug An easily obtained legal or illegal drug that represents a user's first experience with a mind-altering drug

gender General term reflecting a biological basis of sexuality; the male gender or the female gender

gender adoption Lengthy process of learning the behaviour that is traditional for one's gender

gender identification Achievement of a personally satisfying interpretation of one's masculinity or femininity

gender identity Recognition of one's gender

gender preference Emotional and intellectual acceptance of one's own gender

general adaptation syndrome a sequenced physiological response to the presence of a stressor; the alarm, resistance, recovery, and exhaustion stages of the stress response

generalized anxiety disorder (GAD) An anxiety disorder that involves experiencing intense and nonspecific anxiety for at least six months, in which the intensity and frequency of worry is excessive and out of proportion to the situation

generic name Common or nonproprietary name of a drug

genetic predisposition An inherited tendency to develop a disease process if necessary environmental factors exist

greenhouse effect Warming of the earth's surface that is produced when solar heat becomes trapped by layers of carbon dioxide and other gases

gonads Male or female sex glands; testes produce sperm and ovaries produce eggs

H

hallucinogens Psychoactive drugs capable of producing hallucinations (distortions of reality)

health claims Regulated statements attesting to a food's contribution to the improvement/prevention of specific health problems

health education movement in which knowledge, practices, and values are transmitted to people for their use in lengthening their lives, reducing the incidence of illness, and feeling better

health promotion Movement in which knowledge, practices, and values are transmitted to people for use in lengthening their lives, reducing the incidence of illness, and feeling better

herbalism An ancient form of healing in which herbal preparations are used to treat illness and disease

high-density lipoprotein (HDL) The type of lipoprotein that transports cholesterol from the bloodstream to the liver, where it is eventually removed from the body; high levels of HDL are related to a reduction in heart disease

high-risk health behaviour A behavioural pattern, such as smoking, associated with a high risk of developing a chronic illness

holistic health A view of health in terms of its physical, emotional, social, intellectual, spiritual, and occupational makeup

homeopathy The use of minute doses of herbs or minerals to stimulate healing

homicide The intentional killing of one person by another person

hormone replacement therapy (HRT) Medically administered estrogen and progestin to replace hormones lost as the result of menopause

hospice A residence in which people with terminal illnesses and their loved ones can receive palliative care; hospice is also a philosophy of providing comprehensive palliative care to the dying

host An infected person capable of infecting others

host negligence A legal term that reflects the failure of a host to provide reasonable care and safety for people visiting the host's residence or business

hot flashes Temporary feelings of warmth experienced by women during and after menopause; caused by blood vessel dilation

Human Genome Project International quest by geneticists to identify the location and composition of every gene within the human cell

human papillomavirus (HPV) Sexually transmitted virus capable of causing precancerous changes in the cervix; causative agent for genital warts

hypercellular obesity A form of obesity seen in individuals who possess an abnormally large number of fat cells

hypertonic saline solution A salt solution with a concentration higher than that found in human fluids

hypertrophic obesity A form of obesity in which fat cells are enlarged but not excessive in number

I

ICSH (interstitial cell-stimulating hormone) A gonadotropic hormone of the male required for the production of testosterone

identity theft A crime involving the fraudulent use of a person's name, social insurance number, credit line, or other personal financial or identifying information

immune system System of cellular elements that protects the body from invading pathogens and foreign materials

infatuation A relatively temporary, intensely romantic attraction to another person

inhalants Psychoactive drugs that enter the body through inhalation

inhibitions Inner controls that prevent a person from engaging in certain types of behaviour

insulin A pancreatic hormone required by the body for the effective metabolism of glucose (blood sugar)

intensity The level of effort put into an activity

intentional injuries Injuries that are purposely committed by a person

intimacy Any close, mutual, verbal, or nonverbal behaviour within a relationship

intimate partner abuse Violence committed against a person by her or his current or former spouse, boyfriend, or girlfriend

intrauterine contraceptive device (IUCD) A small, plastic, medicated or unmedicated device that prevents continued pregnancy when inserted in the uterus

ionizing radiation Form of radiation capable of releasing electrons from atoms

isokinetic exercises Muscular strength training exercises in which machines are used to provide variable resistances throughout the full range of motion

isometric exercises Muscular strength training exercises in which the resistance is so great that the object cannot be moved

J

joule The System International (SI) unit for measuring the energy value of foods; 1 kilocalorie (kcal) = 4.2 kilojoules (kj); also see "calorie"

L

lactating Breastfeeding; nursing

lead toxicity Blood lead level above 25 micrograms/decilitre

legumes Include dried beans, dried peas, lentils, chick peas (garbanzo beans), and peanuts

low-density lipoprotein (LDL) The type of lipoprotein that transports the largest amount of cholesterol in the bloodstream; high levels of LDL are related to heart disease

luteinizing hormone (LH) A gonadotropic hormone of the female required for fullest development and release of ova; ovulating hormone

lyme disease A bacterial infection transmitted by deer ticks

M

mainstream smoke The smoke inhaled and then exhaled by a smoker

masculinity Behavioural expressions traditionally observed in males

massotherapy The therapeutic use of massage

masturbation Self-stimulation of the genitals

mausoleum An above-ground structure, which frequently resembles a small stone house, into which caskets can be placed for disposition

meltdown The overheating and eventual melting of the uranium fuel rods in the core of a nuclear reactor

menarche Time of a female's first menstrual cycle

menopause Decline and eventual cessation of hormone production by the female reproductive system

metabolite A breakdown product of a drug

metastasis The spread of cancerous cells from their site of origin to other areas of the body

misuse Inappropriate use of legal drugs intended to be medications

monogamous Paired relationship with one partner

mononucleosis ("mono") Viral infection characterized by weakness, fatigue, swollen glands, sore throat, and low-grade fever

morbidity Illness or disease

mortality Death

mucus Clear, sticky material produced by specialized cells within the mucous membranes of the body; mucus traps much of the suspended particulate matter within tobacco smoke

multiorgasmic capacity Potential to have several orgasms within a single period of sexual arousal

muscular endurance The ability of a muscle or muscle group to function over time; supported by the respiratory and circulatory systems

muscular strength The ability to contract skeletal muscles to engage in work; the force that a muscle can exert

mutagenic Capable of promoting genetic alterations in cells

myocardial infarction heart attack; the death of heart muscle as a result of a blockage in one of the coronary arteries

N

narcolepsy A sleep disorder in which a person has a recurrent, overwhelming, and uncontrollable desire to sleep

narcotics Opiates; psychoactive drugs derived from the Oriental poppy plant; narcotics relieve pain and induce sleep

naturally acquired immunity (NAI) Type of acquired immunity resulting from the body's response to naturally occurring pathogens

naturopathy A system of treatment that avoids drugs and surgery and emphasizes the use of natural agents to correct underlying imbalances

neuron A nerve cell

neurophysiological Pertaining to nervous system functioning; processes through which the body senses and responds to its internal and external environments

nocturnal emission Ejaculation that occurs during sleep; "wet dream"

norepinephrine Adrenaline-like neurotransmitter produced within the nervous system

nutrient density The nutritional quality of food, relative to its energy value; a food that is abundant in nutrients yet low in calories has a high nutrient density

nutrients Elements in foods that are required for the energy, growth, and repairs of tissues and regulation of body processes

O

obsessive-compulsive disorder (OCD) An anxiety disorder characterized by obsessions—intrusive thoughts, images, or impulses causing a great deal of distress—and compulsions—repetitive behaviours aimed at reducing anxiety or stress that is associated with the obsessive thoughts

oncogenes Genes that are believed to activate the development of cancer

oral contraceptive pill A pill taken orally, composed of synthetic female hormones that prevent ovulation or implantation; "the pill"

orgasmic platform Expanded outer third of the vagina that grips the penis during the plateau phase of the sexual response pattern

orgasmic stage Third stage of the sexual response pattern; the stage during which neuromuscular tension is released

orthodontics Dental specialty that focuses on the proper alignment of the teeth

osteoarthritis Arthritis that develops with age; largely caused by weight bearing and deterioration of the joints

osteopathy System of medical practice that combines allopathic principles with specific attention to postural mechanics of the body

osteoporosis Loss of calcium from the bone, seen primarily in postmenopausal women

outercourse Sexual activity that does not involve intercourse

overload principle The principle whereby a person gradually increases the resistance load that must be moved or lifted; this principle also applies to other types of fitness training

ovolactovegetarian diet A diet that excludes all meat but does include the consumption of eggs and dairy products

ovulation The release of a mature egg from the ovary

oxidation The process that removes alcohol from the bloodstream

oxygen debt The physical state that occurs when the body can no longer process and transport sufficient amounts of oxygen for continued muscle contraction

ozone layer Layer of triatomic oxygen that surrounds the earth and filters much of the sun's radiation before it can reach the earth's surface

P

palatability Pleasing to the palate

panic disorder An anxiety disorder characterized by panic attacks, in which individuals experience severe physical symptoms; these episodes can seemingly occur "out of the blue" or because of some trigger, and can last for a few minutes or for hours

Pap test A cancer-screening procedure in which cells are removed from the cervix and examined for precancerous changes

particulate phase Portion of tobacco smoke composed of small suspended particles

passively acquired immunity (PAI) Temporary immunity achieved by providing antibodies to a person exposed to a particular pathogen

pathogen Disease-causing agent

pelvic inflammatory disease (PID) Acute or chronic infection of the peritoneum or lining of the abdominopelvic cavity; associated with a variety of symptoms—and a potential cause of sterility

periodic abstinence Birth control methods that rely on a couple's avoidance of intercourse during the ovulatory phase of a woman's menstrual cycle; also called fertility awareness or natural family planning

periodontal disease Destruction of soft tissue and bone that surround the teeth

peritonitis Inflammation of the peritoneum or lining of the abdominopelvic cavity

pesticide Agent used to destroy insects and other pests

physical activity All leisure and non-leisure body movement produced by the skeletal muscles resulting in an increase in energy expenditure

physical fitness A set of attributes that are either health related or performance (or skill) related (health-related fitness comprises those components of fitness that exhibit a relationship with health status; performance/skill-related fitness involves those components of fitness that enable optimal work or sport performance

phytosterol A lipid-like material (sterol) found in plants

placebo pills Pills that contain no active ingredients

placenta The structure through which nutrients, metabolic wastes, and drugs (including alcohol) pass from the bloodstream of the mother into the bloodstream of the developing fetus

plateau stage Second stage of the sexual response pattern; a levelling off of arousal immediately before orgasm

platelet adhesiveness Tendency of platelets to clump together, thus enhancing speed at which the blood clots

platonic Close association between two people that does not include a sexual relationship

pollution The introduction into the biosphere of materials that, because of their quantity, chemical nature, or temperature, have a negative impact on the ecosystem or that cannot be readily absorbed by natural recycling processes

positive caloric balance Caloric intake greater than caloric expenditure

post-abortion syndrome Long-term negative psychological effects of abortion experienced by some women

postpartum The period after the birth of a baby, during which the uterus returns to its prepregnancy size

potentiated effect Phenomenon whereby the use of one drug intensifies the effect of a second drug

preventive or prospective medicine Physician-centred medical care in which areas of risk for chronic illnesses are identified so that they might be lowered

problem drinking An alcohol-use pattern in which a drinker's behaviour creates personal difficulties or difficulties for other people

Prochaska's stages of change The six predictable stages—precontemplation, contemplation, preparation, action, maintenance, and termination—people go through in establishing new habits and patterns of behaviour

procreation Reproduction

progesterone-only pills (POPs) Low-dose progesterone oral contraceptives

progressive resistance exercises Muscular strength-training exercises in which traditional barbells and dumbbells with fixed resistances are used

prosthodontics Dental specialty that focuses on the construction and fitting of artificial appliances to replace missing teeth

proteins Compounds composed of chains of amino acids; primary components of muscle and connective tissue

protooncogenes Normal regulatory genes that may become oncogenes

psychoactive drug Any substance capable of altering one's feelings, moods, or perceptions

psychogenic Pertaining to mind-induced (emotional) changes in physical function, without evidence of structural change to body tissues

psychoneuroimmunology A newly emerging field of human biology and clinical medicine that studies the functional interfaces among the mind, nervous system, and immune system

psychosocial sexuality Masculine and feminine aspects of sexuality

psychosomatic Pertaining to mind-induced (emotional) changes in both physical function and the normal structure of body tissues

puberty Achievement of reproductive ability

pulmonary emphysema Irreversible disease process in which the alveoli are destroyed

purging Using vomiting or laxatives to remove undigested food from the body

putrefaction decomposition of organic matter

R

radiation sickness Illness characterized by fatigue, nausea, weight loss, fever, bleeding from mouth and gums, hair loss, and immune deficiencies, resulting from overexposure to ionizing radiation

radon gas A naturally occurring radioactive gas produced by the decay of uranium

recycling Converting disposable items into reusable materials

reflexology Massage applied to specific areas of the feet to treat illness and disease in other areas of the body

refractory phase That portion of the male's resolution stage during which sexual arousal cannot occur

regulatory genes Genes within the cell that control cellular replication, or doubling

resolution stage Fourth stage of the sexual response pattern; the return of the body to a pre-excitement state

retinal hemorrhage Uncontrolled bleeding from arteries within the eye's retina

rigor mortis Rigidity of the body that occurs after death

risk factor A biomedical index such as serum cholesterol level, or a behavioural pattern such as smoking, associated with a chronic illness

rubella German or three-day measles

rubeola Red or common measles

S

salt sensitive Term used to describe people whose bodies overreact to the presence of sodium by retaining fluid, thus experiencing an increase in blood pressure

saturated fats Fats that are difficult for the body to use; they are in solid form at room temperature; primarily animal fats

sclerotic changes Thickening or hardening of tissues

self-actualization The highest level of personality development; self-actualized people recognize their roles in life and use personal strengths to reach their fullest potential

self-care movement Trend toward individuals taking increased responsibility for prevention or management of certain health conditions

semen Secretion containing sperm and nutrients discharged from the urethra at ejaculation

senescence A gradual decline in the functional capacity of the body's systems, including an increased vulnerability to disease

set point A genetically programmed range of body weight beyond which a person finds it difficult to gain or lose additional weight

sex flush The reddish skin response that results from increasing sexual arousal

sex reassignment operation Surgical procedure designed to remove the external genitalia and replace them with genitalia appropriate to the opposite gender

sexual fantasies Fantasies with sexual themes; sexual daydreams or imaginary events

sexuality The quality of being sexual; can be viewed from many biological and psychosocial perspectives

sexually transmitted infections (STIs) Infectious diseases that are spread primarily through intimate sexual contact

shingles Viral infection affecting the nerve endings of the skin

shock Profound collapse of many vital body functions; evident during acute alcohol intoxication and other health emergencies

sidestream smoke The smoke that comes from the burning end of a cigarette, pipe, or cigar

smegma Cellular discharge that can accumulate beneath the clitoral hood and the foreskin of an uncircumcised penis

smog Air pollution made up of a combination of smoke, photochemical compounds, and fog

social phobia A phobia characterized by feelings of extreme dread and embarrassment in situations in which public speaking or social interaction is involved

spermatogenesis Process of sperm production

spermicides Chemicals capable of killing sperm

stalking A crime involving an assailant's planned efforts to pursue an intended victim

static stretching The slow lengthening of a muscle group to an extended level of stretch; followed by holding the extended position for a recommended time period

sterilization Generally permanent birth control techniques that surgically disrupt the normal passage of ova or sperm

stimulants Psychoactive drugs that stimulate the function of the central nervous system

stress The physiological and psychological state of disruption caused by the presence of an unanticipated, disruptive, or stimulating event

stressors Factors or events, real or imagined, that elicit a state of stress

sudden cardiac death Immediate death caused by a sudden change in the rhythm of the heart

synapse The location at which an electrical impulse from one neuron is transmitted to an adjacent neuron; also referred to as a *synaptic junction*

synergistic drug effect Heightened, exaggerated effect produced by the concurrent use of two or more drugs in the same general category

systolic pressure Blood pressure against blood vessel walls when the heart contracts

T

target heart rate (THR) The number of times per minute that the heart must contract to produce a training effect

teratogenic Capable of promoting birth defects

titration Particular level of a drug within the body; adjusting the level of nicotine by adjusting the rate of smoking

tolerance An acquired reaction to a drug; continued intake of the same dose has diminished results

toxic shock syndrome (TSS) Potentially fatal condition resulting from the proliferation of certain bacteria in the vagina that enter the general blood circulation

trace elements Minerals present in very small amounts in the body; micronutrient elements

transcenders Self-actualized people who have achieved a quality of being ordinarily associated with higher levels of spiritual growth

transcervical balloon tuboplasty The use of inflatable balloon catheters to open blocked fallopian tubes; a procedure used for some women with fertility problems

trimester A three-month period; human pregnancies encompass three trimesters

tsunami A sea wave of local or distant origin that results from large-scale seafloor displacements associated with large earthquakes, major submarine slides, or exploding volcanic islands

U

unintentional injuries Injuries that have occurred without anyone's intending that harm be done

urethra Passageway through which urine leaves the urinary bladder

V

vasectomy Surgical procedure in which the vasa deferentia are cut to prevent the passage of sperm from the testicles; the most common form of male sterilization

vegan diet A vegetarian diet that excludes the use of all animal products, including eggs and dairy products

virulent Capable of causing disease

vitamins Organic compounds that facilitate the action of enzymes

W

wellness The promotion and achievement of optimal health, including physical, emotional, social, spiritual, intellectual, and occupational well-being

withdrawal (coitus interruptus) A contraceptive practice in which the erect penis is removed from the vagina before ejaculation

withdrawal illness Uncomfortable, perhaps toxic response of the body as it attempts to maintain homeostasis in the absence of a drug; also called *abstinence syndrome*

Y

Yerkes-Dodson law A bell-shaped curve demonstrating that there is an optimal level of stress for peak performance; this law states that too little and too much stress is not helpful, while a moderate amount of stress is positive and beneficial

Z

zero tolerance laws Laws that severely restrict the right to drive for drinkers who have been convicted of driving under any influence

zoonosis The transmission of diseases from animals to humans

Credits

Chapter 1: p. 2 (Figure 1-1), Men's Health Magazine/CNN; **p. 6 (Table 1-1),** Adapted from the Statistics Canada publication "The Daily," Catalogue 11-001, *Deaths 2002*, Monday, September 27, 2004, available at **www.statcan.ca/Daily/English/040927/d040927a.htm**; **p. 8 (Star Box),** Adapted from The status of Canada's youth, *The Ottawa charter for health promotion 1986*, 1986, World Health Organization and Health and Welfare Canada.

Chapter 2: p. 22 (Star Box), From Depression is a sign of illness, not a sign of weakness, *Ball State University Campus Update*, Dec 12, 1988, p. 1; **p. 30 (Figure 2-2),** "HIERARCHY OF NEEDS" from MOTIVATION AND PERSONALITY, 3RD 3D. by ABRAHAM H. MASLOW. Revised by Robert Frager, James Fadiman, Cynthia McReynolds, and Ruth Cox. Copyright 1954, © 1987, Harper and Row, Publishers, Inc. Copyright © 1970 by Abraham H. Maslow. Reprinted by permission of HarperCollins Publishers Inc.; **p. 35,** From Study Guide and Personal Explorations for *Psychology applied to modern life; adjustment in the 80s*, by Wayne Weiten. Copyright © 1983 by Wadsworth, Inc. Reprinted by permission of Brooks/Cole Publishing, Pacific Grove, CA 93950; **p. 36 (Figure),** Yankelovich Partners for Lutheran Brotherhood.

Chapter 3: p. 44 (Figure 3.2), The Wirthlin Report; **p. 53 (Making Headlines),** Adapted from *The Canadian Mental Health Association*, found at www.cmha.ca; **p. 54,** Modified from Holmes TH and Rahe RH: The social adjustment rating scale, *Journal of Psychosomatic Research* 11:213-218, 1967; **p. 55,** Source: Self-Development Center, A service of the Counseling and Students Development Center, George Mason University: *Time Management Tips*.

Chapter 4: p. 58 (Star Box), Health Canada. For complete credit information, visit our web site at **www.mcgrawhill.ca/college/hahn**; **p. 59 (Figure 4-1),** Adapted from *2000 Physical Activity Monitor*, Canadian Fitness and Lifestyle Research Institute, 2000, **www.cflri.ca/cflri/pa/surveys/2000survey/2000survey.html**. Reprinted with permission of the Canadian Fitness and Lifestyle Institute, **www.cflri.ca**; **p. 61 (Star Box),** *Terry's Journey: The Marathon of Hope*, **www.terryfoxrun.org/terry/introduction.htm**, reprinted with permission of The Terry Fox Foundation; **pp. 62, 68 (Star Boxes),** From Prentice WE: *Fitness for college and life*, ed 4, St. Louis, 1994, Mosby; **p. 67 (Diversity),** Adapted from "The Birth of the Special Olympics in Canada," found at **www.sco.on.ca**, © The Canadian Special Olympics. Reprinted with permission of Special Olympics Canada; **p. 70 (Star Box),** Health Canada. For complete credit information, visit our web site at **www.mcgrawhill.ca/college/hahn**. Adapted from *Par-Q & You. Physical Activity Readiness Questionnaire*, © The Government of Ontario, found at **www.gov.on.ca**; **p. 71 (Star Box),** *The Rick Hansen Story*, Rick Hansen Institute, **www.rickhansen.com/RHStory/RHStory.htm,** reprinted with permission of the Rick Hansen Man In Motion Foundation; **p. 74 (Figure 4-2),** Copyright 1984, *USA Today*, excerpted with permission, art by Donald O'Connor; **p. 75 (Table 4-1),** From Prentice WE: *Fitness for college and life*, ed 5, St. Louis, 1997, McGraw Hill; **pp. 79–80,** Data from the National Fitness Foundation.

Chapter 5: p. 91 (Figure 5-1), Health Canada. For complete credit information, visit our web site at **www.mcgrawhill.ca/college/hahn**. Reproduced with permission from *Canada's Food Guide to Healthy Eating*, Health Canada 1992, **www.hc-sc.gc.ca/hppb/nutrition/pube/foodguid**, Minister of Public Works and Government Services Canada, 2002; **p. 92 (Figure 5-2),** Health Canada. For complete credit information, visit our web site at **www.mcgrawhill.ca/college/hahn**. Reproduced with permission from *Canada's Food Guide to Healthy Eating*, Health Canada 1992, **www.hc-sc.gc.ca/hppb/nutrition/pube/foodguid/e_guideb.html**, Minister of Public Works and Government Services Canada, 2002; **p. 93 (Table 5-1),** Adapted from The Food and Nutrition Board, Institute of Medicine, The National Academy of Sciences; **p. 94 (Table 5-2),** Modified from Hegarty V: *Decisions in nutrition*, St. Louis, 1988, Mosby, 132–133; **p. 96 (Figure 5-3),** Health Canada. For complete credit information, visit our web site at **www.mcgrawhill.ca/college/hahn**. Reproduced with permission from *New and improved nutrition labelling: the "Nutrition Facts" box*, Health Canada 2001, **www.hc-sc.gc. ca/hppb/nutrition/labels/pdf/2_consultation.pdf**, Minister of Public Works and Government Services Canada, 2002; **p. 98 (Table 5-3),** US Department of Health and Human Services, Public Health Service: *The Surgeon General's report on nutrition and health*, Washington, DC, 1988, US Government Printing Office; **p. 100 (Figure 5-5),** National Dairy Council, Rosemont, IL; **p. 104, (Making Headlines),** *The Lancet* 2002; *360*: 7–22; **pp. 105–106,** From *Nutrition for a healthy life*, courtesy of March Leeds; **p. 108 (Focus On),** Reprinted with permission of the Canadian Broadcasting Corporation.

Chapter 6: p. 111 (Table 6-1), Health Canada. For complete credit information, visit our web site at **www.mcgrawhill.ca/college/hahn**; **p. 111 (Table 6-2),** Health Canada. For complete credit information, visit our web site at **www.mcgrawhill.ca/college/hahn**; **p. 112 (Figure 6-1),** Health Canada. For complete credit information, visit our web site at **www.mcgrawhill.ca/college/hahn**; **p. 118 (Table 6-3),** Based on data from Bannister EW, Brown SR: The relative energy requirements of physical activity. In HB Falls, editor: *Exercise Physiology*, New York, 1968, Academic Press Inc.; Howley ET, Glover ME: The caloric costs of running and walking a mile for men and women, *Medicine and Science in Sports* 6:235, 1984; and Passmore R, Durnin JVGA: Human energy expenditure, *Physiological Reviews* 35:801, 1955; **p. 121 (Figure 6-4),** Opinion Research Corporation for *Simply Lite Foods*; **pp. 122–123 (Table 6-4),** Adapted from Guthrie H: *Introductory nutrition*, ed 7, St. Louis, 1989, Mosby, pp. 226–227; **p. 132,** Data from *Energy and protein requirements: report of a joint FAO/WHO/UNU expert consultation*, Technical Report Series 724, World Health Organization, 1985; **p. 133,** Modified from Foreyt J, Goodrick GK: Living without dieting, Houston: Harrison Publishing; **p. 134–135 (Focus On),** Brooke E. Bryant and Sara Krupp, *Napa Valley Register*. Reprinted with permission of the *Napa Valley Register*.

Chapter 7: pp. 145–146 (Table 7-1), Modified from Muncie Star © 1987. Reprinted with permission; **p. 147 (Figure 7-2),** Source: American Management Association Survey; **p. 149 (Star Box),** Health Canada. For complete credit information, visit our web site at **www.mcgrawhill.ca/college/hahn**. Reprinted with permission from the Centre for Addiction and Mental Health - Date Rape Drug Information **http://sano.camh.net/geninfo/rohypnol.html**, The Metro Research Group on Drug Use; **p. 151 (Star Box),** Health Canada. For complete credit information, visit our web site at **www.mcgrawhill.ca/college/hahn**. Adapted from *Cannabis Quick Facts*, The Canadian Centre on Substance Abuse, **www.ccsa.ca/cannfax**; **p. 153 (Star Box),** Adapted from *CannAmm Drug and Alcohol Testing for the Workplace Inc*, found at **www.cannamm.com/humanrights.html**; **p. 155 (Star Box),** Adapted from The Canadian Health Network; **p. 158,** US Department of Education, *A Parents' Guide to Prevention*.

Chapter 8: pp. 162–163 (Media Pulse), From Mullens A: Cheers to tears: a cautionary tale of wasted youth, *University Affairs* March 2001, p. 3, Association of Universities and Colleges of Canada. **www.aucc.ca/en/uaoindex.html**; **p. 164 (Figure 8-1),** Adapted from Core Institute: *2000 Statistics on alcohol and other drugs on American Campuses Center for Alcohol and Other Drug Studies*, Student Health Programs, Southern Illinois University at Carbondale, 2000; **p. 164 (Table 8-1),** US Department of Health and Human Services: Alcohol and health: fourth special report to the US Congress, Washington, DC, 1981, DHS Pub. No. ADM 81-1080; **p. 165 (Star Box),** Health Canada. For complete credit information, visit our web site at **www.mcgrawhill.ca/college/hahn**. Adapted from The Centre for Addiction and Mental Health Toronto, found at **www.camh.net**; **p. 167 (Figure 8-2),** From Core Institute: *2000 Statistics on alcohol and other drugs on American Campuses Center for Alcohol and Other Drug Studies*, Student Health Programs, Southern Illinois University at Carbondale, 2000; **p. 167 (Table 8-2),** US Department of Transportation, National Highway Safety Administration: Adapted from alcohol and the impaired driver (AMA); **p. 171 (Figure 8-3),** From Wardlaw G: *Perspectives in nutrition*, ed 3, St. Louis, 1996, Mosby; **p. 173 (Figure 8-5),** Adapted from Canadian Institute for Health Information: National Trauma Registry/CIHI 2001. **http://secure.cihi.ca/cihiweb/dispPage.jsp?cw_page=statistics_results_topic_injuries_e**; **p. 174 (Star Box),** Source: Based on Jourard R: *Impaired Driving: what you need to know*. **http://www.criminal-lawyer.on.ca**; **p. 176 (Changing Box),** AADAC-ABC'S: *Being a good host*, October, 2000. **http://corp.aadac.com/alcohol/factsheets/good_host.asp**; **p. 178,** Modified from brochure of the Indiana Alcohol Countermeasure Program; **p. 180 (Star Box),** Modified from Woititz JG: *Adult children of alcoholics*, Pompano Beach, FL, 1983, Health Communications, Inc. In Pinger R, Payne W, Hahn D, Hahn E; *Drugs: issues for today*, St. Louis, 1991, Mosby; **p. 185,** From *Are You Troubled By Someone's Drinking?*, 1980, by Al-Anon Family Group Headquarters, Inc. Reprinted by permission of Al-Anon Family Group Headquarters, Inc.

Chapter 9: p. 188 (Media Pulse), Courtesy of CTV.ca. Reprinted with permission; **p. 189 (Figure 9-1),** Health Canada. For complete credit information, visit our web site at **www.mcgrawhill.ca/college/hahn**; **p. 190 (Star Box),** Health Canada. For complete credit information, visit our web site at **www.mcgrawhill.ca/college/hahn**. Reproduced with permission from *Legislation, Regulation and Compliance: Cigarettes cause mouth diseases*, Health Canada website **www.hc-sc.gc.ca/hecs-sesc/tobacco/legislation/warnings/e_h.html,** Minister of Public Works and Government Services Canada, 2002; **p. 198 (Star Box),** Health Canada. For complete credit information, visit our web site at **www.mcgrawhill.ca/college/hahn**. Adapted with permission from *Legislation, Regulation, and Compliance: Cigarettes cause lung cancer* Health Canada Tobacco Control Program, Tobacco Control Archive, **www.hc-sc.gc.ca/hecs-sesc/tobacco/legislation/warnings/e_m.html,** accessed July 11, 2002; **p. 208–209 (Making Headlines),** Reprinted with permission of the Canadian Broadcasting Corporation.

Chapter 10: p. 217 (Table 10-1), Heart and Stroke Foundation Fact Sheet. © Reproduced with the permission of the Heart and Stroke Foundation of Canada, 2005, **www.heartandstroke.ca**; **p. 221 (Figure 10-2),** Reproduced with permission, © 1988, American Heart Association: Heart Facts; **p. 227 (Figure 10-4),** National Cancer Institute: *Horizons of cancer research*, NIH Pub No 89-3011, © 1989; **p. 228 (Figure 10-5),** data from National Cancer Institute of Canada: *Canadian Cancer Statistics 2001*, Toronto, Canada, 2001; **p. 229 (Changing Box)** Adapted from *Canadian Cancer Society's Guidelines for Early Detection & Screening for Cancer*, September 2001. © Canadian Cancer Society; **p. 230 (Changing Box)** and **p. 232 (Changing Box),** Reprinted with permission of the American Cancer Society, Inc.; **p. 233 (Melanoma box),** American Academy of Dermatology; **p. 237 (Star Box),** Reprinted with permission from the Canadian Diabetes Association; **pp. 242–243,** Adapted from Howard E: *Health Risks*, Tucson, 1985, Body Press.

Chapter 11: p. 252 (Figure 11-2), Sources: Centers for Disease Control and Prevention and American Academy of Pediatrics; **p. 258 (Table 11-2),** Courtesy of the National Institute of Allergy and Infectious Diseases; **p. 264 (Figure 11-4),** Adapted from UNAIDS and World Health Organization; **p. 267 (Figure 11-5),** Source: RT Michael, JH Gagnon, EO Laumann, G Kolata: *Sex in America: A Definitive Study*; **p. 275 (Making Headlines),** "AIDS Death Hits Mandela Family." Taken from *The Chronicle Herald*, World section, p. A4, by Michael Wines, *The New York Times*. Copyright © 2005 by The New York Times Co. Reprinted with permission. **p. 276,** Centers for Disease Control and Prevention, Atlanta.

Chapter 12: p. 279 (Media Pulse), Adapted from **www.wnetwork.com/shows/sunday_night_sex_show/index/asp**, © The Women's Television Network; **p. 299 (Diversity),** Canadian data from **http://www.religioustolerance.org/hom_marb0.htm**; **p. 300 (Changing Box),** Adapted from Haas K, Haas A: *Understanding sexuality*, ed 3, St. Louis, 1993, Mosby; **p. 304 (Making Headlines),** Adapted from *Canadian Court Rules for Gay Teenager*, British Broadcasting Corporation © 2001, Broadcasting House, Portland Place, London, W1A 1AA; **p. 306,** Modified from *USA Today*.

Chapter 13: p. 313 (Table 13-1), Adapted from Hatcher et al: "Contraceptive Technology", 17th rev. ed, 1998, Ardent Media, Inc; **p. 331 (Diversity),** Sources: Adapted from the Statistics Canada publication "Families and Household Living Arrangements: Highlight Tables, 2001 Census," Catalogue 97F0024XIE, October 22, 2002, available at **www12.statcan.ca/english/census01/products/highlight/Private-Households/Index.cfm?Lang=E**; Patterson C: Children of lesbian and gay parents, *Child development*, 63, 1025 1042, 1992; Patterson C: Lesbian mothers and their children: findings from the Bay Area Families Study, in J. Laird & R. Green, eds., *Lesbians and gays in couples and families*, pp. 420–438, 1996, San Francisco: Jossey-Bass; Kirkpatrick, M: Lesbians as parents, in R. P. Cabaj & T. S. Stein, eds., *Textbook of homosexuality and mental health*, 1996,Washington, D.C.: American Psychiatric Press; Tasker F, Golombok S: *Growing up in a lesbian family: effects on child development*, 1997, New York: Guilford; Vanier Institute of the Family website, **http://www.vifamily.ca/faqs/faq.htm**; **p. 338**; From Haas K. Haas A: *Understanding sexuality*, ed 3, St. Louis, 1993, Mosby; **p. 339–340 (Focus On),** Health Canada. For complete credit information, visit our web site at **www.mcgrawhill.ca/college/hahn**.

Chapter 14: p. 353 (Star Box), Source: Health Canada: Canada's national organ and tissue information website, **www.organandtissue.ca.** Accessed March 2002.

Chapter 15: p. 368 (Changing Box), Pell AR: *Making the Most of Medicare*, DCI Publishing, 1990, in *in-synch*, Erie, PA, Spring, 1994, Erie Insurance. **p. 374 (Star Box),** Health Canada. For complete credit information, visit our web site at **www.mcgrawhill.ca/college/hahn**; **p. 377 (Changing Box),** Health Canada. For complete credit information, visit our web site at **www.mcgrawhill.ca/college/hahn**; **p. 380 (Making Headlines),** Health Canada. For complete credit information, visit our web site at **www.mcgrawhill.ca/college/hahn**.

Chapter 16: p. 386–387, Adapted from the Statistics Canada publication "Canada e-Book," Catalogue 11-404, May 26, 2003, available at **http://142.206.72.67/04/04b/04b_002a_e.htm**; **p. 387 (Star Box),** Reprinted with permission of the Canada Safety Council, **www.safety-council.org**; **p. 388 (Star Box),** Based on "Cause and effect: ribbons tie supporters to issues," © The Republic, found at **http://www.therepublic.com**; **p. 388,** Adapted from the Statistics Canada publication "The Daily," Catalogue 11-001, *Homicides* 2003, Wednesday, September 29, 2004, available at **www.statcan.ca/Daily/English/040929/d040929a.htm**; **p. 392 (Star Box),** Reprinted with permission of the Canadian Broadcasting Corporation; **p. 395 (Star Box),** Fact Sheet: *Identity Theft: What it is and what you can do about it*, Privacy Commissioner of Canada, 2004. Reproduced with the permission of the Minister of Public Works and Government Services Canada, 2005; **p. 396 (Changing Boxes),** From the American College Health Association; **p. 400 (Figure 16-1, left),** *Road Safety in Canada—An Overview*, Transport Canada, 2004, **www.tc.gc.ca/roadsafety/stats/overview/2004/pdf/overview.pdf.htm**. Reproduced with the permission of the Minister of Public Works and Government Services Canada, 2005; **p. 400 (Figure 16-1, right),** *Canadian Motor Vehicle Traffic Collision Statistics: 2003*, Transport Canada, 2004, **www.tc.gc.ca/roadsafety/tp/tp3322/2003/page2.htm**. Reproduced with the permission of the Minister of Public Works and Government Services Canada, 2005; **p. 401 (Changing Box),** Adapted from Pynoos J, Cohen E: *Creative ideas for a safe and livable home*, Washington, DC, American Association of Retired Persons, 1992; and Van Tassel D: *Home, safe home*, St. Louis, 1996, GenCare Health Systems; **p. 405 (Making Headlines),** Adapted from the Statistics Canada publication "The Daily," Catalogue 11-001, *Crime Statistics 2003*, Wednesday, July 28, 2004, available at **www.statcan.ca/Daily/English/040728/d040728.htm**; **p. 407–408 (Focus On),** Health Canada. For complete credit information, visit our web site at **www.mcgrawhill.ca/college/hahn**.

Photo Credits

Chapter 1: p. 11, Rob Melnychuk/Getty Images; **p. 13,** CORBIS

Chapter 2: p. 21, Doug Menuez/Getty Images; **p. 31,** Doug Menuez/Getty Images; **p. 37,** © David Schmidt/Masterfile

Chapter 3: p. 50, Ryan McVay/PhotoDisc/Getty Images

Chapter 4: p. 61, CP; **p. 63,** Ryan McVay/PhotoDisc/Getty Images; **p. 65,** Ryan McVay/PhotoDisc/Getty Images; **p. 69,** Karl Weatherly/Getty Images; **p. 70,** Jack Hollingsworth/Getty Images; **p. 71,** COC/J. Merrithew; **p. 79 (top, middle, and bottom),** Courtesy Stewart Halperin; **p. 80 (top, middle, and bottom),** Courtesy Stewart Halperin; **p. 81,** Ryan McVay/PhotoDisc/Getty Images

Chapter 6: p. 114, © Custom Medical Stock Photo

Chapter 7: p. 138, Image100; **p. 143,** PhotoDisc/Getty Images; **p. 148,** Jack Star/PhotoLink/PhotoDisc/Getty Images; **p. 150,** Doug Menuez/PhotoDisc/Getty Images

Chapter 8: p. 166, Ryan McVay/Getty Images; **p. 168,** SW Productions/PhotoDisc/Getty Images; **p. 172,** © George Steinmetz

Chapter 9: p. 190, © Custom Medical Stock Photo; **p. 198 (left and right),** Courtesy Wayne Jackson

Chapter 10: p. 228, © Kevin Laubacher/Getty Images/Taxi; **p. 234 (left and right),** From Thibeodeau G., Patton, K. *Anatomy and Physiology*, 3/e, St. Louis, 1996, Mosby

Chapter 11: p. 257, Janis Christie/PhotoDisc/Getty Images; **p. 265,** ABACA; **p. 268,** © Phototake; **p. 270,** © Custom Medical Stock Photo

Chapter 12: p. 283, Digital Vision

Chapter 13: p. 316, The McGraw-Hill Companies/Jill Braaten, photographer; **p. 317 (top),** Courtesy Stewart Halperin; **p. 317 (bottom left),** Linsley Photographics; **p. 317 (bottom right),** Courtesy Stewart Halperin; **p. 319 (left and right),** © Laura J. Edwards; **p. 320,** Courtesy Stewart Halperin; **p. 321,** Courtesy of Alza Corp.; **p. 322 (left and right),** Courtesy of Organon USA

Chapter 14: p. 347, CP/Richard Sheinwald; **p. 352,** CP/Adrian Wyld

Chapter 15: p. 367, Anthony Saint James/PhotoDisc/Getty Images; **p. 368,** PhotoLink/Getty Images; **p. 382,** Javier Pierini/Getty Images

Chapter 16: p. 391, CORBIS; **p. 393,** SW Productions/Getty Images; **p. 395,** Mitch Hrdlicka/PhotoDisc/Getty Images

Chapter 17: p. 411, AP/Manish Swarup; **p. 419,** AP/Douglas Engle; **p. 420,** AP/Tsugufumi Matsumoto; **p. 427,** CP/Jack Branswell

Index

D

H

I

P

T

URL Index